LIBERTY
EQUALITY
POWER

LIBERTY EQUALITY POWER

A History of the American People

CONCISE SECOND EDITION

JOHN M. MURRIN
Princeton University

PAUL E. JOHNSON
University of South Carolina

JAMES M. MCPHERSON
Princeton University

GARY GERSTLE
University of Maryland

EMILY S. ROSENBERG
Macalester College

NORMAN L. ROSENBERG
Macalester College

HARCOURT COLLEGE PUBLISHERS
Fort Worth Philadelphia San Diego New York Orlando Austin San Antonio
Toronto Montreal London Sydney Tokyo

Publisher	Earl McPeek
Executive Editor	David C. Tatom
Executive Market Strategist	Steve Drummond
Developmental Editor	Margaret McAndrew Beasley
Project Editor	Charles J. Dierker
Art Director	Brian Salisbury
Production Manager	Diane Gray
Art & Design Coordinator	Florence Fujimoto

Cover Image: Colin Campbell Cooper (1856–1937), *Fifth Avenue in New York,* 1913. Musee d'Orsay, Paris, France. Giraudon/Art Resource, NY.

ISBN: 0-15-508262-0

Library of Congress Catalog Card Number: 00-103388

Address for Domestic Orders
Harcourt College Publishers, 6277 Sea Harbor Drive, Orlando, FL 32887-6777. 800-782-4479

Address for International Orders
International Customer Service, Harcourt, Inc., 6277 Sea Harbor Drive, Orlando, FL 32887-6777. 407-345-3800. (fax) 407-345-4060. (e-mail) hbintl@harcourt.com

Address for Editorial Correspondence
Harcourt College Publishers, 301 Commerce Street, Suite 3700, Fort Worth, TX 76102

Web Site Address
http://www.harcourtcollege.com

Harcourt College Publishers will provide complimentary supplements or supplement packages to those adopters qualified under our adoption policy. Please contact your sales representative to learn how you qualify. If as an adopter or potential user you receive supplements you do not need, please return them to your sales representative or send them to: Attn: Returns Department, Troy Warehouse, 465 South Lincoln Drive, Troy, MO 63379.

Printed in the United States of America

0   1   2   3   4   5   6   7   8   9   039   10   9   8   7   6   5   4   3   2   1

∽ ABOUT THE AUTHORS ∼

JOHN M. MURRIN, *Princeton University*

John M. Murrin, a specialist in American colonial and revolutionary history, is the author of the first section (Chapters 1–6) of *Liberty, Equality, Power,* Concise Second Edition. He has edited one multivolume series and five books, including *Colonial America: Essays in Politics and Social Development,* Fourth Edition (1993) and *Saints and Revolutionaries* (1984). His many essays on early American history show a diversity of interests that range from ethnic tensions, the early history of trial by jury, and the political culture of Revolutionary America, to the rise of professional baseball and college football. Professor Murrin was elected president of the Society of Historians of the Early American Republic (SHEAR) for 1998–99.

PAUL E. JOHNSON, *University of South Carolina*

Paul E. Johnson authored the second section of the text (Chapters 7–12). A specialist in early national social and religious history, he is also the author of *A Shopkeeper's Millennium: Society and Revivals in Rochester, New York, 1815–1837* (1978); coauthor (with Sean Wilentz), of *The Kingdom of Matthias: Sex and Salvation in 19th-Century America* (1994); and editor of *African-American Christianity: Essays in History* (1994). He has been awarded the Merle Curti Prize of the Organization of American Historians (1980), and a John Simon Guggenheim Memorial Fellowship (1995).

JAMES M. McPHERSON, *Princeton University*

James M. McPherson is the author of the third section of the text (Chapters 13–19). A distinguished Civil War historian, he won the 1989 Pulitzer Prize for his book *Battle Cry of Freedom: The Civil War Era.* His other publications include *Marching Toward Freedom: Blacks in the Civil War,* Second Edition (1991), *Ordeal by Fire: The Civil War and Reconstruction,* Second Edition (1992), *Abraham Lincoln and the Second American Revolution* (1991), and *For Cause and Comrades: Why Men Fought in the Civil War* (1997). In addition, he is, along with Gary Gerstle, a consulting editor of *American Political Leaders: From Colonial Times to the Present* (1991) and *American Social Leaders: From Colonial Times to the Present* (1993).

GARY GERSTLE, *University of Maryland*

Gary Gerstle is the author of the fourth section of the text (Chapters 20–25). A specialist in labor, immigration, and political history, he has published *Working-Class Americanism: The Politics of Labor in a Textile City, 1914–1960* (1989), *The Rise and Fall of the New Deal Order, 1930–1980* (1989) and articles in the *American Historical Review, Journal of American History, American Quarterly,* and many other journals. He is a consulting editor, along with James M. McPherson, of *American Political Leaders: From Colonial Times to the Present* (1991) and *American Social Leaders: From Colonial Times to the Present* (1993). He has been awarded many honors, including a National Endowment for the Humanities Fellowship for University Teachers, an Institute for Advanced Study Membership, and a John Simon Guggenheim Memorial Fellowship.

EMILY S. ROSENBERG, *Macalester College*

Emily S. Rosenberg is the author, along with Norman L. Rosenberg, of the last section of the text (Chapters 26–31). She specializes in United States foreign relations in the 20th century and is the author of the widely used book *Spreading the American Dream: American Economic and Cultural Expansion, 1890–1945* (1982). Her other publications include (with Norman L. Rosenberg) *In Our Times: America Since 1945,* Fifth Edition (1995) and numerous articles on subjects such as international finance, gender issues, and foreign relations. She has served on the board of the Organization of American Historians, on the board of editors of the *Journal of American History,* and as president of the Society for Historians of American Foreign Relations.

NORMAN L. ROSENBERG, *Macalester College*

Norman L. Rosenberg is coauthor, along with Emily S. Rosenberg, of the final section of the text (Chapters 26–31). He specializes in legal history with a particular interest in legal culture and First Amendment issues. His books include *Protecting the "Best Men": An Interpretive History of the Law of Libel* (1990) and (with Emily S. Rosenberg) *In Our Times: America Since 1945,* Fifth Edition (1995). He has published articles in the *Rutgers Law Review, Constitutional Commentary, Law & History Review,* and many other legal journals.

∼ PREFACE ∼

Why take a course in American history? This is a question that many college and university students ask. In many respects, students today are like the generations of Americans who have gone before them: optimistic and forward looking, far more eager to imagine where we as a nation might be going than to reflect on where we have been. If anything, this tendency has become more pronounced in recent years, as the Internet revolution has accelerated the pace and excitement of change and made even the recent past seem at best quaint, at worst uninteresting and irrelevant.

But it is precisely in these moments of great change that a sense of the past can be indispensable in terms of guiding our actions in the present and future. We can find in other periods of American history moments, like our own, of dizzying technological change and economic growth, rapid alterations in the concentration of wealth and power, and basic changes in patterns of work, residence, and play. How did Americans at those times create, embrace, and resist these changes? In earlier periods of American history, the United States was home, as it is today, to a remarkably diverse array of ethnic and racial groups. How did earlier generations of Americans respond to the cultural conflicts and misunderstandings that often arise from conditions of diversity? How did immigrants perceive their new land? How and when did they integrate themselves into American society? To study how ordinary Americans of the past struggled with these issues is to gain perspective on the opportunities and problems that we face today.

History also provides an important guide to affairs of state. What should the role of America be in world affairs? Should we participate in international bodies such as the United Nations or insist on our ability to act autonomously and without the consent of other nations? What is the proper role of government in economic and social life? Should the government regulate the economy? To what extent should the government enforce morality regarding religion, sexual practices, drinking and drugs, movies, TV, and other forms of mass culture? And what are our responsibilities as citizens to each other and to the nation? Americans of past generations have debated these issues with verve and conviction. Learning about these debates and how they were resolved will enrich our understanding of the policy possibilities for today and tomorrow.

History, finally, is about stories—stories that we all tell about ourselves, our families, our communities, our ethnicity, race, region, and religion, and our nation. They are stories of triumph and tragedy, of engagement and flight, and of high ideals and high comedy. When telling these stories, "American history" is often the furthest thing from our minds. But, often, an implicit sense of history informs what we say about grandparents who immigrated many years ago, the suburb in which we live, the church, synagogue, or mosque that we attend, or the ethnic or racial group to which we belong. But how well do we really understand these individuals, institutions, and groups? Do we tell the right stories about them, ones that capture the complexities of their past? Or have we wittingly or unwittingly simplified, altered, or flattened them? A study of American history first helps us to ask these questions and then to answer them. In the process, we can engage in a fascinating journey of intellectual and personal discovery and situate ourselves more firmly than we had ever thought possible in relation to those who came before us. We can gain firmer self-knowledge and a greater appreciation for the richness of our nation and, indeed, of all humanity.

THE *LIBERTY EQUALITY POWER* APPROACH

In this book we tell many small stories, and one large one: how America transformed itself, in a relatively brief era of world history, from a land inhabited by hunter-gatherer and agricultural Native American societies into the most powerful industrial nation on earth. This story has been told many times before, and those who have told it in the past have usually emphasized the political experiment in liberty and equality that took root here in the 18th century. We, too, stress the extraordinary and transformative impact that the ideals of liberty and equality exerted on American politics, society, and economics during the American Revolution and after. We show how the creation of a free economic environment—one in which entrepreneurial spirit, technological innovation, and industrial production has flourished—underpinned American industrial might. We have emphasized, too, the successful struggles for freedom that, over the course of the last 225 years, have brought—first to all white men, then to men of color and finally to women—rights and opportunities that they had not previously known.

But we have also identified a third factor in this pantheon of American ideals—that of power. We examine power in many forms: the accumulation of vast economic fortunes that dominated the economy and politics; the dispossession of native Americans from land that they regarded as theirs; the enslavement of millions of Africans and their African American descendants for a period of almost 250 years; the relegation of women and of racial, ethnic, and religious minorities to subordinate places in American society; and the extension of American control over foreign peoples, such as Latin Americans and Filipinos, who would have preferred to have been free and self-governing. We do not mean to suggest that American power has always been turned to these negative purposes. Subordinate groups have themselves marshaled power to combat oppression, as in the abolitionist and civil rights crusades, the campaign for woman's suffrage, and the labor movement. The state has used its power to moderate poverty and to manage the economy in the interests of general prosperity. And it has used its military power to defeat Nazi Germany, World War II Japan, the Cold War Soviet Union, and other enemies of freedom.

The invocation of power as a variable in American history forces us to widen the lens through which we look at the past and to complicate the stories we tell. Ours has been a history of freedom and domination; of progress toward realizing a broadly democratic polity and of delays and reverses; of abundance and poverty; of wars for freedom and justice and for control of foreign markets.

In complicating our master narrative in this way, we think we have rendered American history more exciting and intriguing. Progress has not been automatic, but the product of ongoing struggles.

In this book we have also tried to capture the diversity of the American past, both in terms of outcomes and in terms of the variety of groups who have participated in America's making. Native Americans, in this book, are not presented simply as the victims of European aggression but as a people remarkably diverse in their own ranks, with a variety of systems of social organization and cultural expression. We give equal treatment to the industrial titans of American history—the likes of Andrew Carnegie and John D. Rockefeller—and to those, such as small farmers and poor workers, who resisted the corporate reorganization of economic life. We celebrate the great moments of 1863, when African Americans were freed from slavery, and of 1868, when they were made full citizens of the United States. But we also note how a majority of African Americans had to wait another 100 years, until the civil rights movement of the 1960s, to gain full access to American freedoms. We tell similarly complex stories about women, Latinos, and other groups of ethnic Americans.

Political issues, of course, are only part of America's story. Americans have always loved their leisure and have created the world's most vibrant popular culture. They have embraced technological innovations, especially those promising to make their lives easier and more fun. We have, therefore, devoted considerable space to a discussion of American popular culture, from the founding of the first newspapers in the 18th century to the rise of movies, jazz, and the comics in the 20th century, to the cable television and Internet revolutions in recent years. We have pondered, too, how American industry has periodically altered home and personal life by making new products—such as clothing, cars, refrigerators, and computers—available to consumers. In such ways we hope to give our readers a rich portrait of how Americans lived at various points in our history.

This book is a brief version of the much admired, *Liberty, Equality, Power,* second edition. We have reduced the length of that volume the hard way—not by cutting whole sections but by carefully eliminating single phrases, lines, and sentences on every page. Thus readers can be assured that all the topics covered in the longer version are covered here; indeed all the headings and subheadings remained unchanged. And the high quality of the writing in *Liberty Equality Power,* a feature much valued by its users, has been preserved. And yet, the text is significantly shorter, thus giving instructors more flexibility in determining how to use it in their courses. With this brief edition, it becomes easier to give students supplementary reading assignments or to expand a Web-based portion of the course.

In a brief edition of this sort, the art and photography program of the longer edition must inevitably be reduced. Nevertheless, we have included a significant number of visuals, and we have carried over from the larger work its highly popular "American Album" feature. More than half of the chapters include an "American Album," a brief essay illustrated with historic photos or artwork that offers a visual excursion into a fascinating moment of the American past. In addition to the themes of liberty, equality, and power, these features explore subjects especially intriguing to students—sports, the environment, gender roles, religion, popular and material culture, war, and race. They can be easily integrated into lectures and classroom discussion or left for students to discover on their own.

We have also carried over into this work most of the graphs and charts from the second edition as well as the chapter-ending chronologies of major events and movements that users of the comprehensive volume have found so useful.

ACKNOWLEDGMENTS

We recognize the contributions of reviewers who read portions of the manuscript in various stages:

Janet Brantley, *Texarkana College*
Sally Hadden, *Florida State University*
Terry Isaacs, *South Plains College*
Thomas Ott, *University of North Alabama*
Geoffrey Plank, *University of Cincinnati*
Stephen Webre, *Louisiana Tech University*

We also appreciate the comments of students at South Plains College who read selected chapters: Anna-Marie Darden, Samuel Hinojosa, and Gwen W. McEntire.

We have once again benefited from the excellent work of the veteran Harcourt staff, and we would like to thank these individuals in particular: David C. Tatom, executive editor; Margaret McAndrew Beasley, senior developmental editor; Charles Dierker, senior project editor; Diane Gray, production manager; Brian Salisbury, senior art director; Steve Drummond, executive market strategist; and Carolyn D. Smith, freelance manuscript editor. Several of these individuals have probably read the various versions of this textbook almost as many times as we have, and yet their enthusiasm for and commitment to this project remain undiminished. Their skills at editing, production, and promotion, and at keeping a dispersed group of authors focused on the tasks at hand are as sharp as ever. We are deeply in their debt.

John M. Murrin
Paul E. Johnson
James M. McPherson
Gary Gerstle
Emily S. Rosenberg
Norman L. Rosenberg

≈ CONTENTS IN BRIEF ≈

~ Contents in Detail ~

~ LIST OF MAPS ~

⁓ AMERICAN ALBUMS ⁓

1

WHEN OLD WORLDS COLLIDE: CONTACT, CONQUEST, CATASTROPHE

PEOPLES IN MOTION ⟋ EUROPE AND THE WORLD IN THE 15TH CENTURY

SPAIN, COLUMBUS, AND THE AMERICAS

THE EMERGENCE OF COMPLEX SOCIETIES IN THE AMERICAS

CONTACT AND CULTURAL MISUNDERSTANDING

CONQUEST AND CATASTROPHE

EXPLANATIONS: PATTERNS OF CONQUEST, SUBMISSION, AND RESISTANCE

When Christopher Columbus crossed the Atlantic, he did not know where he was going, and until his death he never figured out where he had been. Yet he changed history forever. In the 40 years after 1492, European invaders conquered the Americas, not just with sails, gunpowder, and steel, but also with their plants and livestock and, most of all, their diseases. By 1600 they had created the first global economy in the history of mankind and had inflicted upon the Indian peoples of the Americas the greatest known catastrophe that human societies have ever experienced.

In the 15th century, when all of this started, the Americas were in some ways a more ancient world than western Europe. For example, the Portuguese, Spanish, French, and English languages were only beginning to assume their modern forms. But centuries earlier, at a time when Paris and London were little more than hamlets, huge cities were thriving in the Andes and Mesoamerica (the area embracing Central America and southern and central Mexico). Which world was old and which was new is a matter of perspective. Each already had its own distinctive past.

PEOPLES IN MOTION

Long before Europeans discovered and explored the wide world around them, many different peoples had migrated thousands of miles across oceans and continents. Before Columbus sailed west from Spain in 1492, five distinct waves of immigrants had already swept over the Americas. Three came from Asia. The fourth, from the Pacific Islands, or Oceana, may have just brushed America. The last, from northern Europe, decided not to stay.

FROM BERINGIA TO THE AMERICAS

Before the most recent Ice Age ended, glaciers covered huge portions of the Americas, Europe, and Asia. The ice captured so much of the world's water that sea level fell drastically, enough to create a land bridge 600 miles wide across the Bering Strait between Siberia and Alaska. For several thousand years around 50,000 B.C., and again for more than 10,000 years after 23,000 B.C., this exposed area—called Beringia—was dry land on which plants, animals, and humans could live. People drifted in small bands from Asia to North America. No doubt many generations lived on Beringia itself, although its harsh environment on the edge of the Arctic Circle would have required unusual skills just to survive. These first immigrants to the Americas hunted animals for meat and furs and probably built small fishing vessels that could weather the Arctic storms. They made snug homes to keep themselves warm through the fierce winters.

Exactly when they arrived remains controversial. Many archaeologists believe that humans crossed Beringia and began spreading through the Americas more than 40,000 years ago. Canadians digging at the Old Crow site in the Yukon claim they have found evidence of human habitation that may be 50,000 years old. A French team working in northeastern Brazil is examining a site that may be 48,000 years old. Other experts remain skeptical, however. Until the Brazilian find, which is still being evaluated, all very old sites have had something wrong with them, archaeologically speaking. For example, natural forces might have disturbed the setting or carried the artifacts away from their original environment. Moreover, no evidence has yet been found that humans were living in eastern Siberia as far back as 30,000 years ago. Even if some people did make it from there to the Americas at that time, they did not multiply very rapidly.

AN INDIAN WALL PAINTING   Found in northeastern Brazil, this painting may be 32,000 years old. If so, it is one of the oldest in the world.

The record becomes clearer toward the end of the last Ice Age, about 12,000 years ago. By then, humans definitely were living in eastern Siberia, western Alaska, and Beringia. As the glaciers receded for the last time, these people spread throughout the Americas. By 8000 B.C. they had reached all the way to Tierra del Fuego off the southern tip of South America.

These Asians probably came in three waves. Those in the first wave, which began more than 14,000 years ago, spread over most of the two continents and spoke "Amerind," the forerunner of the vast majority of Indian languages on both continents. The Algonquian, Iroquoian, Muskogean, Siouan, Nahuatl (Aztec), Mayan, and all South American tongues derive from this source. Those in the middle wave, which came a few thousand years later, spoke what linguists call "Na-Déné," which eventually gave rise to the various Athapaskan languages of the Canadian Northwest as well as the Apache, Navajo, and related tongues in the American Southwest. The last to arrive, the ancestors of the Inuits (called Eskimos by other Indians), crossed after 7000 B.C., when Beringia was again under water. About 4,000 years ago, these people began to migrate from the Aleutian Islands and Alaska to roughly their present sites in the Americas. They migrated across the northern rim of North America and then across the North Atlantic to Greenland, where they encountered the first Europeans migrating westward—the Norsemen.

The Great Extinction and the Rise of Agriculture

As the glaciers receded and the climate warmed, the people who had wandered south and east found an attractive environment teeming with game. Imperial mammoths, huge mastodons, woolly rhinoceroses, a species of enormous bison, and giant ground sloths roamed the plains and forests, along with camels and herds of small horses. These animals had no instinctive fear of the two-legged intruders, who became ever more skillful at hunting them. A superior spear point, the Clovis tip, appeared in the area around present-day New Mexico and Texas some time before 9000 B.C. and within a thousand years its use had spread throughout North and South America. As it spread, the big game died off. Overhunting cannot explain the entire extinction, but it was a major factor, along with climatic change.

The hemisphere was left with a severely depleted number of animal species. The largest beasts were bears, buffalo, and moose; the biggest cat was the jaguar. The human population had multiplied and spread with ease so long as the giant species lasted. Their extinction probably led to a sharp decline in population. Some Indians raised guinea pigs, turkeys, or ducks, but apart from dogs they domesticated no large animals except for llamas (useful for hauling light loads in mountainous terrain) and alpacas (valued for their wool) in South America.

About 5000 B.C., along the northeast coast of North America, a gifted maritime people emerged who ventured out onto the North Atlantic to catch swordfish and, probably, whales. They carried on a vigorous trade from Labrador to Maine and perhaps as far south as New Jersey. They are sometimes called the Red Paint People because of their use of red ocher in funeral ceremonies. Their burial mounds are the oldest yet found in America. They lived in multiroom houses up to 100 yards long. Most remarkable of all, the motifs on their religious monuments—mounds and stone markers—resemble others found in Brittany and Norway, but the American monuments are several hundred years older than the most ancient ones yet found in Europe. It is just possible that these Indian seafarers followed the Gulf Stream across the Atlantic to Europe thousands of years before Europeans voyaged to America. This culture collapsed 4,000 years ago. No one knows why.

Meanwhile, the peoples of the Pacific Northwest, who developed complex art forms that fascinate modern collectors, sustained themselves through fishing, hunting, and the gathering of nuts, berries, and other edible plants. Men fished and hunted; women gathered. California Indians sustained some of the densest populations north of Mexico by collecting acorns and processing them into meal, which they then baked into cakes. Hunter-gatherers also lived in the rain forests of Brazil, in south and central Florida, and in the cold woodlands of northern New England.

But most Indians could not depend solely on hunting and gathering food. In a few places some of them, probably women, began to plant and harvest crops instead of simply gathering and eating what they found. In Asia and Africa, this practice was closely linked to the domestication of animals and happened quickly enough to be called the neolithic (new or late Stone Age) revolution. But in the Americas the rise of farming had little to do with animals, occurred over a period of about 3,500 years, and might better be termed the ne-olithic *evolution*. Somewhere between 4000 and 1500 B.C., permanent farm villages began to dominate parts of Peru, south-central Mexico, northeast Mexico, and the southwestern United States. The first American farmers grew amaranth (a cereal), manioc (tapioca), chili peppers, pumpkins, sweet potatoes, several varieties of beans, and, above all, maize, or Indian corn.

The Polynesians and Hawaii

Asians migrating across Beringia were not the only people on the move. Polynesians sailed out from Southeast Asia into the Pacific after 1600 B.C. and settled hundreds of islands scattered across more than 30 million square miles of ocean. Nearly all of their settlements were on tropical islands. By the 1st century A.D., with Fiji as a kind of cultural and linguistic center, they had reached as far as Hawaii, nearly 2,500 miles to the northeast, and by A.D. 300 they had colonized Easter Island, more than 4,000 miles to the east and only 2,000 miles off the coast of South America. Before A.D. 1000 they had also settled New Zealand, far to the south of Fiji. Hawaii's population, organized into stratified societies and multiple chiefdoms, would grow to 800,000 before the first Europeans arrived in the 1770s.

It seems hard to believe that such daring mariners would not have sailed on beyond Hawaii and Easter Island. And yet, if some of them did reach the Americas, they left no dis-cernible influence on the Indian societies already there. Someone—either an Indian or a Polynesian—must have brought the sweet potato from South America to Easter Island. Yet the culture of Easter Island was Polynesian, while that of South America remained thoroughly Indian.

The Norsemen

About the time that Polynesians were settling Easter Island, Europeans also began trekking long distances. Pushed by fierce invaders from central Asia, various Germanic tribes overran the western provinces of the Roman Empire. The Norse, a Germanic people who had occu-pied Scandinavia, were among the most innovative of these invaders. For centuries their Viking warriors raided the coasts of the British Isles and France. Their sleek longboats, pro-pelled by both sails and oars, enabled them to challenge the contrary currents of the North Atlantic.

Beginning in A.D. 874, Vikings occupied Iceland. In 982 and 983 Erik the Red, accused of manslaughter in Norway and then outlawed for committing more mayhem in Iceland, led his Norse followers farther west to Greenland. There they established permanent settlements.

Leif, Erik's son, sailed west from Greenland in 1001 and began to explore the coast of North America. He made three more voyages, the last in 1014, and started a colony that he called "Vinland" on the northern coast of Newfoundland at a place now named L'Anse aux Meadows. The local Indians resisted vigorously. In one engagement, just as the Norse were about to be routed, Freydis, the bastard daughter of old Erik, saved the day by baring her breasts, slapping them with a sword, and screaming ferociously. Awed, the Indians fled. But the Norse soon quarreled among themselves and destroyed the colony. They abandoned Vinland, but they continued to visit North America for another century, probably to get wood.

About 500 years after Erik the Red's settlement, the Norse also lost Greenland. There, not long before Columbus sailed in 1492, the last Norse settler died a lonely death. In the chaos that followed the Black Death in Europe and Greenland after 1350, the colony had suffered a severe population decline and had gradually lost regular contact with the homeland. Then it slowly withered away. Despite their spectacular exploits, the Norse had no impact on the later course of American history.

Europe and the World in the 15th Century

Nobody in the year 1400 could have foreseen the course of European expansion that was about to begin. Europe stood at the edge, not the center, of world commerce.

China: The Rejection of Overseas Expansion

By just about every standard, China under the Ming dynasty was the world's most complex culture. In the 15th century the government of China, staffed by well-educated bureaucrats, ruled 100 million people. The Chinese had invented the compass, gunpowder, and early forms of printing and paper money. Foreigners coveted the silks, teas, and other fine products available in China, but they had little to offer in exchange. Most of what Europe knew about China came from *The Travels* of Marco Polo, a merchant from the Italian city-state of Venice who reached the Chinese court in 1271 and served the emperor, Kublai Khan, for the next 20 years. The Khan's capital city (today's Beijing) was the world's largest and grandest, Marco reported, and received 1,000 cartloads of silk a day. China outshone Europe and all other cultures, he insisted.

The Chinese agreed. Between 1405 and 1434 a royal eunuch, Cheng Ho, led six large fleets from China to the East Indies and the coast of East Africa, trading and exploring along the way. His ships were large enough to sail around the southern tip of Africa and "discover" Europe. Had China thrown its resources and talents into overseas expansion, the subsequent history of the world would be vastly different. But most of what the Chinese learned about the outside world merely confirmed their belief that other cultures had little to offer their Celestial Kingdom. No one followed Cheng Ho's lead after he died. The emperor banned the construction of oceangoing ships and later forbade anyone to own a vessel with more than two masts. China, a self-contained economic and political system, did not need the rest of the world.

EUROPE VERSUS ISLAM

Western Europe was a rather backward place in 1400. Its location on the Atlantic rim of the Eurasian continent had always made access to Asian trade difficult and costly. Islam controlled overland trade with Asia and the only known seaborne route to Asia through the Persian Gulf. As of 1400, Arab mariners were the world's best. Europeans coveted East Indian spices, but because they produced little that Asians wished to buy, they had to pay for these imports with scarce silver or gold.

In fact, while Europe's sphere of influence was shrinking and while China seemed content with what it already had, Islam was well embarked on another great phase of expansion. The Ottoman Turks took Constantinople in 1453, overran the Balkans by the 1520s, and even threatened Vienna. The Safavid Empire in Iran (Persia) rose to new splendor at the same time. Other Moslems carried the Koran to Indonesia and northern India.

Yet the European economy had made impressive gains in the Middle Ages, primarily owing to agricultural advances, such as improved plows, that also fostered rapid population growth. By 1300, more than 100 million people were living in Europe. Europe's farms could not sustain further growth, however. Lean years and famines ensued, leaving people undernourished. Then in the late 1340s, the Black Death (bubonic plague) reduced the population by more than a third. Recurring bouts of plague kept population low until about 1500. Meanwhile, overworked soil regained its fertility, and per capita income rose considerably among people who now had stronger immunity to disease.

By then European metallurgy and architecture were quite advanced. The Renaissance, which revived interest in the literature of ancient Greece and Rome, also gave a new impetus to European culture, especially after Johannes Gutenberg invented the printing press and movable type in the 1430s. This revolution in communications permitted improvements in ship design and navigational techniques to build on each other and become a self-reinforcing process. The Arabs, by contrast, had borrowed printing from China in the 10th century, only to give it up by 1400.

Unlike China, none of Europe's kingdoms was a self-contained economy. All needed to trade with one another and with the non-Christian world. No single state had a monopoly on the manufacture of firearms or on the flow of capital—a situation that proved advantageous in the long run. During the 15th century, European societies began to compete with one another in gaining access to these resources and in mastering new maritime and military techniques. European armies were far more formidable in 1520 then they had been in 1453, and by then European fleets could outsail and outfight all rivals.

THE LEGACY OF THE CRUSADES

Quite apart from the Norse explorers, Europe had a heritage of expansion that derived from the efforts of the crusaders to conquer the Holy Land from Islam. Crusaders had established their own Kingdom of Jerusalem, which survived for more than a century but was finally retaken in 1244. This overseas venture taught Europeans some important lessons. To make Palestine profitable, the crusaders had taken over sugar plantations and worked them with a combination of free and slave labor. After they were driven from the Holy Land, they retreated to the Mediterranean islands of Cyprus, Malta, Crete, and Rhodes, where they used slaves to grow sugar cane or grapes.

Long before Columbus, these planters had created the economic components of overseas expansion. They assumed that colonies should produce a staple crop, at least partly through slave labor, for sale in Europe. The first slaves were Moslem captives. In the 14th and 15th centuries, planters turned to pagan Slavs (hence the word "slave") from the Black Sea area and the Adriatic. Some black Africans were also acquired from Arab merchants who controlled the caravan trade across the Sahara desert.

The crusades also left a cultural legacy in the legend of Prester John. For centuries after the loss of Jerusalem, many Europeans still cherished the hope of linking up somewhere deep in the African interior with this mythical Christian king, whose legend reflected the garbled information that Europe had acquired about the Coptic Christian kingdom of Ethiopia. As late as the 15th century, Europeans still hoped to inflict a mortal blow upon Islam by uniting with the descendants of that powerful prince.

THE UNLIKELY PIONEER: PORTUGAL

It seemed highly improbable in 1400 that Europe was standing on the threshold of a dramatic expansion. That Portugal would lead the way seemed even less likely. Portugal, a small kingdom of fewer than a million people, had been united for less than a century. Its maritime traditions lagged well behind those of the Italian states, France, and England, and it had little capital.

Yet Portugal enjoyed internal peace and an efficient government at a time when its neighbors were beset by war and internal upheaval. Moreover, it was located at the intersection of the Mediterranean and Atlantic worlds. At first, Portuguese mariners were interested in short-term gains, rather than in some all-water route to Asia. The Portuguese knew that Arab caravans crossed the Sahara to bring gold, slaves, and ivory from black Africa to Europe. The Portuguese believed that an Atlantic voyage to coastal points south of the Sahara would undercut Arab traders and bring large profits. The greatest problem they faced in this quest was Cape Bojador, with its treacherous shallows, awesome waves, and strong northerly winds.

THE CARAVEL: A SWIFT OCEANGOING VESSEL   Shown here is a 15th century caravel—in this case a modern reconstruction of the *Niña*, which crossed the Atlantic with Columbus in 1492.

In 1420 a member of the Portuguese royal family, Prince Henry, became head of the crusading Order of Christ and used its revenues to sponsor 15 voyages along the African coast. In 1434 one of his captains, Gil Eannes, finally succeeded. After passing the cape and exploring the coastline, Eannes sailed west into the Atlantic beyond the sight of land until he met favorable winds and currents that carried him back to Europe. Other captains pushed farther south along the African coast. But only after they made it beyond the Sahara did their efforts begin to pay off.

During the 15th century Portugal vaulted past all rivals in the ability to navigate the high seas beyond sight of land. Portuguese navigators mapped the prevailing winds and currents on the high seas over most of the globe. They collected geographical information. They studied the superior designs of Arab vessels, copied them, and then improved on them. They borrowed the lateen (triangular) sail from the Arabs, and combined it with square rigging in the right proportion to produce a superb oceangoing vessel, the caravel. A caravel could make from 3 to 12 knots and could beat closer to a head wind than any other sailing ship. Portuguese captains also used the compass and adopted the Arabs' astrolabe, a device that permits accurate calculation of latitude, or distances north and south. As they skirted the African coast, they made precise charts and maps.

The Portuguese also learned how to mount heavy cannon on the decks of their ships—a formidable advantage in an age when others fought naval battles by grappling and boarding enemy vessels. Portuguese ships were able to stand farther off and literally blow their opponents out of the water.

As the 15th century advanced, Portuguese mariners explored ever farther along the African coast. South of the Sahara they found the wealth they had been seeking—gold, ivory, and slaves.

AFRICA, COLONIES, AND THE SLAVE TRADE

West Africans had been supplying Europe with most of its gold for hundreds of years through indirect trade across the Sahara. West Africa's political history had been marked by the rise and decline of a series of large inland states. The most recent of these was the empire of Mali. As the Portuguese advanced past the Sahara, their commerce began to pull trade away from the desert caravans, weakening Mali and other interior states. By 1550, the empire had fallen apart.

The Portuguese also founded offshore colonies along the way. They began to settle the uninhabited Madeira Islands in 1418, took possession of the Azores between 1427 and 1450, occupied the Cape Verde group in the 1450s, and took over São Tomé in 1470. Like exploration, colonization also turned a profit. Beginning in the 1440s, Portuguese planters on the islands produced sugar or wine, increasingly with slave labor imported from nearby Africa.

At first the Portuguese acquired their slaves by landing on the African coast, attacking villages, and carrying off everyone they could catch. But these raids enraged coastal peoples and made other forms of trade more difficult. In the decades after 1450, the slave trade assumed its classic form. The Portuguese established small posts, or "factories," along the coast or on small offshore islands, such as Arguin Island near Cape Blanco, where they built their first African fort in 1448. Operating out of these bases, traders would buy slaves from the local rulers, who usually acquired them by waging war. During the long history of the Atlantic slave trade, nearly every African shipped overseas had first been enslaved by other Africans.

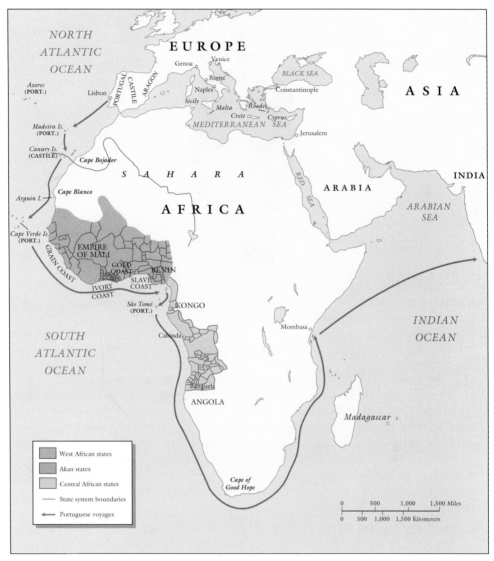

AFRICA AND THE MEDITERRANEAN IN THE 15TH CENTURY

Slavery had long existed in Africa, but in a form less brutal than what the Europeans would impose. In Africa, slaves were not forced to toil endlessly to produce staple crops, and their descendants often became fully assimilated into the captors' society. Slaves were not isolated as a separate caste. By the time African middlemen learned about the cruel conditions of slavery under European rule, the trade had become too lucrative to stop. When the rulers of the Kongo embraced Catholicism in the 16th century, they protested against the Atlantic slave trade, only to see their own people become vulnerable to enslavement by others. The non-Christian kingdom of Benin learned the same lesson.

BRONZE PORTRAIT HEAD   This bronze head is of an Oni, or West African ruler, of 13th century Ife (now Nigeria), two centuries before Europeans arrived.

The Portuguese made the slave trade profitable by exploiting rivalries among the more than 200 small states of West and Central Africa. Despite many cultural similarities among these groups, West Africans had never thought of themselves as a single people. Nor did they share a universal religion that might have restrained them from selling other Africans into slavery. Moslems believed it sinful to enslave a fellow believer. Western Europeans strongly believed that enslaving fellow Christians was immoral. Enslaving pagan or Moslem Africans was another matter. Some Europeans even persuaded themselves that they were doing Africans a favor by buying them and making their souls eligible for salvation.

PORTUGAL'S ASIAN EMPIRE

Because it paid for itself through gold and slaves, Portuguese exploration continued. In the 1480s the Portuguese government supported the quest for an all-water route to Asia. In 1487 Bartolomeu Dias reached the Cape of Good Hope at the southern tip of Africa and headed east toward the Indian Ocean, but his crew rebelled in those stormy waters, and he turned back. Ten years later Vasco da Gama led a small fleet around the Cape of Good Hope and sailed on to the Malibar Coast of southwestern India. In a voyage that lasted more than two years (1497–1499), he bargained and fought for spices that yielded a 20-to-1 profit for his investors.

To secure their Asian trade, the Portuguese established a chain of naval bases that extended from East Africa to the mouth of the Persian Gulf, then to Goa on the west coast of India, and from there to the Moluccas, or East Indies. Portuguese missionaries even penetrated Japan. The Moluccas became the Asian center of the Portuguese seaborne empire, with their spices yielding most of the wealth that Portugal extracted from its eastern holdings.

Beyond assuring its continued access to spices, Portugal made little effort to govern its colonies. In all their Asian holdings, the Portuguese remained heavily outnumbered by native peoples. Only in the other hemisphere—in Brazil, discovered accidentally by Pedro Álvares Cabral in 1500 when he was blown off course while trying to round the Cape of Good Hope—had settlement become a major goal by the late 16th century.

Early Lessons

As the Norse failure showed, the ability to navigate the high seas gave no guarantee of lasting success. Sustained expansion overseas required the support of a home government and ready access to what other states had learned. The experience acquired by Italian merchants in nearby Rhodes or Cyprus could be passed on to the Portuguese and applied in the Atlantic islands of Madeira or the Azores. And the lessons learned there could be relayed to distant Brazil. The Portuguese drew on Italian capital and maritime skills, as well as on Arab learning and technology, in launching their ventures. Spaniards, in turn, would learn much from the Portuguese, and the French, Dutch, and English would borrow from Italians, Portuguese, and Spaniards.

The economic impulse behind colonization was thus in place long before Columbus sailed west. The desire for precious metals provided the initial stimulus, but staple crops and slavery kept that impetus alive. Before the 19th century, about two-thirds of the people who crossed the Atlantic were slaves, not free European settlers.

Few Europeans who crossed the ocean expected to work. Early modern Europe was a hierarchical society in which men with prestige and wealth did virtually no physical labor. Upward social mobility meant advancing toward the goal of "living nobly." In both Portugal and Spain, professional men, famous soldiers, and rich merchants could acquire titles and begin to "live nobly." The opening of the Americas offered even greater possibilities for men to succeed by forcing others to toil for them.

Spain, Columbus, and the Americas

While the Portuguese surged east, Spaniards moved more sluggishly to the west. The Spanish kingdom of Castile sent its first settlers to the Canary Islands just after 1400. They spent the last third of the 15th century conquering the local inhabitants, the Guanches, a Berber people who had left North Africa before the rise of Islam and had been almost completely cut off from Africa and Europe for a thousand years. By the 1490s the Spanish had all but exterminated them.

Except for seizing the Canaries, the Spaniards devoted little attention to exploration or colonization. But in 1469 Prince Ferdinand of Aragon married Princess Isabella of Castile. They soon inherited their respective thrones and formed the modern kingdom of Spain. Aragon, a Mediterranean society, had made good an old claim to the Kingdom of Naples and Sicily and thus already possessed a small imperial bureaucracy with experience in administering overseas possessions. Castile, landlocked on three sides, had turned over much of its small overseas trade to merchants and mariners from Genoa in northern Italy who had settled in the port of Seville. Castilians were more likely than the Portuguese to identify expansion with conquest rather than trade.

In January 1492 Isabella and Ferdinand completed the reconquest of Spain by taking Granada, the last outpost of Islam on the Iberian peninsula. They gave unconverted Jews six months to become Christians or be expelled from Spain. Just over half of Spain's 80,000 Jews fled. A decade later Ferdinand and Isabella also evicted all unconverted Moors. Spain entered the 16th century as Europe's most fiercely Catholic society, and this attitude accompanied its soldiers and settlers to America.

COLUMBUS

A talented navigator from Genoa named Christopher Columbus promptly sought to bene-fit from the victory at Granada. He had been pleading for years with the courts of Portugal, England, France, and Spain to give him the ships and men to attempt an unprecedented feat: He believed he could reach eastern Asia by sailing west across the Atlantic. Colum-bus's proposed voyage was controversial, but not because he assumed the earth is round. Learned men at that time agreed on that point, but they disagreed about the earth's size. Columbus put its circumference at only 16,000 miles, whereas the Portuguese calculated it, correctly, at about 26,000 miles and warned Columbus that he would perish on the vast ocean if he tried his mad scheme. Nevertheless, the fall of Granada gave Columbus another chance to plead his case. Isabella, who now had men and resources to spare, appointed him "Admiral of the Ocean Sea" in charge of a fleet of two caravels, the *Niña* and the *Pinta*, together with a larger, square-rigged vessel, the *Santa María*, which Columbus made his flagship.

Columbus's motives were both religious and practical. As the "Christ-bearer" (the literal meaning of his first name), Columbus was convinced that he had a role to play in bringing on the Millennium, the period at the end of history when Christ would return, perhaps as early as 1648, and rule with his saints for 1,000 years. But he was not at all averse to acquiring wealth and glory along the way.

Embarking from the port of Palos in August 1492, Columbus headed south to the Canaries, picked up provisions, and then sailed west across the Atlantic. He promised a prize to the first sailor to sight land. Despite his assurances that they had not sailed very far, the crews grew restless in early October. Columbus pushed on. When land was spotted, on Octo-ber 12, he claimed the prize for himself. He said he had seen a light in the distance the previ-ous night.

The Spaniards splashed ashore on San Salvador, now Watling's Island in the Bahamas. Convinced that he was somewhere in the East Indies, Columbus called the local inhabitants "Indians." When the peaceful Tainos (or Arawaks) claimed that the Carib Indians on nearby islands were cannibals, Columbus interpreted their word for "Carib" to mean the great "Khan" or emperor of China, known to him through Marco Polo's *Travels*. Columbus set out to find the Caribs. For several months he poked about the Caribbean. Then, on Christmas, the *Santa María* ran onto rocks and had to be abandoned. A few weeks later Columbus sailed for Spain on the *Niña*, leaving some of the crew as a garrison on the island of Hispaniola. But the Tainos had seen enough of the Europeans' tactics. By the time Columbus returned on his second voyage in late 1493, they had killed every man he had left behind.

The voyage had immediate consequences. In 1493 Pope Alexander VI (a Spaniard) issued a bull, *Inter Caeteras*, which divided all non-Christian lands between Spain and Portugal. A year later, in the Treaty of Tordesillas, the two kingdoms adjusted the dividing line, with Spain eventually claiming most of the Western Hemisphere, plus the Philippines, and Portugal most of the Eastern Hemisphere, including the African coast, plus Brazil. As a result, Spain never acquired direct access to the African slave trade.

Columbus made three more voyages in quest of China and also served as governor of the Spanish Indies. But Castilians never really trusted him. The colonists often defied him, and after his third voyage they shipped him back to Spain in chains in 1500. Although later restored to royal favor, he died in 1506, a bitter, disappointed man.

Spain and the Caribbean

By then overseas settlement had acquired a momentum of its own as thousands of ex-soldiers, bored *hidalgos* (minor nobles with little wealth), and assorted adventurers drifted across the Atlantic. They carried with them seeds for Europe's cereal crops and livestock, including horses, cows, sheep, goats, and pigs. On islands without fences, the animals roamed freely, eating everything in sight, and soon threatened the Tainos' food supply. Unconcerned, the Spaniards forced the increasingly malnourished Indians to work for them, mostly panning for gold. Under these pressures, even before the onset of major infectious diseases, the Indian population declined catastrophically throughout the Caribbean. A whole way of life all but vanished from the earth to be replaced by sugar, slaves, and livestock. African slaves, acquired from the Portuguese, soon arrived to replace the dead Indians as a labor force.

The Spaniards continued their explorations, however. Juan Ponce de León tramped through Florida in quest of a legendary fountain of youth. Vasco Núñez de Balboa became the first European to reach the Pacific Ocean, after crossing the Isthmus of Panama in 1513. But as late as 1519 Spain had gained little wealth from these new possessions. One geographer concluded that Spain had found a whole new continent, which he named "America" in honor of his informant, the explorer Amerigo Vespucci. For those who doubted, Ferdinand Magellan, a Portuguese mariner serving the king of Spain, settled the issue when his fleet sailed around the world between 1519 and 1522.

But during the same three years, Hernán Cortés sailed from Cuba, conquered Mexico for Spain, and found the treasure that Spaniards had been seeking. In 1519 he landed at a place he named Vera Cruz ("The True Cross") and over the next several months succeeded in tracking down the fabulous empire of the Aztecs, high in the Valley of Mexico. When his small army of 400 men first laid eyes on the Aztec capital of Tenochtitlán (a metropolis of 200,000, much larger than any city in Western Europe), they wondered if they were dreaming. But they marched on. Moctezuma, the Aztec "speaker," or ruler, sent rich presents to persuade the Spaniards to leave, but the gesture had the opposite effect. The Spaniards pushed onward.

The Emergence of Complex Societies in the Americas

The high cultures of the Americas had been developing for thousands of years before Cortés found one of them. Their wealth fired the imagination of Europe and aroused the envy of Spain's enemies. The fabulous Aztec and Inca empires became the magnets that turned European exploration into empires of permanent settlement.

GLOBAL EMPIRE AND THE
AESTHETICS OF POWER

The Portuguese Empire brought together peoples who, in the past, had made contact with each other only through numerous intermediaries. Thus, after Vasco da Gama's 1497–1499 voyage to India, the Portuguese also reached China, the East Indies, and Japan and became the means through which other Europeans obtained goods from the Far East. The Spanish explorers, by contrast, established contact with peoples that Europeans did not even know existed—and who had never heard of Europeans, Asians, or Africans. When King Philip II of Spain took over the Portuguese throne in 1580, he united the two empires. His overseas possessions stretched from the Philippines and the Spice Islands in the Far East to a string of bases in Japan and India, to the Portuguese slave factories in West Africa and Angola, and on to the West Indies, Mexico, and Peru. Only Spain's American silver permitted Europe to pay for the silks and spices it imported from the Far East.

Even in colonial Mexico, far from the seats of imperial power in Seville and Madrid, Spanish artists knew that they were part of a global empire without precedent in the history of the world. A good example is *The Martyrdom of San Felipe de Jesús* (St. Philip of Jesus). This event, which occurred in Nagasaki, Japan, in 1597, is depicted here by an unknown Mexican sculptor in the 17th century.

The Rise of Sedentary Cultures

After 4000 B.C., agriculture transformed the lives of most Indians. As farming slowly became the principal source of food in the Americas, settled villages in a few locations grew into large cities. Most of them appeared in the Valley of Mexico, Central America, or the Andes. For centuries, however, dense settlements also thrived in Chaco Canyon in present-day New Mexico and in the Mississippi River valley.

Indians became completely sedentary (nonmigratory) only in the most advanced cultures. Most of those north of Mexico were migratory for part of each year. After a tribe chose a site, the men chopped down some trees, girdled others, burned away the underbrush, and often planted tobacco, a mood-altering sacred crop grown exclusively by men. Burning the underbrush fertilized the soil with ash and gave the community years of high productivity. Indian women usually erected the dwellings and planted and harvested food crops. In the fall, either the men alone or entire family groups went off hunting or fishing.

Because this "slash and burn" system of agriculture slowly depleted the soil, the whole tribe had to move to new fields after a number of years. In this semisedentary way of life, few Indians cared to acquire more personal property than the women could carry from one place to another. This limited interest in consumption would profoundly condition their response to capitalism after contact with Europeans.

Even sedentary Indians did not own land as individuals. Clans or families guarded their "use rights" to land that had been allocated to them by their chiefs. In sedentary societies both

Indian Women as Farmers In this illustration, a French artist depicted 16th century Indian women in southeastern North America.

men and women worked in the fields, and families accumulated surpluses for trade. Not all sedentary peoples developed monumental architecture and elaborate state forms. But, with a few striking exceptions, such examples of cultural complexity emerged only among sedentary populations. In Mesoamerica and the Andes, intensive farming, cities, states, and monumental architecture came together at several different times to produce distinctive high cultures.

The spread of farming produced another population surge among both sedentary and semisedentary peoples. Estimates vary greatly, but according to the more moderate ones, at least 50 million people were living in the Western Hemisphere by 1492—and there may well have been as many as 70 million, which was one-seventh of the world's population.

Despite their large populations, even the most complex societies in the Americas remained Stone Age cultures. The Indians made some use of metals, although more for decorative than practical purposes. This metalworking skill originated in South America and spread to Mesoamerica a few centuries before Columbus. As far north as the Great Lakes, copper had been mined and fashioned into fishing tools and art objects since the first millennium B.C. It was traded over large areas of North America. But Indians had not learned how to make bronze (a compound of copper and tin), nor found any use for iron. Nearly all of their tools were made of stone or bone, and their sharpest weapons were made from obsidian, a hard, glassy, volcanic rock. Nor did they use the wheel or devices based on the wheel, such as pulleys or gears.

THE ANDES: CYCLES OF COMPLEX CULTURES

During the second millennium B.C., elaborate urban societies began to take shape both in the Andes and along Mexico's gulf coast. Ancient Andean societies devised extremely productive agricultural systems at 12,000 feet above sea level, far above the altitude at which anyone else has ever been able to raise crops. The Andean system could produce 10 metric tons of potatoes per hectare (about 2.4 acres), as against 1 to 4 tons on nearby modern fields. Lands using the Andean canal system never had to lie fallow. This type of irrigation took hold around Lake Titicaca about 1000 B.C. and spread throughout the region. It was abandoned around A.D. 1000, apparently in response to a drought that endured almost continuously for two centuries.

Between 3000 and 2100 B.C., monumental architecture and urbanization took hold along the Peruvian coast and in the interior. The new communities were built around a U-shaped temple about three stories high. Some of the earliest temples were pyramids. As more people moved into the mountains, some pyramids became immense, such as the one at Sechin Alto near Lima, more than 10 stories high, which was built between 1800 and 1500 B.C. This "Pre-Classic" Chavin culture was well established by 1000 B.C., only to collapse suddenly around 300 B.C.

Chavin culture had two offshoots, one on the coast, one in the mountains. Together they constitute the "Classic" phase of pre-Columbian history in South America. The Mochica culture, which emerged around A.D. 300 on the northwest coast of Peru, produced finely detailed pottery, much of it erotic, and built pyramids as centers of worship. At about the same time, another Classic culture arose in the mountains around the city of Tiwanaku, 12,000 feet above sea level. The people of this society grew a great variety of food plants. Terraces at various altitudes enabled the community to raise crops from different climatic zones. At the lowest levels, Tiwanakans planted cotton in the hot, humid air. Farther up the mountain, they raised maize (corn) and other crops suitable to a temperate zone. At still higher elevations, they grew potatoes and grazed their alpacas and llamas.

COMPLEX CULTURES OF PRE-COLUMBIAN AMERICA

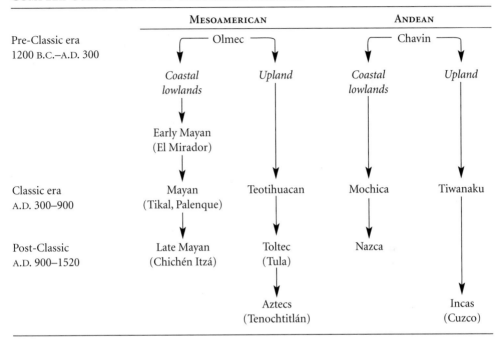

	MESOAMERICAN		ANDEAN	
Pre-Classic era 1200 B.C.–A.D. 300	Olmec		Chavin	
	Coastal lowlands	*Upland*	*Coastal lowlands*	*Upland*
	Early Mayan (El Mirador)			
Classic era A.D. 300–900	Mayan (Tikal, Palenque)	Teotihuacan	Mochica	Tiwanaku
Post-Classic A.D. 900–1520	Late Mayan (Chichén Itzá)	Toltec (Tula)	Nazca	
	Aztecs (Tenochtitlán)			Incas (Cuzco)

The Tiwanaku Empire, with its capital on the southern shores of Lake Titicaca, flourished until the horrendous drought that began at the end of the 10th century A.D. The Classic Andean cultures collapsed between the 6th and 11th centuries A.D., possibly after a conquest of the Mochica region by the Tiwanakans, who provided water to the coastal peoples until they too were overwhelmed by the drought.

The disruption that followed this decline was not permanent, for complex Post-Classic cultures soon thrived both north and west of Tiwanaku. The coastal culture of the Nazca people has long fascinated both scholars and tourists because of a unique network of lines that they etched in the desert. Some lines form the outlines of birds or animals, but others simply run straight for miles until they disappear at the horizon. Only from the air are these patterns fully visible.

INCA CIVILIZATION

Around A.D. 1400 the Inca (the word applies both to the ruler and to the empire's dominant nation) emerged as the new imperial power in the Andes. They built their capital at Cuzco, high in the mountains. From that upland center, the Inca controlled an empire that eventually extended more than 2,000 miles from south to north, and they bound it together with an efficient network of roads and suspension bridges. They had no written language, but high-altitude runners, who memorized the Inca's oral commands with perfect accuracy, raced along the roads to deliver their ruler's decrees over vast distances. The Incas also invented a decimal

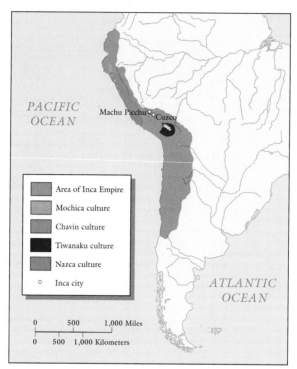

PACIFIC
OCEAN

Machu Picchu ⚬⚬ Cuzco

ATLANTIC
OCEAN

- Area of Inca Empire
- Mochica culture
- Chavin culture
- Tiwanaku culture
- Nazca culture
- ⚬ Inca city

0   500   1,000 Miles

0   500   1,000 Kilometers

INCA EMPIRE AND PRINCIPAL EARLIER CULTURES

system and used it to keep accounts on a device they called a *quipu.* By 1500 the Inca Empire ruled perhaps 8 to 12 million people. No other nonliterate culture has ever matched that feat.

MESOAMERICA: CYCLES OF COMPLEX CULTURES

Mesoamerica experienced a similar cycle of change. It had its own Pre-Classic, Classic, and Post-Classic cultures comprising both upland and lowland societies.

The Olmecs, who appeared along the Gulf Coast around 1200 B.C., centered on three cities. The oldest, San Lorenzo, flourished from 1200 to 900 B.C., when it was conquered by invaders. Olmec influence reached its zenith during the domination of La Venta, which became an urban center around 1100 B.C., reached its peak 300 years later, and then declined. After La Venta was demolished between 500 and 400 B.C., leadership passed to the city of Tres Zapotes, which thrived for another four centuries.

These three Olmec centers were small, with permanent populations of only about 1,000, not enough to sustain large armies. The colossal stone heads that honored their rulers were the most distinctive Olmec artifacts, but they appeared only in the homeland. Other aspects of Olmec culture became widely diffused throughout Mesoamerica. The Olmecs built the first pyramids and the first ballparks in Mesoamerica.

The Olmecs also learned how to write and developed a dual calendar system. It took 52 years for the two calendars to complete a full cycle, after which the first day of the "short" calendar

OLMEC STONE HEAD   This giant head of stone is 9 feet 4 inches tall.

would again coincide with the first day of the "long" one. Olmecs faced the closing days of each cycle with dread, lest the gods allow the sun to be destroyed—something that, Olmecs believed, had already happened several times. They believed that the sacrifice of a god had been necessary to set the sun in motion once again, and that only human sacrifice could placate the gods and keep the sun moving. These beliefs endured for perhaps 3,000 years and retained immense power. The arrival of Cortés created a religious as well as a political crisis, because 1519 marked the end of a 52-year cycle.

The Olmecs were succeeded by two Classic cultures. The city and empire of Teotihuacan emerged in the mountains not far from modern Mexico City. Mayan culture took shape mostly in the southern lowlands of Yucatán.

Teotihuacan was already a city of 40,000 by A.D. 1. Its most impressive art form was its brightly painted murals, of which only a few survive. Teotihuacan invested resources in comfortable apartment dwellings for ordinary residents, not in monuments or inscriptions to rulers. It was probably governed by something like a senate, not by a monarch. The city was able to extend its influence throughout Mesoamerica and remained a powerful force until its sudden destruction around A.D. 750, when its shrines were toppled and the city was abandoned. In all likelihood, Teotihuacan's growth had so depleted the resources of the area that the city could not have sustained itself much longer.

In the lowlands, Classic Mayan culture went through a similar cycle from expansion to ecological crisis. It was also urban but less centralized than that of Teotihuacan. For more than 1,000 years, Mayan culture rested upon a network of competing city-states. One of the largest Mayan cities, Tikal, controlled commerce with Teotihuacan. Tikal housed 100,000 at its peak before A.D. 800. Twenty other cities, most about one-fourth the size of Tikal, flourished throughout the region. Mayan engineers built canals to water the crops needed to support this urban system, which was well established by the 1st century B.C.

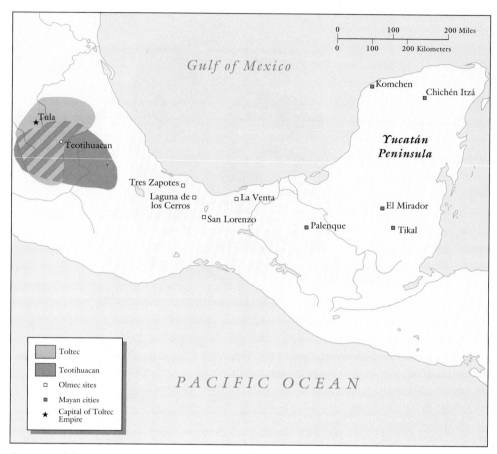

ANCIENT MESOAMERICA

The earliest Mayan writings date to 50 B.C., but few survive from the next 300 years. Around A.D. 300, Mayans began to record their history in considerable detail. Since 1960 scholars have been able to decipher most Mayan inscriptions. Mayan art and writings reveal the religious beliefs of these people, including the place of human sacrifice and the role of ritual self-mutilation in their worship. Scholars have learned, for example, about the long reign of Pacal the Great, king (or "Great Sun") of the elegant city of Palenque, who was born on March 26, 603, and died on August 31, 683. His sarcophagus lists his ancestors through six generations. Other monuments tell of the Great Suns of other cities whom Pacal vanquished and sacrificed to the gods.

Classic Mayan culture began to collapse about 50 years after the fall of Teotihuacan, which disrupted Mayan trade with the Valley of Mexico. The crisis spread rapidly. Palenque and a half-dozen other cities were abandoned between 800 and 820. The last date recorded at Tikal was in 869; the last in the southern lowlands came 40 years later. The Mayan aristocracy had grown faster than the ability of commoners to support it, until population outstripped local resources.

MAYAN SACRIFICIAL VICTIM   Human sacrifice played a major role in Mesoamerican religion. The artist who crafted this disemboweled man recognized the agony of the victim.

Frequent wars hastened the decline. Trade with the Valley of Mexico shifted north to other cities. With the collapse of the southern cities, the population of the region fell drastically.

After A.D. 900, the Post-Classic era saw a kind of Mayan renaissance in the northern lowlands of the Yucatán, where many refugees from the south had fled. Chichén Itzá, a city that had existed for centuries, preserved many distinctive Mayan traits but now merged them with new influences from the Valley of Mexico, where the Toltecs had become dominant in the high country and may even have conquered Chichén Itzá. The Toltecs were a fierce warrior people whose capital at Tula, with 40,000 people, was one-fifth as large as Teotihuacan at its peak. They prospered from the cocoa trade with tropical lowlands but otherwise did nothing to expand the region's food supply. They controlled the Valley of Mexico for almost three centuries, until about A.D. 1200 when they too declined.

THE AZTECS AND TENOCHTITLÁN

By 1400 power in the Valley of Mexico was passing to the Aztecs, a warrior people who had migrated from the north about two centuries earlier and had settled on the shore of Lake Texcoco. They then built a great city, Tenochtitlán, out on the lake itself. Its only connection with the mainland was by several broad causeways. The Aztecs raised their agricultural productivity by creating highly productive *chinampas,* or floating gardens, right on the lake. Yet their mounting population strained the food supply. In the 1450s the threat of famine was severe.

As newcomers to the region, the Aztecs felt a need to prove themselves worthy heirs to the ancient culture of the Valley of Mexico. They adopted the old religion but practiced it with a terrifying intensity. They waged perpetual war to gain captives for their ceremonies. They built and constantly rebuilt and enlarged their Great Pyramid of the Sun. At its dedication in 1487, they sacrificed—if we can believe later accounts—about 14,000 people. Each captive climbed the steep steps of the pyramid and was held by his wrists and ankles over the sacrificial slab while a priest cut open his breast, ripped out his heart, held it up to the sun, placed it inside the statue of a god, and then rolled the carcass down the steps so that parts of the body could be eaten, mostly by members of the captor's family, but never by the captor himself. He fasted instead, and mourned the death of a worthy foe.

Human sacrifice was an ancient ritual in Mesoamerica, familiar to everyone. But the Aztecs practiced it on a scale that had no parallel anywhere else in the world. The need for thousands of victims each year created potential enemies everywhere. After 1519, many Indians in Mesoamerica would help the Spaniards bring down the Aztecs. By contrast, the Spanish found few allies in the Andes, where resistance in the name of the Inca would persist for most of the 16th century.

NORTH AMERICAN MOUND BUILDERS

North of Mexico, from 3000 B.C. to about A.D. 1700, three distinct cultures of "mound builders" exerted a powerful influence over the interior of North America. These cultures arose near the Ohio and Mississippi Rivers and their tributaries. The earliest mound builders became semi-sedentary even before learning to grow crops. Fish, game, and the lush vegetation of the river valleys sustained them for most of the year and enabled them to erect permanent dwellings.

The oldest mound building culture appeared among a preagricultural people in what is now northeastern Louisiana around 3400 B.C., at a site called Watson Break. Later, just 40 miles away, early mound builders flourished from 1500 B.C. to 700 B.C. at Poverty Point, a center that contained perhaps 5,000 people at its peak around 1000 B.C. The second mound building culture, the Adena-Hopewell, emerged between 500 B.C. and A.D. 400 in the Ohio River valley. Its mounds were increasingly elaborate burial sites, indicating belief in an afterlife. Mound building communities participated in a commerce that spanned most of the continent between the Appalachians and the Rockies, the Great Lakes and the Gulf of Mexico. Obsidian from the Yellowstone Valley in the Far West, copper from the Great Lakes basin, and shells from the Gulf of Mexico have all been found buried in the Adena-Hopewell mounds. Both the mound building and the long-distance trade largely ceased after A.D. 400, for reasons that remain unclear.

Mound building revived in a third and final Mississippian phase between A.D. 1000 and 1700. This culture dominated the Mississippi River valley from modern St. Louis to Natchez, with the largest center at Cahokia in present-day Illinois, and another important one at Moundville in Alabama. In this culture, the "Great Sun" ruled and was transported by litter from place to place. When he died, some of his wives, relatives, and retainers even volunteered to be sacrificed at his funeral and join him in the afterlife. Burial mounds thus became much grander in Mississippian communities.

The city of Cahokia, near modern St. Louis, flourished from A.D. 900 to 1250 and may have had 30,000 residents at its peak, making it the largest city north of Mexico. Cahokia's enormous central mound, 100 feet high, is the world's largest earthen work. Similarities with Mesoamerican practices and artifacts have led many scholars to look for direct links between

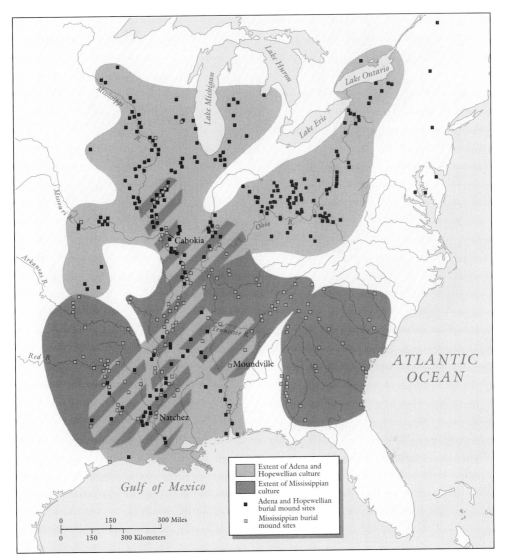

MOUND BUILDING CULTURES OF NORTH AMERICA

the two cultures. But although travel was possible between Mesoamerica and the Mississippi valley, no Mesoamerican artifacts have yet been found in the southeastern United States.

URBAN CULTURES OF THE SOUTHWEST

Other complex societies emerged in North America's semiarid Southwest—among them the Hohokam, the Anasazi, and the Pueblo. The Hohokam Indians settled in what is now central Arizona somewhere between 300 B.C. and A.D. 300. Their irrigation system, consisting of several hundred miles of canals, produced two harvests a year. They wove cotton cloth and made

Modern Restoration of an Anasazi *Kiva* This *kiva,* or meeting room of the Anasazi, was located underground and was accessed by ladder through a hole in the ceiling.

pottery with a distinctive red color. They traded with places as distant as California and Mesoamerica. Perhaps because unceasing irrigation had increased the salinity of the soil, this culture declined by 1450.

Even more tantalizing and mysterious is the brief flowering of the Anasazi, a cliff-dwelling people who have left behind some remarkable artifacts at Chaco Canyon in New Mexico, at Mesa Verde in Colorado, and at other sites. In their caves and cliffs they constructed apartment houses five stories high with as many as 500 dwellings and with elegant and spacious *kivas,* or meeting rooms for religious functions. The Anasazi were superb astronomers. Through an arrangement of rock slabs, open to the sun and moon at the mouth of a cave, and of spirals on the interior wall that plotted the movement of the sun and moon, they created a calendar that could track the summer and winter solstices and even the 19-year cycles of the moon. To get to their fields and to bring in lumber and other distant supplies, they built a network of roads that ran for scores of miles in several directions. They flourished for about two centuries and then, in the last quarter of the 13th century, apparently overwhelmed by a prolonged drought and by hostile invaders, they abandoned their principal sites. Pueblo architecture resembles that of the Anasazi, and the Pueblo Indians claim descent from them.

Contact and Cultural Misunderstanding

After the voyage of Columbus, the peoples of Europe and America, both with ancient pasts, confronted each other. Nothing in the histories of Europeans or Indians had prepared either of them for the encounter.

AZTEC SKULL RACK ALTAR   This rack held the skulls of hundreds of sacrificial victims and shocked the invading Spaniards.

RELIGIOUS DILEMMAS

Christians had trouble understanding how Indians could exist at all. The Bible never mentioned the Indians. Were they the "lost 10 tribes" of Israel, perhaps? Some theologians, such as the Spaniard Juan Ginés de Sepúlveda, tried to resolve this dilemma by arguing that Indians were animals without souls, not human beings at all. The pope and the royal courts of Portugal and Spain listened instead to a Dominican missionary, Fray Bartolomé de Las Casas, who insisted on the Indians' humanity. But, asked Europeans, if Indians did possess immortal souls, would a compassionate God have failed to make the Gospel known to them? Some early Catholic missionaries concluded that one of the apostles must have visited America (and India) and that the Indians must have rejected his message. The Portuguese announced in the 1520s that they had discovered the tomb of St. Thomas the Doubter in India, and then in 1549 a Jesuit claimed to have found Thomas's footprint in Brazil. If only to satisfy the spiritual yearnings of Europeans overseas, St. Thomas got around!

To Europeans, the sacrificial temples, skull racks, and snake motifs of Mesoamerica led to only one conclusion: The Aztecs worshiped Satan himself. Human sacrifice and ritual cannibalism were indeed widespread throughout the Americas. The Incas, whose creation myth resembled that of Mesoamerica, offered an occasional victim to the sun or to some other god. The Indians of eastern North America frequently tortured to death their adult male captives. Christians were shocked by human sacrifice and found cannibalism revolting, but Indians regarded certain European practices with equal horror. Between 1500 and 1700, Europeans burned or hanged perhaps 100,000 people, usually old women, for conversing with the wrong spirits—that is, for witchcraft. The Spanish Inquisition burned thousands of heretics. To the Indians, such executions looked like human sacrifices.

On his second voyage, Columbus brought the first missionaries to the Americas. After one of them preached to a group of Tainos and presented them with some holy images, the Indians "left the chapel, . . . flung the images to the ground, covered them with a heap of earth, and pissed upon it." The governor had them burned alive. The Indians probably saw this punishment as a form of human sacrifice to a vengeful god.

Even the moral message conveyed by Christians was ambiguous. Missionaries eagerly brought news of how Christ had died to save mankind from sin. Catholic worship, then as now, centered on the Mass and the Eucharist, in which a priest transforms bread and wine into the literal body and blood of Christ. Most Protestants also accepted this sacrament but interpreted it symbolically, not literally. To the Indians, Christians seemed to be a people who ate their own god but grew outraged at the lesser matter of sacrificing a human being to please an Indian god.

When Europeans tried to convert Indians to Christianity, the Indians concluded that the converts would spend the afterlife with the souls of Europeans, separated forever from their own ancestors, whose memory they revered. Neither side fully recognized these obstacles to mutual understanding. Although early Catholic missionaries converted thousands of Indians, the results were, at best, mixed. Most converts adopted some Christian practices while continuing many of their old rituals, often in secret.

War as Cultural Misunderstanding

Such misunderstandings multiplied as Indians and Europeans came into closer contact. Both waged war, but with different objectives. Europeans tried to settle matters on the battlefield and expected to kill many enemies. Indians fought mostly to obtain captives, whether for sacrifice (as with the Aztecs) or to replace tribal losses through adoption (as with the Iroquois). To them, massive deaths on the battlefield were an appalling waste of life that could in no way appease the gods. Europeans and Indians also differed profoundly on what acts constituted atrocities. The torture and ritual sacrifice of captives horrified Europeans; the slaughter of women and children, which Europeans brought to America, appalled Indians.

Gender and Cultural Misunderstanding

Indian social organization also differed fundamentally from that of Europeans. European men owned almost all property, set the rules of inheritance, farmed the land, and performed nearly all public functions. Among many Indian peoples, descent was matrilineal (traced through the maternal line) and women owned nearly all movable property. European men felt incomplete unless they acquired authority over other people, usually the other members of their households. Indian men had no patriarchal ambitions. Women did the farming in semisedentary Indian cultures, and they often could demand a war or try to prevent one, although the final decision rested with men. When Europeans tried to change warriors into farmers, Indian males protested that they were being turned into women. Only over fully sedentary peoples were Europeans able to impose direct rule, because there they could build upon the social hierarchy, division of labor, and system of tribute already in place.

CONQUEST AND CATASTROPHE

Spanish *conquistadores,* or conquerors, led small armies that rarely exceeded 1,000 men. Yet they subdued two empires much larger than Spain itself and then looked around for more worlds to overrun. There, beyond the great empires, Indians had more success in resisting them.

THE CONQUEST OF MEXICO AND PERU

When Cortés entered Tenochtitlán in 1519, he seized Moctezuma, the Aztec ruler, as prisoner and hostage. Though overwhelmingly outnumbered, Cortés and his men began to destroy Aztec religious objects, replacing them with images of the Virgin Mary or other Catholic saints. In response, while Cortés was away, the Aztecs rose against the intruders, Moctezuma was killed, and the Spaniards were driven out with heavy losses. But the smallpox the Spaniards left behind was soon killing Aztecs by the thousands. Cortés found refuge with the nearby Tlaxcalans, a proudly independent people. With thousands of their warriors,

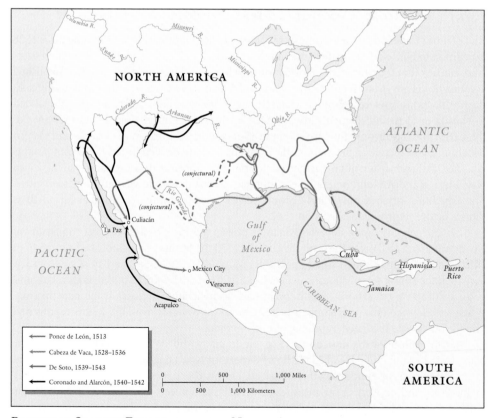

PRINCIPAL SPANISH EXPLORATIONS OF NORTH AMERICA

he returned the next year and destroyed Tenochtitlán. With royal support from Spain, the *conquistadores* established themselves as new imperial rulers in Mesoamerica, looted all the silver and gold they could find, and built Mexico City on the ruins of Tenochtitlán.

Rumors abounded about an even richer empire far to the south, and in 1531 and 1532 Francisco Pizarro finally located the Inca Empire high in the Andes. Smallpox had preceded him and had killed the reigning Inca. In the civil war that followed, Atahualpa had defeated his brother to become the new Inca. Pizarro captured Atahualpa, held him hostage, and managed to win a few allies from among the Inca's recent enemies. Atahualpa paid a huge ransom, but Pizarro had him strangled anyway. Tens of thousands of angry Indians besieged the Spaniards for months in Cuzco, the Inca capital, but Pizarro, though vastly outnumbered, managed to hold out and finally prevailed. After subduing the insurgents, the Spanish established a new capital at Lima on the coast.

In a little more than 10 years, some hundreds of Spanish soldiers with thousands of Indian allies had conquered two enormous empires with a combined population perhaps five times greater than that of all Spain. But only in the 1540s did the Spanish finally locate the bonanza they had been seeking. The fabulous silver mines at Potosí in present-day Bolivia and other smaller lodes in Mexico became the source of Spain's wealth and power for the next 100 years.

North American *Conquistadores* and Missionaries

Alvar Núñez Cabeza de Vaca was one of four survivors of Pánfilo de Narváez's disastrous 1528 expedition to Florida. Cabeza de Vaca made his way back to Mexico City in 1536 after an overland journey that took him from Florida through Texas and northern Mexico. In a published account of his adventures, he briefly mentioned Indian tales of great and populous cities to the north, and this reference soon became stories of "golden cities." Hernando de Soto landed in Florida in 1539 and roamed through much of the southeastern United States in quest of these treasures. He crossed the Mississippi in 1541, wandered through the Ozarks and eastern Oklahoma, and then marched back to the great river, where he died in 1542. His companions returned to Spanish territory. Farther west, Francisco Vasquez de Coronado marched into New Mexico and Arizona, where he encountered several Pueblo towns but no golden cities. The expedition reached the Grand Canyon, then headed east into Texas and as far north as Kansas before returning to Mexico in 1542.

After the *conquistadores* departed, Spanish priests did their best to convert thousands of North American Indians to the Catholic faith. In 1570 the Jesuits even established a mission in what is now Virginia. When some Spaniards reconnoitered Chesapeake Bay at midcentury, they took the young son of a local chief back to Spain, where he was baptized as Don Luis and given a European education. Then he went back to his people to assist at the new mission. When he celebrated his homecoming in 1571 by taking several wives, the Jesuits reproached him for his sin. He retaliated by wiping out the mission.

After the failure of the mission in 1571, the Jesuits withdrew and Franciscans took their place. In 1573 King Philip II issued the Royal Orders for New Discoveries, which made it illegal to enslave Indians or even attack them. Instead, unarmed priests were to bring them together in missions and convert them into peaceful Catholic subjects of Spain. The Franciscans quickly discovered that, without military support, they were more likely to win martyrdom than converts. They reluctantly accepted military protection.

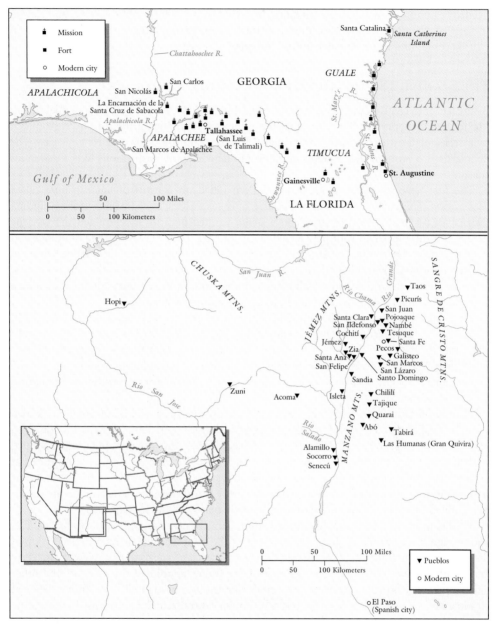

Mission
■ **Fort**
○ **Modern city**

SANTA CATALINA ▪ *Santa Catherines Island*
Chattahoochee R.
GEORGIA
GUALE
APALACHICOLA
San Nicolás ▪ San Carlos
ATLANTIC OCEAN
La Encarnación de la Santa Cruz de Sabacola
Apalachicola R.
Tallahassee
APALACHEE (San Luis de Talimali)
San Marcos de Apalachee
St. Marys R.
St. Johns R.
TIMUCUA
Gulf of Mexico
Gainesville ○
▪ **St. Augustine**
LA FLORIDA

0 50 100 Miles
0 50 100 Kilometers

CHUSKA MTNS.
San Juan R.
SANGRE DE CRISTO MTNS.
Hopi ▼
JÉMEZ MTNS.
Rio Chama
Rio Grande
▼ Taos
▼ Picurís
San Juan ▼
Santa Clara ▼ Pojoaque ▼
San Ildefonso ▼ Nambé ▼
Cochití ▼ Tesuque ▼
Jémez ▼ ○ ▼ Santa Fe
Zia ▼ Pecos ▼
Santa Ana ▼ ▼ Galisteo
San Felipe ▼ San Marcos
Sandia ▼ San Lázaro
Santo Domingo
Rio San Jose
Zuni ▼
Acoma ▼ Isleta ▼
MANZANO MTS.
▼ Chililí
▼ Tajique
▼ Quarai
Abó ▼ ▼ Tabirá
▼ Las Humanas (Gran Quivira)
Rio Salado
Alamillo ▼
Socorro ▼
Senecú ▼

0 50 100 Miles
0 50 100 Kilometers

▼ **Pueblos**
○ **Modern city**

○ El Paso (Spanish city)

SPANISH MISSIONS IN FLORIDA AND NEW MEXICO, CIRCA 1675

Franciscans had no success among the nomadic residents of central and southern Florida. They had to build their missions within the permanent villages of northern Florida or the Pueblo communities of New Mexico. At first Indian women willingly supplied the labor needed to build and sustain these missions. By 1630 about 86,000 Pueblo, Apache, and Navajo Indians of New Mexico had accepted baptism. By midcentury there were 30 missions in Florida containing about 26,000 baptized Indians.

THE SPANISH EMPIRE AND DEMOGRAPHIC CATASTROPHE

By the late 16th century, the Spanish Empire had emerged as a system of direct colonial rule in Mexico and Peru, protected by a strong defensive perimeter in the Caribbean, and surrounded by a series of frontier missions, extending in the north into Florida and New Mexico. The Spaniards also brought new systems of labor and new religious institutions to their overseas colonies.

The first Spanish rulers in Mexico and Peru relied on a form of labor tribute called *encomienda.* This system permitted the holder, or *encomendero,* to claim labor from an Indian district for a stated period of time. *Encomienda* worked because it resembled the way the Aztecs and the Incas had routinely levied labor for their own massive public buildings and irrigation projects. In time, the king intervened to correct abuses and to limit labor tribute to projects that the Crown initiated, such as mining. Spanish settlers resisted the reforms at first but then shifted from demanding labor to claiming land. In the countryside the *hacienda,* a large estate with its own crops and herds, became a familiar institution.

The Church became a massive presence during the 16th century, but America changed it, too. As missionaries acquired land and labor, they began to exhibit less zeal for Indian souls. The Franciscans—in Europe, the gentlest of Catholic religious orders—systematically tortured their Mayan converts whenever they caught them worshiping their old gods. To the Franciscans, the slightest lapse could signal a reversion to Satan-worship, with human sacrifice a likely consequence.

Most important of all, the Spaniards brought deadly microbes with them. Smallpox, which could be fatal but which most Europeans survived in childhood, devastated the Indians, who had almost no immunity to it. When Cortés arrived in 1519, the Indian population of Mexico probably exceeded 15 million. In the 1620s, after waves of killing epidemics, it bottomed at 700,000. For the hemisphere as a whole, any given region probably lost 90 or 95 percent of its population within a century of sustained contact with Europeans. Lowland tropical areas usually suffered the heaviest casualties; in some of these places, all the Indians died.

The Spanish Crown eventually imposed administrative order on the unruly *conquistadores* and brought peace to its colonies. At the center of the imperial bureaucracy, in Seville, stood the Council of the Indies. It administered the three American viceroyalties of New Spain, Peru, and eventually New Granada. The Council of the Indies appointed the viceroys and other major officials, who ruled from the new cities that the Spaniards built with Indian labor at Havana, Mexico City, Lima, and elsewhere. Although centralized and autocratic in theory, the Spanish Empire allowed local officials a fair degree of initiative, if only because months or even years could elapse in trying to communicate across its immense distances.

BRAZIL

Portuguese Brazil was divided into 14 "captaincies," or provinces, and thus was far less centralized. After the colonists on the northeast coast turned to raising sugar in the late 16th century, Brazilian frontiersmen, or *bandeirantes,* foraged deep into the continent to enslave thousands of Indians. They even raided remote Spanish Andean missions, rounded up the converts, and dragged them thousands of miles to be worked to death on the sugar plantations. In the 17th century Africans gradually replaced Indians as the dominant labor force. Brazil was the major market for African slaves until the 1640s, when Caribbean demand became even greater.

GLOBAL COLOSSUS, GLOBAL ECONOMY

American silver made the king of Spain the most powerful monarch in Christendom. Philip II (1556–1598) commanded the largest army in Europe. In 1580, when the king of Portugal died with no direct heir, Philip claimed his throne, thus uniting under his own rule Portugal's Asian empire, Brazil, Spain's American possessions, and the Philippines. This colossus was the greatest empire the world had ever seen. It also sustained the first truly global economy, because the Portuguese used Spain's American silver to pay for the spices and silks they imported from Asia.

The Spanish colossus became part of an even broader economic pattern. Serfdom, which tied peasants to their lords and to the land, had been declining in western Europe since the 12th century and was nearly gone by 1500. A system of free labor arose in its place, and overseas expansion strengthened that trend within western Europe. Although free labor prevailed in the western European homeland, unfree labor systems took root all around

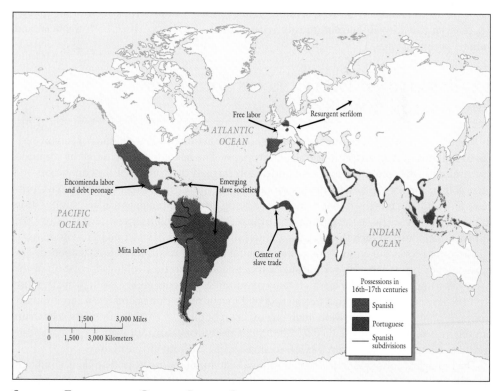

SPANISH EMPIRE AND GLOBAL LABOR SYSTEM

Europe's periphery, and the two were structurally linked. In general, free labor reigned where populations were dense and still growing. Large pools of labor kept wages low. But around the periphery of western Europe, where land was cheap and labor expensive, coercive systems became the only efficient way for Europeans to extract from those areas the goods they desired.

The forms of unfree labor varied greatly across space and time. In New Spain, the practice of *encomienda* slowly yielded to debt peonage. Debts that could not be paid kept Indians tied to the *haciendas* of the countryside. The mining of precious metals, on the other hand, was so dangerous and unpleasant that it almost always required a coercive system of labor tribute that was called *mita* in the Andes. Similarly, any colonial region that devoted itself to the production of staple crops for sale in Europe also turned to unfree labor and eventually to overt slavery. The production of sugar first reduced Indians to bondage in the Caribbean and Brazil and then, as they died off, led to the importation of African slaves by the millions. Tobacco, rice, cotton, and coffee followed similar patterns. At first these crops were considered luxuries and commanded high prices. But as they became widely available on the world market, their prices fell steeply, profit margins contracted, and planters turned overwhelmingly to coerced labor. Even in eastern Europe, which began to specialize in producing cereal crops for sale in the more diversified West, serfdom vigorously revived.

Spain's rise had been spectacular, but its empire was vulnerable. The costs of continuous conflict, the inflation generated by a steady influx of silver, and the need to defend a much greater perimeter absorbed Spain's new resources and a great deal more. Between 1492 and 1580 Spain's population grew from 4.9 million to 8 million. But over the course of the following century, it fell by 20 percent, mostly because of the escalating costs, both financial and human, of Spain's wars.

EXPLANATIONS: PATTERNS OF CONQUEST, SUBMISSION, AND RESISTANCE

By the middle of the 18th century, conquest and settlement had killed millions of Indians, enslaved millions of Africans, and degraded Europeans. The benefits seemed small by comparison, even though economic gains were undeniably large. If the cruelest of the conquerors had been able to foresee the results of this process, asked the Abbé Raynal, would he have proceeded? "Is it to be imagined that there exists a being infernal enough to answer this question in the affirmative!" The success of the American Revolution, with its message of freedom and human rights, quieted such thinking for a time, but the critique has revived in recent years.

Modern historians are more interested in asking how and why these things happened. The most compelling explanation for European success focuses on the prolonged isolation of the Americas from the rest of the world. If two communities of equal ability are kept apart, those with the larger and more varied population will invent more things and learn more rapidly from one another over time. More than any other technological edge, far more than firearms or even horses, steel made military conquest possible. European armor stopped Indian spears and arrows, and European swords killed enemies swiftly without any need to reload.

The biological consequences of isolation were even more momentous than the technological. The Indians' genetic makeup was more uniform than that of Europeans, Africans, or Asians. Indians were descended from a rather small sample of the total gene pool of Eurasia.

CHRONOLOGY

50,000–40,000 B.C.	Possible early migration across Beringia to America
23,000–10,000 B.C.	Migration across Beringia to America
9000–7000 B.C.	Most large American mammals become extinct
5000–700 B.C.	Cultures of the Red Paint People and the Louisiana mound builders thrive
1600 B.C.	Polynesian migrations begin (reaching Hawaii by 100 A.D.)
500 B.C.–A.D. 400	Adena-Hopewell mound builders emerge in Ohio River valley
874	Norsemen reach Iceland
900–1250	Toltecs dominate the Valley of Mexico • Cahokia becomes largest Mississippian mound builders' city • Anasazi culture thrives in American Southwest
982	Norse settle Greenland
1001–1014	Norse found Newfoundland colony
1400s	Incas begin to dominate the Andes; Aztecs begin to dominate Mesoamerica (1400–1450) • Cheng Ho makes voyages of exploration for China (1405–1434) • Portuguese begin to master the Atlantic coast of Africa (1434) • First Portuguese slave factory established on African coast (1448) • Dias reaches Cape of Good Hope (1487) • Columbus reaches the Caribbean (1492) • Treaty of Tordesillas divides non-Christian world between Portugal and Spain (1494) • da Gama rounds Cape of Good Hope and reaches India (1497–1499)
1500s	Portuguese discover Brazil (1500) • Balboa crosses Isthmus of Panama to the Pacific (1513) • Magellan's fleet circumnavigates the globe; Cortés conquers the Aztec Empire (1519–1522) • de Vaca makes overland journey from Florida to Mexico (1528–1536) • Pizarro conquers the Inca Empire (1531–1532) • de Soto's expedition explores the American Southeast (1539–1543) • Coronado's expedition explores the American Southwest (1540–1542) • Jesuit mission established at Chesapeake Bay (1570–1571) • Philip II issues Royal Order for New Discoveries (1573) • Philip II unites Spanish and Portuguese empires (1580)

The Indians first encountered by Europeans were bigger, stronger, and—at first contact—healthier than the newcomers. But they died in appalling numbers because they had almost no resistance to European diseases.

European plants also thrived at the expense of native vegetation. For example, when British settlers first crossed the Appalachian Mountains, they marveled at the lush Kentucky blue-grass. They did not realize that they were looking at an accidental European import that had conquered the landscape even faster than they had. European animals also prevailed over potential American rivals. Horses multiplied at an astonishing rate in America, and wild herds moved north from Mexico faster than the Spaniards, transforming the way of life of the Apaches and the Sioux. But some life-forms also moved from the Americas to Europe, Asia, and Africa. Indians probably gave syphilis to the first Europeans they met. Other American exports, such as corn, potatoes, and tomatoes, were far more benign and have enriched the diet of the rest of the world.

CONCLUSION

For thousands of years the Americas had been cut off from the rest of the world. The major cultures of Eurasia and Africa had existed in relative isolation, engaging in direct contact only with their immediate neighbors. Islam, which shared borders with India, the East Indies, black Africa, and Europe, had been the principal mediator among these cultures. Then suddenly, in just 40 years, daring European navigators joined the world together and challenged Islam's mediating role. Between 1492 and 1532 Europe, Africa, Asia, the Spice Islands, the Philippines, the Caribbean, Aztec Mexico, Inca Peru, and other parts of the Americas came into intense and often violent contact with one another. Spain acquired a military advantage within Europe that would last for a century. Nearly everybody else suffered, especially in the Americas and Africa. And Spain spent the rest of the 16th century trying to create an imperial system that could impose order on this turbulent reality.

But Spain had many enemies. The lure of wealth and land overseas would be just as attractive to them as it was to Spaniards.

THE CHALLENGE TO SPAIN
AND THE SETTLEMENT OF
NORTH AMERICA

Catholic France and two Protestant countries, the Dutch Republic and England, challenged Spanish power in Europe and then overseas. Before 1600 none of them planted a permanent settlement in North America. In the quarter-century after 1600, they all did. The French converted thousands of Indians. The French and Dutch traded European goods for furs. By 1700 the English, who coveted the land itself, had founded 12 permanent colonies in North America and others in the West Indies.

In Mexico and Peru, the Spaniards had set themselves up as a European ruling class over a much larger Indian population of farmers, artisans, and miners. Spain's rivals created colonies of different kinds. Some, such as Virginia and Barbados, grew staple crops with indentured servants and African slaves. New France and New Netherland prospered from a thriving trade with the Indians without trying to rule them. In New England, the Puritans relied on free labor provided by hard-working family members. After 1660 the English state conquered New Netherland, and English Quakers created another free-labor society in the Delaware valley.

THE PROTESTANT REFORMATION AND
THE CHALLENGE TO SPAIN

By the time Spain's enemies felt strong enough to challenge Spain overseas, the Protestant Reformation had shattered the religious unity of Europe. In November 1517 Martin Luther

35

nailed his 95 Theses to the cathedral door at Wittenberg in the German electorate of Saxony and touched off the Reformation. No human act, or "good work," Luther insisted, can be meritorious in the sight of God. Salvation comes through faith alone, and God grants saving faith only to those who admit that, without God's grace, they are damned. Within a generation, the states of northern Germany and Scandinavia had embraced Lutheranism.

John Calvin, a French Protestant, also embraced justification by faith alone and put his own militant principles into practice in the Swiss canton of Geneva. The Huguenot movement in France, the Dutch Reformed Church in the Netherlands, and the Presbyterian Kirk (or Church) of Scotland all embraced Calvin's principles. In England the formal doctrine (but not the liturgy) of the Anglican Church became Calvinist, prompting a reform movement, Puritanism, that challenged the English church as insufficiently Calvinist. Calvinists won major victories over Catholics in Europe in the last half of the 16th century. After 1620 Puritans carried their religious vision across the Atlantic to New England.

Calvinists rejected papal supremacy, the seven sacraments (they kept only baptism and the Lord's Supper), clerical celibacy, veneration of the saints, and the acts of charity and the penitential rituals by which Catholics tried to earn grace and store up merits. Calvin gave central importance to predestination. According to that doctrine, God has already decreed who will be saved and who will be damned. Christ died not for all humankind, but only for God's elect. Because salvation and damnation were beyond human power to alter, Calvinists—especially English Puritans—felt a compelling inner need to find out whether they were saved. They struggled to recognize in themselves a conversion experience, the process by which God's elect discovered that they had been chosen.

France, the Netherlands, and England, all with powerful Protestant movements, challenged Spanish power in Europe. Until 1559 France was the main threat, but Spain won that phase. Then in the 1560s, with France embroiled in its own Wars of Religion, a new challenge came from a rebellion in the 17 provinces of the Netherlands, which Spain ruled. As Spanish armies put down the revolt in the 10 southern provinces (modern Belgium), merchants and Protestants fled north. Many went to Amsterdam, which replaced Spanish-controlled Antwerp as the economic center of northern Europe. The seven northern provinces gradually took shape as the Dutch Republic, or the United Provinces of the Netherlands. The Dutch turned their resistance into a war for independence from Catholic Spain. The conflict went on for 80 years, drained Spanish resources, and spread to Asia, Africa, and America.

NEW FRANCE

About 16 million people lived in France in 1500, more than three times the population of Spain. The French made a few stabs at overseas expansion before 1600, but with little success.

EARLY FRENCH EXPLORERS

In 1524 King Francis I (1515–1547) sent Giovanni da Verrazano, an Italian, to America in search of a northwest passage to Asia. Verrazano explored the North American coast from the Carolinas to Nova Scotia but found no passage to Asia. Between 1534 and 1543, Jacques Cartier made three voyages to North America. He sailed up the St. Lawrence River in search of a wealthy kingdom, Saguenay, rumored to be in the interior. Instead he discovered the severity of a Canadian winter and gave up. For the rest of the century, the French ignored Canada.

After 1550 the French turned to warmer climates. Some Huguenots briefly challenged the Portuguese in Brazil. Others sacked Havana, prompting Spain to turn it into a fortified, year-round naval base under the command of Admiral Pedro Menéndez de Avilés. Still others planted a settlement on the Atlantic coast of Florida. Menéndez attacked them in 1565, talked them into surrendering, and then executed every man who refused to accept the Catholic faith.

In France the Wars of Religion blocked further efforts at expansion for the rest of the century. King Henry IV (1589–1610), a Protestant, converted to Catholicism and granted limited toleration to Huguenots through the Edict of Nantes in 1598, thus ending the civil wars. Henry was a *politique,* someone who insisted that the survival of the state must take precedence over religious differences. Another *politique* was the Catholic soldier and explorer, Samuel de Champlain.

MISSIONS AND FURS

Champlain believed that Catholics and Huguenots could work together and even convert the Indians. Before his death in 1635, he made 11 voyages to Canada. During his second trip (1604–1606), he planted a predominantly Huguenot settlement in Acadia (Nova Scotia). In 1608 he sailed up the St. Lawrence River, established friendly relations with the Montagnais, Algonquin, and Huron Indians, and founded Quebec. "Our sons shall wed your daughters," he told them, "and we shall be one people." Many Frenchmen cohabited with Indian women, but only 15 formal marriages took place between them in the 17th century. Champlain's friendliness toward the local Indians drew him into their wars against the Iroquois Five Nations farther south. At times, the hostility of the Iroquois almost destroyed New France.

Champlain failed to unite Catholics and Protestants in mutual harmony. Huguenots in France were eager to trade with Canada, but few settled there. Their ministers showed no interest in converting the Indians, whereas Catholic priests became zealous missionaries. In 1625 the French Crown declared that only the Catholic faith could be practiced in New France, thus ending Champlain's dream. Acadia soon became Catholic as well.

Early New France is a tale of missionaries and furs, of attempts to convert the Indians and of efforts to trade with them. The carousing habits of the first *coureurs de bois* (roamers of the woods), or fur traders, did much for the colonies' commerce but made life difficult for the missionaries.

After 1630 Jesuit missionaries made heroic efforts to bring Christ to the wilderness. Uncompromising in their opposition to Protestants, Jesuits proved remarkably flexible in dealing with non-Christian peoples, from China to North America. Other missionaries insisted that Indians must be Europeanized before they could be converted, but the Jesuits disagreed. They saw nothing contradictory about a nation of Christians that retained its Indian customs.

The Jesuits converted 10,000 Indians in 40 years. After learning to speak several Algonquian and Iroquoian dialects, the Jesuits began to convert the five confederated Huron nations and baptized several thousand of their members. But this success antagonized Indians who were still attached to their own rituals. When smallpox devastated the Hurons in the 1640s, Jesuits baptized hundreds of dying victims to assure their salvation. Many of the Indian survivors noticed that death usually followed this mysterious rite, and their resistance grew stronger. A second disaster occurred when the Iroquois attacked, defeated, and scattered the Hurons. Despite these setbacks, the Jesuits' courage remained strong. They were the only Europeans who measured up to Indian standards of bravery under torture. Some of them, such as Isaac Jogues and Jean de Brebeuf, died as martyrs. But their efforts slowly lost ground to the fur trade, especially after the Crown assumed control of New France in 1663.

NEW FRANCE UNDER LOUIS XIV

Royal intervention transformed Canada after 1663 when Louis XIV and his minister, Jean-Baptiste Colbert, took charge of the colony and tried to turn it into a model absolutist society—peaceful, orderly, deferential. Government was in the hands of two appointive officials, a governor-general responsible for military and diplomatic affairs, and an *intendant* who administered justice.

The governor appointed all militia officers, who earned promotion through merit, not by purchasing a commission. When the Crown sent professional soldiers to New France after 1660, the governor put them under the command of Canadian officers, who knew the woodlands. Colbert also sent 774 young women to the St. Lawrence, to provide brides for settlers

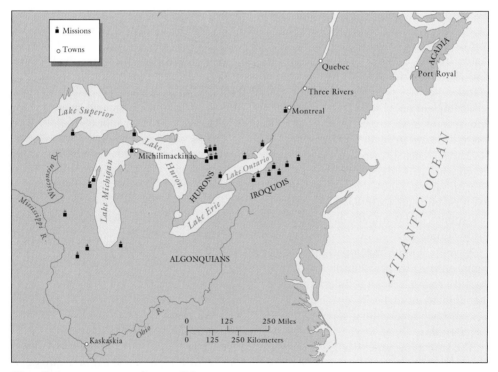

NEW FRANCE AND THE JESUIT MISSIONS

and soldiers. He offered bonuses to couples who produced large families and fined fathers whose children failed to marry while still in their teens. Between 1663 and 1700, the population of New France increased from 3,000 to about 14,000. About one-fourth of the population concentrated in three cities—Quebec, Three Rivers, and Montreal. Montreal, the largest, became the center of the fur trade.

Farming took hold in the St. Lawrence valley, and by the 1690s Canada was growing enough wheat to feed itself and to give its *habitants,* or settlers, a level of comfort about equal to that of contemporary New Englanders. A new class of *seigneurs,* or gentry, claimed most of the land between Quebec and Montreal, but they never exercised the kind of power wielded by aristocrats in France. Yet when the Church was also the *seigneur,* the obligations imposed on farmers could be heavy.

Colbert even tried to ban Frenchmen from Indian territory by limiting the fur trade to annual fairs at Montreal and Quebec. The Indians would have to come to the settlers. But Colbert's policy failed and, by 1700, even led to a quiet rebellion in the west. Hundreds of Frenchmen settled in the Mississippi River valley in what became the Illinois country. By 1750 these communities contained 3,000 residents. The settlers rejected *seigneurs,* feudal dues, and compulsory militia service. They did, however, import African slaves from Louisiana.

But Canada did not long remain the center of French overseas activity. Like other Europeans, most of the French who crossed the Atlantic preferred the warmer climes of the Caribbean. At first the French in the West Indies joined with other enemies of Spain to prey upon Spanish colonies and ships. Then they transformed the island colonies of St. Domingue (modern Haiti), Guadeloupe, and Martinique into centers of sugar production, where a small planter class prospered from the labor of thousands of slaves. In the late 18th century, St. Domingue became the world's richest colony.

THE DUTCH AND SWEDISH SETTLEMENTS

For most of the 17th century, the Dutch were more active overseas than the French. In alliance with France during Europe's Thirty Years' War (1618–1648), the Dutch wore down and finally destroyed Spain's bid for "universal monarchy" in Europe. The Netherlands, the most densely populated part of Europe, surpassed northern Italy in manufacturing and moved ahead of all competitors in finance, shipping, and trade. The Dutch Republic offered an ideological as well as a political challenge to Spanish absolutism.

In contrast to Spain, which stood for Catholic orthodoxy and the centralizing tendencies of Europe's "new monarchies," Dutch republicanism emphasized local liberties, prosperity, and religious toleration. Political power was decentralized to the cities and their wealthy merchants, who favored religious toleration, tried to keep trade as free as possible, and resisted the monarchical ambitions of the House of Orange. The prince of Orange usually served as *stadholder* (captain general) of Holland, the richest province, and commanded its armies.

The Dutch Republic—with numerous Protestant dissenters, a sizable Jewish community, and a Catholic minority—was actually a polyglot confederation. Amsterdam's merchant republicanism competed with Calvinist orthodoxy for the allegiance of the Dutch people. Only during a military crisis could the prince of Orange mobilize the Dutch Reformed clergy and impose something like Calvinist orthodoxy. The States General, to which each province sent representatives, became a weak central government for the republic. The tension between tolerant merchant republicanism and Calvinist orthodoxy carried over into New Netherland.

Profit was the dominant motive in Dutch expansion overseas. By 1600 Dutch commercial assets were already enormous. By 1620 Dutch foreign trade probably exceeded that of the rest of Europe combined. Even during the long war with Spain, the Dutch traded with Lisbon and Seville for products from the East Indies and America. This effrontery so annoyed Philip II that he twice committed a grave blunder in the 1590s, when he confiscated all the Dutch ships crowding his ports. The Dutch retaliated by sailing into the Atlantic and Indian Oceans to acquire colonial goods at the source. The Dutch threat forced Spain to use expensive convoys to protect the silver fleets crossing the Atlantic.

THE EAST AND WEST INDIA COMPANIES

In 1602 the States General chartered the Dutch East India Company, the richest corporation the world had yet seen. It pressured Spain where it was weakest, in the Portuguese East Indies. Elbowing the Portuguese out of the Spice Islands and even out of Nagasaki in Japan, the Dutch set up their own capital at Batavia (now Jakarta) on the island of Java.

The Atlantic and North America also attracted the Dutch. In 1609, Henry Hudson, an Englishman in Dutch service, sailed up what the Dutch called the North River (the English later renamed it the Hudson) and claimed the whole area for the Netherlands. In 1614 some Lutheran refugees from Amsterdam built a fort near modern Albany to trade with the Mahicans and Iroquois for furs.

In 1621 the States General chartered the Dutch West India Company and gave it jurisdiction over the African slave trade, Brazil, the Caribbean, and North America. The West India Company harbored strong Orangist sympathies and even some Calvinist fervor, sustained by refugees from the Spanish army. The company took over Portugal's slave-trading posts in West Africa and for a while even dominated Angola. It also occupied the richest sugar-producing region of Brazil until the Portuguese took it back, as well as Angola, in the 1640s.

In North America the Dutch claimed the Delaware, the Hudson, and the Connecticut river valleys. The company put most of its effort, and some of its religious fervor, into the Hudson valley. The first permanent settlers arrived in 1624. Two years later, Deacon Pierre Minuit, leading 30 Walloon (French-speaking) Protestant refugee families, bought Manhattan Island from the Indians and founded the port of New Amsterdam. The Dutch established Fort Orange (modern Albany) 150 miles upriver for trade with the Iroquois. Much like New France, New Netherland depended on the goodwill of nearby Indians, and the fur trade gave the colony a similar urban flavor. But in contrast to the settlers of New France, few Dutchmen ventured into the deep woods. The Indians brought their furs to Fort Orange and exchanged them for firearms and other goods.

New Netherland resembled New France in other ways. In the 1630s, decades before the French created *seigneuries* in the St. Lawrence valley, the Dutch established "patroonships," vast estates under a single landlord, mostly along the Hudson. But few Dutch settlers had much interest in becoming peasants, and the system never thrived. The one exception was Rensselaerswyck, a gigantic estate on both banks of the Hudson above and below Fort Orange, which exported wheat and flour to the Caribbean.

New Netherland as a Pluralistic Society

New Netherland became North America's first experiment in ethnic and religious pluralism. The Dutch themselves were a mixed people with a Flemish majority and a Walloon minority. Both came to the colony. So did Danes, Norwegians, Swedes, Finns, Germans, and Scots.

The government of the colony tried to utilize this diversity by drawing upon two conflicting precedents from the Netherlands. On the one hand, it appealed to religious refugees by emphasizing the company's militant Calvinist role in the struggle against Spain. This policy, roughly speaking, reflected the Orangist position in the Netherlands. On the other hand, the government recognized that a frank acceptance of religious diversity might stimulate trade. The pursuit of prosperity through toleration was the normal role of the city of Amsterdam in Dutch politics. Minuit and Pieter Stuyvesant represented the religious formula for unity, other governors the commercial alternative. Neither policy worked very well.

After Minuit returned to Europe in 1631, the emphasis shifted rapidly from piety to trade. The Dutch sold muskets to the Iroquois to expand their own access to the fur trade. They began to export grain to the Caribbean. But Willem Kieft, a stubborn and quarrelsome governor, slaughtered a tribe of Indian refugees to whom he had granted asylum from other Indians. This Pavonia Massacre of 1643, which took place across the Hudson from Manhattan, set off a war with nearby Algonquian nations that nearly destroyed New Netherland. By the time Stuyvesant replaced Kieft in 1647, the colony's population had fallen to about 700 people. Stuyvesant made peace and then strengthened town governments and the Dutch Reformed Church. During his administration, the population rose to more than 6,000. Most newcomers arrived as members of healthy families who reproduced readily, enabling the population to double every 25 years.

Swedish and English Encroachments

Minuit, back in Europe, organized another refugee project, this one for Flemings who had been uprooted by the Spanish war. When Dutch authorities refused to back him, he turned for support to the Protestant kingdom of Sweden. He returned to America in 1638 with Flemish and Swedish settlers to found New Sweden, with its capital at Fort Christina (modern Wilmington) near the mouth of the Delaware River, on land claimed by New Netherland. After Minuit died on his return trip to Europe, the colony became less Flemish and Calvinist and more Swedish and Lutheran, at a time when Stuyvesant was trying to make New Netherland an orthodox Calvinist society. In 1654 the Swedes seized Fort Casimir, a Dutch post that provided access to the Delaware. In response, Stuyvesant took over all of New Sweden the next year, and Amsterdam sent over settlers to guarantee Dutch control. Stuyvesant actively persecuted Lutherans in New Amsterdam. Orthodoxy and harmony were not easily reconciled.

The English, already entrenched around Chesapeake Bay to the south and New England to the east (discussed in the next section), threatened to overwhelm the Dutch as they moved from New England onto Long Island and into what is now Westchester County, New York. Kieft welcomed them in the 1640s and gave them local privileges greater than those enjoyed by the Dutch, in the hope that their farms and herds would give the colony valuable exports to the Caribbean. Stuyvesant regarded these "Yankees" (a Dutch word that probably meant "land pirates") as good Calvinists, English-speaking equivalents of his Dutch Reformed settlers. They agitated for a more active role in government, but their loyalty was questionable.

If England attacked the colony, would these Puritans side with the Dutch Calvinists or the Anglican invaders? Stuyvesant learned the unpleasant answer when England attacked him in 1664.

THE CHALLENGE FROM ELIZABETHAN ENGLAND

England's interest in America emerged slowly. In 1497 Henry VII (1485–1509) sent Giovanni Cabato (John Cabot), an Italian mariner, to search for a northwest passage to Asia. Cabot probably reached Newfoundland, which he took to be part of Asia. He sailed again in 1498 with five ships but was lost at sea. Only one vessel returned, but Cabot's voyages gave England a vague claim to portions of the North American coast.

THE ENGLISH REFORMATION

When interest in America revived during the reign of Elizabeth I (1558–1603), England was rapidly becoming a Protestant kingdom. Elizabeth's father, Henry VIII (1509–1547), had broken with the pope to divorce his queen and proclaimed himself the "Only Supreme Head" of the Church of England. Under Elizabeth's younger brother Edward VI (1547–1553), the government embraced Protestantism. Then when Edward died, Elizabeth's older sister Mary I (1553–1558) reimposed Catholicism, burned hundreds of Protestants at the stake, and drove thousands into exile, where many of them became Calvinists. Elizabeth, however, accepted Protestantism, and the exiles returned. The Church of England became Calvinist in doctrine and theology, while still largely Catholic in structure, liturgy, and ritual.

Some Protestants demanded the eradication of Catholic vestiges and the replacement of the Anglican *Book of Common Prayer* with sermons and psalms as the dominant mode of worship. These "Puritans" played a major role in English expansion overseas. More extreme Protestants, called Separatists, denied that the Church of England was a true church and began to set up independent congregations of their own. Some of them would found the small colony of Plymouth.

HAWKINS AND DRAKE

In 1560 England was a rather backward country of 3 million people. Its chief export was coarse woolen cloth, most of which was shipped to the Netherlands. During the 16th century the numbers of both people and sheep grew rapidly, and they sometimes competed for the same land. When farms were enclosed for sheep pasture, laborers were set adrift. Thousands headed for London. Although deaths greatly outnumbered births in London, new arrivals lifted the city's population from 50,000 in 1500 to 200,000 in 1600 and, including the suburbs, to 575,000 by 1700. By then London was the largest city in western Europe. After 1600 internal migration fueled overseas settlement. But before then interest in America was centered not in London, but in the ports of southwestern England that were already involved in the Newfoundland fisheries.

Taking advantage of friendly relations that still prevailed between England and Spain, John Hawkins of Plymouth made three voyages to New Spain between 1562 and 1569. On his first trip he bought slaves from the Portuguese in West Africa and then sold them to the Spaniards in Hispaniola, where he tried to set himself up as a legitimate trader. Spanish authorities disapproved, and on his second voyage he had to trade at gunpoint. On his third trip his six vessels were caught in a Mexican port by the Spanish viceroy, who sank four of them. Hawkins and his young kinsman Francis Drake escaped, both vowing vengeance.

Drake even began to talk of freeing slaves from Spanish tyranny. His most dramatic exploit came between 1577 and 1580 when he rounded Cape Horn and plundered Spanish possessions along the undefended Pacific coast of Peru. Knowing that the Spaniards would be waiting for him if he returned by the same route, he sailed north, explored San Francisco Bay, and continued west around the world to England—the first circumnavigation since Magellan's voyage more than half a century earlier.

Gilbert, Ireland, and America

By the 1560s the idea of permanent colonization intrigued several Englishmen. England had a model close at hand in Ireland, which the English Crown had claimed for centuries. The English formed their preconceptions about Indians largely from contact with the Irish who, claimed one Elizabethan, "live like beasts, void of law and all good order." The English tried to conquer Ulster in the northeast and Munster in the southwest. In Ulster the Protestant invaders drove out most of the residents and took over the land. In Munster they ejected the Catholic leaders and tried to force the remaining Catholic Irish to become tenants under Protestant landlords. Terror became an acceptable tactic, as when the English slaughtered 200 Irish at a Christmas feast in 1574.

Sir Humphrey Gilbert, a well-educated humanist, was one of the most brutal of Elizabeth's captains in the Irish wars of the 1560s. In pacifying Munster in 1569, Gilbert killed nearly everyone in his path and destroyed all the crops, a strategy that the English later employed against Indians. Massacring women and children "was the way to kill the men of war by famine," explained one apologist. For 80 years after 1560, Ireland attracted more English settlers than all American and Caribbean colonies combined. Only after 1641, when the Irish rose and killed thousands of English settlers, did the Western Hemisphere replace Ireland as a preferred site for English colonization.

Fresh from his Irish exploits, Gilbert began to think about colonizing America. In an essay titled "A Discourse How Her Majesty May Annoy the King of Spain" (1577), he proposed that England grab control of the Newfoundland fisheries and urged the founding of settlements close enough to New Spain to provide bases for plundering. He obtained a royal patent in 1578 and sent out a fleet, but his ships got into a fight somewhere short of America and limped back to England. He tried again in 1583. This time his fleet sailed north to claim Newfoundland. The crews of 22 Spanish and Portuguese fishing vessels and 18 French and English ships listened in astonishment as he read his royal patent to them, divided up the land among them, assigned them rents, established the Church of England among this mostly Catholic group, and then sailed away to explore more of the American coast. His own ship went under during a storm.

Ralegh, Roanoke, and War with Spain

Gilbert's half-brother, Sir Walter Ralegh, obtained his own patent from the queen and tried twice to plant a colony in North America. In 1585 he sent a large expedition to Roanoke Island in Pamlico Sound, but the settlers planted no crops and exasperated the Indians with demands for food. In June 1586 the English killed the local chief, Wingina, whose main offense was apparently a threat to resettle his people on the mainland and leave the colonists to starve—or work. Days later, when the expected supply vessels did not arrive on schedule, the colonists sailed back to England on the ships of Sir Francis Drake, who had just burned the Spanish city of St. Augustine. The supply ships reached Roanoke a little later, only to find the site abandoned. They left a small garrison there and sailed off in quest of Spanish plunder. The garrison was never heard from again.

Ralegh sent a second expedition to Roanoke in 1587, one that included women—an indication that he envisioned a permanent colony. When Governor John White went back to England for more supplies, his return to Roanoke was delayed by the assault of the Spanish Armada on England in 1588. By the time he reached Roanoke in 1590, the settlers had vanished, leaving a cryptic message—"CROATOAN"—carved on a tree. The colonists may have settled among the Chesapeake nation of Indians near the entrance to Chesapeake Bay. Sketchy evidence suggests that the Powhatans, the most powerful Indians in the area, wiped out the Chesapeakes, along with any English living with them, in the spring of 1607, just as an English fleet arrived in the bay.

The Spanish Armada touched off a war that lasted until 1604. The exploits of Hawkins, Drake, and Ralegh helped provoke this conflict, as did Elizabeth's intervention in the Dutch war against Spain. The loss of the Armada, first to nimbler English ships in the English Channel and then to fierce storms off the Irish coast, crippled Spain. The war also strained the resources of England.

By 1600 Richard Hakluyt the elder and Richard Hakluyt the younger, his cousin, were publishing accounts of English exploits overseas and offering advice on how to make future colonization efforts more successful. The Hakluyts celebrated the deeds of Hawkins, Drake, Gilbert, and Ralegh, who were all West Country men with large ambitions and limited financial resources. Although their plundering exploits continued to pay, they could not afford to sustain a colony like Roanoke until it could return a profit. Beginning in the 1590s, however, London became involved in American affairs by launching privateering fleets against Spain. The continuation of West Country experience and London capital would make permanent colonization possible.

THE SWARMING OF THE ENGLISH

In the 17th century, more than 700,000 people sailed from Europe or Africa to the English colonies in North America and the Caribbean. Most of the European migrants were unmarried younger sons with no inheritance in England. Most of them arrived as servants. Indeed, at first even many of the Africans were regarded as servants rather than slaves.

THE PATTERN OF SETTLEMENT IN THE ENGLISH COLONIES UP TO 1700

| | WHO CAME (IN THOUSANDS) | | POPULATION IN 1700 (IN THOUSANDS) | |
Region	Europeans	Africans	Europeans	Africans
West Indies	220 (29.6%)	316 (42.5%)	33 (8.3%)	115 (28.8%)
South	135 (18.1%)	30 (4.0%)	82 (20.5%)	22 (5.5%)
Mid-Atlantic	20 (2.7%)	2 (0.3%)	51 (12.8%)	3 (0.8%)
New England	20 (2.7%)	1 (0.1%)	91 (22.8%)	2 (0.5%)
Total	395 (53.1%)	349 (46.9%)	257 (64.4%)	142 (35.6%)

The Europeans who settled in New England or the Hudson and Delaware valleys were the most fortunate. Because Puritans and Quakers migrated as families into wholesome and healthy regions, their population expanded at a rate far beyond anything known in Europe. The descendants of this small, idealistic minority soon became a substantial part of the total population. As the accompanying table shows, the New England and Middle Atlantic colonies together attracted only 5.4 percent of the immigrants, but by 1700 they contained 37 percent of all the people in the English colonies and 55 percent of the Europeans.

THE CHESAPEAKE AND WEST INDIAN COLONIES

In 1606 King James I of England (1603–1625) chartered the Virginia Company with authority to colonize North America between the 34th and 45th parallels. The company had two head-quarters. One, in the English city of Plymouth, raised only a small amount of capital but won jurisdiction over the northern portion of the grant. Known as the Plymouth Company, it carried on the West Country expansionist traditions of Gilbert and Ralegh. In 1607 it planted a colony at Sagadahoc on the coast of Maine. But the colonists found the cold winter and the Abenaki Indians intimidating and abandoned the site in September 1608.

The other branch, which had its offices in London, decided to colonize the Chesapeake Bay area. In 1607 the London Company sent out three ships carrying 104 settlers. They sailed up the Powhatan River (which they renamed the James), landed at a defensible peninsula, built a fort and other crude buildings, and called the place Jamestown. The settlers expected to get local Indians to work for them, much as the Spanish had done. If the Indians proved hostile, the settlers were told to form alliances with more distant Indians and subdue those who resisted. Company officials did not realize that a war chief named Powhatan ruled virtually all of the Indians below the fall line.[1]

THE JAMESTOWN DISASTER

Jamestown was a deathtrap. Only 38 of the original 104 settlers survived the first year. Of the 325 who came before 1609, fewer than 100 remained alive in the spring of that year. Every summer the James River became contaminated around Jamestown and sent out killing waves of dysentery and typhoid fever. Before long malaria also set in.

The survivors owed their good fortune to the resourcefulness of Captain John Smith, a soldier and adventurer. When his explorations uncovered no gold or silver nor any quick route across the continent to Asia, he concentrated instead on sheer survival. He tried to awe Powhatan, maintain friendly relations with him, and buy corn. Through the help of Pocahontas, Powhatan's 12-year-old daughter, he avoided war. Smith clearly believed that Pocahontas saved his life in December 1607. But food remained scarce. The colony had too many gentlemen and specialized craftsmen who considered farming beneath their dignity. Over their protests, Smith set them to work raising grain for four hours a day.

In 1609 the London Company sent out 600 more settlers under Lt. Governor Thomas Gates, but his ship ran aground on Bermuda, and the crew spent a year building another

---

[1] The fall line, defined by the first waterfall encountered on each river by a vessel sailing inland from the sea, marked a significant barrier to penetration of the continent. In the South, the area below the falls is called the tidewater. The land between the falls and the Appalachians is called the piedmont.

CAPTAIN JOHN SMITH SUBDUING OPECHANCANOUGH, THE WARRIOR CHIEF OF THE PAMUNKEY INDIANS, 1608   Note the difference in height between Opechancanough and Smith, even as depicted by a European artist.

vessel. About 400 new settlers reached Virginia before Gates arrived. Smith, after suffering a severe injury in an explosion, was shipped back to England, and the colony lacked firm leadership for the next year. Wearying Powhatan with their endless demands for corn, the settlers provoked the Indian war that Smith had avoided. They almost starved during the winter of 1610. Some escaped to the Indians, but those who were caught fleeing were executed.

When Gates finally reached Jamestown with 175 colonists in June 1610, he found only 60 settlers alive and the food supply nearly exhausted. Gates despaired, packed everyone aboard ship, and started downriver. The small fleet came abreast of the new governor, Thomas West, baron de la Warr, sailing up the James with 300 new colonists. They all went back to Jamestown, and the colony managed to survive.

De la Warr and Gates found themselves in the middle of the colony's first Indian war, which lasted from 1609 to 1614. Powhatan's warriors picked off any settlers who strayed far from Jamestown. The English retaliated by slaughtering whole villages and destroying crops. Their strategy was terroristic. The slaughter of one tribe might intimidate others. The war finally ended after the English captured Pocahontas and used her as a hostage to negotiate peace. She converted to Christianity and in 1614 married John Rolfe, a widower who had fallen in love with her.

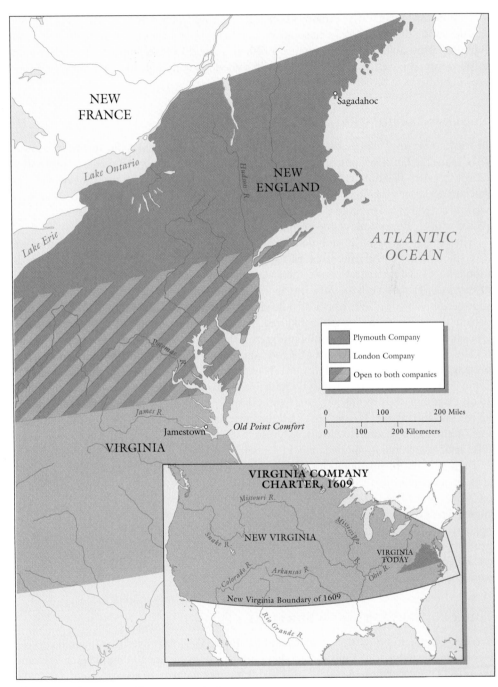

VIRGINIA COMPANY CHARTER, 1606

Despite the Indian war, the colony's prospects improved after 1610. The governors imposed martial law on the settlers and sent some of them to healthier locations. Through the efforts of John Rolfe, the colony began to produce a cash crop. In 1613 Rolfe imported a mild strain of tobacco from the West Indies. It brought such a good price in England that settlers were soon growing tobacco in the streets of Jamestown.

REORGANIZATION, REFORM, AND CRISIS

In 1609 a new royal charter extended Virginia's boundaries to the Pacific. A third charter in 1612 made the London Company a joint-stock company. It resembled a modern corporation except that each stockholder had only one vote regardless of how many shares he owned. The stockholders met quarterly but entrusted everyday management to the company's treasurer, who until 1618 was Sir Thomas Smyth, a wealthy London merchant. In 1618 Smyth was replaced with Sir Edwin Sandys, the Puritan son of the archbishop of York.

The company adopted an ambitious reform program for Virginia. It encouraged economic diversification, such as glassblowing, planting grape vines, and raising silkworms. English common law replaced martial law. The settlers were allowed to elect their own assembly, the House of Burgesses, to meet with the governor and his council and to make local laws. Finally, settlers were permitted to own land. Under this "headright" system, a colonist received 50 acres for each person whose passage to Virginia he financed. By 1623 Sandys had shipped 4,000 settlers to Virginia, but the economic diversification program failed. Only tobacco found a market.

The flood of newcomers strained the food supply and soured relations with the Indians, especially after Powhatan died and was succeeded by his militant brother, Opechancanough. On Good Friday in March 1622, the new chief launched an attack intended to wipe out the whole colony. Without a last-minute warning from a friendly Indian, Jamestown might not have survived. As it turned out, 347 settlers were killed that day, and most of the outlying settlements were destroyed. Newcomers who arrived in subsequent months had nowhere to go and, with food again scarce, hundreds died over the winter.

Back in London, Smyth and his allies turned against Sandys and asked the king to intervene. A royal commission visited the colony and found only 1,200 settlers alive out of the 6,000 sent over since 1607. In 1624 the king declared the London Company bankrupt and assumed direct control of Virginia, making it the first royal colony, with a governor and council appointed by the Crown. The London Company had invested some £200,000 in the enterprise, equal to £1,400 or £1,500 for every surviving settler, at a time when skilled English craftsmen were lucky to earn £50 a year. Such extravagance guaranteed that future colonies would be organized in different ways.

TOBACCO, SERVANTS, AND SURVIVAL

Between Opechancanough's 1622 attack and the 1640s, Virginia proved that it could survive. Despite an appalling death rate, about a thousand new settlers came to Virginia each year, and population grew slowly, to 5,200 by 1634 and 8,100 by 1640. For 10 years the settlers warred against Opechancanough. In 1623 they poisoned 200 Indians they had invited to a peace conference. In most years they attacked the Indians just before harvest time, destroying their crops and villages. By the time both sides made peace in 1632, all Indians had been expelled from the peninsula between the James and York Rivers below Jamestown.

That area became secure for tobacco, and the export of tobacco financed the importation of indentured servants. Most servants were young men who agreed to work for a term of years in exchange for the cost of passage, for bed and board during their years of service, and for modest freedom dues when their terms expired. Those signing indentures in England usually had valuable skills and negotiated terms of four or five years. Those arriving without an indenture, most of whom were younger and less skilled, were sold by the ship captain to a planter. Those over age 19 served five years. Those under 19 served until age 24. The system turned servants into freemen who hoped to prosper on their own. Most former servants became tenants for several years while they tried to save enough to buy their own land.

In 1634 Virginia was divided into counties, each with its own justices of the peace, who sat together as the county court and, by filling their own vacancies, soon became a self-perpetuating oligarchy. Most counties also became Anglican parishes, with a church and a vestry of prominent laymen, usually the justices. The vestry managed temporal affairs for the church, including the choice of the minister. Though the king did not recognize the House of Burgesses until 1639, it met almost every year after 1619 and by 1640 was well established. Before long, only a justice could hope to be elected as a burgess.

Until 1660 many former servants managed to acquire land. Some even served on the county courts and in the House of Burgesses. But as tobacco prices fell after 1660, upward mobility became more difficult. Political offices usually went to the richest 15 percent of the settlers, those able to pay their own way across the Atlantic. They monopolized the posts of justice of the peace and vestryman, the pool from which burgesses and councillors were normally chosen. Virginia was becoming an oligarchy.

MARYLAND

Maryland grew out of the social and religious vision of Sir George Calvert and his son Cecilius, both of whom looked to America as a refuge for persecuted English and Irish Catholics. Sir George had invested in the London Company. When he resigned his royal office after becoming a Catholic, King James I made him baron Baltimore in the Irish peerage.

The Maryland charter of 1632 made Baltimore "lord proprietor" of the colony, the most sweeping delegation of power that the Crown could make. After 1630 most new colonies were proprietary projects. Many of them embodied the distinctive social ideals of their founders.

George Calvert died as the Maryland patent was being issued, and Cecilius inherited Maryland and the peerage. Like Champlain, he believed that Catholics and Protestants could live in peace in the same colony. But he expected the servants, most of whom were Protestants, to continue to serve the Catholic gentlemen of the colony (who became manor lords) after their indentures expired.

Those plans were never fulfilled. The condition of English Catholics improved under Charles I (1625–1649) and his queen, Henrietta Maria, a French Catholic. Because few Catholics emigrated, most settlers were Protestants. The civil war that erupted in England in 1642 (discussed later in the chapter) soon spread to Maryland. Protestants overthrew Lord Baltimore's regime several times between 1642 and 1660, but the English state always sided with him. During these struggles, Baltimore conceded a bicameral legislature to the colony, knowing that Protestants would dominate the elective assembly and that Catholics would control the appointive council. He also approved the Toleration Act of 1649, which granted freedom of worship to Christians (but not to Maryland's tiny Jewish minority).

The manorial system did not survive these upheavals. Protestant servants, after their indentures expired, acquired their own land rather than become tenants under Catholic manor lords, most of whom died or returned to England. When Maryland's unrest ended around 1660, the colony was raising tobacco, corn, and livestock and was governed by county courts similar to those in Virginia. In fact, religion provided the biggest difference between the two colonies. Virginia was Anglican, but Maryland had no established church and no vestries. Most Maryland Protestants had to make do without ministers until the 1690s.

CHESAPEAKE FAMILY LIFE

At first, men outnumbered women in Virginia and Maryland by 5 to 1. Among new immigrant servants as late as the 1690s, the ratio was still 5 to 2. Population did not become self-sustaining until about 1680, when live births finally began to outnumber deaths. Among adults this transition was felt only after 1700.

CRUDE HOUSING FOR SETTLERS IN NORTH AMERICA   When the first settlers came to North America, their living quarters were anything but luxurious. The crude housing shown in this modern reconstruction of Jamestown remained typical of Virginia and Maryland through the 17th century.

Life expectancy slowly improved, but it still remained much lower than in England. The Chesapeake immigrants had survived childhood diseases in Europe, but men at age 20 could expect to live only to about 45, with 70 percent dead by age 50. Women died at even younger ages, especially in areas ravaged by malaria, a dangerous disease for pregnant women. In those places women rarely lived to age 40. England's patriarchal families found it hard to survive in the Chesapeake. About 70 percent of the men never married or, if they did, produced no children. Most men waited years after completing their service before they could marry. Because women could not marry until they had finished their indentures, most spent a good part of their childbearing years unwed. About one-fifth had illegitimate children, and roughly one-third were pregnant on their wedding day. Virtually all women married.

In a typical Chesapeake marriage, the groom was in his thirties and the bride eight or ten years younger. This age gap meant that the husband usually died before his wife, who then quickly remarried. Native-born settlers married at a much earlier age than immigrants; women were often in their middle to late teens when they wed. Orphans were a major community problem. Stepparents were common; surviving spouses with property usually remarried. Few lived long enough to become grandparents.

Under these circumstances, family loyalties tended to focus on other kin—on uncles, aunts, cousins, older stepbrothers or stepsisters—thus contributing to the value that Virginia and Maryland placed upon hospitality. Patriarchalism remained weak. Because fathers died young, even members of the officeholding elite that took shape after 1650 had difficulty passing on their status to their sons. Only toward the end of the century were the men holding office likely to be descended from fathers of comparable distinction.

The West Indies and the Transition to Slavery

Before 1700, far more Englishmen went to the West Indies than to the Chesapeake. Between 1624 and 1640 they settled the Leeward Islands (St. Christopher, Nevis, Montserrat, and Antigua) and Barbados, tiny islands covering just over 400 square miles. In the 1650s England seized Jamaica from Spain. At first English planters grew tobacco, using the labor of indentured servants. Then, beginning around 1645 in Barbados, sugar replaced tobacco, with dramatic social consequences. The Dutch provided some of the capital for this transition, showed the English how to raise sugar, introduced them to slave labor on a massive scale, and for a time dominated the exportation and marketing of the crop. Sugar became so valuable that planters imported most of their food from North America rather than divert land and labor from the cash crop.

Sugar required a heavy investment in slaves and mills, and large planters with many slaves soon dominated the islands. There was little need for ex-servants, and many joined the buccaneers or moved to the mainland. Their exodus hastened the transition to slavery. In 1660, Europeans outnumbered slaves in the islands by 33,000 to 22,000. By 1700, the white population had stagnated, but the number of slaves had increased sixfold. By 1775 they would triple again. Planters often worked their slaves to death and then bought others to replace them. Of the 316,000 Africans imported before 1700, only 115,000 remained alive in that year.

Observers were depressed by the moral climate on the islands, where underworked and overfed planters arrogantly dominated their overworked and underfed slaves. Yet the islands generated enormous wealth for the English empire, far more than the mainland colonies well into the 18th century.

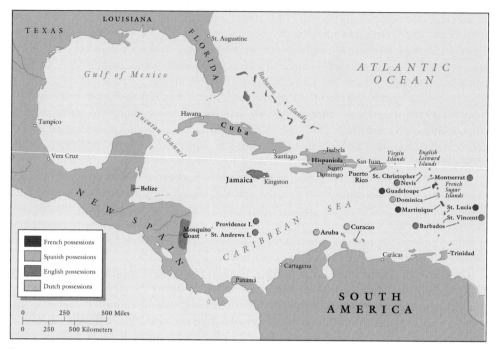

PRINCIPAL WEST INDIAN COLONIES IN THE 17TH CENTURY

THE RISE OF SLAVERY IN NORTH AMERICA

Africans appeared in Virginia sometime before 1619 when, John Rolfe reported, a Dutch ship "sold us twenty Negars." Their status remained ambiguous for decades. In the Chesapeake some Africans were treated as servants and won their freedom after several years. But other Africans were already serving for life, a pattern that finally prevailed.

This uncertainty about status is not surprising. Because the English had no experience with slavery at home, a rigid caste system took time to crystallize. When Hugh Davis was whipped in 1630 "for abusing himself to the dishonor of God and shame of Christians, by defiling his body in lying with a negro," his offense may have been sodomy rather than miscegenation. Fifty years later when Katherine Watkins, a white woman, accused John Long, a mulatto, of raping her, the neighbors blamed her, not him, for engaging in blatantly seductive behavior. The case of Elizabeth Key, the bastard mulatto daughter of Thomas Key, shows similar ambiguity. In 1655 when she claimed her freedom, her new owner fought to keep her enslaved. William Greensted, who had fathered two children by her, sued on her behalf, won, and then married her.

In the generation after 1680, the caste structure of the Chesapeake colonies became firmly set. Fewer indentured servants reached the Chesapeake from England, as the Delaware valley and the expanding English army and navy competed more successfully for the same young men. Slaves took their place. They cost more to buy, but they served for life. In 1705 the Virginia legislature forbade the whipping of a white servant without a court's permission, a restriction that did not apply to the punishment of slaves. To attract more whites, Virginia also promised every ex-servant 50 acres of land. The message was obvious. Every white was now superior to any black.

THE NEW ENGLAND COLONIES

Other Europeans founded colonies to engage in economic activities they could not pursue at home. But the New England settlers reproduced the mixed economy of old England, with minor variations. Their family farms raised livestock and European grains, as well as corn. Their artisans specialized in many crafts, from carpentry and shipbuilding to printing. Their quarrel with England was over religion, not economics. They came to America, they insisted, to worship as God commanded, not as the Church of England required. Later generations were less certain of their place in the world, less eager to question English ways, and more inclined to drift back toward English models.

THE PILGRIMS AND PLYMOUTH

As mentioned earlier, the Pilgrims were Separatists who left England for the Netherlands between 1607 and 1609. After 10 years there, they realized that their children were growing up Dutch, not English. That fear prompted a minority of the congregation to move to America. In 1620 they sailed for Virginia on the *Mayflower,* but the ship was blown off course, landing first on Cape Cod, and then on the mainland well north of the charter boundaries of Virginia, at a place they named Plymouth. Before landing, the 100 passengers agreed to the Mayflower Compact, which bound them all to obey the decisions of the majority.

Short on supplies, the colonists suffered keenly during the first winter. Half of them died. The settlers fared much better when spring came. The Patuxet Indians of the area had been wiped out by disease in 1617, but their fields were ready for planting. Squanto, the only Patuxet to survive, had been kidnapped in 1614 by coastal traders and carried to England. He had just made his way home and showed up at Plymouth one day in March 1621. He taught the settlers Indian methods of fishing and growing corn. He also introduced them to Massasoit, the powerful Wampanoag sachem (or chief), whose people celebrated the first thanksgiving feast with the settlers after the 1621 harvest. After a decade the settlers numbered about 300. By paying off their London creditors, they gained political autonomy and private ownership of their flourishing farms.

COVENANT THEOLOGY

A much larger Puritan exodus settled Massachusetts Bay between 1630 and 1641. To Puritans the stakes were high indeed by the late 1620s. During that early phase of the Thirty Years' War (1618–1648), Catholic armies seemed about to crush the German Reformation. Charles I blundered into a brief war against both Spain and France, raised money for the war by dubious methods, and dissolved Parliament when it protested. Puritans warned that God's wrath would soon descend on England.

These matters were of genuine urgency to Puritans, who embraced what they called "covenant theology." According to this system, God had made two personal covenants with humans, the covenant of works and the covenant of grace. In the covenant of works God had promised Adam that if he kept God's law he would never die—but Adam ate of the forbidden fruit, was expelled from the Garden of Eden, and died. All of Adam's descendants remain under the same covenant, but because of his fall none will ever be capable of keeping the law. All humans deserve damnation. But God is merciful, and he answered sin with the covenant of grace. God will save those whom he has chosen; everyone else is damned. Even though the covenant of works can no longer bring eternal life, it establishes the strict moral standards that every Christian must strive to follow, before and after conversion. A Christian's inability to keep the law usually triggered the conversion experience by demonstrating that only faith, not works, could save.

At this level, covenant theology merely restated Calvinist orthodoxy. But the Puritans gave it a novel social dimension by pairing each personal covenant with a communal counterpart. The social equivalent of the covenant of grace was the church covenant. Each congregation organized itself into a church, a community of the elect. The founders, or "pillars," of each church, after satisfying one another of their own conversions, agreed that within their church the Gospel would be properly preached and discipline would be strictly maintained. God, in turn, promised to bestow saving grace within that church—not to everyone, of course, but presumably to most of the children of the elect. The communal counterpart of the covenant of works was called the "national" covenant. It determined not who was saved or damned, but the rise and fall of nations or peoples. As a people, New Englanders agreed to obey the law, and God promised to prosper them. They, in turn, covenanted with their magistrates to punish sinners. If magistrates enforced God's law and the people did not resist these efforts, God would not punish the whole community for the misdeeds of individuals. But if sinners were not called to public account, God's anger would be terrible. For New Englanders the idea of the covenant thus became a powerful social metaphor, explaining everything from crop failures and untimely deaths to Indian wars and political contention.

In England the government had refused to assume a godly role. Puritans fleeing to America hoped to escape the divine wrath that threatened England and to create in America the kind of churches that God demanded. A few hoped to erect a model "city upon a hill" to inspire all humankind. Governor John Winthrop developed this idea in a famous sermon of 1630, but this theme seldom appeared in the writings of other founders. It became more common a generation later when, ironically, any neutral observer could see that the rest of the world no longer cared what New Englanders were doing.

Massachusetts Bay

In 1629 several English Puritans obtained a charter for the Massachusetts Bay Company, a typical joint-stock corporation except for one feature: The charter did not specify where the company was to be located. Puritan investors going to New England bought out the other stockholders. Led by Winthrop, they carried the charter to America, beyond the gaze of Charles I. They used it not to organize a business corporation, but as the constitution for the colony. In the 1630s the General Court created by the charter became the Massachusetts legislature.

New England settlers came from the broad middle range of English society. Most had owned property in England. When they sold it to go to America, they probably liquidated far more capital than the London Company had invested in Virginia.

An advance party that sailed in 1629 took over a fishing village on the coast and renamed it Salem. The Winthrop fleet brought 1,000 settlers in 1630. In small groups they scattered around the bay, founding Dorchester, Roxbury, Boston, Charlestown, and Cambridge. Each town formed around a minister and a magistrate. The local congregation was the first institution to take shape. From it evolved the town meeting. Soon the colonists were raising European livestock and growing English wheat and other grains, along with corn. Perhaps 30 percent of them perished during the first winter, but then conditions rapidly improved. About 13,000 settlers came to New England by 1641, most as families—a unique event in Atlantic empires to that time.

Settlers did a brisk business selling grain to the newcomers arriving each year. When the flow of immigrants ceased in 1641, that trade collapsed, creating a crisis that ended only as Boston merchants opened up West Indian markets for New England grain, lumber, and fish. New Englanders possessed this flexibility because they had started to build ships in 1631, and shipbuilding soon became a major industry. The economic success of the region depended on its ability to ship food and lumber products to colonies that grew staple crops.

The region's economy imperiled Puritan orthodoxy. Few Boston merchants and almost no fishermen could meet the religious standards of a Puritan society. Not many of them became church members in the first generation. But the colony needed their services and had to put up with them. The fishing towns of Marblehead and Gloucester did little to implement Puritan values or even to found churches in the early decades, while Boston merchants favored toleration of Protestant dissenters because it would be good for business. Although these contrasts softened with time, Puritan orthodoxy was mostly a rural phenomenon.

PURITAN FAMILY LIFE

In rural areas, New Englanders soon observed a remarkable fact. After the first winter, deaths were rare. "The air of the country is sharp, the rocks many, the trees innumerable, the grass little, the winter cold, the summer hot, the gnats in summer biting, the wolves at midnight howling," one woman complained. But the place was undeniably healthy, and families grew rapidly as 6 or even 10 children reached maturity. The settlers had left most European diseases behind and had encountered no new ones in the bracing climate. For the founders and their children, life expectancy far exceeded the European norm. More than one-fifth of the men who founded Andover lived past age 80. Infant mortality fell, and few mothers died in childbirth. Because people lived so long, New England families became intensely patriarchal. Many fathers refused to grant land titles to their sons before their own deaths. In the early years settlers often moved, looking for the richest soil, the best neighbors, and the most inspiring minister. By about 1645 most of them had found what they wanted, and the New England town settled into a tight community that slowly became an intricate web of cousins. Once the settlers had formed a typical farming town, they grew reluctant to admit "strangers" to their midst, not even slaves.

CONVERSION, DISSENT, AND EXPANSION

Among serious Puritans, competing visions of the godly society became divisive enough to spawn several new colonies. The vital force behind Puritanism was the quest for conversion. Probably because of John Cotton's stirring sermons in Boston, the settlers crossed an invisible boundary in the mid-1630s. As Cotton's converts described their religious experiences, their

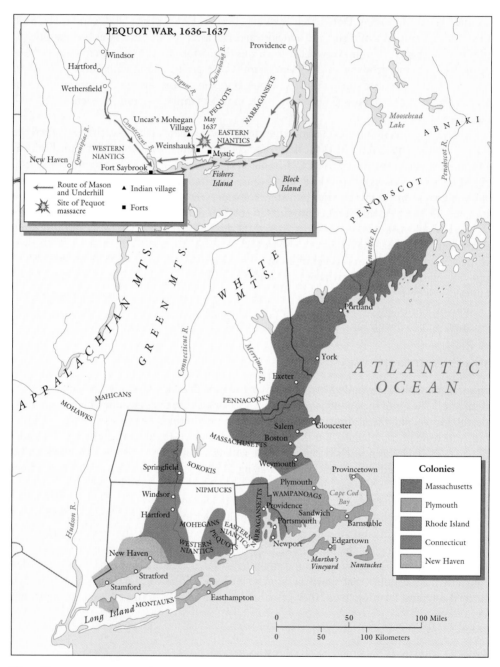

NEW ENGLAND IN THE 1640S

neighbors turned from analyzing the legitimacy of their own conversions to assessing the validity of someone else's. Churches began to test for regeneracy, and the standards of acceptance escalated rapidly.

The conversion experience was deeply ambiguous to a Puritan. Anyone who found no inner trace of saving grace was damned. Anyone absolutely certain of salvation had to be relying on personal merit and was also damned. Conversion began with the discovery that one could not keep God's law and that one *deserved* damnation. It progressed through despair to hope, which always arose from passages of scripture that spoke to that person's condition. A "saint" at last found reason to believe that God had saved him or her. The whole process involved a painful balance between assurance and doubt. A saint was sure of salvation, but never too sure.

This quest for conversion generated dissent and new colonies. The founders of Connecticut feared that Massachusetts was too strict in certifying church members. The founders of New Haven Colony worried that the Bay Colony was much too lenient. The first Rhode Islanders disagreed with all of them.

In the mid-1630s, Reverend Thomas Hooker, alarmed by Cotton's preaching, led his people west to the Connecticut River where they founded Hartford and other towns south of the charter boundary of Massachusetts. John Winthrop Jr. built Saybrook Fort at the mouth of the river, and it soon merged with Hooker's towns into the colony of Connecticut. In 1639 an affluent group planted New Haven Colony on Long Island Sound. New Hampshire and Maine had independent origins under their own charters, but when England fell into civil war after 1642, Massachusetts took control of both of them.

The residents of most towns agreed on the kind of worship they preferred. But some settlers, such as Roger Williams and Anne Hutchinson, made greater demands. Williams was a Separatist who refused to worship with anyone who did not explicitly repudiate the Church of England. Nearly all Massachusetts Puritans were Nonseparatists who claimed only to be reforming the Anglican Church. In 1636, after Williams challenged the king's right as a Christian to grant Indian lands to anyone at all, the colony banished him. He fled to Narragansett Bay with a few disciples and founded Providence. He developed eloquent arguments for religious liberty and the complete separation of church and state.

Anne Hutchinson, an admirer of John Cotton, claimed that virtually all other ministers were preaching only the covenant of works, not the covenant of grace, and were leading people to hell. She won a large following in Boston. At her trial there, she claimed to have received direct messages from God (the "Antinomian" heresy). Banished in 1638, she and her followers also fled to Narragansett Bay, where they founded Newport and Portsmouth. These towns united with Providence to form the colony of Rhode Island and accepted both the religious liberty and the separation of church and state that Williams advocated.

Much of this territorial expansion reflected not just religious idealism, but a quest for more land that threatened the neighboring Indians. Connecticut and Massachusetts waged a war of terror and annihilation against the Pequot Indians, who controlled the fertile Thames River valley in Connecticut. In May 1637 New England soldiers debated with their chaplain which of two Pequot forts to attack, the one held by warriors or the one with women children, and the elderly. He probably told them to remember Saul and the Amalekites because, with horrified Narragansett Indians looking on as nominal allies of the settlers, the Puritan army chose the second fort, set fire to all the wigwams, and shot everyone who tried to flee. The godly had their own uses for terrorism.

CONGREGATIONS, TOWNS, AND COLONY GOVERNMENTS

These struggles helped to shape New England's basic institutions. Congregations abolished the distinctive rites of Anglicanism—vestments, incense, the *Book of Common Prayer,* church courts, bishops. The sermon became the center of worship, and each congregation chose and ordained its own minister. No singing was permitted, except of psalms. Congregations sometimes sent ministers and laymen to a synod, but its decisions were advisory, not binding. A 1648 synod issued the Cambridge Platform, which defined "Congregationalist" worship and church organization.

By then the town had become something distinct from the congregation. Some towns chose independent farms at the outset, but many adopted open-field agriculture, a medieval system that appeared nowhere else in colonial America. In that system farmers owned scattered strips of land within a common field, and the town decided what crops to grow. This emphasis on communal cooperation may have appealed to the founders, who were also short of oxen and plows at first, but it did not survive the first generation.

Town meetings decided who got how much land. It was distributed broadly but never equally. In some villages, town meetings occurred often, made most of the decisions, and left only the details to a board of elected "selectmen." In others the selectmen did most of the governing. All adult males usually participated in local decisions, but Massachusetts and New Haven restricted the vote for colonywide offices to men who were full church members, a decision that greatly narrowed the electorate by the 1660s.

Massachusetts had a bicameral legislature by the 1640s. Voters in each town chose representatives who met as the Chamber of Deputies, or lower house. They also voted for the governor and the magistrates, or upper house (the Council or, in its judicial capacity, the Court of Assistants). The magistrates also staffed the county courts. The Court of Assistants heard appeals from the counties and major criminal cases. Final appeals were heard by the General Court, with both houses sitting together to decide judicial questions.

Massachusetts defined its legal system in the "Body of Liberties" of 1641 and in a comprehensive law code of 1648. It sharply reduced the number of capital offenses under English law. Other distinctive features of the legal system included an explicit recognition of the liberties of women, children, servants, foreigners, and even "the Bruite Creature," or animals.

New England also transformed the traditional English jury system. New Haven abolished juries altogether because the Bible does not mention them. But the other colonies vastly expanded the role of civil (noncriminal) juries, using them even to decide appeals. Except in capital trials, however, the criminal jury almost disappeared in New England. Most offenders appeared in court and accepted their punishments. Acquittals were rare, yet hardly anyone ran away to avoid trial or punishment.

INFANT BAPTISM AND NEW DISSENT

Although most of the founders of the New England colonies became church members during the fervor of the 1630s, their children had trouble achieving conversion. They had never lived as part of a beleaguered minority in England, nor had they experienced the joy of joining with other holy refugees in founding their own church. They had to find God on their own and then persuade their elders that their conversions were authentic. Most could not do it. They grew up, married, and requested baptism for their children. The Cambridge Platform declared that only "saints" (the converted) and their children could be baptized. Other children could not be. But what about grandchildren of "saints" whose own parents had not yet experienced conversion? By 1660 this problem was becoming acute.

Dissenters offered two answers, the ministers a third. In the 1640s some settlers became Baptists. Noting that scripture contains no mandate to baptize infants, they argued that only converted adults should receive that rite. Samuel Gorton, a Baptist expelled from Massachusetts and Plymouth, founded Warwick, Rhode Island, in the 1640s. When Massachusetts arrested him, accused him of blasphemy, and put him on trial for his life, Gorton appealed to Parliament in England, and Massachusetts backed down.

Even more alarming to the Puritan establishment were the Quakers, who invaded the region from England in the 1650s (to be discussed later in the chapter). Quakers found salvation within themselves—through God, the Inner Light present in all people if they will only let it shine forth. To Puritans the Quaker answer to the conversion dilemma seemed blasphemous. Massachusetts hanged four Quakers, including Mary Dyer, once a disciple of Anne Hutchinson.

The clergy's answer to the lack of conversions, worked out at a synod in 1662, became known as the Half-Way Covenant. Parents who had been baptized but had not yet experienced conversion could bring their children before the church, "own the covenant" (that is, subject themselves and their offspring to the doctrine and discipline of the church), and have their children baptized. Despite the urging of the clergy, aging church members resisted the Half-Way Covenant. But as the founders died off in the 1670s and 1680s, it took hold and soon led to something like universal baptism. Almost every child had an ancestor who had been a full church member.

But dissent persisted. The orthodox colonies were divided over whether to persecute or to ignore their Baptist and Quaker minorities. Ministers preached "jeremiads," shrill warnings against any backsliding from the standards of the founding generation. Many laypeople disliked the persecution of conscientious Protestants, however. By the 1670s, innovation seemed dangerous and divisive, but the past was also becoming a burden that no one could shoulder.

THE ENGLISH CIVIL WARS

The 1640s were a critical decade in England and the colonies. From 1629 to 1640 Charles I governed without Parliament. But when he tried to impose the Anglican *Book of Common Prayer* on Presbyterian Scotland, his Scottish subjects rebelled and even invaded England. Needing revenue, Charles summoned two Parliaments in 1640 only to find that many of its members, especially the Puritans, sympathized with the Scots. In 1641 Irish Catholics launched a massive revolt against the Protestant colonizers of their land. King and Parliament agreed that the Irish must be crushed, but neither dared trust the other with the men and resources to do the job. Instead, they began to fight each other.

In 1642 the king and Parliament raised separate armies and went to war. Parliament gradually won the military struggle. It then had to govern most of England without a king. In January 1649, after its moderate members had been purged by its own "New Model Army," Parliament beheaded Charles, abolished the House of Lords, and proclaimed England a Commonwealth (or republic). Within a few years Oliver Cromwell, Parliament's most successful general, dismissed Parliament, and the army then proclaimed him "Lord Protector" of England. He convened several of his own Parliaments, but these experiments failed. The army could not win legitimacy for a government that ruled without the ancient trinity of "King, Lords, and Commons." Cromwell also faced a challenge outside Parliament from "levelers," "diggers," and "ranters" who demanded sweeping social reforms.

Cromwell died in September 1658, and his regime collapsed. Part of the army then invited Charles II (1660–1685) back from exile to claim his throne. This "Restoration" government did its best to restore the old order. It brought back the House of Lords. The Church of England was reestablished and the state persecuted both Catholics and Protestant dissenters: Presbyterians, Congregationalists, Baptists, and Quakers. This persecution drove thousands of Quakers to the Delaware valley after 1675.

THE FIRST RESTORATION COLONIES

England had founded six of the original 13 colonies before 1640. Six others were founded or came under English rule during the Restoration Era (1660–1688). The last, Georgia, was settled in the 1730s (see Chapter 4). All of the new colonies were proprietary in form, allowing the organizers to pursue daring social experiments. The proprietors tried to attract settlers from the older colonies because importing them from Europe was too expensive.

The most prized settlers were New Englanders, who had built the most thriving colonies in North America. But few New Englanders would go farther south than New York or New Jersey. Settlers from the West Indies populated South Carolina.

The Restoration colonies made it easy for settlers to acquire land, and they competed with one another by offering newcomers strong guarantees of civil and political liberties. They all promised either toleration or full religious liberty, at least for Christians. Whereas Virginia and New England (except Rhode Island) were still homogeneous societies, all the Restoration colonies attracted a mix of religious and ethnic groups. None of them found it easy to translate this human diversity into political stability.

Most of the new proprietors were "cavaliers" who had supported Charles II and his brother James, duke of York, during their long exile. Charles owed them something, and a colonial charter cost nothing to grant. Many proprietors took part in more than one project. The eight who obtained charters for Carolina in 1663 and 1665 were also prominent in organizing the Royal African Company, which soon made England a major participant in the African slave trade. Two of the Carolina proprietors obtained a charter from the duke of York for New Jersey as well. William Penn invested in New Jersey before acquiring Pennsylvania from the king.

CAROLINA, HARRINGTON, AND THE ARISTOCRATIC IDEAL

In 1663 eight courtiers obtained a charter by which they became the board of proprietors for a colony called "Carolina" in honor of the king. Most of the settlers came from two sources. Former servants from Virginia and Maryland, many in debt, claimed land around Albemarle Sound in what eventually became North Carolina. Another wave of former servants came from Barbados. They settled the area that became South Carolina.

To the proprietors in England, these scattered settlements made up a single colony. Led by Anthony Ashley-Cooper, the proprietors drafted the Fundamental Constitutions of Carolina in 1669, an incredibly complex plan for organizing the new colony. The philosopher John Locke, Shaftesbury's young secretary, helped write the document.

The Fundamental Constitutions drew on the work of James Harrington, author of *Oceana* (1656). He tried to design a republic that could endure—unlike ancient Athens or Rome, which had finally become despotic states. Harrington argued that how land was distributed ought to determine whether power should be lodged in one man (monarchy), a few men (aristocracy), or many (a republic). Where ownership of land was widespread, he insisted, absolute government could not prevail. He proposed several other devices to prevent one man, or a few, from undermining a republic, such as frequent rotation of officeholders (called "term limits" today), the secret ballot, and a bicameral legislature in which the smaller house would propose laws and the larger house approve or reject them. Harrington had greater impact on colonial governments than any other thinker of his time.

Shaftesbury believed that Harrington had uncovered the laws of history. By emphasizing Henry VIII's confiscation of monastic lands and their sale to an emerging gentry, Harrington seemed to have an explanation for the decline of the monarchy, England's civil wars, and the execution of Charles I—an explanation that was anathema to the king because, if Harrington was correct, the dynasty was still in trouble. English writers did not dare to discuss these ideas openly in the 1660s. But by applying Harrington's principles at a safe distance of 3,000 miles, the Carolina proprietors could choose the kind of society they desired and then devise institutions to ensure its success. Well aware that the House of Lords had been abolished for 11 years after 1649, they were not yet certain whether the English aristocracy could survive at home. In Carolina they hoped to create an aristocratic society that would really work.

The Fundamental Constitutions proposed a government far more complex than any colony could sustain. England had three supreme courts; Carolina would have eight. A Grand Council of proprietors and councillors would exercise executive power and propose all laws. Their bills would have to be approved by a Parliament of commoners and nobles (called "landgraves" and "casiques"). The nobles would control 40 percent of the land. A distinct group of manor lords would also have large estates. The document guaranteed religious toleration to all who believed in God, but everyone had to join a church or lose his citizenship. The document also envisioned a class of lowly whites, "leetmen," who would live on small tracts and serve the great landlords—and it took slavery for granted.

Between 1670 and 1700, the proprietors tried several times, without success, to win approval of the document by the ex-servants in South Carolina. In the 1680s, weary of resistance, they shipped 1,000 dissenters from England and Scotland to South Carolina. These newcomers formed the nucleus of a proprietary party in South Carolina politics and made religious diversity a social fact. But their influence was never strong enough to win approval for the Fundamental Constitutions. The Barbadians formed, in effect, an antiproprietary party and remained in control.

Carolina presented other obstacles to these aristocratic goals. The proprietors assumed that land ownership would be the key to wealth and status. But many settlers prospered in other ways. Some of them exploited the virgin forests to produce masts, turpentine, tar, and pitch for sale to English shipbuilders. Other settlers raised cattle and hogs by letting them run free on open land. Some of South Carolina's early slaves were probably America's first cowboys. The settlers also traded with the Indians, usually for deerskins. The Indian trade sustained a genuine city, Charleston, founded in 1680 at the confluence of the Ashley and Cooper Rivers. The Indian trade also became something more dangerous than hunting or trapping animals. Carolina traders allied themselves with some Indians to attack others and drag the captives, mostly women and children, to Charleston for sale as slaves.

In the early 18th century, South Carolina and North Carolina became separate colonies, and South Carolina's economy moved in a new direction. For two decades, until 1720, a parliamentary subsidy sustained a boom in the naval stores industry. But Charleston merchants increasingly invested their capital, acquired in the Indian trade, in rice plantations. In the 1690s planters learned how to grow rice from slaves who had cultivated it in West Africa. It quickly became the staple export of South Carolina and triggered a massive growth of slavery. By 1730 two-thirds of the colony's 30,000 people were African slaves, most of whom toiled on rice plantations.

NEW YORK: AN EXPERIMENT IN ABSOLUTISM

In 1664 James, duke of York, obtained a charter from his royal brother for a colony between the Delaware and Connecticut Rivers. Charles II claimed that the territory of New Netherland was rightfully England's because it was included in the Virginia charter of 1606. James sent a fleet to Manhattan, and the English settlers on western Long Island rose in arms to support his claim. Reluctantly, Stuyvesant surrendered without resistance. The English renamed the province New York. New Amsterdam became New York City, and Fort Orange became Albany. New York took over all of Long Island, most of which had been ruled by Connecticut, but never made good its claim to the Connecticut River as its eastern boundary.

Richard Nicolls, the first English governor of New York, planned to lure Yankees to the Jersey coast as a way of offsetting the preponderance of Dutch settlers in the Hudson valley. Official policy toward the Dutch was conciliatory. Those who chose to leave could take their property with them. Those who stayed retained their property and were assured of religious toleration. Most stayed. Except in New York City and the small Dutch portion of Long Island, Dutch settlers still lived under Dutch law. England also expected to take over the colony's trade with Europe, but New York's early governors realized that a total ban on commerce with Amsterdam could ruin the colony. Under various legal subterfuges, they allowed this trade to continue.

The duke boldly tried to do in New York what he and the king did not dare attempt in England—to govern without an elective assembly. This policy upset English settlers on Long Island far more than the Dutch, who had no experience with representative government. Governor Nicolls compiled a code of laws ("the Duke's Laws") culled mostly from New England statutes. With difficulty, he secured the consent of English settlers to this code in 1665, but thereafter he taxed and governed on his own, seeking only the advice and consent of his appointed council and of a somewhat larger court of assize, also appointive, that dispensed justice, mostly to the English settlers.

This policy made it difficult to attract English colonists to New York, especially after New Jersey became a separate proprietary colony in 1665. The two proprietors, Sir George Carteret and John, baron Berkeley, granted settlers the right to elect an assembly, which made New Jersey far more attractive to English settlers than New York. The creation of New Jersey also slowed the flow of Dutch settlers across the Hudson and thus helped to keep New York Dutch.

The transition from a Dutch to an English colony did not go smoothly. James expected his English invaders to assimilate the conquered Dutch, but the reverse was more common for two or three decades. Most Englishmen who settled in New York after the conquest married Dutch women and sent their children to the Dutch Reformed Church. In effect, the Dutch were assimilating the English. Nor did the Dutch give up their loyalty to the Netherlands. In 1673 when a Dutch fleet threatened Manhattan, the Dutch refused to assist the English garrison of Fort James. Much as Stuyvesant had done nine years earlier, the English garrison gave up without resistance. New York City now became New Orange and Fort James was renamed Fort William, both in honor of young William III of Nassau, Prince of Orange, the new *stadholder* (military leader) of the Dutch Republic in its struggle with France.

New Orange survived for 15 months. But once again, the Dutch Republic concluded that the colony was not worth what it cost and gave it back to England at the end of the war. The new governor, Major Edmund Andros, arrested seven prominent Dutch merchants and tried them as aliens after they refused to swear an oath of loyalty to England that might oblige them to fight other Dutchmen. Faced with the confiscation of their property, they gave in. Andros also helped secure bilingual ministers for Dutch Reformed pulpits. Ordinary Dutch settlers looked with suspicion on the new ministers and on wealthier Dutch families who socialized with the governor or sent their sons to New England to learn English.

English merchants in New York City resented the continuing Amsterdam trade and the staying power of the Dutch elite. They believed the colony had to become more English to attract newcomers. When Andros did not renew the colony's basic revenue act before returning to England in 1680, the merchants refused to pay any duties that had not been voted by an elective assembly. The court of assize, supposedly a bastion of absolutism, supported the tax strike, convicted the duke's customs collector of usurping authority, and sent him to England for punishment where, of course, James exonerated him. The justices also fined several Dutch officeholders for failing to respect English liberties. The English (but not Dutch) towns on Long Island joined in the demand for an elective assembly, an urgent matter now that William Penn's much freer colony on the Delaware threatened to drain away the small English population of New York. Several prominent merchants did move to Philadelphia.

The duke finally relented and conceded an assembly. When it met in 1683, it adopted a Charter of Liberties that proclaimed government by consent. It also imposed English law on the Dutch parts of the province. Although the drain of English settlers to Pennsylvania declined, few immigrants came to New York at a time when thousands were landing in Philadelphia. Philadelphia's thriving trade cut into New York City's profits. New York remained a Dutch society with a Yankee enclave, governed by English intruders. In 1689, when James and William fought for the English throne, their struggle would tear the colony apart.

BROTHERLY LOVE: THE QUAKERS AND AMERICA

The most fascinating social experiment of the Restoration era took place in the Delaware valley where Quakers led another family-based, religiously motivated migration of more than 10,000 people between 1675 and 1690. Founded by George Fox during England's civil wars, the Society of Friends expanded dramatically in the 1650s. After the Restoration, Quakers faced harsh persecution in England and began to think about finding refuge in America.

QUAKER BELIEFS

Quakers insisted that God, in the form of the Inner Light, is present in all people, who can become good—even perfect—if only they will let it shine forth. They became pacifists, enraging

Catholics and most other Protestants, all of whom had found ways to justify war. Quakers also denounced oaths as sinful. Again, other Christians reacted with horror because their judicial systems rested on oaths.

Although orderly and peaceful, Quakers struck others as dangerous radicals whose beliefs would bring anarchy. For instance, slavery made them uncomfortable, although the Friends did not embrace abolitionism until a century later (see Chapter 5). Further, in what they called "the Lamb's war" against human pride, Quakers refused to doff their hats to social superiors. Hats symbolized the social hierarchy of Europe. Every man knew his place so long as he understood whom to doff to, and who should doff to him. Quakers also refused to accept or to confer titles. They called everyone "thee" or "thou," familiar terms used by superiors when addressing inferiors, especially servants.

The implications of the Quakers' beliefs appalled other Christians. The Inner Light seemed to obliterate predestination, original sin, maybe even the Trinity. Quakers had no sacraments, not even an organized clergy. They denounced Protestant ministers as "hireling priests." Other Protestants retorted that the Quakers were conspiring to return the world to "popish darkness" by abolishing a learned ministry. (The terms "papists" and "popish" were abusive labels applied to Catholics by English Protestants.) Quakers also held distinctive views about revelation. If God speaks directly to Friends, that Word must be every bit as inspired as anything in the Bible. Quakers compiled books of their "sufferings," which they thought were the equal of the "Acts of the Apostles," a claim that seemed blasphemous to others.

Contemporaries expected the Society of Friends to fall apart as each member followed his or her own Light in some unique direction. However, the Quakers found ways to deal with discord. The heart of Quaker worship was the "weekly meeting" of the local congregation. There was no sermon or liturgy. People spoke whenever the Light moved them. But because a few men and women spoke often and with great effect, they became recognized as "public friends," the closest the Quakers came to having a clergy. Public friends occupied special, elevated seats in some meetinghouses, and many went on missionary tours in Europe or America. The weekly meetings within a region sent representatives to a "monthly meeting," which resolved questions of policy and discipline. The monthly meetings sent delegates to the "yearly meeting" in London. At every level, decisions had to be unanimous. There is only one Inner Light, and it must convey the same message to every believer. This insistence on unanimity provided strong safeguards against schism.

QUAKER FAMILIES

Quakers transformed the traditional family as well. Women enjoyed almost full equality with men. They held their own formal meetings and made important decisions about discipline and betrothals. Quaker reforms also affected children, whom most Protestants saw as tiny sinners whose will had to be broken by severe discipline. But once Quakers stopped worrying about original sin, their children became innocents who must be protected from worldly corruption. In America, Quakers created affectionate families and worked hard to acquire land for all their children. Earlier than other Christians, they began to limit family size. They seldom associated with non-Quakers. To marry an outsider meant expulsion from the Society.

Persecution in England helped to drive Quakers across the ocean, but the need to provide for their children was another powerful motive for emigration. By 1700, half of all the Quakers in England and Wales had moved to America.

West New Jersey

In 1674 the New Jersey proprietors split their holding into two colonies. Sir George Carteret claimed what he now called East New Jersey, a province near New York City with half a dozen towns populated by Baptist, Quaker, Puritan, and Dutch Reformed settlers. Lord Berkeley claimed West New Jersey and promptly sold it to the Quakers, who founded West New Jersey and Pennsylvania. In the 1680s Quakers bought out the proprietor of East New Jersey and also gained power in Delaware (formerly New Sweden). The West Jersey purchasers divided their proprietary into 100 shares. Two of them were Edward Byllinge, a former "leveler," and William Penn.

In 1676 Byllinge drafted the West Jersey Concessions and Agreements, which was approved by the first settlers in 1677. It lodged legislative power in a unicameral assembly, elected by secret ballot. In the court system, juries would decide both fact and law. Judges would merely preside over the court and, if asked by a juror, offer advice. Although the document was never fully implemented, it made West Jersey the most radical political experiment attempted in America before the Revolution. The Quakers believed that godly people could live together in love—without war, lawyers, or internal conflict. They made land easy to acquire and promised freedom of worship to everyone. In the 1680s lawsuits often ended with one litigant forgiving the other, and criminal trials sometimes closed with the victim embracing the perpetrator. But as social and religious diversity grew, the system broke down. Non-Quakers increasingly refused to cooperate. In the 1690s the courts became impotent, and Quaker rule collapsed some years before the Crown took over the colony in 1702.

Pennsylvania

By 1681 Quaker attention was already shifting to the west bank of the Delaware River. There William Penn launched a much larger "Holy Experiment." The son of a Commonwealth admiral, Penn grew up surrounded by privilege. He attended Oxford and the Inns of Court (England's law schools), went on the grand tour of Europe, and began to manage his father's Irish estates. Then, to his father's horror, he became a Quaker. Penn often traveled to the European continent on behalf of the Society of Friends, winning converts and recruiting settlers in the Netherlands and Germany. In England he was jailed several times for his beliefs, and in the so-called Penn-Meade trial of 1670 he challenged a judge's right to compel a jury to reconsider its verdict. In a landmark decision, a higher court vindicated him.

Penn was no ordinary colonizer. Using his contacts at court, he converted an old debt (owed to his father by the king) into a charter for a proprietary colony that Charles named "Pennsylvania" in honor of the deceased admiral. Penn agreed to enforce the Navigation Acts (see Chapter 3), to let the Crown approve his choice of governor, to submit all legislation to the English Privy Council for approval, and to allow appeals from Pennsylvania courts to the Privy Council in England.

Friendly relations with Indians were essential to the project's success, and Penn was careful to deal fairly with the Lenni Lenape, or Delaware Indians. They liked him and called him "Miquon," their word for "quill" and thus a pun on "Penn."

Under the First Frame of Government, Penn's 1682 constitution for the province, the settlers would elect a council of 72 men to staggered three-year terms. The council would draft all legislation and submit copies to the voters. In the early years the voters would meet to approve

***Penn's Treaty with the Indians,* by Benjamin West**   This 1771 painting celebrates William Penn's efforts, nearly a century earlier, to establish peaceful relations with the Delaware Indians.

or reject these bills in person. But as the province expanded, such meetings would become impractical. Voters would then elect an assembly of 200, which would increase gradually to 500. Penn gave up the power to veto bills but retained control of the distribution of land. Capital punishment for offenses other than murder was abolished. Religious liberty, trial by jury, and habeas corpus all received strong guarantees.

Settlers had been arriving in Pennsylvania for a year when Penn landed in 1682. Some lived in caves along the river. Others built log cabins. The colonists persuaded Penn that the First Frame was too cumbersome for a small colony. In what became known as the Second Frame, or the Pennsylvania Charter of Liberties of 1683, the council was reduced to 18 men and the assembly to 36. The assembly's inability to initiate legislation soon became a major grievance.

Penn laid out Philadelphia and organized other settlements. Then, in 1684, he returned to England to answer Lord Baltimore's complaint that Philadelphia fell within the charter boundaries of Maryland. This dispute troubled the Penn family until the 1760s, when the Mason-Dixon line finally established the modern boundary.

Penn expected his settlers to defer to the leaders among them. He created the Free Society of Traders to control commerce with England and gave high offices to its members. But from the start, wealth in Pennsylvania rested on trade with other colonies, especially in the Caribbean, not with England. That trade was dominated by Quakers from Barbados, Jamaica,

CHRONOLOGY

1517	Luther begins the Protestant Reformation
1577–1580	Drake circumnavigates the globe
1580s	Gilbert claims Newfoundland for England (1583) • Ralegh twice fails to colonize Roanoke Island (1585–1587) • England repels attack by the Spanish Armada
1607	English settlement established at Jamestown
1608	Champlain founds Quebec
1609	Virginia receives sea-to-sea charter
1613–1614	Rolfe grows tobacco, marries Pocahontas
1618	Sandys implements London Company reforms
1619	First Africans arrive in Virginia • House of Burgesses and Headright system created
1620s	Pilgrims adopt Mayflower Compact, land at Plymouth (1620) • Dutch West India Company chartered (1621) • Opechancanough launches war of extermination in Virginia (1622) • King assumes direct control of Virginia (1624) • Minuit founds New Amsterdam (1626)
1630s	Puritans settle Massachusetts Bay (1630) • Maryland chartered (1632) • Williams founds Providence; Hooker founds Hartford (1636) • Anne Hutchinson banished to Rhode Island; Minuit founds New Sweden (1638) • New Haven Colony founded (1639)
1640s	Massachusetts "Body of Liberties" passed (1641) • English civil wars begin (1642) • Pavonia Massacre in New Netherland (1643) • Charles I beheaded (1649)
1655	New Netherland conquers New Sweden
1660s	Charles II restored to English throne (1660) • Puritans institute Half-Way Covenant (1662) • First Carolina charter granted (1663) • New Netherland surrenders to the English (1664) • New Jersey becomes a separate colony (1665) • Carolina's Fundamental Constitutions proposed (1669)
1670s	First permanent English settlement established in South Carolina (1670) • Dutch retake New York (1673–1674) • West New Jersey approves Concessions and Agreements (1677)
1680s	Charleston founded (1680) • Pennsylvania charter granted (1681) • New York and Pennsylvania each adopt a Charter of Liberties (1683)
1705	Virginia adopts comprehensive slave code

New York, and Boston. These men owed little to Penn and became an opposition faction in the colony. They claimed that they could not afford to pay Penn's quitrents,[2] and quarreled more often than was seemly for men of brotherly love.

In exasperation, Penn finally appointed John Blackwell, a friend and old Cromwellian soldier, as governor in 1688, ordering him to end the quarrels and collect quitrents but to rule

---

[2] A feudal relic, a quitrent was an annual fee, usually small, required by the patent that gave title to a piece of land. It differed from ordinary rents in that nonpayment led to a suit for debt, not ejection from the property.

"tenderly." Boys jeered Blackwell as he tried to enter Penn's Philadelphia house, and the council refused to let him use the colony's great seal. Debate in the legislature became angrier than ever. After 13 months, Blackwell resigned.

In 1691, the Society of Friends suffered a brief schism in the Delaware valley. A Quaker schoolteacher, George Keith, urged all Quakers to systematize their beliefs and even wrote his own catechism, only to encounter the opposition of the public friends, who included the colony's major officeholders. When he attacked them directly, he was convicted and fined for abusing civil officers. He claimed that he was being persecuted for his religious beliefs, but the courts insisted that his only crime was his attack on public authority. In contrast to Massachusetts in the 1630s, no one was banished, and Pennsylvania remained a haven for all religions. The colony's government changed several more times before 1701, when Penn and the assembly finally agreed on the Fourth Frame, or Charter of Privileges, which gave Pennsylvania a unicameral legislature. But its politics remained turbulent and unstable into the 1720s.

Despite these controversies, Pennsylvania quickly became an economic success, well established in the Caribbean trade as an exporter of wheat and flour. Quaker families were thriving, and the colony's policy of religious freedom attracted thousands of outsiders. Some were German pacifists who shared the social goals of the Society of Friends. Others were Anglicans and Presbyterians who warned London that Quakers were unfit to rule—anywhere.

CONCLUSION

In the 16th century, France, the Netherlands, and England all challenged Spanish power in Europe and across the ocean. After 1600 all three founded their own colonies in North America and the Caribbean. New France became a land of missionaries and traders and developed close ties with most nearby Indians. New Netherland also was founded to participate in the fur trade. Both colonies slowly acquired an agricultural base.

The English, by contrast, desired the land itself. They founded colonies of settlement that threatened nearby Indians, except in the Delaware valley where Quakers insisted on peaceful relations. The southern mainland and Caribbean colonies produced staple crops for sale in Europe, first with the labor of indentured servants and then with enslaved Africans. The Puritan and Quaker colonies became smaller versions of England's mixed economy, with an emphasis on family farms. Maintaining the fervor of the founders was a problem for both. After conquering New Netherland, England controlled the Atlantic seaboard from Maine to South Carolina, and by 1700 the population of England's mainland colonies was doubling every 25 years. England was beginning to emerge as the biggest winner in the competition for empire.

3

ENGLAND DISCOVERS ITS COLONIES: EMPIRE, LIBERTY, AND EXPANSION

THE SPECTRUM OF SETTLEMENT ∾ THE BEGINNINGS OF EMPIRE

INDIANS, SETTLERS, UPHEAVAL

CRISIS IN ENGLAND AND THE REDEFINITION OF EMPIRE

THE GLORIOUS REVOLUTION

CONTRASTING EMPIRES: SPAIN AND FRANCE IN NORTH AMERICA

AN EMPIRE OF SETTLEMENT: THE BRITISH COLONIES

In 1603 England was still a weak power on the fringes of Europe. By 1700 England was a global giant. It possessed 20 colonies in North America and the Caribbean, controlled much of the African slave trade, and had muscled its way into distant India. Commerce and colonies had vastly magnified England's power in Europe.

This transformation occurred during a century of political and religious upheaval at home. King and Parliament fought over their respective powers—a long struggle that led to civil war and the execution of one king in 1649 and to the overthrow of another in 1688. The result was a unique constitution that rested upon parliamentary supremacy and responsible government under the Crown.

By 1700 England and the colonies had begun to converge around the newly defined principles of English constitutionalism. All of them adopted representative government at some point during the century. All of them affirmed the values of liberty and property under the English Crown.

England also quarreled with the colonies. The sheer diversity of the colonies daunted anyone who hoped to govern them. The colonies formed not a single type, but a spectrum of settlement with contrasting economies, social relationships, and institutions. Yet by 1700 England had created a system of regulation that respected colonial liberties while asserting imperial power.

THE SPECTRUM OF SETTLEMENT

Over thousands of years, the Indians of the Americas had become diversified into hundreds of distinct cultures and languages. The colonists of 17th century North America and the

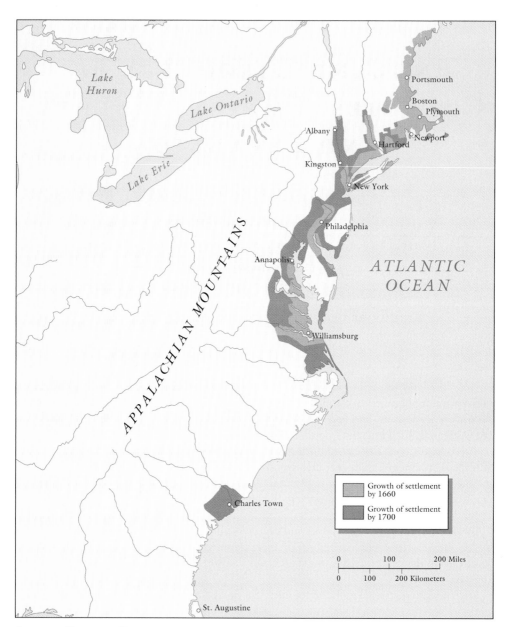

AREA OF ENGLISH SETTLEMENT BY 1700

Caribbean were following much the same course. America divided them. The Atlantic united them. Their connection with England gave them what unity they could sustain.

As long as population remained small, no colony could duplicate the complexity of England. The settlers had to choose what to bring with them and what to leave behind, what they could do for themselves and what they would have to import—choices dictated both by their motives for crossing the ocean and by what the new environment would permit. The colonists sorted themselves out along a vast arc from the cold North to the subtropical Caribbean. If we imagine England as a source of white light and the Atlantic as a prism refracting that light, 17th century America becomes a spectrum of settlement, with each color merging imperceptibly into the shade next to it. Each province had much in common with its neighbors, but shared few traits with more distant colonies. At the extremes, the sugar and slave society of Barbados had almost nothing in common with Puritan Massachusetts. Nor did Canada with the French West Indies.

DEMOGRAPHIC DIFFERENCES

The most pronounced differences involved the sex ratio (the ratio of men to women in any society) and family structure. At one extreme were the all-male, multiethnic societies in the Caribbean that lived only for plunder. Because women settlers were scarce at first, the family itself seemed an endangered institution. Even when the sex ratio evened out and families began to emerge, couples had few children. In Virginia and Maryland, as natural increase replaced immigration as the main source of population growth after 1680, women became more numerous, married much earlier, and raised larger families.

There were also significant differences in life expectancy. In the sugar colonies, men often died by age 40. In the Chesapeake colonies, for men who survived childhood diseases, life expectancy was about 45. The northern colonies were much healthier. In the Delaware valley, a man who reached adulthood could expect to live past 60.

New England was one of the healthiest places in the world. Because the sex ratio rapidly approached equality and because the thriving economy permitted couples to marry perhaps two years earlier than in England, population growth exploded. Canada followed a similar pattern. In the late 17th century, the birth rate in New France caught up with New England's, and population grew at a comparable pace.

These demographic differences had significant consequences. For example, the Caribbean and southern colonies were youthful societies in which men with good connections could expect to achieve high office while in their thirties, or even their twenties. By contrast, the New England colonies gradually became dominated by grandfathers. A man was not likely to become even a selectman before his forties. Simon Bradstreet was 90 when he completed his last term as governor of Massachusetts in 1692. Despite the appalling death rate in the sugar and tobacco colonies, young men remained optimistic and upbeat, as they looked forward to challenging the world and making their fortunes. But in New England, people grew ever more despondent as the century progressed, even though they lived much longer.

RACE, ETHNICITY, AND ECONOMY

The degree of racial and ethnic mixture also varied from region to region, along with economic priorities. The West Indies already had a large slave majority by 1700. In 1700 English settlers were still a clear majority in the southern mainland colonies, but African slaves became a majority in South Carolina around 1710 and were increasing rapidly. They would comprise 40 percent of Virginia's population by the 1730s. Africans were less numerous in the Delaware and Hudson valleys, although slavery became deeply entrenched in New York City and parts of New Jersey.

THE SPECTRUM OF SETTLEMENT: *Demography, Ethnicity, Economy, 1650–1700*

CATEGORY	WEST INDIES	LOWER SOUTH	CHESAPEAKE	MID-ATLANTIC	NEW ENGLAND	NEW FRANCE
Life expectancy for men, age 20	40	42	45	60+	Late 60s	60s
Family size	Below replacement rate	About two children	Rising after 1680	Very large	Very large	Very large
Race and ethnicity	Black majority by circa 1670s	Black majority by circa 1710	Growing black minority	Ethnic mix, N.W. Europe, English a minority	Almost all English	Almost all French
Economy	Sugar	Rice, 1690s ff	Tobacco	Furs, farms	Farms, fishing, shipbuilding	Furs, farms

In the Middle Atlantic region, settlers from all over northwestern Europe were creating a new ethnic mosaic. English colonists were probably always a minority, outnumbered at first by the Dutch, and later by Germans, Scots, and Irish. But New England was in every sense the most English of the colonies. New France was as French as New England was English. The farther south one went, the more diverse the population; the farther north, the more uniform.

Slavery and staple crops went together. The slave societies raised sugar, rice, or tobacco for sale in Europe. General farming and family labor also went together. By 1700 the Middle Atlantic was the wheat belt of North America. The New Englanders farmed and exported fish and lumber to the West Indies.

RELIGION AND EDUCATION

The intensity of religious observance varied immensely across the spectrum of settlement, ranging from irreverence and indifference in the West Indies to intense piety in Pennsylvania, New England, and New France. Because formal education in the 17th century nearly always had a religious base, literacy followed a similar pattern. Colonists everywhere tried to prevent slaves from learning to read, and low literacy prevailed wherever slavery predominated. Chesapeake settlers provided almost no formal schooling for their children prior to 1693. By contrast, the Dutch maintained several good schools in New Netherland. Massachusetts required every town to have a writing school, and larger towns to support a Latin grammar school, in order to frustrate "ye old deluder Satan." In New France a seminary (now Laval University) was established in the 1660s. Along the spectrum, piety, literacy, and education all grew stronger from south to north.

Public support for the clergy followed the same pattern. By 1710 the established church of the mother country was the legally established church in the West Indies and in the southern mainland colonies. Toleration prevailed in New York and full religious liberty in Pennsylvania. In New England, Old World dissent became the New World establishment. Public support for

THE SPECTRUM OF SETTLEMENT: *Religion and Government, circa 1675–1700*

CATEGORY	WEST INDIES	LOWER SOUTH	CHESAPEAKE	MID-ATLANTIC	NEW ENGLAND	NEW FRANCE
Formal religion	Anglican Church establishment	Anglican Church establishment by circa 1710	Anglican Church establishment (after 1692 in Md.)	Competing sects, no established church	Congregational Church established	Catholic Church established
Religious tone	Irreverent	Contentious	Low-church Anglican	Family-based piety, sectarian competition	Family-based piety, intensity declining	Intensely Catholic
Local government	Parish	Parish and phantom counties (i.e., no court)	County and parish	County and township	Towns and counties; parishes after 1700	Cities
Provincial government	Royal	Proprietary	Royal (Va.), proprietary (Md.)	From proprietary to royal, except in Pa.	Corporate, with Mass. & N.H. becoming royal	Royal absolutism

the clergy was much greater in the north than in the south. The sugar islands had the most wealth, but they maintained only one clergyman for every 3,000 to 9,000 people, depending on the island. In the Chesapeake the comparable ratio was about one for every 1,500 people by 1700. It was perhaps one for every 1,000 in New York, one for every 600 in New England, and still lower in New France.

Moral standards also rose from south to north. New Englanders boasted that they were far more godly than all other colonists. As early as 1638 one Marylander quipped that a neighbor deserved to be "whippt at virginea" or "hanged in new England."

LOCAL AND PROVINCIAL GOVERNMENTS

Forms of government also varied. Drawing on their English experience, settlers could choose from among parishes, boroughs (towns), and counties.

The only important local institution in the sugar islands and in South Carolina was the parish, which took on many secular functions, such as poor relief. The Chesapeake colonies relied primarily on the county but also made increasing use of the parish. Few parishes were ever organized in the Middle Atlantic colonies, but the county as a form of government became a powerful institution after 1664. New England's most basic local institution was the town. Massachusetts created counties in the 1640s, followed 20 years later by Connecticut and in the 1680s by Plymouth. After 1700, towns large enough to support more than one church also adopted the parish system. In local government as in its economy, New England's use of the full range of parishes, towns, and counties made the region more fully English than other colonies were.

The West Indian colonies all had royal governments by the 1660s. Proprietary forms dominated the mainland south of New England, except for royal Virginia. Until the 1680s New England relied on corporate forms of government in which all officials, even governors, were elected. This system survived in Connecticut and Rhode Island until independence and beyond.

UNIFYING TRENDS: LANGUAGE, WAR, LAW, AND INHERITANCE

Despite all this diversity, a few trends toward greater homogeneity developed in the 17th century. For instance, language became more uniform in America than in England. True, the New England dialect derived mostly from East Anglia, the southern accent from southern and western England, and Middle Atlantic speech from north-central England. But Londoners went to all the colonies, and London English affected every colony and softened the contrasts among the emerging regional dialects.

Another area of uniformity was the manner in which the settlers waged war: They did it with short-term volunteers for whom terror against Indian women and children was often the tactic of choice. Europe was moving toward limited wars; the colonists demanded quick and total victories.

In the colonies, law became a simpler version of England's complex legal system. Justice was local and uncomplicated—in fact, an organized legal profession did not emerge until the 18th century.

Finally, no mainland American colony rigidly followed English patterns of inheritance. Instead, some women had a chance to acquire property, usually by inheritance from a deceased husband, particularly in the Chesapeake colonies. The single women who went there as servants were desperate people who had hit bottom in England. Those who stayed alive enjoyed a fantastic chance at upward mobility. Many won a respectability never available to them in England. In every colony younger sons also found their situation improved. They played a huge role in settling the colonies, and they showed little inclination to preserve institutions that had offered them no landed inheritance in England. Most families made no distinction between the eldest and other sons, except in New England. The Puritan colonies honored a biblical mandate to give the eldest son a double share. That practice strengthened patriarchy in the region, but it was much less discriminatory than primogeniture, which gave all land to the eldest son in England.

THE BEGINNINGS OF EMPIRE

In the chaotic 1640s, the English realized that their colonies overseas were bringing them very few benefits. England had no coherent colonial policy.

UPHEAVAL IN AMERICA: THE CRITICAL 1640S

England's civil wars rocked its emerging empire, politically and economically. As royal power collapsed in the 1640s, the West Indian colonies demanded and received elective assemblies. Then the Dutch, taking advantage of the chaos in England, helped finance the sugar revolution in Barbados and seized control of trade in and out of England's West Indian and Chesapeake colonies. By 1650 most sugar and tobacco exports were going to Amsterdam, not London.

During the civil wars, nobody in England exercised effective control over the colonies. The king had declared that their trade was to remain in English hands, but no agency existed to enforce that claim. The new elective assemblies of Barbados and the Leeward Islands preferred to trade with the Dutch, even after the English Crown took over those colonies in 1660. The mainland colonies had been organized by joint-stock companies or proprietary lords under royal charters, but there the colonists governed themselves. As the New England settlements expanded, the new colonies of Connecticut, Rhode Island, and New Haven did not even bother to obtain royal charters. On the mainland, only Virginia had a royal governor.

The chaos of the 1640s gave Indians a unique opportunity to resist the settlers. The disruption of trade with England during the civil wars threatened to cut off the settlements from regular supplies of muskets and gunpowder, giving the Indians a powerful advantage. Although the Indians of the eastern woodlands never united into an effective league, many of them began to think of driving the Europeans out altogether. Between 1643 and 1647, the Iroquois nearly wiped out New France, and the Hudson valley Algonquians almost destroyed New Netherland. Maryland, beset by conflicts with Susquehannock Indians and by civil war among its colonists, nearly ceased to exist. In Virginia in 1644 the aging warrior Opechancanough staged another massacre, killing 500 settlers without warning. This time the settlers recovered more quickly, murdered Opechancanough after he surrendered, broke up his chiefdom, and made its member tribes accept treaties of dependency.

Only New England avoided war with the Indians—just barely. Miantonomo, sachem of the Narragansetts, called for a war of extermination against the settlers, to be launched by a surprise attack in 1642. He abandoned the plan when settlers got wind of it. The colonists created their own defensive alliance in 1643, the New England Confederation, which united the four orthodox colonies of Massachusetts, Plymouth, Connecticut, and New Haven. The confederation persuaded the Mohegans to kill Miantonomo, and tensions with the Narragansett Indians remained high. The Narragansetts controlled some of the finest land in New England. Massachusetts, Plymouth, and Connecticut all wanted that land, but the Narragansetts were still too powerful to intimidate.

What happened in the colonies seemed of little interest to the English people in the turbulent 1640s. But as the civil wars ended and the extent of Dutch commercial domination became obvious, the English turned their eyes westward once again. In a sense, England first discovered its colonies and their importance around 1650.

Mercantilism as a Moral Revolution

During the 17th century, most of the European powers followed a set of policies now usually called "mercantilism." Mercantilists argued that power derived ultimately from the wealth of a country, that the increase of wealth required vigorous trade, and that colonies had become essential to that growth. Clearly, a state had to control the commerce of its colonies. But mercantilists disagreed over the best ways to promote economic growth. The Dutch favored virtual free trade within Europe. England preferred some kind of state regulation of the domestic and imperial economy.

European philosophers agreed that the major passions are glory, love, and greed. In an age of religious wars, statesmen began to see glory and love as dangerous and to look more favorably

A PICTISH MAN HOLDING A HUMAN HEAD, BY JOHN WHITE, LATE 16TH CENTURY   In the ancient world, the Picts were among the ancestors of the English and the Scots. John White, who painted many Indian scenes on Roanoke Island in the 1580s, believed that the English had been "savages" not all that long ago and that American Indians, like the English, could progress to "civility." America made him think of "progress."

upon greed. The pursuit of glory or love inspired intense, often unpredictable and destructive activity, followed by relaxation or even exhaustion. But greed, because it can never be satiated, fostered *predictable* behavior—namely, the pursuit of self-interest. By creating economic incentives, then, a state could induce its people to engage in activities that would increase not just their own wealth and power but that of the whole country. And through the imposition of import duties and other disincentives, the state could discourage actions detrimental to its power.

Early mercantilists assumed that the world contained a fixed supply of wealth. A state, to augment its own power, would have to expropriate the wealth of a rival. Trade wars would replace religious wars. Gradually, however, a more radical idea took hold: The growth of trade might multiply the wealth of the whole world, with all nations benefiting and becoming so interdependent that war between them would be recognized as suicidal.

Mercantilism gradually became associated with the emerging idea of unending progress. Europeans were already familiar with two kinds of progress, one associated with Renaissance humanism, the other explicitly Christian. The opening of the Americas had already reinforced both visions. Humanists knew that the distant ancestors of Europeans had all been "barbarians" who had advanced over the centuries toward "civility." Their own encounters with the indigenous peoples of Africa, Ireland, and America underscored this dualistic view by revealing new "savages" who seemed morally and culturally inferior to the "civilized" colonists. Most Christians shared these convictions, but they also believed that human society was progressing toward a future Millennium in which Christ would return to earth and reign with his saints in perfect harmony for 1,000 years. To missionaries the discovery of millions of "heathens" in the Americas stimulated millennial thinking. God had chosen this moment to open a new hemisphere to Christians, they explained, because the Millennium was near. But both the humanist and the Christian notions of progress were static concepts. Humanity would advance to a certain level, and then change would cease. Mercantilism, by contrast, marked a revolution of the human imagination precisely because it could arouse visions of endless progress.

Mercantilism also promoted a more modern concept of law. In the past, most jurists believed that legislation merely restated natural laws or ancient customs in written form. They did not see it as an agent of change. Mercantilists did. They intended to modify behavior. At first, they probably considered anything a triumph that made their exhausted world less terrible. But as the decades passed, mercantilists became more confident of their ability to improve society.

THE FIRST NAVIGATION ACT

English merchants began debating trade policy during a severe depression in the 1620s. They agreed that a nation's wealth depended on its balance of trade, that a healthy nation ought to export more than it imports, and that the difference—or balance—could be converted into military strength. They also believed that a state needed colonies to produce essential commodities unavailable at home. And they argued that a society ought to export luxuries, not import them. English merchants observed Dutch commercial success and determined that it seemed to rest on a mastery of these principles. For England to catch up, Parliament would have to intervene.

London merchants clamored for measures to stifle Dutch competition. In 1650 Parliament responded by banning foreign ships from English colonies. A year later, it passed the first comprehensive Navigation Act. Under this act, Asian and African goods could be imported into the British Isles or the colonies only in English-owned ships, and the master and at least half of each crew had to be Englishmen. European goods could be imported into Britain or the colonies in either English ships or the ships of the producing country, but foreigners could not trade between one English port and another.

This new attention from the English government angered the colonists in the West Indies and North America. Mercantilists assumed that the colonies existed only to enrich the mother country. Why else had England permitted them to be founded? But the young men growing sugar in Barbados or tobacco in Virginia intended to prosper on their own. Selling their crops to the Dutch, who offered the lowest freight rates, added to their profits. Although New England produced no staple that Europeans wanted except fish, Yankee skippers cheerfully swapped their fish or forest products in the Chesapeake for tobacco, which they then carried directly to Europe, usually to Amsterdam.

Barbados greeted the Navigation Act by proclaiming virtual independence. Virginia recognized Charles II as king and continued to welcome Dutch and Yankee traders. In 1651 Parliament dispatched a naval force to America. It compelled Barbados to submit to Parliament and then sailed to the Chesapeake, where Virginia and Maryland capitulated in 1652. But in the absence of resident officials to enforce English policy, trade with the Dutch continued.

By 1652 England and the Netherlands were at war. For two years the English navy dealt heavy blows to the Dutch. Finally, in 1654, Oliver Cromwell sent Parliament home and made peace. A militant Protestant, he preferred to fight Catholic Spain rather than the Netherlands. He sent a fleet to take Hispaniola. It failed, but it did seize Jamaica in 1655.

RESTORATION NAVIGATION ACTS

By the Restoration era, mercantilist thinking had become widespread. Although the new royalist Parliament invalidated all legislation passed during the Commonwealth period, these "Cavaliers" promptly reenacted and extended the original Navigation Act. The Navigation Act of 1660 required that all colonial trade be carried on English ships (a category that included colonial vessels but now excluded the Scots), but the master and *three-fourths* of the crew had to be English. The act also created a category of "enumerated commodities," of which sugar and tobacco were the most important, permitting these products to be shipped from the colony of origin *only* to England or to another English colony. The colonists could still export unenumerated commodities elsewhere. New England could send fish to a French sugar island, for example, and Virginia could export wheat to Cuba, provided the French and the Spanish would let them.

In a second measure, the Staple Act of 1663, Parliament regulated goods going to the colonies. With few exceptions, products from Europe, Asia, or Africa could not be delivered to the settlements unless they had first been landed in England.

A third measure, the Plantation Duty Act of 1673, required captains of colonial ships to post bond in the colonies that they would deliver all enumerated commodities to England, or else pay on the spot the duties that would be owed in England (the "plantation duty"). This measure, England hoped, would eliminate all incentives to smuggle. To make it effective, England for the first time sent customs officers to the colonies to collect the duty and prosecute all violators. Most of them won little compliance at first.

Properly enforced, the Navigation Acts would dislodge the Dutch and establish English hegemony over Atlantic trade, and that is what happened by the end of the century. In 1600, about 90 percent of England's exports consisted of woolen cloth. By 1700, colonial and Asian commerce accounted for 30 to 40 percent of England's overseas trade, and London had become the largest city in western Europe.

In the 1670s a war between France and the Netherlands diverted critical Dutch resources from trade to defense, thus helping England to catch up with the Dutch. The British navy soon became the most powerful fleet in the world. By 1710 or so, virtually all British colonial trade was carried on British ships. Sugar, tobacco, and other staple crops all passed through Britain on their way to their ultimate destination. Nearly all of the manufactured goods consumed in the colonies were made in Britain. Most products from Europe or Asia destined for the colonies passed through Britain first, although some smuggling of these goods continued.

Few government policies have ever been as successful as England's Navigation Acts, but England achieved these results without pursuing a steady course toward increased imperial control. For example, in granting charters to Rhode Island in 1662 and to Connecticut in 1663, Charles II approved elective governors and legislatures in both colonies. (The Connecticut charter also absorbed the New Haven Colony into the Hartford government.) These elective officials could not be dismissed or punished for failure to enforce the Navigation Acts. Moreover, the Crown also chartered several new Restoration colonies (see Chapter 2), whose organizers had few incentives to obey the new laws.

INDIANS, SETTLERS, UPHEAVAL

As time passed, the commercial possibilities and limitations of North America were becoming much clearer. The French and Dutch mastered the fur trade because they controlled the two all-water routes to the interior, via the St. Lawrence system and the Hudson and Mohawk valleys. South Carolinians could go around the southern extreme of the Appalachians. They all needed Indian trading partners.

As of 1670, there were still no sharp boundaries between Indian lands and colonial settlements. Boston, the largest city north of Mexico, was only 15 miles from an Indian village. The outposts on the Delaware River were islands in a sea of Indians. In the event of war, nearly every European settlement was vulnerable to attack.

INDIAN STRATEGIES OF SURVIVAL

By the 1670s most of the coastal tribes in regular contact with Europeans had already been devastated by disease or soon would be. European diseases, by magnifying the depleted tribes' need for captives, also increased the intensity of wars among Indian peoples. The Iroquois, hard hit by smallpox and other ailments, acquired muskets from the Dutch and used them, first to attack other Iroquoian peoples, and then Algonquians. These "mourning wars" were often initiated by the widow or bereaved mother or sister of a deceased loved one, who insisted that her male relatives repair the loss. Her warrior relatives then launched a raid and brought back captives. Although adult male prisoners were usually tortured to death, most of the women and children were adopted and assimilated. Adoption worked because the captives shared the cultural values of their captors. They became Iroquois. As early as the 1660s, a majority of the Indians in the Five Nations were adoptees, not native-born Iroquois. In this way the confederacy remained strong while its rivals declined. In the southern piedmont, the warlike, Sioux-speaking Catawba Indians also assimilated thousands from other tribes. Further into the southern interior, the Creeks assimilated adoptees from a wide variety of ethnic backgrounds.

In some ways, America became as much a new world for the Indians as it did for the colonists. European cloth, muskets, hatchets, knives, and pots were welcomed among the Indians and spread far into the interior, but Indians who learned to use them gradually abandoned traditional skills and became increasingly dependent on trade with Europeans. Alcohol, the one item always in demand, was also dangerous. Indian men drank to alter their mood and achieve visions, not for sociability. Drunkenness became a major, if intermittent, social problem.

Settlers who understood that their future depended on the fur trade tried to stay on good terms with the Indians. Pieter Stuyvesant put New Netherland on such a course, and the English governors of New York followed his lead. Edmund Andros, governor from 1674 to 1680, cultivated the friendship of the Iroquois League, in which the five member nations had promised not to wage war against one another. In 1677 Andros and the Five Nations agreed to make New York the easternmost link in what the English called the "Covenant Chain" of peace, a huge defensive advantage for a lightly populated colony. Thus, while New England and Virginia fought bitter Indian wars in the 1670s, New York avoided conflict. The Covenant Chain later proved flexible enough to incorporate other Indians and colonies as well.

Where the Indian trade was slight, war became more likely. In 1675 it erupted in both New England and the Chesapeake. In the 1640s Virginia had negotiated treaties of dependency with the member nations of the Powhatan chiefdom. The New England colonies had similar understandings with the large non-Christian nations of the region. But the Puritan governments placed even greater reliance on a growing number of Christianized Indians.

PURITAN INDIAN MISSIONS

Serious efforts to convert Indians to Protestantism began in the 1640s on the island of Martha's Vineyard under Thomas Mayhew Sr. and Thomas Mayhew Jr., and in Massachusetts under John Eliot, pastor of the Roxbury church. Eliot tried to make the nearby Indian town of Natick into a model mission community.

The Mayhews were more successful than Eliot, although he received most of the publicity. They worked with local sachems and challenged only the tribal powwows (prophets or medicine men). The Mayhews encouraged Indian men to teach the settlers of Martha's Vineyard and Nantucket how to catch whales, an activity that made them a vital part of the settlers' economy without threatening their identity as males. Eliot, by contrast, attacked the authority of the sachems as well as the powwows and insisted on turning Indian men into farmers, a female role in Indian society. Yet he did translate the Bible and a few other religious works into the Wampanoag language.

By the early 1670s more than 1,000 Indians, nearly all of them survivors of coastal tribes that had been decimated by disease, lived in a string of seven "praying towns," and Eliot was busy organizing five more. By 1675 about 2,300 Indians, perhaps one-quarter of all those living in southeastern New England, were in various stages of conversion to Christianity. But only 160 of them had achieved the kind of conversion experience that Puritans required for full membership in a church. Indians did not share the Puritan sense of sin. The more powerful nations felt threatened by this pressure to convert, and resistance to Christianity became one cause of the war that broke out in 1675. Other causes were the settlers' lust for Indian lands and the Indian fear that their way of life was in danger of extinction.

METACOM'S (OR KING PHILIP'S) WAR

Metacom (whom the English called King Philip) shared these fears. He was sachem of the Wampanoags and the son of Massasoit, who had celebrated the first thanksgiving feast with the Pilgrims. What came to be known as Metacom's War began in the frontier town of Swansea in June 1675, after settlers killed an Indian they found looting an abandoned house. When the Indians demanded satisfaction the next day, the settlers laughed in their faces. The Indians took revenge, and the violence escalated into war.

The settlers were confident of victory. But since the 1630s the Indians had acquired firearms. They had built forges to make musket balls and repair their weapons. They had even

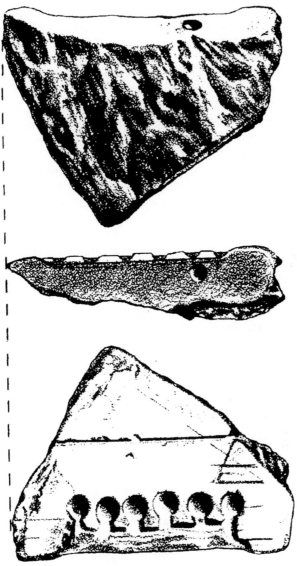

Bullet Mold in Use among New England Indians, circa 1675 Indians could make bullets and repair muskets, but they remained dependent on Europeans for their supply of gunpowder. In early 1676, the Indian leader Metacom ran out of gunpowder after failing to acquire more from New France. Over the next several months, he lost his war against the settlers.

become marksmen with the smoothbore musket by firing several smaller bullets, instead of a single musketball, with each charge. The settlers were terrible shots. In the tradition of European armies, they discharged volleys without aiming. To the shock of the colonists, Metacom won several engagements against Plymouth militia, usually by ambushing the noisy intruders.

He then escaped from Plymouth Colony and headed toward the upper Connecticut valley, where he burned five Massachusetts towns in three months.

Massachusetts and Connecticut joined the fray. Rather than attack Metacom's Wampanoags they went after the Narragansetts, who were trying hard to remain neutral but whose fertile lands many settlers dreamed of acquiring. In the Great Swamp Fight of December 1675, a Puritan army attacked an unfinished Narragansett fort and massacred hundreds of Indians, most of them women and children, but not before the Indians had picked off a high percentage of the officers. The surviving warriors joined Metacom and showed that they too could use terror. They torched more frontier settlements. Altogether about 800 settlers were killed, and two dozen towns were destroyed or badly damaged.

Atrocities were common on both sides. When one settler boasted that his Bible would save him from harm, the Indians disemboweled him and stuffed the sacred book in his belly. At least 17 friendly Indians were murdered by settlers, some in cold blood before dozens of witnesses, but for more than a year New England juries refused to convict anyone.

Frontier settlers demanded the annihilation of all nearby Indians, even the Christian converts. The Massachusetts government, shocked to realize that it could not win the war without Indian allies, did what it could to protect the "praying" Indians. The magistrates evacuated them to a bleak island in Boston harbor where they spent a miserable winter of privation but then enlisted to fight against Metacom in the spring campaign.

The war split the clergy. Increase Mather, a prominent Boston minister, saw the conflict as God's judgment on a sinful people and warned that no victory would come until New England repented and reformed. At first the Massachusetts General Court agreed. It blamed the war on young men who wore their hair too long, on boys and girls who took leisurely horse rides together, on people who dressed above their station in life, and on blaspheming Quakers. Another Boston minister, William Hubbard, insisted that the war was only a brief testing time, after which the Lord would lead his saints to victory over the heathen. To Daniel Gookin, a magistrate committed to Eliot's mission work, the war was an unspeakable tragedy for both settlers and Indians.

Despite their disagreements, the settlers pulled together and won the war in 1676. Governor Andros of New York persuaded the Mohawks to attack Metacom's winter camp and disperse his people, who by then were short of gunpowder. The New Englanders, working closely with Mohegan and Christian Indian allies, then hunted down Metacom's war parties, killed hundreds of Indians, including Metacom, and sold hundreds more into West Indian slavery. Some of those enslaved had not even been party to the conflict and had actually requested asylum from it.

VIRGINIA'S INDIAN WAR

In Virginia, Governor Sir William Berkeley rejoiced in the New Englanders' woes. Metacom's War was the least they deserved for the way the Puritans had ripped England apart and executed Charles I during the civil wars. Then Virginia began to have troubles of its own.

In 1675 the Doegs, a dependent Indian nation in the Potomac valley, demanded payment of an old debt from a local planter. When he refused, they ran off some of his livestock. After his overseer killed one of them, the others fled but later returned to ambush and kill the man. The county militia mustered and followed the Doegs across the Potomac into Maryland. At a fork in the trail, the militia split into two parties. Each found a group of Indians in a shack a few hundred yards up the path it was following. Both parties fired at point-blank range, killing 11 at one cabin and 14 at the other. One of the bands was indeed Doeg; the other was not: "Susquehannock friends," blurted one Indian as he fled.

The Susquehannocks were a strong Iroquoian-speaking people with firearms who had moved south to escape Iroquois attacks. At Maryland's invitation, they had recently occupied land north of the Potomac. Berkeley, still hoping to avoid war, sent John Washington (ancestor of George) with some Virginia militia to investigate the killings and, if possible, to set things right.

Washington preferred vengeance. His Virginia militia joined with a Maryland force, and together they besieged a formidable Susquehannock fort on the north bank of the Potomac. When the Indians sent out five or six sachems to negotiate, the militia murdered them and then laid siege to the fort for the next six weeks. The Indians, short of provisions, finally broke out one night with all their people, killing several militiamen. After hurling taunts of defiance and promises of vengeance, they disappeared into the forest. Apparently blaming Virginia more than Maryland, they killed more than 30 Virginia settlers in January 1676. The colonists began to panic.

Berkeley favored a defensive strategy against the Indians; most settlers wanted to attack. In March 1676 the governor summoned a special session of the Virginia legislature to approve the creation of a string of forts above the fall line of the major rivers, with companies of "rangers" to patrol the stretches between them. Berkeley also hoped to maintain a distinction between the clearly hostile Susquehannocks and other Indians who might still be neutral or friendly. Frontier settlers demanded war against them all. Finally, to avoid further provocation, Berkeley restricted the fur trade to a few of his close associates. To the men excluded from that circle, his actions looked like favoritism. To new settlers in frontier counties, whose access to land was blocked by the Indians and who now had to pay higher taxes, Berkeley's strategy seemed intolerable.

In both the Second (1665–1667) and Third (1672–1674) Anglo-Dutch Wars, Berkeley had built costly forts to protect the colony from the Dutch navy, but Dutch warships had sailed around the forts and mauled the tobacco fleet anyway. Accordingly, colonists denounced the building of any more forts and demanded an offensive campaign waged by unpaid volunteers, who would take their rewards by plundering and enslaving Indians. In April the frontier settlers found a reckless leader in newcomer Nathaniel Bacon. Using his political connections (he was the governor's cousin by marriage), he got himself appointed to the council soon after his arrival in the colony in 1674, but was now excluded from the Indian trade under Berkeley's new rules.

BACON'S REBELLION

Ignoring Berkeley's orders, Bacon marched his frontiersmen south in search of the elusive Susquehannocks. After several days his weary men reached a village of friendly Occaneechees, who offered them shelter, announced that they knew where to find a Susquehannock camp, and even offered to attack it. The Occaneechees surprised and defeated the Susquehannocks and returned with their captives to celebrate the victory with Bacon. But after they had fallen asleep, Bacon's men massacred them and seized their furs and prisoners.

By then, Berkeley had outlawed Bacon, dissolved the legislature, and called the first general election since 1661. He asked the burgesses to bring their grievances to Jamestown for redress at the June assembly.

Local voters elected Bacon to the House of Burgesses. Berkeley had him arrested when he reached Jamestown and made him go down on his knees before the governor and council and apologize for his disobedience. Berkeley then forgave him and restored him to his seat in the council. While the burgesses were passing laws to reform the county courts, the vestries, and the tax system, Bacon slipped home, summoned his followers again, and marched on Jamestown. At gunpoint, he forced Berkeley to commission him as general of volunteers and compelled the legislature to authorize another expedition against the Indians.

Berkeley retreated down river to Gloucester County and mustered its militia, but they refused to follow him against Bacon. They would fight only Indians. Mortified, Berkeley fled to the eastern shore, the only part of the colony that was still loyal to him. Bacon hastened to Jamestown, summoned a meeting of planters at the governor's Green Spring mansion, and ordered the confiscation of the estates of Berkeley's supporters. Meanwhile, Berkeley raised his own force on the eastern shore by promising the men an exemption from taxes for 21 years and the right to plunder the rebels.

Royal government collapsed. During the summer of 1676, hundreds of settlers set out to make their fortunes by plundering Indians, other colonists, or both. Bacon's Rebellion was the largest upheaval in the American colonies before 1775.

Bacon never did kill a hostile Indian. While he was slaughtering and enslaving the unresisting Pamunkeys along the frontier, Berkeley assembled a small fleet and retook Jamestown in August. Bacon rushed east and laid siege to Jamestown. After suffering only a few casualties, the governor's men grew discouraged, and in early September the whole force returned to the eastern shore. Bacon then burned Jamestown to the ground. He also boasted of his ability to hold off an English army, unite Virginia with Maryland and North Carolina, and win Dutch support for setting up an independent Chesapeake republic. Instead he died of dysentery in October.

Berkeley soon regained control of Virginia. Using the ships of the London tobacco fleet, he overpowered the plantations that Bacon had fortified. Ignoring royal orders to show clemency, Berkeley hanged 23 of the rebels. A new assembly repudiated the reforms of 1676, and in many counties the governor's men used their control of the courts to continue plundering the Baconians through confiscations and fines. Berkeley, summoned to England to defend himself, died there in 1677 before he could present his case.

CRISIS IN ENGLAND AND THE REDEFINITION OF EMPIRE

Bacon's Rebellion helped trigger a political crisis in England. Because Virginia produced little tobacco in 1676 during the uprising, English customs revenues fell sharply, and the king was obliged to ask Parliament for more money. Parliament's response was tempered by the much deeper problem of the royal succession. Charles II had fathered many bastards, but his royal marriage was childless. After the queen reached menopause in the mid-1670s, his brother James, duke of York, became his heir. By then James had become a Catholic. When Charles dissolved the Parliament that had sat from 1661 until 1678, he knew he would have to deal with a new House of Commons terrified by the prospect of a Catholic king.

THE POPISH PLOT, THE EXCLUSION CRISIS, AND THE RISE OF PARTY

In this atmosphere of distrust, a cynical adventurer, Titus Oates, fabricated the sensational story that he had uncovered a sinister "Popish Plot" to kill Charles and bring James to the throne. In the wake of these accusations, the king's ministry fell, and the parliamentary opposition won majorities in three successive elections between 1678 and 1681. Organized by Lord Shaftesbury (the Carolina proprietor), the opposition demanded that James, a Catholic, be excluded from the throne in favor of his Protestant daughters, Mary and Anne. It also called for a guarantee of frequent elections and for an independent electorate not under the influence of wealthy patrons. The king's men began castigating Shaftesbury's followers as "Whigs," the name of an obscure sect of Scottish religious extremists who favored the assassination of both Charles and James. Whigs in turn denounced Charles's courtiers as "Tories," a term for Irish Catholics who murdered Protestant landlords. Both labels stuck.

England's party struggle reflected a deep rift between "Court" and "Country" forces. As of 1681 Tories were a Court party. They favored the legitimate succession, a standing army with adequate revenues to maintain it, the Anglican Church without toleration for Protestant dissenters, and a powerful monarchy. The Whigs were a Country opposition that stood for the exclusion of James from the throne, a decentralized militia rather than a standing army, toleration of Protestant dissenters but not of Catholics, and an active role in government for a reformed Parliament. During this struggle, James fled to Scotland in virtual exile. But Charles, after getting secret financial support from King Louis XIV of France, dissolved Parliament in 1681 and ruled without one for the last four years of his reign.

THE LORDS OF TRADE AND IMPERIAL REFORM

English politics of the 1670s and 1680s had a profound impact on the colonies. The duke of York emerged from the Third Anglo-Dutch War as the most powerful shaper of imperial policy. At his urging the government created a new agency in 1675, the Lords Committee of Trade and Plantations, or more simply, the Lords of Trade. This agency enforced the Navigation Acts and administered the colonies. The West Indies became the object of most of the new policies. The instruments of royal government first took shape in the islands and were then extended to the mainland.

In the 1660s the Crown took control of the governments of Barbados, Jamaica, and the Leeward Islands. The king appointed the governor and upper house of each colony; the settlers elected an assembly. The Privy Council in England reserved to itself the power to hear appeals from colonial courts and to disallow colonial legislation after the governor had approved it. The Privy Council also issued a formal commission and a lengthy set of instructions to each royal governor. In the two or three decades after 1660, these documents became standardized.

From the Crown's point of view, the governor's commission *created* the constitutional structure of each colony, a claim that few settlers accepted. The colonists believed they had an inherent right to constitutional rule.

Written instructions told each royal governor how to use his broad powers. They laid out things he must do, such as command the militia, and things he must avoid, such as approve laws detrimental to English trade. Crown lawyers eventually agreed that these instructions were binding only on the governor, not on the colony as a whole. In other words, royal instructions never acquired the force of law.

London also insisted that each colony pay the cost of its own government. This requirement, ironically, strengthened colonial claims to self-rule. After a long struggle in Jamaica, the Crown imposed a compromise in 1681 that had broad significance for all the colonies. The Lords of Trade threatened to make the Jamaica assembly as weak as the Irish Parliament, which could debate and approve only those bills that had first been adopted by the English Privy Council. Under the compromise, the Jamaica assembly retained its power to initiate and amend legislation, in return for agreeing to a permanent revenue act, a measure that freed the governor from financial dependence on the assembly.

Metacom's War and Bacon's Rebellion lent urgency to these reforms. The Lords of Trade ordered soldiers to Virginia along with a royal commission to investigate grievances there. In 1676 they also sent an aggressive customs officer, Edward Randolph, to Massachusetts. He recommended that the colony's charter be revoked. The Lords of Trade viewed New England and all proprietary colonies with deep suspicion. They had reason for concern. As late as 1678, Virginia remained the only royal colony on the mainland. The Lords of Trade possessed no effective instruments for punishing violators of the Navigation Acts in North America. The king could demand and reprimand, but not command.

The Jamaica model assumed that each royal governor would summon an assembly on occasion, though not very often. In the 1680s the Crown imposed a similar settlement on Virginia. James conceded an assembly to New York, too. The Jamaica model was becoming the norm for the Lords of Trade. James's real preference emerged after the English Court of Chancery revoked the Massachusetts Charter in 1684. Charles II died and his brother became King James II in early 1685. The possibility of a vigorous autocracy in America suddenly reappeared.

THE DOMINION OF NEW ENGLAND

Absolutist New York now became the king's model for reorganizing New England. James disallowed the New York Charter of Liberties of 1683 (see Chapter 2) and abolished the colony's assembly but kept the permanent revenue act in force. In 1686 he sent Sir Edmund Andros, the autocratic governor of New York from 1674 to 1680, to Massachusetts to take over a new government called the Dominion of New England. James added New Hampshire, Plymouth, Rhode Island, Connecticut, New York, and both Jerseys to the Dominion. Andros governed this vast domain through an appointive council and a superior court that rode circuit dispensing justice. There was no elective assembly. Andros also imposed religious toleration on the Puritans.

At first, Andros won support from merchants who had been excluded from politics by the Puritan requirement that they be full church members, but his rigorous enforcement of the Navigation Acts soon alienated them. When he tried to compel New England farmers to take out new land titles that included annual quitrents, he enraged the whole countryside. His suppression of a tax revolt in Essex County, Massachusetts, started many people thinking more highly of their rights as Englishmen than of their peculiar liberties as Puritans. By 1688, government by consent probably seemed more valuable than it ever had before.

THE GLORIOUS REVOLUTION

Events in England and France undermined the Dominion of New England. James II proclaimed toleration for Protestants and Catholics and began to name Catholics to high office.

LE ROY DE FRANCE.
l'Home immortel Chef de la S.te Ligue.

Mon soleil par sa force eclaira l'heretique.
Il chassa tout d'un coup les brouillards de Calvin:
Non pas par un Zele divin.
Mais afin de cacher ma fine Politique.

THE SUN KING AS DEATH This Dutch cartoon, "Le Roy de France" ("the King of France"), responded to French persecution of the Huguenots by portraying the illustrious "Sun King" as death carrying his ominous scythe. Few early modern cartoons were able to make so dramatic a point as concisely and graphically as this one.

In 1685 Louis XIV revoked the 1598 Edict of Nantes that had granted toleration to Protestants and launched a vicious persecution of the Huguenots. About 160,000 fled the kingdom. Many went to England; several thousand settled in the English mainland colonies. James II tried to suppress the news of Louis's persecution, which made his own professions of toleration seem hypocritical, even though his commitment was probably genuine. Then in 1688 James II's queen gave birth to a son who would clearly be raised Catholic, thus imposing a Catholic *dynasty* on England. Several Whig and Tory leaders swallowed their mutual hatred and invited William of Orange, the *stadholder* of the Netherlands, to England. The husband of the king's older Protestant daughter Mary (by James's first marriage), William had become the most prominent Protestant soldier in Europe during a long war against Louis XIV.

William landed in England in November 1688. Most of the English army sided with him, and James fled to France in late December. Parliament declared that James had abdicated the throne and named William III (1689–1702) and Mary II (1689–1694) as joint sovereigns. It also passed a Toleration Act that gave Protestant dissenters (but not Catholics) the right to worship publicly, and a Declaration of Rights that guaranteed a Protestant succession and condemned as illegal many of the acts of James II. This "Glorious Revolution" also brought England and the Netherlands into war against Louis XIV, who supported James.

THE GLORIOUS REVOLUTION IN AMERICA

The Boston militia overthrew Andros on April 18 and 19, 1689. Andros's attempt to suppress the news that William had landed in England convinced the Puritans that he was part of a global "Popish Plot" to undermine Protestant societies everywhere.

In May and June, the New York City militia took over Fort James at the southern tip of Manhattan and renamed it Fort William. Francis Nicholson, lieutenant governor in New York under Andros, refused to proclaim William and Mary as sovereigns without direct orders from England and soon sailed for home. The active rebels in New York City were nearly all Dutch who had little experience with traditional English liberties. Few had held high office. Their leader, Jacob Leisler, dreaded conquest by Catholics from New France and began to act like a Dutch *stadholder* in a nominally English colony.

Military defense became Leisler's highest priority, but his demands for supplies soon alienated even his Yankee supporters on Long Island. Although he summoned an elective assembly, he made no effort to revive the Charter of Liberties of 1683 while continuing to collect duties under the permanent revenue act of that year. He showed little respect for the legal rights of his opponents, most of whom were English or were Dutch merchants who had served the Dominion of New England. Loud complaints against his administration reached the Crown in London.

In Maryland, Protestants overthrew Lord Baltimore's Catholic government in 1689. The governor of Maryland refused to proclaim William and Mary, even after all the other colonies had done so. To Lord Baltimore's dismay, the messenger he sent from London to Maryland with orders to accept the new monarchs died en route. Had he arrived, the government probably would have survived the crisis.

THE ENGLISH RESPONSE

England responded in different ways to each of these upheavals. The Maryland rebels won the royal government they requested from England and soon established the Anglican Church in the colony. Catholics could no longer worship in public, hold office, or even expect toleration. Most prominent Catholic families, however, remained loyal to their faith. In 1716, when Lord Baltimore became a Protestant, the Crown restored proprietary government.

In New York, the Leislerians suffered a deadly defeat. Leisler and his Dutch followers, who had no significant contacts at the English Court, watched helplessly as their enemies, working through the imperial bureaucracy that William inherited from James, manipulated the Dutch king of England into undermining his loyal Dutch supporters in New York. The new governor, Henry Sloughter, arrested Leisler and his son-in-law in 1691, tried both for treason, and had them hanged, drawn, and quartered. The assembly elected that year was controlled by Anti-Leislerians, most of whom were English. It passed a modified version of the Charter of Liberties of 1683, this time denying toleration to Catholics. Like its predecessor, it was later disallowed. Bitter struggles between Leislerians and Anti-Leislerians raged until after 1700.

Another complex struggle involved Massachusetts. In 1689 Increase Mather, acting as the colony's agent in London, failed to get Parliament to restore the charter of 1629. Over the next two years he negotiated a new charter, which gave the Crown the power to appoint governors, justices, and militia officers, and the power to veto laws and to hear judicial appeals. The 1691 charter also granted toleration to all Protestants and based voting rights on property qualifications, not church membership. In effect, liberty and property had triumphed over godliness.

While insisting on these concessions, William also accepted much of the previous history of the colony. The General Court, not the governor as in other royal colonies, retained control over the distribution of land. The council remained an elective body, although it was chosen annually by the full legislature, not directly by the voters. The governor could veto any councillor. Massachusetts also absorbed the colonies of Plymouth and Maine. New Hampshire regained its autonomy, but until 1741 it usually shared the same royal governor with Massachusetts. Rhode Island and Connecticut resumed their charter governments.

THE SALEM WITCH TRIALS

When Mather sailed into Boston harbor with the new charter in May 1692, he found the province besieged by witches. The accusations arose in Salem Village (modern Danvers) among a group of girls, most of whom had been orphaned during the Indian wars and had been adopted into households more pious than their original families. Uncertain whether anyone was responsible for finding husbands for them, they probably asked Tituba, a Carib Indian slave in the household of Reverend Samuel Parris, to tell their fortunes. This occult activity imposed a heavy burden of guilt on the girls and, beginning with the youngest, they broke under the strain. They howled, barked, and stretched themselves into frightful contortions. With adult encouragement, they accused many of their neighbors of witchcraft. Most of the accused were old women in families that had opposed the appointment of Parris as village minister.

The trials began in June. The court hanged 19 people, pressed one man to death because he refused to stand trial, and allowed several other people to die in jail. Many of those hanged were grandmothers, several quite conspicuous for their piety. One victim was a former minister at Salem Village who had become a Baptist. The governor finally halted the trials after the girls accused his wife of being a witch.

The witch trials provided a bitter finale to the era of political upheaval that had afflicted Massachusetts since the loss of the colony's charter in 1684. Along with the new charter, the trials brought the Puritan era to a close.

THE COMPLETION OF EMPIRE

The Glorious Revolution killed absolutism in English America and guaranteed that royal government would be representative government in the colonies. Both Crown and colonists took it for granted that any colony settled by the English would elect an assembly to vote on all taxes and consent to all local laws. Governors would be appointed by the Crown or a lord proprietor. (Governors were elected in Connecticut and Rhode Island.) But royal government soon became the norm especially after the New Jersey and Carolina proprietors surrendered their powers of government to the Crown. By the 1720s Maryland and Pennsylvania (along with Delaware, which became a separate colony under the Penn proprietorship in 1704) were the only surviving proprietary provinces on the mainland.

This transition to royal government seems smoother in retrospect than it did at the time. London almost lost control of the empire in the 1690s. Overwhelmed by the pressures of the

French war, the Lords of Trade could not keep pace with events in the colonies. When French privateers disrupted the tobacco trade, Scottish smugglers stepped in and began to divert it to Glasgow in defiance of the Navigation Acts. New York became a haven for pirates. Parliament, suspecting William of favoring Dutch interests over English, even threatened to take control of the colonies away from the king.

William took action in 1696. With his approval Parliament passed a new, comprehensive Navigation Act that plugged several loopholes in earlier laws and extended to America the English system of vice admiralty courts, which dispensed quick justice without juries. When the new courts settled routine maritime disputes or condemned enemy merchant ships captured by colonial privateers, their services were highly regarded by the settlers. But when the courts tried to assume jurisdiction over the Navigation Acts, they aroused controversy.

William also replaced the Lords of Trade in 1696 with a new agency, the Board of Trade. Its powers were almost purely advisory. It corresponded with governors and other officials in the colonies, listened to lobbyists in England, and made policy recommendations to appropriate governmental bodies. The board tried to collect information on complex questions and to offer helpful advice. It was, in short, an early attempt at government by experts.

Another difficult problem was resolved in 1707 when England and Scotland agreed to merge their separate parliaments and become the single kingdom of Great Britain. At a stroke, the Act of Union placed Scotland inside the Navigation Act system, legalized Scottish participation in the tobacco trade, and opened numerous colonial offices to ambitious Scots. By the middle of the 18th century most of Scotland's growing prosperity derived from its trade with the colonies.

IMPERIAL FEDERALISM

The transformations that took place between 1689 and 1707 defined the structure of the British Empire until the American Revolution. Although Parliament claimed full power over the colonies, in practice it seldom regulated anything colonial except Atlantic commerce. Even the Woolens Act of 1699 did not prohibit the manufacture of woolen textiles in the colonies. It simply prohibited their export. The Hat Act of 1732 was similarly designed.

When Parliament regulated oceanic trade, its measures were usually enforceable. But compliance was minimal to nonexistent when Parliament tried to regulate inland affairs through statutes protecting white pines (needed as masts for the navy) or through the Iron Act of 1750, which prohibited the erection of certain types of new iron mills. To get things done within the colonies, the Crown had to win the settlers' agreement through their lawful assemblies and unsalaried local officials. In effect, the empire had stumbled into a system of de facto federalism, an arrangement that no one could quite explain or justify. Parliament exercised only limited powers, and the colonies controlled the rest. What seemed an arrangement of convenience in London soon acquired overtones of right in America, the right to consent to all taxes and local laws.

THE MIXED AND BALANCED CONSTITUTION

The Glorious Revolution transformed British politics. Britain, whose government had seemed wildly unstable for half a century, quickly became a far more powerful state than the Stuart kings had been able to sustain with their pretensions to absolute monarchy. The British constitution, which made ministers legally responsible for their public actions, proved remarkably stable. In the ancient world, free societies had degenerated into tyrannies. Liberty had always been fragile and was easily lost. Yet England had retained its liberty and grown stronger in the process. England had defied history.

The explanation, everyone agreed, lay in England's "mixed and balanced" constitution. Government by "King, Lords, and Commons" mirrored society itself—the monarchy, aristocracy, and commonality. As long as each freely consented to government measures, English liberty would be secure because each had voluntarily placed the public good ahead of its own interests. But if one of the three acquired the power to dominate or manipulate the other two, English liberty would indeed be in peril. That danger fueled an unending dialogue in 18th century Britain. The underlying drama was always the struggle of power against liberty, and liberty usually meant a limitation of governmental power.

Power had to be controlled, or liberty would be lost. Nearly everyone agreed that a direct assault on Parliament through a military coup was highly unlikely. The real danger lay in corruption, in the ability of Crown ministers to undermine the independence of the House of Commons.

The wars with France aroused acute constitutional anxieties. After 1689 England raised larger fleets and armies than the kingdom had ever mobilized before. To support them the kingdom created for the first time a funded national debt, in which the state agreed to pay the interest due to its creditors ahead of all other obligations. This simple device gave Britain enormous borrowing power. In 1694 the government created the Bank of England to facilitate its own finances; the London Stock Exchange also emerged in the 1690s. Parliament levied a heavy land tax on the gentry and excises on ordinary people to meet wartime expenses. These actions amounted to a financial revolution that enabled England to outspend France, despite having only one-fourth of France's population. And by giving public offices to members of Parliament, Crown ministers were almost assured of majority support for their measures.

As during the controversy over the "Popish Plot," public debates still pitted the "Court" against the "Country." The Court favored policies that strengthened its warmaking capacity. The Country stood for liberty. Each of the parties, Whig and Tory, had Court and Country wings. But between 1680 and 1720 they reversed their polarities. Although the Tories had begun as Charles II's Court party, by 1720 most of them were a Country opposition. Whigs had defended Country positions in 1680, but by 1720 most of them were strong advocates for the Court policies of George I (1714–1727). Court spokesmen defended the military buildup, the financial revolution, and the new patronage as essential to victory over France. Their Country opponents denounced standing armies, attacked the financial revolution as an engine of corruption, favored an early peace with France, demanded more frequent elections, and tried to ban "placemen" (officeholders who sat in Parliament) from the House of Commons.

Court Whigs emerged victorious during the long ministry of Sir Robert Walpole (1721–1742), but their opponents were more eloquent and controlled more presses. By the 1720s, the opposition claimed many of the kingdom's best writers, especially the Tories Alexander Pope, Jonathan Swift, John Gay, and Henry St. John, viscount Bolingbroke. Their detestation of Walpole was shared by a smaller band of radical Whigs, including John

Trenchard and Thomas Gordon, who wrote *Cato's Letters,* four volumes of collected newspaper essays. The central theme of the opposition was corruption—and insidious means by which ministers threatened the independence of Parliament and English liberty. This debate over liberty soon reached America. *Cato's Letters* were especially popular in the northern colonies, while Bolingbroke won numerous admirers in the southern colonies.

CONTRASTING EMPIRES: SPAIN AND FRANCE IN NORTH AMERICA

After 1689, Britain's enemies were France and Spain, Catholic powers with their own American empires. Until 1689 the three empires had coexisted in America without much contact among them. But Europe's wars soon engulfed them all. Spain and France shared a zeal for converting Indians that exceeded anything displayed by English Protestants. But their American empires had little else in common.

THE PUEBLO REVOLT

In the late 17th century, the Spanish missions of North America entered a period of crisis. Fewer priests took the trouble to master Indian languages, insisting instead that the Indians learn Spanish. For all of their good intentions, the missionaries often whipped or shackled Indians for minor infractions. Disease also took a heavy toll. A declining Indian population made labor demands by the missionaries a heavier burden, and despite strong prohibitions, some Spaniards enslaved Indians in Florida and New Mexico. After 1670 Florida also feared encroachments by English Protestants out of South Carolina, eager to enslave unarmed Indians, whether or not they had embraced Christianity. By 1700, the European refusal to enslave other Christians protected only white people. Spain also refused to arm its Indians.

But the greatest challenge to the Spanish arose in New Mexico, where the Pueblo population had fallen from 80,000 to 17,000 since 1598. A prolonged drought, together with Apache and Navajo attacks, prompted many Pueblos to abandon the Christian God and resume their old forms of worship. Missionaries responded with whippings and even several executions in 1675. Popé, a San Juan Pueblo medicine man who had been whipped for his beliefs, moved north to Taos Pueblo, where he organized the most successful Indian revolt in American history. In 1680, in a carefully timed uprising, the Pueblos killed 400 of the 2,300 Spaniards in New Mexico and destroyed or plundered every Spanish building in the province (see the Chapter 1 map, Spanish Missions in Florida and New Mexico, circa 1675). They desecrated every church and killed 21 of New Mexico's 33 missionaries. Spanish survivors fled from Santa Fe down the Rio Grande to El Paso.

Popé lost his influence when the traditional Pueblo rites failed to end the drought or stop the attacks of hostile Indians. When the Spanish returned in the 1690s, the Pueblos were badly divided. Most villages yielded without much resistance, but Santa Fe held out until December 1693. When it fell, the Spanish executed 70 men and gave 400 women and children to the returning settlers as their slaves.

In both Florida and New Mexico, missionaries had often resisted the demands of Spanish governors. By 1700 the state ruled and missionaries obeyed. Spain's daring attempt to create a demilitarized Christian frontier was proving a tragic failure for both Indians and missionaries.

NEW FRANCE AND THE MIDDLE GROUND

A different story unfolded along the western frontier of New France. There the Iroquois menace made possible an unusual accommodation between the colony and the Indians of the Great Lakes region. The survival of the Iroquois Five Nations depended on their ability to assimilate captives. Their raiders, armed with muskets, terrorized western Indians and carried away thousands of captives. The Iroquois wars depopulated nearly all of what is now the state of Ohio and much of the Ontario peninsula. The Indians around Lakes Erie and Huron either fled west or were absorbed by the Iroquois. The refugees, mostly Algonquian-speaking peoples, founded new communities farther west. Most of these villages contained families from several different tribes, and village loyalties gradually supplanted older tribal (or ethnic) loyalties. But when the refugees disagreed with one another or came into conflict with the Sioux to their west, the absence of traditional tribal structures made it difficult to resolve their differences. Over time, French soldiers, trappers, and missionaries stepped in as mediators.

The French were not always welcome. In 1684, the only year for which we have a precise count, the Algonquians killed 39 French traders. Yet the leaders of thinly populated New France were eager to erect an Algonquian shield against the Iroquois. They began by easing tensions among the Algonquians while supplying them with firearms, brandy, and other European goods. New France provided the resources that the Algonquians needed to strike back against the Iroquois. By 1701 Iroquois losses had become so heavy that the Five Nations negotiated a peace treaty with the French and the western Indians. The Iroquois agreed to remain neutral in any war between France and England. France's Indian allies, supported by a new French fort erected at Detroit in 1701, began returning to the fertile lands around Lakes Erie and Huron. That region became a "Middle Ground" over which no one could wield sovereign power, although New France exercised great influence within it.

France's success in the interior rested more on intelligent negotiation than on force. Hugely outnumbered, the French knew that they could not impose their will on the Indians. But Indians respected those Frenchmen who honored their ways. The French conducted diplomacy according to Indian, not European, rules. The governor of New France became a somewhat grander version of a traditional Indian chief. Algonquians called him Onontio ("Great Mountain"), the supreme alliance chief who had learned that, among the Indians, persuasion was always accompanied by gifts. The respect accorded to peacetime chiefs was roughly proportionate to how much they gave away, not to how much they accumulated. The English, by contrast, tried to "buy" land from the Indians and regarded the sale of the land and of the Indians' right to use it as irrevocable. The French understood that this idea had no place in Indian culture. Agreements were not final contracts, never to be altered. They required regular renewal, always with an exchange of gifts.

FRENCH LOUISIANA AND SPANISH TEXAS

The pattern worked out by the French and the Indians on the Great Lakes Middle Ground also took hold in the lower Mississippi valley. In quest of a passage to Asia, Father Jacques

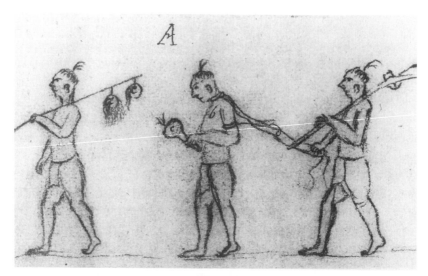

IROQUOIS WARRIORS LEADING AN INDIAN PRISONER INTO CAPTIVITY, 1660S   Because Indian populations had been depleted by war and disease, a tribe's survival became dependent on its ability to assimilate captives. This is a French copy of an Iroquois pictograph.

Marquette and trader Louis Joliet paddled down the Mississippi to its juncture with the Arkansas River in 1673. But once they became convinced that the Mississippi flowed into the Gulf of Mexico and not the Pacific, they turned back. Then, in 1682, René-Robert Cavelier, *sieur* de La Salle traveled down the Mississippi to its mouth, claiming possession of the entire area for France and calling it Louisiana (for Louis XIV).

In 1699, during a brief lull in the wars between France and England, the French returned to the Gulf of Mexico. Pierre le Moyne d'Iberville, a Canadian, landed with 80 men at Biloxi, built a fort, and began trading with the Indians. In 1702 he moved his headquarters to Mobile to get closer to the more populous nations of the interior, especially the Choctaws. The Choctaws could still field 5,000 warriors but had suffered heavy losses from slaving raids organized by South Carolinians and carried out mostly by that colony's Chickasaw and Creek allies. About 1,800 Choctaws had been killed and 500 enslaved during the preceding decade. Using the Choctaws to anchor their trading system, the French created a weaker, southern version of the Great Lakes Middle Ground, acting as mediators and trading brandy, firearms, and other European products for furs and food. Often, during the War of the Spanish Succession (1702–1713), the French were unable to get European supplies, and they remained heavily outnumbered by the Indians. Although European diseases had been ravaging the area since the 1540s, the Indians of the lower Mississippi valley still numbered about 70,000. In 1708 the French numbered fewer than 300, including 80 Indian slaves. The French were lucky to survive at all.

Spain, alarmed at any challenge to its monopoly on the Gulf of Mexico, founded Pensacola in 1698. Competition from France prompted the Spanish to move into Texas in 1690, where

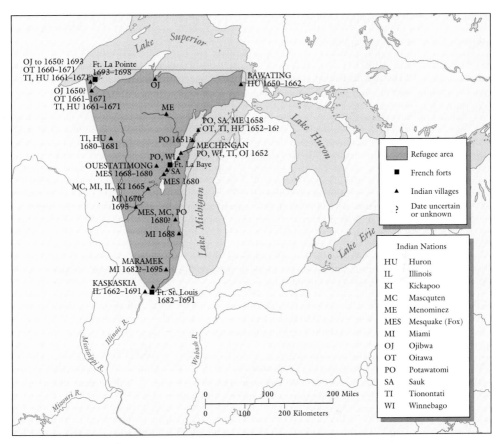

OJ to 1650? 1693
OT 1660–1671   Ft. La Pointe
TI, HU 1661–1671 1693–1698

OJ 1650?
OT 1661–1671
TI, HU 1661–1671   ME

OJ

BAWATING
HU 1650–1662

PO, SA, ME 1658
OT, TI, HU 1652–16?

TI, HU
1680–1681   PO 1651
MECHINGAN
PO, WI, TI, OJ 1652
PO, WI
OUESTATIMONG   Ft. La Baye
MES 1668–1680   SA
MES 1680
MC, MI, IL, KI 1665
MI 1670
1695
MES, MC, PO
1680?

MI 1688

MARAMEK
MI 1682?–1695

KASKASKIA
IL 1662–1691   Ft. St. Louis
1682–1691

Refugee area

■ **French forts**

▲ **Indian villages**

? **Date uncertain or unknown**

Indian Nations	
HU	Huron
IL	Illinois
KI	Kickapoo
MC	Mascquten
ME	Menominez
MES	Mesquake (Fox)
MI	Miami
OJ	Ojibwa
OT	Oitawa
PO	Potawatomi
SA	Sauk
TI	Tionontati
WI	Winnebago

0   100   200 Miles

0   100   200 Kilometers

FRENCH MIDDLE GROUND, CIRCA 1700

they established missions near the modern Texas-Louisiana border. At first, the missionaries were cordially received by the Tejas (Texas) Indians, but they brought smallpox with them. Their explanation, that the epidemic was God's "holy will," did not mollify the Indians, who told the missionaries to get out or be killed. They departed in 1693, leaving Texas to the Indians for 20 more years.

AN EMPIRE OF SETTLEMENT: THE BRITISH COLONIES

By 1700, when 250,000 settlers and slaves were already living in England's mainland colonies, the population was doubling every 25 years. New France matched that pace, but with only 14,000 people in 1700, it could not close the gap. By contrast, the population of the Spanish missions continued to decline. In the struggle for empire, a growing population became Britain's greatest advantage.

THE ENGINE OF BRITISH EXPANSION: THE COLONIAL HOUSEHOLD

With few exceptions, colonial families did not adopt the English customs of entail and primogeniture. Entail prohibited a landowner, or his heir, from dividing up his landed estate (that is, selling part of it) during his lifetime. Primogeniture obliged him to leave all of his land to his eldest surviving son. Under this system, younger sons were clearly not equal to the oldest son, and daughters ranked behind both.

Primogeniture and entail became more common in the 18th century colonies than they had been before, but until the late colonial period they failed to structure social relations the way they did in England. A Virginia planter, for example, might entail his home plantation (the one on which he had erected his big house) and bequeath it to his oldest son, but he would also leave land and slaves, sometimes whole plantations, to his other sons. The patriarchs of most colonial households tried to pass on their status to *all* their sons, and to provide dowries that would enable all their daughters to marry men of equal status. Until 1750 or so, these goals were usually realistic.

English households had become "Americanized" in the colonies as soon as Virginia and Plymouth made land available to nearly all male settlers. Yet by the mid-18th century, social change was beginning to drive American households back toward English practices. Without continual expansion onto new lands, the colonial household could not provide equal opportunity for all sons, much less for all daughters.

Colonial households were patriarchal. A mature male was expected to be the master of others. Above all, a patriarch strove to perpetuate the household itself into the next generation and to preserve his own economic "independence." Of course, complete independence was impossible. Every household owed small debts or favors to its neighbors, but these obligations seldom compromised the family's standing in the community.

Although farmers rarely set out to maximize profits, they did try to grow an agricultural surplus, if only as a hedge against drought, storms, and other unpredictable events. For rural Pennsylvanians this surplus averaged about 40 percent of the total crop. With the harvest in, farmers marketed their produce, often selling it for cash to merchants in Boston, New York, or Philadelphia. Farmers used the cash to pay taxes or their ministers' salaries and to buy British imports. Although these arrangements sometimes placed families in short-term debt to merchants, most farmers and artisans managed to avoid long-term debt. Settlers accepted temporary dependency among freemen—of sons on their parents, indentured servants on their masters, or apprentices and journeymen on master craftsmen. Sons often worked as laborers on neighboring farms, as sailors, or as journeymen craftsmen, provided that such dependence was temporary. But a man who became permanently dependent on others lost the respect of his community.

THE VOLUNTARISTIC ETHIC AND PUBLIC LIFE

Householders carried their quest for independence into public life. In entering politics and in waging war, their autonomy became an ethic of voluntarism. Few freemen could be coerced into doing something of which they disapproved. They had to be persuaded or induced. "Obedience by compulsion is the Obedience of Vassals, who without compulsion would disobey," explained one essayist. Local officials serving without pay frequently ignored orders that did not serve their own interests or the interests of their community.

Most young men accepted military service only if it fitted in with their future plans. They would serve only under officers they knew, and then for only a single campaign. Few reenlisted. After serving, they used their bonus and their pay, and often the promise of a land grant, to speed their way to becoming masters of their own households. Military service, for those who survived, could lead to the ownership of land and an earlier marriage. For New England women, however, war reduced the supply of eligible males and raised the median age of marriage by about two years, which usually meant one fewer pregnancy per marriage.

THREE WARRING EMPIRES, 1689–1716

When the three empires went to war after 1689, the Spanish and French fought mostly to survive. The British fought to expand their holdings. None of them won a decisive advantage in the first two wars, which ended with the Treaty of Utrecht in 1713.

Smart diplomacy with the Indians protected the western flank of New France, but the eastern parts of the colony were vulnerable to English invasion. The governors of New France knew that Indian attacks against English towns would keep the English colonies disorganized and make them disperse their forces. Within a year after the outbreak of war between France and England in 1689, Indians had devastated most of coastal Maine and had attacked the Mohawk valley town of Schenectady, carrying most of its inhabitants into captivity.

In each of the four colonial wars between Britain and France, New Englanders called for the conquest of New France, usually through a naval expedition against Quebec, combined with an overland attack on Montreal. In King William's War (1689–1697), Sir William Phips of Massachusetts forced Acadia to surrender in 1690 (although the French soon regained it) and then sailed up the St. Lawrence. At Quebec, he was bluffed into retreating by the French governor, the comte de Frontenac, who kept marching the same small band of soldiers around his ramparts until the attackers became intimidated and withdrew.

In 1704, during Queen Anne's War (1702–1713), the French and Indians destroyed Deerfield, Massachusetts, in a winter attack and marched most of its people off to captivity in Canada. Hundreds of New Englanders spent months or even years as captives. As the war dragged on, New Englanders twice failed to take Port Royal in Acadia, but a combined British

BRITISH WARS AGAINST FRANCE (AND USUALLY SPAIN), 1689–1763

EUROPEAN NAME	AMERICAN NAME	YEARS	PEACE
War of the League of Augsburg	King William's War	1689–1697	Ryswick
War of the Spanish Succession	Queen Anne's War	1702–1713	Utrecht
War of Jenkins' Ear, merging with		1739–1748	
War of the Austrian Succession	King George's War	1744–1748	Aix-la-Chapelle
Seven Years' War	French and Indian War	1754–1763*	Paris

*The French and Indian War began in America in 1754 and then merged with the Seven Years' War in Europe, which began in 1756.

CHRONOLOGY

1642	Civil war erupts in England • Miantonomo abandons planned war of extermination
1643	New England Confederation created
1644	Opechancanough's second massacre in Virginia
1649	England becomes a Commonwealth
1651	Parliament passes first Navigation Act
1652–1654	First Anglo-Dutch War
1660	Charles II restored to English throne • Parliament passes new Navigation Act
1662	Charles II grants Rhode Island Charter
1663	Staple Act passed • Charles II grants Connecticut Charter
1673	Plantation Duty Act passed • Dutch retake New York for 15 months
1675	Lords of Trade established • Metacom's War breaks out in New England
1676	Bacon's Rebellion breaks out in Virginia
1678	"Popish Plot" crisis begins in England
1680	Pueblos revolt in New Mexico
1684	Massachusetts Charter revoked
1685	Louis XIV revokes Edict of Nantes
1686	Dominion of New England established
1688–1689	Glorious Revolution occurs in England
1689	Anglo-French wars begin • Glorious Revolution spreads to Massachusetts, New York, and Maryland
1691	Leisler executed in New York
1692	19 witches hanged in Salem
1696	Parliament passes comprehensive Navigation Act • Board of Trade replaces Lords of Trade
1699	French found Louisiana • Woolens Act passed
1701	Iroquois make peace with New France
1702–1704	Carolina slavers destroy Florida missions
1707	Anglo-Scottish union creates kingdom of Great Britain
1713	Britain and France make peace
1714	George I ascends British throne
1715	Yamasee War devastates South Carolina

and colonial force finally succeeded in 1710, renaming the colony Nova Scotia. An effort to subdue Quebec the following year met with disaster when many of the British ships ran aground in a treacherous stretch of the St. Lawrence River.

Farther south, the imperial struggle was grimmer and even more tragic. The Franciscan missions of Florida were already in decline. But mission Indians still attracted Carolina slavers, who invaded Florida between 1702 and 1704 with a large force of Indian allies, dragged off 4,000 women and children as slaves, drove 9,000 Indians from their homes, and wrecked the missions. The invaders failed to take the Spanish fortress of St. Augustine, but slaving raids spread devastation as far west as the lands of the Choctaws and far south along the Florida peninsula.

South Carolina's greed for Indian slaves finally alienated the colony's strongest Indian allies, the Yamasees, who, fearing that they would be the next to be enslaved, attacked South Carolina in 1715 and almost destroyed the colony before being thrust back and nearly exterminated. Some of the Yamasees and a number of escaped African slaves fled as refugees to Spanish Florida.

The wars of 1689–1716 halted the movement of British settlers onto new lands in New England and the Carolinas. Only four Maine towns survived the wars; after half a century, South Carolina still had fewer than 6,000 settlers in 1720. But in Pennsylvania, Maryland, and Virginia—colonies that had not been deeply involved in the wars—the westward thrust continued.

CONCLUSION

The variety and diversity of the colonies posed a huge challenge to the English government. After 1650 it found ways to regulate their trade, mostly for the mutual benefit of both England and the colonies. The colonies, beset by hostile Indians and internal discord, began to recognize that they needed protection that only England could provide. Once the Crown gave up its claims to absolute power, the two sides discovered much on which they could agree.

Political values in England and the colonies began to converge during the Glorious Revolution and its aftermath. Englishmen throughout the empire insisted that the right to property was sacred, that without it liberty could never be secure. They celebrated liberty under law, government by consent, and the toleration of all Protestants. They barred Catholics from succession to the throne, disfranchised them, and barred them from public office. In an empire dedicated to "liberty, property, and no popery," Catholics became big losers.

By the 18th century, the British colonists had come to believe they were the freest people on earth. They attributed this fortune to their widespread ownership of land and to the English constitutional principles that they had incorporated into their own governments. When George I became king in 1714, they proudly proclaimed their loyalty to the Hanoverian dynasty that guaranteed a Protestant succession to the British throne. In their minds, the British Empire had become the world's last bastion of liberty.

4

PROVINCIAL AMERICA AND THE STRUGGLE FOR A CONTINENT

The British colonists believed they were the freest people on earth. Yet during the 18th century they faced a growing dilemma. To maintain the opportunity that settlers had come to expect, the colonies had to expand onto new lands. But provincial society also emulated the cultural values of Great Britain—its architecture, polite learning, evangelical religion, and politics. Relentless expansion made this emulation difficult because frontier areas were not very genteel. An anglicized province would become far more hierarchical than the colonies had been and might not even try to provide a rough equality of opportunity. The settlers tried to sustain both, an effort that also brought brutal conflict with the Indians, the Spanish, and the French as the settlers coveted their lands.

When the British again went to war against Spain and France after 1739, the settlers joined in the struggle and declared that liberty itself was at stake. But less fortunate people among them disagreed. Slaves in the southern colonies saw Spain, not Britain, as a beacon of liberty. In the eastern woodlands, most Indians identified France, not Britain, as the one ally genuinely committed to their survival and independence.

EXPANSION VERSUS ANGLICIZATION

In the 18th century, as the British colonists sought to emulate their homeland, many of the things they had left behind in the 17th century began to reappear. After 1740, for example, imports of British goods grew spectacularly. The gentry and the merchants dressed in the latest London fashions and embraced that city's standards of taste and elegance. Southern planters erected "big houses" such as Mount Vernon. Newspapers and learned professions based on English models proliferated, and colonial seaports began to resemble Bristol and other provincial cities in England.

But the population of British North America doubled every 25 years. That meant that each generation required twice as many colleges, ministers, lawyers, physicians, craftsmen, printers, sailors, and unskilled laborers as the preceding generation. None of these institutions could meet colonial needs unless it continued to grow. As the 18th century progressed, the colonies became the scene of a contest between the unrelenting pace of expansion and these anglicizing tendencies.

The southern colonies, which looked only to England, or even Europe, to satisfy their needs for skilled talent, could no longer attract as many people as they needed. In 1700, for example, Oxford and Cambridge Universities in England had managed to fill the colonies' needs for Anglican clergymen by sending over those graduates who could not find parishes at home. By 1750 the colonial demand far exceeded what Oxford and Cambridge could supply, and the colonies were also trying to attract Scottish and Irish clergymen. By contrast, northern colonies founded their own colleges and trained their own ministers, lawyers, and doctors, as well as their own printers, shipwrights, and other skilled craftsmen.

Much of this change occurred during prolonged periods of warfare. War interrupted expansion, which resumed at an even more frantic pace with the return of peace. By midcentury, the wars were becoming a titanic struggle for control of the North American continent. Gradually Indians realized that constant expansion for British settlers meant unending retreat for them.

THREATS TO HOUSEHOLDER AUTONOMY

As population rose, some families acquired more prestige than others. "Gentlemen" performed no manual labor, and such men began to dominate public life. Before 1700 ordinary farmers and small planters had often sat in colonial assemblies. In the 18th century the assemblies grew much more slowly than the overall population. In the five colonies from New York to Maryland, they remained almost unchanged in size despite the enormous growth of the population. The men who took part in public life above the local level came, more and more, from a higher social status. They had greater wealth, a more impressive lineage, and a better education than ordinary farmers or craftsmen.

By midcentury, despite the high value that colonists placed on householder autonomy, patterns of dependency were beginning to emerge. In one Maryland county, 27 percent of the householders were tenants who worked small tracts of land without slaves, or were men who owned a slave or two but had no claim to land. Such families could not satisfy the ambitions of all their children. In Pennsylvania's Chester County, a new class of married farm laborers arose. Their employers would let them use a small patch of land on which they could build a cottage and raise some food. Called "inmates" (or "cottagers" in England), such people made up 25 percent of the county population. Tenants on New York manors had to accept higher rents and shorter leases after 1750. In Chebacco Parish in Ipswich, Massachusetts, half of the farmers had only enough land for some of their sons by 1760.

Families that could not provide for all of their children reverted to English social norms. A father favored his sons over his daughters. In Connecticut, from the 1750s to the 1770s, about 75 percent of eligible sons inherited some land, but for daughters the rate fell from 44 to 34 percent. When a father could not support all his sons, he favored the eldest over the younger sons. The younger sons took up a trade or headed for the frontier. To increase their resources, many New England farmers added a craft or two to the household. The 300 families of Haverhill, Massachusetts, supported 44 workshops and 19 mills by 1767. Most families added a craft

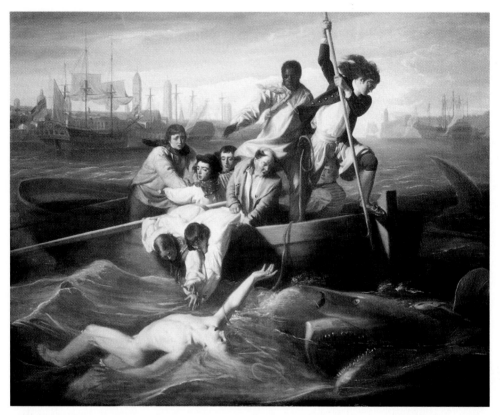

WATSON AND THE SHARK John Singleton Copley's 1778 painting, dramatically depicting a young man's rescue from shark attack, began the democratization of heroism. Note that a black man holds the traditional central and elevated place of honor in the painting, and that only one on the rescue boat is a "gentleman." In this graphic work, Copley used the most refined techniques of English painting to suggest a colonial theme, that even ordinary men can become heroes.

in order to sustain household autonomy. The goal of independence continued to exercise great power, but it was under siege.

ANGLICIZING THE ROLE OF WOMEN

The changing role of women provides a dramatic example of the anglicizing tendencies of the 18th century. When they married, most women received a dowry from their father, usually in cash or goods, not land. Under the common law doctrine of coverture, the legal personality of the husband "covered" the wife, and he made all legally binding decisions. If he died first, his widow was entitled to dower rights, usually one-third of the estate, which passed, after her death, to the couple's surviving children.

To maintain the family status, women in many households had to work harder—at the spinning wheel, for example. In a sense, women were becoming more English. Until 1700 many Chesapeake widows inherited all of their husbands' property and administered their own estates. After 1700 such arrangements were rare. In New England too, women suffered losses. Before 1700, courts had routinely punished men for sexual offenses, and many men had pleaded guilty and accepted their sentence. After 1700 almost no man would plead guilty to a sexual offense, except perhaps to making love to his wife before their wedding day. However, to avoid a small fine, some husbands humiliated their wives by denying that charge, even if their wives had already pleaded guilty after giving birth to a child that had obviously been conceived before their wedding day. The European double standard of sexual behavior, which punished women for their indiscretions while tolerating male infractions, had been in some jeopardy under the Puritan regime. It now revived.

EXPANSION, IMMIGRATION, AND REGIONAL DIFFERENTIATION

After 1715, the settled portions of North America enjoyed their longest era of peace since the arrival of Europeans. The wars had emptied the borderlands of most of their inhabitants. Until midcentury, people poured into these areas. As they expanded, the colonies evolved into distinct regions, although only New Englanders had acquired a self-conscious sense of regional identity before independence.

THE EMERGENCE OF THE OLD SOUTH

Renewed immigration drove much of the postwar expansion. After 1730 the flow became enormous. In that year, about 630,000 settlers and slaves lived in the mainland colonies. By 1775 another 248,000 Africans and 284,000 Europeans had landed, including 50,000 British convicts, shipped mostly to Maryland and Virginia, where they served long indentures. Most of the 210,000 voluntary immigrants settled in the middle or southern colonies.

During this period, the African slave trade to North America reached its peak. Almost 90 percent of the slaves went to the southern colonies. One-eighth of the slaves went to northern colonies. About 80 percent of the slaves arrived from Africa on British-owned vessels. Most of the rest came, a few at a time, from the West Indies on New England ships. This massive influx of slaves created the Old South, a society consisting of wealthy slaveholding planters, a much larger class of small planters, and thousands of slaves. By 1720 slaves made up 70 percent of South Carolina's population. By 1740 they made up 40 percent of Virginia's and 30 percent of Maryland's.

Slaves performed most of the manual labor in the southern colonies. Their arrival transformed the social structure of the southern colonies. In 1700 most members of Virginia's House of Burgesses were small planters who raised tobacco with a few indentured servants and perhaps a slave or two. After 1730 the typical burgess was a great planter who owned at least 20 slaves. And by 1750 the rice planters of South Carolina were richer than any other group in British North America. But tobacco and rice planters had few contacts with each other and did not yet think of themselves as "southerners."

The life of slaves in the upper South (Maryland, Virginia, and the Albemarle region of North Carolina) differed considerably from the life of slaves in the lower South (from Cape Fear in North Carolina through South Carolina and eventually Georgia). The Chesapeake tobacco planters organized their slaves into gangs, supervised them closely, and kept them in the fields all day, weather permitting. But to make their plantations more self-sufficient, they trained perhaps 10 percent of their slaves as blacksmiths, carpenters, coopers, or as other skilled artisans. The planters, who saw themselves as benevolent paternalists, also encouraged family life among their workers, who by the 1720s were beginning to achieve a rate of reproduction that almost equaled that of the settlers. Slaveholders even explained brutal whippings as fatherly efforts to correct the behavior of members of their household.

South Carolina planters began with similar paternalistic inclinations, but the rice swamps and mosquitoes defeated them. Whites who supervised slave gangs in the rice fields quickly caught malaria, which left them vulnerable to other diseases that often killed them.

Africans fared much better than whites in the marshy rice fields. (According to modern medicine, many Africans possess a "sickle cell" in the blood that grants them protection against malaria but can also expose their children to a deadly form of inherited anemia.) As the ability of Africans to resist malaria became evident, Carolina planters seldom ventured near the rice fields. Many rice planters relocated their big houses to higher ground. After midcentury, many of them chose to spend their summers in Charleston or else found summer homes on high ground in the interior. A wealthy few summered in Newport, Rhode Island.

This situation altered work patterns. To produce a crop of rice, planters devised the task system, in which the slaves had to complete certain chores each day, after which their time was their own. Slaves used their free time to raise crops, hunt, or fish. To get local manufactures, the planters relied on a large class of white artisans in Charleston.

Thus, while many Chesapeake slaves were acquiring the skills of artisans, Carolina slaves were heading in the other direction. Before rice became the colony's staple, they had performed a wide variety of tasks. But the huge profits from rice now condemned nearly all of them to monotonous, unpleasant labor in the swamps, even though they were freed from the direct oversight of their masters. Yet because the task system gave them more control over their own lives, slaves preferred it to gang labor.

This freedom meant slower assimilation into the British world. African words and customs survived longer in South Carolina than in the Chesapeake colonies. Newly imported slaves spoke Gullah, originally a pidgin language (that is, a simple second language for everyone who spoke it). Gullah began with a few phrases common to many West African languages, gradually added English words, and became the natural language of subsequent generations, eventually evolving into modern black English.

Rice culture also left Africans with low rates of reproduction. The South Carolina slave population was unable to grow by natural increase until perhaps the 1770s, half a century later than in the tobacco colonies. But by the Revolution, the American South was becoming the world's most self-sustaining slave society. Nowhere else were staple colonies able to reproduce their labor force without continuous imports from Africa.

The southern colonies prospered in the 18th century by exchanging their staple crops for British imports. By midcentury much of this trade had been taken over by Scots. Glasgow became the leading tobacco port of the Atlantic. Although the profits on tobacco were precarious before 1730, they improved in later decades, partly because Virginia guaranteed a high-quality leaf by passing an inspection law and partly because a tobacco contract between Britain and France opened up a vast continental market for Chesapeake planters. By 1775, more than 90 percent of their tobacco was reexported to Europe from Britain.

Other exports and new crafts also contributed to rising prosperity. South Carolina continued to export provisions to the sugar islands and deerskins to Britain. Indigo, used as a dye by the British textile industry, emerged at midcentury as a second staple crop, pioneered by a woman planter, Eliza Lucas Pinckney. North Carolina sold naval stores (pitch, resin, turpentine) to British shipbuilders. Many Chesapeake planters turned to wheat as a second cash crop. Wheat required mills to grind it into flour, barrels in which to pack it, and ships to carry it away. The result was the growth of cities. Norfolk and Baltimore had nearly 10,000 people by 1775, and smaller cities, such as Alexandria and Georgetown, were also thriving. Shipbuilding, closely tied to the export of wheat, became an important Chesapeake industry.

THE MID-ATLANTIC COLONIES: THE "BEST POOR MAN'S COUNTRY"

The Mid-Atlantic colonies had been pluralistic societies from the start. Immigration added to this ethnic and religious complexity after 1700. The region had the most prosperous family farms in America and, by 1760, the two largest cities, Philadelphia and New York. Enormous manors, granted by New York governors to political supporters, dominated the Hudson valley and discouraged immigration. As late as 1750, the small colony of New Jersey had as many settlers as New York, but fewer slaves. Pennsylvania's growth exploded, driven by both natural increase and a huge surge of immigration.

After 1720 Ireland and Germany replaced England as the source of most free immigrants. About 70 percent of Ireland's emigrants came from Ulster. They were Presbyterians whose forebears had come to Ireland from Scotland in the 17th century. (Historians now call them the Scots-Irish, a term seldom used at the time.) Most of them left for America to avoid an increase in rents and to enjoy greater trading privileges than the British Parliament allowed Ireland. The first Ulsterites sailed for New England in 1718. They expected a friendly reception from fellow Calvinists, but the Yankees treated them with suspicion. Some of them stayed and introduced linen manufacturing in New Hampshire, but after 1718 most immigrants from Ulster headed for the Delaware valley. About 30 percent of Irish immigrants came from southern Ireland. Most of them were Catholics, but perhaps a quarter were Anglicans. They too headed for the Mid-Atlantic colonies. Altogether, some 80,000 Irish reached the Delaware valley before 1776.

About 70,000 of the free immigrants were Germans. Most of them arrived as families, often as "redemptioners," a new form of indentured service attractive to married couples because it allowed them to find and bind themselves to their own masters. After redemptioners completed their service, most of them streamed into the interior of Pennsylvania, where Germans outnumbered the original English and Welsh settlers by 1750. Other Germans moved to the southern backcountry with the Irish. The Mid-Atlantic colonies were the favored destination of free immigrants because the expanding economies of the region offered many opportunities. These colonies grew excellent wheat and built their own ships to carry it abroad. When Europe's population started to surge around 1740, the middle colonies began to ship flour across the Atlantic. Around 1760 both Philadelphia and New York City overtook Boston's stagnant population of 15,000. Philadelphia, with 32,000 people, was the largest city in British North America by 1775.

THE BACKCOUNTRY

Many of the Scots-Irish, together with some of the Germans, pushed west into the mountains and then up the river valleys into the interior parts of Virginia and the Carolinas. Most of the English-speaking colonists were immigrants from Ulster, northern England, or lowland Scotland who brought their folkways with them and soon gave the region its own distinctive culture. Although most of them farmed, many turned to hunting or raising cattle. Unlike the coastal settlements, the backcountry had no newspapers, few clergymen or other professionals, and little elegance. Some parts, especially in South Carolina, had almost no government. A visiting Anglican clergyman bemoaned "the abandon'd Morals and profligate Principles" of the settlers. To refined easterners, the backcountry seemed more than a little frightening.

Backcountry settlers were clannish and violent. They drank heavily and hated Indians. After 1750 the situation became quite tense in Pennsylvania where the Quaker legislature insisted on handling differences with the Indians through peaceful negotiation. Once fighting broke out against the Indians, most backcountry residents demanded their extermination. Virginia and South Carolina faced the same problem.

New England: A Faltering Economy and Paper Money

New England, a land of farmers, fishermen, lumberjacks, shipwrights, and merchants, still considered itself more pious than the rest of the British Empire. But the region faced serious new problems. Since about 1660 more people had been leaving the region than had been arriving.

New England's relative isolation in the 17th century began to have negative social and economic effects after 1700. Life expectancy declined as diseases from Europe invaded the region by way of Atlantic commerce. The first settlers had left these diseases behind, but lack of exposure in childhood made later generations vulnerable. When smallpox threatened to devastate Boston in 1721, Zabdiel Boylston, a self-taught doctor, began inoculating people with it on the theory that healthy people would survive the injection and become immune. Although the city's leading physicians opposed the experiment as too risky, it worked. But a diphtheria epidemic in the 1730s and high military losses after 1740 reduced population growth. New England could not keep pace with other regions.

After the wars ended in 1713, New England's economy began to weaken. The region had prospered in the 17th century, mostly by exporting cod, grain, and barrel staves to the West Indies. But a blight called the "wheat blast" appeared in the 1660s and slowly spread until cultivation of wheat nearly ceased. Because Yankees preferred wheat bread to corn bread, they had to import flour from New York and Pennsylvania and, eventually, wheat from Chesapeake Bay. Poverty became a huge social problem in Boston, where by the 1740s about one-third of all adult women were widows, mostly poor.

After grain exports declined, the once-profitable West Indian trade barely broke even. Yet its volume remained large, especially after enterprising Yankees opened up new markets in the lucrative French sugar islands. Within the West Indian market, competition from New York and Philadelphia grew almost too severe for New Englanders to meet, because those cities had flour to export and shorter distances over which to ship it. Mostly, the Yankees shipped fish and forest products to the islands in exchange for molasses, which they used as a sweetener or distilled into rum. However, British West Indian planters, alarmed by the flood of cheap French molasses, urged Parliament to stamp out New England's trade with the French West Indies. Parliament passed the Molasses Act of 1733, which placed a prohibitive duty of six pence per gallon on all foreign molasses. Strictly enforced, the act could have strangled New England trade; instead it gave rise to bribery and smuggling, and the molasses continued to flow.

Shipbuilding gave New England most of its leverage in the Atlantic economy. Yankees made more ships than all the other colonies combined. These ships earned enough from freight in most years to offset losses elsewhere, but New England ran unfavorable balances with nearly every trading partner, especially England. Yankees imported many British products but produced little that anybody in Britain wanted to buy. Whale oil, used in lamps, was an exception. A prosperous whaling industry emerged on the island of Nantucket. But the grain trade with the Mid-Atlantic and Chesapeake colonies was not profitable, although settlers there eagerly bought rum and a few slaves from Yankee vessels that stopped on their way back from the West Indies. Newport even became deeply involved in slave trading along the African coast. Although that traffic never supplied a large percentage of North America's slaves, it contributed to the city's growth.

New England's experience with paper money illustrates these economic difficulties. In response to a military emergency in 1690, Massachusetts invented fiat money—that is, paper money the value of which was not tied to silver or gold but was backed only by the promise of government acceptance for the payment of taxes. It worked well enough until serious depreciation set in after the Treaty of Utrecht. The declining value of money touched off a fierce debate in 1714 that raged until 1750. Creditors attacked paper money as fraudulent: Only gold and silver, they claimed, had real value. Defenders retorted that, in most other colonies, paper was holding its value. The problem, they insisted, lay with the New England economy, which could not generate enough exports to pay for the region's imports. The elimination of paper, they warned, would only deepen New England's problems. War disrupted shipping in the 1740s, and military expenditures sent New England currency to a new low. Then, in 1748, Parliament agreed to reimburse Massachusetts for these expenses at the 1745 exchange rate. Governor William Shirley and House Speaker Thomas Hutchinson, an outspoken opponent of paper money, barely persuaded the legislature to use the grant to retire all paper and convert to silver money. That decision was a drastic example of anglicization. Although fiat money was the colony's own invention, Massachusetts repudiated its own offspring in 1750 in favor of orthodox methods of British public finance. As Hutchinson's critics had warned, however, silver gravitated to Boston and back to London to pay for imports. New England's economy entered a deep depression in the early 1750s from which it did not revive until after 1755, when the wars resumed.

ANGLICIZING PROVINCIAL AMERICA

What made these diverse regions more alike was what they retained or acquired from Britain. Although each exported its own distinctive products, their patterns of consumption became quite similar. In the 18th century, printing and newspapers, the learned professions, and the intellectual movement known as the Enlightenment all made their impact on British North America. A powerful transatlantic religious revival, the Great Awakening, swept across Britain and the colonies in the 1730s and 1740s. And colonial political systems tried to recast themselves in the image of Britain's mixed and balanced constitution.

THE WORLD OF PRINT

In 17th century America, few settlers owned books, and except in New England, even fewer engaged in the intellectual debates of the day. Only Massachusetts had printing presses. For the next century, Boston was the printing capital of North America. By 1740 Boston had eight printers; New York and Philadelphia each had two. No other community had more than one.

Not surprisingly, Boston also led the way in newspaper publishing. John Campbell, the city's postmaster, established the *Boston News-Letter* in 1704. By the early 1720s two more papers had opened in Boston, and Philadelphia and New York City had each acquired one. The *South Carolina Gazette* was founded in Charleston in 1732 and the *Virginia Gazette* at Williamsburg in 1736. Benjamin Franklin took charge of the *Pennsylvania Gazette* in 1729, and John Peter Zenger launched the *New York Weekly Journal* in 1733. In 1735, after attacking Governor William Cosby, Zenger won a major victory for freedom of the press when a jury acquitted him of "seditious libel," the crime of criticizing government officials.

These papers were weeklies that devoted nearly all of their space to European affairs. At first, they merely reprinted items from the *London Gazette*. But beginning in the 1720s, the *New England Courant* also began to reprint Richard Steele's essays from *The Spectator,* Joseph Addison's pieces from *The Tatler,* and the angry, polemical writings, mostly aimed at religious bigotry and political and financial corruption, of "Cato," a pen name used jointly by John Trenchard and Thomas Gordon. *Cato's Letters* became immensely popular among colonial printers and readers.

Benjamin Franklin seemed to personify the concepts of Enlightenment that the newspapers were spreading. As a boy, although raised in Puritan Boston, he skipped church on Sundays to read Addison and Steele and to perfect his prose style. As a young printer with the *New England Courant* in the 1720s, he helped to publish the writings of John Checkley, an Anglican whom the courts twice prosecuted in a vain attempt to silence him. In 1729 Franklin took over the *Pennsylvania Gazette* and made it the best-edited paper in America. It reached 2,000 subscribers, four times the circulation of a Boston weekly.

Franklin was always looking for ways to improve society. In 1727 he and some friends founded the Junto, a debating society that later evolved into the American Philosophical Society. Franklin was a founder of North America's first Masonic lodge in 1730, the Library Company of Philadelphia a year later, the Union Fire Company in 1736, the Philadelphia Hospital in 1751, and an academy that became the College of Philadelphia (now the University of Pennsylvania) in the 1750s. But his greatest fame came from his electrical experiments during the 1740s and 1750s, which brought him honorary degrees from Harvard, Yale, William and Mary, Oxford, and St. Andrews University in Scotland. He invented the Franklin stove and the lightning rod. By the 1760s he had become the most celebrated North American in the world.

THE ENLIGHTENMENT IN AMERICA

The English Enlightenment, which exalted man's capacity for knowledge and social improvement, grew out of the rational and benevolent piety favored by Low Church (latitudinarian) Anglicans in Restoration England. These Anglicans disliked rigid doctrine, scoffed at conversion experiences, attacked superstition, and rejected all "fanaticism," whether that of High Church Laudians or that of the Puritans. High Church men, a small group after 1689, stood for orthodoxy, ritual, and liturgy.

Enlightened writers greeted Sir Isaac Newton's laws of motion as one of the greatest intellectual achievements of all time and joined the philosopher John Locke in looking for ways to improve society. John Tillotson, archbishop of Canterbury until his death in 1694, embodied this "polite and Catholick [i.e., universal] spirit," preaching morality rather than dogma. He had a way of defending the doctrine of eternal damnation that left his listeners wondering how a merciful God could possibly have ordained such a cruel punishment.

Enlightened ideas won an elite constituency in the mainland colonies. Tillotson's sermons appeared in numerous southern libraries and made a deep impression at Harvard College, beginning with two young tutors, William Brattle and John Leverett Jr. After Leverett replaced Increase Mather as college president in 1707, Tillotson's ideas became entrenched in the curriculum. For the rest of the century most Harvard-trained ministers embraced Tillotson's latitudinarian piety. They stressed the similarities between Congregationalists and Anglicans and favored broad religious toleration. After 1800 most Harvard-educated ministers became Unitarians who no longer believed in hell or the divinity of Jesus.

In 1701, largely in reaction to this trend at Harvard, a new college was founded in Connecticut. When it finally settled in New Haven, it was named Yale College in honor of a wealthy English benefactor, Elihu Yale, who donated his library to the school. Those Anglican books did to the Yale faculty what Tillotson had done at Harvard—and more. At the commencement of 1722, the entire Yale faculty, except for a 19-year-old tutor, Jonathan Edwards, announced their conversion to the Church of England and sailed for England to be ordained by the bishop of London. Their leader, Timothy Cutler, became the principal Anglican spokesman in Boston. Samuel Johnson, another defector, became the first president of King's College (now Columbia University) in New York City in the 1750s.

LAWYERS AND DOCTORS

The rise of the legal profession helped to spread Enlightenment ideas. Most Massachusetts lawyers before 1760 were either Anglicans or young men who had rejected the ministry as a career. Most probably thought of themselves as a new learned elite. By the 1790s, lawyers saw themselves as the cultural vanguard of the new republic. Poet John Trumbull, playwright Royall Tyler, and novelist Hugh Henry Brackenridge all continued to practice law while writing on the side. Others turned from the law to full-time writing, including the poet William Cullen Bryant, the writer Washington Irving, and the novelist Charles Brockden Brown.

Medicine also became an enlightened profession, with Philadelphia setting the pace. William Shippen earned degrees at Princeton and Edinburgh, the best medical school in the world at the time, before returning to Philadelphia in 1762, where he became the first American to lecture on medicine, publish a treatise on chemistry, and dissect human cadavers. His student, John Morgan, became the first professor of medicine in North America when the College of Philadelphia established a medical faculty a few years later. Benjamin Rush, who also studied at Princeton and Edinburgh, brought the latest Scottish techniques to the Philadelphia Hospital. He too became an enlightened reformer. He attacked slavery and alcohol and supported the Revolution. Many colonial physicians embraced radical politics.

GEORGIA: THE FAILURE OF AN ENLIGHTENMENT UTOPIA

In the 1730s Anglican humanitarianism and the Enlightenment belief in social improvement converged and led to the founding of Georgia, named for King George II (1727–1760). The sponsors of this project hoped to create a society that could make productive use of England's "worthy" poor. Believing that South Carolina might well be helpless if attacked by Spain, they also intended to shield that colony's slave society from Spanish Florida by populating Georgia with disciplined, armed free men. They hoped to produce silk and wine, items that no other British colony had yet succeeded in making. They prohibited slavery and hard liquor. Slaves would make Georgia a simple extension of South Carolina, with all of its vulnerabilities. And the founders of Georgia were appalled by what cheap English gin was doing to the sobriety and industry of the working people of England.

A group of distinguished trustees set themselves up as a nonprofit corporation and announced that they would give land away, not sell it. Led by James Oglethorpe, the trustees obtained a 20-year charter from Parliament in 1732, raised money from Anglican friends, and launched the colony on land claimed by both Spain and Britain. The trustees recruited foreign Protestants, including some Germans who had just been driven out of Salzburg by its Catholic bishop, a small number of Moravian Brethren (a German pacifist sect, led by Count Nicholas von Zinzendorf), and French Huguenots. In England, they interviewed many prospective settlers to distinguish the worthy poor from the unworthy. They engaged silk and wine experts and recruited Scottish Highlanders as soldiers.

But the trustees refused to consult the settlers on what might be good for them or for Georgia. They created no elective assembly, nor did they give the British government much chance to supervise them. Under their charter, Georgia laws had to be approved by the British Privy Council. So the trustees passed only three laws during their 20 years of rule. One laid out the land system, and the others prohibited slavery and hard liquor. The trustees governed through "regulations" instead of laws.

In 1733 the first settlers laid out Savannah, a town with spacious streets. Within 10 years, 1,800 charity cases and just over 1,000 self-supporting colonists reached Georgia. The most successful were the Salzburgers, who agreed with the prohibitions on slavery and alcohol and built a thriving settlement at Ebenezer, farther up the Savannah River. The Moravian Brethren left for North Carolina after five years rather than bear arms. A group of Lowland Scots known as the Malcontents grew disgruntled and left for South Carolina.

The land system never worked as planned. The trustees gave 50 acres to every male settler whose passage was paid for out of charitable funds. Those who paid their own way could claim up to 500 acres. Ordinary farmers did poorly, because they could not support a family on 50 acres of the sandy soil around Savannah. Because the trustees envisioned every landowner as a soldier, women could not inherit land, nor could landowners sell their plots.

The settlers were unable to grow grapes or produce silk. They clamored for rum, smuggled it into the colony when they could, and insisted that Georgia would never thrive until it had slaves. By the mid-1740s, enough people had died or left to reduce the population by more than half.

Between 1750 and 1752 the trustees dropped their ban on alcohol, allowed the importation of slaves, summoned an elective assembly (but only to consult, not legislate), and finally surrendered their charter to Parliament. With the establishment of royal government in 1752 Georgia finally got an elective assembly with full powers of legislation. Thus Georgia became what it was never meant to be, a smaller version of South Carolina, producing rice and indigo with slave labor. But by then, in one of the supreme ironies of the age, the colony had done more to spread religious revivalism than to vindicate Enlightenment ideals. Georgia helped to turn both John Wesley and George Whitefield into the greatest revivalists of the century.

The Great Awakening

Between the mid-1730s and the early 1740s, an immense religious revival, the Great Awakening, swept across the Protestant world. England, Scotland, Ulster, New England, the Mid-Atlantic colonies, and for a time South Carolina responded warmly to emotional calls for a spiritual rebirth. Southern Ireland, the West Indies, and the Chesapeake colonies remained on the margins until Virginia and Maryland were drawn into a later phase of revivalism in the 1760s and 1770s.

Origins of the Revivals

Some of the earliest revivals arose among the Dutch in New Jersey. Guiliam Bertholf, a farmer and cooper (barrelmaker), was a lay reader who had been ordained in the Netherlands in 1694 and returned to preach in Hackensack and Passaic. His emotional piety won many adherents. After 1720 Theodorus Jacobus Frelinghuysen sparked several revivals in his congregation in New Brunswick, New Jersey. The local Presbyterian pastor, Gilbert Tennent, watched and learned.

Tennent was a younger son of William Tennent Sr., a Presbyterian minister from Ulster who had moved to America. At Neshaminy, Pennsylvania, he set up the Log College, where he trained his sons and other young men as evangelical preachers. The Tennent family dominated the Presbytery of New Brunswick, used it to ordain ministers, and sent them off to any congregation that requested one, even in other presbyteries. That practice angered the Philadelphia Synod, the governing body of the Presbyterian church in the colonies. Most of its ministers emphasized orthodoxy over a personal conversion experience. In a 1740 sermon, *The Dangers of an Unconverted Ministry*, Gilbert Tennent denounced those preachers for leading their people to hell. His attack split the church. In 1741 the outnumbered revivalists withdrew and founded their own Synod of New York.

In New England, Solomon Stoddard of Northampton presided over six revivals between the 1670s and his death in 1729. Jonathan Edwards, his grandson and successor—the only

The Synod of Philadelphia by 1738   In actuality, some presbyteries had more churches than others. Arrows indicate descending lines of authority.

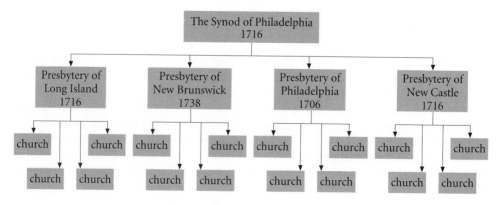

member of the Yale faculty who had not defected to the Anglicans in 1722—touched off a revival in 1734 and 1735 that rocked dozens of Connecticut valley towns. Edwards's *A Faithful Narrative of the Surprising Work of God* (1737) explained what a revival was—an emotional response to God's Word that brought sudden conversions to scores of people. He described these conversions in acute detail and won admirers in Britain as well as in New England.

In England, John Wesley and George Whitefield set the pace. At worldly Oxford University, Wesley and his brother founded the Holy Club, a High Church society whose members sometimes fasted until they could barely walk. These methodical practices prompted scoffers to call them "Methodists." Wesley went to Georgia as a missionary in 1735, but the settlers rejected his ascetic piety. In 1737, on the return voyage to England, some Moravians convinced him that he had never grasped the central Protestant message, justification by faith alone. Some months later he was deeply moved by Edwards's *Faithful Narrative*. Soon, Wesley found his life's mission, the conversion of sinners, and it launched him on an extraordinary preaching career of 50 years.

George Whitefield, who had been a talented amateur actor in his youth, joined the Holy Club at Oxford and became an Anglican minister. He followed Wesley to Georgia, founded an orphanage, then returned to England and preached all over the kingdom to raise money for it. He too began to preach the "new birth"—the necessity of a conversion experience. When many pastors banned him from their pulpits, he responded by preaching in open fields to anyone who would listen. Newspapers reported the controversy, and soon Whitefield's admirers began to notify the press where he would be on any given day. Colonial newspapers, keenly sensitive to the English press, also reported his movements.

WHITEFIELD LAUNCHES THE TRANSATLANTIC REVIVAL

In 1739 Whitefield made his second trip to America, ostensibly to raise funds for his orphanage at Bethesda, Georgia. Everyone knew who he was from newspaper accounts, and thousands flocked to hear him preach. After landing in Delaware, he preached his way northward through Philadelphia, New Jersey, and New York City, and then headed south through the Chesapeake colonies and into South Carolina. In September 1740 he sailed to Newport and for two months toured New England. Using his acting skills, he imitated Christ on the cross, shedding "pious tears" for poor sinners. When he wept, his audience wept with him. When he condemned them, they fell to the ground in agony.

Although Whitefield wore the surplice of an Anglican minister and carried the *Book of Common Prayer* when he preached, Anglicans treated him with reserve or hostility. In Charleston and New York City, he was denounced by the official spokesmen for the bishop of London. But Presbyterians, Congregationalists, and Baptists embraced him, at least until some of them began to fear that he was doing more harm than good. To many he embodied the old nonseparatist ideal that all English Protestants were really members of the same church.

DISRUPTIONS

When other preachers tried to take up Whitefield's role, they aroused fierce controversy. In South Carolina Hugh Bryan, a Savannah River planter, began preaching the evangelical message to his slaves. Then in 1742, not long after a major slave revolt had rocked the colony, he denounced slavery as a sin. Proclaiming himself an American Moses, he attempted to part the waters of the Savannah River and lead the slaves to freedom in Georgia. Instead, he almost drowned. He then confessed publicly that he had been deluded. This fiasco discredited evangelicalism among the settlers of the lower South for another generation, but Bryan and his family continued to convert their own slaves. African American evangelical piety, including some of the first black preachers, took root as a result of their efforts.

Whitefield's successors also caused severe disturbances in New England. Gilbert Tennent preached there for months. He specialized in "Holy Laughter," the scornful peals of a triumphant God as sinners tumble into hell. He abandoned the usual garb of a minister for a robe and sandals and let his hair grow long, thereby proclaiming himself a new John the Baptist heralding the Second Coming of Christ. Many ecstatic followers believed that the Millennium was at hand.

James Davenport, who succeeded Tennent, liked to preach by eerie candlelight, roaring damnation at his listeners, even grabbing Satan and wrestling him back to hell. In 1743 he established the "Shepherd's Tent" in New London to train awakened preachers. This outdoor school abandoned the classical curriculum of colleges and insisted only on a valid conversion experience. He organized a book-burning (in which titles by Increase Mather and other New England dignitaries went up in flames) and threw his britches on the fire, declaring them a mark of human vanity. A New England grand jury, asked to indict him, proclaimed him mad instead. Like Bryan in South Carolina, he repented and claimed that he had been deluded. The Shepherd's Tent collapsed.

LONG-TERM CONSEQUENCES OF THE REVIVALS

As time passed, the revivals feminized evangelical churches. Amid the enthusiasm of Whitefield's tour, more men than usual had joined a church, but after another year or two, men became hard to convert. The number of women church members began to soar, however, and in some congregations they acquired an informal veto over the choice of the minister.

Partly in reaction to the revivals, thousands of men became Freemasons. During and after the Revolution the Masons' membership grew spectacularly. Appealing to men of all denominations, they very nearly turned their order into a religion of manliness, complete with secret rituals. They extolled sobriety, industry, brotherhood, benevolence, and citizenship. At first most clergymen saw Masons as a force for good. But by the 1820s the order would be drawing angry criticism.

The revivals shattered the unity of New England's Congregational Church. Evangelicals seceded from dozens of congregations to form their own "Separate" churches. Many of those that survived went Baptist by the 1760s. In the middle colonies, the revivals strengthened denominational loyalties and energized the clergy. In the 1730s most people in the region had never joined a church. But the revivals prompted many of them to become New Side (evangelical) Presbyterians, Old Side (anti-revival) Presbyterians, or unevangelical Anglicans. The southern colonies were less affected, although evangelical Presbyterians made modest gains in the Virginia backcountry after 1740. Finally, in the 1760s, the Baptists began to win thousands of converts, to be followed and overtaken by the Methodists a decade or two later.

The revivals created new links with Britain and between colonies. Whitefield ran the most efficient publicity machine in the Atlantic world. In London, Glasgow, and Boston, periodicals called *The Christian History* carried news of revivals occurring anywhere in the empire. For years, London evangelicals held regular "Letter Days," at which they read accounts of revivals in progress. When fervor declined in New England, Jonathan Edwards organized a Concert of

Prayer with his Scottish correspondents, setting regular times for them all to beseech the Lord to pour out his grace once more. As Anglicans split into Methodists and Latitudinarians, Congregationalists into New Lights (pro-revival) and Old Lights (anti-revival), and Presbyterians into comparable New Side and Old Side synods, evangelicals discovered that they had more in common with revivalists in other denominations than with anti-revivalists in their own.

Jonathan Edwards was the ablest apologist for revivals in Britain or America. When Boston's Charles Chauncy (very much a man of the Enlightenment) attacked the revivals as frauds because of their emotional excesses, Edwards replied with *A Treatise Concerning Religious Affections* (1746), which displayed his own mastery of Enlightenment sources, including Newton and Locke. Although admitting that no emotional response, however intense, was proof by itself of the presence of God in a person's soul, he insisted that intense feeling must always accompany the reception of divine grace. That view upset people who believed that a rational God must have established a polite and genteel religion. For Edwards, an unemotional piety could never be the work of God. In effect, Edwards countered Chauncy's emotional defense of reason with his own rational defense of emotion.

New Colleges

The Great Awakening also created several new colleges. Each was set up primarily by a single denomination, but all were willing to admit other Protestants. In 1740 North America had only three colleges: Harvard, William and Mary, and Yale. Although Yale eventually embraced the revivals, all three opposed them at first. In 1746 middle colony evangelicals, eager to show their commitment to classical learning after the fiasco of the Shepherd's Tent, founded the College of New Jersey. It graduated its first class in 1748 and settled in Princeton in 1756. Unlike the older colleges, it drew students from all 13 colonies and sent its graduates throughout America. It also reshaped the Presbyterian Church. When Presbyterians healed their schism and reunited in 1758, the New Siders set the terms. Outnumbered in 1741, the New Siders held a large majority of ministers by 1758. Through control of Princeton, their numbers had increased rapidly. The Old Side, still dependent on the University of Glasgow in Scotland, could barely replace those who died.

New Light Baptists founded the College of Rhode Island (now Brown University) in the 1760s. Dutch Reformed revivalists established Queens College (now Rutgers University) in New Jersey, mostly to train evangelical ministers who could preach in English. Eleazer Wheelock opened an evangelical school for Indians in Lebanon, Connecticut. After his first graduate, Samson Occum, raised £12,000 in England for the school, Wheelock moved to New Hampshire and used most of the money to found Dartmouth College instead.

In the 1750s Anglicans countered with two new colleges of their own: the College of Philadelphia (now the University of Pennsylvania), which also had Old Side Presbyterian support, and King's College (now Columbia University) in New York. Their undergraduate programs remained small, however, and few of their students chose a ministerial career.

The Denominational Realignment

The revivals transformed American religious life. In 1700, the three strongest denominations had been the Congregationalists in New England, the Quakers in the Delaware valley, and the Anglicans in the South. By 1800, all three had lost ground to newcomers: the Methodists, who grew at an astonishing rate as the Church of England collapsed during the Revolution; the Baptists, who leaped into second place; and the Presbyterians. Methodists and Baptists did not expect their preachers to attend college, and they recruited ministers from a much broader segment of the population than their rivals could tap. Although they never organized their own Shepherd's Tent, they embraced similar principles, demanding only personal conversion, integrity, knowledge of the Bible, and a talent for preaching. Anti-revivalist denominations, especially Anglicans and Quakers, lost heavily. New Light Congregationalists made only slight gains because, when their people left behind the established churches of New England and moved west, they usually joined a Presbyterian church, which provided a structure and network of support that isolated congregations in a pluralistic society could not sustain.

POLITICAL CULTURE IN THE COLONIES

In politics as in other activities, the colonies became more like Britain during the 18th century. A quarter-century of warfare after 1689 convinced the settlers that they needed the protection of the British state and strengthened their admiration for its parliamentary system. Most colonial voters and assemblymen were more "independent" than their British counterparts. Still, provincial politics began to absorb many of the values and practices that had taken hold in Britain after the Glorious Revolution. Colonists agreed that they were free because they were British, because they too had mixed constitutions that united monarchy, aristocracy, and democracy in almost perfect balance.

By the 1720s every colony except Connecticut and Rhode Island had an appointive governor, either royal or proprietary, plus a council and an elective assembly. The governor stood for monarchy and the council for aristocracy. In Massachusetts, Rhode Island, and Connecticut the council or upper house was elected (indirectly in Massachusetts). In all other colonies except Pennsylvania, an appointive council played an active legislative role. The office of councillor was not hereditary, but many councillors served for life, especially in Virginia, and some were succeeded by their sons.

THE RISE OF THE ASSEMBLY AND THE GOVERNOR

In all 13 colonies the settlers elected the assembly, which embodied a colony's "democratic" elements. The right to vote was more widely shared than in England, where two-thirds of adult males were disfranchised. By contrast, something like three-fourths of free adult white males could vote in the colonies. The frequency of elections varied—every seven years in New York and Virginia, as well as in Britain; every three years in New Hampshire, Maryland, and South Carolina; irregular but fairly frequent by midcentury in New Jersey, North Carolina and Georgia; and every year in the other five colonies. As the century advanced, legislatures sat longer and passed more laws, and the lower house—the assembly—usually initiated major bills. The rise of the assembly was a major political fact of the era.

Every royal colony except New York and Georgia already had an assembly with a strong sense of its own privileges when the first royal governor arrived, but the governors also grew more powerful. Because the governor's instructions usually challenged some existing practices, the result was often a clash in which the first royal governors never got all of their demands. But they did win concessions over the years. In almost every colony the most

THE GOVERNOR'S PALACE AT WILLIAMSBURG, VIRGINIA The governor's palace was built under Governor Alexander Spotswood (1710–1722) and restored in the 20th century. For Spotswood, the palace was an extension of royal might and splendor across the ocean. He set a standard of elegance that many planters imitated when they built their own great houses in the second quarter of the 18th century.

successful governors were those who served between 1730 and 1765. Most of them had learned by then that their success depended less on their royal prerogatives than on their ability to win over the assembly through persuasion or patronage.

Early in the century, conflicts between the governor and an assembly majority tended to be legalistic. Each side cited technical precedents to justify the governor's prerogatives or the assembly's traditional privileges. Later on, when conflict spilled over into the newspapers, it often pitted an aggrieved minority (unable to win an assembly majority) against both governor and assembly. These contests were ideological. The opposition accused the governor of corruption, and he denounced the opposition as a "faction." Everyone condemned factions, or political parties, as self-interested and destructive.

"COUNTRY" CONSTITUTIONS: THE SOUTHERN COLONIES

In most southern colonies, the "Country" principles of the British opposition (see Chapter 3) became the common assumptions of public life, acceptable to both governor and assembly, typically after an attempt to impose the "Court" alternative had failed. When a governor, such as Virginia's Alexander Spotswood (1710–1722), used his patronage to fill the assembly with his own "placemen," the voters turned them out at the next election. Just as Spotswood learned

THE SPECTRUM OF COLONIAL POLITICS

CONSTITUTIONAL TYPE	SUCCESSFUL	UNSUCCESSFUL
Northern "Court"	New York, circa 1710–1728 New Hampshire after 1741 Massachusetts after 1741 New Jersey after 1750	New York after 1728 Pennsylvania (successful in peace, ineffective in war)
Southern "Country"	Virginia after 1720 South Carolina after 1730 Georgia after 1752	Maryland North Carolina

Connecticut and Rhode Island never really belonged to this system.

that he could not manipulate the house through patronage, the assembly discovered that it could not coerce a governor who had a permanent salary. Accordingly, Virginia and South Carolina cultivated a "politics of harmony." Governors found that they could get more done through persuasion than through patronage, and the assemblies responded by showing their appreciation. Factions disappeared, allowing the governor and the assembly to pursue the common good in an atmosphere free of rancor or corruption. Georgia adopted the same practices in the 1750s.

This system worked well because the planters were doing what Britain wanted them to do: shipping staple crops to Britain. Both sides could agree on measures that would make this process more efficient, such as the Virginia Tobacco Inspection Act of 1730. In Virginia, public controversy actually ceased. Between 1720 and 1765 the governor and House of Burgesses engaged in only one public quarrel, an unparalleled record of political harmony. South Carolina's politics became almost as placid from the 1730s into the 1760s, but harmony there masked serious social problems that were beginning to emerge in the unrepresented backcountry. By contrast, the politics of harmony never took hold in Maryland, where the lord proprietor always tried to seduce assemblymen with his lavish patronage, nor in factional North Carolina, where the tobacco and rice planters could not get along with each other, and the backcountry disliked both.

"COURT" CONSTITUTIONS: THE NORTHERN COLONIES

With many economic interests and ethnic groups to satisfy, the northern colonies were more likely to give rise to political factions. Governors could win support by using patronage to reward some groups and to discipline others. William Shirley, governor of Massachusetts from 1741 to 1756, used judicial and militia appointments and war contracts to build a majority in the assembly. Like Sir Robert Walpole in Britain, he was a master of "Court" politics. In New Hampshire, Benning Wentworth created a political machine that rewarded just about every assemblyman between 1741 and 1767. An ineffective opposition in both colonies accused the governors of corrupting the assembly, but Shirley and Wentworth each claimed that what he did was essential to his colony's needs.

The opposition, though seldom able to implement its demands at the provincial level, was important nonetheless. It kept settlers alert to any infringements on their liberties. It dominated the town of Boston from 1720 on, and it reminded people that resistance to authority might be the only means to preserve liberty. Boston artisans engaged in ritualized mob activities that had a sharp political edge. On Guy Fawkes's Day (November 5) every year, a North End mob and a South End mob bloodied each other for the privilege of burning effigies of the pope, the devil, and the Stuart pretender to the British throne. These men were celebrating liberty, property, and no popery—the British constitution as they understood it. The violence made many wealthy merchants nervous, and by 1765 some of them would become its targets.

New York's governors, particularly Robert Hunter (1710–1719), achieved great success even before 1720, mostly by playing off one faction against another in a colony that had been fiercely divided since Leisler's rebellion of 1689. Hunter's salary and perquisites became more lucrative than those attached to any other royal office in North America, and after 1716 he and his successor were so satisfied with their control of the assembly that they let 10 years pass without calling a general election. During the 25 years after 1730, later governors lost these advantages, primarily because London gave the governorship to a series of men eager to rebuild their tattered fortunes at New York's expense. This combination of greed and need gave new leverage to the assembly, which attacked many royal prerogatives during the 1740s. Of the mainland colonies, only the governor of New York emerged weaker by 1760 than he had been in 1730.

Pennsylvania, by contrast, kept its proprietary governor weak well into the 1750s. A unified Quaker Party won undisputed control of the assembly during the 1730s. The governor, who by this time was never a Quaker, had a lot of patronage to dispense. But it was of no use to him in controlling the Quaker assemblymen, who had lost interest in becoming judges if that meant administering oaths. Nor could these pacifists be won over with military contracts, no matter how lucrative.

The colonists, both north and south, absorbed the ideology of the British opposition, which warned that those in power were always trying to destroy liberty and that corruption was their most effective weapon. By 1776 that view would justify independence and the repudiation of a "corrupt" king and Parliament. Before the 1760s, however, it served different purposes. In the south, this ideology celebrated Anglo-American harmony. In the north, it became the language of frustrated minorities unable to defeat the governor or control the assembly.

THE RENEWAL OF IMPERIAL CONFLICT

A new era of imperial war began in 1739 and continued, with only a brief interruption, until 1763. The British colonies, New Spain, and New France all became involved, and eventually so did all the Indians of the eastern woodlands. By 1763 France had been expelled from North America. Britain controlled the continent east of the Mississippi, and Spain claimed the land west of it.

CHALLENGES TO FRENCH POWER

In the decades of peace after 1713, the French tried to strengthen their position in North America. They erected the continent's most formidable fortress, Louisbourg, on Cape Breton Island. The naval force stationed there could protect the French fishery and guard the approaches to the St. Lawrence River. The French also built Fort St. Frédéric (the British called it

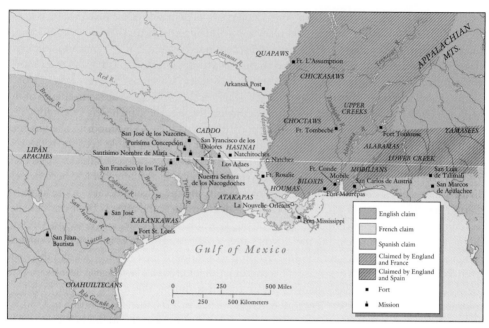

FRENCH LOUISIANA AND SPANISH TEXAS, CIRCA 1730

Crown Point) on Lake Champlain and maintained their Great Lakes posts at Forts Frontenac, Michilimackinac, and Detroit. To bolster its weak hold on the Gulf of Mexico, France created the Company of the Indies, which shipped 7,000 settlers and 2,000 slaves to Louisiana between 1717 and 1721 but then was unable to supply them. By 1726 half of them had starved to death or had fled. In 1718 the French founded New Orleans, which became the capital of Louisiana in 1722.

Despite these efforts, the French hold on the interior began to weaken. Indians returned to the Ohio valley, mostly to trade with pacifist Pennsylvania or with Fort Oswego, a new British post on Lake Ontario. The British were often clumsy in their dealings with Indians, but British goods were cheaper than French trade goods. Many of the Indians founded what the French disparagingly called "republics," villages outside the French alliance system that were willing to trade with the British. They accepted people from all tribes—Delawares from the east, Shawnees from the south and east, Mingoes (Iroquois who had left their homeland) from the north, and other Algonquians of the Great Lakes region to the west. Because the inhabitants of each new village had blood relatives living among all the nearby nations, the chiefs hoped that none of their neighbors would attack them.

Sometimes even the French system of mediation broke down. In the northwest from 1712 to 1737, the French and their Algonquian allies fought a long, intermittent war with the Fox nation. In the southwest an arrogant French officer decided to take over the lands of the Natchez Indians (the last of the Mississippian mound builders) and ordered them to move. While pretending to comply, the Natchez planned a counterstroke and on November 28, 1729, killed every French male in the vicinity. In the war that followed, the French and their Choctaw allies destroyed the Natchez as a distinct people, although some Natchez refugees found homes among the Chickasaws and the Creeks.

In 1730 the French barely averted a massive slave uprising in New Orleans. To stir up hatred between Indians and Africans, the French turned over some of the African leaders of the revolt to the Choctaws to be burned alive. Unable to afford enough gifts to hold an alliance with both the Choctaws and the Chickasaws, they encouraged hostilities between both nations. This policy did serious damage to the French. Instead of weakening the pro-British Chickasaws, it touched off a civil war among the Choctaws, and France lost both influence and prestige.

THE DANGER OF SLAVE REVOLTS AND WAR WITH SPAIN

To counter the French, Spain sent missionaries and soldiers into Texas between 1716 and 1720 and founded a capital at Los Adaes, a few miles from the French trading post at Natchitoches. To prevent smuggling, Spain refused to open a seaport on the Gulf Coast. As a result, its tiny outposts had to depend on French trade goods for supplies. The Texas missions won few converts and suffered frequent depredations by Indians. In 1719 the survivors of these attacks abandoned their missions in eastern Texas and fled west to San Antonio, which eventually became the capital.

The Spanish presence proved troublesome to the British as well, especially in South Carolina. In the 16th century, Francis Drake had proclaimed himself a liberator when he attacked St. Augustine and promised freedom to Indians and Africans. By the 1730s the roles had been reversed. On several occasions after 1680, Spanish Florida had promised freedom to any slaves who escaped from Carolina and were willing to accept Catholicism. In 1738 the governor established, just north of St. Augustine, a new town, Gracia Real de Santa Teresa de Mose (or Mose for short, pronounced *Moe*-shah). He put a remarkable African in charge, a man who took the name Francisco Menéndez at baptism. He had escaped from slavery, had fought with the Yamasees against South Carolina in 1715, and had fled to Florida, only to be enslaved again. Yet he became literate in Spanish and, while still a slave, rose to the rank of militia captain. After winning his freedom, he took charge of Mose in 1738 and made it the first community of free blacks in what is now the United States. The very existence of Mose acted as a magnet for Carolina slaves.

In 1739, the governor of Spanish Florida offered liberty to any slaves from the British colonies who could make their way to Florida. This manifesto, and rumors about Mose, touched off the Stono Rebellion in South Carolina, the largest slave revolt in the history of the 13 colonies. On September 9, 1739, a force of 20 slaves attacked a store at Stono (south of Charleston), killed the owner, seized weapons, and moved on to assault other houses and to attract new recruits. Heading toward Florida, they killed about 25 settlers that day. When the rebels reached the Edisto River, they stopped, raised banners, and shouted "Liberty," hoping to begin a general uprising. There the militia caught them and killed about two-thirds of the growing force. In the weeks that followed, the settlers killed another 60. None of the rebels reached Florida, but, as the founders of Georgia had foreseen, South Carolina was vulnerable in any dispute with Spain.

The War of Jenkins's Ear, derisively named for a ship captain who displayed his severed ear to Parliament as proof of Spanish cruelty, then broke out between Britain and Spain. Some 3,000 men from the 13 colonies, eager for plunder, joined expeditions in 1741 and 1742 against Cartegena in South America, then against Cuba and Panama. All were disasters. Most of the men died of disease; only 10 percent of the volunteers returned home. But Britain got a surge of patriotic fervor from the war. Both "God Save the King" and "Rule Britannia" were written during the struggle.

Savages of Several Nations, New Orleans, 1735   This painting by Alexandre de Batz depicts a multiethnic Indian village near New Orleans. The woman at lower left was a Fox Indian who had been captured and enslaved. The African boy was an adoptee.

Georgia was supposed to protect South Carolina. General Oglethorpe, its governor, retaliated against the Spanish by invading Florida in 1740. He dispersed the black residents of Mose and occupied the site, but the Spaniards mauled his garrison in a surprise counterattack. Oglethorpe retreated without taking St. Augustine and brought some disturbing reports back to Georgia. Spain, he said, was sending blacks into the British colonies to start slave uprisings. And Spanish priests in disguise were intermingled with the black conspirators. This news set off panics in the rice and tobacco colonies, but it had its biggest impact in New York City.

Back in 1712 a slave revolt had shaken the city. After setting fire to a barn one night, slaves had shot 15 settlers who rushed to put out the blaze, killing nine. Twenty-one slaves were executed. By 1741 New York City's 2,000 slaves were the largest concentration of blacks in British North America outside of Charleston. When a series of suspicious fires broke out, the settlers grew nervous. Some of the fires probably provided cover for an interracial larceny ring that operated out of the tavern of John Hughson, a white man. When the New York Supreme Court offered freedom to Mary Burton, a 16-year-old Irish servant girl at the tavern, in exchange for her testimony, she swore that the tavern was the center of a hellish "Popish Plot" to murder the city's whites, free the slaves, and make Hughson king of the Africans. Several free black Spanish sailors, who had been captured and enslaved by privateers, also were accused, though apparently their only crime was to insist that they were free men. After Oglethorpe's warning reached New York in June, the number of the accused escalated, and John Uty, a High Churchman and a Latin teacher who had arrived recently, was hanged as a likely Spanish priest.

The New York conspiracy trials continued from May into August of 1741. Four whites and 18 slaves were hanged, 13 slaves were burned alive, and 70 were banished to the West Indies.

In 1742 King Philip V of Spain nearly accomplished what Oglethorpe had dreaded. He sent 36 ships and 2,000 soldiers from Cuba with orders to devastate Georgia and South Carolina and free the slaves. Although the invaders probably outnumbered the entire population of Georgia, Oglethorpe raised 900 men and met them on St. Simons Island in July. After he ambushed two patrols, Spanish morale collapsed. The Spanish force departed, leaving British North America as a safe haven once more for liberty, property, no popery—and slavery.

FRANCE VERSUS BRITAIN: KING GEORGE'S WAR

In 1744 France joined Spain in the war against Britain. The main action then shifted to the north. When the French laid siege to Port Royal, the capital of Nova Scotia, Governor William Shirley of Massachusetts intervened just in time to save the small garrison, and the French withdrew. Shirley then planned a rash attack on Fort Louisbourg. With only a few lightly armed Yankee vessels at his disposal, he asked the commander of the British West Indian squadron, Sir Peter Warren, for assistance. But Shirley's expedition, which included about one-sixth of all the adult males of Massachusetts, set out before Warren could respond. With no heavy artillery of his own, Shirley ordered the expedition to take the outer batteries of the fortress, capture their guns, and use them to knock down its walls. Had the Yankees met a French fleet instead of the Royal Navy, which arrived in the nick of time, nearly every family in New England might have lost a close relative. The most amazing thing about this venture is that it worked. The British navy drove off the French, and untrained Yankee volunteers subdued the mightiest fortress in America with its own guns. Louisbourg fell on June 16, 1745.

After that, however, nothing went right. Hundreds of volunteers died of disease before regular troops arrived to take over. Plans to attack Quebec by sea in 1746 and 1747 came to nothing. French and Indian raiders devastated the frontier, which was weakly defended because Shirley held back most of his men for a Canada offensive that never took place. Bristol County farmers rioted against high taxes. When the Royal Navy finally got to Boston in late 1747, its commander sent gangs of sailors ashore to compel anyone they could seize into serving with the fleet. An angry crowd descended on the sailors, took some officers hostage, and controlled the streets of Boston for three days before the naval commander relented and released all the Massachusetts men he had impressed. Finally, Britain had to return Louisbourg to France under the Treaty of Aix-la-Chapelle, which ended the war in 1748. New England had suffered enormous losses and had gained nothing except pride.

THE IMPENDING STORM

The war had driven back the frontiers of British settlement in North America, but the colonies had promised land grants to many volunteers. Thus peace touched off a frenzy of expansion. The British, aware that their hold on Nova Scotia was feeble, recruited 2,500 Protestants from Europe to populate the colony and sent four regiments of redcoats to accompany them. In 1749 they founded the town of Halifax, which became the new capital of Nova Scotia.

In the 13 colonies, settlers eagerly pressed on to new lands. Yankees swarmed north into Maine and New Hampshire and west into the middle colonies. By refusing to pay rent to the manor lords of the Hudson valley, they sparked a tenant revolt in 1753 that was subdued only with difficulty. A year later, Connecticut's delegation to the Albany Congress (discussed in the next section) used bribes to acquire an Indian title to all of northern Pennsylvania, which Connecticut claimed on the basis of its sea-to-sea charter of 1663. The blatant encroachments of New York speculators and settlers on Mohawk lands so infuriated the Mohawks' Chief Hendrik that he bluntly told the governor of New York that "the Covenant Chain is broken between you and us [the Iroquois League]." New York, Pennsylvania, and Virginia competed for the trade with the new Indian "republics" between Lake Erie and the Ohio River.

Virginians, whom the Indians called "long knives," were particularly aggressive. Citing their own 1609 sea-to-sea charter, they organized the Ohio Company of Virginia in 1747 to settle the Ohio valley and established their first outpost at the place where the Monongahela and Allegheny Rivers converge to form the Ohio River (the site of modern Pittsburgh). Farther south, encroachments upon the Cherokees almost flared into war with South Carolina in 1750.

The French response to these intrusions verged on panic. The fall of Louisbourg had interrupted the flow of French trade goods to the Ohio country for several years. And the men who had long been conducting Indian diplomacy had either died or left office by the late 1740s. Authoritarian newcomers from France replaced them and began giving orders to Indians instead of negotiating with them. The French rebuilt Louisbourg and erected Fort Beauséjour on the neck that connects mainland Canada to Nova Scotia. In 1755 they erected Fort Carillon (Ticonderoga to the British) on Lake Champlain to protect Crown Point.

Far more controversial was the policy the French now implemented in the area between the Great Lakes and the Ohio. Without trying to explain themselves to the Indians, they launched two expeditions into the area. In 1749 Pierre-Joseph Céloron de Blainville led several hundred men down the Allegheny to the Ohio, then up the Miami and back to Canada. He ordered western Indians to join him, but most of them refused. To them, the French were acting like British settlers, intruding on their lands. Along the way Blainville buried plaques, claiming the area for France. The Indians removed them. Marquis Duquesne sent 2,000 Canadians, with almost no Indian support, to erect a line of posts from Fort Presque Isle (now Erie, Pennsylvania) to Fort Duquesne (now Pittsburgh).

The French intended to prevent British settlement west of the Alleghenies. To Duquesne, this policy was so obviously beneficial to the Indians that it needed no explanation. Yet the Mingoes warned him not to build a fort in their territory, and a delegation of Delawares and Shawnees asked the Virginians if they would be willing to expel the French from the Ohio country and then go back home. The Indians did not like Virginia's response. In 1753 Virginia sent George Washington to the Ohio country to warn Duquesne to withdraw, and a small Virginia force began building its own fort at the forks of the Ohio. Duquesne ignored Washington, advanced toward the Ohio, expelled the Virginians, took over their fort, and finished building it. Virginia sent Washington back to the Ohio in 1754. On May 28, after discovering a French patrol nearby, Washington launched an attack. That command set off a world war.

THE WAR FOR NORTH AMERICA

At first, the war with France generated fierce tensions between Britain and the colonies, but both sides learned to cooperate effectively until they achieved victory together. Of the four wars fought between Britain and France from 1689 to 1763, only the last began in America. That conflict, popularly known as the French and Indian War, was also the biggest and produced the most sweeping results. Only World War II, the Civil War, and the Revolution put a higher percentage of men under arms. Only the Civil War and the Revolution killed a higher percentage of those mobilized.

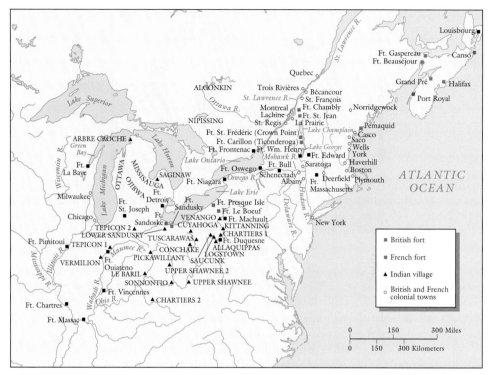

France versus Britain in North America by 1755

The Albany Congress and the Onset of War

In the spring of 1754 both New France and Virginia were expecting a clash at the forks of the Ohio. But neither anticipated the titanic struggle that clash would set off. Nor did the French and British governments, which hoped to limit any conflict to a few strategic points in North America. But New Englanders saw an apocalyptic struggle in the making between "Protestant freedom" and "popish slavery," with the North American continent as the battleground. The only purpose of all the new French forts, suggested Jonathan Mayhew, a Boston preacher, must be to serve as bases for the conquest of the British colonies.

Britain ordered New York to host an intercolonial congress at Albany to meet with the Iroquois and redress their grievances. The governor invited every colony as far south as Virginia, except nonroyal Connecticut and Rhode Island. Virginia and New Jersey declined to attend, but Governor Shirley of Massachusetts invited Connecticut and Rhode Island to participate, and the Massachusetts legislature instructed its delegates to work for a plan of intercolonial union.

In Philadelphia, Benjamin Franklin too was thinking about colonial union. On May 9, 1754, his *Pennsylvania Gazette* printed the first political cartoon in American history, with the caption, "Unite or die!" A month later he drafted his "Short Hints towards a Scheme for Uniting the Northern Colonies," which he presented to the Albany Congress in June. His plan called for a "President General" to be appointed by the Crown as commander in chief and to administer

BENJAMIN FRANKLIN'S SNAKE CARTOON   The first newspaper cartoon in colonial America, this device appeared in the *Pennsylvania Gazette* in the spring of 1754. It was a call for colonial union on the eve of the Albany Congress. It drew on the folk legend that a snake, cut into pieces, could revive and live if it somehow joined its severed parts together before sundown.

the laws of the union, and for a "Grand Council" to be elected for three-year terms by the lower houses of each colony. The union would have power to raise soldiers, build forts, levy taxes, regulate the Indian trade, purchase land from the Indians, and supervise western settlements until the Crown organized them as new colonies. To take effect, the plan would have to be approved by the Crown and by each colonial legislature and then be presented to Parliament for its consent. The Albany Congress adopted an amended version of Franklin's proposal.

Both Shirley and Franklin were far ahead of public opinion. Newspapers did not even discuss the Albany Plan. Every colony rejected it. As Franklin later explained, the colonies feared that the President General might become too powerful. But they also distrusted one another. Despite the French threat, they were not ready to patch up their differences and unite. They did not yet see themselves as "Americans."

The Board of Trade responded by drafting its own plan of union. Its plan resembled Franklin's, except that the Grand Council could only requisition—instead of tax—and colonial union would not require Parliament's approval. Then, after news arrived that Washington had surrendered his small force to the French at Great Meadows in July 1754, Britain decided that the colonies were incapable of uniting in their own defense. Even if they could, the precedent would be dangerous. So London sent redcoats to Virginia instead—two regiments, commanded by Edward Braddock. For Britain, colonial union and direct military aid were policy *alternatives*. Although military aid was more expensive to the British government than the proposed union, it seemed the safer choice.

Yet the Albany Congress achieved one major objective: It urged the Crown to take charge of relations with all western Indians. London responded by creating two Indian superintendencies—one south of the Ohio, which went to Edmund Atkin; and one north of the Ohio, which went to William Johnson, an Irish immigrant to New York who had influence with the Mohawks.

BRITAIN'S YEARS OF DEFEAT

In 1755, London hoped that a quick victory by Braddock at the forks of the Ohio would keep the war from spreading. Braddock's regiments landed in Virginia. At a council of high officials called by Braddock at Alexandria, Virginia, Governor Shirley persuaded him to accept New England's much broader war objectives. Instead of a single expedition aimed at one fort, to be followed by others if time permitted, the campaign of 1755 became four distinct offensives designed to crush the outer defenses of New France and leave it open to British invasion.

The redcoats were highly disciplined professional soldiers who served long terms and had been trained to fight other professional armies. Irregular war in the forests of North America made them uncomfortable. Provincial soldiers, by contrast, were volunteers, often quite young, who usually enlisted only for a single campaign. They knew little about military drill, expected to serve under the officers who had recruited them, and sometimes refused to obey orders that they disliked. Provincials admired the courage of the redcoats but were shocked by the brutal discipline imposed on them. Nevertheless, several thousand colonists also enlisted in the British army.

Under the enlarged plan, the redcoats in Nova Scotia together with New England provincials would assault Fort Beauséjour. New England and New York provincials would attack Crown Point, while Shirley, who had been commissioned as a British colonel, would lead two regiments of redcoats (recently recruited in New England) to Niagara and cut off New France from the western Indians. Braddock, with the strongest force, would attack Fort Duquesne.

Instead, Braddock alienated the Indians and marched to disaster on the Monongahela. In April the western Delawares asked him whether their villages and hunting rights would be secure under British protection. He replied, "No Savage Should Inherit the Land." The chiefs retorted that "if they might not have Liberty To Live on the Land they would not Fight for it." It took Braddock several months to hack a road through the wilderness wide enough for his artillery.

At Fort Duquesne the French commander, Liénard, *sieur* de Beaujeu, could muster only 72 French, 146 Canadians, and 637 Indians against the 1,400 regulars under Braddock and 450 Virginia provincials. Beaujeu had planned to attack the British at the fords of the Monongahela, but the Indians thought such an assault would be suicidal and refused. "Will you allow your father to act alone?" he finally asked melodramatically. "I am sure to defeat them." As Beaujeu marched out, the reluctant Indians followed. Too late to attack at the fords, the French ran into the British vanguard a few miles southeast of the fort. They clashed along a narrow path with thick forest and brush on either side. Beaujeu was killed at once, and his men almost broke. But then they rallied and took cover on the British flanks. Braddock's rear elements rushed toward the sound of the guns and there, massed together, they formed a gigantic red bull's-eye. The Indians and the French poured round after round into them, while the British fired wild volleys at the invisible enemy. The British lost 977 killed or wounded, along with their artillery. Braddock was killed. Only 39 French and Indians were killed or wounded. The redcoats finally broke and ran. Washington, who had fought as a Virginia volunteer, reported that offensive operations would be impossible for the rest of the year. Braddock's road through the wilderness now became a highway for the enemy. For the first time in the history of Quaker Pennsylvania, its settlers faced the horrors of a frontier war.

In Nova Scotia, Fort Beauséjour fell on June 17, 1755. Then, when the Acadians refused to take an oath that might have obliged them to bear arms against other Frenchmen, the British and Yankees responded with an 18th century version of ethnic cleansing. They rounded up between 6,000 and 7,000 Acadians, forced them aboard ships, and expelled them from the province, to be scattered among the 13 colonies, none of which was prepared for the influx. A second roundup in 1759 caught most of the families that had evaded the first one.

Reasoning that the Acadians were not British subjects because they had not taken the oath, and that only British subjects could own land in a British colony, the government of Nova Scotia confiscated the Acadians' land and redistributed it to Protestant settlers, mostly from New England. About 3,000 of the Acadian refugees, after spending miserable years as unwanted Catholic exiles in a Protestant world, finally made it to French Louisiana, where their descendants became known as Cajuns.

Meanwhile William Johnson led his provincials against Crown Point. The French commander, Jean-Armand, baron Dieskau, attacked a body of provincials on September 8 and drove it back in panic to the improvised Fort William Henry near Lake George. French regulars then assailed the fort but were driven off with heavy losses in a six-hour struggle. Colonial newspapers proclaimed the battle a great victory because the provincials had not only held the field but had also wounded and captured Dieskau. But Johnson failed to take Crown Point.

Shirley's Niagara campaign got no farther than Oswego on Lake Ontario and then stopped for the winter, held in check by the French at Fort Frontenac on the lake's northern shore. Oswego was soon cut off by heavy snows. Malnutrition and disease ravaged the garrison.

A WORLD WAR

With the death of Braddock and the capture of Dieskau, military amateurs took over both armies: Shirley in the British colonies and Governor-General Pierre de Rigaud de Vaudreuil in New France. Vaudreuil was a Canadian who understood his colony's weakness without Indian support. The white population of the 13 colonies outnumbered that of New France by 13 to 1; Massachusetts alone had nearly three times as many settlers as New France. Vaudreuil knew that if the British colonies could concentrate their resources in a few places, they had a good chance of overwhelming New France. Therefore, a frontier war waged by New France primarily against ordinary settlers remained the most effective way to force the British colonies to disperse their resources over a vast area.

As long as Vaudreuil was in charge, New France kept winning. Oswego fell in the summer of 1756. When Fort William Henry fell the next year, the French promised to let the garrison march unmolested to Fort Edward. But France's Indian allies killed or carried off 308 of the 2,300 prisoners, an event that colonial newspapers called the Fort William Massacre. Vaudreuil's attacks devastated Pennsylvania's frontier settlements. Even so, the French government decided that New France needed a professional general and sent Louis-Joseph, marquis de Montcalm, in 1756. Shocked and repelled by the brutality of frontier warfare, Montcalm tried to turn the conflict into a traditional European struggle of sieges and battles in which the advantage (as Vaudreuil well understood) would pass to the British.

Meanwhile, Braddock's defeat convinced the British government that the struggle with France could not be limited to a few outposts. Britain declared war on France in 1756, and the French and Indian War in the colonies merged with a general European struggle—the Seven Years' War (1756–1763)—involving France, Austria, and Russia against Prussia, which was heavily subsidized by Britain.

For most of the war, Spain remained neutral, a choice that had huge implications within North America. In the previous war, Spain had been able to turn the slaves of South Carolina against their masters and to create unrest even in New York. At a minimum, Spanish hostilities early in the war would have forced the British to fight in another theater of conflict. Instead, Spain's neutrality permitted Britain to concentrate its resources against New France. By 1762, when Spain finally entered the war in a vain effort to prevent a total British victory, the French had already surrendered Canada, and Britain's seasoned army and navy easily rolled over Spain's less experienced forces.

IMPERIAL TENSIONS: FROM LOUDOUN TO PITT

When London suddenly realized in 1755 that Shirley, an amateur, had taken command of the British army in North America, it dispatched John Campbell, earl of Loudoun, to replace him and began pouring in reinforcements. Loudoun had a special talent for alienating provincials. Colonial units did not care to serve under his command and sometimes bluntly rejected his orders. Provincial volunteers believed they had a contractual relationship with *their* officers; they had never agreed to serve under Loudoun's professionals. They refused to serve beyond their term of enlistment. Even when the British ordered them to stay longer, many of them marched defiantly home.

In fact, many British officers despised the provincials, especially their officers. "The Americans are in general the dirtiest most contemptible cowardly dogs that you can conceive," snarled General James Wolfe. A few British officers held more favorable opinions. Horatio Gates, Richard Montgomery, Hugh Mercer, and Arthur St. Clair all remained in America after the war and became generals in the American army during the Revolution. Colonel Isaac Barré praised American courage in the House of Commons in 1765 and even coined the phrase "Sons of Liberty," to describe them—a label instantly adopted by men who resisted Britain's postwar policies.

As the new commander in chief, Loudoun faced other problems—the quartering (or housing) of British soldiers, the relative rank of British and provincial officers, military discipline, revenue, and smuggling. He tried to impose authoritarian solutions on them all. When he sent redcoats into a city, he demanded that the assembly pay to quarter them or else he would take over buildings by force. He tried to make any British major superior in rank to any provincial officer. Loudoun ordered New England troops to serve directly under British officers, an arrangement that New Englanders thought violated the terms of their enlistment. When some colonial assemblies refused to vote adequate supplies, Loudoun urged Parliament to tax the colonies directly. Shocked that the molasses trade with the French West Indies was proceeding as usual, he urged the navy to stamp it out and sometimes imposed embargoes on colonial shipping. Loudoun did build up his forces, but otherwise he accomplished little.

In 1757 William Pitt came to power as Britain's war minister and found workable voluntaristic solutions to the problems that had defeated Loudoun's authoritarian methods. Pitt understood that consent worked better than coercion in the colonies. Colonial assemblies built barracks to house British soldiers. Pitt declared that every provincial officer would rank immediately behind the equivalent British rank but above all lesser officers, British or provincial. He then promoted every British lieutenant colonel to the rank of "colonel in America only." That decision left only about 30 British majors vulnerable to being ordered about by a provincial colonel, but few of them had independent commands anyway. Provincial units under the command of their own officers cooperated with the British army, and the officers began to impose something close to British discipline on them, including hundreds of lashes for routine offenses. Rather than impose a parliamentary tax, Pitt set aside £200,000 beginning in 1758 (later reduced to £133,000) and told the colonies that they could claim a share of it in proportion to their contribution to the war effort. In effect, he got the colonies to compete voluntarily in support of his stupendous war effort. The subsidies covered slightly less than half of the cost of fielding 20,000 provincials each year from 1758 to 1760, and somewhat smaller numbers in 1761 and 1762 as operations shifted to the Caribbean. Smuggling angered Pitt as much as it did anyone else, but British conquests soon reduced that problem. By 1762 Canada, Martinique, and Guadeloupe, as well as Spanish Havana, were all in British hands. Few places were any longer worth smuggling to, except St. Domingue.

Pitt had no patience with military failure. After Loudoun called off his attack on Louisbourg in 1757, Pitt replaced him with James Abercrombie. He also put Jeffrey Amherst in charge of a new Louisbourg expedition. By 1758 the British Empire had finally put together a military force capable of overwhelming New France and had learned how to use it. In the last years of the war, cooperation between redcoats and provincials became routine and devastatingly effective.

THE YEARS OF BRITISH VICTORY

By 1758 the Royal Navy had cut off Canada from reinforcements and supplies. Britain had sent more than 30 regiments to North America. Combined with 20,000 provincials, thousands of bateau men rowing supplies into the interior, and swarms of privateers preying on French commerce, Britain had mustered perhaps 60,000 men in North America and in nearby waters. Most of them now closed in on the 75,000 people of New France. Montcalm refused to encourage more Indian attacks on the frontier and prepared to defend the approaches to Canada at Forts Duquesne, Niagara, Frontenac, Ticonderoga, Crown Point, and Louisbourg.

Spurred on by Quaker mediators, the British and colonial governments came to terms with the western Indians in 1758, promising not to seize their lands after the war and arranging an uneasy peace. Few settlers or officials had yet noticed a new trend that was emerging during the conflict: Few Indians in the northeastern woodlands were willing to attack others. In 1755, for example, some Senecas fought with New France and some Mohawks with the British, but they maneuvered carefully to avoid confronting each other. This Iroquois sense of solidarity was beginning to spread.

Peace with the western Indians in 1758 permitted the British to revive the grand military plan of 1755, except that this time the overall goal was clear—the conquest of New France. Amherst and James Wolfe, with 9,000 regulars and 500 provincials, besieged Louisbourg for 60 days. It fell in September, thus adding Cape Breton Island to the British province of Nova Scotia. A force of 3,000 provincials under Colonel John Bradstreet advanced to Lake Ontario, took Fort Frontenac, and began building a fleet. This victory cut off the French in the Ohio valley from their supplies. A powerful force of regulars under John Forbes and provincials under Washington marched west through Pennsylvania, to attack Fort Duquesne, but the French blew up the fort and retreated north just before they arrived. The British erected Fort Pitt on the ruins.

The only British defeat in 1758 occurred in northern New York when Abercrombie sent 6,000 regulars and 9,000 provincials against Ticonderoga (Carillon), which was defended by Montcalm and 3,500 troops. Instead of waiting for his artillery to arrive or trying to outflank the French, Abercrombie ordered a frontal assault against a heavily fortified position. His regulars were butchered by the withering fire, and the provincials fled. When Pitt heard the news, he sacked Abercrombie, put Amherst in charge of the New York theater of war, and left Wolfe at Louisbourg to plan an attack up the St. Lawrence against Quebec.

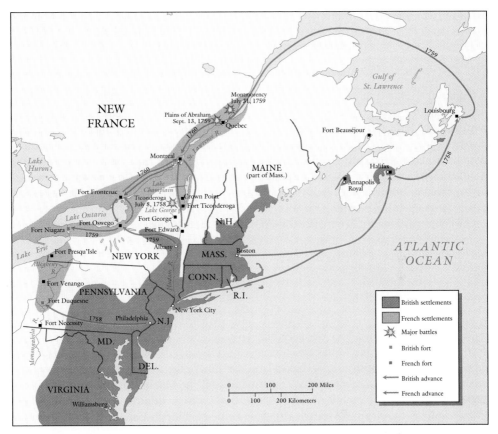

CONQUEST OF CANADA, 1758–1760

In 1759, while the provincials on Lake Ontario moved west and took Niagara, Amherst spent the summer cautiously reducing Ticonderoga and Crown Point. The most dramatic campaign occurred farther east. In June, Wolfe ascended the St. Lawrence with 8,000 redcoats and colonial rangers and laid siege to Quebec, defended by Montcalm with 16,000 regulars, Canadian militia, and Indians. Wolfe mounted howitzers on high ground across the river from Quebec and began reducing most of the city to rubble. Frustrated by the French refusal to come out and fight, he turned loose his American rangers, who ravaged and burned more than 1,400 farms. Still the French held out.

By September both Wolfe and Montcalm realized that the British fleet would soon have to depart or risk being frozen in during the long winter. Wolfe made a last desperate effort. His men silently sailed up the river, climbed a formidable cliff above the city in darkness, and on the morning of September 13, 1759, deployed on the Plains of Abraham behind Quebec. Montcalm panicked. Instead of using his artillery to defend the walls from inside (Wolfe's force had been able to drag only two guns with them), he marched out of Quebec onto the plains. Both generals now had what they craved most, a set-piece European battle that lasted about 15 minutes.

Wolfe and Montcalm were both mortally wounded, but the British drove the French from the field and took Quebec. After the fall of Montreal in 1760, Canada surrendered.

THE CHEROKEE WAR AND SPANISH INTERVENTION

In January 1760 the Cherokees, who had been allies and trading partners of South Carolina, reacted to a long string of violent incidents by attacking backcountry settlers. Within a year, they drove the settlers back 100 miles. South Carolina had to appeal to Amherst for help, and he sent regular soldiers who laid waste the Cherokee Lower Towns in the Appalachian foothills. When that expedition failed to bring peace, another one the next year devastated the Middle Towns farther west, while Virginia threatened the Overhill Towns. The Cherokees made peace in December 1761, but the backcountry settlers, left brutalized and lawless, soon became severe political problems for South Carolina's government.

Only then, in January 1762, after the French and the Cherokees had been defeated, did Spain finally enter the war. British forces quickly took Havana and even Manila in the distant Philippines. France and Spain sued for peace.

THE PEACE OF PARIS

In 1763 the Peace of Paris ended the war. Britain returned Martinique and Guadeloupe to France. France surrendered to Great Britain several minor West Indian islands and all of North America east of the Mississippi, except New Orleans. In exchange for Havana, Spain ceded Florida to the British and also paid a large ransom for the return of Manila. To compensate its Spanish ally, France gave all of Louisiana west of the Mississippi and New Orleans to Spain. Most of the Spanish and African occupants of Florida withdrew to other parts of the Spanish Empire, but nearly all French settlers remained behind in Canada, the Illinois country, and what was now Spanish Louisiana.

The colonists were jubilant. Britain and the colonies could now develop their vast resources in an imperial partnership and would share unprecedented prosperity. But the western Indians angrily rejected the peace settlement. No one had conquered them, and they denied the right or the power of France to surrender their lands to Great Britain. They began to plan their own war of liberation.

CONCLUSION

Between 1713 and 1754, expansion and renewed immigration pushed the edge of North American settlement ever farther into the interior. With a population that doubled every 25 years, many householders no longer enjoyed the opportunity to give all their sons and daughters the level of economic success that they themselves enjoyed. By midcentury many families took up a trade or moved west. Women had to work harder just to sustain levels of opportunity for their households. Many families had to favor sons over daughters and the eldest son over his younger brothers, following the practice in England. The colonies anglicized in other ways as well. Newspapers and the learned professions spread the English Enlightenment to the colonies. English revivalists had a tremendous impact in North America. The northern colonies borrowed "Court" politics from Britain, while most southern colonies favored the

CHRONOLOGY

1690	Massachusetts invents fiat money
1704	*Boston News-Letter* founded
1712	Slaves revolt in New York City
1716	Spanish begin to settle Texas
1718	Beginning of Scots-Irish emigration to North America
1721	Boylston introduces smallpox inoculation in Boston
1732	Georgia charter granted by Parliament
1733	Molasses Act passed
1734	Edwards launches massive religious revival in the Connecticut valley
1735	Zenger acquitted of seditious libel in New York
1738	Spanish found Mose in Florida
1739	Slaves revolt in Stono, South Carolina
1739–1741	Whitefield launches Great Awakening
1741	New York slave conspiracy trials lead to 35 executions
1745	New England volunteers take Louisbourg
1747	Ohio Company of Virginia founded • Anti-impressment rioters in Boston resist Royal Navy
1750	Massachusetts converts from paper money to silver
1754	Washington attacks French patrol near the forks of the Ohio River • Albany Congress proposes plan for colonial union
1755	Braddock suffers disaster near Fort Duquesne • British expel Acadians from Nova Scotia
1756–1757	Loudoun antagonizes the colonies as commander in chief
1756	French take Oswego
1757	French take Fort William Henry • Pitt becomes Britain's war minister
1758	British take Fort Duquesne • British take Fortress Louisbourg and Fort Frontenac • French repel British attack at Ticonderoga
1759	British take Ticonderoga and Crown Point • Wolfe dies taking Quebec; Montcalm also killed
1760	Montreal falls; Canada surrenders to the British
1760–1761	Cherokee War devastates South Carolina backcountry
1762	Spain enters war, loses Havana and Manila
1763	Peace of Paris ends Seven Years' War

kind of political system envisioned by the "Country" opposition in Britain. Both thought they were the freest people on earth. But when expansion and imperial rivalries again led to war after 1739, the colonists discovered that enslaved Africans associated Spain with liberty, while most eastern woodland Indians looked to New France for support. The threat of internal upheaval kept King George's War indecisive in the 1740s. But when Spain remained neutral as Britain and France went to war after 1754, the British Empire mobilized its full resources and conquered New France, thus opening more lands to settlement.

The French and Indian War left powerful memories behind. Provincials admired the courage of the redcoats and the victories they won but hated their arrogant officers. The concord and prosperity that were supposed to follow Britain's great imperial victory yielded instead to bitter political strife.

5

REFORM, RESISTANCE, REVOLUTION

IMPERIAL REFORM ∼ THE STAMP ACT CRISIS

THE TOWNSHEND CRISIS

INTERNAL CLEAVAGES: THE CONTAGION OF LIBERTY

THE LAST IMPERIAL CRISIS ∼ THE IMPROVISED WAR

Britain left an army in North America after 1763 and taxed the colonies to pay part of its cost. The colonists agreed that they should contribute to their own defense but insisted that taxation without representation violated their rights as Englishmen. During the next 12 years, three successive crises shattered Britain's Atlantic empire.

In the first, the Stamp Act crisis, the colonists began by petitioning for a redress of grievances. When that effort failed, they nullified the Stamp Act and continued their resistance until Parliament repealed the tax in 1766. The jubilant colonists celebrated their victory. In the second, the Townshend crisis of 1767–1770, Parliament imposed new taxes on certain imported goods. The colonists petitioned and resisted simultaneously, mostly through an intercolonial nonimportation movement. The British sent troops to Boston. After several violent confrontations, the soldiers withdrew, and Parliament modified the Townshend Revenue Act, retaining the duty on tea. That gesture broke the back of the nonimportation movement, but nobody celebrated the result. The third crisis began with the Tea Act of 1773 and quickly escalated. Boston destroyed British tea without bothering to petition first. When Parliament responded with the Coercive Acts of 1774, the colonists created the Continental Congress to organize further resistance. Neither side dared back down, and the confrontation careened toward military violence. The war broke out in April 1775. Fifteen months later the colonies declared their independence.

IMPERIAL REFORM

In 1760 George III (1760–1820) inherited the British throne at the age of 22. The king's pronouncements on behalf of religion and virtue at first won him many admirers in North America. But the political coalition leading Britain to victory over France fell apart. The king's new ministers set out to reform the empire.

THE BUTE MINISTRY

The king, along with his tutor and principal adviser, John Stuart, earl of Bute, feared that the Seven Years' War would bankrupt Britain. From 1758 on, George and Bute grew more and more despondent. When William Pitt, the king's war minister, urged a preemptive strike on Spain before Spain could attack Britain, Bute forced him to resign in October 1761. Bute soon learned that Pitt had been right. Spain declared war on Britain in January 1762.

In May 1762, Bute forced Thomas Pelham-Holles, duke of Newcastle, to resign as first lord of the treasury. To economize, Bute then reduced Britain's subsidies to Prussia, its only major ally in Europe. So eager were the king and Bute to end the war that they gave back to France the wealthy West Indian islands of Guadeloupe and Martinique.

The British press harshly denounced Bute. As soon as Parliament approved the Treaty of Paris, Bute dismayed the king by resigning. Thus in April 1763, George Grenville became first lord of the treasury, though the king did not trust him and found him only marginally acceptable.

THE GRENVILLE MINISTRY

Britain's national debt had nearly doubled during the last war with France and stood at £130 million. The sheer scale of Britain's victory required more revenue just to police the conquered colonies. In 1762 and 1763 Bute and Grenville decided to leave 20 battalions with about 7,000 men in America. Because the colonists would receive the benefit of this protection, Grenville argued, they ought to pay a reasonable portion of the cost, and eventually all of it.

Instead of building on the voluntaristic measures that Pitt had used to win the war, then, Grenville was reverting to the demands for coercive reforms that had crisscrossed the Atlantic during Britain's years of defeat from 1755 to 1757. London, he believed, had to gain effective centralized control over the colonies. To the settlers, victory over France would mean new burdens, not relief.

To Grenville, the willing cooperation of the colonies after 1758 reflected the empire's weakness, not its strength. He believed that the British government had to act quickly to establish its authority before the colonies slipped completely out of control. In effect, he set in motion a self-fulfilling prophecy in which the British government brought about precisely what it was trying to prevent.

INDIAN POLICY AND PONTIAC'S WAR

Britain's Proclamation of 1763 set up governments in Canada, Florida, and other conquered colonies. It tried to set the pace of western settlement by establishing the so-called Proclamation Line along the Appalachian watershed. No settlements could be planted west of that line unless Britain first purchased the land by treaty from the Indians. Settlers would be encouraged to move instead to Nova Scotia, northern New England, Georgia, or Florida. Because most Iroquois land lay east of the line, the Six Nations felt threatened by the new policy. General Amherst's contempt for Indian customs deprived British officials of most of their leverage with them, at a time when their ability to unite had become stronger than ever.

In 1761 Neolin, a western Delaware, reported a vision in which God commanded Indians to return to their ancestral ways. Neolin called for an end to Indian dependence on the Anglo-

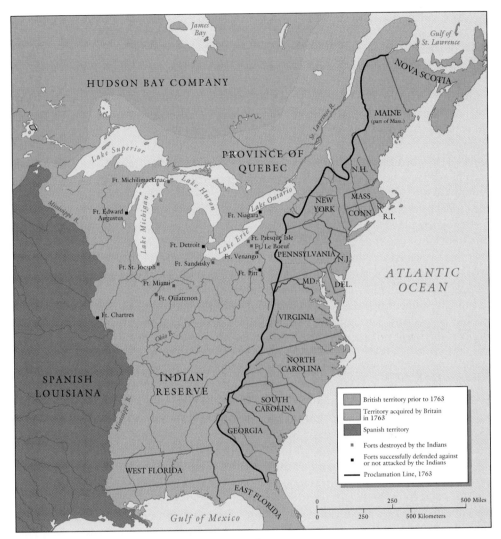

PONTIAC'S WAR AND THE PROCLAMATION LINE OF 1763

Americans. European vices, he said, especially drinking rum, blocked the path to heaven. God was punishing Indians for accepting European ways: "If you suffer the English among you, you are dead men. Sickness, smallpox, and their poison will destroy you entirely." But Neolin's condemnation did not extend to the French who were still living in the Great Lakes region.

With a unity never seen before, the Indians struck in 1763. The conflict became known as Pontiac's War, named for an Ottawa chief. Senecas, Mingos, Delawares, Shawnees, Wyandots, Miamis, Ottawas, and other nations attacked 13 British posts in the West. Between May 16 and June 20, all of the forts fell except Niagara, Fort Pitt, Detroit, and a tiny outpost on Green Bay that the Indians did not bother to attack. For months the Indians kept Detroit and Fort Pitt under close siege. They hoped to drive British settlers back to the eastern seaboard.

These Indian successes enraged Amherst. In retaliation, he ordered Colonel Henry Bouquet, commander at Fort Pitt, to distribute smallpox-infested blankets among the western nations, touching off a lethal epidemic. However, not until 1764 did British and provincial forces end resistance and restore peace. The British then reluctantly accepted the role that the French had played in the Great Lakes region by distributing gifts and mediating differences.

But 10 years of conflict had brutalized the frontiersmen. Perhaps sensing the Indians' growing revulsion against warring with one another, many settlers began to assume that all Indians must be the enemies of all whites. In December 1763 the Scots-Irish of Paxton Township, Pennsylvania, murdered six unarmed Christian Indians—two old men, three women, and a child—at nearby Conestoga. Two weeks later the "Paxton Boys" slaughtered 14 more Christian Indians who had been brought to Lancaster for protection. When Governor John Penn removed 140 Moravian mission Indians to Philadelphia for safety, the Paxton Boys marched on the capital determined to kill them all.

Denouncing the Paxton Boys as "Christian white Savages," Benjamin Franklin led a delegation from the assembly that met the marchers at Germantown and persuaded them to go home after they presented a list of their grievances. The Moravian Indians had been spared. But all efforts to bring the murderers to justice failed, and the frontiersmen of Pennsylvania and Virginia virtually declared an open season on Indians that continued for years. London had hoped that its officials would bring evenhanded justice to the frontier. Indians had won real benefits from the superintendents, such as protection from land speculators. But otherwise they found little to choose between Amherst's smallpox blankets and the murderous rage of the Paxton Boys.

THE SUGAR ACT

In a step that settlers found ominous, Grenville's Sugar Act of 1764 placed duties on Madeira wine, coffee, and other products, but Grenville expected the greatest revenue to come from the molasses duty of three pence per gallon. The Molasses Act of 1733 had been designed to keep French molasses out of North America by imposing a prohibitive duty of six pence per gallon. Instead, by paying a bribe of about a penny a gallon, merchants were able to get French molasses certified as British. By 1760, more than 90 percent of all molasses imported into New England came from the French islands. Planters in the British islands gave up, lost interest in New England markets, and turned their molasses into quality rum for sale in Britain and Ireland. Nobody, in short, had any interest in stopping the trade in French molasses. New England merchants said they were willing to pay a duty of one pence (what bribes were costing them), but Grenville insisted on three.

The Sugar Act also launched Grenville's war against smugglers. It vastly increased the amount of paperwork required of ship captains and permitted seizures of ships for what owners considered mere technicalities. In effect, Grenville tried to make it more profitable for customs officers to hound the merchants than to accept bribes from them. The Sugar Act encouraged them to prosecute violators in vice admiralty courts, which did not use juries, rather than in common law courts, which did.

THE CURRENCY ACT AND THE QUARTERING ACT

Grenville passed several other imperial measures. The Currency Act of 1764 responded to wartime protests of London merchants against Virginia's paper money, which had lost almost

15 percent of its value between 1759 and 1764. The Currency Act forbade the colonies to issue any paper money as legal tender. The money question had become urgent because the Sugar Act (and, later, the Stamp Act) required that all duties be paid in specie (silver or gold). Supporters of those taxes argued that the new duties would keep the specie in America to pay the army, but the colonists replied that the drain of specie from some of the colonies would put impossible constraints on trade. Boston and Newport, for instance, would pay most of the molasses tax, but the specie collected there would follow the army to Quebec, New York, the Great Lakes, and Florida. Grenville saw "America" as a single region in which specie would circulate to the benefit of all. The colonists knew better. As of 1765, "America" existed only in British minds, not yet in colonial hearts.

Another reform measure was the Quartering Act of 1765, which was requested by Sir Thomas Gage, Amherst's successor as army commander. Gage asked for parliamentary authority to quarter soldiers in private homes, if necessary, when on the march and away from their barracks. Grenville turned the problem over to Thomas Pownall, the governor of Massachusetts during its 1757 quartering crisis, which had been resolved by building the barracks that Gage now feared might not be adequate. Pownall came up with a bill that addressed the old problem, not the new one. It ordered colonial assemblies to vote specific supplies, such as beer and candles, for the troops, which the assemblies were willingly doing already. But it also required the army to quarter its soldiers only in public buildings, such as taverns, which existed in large numbers only in cities. The Quartering Act solved no problems, but it created several new ones.

THE STAMP ACT

When Parliament passed the Sugar Act early in 1764, Grenville announced that it might also be necessary to impose a stamp tax on legal documents and publications in the colonies. No one in the House of Commons, he declared, doubted that Parliament had the right to impose such a tax. Because Parliament had never imposed a direct tax on the colonies, however, he also knew that he had to persuade the settlers that a stamp tax would not be an innovation. His supporters insisted that the measure did not violate the principle of no taxation without representation. Each member of Parliament, they argued, represented the entire empire, not just a local constituency. The colonists were no different from the large nonvoting majority of subjects within Great Britain. All were "virtually" represented in Parliament. Grenville also denied that there was any legal difference between external taxes (port duties, such as that on molasses) and internal (or inland) taxes, such as the proposed stamp tax.

Grenville indicated that, if the colonies could devise a revenue plan better than a stamp tax, he would listen. His offer created confusion. All 13 colonial assemblies drafted petitions objecting to the Stamp Act as a form of taxation without representation. Most of them also attacked the duties imposed by the Sugar Act. They too rejected the distinction between internal and external taxes. Both kinds, they declared, would violate the British constitution. While agreeing that they ought to contribute to their own defense, they urged the government to return to the traditional method of requisitions, in which the Crown asked a colony for a specific sum, and the assembly decided how (or whether) to raise it. Colonists feared that taxation by Parliament might tempt Britain to rule them without consulting their assemblies.

But when the first round of these petitions reached London early in 1765, Parliament refused to receive them. To Grenville, requisitions were not a better idea. They had often been tried, had never worked efficiently, and never would. He rejected the petitions with a clear conscience. But to the colonists, he seemed to have acted in bad faith all along. He had asked their advice and had then refused even to consider it.

The Stamp Act passed in February 1765, to go into effect on November 1. Under this law, all contracts, licenses, commissions, and most other legal documents would be void unless they were executed on officially stamped paper. Law courts would not recognize any document that lacked the proper stamp. A stamp duty was also put on all newspapers and pamphlets, a requirement likely to anger every printer in the colonies. Playing cards and dice were also taxed.

When the Stamp Act became law, most colonial leaders resigned themselves to a situation that seemed beyond their power to change. For instance, Daniel Dulany, a Maryland lawyer, refuted the argument for virtual representation but drew a line short of overt resistance: "At the same Time that I invalidate the Claim upon which [the Stamp Act] is founded, I may very consistently recommend a Submission to the Law, whilst it endures." But ordinary settlers began to take direct action to prevent the implementation of the act.

THE STAMP ACT CRISIS

Resistance to the Stamp Act began in the spring of 1765 and continued for a year, until it was repealed. Patrick Henry, a newcomer to the Virginia House of Burgesses, launched the first wave by introducing five resolutions on May 30 and 31, 1765. His resolves passed by narrow margins, and one was rescinded the next day. Henry had two more in his pocket that he decided not to introduce. But over the summer the *Newport Mercury* printed six of Henry's seven resolutions, and the *Maryland Gazette* printed all of them. Neither paper reported that some of the seven had not passed. To other colonies, Virginia seemed to have taken a far more radical position than it actually had. The last two resolves printed in the *Maryland Gazette* claimed that Virginians "are not bound to yield Obedience to any Law . . . designed to impose any Taxation upon them" except those passed by their own assembly, and that anyone defending Parliament's right to tax Virginia "shall be Deemed, an Enemy to this his Majesty's Colony."

In their fall or winter sessions, eight colonial legislatures passed new resolutions condemning the Stamp Act. Nine colonies sent delegates to the Stamp Act Congress, which met in New York in October. It passed resolutions affirming colonial loyalty to the king and "all due subordination" to Parliament but condemned the Stamp and Sugar Acts. By 1765 nearly all colonial spokesmen agreed that the Stamp Act was unconstitutional, that colonial representation in Parliament (urged by a few writers) was impractical because of the distance and the huge expense, and that therefore the Stamp Act had to be repealed. They accepted the idea of virtual representation *within* the colonies—their assemblies, they said, represented both voters and nonvoters—but the colonists ridiculed the argument when it was applied across the Atlantic. A disfranchised Englishman who acquired sufficient property could become a voter, pointed out Daniel Dulany. But, Dulany explained, no colonist, no matter how wealthy he became, could vote for a member of Parliament. Members of Parliament paid the taxes that they levied on others within Britain. But they would never pay any tax imposed on the colonies.

NULLIFICATION

No matter how eloquent, resolutions and pamphlets alone could not defeat the Stamp Act. Street violence might, however, and Boston showed the way, led by men calling themselves the "Sons of Liberty." On August 14 the town awoke to find an effigy of Andrew Oliver, the stamp distributor, hanging on what became the town's Liberty Tree (the gallows on which enemies of the people deserved to be hanged). The sheriff admitted that he dared not remove the effigy, and after dark a crowd of men roamed the streets, shouted defiance at the governor and council, demolished a new building Oliver was erecting that "they called the Stamp Office," beheaded and burned Oliver's effigy, and finally invaded Oliver's home. Oliver had already fled. Thoroughly cowed, he resigned.

On August 26 an even angrier crowd all but demolished the elegant mansion of Lt. Governor Thomas Hutchinson. Most Bostonians believed that Hutchinson had defended and even helped to draft the Stamp Act in letters to British friends. In fact, he had opposed it, although quietly. Shocked by the destruction of property, the militia finally appeared to police the streets. But when Governor Sir Francis Bernard tried to arrest those responsible for the first riot, he got nowhere. Bostonians deplored the events of August 26 but approved those of August 14. No one was punished for either event.

Everywhere except Georgia, the stamp master was forced to resign before the law took effect on November 1. With no one to distribute the stamps, the act could not be implemented. Merchants adopted nonimportation agreements to pressure the British into repeal. Following Boston's lead, the Sons of Liberty took control of the streets in other cities. After November 1, they agitated to open the ports and courts, which had closed down rather than operate without stamps. As winter gave way to spring, most ports and some courts resumed business. Violent resistance worked. The Stamp Act was nullified—even in Georgia, eventually. Neither the courts nor the customs officers had any stamps to use because nobody dared distribute them.

REPEAL

Clearly, the next move was up to Britain. For reasons that had nothing to do with the colonies, the king dismissed Grenville in the summer of 1765 and replaced his ministry with a narrow coalition organized primarily by William Augustus, duke of Cumberland, the king's uncle. An untested young nobleman, Charles Watson-Wentworth, marquess of Rockingham, took over the treasury. This "Old Whig" ministry had to deal with the riots in America, and Cumberland—the man who had sent Braddock to America in the winter of 1754–1755—may have favored a similar use of force in late 1765. If so, he never had a chance to issue the order. On October 31, minutes before an emergency cabinet meeting on the American crisis, he died of a heart attack, leaving Rockingham in charge of the government. At first, Rockingham favored amending the Stamp Act, but by December he had decided on repeal. To win over the other ministers, the king, and Parliament would demand great skill.

To Rockingham, the only alternative to repeal seemed to be a ruinous civil war in America. But as the king's chief minister, he could hardly tell Parliament that the world's greatest empire had to yield to unruly mobs. He needed a better reason for repeal. Even before news of the nonimportation agreements reached London, he began to mobilize the British merchants and manufacturers who traded with America. They petitioned Parliament for repeal of the

"THE REPEAL OR THE FUNERAL OF MISS AMERIC-STAMP"   This London cartoon of 1766 shows George Grenville carrying the coffin of the Stamp Act with Lord Bute behind him. Contemporaries would easily have identified the other personalities.

Stamp Act. To them the Grenville program had been an economic disaster, and their arguments gave Rockingham the leverage he needed.

Rockingham won the concurrence of the other ministers by promising his support for a Declaratory Act that would affirm the sovereignty of Parliament over the colonies. When William Pitt eloquently demanded repeal in the House of Commons on January 14, 1766, Rockingham gained a powerful, though temporary, ally. Parliament "may bind [the colonists'] trade, confine their manufactures, and exercise every power whatsoever," Pitt declared, "except that of taking their money out of their pockets without their consent."

Rockingham still had to overcome resistance from the king, who hinted that he favored "modification" rather than repeal. George III was apparently willing to repeal all the stamp duties except those on dice and playing cards. But because only Grenville was ready to use the army to enforce even an amended Stamp Act, Rockingham brought the king around by threatening to resign.

Three pieces of legislation ended the crisis. The first repealed the Stamp Act because it had been "greatly detrimental to the commercial interests" of the empire. The second, the Declaratory Act, affirmed that Parliament had "full power and authority to make laws and statutes of sufficient force and validity to bind the colonies and people of America . . . in all cases whatsoever." Rockingham resisted pressure to insert the word "taxes" along with "laws and statutes." That omission permitted the colonists, who drew a sharp distinction between legislation (which, they conceded, Parliament had a right to pass) and taxation (which it could not), to interpret the act as an affirmation of their position, while nearly everyone in Britain read precisely the opposite meaning into the phrase "laws and statutes." The Colonists read the Declaratory Act as a face-saving gesture that made repeal of the Stamp Act possible.

The third measure, the Revenue Act of 1766, reduced the duty on molasses from three pence per gallon to one penny. But the duty was imposed on all molasses, British or foreign, imported into the mainland colonies. Although the act was more favorable to the molasses trade than any other measure yet passed by Parliament, it was also, beyond any doubt, a revenue measure, and it generated more income for the empire than any other colonial tax. Few colonists attacked it for violating the principle of no taxation without representation. In Britain it seemed that the colonists objected only to internal taxes but would accept external duties.

In the course of the struggle, both sides, British and colonial, had rejected the distinction between "internal" and "external" taxes. They could find no legal or philosophical basis for condemning the one while approving the other. Hardly anyone except Franklin noticed in 1766 that the difference was quite real and that the crisis had in fact been resolved according to that distinction. Parliament had tried to extend its authority over the internal affairs of the colonies and had failed. But it continued to collect port duties in the colonies, some to regulate trade, others explicitly for revenue. Although no one knew how to justify this division of authority, the internal-external cleavage marked the boundary between what Parliament could do on its own and what the Crown could accomplish only with the consent of the colonists.

Another misunderstanding was equally grave. Only the riots had created a crisis severe enough to push Parliament into repeal. Both sides, however, preferred to believe that economic pressure had been decisive. For the colonies, this conviction set the pattern of resistance for the next two imperial crises.

THE TOWNSHEND CRISIS

The goodwill created by repeal did not last long. In 1766 the king again replaced his ministry. This time he persuaded William Pitt to form a government. Pitt appealed to men of goodwill from all parties, but few responded. His ministry faced serious opposition within Parliament. Pitt compounded that problem by accepting a peerage as earl of Chatham, a decision that removed his magnificent oratory from the House of Commons and eventually left Charles Townshend as his spokesman in that chamber. A witty, extemporaneous speaker, Townshend had betrayed every leader he ever served. The only point of real consistency in his political career had been his attitude toward the colonies: He always took a hard line.

THE TOWNSHEND PROGRAM

New York had already created a small crisis for the new earl of Chatham by objecting to the Quartering Act as a disguised form of taxation without consent. Under the old rules, when the army had asked for quarters and supplies and the assembly had voted them, consent had been an integral part of the process. Now one legislature (Parliament) was telling others (the colonial assemblies) what they must do. New York refused. In 1767 Parliament passed the New York Restraining Act, which forbade New York's governor from signing any law until the assembly complied with the Quartering Act. The crisis fizzled out when the governor bent the rules and announced that the assembly had already complied with the substance of the Quartering Act before the Restraining Act went into effect.

Chatham soon learned that he could not control the House of Commons from his position in the House of Lords. During the Christmas recess of 1766–1767, Chatham began to slip into an acute depression that lasted more than two years. He refused to communicate with other ministers or even with the king. The colonists expected sympathy from his administration. Instead they got Townshend, who took charge of colonial policy in the spring of 1767.

As chancellor of the exchequer, Townshend had to present the annual budget to the House of Commons. A central aspect of it was the Townshend Revenue Act of 1767, which imposed new duties in colonial ports on certain imports that the colonies could legally get only from Britain: tea, paper, glass, red and white lead, and painter's colors. At the same time, Townshend removed more duties on tea within Britain than he could offset with the new revenue collected in the colonies. Revenue, clearly, was not his object. The statute's preamble stated his real goal: to use the new revenues to pay the salaries of governors and judges in the colonies, thereby freeing them from dependence on the assemblies. This rather devious strategy aroused suspicions of conspiracy in the colonies. Many sober provincials began to believe that, deep in the recesses of the British government, men really were plotting to deprive them of their liberties.

Other measures gave appellate powers to the vice admiralty courts in Boston, Philadelphia, and Charleston and created a separate American Board of Customs Commissioners to enforce the trade and revenue laws in the colonies. The board was placed in Boston, where resistance to the Stamp Act had been fiercest, rather than in Philadelphia, which had been rather quiet in 1765 and would have been a much more convenient location. Townshend was eager for confrontation.

The British army also began to withdraw from nearly all frontier posts and concentrate near the coast. Although the primary motive was to save money, the implications were striking. It was one thing to keep an army in America to guard the frontier and then ask the colonists to pay part of its cost. But an army far distant from the frontier presumably existed only to police the colonists themselves. Why should they pay any part of its cost if its role was to enforce policies that would deprive them of their liberties?

Townshend ridiculed the distinction between internal and external taxes, a distinction that he attributed to Chatham and the colonists, but declared that he would honor it anyway. Then, having won approval for his program, he died suddenly in September 1767, passing on to others the dilemmas he had created. Frederick, Lord North, became chancellor of the exchequer. Chatham resigned, and Augustus Henry Fitzroy, duke of Grafton, became prime minister.

RESISTANCE: THE POLITICS OF ESCALATION

The internal-external distinction was troublesome for the colonists. Since 1765 they had been objecting to all taxes for revenue, but in 1766 they had accepted the penny duty on molasses with few complaints. Defeating the Revenue Act of 1767 would prove tougher than nullifying the Stamp Act. Parliament had never been able to impose its will on the internal affairs of the colonies, as the Stamp Act fiasco demonstrated, but it did control the seas. Goods subject to duties might be aboard any of hundreds of ships arriving from Britain each year, but screening the cargo of every vessel threatened to impose an enormous burden on the Sons of Liberty. A policy of general nonimportation would be easier to implement, but British trade played a bigger role in the colonial economy than North American trade did in the British economy. To hurt Britain a little, the colonies would have to harm themselves a lot.

The colonists divided over strategies of resistance. On August 31, 1767, the radical *Boston Gazette* called for complete nonimportation of all British goods. The merchants' paper, the *Boston Evening Post*, disagreed. In October, the Boston town meeting encouraged greater use of home manufactures and authorized the voluntary nonconsumption of British goods. But there was no organized resistance to the new measures, and the Townshend duties became operative in November 1767 with little opposition. A month later, John Dickinson, a Philadelphia lawyer writing as a Pennsylvania farmer, tried to rouse his fellow colonists to action through 12 urgent letters that were reprinted in nearly every colonial newspaper. These *Letters from a Farmer in Pennsylvania* denied the distinction between internal and external taxes and insisted that all parliamentary taxes for revenue violated the rights of the colonists.

Massachusetts again set the pace of resistance. In February 1768 its assembly petitioned the king, but not Parliament, against the new measures. Without waiting for a reply, it also sent a Circular Letter to the other assemblies, urging them to pursue "constitutional measures" of resistance against the Quartering Act, the new taxes, and the use of Townshend revenues to pay the salaries of governors and judges.

Wills Hill, earl of Hillsborough and secretary of state for the American colonies (an office created in 1768), responded so sharply that he turned tepid opposition into serious resistance. He told the Massachusetts assembly to rescind the Circular Letter and ordered all governors to dissolve any assembly that dared to accept it. The Massachusetts House voted 92 to 17 in June 1768 not to rescind. Most other assemblies had shown little interest in the Townshend program, particularly in the southern colonies where governors already had fixed salaries. But they bristled when told what they could or could not debate. All of them took up the Circular Letter or began to draft their own. One by one, the governors dissolved their assemblies until government by consent did indeed seem endangered.

By January 1769, nonimportation at last began to take hold. Spurred on by the popular but mistaken belief that the nonimportation agreements of 1765 had forced Parliament to repeal the Stamp Act, the colonists again turned to a strategy of economic sanctions. Nonimportation affected only imports from Britain. No one tried to block the importation of West Indian molasses, which was essential to the rum industry of Boston and Newport. On the other hand, the Sons of Liberty knew that virtually all molasses came from the French islands, and that nonimportation would injure only French planters and American manufacturers and consumers, while putting no pressure on Parliament or British merchants. The only proven way to resist the penny duty was through smuggling.

The next escalation again came from Boston. On March 18, 1768, the town's celebration of the anniversary of the Stamp Act's repeal grew so raucous that the governor and the new American Board of Customs Commissioners asked Hillsborough for troops. He ordered General Gage, based in New York, to send two regiments to Boston. But on June 10, before Gage could respond, a riot broke out in Boston after customs collectors seized John Hancock's sloop *Liberty* for having smuggled Madeira wine (taxed under the Sugar Act) on its *previous* voyage. By waiting until the ship had a new cargo, informers and customs officials would be able to split larger shares when the sloop was condemned. Terrified by the fury of the popular response, the commissioners fled to Castle William in Boston harbor and again petitioned Hillsborough for troops. He then sent two regiments from Ireland.

Believing that he held the edge with the army on its way, Governor Bernard leaked this news in late August 1768. The public response flabbergasted him. The Boston town meeting asked him to summon the legislature, which Bernard had dissolved in June after it stood by its Circular Letter. When Bernard refused, the Sons of Liberty asked the other towns to elect delegates to a "convention" in Boston. The convention had no legal standing in the colony's royal

PAUL REVERE'S ENGRAVING OF THE BRITISH ARMY LANDING IN BOSTON, 1768   The navy approached the city in battle array, a sight familiar to veterans of the French wars. To emphasize the peaceful, Christian character of Boston, Revere exaggerated the height of the church steeples.

government. When the convention met, it accepted Boston's definition of colonial grievances but refused to sanction violence. Boston had no choice but to go along.

AN EXPERIMENT IN MILITARY COERCION

The British fleet entered Boston harbor in battle array by October 2, 1768, and landed 1,000 soldiers, sent by General Gage from Nova Scotia. Massachusetts had built barracks in Castle William, miles away on an island in Boston harbor, where the soldiers could hardly function as a police force. According to the Quartering Act, any attempt to quarter soldiers on private property would expose the officer responsible to being cashiered from the army. The soldiers pitched their tents on Boston Common. Eventually they took over a building that had been the Boston poorhouse. The regiments from Ireland joined them later.

To warn the public against the dangers posed by a standing army in time of peace, the patriots compiled a "Journal of the Times" describing how British soldiers were undermining public order in Boston—clashing with the town watch, endangering the virtue of young women, disturbing church services, and starting fights. The "Journal" always appeared first as a newspaper column in some other city, usually New York. Only later was it reprinted in Boston, after memories of any specific incident had grown hazy. Yet violence against customs officers ceased for many months. John Mein (pronounced "mean"), loyalist editor of the *Boston Chronicle,* caricatured leading patriots and began to publish customs records that exposed merchants who were violating the nonimportation agreement. Yet Britain's experiment in military coercion seemed successful enough to justify withdrawal of half the soldiers in the summer of 1769.

Meanwhile, when news of the Massachusetts convention of towns reached Britain, the House of Lords passed a set of resolutions calling for the deportation of colonial political offenders to England for trial. Instead of quashing dissent, this threat to colonial political autonomy infuriated the southern colonies. Virginia, Maryland, and South Carolina now adopted nonimportation agreements. In the Chesapeake, no enforcement mechanism was ever put in place. But Charleston took nonimportation seriously. Up and down the continent, the feeble resistance of mid-1768 was becoming formidable by 1769.

THE WILKES CRISIS

John Wilkes, a member of Parliament and a radical opposition journalist, had fled into exile in 1763 and had been outlawed for publishing an attack on the king in *The North Briton* No. 45, his newspaper.

In 1768 George III dissolved Parliament and issued writs for the usual septennial elections. Wilkes returned from France and won a seat for the county of Middlesex. He then received a sentence of one year in King's Bench Prison. Hundreds of supporters gathered to chant "Wilkes and Liberty!" On May 10, 1768, Wilkites just outside the prison clashed with soldiers who fired into the crowd, killing six and wounding 15. Wilkes denounced "the Massacre of St. George's Fields."

The House of Commons expelled Wilkes and ordered a new election, but the voters chose him again. Two more expulsions and two more elections took place the next year, until in April 1769, after Wilkes had won again by 1,143 votes to 296, the exasperated House of Commons voted to seat the loser.

Wilkes had created a constitutional crisis. His adherents founded "the Society of Gentlemen Supporters of the Bill of Rights," which raised money to pay off his huge debts and organized a national campaign on his behalf. Wilkites called for a reduction of royal patronage and major reforms of the electoral system. And they sympathized openly with North American protests. Colonial Sons of Liberty began to identify strongly with Wilkes. Boston even printed a Wilkite parody of the Apostles' Creed. It began: "I believe in Wilkes, the firm patriot, . . . Who was born for our good. Suffered under arbitrary power. Was banished and imprisoned." It ended with a hope for "the resurrection of liberty, and the life of universal freedom forever. Amen."

In 1769 the South Carolina assembly borrowed £1,500 sterling from the colony's treasurer and donated it to Wilkes. When the assembly passed an appropriation to cover the gift, the council rejected the bill. Because neither side would back down, the assembly voted no taxes after 1769 and passed no laws after 1771. Royal government broke down over the Wilkes question.

The Townshend crisis and the Wilkite movement became an explosive combination. For the first time, many colonists began to question the decency of the British government and its commitment to liberty. That a conspiracy existed to destroy British and colonial liberty began to seem quite credible.

THE BOSTON MASSACRE

In late 1769, the Boston Sons of Liberty turned to direct confrontation with the army, and the city again faced a serious crisis. The town watch clashed with the army's guardposts because the watch, when challenged by the redcoats' call "Who goes there?" refused to give the required answer: "Friends." Under English common law, soldiers could not fire on civilians without an order from a civil magistrate, except in self-defense when their lives were in danger. By the fall of 1769 no magistrate dared to issue such a command. Clashes between soldiers and civilians grew frequent.

By 1770 the soldiers often felt under siege. When rioters drove editor John Mein out of town, the army offered him no protection. Once again the Sons of Liberty felt free to intimidate merchants who violated nonimportation. They nearly lynched Ebenezer Richardson, a customs informer who fired shots from his home into a stone-throwing crowd and killed an 11-year-old boy. The lad's funeral on February 26, 1770, became an enormous display of public mourning. Richardson, although convicted of murder, was pardoned by George III.

After the funeral, tensions between soldiers and citizens reached a fatal climax. Off-duty soldiers tried to supplement their meager wages with part-time employment, a practice that angered local artisans who resented the competition. On Friday, March 2, 1770, three soldiers came to John Hancock's wharf looking for work. "Soldier, will you work?" asked Samuel Gray, a rope maker. "Yes," replied one. "Then go and clean my shit house," sneered Gray. The soldiers attacked him but were repelled. They returned with 10 others but were again repulsed. Forty soldiers had no better luck. Then Gray's employer persuaded Colonel William Dalrymple to confine his men to barracks. Peace prevailed through the Puritan sabbath that ran from Saturday night to sunrise on Monday, but everyone expected trouble on Monday, March 5.

After dark on Monday, civilians and soldiers clashed at several places. A crowd hurling snowballs and rocks closed in on the lone sentinel guarding the customs house. The guard called for help. A corporal and seven soldiers rushed to his aid and loaded their weapons. Captain Thomas Preston then took command and ordered the soldiers to drive the attackers slowly back with fixed bayonets. The crowd taunted the soldiers, daring them to fire. One soldier apparently slipped, discharging his musket into the air as he fell. The others then fired into the crowd, killing five and wounding six.

With the whole town taking up arms, the soldiers were withdrawn to Castle William. Preston and six of his men stood trial for murder and were defended, brilliantly, by two radical patriot lawyers, John Adams and Josiah Quincy Jr., who believed that every accused person ought to have a proper defense. Preston and four of the soldiers were acquitted. The other two were convicted only of manslaughter, branded on the thumb, and released.

The Boston Massacre, as the Sons of Liberty called this encounter, became the colonial counterpart to the Massacre of St. George's Fields in England. It marked the failure of Britain's first attempt at military coercion.

PARTIAL REPEAL

The day of the massacre marked a turning point in Britain as well, for on that day Lord North (who had become prime minister in January 1770) asked Parliament to repeal the Townshend duties, except the one on tea. North wanted them all repealed, but the cabinet had rejected complete repeal by a 5-to-4 vote on May 1, 1769. As with the Stamp Act, Britain had three choices: enforcement, repeal, or modification. North chose the middle ground—modification instead of full repeal or enforcement. In public, he claimed to be retaining only a preamble without a statute, a vestige of the Townshend Revenue Act, while repealing the substance. In fact, he did the opposite. Tea provided nearly three-fourths of the revenue under the act. North kept the substance but gave up the shadow.

This news reached the colonies just after nonimportation had achieved its greatest success in 1769 (see the accompanying table). The colonies reduced imports by about one-third from what they had been in 1768, but the impact on Britain was slight. North had hoped that partial repeal, although it would not placate all the colonists, would at least divide them. It did.

Most merchants favored renewed importation of everything but tea, while the Sons of Liberty, most of whom were artisans, still supported complete nonimportation, a policy that would increase demand for their own manufactures.

Resistance collapsed first in Newport, where smuggling had always been the preferred method of challenging British authority. It spread to New York City, where the boycott on imports had been most effective. Soon Philadelphia caved in, followed by Boston in October 1770. By contrast, nonimportation had hardly caused a ripple in the import trade of the Chesapeake colonies. North's repeal was followed everywhere by an orgy of importation of British goods, setting record highs in all the colonies.

DISAFFECTION

The Quartering Act expired quietly in 1770; some of the more objectionable features of the vice admiralty courts were softened; and the Currency Act of 1764 was repealed in stages between 1770 and 1773, as even London began to recognize that it was harming trade. Yet North had not restored confidence in the justice and decency of the British government. To a degree hard to appreciate today, the empire ran on voluntarism, on trust, or what people at the time called "affection." Its opposite was *dis*affection, which meant something more literal and dangerous to them than it does now.

Many colonists blamed one another for failing to win complete repeal of the duties. Bostonians lamented the "immortal shame and infamy" of New Yorkers for abandoning resistance. A New Yorker retaliated by calling Boston "the common sewer of America into which every beast that brought with it the unclean thing has disburthened itself."

These recriminations, gratifying as they must have been to British officials, actually masked a vast erosion of trust in the imperial government. The colonists were angry with one another

EXPORTS IN £000 STERLING FROM ENGLAND AND SCOTLAND TO THE AMERICAN COLONIES, 1766–1775

COLONY	1766	1767	1768	1769	1770	1771	1772	1773	1774	1775
New England	419	416	431	224	417	1,436*	844	543	577	85.0
New York	333	424	491	76	480	655*	349	296	460	1.5
Pennsylvania	334	383	442	205	140	747*	526	436	646	1.4
Chesapeake†	520	653	670	715	997*	1,224*	1,016	589	690	1.9
Lower South‡	376	292	357	385*	228	515*	575*	448	471	130.5
Totals	1,982	2,168	2,391	1,605	2,262	4,577*	3,310	2,312	2,844	220.3

Average total exports, 1766–1768 = £2,180

1769 = 73.6% of that average, or 67.1% of 1768 exports

1770 = 103.8% of that average, or 94.6% of 1768 exports

*These totals surpassed all previous highs

†Chesapeake = Maryland and Virginia

‡Lower South = Carolinas and Georgia

for failing to appreciate how menacing British policy still was. The tea duty remained a sliver in a wound that would not heal.

That fear sometimes broke through the surface calm of the years from 1770 to 1773. Rhode Islanders had often clashed with customs officers. Then, in 1772, a predatory customs vessel, the *Gaspée,* ran aground near Providence while pursuing some peaceful coastal ships. After dark, men with blackened faces boarded the *Gaspée,* wounded its captain, and burned the ship. Britain sent a panel of dignitaries to the colony with instructions to send the perpetrators to England for trial. The inquiry failed because no one would talk.

Twelve colonial assemblies considered this threat so ominous that they created permanent committees of correspondence to keep in touch with one another and to *anticipate* the next assault on their liberties. Even colonial moderates now believed that the British government was conspiring to destroy liberty in America. When Governor Hutchinson announced in 1773 that Massachusetts Superior Court justices would receive their salaries from the imperial treasury, Boston created its own committee of correspondence and urged other towns to do the same. Hutchinson grew alarmed when most towns of any size followed Boston's lead. That there was a plot to destroy their liberties seemed plausible to them.

The Boston Massacre trials and the *Gaspée* affair convinced London that it was pointless to prosecute individuals for politically motivated crimes. Whole communities would have to be punished. That choice brought the government to the edge of a precipice. The use of force against entire communities could lead to outright war. The spread of committees of correspondence throughout the colonies suggested that settlers who had been unable to unite against New France at Albany in 1754 now deemed unity against Britain essential to their liberties. By 1773 several New England newspapers were calling on the colonies to create a formal union.

In effect, the Townshend crisis never ended. With the tea duty standing as a symbol of Parliament's right to tax the colonies without their consent, genuine imperial harmony was becoming impossible. North's decision to retain the tea tax in 1770 did not guarantee that armed resistance would break out five years later, but it severely narrowed the ground on which any compromise could be built.

INTERNAL CLEAVAGES: THE CONTAGION OF LIBERTY

Any challenge to British authority carried high risks for prominent families in the colonies. They depended on the Crown for their public offices and government contracts. Since the Stamp Act crisis, these families had faced a dilemma. The Hutchinsons of Massachusetts kept on good terms with Britain while incurring the scorn and even hatred of many of their neighbors. John Hancock championed the grievances of the community but alienated British authorities. So did the Livingstons of New York and most of the great planters in the southern colonies. The Townshend crisis was a far more accurate predictor of future behavior than response to the Stamp Act had been. Nearly everyone had denounced the Stamp Act. By contrast, the merchants and lawyers who resisted nonimportation in 1768 were likely to become loyalists by 1775. Artisans, merchants, and lawyers who supported the boycotts became patriots.

But the patriot leaders also faced challenges from within their own ranks. Artisans demanded more power, and tenant farmers in the Hudson valley protested violently against their landlords. Discontent ran high in Boston, where the economy had been faltering since the 1740s while taxes remained high. Boston set the pace of resistance in every imperial crisis. In New York City, Philadelphia, and Charleston, artisans also began to play a much more assertive role in public affairs.

THE FEUDAL REVIVAL AND RURAL DISCONTENT

Tensions increased in the countryside as well as in the cities. Three processes intensified discontent in rural areas: a revival of old proprietary charters, massive foreign immigration, and the settlement of the backcountry.

Between about 1730 and 1750, the men who owned 17th century proprietary or manorial charters began to see the prospect of huge profits by enforcing these old legal claims. The great estates of the Hudson valley had attracted few settlers before the middle of the 18th century, and those who arrived first had received generous leases. But as leases became more restrictive and as New Englanders swarmed into New York, discontent increased. In 1766 several thousand angry farmers took to the fields and the roads to protest the terms of their leases. The colony had to call in redcoats to suppress them. But when New York landlords also tried to make good their claims to the upper Connecticut valley, the Yankee settlers utterly defied them, set up their own government and, after a long struggle, became the independent state of Vermont.

The proprietors of East New Jersey claimed much of the land that was being worked by descendants of the original settlers of Newark and Elizabethtown, who thought they owned their farms. The proprietors, in firm control of the law courts, planned to sell or lease the land, either to the current occupants or to newcomers. After they expelled several farmers and replaced them with tenants, a succession of land riots rocked much of northern New Jersey for 10 years after 1745. The proprietary intruders were driven out, and the riots stopped. But tensions remained high.

In Maryland, Frederick, seventh and last Lord Baltimore, received the princely income of £30,000 sterling per year until his death in 1771. The Penns enjoyed similar gains in Pennsylvania, though more slowly. Their landed income rose to about £15,000 or £20,000 in the 1760s and then soared to £67,000 in 1773. With more than half of their land still unsettled, they seemed about to turn their colony into the most lucrative piece of real estate in the Atlantic world. But their reluctance to contribute to the war effort in the 1750s had so angered Benjamin Franklin at the time that, with the assembly's support, he went to London to urge the Crown to make Pennsylvania a royal colony. Meanwhile Connecticut settlers claimed all of northern Pennsylvania on the basis of Connecticut's sea-to-sea charter and set off a small civil war in the 1770s.

In Virginia, Thomas, sixth baron Fairfax, acquired title to the entire northern neck of the colony (the land between the Potomac and the Rappahannock Rivers). By 1775, the Fairfax estate's 5 million acres contained 21 counties. He received £5,000 a year from his holdings, but he muted criticism by moving to the colony and setting himself up as a great planter.

In North Carolina, John Carteret, earl of Granville, consolidated his claim as the Granville District after 1745. Although still living in England, he received an income of about £5,000 per year. The Granville District embraced more than half of North Carolina's land and two-thirds of its population, deprived the colony of revenue from land sales and quitrents within the district, and forced North Carolina to resort to direct taxation. For several years after Granville's death in 1763, his land office remained closed. Disgruntled settlers often rioted when they could not get title to their lands.

Taken together, the New York manor lords, the New Jersey proprietors, and the Penn, Baltimore, Fairfax and Granville claims blanketed the colonies from New York to North Carolina. They were the biggest winners in America's "feudal revival," the use of old charters to pry income from the settlers.

THE REGULATOR MOVEMENTS IN THE CAROLINAS

Massive immigration from Europe and the settlement of the backcountry created severe social tensions. Most immigrants were Scottish or Scots-Irish Presbyterians, Lutherans, or German Reformed Protestants. They were dissenters from the prevailing faith in the colonies they entered. They angered Indians by squatting on their land and, quite often, by murdering those who were in their way. In the Carolina backcountry, the newcomers provoked the Cherokee War of 1760–1761, which in turn brutalized and demoralized the whole region.

Following the Cherokee War, great bands of outlaws, men who had been dislocated by the war, began roaming the countryside, plundering the more prosperous farmers and often raping their wives and daughters. As the violence peaked between 1765 and 1767, the more respectable settlers organized themselves as "regulators" (a later generation would call them "vigilantes") to impose order in the absence of any organized government. Although South Carolina claimed jurisdiction over the backcountry, the colony's law courts were located in Charleston, more than 100 miles to the east. Even though most of the white settlers now lived in the backcountry, they elected only 2 of the 48 members of South Carolina's assembly. In effect, they had no local government.

After obtaining commissions from Charleston as militia officers and justices of the peace, the regulators chased the outlaws out of the colony. They then imposed order on what they called the "little people," poor settlers who may have aided the outlaws. The discipline imposed by the regulators, typically whippings and forced labor, outraged their victims, who organized as "moderators" and got their own commissions from the governor. With both sides claiming legality, about 600 armed regulators confronted an equal force of moderators at the Saluda River in 1769. Civil war was avoided only by the timely arrival of an emissary from the governor bearing a striking message: South Carolina would finally bring government to the backcountry by providing a circuit court system for the entire colony. Violence ebbed, but tensions remained.

In North Carolina, the backcountry's problem was corruption, not the absence of government. The settlers, mostly immigrants pushing south from Pennsylvania, found the county courts under the control of men with strong ties to powerful families in the eastern counties. Because county officials were appointed by the governor, getting ahead required gaining access to his circle. These justices, lawyers, and merchants seemed to regard county government as an engine for fleecing farmers through taxes, fees, court costs, and suits for debt. North Carolina's regulator movement arose to reform these abuses.

In 1768 the regulators refused to pay taxes in Orange County. Governor William Tryon mustered 1,300 eastern militiamen. This force overawed the regulators for a time. Then, in a bid for a voice in the 1769 assembly, the regulators managed to capture six seats. These new assemblymen called for the secret ballot, fixed salaries (instead of fees) for justices and other officials, and a land tax rather than poll taxes. But they were outvoted by the eastern majority. After losing ground in the 1770 election, they stormed into Hillsborough, closed the Orange County Court, and whipped Edmund Fanning, whose lust for fees had made him the most

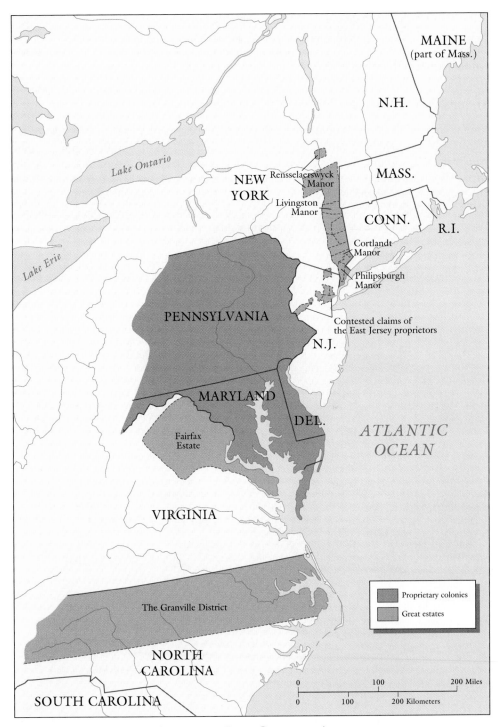

FEUDAL REVIVAL: GREAT ESTATES OF LATE COLONIAL AMERICA

detested official in the backcountry. Tryon responded by marching 1,000 militiamen westward, who defeated a force of more than 2,000 poorly armed regulators in early 1771 at the battle of Alamance Creek. Seven regulators were hanged, and many fled the colony. North Carolina entered the struggle for independence as a bitterly divided society.

SLAVES AND WOMEN

Around the middle of the 18th century, an antislavery movement arose on both sides of the Atlantic and attracted both patriots and loyalists. In the 1740s and 1750s, Benjamin Lay, John Woolman, and Anthony Benezet urged fellow Quakers to free their slaves. In the 1750s the Quaker Yearly Meeting placed the slave trade off limits and finally, in 1774, forbade slaveholding altogether. Any Friend who did not comply by 1779 was disowned. Britain's Methodist leader John Wesley also attacked slavery, as did several colonial disciples of Jonathan Edwards. Two and three decades after the Great Awakening, many evangelicals began to agree that slavery was a sin.

By the 1760s, supporters of slavery found that they had to defend the institution. Hardly anyone had bothered to do so earlier, but as equal rights became a popular topic, some began

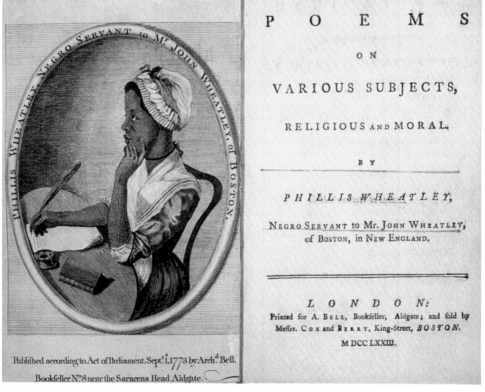

PHILLIS WHEATLEY   Engraving of Phillis Wheatley opposite the title page of her collected poems, published in 1773.

to suggest that *all* people could claim these rights, and slavery came under attack. Arthur Lee, a Virginian, discovered that he could not justify slavery, "always the deadly enemy to virtue and science." Patrick Henry agreed. Slavery, he wrote, "is as repugnant to humanity as it is inconsistent with the Bible and destructive of liberty." In England, Granville Sharp, an early abolitionist, brought the Somerset case before the Court of King's Bench in 1771 and compelled a reluctant Chief Justice William Murray, baron Mansfield, to declare that slavery was incompatible with the "free air" of England. That decision gave England's 10,000 or 15,000 blacks a chance to claim their freedom. With the courts challenging slavery in Britain, with Quakers taking steps against it in the Mid-Atlantic colonies, and with even great planters expressing doubts about it, New Englanders began to move as well.

Two women, Sarah Osborn and Phillis Wheatley, played leading roles in the movement. Osborn, an English immigrant to Newport, Rhode Island, and a widow, opened a school in 1744 to support her family. A friend of the revivalist George Whitefield, she also taught women and blacks and began holding evening religious meetings, which turned into a big local revival. At one point in the 1760s, about one-sixth of Newport's Africans were attending her school. Osborn's students supported abolition of the slave trade and, later, slavery itself.

Meanwhile, an 8-year-old girl who would become known as Phillis Wheatley arrived in Boston from Africa in 1761; she was purchased by wealthy John Wheatley as a servant for his wife Susannah, who treated her more like a daughter than a slave, taught her to read and write, and emancipated her when she came of age. In 1767 Phillis published her first poem in Boston, and in 1773 a volume of her poetry was printed in London. Her poems deplored slavery but rejoiced in the Christianization of Africans.

Soon many of Boston's blacks sensed an opportunity for emancipation. On several occasions in 1773 and 1774, they petitioned the legislature or the governor for freedom, pointing out that, although they had never forfeited their natural rights, they were being "held in slavery in the bowels of a free and Christian Country." When the legislature passed a bill on their behalf, Governor Hutchinson vetoed it. Boston slaves made it clear to General Gage, Hutchinson's successor, that they would serve him as a loyal militia in exchange for their freedom. In short, they offered allegiance to whichever side supported their emancipation. Many patriots began to rally to their cause.

The patriots could look to another group of allies, as well. Many women became an indispensable part of the broader resistance movement. They could not vote or hold office, but without their willing support nonimportation would have been not just a failure, but a fiasco. In thousands of households, women joined the intense discussions about liberty and agreed to make homespun clothing to take the place of imported British textiles.

Freedom's ferment made a heady wine. After 1773, any direct challenge to British power would trigger enormous social changes within the colonies.

THE LAST IMPERIAL CRISIS

The surface calm between 1770 and 1773 ended when Lord North moved to save the East India Company from bankruptcy. The company was being undersold in southeastern England and the colonies by smuggled Dutch tea. Without solving the company's problems, North created a crisis too big for Britain to handle.

THE TEA CRISIS

North decided to rescue the East India Company by empowering it to undersell its rivals, the smugglers of Dutch tea. His Tea Act of 1773 repealed import duties on tea in England but retained the Townshend duty in the colonies. In both places, North estimated, legal tea would be cheaper than anyone else's. The company would be saved, and the settlers, by willingly buying legal tea, would accept Parliament's right to tax them.

Another aspect of the Tea Act antagonized most merchants in the colonies. The company had been selling tea to all comers at public auctions in London, but the Tea Act gave it a monopoly on the shipping and distribution of tea in the colonies. Only company ships could carry it, and a few consignees in each port would have the exclusive right to sell it. The combined dangers of taxation and monopoly again forged the coalition of artisans and merchants that had helped to defeat the Stamp Act in 1765 and resisted the Townshend Act in 1769. Patriots saw the Tea Act as a Trojan horse that would destroy liberty by seducing the settlers into accepting Parliamentary sovereignty. Unintentionally, North also gave a tremendous advantage to those determined to resist the Tea Act. He had devised an oceanic, or "external," measure that the colonists could actually nullify despite British control of the seas. No one would have to police the entire waterfront looking for tea importers. The patriots had only to wait for the specially chartered tea ships and then prevent them from landing their tea.

Direct threats usually did the job. As the first tea ship approached Philadelphia, the Sons of Liberty greeted the skipper with a rude welcome: "What think you Captain, of a halter around your neck—ten gallons of liquid tar decanted on your pate—with the feathers of a dozen wild geese laid over that to enliven your appearance?" The ship quickly departed.

Similar scenes took place in every port except Boston. There, Governor Hutchinson decided to face down the radicals. He refused to grant clearance papers to three tea ships which, under the law, had to pay the Townshend duty within 21 days of arrival or face seizure. Hutchinson meant to force them to land the tea and pay the duty. This timetable led to urgent mass meetings for several weeks and generated a major crisis. Finally convinced that there was no other way to block the landing of the tea, Boston radicals, disguised as Indians, threw 342 chests of tea, worth about £11,000 sterling (more than $700,000 in 1999 dollars), into Boston harbor on the night of December 16, 1773.

BRITAIN'S RESPONSE: THE COERCIVE ACTS

This willful destruction of private property shocked both Britain and America. Convinced that severe punishment was essential to British credibility, Parliament passed four Coercive Acts during the spring of 1774. The Boston Port Act closed the port of Boston until Bostonians paid for the tea. A new Quartering Act allowed the army to quarter soldiers on civilian property if necessary. The Administration of Justice Act permitted a British soldier or official who was charged with a crime while carrying out his duties to be tried either in another colony or in England. Most controversial of all was the Massachusetts Government Act. It overturned the Massachusetts Charter of 1691, made the council appointive, and restricted town meetings. In effect, it made Massachusetts like other royal colonies. Before it passed, the king named General Gage, already the commander of the British army in North America, as the new governor of Massachusetts.

Parliament also passed a fifth law, unrelated to the Coercive Acts but significant nonetheless. The Quebec Act established French civil law and the Roman Catholic Church in the Province of Quebec, provided for trial by jury in criminal but not in civil cases, gave legislative power to an appointive governor and council, and extended the administrative boundaries of Quebec to the area between the Great Lakes and the Ohio River. Settlers from New England to Georgia were appalled. Instead of conciliation and toleration, they saw a deliberate revival of the power of New France and the Catholic Church on their northern border, this time bolstered by Britain's naval and military might. The Quebec Act added credibility to the fear that evil ministers in London were conspiring to destroy British and colonial liberties. The settlers lumped the Quebec Act together with the Coercive Acts and coined their own name for all of them: the Intolerable Acts.

THE RADICAL EXPLOSION

The interval between the passage of the Boston Port Act in March 1774 and the Massachusetts Government Act in May permits us to compare the response that each provoked. The Port Act was quite enforceable and could not be nullified by the colonists. It led to another round of nonimportation and to the summoning of the First Continental Congress. But the Government Act *was* nullified by the colonists. It led to war. The soldiers marching to Concord on April 19, 1775, were trying to enforce it against settlers who absolutely refused to obey it.

Gage took over the governorship of Massachusetts in May 1774, before the Massachusetts Government Act was passed. In June he closed the ports of Boston and Charlestown, just north of Boston. At first, Boston split over the Port Act. Many merchants wanted to abolish the Boston Committee of Correspondence and pay for the tea to avoid an economic catastrophe. But they were badly outvoted in a huge town meeting. Boston then called for a colonial union and for immediate nonimportation and nonconsumption of British goods. By then some radicals were losing patience with nonimportation as a tactic. Parliament had already shut Boston down.

Discouraging news arrived from elsewhere. A mass meeting in New York City rejected immediate nonimportation in favor of an intercolonial congress. Philadelphia followed New York's lead. In both cities, cautious merchants hoped that a congress might postpone or prevent radical measures of resistance.

Despite this momentary success, Gage quickly learned that none of his major objectives was achievable. Contributions began pouring in from all the colonies to help Boston survive. When royal governors outside Massachusetts dismissed their assemblies to prevent them from joining the resistance movement, the colonists elected "provincial congresses," or conventions, to organize resistance. As the congresses took hold, royal government began to collapse almost everywhere.

Numerous calls for a continental congress made the movement irresistible. By June it was obvious that any congress would adopt nonimportation.

Despite all this activity, Gage remained optimistic through most of the summer. Then news of the Massachusetts Government Act arrived on August 6. Gage's authority disintegrated when he tried to enforce the act. The "mandamus councillors," whom Gage appointed to the new upper house under the act, either resigned their seats or fled to Boston to seek the protection of the army. The Superior Court could not hold its sessions because jurors refused to take an oath under the new act. At the county level (the real center of royal power in the colony), popular conventions closed the courts and took charge in August and September.

AMERICAN ARTISTS AND THE REVOLUTION IN PAINTING

Protestant England sustained few painters before the 18th century. Then William Hogarth and Sir Joshua Reynolds established international reputations for their highly original creations. They were soon joined by several North Americans. Benjamin West, a self-taught Pennsylvanian, established his own studio in Philadelphia in the 1750s, then went to Italy from 1760 to 1763 to study the Renaissance masters before settling in London, where Reynolds gave him strong encouragement. Until West's arrival, heroic contemporaries were always depicted in classical grab. West's *Death of General Wolfe* (1771) depicts James Wolfe after he has fallen on the battlefield of the Plains of Abraham outside Quebec in 1759. All the participants are wearing their appropriate uniforms. George III spent hours study-

Before this explosion of radical activity, Gage had called for a new General Court to meet in Salem in October. Many towns sent representatives. But others followed the lead of the Worcester County Convention, which in August urged all towns to elect delegates to a provincial congress in Concord. Although Gage revoked his call for a General Court, about 90 representatives met at Salem anyway. When Gage refused to recognize them, they adjourned to Concord in early October and joined the 200 delegates who had already gathered there as the

ing the painting and was so impressed that he created a special position for West as historical painter to the royal court. West's breakthrough soon established a new tradition.

West was a moderate loyalist, although he did, on occasion, quietly donate money to American prisoners of war who had escaped and were trying to get back home. But he also attracted patriots as students. John Trumbull of Connecticut, who had fought on the American side in the Revolution, began studying with West before the war was over and painted *Death of General Warren at Bunker's Hill* (1786). Trumbull also painted scenes of other battles and of the signing of the Declaration of Independence, as well as numerous portraits, including George Washington's. In an effort that transcended the bitterness of the war, these Americans transformed painting in their own day. That feat was the greatest cultural accomplishment that any American artists had yet made in any field—literature, music, architecture, sculpture, or painting.

Massachusetts Provincial Congress. That body became the de facto government of the colony and implemented the radical demands of the Suffolk County Convention, which included the creation of a special force of armed "minutemen" and the payment of taxes to the congress in Concord, not to Gage in Boston. The Provincial Congress also collected military stores at Concord. North assumed that Gage's army would uphold the new Massachusetts government. Instead, Gage's government survived only where the army could protect it.

By October, Gage's power was limited to the Boston area, which the army held. Unable to put his 3,000 soldiers to any positive use, he wrote North on October 30 that "a small Force rather encourages Resistance than terrifys." He then stunned North by asking for 20,000 redcoats, as many as Britain had needed to conquer New France.

THE FIRST CONTINENTAL CONGRESS

From 1769 into 1774, colonial patriots had looked to John Wilkes in London for leadership. At the First Continental Congress, they began relying on themselves. Twelve colonies (all but Georgia) sent delegates. They met at Philadelphia's Carpenters' Hall in September 1774. They scarcely even debated nonimportation. The southern colonies insisted, and the New Englanders agreed, that nonimportation finally be extended to molasses. The delegates were almost unanimous in adopting nonexportation if Britain had not redressed colonial grievances by September 1775. Nonexportation was a much more radical tactic than nonimportation because it contained the implicit threat of repudiating debts to British merchants, which were normally paid off with colonial exports. Joseph Galloway, a Pennsylvania loyalist, submitted a plan of imperial union that would have required all laws affecting the colonies to be passed by both Parliament and an intercolonial congress, but his proposal was tabled by a 6-to-5 vote. The Congress spent three weeks trying to define colonial rights. Everyone agreed that the Coercive Acts, the Quebec Act, and all surviving revenue acts had to be repealed and that infringements on trial by jury had to be rejected. The delegates generally agreed on what would break the impasse, but they had trouble finding the precise language for their demands. They finally affirmed the new principle of no *legislation* without consent—but added a saving clause that affirmed colonial assent to the empire's navigation and trade acts, passed as far back as 1650.

The Congress petitioned the king rather than Parliament, because patriots no longer recognized Parliament as a legitimate legislature for the colonies. Congress explained its position in separate addresses to the people of the 13 colonies, the people of Quebec, and the people of Great Britain. It agreed to meet again in May 1775 if the British response was not satisfactory. And it created the Association—citizen committees in every community—to enforce its trade sanctions against Britain. In approving the Association, Congress was beginning to act as a central government for the United Colonies.

TOWARD WAR

The news from Boston and Philadelphia shook the North ministry. Although Franklin kept assuring the British that Congress meant exactly what it said, both North and the opposition assumed that conciliation could be achieved on lesser terms. Lord Chatham (William Pitt) introduced a bill to prohibit Parliament from taxing the colonies, to recognize the Congress, and even to ask Congress to provide revenue for North American defense and to help pay down the national debt. It was voted down.

The initiative lay, of course, with Lord North, who still hoped for a peaceful solution. But in January 1775 he took a step that made war inevitable. He ordered Gage to send troops to Concord, destroy the arms stored there, and arrest John Hancock and Samuel Adams. Only after sending this dispatch did he introduce his own Conciliatory Proposition, in which Parliament pledged that it would not tax any colony that met its share of the

A VIEW OF THE SOUTH PART OF LEXINGTON, APRIL 19, 1775   This painting by Ralph Earl, done in 1775, shows the retreat of the British toward Boston, under heavy fire, on the first day of the Revolutionary War.

cost of imperial defense and paid proper salaries to its royal officials. But Britain would use force against delinquent colonies. To reassure hard-liners that he was not turning soft, he introduced the New England Restraining Act on the same day. It barred New Englanders from the Atlantic fisheries and banned all commerce between New England and any place except Britain and the British West Indies, precisely the trade routes that Congress had resolved to block through nonimportation. Both sides were now committed to economic sanctions.

North's orders to Gage arrived before his Conciliatory Proposition reached America, and Gage obeyed. He hoped to surprise Concord with a predawn march, but Boston radicals knew about the expedition almost as soon as the orders were issued. They had already made careful preparations to alert the whole countryside. Their informant, in all likelihood, was Gage's wife, Margaret Kemble Gage, a New Jerseyan by birth. At 2 A.M. on the night of April 18–19, about 700 grenadiers and light infantry began their march toward Concord. Paul Revere, a Boston silversmith, went dashing west with the news that "The redcoats are coming!" When he was captured past Lexington by a British patrol, Dr. Samuel Prescott, returning from a lady friend's house, managed to get the message through to Concord. As the British approached Lexington Green at dawn, they found 60 to 70 militiamen drawn up to face them. The outnumbered militia began to withdraw when somebody fired the first shot. Without orders, the British line opened fire, killing eight and wounding nine. Behind and ahead of them, like angry bees, the whole countryside surged toward them. The British continued their march to Concord.

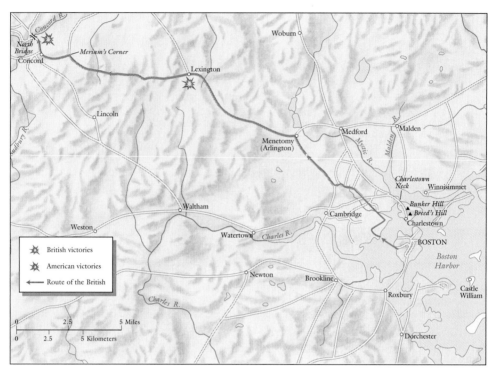

LEXINGTON, CONCORD, AND BOSTON, 1775–1776

THE IMPROVISED WAR

In April 1775 neither side had a plan for winning a major war. Gage's soldiers were trying to enforce acts of Parliament. The militia were fighting for a political regime that Parliament was trying to change. They drove the British from Concord Bridge and pursued them all the way to Boston. Had a relief force not met the battered British survivors east of Lexington, all of them might have been lost.

Without an adequate command or supply structure, the colonists besieged Boston. After two months, Gage finally declared that all settlers bearing arms, and those who aided them, were rebels and traitors. He offered to pardon anyone who returned to his allegiance, except John Hancock and Samuel Adams. Instead of complying, the besiegers escalated the struggle two days later. They fortified the high ground on Breed's Hill (next to Bunker Hill) near Charlestown and overlooking Boston. The British sent 2,400 men, one-fifth of the garrison, to take the hills on June 17. Secure behind their defenses, the settlers shot more than 1,000 of the attackers before they ran out of ammunition and withdrew. The defenders suffered about 370 casualties, nearly all during the retreat.

Well into 1776 both sides fought an improvised war. In May 1775 Vermont and Massachusetts militia took Ticonderoga on Lake Champlain and seized the artillery and gunpowder that would be used months later in the siege of Boston. Crown Point also fell. With nearly all of their forces in Boston, the British were too weak to defend other positions. The collapse of royal government meant that the rebels now controlled the militia and most of the royal powderhouses.

During the Revolutionary War, the militia became the key to political allegiance. Compulsory service with the militia politicized many waverers, who decided that they really were patriots when a redcoat shot at them or when they drove a loyalist into exile. The militia kept the countryside committed to the Revolution wherever the British army was too weak to overwhelm them.

The Second Continental Congress

When the Second Continental Congress met in May 1775, it inherited the war. For months it pursued the conflicting strategies of resistance and conciliation. It voted to turn the undisciplined men besieging Boston into a "Continental Army."

On June 15, at the urging of John Adams of Massachusetts, Congress made George Washington of Virginia commanding general. When Washington took charge of the Continental Army, he was appalled at the poor discipline among the soldiers and their casual familiarity with their officers. He insisted that officers behave with a dignity that would instill obedience, and as the months passed, most of them won his respect. But as the year ended, nearly all the men went home, and Washington had to train a new army for 1776. Enthusiasm for the cause remained strong, however, and fresh volunteers soon filled his camp.

In June 1775, Congress, fearing that the British might recruit French Canadians to attack New York or New England, authorized an invasion of Canada. Two forces of 1,000 men each moved northward. One, under General Richard Montgomery, took Montreal in November. The other, commanded by Colonel Benedict Arnold, advanced on Quebec through the Maine wilderness and laid siege to the city, where Montgomery joined Arnold in December. With enlistments due to expire at year's end, they decided to assault the city. Their attack on December 31 was a disaster. Nearly half of the 900 men still with them were killed, wounded, or captured. Montgomery was killed and Arnold wounded. Both were hailed as American heroes.

The colonial objective in this fighting was still to restore government by consent under the Crown. After rejecting Lord North's Conciliatory Proposition out of hand, Congress approved an "Olive Branch Petition" to George III on July 5 in the hope of ending the bloodshed. Moderates, led by John Dickinson, strongly favored the measure. The petition affirmed the colonists' loyalty to the Crown, did not even mention "rights," and implored the king to take the initiative in devising "a happy and permanent reconciliation." Another document written mostly by Thomas Jefferson, "The Declaration of the Causes and Necessities of Taking Up Arms," set forth the grievances of the colonies and justified their armed resistance. Like the Olive Branch Petition, the declaration assured the British people "that we mean not to dissolve that Union which has so long and so happily subsisted between us." The king's refusal even to receive this moderate petition strengthened colonial radicals. It reached London along with news of Bunker Hill. George III replied with a formal proclamation of rebellion on August 23.

Congress began to function more and more like a government. But, with few exceptions, it assumed royal rather than parliamentary powers, which were taken over by the individual colonies. Congress did not tax or regulate trade, beyond encouraging nonimportation. It did not pass laws. It took command of the Continental Army, printed paper money, opened diplomatic relations with Indian nations, took over the royal post office, and decided which government was legitimate in individual colonies—all functions that had been performed by the Crown. In short, Congress thought of itself as a temporary plural executive for the continent, not as a legislature.

WAR AND LEGITIMACY, 1775–1776

Throughout 1775 the British reacted with fitful displays of violence and grim threats of turning slaves and Indians against the settlers. When the weak British forces could neither restore order nor make good their threats, they conciliated no one, enraged thousands, and undermined British claims to legitimacy. The navy burned Falmouth (now Portland), Maine, in October. On November 7, John Murray, earl of Dunmore and governor of Virginia, offered freedom to any slaves of rebel planters who would join his 200 redcoats. About 800 slaves mustered under his banner only to fall victim to smallpox after the Virginia militia defeated them in a single action. Dunmore bombarded Norfolk in retaliation on January 1, setting several buildings ablaze. The patriot militia, who considered Norfolk a loyalist bastion, burned the rest of the city and then blamed Dunmore for its destruction.

The British efforts suffered other disasters in Boston and the Carolinas. The greatest colonial victory came at Boston. On March 17, 1776, after Washington fortified Dorchester Heights south of the city and brought heavy artillery to bear on it, the British pulled out and sailed for Nova Scotia. A loyalist uprising by Highland Scots in North Carolina was crushed at Moore's Creek Bridge on February 27, and a British naval expedition sent to take Charleston was repulsed with heavy losses in June. Cherokee attacks against Virginia in 1776 were defeated because they occurred after Dunmore had left and did not fit into any larger general strategy. Before spring turned to summer, patriot forces had won control of the territory of all 13 colonies.

INDEPENDENCE

George III's dismissal of the Olive Branch Petition left moderates no option but to yield or fight. In late 1775, Congress created a committee to correspond with foreign powers. By early 1776 the delegates from New England, Virginia, and Georgia already favored independence, but they knew that unless they won over all 13 colonies, the British would have the leverage to divide them. The British attack on Charleston in June nudged the Carolinas toward independence.

Resistance to independence came mostly from the mid-Atlantic colonies, from New York through Maryland. None of the five legal assemblies in the mid-Atlantic region ever repudiated the Crown. All of them had to be overthrown along with royal (or proprietary) government itself.

In the struggle for middle colony loyalties, Thomas Paine's pamphlet, *Common Sense,* became a huge success. First published in Philadelphia in January 1776, it sold more than 100,000 copies within a few months. Paine wasted no reverence on Britain's mixed and balanced constitution. To him, George III was "the Pharaoh of England" and "the Royal Brute of Great Britain." Paine attacked monarchy and aristocracy as degenerate institutions and urged Americans to unite under a simple republican government of their own. "Reconciliation and ruin are nearly related," he insisted. "There is something very absurd, in supposing a Continent to be perpetually governed by an island."

CHRONOLOGY

1745–1755	Land riots rock New Jersey
1760–1761	Cherokee War occurs in South Carolina
1760	George III becomes king of Great Britain
1761	Pitt resigns as war minister
1763	Grenville ministry takes power • Wilkes publishes *North Briton* No. 45 • Pontiac's War begins • King issues Proclamation of 1763
1764	Parliament passes Currency and Sugar Acts
1765	Parliament passes Quartering Act • Stamp Act passed and nullified • Rockingham ministry replaces Grenville's
1766	Parliament repeals Stamp Act, passes Declaratory Act and Revenue Act of 1766 • Chatham (Pitt) ministry takes power
1767	Parliament passes New York Restraining Act and Townshend Revenue Act
1768	Massachusetts assembly dispatches Circular Letter • Wilkes elected to Parliament • Massacre of St. George's Fields occurs in England • Massachusetts refuses to rescind Circular Letter • *Liberty* riot occurs in Boston • Governors dissolve assemblies that support Circular Letter • Redcoats sent to Boston
1769	Nonimportation becomes effective • Regulators achieve major goals in South Carolina
1770	North becomes prime minister • Boston Massacre • Townshend Revenue Act partially repealed • Nonimportation collapses
1771	North Carolina regulators defeated at Alamance Creek
1772	*Gaspée* affair in Rhode Island increases tensions
1772–1773	Twelve colonies create committees of correspondence
1773	Tea Act passed • Boston Tea Party protests tea duty • Wheatley's poetry published in London
1774	American Quakers prohibit slaveholding • Parliament passes Coercive Acts • First Continental Congress convenes in Philadelphia
1775	Revolutionary War begins at Lexington and Concord • Second Continental Congress creates Continental Army • George III issues Proclamation of Rebellion
1775–1776	Americans invade Canada
1776	Paine publishes *Common Sense* • British evacuate Boston • Continental Congress approves Declaration of Independence

The British continued to alienate the colonists. The king named Lord George Germain, a hard-liner, as secretary of state for the American colonies. The British bought 17,000 soldiers from Hesse and other north German states (they were all called "Hessians" by the colonists). Disturbing (though false) rumors suggested that Britain and France were about to sign a "partition treaty" dividing the eastern half of North America between them. Many congressmen concluded that only independence could counter these dangers by engaging Britain's European enemies on America's side. As long as conciliation was the goal, France would not participate, because American success would mean restoring the British Empire to its former glory. But Louis XVI (1774–1793) might well help the colonies win their independence if that meant crippling Britain permanently.

From April to June, about 90 communities issued calls for independence. Most of them did not look further back than 1775 to justify their demand. The king had placed the colonists outside his protection, was waging war against them, and had hired foreigners to kill them. Self-defense demanded a permanent separation.

On May 15, 1776, Congress voted to suppress "every kind of authority" under the British Crown, thus giving radicals an opportunity to seize power in Pennsylvania and New Jersey. Moderates remained in control in New York, Delaware, and Maryland, but they reluctantly accepted independence as inevitable. In early June, Congress postponed a vote on independence but named a committee of five, including Jefferson, John Adams, and Franklin, to prepare a declaration that would vindicate America's decision to the whole world. Jefferson's draft justified independence on the lofty ground of "self-evident truths," including a natural right to "life, Liberty, and the pursuit of happiness." The longest section indicted George III as a tyrant.

With the necessary votes in place, Congress on July 2 passed Richard Henry Lee's resolution "that these United colonies are, and of right, ought to be, Free and Independent States; . . . and that all political connexion between them, and the state of Great Britain, is, and ought to be, totally dissolved." On the same day, the first ships of the largest armada yet sent across the Atlantic by any European state began landing British soldiers on Staten Island. Two days later, 12 colonies, with New York abstaining for the time being, unanimously approved Jefferson's Declaration of Independence.

CONCLUSION

Between 1763 and 1776 Britain and the colonies became trapped in a series of self-fulfilling prophecies. The British feared that without major reforms to guarantee Parliament's control of the empire, the colonies would drift toward independence. Colonial resistance to the new policies convinced the British that a movement for independence was indeed under way. The colonists denied that they desired independence, but they began to fear that the British government was determined to deprive them of their rights as Englishmen. Britain's policy drove them toward a closer union with one another and finally provoked armed resistance. With the onset of war, both sides felt vindicated.

Both sides were wrong. The British had no systematic plan to destroy liberty in North America, and until the winter of 1775–1776 hardly any colonists favored independence. But the three imperial crises undermined mutual confidence and brought about an independent American nation. Unable to govern North America, Britain now faced the grim task of conquering it instead.

THE REVOLUTIONARY REPUBLIC

HEARTS AND MINDS: THE NORTHERN WAR, 1776–1777

THE CAMPAIGNS OF 1777 AND FOREIGN INTERVENTION

THE RECONSTITUTION OF AUTHORITY

THE CRISIS OF THE REVOLUTION, 1779–1783

THE BRITISH OFFENSIVE IN THE SOUTH ∼ A REVOLUTIONARY SOCIETY

A MORE PERFECT UNION

The Revolutionary War was a civil war. Neighbors were more likely to shoot at neighbors during the Revolution than they were between 1861 and 1865, when the geographical line separating the two sides would be much sharper. Twice, in 1776 and again in 1780, the British had a chance to win a decisive military victory, but in both campaigns the Americans somehow rallied. The Americans won only by bringing in France as an ally. France brought in Spain.

During the war, more and more Americans began to think in crude racial categories. As settlers and Indians, whites and blacks redefined their differences, they often resorted to racial stereotypes. Most Indians and slaves hoped that Britain would win the war.

Even as the war raged and the economy disintegrated, Americans drafted state constitutions and eloquent bills of rights. They knew they were attempting something daring—the creation of a stable, enduring republic. In the Atlantic world, political stability seemed to require a monarchy. The English monarchy, for example, was about 1,000 years old, older than any republic in history. Educated people knew a great deal about the city-states of classical Greece and about republican Rome—how they had called forth the noblest sentiments of patriotism for a time and had then decayed into despotisms. Still, once Americans broke with Britain, they warmly embraced republicanism. They were able to build viable republican governments because they grasped the voluntaristic dynamics of their society. They knew they had to restructure their governments through persuasive means. The use of force against armed fellow patriots would be self-defeating.

The war also demonstrated how weak Congress was, even after ratification of the Articles of Confederation in 1781. It could not pay its debts. It could not expel the British from their western military posts or defeat the Indians of the Ohio country, Congress nevertheless announced plans to create new western states. During the summer of 1787, the Philadelphia Convention drafted a new Constitution for the United States. After ratification by 11 states, it went into effect in April 1789.

HEARTS AND MINDS: THE NORTHERN WAR, 1776–1777

Because the men who ruled Britain believed that the loss of the colonies would be a fatal blow to British power, the price of patriotism escalated once independence became the goal. Britain raised more soldiers and larger fleets than ever before and more than doubled its national debt. Americans, too confident after their early successes, staggered under the onslaught.

THE BRITISH OFFENSIVE

The first setback came in Canada. Americans had to retreat from Quebec when a fresh British force sailed up the St. Lawrence in May 1776. By July, Sir Guy Carleton drove them back into northern New York, to Ticonderoga on Lake Champlain. Both sides built ships to control that strategic waterway. Largely through Benedict Arnold's efforts, the Americans held, and Carleton returned to Canada for the winter.

Farther south, Richard viscount Howe, admiral of the British fleet, and his brother General William Howe prepared an awesome striking force on Staten Island. The Howes also acted as peace commissioners, with power to restore whole colonies to the king's peace. They hoped they would not have to use their huge army, but when they wrote George Washington to open negotiations, he refused to accept the letter because it did not address him as "General." To do so would have recognized the legitimacy of his appointment. Unable to negotiate, the Howes had to fight.

Since spring, Washington had moved his army from Boston to New York City. Early successes had kept morale high among American forces. Although some volunteers served in the Continental Army and others with state militia units, the difference between the two forces was not yet large. Neither of them received formal military training, and the men in both served only for short terms.

Washington was reluctant to abandon any large city. He therefore divided his inferior force and sent half of it from Manhattan to Long Island. Most of the men dug in on Brooklyn Heights and waited for a frontal attack. The British invaded Long Island and on August 27, 1776, sent a force around the American left flank through unguarded Jamaica Pass. While Hessians feinted a frontal assault, the flanking force crushed the American left and rear and sent the survivors reeling.

The Howes did nothing to prevent the evacuation of the rest of the American army to Manhattan, even though the navy could have cut them off. Instead, the British opened informal talks with several members of Congress on Staten Island on September 11. But when the Americans insisted that the British recognize their independence, no progress was possible. Washington evacuated lower Manhattan and the British took New York City, much of which was destroyed by an accidental fire on September 21. The Howes then appealed directly to the people to lay down their arms and return to British allegiance within 60 days in exchange for a full pardon. In southern New York state, thousands complied.

In October, the Howes drove Washington out of Manhattan and Westchester and then turned on two garrisons he had left behind. On November 16, at a cost of 460 casualties, the British forced 3,000 men to surrender at Fort Washington on the Manhattan side of the Hudson River. General Nathanael Greene, a lame Rhode Island Quaker who had given up pacifism

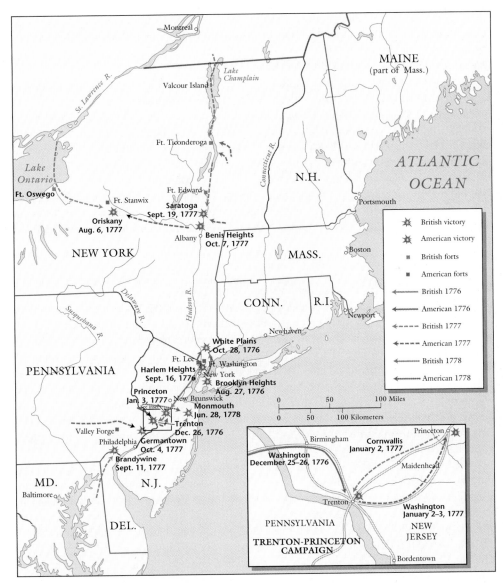

REVOLUTIONARY WAR IN THE NORTHERN STATES

for soldiering, saved his men on the New Jersey side by abandoning Fort Lee. But he lost all his supplies.

British victories and the American reliance on short-term volunteers were destroying Washington's army. British success seemed to prove that no American force could stand before a properly organized British army. But to capture Washington's entire army would have been a political embarrassment, leading to massive treason trials, executions, and great bitterness.

Instead, Britain's impressive victories demoralized Americans and encouraged them to go home. In September, there were 27,000 Americans fit for duty in the northern theater (including the Canadian border); by December, only 6,000 remained. And most of those intended to leave when their enlistments expired on December 31.

The Howes' strategy nearly worked. In December British forces swept across New Jersey as far south as Burlington. They captured Charles Lee, next in command after Washington, and Richard Stockton, a signer of the Declaration of Independence. Several thousand New Jersey residents, including Stockton, took the king's oath. To seal off Long Island Sound from both ends, the Howes also captured Newport, Rhode Island. Many observers thought the war was all but over as sad remnants of the Continental Army crossed the Delaware River into Pennsylvania, confiscating all boats along the way so that the British could not follow them. One general believed that the time had come to "bargain away the Bubble of Independency for British Liberty well secured." Charles Carroll, another signer of the Declaration, agreed. Even Jefferson began to think about the terms on which a restoration of the monarchy might be acceptable.

THE TRENTON-PRINCETON CAMPAIGN

Washington knew he had to do something dramatic to restore morale and encourage his soldiers to reenlist. On the night of December 25, 1776, he crossed the ice-choked Delaware and marched south, surprising the Trenton garrison at dawn. At almost no cost to the attackers, 1,000 Hessians surrendered. The British sent their most energetic general, Charles, earl Cornwallis, south with 8,000 men. They caught Washington at Trenton near sunset on January 2 but decided to wait until dawn before attacking. British patrols watched the Delaware to prevent another escape across the river, but Washington left his campfires burning, muffled the wheels of his wagons and guns, and stole around the British left flank, heading north. At dawn, he met a British regiment that was just beginning its march from Princeton to Trenton. The Battle of Princeton amounted to a series of sharp clashes in which the Americans, with a 5-to-1 edge, mauled yet another outpost.

Washington's two quick victories had an enormous impact on the war. The Howes, who until January had shown a firm grasp of revolutionary warfare, blundered in not hounding Washington's remnant of an army to its destruction after Princeton. Instead, they called in their garrisons and concentrated the army along the Raritan River from New Brunswick to the sea. As the British departed, the militia returned, asking who had sworn oaths to the king. Those who had taken the oath now groveled, as the price of acceptance, or fled to British lines. The Howes had encouraged loyalists to come forward, and had then abandoned them to the king's enemies. The Hessians had aroused fierce hatred by looting and raping their way across New Jersey. Together, the British and the Hessians had lost the hearts and minds of the settlers. In 1777, very few would be willing to declare for the Crown. The Revolution survived.

THE CAMPAIGNS OF 1777 AND FOREIGN INTERVENTION

In 1777 the Howes again had a plan for winning the war, but it required 20,000 reinforcements that did not exist. Instead, Lord George Germain, Britain's war minister, ordered the Howes to take Philadelphia. He also sent General John Burgoyne to Canada with orders to march his army south and link up with the garrison of New York City, commanded by Sir Henry Clinton.

A small force under Barry St. Leger was to march down the Mohawk valley and threaten Albany from the west. When few reinforcements reached the Howes, they decided to invade by sea, a decision that allowed Washington to shift men north to oppose Burgoyne.

The British campaign made little sense. If the point of Burgoyne's march was to get his army to New York City, he should have gone by sea. If the point was to force a battle with New Englanders, his army should have been larger. And if Howe's army—Britain's biggest—would not challenge Washington's, who would?

The Loss of Philadelphia

After Trenton and Princeton, Washington demanded stricter discipline and longer terms of enlistment. Congress responded by raising the number of lashes a soldier could receive from 39 to 100, and by promising a cash bonus to anyone enlisting for three years and a land bounty to anyone serving for the duration. Congress never came close to raising the 75,000 men it

Congress Fleeing Philadelphia by Balloon, 1777   This British cartoon mocked Congress as it fled from the British army in the 1777 campaign. Hot air balloon flights were still in an experimental phase but were becoming a popular rage in France and Britain. The first flight across the English Channel would occur in 1783.

hoped for, but these new policies did create the foundation for the Continental Line, or Army. Longer terms made military training a real possibility, which in turn made the Continentals much more professional than the militia.

The Continental Army acquired its own distinctive character. The men who signed up were often poor. Some recruits were British deserters. Short-term militia, by contrast, usually held a secure place in their communities. As the 1777 recruits came in, the two northern armies, swelled by militia, grew to about 28,000 men fit for duty—17,000 in northern New York, and 11,000 under Washington.

The Howes sailed south from New York with 13,000 men. When river pilots were unable to guarantee a safe ascent up the Delaware against American fire, the fleet sailed on to Chesapeake Bay and landed the troops at Head of Elk, Maryland, on August 24. The British marched on Philadelphia through southeastern Pennsylvania, a region thickly populated with loyalists and neutral Quakers. Few militia turned out to help Washington, but most residents, aware of the atrocities committed by the Hessians in New Jersey, fled rather than greet the British army as liberators. The British burned many of their abandoned farms.

After his experience in New York, Washington was wary of being trapped in a city. Instead of trying to hold Philadelphia, he took up strong positions at Brandywine Creek along the British line of march. On September 11, Howe again outmaneuvered him, drove in his right flank, and forced the Americans to retreat. Congress fled to Lancaster, and the British occupied Philadelphia on September 26.

Washington headed west to Valley Forge, where the army endured a miserable winter. There, Frederick Wilhelm, baron von Steuben, a Prussian serving with the Continental Army, devised a drill manual based on Prussian standards. Through his efforts, the Continentals became far more soldierly. Other European volunteers also helped. From France came marquis de Lafayette and Johann, baron de Kalb. The Poles sent Thaddeus Kosciuszko (a talented engineer) and Casimir, count Pulaski. By the last years of the war, more than one-fifth of all Continental officers were professional soldiers from Europe.

SARATOGA

In northern New York, Ticonderoga fell to Burgoyne on June 2, 1777, but little went right for the British after that. Colonel St. Leger, with 900 soldiers and an equal number of Indians, reached Fort Schuyler in the Mohawk valley in August and defeated 800 militia at Oriskany. But when Benedict Arnold approached with an additional 1,000 men, the Indians fled, and St. Leger withdrew to Oswego.

Burgoyne's army of 7,800, advancing from Ticonderoga toward Albany, was overwhelmed in the upper Hudson valley. As his supply line to Canada grew longer, American militia swarmed to his rear and cut it. When he detached 700 Hessians to forage in the Green Mountains, they ran into 2,600 militia raised by John Stark of New Hampshire. On August 16 at Bennington, Vermont, Stark killed or captured nearly all of them. A relief force of 650 Hessians was also mauled. By the time Burgoyne's surviving soldiers reached the Hudson and started toward Albany, the Americans under Horatio Gates outnumbered them 3 to 1. The British got as far as Bemis Heights, 30 miles north of Albany, but failed to break through in two costly battles on September 19 and October 7, with Arnold again distinguishing himself. Burgoyne retreated 10 miles to Saratoga, where he surrendered his entire army on October 17.

FRENCH INTERVENTION

In May 1776, Louis XVI authorized secret aid to the American rebels. A French dramatist, Pierre-Augustin Caron de Beaumarchais, set up the firm of Roderique Hortalez et Compagnie to smuggle supplies through Britain's weak blockade of the American coast. Without this aid, the Americans could not have continued the war.

In December 1776 Benjamin Franklin arrived in France as an agent of the American Congress. The 70-year-old Franklin took Parisian society by storm by adopting simple clothes, replacing his wig with a fur cap, and playing to perfection the role of an innocent man of nature. Through Beaumarchais, he kept the supplies flowing and organized privateering raids on British commerce, which the French court claimed it was unable to stop.

The fall of Philadelphia alarmed Foreign Minister Charles Gravier, comte de Vergennes. He feared that Congress might give up unless France entered the war. But Burgoyne's defeat convinced Louis that the Americans could win and that intervention was a good risk. Franklin and Vergennes signed two treaties in February 1778. One, a commercial agreement, granted Americans generous trading terms with France. In the other, France made a perpetual alliance with the United States, recognized American independence, agreed to fight until Britain conceded independence, and disavowed all territorial ambitions on the North American continent. Vergennes also brought Spain into the war a year later.

The Franco-American treaties stunned London. Lord North tried to resign, but the king would not let him. Lord Chatham, warning that American independence would be a disaster for Britain, collapsed in the House of Lords after finishing his speech and died a month later. North put together a plan of conciliation that conceded virtually everything but independence and sent a distinguished group of commissioners under Frederick Howard, earl of Carlisle, to present it to Congress and block the French alliance. Congress recognized the proposals as a sign of desperation and rejected them out of hand.

Americans now expected a quick victory, while the British regrouped. George III declared war on France, recalled the Howe brothers, and ordered General Clinton to abandon Philadelphia. Wary of being caught at sea by the French, Clinton marched overland to New York in June 1778. Washington's newly disciplined army attacked his rear at Monmouth, New Jersey, and almost drove the British from the field, but the redcoats rallied and won the day. Fearing a French invasion of the British Isles while most of the Royal Navy was in American waters, the British redeployed their forces on a global scale. They stood on the defensive in America through most of 1778 and 1779.

SPANISH EXPANSION AND INTERVENTION

Like France, Spain was eager to avenge old defeats against Britain. The Spanish king, Charles III (1759–1788), had endured the loss of Florida shortly after ascending the throne but had received Louisiana from France in compensation. The province attracted 2,000 immigrants from the Canary Islands, perhaps 3,000 Acadian refugees, and other French settlers from the Illinois country. Louisiana remained heavily French even under Spanish rule.

During this time, Spaniards also moved into California. They explored the Pacific coastline as far north as southern Alaska, set up an outpost at San Francisco Bay, and built a series of Franciscan missions under Junípero Serra. With little danger from other Europeans, Spain sent relatively few soldiers to California. In fact, its California frontier duplicated many aspects of the earlier Florida missions. For the last time in the history of North America, missionaries set the tone for a whole province. As in Florida, the Indians died in appalling numbers from European diseases, and many objected to the harsh discipline of the missions.

Charles III never made a direct alliance with the United States. But in 1779 he joined France in its war against Britain, hoping to retake Gibraltar and to stabilize Spain's North American borders. Although Spain failed to take Gibraltar, it overran British West Florida, and at the end of the war Britain ceded East Florida as well. By 1783, for the first time in a century, Spain once again controlled the entire coastline of the Gulf of Mexico.

THE RECONSTITUTION OF AUTHORITY

In 1776 the prospect of independence touched off an intense debate among Americans on constitutionalism. They agreed that every state needed a written constitution to limit the powers of government, something more explicit than the precedents, statutes, and customs that made up Britain's unwritten constitution. They moved toward ever fuller expressions of popular sovereignty—the theory that all power must be derived from the people themselves. For four years, these lively debates sparked a learning process. By 1780, Americans knew what they meant when they insisted that the people must be their own governors.

JOHN ADAMS AND THE SEPARATION OF POWERS

No one learned more from this process than John Adams. When Thomas Paine advocated a simple, unicameral legislature to carry out the people's will, Adams took alarm. He replied in *Thoughts on Government,* a tract that influenced the men drafting Virginia's constitution.

In 1776 Adams was already moving away from the British notion of a "mixed and balanced" constitution, in which the government embodied the distinct social orders of British society—"King, Lords, and Commons." He was groping toward a very different notion, the separation of powers. Government, he affirmed, should be divided into three branches—an executive armed with veto power, a legislature, and a judiciary independent of both. The legislature, he insisted, must be bicameral, so that each house could expose the failings of the other. A free government need not embody distinct social orders to be stable. It could uphold republican values by being properly balanced within itself.

Governments exist to promote the happiness of the people, Adams declared, and happiness depends on "virtue," both public and private. Public virtue meant "patriotism," the willingness of independent householders to value the common good above their personal interests. The form of government that rests entirely on virtue, Adams argued, is a republic. Americans must elect legislatures that would mirror the diversity of society. Britain had put the nobility in one house and the commoners in another. But in America, everyone was a commoner. There were no "social orders." In what sense, then, could any government reflect American society?

In 1776 Adams knew only that the legislature should mirror society and that the structure of a republic should be more complex and balanced than what Paine advocated. Unicameral legislatures, which Georgia, Pennsylvania, and Vermont all adopted, horrified him: "A single assembly, possessed of all the powers of government, would make arbitrary laws for their own interest, execute all laws arbitrarily for their own interest, and adjudge all controversies in their own favor," he warned.

Adams had not yet found a way to distinguish between everyday legislation and the power to create a constitution. A few ordinary settlers had already spotted the dangers of having the two functions performed by the same body. As the citizens of Concord, Massachusetts, warned in October 1776, "A Constitution alterable by the Supreme Legislative [Power] is no Security at all to the Subject against any Encroachment of the Governing part on . . . their Rights and Privileges."

This concern would eventually prompt Americans to invent the embodiment of popular sovereignty in its purest form, the constitutional convention. But in 1776 most Americans still assumed that governments must be sovereign. In the early state constitutions, every state lodged sovereign power in its legislature and let the legislature define the rights of citizens. In 1776 the American reply to Britain's sovereign Parliament was 13 sovereign state legislatures—or 14, if Vermont is included.

THE VIRGINIA CONSTITUTION

In June 1776 Virginia became the first state to adopt a permanent, republican constitution. The provincial congress (called a "convention" in Virginia), which had assumed full legislative powers, affirmed "that the legislative and executive powers . . . should be separate and distinct from the judiciary"—but then wrote a constitution that made the legislature sovereign. The legislature chose the governor, the governor's council, and all judges above the level of justice of the peace. The governor had no veto and hardly any patronage. The lower house faced annual elections, but members of the upper house served four-year terms.

George Mason drafted a declaration of rights that the Virginia delegates passed before approving the constitution itself, on the theory that the people should define their rights before empowering the government. Mason's text affirmed the right to life, liberty, property, and the pursuit of happiness. It condemned hereditary privilege, called for rotation in office, provided strong guarantees for trial by jury and due process, and extolled religious liberty.

Other states adopted variations of the Virginia model. Because America had no aristocracy, uncertainty about the makeup of the upper house was widespread. Some states imposed higher property qualifications on "senators" than on "representatives." In three states the lower house elected the upper house. Maryland chose state senators through an electoral college, but most states created separate election districts for senators. Most states also increased the number of representatives in the lower house. Inland counties, underrepresented in most colonial assemblies, became better represented, and men of moderate wealth won a majority of seats in most states, displacing the rich who had won most colonial elections. Most states also stripped the governor of patronage and of royal prerogatives, such as the power to dissolve the legislature. Only New York empowered the governor, as part of a "Council of Revision," to override bills passed by the legislature.

THE PENNSYLVANIA CONSTITUTION

In Pennsylvania, radicals overthrew Crown, proprietor, and assembly in June 1776, rejected the leadership of both the old Quaker and Proprietary Parties, and elected artisans to office in Philadelphia and ordinary farmers in rural areas. Until 1776 most officeholders had either been Quakers or Anglicans. Now, Scots-Irish Presbyterians and German Lutherans or Calvinists replaced them and drafted a new constitution.

In 1776, Pennsylvania came closer than any other state to recognizing the constitutional dangers of resting sovereignty solely in the legislature rather than in the citizens. The radicals even summoned a special convention whose only task was to write a constitution. That document established a unicameral assembly and a plural executive of 12 men, one of whom would preside and thus be called "president." All freemen who paid taxes, and their adult sons living at home, could vote. Elections were annual, voting was by secret ballot, legislative sessions were open to the public, and no representative could serve for more than four years out of any seven. All bills were to be published before passage for public discussion throughout the state. Only at the next session of the legislature could they be passed into law, except in emergencies. Pennsylvania also created a "Council of Censors" to meet every seven years to determine whether the constitution had been violated. It could also recommend amendments.

The Pennsylvania constitution, however, generated intense conflict in late 1776 as the British army drew near. In this emergency, the convention that drafted the constitution also began to pass laws, destroying any distinction between itself and the legislature it had created. Likewise, the convention and the legislatures that eventually succeeded it rarely delayed the enactment of a bill until after the voters had had time to discuss it. The war lent a sense of emergency to almost every measure. Even more alarming, many residents condemned the new constitution as illegitimate. The men driven from power in 1776 never consented to it and saw no good reason why they should accept it. The radicals, calling themselves "Constitutionalists," imposed oaths on all citizens obliging them to uphold the constitution and then disfranchised Quakers, German pacifists, and anyone else who refused to support it.

These illiberal measures gave radicals a majority in the legislature into the 1780s and kept voter turnout low in most elections, although some men (mostly leaders of the old Proprietary Party) took the oaths only to form an opposition party. Called "anti-Constitutionalists" at first (that is, opponents of the 1776 constitution), they soon took the name "Republicans." After the war, as the disfranchised regained the right to vote, Republicans won a solid majority in the legislature. In 1787 they won ratification of the federal Constitution, and then, in 1790 they replaced the 1776 state constitution with a new one that created a bicameral legislature and an elective governor.

MASSACHUSETTS REDEFINES CONSTITUTIONALISM

Another bitter struggle occurred in Massachusetts. After four years of intense debate, Massachusetts found a way to lodge sovereignty with the people and not with government—that is, a way to distinguish a constitution from simple laws.

In response to the Massachusetts Government Act, passed by Parliament in 1774 (see Chapter 5), the colonists had prevented the royal courts from sitting. The courts remained closed until the British withdrew from Boston in March 1776 and the provincial congress moved into the city and reestablished itself as the General Court under the royal charter of 1691. The legislature then reapportioned itself. The new system let towns choose representatives in proportion to population. It rewarded the older, populous eastern towns at the expense of the lightly settled western towns.

When the General Court also revived royal practice by appointing its own members as county judges and justices of the peace, the western counties exploded. They attacked the reapportionment act and refused to reopen the courts in Hampshire and Berkshire counties. Berkshire's radicals insisted on contracts or compacts as the basis of authority in both church and state and continued to use county conventions in place of the courts. To these Berkshire Constitutionalists a "convention" was becoming the purest expression of the will of the people, superior to any legislature. These uneducated farmers set the pace in demanding a formal constitution for the state.

In the fall of 1776 the General Court asked the towns to authorize it to draft a constitution. By a 2-to-1 margin the voters agreed, a result that reflected growing *distrust* of the legislature. Six months earlier hardly anyone would have questioned such a procedure. The legislature drafted a constitution over the next year and then, in an unusual precaution, asked the towns to ratify it. The voters rejected it by the stunning margin of 5 to 1. Voters angry with a particular clause had apparently condemned the whole document.

Chastened, the General Court urged the towns to postpone the question until after the war. Hampshire County reopened its courts in April 1778, but Berkshire County threatened to secede from the state unless it summoned a constitutional convention. Citing John Locke, these farmers insisted that they were now in a "state of nature," subject to no legitimate government. They might even join a neighboring state that had a proper constitution. At a time when Vermont was making good its secession from New York, this was no idle threat.

The General Court gave in, and a convention met in Boston in December 1779. John Adams drafted a constitution for it to consider, and the convention used his text as its starting point. A constitution now had to be drafted by a convention, elected for that specific purpose, and then be ratified by the people.

Like the Virginia constitution, the Massachusetts constitution began with a bill of rights. Both houses would be elected annually. The House of Representatives would be chosen by the towns. Senators were to be elected by counties and apportioned according to property values, not population. The governor was to be popularly elected and would have a veto that two-thirds of both houses could override. Property qualifications rose as a man's civic duties increased. Voters had to own £50 of real property or £100 of personal property, representatives £100 in land or £200 in other property, senators £300 or £600 respectively, and the governor had to own £1,000 in landed property. For purposes of ratification only, all free adult males were eligible to vote. In accepting the basic social compact, everyone (that is, all free men) would have a chance to consent. Voters were asked to vote on each article separately, not on the document as a whole.

During the spring of 1780 town meetings began the ratification process. The convention tallied the results and declared that the constitution had received the required two-thirds majority. The new constitution promptly went into effect and, though it has often been amended, is still in force today, making it the oldest constitution in the world. Starting with New Hampshire in 1784, other states adopted the Massachusetts model.

CONFEDERATION

Before independence, hardly anyone had given serious thought to how an American nation ought to be governed. Dozens of colonists had drafted plans of conciliation with Britain, some quite innovative. But through 1775 only Benjamin Franklin and Connecticut's Silas Deane had presented plans for an American union. Franklin's was an updated version of the Albany Plan of 1754 (see Chapter 4). Another proposal appeared in an American newspaper, but none of the three attracted public comment. Colonists passionately debated the empire and their state governments, but not America.

Congress began discussing the American union in the summer of 1776 but then took a year and a half to draft the final text of what became the "Articles of Confederation and perpetual Union." Congress had been voting by state ever since the First Continental Congress in 1774. Delegates from large states favored representation according to population, but no census existed to give precise numbers, and the small states insisted on being treated as equals. As long as Britain was ready to embrace any state that defected, small states had great leverage: The tail could wag the dog. In one early draft of the Articles of Confederation, John Dickinson rejected proportional representation in favor of state equality. He enumerated the powers of Congress, which did not include levying taxes or regulating trade. To raise money, Congress would have to print it or requisition specific amounts from the states. Congress then split over how to apportion these requisitions. Northern states wanted to count slaves in computing the ratios. Southern states wanted to apportion revenues on the basis of each state's free population. Western lands were another tough issue. States with fixed borders pressured states with boundary claims stretching into the Ohio or Mississippi valleys to surrender their claims to Congress. Congress could not resolve these issues in 1776.

Debate resumed after Washington's victories at Trenton and Princeton. Thomas Burke of North Carolina introduced a resolution that eventually became part of the Articles of Confederation: "Each state retains its sovereignty, freedom and independence, and every power, jurisdiction, and right, which is not by this confederation expressly delegated to the United States in Congress assembled." The acceptance of Burke's resolution, with only Virginia dissenting, ensured that the Articles would contain a firm commitment to state sovereignty. In the final version, Congress was given no power over western land claims, and requisitions would be based on each state's free population.

In November 1777 Congress asked the states to ratify the Articles by March 10, 1778, but only Virginia met the deadline. By midsummer 10 had ratified. The three dissenters were Delaware, New Jersey, and Maryland—all states without western land claims who feared their giant neighbors. Maryland held out for more than three years, until Virginia agreed to cede its land claims north of the Ohio River to Congress. The Articles finally went into force on March 1, 1781.

By then, the Continental Congress had lost most of its power. The congressional effort to manage everything through committees created impossible bottlenecks. In 1776 the states had looked to Congress to confer legitimacy on their new governments. But as the states adopted their own constitutions, their legitimacy became more obvious than that of Congress. Even more alarming, by the late 1770s Congress simply could not pay its bills.

THE CRISIS OF THE REVOLUTION, 1779–1783

Americans expected a quick victory under the French alliance. Instead, the struggle turned into a grim war of attrition, testing which side would first exhaust its resources or lose the will to fight. Loyalists became much more important to the British war effort, both as a source of manpower and as the main justification for continuing the war. Most settlers, argued Lord North, were still loyal to Britain. The British began to look to the Deep South as the likeliest recruiting ground for armed loyalists. The Carolinas, bitterly divided by the regulator movements and vulnerable to massive slave defections, seemed a promising source.

THE LOYALISTS

Most loyalists were committed to English ideas of liberty. They also thought that creating a new American union was a far riskier venture than remaining part of the British Empire. For many, the choice of loyalties was painful. Some waited until the fighting reached their neighborhood before deciding which soldiers to flee from, which to shoot.

The British, in turn, were slow to take advantage of the loyalists. But as the war continued, the loyalists, who stood to lose everything in an American victory, showed that they could be fierce soldiers.

About one-sixth of the white population chose the British side in the war. Unlike most patriots, loyalists served long terms, because they could not go home unless they won. By 1780 the number of loyalists under arms probably exceeded the number of Continentals by 2 to 1. State governments retaliated by banishing prominent loyalists under pain of death and by confiscating their property.

LOYALIST REFUGEES, BLACK AND WHITE

When given the choice, most slaves south of New England sided with Britain. In New England, where they sensed that they could gain freedom by joining the rebels, many volunteered for military service. Elsewhere, although some fought for the Revolution, they realized that their best chance of emancipation lay with the British army. During the war, more than 50,000 slaves (about 10 percent) fled their owners; of that total, about 20,000 were evacuated by the British. The decision to flee carried risks. In South Carolina, hundreds reached the sea islands in an effort to join the British during Clinton's 1776 invasion, only to face their owners' wrath when the British failed to rescue them. Others approached British units only to be treated as contraband (property) and to face possible resale. But most slaves who reached British lines won their freedom. When the British withdrew after the war, blacks went with them, many to Jamaica, some to Nova Scotia, others to London.

Extract of a letter from Monmouth county, June 12.
" Ty, with his party of about 20 blacks and whites, laſt Friday afternoon took and carried off priſoners, Capt. Barns Smock and Gilbert Vanmater; at the fame time ſpiked up the iron four pounder at Capt. Smock's houſe, but took no ammunition : Two of the artillery horſes, and two of Capt. Smock' horſes, were likewiſe taken off."
The above-mentioned Ty is a Negroe, who bears the title of Colonel, and commands a motly crew at Sandy-Hook.

AN OFFER OF FREEDOM An American newspaper reported on the efforts of the British to gain the support of slaves by offering them freedom.

The war, in short, created an enormous stream of refugees, black and white. In addition to 20,000 former slaves, some 60,000 to 70,000 colonists left the states for other parts of the British Empire. The American Revolution created 30 refugees for every 1,000 people, compared with 5 per 1,000 created by the French Revolution in the 1790s. About 35,000 settlers found their way to the maritime provinces. Another 6,000 to 10,000 fled to Quebec, settled upriver from the older French population, and in 1791 became the new province of Upper Canada (later Ontario). A generous land policy, which required an oath of allegiance to George III, attracted thousands of new immigrants to Canada from the United States in the 1780s and 1790s. By the War of 1812, four-fifths of Upper Canada's 100,000 people were American-born. Though only one-fifth of them could be traced to loyalist resettlement, the settlers supported Britain in that war. In a very real sense the American Revolution laid the foundation of two new nations—the United States and Canada—and competition between them for settlers and loyalties continued long after the fighting stopped.

THE INDIAN STRUGGLE FOR UNITY AND SURVIVAL

Indians of the eastern woodlands also began to play a more active role in the war. Most of them saw that an American victory would threaten their survival as a people on their ancestral lands. Nearly all of them sided with Britain in the hope that a British victory might stem the flood of western expansion. In the final years of the war, they achieved a level of unity without precedent in their history.

At first, most Indians tried to remain neutral. Only the Cherokees took up arms in 1776. Short on ammunition and other British supplies, they took heavy losses before making peace and accepting neutrality. The Chickamaugas, a splinter group, continued to resist. In the Deep South, only the Catawbas fought on the American side.

Burgoyne's invasion brought the Iroquois into the war in 1777. The Mohawks in the east and the Senecas in the west sided with Britain under the leadership of Joseph Brant, a literate and educated Mohawk and a Freemason. His sister, Mary Brant, emerged as a skillful diplomat in the alliance between the Iroquois and the loyalists. A minority of Oneidas and some Tuscaroras fought with the Americans, thus rupturing the Iroquois League.

A minority of Shawnees, led by Cornplanter, and of Delawares, led by White Eyes and Killbuck, also pursued friendly relations with the Americans, but they refused to fight other Indians. Christian Moravian Indians in the Ohio country took a similar stance. Loyalists and patriots were far more willing than Indians to kill one another.

Frontier racism made Indian neutrality all but impossible. Backcountry settlers from Carolina through New York refused to accept the neutrals on their own terms. Indian warriors, especially young men strongly influenced by nativist prophets, increasingly believed that the Great Spirit had created whites, Indians, and blacks as separate peoples who ought to remain apart. Their militancy further enraged the settlers. Young white hunters, disdained by many easterners as "near savages," proved their worth as "whites" by killing Indians.

The hatred of Indians grew so extreme that it threatened to undercut the American war effort. In 1777 a Continental officer had Cornplanter murdered. In 1778 American militia killed White Eyes. Four years later Americans massacred 100 unarmed Moravian mission Indians at Gnadenhutten, Ohio. Nearly all of them were women and children, who knelt in prayer as, one by one, their skulls were crushed with mallets. Until then, most Indians had refrained from the ritual torture of prisoners. But after Gnadenhutten they resumed the custom. When they captured known leaders of the massacre, they burned them alive.

Faced with hatred, Indians united to protect their lands. They won the frontier war north of the Ohio River. The Iroquois ravaged the Wyoming valley of Pennsylvania in 1778. When an American army devastated Iroquoia in 1779, the Indians fell back on the British post at Niagara and continued the struggle. In 1779 nearly all Indians, from the Creeks on the Gulf Coast to the nations of the Great Lakes, exchanged emissaries and planned an all-out war along the frontier. George Rogers Clark of Virginia thwarted their offensive with a daring winter raid in which he captured Vincennes and cut off the western nations from British supplies. But the Indians regrouped and by 1782 drove the Virginia "Long Knives" out of the Ohio country.

ATTRITION

After 1778, George III's determination to continue the war bitterly divided his country. Trade was disrupted, thousands of ships were lost to privateers, taxes and the national debt soared, military recruits became harder to find, and a French invasion became a serious threat. Much of the British public doubted that the war could be won. Political dissent rose and included widespread demand for the reduction of royal patronage and for electoral reforms. A proposal to abolish Lord George Germain's office, clearly an attack on the American war, failed in the House of Commons by only 208 votes to 201 in March 1780. A resolve condemning the influence of the Crown carried in April, 233 to 215. The king had great difficulty persuading North not to resign.

Desperate for men, the British army had been quietly recruiting Irish Catholics, and North supported a modest degree of toleration for English and Scottish Catholics. This leniency produced a surge of Protestant violence culminating in the Gordon riots, named for Lord George Gordon, an agitator. For a week in June 1780 crowds roared through the streets of London, smashing Catholic chapels attached to foreign embassies, liberating prisoners from city jails, and finally attacking the Bank of England. The army, supported by Lord Mayor John Wilkes, put down the rioters. This spectacular violence discredited the demands for reform that had seemed on the verge of toppling North. The riots gave him one more chance to win the war, this time with strong support from loyalists.

Attrition also weakened the United States. Indian raids reduced harvests, and military levies kept thousands of men away from productive work. British and Loyalist raids into Connecticut, New Jersey, and Virginia wore down the defenders and destroyed a great deal of property. Merchants lost most of their European and West Indian markets. Average household income plunged by more than 40 percent. Even some American triumphs came at a high price. Burgoyne's surrender left Americans with the burden of feeding his army for the rest of the war. Provisioning the French fleet in American waters put enormous strain on American resources.

These heavy demands led to the collapse of the Continental dollar in 1779–1780. Congress had been printing money to pay its bills, using the Spanish dollar as its basic monetary unit. With the French alliance bolstering American credit, this practice worked reasonably well into 1778. The money depreciated but without causing widespread dissatisfaction. But as the war ground on, the value of Continental money fell to less than a penny on the dollar in 1779. Congress agreed to stop the printing presses and to rely instead on requisitions from the states and on foreign and domestic loans. But it found that, without paper, it could not even pay the army. Congress and the army had to requisition supplies directly from farmers in exchange for certificates geared to an inflation rate of 40 to 1, well below what it really was. Many farmers, rather than lose money on their crops, simply cut back production.

Continental soldiers—unpaid, ill-clothed, and often poorly fed—grew mutinous. As they became more professional through frequent drill, they also became contemptuous of civilians. The winter 1779–1780, the worst of the century, marked a low point in morale among the main force of Continentals snowed in with Washington at Morristown, New Jersey. Many deserted. In May 1780 two Connecticut regiments of the Continental Line, without food for three days, threatened to go home, raising the danger that the whole army might dissolve. Their officers were barely able to restore control. On paper, Washington had 16,000 men. His real strength was 3,600, and he did not have enough horses to move his artillery.

THE BRITISH OFFENSIVE IN THE SOUTH

In 1780 the British attacked in the Deep South with great success. The Revolution almost collapsed. In December 1778 a small British amphibious force had taken Savannah and had held it through 1779 against an American and French counterthrust. By early 1780 they were ready to launch a general offensive. Their commander, General Clinton, had devised a strategy for winning the war, but he revealed its details to no one.

Clinton's New York army would invade South Carolina and take Charleston. Part of the regular forces would remain to pacify the Carolinas. Clinton would sail with the rest back to New York and land on the Jersey coast with a force three times larger than Washington's at Morristown. By dividing this army into two columns, Clinton could break through both passes of the Watchung Mountains leading to Morristown. Washington would either have to hold fast and be overwhelmed, or else abandon his artillery for lack of horses and attack one of the invading columns on unfavorable terms. Either way, Clinton reasoned, the Continental Army would be destroyed. He was also negotiating secretly with Benedict Arnold for the surrender of West Point, which would open the Hudson River to British ships as far north as Albany. Finally, if the French landed in Newport, as everyone expected, Clinton would then move against them with nearly his entire New York fleet and garrison. If he succeeded there too, he would have smashed every professional force in North America within a year's time. His remaining task would then be pacification, which he could pretty much leave to loyalists.

Clinton's invasion of South Carolina began with awesome successes. While the British navy sealed off Charleston from the sea, an army of 10,000 closed off the land approaches to the city, which surrendered on May 12. A force of loyalists under Banastre Tarleton caught the 350 remaining Continentals near the North Carolina border on May 29 and killed them all, even those who surrendered.

Such calculated brutality was designed to terrorize civilians into submission. It succeeded at first. But Thomas Sumter began to fight back after loyalists burned his plantation. His mounted raiders attacked British outposts and terrorized loyalists. At Hanging Rock on August 6, Sumter's 800 men scattered 500 loyalists, killing or wounding nearly half of them. All the participants on both sides were colonists.

Leaving Cornwallis in command of 8,300 men in South Carolina, Clinton sailed north with one-third of his Carolina army, only to learn that loyalists had persuaded Wilhelm, baron von

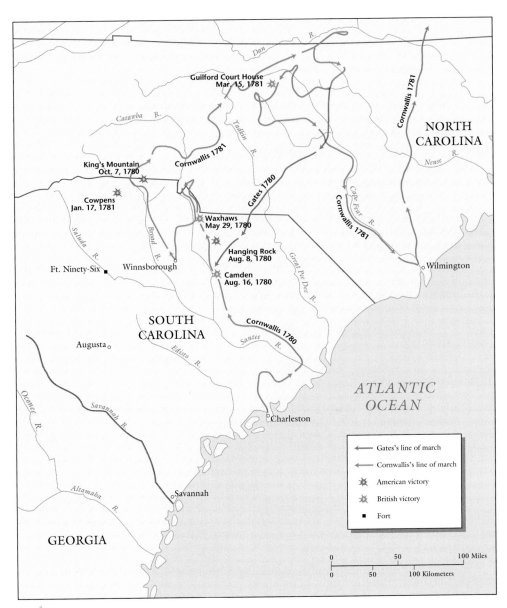

NORTH
CAROLINA

Guilford Court House
Mar. 15, 1781

King's Mountain
Oct. 7, 1780

Cowpens
Jan. 17, 1781

Waxhaws
May 29, 1780

Hanging Rock
Aug. 8, 1780

Camden
Aug. 16, 1780

Ft. Ninety-Six   Winnsborough

SOUTH
CAROLINA

Augusta

ATLANTIC
OCEAN

Charleston

Savannah

GEORGIA

Cornwallis 1781

Cornwallis 1781

Gates 1780

Cornwallis 1781

Wilmington

Cornwallis 1780

- Gates's line of march
- Cornwallis's line of march
- American victory
- British victory
- Fort

| 0 | 50 | 100 Miles |
| 0 | 50 | 100 Kilometers |

WAR IN THE LOWER SOUTH, 1780–1781

Knyphausen, the temporary commander, to land in New Jersey with 6,000 men on the night of June 6–7, 1780. Even a force that small would pose a grave threat to Washington unless the militia came to his aid. Most loyalists hoped that the militia was so weary from the harsh winter and numerous raids that they would not turn out. Some companies had even begun to muster women. To the dismay of the British, however, the militia appeared in force on June 7.

Only then, after an inconclusive engagement, did Knyphausen learn that Clinton was on his way. The British pulled back to the coast and waited, but they had lost the element of surprise. Clinton attacked at Springfield on June 23. The battle became America's civil war in miniature. New Jersey loyalist regiments attacked the New Jersey regiments of the Continental Line, who were assisted by New Jersey militia. The defense was stout enough to persuade Clinton to withdraw to New York. With Washington's army still intact, the British ignored the French when the French landed at Newport; after June 1780 the British put all their hopes on the southern campaign. Even Arnold's attempt to betray West Point was thwarted, although Arnold escaped to British lines and became a general in the British army.

Despite Sumter's harassment, Cornwallis's conquest of the Carolinas proceeded rapidly. Congress scraped together 900 tough Maryland and Delaware Continentals, put Horatio Gates in command, and sent them south against Cornwallis. Bolstered by 2,000 Virginia and North Carolina militia, Gates rashly offered battle at Camden on August 16. The militia, who lacked bayonets, fled in panic at the first British charge. The exposed Continentals fought bravely but were crushed. Gates informed Congress that he had suffered "total Defeat." Two days after Camden, Tarleton surprised Sumter's camp at Fishing Creek, killing 150 men and wounding 300.

In four months the British had destroyed all the Continental forces in the Deep South, mauled Sumter's band of partisans, and left North Carolina exposed. Cornwallis turned the pacification of South Carolina over to his loyalists and marched confidently on to "liberate" North Carolina.

The Partisan War

But resistance continued. Tarleton and Sumter fought one engagement to a draw. Farther west, frontier riflemen crossed the Blue Ridge to challenge Patrick Ferguson's loyalists at King's Mountain near the North Carolina border on October 7, 1780. Losing only 88 men, rebel marksmen picked off many defenders, advanced from tree to tree, and finally overwhelmed the loyalists. They shot many prisoners and hanged a dozen. This victory stung Cornwallis, who halted his drive into North Carolina.

In October 1780, Congress sent Nathanael Greene to the Carolinas with a small Continental force. When Sumter withdrew for several months to nurse a wound, Francis Marion took his place. A much abler leader, Marion operated from remote bases in the swampy low country. Yet Greene's prospects seemed desperate. The ugliness of the partisan war and the condition of his own soldiers appalled him. Yet Greene and Marion devised a masterful strategy of partisan warfare that finally wore out the British.

In the face of a greatly superior enemy, Greene ignored a standard maxim of war and split up his force of 1,800 Continentals. In smaller bands they would be easier to feed, but Greene's decision involved more than supplies. He sent 300 men east to bolster Marion, and ordered Daniel Morgan and 300 riflemen west to threaten the British outpost of Ninety-Six. Cornwallis, worried that after King's Mountain Morgan might raise the entire backcountry against the British, divided his own army. He sent Tarleton with a mixed force of 1,100 British and loyalists after Morgan, who decided to stand with his back to a river at a place called Cowpens. Including militia, Morgan had 1,040 men.

Tarleton attacked on January 17, 1781. In another unorthodox move, Morgan sent his militia out front as skirmishers. He ordered them to fire two rounds and then redeploy in his rear as a reserve. Relieved of their fear of a bayonet charge, they obeyed. As they pulled back, the British rushed forward into the Continentals, who also retreated at first, then wheeled and discharged a lethal volley. After Morgan's cavalry charged into the British left flank, the militia returned to the fray. Although Tarleton escaped, Morgan annihilated his army.

As Morgan rejoined Greene, Cornwallis staked everything on his ability to find Greene and crush him. But Greene placed flatboats in his rear at major river crossings and then lured Cornwallis into a march of exhaustion. In a race to the Dan River, Cornwallis burned his baggage in order to travel lightly. Greene escaped on his flatboats across the Yadkin River, flooded with spring rains, just ahead of Cornwallis—who had to march to a ford 10 miles upstream, cross the river, and then march back while Greene rested. Greene repeated this stratagem all the way to the Dan until he judged that Cornwallis was so weak that the Americans could offer battle at Guilford Court House on March 15, 1781. With militia, he outnumbered Cornwallis 4,400 to 1,900. Even though the British retained possession of the battlefield, they lost one-quarter of their force along with the strategic initiative.

Cornwallis retreated to the coast at Wilmington to refit. He then marched north into Virginia—the seat of southern resistance, he told Clinton, the one place where Britain could achieve decisive results. Instead of following him, Greene returned to South Carolina, where he and Marion took the surviving British outposts one by one. After the British evacuated Ninety-Six on July 1, 1781, they held only Savannah and Charleston in the Deep South. Against heavy odds, Greene had reclaimed the region for the Revolution.

Mutiny and Reform

After the Camden disaster, army officers and state politicians demanded reforms to strengthen Congress and win the war. State legislatures sent their ablest men to Congress. Maryland, the last state to hold out, finally completed the American union by ratifying the Articles of Confederation.

Before any reforms could take effect, discontent again erupted in the army. Insisting that their three-year enlistments had expired, 1,500 men of the Pennsylvania Line got drunk on New Year's Day 1781, killed three officers, and marched out of their winter quarters at Morristown. General Clinton sent agents to promise them a pardon and their back pay if they defected to the British. But the mutineers marched south toward Princeton instead and turned Clinton's agents over to Pennsylvania authorities, who executed them. Congress, reassured, negotiated with the soldiers. More than half of them accepted discharges, and those who remained in service got furloughs and bonuses for reenlistment. Encouraged by this treatment, 200 New Jersey soldiers at Pompton also mutinied, but Washington used New England units to disarm them and had two of the leaders executed. The army somehow held together, but well into 1781 there were still more loyalists serving with the British than there were Continentals with Washington.

Civilian violence, such as the "Fort Wilson" riot in Philadelphia, also prompted Congress to change policies. Radical artisans blamed rich merchants for the inflation of 1779 and demanded price controls. The merchants blamed paper money. In October, several men were killed when the antagonists exchanged shots near the fortified home of James Wilson, a wealthy lawyer. Spokesmen for the radicals deplored the violence and abandoned the quest for price controls. For city dwellers rich and poor, sound money was becoming the only solution to the inflation.

Congress interpreted these disturbances as a call for reform. It stopped printing money, abandoned its cumbersome committee system, and created separate executive departments of foreign affairs, finance, war, and marine. Robert Morris, a Philadelphia merchant, became the first secretary of finance, helped to organize the Bank of North America (America's first), and made certain that the Continental Army was clothed and well fed. Congress began to requisition revenue from the states. The states began to impose heavy taxes, but they never collected enough to meet both their own and national needs. Congress tried to amend the Articles of Confederation in 1781 and asked the states for a 5 percent duty on all imports. Most states quickly ratified the "impost," but Rhode Island rejected it in 1783. Amendments to the Articles needed unanimous approval by the states, and this opposition killed the impost. A new impost in 1783 was defeated by New York in 1786.

The reforms of 1781 just barely kept a smaller army in the field for the rest of the war, but the new executive departments had an unforeseen effect. Congress had been a plural executive, America's answer to the imperial Crown. But once Congress created its own departments, it looked more like a national legislature, and a feeble one at that, for it still had no power to compel obedience. It began to pass, not just "orders" and "resolves," but also "ordinances," which were meant to be permanent and binding. But it could not punish anyone for noncompliance, which may be why it never passed any "laws."

FROM THE RAVAGING OF VIRGINIA TO YORKTOWN AND PEACE

Both Cornwallis and Washington believed that events in Virginia would decide the war. When a large British force raided the state in late 1780, Governor Thomas Jefferson called up enough militia to keep the British bottled up in Portsmouth, while he continued to ship men and supplies to Greene in the Carolinas. Thereafter, the state's ability to raise men and supplies almost collapsed.

In January 1781, Clinton sent Arnold by sea from New York with 1,600 men, mostly loyalists. They sailed up the James, took the new capital of Richmond almost without resistance, and gutted it. When Jefferson called out the militia, few responded. Most Virginia freemen had already done service, if only as short-term militia. In 1781 they thought it was now someone else's turn.

For months, there was no one else. Cornwallis took command in April, and Arnold departed for New York. But the raids continued into summer, sweeping as far west as Charlottesville, where Tarleton scattered the ∽ Virginia legislature and came within minutes of capturing Jefferson on June 3. Many of Jefferson's slaves greeted the British as liberators. Washington sent Lafayette with 1,200 New England and New Jersey Continentals to contain the damage, and Cornwallis withdrew to Yorktown.

At last, Washington saw an opportunity to launch a major strike. He learned that a powerful French fleet under François, comte de Grasse, would sail with 3,000 soldiers from St. Domingue on August 13 for Chesapeake Bay. Cooperating closely with the French army commander, Jean Baptiste Donatien, comte de Rochambeau, Washington sprang his trap. Rochambeau led his 5,000 soldiers from Newport to the outskirts of New York, where they joined Washington's 5,000 Continentals. After feinting an attack to freeze Clinton in place, Washington marched the combined armies 400 miles south to tidewater Virginia, where they linked up with Lafayette's Americans and the other French army brought by de Grasse. After de Grasse's fleet beat off a British relief force at the Battle of the Capes on September 5,

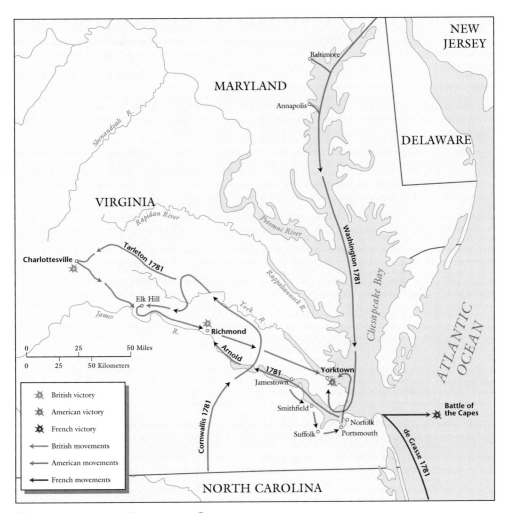

VIRGINIA AND THE YORKTOWN CAMPAIGN

Washington cut off all retreat routes and besieged Cornwallis in Yorktown. On October 19, 1781, Cornwallis surrendered his entire army of 8,000 men.

Yorktown brought down the British government in March 1782. Lord North resigned. The new ministry continued to fight the French in the Caribbean and the Spanish at Gibraltar, but the British evacuated Savannah and Charleston and concentrated their remaining forces in New York City.

Contrary to the French Treaty of 1778, John Jay and John Adams opened secret peace negotiations in Paris with the British. They won British recognition of the Mississippi, though without New Orleans, as the western boundary of the new republic. New Englanders retained the right to fish off Newfoundland. The treaty recognized the validity of prewar transatlantic debts, and Congress promised to urge the states to restore confiscated loyalist property. After the negotiations were far advanced, the Americans told Vergennes, the French foreign minister, what they were doing. He feigned indignation, but the threat of a separate peace gave him the leverage he needed with Spain. Spain stopped demanding that France keep fighting until Gibraltar surrendered. The Treaty of Paris, though not ratified for months, ended the war in February 1783.

Western Indians were appalled to learn that the treaty gave their lands to the United States. They knew that they had not been conquered, whatever European diplomats might say. Their war for survival continued with few breaks into 1795.

Congress still faced ominous problems. In March 1783 many Continental officers threatened a coup d'état unless Congress granted them generous pensions. Washington, confronting them at their encampment at Newburgh, New York, fumbled for his glasses and remarked, "I have grown old in the service of my country, and now find that I am growing blind." Tears filled the eyes of his comrades in arms, and the threat of a coup vanished.

In Philadelphia two months later, unpaid Pennsylvania soldiers marched on the statehouse where both Congress and the state's executive council sat. Ignoring Congress, they demanded that Pennsylvania redress their grievances. Congress felt insulted and left the city for Princeton, where it reconvened in Nassau Hall. "I confess I have great apprehensions for the union of the states," wrote Charles Thomson, secretary to Congress since 1774. The British threat, Thomson knew, had created the American Union. He feared that the Union would dissolve with the return of peace. Congress moved on from Princeton to Annapolis and eventually settled in New York, but the Union's survival remained uncertain.

A REVOLUTIONARY SOCIETY

Independence transformed American life. The biggest winners were free householders, who gained enormous benefits from the democratization of politics and the chance to colonize the Great West. Besides the loyalists, the biggest losers were the Indians, who continued to resist settler expansion. Many slaves won their freedom, and women struggled for greater dignity. Both succeeded only when their goals proved compatible with the ambitions of white householders.

RELIGIOUS TRANSFORMATIONS

After independence, the Anglican Church became vulnerable. Although most Anglican clergymen had supported the Revolution or had remained neutral, an aggressive loyalist minority had stirred the wrath of patriots. Religious dissenters disestablished the Anglican Church in every southern state. They deprived it of its tax support and other privileges, such as the sole right to perform marriages. In 1786 Virginia passed Thomas Jefferson's eloquent Statute for Religious Freedom, which declared that "God hath created the mind free" and that efforts to use coercion in matters of religion "tend only to beget habits of hypocrisy and meanness." In Virginia, church attendance and the support of ministers became voluntary activities.

Other states moved more slowly. In New England, the Congregational churches had strongly supported the Revolution and were less vulnerable to attack. Their ministers' salaries (except in Rhode Island) continued to be paid out of public taxes. The Congregational Church exercised other public or quasi-public functions. Disestablishment did not become complete until 1818 in Connecticut and 1833 in Massachusetts.

Although most states still restricted officeholding to Christians or Protestants, many people were coming to regard the coercion of anyone's conscience as morally wrong. Jews and Catholics both gained from the new atmosphere of tolerance. When John Carroll of Maryland became the first Roman Catholic bishop in the United States, hardly anyone protested. And in the 1780s the Church of England reorganized itself as the Protestant Episcopal Church and quietly began to consecrate its own bishops.

THE FIRST EMANCIPATION

The Revolution freed tens of thousands of slaves. But it also gave new vitality to slavery in the region that people were beginning to call "the South." Within a generation, slavery was abolished in the emerging "North." Race became a defining factor in both regions: In the South, most blacks remained slaves; in the North, they became free but not equal.

Many slaves freed themselves. The British army enabled more than half the slaves of Georgia and perhaps one-quarter of those in South Carolina to win their freedom. A similar process was under way in Virginia in 1781, only to be cut off at Yorktown. Hundreds of New England slaves won their freedom through military service. After the Massachusetts bill of rights proclaimed that all people were "born free and equal," Elizabeth (Bett) Freeman sued her master in 1781 and won her liberty. Thereafter, most of the slaves in Massachusetts and New Hampshire simply walked away from their masters.

Elsewhere, legislative action was necessary. Pennsylvania led the way in 1780 with the modern world's first gradual emancipation statute. Instead of freeing current slaves, it declared that all children born to Pennsylvania slaves would become free at age 28. This requirement left former slaves unable to compete on equal terms with free whites, who usually entered adult life with inherited property. Some masters shipped their slaves south before the moment of emancipation, and some whites kidnapped freedmen and sent them south. The Pennsylvania Abolition Society was organized largely to fight these abuses. By 1800 Philadelphia had the largest community of free blacks in America.

The Pennsylvania pattern was followed, with variations, in most other northern states. Where slaves constituted more than 10 percent of the population, as in southern New York and northeastern New Jersey, slaveholders' resistance delayed legislation for years. New York yielded in 1799, and finally so did New Jersey in 1804.

In the upper South, many Methodists and Baptists supported emancipation in the 1780s, only to retreat in later years. Maryland and Virginia authorized the manumission of individual slaves. By 1810 more than one-fifth of Maryland's slaves had been freed, as had 10,000 of Virginia's 300,000 slaves. But slaves were essential to the plantation economy. In the South, emancipation would have amounted to a social revolution. Planters resisted it, but they supported the Christianization of their slaves and other humane reforms.

Maryland and Virginia, where population growth among the slaves exceeded what the tobacco economy could absorb, banned the Atlantic slave trade, as had all states outside the Deep South. However, Georgia and South Carolina reopened the Atlantic slave trade. South Carolina imported almost 60,000 more Africans before Congress prohibited the Atlantic slave trade in 1808.

THE CHALLENGE TO PATRIARCHY

Nothing as dramatic as emancipation altered relations between the sexes. With the men away fighting, many women were left in charge of the household. But while some women acquired new authority, nearly all of them had to work harder to keep their households functioning. The war cut them off from most European consumer goods. Household manufactures, mostly the task of women, filled the gap. Women accepted these duties without insisting on broader legal or political rights.

Attitudes toward marriage were also changing. The common-law rule of coverture (see Chapter 4) still denied wives any legal personality, but some of them persuaded state governments not to impoverish them by confiscating the property of their loyalist husbands. Many writers insisted that good marriages rested on mutual affection, not on property settlements. Parents were urged to respect the personalities of their children and to avoid severe discipline. Traditional reverence for the elderly was giving way to an idealization of youth and energy.

Esther de Berdt Reed organized the Philadelphia Ladies Association in 1780 to relieve the sufferings of Continental soldiers. It was the first women's society in American history to take on a public role. Although few women demanded equal political rights during the Revolution, the New Jersey Constitution of 1776 let them vote if they headed a household (usually as a widow) and paid taxes. This right was revoked in 1807.

Philosophers, clergymen, and even popular writers began treating women as morally superior to men. Especially in the Northeast, more women learned to read and write. By 1830 nearly all native-born women in the Northeast had become literate. The ideal of the "republican wife" and the "republican mother" took hold, giving wives and mothers an expanding educational role within the family. They encouraged diligence in their husbands and patriotism in their sons. The novel became a major cultural form in the United States. Its main audience

26. Women Voting in Late Eighteenth-Century New Jersey (Courtesy of *the Constitution* and Project '87)

WOMEN VOTING IN LATE 18TH CENTURY NEW JERSEY   Alone among the 13 states, the New Jersey constitution of 1776 permitted women to vote if they were the heads of their households, a category that included mostly widows. This privilege was revoked in 1807.

was female, as were many of the authors. Novels cast women as central characters and warned young women to beware of suitors motivated only by greed or lust.

WESTERN EXPANSION, DISCONTENT, AND CONFLICT WITH INDIANS

Westward expansion had continued during the Revolutionary War. With 30 axmen, Daniel Boone, a North Carolina hunter, hacked out the Wilderness Road from Cumberland Gap to the Kentucky bluegrass country in early 1775. The first settlers to arrive called Kentucky "the best poor-man's country" and claimed it should belong to those who tilled its soil, not to the speculative Transylvania Company, which claimed title to the land.

Although few Indians lived in Kentucky, it was the favorite hunting ground of the Shawnees and other nations. Their raids often prevented the settlers from planting crops. The settlers put up log cabins against the inside walls of large rectangular stockades, 10 feet high and built from oak logs. At each corner, a blockhouse with a protruding second story permitted the defenders to fire along the outside walls. Three of these "Kentucky stations" were built—at Boonesborough, St. Asaph, and Harrodsburg—and they withstood Indian attacks until late in the war.

Kentucky lived up to its old Indian reputation as the "dark and bloody ground." Only a few thousand settlers stuck it out until the war ended, but then they were joined by swarms of newcomers. Speculators and absentees were already trying to claim the best bluegrass land. The Federal Census of 1790 listed 74,000 settlers and slaves in Kentucky and about half that many in Tennessee, where the Cherokees had ceded a large tract after their defeat in 1776. These settlers thrived both because few Indians lived there and because British and Spanish raiders found it hard to reach them.

To the south and north, settlement was much riskier. After the war, Spain supplied arms and trade goods to Creeks, Cherokees, Choctaws, and Chickasaws willing to resist Georgia's attempt to settle its western lands. North of the Ohio River, Britain refused to withdraw its garrisons and traders from Niagara, Detroit, and a few other posts, even though, according to the Treaty of Paris, those forts now lay within the boundaries of the United States. To justify their refusal, the British pointed to the failure of Congress to honor America's obligations to loyalists and British creditors under the treaty.

During the Revolutionary War, many states and Congress had raised soldiers by promising them land after it was over, and now they needed Indian lands to fulfill these pledges. The few Indian nations that had supported the United States suffered the most. In the 1780s, after Joseph Brant led most of the Iroquois north to Canada, New York confiscated much of the land of the friendly Iroquois who stayed. South Carolina dispossessed the Catawbas of most of their ancestral lands. The states had a harder time seizing the land of hostile Indians, who usually had Spanish or British allies.

Secessionist movements arose in the 1780s when neither Congress nor eastern state governments seemed able to solve western problems. Some Tennessee settlers seceded from North Carolina and for a time maintained a separate state called Franklin. Separatist sentiment also ran strong in Kentucky. Even the settlers of western Pennsylvania thought of setting up on their own after Spain closed the Mississippi to American traffic in 1784. James Wilkinson explored the possibility of creating an independent republic west of the Appalachians under Spanish protection. When Congress refused to recognize Vermont's independence from New York, even the radical Green Mountain Boys sounded out Canadian officials about readmission to the British Empire as a separate province.

TOWARD EQUALITY: THE AFFECTIONATE FAMILY

Well into the 18th century, family portraits reflected the prevailing patriarchal values of British and colonial society. In Robert Feke's 1741 painting of *Isaac Royall and His Family* (top), notice that the figure of the New England father is elevated above other members of the household and is dressed more resplendently than anyone else.

This pattern changed dramatically in the Northeast after independence. In the 1849 *Portrait of the Haight Family,* the father and mother share equal elevation, but the mother, the keeper of domestic space, is closer to the viewer and more prominent. The oldest daughter, soon to be of marriageable age, has the most elevated position in the portrait, which suggests a family strongly oriented toward the welfare of its children. The classical statuary and the portrait in the background indicate taste and refinement.

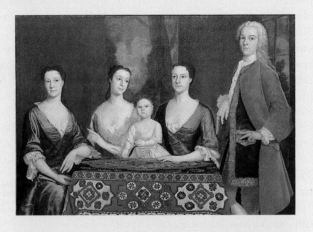

THE NORTHWEST ORDINANCE

Congress did, however, persuade states to cede to it their charter claims to land north of the Ohio River. Virginia's compliance in early 1781 prompted other states to follow suit. In the Land Ordinance of 1785, Congress authorized the survey of the Northwest Territory and its division into townships 6 miles square, each composed of 36 "sections" of 640 acres. Surveyed land would be sold at auction starting at a dollar an acre. Alternate townships would be sold in sections or as a whole, to satisfy settlers and speculators, respectively.

In July 1787, while the Constitutional Convention met in Philadelphia, Congress (sitting in New York) returned to the problem of governing the Northwest Territory. By then,

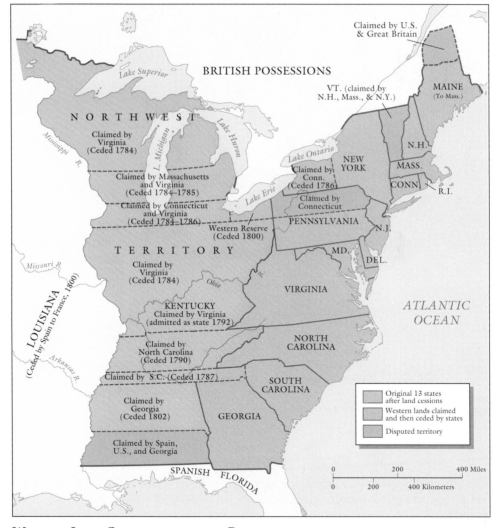

WESTERN LAND CLAIMS DURING THE REVOLUTION

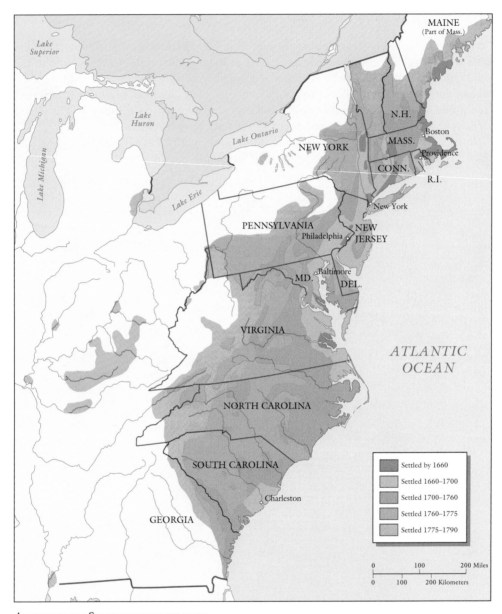

ADVANCE OF SETTLEMENT TO 1790

Massachusetts veterans were organizing the Ohio Company under Manassah Cutler to obtain a huge land grant from Congress. Cutler joined forces with William Duer, a New York speculator who was organizing the Scioto Company. Together they pried from Congress 1.5 million acres for the Ohio Company veterans and an option on 5 million more acres, which the Ohio Company assigned to the Scioto Company. The Ohio Company agreed to pay Congress two installments of $500,000 in depreciated securities. To meet the first payment, Duer's backers lent Cutler's $200,000. Once again speculators, rather than settlers, seemed to be winning the West.

In the same month Congress passed the Northwest Ordinance to provide government for the region. The ordinance authorized the creation of from 3 to 5 states, to be admitted to the Union as full equals of the original 13. The ordinance thus rejected colonialism among white people except as a temporary phase through which a "territory" would pass on its way to statehood. Congress would appoint a governor and a council to rule until population reached 5,000. At that point, the settlers could elect an assembly empowered to pass laws, although the governor had an absolute veto. When population reached 60,000, the settlers could adopt their own constitution and petition Congress for statehood. The ordinance protected civil liberties, made provision for public education, and prohibited slavery within the region.

Southern delegates all voted for the Northwest Ordinance despite its antislavery clause. They probably hoped that Ohio would become what Georgia had been in the 1730s, a society of armed free men able to protect vulnerable slave states, such as Kentucky, from hostile invaders. Southern delegates also thought that most settlers would come from Maryland, Virginia, and Kentucky. Even if they could not bring slaves with them, they would have southern loyalties. New Englanders, by contrast, were counting on the Ohio Company to lure their own veterans to the region.

Finally, the antislavery clause may have been part of a larger "Compromise of 1787," involving both the ordinance and the clauses on slavery in the federal Constitution. The Philadelphia Convention permitted states to count three-fifths of their slaves for purposes of representation. The antislavery concession to northerners in the ordinance was made at the same time that southern states won this concession in Philadelphia. Several congressmen were also delegates to the Constitutional Convention and traveled back and forth between the two cities while these decisions were being made. They may have struck a deal.

Congress had developed a coherent western policy. After 1787 only the Indians stood in the way. When the first townships in Ohio were offered for sale in late 1787, there were few buyers. Yet by 1789, the Ohio Company had established the town of Marietta, Kentuckians had founded a town that would soon be called Cincinnati, and tiny outposts had been set up at Columbia and Gallipolis. But without massive help from the new federal government, the settlers had little chance of defending themselves against the Indians.

A More Perfect Union

The 1780s were difficult times. The economy failed to rebound, debtors fought creditors, and state politics became bitter and contentious. Out of this ferment arose the demand to amend or even replace the Articles of Confederation.

Commerce, Debt, and Shays's Rebellion

In 1784 British merchants flooded American markets with exports worth £3.7 million, the greatest volume since 1771. But Americans could not pay for them. Exports to Britain that year were £750,000—less than half of the £1.9 million of 1774, the last year of peace. When Britain invoked the Navigation Acts to close the British West Indies to American ships (but not to American goods), indirect returns through this once profitable channel also faltered. Trade with France closed some of the gap, but because the French could not offer the long-term credit that the British had provided, it remained disappointing. The American economy entered a deep depression. Imports from Britain fell by 40 percent in 1785. Exports rose to almost £900,000 but remained far below prewar levels.

Private debts became a huge social problem. Merchants, dunned by British creditors, sued their customers, many of whom could not even pay their taxes. Farmers, faced with the loss of their crops, livestock, and even their farms, resisted foreclosures and looked to their state governments for relief.

About half of the states issued paper money in the 1780s, and many passed stay laws to postpone the date on which a debt would come due. Massachusetts rejected both options and raised taxes to new highs. In 1786 many farmers in Hampshire County took matters into their own hands. Crowds gathered to prevent the courts from conducting business. In early 1787 the protestors, loosely organized under a Continental Army veteran, Captain Daniel Shays, attacked the federal arsenal at Springfield. An army of volunteers under Benjamin Lincoln marched west with artillery and scattered the Shaysites. Yet, in the May assembly elections, Shaysites won enough seats to pass a stay law. In Massachusetts, Shays's Rebellion converted into nationalists many gentlemen and artisans who until then had opposed strengthening the central government.

COSMOPOLITANS VERSUS LOCALISTS

The tensions racking Massachusetts surfaced elsewhere as well. Crowds of debtors in other states closed law courts or even besieged the legislature. State politics reflected a persistent cleavage between "cosmopolitan" and "localist" coalitions. Merchants, urban artisans, commercial farmers, southern planters, and former Continental Army officers made up the cosmopolitan bloc. They looked to energetic government to solve their problems. They favored aggressive trade policies, hard money, payment of public debts, good salaries for executive officials and judges, and leniency to returning loyalists. The "localists" were farmers, rural artisans, and militia veterans who distrusted those policies. They demanded paper money and debtor relief. They supported generous salaries for representatives, so that ordinary men could serve, which cosmopolitans resisted.

In most states, localists defeated their opponents most of the time. During and after the war, they destroyed the feudal revival (see Chapter 5) by confiscating the gigantic land claims of the Granville District, the Fairfax estate, the Calvert and Penn proprietaries, and the manorial estates of New York loyalists. Except in Vermont, localists were much less adept at blocking the claims of land speculators. Yet cosmopolitans lost so often that many of them despaired of state politics and looked to a strengthened central government for relief.

Congress faced its own fiscal problems. Its annual income had fallen to $400,000 at a time when interest on its debt approached $2.5 million and when the principal on the foreign debt was about to come due. Requisitions were beginning to seem as hopelessly inefficient as George Grenville had proclaimed them to be when he proposed the Stamp Act.

Foreign relations also took an ominous turn. In 1786 Foreign Secretary John Jay negotiated a treaty with Don Diego de Gardoqui, the Spanish minister to the United States. It offered northern merchants trading privileges with Spanish colonies, in exchange for the closure of the Mississippi to American traffic for 25 years. Seven northern states voted for it, but all five southern states in Congress rejected these terms—thus defeating the treaty, which needed nine votes for ratification under the Articles of Confederation. Angry talk of disbanding the Union soon filled Congress. Delegates began haggling over which state would join what union if the breakup occurred. The quarrel became public in February 1787 when a Boston newspaper endorsed a dissolution of the Union.

By the mid-1780s many cosmopolitans were becoming nationalists eager to strengthen the Union. In 1785 some of them tried to see what could be done outside Congress. To resolve disputes about navigation rights on the Potomac River, Washington invited Virginia and Maryland delegates to a conference at Mount Vernon, where they drafted an agreement acceptable to both states and to Congress. Prompted by James Madison, a former congressman, the Virginia legislature urged all the states to participate in a convention at Annapolis to explore ways to improve American trade.

Four states, including Maryland, ignored the call, and the New Englanders had not yet arrived when, in September 1786, the delegates from the four middle states and Virginia accepted a report drafted by Alexander Hamilton of New York. It asked all of the states to send delegates to a convention at Philadelphia the next May "to devise such further provisions as shall appear to them necessary to render the constitution of the Federal Government adequate to the exigencies of the Union." Seven states responded positively before Congress endorsed the convention on February 21, 1787, and five accepted later. Rhode Island refused to participate. Madison used the winter months to study the defects of classical and European confederacies and to draft a plan for a stronger American union.

THE PHILADELPHIA CONVENTION

The convention opened in May 1787 with a plan similar to the Virginia constitution of 1776. It proposed an almost sovereign Parliament for the United States. By September the delegates had produced a document much closer to the Massachusetts constitution of 1780, with a clear separation of powers. The delegates, in four months of secret sessions, repeated the constitutional learning process that had taken four years at the state level after 1776.

With Washington presiding, Governor Edmund Randolph proposed the Virginia, or "large state," Plan. Drafted by Madison, it proposed a bicameral legislature, with representation in both houses apportioned according to population. The legislature would choose the executive and the judiciary. It would possess all powers currently lodged in Congress and the power "to legislate in all cases to which the separate States are incompetent." It could make "negative all laws passed by the several States, contravening in [its] opinion . . . the articles of Union." Remarkably, the plan did not include specific powers to tax or regulate trade. Madison apparently believed it wiser to be vague and sweeping, rather than explicit.

Within two weeks, the delegates agreed on three-year terms for members of the lower house and seven-year terms for the upper house. The legislature would choose the executive for a single term of seven years. But in mid-June delegates from the small states struck back. William Paterson proposed the New Jersey Plan, which gave the existing Congress the power to levy import duties and a stamp tax (as in Grenville's imperial reforms of 1764 and 1765), to regulate trade, and to use force to collect delinquent requisitions from the states (as Lord North had proposed in 1775). Each state would have one vote.

As another alternative, perhaps designed to terrify the small states, Hamilton suggested a government in which both the senate and the executive would serve "on good behavior"—that is, for life! To him, the British constitution still seemed the best in the world. But he never formally proposed his plan.

All the options before the convention seemed counterrevolutionary at that point. Madison's Parliament for America, Paterson's emulation of Grenville and North, and Hamilton's enthusiasm for the British Empire all challenged in major ways the principles of 1776. But as the summer progressed, the delegates asked themselves what the voters would or would not accept and relearned the hard lessons of popular sovereignty that the state constitutions had taught. The result was a federal Constitution that was indeed revolutionary.

Before the Constitution took its final shape, however, the debate grew as hot as the summer weather. The small states warned that their voters would never accept a constitution that let the large states swallow them. The large states insisted on proportional representation in both houses. Then the Connecticut delegates announced that they would be happy with proportional representation in one house and state equality in the other.

In July, the delegates accepted this "Connecticut Compromise" and then completed the document by September. They finally realized that they were creating a government of laws, to be enforced on individuals through federal courts, and were not propping up a system of congressional resolutions to be carried out (or ignored) by the states. Terms for representatives were reduced to two years, and terms for senators to six, with each state legislature choosing two senators. The president would serve four years, could be reelected, and would be chosen by an Electoral College. Each state received as many electors as it had congressmen and senators combined, and the states were free to decide how to choose their electors.

In other provisions, free and slave states agreed to count only three-fifths of the slaves in apportioning both representation and direct taxes. The enumeration of congressional powers became lengthy and explicit and included taxation, the regulation of foreign and interstate commerce, and the catchall "necessary and proper" clause. Madison's negative on state laws was replaced by the gentler "supreme law of the land" clause. Over George Mason's last-minute objection, the delegates voted not to include a bill of rights.

With little debate, the convention approved a revolutionary proposal for ratifying the Constitution. This clause called for special conventions in each state and declared that the Constitution would go into force as soon as any nine states had accepted it, even though the Articles of Confederation required unanimous approval for all amendments. The delegates were proposing an illegal but peaceful overthrow of the existing legal order—that is, a revolution. If all the states approved, it would, they hoped, become both peaceful and legal. The Constitution would then rest on popular sovereignty in a way that the Articles never had. The "Federalists," as supporters of the Constitution now called themselves, were willing to risk destroying the Union in order to save it.

RATIFICATION

When the Federalist delegates returned home, they made a powerful case for the Constitution in newspapers. Most "Anti-Federalists," or opponents of the Constitution, were localists with little access to the press. The first ratifying conventions met in December. Delaware ratified unanimously on December 7, Pennsylvania by a 46-to-23 vote five days later, and New Jersey unanimously on December 18. Georgia ratified unanimously on January 2, and Connecticut soon approved, also by a lopsided margin.

Except in Pennsylvania, these victories were in small states. Once they had equality in the senate, they saw many advantages in a strong central government. Under the new Constitution, import duties would go to the federal government, not to neighboring states, a clear gain for every small state but Rhode Island, which stood to lose import duties at both Providence and Newport.

By contrast, Pennsylvania was the only large state with a solid majority for ratification. But Anti-Federalists there eloquently demanded a federal bill of rights and major changes in the structure of the new government. Large states could think of going it alone. Small states could not—except for Rhode Island with its two cities and its long history of defying its neighbors.

The first hotly contested state was Massachusetts. Federalists there won by a slim margin (187 to 168) in February 1788. They blocked Anti-Federalist attempts to make ratification conditional on the adoption of specific amendments. Instead they promised to support a bill of rights by constitutional amendment after ratification. The Rhode Island legislature voted overwhelmingly not even to summon a ratifying convention. Maryland and South Carolina ratified easily in April and May, bringing the total to eight of the nine states required. Then conventions met almost simultaneously in New Hampshire, Virginia, New York, and North Carolina. In each, a majority at first opposed ratification.

As resistance stiffened, the ratification controversy turned into the first great debate on what kind of a national government America ought to have. The Anti-Federalists argued that the new government would be too remote from the people to be trusted with the broad powers specified in the Constitution. They warned that in a House of Representatives divided into districts of 30,000 people, only prominent and wealthy men would be elected and the new government would become an aristocracy or oligarchy. The absence of a bill of rights also troubled them.

During the struggle over ratification, Hamilton, Madison, and Jay wrote a series of 85 essays, published first in New York newspapers and widely reprinted elsewhere, in which they defended the Constitution almost clause by clause. Signing themselves "Publius," they later published the collected essays as *The Federalist.* In *Federalist No. Ten,* Madison argued that a large republic would be far more stable than a small one. He challenged 2,000 years of accepted wisdom, which insisted that only small republics could survive. Small republics were inherently unstable, Madison insisted, because majority factions could easily gain power within them, trample upon the rights of minorities, and ignore the common good. But in a republic as huge and diverse as the United States, factions would seldom be able to forge a majority. "Publius" hoped that the new government would draw on the talents of the wisest and the best-educated citizens. To those who accused him of trying to erect an American aristocracy, he pointed out that the Constitution forbade titles and hereditary rule.

Federalists won a narrow majority (57 to 46) in New Hampshire on June 21, and Madison guided Virginia to ratification (89 to 79) five days later. New York approved, by 30 votes to 27, a month later, bringing 11 states into the Union, enough to launch the new government. North Carolina rejected the Constitution in July 1788 but finally ratified in November 1789 after the first Congress had drafted the Bill of Rights and sent it to the states. Rhode Island, after voting seven times not to call a ratifying convention, finally summoned one that ratified by a vote of only 34 to 32 in May 1790.

CONCLUSION

Americans survived the most devastating war they had yet fought and won their independence, but only with massive aid from France. Most blacks and Indians sided with Britain. During the struggle white Americans affirmed liberty and equality for themselves in their new state constitutions and bills of rights, but they rarely applied these values to blacks and Indians, even though every northern state adopted either immediate or gradual emancipation. The discontent of the postwar years created the Federalist coalition, which drafted and ratified a new national Constitution to replace the Articles of Confederation. Federalists endowed the new central government with more power than Parliament had ever successfully exercised

CHRONOLOGY

1775	Settlement of Kentucky begins
1776	Virginia becomes first state to adopt a permanent constitution and bill of rights • British forces land on Staten Island • Declaration of Independence adopted • Pennsylvania constitution creates unicameral legislature • British win battle of Long Island; New York City falls • Washington wins at Trenton
1777	Washington wins at Princeton • Howe takes Philadelphia • Burgoyne surrenders at Saratoga • Congress completes the Articles of Confederation
1778	Franco-American alliance negotiated
1779	Indians form confederation from the Gulf to the Great Lakes • Spain declares war on Britain • Continental dollar collapses
1780	Massachusetts constitution approved • Pennsylvania adopts gradual emancipation • British take Charleston and overrun South Carolina • Gordon riots in London discredit other reformers • Arnold's treason uncovered • Americans win at King's Mountain
1781	Continental Army mutinies • Americans win at Cowpens • Congress creates executive departments • Articles of Confederation ratified • Cornwallis surrenders at Yorktown
1782	Gnadenhutten massacre leaves 100 unarmed Indians dead
1783	Peace of Paris recognizes American independence
1785	Congress passes Land Ordinance
1786	Annapolis convention meets • Virginia passes Statute for Religious Freedom
1786–1787	Shays's Rebellion in Massachusetts protests taxes and economic woes
1787	Congress passes the Northwest Ordinance • Philadelphia Convention drafts a new federal Constitution
1787–1788	Eleven states ratify the Constitution
1789	First federal Congress sends Bill of Rights to the states
1799	New York adopts gradual emancipation
1804	New Jersey adopts gradual emancipation

over the colonies but insisted that the Constitution was fully compatible with the liberty and equality proclaimed during the Revolution.

Nothing resembling the American federal system had ever been tried before. Under this new system, sovereignty was removed from government and bestowed on the people, who then empowered separate levels of government through their state and federal constitutions. As the Great Seal of the United States proclaimed, it was a *novus ordo seclorum,* a new order for the ages.

THE DEMOCRATIC REPUBLIC, 1790–1820

In 1789 Americans were an overwhelmingly rural people. Some were planters who sent crops onto world markets. Most, however, owned small farms. Whatever their level of prosperity, most households in the American countryside were headed by men who owned land, and who enjoyed the liberty and civil equality for which they had fought the Revolution. They also wielded power—both as citizens and as governors of families that included their wives, children, slaves, and other dependents.

In the first 30 years of government under the Constitution the Americans consolidated their republic and seized opportunities to expand their commerce with a war-torn Europe. In these years their population shot from 4 million to 10 million persons; their agrarian republic spilled across the Appalachians and reached the Mississippi River; their exports rose; and their seaport towns became cities. In the midst of this rapid change, increasing thousands of white men found it hard to maintain their status as propertied citizens or to pass that status on to new generations; others simply grew impatient with the responsibilities and limits of rural patriarchy. The resultant erosion of authority encouraged women, slaves, and the growing ranks of propertyless white men to imagine that the revolutionary birthrights of liberty and equality—perhaps even power—might also belong to them. By 1820 the agrarian republic, with its promise of widespread proprietorship and well-ordered paternal authority, was in deep trouble. A more individualistic, democratic, and insecure order was taking its place.

THE FARMER'S REPUBLIC

In 1782 J. Hector St. John de Crèvecoeur, a French soldier who had settled in rural New York, explained American agrarianism through the words of a fictionalized farmer. First of all, he said, the American farmer owns his own land and bases his claim to dignity and citizenship on that fact: "This formerly rude soil has been converted by my father into a pleasant farm, and in return, it has established all our rights; on it is founded our rank, our freedom, our power as citizens, our importance as inhabitants of [a rural neighborhood]...." Second, farm ownership endows the American farmer with the powers and responsibilities of fatherhood: "I am now doing for [my son] what my father did for me; may God enable him to live that he may perform the same operations for the same purposes when I am worn out and old!"

Crèvecouer's farmer was a proud citizen of America's revolutionary republic. From New England through the mid-Atlantic and on into the southern Piedmont and backcountry, few farmers in 1790 thought of farming as a business. Their first concern was to provide a subsistence for their households. Their second was to achieve long-term security and the ability to pass their farm on to their sons. The goal was to create what rural folks called a "competence": the ability to live up to neighborhood standards of material decency while protecting the long-term independence of their household—and thus the dignity and political rights of its head. Most of these farmers raised a variety of animals and plants, ate most of what they grew, traded much of the rest within their neighborhoods, and sent small surpluses into outside markets.

The world's hunger for American food, however, was growing. West Indian and European markets for American meat and grain expanded dramatically between 1793 and 1815, when war disrupted farming in Europe. American farmers took advantage of these markets, but most continued to rely on family and neighbors for subsistence, and risked little by sending increased surpluses overseas. Thus they profited from world markets without becoming dependent on them.

HOUSEHOLDS

Production for overseas markets did, however, alter relationships within rural households. Farm labor in postrevolutionary America was carefully divided by sex. Men worked in the fields, and production for markets both intensified that labor and made it more exclusively male. In the grain fields, for instance, the long-handled scythe was replacing the sickle as the principal harvest tool. Women could use the sickle efficiently, but the long, heavy scythe was designed to be wielded by men. At the same time, farmers completed the substitution of plows for hoes as the principal cultivating tools—not only because plows worked better but because rural Americans had developed a prejudice against women working in the fields.

At the same time, household responsibilities fell more exclusively to women. It was farm women's labor and ingenuity that helped create a more varied and nutritious rural diet in these years. Bread and salted meat were still the staples. The bread was the old mix of Indian corn and coarse wheat. A variety of other foods were now available, however. By the 1790s, improved winter feeding for cattle and better techniques for making and storing butter and cheese kept dairy products on the tables of the more prosperous farm families throughout the year. Chickens became more common, and farm women began to plant potatoes, turnips, cabbages, squashes, beans, and other vegetables that could be stored.

RURAL INDUSTRY

Industrial outwork provided many farmers with another means of protecting their independence. From the 1790s onwards, city merchants provided country workers with raw materials and paid them for finished shoes, furniture, cloth, brooms, and other handmade goods. In Marple, Pennsylvania, a farming town near Philadelphia, fully one-third of households were engaged in weaving, furniture making, and other household industry in the 1790s.

Most of the outwork was taken on by large, relatively poor families, with the work organized in ways that shored up the authority of fathers. When New Hampshire women and girls fashioned hats, for example, the accounts were kept in the name of the husband or father. In general, household industry was part-time work performed only by the dependent women and children of the household. And when it was the family's principal means of support, the work was arranged in ways that supported traditional notions of fatherhood and proprietorship. In eastern Massachusetts in the 1790s, for instance, when thousands of farmers on small plots of worn-out land became household shoemakers, skilled men cut the leather and shaped the uppers, while the more menial tasks of sewing and binding were left to the women.

Neighbors

Few farmers possessed the tools, the labor, and the food they would have needed to be truly independent. They regularly worked for one another, borrowed oxen and plows, and swapped surpluses of one kind of food for another. Women traded ashes, herbs, butter and eggs, vegetables, seedlings, baby chicks, goose feathers, and the products of their spinning wheels and looms. Some cooperative undertakings—house and barn-raisings and husking bees, for example—brought the whole neighborhood together, transforming a chore into a pleasant social event.

Few neighborhood transactions called for the use of money. In New England, farmers kept careful accounts of neighborhood debts. In the South and West, on the other hand, farmers used a "changing system" in which they simply remembered what they owed. Yet farmers everywhere relied more on barter than on cash. A French visitor noted that "[Americans] supply their needs in the countryside by direct reciprocal exchanges. The tailor and the bootmaker go and do their work at the home of the farmer . . . who most frequently provides the raw material for it and pays for the work in goods. They write down what they give and receive on both sides, and at the end of the year they settle a large variety of exchanges with a very small quantity of coin." The result was an elaborate network of neighborhood debt, which was part of a highly structured and absolutely necessary system of neighborly cooperation.

Inheritance

After 1790 overcrowding and the growth of markets caused the price of good farmland to rise sharply throughout the older settlements. Most young men could expect to inherit only a few acres of exhausted land, or to move to wilderness land in the backcountry. Failing those, they would quit farming altogether.

In Revolutionary America, fathers had been judged by their ability to support and govern their households, to serve as good neighbors, and to pass land on to their sons. After the war, fewer farm fathers were able to do that. Those in the old settlements had small farms and large families, which made it impossible for them to provide a competence for all their offspring. Sons, with no prospect of an adequate inheritance, were obliged to leave home. Most fathers tried valiantly to provide for all their heirs (generally by leaving land to their sons and personal property to their daughters). Few left all their land to one son, and many stated in their wills that the sons to whom they left the land must share barns and cider mills—even the house—on farms that could be subdivided no further.

Outside New England, farm tenancy was on the increase. Farmers often bought farms when they became available in the neighborhood, rented them to tenants, and then gave them to their sons when they reached adulthood. The sons of poorer farmers often rented a farm in the hope of saving enough money to buy it. Some fathers bought tracts of unimproved land in the backcountry—sometimes on speculation, more often to provide their sons with land they could make into a farm. Others paid to have their sons educated, or arranged an apprenticeship to provide them with an avenue of escape from a declining countryside. As a result, more and more young men left home. The populations of the old farming communities grew older and more female, while the populations of the rising frontier settlements and seaport cities became younger and more male.

STANDARDS OF LIVING

The rise of markets in the late 18th and early 19th centuries improved living standards for some families but not for all. Most farmhouses in the older rural areas were small, one-story structures. Few farmers, especially in the South and West, bothered to keep their surroundings clean or attractive. They repaired their fences only when they became too dilapidated to function. They rarely planted trees or shrubs, and housewives threw out garbage to feed the chickens and pigs that foraged near the house.

Inside, there were few rooms and many people. Beds stood in every room, and few family members slept alone. The hearth remained the source of heat and light in most farmhouses.

THE DINING ROOM OF DR. WHITBRIDGE, A RHODE ISLAND COUNTRY DOCTOR, CIRCA 1815
It is a comfortable, neatly furnished room, but there is little decoration, and the doctor must sit near the fire in layered clothing to ward off the morning chill.

One of the great disparities between wealthy families and their less affluent neighbors was that the wealthy families could light their houses at night. Another disparity was in the outward appearance of houses. The wealthier families painted their houses white as a token of pristine republicanism. But their bright houses stood apart from the weathered gray-brown clapboard siding of their neighbors in stark and unrepublican contrast.

Some improvements emerged in personal comfort. As time passed more beds had mattresses stuffed with feathers. At mealtimes, only the poorest families continued to eat with their fingers or with spoons from a common bowl. By 1800 individual place settings with knives and forks and china plates, along with chairs instead of benches, had become common in rural America. Although only the wealthiest families had upholstered furniture, ready-made chairs were widely available, and clocks appeared in the more prosperous rural households.

FROM BACKCOUNTRY TO FRONTIER

The United States was a huge country in 1790, but most white Americans were still living on a thin strip of settlement along the Atlantic coast and along the few navigable rivers that emptied into the Atlantic. Some were pushing their way into the wilds of Maine and northern Vermont, and in New York they had set up communities as far west as the Mohawk valley. Pittsburgh was a struggling new settlement, and two outposts had been established on the Ohio River—at Marietta and at what would become Cincinnati. Farther south, farmers had occupied the Piedmont lands up to the eastern slope of the Appalachians and were spilling through the Cumberland Gap into the new lands of Kentucky and Tennessee. But north of the Ohio River the Shawnee, Miami, Delaware, and Potawatomie nations, along with smaller tribes, controlled nearly all the land. To the south, the "Five Civilized Tribes" still occupied much of their ancestral land. Taken together, Indian peoples occupied most of the land that treaties and maps showed as the interior of the United States.

THE DESTRUCTION OF THE WOODLANDS INDIANS

Though many of the woodland tribes were still intact and still living on their ancestral lands in 1790, they were in serious trouble. The members of the old Iroquois Federation had been restricted to reservations in New York and Pennsylvania; many had fled to Canada. The once-powerful Cherokees had been severely punished for fighting on the side of the British during the Revolution and by 1790 had ceded three-fourths of their territory to the Americans.

In the Old Northwest, the Shawnee, Miami, and other tribes—with the help of the British who still occupied seven forts within what was formally the United States—continued to trade furs and to impede white settlement. Skirmishes with settlers, however, brought reprisals, and the Indians faced not only hostile pioneers but the United States Army as well. In the Ohio country, expeditions led by General Josiah Harmar and General Arthur St. Clair failed in 1790 and 1791. In 1794 President Washington sent a third army, under General "Mad Anthony" Wayne, which defeated the Indians at Fallen Timbers, near present-day Toledo. The Treaty of Greenville forced the Native Americans to cede two-thirds of what now makes up Ohio and southeastern Indiana. It was at this point that the British decided to abandon their forts in the Old Northwest. Whites filtered into what remained of Indian lands.

Relegated to smaller territory but still dependent on the European fur trade, the natives of the Northwest now fell into competition with settlers and other Indians for the diminishing supply of game. The Creeks, Choctaws, and other tribes of the Old Southwest faced the same problem: Even when they chased settlers out of their territory, the settlers managed to kill or scare off the deer and other wildlife, thus ruining the old hunting grounds. When the Shawnee sent hunting parties farther west, they were opposed by western Indians. The Choctaws also sent hunters across the Mississippi, where they found new sources of furs, along with the angry warriors of the Osage and other peoples of Louisiana and Arkansas.

Faced with shrinking territories, the disappearance of wildlife, and diminished opportunities to be traditional hunters and warriors, many Indian societies sank into despair. Epidemics of European diseases (smallpox, influenza, measles) attacked peoples who were increasingly sedentary and vulnerable. Murder and clan revenge plagued the tribes, and depression and suicide became more common. The use of alcohol, which had been a scourge on Indian societies for two centuries, increased.

THE FAILURE OF CULTURAL RENEWAL

Out of this cultural wreckage emerged visionary leaders who spoke of a regenerated native society and the expulsion of all whites from the old tribal lands. One of the first was Chief Alexander McGillivray, a mixed-blood Creek who had sided with the British during the Revolution. Between 1783 and 1793, McGillivray tried to unite the Creeks under a national council that could override local chiefs, and to form alliances with other tribes and with Spanish Florida. McGillivray's premature death in 1793 prevented the realization of his vision.

The Cherokees north and east of the Creeks did succeed in making a unified state. Angered by the willingness of village chiefs to be bribed and flattered into selling land, a group of young chiefs staged a revolt between 1808 and 1810. Previously, being a Cherokee had meant loyalty to one's clan and kin group and adherence to the tribe's ancient customs. Now it meant remaining on the tribe's ancestral land (migration across the Mississippi was regarded as treason) and unquestioning acceptance of the laws, courts, and police controlled by the national council.

Among the many prophets who emerged during these years, the one who came closest to military success was Tenskwatawa, a fat, one-eyed, alcoholic Shawnee. When he went into a deep trance in 1805, the people thought he was dead and prepared his funeral. But he awoke and told them he had visited heaven and hell and had received a prophetic vision. First, all the Indians must stop drinking and fighting among themselves. They must also return to their traditional food, clothing, tools, and hairstyles, and must extinguish all their fires and start new ones without using European tools. All who opposed the new order (including local chiefs, medicine men, shamans, and witches) must be put down by force. When all that had been done, God (a monotheistic, punishing God borrowed from the Christians) would restore the world that Indians had known before the whites came over the mountains.

Tenskwatawa's message soon found its way to the native peoples of the Northwest. When converts flooded into the prophet's home village, he moved to Prophetstown (Tippecanoe) in what is now Indiana. There, with the help of his brother Tecumseh, he created an army estimated by the whites at anywhere between 650 and 3,000 warriors, and pledged to end further encroachment by whites. Tecumseh, who took control of the movement, announced to the whites that he was the sole chief of all the Indians north of the Ohio River; land cessions by anyone else would be invalid.

TENSKWATAWA The Shawnee prophet Tenskwatawa ("The Open Door"), brother of Tecumseh, was painted by George Catlin in 1836—long after the defeat of his prophetic attempt to unify Native America.

Tecumseh's confederacy posed a threat to the United States. A second war with England was looming, and Tecumseh was receiving supplies and encouragement from the British in Canada. He was also planning to visit the southern tribes in an attempt to bring them into his confederacy. The prospect of unified resistance by the western tribes in league with the British jeopardized every settler west of the Appalachians. In 1811 William Henry Harrison led an army toward Prophetstown. With Tecumseh away, Tenskwatawa ordered an unwise attack on Harrison's army and was beaten at the Battle of Tippecanoe.

Tecumseh's still-formidable confederacy, joined by the traditionalist wing of the southern Creeks, fought alongside the British in the War of 1812 and lost (see Chapter 8). With that, the military power of the Indians east of the Mississippi River was destroyed. General Andrew Jackson forced the Creeks (including those who had served as his allies) to cede millions of acres of land in Georgia and Alabama. The other southern tribes, along with the members of Tecumseh's northern confederacy, watched helplessly as new settlers took over their hunting lands. Some of the Indians moved west, and others tried to farm what was left of their old land. All of them had to deal with settlers and government officials who neither feared them nor took their sovereignty seriously.

THE BACKCOUNTRY, 1790–1815

To easterners, the backcountry whites who were displacing the Indians were no different from the defeated aborigines. Indeed, in accommodating themselves to a borderless forest used by both Indians and whites, many settlers had melded Indian and white ways. To clear the land, backcountry farmers simply girdled the trees and left them to die and fall down by themselves. Then they ploughed the land by navigating between the stumps. Like the Indians, backcountry whites depended on game for food and animal skins for trade. And like the Indians, they often spent long periods away on hunting trips, leaving the women to tend the fields.

Eastern visitors were appalled not only by the poverty, lice, and filth of frontier life but by the drunkenness and violence of the frontiersmen. Travel accounts tell of no-holds-barred fights in which frontiersmen gouged the eyes and bit off the noses and ears of their opponents. Stories arose of half-legendary heroes like Davy Crockett of Tennessee, who wrestled bears and alligators, and Mike Fink, a Pennsylvania boatman who brawled and drank his way along the rivers of the interior until he was shot and killed in a drunken episode. Samuel Holden Parsons, a New Englander serving as a judge in the Northwest Territory, called the frontiersmen "our white savages."

After 1789 settlers of the western backcountry made two demands of the new national government: protection from the Indians and a guarantee of the right to navigate the Ohio and Mississippi Rivers. The Indians were pushed back in the 1790s and finished off in the War of 1812, and in 1803 Jefferson's Louisiana Purchase (see Chapter 8) ended the European presence on the rivers. Over these years the pace of settlement quickened. In 1790 only 10,000 settlers were living west of the Appalachians—about 1 American in 40. By 1820, 2 million Americans were westerners–1 in 5.

The new settlers bought land, built frame houses surrounded by cleared fields, planted marketable crops, and settled into the struggle to make farms out of the wilderness. By 1803 four frontier states had entered the union: Vermont (1791), Kentucky (1792), Tennessee (1796), and Ohio (1803). Louisiana soon followed (1812), and with the end of the war in 1815 one frontier state after another gained admission: Indiana (1816), Mississippi (1817), Illinois (1818), Alabama (1818), Maine (1820), and Missouri (1821).

As time passed, the term "backcountry," which easterners had used to refer to the wilderness, fell into disuse. By 1820 the term "frontier" had replaced it. The new settlements were no longer in the backwash of American civilization. They were on its cutting edge.

THE PLANTATION SOUTH, 1790–1820

In 1790 the future of slavery in the Chesapeake was uncertain. The tobacco market had been precarious since before the Revolution. Tobacco depleted the soil, and by the late 18th century tidewater farms and plantations were giving out. As lands west of the Appalachians were opened to settlement, white tenants, laborers, and small farmers left the Chesapeake in droves. Many of them moved to Kentucky, Tennessee, or the western reaches of Virginia. But many others found new homes in nonslave states north of the Ohio River.

SLAVERY AND THE REPUBLIC

With slave labor becoming less necessary, Chesapeake planters continued to switch to grain and livestock. Some planters divided their land into small plots and rented both the plots and

their slaves to white tenant farmers. Others hired out their slaves as artisans and urban laborers. These solutions, however, could not employ the great mass of slaves or repay the planters'
huge investment in slave labor.

In this situation many Chesapeake planters began to manumit their slaves. The farmers of
Maryland and Delaware in particular set their slaves free. Virginia's economic and cultural
commitment to the plantation was stronger, but there was a strong movement to manumit
slaves there as well. George Washington manumitted his slaves by will. Robert Carter, reput-
edly the largest slaveholder in Virginia, also freed his slaves, as did many others.

There were, however, limits on the manumission of Virginia slaves. First, few planters could
afford to free their slaves without compensation. Second, white Virginians feared the social
consequences of black freedom. Thomas Jefferson, for instance, owned 175 slaves when he
penned the phrase that "all men are created equal." He lived off their labor, sold them to pay
his debts, gave them as gifts, and sometimes sold them away from their families as a punishment. Through it all he insisted that slavery was wrong. He could not imagine emancipation,
however, without the colonization of freed slaves far from Virginia. A society of free blacks
and whites, Jefferson insisted, would end in disaster.

THE RECOMMITMENT TO SLAVERY

Jefferson's dilemma was eased by the rise of cotton cultivation further south. British industrialization created a demand for cotton from the 1790s onward, and planters knew they could
sell all the cotton they could grow. But long-staple cotton, the only variety that could be profitably grown, was a delicate plant that thrived only on the Sea Islands off Georgia and South

DISTRIBUTION OF SLAVE POPULATION, 1790–1820

Carolina. The short-staple variety was hardier, but its sticky seeds had to be removed by hand before the cotton could be milled.

In 1793 Eli Whitney, a Connecticut Yankee who had come south to work as a tutor, set his mind to the problem. Within a few days he had made a model of a cotton "gin" (a southern contraction of "engine") that combed the seeds from the fiber with metal pins fitted into rollers. Working with Whitney's machine, a slave could clean 50 pounds of short-staple cotton in a day. At a stroke, cotton became the great American cash crop and plantation agriculture was rejuvenated.

Short-staple cotton grew well in the hot, humid climate and the long growing season of the Lower South, and it grew almost anywhere. It was also a labor-intensive crop that could be grown in either small or large quantities; farmers with few or no slaves could make a decent profit, and planters with extensive land and many slaves could make enormous amounts of money. Best of all, the factories of England and, eventually, of the American Northeast, had a seemingly insatiable appetite for southern cotton.

The result was the rejuvenation of plantation slavery and its rapid spread into the new cotton-growing regions of the South. Meanwhile, Chesapeake planters sold their excess slaves to planters in the cotton frontier. After 1810, most of the slaves who left Virginia were commodities in the burgeoning interstate slave trade, headed for the new plantations of Georgia, Alabama, and Mississippi.

The movement of slaves out of the Chesapeake was immense. In the 1790s about 1 in 12 Virginia and Maryland slaves was taken south and west. The figure rose to 1 in 10 between 1800 and 1810, and to 1 in 5 between 1810 and 1820. In 1790 planters in Virginia and Maryland had owned 56 percent of all American slaves; by 1860 they owned only 15 percent. The demand for slaves in the new cotton lands had thus provided many Chesapeake planters with a means of disposing of an endangered investment and with cash to pay for their transition to new crops.

The other region that had been a center of slavery during the 18th century—coastal South Carolina and Georgia—made a massive recommitment to slave labor in the years after the Revolution. There the principal crop was rice, which was experiencing a sharp rise in international demand. For their secondary crop, most planters in this region were switching from indigo (a source of blue dye) to cotton, creating an increase in the demand for slaves. With slave prices rising and slave-produced crops becoming steadily more profitable, they rushed to import as many African slaves as they could before the African slave trade ended in 1808. Between 1788 and 1808, some 250,000 slaves were brought directly from Africa to the United States—nearly all of them to Charleston and Savannah.

RACE, GENDER, AND CHESAPEAKE LABOR

The transition to grain and livestock raising in the Chesapeake and the rise of the cotton belt in the Lower South imposed new kinds of labor upon the slaves. Wheat cultivation, for example, meant a switch from the hoes used for tobacco to the plow and grain cradle—both of which called for the upper-body strength of adult men. The grain economy also required carts, wagons, mills, and good roads, and thus created a need for greater numbers of slave artisans—nearly all of whom were men. Many of these were hired out to urban employers. In the diversifying economy of the Chesapeake, male slaves did the plowing, mowing, sowing, ditching, and carting and performed most of the tasks requiring artisanal skills.

An Overseer Doing His Duty In 1798 the architect and engineer Benjamin Latrobe sketched a white overseer smoking a cigar and supervising slave women as they hoed newly cleared farmland near Fredricksburg, Virginia. A critic of slavery, Latrobe sarcastically entitled the sketch *An Overseer Doing His Duty.*

Slave women were left with all the lesser tasks. A few of them were assigned to such chores as cloth manufacture, sewing, candle molding, and the preparation of salt meat. But most female slaves still did farm work—hoeing, weeding, spreading manure, cleaning stables—that was monotonous, called for little skill, and was closely supervised. This new division of labor was clearly evident during the wheat harvest. On George Washington's farm, for example, male slaves, often working alongside temporary white laborers, moved in a broad line as they mowed the grain. Following them came a gang of children and women bent over and moving along on their hands and knees as they bound wheat into shocks.

THE LOWLAND TASK SYSTEM

On the rice and cotton plantations of South Carolina and Georgia, planters faced different labor problems. Slaves made up 80 percent of the population in this region. Farms were large, and the two principal crops demanded skilled, intensive labor. The environment encouraged deadly summer diseases and kept white owners and overseers out of the fields. Planters solved these problems by organizing slaves according to the so-called "task system." Each morning the owner or overseer assigned a specific task to each slave, and allowed him to work at his own pace. When the task was done, the rest of the day belonged to the slave. Slaves who did not finish their task were punished, and when too many slaves finished early the owners assigned heavier tasks.

The task system encouraged slaves to work hard without supervision, and they turned the system to their own uses. Often several slaves would work together, until all their tasks were completed. And strong young slaves would sometimes help older and weaker slaves after they had finished their own tasks. Once the day's work was done, the slaves would share their hard-earned leisure out of sight of the owner.

Slaves under the task system won the right to cultivate land as "private fields"—farms of up to 5 acres on which they grew produce and raised livestock for market. There was a lively trade in slave-produced goods, and by the late 1850s slaves in the low-country not only produced and exchanged property but passed it on to their children. The owners tolerated such activity because slaves on the task system worked hard, required minimal supervision, and made money for their owners.

THE SEAPORT CITIES, 1790–1815

When the first federal census takers made their rounds in 1790, they found that 94 percent of the population was living on farms and in rural villages. The remaining 6 percent lived in the 24 towns that had populations of more than 2,500. Only five communities had a population over 10,000: Boston (18,038), New York (33,131), Philadelphia (42,444), Baltimore (13,503), and Charleston (16,359). All five were seaport cities.

COMMERCE

These cities had grown steadily during the 18th century, handling imports from Europe and farm exports from America. With the outbreak of war between Britain and France in 1793, the overseas demand for American foodstuffs and for shipping to carry products from the Caribbean islands to Europe further strengthened the seaport cities. Foreign trade during these years was risky and uneven. French seizures of American shipping and the resulting un-declared war of 1798–1800, the British ban on America's reexport trade in 1805, Jefferson's importation ban of 1806 and his trade embargo of 1807, and America's entry into war in 1812 all disrupted the maritime economy. But by 1815, it was clear that wartime commerce had transformed the seaports and the institutions of American business. New York City had become the nation's largest city, with a population of 96,373 in 1810. Philadelphia's population had risen to 53,722; Boston's to 34,322; and Baltimore's to 46,555.

Seaport merchants in these years amassed huge personal fortunes. To manage those fortunes, new institutions emerged. Docking and warehousing facilities expanded dramatically. Bookkeepers were replaced by accountants familiar with the new double-entry system of accounting, and insurance and banking companies were formed to handle the risks and rewards of wartime commerce.

The bustle of prosperity was evident on the waterfronts and principal streets of the seaport cities. An Englishman who visited the New York City docks during the wartime boom left this description:

> The carters were driving in every direction; and the sailors and labourers upon the wharfs, and on-boards the vessels, were moving their ponderous burdens from place to place. The merchants and their clerks were busily engaged in their counting-houses, or upon the piers. The Tontine coffee-

house was filled with underwriters, brokers, merchants, traders, and politicians. . . . The steps and balcony of the coffee-house were crowded with people bidding, or listening to the several auction-eers, who had elevated themselves upon a hogshead of sugar, a puncheon of rum, or a bale of cot-ton. . . . Everything was in motion; all was life, bustle, and activity.

POVERTY

Away from the waterfront, the main thoroughfares and a few of the side streets were paved with cobblestones and lined with fine shops and townhouses. But in other parts of the cities, visitors learned that the boom was creating unprecedented poverty as well as wealth. A few steps off the handsome avenues were narrow streets crowded with ragged children, browsing dogs, pigs, horses, and cattle, with garbage and waste filling the open sewers. Epidemics had become more frequent and deadly. New York City, for example, experienced six severe epidemics of yellow fever between 1791 and 1822.

The slums were evidence that money created by commerce was being distributed in undemocratic ways. Per capita wealth in New York rose 60 percent between 1790 and 1825, but the wealthiest 4 percent of the population owned more than half of that wealth. The wages of skilled and unskilled labor rose in these years, but the increase in seasonal and temporary employment, together with the recurring interruptions of foreign commerce, cut deeply into the security and prosperity of ordinary women and men.

THE STATUS OF LABOR

Meanwhile, the status of artisans in the big cities was undergoing change. In 1790, indepen-dent artisans demanded and usually received the respect of their fellow citizens. Artisans con-stituted about half the male workforce of the seaport cities, and their respectability and usefulness, together with the role they had played in the Revolution (see Chapter 6), had earned them an honorable status.

That status rested in large part on their independence. In 1790 most artisan workshops had been household operations with at most one or two apprentices and hired journeymen, who looked forward to owning their own shops one day. Most master craftsmen lived modestly (on the borderline of poverty in many cases) and aspired only to the ability to support their household in security and decency. They identified their way of life with republican virtue.

As in the countryside, however, the patriarchal base of that republicanism was being eroded. Accompanying the growth of the maritime economy was a change in the nature of construction work, shipbuilding, the clothing trades, and other specialized crafts. Artisans were being replaced by cheaper labor and were being undercut by subcontracted "slop work" performed by semiskilled outworkers. Perhaps one in five master craftsmen entered the newly emerging business class. The others took work as laborers or journeymen (the term for wage-earning craftsmen). By 1815 most young craftsmen could no longer hope to own their own shops. In the seaport cities between 1790 and 1820, the world of artisans like Paul Revere, Ben-jamin Franklin, and Thomas Paine was passing out of existence and was being replaced by wage labor.

The loss of independence undermined the paternal status of artisan husbands and fathers. As wage earners few could support their family unless the wife and children earned money to augment family income. Working-class women took in boarders and did laundry and found work as domestic servants or as peddlers of fruit, candy, vegetables, cakes, or hot corn. The descent into wage labor and the reliance on the earnings of women and children violated the republican, patriarchal assumptions of fathers.

THE ASSAULT ON AUTHORITY

In the 50 years following the Declaration of Independence, the patriarchal republic created by the Founding Fathers became a democracy. Most Americans witnessed the initial stirrings of change as a withering of paternal authority in their own households. For some—slaves and many women in particular—the decline of patriarchy could be welcomed. For others (the fathers themselves, disinherited sons, and women who looked to the security of old ways) it was a disaster of unmeasured proportions. But whether they experienced the transformation as a personal rise or fall, Americans by the early 19th century had entered a world where received authority and the experience of the past had lost their power.

PATERNAL POWER IN DECLINE

From the mid-18th century onward, especially after the Revolution, many young people grew up knowing that their father would be unable to help them, and that they would have to make their own way in the world. The consequent decline of parental power became evident in many ways—perhaps most poignantly in changing patterns of courtship and marriage. In the countryside, young men knew that they would not inherit the family farm, and young women knew that their father would be able to provide only a small dowry. As a result, fathers had less control over marriage choices than they had had when marriage was accompanied by a significant transfer of property. Young people now courted away from parental scrutiny and made choices based on affection and personal attraction rather than on property or parental pressure. One sign of the independence of young people (and of their lack of faith in their future) was the high number of pregnancies outside of marriage. In the second half of the 18th century and in the first decades of the 19th, the number of first births that occurred within eight months of marriage averaged between 25 and 30 percent—with the rates running much higher among poor couples.

THE ALCOHOLIC REPUBLIC

The erosion of the old family economy was paralleled by a dramatic rise in alcohol consumption. Americans had been drinking alcohol since the time of the first settlements. But drinking, like everything else that was "normal," took place within a structure of paternal authority. Americans tippled every day in the course of their ordinary activities: at family meals and around the fireside, at work, and at barn-raisings, militia musters, dances, weddings, funerals—even at the ordination of ministers. Under such circumstances, drinking—even drunkenness—seldom posed a threat to authority or to the social order.

That old pattern of communal drinking persisted into the 19th century. But during the 50 years following the Revolution it gradually gave way to a new pattern. Farmers, particularly those in newly settled areas, regularly produced a surplus of grain that they turned into

INTERIOR OF AN AMERICAN INN, 1813   In this democratic, neighborly scene in a country inn in the early republic, men of varying degrees of wealth, status, and inebriety are drinking and talking freely with each other. One man's wife and daughter have invaded this male domain, perhaps to question the time and money spent at the inn.

whiskey. Whiskey was safer than water and milk, which were often tainted, and it was cheaper than coffee or tea. It was also cheaper than imported rum. So Americans embraced whiskey as their national drink and consumed extraordinary quantities of it. By 1830 per capita consumption of distilled spirits was more than 5 gallons per year—the highest it has ever been. The United States had indeed become, as one historian has said, an "alcoholic republic."

The nation's growing thirst was driven not by conviviality or neighborliness but by a desire to get drunk. Most Americans drank regularly, though there were wide variations. Men drank far more than women, the poor and the rich drank more than the emerging middle class, city dwellers drank more than farmers, westerners drank more than easterners, and southerners drank a bit more than northerners. Throughout the nation, the heaviest drinking took place among the increasing numbers of young men who lived away from their family and outside the old social controls: soldiers and sailors, boatmen and other transport workers, lumberjacks, schoolmasters, journeyman craftsmen, college students. Among such men the controlled tippling of the 18th century gave way to the binge and to solitary drinking. By the 1820s social reformers branded alcohol as a threat to individual well-being, to social peace, and to the republic itself.

THE DEMOCRATIZATION OF PRINT

Of course, Americans freed from the comforts and constraints of patriarchal authority did more than fornicate and drink. Many seized more constructive opportunities to think and act for themselves. That tendency was speeded by a rise in literacy and by the emergence of a print culture that catered to popular tastes. The literacy rate in the preindustrial United States was among the highest ever recorded. By 1820 all but the poorest white Americans, particularly in the North, could read and write. The rise in literacy was accompanied by an explosive growth in the amount and kinds of reading matter available to the public. At its simplest and most intimate, this took the form of personal letters. Increased mobility separated families and friends and encouraged letter writing, especially by women. Women were also the principal readers of novels. The first best-selling novel in the United States was *The Power of Sympathy,* a morally ambiguous tale of seduction and betrayal that exposed hypocrisy in male authorities who punished (generally poor and vulnerable) women for their own seductions.

The most widely distributed publications, however, were newspapers. In 1790, there were 90 newspapers being published in the United States. In 1830 there were 370, and they had grown chattier and more informal. Still, even in New England, only 1 household in 10 or 12 subscribed to a newspaper. The papers were passed from hand to hand, read aloud in groups, and made available at taverns and public houses.

The increase in literacy and in printed matter accelerated the democratizing process. In the 18th century, when books and newspapers were scarce, most Americans had experienced the written word only as it was read aloud by fathers, ministers, or teachers. Between 1780 and 1820 private, silent reading of new kinds of texts became common— religious tracts, inexpensive Bibles, personal letters, novels, newspapers, and magazines. No longer were authority figures the sole interpreters of the world for families and neighborhoods. The new print culture encouraged Americans to read and think for themselves, and to interpret information without the mediation of the old authorities.

CITIZENSHIP

The transition from republic to democracy—and the relation of that transition to the decline of rural patriarchy—took on formal, institutional shape in a redefinition of republican citizenship.

The revolutionary constitutions of most states retained the colonial freehold (property) qualifications for voting. These granted the vote to from one-half to three-quarters of adult white men. Many of the disenfranchised were dependent sons who expected to inherit citizenship along with land. Some states dropped the freehold clause and gave the vote to all adult men who paid taxes, but with little effect on the voting population. Both the freehold and taxpaying qualifications tended to grant political rights to adult men who headed households, thus reinforcing classical republican notions that granted full citizenship to independent fathers and not to their dependents.

Between 1790 and 1820 republican notions of citizenship grounded in fatherhood and proprietorship gave way to a democratic insistence on equal rights for all white men. In 1790 only Vermont granted the vote to all free men. Kentucky entered the Union in 1792 without property or taxpaying qualifications; Tennessee followed with a freehold qualification, but only for newcomers who had resided in their counties for less than six months. The federal government dropped the 50-acre freehold qualification in the territories in 1812; of the eight territories that became states between 1796 and 1821 none kept a property qualification, only three maintained a taxpaying qualification, and five explicitly granted the vote to all white men. In the same years, one eastern state after another widened the franchise. By 1840 only Rhode Island retained a propertied electorate—primarily because Yankee farmers in that state wanted to retain power in a society made up more and more of urban, immigrant wage earners.

Early 19th century suffrage reform gave political rights to propertyless men, and thus took a long step away from the Founding Fathers' republic and toward mass democracy. At the same time, however, reformers explicitly limited the democratic franchise to those who were white and male. New Jersey's revolutionary constitution, for instance, had granted the vote to "persons" who met a freehold qualification. This loophole enfranchised property-holding widows, many of whom exercised their rights. A law of 1807 abolished property restrictions and gave the vote to all white men; the same law closed the loophole that had allowed propertied women to vote. The question of woman suffrage would not be raised again until women raised it in 1848 (see Chapter 11); it would not be settled until well into the 20th century.

New restrictions also applied to African Americans. The revolutionary constitutions of Massachusetts, New Hampshire, Vermont, and Maine granted the vote to free blacks. New York and North Carolina laws gave the vote to "all men" who met the qualifications, and propertied African Americans in many states routinely exercised the vote. Postrevolutionary laws that extended voting rights to all white men often specifically excluded or severely restricted votes for blacks. Free blacks lost the suffrage in New York, New Jersey, Pennsylvania, Connecticut, Maryland, Tennessee, and North Carolina. By 1840 fully 93 percent of blacks in the North lived in states that either banned or severely restricted their right to vote.

Thus the "universal" suffrage of which many Americans boasted was far from universal: New laws dissolved the old republican connections between political rights and property, and thus saved the citizenship of thousands who were becoming propertyless tenants and wage earners; the same laws that gave the vote to all white men, however, explicitly barred other Americans from political participation. Faced with the disintegration of Jefferson's republic of proprietors, the wielders of power had chosen to blur the emerging distinctions of social class while they hardened the boundaries of sex and race.

REPUBLICAN RELIGION

The Founding Fathers had been largely indifferent to organized religion. Some attended church out of a sense of obligation. Many of the better educated subscribed to deism, the belief that God had created the universe but did not intervene in its affairs. Many simply did not bother themselves with thoughts about religion. When asked why the Constitution mentioned neither God nor religion, Alexander Hamilton is reported to have smiled and answered, "We forgot."

THE DECLINE OF THE ESTABLISHED CHURCHES

In state after state, postrevolutionary constitutions withdrew government support from religion, and the First Amendment to the U.S. Constitution clearly prescribed the national separation of church and state. Reduced to their own sources of support, the established churches went into decline. The Episcopal Church, which until the Revolution had been the established

Church of England in the southern colonies, began to lose members. In New England, the old churches fared little better. About one-third of New England's Congregational pulpits were vacant in 1780, and the situation was worse to the north and west. In 1780 there were 750 Congregational churches in the United States (nearly all of them in New England) and the total was only 1,100 in 1820—this over a period when the nation's population was rising from 4 to 10 million. Ordinary women and men were leaving the churches that had dominated the religious life of colonial America.

THE RISE OF THE DEMOCRATIC SECTS

The collapse of the established churches, the social dislocations of the postrevolutionary years, and the increasingly antiauthoritarian, democratic sensibilities of ordinary Americans provided fertile ground for the growth of new democratic sects. These were the years of camp-meeting revivalism, years in which Methodists and Baptists grew from small, half-organized sects into the great popular denominations they have been ever since. They were also years in which fiercely independent dropouts from older churches were putting together a loosely organized movement that would become the Disciples of Christ. At the same time, ragged, half-educated preachers were spreading the Universalist and Freewill Baptist messages in up-country New England, while in western New York young Joseph Smith was receiving the visions that would lead to Mormonism (see Chapter 10).

The result was, first of all, a vast increase in the variety of choices on the American religious landscape. But within that welter of new churches was a roughly uniform democratic style shared by the fastest-growing sects. First, they renounced the need for an educated, formally authorized clergy. Religion was now a matter of the heart and not the head; crisis conversion (understood in most churches as personal transformation that resulted from direct experience of the Holy Spirit) was a necessary credential for preachers; a college degree was not. The new preachers substituted emotionalism and storytelling for Episcopal ritual and Congregational theological lectures; stories attracted listeners, and they were harder for the learned clergy to refute. The new churches also held up the Bible as the one source of religious knowledge, thus undercutting all theological knowledge and placing every literate Christian on a level with the best-educated minister. These tendencies often ended in Restorationism—the belief that all theological and institutional changes since the end of biblical times were man-made mistakes, and that religious organizations must restore themselves to the purity and simplicity of the church of the Apostles. In sum, this loose democratic creed rejected learning and tradition and raised up the priesthood of all believers.

Baptists and Methodists were by far the most successful at preaching to the new populist audience. In 1820, they outnumbered Episcopalians and Congregationalists by 3 to 1. Baptists based much of their appeal in localism and congregational democracy. Methodist success, on the other hand, was due to skillful national organization. Bishop Francis Asbury, the head of the church in its fastest-growing years, built an episcopal bureaucracy that seeded churches throughout the republic, and sent circuit-riding preachers to places that had none. Asbury demanded much of his itinerant preachers, and until 1810 he strongly suggested that they remain celibate.

The Methodist preachers were common men who spoke plainly, listened carefully to others, and carried hymnbooks with simple tunes that anyone could sing. They also, particularly in the early years, shared traditional folk beliefs with their humble flocks. Some of the early circuit riders relied heavily on dreams; some could predict the future; many visited heaven and hell and returned with full descriptions. But in the end it was the hopefulness and simplicity of the Methodist message that attracted ordinary Americans. The Methodists rejected the old terrors of Calvinist determinism and taught that while salvation comes only through God, men and women can decide to open themselves to divine grace and thus play a decisive role in their own salvation.

THE CHRISTIANIZATION OF THE WHITE SOUTH

It was during these same years that evangelical Protestantism became the dominant religion of the white South. That triumph constituted a powerful assault on the prerevolutionary structure of authority. The essence of southern evangelicalism was a violent conversion experience followed by a life of piety and a rejection of what evangelicals called "the world." To no small degree, "the world" was the economic, cultural, and political world controlled by the planters.

Southern Baptists, Methodists, and Presbyterians spread their democratic message in the early 19th century through the camp meeting. Though its origins stretched back into the 18th century, the first full-blown camp meeting took place at Cane Ridge, Kentucky, in 1801. Here

CAMP MEETING   Painted in 1839, when camp meetings had become routine, this striking watercolor depicts swooning, crying, and other "exercises" of converts (most of them women) under the sway of revival preachers.

the annual "Holy Feast," a three-day communion service of Scotch-Irish Presbyterians, was transformed into an outdoor, interdenominational revival at which hundreds experienced conversion. Estimates of the crowd at Cane Ridge ranged from 10,000 to 20,000 persons, and by all accounts the enthusiasm was nearly unprecedented. Some converts fainted; others succumbed to uncontrolled bodily jerkings, while a few barked like dogs—all of them visibly taken by the Holy Spirit. Such exercises fell upon women and men, whites and blacks, rich and poor, momentarily erasing southern social distinctions in moments of profound and very public religious ecstasy.

EVANGELICALS AND SLAVERY

Despite its critique of worldliness and its antiauthoritarian emphasis, southern evangelicalism was at bottom conservative, for it seldom questioned the need for social hierarchy. As the 19th century progressed, the Baptists, Methodists, and Presbyterians of the South, though they never stopped railing against greed and pride, learned to live comfortably within a system of fixed hierarchy and God-given social roles.

Slavery became the major case in point. For a brief period after the Revolution, evangelicals included slavery on their list of worldly sins. Methodists and Baptists preached to slaves as well as to whites. In 1780 a conference of Methodist preachers ordered circuit riders to free their slaves and advised all Methodists to do the same. In 1784 the Methodists declared that they would excommunicate members who failed to free their slaves within two years. Other evangelicals shared their views. As early as 1787, southern Presbyterians prayed for "final abolition," and two years later Baptists condemned slavery as "a violent deprivation of the rights of nature and inconsistent with a republican government."

The period of greatest evangelical growth, however, came during the years in which the South was committing irrevocably to plantation slavery. As increasing numbers of both slaves and slaveowners came within the evangelical fold, the southern churches had to rethink their position on slavery. The Methodists never carried out their threat to excommunicate slaveholders. Similarly, the Baptists and Presbyterians never translated their antislavery rhetoric into action. By 1820, evangelicals were coming to terms with slavery. Instead of demanding freedom for slaves, they suggested, as the Methodist James O'Kelly put it, that slaveowners remember that slaves were "dear brethren in Christ" who should not be treated cruelly and who should be allowed to attend religious services.

THE BEGINNINGS OF AFRICAN AMERICAN CHRISTIANITY

In the South Carolina and Georgia low-country there were few slave Christians before 1830. But in the slave communities of the Upper South, as well as the burgeoning free and semifree urban black populations of both the North and South, the evangelical revivals of the late 18th and early 19th centuries appealed powerfully to African Americans who sensed that the bonds of slavery were loosening. During the years from 1780 to 1820, for the first time, thousands of slaves embraced Christianity and began to turn it into a religion of their own. Slaves attended camp meetings, listened to itinerant preachers, and joined the Baptist and Methodist congregations of the southern revival.

Blacks were drawn to revival religion for many of the same reasons as whites. They found the informal, storytelling evangelical preachers more attractive than the old Anglican missionaries. The revivalists, in turn, welcomed slaves and free blacks to their meetings, and sometimes recruited them as preachers. Evangelical, emotional preaching, the falling, jerking, and other camp-meeting "exercises," and the revivalists' emphasis on singing and other forms of audience participation were much more attractive than the cold, high-toned preaching of the Anglicans. So were the humility and suffering of the evangelical whites. Slaves respected Methodist missionaries who entered their cabins and talked with them on their own terms. Finally, the slaves gloried in the evangelicals' assault on the slaveholders' culture and in the antislavery sentiments of many white evangelicals. The result was a huge increase in the number of African American Christians.

Neither antislavery beliefs nor openness to black participation, however, persisted long among white evangelicals. Although there were exceptions, most "integrated" congregations in both the North and South were in fact internally segregated. Blacks began organizing independent churches. In Philadelphia, the black preachers Richard Allen and Absalom Jones rebelled against segregated seating in St. George's Methodist Church and, in 1794, founded two separate black congregations. Similar secessions resulted in new churches farther south: in Baltimore; in Wilmington, Delaware; in Richmond; in Norfolk; and in the cluster of villages that had risen to serve the Chesapeake's new mixed economy. By 1820 there were roughly 700 independent black churches in the United States; 30 years earlier there had been none at all. The creation of an independent Christian tradition among the majority of blacks who remained plantation slaves took place only after 1830 (see Chapter 10). But the democratic message of the early southern revival, the brief attempt of white and black Christians to live out the implications of that message, and the independent black churches that rose from the failure of that attempt all left a permanent stamp on southern Protestantism, black and white.

Black Republicanism: Gabriel's Rebellion

Masters who talked of liberty and natural rights sometimes worried that slaves might imagine that such language could apply to themselves. The Age of Democratic Revolution took a huge step in that direction with the French Revolution in 1789. Among the first repercussions outside of France was a revolution on the Caribbean island of Saint Dominque. That island's half-million slaves fought out a complicated political and military revolt that eventually led to the creation of the independent black republic of Haiti. Slave societies throughout the hemisphere heard tales of terror from refugee French planters and stories of hope from the slaves they brought with them.

Slaves from the 1790s onward whispered of natural rights and imagined themselves as part of the Democratic Revolution. This covert republic of the slaves sometimes came into the open, most ominously in Richmond in 1800, where a slave blacksmith named Gabriel hatched a well-planned conspiracy to overthrow Virginia's slave regime. Gabriel had been hired out to Richmond employers for most of his adult life; he was shaped less by plantation slavery than by the democratic, loosely interracial underworld of urban artisans. Working with his brother and other hired-out slave artisans, Gabriel planned his revolt with military precision. They recruited soldiers among slave artisans, adding plantation slaves only at the last moment. Gabriel planned to march an army of 1,000 men on Richmond in three columns. The outside columns would set diversionary fires in the warehouse district and prevent the militia from entering the town. The center would seize Capitol Square, including the treasury, the arsenal, and Governor James Monroe.

Although his army would be made up of slaves, and although his victory would end slavery in Virginia, Gabriel hoped to make a republican revolution, not a slave revolt. His chosen enemies were the Richmond "merchants" who had controlled his labor. Later, a coconspirator divulged the plan: The rebels would hold Governor Monroe hostage and split the state treasury among themselves, and "if the white people agreed to their freedom they would then hoist a white flag, and [Gabriel] would dine and drink with the merchants of the city on the day when it would be agreed to." Gabriel expected what he called "the poor white people" and "the most redoubtable republicans" to join him. He would kill anyone who opposed him, but he would spare Quakers, Methodists, and Frenchmen, for they were "friendly to liberty." Unlike those of earlier slave insurgents, Gabriel's dreams did not center on violent retribution or a return to or reconstruction of West Africa. He was an American revolutionary, and he dreamed of a truly democratic republic for Virginia. His army would march into Richmond under the banner "Death or Liberty."

Gabriel and his coconspirators recruited at least 150 soldiers who agreed to gather near Richmond on August 30, 1800. The leaders expected to be joined by 500 to 600 more rebels as they marched upon the town. But on the appointed day it rained heavily. Rebels could not reach the meeting point, and amid white terror and black betrayals Gabriel and his henchmen were hunted down, tried, and sentenced to death. In all, the state hanged 27 supposed con-

CHRONOLOGY

1789	National government under the Constitution begins
1791	Vermont enters the union as the 14th state
1792	Kentucky enters the union as the 15th state
1793	Beginning of Anglo-French War • Eli Whitney invents the cotton gin
1794	Anthony Wayne defeats the northwestern Indians at Fallen Timbers • British abandon their forts in the Old Northwest
1795	Northwestern Indians cede most of Ohio at Treaty of Greenville
1796	Tennessee enters the union as the 16th state
1799	Successful slave revolution in Haiti
1800	Gabriel's Rebellion in Virginia
1801	First camp meeting at Cane Ridge, Kentucky
1803	Jefferson purchases the Louisiana Territory from France • Ohio enters the union as the 17th state
1805	Tenskwatawa's first vision
1810	Nationalist Cherokee chiefs depose old local leaders
1811	Battle of Tippecanoe
1812	Second war with Britain begins

spirators, while others were sold and transported out of Virginia. A white Virginian marveled that the rebels on the gallows displayed a "sense of their [natural] rights, [and] a contempt of danger."

Conclusion

Between 1790 and 1820 Americans had transformed their new republic—with paradoxical results. The United States more than doubled in both size and population during these years. American trade with Britain, continental Europe, and the Caribbean skyrocketed. Some Americans amassed fortunes; others made more modest gains; others saw their positions deteriorate. Indians between the Appalachians and the Mississippi River lost everything; their hunting grounds became American farmland, much of it worked by slaves who now knew that their masters would never voluntarily free them.

The transformation stemmed both from American independence and from the expansion of agriculture and increased exports of American farm products. When Americans traded plantation staples and surplus food for European (largely British) manufactured goods and financial services, however, they deepened their colonial dependence on the old centers of the world economy—even as they insisted on their independence. It was against this cluttered backdrop of social change, economic and geographic growth, and continuing vulnerability to the whims and needs of the Old World powers that Federalists and Jeffersonian Republicans fought each other to determine the ultimate outcome of the American Revolution.

COMPLETING THE
REVOLUTION, 1789–1815

ESTABLISHING THE GOVERNMENT

THE REPUBLIC IN A WORLD AT WAR, 1793–1800

THE JEFFERSONIANS IN POWER

THE REPUBLIC AND THE NAPOLEONIC WARS, 1804–1815

Almost by acclamation, George Washington became the first president under the Constitution. Washington and his closest advisers (they would soon call themselves Federalists) believed that the balance between power and liberty had tipped toward anarchy after the Revolution. They had made the Constitution to counter democratic excesses, and they came into office determined to make the national government powerful enough to command respect abroad and to impose order at home. For the most part, they succeeded. But in the process they aroused a determined opposition that swung the balance back toward liberty and limited government. These self-styled Democratic Republicans (led almost from the beginning by Thomas Jefferson) were as firmly tied to revolutionary ideals of limited government and the yeoman republic as the Federalists were tied to visions of an orderly commercial republic with a powerful national state. The fight between Federalists and Democratic Republicans was conducted against an ominous backdrop of international intrigue and war between France and Britain.

ESTABLISHING THE GOVERNMENT

George Washington left Mount Vernon for the temporary capital in New York City in April 1789. Militia companies and local dignitaries escorted him from town to town, crowds cheered, church bells marked his progress, and lines of girls in white dresses waved demurely as he passed. At Newark Bay he boarded a flower-bedecked barge and crossed to New York City. There he was welcomed by jubilant citizens as he made his way to the president's house. He arrived on April 23 and was inaugurated seven days later.

THE "REPUBLICAN COURT"

Reporting for work, President Washington found the new government embroiled in its first controversy—an argument over the dignity that would attach to his office. Vice President John Adams had asked the Senate to create a title of honor for the president. Adams, along

227

GEORGE WASHINGTON IN 1796, NEAR THE END OF HIS PRESIDENCY   The artist here captured the formal dignity of the first president, and surrounded him with gold, red velvet, a presidential throne, and other emblems of kingly office.

with many of the senators, wanted a resounding title that would reflect the power of the new executive. They rejected "His Excellency" because that was the term used for ambassadors, colonial governors, and other minor officials. Among the other titles they considered were "His Highness," "His Mightiness," "His Elective Highness," "His Most Benign Highness," "His Majesty," and "His Highness, the President of the United States, and Protector of Their Liberties." The Senate debated the question for a full month, then gave up when it became clear that the more democratic House of Representatives disliked titles. They settled on the austere dignity of "Mr. President."

Much was at stake in the argument over titles. The Constitution provided a blueprint for the republic, but it was George Washington's administration that would translate the blueprint into a working state. Members of the government knew their decisions would set precedents. It mattered very much what citizens called their president, for that was part of the huge constellation of laws, customs, and forms of etiquette that would give the new government either a republican or a courtly tone. Many of those close to Washington wanted to protect presidential power from the localism and democracy that, they believed, had nearly killed the republic in the 1780s. Washington's stately inaugural tour, the endless round of formal balls and presidential dinners, the appearance of Washington's profile on some of the nation's coins—all were meant to bolster the power and grandeur of the new government. Thus the battle over presidential titles was a revealing episode in the argument over how questions of power and liberty that Americans had debated since the 1760s would finally be answered.

THE FIRST CONGRESS

Leadership of the First Congress fell to James Madison. Under his guidance Congress strengthened the new national government at every turn. First it passed a tariff on imports, which would be the government's chief source of income. Then it turned to amendments to the Constitution that had been demanded by the state ratifying conventions.

Madison proposed 19 constitutional amendments to the House. The 10 that survived congressional scrutiny and ratification by the states became the Bill of Rights. The First Amendment guaranteed the freedoms of speech, press, and religion against federal interference. The Second and Third Amendments guaranteed the continuation of a militia of armed citizens and stated the specific conditions under which soldiers could be quartered in citizens' households. The Fourth, Fifth, Sixth, Seventh, and Eighth Amendments protected and defined a citizen's rights in court and when under arrest. The Ninth Amendment stated that the enumeration of specific rights in the first eight amendments did not imply a denial of other rights; the Tenth stated that powers not assigned to the national government by the Constitution remained with the states and the citizenry.

Many doubters at the ratifying conventions had called for amendments that would change the government detailed in the Constitution. By channeling their fears into the relatively innocuous area of civil liberties, Madison soothed their mistrust while preserving the government of the Constitution. The Bill of Rights was an important guarantee of individual liberties. But in the context in which it was written and ratified, it was an even more important guarantee of the power of the national government.

To fill out the framework of government outlined in the Constitution, Congress then created the executive departments of War, State, and Treasury and guaranteed that the heads of those departments and their assistants would be appointed solely by the president, thus removing them from congressional control. Congress then created the federal courts that were demanded but not specified in the Constitution. The Judiciary Act of 1789 established a Supreme Court with six members, along with 13 district courts and 3 circuit courts of appeal. The act made it possible for certain cases to be appealed from state courts to federal circuit courts, which would be presided over by traveling Supreme Court justices.

HAMILTONIAN ECONOMICS: THE NATIONAL DEBT

Washington chose Henry Knox, an old comrade from the Revolution, to be secretary of war. The State Department went to his fellow Virginian, Thomas Jefferson. He chose Alexander Hamilton of New York to head the Department of the Treasury.

Hamilton was a brilliant economic thinker, an admirer of the British system of centralized government and finance, and a supremely arrogant and ambitious man. More than any other cabinet member, Hamilton directed the making of a national government.

In 1789 Congress asked Secretary of the Treasury Hamilton to report on the public debt. The debt fell into three categories, Hamilton reported. The first was the $11 million owed to foreigners—primarily debts to France incurred during the Revolution. The second and third—roughly $24 million each—were debts owed by the national and state governments to American citizens who had supplied food, arms, and other resources to the revolutionary cause. Congress agreed that both justice and the credibility of the new government dictated that the foreign debts be paid in full. But the domestic debts raised troublesome questions. Those debts consisted of notes issued during the Revolution to soldiers, and to merchants, farmers, and others who had helped the war effort. Over the years, speculators had purchased many of these notes at a fraction of their face value; when word spread that the Constitution would create a government likely to pay its debts, speculators and their agents fanned out across the countryside buying up all the notes they could find. By 1790 the government debt was concentrated in the hands of businessmen and speculators who had bought notes at prices only 10 to 30 percent of their original value. Full payment would bring them enormous windfall profits.

The Revolutionary War debts of the individual states were another source of contention. Nationalists wanted to assume the debts of the states as part of a national debt. The state debts had also been bought up by speculators, and they posed another problem as well: Many states had paid off most of their notes in the 1780s; the other states still had significant outstanding debts. If the federal government assumed the state debts and paid them off at the face value of the notes, money would flow out of the southern, middle, and western states—which had paid most of their debts—into the Northeast.

That is precisely what Hamilton proposed in his Report on Public Credit, issued in January 1790. He urged Congress to assume the state debts and to combine them with the federal government's foreign and domestic debts into a consolidated national debt. He agreed that the foreign debt should be paid promptly and in full, but he insisted that the domestic debt be a permanent, tax-supported fixture of government. Under his plan, the government would issue securities to its creditors and would pay an annual rate of interest of 4 percent. A permanent debt would attract the wealthiest financiers in the country as creditors and would render them loyal and dependent on the federal government. It would bring their economic power to the government, and at the same time would require a significant enlargement of the federal civil service, national financial institutions, and increased taxes. The national debt, in short, was at the center of Alexander Hamilton's plan for a powerful national state.

HAMILTONIAN ECONOMICS: THE BANK AND THE EXCISE

As part of that plan, Hamilton asked Congress to charter a Bank of the United States. The government would store its funds in the bank and would supervise its operations, but the bank would be controlled by directors representing private stockholders. The Bank of the United States would print and back the national currency and would regulate other banks. Hamilton's proposal also made stock in the bank payable in government securities, thus giving the bank a powerful interest in the fiscal stability of the government.

To fund the national debt, Hamilton called for a federal excise tax on wines, coffee, tea, and spirits. The tax on spirits would fall most heavily on the whiskey produced in abundance on the frontier. Its purpose was not only to produce revenue but to establish the government's power to create an internal tax and to collect it in the most remote regions in the republic. The result, as we shall see later in this chapter, was a "Whiskey Rebellion" in the west and an overwhelming display of federal force.

THE RISE OF OPPOSITION

In 1789 nearly everyone in the national government was committed to making the new government work. In particular, Alexander Hamilton at Treasury and James Madison in the House of Representatives expected to continue their political and personal friendship. Yet in the debate over the national debt, Madison led congressional opposition to Hamilton's proposals. In 1792 Thomas Jefferson joined the opposition. Within a few short years the consensus of 1789 had degenerated into an angry argument over what sort of government would finally result from the American Revolution.

Hamilton presented his national debt proposal to Congress as a solution to specific problems of government finance. Madison and other southerners opposed it because they did not want northern speculators—many of whom had received information from government insiders—to reap fortunes from notes bought at rock-bottom prices from soldiers, widows, and orphans.

At the urging of Jefferson and others, the congressional opposition compromised with Hamilton. In exchange for accepting his proposals on the debt, they won his promise to locate the permanent capital of the United States at a site on the Potomac River. The compromise went to the heart of American revolutionary republicanism. Hamilton intended to tie northeastern commercial interests to the federal government. If New York or Philadelphia became the permanent capital, political and economic power might be concentrated there as it was in Paris and London. Benjamin Rush, a Philadelphian, condemned the "government which has begun so soon to ape the corruption of the British Court, conveyed to it through the impure channel of the City of New York." Madison and other agrarians considered Philadelphia just as bad, and supported Hamilton's debt only on condition that the capital be moved south. The compromise would distance the commercial power of the cities from the federal government and would put an end to the "republican court" that had formed around Washington.

JEFFERSON VERSUS HAMILTON

When Hamilton proposed the Bank of the United States, republicans in Congress immediately noted its similarity to the Bank of England and voiced deep suspicion of Hamilton's economic and governmental plans. It was at this point that Thomas Jefferson joined the opposition, arguing that the Constitution did not grant Congress the right to charter a bank. Hamilton responded with the first argument for expanded federal power under the clause in the Constitution empowering Congress "to make all laws which shall be necessary and proper" to the performance of its duties. President Washington and a majority in Congress ultimately sided with Hamilton.

Jefferson argued that the federal bank was unconstitutional, that a federal excise tax was certain to arouse public opposition, and that funding the debt would reward speculators and penalize ordinary citizens. But more important, Jefferson argued, Hamilton used government securities and stock in the Bank of the United States to buy the loyalty not only of merchants and speculators but of members of Congress. "The ultimate object of all this," insisted Jefferson, "is to prepare the way for a change, from the present republican form of government, to that of a monarchy, of which the English constitution is to be the model."

For their part, Hamilton and his supporters (who by now were calling themselves Federalists) insisted that the centralization of power and a strong executive were necessary to the survival of the republic. The alternative was a return to the localism and public disorder of the 1780s. The argument drew its urgency from the understanding of both Hamilton and his detractors that republics had a long history of failure. Until late 1792, however, the argument over Hamilton's centralizing schemes was limited very largely to members of the government. Hamilton and his supporters tried to mobilize the commercial elite on the side of government, while Madison and Jefferson struggled to hold off the perceived monarchical plot until the citizens could be aroused to defend their liberties. Then, as both sides began to mobilize popular support, events in Europe came to dominate the politics of the American republican experiment.

THE REPUBLIC IN A WORLD AT WAR, 1793–1800

Late in 1792 French revolutionaries rejected monarchy and proclaimed the French Republic. They beheaded Louis XVI in January 1793. Eleven days later the French declared war on conservative Britain, thus launching a war between French republicanism and British-led reaction that, with periodic outbreaks of peace, would embroil the Atlantic world until the defeat of France in 1815.

AMERICANS AND THE FRENCH REVOLUTION

Americans could not have escaped involvement even had they wanted to. Treaties signed in 1778 allied the United States with France. Americans had overwhelmingly supported the French Revolution of 1789 and had applauded the progress of French republicanism during its first three years. But American hopes for international republicanism were put to severe tests in 1793, when the French Republic began to execute thousands of aristocrats, priests, and other "counterrevolutionaries." The argument between Jeffersonian republicanism and Hamiltonian centralization was no longer a squabble within the United States government. National politics was now subsumed within the struggle over international republicanism.

As Britain and France went to war in 1793, President Washington declared American neutrality, thereby abrogating obligations made in the 1778 treaties with the French. Washington and most of his advisers realized that the United States was in no condition to fight a war. They also wanted to stay on good terms with Great Britain. The nation's commerce and the financial health of the government both depended on good relations with Great Britain. Moreover, Federalists genuinely sympathized with the British in the war with France. They viewed Britain as the defender of hierarchial society and ordered liberty against the homicidal anarchy of the French.

Jefferson and his friends saw things differently. They applauded the French for carrying on the republican revolution Americans had begun in 1776, and they had no affection for the "monarchical" politics of the Federalists or for Americans' continued neocolonial dependence upon British trade. The faction led by Jefferson and Madison wanted to abandon the English mercantile system and trade freely with all nations. They did not care if that course of action hurt commercial interests (most of which supported the Federalists) or impaired the government's ability to centralize power in itself. While they agreed that the United States should stay out of the war, the Jeffersonians sympathized as openly with the French as the Federalists did with the British.

THE CAPITAL OF THE REPUBLIC

Having determined to build its capital city on the Potomac, Congress commissioned the French architect and engineer Pierre Charles L'Enfant to plan the city. The Americans dismissed L'Enfant's suggestions for ornamentation and for a national church at the center of town, but with these alterations the Frenchman's plan became the plan of Washington, D.C. L'Enfant inscribed the Constitution on the landscape: Congress sat in the Capitol Building, situated on high ground looking down what would become the Capitol Mall; the President's House stood a mile and a half away (neither could be seen from the other), and the Court was equidistant between them. Most striking to those who had seen European capitals, the city had no function other than republican government. There were no mercantile or financial establishments, no theaters, and no military fortress. Broad, straight streets stretched beyond the built-up areas of the town; visually as well as politically, the capital was dependent upon and vulnerable to the countryside—the opposite of European court cities. Foreign diplomats complained that Washington was swampy and unpleasant, and that the city provided few amusements. As late as 1842, the English writer Charles Dickens found Washington unfinished and uncivilized: "It is sometimes called the City of Magnificent Distances, but it might with greater propriety be termed the City of Magnificent Intentions. . . . Spacious avenues that begin in nothing, and lead

nowhere; streets, mile-long, that only want houses, roads and inhabitants; public buildings that need only a public to be complete." What Dickens and earlier visitors missed, however, was that American republicans had built precisely the capital city that most of them wanted.

CITIZEN GENÊT

In April 1793 the French sent Citizen Edmond Genêt to the United States to enlist American aid with or without the Washington administration's consent. After the president's proclamation of neutrality, Genêt openly commissioned American privateers to harass British shipping and enlisted Americans in intrigues against the Spanish outpost of New Orleans. Genêt then opened France's Caribbean colonies to American shipping, providing American shippers a choice between French free trade and British mercantilism.

The British responded to Genêt's free-trade declaration with a promise to seize any ship trading with French colonies in the Caribbean. Word of these Orders in Council reached the Royal Navy before American merchant seamen had learned of them, with the result that 250 American ships fell into British hands. The Royal Navy also began searching American ships for English sailors who had deserted or who had switched to safer, better-paying work in the American merchant marine. Inevitably, some American sailors were kidnapped into the British navy. Meanwhile the British began promising military aid to the Indians north of the Ohio River. Thus, while the French ignored the neutrality of the United States, the English engaged in both overt and covert acts of war.

WESTERN TROUBLES

In the Northwest the situation came to a head in the summer and fall of 1794. The Shawnee and allied tribes plotted with the British and talked of driving all settlers out of their territory. At the same time, frontier whites grew increasingly contemptuous of a national government that could neither pacify the Indians nor guarantee their free use of the Mississippi River. President Washington heard that 2,000 Kentuckians were armed and ready to attack New Orleans—a move that would have started a war between the United States and Spain. Settlers in Georgia were making unauthorized forays against the Creeks. Worst of all, settlers up and down the frontier refused to pay the Federalists' excise tax on whiskey—a direct challenge to federal authority. In July 1794 near Pittsburgh, 500 militiamen marched on the house of General John Neville, one of the most hated of the federal excise collectors. Neville, his family, and a few federal soldiers fought the militiamen, killing two and wounding six before they abandoned the house to be looted and burned. Two weeks later, 6,000 "Whiskey Rebels" met at Braddock's Field near Pittsburgh, threatening to attack the town.

Faced with serious international and domestic threats to his new government, Washington determined to defeat the Indians and the Whiskey Rebels by force. He sent General "Mad" Anthony Wayne against the northwestern tribes. Wayne's decisive victory at Fallen Timbers in August 1794 ended the Indian-British challenge in the Northwest for many years (see Chapter 7).

In September, Washington ordered 12,000 federalized militiamen from eastern Pennsylvania, Maryland, Virginia, and New Jersey to quell the Whiskey Rebellion. The president promised amnesty to rebels who pledged to support the government and prison terms to those who did not. As the army marched west from Carlisle, they found no armed resistance. Arriving at Pittsburgh, the army arrested 20 suspected rebels and marched them back to Philadelphia for trial. In the end only two "rebels," both of them feebleminded, were convicted. President Washington pardoned them and the Whiskey Rebellion was over.

THE JAY TREATY

In 1794 President Washington sent John Jay, chief justice of the Supreme Court, to negotiate the conflicts beween the United States and Britain. Armed with news of Wayne's victory, Jay extracted a promise from the British to remove their troops from American territory in the Northwest. But on every other point of dispute he agreed to British terms. The Jay Treaty made no mention of impressment or other violations of American maritime rights, nor did it refer to the old issue of British payments for slaves carried off during the Revolution. The treaty did allow small American ships back into the West Indies, but only on terms that the Senate would reject. Given the power of Great Britain, it was the best that Americans could expect. Washington passed it on to the Senate, which in June 1795 ratified it by a bare two-thirds majority.

The seaport cities and much of the Northeast reacted favorably to the treaty. It ruled out war with England and cemented an Anglo-American trade relationship that strengthened both Hamilton's national state and the established commercial interests that supported it. Moreover, there was little enthusiasm for the French Revolution in the Northeast. The South, on the other hand, saw Jay's Treaty as a blatant sign of the designs of Britain and the Federalists to subvert republicanism in both France and the United States. The Virginia legislature branded the treaty unconstitutional, and Republican congressmen demanded to see all documents relating to Jay's negotiations. Washington responded by telling them that their request could be legitimate only if the House was planning to initiate impeachment proceedings—thus tying approval of the treaty to his enormous personal prestige.

Meanwhile, on March 3, 1796, Washington released the details of a treaty that Thomas Pinckney had negotiated with Spain. In this treaty, Spain recognized American neutrality and set the border between the United States and Spanish Florida on American terms. Most important, the Pinckney Treaty put an end to Spanish claims to territory in the Southwest and gave Americans the unrestricted right to navigate the Mississippi River and to transship produce at the Spanish port of New Orleans. Pinckney's Treaty helped turn the tide in favor of the unpopular Jay's Treaty. With a diminishing number of hotheads willing to oppose Washington, western representatives joined the Northeast and increasing numbers of southerners to ratify Jay's Treaty.

WASHINGTON'S FAREWELL

George Washington refused to run for reelection in 1796. He could be proud of his accomplishment. He had presided over the creation of a national government. He had secured American control over the western settlements by ending British, Spanish, and Indian military threats and by securing free use of the Mississippi River for western produce. Those policies, together with the federal invasion of western Pennsylvania, had made it evident that the government could and would control its most distant regions. He had also avoided war with Great Britain—though not without overlooking assaults on American sovereignty. As he was about to leave government he gave a farewell address in which he warned against long-term "entangling alliances" with other countries; America, he said, should stay free to operate on its own in international affairs. Washington also warned against internal political divisions. Of course, he did not regard his own Federalists as a "party"—they were simply friends of the government. But he saw the Democratic Republicans as a self-interested, irresponsible "faction." Washington's call for national unity and an end to partisanship was in fact a parting shot at the Democratic Republican opposition.

THE ELECTION OF 1796

Washington's retirement opened the way to the fierce competition for public office that he had feared; in 1796 Americans experienced their first contested presidential election. The Federalists chose as their candidate John Adams, an upright conservative from Massachusetts who had served as vice president. The Democratic Republicans nominated Thomas Jefferson. According to the gentlemanly custom of the day, neither candidate campaigned in person. But the friends of the candidates, the newspaper editors who enjoyed their patronage, and even certain European governments ensured that the election would be intensely partisan.

Since it was clear that Adams would carry New England and that Jefferson would carry the South, the election would be decided in Pennsylvania and New York. Some states, most of them in the South, chose presidential electors by direct vote. But in most states, including the crucial mid-Atlantic states, state legislatures selected the presidential electors. The election of 1796 would be decided in elections to the legislatures of those states, and in subsequent intriguing within those bodies. John Beckley, clerk of the House of Representatives, devised the Republican strategy in Pennsylvania. He secretly circulated a list of well-known and respected candidates for the state legislature who were committed to Jefferson's election as president. Discovering the Republican slate only when it was too late to construct a similar list, the Federalists lost the elections. In New York, however, there was no John Beckley. Adams took the state's electoral votes and won the national election. The distribution of electoral votes revealed the bases of Federalist and Republican support: Adams received only 2 electoral votes south of the Potomac, and Jefferson received only 18 (all but 5 of them in Pennsylvania) north of the Potomac.

The voting was over, but the intriguing was not. Alexander Hamilton, who since his retirement from the Treasury in 1795 had directed Federalist affairs from his New York law office, knew that he could not manipulate Adams. So he secretly instructed South Carolina's Federalist electors to withhold their votes from Adams. That would have given the presidency to Adams's running mate, Thomas Pinckney, relegating Adams to the vice presidency. (Prior to the ratification of the Twelfth Amendment in 1804, the candidate with a majority of the electoral votes became president, and the second-place candidate became vice president.) Like some of Hamilton's other schemes, this one backfired. New England electors heard of the plan and angrily withheld their votes from Pinckney. As a result, Adams was elected president and his opponent Thomas Jefferson became vice president.

TROUBLES WITH FRANCE, 1796–1800

As Adams entered office an international crisis was already in full swing. France, regarding Jay's Treaty as an Anglo-American alliance, had broken off relations with the United States. During the crucial elections in Pennsylvania, the French had stepped up their seizures of American ships trading with Britain, giving the Americans a taste of what would happen if they did not elect a government friendlier to France. When the election went to John Adams, the French gave up on the United States and set about denying Britain its new de facto ally. In 1797 France expelled the American minister. The French ordered that American ships carrying "so much as a handkerchief" made in England be confiscated without compensation and announced that American seamen serving in the British navy would be summarily hanged if captured.

President Adams wanted to protect American commerce, but he knew that the United States might not survive a war with France. He also knew that French grievances (including

Jay's Treaty and the abrogation of the French-American treaties of 1778) were legitimate. So he decided to send a mission to France, made up of Charles Cotesworth Pinckney of South Carolina, John Marshall of Virginia, and Elbridge Gerry of Massachusetts. But when these prestigious delegates reached Paris, they were ignored. At last three French officials (the correspondence identified them only as "X, Y, and Z"—and the incident later became known as the XYZ affair) discreetly hinted that France would receive them if they paid a bribe of $250,000, arranged for the United States to loan $12 million to the French government, and apologized for unpleasant remarks that John Adams had made about France. The delegates refused, saying "No, not a sixpence," and returned home. There a journalist transformed their remark into "Millions for defense, but not one cent for tribute."

President Adams asked Congress to prepare for war, and the French responded by seizing more American ships. Thus began, in April 1798, an undeclared war between France and the United States in the Caribbean. While the French navy dealt with the British in the North Atlantic, French privateers inflicted costly blows on American shipping. After nearly a year of fighting, with the British providing powder and shot for American guns, the U.S. Navy chased the French privateers out of the Caribbean.

THE CRISIS AT HOME, 1798–1800

The troubles with France precipitated a crisis at home. The disclosure of the XYZ correspondence, together with the quasi-war in the Caribbean, produced a surge of public hostility toward the French and, to some extent, toward their Republican friends in the United States. Many Federalists, led by Alexander Hamilton, wanted to use the crisis to destroy their political opponents. Without consulting President Adams, the Federalist-dominated Congress passed a number of wartime measures. The first was a federal property tax—justified by military necessity, but a direct federal tax nonetheless. Congress then passed four laws known as the Alien and Sedition Acts. The first three were directed at immigrants: They extended the naturalization period from 5 to 14 years and empowered the president to detain enemy aliens during wartime and to deport those he deemed dangerous to the United States. The fourth law—the Sedition Act—set jail terms and fines for persons who advocated disobedience to federal law or who wrote, printed, or spoke "false, scandalous, and malicious" statements against "the government of the United States, or the President of the United States, with intent to defame . . . or to bring them or either of them, into contempt or disrepute."

President Adams never used the powers granted under the Alien Acts. But the Sedition Act resulted in the prosecution of 14 Republicans, most of them journalists. William Duane, editor of the *Philadelphia Aurora,* was indicted when he and two Irish friends circulated a petition against the Alien Act on the grounds of a Catholic church. James Callendar, editor of a Jeffersonian newspaper in Richmond, was arrested, while another prominent Republican went to jail for statements made in a private letter. Jedediah Peck, a former Federalist from upstate New York, was arrested when he petitioned Congress to repeal the Alien and Sedition Acts. Matthew Lyon, a scurrilous and uncouth Republican congressman from Vermont, had brawled with a Federalist representative in the House chamber; he went to jail for his criticisms of President Adams, Federalist militarism, and what he called the "ridiculous pomp" of the national administration.

Republicans, charging that the Alien and Sedition Acts violated the First Amendment, turned to the states for help. Southern states took the lead. Jefferson provided the Kentucky legislature with draft resolutions, and Madison did the same for the Virginia legislature. Jefferson's Kentucky Resolves reminded Congress that the Alien and Sedition Acts gave the national government powers not mentioned in the Constitution and that the Tenth Amendment reserved such powers to the states. He also argued that the Constitution was a "compact" between sovereign states, and that state legislatures could "nullify" federal laws they deemed unconstitutional.

The Virginia and Kentucky Resolves had few immediate effects. Opposition to the Sedition Act ranged from popular attempts to obstruct the law to fistfights in Congress. But no other states followed the lead of Virginia and Kentucky, and talk of armed opposition to Federalist policies was limited to a few areas in the South.

THE POLITICIANS AND THE ARMY

Federalists took another ominous step by implementing President Adams's request that Congress create a military prepared for war. Adams wanted a stronger navy; Hamilton and others (who were becoming known as "High Federalists") preferred a standing army. At the urging of Washington and against his own judgment, Adams had appointed Hamilton inspector general. As such, Hamilton would be the de facto commander of the U.S. Army. Congress authorized a 20,000-man army and Hamilton proceeded to raise it. Congress also provided for a much larger army to be called up in the event of a declaration of war. When he expanded the officer corps in anticipation of such an army, Hamilton excluded Republicans and commissioned only his political friends. High Federalists wanted a standing army to enforce the Alien and Sedition Acts and to put down an impending rebellion in the South. Beyond that, there was little need for such a force. The Republicans, President Adams himself, and many other Federalists now became convinced that Hamilton and his High Federalists were determined to destroy their political opponents, enter into an alliance with Great Britain, and impose Hamilton's statist designs on the nation by force.

Adams was both fearful and angry. First the Hamiltonians had tried to rob him of the presidency, and then had passed the Alien and Sedition Acts, the direct tax, and plans for a standing army without consulting him. None of this would have been possible had it not been for the crisis with France. Adams began looking for ways to declare peace. He opened negotiations with France and stalled the creation of Hamilton's army while the talks took place. At first the Senate refused to send an envoy to France. The senators relented when Adams threatened to resign and leave the presidency to Vice President Jefferson. In the agreement that followed, the French canceled the obligations that the United States had assumed under the treaties of 1778, but they refused to pay reparations for attacks on American shipping since 1793. Peace with France cut the ground from under the more militaristic and repressive Federalists and intensified discord among the Federalists in general.

THE ELECTION OF 1800

Thomas Jefferson and his Democratic Republicans approached the election of 1800 better organized and more determined than they had been four years earlier. Moreover, events in the months preceding the election worked in their favor. The Alien and Sedition Acts, the direct tax of 1798, and the Federalist military buildup were never popular. Prosecutions under the Sedition Act revealed its partisan origins; and the Federalists showed no sign of abandon-

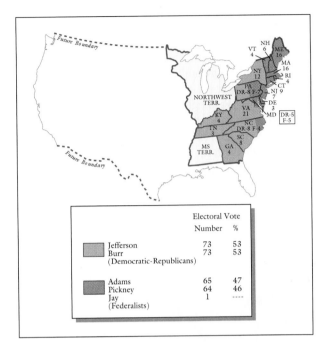

	Electoral Vote	
	Number	%
Jefferson	73	53
Burr	73	53
(Democratic-Republicans)		
Adams	65	47
Pickney	64	46
Jay	1	----
(Federalists)		

PRESIDENTIAL ELECTION, 1800

ing the Alien and Sedition Acts and the new military even when peace seemed certain. Taken together, these events gave credence to the Republicans' allegation that the Federalists were using the crisis with France to destroy their opposition and overthrow the American republic. The Federalists countered by warning that the election of Jefferson and his radical allies would release the worst horrors of the French Revolution onto the streets of American towns.

Jefferson knew that in order to achieve a majority in the electoral college he had to win New York. Jefferson's running mate, Aaron Burr, arranged a truce in New York between Republican factions led by the Clinton and Livingston families and chose candidates for the state legislature who were likely to win. In New York City, Burr played skillfully on the interests and resentments of craftsmen and granted favors to merchants who worked outside the British trade, which was dominated by Federalist insiders. The strategy succeeded. The Republicans carried New York City and won a slight majority in the legislature; New York's electoral votes belonged to Jefferson. The election was decided in South Carolina, which after a brisk campaign cast its votes for Jefferson.

When the electoral votes were counted, Jefferson and Burr had won with 73 votes each. Adams had 65 votes, and his running mate Charles Cotesworth Pinckney had 64. Congress, which was still controlled by Federalists, would have to decide whether Jefferson or Burr was to be president of the United States. After 35 ballots, with most of the Federalists supporting Burr, a compromise was reached whereby the Federalists turned in blank ballots and thus avoided voting for the hated Jefferson.

THE JEFFERSONIANS IN POWER

On the first Tuesday of March 1801, Thomas Jefferson left his rooms at Conrad and McMunn's boarding house in the half-built capital city of Washington and walked up Pennsylvania Avenue. There were military salutes along the way, but Jefferson forbade the pomp and ceremony that had ushered Washington into office. Accompanied by a few friends and a company of artillery from the Maryland militia, he walked up the street and into the unfinished capitol building. There he joined Vice President Burr, other members of the government, and a few foreign diplomats in the newly finished Senate chamber.

THE REPUBLICAN PROGRAM

Jefferson took the oath of office from Chief Justice John Marshall. Then he delivered his inaugural address. Referring to the political discord that had brought him into office, he began

PORTRAIT OF JEFFERSON, BY REMBRANDT PEALE, 1805   A self-consciously plain President Jefferson posed for this portrait in January 1805, near the end of his first term. He wears an unadorned fur-collared coat, is surrounded by no emblems of office, and gazes calmly and directly at the viewer.

with a plea for unity, insisting that "every difference of opinion is not a difference of principle." He did not mean that he and his opponents should forget their ideological differences. He meant only to invite moderate Federalists into a broad Republican coalition.

Jefferson went on to outline the kind of government a republic should have. He declared that Americans were a free people with no need for a national state built on European models. A people blessed with isolation, bountiful resources, and liberty needed only "a wise and frugal Government, which shall restrain men from injuring one another, shall leave them otherwise free to regulate their own pursuits of industry and improvement, and shall not take from the mouth of labor the bread it has earned."

In particular, Jefferson's "wise and frugal" government would respect the powers of the individual states. It would also defend the liberties ensured by the Bill of Rights. It would be made smaller, and it would pay its debts without incurring new ones, thus ending the need for taxation. It would rely for defense on "a disciplined militia" that would fight invaders while regulars were being trained—thus getting rid of Hamilton's standing army. It would protect republican liberties from enemies at home and from the nations of Europe. And, Jefferson promised, it would ensure "the encouragement of agriculture, and of commerce as its handmaiden."

The simplicity of Jefferson's inauguration set the social tone of his administration. The new president reduced the number and grandeur of formal balls, levees, and dinners. He sent his annual messages to Congress to be read by a clerk, rather than delivering them in person. He refused to ride about Washington in a carriage, preferring to carry out his errands on horseback. Abandoning the grand banquets favored by his predecessors, Jefferson entertained senators and congressmen at small dinners—dinners that were served at a round table without formal seating. Jefferson presided over the meals without wearing a wig, and dressed in old homespun and a pair of worn bedroom slippers. The casualness did not extend to what was served, however. The food was prepared by expert chefs and accompanied by fine wines. And it was followed by brilliant conversation. The president's dinners set examples of the unpretentious excellence through which Jefferson hoped to govern the republic that he claimed to have saved from monarchists.

CLEANSING THE GOVERNMENT

Jefferson's first order of business was to reduce the size and expense of government. He reduced the diplomatic corps and replaced officeholders who were incompetent, corrupt, or avowedly antirepublican. He made more substantial cuts in the military. Legislation passed in March 1802 reduced the army to two regiments of infantry and one of artillery—a total of 3,350 officers and men, most of whom were assigned to western posts. Similar cutbacks were made in the navy. The goal, Jefferson explained, was to rely mainly on the militia for national defense but to maintain a small, well-trained professional army as well. At Jefferson's urging, Congress also abolished the direct tax of 1798 and repealed the parts of the Alien and Sedition Acts that had not already expired. Jefferson personally pardoned the 10 victims of those acts who were still in jail and repaid with interest the fines that had been levied under them.

Thus with a few deft strokes, Jefferson dismantled the repressive apparatus of the Federalist state. And by reducing government expenditures he reduced the government's debt. During Jefferson's administration the national debt fell from $80 million to $57 million, and the

"MAD TOM IN A RAGE"   This Federalist cartoon of 1801 portrays Jefferson, with the help of the devil and a bottle of brandy, pulling down the government that Washington and Adams had built.

government built up a treasury surplus. Although some doubted the wisdom of such stringent economy, no one doubted Jefferson's frugality.

THE JEFFERSONIANS AND THE COURTS

Jefferson's demands for a "wise and frugal" government applied to the federal judiciary as well as to other branches. The First Congress had created a system of circuit courts presided over by the justices of the Supreme Court. Only Federalists had served on the Supreme Court under Washington and Adams, and Federalists on the circuit courts had extended federal authority into the hinterland. Thus Jeffersonian Republicans had ample reason to distrust the federal courts. Their distrust was intensified by the Judiciary Act of 1801, which was passed just before Jefferson's inauguration by the lame-duck Federalist Congress. Coupled with President Adams's appointment of the Federalist John Marshall as chief justice in January, the Judiciary Act assured long-term Federalist domination of the federal courts. First, it reduced the number of associate justices of the Supreme Court from six to five when the next vacancy occurred, thus reducing Jefferson's chances of appointing a new member to the Court. The Judiciary Act also took Supreme Court justices off circuit and created a new system of circuit courts. This allowed Adams to appoint 16 new judges, along with a full array of marshals, federal attorneys, clerks, and justices of the peace. He worked until 9 o'clock on his last night in office signing commissions for these new officers. All of them were staunch Federalists.

Jefferson and most in his party wanted the courts shielded from democratic control; at the same time, they deeply resented the uniformly Federalist "midnight judges" created by the Judiciary Act of 1801. Jefferson did replace the new federal marshals and attorneys with Republicans and dismissed some of the federal justices of the peace. But judges were appointed for life and could be removed only through impeachment. The Jeffersonians hit on a simple solution: They would get rid of the new judges by abolishing their jobs. Early in 1802 Congress repealed the Judiciary Act of 1801 and thus did away with the midnight appointees.

The Impeachments of Pickering and Chase

With the federal courts scaled back to their original size, Republicans in Congress went after High Federalists who were still acting as judges. As a first test of removal by impeachment they chose John Pickering, a federal attorney with the circuit court of New Hampshire. Pickering was a notorious alcoholic and clearly insane. The Federalists who had appointed him had long considered him an embarrassment. The House drew up articles of impeachment and Pickering was tried by the Senate, which, by a strict party vote, removed him from office.

On the same day, Congress voted to impeach Supreme Court Justice Samuel Chase. Chase was a much more prominent public figure than Pickering. He had prosecuted sedition cases with real enthusiasm. He had also delivered anti-Jeffersonian diatribes from the bench, and he had used his position and his formidable legal skills to bully young lawyers with whom he disagreed. In short, Chase was an unpleasant, overbearing, and unashamedly partisan member of the Supreme Court. But his faults did not add up to the "high crimes and misdemeanors" that are the constitutional grounds for impeachment.

Moderate Republicans in the government doubted the wisdom of the Chase impeachment, and their uneasiness grew when Congressman John Randolph took over the prosecution. Randolph led a radical states'-rights faction that violently disapproved, among other things, of the way Jefferson had settled a southern land controversy. A corrupt Georgia legislature had sold huge parcels in Mississippi and Alabama to the Yazoo Land Company, which in turn had sold them to private investors—many of them New England speculators. When a new Georgia legislature rescinded the sale and turned the land over to the federal government in 1802, Jefferson agreed to pay off the investors' claims with federal money.

Randolph claimed that Jefferson was double-crossing southern Republicans in an effort to win support in the Northeast. Most of the Republican senators disagreed, and some of them withdrew their support from the impeachment proceedings. With Jefferson's approval, many Republicans in the Senate joined the Federalists in voting to acquit Samuel Chase.

Justice Marshall's Court

Chief Justice John Marshall probably cheered the acquittal of Justice Chase, for it was clear that Marshall was next on the list. Marshall was committed to Federalist ideas of national power, as he demonstrated with his decision in the case of *Marbury* v. *Madison*. William Marbury was one of the justices of the peace whom Jefferson had eliminated in his first few days in office. He sued Jefferson's secretary of state, James Madison, for the nondelivery of his commission. Although Marbury never got his job, Marshall used the case to hand down a number of important rulings. The first ruling, which questioned the constitutionality of Jefferson's refusal to deliver Marbury's commission, helped to convince Republican moderates to repeal the Judiciary Act of 1801. The last ruling, delivered in February 1803, laid the basis for the practice of judicial review—that is, the Supreme Court's power to rule on the constitutionality of acts of Congress.

Some Republicans saw Marshall's ruling as an attempt to arrogate power to the Court. But Marshall was not a sinister man. As secretary of state under John Adams, he had helped to end the undeclared war with France, and he had expressed doubts about the wisdom of the Alien and Sedition Acts. Of more immediate concern, while he disliked Congress's repeal of the 1801 legislation, he did not doubt the right of Congress to make and unmake laws and he was determined to accept the situation. While the decision in *Marbury* v. *Madison* angered many Republicans, Jefferson and the moderate Republicans noted that Marshall was less interested in the power of the judiciary than in its independence. Ultimately, they decided they trusted Marshall more than they trusted the radicals in their own party. With the acquittal of Justice Chase, Jeffersonian attacks on the federal courts ceased.

LOUISIANA

It was Jefferson's good fortune that Europe remained at peace during his first term and stayed out of American affairs. Indeed the one development that posed an international threat to the United States turned into a grand triumph: the purchase of the Louisiana Territory from France in 1803.

By 1801 a half-million Americans lived west of the Appalachians. Republicans saw westward expansion as the best hope for the survival of the republic. Social inequality would almost inevitably take root in the East, but the vast lands west of the mountains would enable the republic to renew itself for many generations to come. To serve that purpose, however, the West needed ready access to markets through the river system that emptied into the Gulf of Mexico at New Orleans.

In 1801 Spain owned New Orleans and under Pinckney's Treaty allowed Americans to transship produce from the interior. The year before, however, Spain had secretly ceded the Louisiana Territory (roughly, all the land west of the Mississippi drained by the Missouri and Arkansas rivers) to France. Napoleon Bonaparte had plans for a new French empire in America with the sugar island of Saint Dominque (present-day Haiti and the Dominican Republic) at its center, and with mainland colonies feeding the islands and thus making the empire self-sufficient. Late in 1802, the Spanish, who had retained control of New Orleans, closed the port to American commerce, giving rise to rumors that they would soon transfer the city to France. To forestall such a move, President Jefferson sent a delegation to Paris early in 1803 with authorization to buy New Orleans for the United States.

By the time the delegates reached Paris, the slaves of Saint Dominque had revolted against the French and had defeated their attempts to regain control of the island (see Chapter 7). At the same time, another war between Britain and France seemed imminent. Napoleon decided to bail out of America and concentrate his resources in Europe. He astonished Jefferson's delegation by announcing that France would sell not only New Orleans but the whole Louisiana Territory for the bargain price of $15 million.

Jefferson faced a dilemma: The Constitution did not give the president the power to buy territory. But the chance to buy Louisiana was too good to refuse. It would assure Americans access to the rivers of the interior; it would eliminate a serious foreign threat on America's western border; and it would give American farmers enough land to sustain the agrarian republic for a long time to come. Swallowing his constitutional scruples, Jefferson told the American delegates to buy Louisiana. Republican senators quickly ratified the Louisiana treaty over Federalist objections. Most Americans agreed that the accidents of French and Haitian history had given the United States a grand opportunity, and Congress's ratification of the Louisiana Purchase met with overwhelming public approval. For his part, Jefferson was certain that the republic had gained the means of renewing itself through time.

As Jefferson stood for reelection in 1804, he could look back on an astonishingly successful first term. He had dismantled the government's power to coerce its citizens, and he had begun to wipe out the national debt. The Louisiana Purchase had doubled the size of the republic at remarkably little cost. Moreover, by eliminating France from North America it had strengthened the argument for reducing the military and the debts and taxes that went with it.

The combination of international peace, territorial expansion, and inexpensive, unobtrusive government left the Federalists without an issue in the 1804 election. They went through the motions of nominating Charles Pinckney of South Carolina as their presidential candidate and then watched as Jefferson captured the electoral votes of every state but Delaware and Connecticut.

THE REPUBLIC AND THE NAPOLEONIC WARS, 1804–1815

In the spring of 1803 Napoleon Bonaparte declared war on Great Britain. This 11-year war dominated the national politics of the United States. Most Americans wanted to remain neutral. Few Republicans supported Bonaparte, and none but the most rabid Federalists wanted to intervene on the side of Great Britain. But neither France nor Britain would permit American neutrality.

THE DILEMMAS OF NEUTRALITY

At the beginning, both Britain and France encouraged the Americans to resume their role as neutral carriers and suppliers of food. For a time, Americans made huge profits. Between 1803 and 1807 U.S. exports rose from $66.5 million to $102.2 million. Reexports—goods produced in the Caribbean, picked up by American vessels and then reloaded in American ports onto American ships bound for Europe—rose even faster, from $13.5 million to $58.4 million.

In 1805 France and Great Britain began systematically to interfere with that trade. In 1805 the Royal Navy under Lord Nelson destroyed the French and Spanish fleets at the Battle of Trafalgar. Later that year Napoleon's armies won a decisive victory over Austria and Russia at the Battle of Austerlitz. The war reached a stalemate: Napoleon's army occupied Europe, the British navy controlled the seas.

Britain decided to use its naval supremacy to blockade Europe and starve the French into submission. In the Essex Decision of 1805, the British ministry dusted off what was known as the Rule of 1756, which stated that a European country could not use a neutral merchant marine to conduct wartime trade with its colonies if its mercantile laws forbade such use during peacetime. Translated into the realities of 1805, the Essex Decision meant that the Royal Navy could seize American ships engaged in the reexport trade with France. In the spring of 1806 Congress, angered by British seizures of American ships, passed the Non-Importation Act forbidding the importation of British goods that could be bought elsewhere or that could be manufactured in the United States. A month after that Britain blockaded long stretches of the European coast. Napoleon responded with the Berlin Decree, which outlawed all trade with the British Isles. The British answered with an Order in Council that demanded that neutral ships trading with Europe stop first for inspection and licensing in a British port. Napoleon responded with the Milan Decree, which stated that any vessel that obeyed the British decrees or allowed itself to be searched by the Royal Navy was subject to seizure by France. Beginning in 1805 and ending with the Milan Decree in December 1807, the barrage of European decrees and counterdecrees meant that virtually all American commerce with Europe had been outlawed by one or the other of the warring powers.

TROUBLE ON THE HIGH SEAS

The Royal Navy maintained a loose blockade of the North American coast and stopped and searched American ships as they left the major seaports. Hundreds of ships were seized, along with their cargoes and crews. Under British law, the Royal Navy during wartime could impress any British subject into service. The British were certain that many British subjects, including legions of deserters from the Royal Navy, were hiding in the American merchant marine. They were right. The danger, low pay, bad food, and draconian discipline on British warships encouraged many British sailors to jump ship and take jobs on American merchantmen. Many of the British warships that stopped American merchant ships on the high seas were undermanned; the sailors their officers commandeered often included Englishmen who had taken out U.S. citizenship (an act the British did not recognize) and, inevitably, native-born Americans. An estimated 6,000 American citizens were impressed into the Royal Navy between 1803 and 1812.

The kidnapping of American sailors enraged the citizens of the United States and brought the country close to war in the summer of 1807. In June the American naval frigate *Chesapeake,* which was outfitting in Norfolk, Virginia, signed on four English deserters from the British navy, along with some Americans who had joined the British navy and then deserted. The British warship H.M.S. *Leopard* also was docked at Norfolk, and some of the deserters spotted their old officers and taunted them on the streets. The *Leopard* left port and resumed its patrol of the American coast. Then, on June 21, its officers caught the *Chesapeake* off Hampton Roads and demanded the return of the British deserters. When the captain refused, the British fired on the *Chesapeake,* killing 3 Americans and wounding 18. The British then boarded the *Chesapeake,* seized the four deserters, and later hanged one of them. The *Chesapeake* limped back into port.

The *Chesapeake* affair set off huge anti-British demonstrations in the seaport towns and angry cries for war throughout the country. President Jefferson responded by barring British ships from American ports and American territorial waters, and by ordering state governors to prepare to call up as many as 100,000 militiamen.

EMBARGO

Jefferson had one more card to play: He could suspend trade with Europe altogether and thus keep American ships out of harm's way. He could use trade as a means of "peaceable coercion" that would both ensure respect for American neutral rights and keep the country out of war. "Our commerce," he wrote just before taking office, "is so valuable to them, that they will be glad to purchase it, when the only price we ask is to do us justice." Convinced that America's yeoman republic could survive without European luxuries more easily than Europe could survive without American food, Jefferson decided to give "peaceable coercion" a serious test. Late in 1807 he asked Congress to suspend all U.S. trade with foreign countries.

Congress passed the Embargo Act on December 22. By the following spring, however, it was clear that peaceable coercion would not work. The British found other markets and other sources of food. They encouraged the smuggling of American goods into Canada. And American merchantmen who had been at sea when the embargo went into effect stayed away from their home ports and functioned as part of the British merchant marine. A loophole in the Embargo Act allowed U.S. ships to leave port in order to pick up American property stranded in other countries, and an estimated 6,000 ships set sail under that excuse. Hundreds of others, plying the coastal trade, were "blown off course" and found themselves thrust into international commerce.

The embargo hurt American commerce badly. The economy slowed in every section of the country, but it ground to a halt in the cities of the Northeast. Unemployed sailors, dockworkers, and other maritime workers and their families sank to levels of economic despair that had seldom been seen in British North America. Federalists accused Jefferson of plotting an end to commerce and a reversion to rural barbarism, and they often took the lead in trying to subvert the embargo through smuggling and other means.

The Federalists gained ground in the elections of 1808. James Madison, Jefferson's old ally and chosen successor, was elected president with 122 electoral votes to 47 for his Federalist opponent, C. C. Pinckney. And although Republicans retained control of both houses of Congress, Federalists made significant gains in Congress and won control of several state legislatures. Federalist opposition to the embargo, and to the supposed southern, agrarian stranglehold on national power that stood behind it, was clearly gaining ground.

THE ROAD TO WAR

When President Madison took office in the spring of 1809 it was clear that the embargo had failed to coerce the British. On the contrary, it had created misery in the seaport cities, choked off the imports that were the source of 90 percent of federal revenue, and revived Federalist opposition to Republican dominance. Early in 1809 Congress passed the Non-Intercourse Act, which retained the ban on trade with Britain and France but reopened trade with other nations. It also gave President Madison the power to reopen trade with either Britain or France once they had agreed to respect American rights. Neither complied, and the Non-Intercourse Act proved nearly as ineffective as the embargo.

In 1810 Congress passed Macon's Bill No. 2, which rescinded the ban on trade with France and Britain but authorized the president to reimpose the Non-Intercourse Act on either belligerent if the other agreed to end its restrictions on U.S. trade. In September 1810 the French foreign minister, the Duc de Cadore, promised that France would repeal the Berlin and Milan Decrees. Though the proposal was a clear attempt to lead the United States into conflict with Great Britain, Madison felt he had no choice but to go along with it. He accepted the French promise and proclaimed in November 1810 that the British had three months to follow suit.

In the end, Madison's proclamation led to war. The French repealed only those sections of the Berlin and Milan Decrees that applied to the neutral rights of the United States. The

British refused to revoke their Orders in Council and told the Americans to withdraw their restrictions on British trade until the French had repealed theirs. The United States would either have to obey British orders or go to war.

THE WARHAWK CONGRESS, 1811–1812

In the congressional session of 1811–1812 the Republicans controlled both houses of Congress. But they were a divided majority. The Federalist minority, which was united against Madison, was joined on many issues by northeastern Republicans who followed the Federalist line on international trade, and by Republicans who wanted a more powerful military. Also opposed to Madison were the self-styled Old Republicans of the South, led by John Randolph.

In this confused situation a group of talented young congressmen took control. Nearly all of them were Republicans from the South or the West. Called the "War Hawks," these men were ardent nationalists who were more than willing to declare war on England to protect U.S. rights. Through their organizational, oratorical, and intellectual power, they won control of Congress. Henry Clay, only 34 years old and serving his first term in Congress, was elected Speaker of the House. More vigorous than his predecessors, Clay controlled debate, packed key committees, worked tirelessly behind the scenes, and imposed order on his fellow congressmen.

In the winter and spring of 1811–1812 the War Hawks led Congress into a declaration of war. In November they voted military preparations, and in April they enacted a 90-day embargo—not to coerce the British but to get American ships safely into port before war began. On June 1, Madison sent a war message to Congress. This was to be the first war declared under the Constitution, and the president stayed out of congressional territory by not asking explicitly for a declaration of war. He did, however, present a list of British crimes that could be interpreted in no other way: the enforcement of the Orders in Council, even within the territorial waters of the United States; the impressment of American seamen; the use of spies and provocateurs within the United States; and the wielding of "a malicious influence over the Indians of the Northwest Territory." Madison concluded that war had in fact begun.

Congress declared war on June 18. The vote was far from unanimous. All 30 Federalists voted against the declaration. So did one in five Republicans, nearly all of them from the Northeast. Thus the war was declared by the Democratic Republican Party, more particularly by the Republicans of the South and the West.

WAR HAWKS AND THE WAR OF 1812

Federalists and many northeastern Republicans expected a naval war. After all, it was on the ocean that the British had committed their atrocities. Yet when Madison asked Congress to prepare for war, the War Hawks led a majority that strengthened the U.S. Army and left the Navy weak. Reasoning that no U.S. naval force could challenge British control of the seas, they prepared instead for a land invasion of British Canada.

The decision to invade Canada led the Federalists, along with many of Randolph's Old Republicans, to accuse Madison and the congressional majority of planning a war of territorial aggression. Some members of Congress did indeed want to annex Canada to the United States. But most saw the decision to invade Canada as a matter of strategy. Lightly garrisoned and with a population of only half a million, Canada seemed the easiest and most logical place in which to damage the British. Moreover, Canada was a valuable colony of Great Britain. The American embargoes, coupled with Napoleon's control of Europe, had impaired Britain's ability to supply her plantation colonies in the West Indies, and Canadian farmers had begun to fill the gap. Thus Canada was both valuable and vulnerable, and American policymakers reasoned that they could take it and hold it hostage while demanding that the British back down on other issues.

THE WAR WITH CANADA, 1812–1813

The United States opened its offensive against Canada in 1812, with disastrous results. The plan was to invade Upper Canada (Ontario) from the Northwest, thus cutting off the pro-British Indian tribes from their British support. When General William Hull, governor of Michigan Territory, took a poorly supplied, badly led army of militiamen and volunteers into Canada from a base in Detroit, he found the area crawling with British troops and their Indian allies. He retreated to the garrison at Detroit. British General Isaac Brock, who knew that Hull was afraid of Indians, sent a note into the fort telling him that "the numerous body of Indians who have attached themselves to my troops, will be beyond my controul the moment the contest commences." Without consulting his officers, Hull surrendered his army of 2,000 to the smaller British force. Though Hull was later court-martialed for cowardice, the damage had been done: The British and their Indian allies occupied many of the remaining American garrisons in the Northwest and transformed the U.S. invasion of Upper Canada into a British occupation of much of the Northwest.

The invasion of Canada from the east went no better. In October a U.S. force of 6,000 faced 2,000 British and Indians across the Niagara River separating Ontario from western New York. The U.S. regular army crossed the river, surprised the British, and established a toehold at Queenston Heights. While the British were preparing a counterattack, New York militiamen refused to cross the river to reinforce the regular troops. The British regrouped and slaughtered the outnumbered, exhausted U.S. regulars.

AMERICAN TROOPS INVADE CANADA   In this painting, a Canadian artist depicts the failed American invasion at Queenston Heights in October 1812. British troops on the right are rushing to repel the Americans who have occupied the cliffs at center.

As winter set in, it was clear that Canada would not fall as easily as the Americans had assumed. Indeed the invasion, which U.S. commanders had thought would knife through an apathetic Canadian population, had the opposite effect: The attacks by the United States turned the ragtag assortment of American loyalist émigrés, discharged British soldiers, and American-born settlers into a self-consciously British Canadian people.

TECUMSEH'S LAST STAND

Tecumseh's Indian confederacy, bruised but not broken in the Battle of Tippecanoe (see Chapter 7), allied itself with the British in 1812. On a trip to the southern tribes Tecumseh

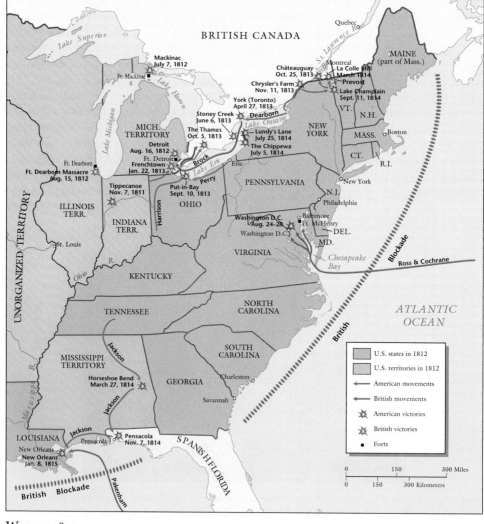

WAR OF 1812

found the traditionalist wing of the Creeks—led by prophets who called themselves Red Sticks—willing to join him. The augmented confederacy provided stiff resistance to the United States throughout the war. The Red Sticks chased settlers from much of Tennessee. They then attacked a group of settlers who had taken refuge in a stockade surrounding the house of an Alabama trader named George Mims. In what whites called the Massacre at Fort Mims, the Red Sticks killed at least 247 men, women, and children. In the Northwest, Tecumseh's warriors, fighting alongside the British, spread terror throughout the white settlements.

A wiser U.S. army returned to Canada in 1813. They raided and burned the Canadian capital at York (Toronto) in April, and then fought inconclusively through the summer. An autumn offensive toward Montreal failed, but the Americans had better luck on Lake Erie. In September 1813 Commodore Oliver Hazard Perry cornered the British fleet at Put-in-Bay and destroyed it. Control of Lake Erie enabled the United States to cut off supplies to the British in the Northwest, and a U.S. army under William Henry Harrison retook the area and continued on into Canada. On October 5 Harrison caught up with a force of British and Indians at the Thames River and beat them badly. In the course of that battle Richard M. Johnson, a War Hawk congressman acting as commander of the Kentucky militia, killed Tecumseh.

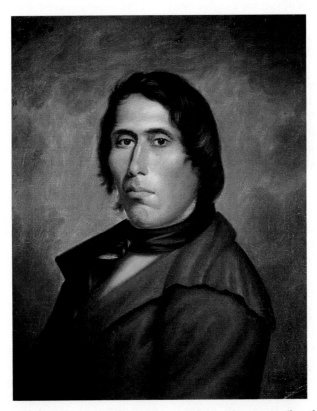

TECUMSEH Tecumseh, military and political leader of the northwestern tribes that sided with the British in 1812, came closer than any other Native American leader to unifying Indian peoples against white territorial expansion.

The following spring General Andrew Jackson's Tennessee militia, aided by Choctaw, Creek, and Cherokee allies, attacked and slaughtered the Red Sticks who had fortified themselves at Horseshoe Bend in Alabama. The military power of the Indian peoples east of the Mississippi River was broken.

THE BRITISH OFFENSIVE, 1814

The British defeated Napoleon in April 1814, thus ending the larger war of which the War of 1812 was a part. The British decided to concentrate their resources on the American war. They had already blockaded much of the American coast. During the summer of 1814 they began to raid the shores of Chesapeake Bay and marched on Washington, D.C. As retribution for the torching of the Canadian capital at York, they chased the army and politicians out of town and then burned down the capitol building and the president's mansion. In September the British attacked the much larger city of Baltimore, but they could not blast their way past the determined garrison that commanded the harbor from Fort McHenry. This was the battle that inspired Francis Scott Key to write "The Star-Spangled Banner." When a British offensive on Lake Champlain stalled during the autumn, the war reached a stalemate: Britain had prevented the invasion of Canada and had blockaded the American coast, but neither side could take and hold the other's territory.

The British now shifted their attention to the Gulf Coast, particularly to New Orleans. A large British amphibious force landed and camped 8 miles south of New Orleans. There they were opposed by an American army made up of U.S. regulars, Kentucky and Tennessee militiamen, clerks, workingmen, and free blacks from the city, and about a thousand French pirates—all under the command of Andrew Jackson of Tennessee. Throughout late December and early January, unaware that a peace treaty had been signed on December 24, the armies exchanged artillery barrages and the British probed and attacked American lines. Then, on January 8, the British launched a frontal assault. A formation of 6,000 British soldiers marched across open ground toward 4,000 Americans concealed behind breastworks. With the first American volley, it was clear that the British had made a mistake. The charge lasted half an hour. At the end, 2,000 British soldiers lay dead or wounded. American casualties numbered only 70. Fought nearly two weeks after the peace treaty, the Battle of New Orleans had no effect on the outcome of the war or on the peace terms. But it salved the injured pride of Americans and made a national hero and a political power of Andrew Jackson.

THE HARTFORD CONVENTION

While most of the nation celebrated Jackson's victory, events in Federalist New England went very differently during the closing months of the war. New Englanders had considered themselves the victims of Republican trade policies, and their congressmen had voted overwhelmingly against going to war. Some Federalist leaders had openly urged resistance to the war. The British had encouraged that resistance by not extending their naval blockade to the New England coast, and throughout the first two years of the war New England merchants and farmers had traded freely with the enemy. In 1814, after the Royal Navy had extended its blockade northward and had begun to raid the towns of coastal Maine, some Federalists talked openly about seceding and making a separate peace with Britain.

CHRONOLOGY

1789	George Washington inaugurated as first president of the United States • Judiciary Act establishes the Supreme Court and federal circuit courts
1790	Hamilton delivers his Report on Public Credit to Congress • Congress drafts the Bill of Rights
1792	Revolutionaries proclaim the French Republic
1793	Anglo-French War begins
1794	Federalists' excise tax triggers Whiskey Rebellion
1796	Jay's Treaty and Pinckney's Treaty ratified • John Adams elected second president
1798	XYZ affair results in undeclared war with France • Alien and Sedition Acts passed by Congress
1799	Slave revolution in Haiti
1800	Thomas Jefferson defeats Adams for the presidency
1803	United States purchases Louisiana Territory from France • *Marbury* v. *Madison* establishes the doctrine of judicial review
1804	Twelfth Amendment to the Constitution passed by Congress
1806	Non-Importation Act forbids importation of many British goods into U.S.
1807	*Chesapeake-Leopard* affair ignites anti-British sentiment • Congress passes Embargo Act
1810	Congress passes Macon's Bill No. 2
1811	Henry Clay elected Speaker of the House
1812	War of 1812 begins
1814	Federalists call Hartford Convention • Treaty of Ghent ends War of 1812
1815	American victory at the Battle of New Orleans

In an attempt to undercut the secessionists, moderate Federalists called a convention at Hartford to air the region's grievances. The Hartford Convention, which met in late December 1814, proposed several amendments to the Constitution. The delegates wanted the "three-fifths" clause, which led to overrepresentation of the South in Congress and the Electoral College (see Chapter 6), stricken from the Constitution; they wanted to deny naturalized citizens—who were strongly Republican—the right to hold office; they wanted to make it more difficult for new states—all of which sided with the Republicans and their southern leadership—to enter the Union; and finally, they wanted to require a two-thirds majority of both houses for a declaration of war—a requirement that would have prevented the War of 1812.

The Federalist leaders of the Hartford Convention took their proposals to Washington in mid-January. They arrived to find the capital celebrating the news of the peace treaty and Jackson's stunning victory at New Orleans. When they aired their proposals, they were branded as negative, selfish, and unpatriotic. Although Federalists continued for a few years to wield power in southern New England, the Hartford debacle ruined any chance of a nation-wide Federalist resurgence after the war.

THE TREATY OF GHENT

Britain's defeat of Napoleon had spurred British and American efforts to end a war that neither wanted. In August 1814 they opened peace talks in the Belgian city of Ghent. Perhaps waiting for the results of their 1814 offensive, the British opened with proposals that the Americans were certain to reject. They demanded the right to navigate the Mississippi. Moreover, they wanted territorial concessions and the creation of the permanent, independent Indian buffer state in the Northwest that they had promised their Indian allies. The Americans ignored these proposals and talked instead about impressment and maritime rights. As the autumn wore on and the war reached stalemate, both sides began to compromise. The British knew that the Americans would grant concessions in the interior only if they were thoroughly defeated, an outcome that most British commanders thought impossible. For their part, the Americans realized that the British maritime depredations were byproducts of the struggle with Napoleonic France. Faced with peace in Europe and a senseless military stalemate in North America, negotiators on both sides began to withdraw their demands. The Treaty of Ghent, signed on Christmas Eve 1814, simply put an end to the war. The border between Canada and the United States remained where it had been in 1812; Indians south of that border—defeated and without allies—were left to the mercy of the United States; and British maritime violations were not mentioned.

CONCLUSION

In 1816 Thomas Jefferson was in retirement at Monticello, satisfied that he had defended liberty against the Federalists' love of power. The High Federalists' attempt to militarize government and to jail their enemies had failed. Their direct taxes were repealed. Their debt and their national bank remained in place, but only under the watchful eyes of true republicans. And their attempt to ally the United States with the antirepublican designs of Great Britain had ended in what many called the "Second War of American Independence."

Yet for all his successes, Jefferson in 1816 saw that he must sacrifice his dreams of agrarianism. Throughout his political life, Jefferson envisioned American yeomen trading farm surpluses for European manufactured goods—a relationship that would ensure rural prosperity, prevent the growth of cities and factories, and thus sustain the landed independence on which republican citizenship rested. Westward expansion, he had believed, would ensure the yeoman republic for generations to come. By 1816 that dream was ended. Arguing as Hamilton had argued in 1790, Jefferson insisted that "we must now place the manufacturer by the side of the agriculturalist." As he wrote, a Republican congress was taking steps that would help transform the yeoman republic into a market society and a boisterous capitalist democracy.

THE MARKET REVOLUTION, 1815–1860

GOVERNMENT AND MARKETS ❧ THE TRANSPORTATION REVOLUTION

FROM YEOMAN TO BUSINESSMAN: THE RURAL NORTH AND WEST

THE INDUSTRIAL REVOLUTION

THE MARKET REVOLUTION IN THE SOUTH

After 1815 a market revolution transformed Jefferson's yeoman republic into the market-oriented, capitalist society that it has been ever since. Improvements in transportation made that transformation possible. But it was decisions made by thousands of farmers, planters, craftsmen, and merchants that pulled farms and workshops out of old household and neighborhood arrangements and into production for distant markets. By the 1830s and 1840s the northern United States was experiencing a full-blown market revolution: New cities and towns provided financing, retailing, manufacturing, and markets for food; commercial farms traded food for what the cities made and sold. The South experienced a market revolution as well. The wealthiest southerners sent mountains of cotton, rice, and other plantation staples onto world markets. But the planters remained provincial grandees who produced for distant markets and purchased shipping, financial services, and manufactured goods from outside the region—increasingly from the Northeast. The planters increased their wealth and local power, the plantation regime spread into vast new lands, and the old slaveholder's republic persisted in the southern states. But now it faced an agressive and expanding capitalist democracy in the North.

GOVERNMENT AND MARKETS

The 14th Congress met in the last days of 1815. Made up overwhelmingly of Jeffersonian Republicans, this Congress nevertheless would reverse many of the positions taken by Jefferson's old party. It would charter a national bank, enact a protective tariff, and debate whether or not to build a national system of roads and canals at federal expense. The War of 1812 had demonstrated that the United States was unable to coordinate a fiscal and military effort. It had also convinced many Republicans that reliance on foreign trade rendered the United States dependent on Europe. The nation, they said, must abandon Jefferson's export-oriented agrarianism and encourage national independence through subsidies to commerce and manufactures.

THE AMERICAN SYSTEM: THE BANK OF THE UNITED STATES

Henry Clay headed the drive for a program of protective tariffs, internal improvements, and a national bank. He called his program the "American System," arguing that it would foster national economic growth and a salutary interdependence between geographical sections.

In 1816 Congress chartered a Second Bank of the United States, headquartered in Philadelphia and empowered to establish branches wherever it saw fit. The government agreed to deposit its funds in the Bank, to accept the Bank's notes as payment for government land, taxes, and other transactions, and to buy one-fifth of the Bank's stock. The fiscal horrors of the War of 1812 had convinced most representatives that it would be a good idea to move toward a national currency and centralized control of money and credit. The alternative was to allow state banks to issue unregulated and grossly inflated notes that might throw the anticipated postwar boom into chaos.

With no discussion of the constitutionality of what it was doing, Congress chartered the Bank of the United States as the sole banking institution empowered to do business throughout the country. Notes issued by the Bank would be the first semblance of a national currency. Moreover, the Bank could regulate the currency by demanding that state banknotes used in transactions with the federal government be redeemable in gold. In 1816 the Bank set up shop in Philadelphia's Carpenter's Hall, and in 1824 moved around the corner to a Greek Revival edifice modeled after the Parthenon—a marble embodiment of the conservatism that directors of the Bank of the United States adopted as their fiscal stance.

THE AMERICAN SYSTEM: TARIFFS AND INTERNAL IMPROVEMENTS

In 1816 Congress drew up the first overtly protective tariff in U.S. history. The Tariff of 1816 raised tariffs an average of 25 percent, extending protection to the nation's infant industries at the expense of foreign trade and American consumers. Again, wartime difficulties had paved the way: Because Americans could not depend on imported manufactures, Congress saw the encouragement of domestic manufactures as a patriotic necessity. The tariff was well supported by the Northeast and the West, with enough southern support to ensure its passage by Congress.

Bills to provide federal money for roads, canals, and other "internal improvements" had a harder time winning approval. The British wartime blockade had hampered coastal shipping and had made Americans dependent on the wretched roads of the interior. Many members of the 14th Congress, after spending days of bruising travel on their way to Washington, were determined to give the United States an efficient transportation network. But consensus was hard to reach. Internal improvements were subject to local ambitions, and they were doubtful constitutionally as well. Congress agreed to complete the National Road linking the Chesapeake with the trans-Appalachian West, but President Madison and his Republican successor James Monroe both refused to support further internal improvements without a constitutional amendment.

With a national government that was squeamish about internal improvements, state governments took up the cause. As a result, the transportation network that took shape after 1815 reflected the designs of the most ambitious states rather than the nationalizing dreams of men like Henry Clay. New York's Erie Canal was the most spectacular accomplishment, but the canal systems of Pennsylvania and Ohio were almost as impressive. Before 1830 most toll roads were built and owned by corporations chartered by state governments. Private entrepreneurs could not have built the transportation network that brought the market economy into being without the active support of state governments—through direct funding, through bond issues, and through the granting of corporate charters that gave the turnpike, canal, and railroad companies the privileges and immunities that made them attractive to private investors.

MARKETS AND THE LAW

The Revolution replaced British courts with national and state legal systems based in English common law—systems that made legal action accessible to most white males. Thus many of the disputes generated in the transition to market society ended up in court. The courts dealt with the conflicts in language that only lawyers understood and resolved them in ways that tended to promote the entrepreneurial use of private property, the sanctity of contracts, and the right to do business shielded from neighborhood restraints and the tumult of democratic politics.

John Marshall, who presided over the Supreme Court from 1801 to 1835, saw the Court as a conservative hedge against the excesses of democratically elected legislatures. His early decisions protected the independence of the courts and their right to review legislation (see Chapter 8). From 1816 onward, his decisions encouraged business and strengthened the national government at the expense of the states. Marshall's most important decisions protected the sanctity of contracts and corporate charters against state legislatures. For example, in *Dartmouth College* v. *Woodward* (1816), Dartmouth was defending a royal charter granted in the 1760s against changes introduced by a Republican legislature that was determined to transform Dartmouth into a state college. Marshall ruled that Dartmouth's corporate charter could not be altered by a state legislature. Though in this case the Supreme Court was protecting Dartmouth's independence and its chartered privileges, the decision also protected the hundreds of turnpike and canal companies, manufacturing corporations, and other ventures that held privileges under corporate charters granted by state governments. Once the charters had been granted, the states could neither regulate the corporations nor cancel their privileges. Thus corporate charters acquired the legal status of contracts, beyond the reach of democratic politics.

Two weeks after the *Dartmouth* decision, Marshall handed down the majority opinion in *McCulloch* v. *Maryland*. The Maryland legislature had attempted to tax the Baltimore branch of the Bank of the United States, and the Bank had challenged the legislature's right to do so. Marshall decided in favor of the Bank. He stated, first, that the Constitution granted the federal government "implied powers" that included chartering the Bank, and he denied Maryland's right to tax the Bank or any other federal agency. "Americans," he said, "did not design to make their government dependent on the states." And yet there were many, particularly in Marshall's native South, who remained certain that that was precisely what the founders had intended.

In *Gibbons* v. *Ogden* (1824) the Marshall Court broke a state-granted steamship monopoly in New York. The monopoly, Marshall argued, interfered with federal jurisdiction over interstate commerce. Like *Dartmouth College* v. *Woodward* and *McCulloch* v. *Maryland*, this decision empowered the national government in relation to the states. And like them, it encouraged private entrepreneurialism. Agreeing with congressmen who supported the American System,

John Marshall's Supreme Court assumed that a natural and beneficial link existed between federal power and market society.

Meanwhile, the state courts were working quieter but equally profound transformations of American law. In the early republic, state courts had often viewed property not only as a private possession but as part of a neighborhood. Thus when a miller built a dam that flooded upriver farms or impaired the fishery, the courts might make him take those interests into account, often in ways that reduced the business uses of his property. By the 1830s, New England courts were routinely granting the owners of industrial millsites unrestricted water rights, even when the exercise of those rights inflicted damage on their neighbors. As early as 1805, the New York Supreme Court in *Palmer* v. *Mulligan* had asserted that the right to develop property for business purposes was inherent in the ownership of property.

The Transportation Revolution

After 1815 dramatic improvements in transportation—more and better roads, steamboats, canals, and finally railroads—tied old communities together and penetrated previously isolated neighborhoods. It was these improvements that made the transition to a market society physically possible.

Transportation in 1815

In 1815 the United States was a rural nation stretching from the old settlements on the Atlantic coast to the trans-Appalachian frontier, with transportation facilities that ranged from primitive to nonexistent. West of the Appalachians, transportation was almost entirely undeveloped. Until about 1830, most westerners were southern yeomen who settled near tributaries of the Ohio-Mississippi River system. Frontier farmers floated their produce downriver on jerry-built flatboats; at New Orleans it was transshipped to New York and other eastern ports. Most boatmen knocked down their flatboats, sold the lumber and then walked home to Kentucky or Ohio over the dangerous path known as the Natchez Trace.

Transporting goods to the western settlements was even more difficult. Keelboatmen like the legendary Mike Fink could navigate upstream—using eddies and back currents, sailing when the wind was right, but usually poling their boat against the current. Skilled crews averaged only 15 miles a day. Looking for better routes, some merchants dragged finished goods across Pennsylvania and into the West at Pittsburgh, but transport costs made these goods prohibitively expensive. Consequently the trans-Appalachian settlements remained marginal to the market economy.

Improvements: Roads and Rivers

In 1816 Congress resumed construction of the National Road (first authorized in 1802) that linked the Potomac River with the Ohio River at Wheeling, Virginia. The smooth, crushed-rock thoroughfare reached Wheeling in 1818. At about the same time, Pennsylvania extended the Lancaster Turnpike to make it run from Philadelphia to the Ohio River at Pittsburgh. The National Road made it easier for settlers and a few merchants' wagons to reach the West. But the cost of moving bulky farm produce over the road remained very high. Eastbound traffic on the National Road consisted largely of cattle and pigs. Farmers continued to float their corn, cotton, wheat, salt pork, and whiskey south by riverboat and thence to eastern markets.

It was the steamboat that first made commercial agriculture feasible in the West. In 1807 an entrepreneur named Robert Fulton launched the *Clermont* on an upriver trip from New York City to Albany. Over the next few years Americans developed flat-bottomed steamboats that could navigate rivers even at low water. The first steamboat reached Louisville from New Orleans in 1815. Two years later, with 17 steamboats already working western rivers, the *Washington* made the New Orleans–Louisville run in 25 days, a feat that convinced westerners that two-way river trade was possible. By 1820, 69 steamboats were operating on western rivers. By the eve of the Civil War 2 million tons of western produce—most of it southwestern cotton—reached the docks at New Orleans. The steamboat had transformed the interior from an isolated frontier into a busy commercial region that traded farm and plantation products for manufactured goods.

IMPROVEMENTS: CANALS AND RAILROADS

In 1817 Governor DeWitt Clinton talked the New York legislature into building a canal linking the Hudson River with Lake Erie—thus opening a continuous water route between the Northwest and New York City. The Erie Canal was a near-visionary feat of engineering: Designed by self-taught engineers and built by gangs of Irish immigrants, local farmboys, and convict laborers, it stretched 364 miles from Albany to Buffalo. Construction began in 1819, and the canal reached Buffalo in 1825. It was clear even before then that the canal would repay New York state's investment of $7.5 million many times over, and that it would transform the territory it served.

The Erie Canal's first and most powerful effects were on western New York, which had been a raw frontier accessible to the East only over a notoriously bad state road. By 1830 the New York corridor of the Erie Canal was one of the world's great grain-growing regions, dotted with market towns and new cities like Syracuse, Rochester, and Buffalo.

The Erie Canal was an immense success, and legislators and entrepreneurs in other states joined a canal boom that lasted for 20 years. Northwestern states, Ohio in particular, built ambitious canal systems that linked isolated areas to the Great Lakes and thus to the Erie Canal. Northeastern states followed suit: A canal between Worcester and Providence linked the farms of central Massachusetts with Narragansett Bay. Another canal linked the coal mines of northeastern Pennsylvania with the Hudson River at Kingston, New York. In 1835 Pennsylvania completed a canal from Philadelphia to Pittsburgh.

The first American railroads connected burgeoning cities to rivers and canals. The Baltimore and Ohio Railroad, for example, linked Baltimore to the rivers of the West. Although the approximately 3,000 miles of railroads built between the late 1820s and 1840 helped the market positions of some cities, they did not constitute a national or even a regional rail network. A national system was created by the 5,000 miles of track laid in the 1840s and by the flurry of railroad building that gave the United States a rail network of 30,000 miles by 1860—a continuous, integrated system that created massive links between the East and the Northwest and that threatened to put canals out of business. In fact, the New York Central,

RIVERS, ROADS, AND CANALS, 1825–1860

which paralleled the Erie Canal, rendered that canal obsolete. Other railroads, particularly in the northwestern states, replaced canal and river transport almost completely, even though water transport remained cheaper.

TIME AND MONEY

The transportation revolution brought a dramatic reduction in the time and money it took to move heavy goods. Overall, the cost of moving goods across long distances dropped 95 percent between 1815 and 1860. Improvements in speed were nearly as dramatic. The overland route from Cincinnati to New York in 1815 (by keelboat upriver to Pittsburgh, then by wagon the rest of the way) had taken a minimum of 52 days. By the 1840s, upriver steamboats carried goods to the terminus of the Main Line Canal at Pittsburgh, which delivered them to Philadelphia, which sent them by train to New York City in a total transit time of 18 to 20 days. At about the same time, the Ohio canal system enabled Cincinnati to send goods north through

THE ERIE CANAL   The complex of locks on the Erie Canal at Lockport, New York, was among the most admired engineering feats of the 1820s and 1830s. The town itself, filled with boatmen and construction workers, had a reputation for violence.

Ohio, across Lake Erie, over the Erie Canal, and down the Hudson to New York City—an all-water route that reduced costs and made the trip in 18 days. Similar improvements occurred in the densely settled and increasingly urbanized Northeast. By 1840 travel time between the big northeastern cities had been reduced to from one-fourth to one-eleventh of what it had been in 1790. It was such improvements in speed and economy that made a national market possible.

By 1840 improved transportation had made a market revolution. Foreign trade, which had driven American economic growth up to 1815, continued to expand. Exports (now consisting more of southern cotton than of northern food crops) increased sixfold to $333.6 million by 1860; imports (mostly European manufactured goods) tripled to $353.6 million. Yet the increases in foreign trade represented vast reductions in the proportion of American market activity that involved other countries. Before 1815 Americans had exported about 15 percent of their total national product; by 1830 exports accounted for only 6 percent of total production. The reason for this shift was that after 1815 the United States developed self-sustaining domestic markets for farm produce and manufactured goods. The great engine of economic growth—particularly in the North and West—was not the old colonial relationship with Europe but a burgeoning internal market.

MARKETS AND REGIONS

Henry Clay and other proponents of the American System dreamed of a market-driven economy that would create a unified United States. But until at least 1840 the market revolution produced greater results within regions than between them. The farmers of New England traded food for finished goods from Boston, Lynn, Lowell, and other towns in what was becoming an urban, industrial region. Although the Erie Canal created a huge potential for interregional trade, until 1839 most of its eastbound tonnage originated in western New York. In the West, market-oriented farmers fed such rapidly growing cities as Rochester, Cleveland, Chicago, and Cincinnati, which in turn supplied the farmers with locally manufactured farm tools, furniture, shoes, and other goods. Farther south, the few plantations that did not produce their own food bought surpluses from farmers in their own region. Thus until about 1840 the market revolution was more a regional than an interregional phenomenon.

In the 1840s and 1850s, however, the new transport networks turned the increasingly industrial Northeast and mid-Atlantic and the commercial farms of the Old Northwest into a unified market society. The earliest settlers in the Northwest were southerners who had carried on a limited trade through the river system that led to New Orleans. From the 1840s onward produce left the Northwest less often by the old Ohio River route than by canal and railroad directly to the Northeast. At the same time, canals and roads from New York, Philadelphia, and Baltimore became the favored passageways for commodities entering the

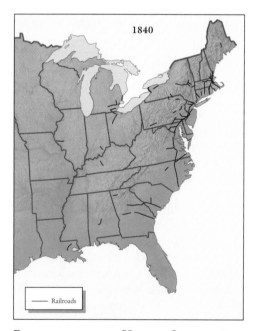

RAILROADS IN THE UNITED STATES, 1840 AND 1860

West. After 1840 the Ohio-Mississippi River system carried vastly increased amounts of goods. But that increase added up to a shrinking share of the expanded total. In short, western farmers and northeastern businessmen and manufacturers were building a national market from which the South was largely excluded.

FROM YEOMAN TO BUSINESSMAN: THE RURAL NORTH AND WEST

In the old communities of the Northeast, the market revolution sent some of the young people off to cities and factory towns and others to the West. Those who remained at home engaged in new forms of agriculture on a transformed rural landscape, while their cousins in the Northwest transformed a wilderness into cash-producing farms.

SHAPING THE NORTHERN LANDSCAPE

An early 19th century New England farm geared toward family subsistence required only 3 acres of cultivated land, 12 acres of pasture and meadow, another acre for the house, outbuildings, and vegetable garden, and a 30-acre woodlot. In the 18th century, overcrowding had encouraged some farmers to turn woodlots into poor farmland. In the 19th century, however, millions of trees were stripped from the New England countryside and livestock raising replaced mixed farming. New Englanders who tried to grow grain on their rocky, worn-out soil could not compete with the farmers of western New York and the Old Northwest, who possessed fertile lands and ready access to markets. At the same time, however, the factories and cities of the Northeast provided Yankee farmers with a market for meat and other perishables. Beef became the great New England cash crop. Dairy products were not far behind, and the proximity to city markets encouraged the spread of poultry and egg farms, fruit orchards, and truck gardens. The burgeoning shoe industry bought leather from the farmers, and woolen mills created a demand for wool.

The rise of livestock specialization reduced the amount of land under cultivation. Early in the century New Englanders still tilled their few acres in the old three-year rotation: corn the first year, rye the second, fallow the third. By the 1820s and 1830s, as farmers raised more livestock and less grain, the land that remained in cultivation was farmed more intensively. Farmers saved manure and ashes for fertilizer, plowed more deeply and systematically, and tended their crops more carefully. These improved techniques, along with cash from the sale of their livestock and the availability of food at stores, encouraged Yankee farmers to allocate less and less land to the growing of food crops.

The transition to livestock raising transformed woodlands into open pastures. As farmers leveled the forests, they sold the wood to fuel-hungry cities. In the 1830s manufacturers began marketing cast-iron stoves that heated houses more cheaply and efficiently than open hearths, and canals brought cheap Pennsylvania anthracite to the Northeast. Farmers who needed pastureland could gain substantial onetime profits from the sale of cut wood. The result was massive deforestation. At the beginning of European settlement, 95 percent of New England had been covered by forest. By 1850 forest covered only 30 percent of Connecticut, 32 percent of Rhode Island, 40 percent of Massachusetts, 45 percent of Vermont, and 50 percent of New Hampshire.

THE MAKING OF RURAL RESPECTABILITY

In 1851 a booster's history of the Phelps-Gorham Purchase in western New York published an idealized sequence of rural progress over the previous half-century. In the first winter a pioneer farmer sets his cabin in a clearing littered with fresh tree stumps where cattle, sheep, and dogs browse up to the doorstep. The second scene represents the following summer, and it is clear that a particular kind of civilization is being imposed upon the land. The farmer and his neighbors clear and plant a new field, while animals nurse their young in the foreground. The labors of the fields and pastures are separated by a rude fence from the house (now decorated with ornamental plants), a rudimentary vegetable garden, and the farmer's wife. Twenty years later the farm family has achieved respectability. Their new frame house dwarfs the pioneer cabin to which it is attached, and an orchard, a solid barn, walkways, and neat gardens share space with the house behind a white picket fence. A road with a sturdy wooden bridge passes by the front gate, giving the farmer and his neighbors access both to markets and to each other, and thus to economic progress and the pleasures of society. The final view culminates this story of rural progress in ways that mix developmental history and myth. The family now lives in a mansion surrounded by an expensive cast iron fence. The road has been widened and a graceful stone bridge has replaced the old wooden one, the forest has been completely replaced by neat, fenced rectangles of farmland and a village with a high church steeple. A railroad—the surest sign of progress and civilization at mid-century—courses through the completed landscape.

THE TRANSFORMATION OF RURAL OUTWORK

On that denuded landscape, poor families with many children continued to supplement their income with industrial outwork (see Chapter 7). But the quickening of market activity brought new kinds of dependence. Before the 1820s outworkers had used local raw materials like wool, leather, and flax and had spent only their spare time on such work. In the 1820s the manufacture of shoes and textiles began to be concentrated in factories, and outworkers who remained were reduced to dependence. Merchants now provided them with raw materials with which to make such items as cloth-covered buttons and palm-leaf hats, and set the pace of labor and the quality of the finished goods. Although outwork still helped poor families to maintain their independence, control of their labor had passed to merchants and other agents of the regional economy.

FARMERS AS CONSUMERS

With the shift to specialized market agriculture, New England farmers became customers for necessities that their forebears had produced themselves or had acquired through barter. They heated their houses with coal dug by Pennsylvania miners. They wore cotton cloth made by the factory women at Lowell. New Hampshire farm girls made straw hats for them, and the craftsmen of Lynn made their shoes. By 1830 or so, many farmers were even buying food. The Erie

A NEW ENGLAND COUNTRY STORE   A Massachusetts country store of the 1830s, as depicted in this reconstruction, was a community gathering place, a market for farm produce, and the source of a growing variety of commodities from the outside world.

Canal and the western grain belt sent flour from Rochester into eastern neighborhoods where grain was no longer grown. Many farmers found it easier to produce specialized crops for market, and to buy butter, cheese, eggs, and vegetables at country stores.

The turning point came in the 1820s. The storekeepers of Northampton, Massachusetts, for instance, had been increasing their stock in trade by about 7 percent per decade since the late 18th century. In the 1820s they increased it 45 percent and now carried not only local farm products and sugar, salt, and coffee, but bolts of New England cloth, sacks of western flour, a variety of necessities and little luxuries from the wholesale houses of New York City and Boston, and pattern samples from which to order silverware, dishes, wallpaper, and other household goods. Those goods were better than what could be made at home and were for the most part cheaper. The price of finished cloth, for instance, declined sixfold between 1815 and 1830; as a result, spinning wheels and handlooms disappeared from the farmhouses of New England. Coal and cast-iron stoves replaced the family hearth.

Material standards of living rose. But more and more families "felt" poor, and many more were incapable of feeding, clothing, and warming themselves in years when the market failed. By the 1820s and 1830s northeastern farmers depended on markets in ways that their fathers and grandfathers would have considered dangerous not only to family welfare but to the welfare of the republic itself.

THE NORTHWEST: SOUTHERN MIGRANTS

One reason the market revolution in the Northeast went as smoothly as it did was that young people with little hope of inheriting land in the old settlements moved away to towns and cities or to the new farmlands of the Northwest. Between 1815 and 1840 migrants from the older areas transformed the Northwest Territory into a working agricultural landscape. By 1830 there were 1,438,379 whites living in Ohio, Indiana, and Illinois. By 1860 the population of those three states, along with that of the new states of Wisconsin and Michigan, numbered 6,926,884—22 percent of the nation's total population.

In the Northwest until about 1830 most settlers were yeomen from Kentucky and Tennessee, usually a generation removed from Virginia, the Carolinas, and western Maryland. They moved along the Ohio and up the Muskingum, Miami, Scioto, Wabash, and Illinois Rivers to set up farms in the southern and central counties of Ohio, Indiana, and Illinois. When southerners moved north of the Ohio River into territory that banned slavery, they often did so saying that slavery blocked opportunities for poor whites. But even those who rejected slavery seldom rejected southern folkways. Like their kinfolk in Kentucky and Tennessee, the farmers of southern and central Ohio, Indiana, and Illinois remained tied to the river trade and to a mode of agriculture that favored free-ranging livestock over cultivated fields. The typical farmer fenced in a few acres of corn and left the rest of his land in woods to be roamed by southern hogs known as "razorbacks" and "land sharks." As late as 1860, southern-born farmers in the Northwest averaged 20 hogs apiece. These animals were thin and tough (they seldom grew to more than 200 pounds), and they could run long distances, leap fences, fend for themselves in the woods, and walk to distant markets.

The southern-born pioneers of the Northwest, like their cousins across the Ohio River, depended more on their families and neighbors than on distant markets. Southerners insisted on repaying debts in kind and on lending tools rather than renting them—thus engaging outsiders in the elaborate network of "neighboring" through which transplanted southerners made their livings. As late as the 1840s, in the bustling town of Springfield, Illinois, barter was the preferred system of exchange.

The Northwest: Northern Migrants

Around 1830 a stream of northeastern migrants entered the Northwest via the Erie Canal and on Great Lakes steamboats. Most of them were New Englanders who had spent a generation in western New York. The rest came directly from New England or—from the 1840s onward—from Germany and Scandinavia. In the Northwest they duplicated the intensive, market-oriented farming they had known at home. They penned their cattle and hogs and fattened them up, making them bigger and worth more than those farther south. They planted their land in grain and transformed the region into one of the world's great wheat-producing regions. In 1820 the Northwest had exported only 12 percent of its agricultural produce. By 1840 that figure had risen to 27 percent, and it stood even higher among northern-born grain farmers. By 1860 the Northwest, intensively commercialized and tied by canals and railways to eastern markets, was exporting 70 percent of its wheat. In that year it produced 46 percent of the nation's wheat crop, nearly all of it north of the line of southern settlement.

The new settlers were notably receptive to improvements in farming techniques. They quickly adopted cast-iron plows, which cut cleanly through oak roots 4 inches thick. By the 1830s the efficient, expensive grain cradle had become the standard harvest tool in northwestern wheat fields. From the 1840s onward, even this advanced hand tool was replaced by mass-produced machinery such as the McCormick reaper. Instead of threshing their grain by driving cattle and horses over it, farmers bought new horse-powered and treadmill threshers and used hand-cranked fanning mills to speed the process of cleaning the grain.

Most agricultural improvements were tailored to grain and dairy farming, and were taken up most avidly by the northern farmers. Others rejected them as expensive and "unnatural." They thought that cast-iron plows poisoned the soil and that fanning mills made a "wind contrary to nater," and thus offended God. John Chapman, an eccentric Yankee who earned the nickname "Johnny Appleseed" by planting apple tree cuttings in southern Ohio and Indiana before the settlers arrived, planted only low-yield, common trees; he regarded grafting, which farmers farther north and east were using to improve the quality of their apples, as "against nature." Southerners scoffed at the Yankee fondness for mechanical improvements, the systematic breeding of animals and plants, careful bookkeeping, and farm techniques learned from magazines and books.

Conflict between intensive agriculture and older, less market-oriented ways reached comic proportions when the Illinois legislature imposed stiff penalties on farmers who allowed their small, poorly bred bulls to run loose and impregnate cows with questionable sperm, thereby depriving the owners of high-bred bulls of their breeding fees and rendering the systematic breeding of cattle impossible. When the poorer farmers refused to pen their bulls, the law was rescinded. A local historian explained that "there was a generous feeling in the hearts of the people in favor of an equality of privileges, even among bulls."

Households

The market revolution transformed 18th century households into 19th century homes. For one thing, Americans began to limit the size of their families. The decline was most pronounced in the North, particularly in commercialized areas. Rural birth rates remained at

18th century levels in the southern uplands, in the poorest and most isolated communities of the North, and on the frontier. These communities practiced the old labor-intensive agriculture and relied on the labor of large families. For farmers who used newer techniques or switched to livestock, large families made less sense. Moreover, large broods hampered the ability of future-minded parents to provide for their children, and conflicted with new notions of privacy and domesticity that were taking shape among an emerging rural middle class.

The commercialization of agriculture was closely associated with the emergence of the concept of housework. Before 1815 farm wives had labored in the house, the barnyard, and the garden while their husbands and sons worked in the fields. With the market revolution came a sharper distinction between "male work" that was part of the cash economy and "female work" that was not. Even such traditional women's tasks as dairying, vegetable gardening, and poultry raising became men's work once they became cash-producing specialties.

At the same time, new kinds of women's work emerged within households. Although there were fewer children to care for, the culture began to demand forms of child-rearing that were more intensive, individualized, and mother-centered. Storebought white flour, butter, and eggs and the new iron stoves eased the burdens of food preparation, but they also created demands for pies, cakes, and other fancy foods that earlier generations had only imagined. And

A SOAP ADVERTISEMENT FROM THE 1850S The rigors of "Old Washing Day" lead the mother in this advertisement to abuse the children and house pets, while her husband leaves the house. With American Cream Soap, domestic bliss returns. The children and cats are happy, the husband returns, and the wife has time to sew.

while farm women no longer spun and wove their own cloth, the availability of manufactured cloth created the expectation that their families would dress more neatly and with greater variety than they had in the past—at the cost of far more time spent by women on sewing, washing, and ironing. Similar expectations demanded greater personal and domestic cleanliness, and farm women from the 1830s onward spent time planting flower beds, cleaning and maintaining prized furniture, mirrors, rugs, and ceramics, and scrubbing floors and children.

Housework was tied to new notions of privacy, decency, and domestic comfort. Before 1820 farmers cared little about how their houses looked, often tossing trash and garbage out the door for the pigs and chickens that foraged near the house. In the 1820s and 1830s, as farmers began to grow cash crops and adopt middle-class ways, they began to plant shade trees and kept their yards free of trash. They painted their houses and sometimes their fences and outbuildings, arranged their woodpiles into neat stacks, surrounded their houses with flowers and ornamental shrubs, and tried to hide their privies from view.

Inside, prosperous farmhouses took on an air of privacy and comfort. Separate kitchens and iron stoves replaced open hearths. The availability of finished cloth permitted the regular use of tablecloths, napkins, doilies, curtains, bedspreads, and quilts. Oil lamps replaced homemade candles, and the more comfortable families began to decorate their homes with wallpaper and upholstered furniture. Farm couples moved their beds away from the hearth and (along with the children's beds that had been scattered throughout the house) put them into spaces designated as bedrooms. They took the washstands and basins, which were coming into more common use, out of the kitchen and put them into the bedroom, thus making sleeping, bathing, and sex more private than they had been in the past. At the center of this new house stood the farm wife—apart from the bustling world of commerce, but decorating and caring for the amenities that commerce bought.

NEIGHBORHOODS: THE LANDSCAPE OF PRIVACY

By the 1830s and 1840s the market revolution had transformed the rural landscape of the Northeast. The forests had been reduced, the swamps had been drained, and most of the streams and rivers were interrupted by mill dams. Bears, panthers, and wolves had disappeared, along with the beaver and many of the fish. Now there were extensive pastures where English cattle and sheep browsed on English grasses dotted with English wildflowers such as buttercups, daisies, and dandelions. Next to the pastures were neatly cultivated croplands that were regularly fertilized and seldom allowed to lie fallow. And at the center stood brightly painted houses and outbuildings surrounded by flowers and shrubs and vegetable gardens. Many towns, particularly in New England, had planted shade trees along the country roads, completing a rural landscape of straight lines and human cultivation—a landscape that made it easy to think of nature as a commodity to be altered and controlled.

Within that landscape, old practices and old forms of neighborliness fell into disuse. Neighbors continued to exchange goods and labor and to contract debts that might be left unpaid for years. But debts were more likely to be owed to profit-minded storekeepers and creditors, and even debts between neighbors were often paid in cash. Traditionally, storekeepers had allowed farmers to bring in produce and have it credited to a neighbor/creditor's account. In the 1830s, storekeepers began to demand cash payment or to charge lower prices to those who paid cash. Neighborly rituals like parties, husking bees, barn-raisings—with their drinking and socializing—were scorned as an inefficient and morally suspect waste of time.

Thus the efficient farmer after the 1820s concentrated on producing commodities that could be marketed outside the neighborhood, and used his cash income to buy material comforts for his family and to pay debts and provide a cash inheritance for his children. Although much of the old world of household and neighborhood survived, farmers created a subsistence and maintained the independence of their households not through those spheres but through unprecedented levels of dependence on the outside world.

THE INDUSTRIAL REVOLUTION

In the 50 years following 1820, American cities grew faster than ever before or since. The fastest growth was in new cities that served commercial agriculture and in factory towns that produced for a largely rural domestic market. Even in the seaports, growth derived more from commerce with the hinterland than from international trade. Paradoxically, the market revolution in the countryside had produced the beginnings of industry and the greatest period of urban growth in U.S. history.

FACTORY TOWNS: THE RHODE ISLAND SYSTEM

Jeffersonians held that the United States must always remain rural. Americans could expand into the rich new agricultural lands of the West, trade their farm surpluses for European finished goods, and thus avoid creating cities with their dependent social classes. Federalists argued that Americans, in order to retain their independence, must produce their own manufactured goods. Neo-Federalists combined those arguments after the War of 1812. They argued that America's abundant water power would enable Americans to build their factories across the countryside instead of creating great industrial cities. Such a decentralized factory system would provide employment for country women and children and thus subsidize the independence of struggling farmers.

The first factories were textile mills. The key to the mass production of cotton and woolen textiles was a water-powered machine that spun yarn and thread. The machine had been invented and patented by the Englishman Richard Arkwright in 1769. The British government forbade the machinery or the people who operated it to leave the country. Scores of textile workers, however, defied the law and made their way to North America. One of them was Samuel Slater, who had served an apprenticeship under Jedediah Strutt, a partner of Arkwright who had improved on the original machine. Working from memory, Slater built the first Arkwright spinning mill in America at Pawtucket, Rhode Island, in 1790.

Slater's first mill was a small frame building tucked among the town's houses and craftsmen's shops. Although its capacity was limited to the spinning of cotton yarn, it provided work for children in the mill and for women who wove yarn into cloth in their homes. As his business grew and he advertised for widows with children, however, Slater was greeted by families headed by landless, impoverished men. Slater's use of children from these families prompted "respectable" farmers and craftsmen to pull their children out of Slater's growing complex of mills. More poor families arrived to take their places, and during the first years of the 19th century Pawtucket grew rapidly into a disorderly mill town.

Soon Slater and other mill owners built factory villages in the countryside. The practice became known as the Rhode Island (or "family") system. At several locations in southern New

England, mill owners built whole villages surrounded by company-owned farmland that they rented to the husbands and fathers of their mill workers. The workplace was closely supervised, and drinking and other troublesome practices were forbidden in the villages. Fathers and older sons either worked on rented farms or as laborers at the mills. By the late 1820s Slater and most of the other owners were getting rid of the outworkers and were buying power looms, thus transforming the villages into disciplined, self-contained factory towns that turned raw cotton into finished cloth.

FACTORY TOWNS: THE WALTHAM SYSTEM

Touring English factory districts in 1811, a wealthy, cultivated Bostonian named Francis Cabot Lowell asked the plant managers questions and made secret drawings of the machines he saw. Returning home, Lowell joined with wealthy friends to form the Boston Manufacturing Company—soon known as the Boston Associates. In 1813 they built their first mill at Waltham, Massachusetts, and then expanded into Lowell, Lawrence, and other new towns

WOMEN IN THE MILLS Two female weavers from a Massachusetts textile mill proudly display the tools of their trade. This tintype was taken in about 1860, when New England farm women such as these were being replaced by Irish immigrant labor.

near Boston during the 1820s. The company, operating under what became known as the Waltham system, built mills that differed from the early Rhode Island mills in two ways: First, they were heavily capitalized and as fully mechanized as possible; they turned raw cotton into finished cloth with little need for skilled workers. Second, the operatives who tended their machines were young, single women recruited from the farms of northern New England. The company provided carefully supervised boardinghouses for them and enforced rules of conduct both on and off the job. The young women worked steadily, never drank, seldom stayed out late, and attended church faithfully. They impressed visitors, particularly those who had seen factory workers in other places, as a dignified and self-respecting workforce.

The brick mills and prim boardinghouses set within landscaped towns and occupied by sober, well-behaved farm girls signified the Boston Associates' desire to build a profitable textile industry without creating a permanent working class. The women would work for a few years in a carefully controlled environment, send their wages back to their family, and return home to live as country housewives. However, these young farm women did not send their wages home or, as was popularly believed, use them to pay for their brothers' college education. Some saved their money to use as dowries that their fathers could not afford. More, however, spent their wages on themselves—particularly on clothes and books.

The Waltham system thus produced a self-respecting sisterhood of independent, wage-earning women. After finishing their stint in the mills, most of them married and became housewives. One in three married Lowell men and became city dwellers. Those who returned home to rural neighborhoods remained unmarried longer than their sisters who had stayed at home, and then married men about their own age who worked at something other than farming. Thus through the 1840s the Boston Associates kept their promise to produce cotton cloth profitably without creating a permanent working class. But they did not succeed in shuttling young women from rural to urban paternalism and back again. Wage labor, the ultimate degradation for agrarian-republican men, opened a road out of rural patriarchy for thousands of young women.

URBAN BUSINESSMEN

The market revolution hit American cities with particular force. Here there was little concern for creating a classless industrial society: Vastly wealthy men of finance, a new middle class that bought and sold an ever-growing range of consumer goods, and the impoverished women and men who produced those goods lived together in communities that unabashedly recognized the reality of social class.

The richest men were seaport merchants who had survived and prospered during the world wars that ended in 1815. They carried on as importers and exporters, took control of banks and insurance companies, and made great fortunes in urban real estate. Below the old mercantile elite (or, in the case of the new cities of the interior, at the top of society) stood a growing middle class of wholesale and retail merchants, master craftsmen who had transformed themselves into manufacturers, and an army of lawyers, salesmen, auctioneers, clerks, bookkeepers, and accountants who took care of the paperwork for the new market society. At the head of this new middle class were the wholesale merchants of the seaports who bought hardware, crockery, and other commodities from importers and then sold them in smaller lots to storekeepers from the interior. Slightly below them were the large processors of farm products. Another step down were specialized retail merchants who dealt in books, furniture, crockery, or some other consumer goods. Alongside the merchants stood master craftsmen who had become manufacturers. With their workers busy in backrooms or in household workshops, they now called themselves shoe dealers and merchant tailors. At the bottom of this new commercial world were hordes of clerks, most of them young men who hoped to rise in the world. Both in numbers and in the nature of the work, this white-collar army formed a new class created by the market revolution.

In the 1820s and 1830s the commercial classes transformed the look and feel of American cities. As retailing and manufacturing became separate activities (even in firms that did both), the merchants, salesmen, and clerks now worked in quiet offices on downtown business streets. Both in the seaports and the new towns of the interior, impressive brick and glass storefronts appeared on the main streets. Perhaps the most striking monuments of the self-conscious new business society were the handsome retail arcades that began going up in the 1820s, providing consumers with comfortable, gracious space in which to shop.

METROPOLITAN INDUSTRIALIZATION

While businessmen were developing a new middle-class ethos, the people who made the consumer goods were growing more numerous while at the same time disappearing from view. With the exception of textiles and a few other commodities, few goods were made in mechanized factories before the 1850s. Most goods were made by hand. City merchants and master craftsmen met the growing demand by hiring more workers. The largest handicrafts—shoemaking, tailoring, and the building trades—were divided into skilled and semiskilled segments and farmed out to subcontractors who could turn a profit only by cutting labor costs. The result was the creation of an urban working class.

Take the case of tailoring. High rents and costly real estate, together with the absence of water power, made it impossible to set up large factories in cities. But the nature of the clothing trade and the availability of cheap labor gave rise to a system of subcontracting that transformed needlework into the first "sweated" trade in America. Merchants kept a few skilled male tailors to take care of the custom trade, and to cut cloth into patterned pieces for ready-made clothing. The pieces were sent out to needleworkers who sewed them together in their homes. Male tailors continued to do the finishing work on men's suits. But most of the work was done by women who worked long hours for piece rates that ranged from 75 cents to $1.50 per week. In 1860, Brooks Brothers kept 70 workers in its shops and used 2,000 to 3,000 outworkers, most of them women. Along with clothing, women in garrets and tenements manufactured the items with which the middle class decorated itself and its homes: embroidery, doilies, artificial flowers, fringe, tassels, fancy-bound books, and parasols. All provided work for ill-paid legions of female workers.

Other trades followed similar patterns. For example, shoes were made in uniform sizes in the Northeast and sent in barrels all over the country. Like tailoring, shoemaking was divided into skilled operations and time-consuming unskilled tasks. The relatively skilled and highly paid work of cutting and shaping the uppers was performed by men; the drudgery of sewing the pieces together went to low-paid women. Skilled shoemakers performed the most difficult work for taskmasters who passed the work along to subcontractors who controlled poorly paid, unskilled workers. Skilled craftsmen could earn as much as $2 a day making custom boots and shoes. Men shaping uppers in boardinghouses earned a little more than half of that; women binders could work a full week and earn as little as 50 cents. In this as in other trades, wage rates and gendered tasks reflected the old family division of labor, which was based on the assumption that female workers lived with an income-earning husband or father. In fact, increasing numbers of them were young women living alone or older women who had been widowed, divorced, or abandoned—often with small children.

Members of the new middle class entertained notions of gentility based on the distinction between manual and nonmanual work. Lowly clerks and wealthy merchants prided themselves on the fact that they worked with their heads and not their hands. They fancied that it was their entrepreneurial and managerial skills that were making the market revolution happen, while manual workers simply performed tasks thought up by the middle class. The men and women of an emerging working class struggled to create dignity and a sense of public worth in a society that hid them from view and defined them as "hands."

THE MARKET REVOLUTION IN THE SOUTH

With the end of war in 1815, the cotton belt of the South expanded dramatically. The resumption of international trade, the revival of textile production in Britain and on the European continent, and the emergence of factory production in the northeastern United States encouraged southern planters to extend the short-staple cotton lands of South Carolina and Georgia into a belt that would stretch across the Old Southwest and beyond the Mississippi into Texas and Arkansas.

The southwestern plantation belt produced stupendous amounts of cotton. In 1810 the South produced 178,000 bales of ginned cotton—more than 59 times the 3,000 bales it had produced in 1790. By 1820 production stood at 334,000 bales. With the opening of southwestern cotton lands, production jumped to 1.35 million bales in 1840 and to 4.8 million on the eve of the Civil War. Over these years cotton accounted for one-half to two-thirds of the value of all U.S. exports. The South produced three-fourths of the world supply of cotton—a commodity that, more than any other, was the raw material of industrialization in Britain and Europe and, increasingly, in the northeastern United States.

THE ORGANIZATION OF SLAVE LABOR

The plantations of the cotton belt were among the most intensely commercialized farms in the world. Many of them grew nothing but cotton—a practice that produced huge profits in good years but in bad years sent planters into debt. Other plantations grew supplementary cash crops and produced their own food. But nearly all of the plantation owners organized their labor in ways that maximized production and reinforced the dominance of the white men who owned the farms.

Cotton, which requires a long growing season and a lot of attention, was well suited to slave labor and to the climate of the Deep South. After the land was cleared and plowed, it was set out in individual plants. Laborers weeded the fields with hoes throughout the hot, humid growing season. In the fall, the cotton ripened unevenly. In a harvest season that lasted up to two months, pickers swept through the fields repeatedly, selecting only the ripe bolls. Plantations that grew their own food cultivated large cornfields and vegetable gardens and kept large numbers of hogs. To cope with diverse growing seasons and killing times that overlapped with the cotton cycle, planters created complex labor systems.

Although this slave force was larger than most, its organization was familiar to every southerner: Gangs of women wielded the hoes and men did the plowing, accompanied, especially

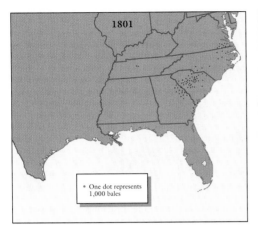
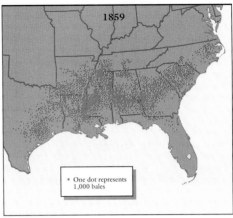

COTTON PRODUCTION, 1801 AND 1859

during the busiest times, by strong women. The division of labor by sex was standard: Even at harvest festivals teams of men shucked the corn while women prepared the meal and the after-supper dance. And during the harvest, when every slave was in the fields, men tended to work beside men, women beside women. Most of the house slaves were women, and female slaves often worked under the direction of the plantation mistress, seeing to the dairy cattle, chickens and geese, and tending vegetable gardens and orchards.

While black women routinely worked in southern fields, white women did so only on the poorest farms and only at the busiest times of the year. They took care of the poultry and cattle and the vegetable gardens—and not the profit-oriented fields. As the larger farms grew into plantations, white women took on the task of supervising the household slaves instead of doing the work themselves.

PATERNALISM

On the whole, the exploitation of slave labor after 1820 became both more systematic and more humane. Planters paid close attention to labor discipline: They supervised the work more closely than in the past, tried (often unsuccessfully) to substitute gang labor for the task system, and forcibly "corrected" slaves whose work was slow or sloppy. At the same time, however, planters clothed the new discipline within a larger attempt to make North American slavery into a system that was both paternalistic and humane. Food and clothing seem to have improved, and individual cabins for slave families became standard. State laws often forbade the more brutal forms of discipline, and they uniformly demanded that slaves not be made to work on Sunday.

The systematic paternalism on 19th century farms and plantations was the result both of planter self-interest and a genuine attempt to exert a kindly, paternal control over slaves. Slaves endured the discipline and accepted the food, clothing, time off, and religious instruction—but used all of them to serve themselves and not the masters (see Chapter 10). But for all that, material standards rose. One rough indicator is physical height. On the eve of the Civil War,

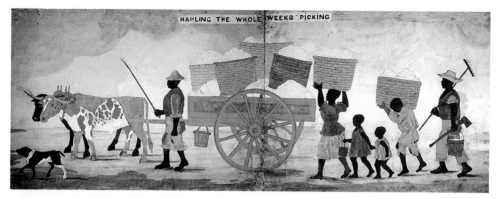

"HAULING THE WHOLE WEEK'S PICKING"   William Henry Brown made this collage of a slave harvest crew near Vicksburg, Mississippi, in 1842. The rigors of the harvest put everyone, including small children, into the fields.

southern slaves averaged about an inch shorter than northern whites. But they were fully 3 inches taller than newly imported Africans, 2 inches taller than slaves on the Caribbean island of Trinidad, and an inch taller than British Marines. While slaves suffered greater infant mortality than whites, those who survived infancy lived out "normal" life spans. Between 1810 and 1860 the slave population of the United States increased threefold, an increase due entirely to the fact that—alone among slave populations of the Western Hemisphere—births outnumbered deaths among North American slaves.

YEOMEN AND PLANTERS

Cotton brought economies of scale: Planters with big farms and many slaves operated more efficiently and more profitably than farmers with fewer resources. And as the price of slaves and good land rose, fewer and fewer owners shared in the profits of the cotton economy, and wealth became more concentrated. The market revolution had commercialized southern agriculture, but a shrinking proportion of the region's white population shared in the benefits. The result was not simply an unequal distribution of wealth, but the creation of a dual economy: plantations at the commercial center and a white yeomanry on the fringes.

There were, of course, small farmers in the plantation counties. They tended to be commercial farmers, growing a few bales of cotton with family labor and perhaps a slave or two. Many of them were poor relatives of prosperous plantation owners. They voted the great planters into office, and used their cotton gins and tapped into their marketing networks. Some of them worked as overseers for their wealthy neighbors, sold them food, and served on local slave patrols. Economic disparities between planters and farmers in the plantation belt continued to widen, but the farmers remained tied to the cotton economy.

Most small farmers, however, lived away from the plantations in what was called the up-country: the eastern slopes of the Appalachians from the Chesapeake through Georgia, the western slopes of the mountains in Kentucky and Tennessee, the pine-covered hill country of northern Mississippi and Alabama, parts of Texas and Louisiana, most of the Ozark Plateau in Missouri and Arkansas. All of these lands were too high, cold, isolated, and heavily wooded to support plantation crops. Here the farmers built a yeoman society that shared many of the characteristics of the 18th century countryside (see Chapter 7). But while northern farmers commercialized, their southern cousins continued in a household- and neighborhood-centered agriculture. Indeed many southern farmers stayed outside the market almost entirely. Farmers in large parts of the up-country South preferred to raise livestock instead of growing cotton or tobacco. They planted cornfields and let their pigs run loose in the woods and on unfenced private land. In late summer and fall they rounded up the animals and sold them to drovers who conducted cross-country drives and sold the animals to flatland merchants and planters. It was a way of life that sustained some of the most fiercely independent neighborhoods in the country.

Yeomen and the Market

A larger group of southern yeomen practiced mixed farming for household subsistence and neighborhood exchange, with the surplus sent to market. Most of these farmers owned their own land. These farmers practiced a "subsistence plus" agriculture. They put most of their land into subsistence crops and livestock, cultivating only a few acres of cotton. They devoted more acreage to cotton as transportation made markets more accessible, but few southern yeomen allowed themselves to become wholly dependent on the market. With the income from a few bales of cotton they could pay their debts and taxes and buy coffee, tea, sugar, tobacco, cloth, and shoes. But they continued to enter and leave the market at will, for their own purposes. The market served the interests of southern yeomen. It seldom dominated them.

Since few farms were self-sufficient, the yeomen farmers routinely traded labor and goods with each other. In the plantation counties, such cooperation tended to reinforce the power of planters who put some of their resources at the disposal of their poorer neighbors. In the up-country, cooperation reinforced neighborliness. Debts contracted within the network of kin and neighbors were generally paid in kind or in labor, and creditors often allowed their neighbors' debts to go unpaid for years.

Among southern neighborly restraints on entrepreneurialism, none was more distinctive than the region's attitude toward fences. In the North, well-maintained fences were a sign of ambitious, hardworking farmers. The poor fences of the South, on the other hand, were interpreted as a sign of laziness. Actually, the scarcity of fences in most southern neighborhoods was the result of local custom and state law. In country neighborhoods where families fished and hunted for food, and where livestock roamed freely, fences conflicted with a local economy that required neighborhood use of privately owned land. The lack of fences in the South reflected neighborhood constraints on the private use of private property, and thus on individual acquisitiveness and ambition. Such constraints, however, were necessary to the subsistence of families and neighborhoods as they were organized in the upland South.

A Balance Sheet: The Plantation and Southern Development

The owners of the South's large farms were among the richest men in the Western Hemisphere. In 1860 the 12 wealthiest counties in the United States were in the South. Southern wealth, however, was concentrated in fewer and fewer hands. The slaves whose labor created the wealth owned nothing. As many as one-third of southern white families lived in poverty, and a declining proportion of the others owned slaves. And huge disparities existed even among the slaveholding minority; in 1860 only one-fifth of the slaveholders owned 20 or more slaves, thus crossing the generally acknowledged line that separated "farmers" from "planters."

In economic terms, the concentration of wealth in the hands of a few planters had profound effects on how the market revolution affected the region. Much of the white population remained marginal to the market economy. Whereas in the North the rural demand for credit, banking facilities, farm tools, clothing, and other consumer goods fueled a revolution in commerce, finance, and industry, the South remained a poor market for manufactured goods. The slaves wore cheap cloth made in the Northeast, and the planters furnished themselves and their homes with finery from Europe. In the North the exchange of farm produce for finished goods was creating self-sustaining economic growth by the 1840s. But the South continued to export its plantation staples and to build only those factories, commercial institutions, and cities that served the plantation.

Not that the South neglected technological innovation and agricultural improvement. Southerners developed Eli Whitney's hand-operated cotton gin into equipment capable of performing complex milling operations. They also developed the cotton press, a machine with a huge wooden screw powered by horses or mules, used to compress ginned cotton into tight bales for shipping. Yet there were few such innovations, and they had to do with the processing and shipping of cotton rather than with its production. The truth is that cotton was a labor-intensive crop that discouraged innovation. Moreover, plantation slaves often resisted their enslavement by sabotaging expensive tools and draft animals, scattering manure in haphazard ways, and passively resisting innovations that would have added to their drudgery. So the cotton fields continued to be cultivated by clumsy, mule-drawn plows that barely scratched the soil, by women wielding hoes, and by gangs who harvested the crop by hand.

Southern state governments spent little on internal improvements. A Virginia canal linked the flour mills at Richmond with inland grain fields, and another connected Chesapeake Bay with the National Road. But planters in the cotton belt had ready access to the South's magnificent system of navigable rivers, while upland whites saw little need for expensive, state-supported internal improvements. Nor did the South build cities. The South used its canals and railroads mainly to move plantation staples to towns that transshipped them out of the region. Southern cities were located on the periphery of the region and served as transportation depots for plantation crops. Southern businessmen turned to New York City for credit, insurance, and coastal and export shipping. And it was from New York that they ordered finished goods for the southern market.

CONCLUSION

In 1858 James H. Hammond, a slaveholding senator from South Carolina, asked:

> What would happen if no cotton was furnished for three years? . . . England would topple headlong and carry the whole civilized world with her save the south. No, you dare not make war on cotton. No power on earth dares to make war on cotton. Cotton is king.

CHRONOLOGY

1790	Samuel Slater builds his first Arkwright spinning mill at Pawtucket, Rhode Island
1801	John Marshall appointed chief justice of the Supreme Court
1807	Robert Fulton launches first steamboat
1813	Boston Associates erect their first textile mill at Waltham, Massachusetts
1815	War of 1812 ends
1816	Congress charters Second Bank of the United States • Congress passes protective tariff • *Dartmouth College* v. *Woodward* defines a private charter as a contract that cannot be altered by a state legislature • *McCulloch* v. *Maryland* affirms Congress's "implied powers" under the Constitution
1818	National Road completed to Ohio River at Wheeling, Virginia
1822	President Monroe vetoes National Road reparations bill
1824	*Gibbons* v. *Ogden* extends power of national government
1825	New York completes the Erie Canal between Buffalo and Albany
1828	Baltimore and Ohio Railroad (America's first) completed
1835	Main Line Canal connects Philadelphia and Pittsburgh

Along with other planter-politicians, Hammond argued that farmers at the fringes of the world market economy could coerce the commercial-industrial center. He was wrong. The commitment to cotton and slavery had not only isolated the South politically, but it had also deepened the South's dependence on the world's financial and industrial centers. The North and West underwent a qualitative market revolution after 1815—a revolution that enriched both, and that transformed the Northeast from a part of the old colonial periphery (the suppliers of food and raw materials) into a part of the core (the suppliers of manufactured goods and financing) of the world market economy. In contrast, the South, by exporting plantation staples in exchange for imported goods, worked itself deeper and deeper into dependence.

10

TOWARD AN AMERICAN CULTURE

THE NORTHERN MIDDLE CLASS ∾ THE PLAIN PEOPLE OF THE NORTH

THE RISE OF POPULAR CULTURE

FAMILY, CHURCH, AND NEIGHBORHOOD: THE WHITE SOUTH

THE PRIVATE LIVES OF SLAVES

Americans after 1815 experienced wave after wave of social and cultural change. Territorial expansion, the market revolution, and the spread of plantation slavery uprooted Americans and broke old social patterns. Americans in these years created distinctive forms of popular literature and art, and they found new ways of having fun. They flocked to evangelical revivals—meetings designed to produce religious conversions and led by preachers who were trained to that task—in which they revived and remade American religious life.

The emerging American culture was more or less uniformly republican, capitalist, and Protestant. But different kinds of Americans made different cultures out of the revolutionary inheritance, the market revolution, and revival religion. Northeastern businessmen and southern planters agreed that economic progress was indeed progress, but they differed radically on its moral implications. Slaveholders, slaves, factory hands, rich and poor farmers, and middle-class women all heard the same Bible stories and learned different lessons. The result, visible from the 1830s onward, was an American national culture composed largely of subcultures based on region, class, and race.

THE NORTHERN MIDDLE CLASS

"The most valuable class in any community," declared the poet-journalist Walt Whitman in 1858, "is the middle class." At that time, the term "middle class" (and the social group that it described) was no more than 30 or 40 years old. Those who claimed the title "middle class" were largely the new kinds of proprietors made by the market revolution—city and country merchants, master craftsmen who had turned themselves into manufacturers, and the mass of market-oriented farmers.

A disproportionate number of them were New Englanders. New England was the first center of factory production, and southern New England farms were thoroughly commercialized by the 1830s. Yankee migrants dominated the commercial heartland of western New York and the northern regions of the Northwest. Even in the seaport cities businessmen from

New England were often at the center of economic innovation. This Yankee middle class invented cultural forms that became the core of an emerging business civilization. They upheld the autonomous and morally accountable individual against the claims of traditional neighborhoods and traditional families. They devised an intensely private, mother-centered domestic life. Most of all, they adhered to a reformed Yankee Protestantism whose moral imperatives became the foundation of American middle-class culture.

THE EVANGELICAL BASE

In November 1830 the evangelist Charles Grandison Finney preached in Rochester, New York, to a church full of middle-class men and women. Most of them were transplanted New Englanders, the heirs of what was left of Yankee Calvinism. In their ministers' weekly sermons, in the formal articles of faith drawn up by their churches, and in the set prayers their children memorized, they reaffirmed the old Puritan beliefs in providence and original sin. The earthly social order (the fixed relations of power and submission between men and women, rich and poor, children and parents, and so on) was necessary because humankind was innately sinful and prone to selfishness and disorder. Christians must obey the rules governing their station in life; attempts to rearrange the social order were both sinful and doomed to failure.

Yet while they reaffirmed those conservative Puritan beliefs in church, the men and women in Finney's audience routinely ignored them in their daily lives. The benefits accruing from the market revolution were clearly the result of human effort. Just as clearly, they added up to "improvement" and "progress." And as middle-class Christians increasingly envisioned an improved material and social world, the doctrines of human inability and natural depravity, along with faith in divine providence, made less and less sense.

It was to such men and women that Charles Finney preached what became the organizing principle of northern middle-class evangelicalism: "God," he insisted, "has made man a moral free agent." Neither the social order, the troubles of this world, nor the spiritual state of individuals was divinely ordained. People would make themselves and the world better by choosing right over wrong, although they would choose right only after an evangelical conversion experience in which they submitted their rebellious wills to the will of God. It was a religion that valued individual holiness over a permanent and sacred social order. It made the spiritual nature of individuals a matter of prayer, submission, and choice.

Yankee evangelists had been moving toward Finney's formulation since the turn of the 19th century. Like Finney, they borrowed revival techniques from the Methodists (weeklong meetings, meetings in which women prayed in public, an "anxious bench" for the most likely converts), but toned them down for their own more "respectable" and affluent audience. While they used democratic methods and preached a message of individualism and free agency, however, middle-class evangelicals retained the Puritans' Old Testament sense of cosmic history: They enlisted personal holiness and spiritual democracy in a fight to the finish between the forces of good and the forces of evil in this world.

DOMESTICITY

The Yankee middle class made crucial distinctions between the home and the world. Men in cities and towns now went off to work, leaving wives and children to spend the day at home. The new middle-class evangelicalism encouraged this division of domestic labor. The public world of politics and economic exchange, said the preachers, was the proper sphere of men; women, on the other hand, were to exercise new kinds of moral influence within households.

The result was a feminization of domestic life. In the old yeoman-artisan republic, the fathers who owned property, headed households, and governed family labor were lawgivers and disciplinarians. Middle-class evangelicals raised new spiritual possibilities for women and children. Mothers replaced fathers as the principle child-rearers, and they enlisted the doctrines of free agency and individual moral responsibility in that task. Middle-class mothers sought to develop their children's conscience and their capacity to love, to teach them to make good moral choices, and to prepare them for conversion and a lifetime of Christian service.

Middle-class mothers were able to do that because they could concentrate their efforts on household duties and because they had fewer children than their mothers or grandmothers had had. Housewives also spaced their pregnancies differently. Unlike their forebears, who gave birth to a child about once every two years throughout their childbearing years, middle-class housewives had their children at five-year intervals, which meant that they could give each child close attention. As a result, households were quieter and less crowded; children learned from their mothers how to govern themselves. Thus mothers assumed responsibility for nurturing the children who would be carriers of the new middle-class culture—and fathers, ministers, and other authorities recognized the importance of that job.

The new ethos of moral free agency was mirrored in the Sunday schools. When Sunday schools first appeared in the 1790s, their purpose was to teach working-class children to read and write by having them copy long passages from the Bible. After the revivals of the 1820s and 1830s, the emphasis shifted to preparing children's souls for conversion. Middle-class children were now included in the schools, corporal punishment was forbidden, and Sunday school teachers now tried to develop the moral sensibilities of their charges. They had the children read a few Bible verses each week and then led them in a discussion of the moral lessons conveyed by the text. Thus Sunday schools became training grounds in free agency and moral accountability—a transformation that made sense only in a sentimental world where children could be trusted to make moral choices.

SENTIMENTALITY

Improvements in the printing, distribution, and marketing of books led to an outpouring of popular literature, much of it directed at the middle class. There were cookbooks, etiquette books, manuals on housekeeping, sermons, and sentimental novels—many of them written and most of them read by women. The works of popular religious writers such as Lydia Sigourney, Lydia Maria Child, and Timothy Shay Arthur found their way into thousands of middle-class homes. Sarah Josepha Hale, whose *Godey's Lady's Book* was the first mass-circulation magazine for women, acted as an arbiter of taste not only in furniture, clothing, and food but in sentiments and ideas. Sentimental novels written by women outsold by wide margins Nathaniel Hawthorne's *The Scarlet Letter* and *The House of Seven Gables,* Ralph Waldo Emerson's essays, Henry David Thoreau's *Walden,* Herman Melville's *Moby Dick,* and Walt Whitman's *Leaves of Grass.* Susan Warner's *The Wide, Wide World* broke all sales records when it appeared in 1850. Harriet Beecher Stowe's *Uncle Tom's Cabin* (1852) broke the records set by Warner.

These sentimental novels sacralized the middle-class home and the trials and triumphs of Christian women. The action takes place indoors, usually in the kitchen or parlor, and the heroines are women (in Stowe's book, docile slave Christians are included). The stories have to do with spiritual struggle, the renunciation of greed and desire, and mother love. The home is a shrine that is juxtaposed to the marketplace and the world of competition, brutality, and power. Unlike the female characters in British and European novels of the time, the women in these American novels are intelligent, generous persons who grow in strength and independence.

In sentimental domestic fiction, women assume the role of evangelical ministers, demonstrating Christian living by precept, example, and moral persuasion. Female moral influence is at war with the male world of politics and the marketplace—areas of power, greed, and moral compromise. The most successful sentimental novel was Harriet Beecher Stowe's *Uncle Tom's Cabin*. (See also the discussion in Chapter 13.) The book's spectacular popularity stemmed from its indictment of slavery as a system of absolute power at odds with the domestic values held dear by Stowe's audience of evangelical women. Based solidly in revival Christianity, the novel lambastes the rational calculation, greed, and power hunger of the "real world" that was made and governed by white men, and upholds domestic space filled with women, slaves, and children who gain spiritual power through submission to Christ. The two most telling scenes—the deaths of the Christian slave Uncle Tom and the perfect child Eva St. Claire—reenact the crucifixion of Jesus. Uncle Tom prays for his tormentors as he is beaten to death, and little Eva extracts promises of Christian behavior from her deathbed. Both are powerless, submissive characters who die in order to redeem a fallen humankind.

Thus *Uncle Tom's Cabin* and other popular sentimental novels were not frivolous fairy tales into which housewives retreated from the "real" world. They were subversive depictions of a higher spiritual reality that would move the feminine ethos of the Christian home to the center of civilization. As we shall see in Chapter 11, that vision was underneath an organized public assault on irreligion, drunkenness, prostitution, slavery, and other practices and institutions that substituted passion and force for Christian love.

A Middle-Class New England Family at Home, 1837   The room is carpeted and comfortably furnished. Father reads his newspaper; books rest on the table. Mother entertains their only child, and a kitten joins the family circle. This is the domestic foundation of sentimental culture on display.

FINE ARTS

Educated Americans of the postrevolutionary generation associated the fine arts with the sensuality, extravagance, and artificiality of European courts and European Catholicism. In making government buildings and monuments, building expensive homes, and painting portraits of wealthy and powerful men, American artists copied the classic simplicity of ancient Greece and Rome—republican styles that had been tested by time and that were free of any hint of sensuality or luxury.

In the 1820s and 1830s, however, educated Americans began to view literature and the arts more favorably. There were a number of reasons for that change. First, American nationalists began to demand an American art that could compete with the arts of the despotic Old World. At the same time, evangelical Christianity and sentimental culture glorified a romantic cult of feeling that was, within its limits, far more receptive to aesthetic experience than Calvinism and the more spartan forms of republicanism had been. Finally, the more comfortable and educated Americans fell into a relationship with nature that called out for aesthetic expression. After 1815, with the agricultural frontier penetrating deep into the interior, educated northeasterners became certain that civilization would supplant wilderness on the North American continent. The result was a multivoiced conversation about the relations between nature and civilization—a conversation that occupied a large portion of a new American art and literature that rose between 1830 and the Civil War.

NATURE AND ART

Much of the new American art went into objects that were lived in and used. Andrew Jackson Downing and other landscape designers and architects created beautiful country cottages surrounded by gardens. At the same time, cities began to build cemeteries in the surrounding countryside. In 1831 several wealthy Boston families put up the money to build Mount Auburn Cemetery. Mount Auburn was situated on rolling ground, with footpaths following the contours of the land. Much of the natural vegetation was left untouched, and wildflowers were planted to supplement it. The headstones were small and dignified. Copied in Brooklyn, Rochester, and other northern cities, the rural cemeteries embodied the faith that nature could teach moral lessons, particularly if nature was shaped and made available to humankind through art.

Not surprisingly, the leading artists of this generation were landscape painters. Thomas Cole, in his "Essay on American Scenery" (1835), reminded readers that the most distinctive feature of America was its wilderness:

> In civilized Europe the primitive features of scenery have long since been destroyed or modified. . . . And to this cultivated state our western world is fast approaching; but nature is still predominant, and there are those who regret that with the improvements of cultivation the sublimity of the wilderness should pass away; for those scenes of solitude from which the hand of nature has never been lifted, affect the mind with a more deep toned emotion than aught which the hand of man has touched. Amid them the consequent associations are of God the creator—they are his undefiled works, and the mind is cast into contemplation of eternal things.

In what became a manifesto of American intellectual and aesthetic life, Cole had found God in nature, and thus endowed art that depicted nature with religious purpose. Among educated persons, art was no longer subversive of the Protestant republic; done right, it was a bulwark of good citizenship and true religion. Educated middle- and upper-class northerners after 1830 built a cultural conversation in which Americans defined themselves by talking about American nature—a nature that had become Christianized and benign.

That conversation was strongest among urban northeasterners who believed that theirs was an age of progress. Indeed some would argue that the feminization of family life, the rise of sentimentality, and the romantic cult of nature could have appeared only when American civilization had turned the tide in its age-old battle with wilderness. The most sensitive and articulate northeasterners warned that the victory might be too complete, and that the United States could become as "unnatural" and "artificial" as an overcultivated Europe. Similarly, ministers and mothers worried that the marketplace could corrupt the "natural" relations of family life, while middle-class women and men cultivated personal "sincerity" as a badge of moral status.

Scenic Tourism: Niagara Falls

In the 1820s rich Americans began to travel for the sole purpose of looking at scenery. Improved transportation and disposable time and money made such journeys possible. But just as important was the determination of the more affluent Americans to re-create themselves as a community of sentiment and taste. They stood beside each other on steamboats and admired the picturesque farms and mountains of the Hudson valley; they traveled to the

NIAGARA FALLS   Frederic Edwin Church, who was among the most renowned of American landscape artists, painted Niagara Falls in 1857. Church's Niagara is immense and powerful, yet somehow ordered, benign, and calming.

Catskills and the White Mountains; but most of all they descended on what became the most venerated spot in all of North America: Niagara Falls.

Niagara was a new attraction in the 1820s. The falls had become part of the border between the United States and British Canada in 1783, but few Americans visited the place, and even fewer settled there. The falls could be reached only by a difficult and expensive voyage up the St. Lawrence River and across Lake Ontario or, after 1804, over New York's notoriously bad state road. The few Americans who wrote about Niagara Falls before the 1820s had stressed the power, wildness, and danger of the place along with its stunning beauty. In 1815 Niagara remained part of an unconquered American wilderness.

Completion of the Erie Canal in 1825 brought civilization to Niagara Falls. Every summer crowds of genteel tourists traveled the easy water route to Buffalo, then took carriages to the falls, where entrepreneurs had built hotels, paths, and stairways and offered boat rides and guided tours. The falls were now surrounded by commerce and viewed comfortably from various sites by well-dressed tourists. In early paintings of the falls, the foreground figure had usually been an Indian hunter or fisherman; now Indians were replaced by tourist couples, the women carrying parasols. The sublime experience of terror and wonder disappeared. Tourists read travel accounts before their trip and, once they arrived, bought guidebooks and took guided tours. Niagara had become controlled, orderly, and beautiful, a grand sermon in which God revealed his benign plan to humankind.

The Plain People of the North

From the 1830s onward, northern middle-class evangelicals proposed their religious and domestic values as a national culture for the United States. But even in their own region they were surrounded and outnumbered by Americans who rejected their cultural leadership. The plain people of the North were a varied lot: settlers in the lower Northwest who remained culturally southern; hill-country New Englanders, New Yorkers, and Pennsylvanians; refugees from the countryside who had taken up urban wage labor; and increasing thousands of Irish and German immigrants. What they shared was a cultural conservatism that rejected sentimentalism and reformist religion out of hand.

Religion and the Common Folk

The doctrines of churches favored by the northern plain folk varied as much as the people themselves. They included the most popular faiths (Baptists and Methodists came to contain two-thirds of America's professing Protestants in both the North and the South) as well as such smaller sects as Hicksite Quakers, Universalists, Adventists, Moravians, and Freewill Baptists. Yet for all their diversity, most of these churches shared an evangelical emphasis on individual experience over churchly authority. Most favored democratic, local control of religious life and distrusted outside organization and religious professionalism. And they rejected middle-class optimism and reformism, reaffirming humankind's duty to accept an imperfect world.

The most pervasive strain was a belief in providence—the conviction that human history was part of God's vast and unknowable plan, and that all events were willed or allowed by

God. Middle-class evangelicals spoke of providence, too, but they seemed to assume that God's plan was manifest in the progress of market society and middle-class religion. Humbler evangelicals believed that the events of everyday life were parts of a vast blueprint that existed only in the mind of God—and not in the vain aspirations of women and men. When making plans, they added the caveat "The Lord willing," and they learned to accept misfortune with fortitude. They responded to epidemics, bad crop years, aches and pains, illness, and early death by praying for the strength to endure, asking God to "sanctify" their suffering by making it an opportunity for them to grow in faith.

In a world governed by providence, the death of a loved one was a test of faith. Plain folk considered it a privilege to witness a death in the family, for it released the sufferer from the tribulations of this world and sent him or her to a better place. The death of children in particular called for a heroic act of submission to God's will; parents mourned the loss but stopped short of displaying grief that would suggest selfishness and lack of faith. Poor families washed and dressed the dead body themselves and then buried it in a churchyard or on a hilltop plot on the family farm. While the urban middle class preferred formal funerals and carefully tended cemeteries, humbler people regarded death as a lesson in the futility of pursuing worldly goals and in the need to submit to God's will.

POPULAR MILLENNIALISM

The plain Protestants of the North seldom talked about the millennium. Middle-class evangelicals were *postmillennialists:* They believed that Christ's Second Coming would occur at the *end* of 1,000 years of social perfection that would be brought about by the missionary conversion of the world. Ordinary Baptists, Methodists, and Disciples of Christ, however, assumed that the millennium would arrive with world-destroying violence, followed by 1,000 years of Christ's rule on earth. But most did not dwell on this terrifying *premillennialism,* assuming that God would end the world in his own time. Now and then, however, the ordinary evangelicals of the North predicted the fiery end of the world. People looked for signs of the approaching millennium in thunderstorms, shooting stars, eclipses, economic panics and depressions, and—especially—in hints that God had placed in the Bible.

An avid student of those hints was William Miller, a rural New York Baptist who, after years of systematic study, concluded that God would destroy the world during the year following March 1843. Miller publicized his predictions throughout the 1830s, and near the end of the decade the Millerites (as his followers were called) gathered together thousands of believers— most of them conservative Baptists, Methodists, and Disciples in hill-country New England and in poor neighborhoods in New York, Ohio, and Michigan. As the end approached, the believers read the Bible, prayed, and attended meeting after meeting. Newspapers published stories alleging that the Millerites were insane and guilty of sexual license. Some of them, the press reported, were busy sewing "ascension robes" in which they would rise straight to heaven without passing through death.

When the end of the year—March 23, 1844—came and went, most of the believers quietly returned to their churches. A committed remnant, however, kept the faith and by the 1860s founded the Seventh-Day Adventist Church. The Millerite movement was a reminder that hundreds of thousands of northern Protestants continued to believe that the God of the Old Testament governed everything from bee stings to the course of human history, and that one day he would destroy the world in fire and blood.

FAMILY AND SOCIETY

Baptists, Methodists, Disciples of Christ, and the smaller popular sects evangelized primarily among persons who had been bypassed or hurt by the market revolution. Often their rhetoric turned to criticism of market society, its institutions, and its centers of power. Elias Hicks, a Long Island farmer who fought the worldliness and pride of wealthy urban Quakers, listed the following among the mistakes of the early 19th century: railroads, the Erie Canal, fancy food and other luxuries, banks and the credit system, the city of Philadelphia, and the study of chemistry. The Baptist millenarian William Miller expressed his hatred of banks, insurance companies, stock-jobbing, chartered monopolies, personal greed, and the city of New York. In short, what the evangelical middle-class identified as the march of progress, poorer and more conservative evangelicals often condemned as a descent into worldliness that would almost certainly provoke God's wrath.

Along with doubts about economic change and the middle-class churches that embraced it, members of the popular sects often held to the patriarchal family form in which they had been raised. For hundreds of thousands of northern Protestants, the erosion of domestic patriarchy was a profound cultural loss and not, as it was for the middle-class, an avenue to personal liberation. For some, religious conversion came at a point of crisis in the traditional family. William Miller, for example, had a strict Calvinist upbringing in a family in which his father, an uncle, and his grandfather were all Baptist ministers. As a young man he rejected his family, set about making money, and became a deist—actions that deeply wounded his parents. When his father died, Miller was stricken with guilt. He moved back to his hometown, took up his family duties, became a leader of the Baptist church, and (after reading a sermon entitled "Parental Duties") began the years of Bible study that resulted in his world-ending prophecies.

THE PROPHET JOSEPH SMITH

The weakening of the patriarchal family and the attempt to shore it up were central to the life and work of one of the most unique and successful religious leaders of the period: the Mormon prophet Joseph Smith (see also Chapter 13). Smith's father was a landless Vermont Baptist who moved his wife and nine children to seven rented farms within 20 years. Around 1820, when young Joseph was approaching manhood, the family was struggling to make mortgage payments on a small farm outside Palmyra, New York. Despite the efforts of Joseph and his brothers, a merchant cheated the Smith family out of the farm. With that, both generations of the Smiths faced lifetimes as propertyless workers. To make matters worse, Joseph's mother and some of his siblings began to attend an evangelical Presbyterian church in Palmyra—apparently against the father's wishes.

Before the loss of the farm, Joseph had received two visions warning him away from existing churches and telling him to wait for further instructions. In 1827 the Angel Moroni appeared to him and led him to golden plates that translated into *The Book of Mormon*. It told of a light-skinned people, descendants of the Hebrews, who had sailed to North America long before Columbus. They had had an epic, violent history, and had been visited by Jesus following his resurrection.

Joseph Smith later declared that his discovery of *The Book of Mormon* had "brought salvation to my father's house" by unifying the family. It eventually unified thousands of others under a patriarchal faith. The good priests and secular leaders of *The Book of Mormon* are farmers who labor alongside their neighbors; the villains are self-seeking merchants, lawyers, and bad priests. Smith carried that model of brotherly cooperation and patriarchal authority into the Church of Jesus Christ of Latter-Day Saints that he founded in 1830. The new church was ruled, not by professional clergy, but by an elaborate lay hierarchy of adult males. On top sat the father of Joseph Smith, rescued from destitution and shame, who was appointed Patriarch of the Church. Below him were Joseph Smith and his brother Hyrum, who were called First and Second Elders. The hierarchy descended through a succession of male authorities that finally reached the fathers of households. An astute observer might have noticed the similarities between this hierarchical structure and the social order of the 18th century North.

THE RISE OF POPULAR CULTURE

Of course, not all the northern plain folk spent their time in church. Particularly in cities and towns, they became both producers and consumers of a commercial popular culture.

BLOOD SPORTS

Urban working-class neighborhoods were particularly fertile ground for the making of popular amusements. Young working men formed a bachelor subculture that contrasted with the piety and self-restraint of the middle class. They organized volunteer fire companies and militia units that spent more time drinking and fighting rival groups than they did drilling or putting out fires. Gathering at firehouses, saloons, and street corners, they drank, joked, and boasted, and nurtured notions of manliness based on physical prowess and coolness under pressure.

They also engaged in such "blood sports" as cock fighting, ratting, and dog fighting, even though many states had laws forbidding such activities. Such contests grew increasingly popular during the 1850s and were often staged by saloonkeepers. One of the best known was Kit Burns of New York City, who ran Sportsman Hall, a saloon frequented by prizefighters, criminals, and their hangers-on. Behind the saloon was a space—reached through a narrow doorway that could be defended against the police—with animal pits and a small amphitheater that seated 250 but that regularly held 400 yelling spectators.

Although most of the spectators were working men, a few members of the old aristocracy who rejected middle-class ways also attended these events. Frederick Van Wyck, scion of a wealthy old New York family, remembered an evening he had spent at Tommy Norris's livery stable, where he witnessed a fight between billy goats, a rat baiting, a cockfight, and a boxing match between bare-breasted women. "Certainly for a lad of 17, such as I," he recalled, "a night with Tommy Norris and his attraction was quite a night."

BOXING

Prize fighting emerged from the same subterranean culture that sustained cockfights and other blood sports. This sport, which was imported from Britain, called for an enclosed ring, clear rules, cornermen, a referee, and a paying audience. The early fighters were Irish or English immigrants, as were many of the promoters and spectators. Boxing's popularity rose during the 1840s and 1850s. Many of the fighters had close ties with ethnic-based saloons, militia units, fire companies, and street gangs, and many labored at occupations with a peculiarly ethnic base. Some of the best American-born fighters were New York City butchers. Butchers usually finished work by 10 A.M. They could then spend the rest of the day idling at a firehouse or a bar and were often prominent figures in neighborhood gangs. A prizefight between an American-born butcher and an Irish day laborer would attract a spirited audience that understood its class and ethnic meaning.

Prizefighting was a way of rewarding courage and skill and, sometimes, of settling scores through contests that were fair and limited to two combatants. Nonetheless, the fights were brutal. Boxers fought with bare knuckles, and a bout ended only when one of the fighters was unable to continue. In an infamous match in 1842, for instance, the Englishman Christopher Lilly knocked down his Irish opponent Thomas McCoy 80 times; the fight ended with round 119, when McCoy died in his corner.

Although boxing was closely associated with ethnic rivalries, the contestants often exhibited a respect for one another that crossed ethnic lines. For example, the native-born Tom Hyer, who had defeated the Irishman James "Yankee" Sullivan in one of the great early fights, later bailed Sullivan out of jail. And when in 1859 Bill Harrington, a retired native-born boxer, disappeared and left a widow and children, his former Irish-born opponent, John Morrisey, arranged a sparring match and sent the proceeds to Harrington's widow.

An American Theater

In the 18th and early 19th centuries, the only theaters were in the large seaport cities. Those who attended were members of the urban elite, and nearly all the plays, managers, and actors were English. After 1815, however, improvements in transportation and communication, along with the rapid growth of cities, created a much broader audience. Theaters and theater companies sprang up not only in New York and Philadelphia but also in Cincinnati, St. Louis, San Francisco, Rochester, and dozens of other new towns west of the Appalachians, and traveling troupes carried theatrical performances to the smallest hamlets. Before 1830 the poorer theatergoers occupied the cheap balcony seats; artisans and other workingmen filled benches in the ground floor area known as "the pit"; wealthier and more genteel patrons sat in the boxes. Those sitting in the pit and balcony ate and drank, talked, and shouted encouragement and threats to the actors.

As time passed, however, rowdyism turned into violence. The less genteel members of theater audiences protested the elegant speech, gentlemanly bearing, and understated performances of the English actors, which happened to match the speech, manners, and bearing of the American urban elite. The first theater riot occurred in 1817 when the English actor Charles Incledon refused a New York audience's demand that he stop what he was doing and sing "Black-Eyed Susan." Such assaults grew more common during the 1820s. By the 1830s there were separate theaters and separate kinds of performances for rich and poor. But violence continued. It culminated in the rivalry between the American actor Edwin Forrest and the English actor William Charles Macready.

Macready was a trained Shakespearean actor, and his restrained style and attention to the subtleties of the text had won him acclaim both in Britain and in the United States. Forrest, on the other hand, played to the cheap seats. With his bombast and histrionics he transformed Shakespeare's tragedies into melodramas. Forrest and Macready carried out a well-publicized feud that led to a mob attack on Macready in 1849. Led by E. Z. C. Judson (who, under the pen name Ned Buntline, wrote scores of dime novels), the mob descended on Macready's performance at the exclusive Astor Place Opera House. The militia was waiting for them, and in the ensuing riot and gunfight 20 persons lost their lives.

Playhouses that catered to working-class audiences continued to feature Shakespearean tragedies, but they now shared the stage with works written in the American vernacular. The stage "Yankee," rustic but shrewd, appeared at this time and so did Mose the Bowery B'hoy, a New York volunteer fireman who performed feats of derring-do. Both frequently appeared in the company of well-dressed characters with English accents—the Yankee outsmarted them; Mose beat them up.

Minstrelsy

The most popular form of theater was the blackface minstrel show, which first appeared in 1831. Although these shows conveyed blatant racism, they were the preferred entertainment of working men in northern cities from 1840 to 1880. The minstrel shows lasted an hour and a half and were presented in three sections. The first consisted of songs and dances performed in a walkaround, in which the audience was encouraged to clap and sing along. This was fol-

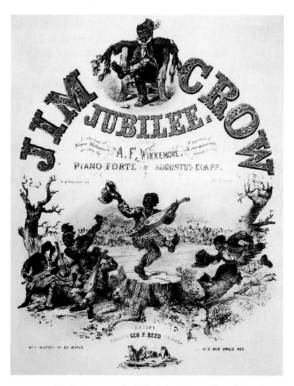

THE VIRGINIA MINSTRELS   In the 1840s, the Virginia Minstrels, white entertainers in absurd black masquerade, claimed in their advertisement to be "able delineators of the sports and pastimes of the Sable Race of the South."

lowed by a longer middle section in which the company sat in a row with a character named Tambo at one end and a character named Bones at the other (named for the tambourine and bones, the instruments they played), with an interlocutor in the middle. The Tambo character, often called Uncle Ned, was a simpleminded plantation slave dressed in plain clothing; the Bones character, usually called Zip Coon, was a dandified, oversexed free black dressed in top hat and tails. The interlocutor was the straight man—fashionably dressed, slightly pretentious, with an English accent. This middle portion of the show consisted of a conversation among the three, which included pointed political satire, skits ridiculing the wealthy and the educated, and sexual jokes that bordered on obscenity. The third section featured songs, dances, and jokes.

The minstrel shows introduced African American song and dance to audiences who would not have permitted black performers onto the stage. They also reinforced racial stereotypes that were near the center of American popular culture. Finally, they dealt broadly with aspects of social and political life that other performers avoided.

Minstrel shows and other theatrical entertainments were among the urban products that the new transportation network carried to rural America. Actors traveled well-established circuits, calling on local amateurs for their supporting casts. Minstrel companies traveled the river system of the interior and played to enthusiastic audiences wherever the riverboats docked. Mark Twain recalled them fondly: "I remember the first Negro musical show I ever saw. It must have been in the early forties. It was a new institution. In our village of Hannibal [Missouri] . . . it burst upon us as a glad and stunning surprise." Among Americans who had been taught to distrust cities, minstrel shows and other urban entertainments gave rural folk a sense of the variety and excitement of city life.

NOVELS AND THE PENNY PRESS

Among the many commodities the market revolution made available, few were more ubiquitous than newspapers and inexpensive books. Improvements in printing and paper making enabled entrepreneurs to sell daily newspapers for a penny. Cheap "story papers" became available in the 1830s, "yellow-back" fiction in the 1840s, and dime novels from the 1850s onward. Although these offerings were distributed throughout the North and the West, they found their first and largest audience among city workers.

Mass-audience newspapers carried political news and local advertisements, but they were heavily spiced with sensationalism. The *Philadelphia Gazette* in late summer of 1829, for instance, treated its eager readers to the following: "Female Child with Two Heads," "Bats," "Another Shark," "Horrid Murder," "Steam Boat Robbery," "Fishes Travelling on Land," "Poisoning by Milk," "Dreadful Steam Boat Disaster," "Raffling for Babies," "Combat with a Bear," "Lake Serpent," and much, much more. Henry David Thoreau commented on the "startling and monstrous events as fill the family papers," while his friend Ralph Waldo Emerson reported that Americans were "reading all day murders & railroad accidents." Such sensational stories portrayed a haunted, often demonic nature that regularly produced monstrosities and ruined the works of humankind, as well as a *human* nature that was often deceptive and depraved.

Working-class readers discovered a similarly untrustworthy world in cheap fiction. George Lippard's *Quaker City* (1845) was a fictional "exposé" of the hypocrisy, lust, and cruelty of Philadelphia's outwardly genteel and Christian elite. Lippard and other adventure writers indulged in a pornography of violence that included cannibalism, blood drinking, and murder by every imaginable means. They also dealt with sex in unprecedentedly explicit ways. The yellow-back novels of the 1840s introduced readers not only to seduction and rape but to transvestitism, child pornography, necrophilia, miscegenation, group sex, homosexuality, and— perhaps most shocking of all—women with criminal minds and insatiable sexual appetites.

Popular fictions were melodramatic contests between good and evil. Heroes met a demonic and chaotic world with courage and guile without hoping to change it. Indeed, melodramatic heroes frequently acknowledged evil in themselves while claiming moral superiority over the hypocrites and frauds who governed the world. A murderer in Ned Buntline's *G'hals of New York* (1850) remarks, "There isn't no *real* witue [virtue] and honesty nowhere, 'cept among the perfessional *dis*honest." (By contrast, in middle-class sentimental novels, the universe is benign; good can be nurtured, and evil can be defeated and transformed. Harriet Beecher Stowe's slavedriver Simon Legree is evil not because of a natural disposition toward evil, but because he had been deprived of a mother's love during childhood.)

FAMILY, CHURCH, AND NEIGHBORHOOD: THE WHITE SOUTH

In the South, farm and plantation labor and the routines of family life were still conducted within the household, and prospects for most whites remained rooted in inherited land and family help. While the new northern middle class nourished a cosmopolitan culture and a domestic sentimentalism that subverted traditional authority, southerners distrusted outsiders and defended rural neighborhoods grounded in the authority of fathers and the integrity of families.

SOUTHERN FAMILIES

Most southern whites regarded themselves less as individuals than as representatives of families. Southern boys often received the family names of heroes as their first names: Jefferson Davis, for example, or Thomas Jefferson (later, "Stonewall") Jackson. More often, however, they took the name of a related family—Peyton Randolph, Preston Brooks, Langdon Cheves. Children learned early on that their first duty was to their family's reputation.

In the white South, reputation and the defense of family honor were everything. A boy with a reputation for cowardice, for ineptness at riding or fighting, or for failure to control his emotions or hold his liquor, was an embarrassment to his family. Among southern white men, wealth generally counted for less than did maintaining one's personal and family honor and thus winning membership in the democracy of honorable males.

The code of honor, while it forged ties of equality and respect among white men, made rigid distinctions between men and women and whites and blacks. Women and girls who misbehaved damaged not only their own reputation but also the honor of the fathers, brothers, or husbands who could not control them. Such a charge could mean social death in a rural community made up of patriarchal households and watchful neighbors. In 1813 Bolling Hall of Alabama advised his daughter, "If you learn to restrain every thought, action, and word by virtue and religion, you will become an ornament."

The southern code of honor blunted attacks upon social hierarchy and inherited status. When sentimental northerners attacked slavery because it denied the freedom of the individual, one southerner responded in a way that was meant to end the argument: "Do you say that the slave is held to involuntary service? So is the wife, [whose] relation to her husband, in the great majority of cases, is made for her and not by her." Few white southerners would have questioned the good sense of that response. Southern life was not about freedom, individual fulfillment, or social progress; it was about honoring the obligations to which one was born.

SOUTHERN ENTERTAINMENTS

Southerners of all classes and races were leisure-loving people. But the rural character of the South threw them upon their own resources rather than on commercial entertainments. They drank, told stories, engaged in wrestling and boxing matches, and danced. For evangelicals who withdrew from such entertainments, church socials and camp meetings filled the gap, while rural southerners engaged in corn-huskings, birthday celebrations, berry-picking expeditions, and so forth. Books were not as readily available as they were in the North. Most southern families owned a Bible, and wealthier families often read histories, religious and political tracts, and English literature—with Shakespeare leading the way and Sir Walter Scott's tales of medieval chivalry not far behind. Hunting and fishing were passionate pursuits among southern men. Fox and deer hunts provided the gentry with an opportunity to display their skill with horses and guns, while the hunts of poorer whites and slaves both provided sport and enhanced their threatened roles as providers.

The commercial entertainments in the South were concentrated in the larger towns and along the major rivers. Showboats brought theatrical troupes, minstrel shows, animal acts,

COLONEL AND MRS. WHITESIDE Colonel and Mrs. James Whiteside, at home in their mansion on the heights above Chattanooga, are properly comfortable and genteel. Their infant son wears the traditional small child's dress, and the slaves who serve them are rendered grotesquely small.

and other entertainment to the river towns. The gentry's love of horses and competition made New Orleans the horse racing capital of the country; New Orleans was also the only southern city where one could watch a professional prizefight. Various violent contests appealed to New Orleans audiences. In 1819 a New Orleans impresario advertised a program that offered a bull vs. six "of the strongest dogs in the country"; six bulldogs vs. a Canadian bear; a "beautiful Tiger" vs. a black bear; and 12 dogs vs. a "strong and furious Opeloussas Bull." Although such events were outlawed in later years, they continued to be held on the sly. In 1852, a crowd of 5,000 gathered outside New Orleans to watch a bull and a grizzly bear fight to the death.

THE CAMP MEETING BECOMES RESPECTABLE

The camp-meeting revivals of the early 19th century had transformed the South into an evangelical Bible Belt (see Chapter 7). Some evangelicals had risen into the slaveholding class, and many of the old families had been converted. As a result, the Anglican gentry of the 18th century became outnumbered by earnest Baptist and Methodist planters.

Southern camp meetings continued throughout the antebellum years, but they were often limited to a single denomination—usually Methodist—and were held on permanent campgrounds maintained by the churches. Conducted with more decorum than in the past, they were routine community events: Women began baking a week ahead of time and looked forward to visiting with neighbors and relatives as much as they did to getting right with God. The goal of camp meetings was still to induce spiritual crisis and conversion, and sinners still wept and fell on their way to being saved. But such manifestations as the barking exercise and the jerks (see Chapter 7) disappeared.

The churches that grew out of southern revivals reinforced localistic neighborhoods and the patriarchal family. Some southern communities began when a whole congregation moved onto new land; others were settled by the chain migration of brothers and cousins, and subsequent revivals spread through family networks. Rural isolation limited most households to their own company during the week, but on Sundays church meetings united the neighborhood's cluster of extended families into a community of believers. In most neighborhoods, social connections seldom extended beyond that.

RELIGIOUS CONSERVATISM

Southern evangelicalism was based, like religious conservatism in the North, on the sovereignty of God, a conviction of human sinfulness, and an acceptance of disappointment and pain as part of God's grand and unknowable design. Southern church people continued to interpret misfortune as divine punishment. When yellow fever was killing 1,000 people every week in New Orleans in 1853, the Episcopal bishop Leonidas Polk asked God to "turn us from the ravages of the pestilence, wherewith for our iniquities, thou are visiting us."

The same view held at home. When the young son of a planter family died, the mother was certain that God had killed the child because the parents had loved him more than God. A grieving South Carolinian received this consolation from a relative: "Hope you are quite reconciled to the loss of your darling babe. As it was the will of God to take him, we must obey, and He will be angry at us if we go past moderate grief." It was a far cry from the middle-class North's garden cemeteries and the romantic, redemptive deaths of children in sentimental fiction.

Southern cultural conservatism was rooted in religion, in the family, and in a system of fixed social roles. Southern preachers assumed that patriarchal social relations were crucial to Christian living within an imperfect and often brutal world. Southerners revered the patriarch and slaveholder Abraham more than any other figure in the Bible. The father must—like Abraham—govern and protect his household; the mother must assist the father; and the women, children, and slaves must faithfully act out the duties of their stations. That meant a Christian must strive to be a good mother, a good father, a good slave; by the same token, a Christian never questioned his or her God-given social role.

Proslavery Christianity

In revolutionary and early national America, white southerners had been the most radical of republicans. Jeffersonian planter-politicians led the fights for equal rights and the absolute separation of church and state, and southern evangelicals were the early republic's staunchest opponents of slavery. By 1830, however, the South was an increasingly conscious minority within a democratic and capitalist nation. The northern middle classes proclaimed a link between material and moral progress, identifying both with individual autonomy and universal rights. A radical northern minority was agitating for the immediate abolition of slavery.

Southerners met this challenge with an "intellectual blockade" against outside publications and ideas and with a moral and religious defense of slavery. The Bible provided plenty of ammunition. Proslavery clergymen constantly stated that the Chosen People of the Old Testament had been patriarchs and slaveholders, and that Jesus had lived in a society that sanctioned slavery and never criticized the institution. Some ministers claimed that blacks were the descendants of Ham and thus deserved enslavement. The most common religious argument, however, was that slavery had given millions of heathen Africans the priceless opportunity to become Christians and to live in a Christian society.

Like their northern counterparts, southern clergymen applauded the material improvements of the age. But they insisted that *moral* improvement occurred only when people embraced the timeless truths of the Bible. Northern notions of progress through individual liberation, equal rights, and universal Christian love were wrong-headed and dangerous. The Presbyterian John Adger asserted that relations of dominance and submission were utterly necessary to both social and individual fulfillment, and that the distribution of rights and responsibilities was unequal and God-given: "The rights of the father are natural, but they belong only to the fathers. Rights of property are natural, but they belong only to those who have property"—and such natural rights were coupled with the awesome duties of fatherhood and proprietorship.

The Private Lives of Slaves

In law, in the census, and in the minds of planters, slaves were members of a plantation household over which the owner exercised absolute authority, not only as owner but also as paternal protector and lawgiver. Yet both slaveholders and slaves knew that slaves could not be treated like farm animals or little children. Wise slaveholders learned that the success of a plantation depended less on terror and draconian discipline (though whippings—and worse—were common) than on the accommodations by which slaves traded labor and obedience for some measure of privilege and autonomy within the bounds of slavery. After achieving privileges, the slaves called them their own: holidays, garden plots, friendships, and social gatherings both on and off the plantation; hunting and fishing rights; and so on. Together, these privileges provided some of the ground on which they made their own lives within slavery.

THE SLAVE FAMILY

The most precious privilege was the right to make and maintain families. As early as the Revolutionary War era, most Chesapeake slaves lived in units consisting of mother, father, and small children. At Thomas Jefferson's Monticello, most slave marriages were for life, and small children almost always lived with both parents. The most common exceptions to this practice were fathers who had married away from their own plantations and who visited "broad wives" and children during their off hours. Owners encouraged stable marriages because they made farms more peaceful and productive and because they flattered the owners' own religious and paternalistic sensibilities. For their part, slaves demanded families as part of the price of their labor.

Yet slave families were highly vulnerable. Many slaveholders assumed that they had the right to coerce sex from female slaves; some kept slaves as concubines, and a few even moved them into the main house. They tended, however, to keep these liaisons within bounds. A far more serious threat to slave marriages was the death, bankruptcy, or depar-

FIVE GENERATIONS OF A SLAVE FAMILY ON A SOUTH CAROLINA SEA ISLAND PLANTATION, 1862   Complex family ties such as those of the family shown here were among the most hard-won and vulnerable cultural accomplishments of enslaved blacks.

ture of the slaveholders. Between one-fifth and one-third of slave marriages were broken by such events.

Slaveholders who encouraged slave marriages knew that marriage implied a form of self-ownership that conflicted with the slaves' status as property. Some conducted ceremonies in which couples "married" by jumping over a broomstick; others had the preacher omit the phrases "let no man put asunder" and "till death do you part" from the ceremony. Slaves knew that such ceremonies had no legal force.

Slaves modified their sense of family and kinship to accommodate such uncertainties. Because separation from father or mother was common, children spread their affection among their adult relatives, treating grandparents, aunts, and uncles almost as though they were parents. In fact, slaves often referred to all their adult relatives as "parents." They also called non-relatives "brother," "sister," "aunt," and "uncle," thus extending a sense of kinship to the slave community at large. Slaves chose as surnames for themselves the names of former owners, Anglicized versions of African names, or names that simply sounded good. They rarely chose the name of their current owner, however. Families tended to use the same given names from one generation to the next, naming boys after their father or grandfather. They seldom named girls after their mother, however. Unlike Southern whites, slaves never married a first cousin. The origins and functions of some of these customs are unknown. We know only that slaves practiced them consistently, usually without the knowledge of the slaveholders.

WHITE MISSIONS

By the 1820s southern evangelicalism had long since abandoned its hostility toward slavery, and slaveholders commonly attended camp meetings and revivals. These prosperous converts faced conflicting duties. Their churches taught them that slaves had immortal souls and that planters were as responsible for the spiritual welfare of their slaves as they were for the spiritual welfare of their own children. A planter on his deathbed told his children that humane treatment and religious instruction for slaves was the duty of slaveowners; if these were neglected, "we will have to answer for the loss of their souls." After Nat Turner's bloody slave revolt in 1831 (discussed shortly), missions to the slaves took on new urgency: If the churches were to help create a family-centered, Christian society in the South, that society would have to include the slaves.

To this end, Charles Colcock Jones, a Presbyterian minister from Georgia, spent much of his career writing manuals on how to preach to slaves. He taught that there was no necessary connection between social position and spiritual worth—that there were good and bad slaveholders and good and bad slaves. But he also taught that slaves must accept the master's authority as God's, and that obedience was their prime religious virtue. Jones warned white preachers never to become personally involved with their slave listeners. "We separate entirely their *religious* from their *civil* condition," he said, "and contend that one may be attended to without interfering with the other."

The evangelical mission to the slaves was not as completely self-serving as it may seem. For to accept one's worldly station, to be obedient and dutiful within that station, and to seek salvation outside of this world were precisely what the planters demanded of themselves and their own families. An important goal of plantation missions was of course to create safe and profitable plantations. Yet that goal was to be achieved by Christianizing both slaveholders and slaves.

SLAVE CHRISTIANS

The white attempt to Christianize slavery, however, depended on the acceptance of slavery by the slaves. But the biblical notion that slavery could be punishment for sin and the doctrine of divinely ordained social orders never took root among the slaves. As one maid boldly told her mistress, *"God never made us to be slaves for white people."*

Although the slaves ignored much of what the missionaries taught, they embraced evangelical Christianity and transformed it into an independent African American faith. Some slaveowners encouraged them by building "praise houses" on their plantations and by permitting religious meetings. Others tried to resist the trend, but with little success. After 1830 most of the southern states outlawed black preachers, but the laws could not be enforced. Sometimes slaves met in a cabin—preaching, praying, and singing in a whisper. At their meetings they rehearsed a faith that was at variance with the faith of the slaveholders.

One way in which slave religion differed from what was preached to them by whites was in the practice of conjuring, folk magic, root medicine, and other occult knowledge—most of it passed down from West Africa. Such practices provided help in areas in which Christianity was useless: They could cure illnesses, make people fall in love, ensure a good day's fishing, or bring harm to one's enemies. Sometimes African magic was in competition with plantation Christianity. Just as often, however, slaves combined the two. For instance, slaves sometimes determined the guilt or innocence of a person accused of stealing by hanging a Bible by a thread, then watching the way it turned. The form was West African; the Bible was not. The slave root doctor George White boasted that he could "cure most anything," but added that "you got to talk wid God an' ask him to help out."

While Christianity could not cure sick babies or identify thieves, it gave slaves something more important: a sense of themselves as a historical people with a role to play in God's cosmic drama. In slave Christianity, Moses the liberator (and not the slaveholders' Abraham) stood beside Jesus. Indeed the slaves' appropriation of the book of Exodus denied the smug assumption of the whites that they were God's chosen people who had escaped the bondage of despotic Europe to enter the promised land of America. To the slaves, America was Egypt, they were the chosen people, and the slaveholders were Pharaoh. The slaves' religious songs, which became known as "spirituals," told of God's people, their travails, and their ultimate deliverance. In songs and sermons the figures of Jesus and Moses were often blurred, and it was not always clear whether deliverance would take place in this world or the next. But deliverance always meant an end to slavery, with the possibility that it might bring a reversal of relations between slaves and masters.

RELIGION AND REVOLT

In comparison with slaves in Cuba, Jamaica, Brazil, and other New World plantation societies, North American slaves seldom went into organized, armed revolt. American plantations were relatively small and dispersed, and the southern white population was large, vigilant, and very well armed. Thousands of slaves demonstrated their hatred of the system by running away. Others fought slaveowners or overseers, sabotaged equipment and animals, stole from planters, and found other ways to oppose slavery. But most knew that open revolt was suicide.

Christianity convinced slaves that history was headed toward an apocalypse that would result in divine justice and their own deliverance, and thus held out the possibility of revolt. But slave preachers almost never told their congregations to become actively engaged in God's divine plan, for they knew that open resistance was hopeless. Slave Christians believed that God hated slavery and would end it, but that their role was to have faith in God, to take care of one another, to preserve their identity as a people, and to await deliverance. Only occasionally did slaves take retribution and deliverance into their own hands.

The most ambitious conspiracy was hatched by Denmark Vesey, a free black of Charleston, South Carolina. Vesey was a leading member of an African Methodist congregation that had seceded from the white Methodists and had been independent from 1817 to 1821. At its height, the church had 6,000 members—most of them slaves. Vesey and some of the other members talked about their delivery out of Egypt, with all white men, women, and children being cut off. They identified Charleston as Jericho and planned its destruction in 1822: A few dozen Charleston blacks would take the state armory, then arm rural slaves who would rise up to help them. They would kill the whites, take control of the city, and then commandeer ships in the harbor and make their getaway. Word of the conspiracy spread secretly into the countryside, largely through the efforts of Gullah Jack, who was both a Methodist and an African conjurer. Jack recruited African-born slaves as soldiers, provided them with charms as protection against whites, and used his spiritual powers to terrify others into keeping silent.

In the end, the Vesey plot was betrayed by slaves. As one coerced confession followed another, white authorities hanged Vesey, Gullah Jack, and 34 other accused conspirators. But frightened whites knew that most of the conspirators (estimates ranged from 600 to 9,000) remained at large and unidentified.

NAT TURNER

In August 1831, in a revolt in Southampton County, Virginia, some 60 slaves shot and hacked to death 55 white men, women, and children. Their leader was Nat Turner, a Baptist lay preacher. Turner was, he told his captors, an Old Testament prophet and an instrument of God's wrath. As a child, he had prayed and fasted often, and the spirit—the same spirit who had spoken to the prophets of the Bible—had spoken directly to him. When he was a young man, he had run away to escape a cruel overseer. But when God said that he had not chosen Nat merely to have him run away, Nat returned. But Turner made it clear that his Master was God, not a slaveowner.

Around 1830, Turner received visions of the final battle in Revelation, recast as a fight between white and black spirits. Convinced by a solar eclipse in February 1831 that the time had come, Turner began telling other slaves about his visions, recruited his force, and launched a bloody and hopeless revolt that ended in mass murder, failure, and the execution of Turner and his followers.

The Vesey and Turner revolts, along with scores of more limited conspiracies, deeply troubled southern whites. Slaveholders were committed to a paternalism that was increasingly tied to the South's attempt to make slavery both domestic and Christian. For their part, slaves recognized that they could receive decent treatment and pockets of autonomy in return for outward docility. Vesey and Turner opened wide cracks in that mutual charade. A plantation mistress who survived Turner's revolt by hiding in a closet listened to the murders of her husband and children, then heard her house servants arguing over possession of her clothes. A Charleston grandee named Elias Horry, upon finding that his coachman was among the Vesey conspirators, asked him, "What were your intentions?" The formerly submissive slave replied that he had intended "to kill you, rip open your belly, and throw your guts in your face."

CHRONOLOGY

1822	Denmark Vesey's slave conspiracy uncovered in Charleston
1830	Charles Grandison Finney leads religious revival in Rochester • Joseph Smith founds the Church of Jesus Christ of Latter-Day Saints
1831	Mount Auburn Cemetery opens near Boston • First minstrel show is presented • Nat Turner leads bloody slave revolt in Southampton County, Virginia
1835	Landscape artist Thomas Cole publishes "Essay on American Scenery"
1843	William Miller's Adventists expect the world to end
1845	George Lippard's lurid novel *Quaker City* becomes a best-seller
1849	Astor Place theater riot in New York City leaves 20 dead
1852	Harriet Beecher Stowe publishes *Uncle Tom's Cabin*

Such stories sent a chill through the white South— a suspicion that despite the appearance of peace, they were surrounded by people who would kill them in an instant. While northerners patronized plays and cheap fiction that dramatized the trickery and horror beneath placid appearances, the nightmares of slaveholding paternalists were both more savage and closer to home.

CONCLUSION

By the second quarter of the 19th century, Americans had made a patchwork of regional, class, and ethnic cultures. The new middle classes of the North and West compounded their Protestant and republican inheritance with a new entrepreneurial faith in progress. The result was a way of life grounded in the self-made and morally accountable individual and the sentimentalized domestic unit. In ways that others often found offensive, they would propose that way of life as a national culture for the United States. The middle class met resistance from poorer urban dwellers and the less prosperous farmers—a northern and western majority that remained grimly loyal to the unsentimental, male-dominated families of their fathers and grandfathers, to new and old religious sects that continued to believe in human depravity and the mysterious workings of providence, and to the suspicion that perfidy and disorder lurked behind the smiling moral order of market economics and sentimental culture. They were also people who enjoyed dark and playful popular entertainments that often mocked middle-class sentimentalism. In the South, most white farmers persisted in a neighborhood-based, intensely evangelical, and socially conservative way of life. Southern planters, while they shared in the northern elite's belief in material progress and the magic of the market, were bound by family values, a system of slave labor, and a code of honor that was strikingly at variance with middle-class faith in an orderly universe and perfectible individuals. Slaves in these years continued to make cultural forms of their own; and despite their exclusion from the white world of liberty and equality, they tied their aspirations to the family, to an evangelical Protestant God, and to the individual and collective dignity that republics promise to their citizens.

11

SOCIETY, CULTURE, AND POLITICS, 1820S–1840S

CONSTITUENCIES ∼ THE POLITICS OF ECONOMIC DEVELOPMENT
THE POLITICS OF SOCIAL REFORM ∼ THE POLITICS OF ALCOHOL
THE POLITICS OF RACE ∼ THE POLITICS OF GENDER AND SEX

Between 1820 and 1845 Thomas Jefferson's agrarian republic became Andrew Jackson's noisy and deeply divided mass democracy. Politicians who built the Whig and Democratic Parties, which helped to bring about that change, were participants in the economic and social transformations of those years; they were both consumers and producers of the new forms of popular culture. John Quincy Adams, Henry Clay, and their National Republican and Whig allies in the states concocted visions of smooth-running, government-sponsored transportation and monetary systems that echoed the faith in cosmic order, material progress, and moral improvement that had become cultural axioms for the more prosperous and cosmopolitan Americans. Democrats, on the other hand, defended Jefferson's republic of limited government and widespread equality and liberty. In the course of that defense, they portrayed a haunted political universe in which trickery, deceit, and special privilege lurked behind the promises and power-hunger of the Whigs.

Politicians constructed the Whig and Democratic coalitions largely at the neighborhood and state levels. At the same time, national debates incorporated Democratic and Whig attitudes on family, religion, race, gender, ethnicity, class, and the proper functions of government that had been shaped by state-level debates. Those local and state issues and the social and cultural constituencies that argued them out are the subjects of this chapter.

CONSTITUENCIES

The Whig and Democratic Parties were national coalitions of ill-matched regional, economic, ethnic, and religious groups. They were united by Whig and Democratic political cultures—consistent attitudes toward government and politics that were embedded in religion, family, and economic life. Support for the Democratic or Whig Party was a matter of personal identity as much as of political preference: A man's vote demonstrated his personal history, his cultural values, and his vision of the good society as clearly as it demonstrated his opinion on any particular political issue. Voters remained loyal to their parties in selecting officeholders. Thus, political parties reduced the stupendous diversity of American society to two political choices.

THE NORTH AND WEST

The broad band of Yankee commercial farms stretching across southern New England, western New York, and the Old Northwest was the northern Whig heartland. Whigs also enjoyed support in northern cities and towns. The wealthiest men in cities were Whigs. The new urban commercial classes created in the market revolution also supported the Whigs. Factory owners were solidly Whig, and native-born factory workers often joined them—in part because Whigs promised opportunities to rise in the world, in part because Whigs protected their jobs by encouraging domestic markets for what they made, and, increasingly, because Whigs pandered to their fears of immigrant labor. For similar reasons, many skilled urban artisans supported the Whigs, as did smaller numbers of dockworkers, day laborers, and others among the unskilled.

Northern Whiggery was grounded in the market revolution, but the Whig political agenda ranged far beyond economic life. Among the urban middle class and in the more market-oriented rural neighborhoods, the inheritors of Puritan theocracy translated the spirit of the late 1820s and early 1830s revivals into an avowedly Christian Whig politics. Whigs called for moral legislation on such issues as Sabbath observance, temperance, and Bible-based public schools. Marching under the banner of activist government, economic development, and moral progress, Whigs set the political agenda in most northern states.

They met a determined Democratic opposition. Democrats found supporters among cultural traditionalists who had gained little from the expansion of national markets and who had no use for the moral agenda of the Whigs. The "Butternuts" (so named for the yellow vegetable dye with which they colored their homespun clothing) of the southern, river-oriented counties of the Northwest joined the Democratic Party. Farmers in the Allegheny Mountains, the Hudson River valley, and northern and western New England also supported the Democrats.

In cities and towns, Democrats made up substantial minorities among businessmen, master craftsmen, and professionals, but most urban Democrats were wage earners. Perhaps the most overwhelmingly Democratic group in the country were immigrant Irish Catholics, who were filling the lower ranks of the urban workforce. Indeed, their presence in the Democratic Party pushed increasing numbers of native Protestant workers into the Whig ranks.

When confronted with opposition to evangelical legislation, Whigs labeled the Democratic Party the party of atheism and immorality. Democrats responded that they opposed theocracy, not religion. True, most freethinkers, atheists, and persons who simply did not care about religion supported the Democratic Party. So did immigrant Catholics, who rightfully feared the militant Protestantism of the Whigs. But Democrats won the support of hundreds of thousands of evangelical Protestants who deeply distrusted what they called "church and state" Whiggery and the mixing of politics and religion. Evangelical Democrats were joined by sectarian Christians who rejected Whig moral legislation as antirepublican and as Yankee cultural imperialism.

THE SOUTH

Throughout the 1830s and 1840s, the southern states divided their votes equally between Whigs and Democrats. But most individual southern localities were either solidly Democratic or solidly Whig. Much more than in the North, southern differences in party preference were tied to differences in economic life.

Isolationist southern neighborhoods tended to support the Democrats. Thus Democrats ran strongest in up-country communities that valued household independence and the society of neighbors and that deeply distrusted intrusions from the outside. The more cosmopolitan southern communities tended to support the Whigs. In general, this meant that Whigs were strongest in plantation counties, where they commanded the votes not only of wealthy planters but of smaller farmers, and of lawyers, storekeepers, and craftsmen in county-seat towns. Upland, non-plantation neighborhoods in which Whigs ran well were places where Whigs promised state-sponsored internal improvements that would link ambitious but isolated farmers to outside markets.

Many exceptions to the link between commerce and the Whig Party were grounded in the prestige and power of local leaders. Southern statesmen who broke with the Jacksonians in the 1830s—John C. Calhoun in South Carolina, Hugh Lawson White in Tennessee, and others— took personal and regional followings with them (see Chapter 12). Political campaigners also had to contend with southerners such as George Reynolds of Pickens County, Alabama, who fathered 17 children and had 234 direct descendants living in his neighborhood, whom he delivered as a bloc to politicians who pleased him. But despite the vagaries of southern kinship, Whigs knew that their core constituency in the South was in communities that were or wanted to be linked to commercial society.

In sharp contrast with the North and West, southern political divisions had little to do with religion. Southern Baptists, Methodists, and Presbyterians seldom combined religion and politics. Although they enforced morality within their own households and congregations, southern evangelicals seldom asked state legislatures to pass moral legislation. Southern evangelicals who embraced the world of the market assumed, along with their northern Whig counterparts, that the new economy encouraged a Christian, civilized life. Other southern churchgoers responded to the Jacksonians' denunciations of greed and the spirit of speculation. Thus, even though many southern communities were bitterly divided over religion, the divisions seldom shaped party politics.

The social, religious, cultural, and economic bases of party divisions formed coherent Whig and Democratic political cultures. Whig voters in the North and South were persons who either were or hoped to become beneficiaries of the market revolution and who wanted government to subsidize economic development. In the North, they also demanded that government help shape market society into a prosperous, orderly, and homogeneous Christian republic. Democrats, North and South, demanded a minimal government that kept taxes low and that left citizens, their families, and their neighborhoods alone.

THE POLITICS OF ECONOMIC DEVELOPMENT

Both the Whigs and the Democrats accepted the transition to market society, but they wanted to direct it into different channels. Whigs wanted to use government and the market to make an economically and morally progressive—albeit hierarchical—republic. Democrats viewed both government and the new institutions of market society with suspicion and vowed to allow neither to subvert the equal rights and rough equality of condition that were, in their view, the preconditions of republican citizenship.

GOVERNMENT AND ITS LIMITS

"The government," remarked a New York City Whig in 1848, "is not merely a machine for making wars and punishing felons, but is bound to do all that is within its power to promote the welfare of the People—its legitimate scope is not merely negative, representative, defensive, but also affirmative, creative, constructive, beneficent." The Whigs insisted that economic development, moral progress, and social harmony were linked and that government should foster them. As long as people developed the work habits and moral discipline required for success, they would be rewarded. To poor farmers and city workers who felt that the market revolution undermined their independence, Whigs promised social mobility within a new system of interdependence—but only to deserving individuals. Whigs believed that the United States exhibited a harmony of class interests and an equality of opportunity that every virtuous person would recognize and that only resentful, mean-spirited, unworthy people would doubt.

Democrats seldom praised or condemned market society per se. Instead, they argued for the primacy of citizenship: Neither government nor the market, they said, should be allowed to subvert the civil and legal equality among independent men on which the republic rested. Democrats saw government not as a tool of progress but as a dangerous—although regrettably necessary—concentration of power in the hands of imperfect, self-interested men. The only safe course was to limit its power. In 1837, *The United States Magazine and Democratic Review* declared: "The best government is that which governs least."

Democrats argued that the Whig belief in benign government and social harmony was absurd. Corporate charters, privileged banks, and subsidies to turnpike, canal, and railroad companies, they said, benefited privileged insiders and transformed republican government into an engine of inequality. George Bancroft, a radical Democrat from Massachusetts, stated that "A republican people should be in an equality in their social and political condition; . . . pure democracy inculcates equal rights—equal laws—equal means of education—and *equal means of wealth* also." By contrast, the government favored by the Whigs would enrich a favored few. Bancroft and other Democrats demanded limited government that was deaf to the demands of special interests.

BANKS

The proper role of banks emerged as a central political issue in nearly every state. Whigs defended banks as agents of economic progress, arguing that they provided credit for roads and canals, loans to businessmen and commercial farmers, and the banknotes that served as the chief medium of exchange. Democrats, on the other hand, regarded banks as government-protected institutions that enabled a privileged few to make themselves rich at the public's expense.

The economic boom of the 1830s and the destruction of the national bank by the Jackson administration (see Chapter 12) created a dramatic expansion in the number of state-chartered banks. Systems varied from state to state. South Carolina, Georgia, Tennessee, Kentucky, and Arkansas had state-owned banks. Many new banks in the Old Northwest were also partially state-owned. Such banks often operated as public service institutions. Georgia's Central Bank, for example, served farmers who could not qualify for private loans, as did other state-owned banks in the South.

Beginning in the 1820s many states had introduced uniform banking laws to replace the unique charters previously granted to individual banks. The new laws tried to stabilize currency and credit. In New York, the Safety-Fund Law of 1829 required banks to pool a fraction of their resources to protect both bankers and small noteholders in the case of bank failures. The result was a self-regulating and conservative community of state banks. Laws in other states required that banks maintain a high ratio of specie (precious metals) to notes in circulation. Such laws, however, were often evaded.

"Hard Money" Democrats (those who wanted to get rid of paper money altogether) regarded banks as centers of trickery and privilege and proposed that they be abolished. Banks, they claimed, with their manipulation of credit and currency, encouraged speculation, luxury, inequality, and the separation of wealth from real work. Jackson himself branded banks "a perfect humbug."

In state legislatures, Whigs defended what had become a roughly standard system of private banks chartered by state governments. They had the right to circulate banknotes and had limited liability to protect directors and stockholders from debts incurred by their bank. Many Democrats proposed abolishing all banks. Others proposed reforms. They demanded a high ratio of specie reserves to banknotes as a guard against inflationary paper money. They proposed eliminating the issuance of banknotes in small denominations, thus ensuring that day-to-day business would be conducted in hard coin, and protecting wage earners and small farmers from speculative ups and downs.

By these and other means, Democrats in the states protected currency and credit from the government favoritism, dishonesty, and elitism that, they argued, enriched Whig insiders and impoverished honest Democrats. Whigs responded that corporate privileges and immunities and an abundant, elastic currency were keys to economic development, and they fought Democrats every step of the way.

INTERNAL IMPROVEMENTS

Democrats in Congress and the White House blocked federally funded roads and canals (see Chapter 12). In response, the states launched the transportation revolution themselves, either by taking direct action or by chartering private corporations to do the work (see Chapter 9). State legislatures everywhere debated the wisdom of direct state action, of corporate privileges, of subsidies to canals and railroads, and of the accumulation of government debt. Whigs, predictably, favored direct action by state governments. Democrats were lukewarm toward the whole idea of internal improvements, convinced that debt, favoritism, and corruption would inevitably result from government involvement in the economy.

Whigs assumed a connection between market society and moral progress—and used that relationship as a basis of their argument for internal improvements. William H. Seward, the Whig governor of New York, supported transportation projects because they broke down neighborhood isolation and hastened the emergence of a market society. In the minds of Whig legislators, a vote for internal improvements was a vote for moral progress and for individual opportunity within a prosperous and happily interdependent market society.

Democratic state legislators supported at least some internal improvements. But they opposed "partial" legislation that would benefit part of their state at the expense of the rest, and they opposed projects that would lead to higher taxes and put state governments into debt. The Democrats made the same argument in every state: Beneath Whig plans for extensive improvements lay schemes to create special privilege, inequality, debt, and corruption—all at the expense of a hoodwinked people.

THE POLITICS OF SOCIAL REFORM

In the North, it was the churchgoing middle class that provided the Whig Party with most of its electoral support. Whig evangelicals believed that with God's help they could improve the world by improving the individuals within it, and they enlisted the Whig Party in that campaign. On a variety of issues including prostitution, temperance, public education, and state-supported insane asylums and penitentiaries, Whigs used government to improve individual morality and discipline. Democrats, on the other hand, argued that attempts to dictate morality through legislation were both antirepublican and wrong.

PUBLIC SCHOOLS

During the second quarter of the 19th century, local and state governments built systems of tax-supported public schools, known as "common" schools. Before that time, most children learned reading, writing, and arithmetic at home, in poorly staffed town schools, in private schools, or in charity schools run by churches or other benevolent organizations. Despite the lack of any "system" of education, most children learned to read and write. That was, however, more likely among boys than among girls, among whites than among blacks, and among northeasterners than among westerners or southerners.

By the 1830s Whigs and Democrats agreed that providing common schools was a proper function of government. And Democrats often agreed with Whigs that schools could equalize opportunity. More radical Democrats, however, wanted public schooling that would erase snobbery. A newspaper declared in 1828 that "the children of the rich and the poor shall receive a national education, calculated to make republicans and banish aristocrats."

The reformers who created the most advanced, expensive, and centralized state school systems were Whigs: Horace Mann of Massachusetts, Henry Barnard of Connecticut, Calvin Stowe (husband of Harriet Beecher) of Ohio, and others. These reformers talked more about character building than about the three R's, convinced that it was the schools' first duty to train youngsters to respect authority, property, hard work, and social order. They wanted schools that would downplay class divisions, but they were interested less in democratizing wealthy children than in civilizing the poor.

The schools taught a basic Whig axiom: that social questions could be reduced to questions of individual character. A textbook entitled *The Thinker, A Moral Reader* (1855) told children to "remember that all the ignorance, degradation, and misery in the world, is the result of indolence and vice." To teach that lesson, the schools had children read from the King James Bible and recite prayers acceptable to all the Protestant sects. Such texts reaffirmed a common Protestant morality while avoiding divisive doctrinal matters.

Political differences centered less on curriculum than on organization. Whigs wanted state-level centralization and proposed state superintendents and state boards of education, normal schools (state teachers' colleges), texts chosen at the state level and used throughout the state, and uniform school terms. They also recruited young women as teachers. In addition to fostering Protestant morality in the schools, these women were a source of cheap labor: Salaries for female teachers in the northern states ranged from 40 to 60 percent lower than the salaries of their male coworkers.

Democrats preferred to give power to individual school districts, thus enabling local school committees to tailor the curriculum, the length of the school year, and the choice of teachers and texts to local needs. Centralization, they argued, would create a metropolitan educational culture that served the purposes of the rich but ignored the preferences of farmers and working people. It was standard Democratic social policy: inexpensive government and local control. Henry Barnard, Connecticut's superintendent of schools, called his Democratic opponents "ignorant demagogues" and "a set of blockheads." Horace Mann denounced them as "political madmen."

ETHNICITY, RELIGION, AND THE SCHOOLS

The argument between Whig centralism and Democratic parsimony dominated the debate over public education until the children of Irish and German immigrants began to enter schools by the thousands in the mid-1840s. Most immigrant families were poor and relied on their children to work and supplement the family income. Consequently, the children's attendance at school was irregular at best. Moreover, most immigrants were Catholics. The Irish regarded Protestant prayers and the King James Bible as heresies and as hated tools of British oppression. Some of the textbooks were worse. Olney's *Practical System of Modern Geography,* a standard textbook, declared that "the Irish in general are quick of apprehension, active, brave and hospitable; but passionate, ignorant, vain, and superstitious."

Many Catholic parents simply refused to send their children to school. Others demanded changes in textbooks, the elimination of the King James Bible, tax-supported Catholic schools, or at least tax relief for parents who sent their children to parish schools. Whigs, joined by many native-born Democrats, saw Catholic complaints as popish assaults on the Protestantism that they insisted was at the heart of American republicanism.

Many school districts, particularly in the rural areas to which many Scandinavian and German immigrants found their way, created foreign-language schools and provided bilingual instruction. In other places, state support for church-run charity schools persisted. But in northeastern cities, where immigrant Catholics often formed militant local majorities, demands for state support led to violence and to organized nativist (anti-immigrant) politics. In 1844 the Native American Party, with the endorsement of the Whigs, won the New York City elections. That same year in Philadelphia, riots that pitted avowedly Whig Protestants against Catholic immigrants, ostensibly over the issue of Bible reading in schools, killed 13 people.

PRISONS

From the 1820s onward, state governments built institutions to house orphans, the dependent poor, the insane, and criminals. Americans in the 18th century (and many in the 19th century as well) had assumed that poverty, crime, insanity, and other social ills were among God's ways of punishing sin and testing the human capacity for both suffering and charity. By the 1820s, however, reformers were arguing that deviance was the result of childhood deprivation. "Normal" people, they suggested, learned discipline and respect for work, property, laws, and other people from their parents. Deviants were the products of brutal, often drunken households devoid of parental love and discipline. The cure was to place them in a controlled setting, teach them work and discipline, and turn them into useful citizens.

In state legislatures, Whigs favored putting deviants in institutions for rehabilitation. Democrats favored institutions that isolated the insane, warehoused the dependent poor, and punished criminals. Most state systems were a compromise between the two positions.

Pennsylvania built prisons at Pittsburgh (1826) and Philadelphia (1829) that put solitary prisoners into cells to contemplate their misdeeds and to plot a new life. The results of such solitary confinement included few reformations and numerous attempts at suicide. Far more common were institutions based on the model developed in New York at Auburn (1819) and Sing Sing (1825). In the "Auburn system," prisoners slept in solitary cells and marched in military formation to meals and workshops; they were forbidden to speak to one another at any time. The rule of silence, it was believed, encouraged both discipline and contemplation.

The Auburn system was designed both to reform criminals and to reduce expenses, for the prisons sold workshop products to the outside. Between these two goals Whigs favored rehabilitation. Democrats favored profit-making workshops, and thus lower operating costs and lower taxes. Robert Wiltse, named by the Democrats to run Sing Sing prison in the 1830s, used harsh punishments (including flogging and starving), sparse meals, and forced labor in order to punish criminals and make the prison pay for itself. In 1839 William Seward, as the newly elected Whig governor of New York, fired Wiltse and appointed administrators who substituted privileges and rewards for punishment and emphasized rehabilitation over profit making. They provided religious instruction; they improved food and working conditions; and they cut back on the use of flogging. When Democrats took back the statehouse in the 1842 elections, they discovered that the Whigs' brief experiment in kindness had produced a $50,000 deficit, so they swiftly reinstated the old regime.

ASYLUMS

The leading advocate of humane treatment for people deemed to be insane was Dorothea Dix, a Boston humanitarian. She traveled throughout the country urging citizens to pressure their state legislatures into building asylums committed to what reformers called "moral treatment." The asylums were to be clean and pleasant places, preferably outside the cities, and the inmates were to be treated humanely. Attendants were not to beat inmates or tie them up, although they could use cold showers as a form of discipline. Dix and other reformers wanted the asylums to be safe, nurturing environments in which people with mental illness could be made well.

By 1860 the legislatures of 28 of the 33 states had established state-run insane asylums. Whig legislators, with minimal support from Democrats, approved appropriations for the more expensive and humane moral treatment facilities. Occasionally, however, Dorothea Dix won Democratic support as well. In North Carolina, she befriended the wife of a powerful Democratic legislator as the woman lay on her deathbed; the dying woman convinced her husband to support the building of an asylum. His impassioned speech won the approval of the lower house for a state asylum to be named Dix Hill. In the North Carolina senate, however, the proposal was supported by 91 percent of the Whigs and only 14 percent of the Democrats—a partisan division that was repeated in state after state.

THE SOUTH AND SOCIAL REFORM

On most economic issues, the legislatures of the southern states divided along the same lines as northern legislatures: Whigs wanted government participation in the economy, Democrats did not. On social questions, however, southern Whigs and Democrats responded in distinctly southern ways. The South was a rural, culturally conservative region of patriarchal households

THE WHIPPING POST AND PILLORY AT NEW CASTLE, DELAWARE   Delaware was a slave state that continued to inflict public, corporal punishment on lawbreakers. Many of the witnesses to the whipping depicted here are small children, who are supposedly learning a lesson.

in which every attempt at government intervention was seen as a threat to independence. Most southern voters, Whigs as well as Democrats, perceived attempts at "social improvement" as expensive and wrong-headed.

The southern states enacted school laws and drew up blueprints for state school systems. But because the white South was culturally homogeneous, it had little need for schools to enforce a common culture. Moreover, the South had less money and less faith in government. Consequently southern schools tended to be locally controlled, to be infused with southern evangelical culture, and to have a limited curriculum and a short school year.

By 1860 every slave state except Florida and the Carolinas operated prisons modeled on the Auburn system. Here, however, prisons stressed punishment and profits over rehabilitation. Though some southerners favored northern-style reforms, they knew that southern voters would reject them. While northern evangelicals were preaching that criminals could be rescued, southern preachers demanded Old Testament vengeance, arguing that hanging, whipping, and branding were sanctioned by the Bible, inexpensive, and more effective than mere incarceration. Other southerners, defending the code of honor, charged that victims and their relatives would be denied vengeance if criminals were tucked away in prisons. Some southern prisons leased prison labor (and sometimes whole prisons) to private entrepreneurs, while dreams of reforming southern criminals were forgotten.

The South did participate in temperance—the all-consuming reform that will be discussed in the next section. By the 1820s Baptists and Methodists had made deep inroads into southern society. Southern ministers preached against dueling, fighting, dancing, gambling, and drinking, while churchgoing women discouraged their husbands, sons, and suitors from drinking. During the 1840s the Washington Temperance Society and other voluntary temperance groups won a solid footing in southern towns. But the religious and temperance organizations of the South were based on individual decisions to abstain. Legal prohibition, which became dominant in the North, got nowhere in the South.

At bottom, southern resistance to social reform stemmed from a conservative, Bible-based acceptance of suffering and human imperfection and a commitment to the power and independence of white men who headed families. Any proposal that sounded like social tinkering or the invasion of paternal rights was doomed to failure. To make matters worse, many reforms—public schools, Sunday schools, prohibitionism, humane asylums—were seen as the work of well-funded and well-organized missionaries from the Northeast who wanted to fashion society in their own self-righteous image. The southern distrust of reform was powerfully reinforced after 1830, when northern reformers began to call for abolition of slavery and equality of the sexes—reforms that were unthinkable to most white southerners.

THE POLITICS OF ALCOHOL

The fight between evangelical Whigs who demanded that government regulate public (and often private) morality and Democrats who feared both big government and the Whig cultural agenda was at the center of party formation in the North. The most persistent issue around which that argument was conducted was the question of alcohol.

ARDENT SPIRITS

Drinking had been a part of social life since the beginning of English settlement. But the withering of authority and the disruptions of the market revolution led to increased consumption, increased public drunkenness, and a perceived increase in the violence and social problems caused by alcohol (see Chapter 7). Beginning in the 1790s, physicians and a few clergymen attacked not only habitual drunkenness but also alcohol itself. And for a short time after 1812, Federalist politicians and Congregational clergymen formed "moral societies" in New England that discouraged strong drink. Their imperious tone, however, doomed them to failure.

The temperance crusade began in earnest in 1826, when northeastern evangelicals founded the American Society for the Promotion of Temperance (soon renamed the American Temperance Society). The movement's manifesto was Lyman Beecher's *Six Sermons on the Nature, Occasions, Signs, Evils, and Remedy of Intemperance* (1826). Addressing the churchgoing middle class, Beecher declared alcohol an addictive drug and warned that even moderate drinkers risked becoming hopeless drunkards. Thus temperance, like other evangelical reforms, was presented as a contest between self-control and slavery to one's appetites. By encouraging total abstinence, reformers hoped to halt the creation of new drunkards while the old ones died out. But even though Beecher pinned his hopes on self-discipline, he wanted middle-class abstainers to spread reform through both example and coercion. As

THE DRUNKARD'S PROGRESS   This popular print describes the drunkard's progression from social drinking to alcoholism, isolation, crime, and death by suicide. His desolate wife and daughter and his burning house are at bottom.

middle-class evangelicals eliminated alcohol from their own lives, they would cease to offer it to their guests, buy or sell it, or provide it to their employees, and they would encourage their friends to do the same.

Charles Grandison Finney (see Chapter 10), in his revival at Rochester, made total abstinence a condition of conversion. Many other ministers and churches followed suit, and by the mid-1830s members of the middle class had largely disengaged themselves from alcohol and from the people who drank it. Hundreds of evangelical businessmen pledged that they would refuse to rent to merchants who sold liquor, sell grain to distillers, or enter a store that sold alcohol. Many of them made abstinence a condition of employment. Abstinence and opposition to the use of distilled spirits had become a badge of middle-class respectability.

By 1835 the American Temperance Society claimed 1.5 million members and estimated that 2 million Americans had renounced ardent spirits (whiskey, rum, and other distilled liquors); 250,000 had formally pledged to completely abstain from alcohol. The society further estimated that 4,000 distilleries had gone out of business. Many politicians no longer bought drinks to win voters to their cause. In 1833, members of Congress formed the American Congressional Temperance Society. The U.S. Army put an end to the age-old liquor ration in 1832, and increasing numbers of militia officers stopped supplying their men with whiskey. The annual consumption of alcohol, which had reached an all-time high in the 1820s, dropped by more than half in the 1830s.

THE ORIGINS OF PROHIBITION

In the middle 1830s Whigs made temperance a political issue. Realizing that voluntary abstinence would not put an end to drunkenness, Whig evangelicals drafted coercive, prohibitionist legislation. First, they attacked the licenses granting grocery stores and taverns the right to sell liquor by the drink and to permit it to be consumed on the premises. The licenses were important sources of revenue for local governments. They also gave local authorities the power to cancel the licenses of troublesome establishments. Militant temperance advocates, usually in association with local Whigs, demanded that the authorities use that power to outlaw all public drinking places. In communities throughout the North, the licensing issue became the issue around which local parties organized. The question first reached the state level in Massachusetts, when in 1838 a Whig legislature passed the "Fifteen-Gallon Law," which decreed that merchants could sell ardent spirits only in quantities of 15 gallons or more—thus outlawing every public drinking place in the state. In 1839 Massachusetts voters sent enough Democrats to the legislature to rescind the law.

Leading Democrats agreed with Whigs that Americans drank too much. But while Whigs insisted that regulating morality was a proper function of government, Democrats warned that government intrusion into areas of private choice would violate republican liberties. In many communities, alcohol was the defining difference between Democrats and Whigs.

THE DEMOCRATIZATION OF TEMPERANCE

Democratic voters held ambiguous attitudes toward temperance. Many of them continued to drink, while many others voluntarily abstained or cut down. Yet almost without exception they resented the coercive tactics of the Whigs and supported their party's pledge to protect them from evangelical meddling in their private lives. In 1830, when Lyman Beecher's Hanover Street Church in Boston caught fire, the volunteer fire companies (which doubled as working-class drinking clubs) arrived, noted that it was the hated Beecher's church, and made no effort to put out the fire.

Democrats, despite their opposition to prohibition, often spoke out against drunkenness. Many craft unions denied membership to heavy drinkers, and hundreds of thousands of rural and urban Democrats quietly stopped drinking. Then, in the late 1830s, former antiprohibitionists launched a temperance movement of their own.

One evening in 1840 six craftsmen were drinking at Chase's Tavern in Baltimore. More or less as a joke, they sent one of their number to a nearby temperance lecture; he came back a teetotaler and converted the others. They then drew up a total abstinence pledge and promised to devote themselves to the reform of other drinkers. Within months, from this beginning a national movement had emerged, called the Washington Temperance Society. The Washingtonians differed from older temperance societies in several ways. First, they identified themselves as members of the laboring classes. Second, they were avowedly nonreligious. Third, the Washingtonians—at least those who called themselves "True Washingtonians"—rejected recourse to politics and legislation and concentrated instead on the conversion of drinkers through compassion and persuasion. Finally, they welcomed "hopeless" drunkards and hailed them as heroes when they sobered up.

Temperance Schisms

Even though Whig reformers welcomed the Washingtonians at first, they soon had second thoughts. The nonreligious character of the movement was disturbing to those who saw temperance as an arm of evangelical reform. While the temperance regulars read pamphlets and listened to lectures by clergymen, lawyers, and doctors, the Washingtonians enjoyed raucous sing-alongs, comedy routines, barnyard imitations, dramatic skits, and even full-dress minstrel shows geared to temperance themes. Meetings were organized around experience speeches offered by reformed drunkards. Speaking extemporaneously, they omitted none of the horrors of an alcoholic life—attempts at suicide, friendships betrayed, fathers and mothers desolated, wives beaten and abandoned, children dead of starvation. Though Washingtonians had given up alcohol, their melodramatic tales, street parades, song books, and minstrel shows were continuous with popular culture. It was temperance, but it was not what Lyman Beecher and the Whigs had had in mind.

Nowhere did the Washingtonians differ more sharply from the temperance regulars than in their visions of the reformed life. The Whig reformers expected men who quit drinking to withdraw from the male world in which drinking was common and retreat into the comfort of the newly feminized middle-class family. Washingtonianism, on the other hand, translated traditional male sociability into sober forms. Moreover they called former drinkers back to the responsibilities of traditional fatherhood. Their experience stories began with the hurt drunkards had caused their wives and children and ended with their transformation into dependable providers and authoritative fathers. While the Whig temperance regulars tried to extend the ethos of individual ambition and the new middle-class domesticity into society at large, Washingtonians sought to rescue the self-respect and moral authority of working-class fathers.

The Washington Temperance Society collapsed toward the end of the 1840s. Yet its legacy survived. Among former drinkers in the North, it had introduced a new sense of domestic responsibility and a healthy fear of drunkenness. Along the way, the Washingtonians and related groups created a self-consciously respectable native Protestant working class in American cities.

Ethnicity and Alcohol

It was into neighborhoods stirred by working-class revivals and temperance agitation that millions of Irish and German immigrants arrived in the 1840s and 1850s. The newcomers had their own time-honored relations to alcohol. The Germans introduced lager beer to the United States, thus providing a wholesome alternative for Americans who wished to give up spirits without joining the teetotalers. The Germans also built old-country beer halls in American cities, complete with sausage counters, oompah bands, group singing, and other family attractions. For their part, the Irish reaffirmed their love of whiskey—a love that was forged in colonial oppression and in a culture that accepted trouble with resignation—a love that legitimized levels of male drunkenness and violence that Americans, particularly the temperance forces, found appalling.

In the 1850s native resentment of Catholic immigrants drove thousands of Baptist and Methodist "respectables" out of the Democratic coalition and into nativist Whig majorities that established legal prohibition throughout New England, in the middle states, and in the

Old Northwest. These were often the Democrats who became part of the North's Republican majority on the eve of the Civil War (see Chapter 14).

THE POLITICS OF RACE

Most whites in antebellum America believed in "natural" differences based on sex and race. God, they said, had given women and men and whites and blacks different mental, emotional, and physical capacities. And, as humankind (women and nonwhites more than others) was innately sinful and prone to disorder, God ordained a fixed social hierarchy in which white men exercised power over others. Slaves and free blacks accepted their subordinate status only as a fact of life, not as something that was natural and just. Some women also questioned patriarchy. But before 1830 hierarchy based on sex and race was seldom questioned in public, particularly by persons who were in a position to change it.

In the antebellum years, southerners and most northerners stiffened their defense of white paternalism. But northern Whig evangelicals were beginning to envision a world based on Christian love and individual worth, not inherited status. They transformed marriage from rank domination into a sentimental partnership—unequal, but a partnership nonetheless. They also questioned the more virulent forms of racism. From among the Whig evangelicals emerged a radical minority that envisioned a world without power. While conservative Christians insisted that relations based on dominance and submission were the lot of a sinful humankind, reformers argued that such relations interposed human power, too often in the form of brute force, between God and the individual spirit. They called for a world that substituted spiritual freedom and Christian love for every form of worldly domination.

FREE BLACKS

Prior to the American Revolution there had been sizable pockets of slavery in the northern states. But revolutionary idealism, coupled with the growing belief that slavery was inefficient and unnecessary, led one northern state after another to abolish it. By 1804 every northern state had taken some action, usually by passing laws that called for gradual emancipation. The first of such laws, and the model for others, was passed in Pennsylvania in 1780. This law freed slaves born after 1780 when they reached their 28th birthday. Slaves born before 1780 would remain slaves, and slave children would remain slaves through their prime working years.

The rising population of northern free blacks gravitated to the cities. In many cities—Philadelphia and New York City in particular—they met a stream of free blacks and fugitive slaves from the Upper South. Thus despite the flood of white immigrants from Europe and the American countryside, African Americans constituted a sizable minority in the rapidly expanding cities.

Blacks in the seaport cities tended to take stable, low-paying jobs. A few became successful entrepreneurs, while some others practiced skilled trades. Many of the others took jobs as waiters or porters in hotels, as barbers, and as butlers, maids, cooks, washerwomen, and coachmen for wealthy families. Others worked as dockworkers, laborers, and sailors. Still others became dealers in used clothing, or draymen with their own carts and horses, or food vendors in the streets and in basement shops.

A Black Street Vendor Selling Oysters in Philadelphia, circa 1814   In early 19th century New York and Philadelphia, African Americans monopolized the public sale of oysters and clams.

DISCRIMINATION

From the 1820s onward, however, the growing numbers of white wage-workers began to edge blacks out of their jobs by underselling them, by pressuring employers to discriminate, and by outright violence. As a result, African Americans were almost completely eliminated from the skilled trades, and many unskilled and semiskilled blacks lost their jobs on the docks, in warehouses, and in the merchant marine. And as their old jobs disappeared, blacks were systematically excluded from the new jobs that were opening up in factories. By the 1830s black workers in Philadelphia were noting "the difficulty of getting places for our sons as apprentices . . . owing to the prejudices with which we have to contend."

By accepting low wages, and by rioting, intimidation, gunplay, and even murder, Irish immigrants displaced most of the remaining blacks from their toehold in the economic life of the northeastern cities. An observer of the Philadelphia docks remarked in 1849 that "when a few years ago we saw none but Blacks, we now see none but Irish."

Meanwhile, official discrimination against blacks was on the rise. Political democratization for white men was accompanied by the disfranchisement of blacks (see Chapter 7). Cities either excluded black children from public schools or set up segregated schools. In 1845, when

Massachusetts passed a law declaring that all children had the right to attend neighborhood schools, the Boston School Committee blithely ruled that the law did not apply to blacks. Blacks were also excluded from white churches or sat in segregated pews.

African Americans responded by building institutions of their own. At one end were black-owned gambling houses, saloons, brothels, and dance halls—the only racially integrated institutions to be found in most cities. At the other end were black churches, schools, social clubs, and lodges. The first independent black church was the African Church of Philadelphia, founded in 1790; the African Methodist Episcopal Church, a national denomination still in existence, was founded in Philadelphia in 1816. Schools and relief societies, usually associated with churches, grew quickly. Black Masonic lodges attracted hundreds of members. It was from this matrix of black businesses and institutions that black abolitionists—David Walker in Boston, Frederick Douglass in New Bedford and Rochester, the itinerant Sojourner Truth, and many others—would emerge to demand abolition of slavery and equal rights for black citizens.

DEMOCRATIC RACISM

Neither the Whigs nor the Democrats encouraged the aspirations of slaves or free blacks. But it was the Democrats, from their beginnings in the 1820s, who incorporated racism into their

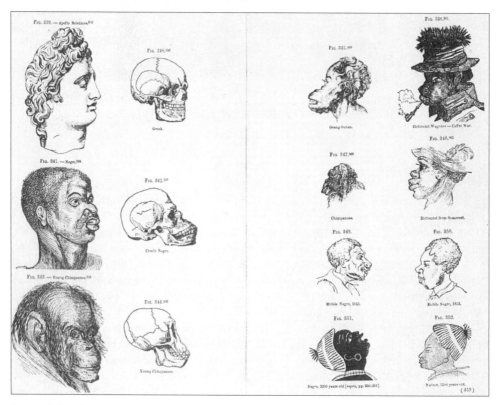

SKULL MEASUREMENTS   This illustration is from *Types of Mankind: or Ethnological Researches* (1845), a "scientific" text that portrayed white men as Greek gods and black men as apes.

political agenda. Minstrel shows, for example, often reflected the Democratic line on current events. By the time of the Civil War, Democrats mobilized voters almost solely with threats of "Negro rule."

Democrats also contributed to the rising tide of antiblack violence. There were plenty of Whig racists, but Democrats seem to have predominated when mobs moved into black neighborhoods, sometimes burning out whole areas. Indeed many Democrats lumped together evangelical reformers, genteel Whigs, and blacks as a unified threat to the white republic. In July 1834 a New York City mob sacked the house of the abolitionist Lewis Tappan, moved on to Charles Finney's Chatham Street Chapel, where abolitionists were said to be meeting, and finished the evening by attacking a British actor at the Bowery Theater. The manager saved his theater by waving two American flags and ordering an American actor to perform popular minstrel routines for the mob.

The first major American race riot broke out in Philadelphia in 1834 between working-class whites and blacks at a street carnival. Although blacks seemed to have won the first round, the whites refused to accept defeat. Over the next few nights, they wrecked a black-owned tavern; broke into black households to terrorize families and steal their property; attacked whites who lived with, socialized with, or operated businesses catering to blacks; wrecked the African Presbyterian Church; and destroyed a black church on Wharton Street by sawing through its timbers and pulling it down.

Conceptions of Racial Difference

Meanwhile, educated whites were being taught to think in racist terms. Among most scientists, biological determinism replaced historical and environmental explanations of racial differences; many argued that whites and blacks were separate species. Democrats welcomed that "discovery." In 1850 the *Democratic Review* confided, "Few or none now seriously adhere to the theory of the unity of the races. The whole state of the science at this moment seems to indicate that there are several distinct races of men on the earth, with entirely different capacities, physical and mental."

As whites came to perceive racial differences as God-given and immutable, they changed the nature of those differences as well. In the 18th and early 19th centuries, whites had stereotyped blacks as ignorant and prone to drunkenness and thievery, but they had also maintained a parallel stereotype of blacks as loyal and self-sacrificing servants. From the 1820s onward, racists continued to regard blacks as incompetent, now they saw all blacks as treacherous, shrewd, and secretive—individuals who only *pretended* to feel loyalty to white families and affection for the white children they took care of, while awaiting the chance to steal from them or poison them. The writer Herman Melville, a lifelong Democrat, dramatized these fears in *Benito Cereno,* a novel about slaves who commandeered a sailing ship and its captain and crew, then (with knives secretly at the throats of their captives) acted out a servile charade for unsuspecting visitors who came aboard.

Above all, Democratic ideologues pronounced blacks unfit to be citizens of the white man's republic. Whigs often supported various forms of black suffrage; Democrats uniformly opposed it. The insistence that blacks were incapable of citizenship reinforced an equally natural white male political capacity. The exclusion of blacks (by Democrats whose own political competence was often doubted by wealthier and better-educated Whigs) protected the republic while extending citizenship to all white men. The most vicious racist assaults were often carried out beneath symbols of the revolutionary republic. Antiblack mobs in Baltimore, Cincinnati, and Toledo called themselves Minute Men and Sons of Liberty.

THE BEGINNINGS OF ANTISLAVERY

Before 1830 only a few whites had thought of slavery as a moral question. Washington, Jefferson, and other Chesapeake gentlemen doubted the wisdom if not the morality of holding slaves; New England Federalists had condemned slavery in the course of condemning Jeffersonian masters. But southerners and most northerners—when they bothered to think about it at all—tended to accept slavery as the result of human (read "black") depravity and God's unknowable plan.

Organized opposition to slavery before 1831 was pretty much limited to the American Colonization Society, founded in 1816. Led by wealthy, generally conservative northern churchmen and a contingent of Chesapeake gentlemen, the society proposed the voluntary, gradual, and compensated emancipation of slaves and the "repatriation" of free blacks to West Africa. Although the society transported a few thousand blacks to Liberia, it never posed a serious threat to slavery. Southerners, who owned 2 million slaves by 1830, opposed emancipation whether compensated or not, and few free blacks were interested in moving to Africa. The society's campaign to deport them so disturbed many free blacks that they substituted "Colored" for "African" in naming their institutions.

But although few white Americans actively opposed slavery before 1830, the writing was on the wall. Emancipation in the North, though it came about quietly, constituted an implicit condemnation of slavery in the South. So did events outside the United States. Toussaint L'Ouverture's successful slave revolution in Haiti in 1804 threatened slavery everywhere (see Chapter 7). The British outlawed the Atlantic slave trade in 1808. Mexico, Peru, Chile, Gran Colombia (present-day Colombia, Venezuela, Equador, and Panama), and other new republics carved out of the Spanish Empire emancipated their slaves. The most powerful blow came in 1830 when the British Parliament emancipated the slaves of Jamaica, Bermuda, and other Caribbean islands ruled by Britain.

ABOLITIONISTS

It was at this time—the late 1820s and early 1830s—that religious revivals created a reform-minded evangelical culture in the northern United States. Radical abolitionism dates from 1831, when William Lloyd Garrison published the first issue of *The Liberator*. Already a veteran reformer, Garrison condemned slavery as a national sin and demanded immediate emancipation—or at least an immediate start toward emancipation.

In 1833 Garrison and like-minded abolitionists formed the American Anti-Slavery Society. Some of them were Unitarians who opposed slavery as an affront to both humanity and rationality; others were Quakers who were happy to join the movement. But abolitionists found their greatest support in southern New England, western New York, northern Ohio, and among the new middle classes of the northeastern cities—ground that Yankee settlement, the market revolution, and Finneyite revivals had turned into the heartland of the northern Whig Party.

Opposition to slavery was a logical extension of middle-class evangelicalism. Whig evangelicals demanded that God's people legislate the behavior of others. But the new evangelicalism was grounded in the morally accountable individual, and not in coercive institutions.

AN ABOLITIONIST VIEW OF SLAVE SOCIETY   This very provocative woodcut appeared in the *Anti-Slavery Almanac for 1840* (Boston, 1839). It pictures the lynching of slaves and their abolitionist allies by a southern mob. Surrounding the hanging tree are men (there are no women in the picture) who are engaged in other activities that northern reformers insisted were a result of the brutal patriarchy of slave society. Men duel with pistols and knives, others engage in an eye-gouging wrestling match, others gamble and drink, and still others cheer for cock fights and horse races. The enemy here is not simply slavery but the debauchery and unbridled passions associated with it.

Whig evangelicals often promised that their reforms would liberate the individual spirit from "slavery" to alcohol, lust, or ignorance—thus phrasing moral legislation as liberation, not coercion. It was not long before some discovered that slavery itself, an institution that obliterated moral choice and encouraged the worst human passions, was America's great national sin.

The American Anti-Slavery Society demanded immediate emancipation of slaves and full civil and legal rights for blacks. Assuming that God had created blacks and whites as members of one human family, abolitionists opposed the "scientific" racism spouted by Democrats and many Whigs. Moderates spoke of inherent racial characteristics but still tended to view blacks in benign (if condescending) ways. Harriet Beecher Stowe, for instance, portrayed blacks as simple, innocent, loving people who possessed a capacity for sentiment and emotionalism that most whites had lost. Radical abolitionists, however, remained committed environmentalists. Lydia Maria Child of New York City declared, "In the United States, colored persons have scarcely any chance to rise. But if colored persons are well treated, and have the same inducements to industry as others, they [will] work as well and behave as well."

AGITATION

Antislavery, unlike other reforms, was a radical attack on one of the nation's central institutions, and the movement attracted a minority even among middle-class evangelicals. Indeed, both Lyman Beecher and Charles Finney opposed the abolitionists in the 1830s, arguing that emancipation would come about sooner or later as a result of the religious conversion of slaveowners; antislavery agitation and the denunciation of slaveholders, they argued, would divide Christians, slow the revival movement, and thus actually delay emancipation.

The American Anti-Slavery Society staged a series of campaigns to force government and the public at large to confront the question of slavery. In 1835 the society launched its "Postal Campaign," flooding the nation's postal system with abolitionist tracts. From 1836 onward, they petitioned Congress to abolish slavery and the slave trade in the District of Columbia and to deny the slaveholding Republic of Texas admission to the Union. These tactics forced President Andrew Jackson to permit southern postal workers to censor the mails; they also forced Democrats and southern Whigs to abridge the right of petition to avoid discussion of slavery in Congress (see Chapter 12).

In these ways, a radical minority forced politicians to demonstrate the complicity of the party system (and the Democrats in particular) in the institution of slavery, brought the slavery question to public attention, and tied it to questions of civil liberties in the North and political power in the South. They were a dangerous minority indeed.

THE POLITICS OF GENDER AND SEX

Whigs valued a reformed masculinity that was lived out in the sentimentalized homes of the northern business classes or in the Christian gentility of the Whig plantation and farm. Jacksonian voters, on the other hand, often defended domestic patriarchy. Democrats often made heroes of men whose flamboyant, rakish lives directly challenged Whig domesticity. Whigs denounced Andrew Jackson for allegedly stealing his wife from her lawful husband; Democrats often admired him for the same reason. Richard M. Johnson of Kentucky, who was vice president under Martin Van Buren, openly kept a mulatto mistress and had two daughters by her; with his pistols always at hand, he accompanied her openly around Washington, D.C. "Prince" John Van Buren, the president's son and himself a prominent New York Democrat, met a "dark-eyed, well-formed Italian lady" who became his "fancy lady," remaining with him until he lost her in a high-stakes card game.

Whigs made Democratic contempt for sentimental domesticity a political issue. William Crane, a Michigan Whig, claimed that Democrats "despised no man for his sins," and went on to say that "brothel-haunters flocked to this party, because here in all political circles, and political movements, they were treated as nobility." Much of the Whig cultural agenda (and much of Democratic hatred of that agenda) was rooted in contests between Whig and Democratic masculine styles.

APPETITES

Many of the reforms urged by Whig evangelicals had to do with domestic and personal life rather than with politics. Their hopes for the perfection of the world hinged more on the character of individuals than on the role of institutions. They hoped to perfect the world by filling it with godly, self-governing individuals.

It was not an easy task, for opportunities to indulge in vanity, luxury, and sensuality were on the rise. Charles Finney, for instance, preached long and hard against vanity. Finney also worried about the effect of money, leisure time, and cheap novels on middle-class homes. He could not, he said, "believe that a person who has ever known the love of God can relish a secular novel" or open his or her home to "Byron, Scott, Shakespeare, and a host of triflers and blasphemers of God." Evangelicals also disdained luxury in home furnishings; they discouraged the use of silks and velvets and questioned the propriety of decorating the home with mahogany, mirrors, brass furnishings, and upholstered chairs and sofas.

Members of the evangelical middle class tried to define levels of material comfort that would separate them from the indulgences of those above and below them. They made similar attempts in the areas of food and sex. Sylvester Graham (now remembered for the cracker that bears his name) gave up the ministry in 1830 to become a full-time temperance lecturer. Before long, he was lecturing on the danger of excess in diet and sex. He claimed that the consumption of red meat, spiced foods, and alcohol produced bodily excitement that resulted in weakness and disease. Sex—including fornication, fantasizing, masturbation, and bestiality—affected the body in even more destructive ways, and the two appetites reinforced each other.

Acting on Graham's concerns, reformers established a system of Grahamite boardinghouses in which young men who were living away from home were provided with diets that helped them control their other appetites. Oberlin College, when it was founded by evangelicals in 1832, banned "tea and coffee, highly seasoned meats, rich pastries, and all unholsome [*sic*] and expensive foods." Reformers who did not actually adopt Graham's system shared his concern over the twin evils of rich food and sexual excess. John Humphrey Noyes set up a community in Oneida, New York, that indulged in plural marriage but at the same time urged sexual self-control; he also believed that in a perfect Christian world there would be no meat-eating.

Moral Reform

Although most middle-class households did not embrace Grahamism, simple food and sexual control became badges of class status. The assumption was that men had the greatest difficulty taming their appetites. The old image of woman as seductress persisted in the more traditionalist churches and in the pulp fiction from which middle-class mothers tried to protect their sons (see Chapter 10). Whig evangelicals, on the other hand, had made the discovery that women were naturally free of desire and that only men were subject to the animal passions. The middle-class ideal combined female purity and male self-control. For the most part it was a private reform, contained within the home. Sometimes, however, evangelical domesticity produced moral crusades to impose that ethos on the world at large. Many of these crusades were led by women.

In 1828 a band of Sunday school teachers initiated an informal mission to prostitutes that grew into the New York Magdalen Society. Taking a novel approach to an age-old question, the society argued that prostitution was created by brutal fathers and husbands who abandoned their young daughters or wives, by dandies who seduced them and turned them into prostitutes, and by lustful men who bought their services. Prostitution, in other words, was not the result of the innate sinfulness of prostitutes; it was the result of the brutality and lust of men. The solution was to remove young prostitutes from their environment, pray with them, and convert them to middle-class morality.

The Magdalen Society's *First Annual Report* (1831) inveighed against male lust and printed shocking life histories of prostitutes. Some men, however, read it as pornography;

others used it as a guidebook to the seamier side of New York City. The wealthy male evangelicals who had bankrolled the Magdalen Society withdrew their support, and the organization fell apart. Thereupon many of the women reformers set up the Female Moral Reform Society, with a House of Industry in which prostitutes were taught morality and household skills to prepare them for new lives as domestic servants in pious middle-class homes. This effort also failed, largely because few prostitutes were interested in domestic service or evangelical religion.

The Female Moral Reform Society was more successful with members of its own class. Its newspaper, *The Advocate of Moral Reform,* circulated throughout the evangelical North. Now, evangelical women fought prostitution by publishing the names of customers. They campaigned against pornography, obscenity, lewdness, and seduction and accepted the responsibility of rearing their sons to be pure, even when it meant dragging them out of brothels. They also publicized the names of adulterers, and they had seducers brought into court. In the process, women reformers fought the sexual double standard and assumed the power to define what was respectable and what was not.

WOMEN'S RIGHTS

From the late 1820s onward, middle-class women in the North assumed roles that would have been unthinkable to their mothers and grandmothers. Evangelical domesticity made loving mothers (and not stern fathers) the principal rearers of children. Housewives saw themselves as missionaries to their families, responsible for the choices their children and husband made between salvation or sin. It was in that role that women became arbiters of fashion, diet, and sexual behavior. That same role motivated them to join the temperance movement and moral reform societies, where they became public reformers while posing as mothers protecting their sons from rum sellers and seducers. Such experiences gave them a sense of spiritual empowerment that led some to question their own subordinate status within a system of gendered social roles.

It was through the antislavery movement that many women became advocates of women's rights. Abolitionists called for absolute human equality and rejection of impersonal institutions and prescribed social roles. It became clear to some female abolitionists that the critique of slavery applied as well to inequality based on sex.

Radical female abolitionists reached the conclusion that they were human beings first and women second. In 1837 Sarah Grimke announced, "The Lord Jesus defines the duties of his followers in his Sermon on the Mount . . . without any reference to sex or condition . . . never even referring to the distinction now so strenuously insisted upon between masculine and feminine virtues. . . . Men and women are CREATED EQUAL!" A women's rights convention put it just as bluntly in 1851: "We deny the right of any portion of the species to decide for another portion . . . what is and what is not their 'proper sphere'; that the proper sphere for all human beings is the largest and highest to which they are able to attain."

Beginning around 1840, women lobbied state legislatures and won significant changes in the laws governing women's rights to property, to the wages of their own labor, and to custody of children in cases of divorce. Fourteen states passed such legislation, culminating in New York's Married Women's Property Act in 1860.

Women's progress in achieving political rights, however, came more slowly. The first Women's Rights Convention, held in 1848 at Seneca Falls, New York, began with a Declaration

CHRONOLOGY

1816	African Methodist Episcopal denomination founded in Philadelphia • American Colonization Society promises to repatriate blacks to Africa
1819	New York state builds the first prison under the Auburn System
1826	Reformers found the American Society for the Promotion of Temperance
1831	William Lloyd Garrison begins publication of the antislavery *Liberator* • New York Magdalen Society publishes its first annual report
1833	Abolitionists found the American Anti-Slavery Society
1834	Antiabolition mob riots in New York City • First major race riot breaks out in Philadelphia
1840	Working-class drinkers found the Washington Temperance Society
1848	First Women's Rights Convention held in Seneca Falls, New York
1851	Maine becomes the first of 17 states to enact statewide prohibition
1860	New York enacts Married Women's Property Act

of Sentiments and Resolutions, based on the Declaration of Independence, that denounced "the repeated injuries and usurpations on the part of man towards woman."

The central issue was the right to vote, for female participation in politics was a direct challenge to a male-ordained women's place. A distraught New York legislator warned: "It is well known that the object of these unsexed women is to overthrow the most sacred of our institutions. . . . Are we to put the stamp of truth upon the libel here set forth, that men and women, in the matrimonial relation, are to be equal?" Later, the feminist Elizabeth Cady Stanton recalled such reactions: "Political rights," she said, "involving in their last results equality everywhere, roused all the antagonism of a dominant power, against the self-assertion of a class hitherto subservient."

CONCLUSION

By the 1830s most citizens in every corner of the republic firmly identified with either the Whig or Democratic Party—so much so that party affiliation was recognized as an indicator of personal history and cultural loyalties. In the states and neighborhoods, Whigs embraced commerce and activist government, arguing that both would foster prosperity, social harmony, and moral progress; faith in progress and improvement led Northern and western Whigs to entertain the hope that liberty and equality might apply to women and blacks. Democrats, on the other hand, were generally more localistic and culturally conservative. They seldom doubted the value of commerce, but they worried that the market revolution and its organization of banking, credit, and monetary supply was creating unprecedented levels of inequality and personal dependence among the republic's white male citizenry. Democrats also looked with angry disbelief at attempts of Whigs to govern the private and public behavior of their neighbors, and sometimes even to tinker with ancient distinctions of gender and race.

In sum, Whigs reformulated the revolutionary legacy of liberty and equality, moving away from classical notions of citizenship and toward liberty of conscience and equality of opportunity within a market-driven democracy; and they often attempted to civilize that new world by using government power to encourage commerce, social interdependence, and cultural homogeneity. When Democrats argued that Whig "interdependence" in fact meant dependence and inequality, Whigs countered with promises of individual success for those who were morally worthy of it. Democrats trusted none of that. Theirs was a Jeffersonian formulation grounded in a fierce defense of the liberty and equality of white men, and in a minimal, inexpensive, decentralized government that protected the liberties of those men without threatening their independence or their power over their households and within their neighborhoods.

12

JACKSONIAN DEMOCRACY

PROLOGUE: 1819 ∾ REPUBLICAN REVIVAL ∾ ADAMS VERSUS JACKSON
JACKSONIAN DEMOCRACY AND THE SOUTH
JACKSONIAN DEMOCRACY AND THE MARKET REVOLUTION
THE SECOND AMERICAN PARTY SYSTEM

National political leaders from the 1820s until the outbreak of the Civil War faced two persistent questions. First, a deepening rift between slave and free states threatened the very existence of the nation. Second, explosive economic development and territorial expansion made new demands upon the political system.

The Whig Party proposed the American System as the answer to both questions. The national government, said the Whigs, should subsidize roads and canals, foster industry with protective tariffs, and maintain a national bank capable of exercising centralized control over credit and currency. The result would be a peaceful, prosperous, and truly national market society. If the South, the West, and the Northeast were profiting by doing business with each other, the argument went, sectional fears and jealousies would quiet down. Jacksonian Democrats, on the other hand, argued that the American System was unconstitutional, that it violated the rights of states and localities, and that it would tax honest citizens in order to benefit corrupt and wealthy insiders. Most dangerous of all, argued the Democrats, Whig economic nationalism would create an activist, interventionist national government that would anger and frighten the slaveholding South. To counter both threats, the Jacksonians resurrected Jefferson's agrarian republic of states' rights and inactive, inexpensive government—all of it deeply inflected in the code of white male equality, domestic patriarchy, and racial slavery that was being acted out in families, neighborhoods, and state legislatures.

PROLOGUE: 1819

Jacksonian Democracy was rooted in two events that occurred in 1819. First, the angry debate that surrounded Missouri's admission as a slave state revealed the centrality and vulnerability of slavery within the Union. Second, a severe financial collapse led many Americans to wonder whether the market revolution was compatible with the Jeffersonian republic. By 1820 politicians were determined to reconstruct the limited-government, states'-rights coalition that had elected Thomas Jefferson. By 1828 they had formed the Democratic Party, with Andrew Jackson at its head.

THE WEST, 1803–1840S

When Jefferson bought the Louisiana Territory in 1803, he knew almost nothing about the new land itself. Only a few French trappers and traders had traveled the plains between the Mississippi and the Rocky Mountains, and no white person had seen the territory drained by the Columbia River. In 1804 Jefferson sent an expedition under Meriwether Lewis and William Clark to explore the land he had bought. To prepare for the expedition, Lewis studied astronomy, zoology, and botany; Clark was already an accomplished mapmaker. The two kept meticulous journals of one of the epic adventures in American history.

In May 1804 Lewis and Clark and 41 companions boarded a keelboat and two large canoes at the village of St. Louis. That spring and summer they poled and paddled 1,600 miles up the Missouri River, passing through rolling plains dotted by the farm villages of the Pawnee, Oto, Missouri, Crow, Omaha, Hidatsa, and Mandan peoples. The villages of the lower Missouri had been cut off from the western buffalo herds and reduced to dependence by mounted Sioux warriors who had begun to establish their hegemony over the northern plains.

Lewis and Clark traveled through Sioux territory and stopped for the winter at the prosperous, heavily fortified Mandan villages at the big bend of the Missouri River in Dakota country. In the spring they hired Toussaint Charbonneau, a French fur trader, to guide them to the Pacific. Although Charbonneau turned out to be useless, his wife, a teenaged Shoshone girl named Sacajawea, was an indispensable guide, interpreter, and diplomat. With her help, Lewis

A BIRDS-EYE VIEW, BY GEORGE CATLIN   The Mandan village at the big bend of the Missouri River hosted the Lewis and Clark party in 1804 and 1805. This bird's-eye view of the village was painted by George Catlin in 1832. Within a few years, the Mandan were nearly extinct, victims of smallpox and the Sioux.

and Clark navigated the upper Missouri, crossed the Rockies to the Snake River, and followed that stream to the Columbia River. They reached the Pacific in November 1805 and spent the winter at what is now Astoria, Oregon. Retracing their steps the following spring and summer, they returned to St. Louis in September 1806. They brought with them many volumes of drawings and notes, along with assurances that the Louisiana Purchase had been worth many, many times its price.

As time passed, Americans began to settle the southern portions of the Louisiana Purchase. Louisiana itself entered the Union in 1812. Settlers were also filtering into northern Louisiana and the Arkansas and Missouri territories. Farther north and west, the Sioux extended their control over the northern reaches of the land that Jefferson had bought.

The Sioux were aided in their conquest by the spread of smallpox. The Mandans were almost completely wiped out. The Sioux and their Cheyenne allies, who lived in small bands and were constantly on the move, fared better. Their horse-raiding parties now grew into armies of mounted invaders numbering as many as 2,000, and they extended their hunting lands south into what is now southern Nebraska and as far west as the Yellowstone River.

The Argument over Missouri

Early in 1819 slaveholding Missouri applied for admission to the Union as the first new state to be carved out of the Louisiana Purchase. New York Congressman James Tallmadge Jr. quickly proposed two amendments to the Missouri statehood bill. The first would bar additional slaves from being brought into Missouri. The second would emancipate Missouri slaves born after admission when they reached their 25th birthday.

The congressional debates on the Missouri question had nothing to do with humanitarian objections to slavery. Rufus King of New York, an old Federalist who led the northerners in the Senate, insisted that he opposed the admission of a new slave state "solely in its bearing and effects upon great political interests, and upon the just and equal rights of the freemen of the nation." Northerners had long chafed at the added representation in Congress and in the Electoral College that the "three-fifths" rule granted to the slave states (see Chapter 6). The rule had, in fact, added significantly to southern power: In 1790 the South, with 40 percent of the white population, controlled 47 percent of the votes in Congress.

In 1819 the North held a majority in the House of Representatives. The South controlled a bare majority in the Senate. Voting on the Tallmadge amendments was starkly sectional: Northern congressmen voted 86 to 10 for the first amendment, 80 to 14 for the second; southerners rejected both, 66 to 1 and 64 to 2. In the Senate, a unanimous South defeated the Tallmadge amendments with the help of the two Illinois senators and three northerners. Deadlocked between a Senate in favor of admitting Missouri as a slave state and a House dead set against it, Congress broke off one of the angriest sessions in its history and went home.

The Missouri Compromise

The new Congress that convened in the winter of 1819–1820 passed the legislative package that became known as the Missouri Compromise. Massachusetts offered its northern counties as the new free state of Maine, thus neutralizing fears that the South would gain votes in the Senate with the admission of Missouri. Senator Jesse Thomas of Illinois then proposed the so-called Thomas Proviso: If the North would admit Missouri as a slave state, the South would agree to outlaw slavery in territories above 36°30′ N latitude—a line extending from the southern border of Missouri to Spanish territory. That line would open Arkansas Territory to slavery and would close to slavery the remainder of the Louisiana Territory.

Congress admitted Maine with little debate. But the admission of Missouri under the terms of the Thomas Proviso met northern opposition. A joint Senate-House committee finally decided to separate the two bills. With half of the southern representatives and nearly all of the northerners supporting it, the Thomas Proviso passed. Congress then took up the admission of Missouri. With the votes of a solid South and 14 compromise-minded northerners, Missouri entered the Union as a slave state.

The Missouri crisis brought the South's commitment to slavery and the North's resentment of southern political power into collision. While northerners vowed to relinquish no more territory to slavery, southerners talked openly of disunion and civil war. A Georgia politician announced that the Missouri debates had lit a fire that "seas of blood can only extinguish."

Viewing the crisis from Monticello, the aging Thomas Jefferson was distraught:

> A geographical line, coinciding with a marked principle, moral and political, once conceived and held up to the angry passions of men, will never be obliterated; every new irritation will mark it deeper and deeper.... This momentous question, like a fire-bell in the night, awakened and filled me with terror.

THE PANIC OF 1819

Politicians debated the Missouri question against a darkening backdrop of economic depression. The origins of the Panic of 1819 were international: European agriculture was recovering from the Napoleonic wars, thereby reducing the demand for American foodstuffs; war and revolution in the New World had cut off the supply of precious metals (the base of the international money supply) from the mines of Mexico and Peru; debt-ridden European governments hoarded the available specie (precious metals); and American bankers and businessmen met the situation by expanding credit and issuing banknotes that were mere dreams of real money. Coming in the first years of the market revolution, this speculative boom was encouraged by American bankers who had little experience with corporate charters, promissory notes, bills of exchange, or stocks and bonds.

One of the reasons Congress had chartered the Second Bank of the United States in 1816 (see Chapter 9) was to impose order on this situation. But the Bank itself became part of the problem: The western branch offices in Cincinnati and Lexington became embroiled in the speculative boom, and insiders at the Baltimore branch hatched criminal schemes to enrich themselves. In 1819 the bank's president resigned and was replaced by Langdon Cheves of South Carolina. Cheves curtailed credit and demanded that state banknotes received by the Bank of the United States be redeemed in specie. By doing so, Cheves rescued the Bank from the paper economy created by state-chartered banks, but at huge expense: When the state banks were forced to redeem their notes in specie, they demanded payment from their own borrowers, and the national money and credit system collapsed.

The depression that followed the Panic of 1819 was the first failure of the market economy. Employers who could not meet their debts went out of business, and hundreds of thousands of wage workers lost their jobs. In Philadelphia, unemployment reached 75 percent; 1,800 workers in that city were imprisoned for debt. A tent city of the unemployed sprang up on the outskirts of Baltimore. Other cities and towns were hit as hard, and the situation was no better in the countryside.

Faced with a disastrous downturn that none could control and that few understood, many Americans directed their resentment onto the banks, particularly on the Bank of the United States. John Jacob Astor, a New York merchant and possibly the richest man in America at that time, admitted that "there has been too much Speculation and too much assumption of Power on the Part of the Bank Directors which has caused [*sic*] the institution to become unpopular . . . ." William Gouge, who would become the Jacksonian Democrats' favorite economist, put it more bluntly: When the Bank demanded that state banknotes be redeemed in specie, he said, "the Bank was saved and the people were ruined."

REPUBLICAN REVIVAL

The crises during 1819 and 1820 prompted demands for a return to Jeffersonian principles. Without opposition, Jefferson's dominant Republican Party had lost its way. The nationalist Congress of 1816 had enacted much of the Federalist program under the name of Republicanism; the result, said the old Republicans, was an aggressive government that helped bring on the Panic of 1819. At the same time, the collapse of Republican Party discipline in Congress had allowed the Missouri question to degenerate into a sectional free-for-all. By 1820 many Republicans were calling for a Jeffersonian revival that would limit government power and guarantee southern rights within the Union.

MARTIN VAN BUREN LEADS THE WAY

The busiest and the most astute of those Republicans was Martin Van Buren, leader of New York's Bucktail Republican faction, who took his seat in the Senate in 1821. Van Buren had built his political career out of a commitment to Jeffersonian principles, personal charm, and party discipline. He hoped to apply his political expertise to what he perceived as a dangerous turning point in national politics.

Van Buren's New York experience, along with his reading of national politics, told him that disciplined political parties were necessary democratic tools. Van Buren insisted that competition and party divisions were inevitable and good, but that they must be made to serve the republic. Working with likeminded politicians, he reconstructed the coalition of northern and southern agrarians that had elected Thomas Jefferson. The result was the Democratic Party and, ultimately, a national two-party system that persisted until the eve of the Civil War.

THE ELECTION OF 1824

With the approach of the 1824 presidential election, Van Buren and his friends supported William H. Crawford, Monroe's secretary of war and a staunch Georgia Republican. The Van Burenites controlled the Republican congressional caucus, the body that traditionally chose the party's presidential candidates. The public distrusted the caucus as undemocratic, for it represented the only party in government and thus could dictate the choice of a president. With most congressmen fearing their constituents, only a minority showed up for the caucus vote. They dutifully nominated Crawford.

With Republican Party unity broken, the list of sectional candidates grew. John Quincy Adams was the son of a Federalist president, successful secretary of state under Monroe, and one of the northeastern Federalist converts to Republicanism who, according to people like Van Buren and Crawford, had blunted the republican thrust of Jefferson's old party. He entered the contest as New England's favorite son. Henry Clay of Kentucky, a nationalist who claimed as his own the American System of protective tariffs, centralized banking, and government-sponsored internal improvements, expected to carry the West. John C. Calhoun of South Carolina announced his candidacy; but when he saw the swarm of candidates, he dropped out and put himself forth as the sole candidate for vice president.

The wild card was Andrew Jackson of Tennessee, who in 1824 was known only as a military hero. He was also a frontier nabob with a reputation for violence. According to Jackson's detractors, impetuosity marked his public life as well. As commander of U.S. military forces in the South in 1818, Jackson had led an unauthorized invasion of Spanish Florida, claiming that it was a hideout for Seminole warriors who raided into the United States. During the action he had occupied Spanish forts, summarily executed Seminoles, and hanged two British subjects. After being appointed governor of newly acquired Florida in 1821, Jackson retired from public life later that year. In 1824 eastern politicians knew Jackson only as a "military chieftain," "the Napoleon of the woods."

Jackson may have been all those things. But what the easterners did not take into account was his immense popularity. Thus, in the election of 1824, in the 16 states that chose presidential electors by popular vote Jackson polled 152,901 votes to Adams's 114,023 and Clay's 47,217. Crawford, who suffered a crippling stroke during the campaign, won 46,979 votes.

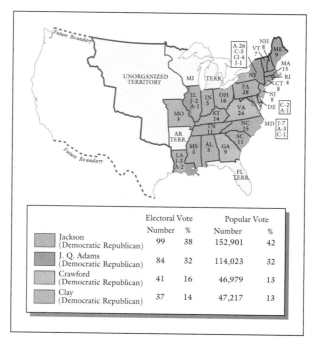

	Electoral Vote		Popular Vote	
	Number	%	Number	%
Jackson (Democratic Republican)	99	38	152,901	42
J. Q. Adams (Democratic Republican)	84	32	114,023	32
Crawford (Democratic Republican)	41	16	46,979	13
Clay (Democratic Republican)	37	14	47,217	13

PRESIDENTIAL ELECTION, 1824

Jackson's support was not only larger but more nearly national than that of his opponents. Jackson carried 84 percent of the votes of his own Southwest, and won victories in Pennsylvania, New Jersey, North Carolina, Indiana, and Illinois, while running a close second in several other states.

"A Corrupt Bargain"

Jackson assumed that he had won the election: He had received 42 percent of the popular vote to his nearest rival's 32 percent, and he was clearly the nation's choice. But his 99 electoral votes were 32 shy of the plurality demanded by the Constitution. And so, acting under the Twelfth Amendment, the House of Representatives would select a president from among the top three candidates. As the candidate with the fewest electoral votes, Henry Clay was eliminated. But he remained Speaker of the House, and he had enough support to throw the election to either Jackson or Adams. Years later, Jackson told a dinner guest that Clay had offered to support him in exchange for Clay's appointment as secretary of state—an office that traditionally led to the presidency. When Jackson turned him down, according to Jacksonian legend, Clay went to Adams and made the same offer. Adams accepted what became known as the "Corrupt Bargain" in January 1825. A month later, the House of Representatives voted: Clay's supporters, joined by several old Federalists, switched to Adams, giving him a one-vote victory. Soon after becoming president, Adams appointed Henry Clay as his secretary of state.

Reaction to the alleged "Corrupt Bargain" between John Quincy Adams and Henry Clay dominated the Adams administration. Before the vote took place in the House of Representatives, Andrew Jackson remarked, "Rumors say that deep intrigue is on foot," and predicted that there would be "bargain & sale" of the presidency. After the election, Jackson declared that the "gamester" Henry Clay had subverted the democratic will to his own purposes, and that "the rights of the people have been bartered for promises of office." Others in Washington were equally appalled. Robert Y. Hayne of South Carolina denounced the "monstrous union between Clay & Adams," while Louis McLane of Delaware declared the coalition of Clay and Adams utterly "unnatural & preposterous."

Jacksonian Melodrama

A frontier planter with a deep distrust of banks, Jackson claimed that the Panic of 1819 had been brought on by self-serving miscreants in the Bank of the United States. He insisted that the national debt was another source of corruption; it must be paid off and never allowed to recur. The federal government under James Monroe was filled with swindlers, and in the name of a vague nationalism they were taking power for themselves and scheming against the liberties of the people. The politicians had been bought off, said Jackson, and had attempted—through "King Caucus"—to select a president by backstairs deals rather than by popular election. Finally, in 1825, they had stolen the presidency outright.

Like hundreds of thousands of other Americans, Jackson sensed that something had gone wrong with the republic—that selfishness and intrigue had corrupted the government. In the language of revolutionary republicanism, a corrupt power once again threatened to snuff out liberty. Unlike most of his revolutionary forebears, however, Jackson believed that government should be subject to the will of popular majorities. An aroused public, he said, was the republic's best hope: "My fervent prayers are that our republican government may be perpetual, and the people alone by their virtue, and independent exercise of their free suffrage can make it perpetual."

More completely than any of his rivals, Jackson had captured the rhetoric of the revolutionary republic. And, with his fixation on secrecy, corruption, and intrigues, he transformed both that rhetoric and his own biography into popular melodrama. Finally, with a political alchemy that his rivals never understood, Jackson submerged old notions of republican citizenship into a firm faith in majoritarian democracy: Individuals might become selfish and corrupt, he believed, but a democratic majority was, by its very nature, opposed to corruption and governmental excess. Thus the republic was safe only when governed by the will of the majority.

ADAMS VERSUS JACKSON

While Jackson plotted revenge, John Quincy Adams assumed the duties of the presidency. He was well prepared. The son of a Federalist president, he had been an extraordinarily successful secretary of state under Monroe, guiding American diplomacy in the postwar world.

NATIONALISM IN AN INTERNATIONAL ARENA

In the Rush-Bagot Treaty of 1817 and the British-American Convention of 1818 Secretary of State John Quincy Adams helped pacify the Great Lakes, restore American fishing rights off of Canada, and draw the U.S.-Canadian boundary west to the Rocky Mountains. He pacified the southern border as well. In 1819, the Adams-Onis Treaty procured Florida for the United States and defined the U.S.-Spanish border west of the Mississippi in ways that gave the Americans claims to the Pacific Coast in the Northwest.

Trickier problems had arisen when Spanish colonies in the Americas declared their independence. Spain could not prevent this, and the powers of Europe, victorious over Napoleon and determined to roll back the republican revolution, talked openly of helping the Spanish or of annexing South American territory for themselves. Both the Americans and the British opposed such a move, and the British proposed a joint statement outlawing the interference of any outside power (including themselves) in Latin America. Adams had thought it better for the United States to make its own policy. In 1823 he wrote what became known as the Monroe Doctrine. It declared American opposition to any European attempt at colonization in the New World without (as the British had wanted) denying the right of the United States to annex new territory. Although the international community knew that the British navy, and not the Monroe Doctrine, kept the European powers out of the Americas, Adams had announced that the United States was determined to become the preeminent power in the Western Hemisphere.

NATIONALISM AT HOME

As president, Adams tried to translate his fervent nationalism into domestic policy. In his first annual message to Congress, Adams outlined an ambitious program for national development under the auspices of the federal government: roads, canals, a national university, a national astronomical observatory ("lighthouses of the skies"), and other costly initiatives:

The spirit of improvement is abroad upon the earth, . . . While foreign nations less blessed with . . . freedom . . . than ourselves are advancing with gigantic strides in the career of public improvement, were we to slumber in indolence or fold up our arms and proclaim to the world that we are palsied by the will of our constituents, would it not . . . doom ourselves to perpetual inferiority?

Congressmen could not believe their ears as they listened to Adams's extravagant proposals. Here was a president who had received only one in three votes and who had entered office accused of intrigues against the democratic will. And yet at the first opportunity he was telling Congress to pass an ambitious program and not to be "palsied" by the will of the electorate. Even members of Congress who favored Adams's program (and there were many of them) were afraid to vote for it. Hostile politicians and journalists never tired of joking about Adams's "lighthouses to the skies." More lasting, however, was the connection they drew between federal public works projects and high taxes, intrusive government, the denial of democratic majorities, and expanded opportunities for corruption, secret deals, and special favors. Congress never acted on the president's proposals, and the Adams administration emerged as little more than a long prelude to the election of 1828.

THE BIRTH OF THE DEMOCRATIC PARTY

As early as 1825, it was clear that the election of 1828 would pit Adams against Andrew Jackson. To the consternation of his chief supporters, Adams did nothing to prepare for the contest. He refused to remove even his noisiest enemies from appointive office, and he built no political organization. The opposition was much more active. Van Buren and like-minded Republicans (with their candidate Crawford hopelessly incapacitated) switched their allegiance to Jackson. They wanted Jackson elected, however, not only as a popular hero but as head of a disciplined and committed Democratic Party that would continue the states'-rights, limited-government positions of the old Jeffersonian Republicans.

The new Democratic Party linked popular democracy with the defense of southern slavery. Van Buren began preparations for 1828 with a visit to John C. Calhoun of South Carolina. Calhoun was moving along the road from postwar nationalism to states'-rights conservatism; he also wanted to stay on as vice president and thus keep his presidential hopes alive. After convincing Calhoun to support Jackson and to endorse limited government, Van Buren wrote to Thomas Ritchie, editor of the *Richmond Enquirer* and leader of Virginia's Republicans, who could deliver Crawford's southern supporters to Jackson. In his letter, Van Buren proposed to revive the alliance of "the planters of the South and the plain Republicans of the North" that had won Jefferson the presidency. A new Democratic Party, committed to an agrarian program of states' rights and minimal government and dependent on the votes of both slaveholding and non-slaveholding states, would ensure democracy, the continuation of slavery, and the preservation of the Union.

THE ELECTION OF 1828

The presidential campaign of 1828 was an exercise in slander rather than a debate on public issues. Jacksonians hammered away at the "Corrupt Bargain" of 1825 and at the dishonesty and weakness that Adams had supposedly displayed in that affair. The Adams forces attacked

RACHEL DONELSON JACKSON AS A MATURE PLANTATION MISTRESS   Andrew Jackson supposedly wore this miniature portrait of his beloved Rachel over his heart after her death in 1829.

Jackson's character. One of Henry Clay's newspaper friends circulated the rumor that Jackson was a bastard and that his mother was a prostitute. But the most egregious slander of the campaign centered on Andrew Jackson's marriage. In 1790 Jackson had married Rachel Donelson, probably aware that she was estranged but not formally divorced from a man named Robards. Branding the marriage an "abduction," the Adams team screamed that Jackson had "torn from a husband the wife of his bosom," and had lived with her in a state of "open and notorious lewdness."

The Adams strategy ultimately backfired. Many voters did agree that only a man who strictly obeyed the law was fit to be president, and that Jackson's "passionate" and "lawless" nature disqualified him. But many others criticized Adams for permitting Jackson's private life to become a public issue. Whatever the legality of their marriage, Andrew and Rachel Jackson had lived as models of marital fidelity and romantic love for nearly 40 years; their neighbors had long ago forgiven whatever transgressions they may have committed. Thus on the one hand, Jackson's supporters accused the Adams campaign of a gross violation of privacy and honor. On the other, they defended Jackson's marriage as a triumph of what was right and just over what was narrowly legal. The attempt to brand Jackson as a lawless man, in fact, enhanced his image as a melodramatic hero who battled shrewd, unscrupulous, legalistic enemies by drawing on his natural nobility and force of will.

The campaign caught the public imagination. Voter turnout was double what it had been in 1824, totaling 56.3 percent. Jackson won the election with 56 percent of the popular vote

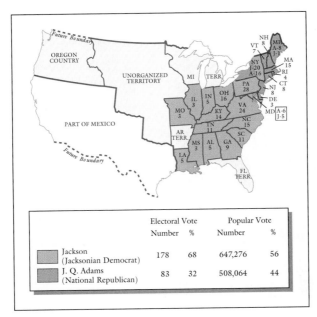

	Electoral Vote		Popular Vote	
	Number	%	Number	%
Jackson (Jacksonian Democrat)	178	68	647,276	56
J. Q. Adams (National Republican)	83	32	508,064	44

PRESIDENTIAL ELECTION, 1828

and with a margin of 178 to 83 in electoral votes. It was a clear triumph of democracy over genteel statesmanship, of limited government over expansive nationalism. Just as clearly, it was a victory of popular melodrama over old forms of cultural gentility.

A PEOPLE'S INAUGURATION

Newspapers estimated that from 15,000 to 20,000 citizens came to Washington to witness Jackson's inauguration on March 4, 1829. They were "like the inundation of the northern barbarians into Rome," remarked Senator Daniel Webster. As members of the Washington establishment watched uneasily, the crowd filled the open spaces and the streets near the east portico of the Capitol Building, where Jackson was to deliver his inaugural address.

Jackson arrived at the Capitol in deep mourning. In December his wife Rachel had gone to Nashville to shop and had stopped to rest in a newspaper office. There, for the first time, she read the accusations that had been made against her. She fainted on the spot. Although she had been in poor health, no one would ever convince Jackson that her death in January had not been caused by his political enemies.

Jackson's inaugural address was vague. He promised "proper respect" for states' rights and a "spirit of equity, caution, and compromise" on the question of the tariff. He promised to reform the civil service by replacing "unfaithful or incompetent" officers, and he vowed to retire the national debt through "a strict and faithful economy." Beyond that, he said very little, though he took every opportunity to flatter the popular majority. He had been elected "by the choice of a free people," and he pledged "the zealous dedication of my humble abilities to their service and their good." He finished by reminding Americans that a benign providence looked over them.

THE PRESIDENT'S LEVEE   Robert Cruikshank drew Jackson's inaugural reception with men and women of all classes, children, dogs, and bucking horses celebrating the Old General's victory. Cruikshank subtitled his lithograph *All Creation Going to the White House.*

The new president traveled slowly from the Capitol to the White House, with the throng following and growing noisier along the way. The crowd followed him into the White House, where refreshments had been provided. Soon Jackson's well-wishers were ranging through the mansion, muddying the carpets, tipping things over, breaking dishes, and standing in dirty boots on upholstered chairs. Jackson had to retreat to avoid being crushed. The White House staff lured much of the crowd outside by moving the punch bowls and liquor to the lawn.

THE SPOILS SYSTEM

Martin Van Buren, who had mobilized much of the support Jackson gained between 1824 and 1828, was the new secretary of state—positioned to succeed Jackson as president. Van Buren quit his newly won post as governor of New York and came to Washington, where he became Jackson's most valued adviser. Other appointments were less promising, for Jackson filled the remaining cabinet posts with old friends and political supporters who in many cases proved unfit for their jobs. The same was true in other areas of the civil service. Early in the administration, opponents complained that Jackson was replacing able, educated, patriotic public servants with some very dubious appointments. They soon had convincing evidence: Samuel Swarthout, whom Jackson had appointed collector of the Port of New York, stole $1.2 million and took off for Europe.

Actually, much of the furor over Jackson's "spoils system" was overwrought and misdirected. All he wanted to do, Jackson claimed, was to get rid of officeholders who expected to hold lifetime appointments. Arguing that most government jobs could be performed by any honest, reasonably intelligent citizen, Jackson proposed ending the long tenures that, he said, turned the civil service into "support of the few at the expense of the many." Jackson removed about 1 in 10 executive appointees during his eight years in office, and his replacements were as wealthy and well-educated as their predecessors. They were, however, *political* appointees. Acting out of his own need for personal loyalty and on the advice of Van Buren and other architects of the Democratic Party, Jackson filled vacancies with Democrats who had worked for his election.

Jackson sought Van Buren's advice on appointments. Van Buren knew the political value of dispensing government jobs; indeed it was one of his henchmen who coined the phrase "To the victor belongs the spoils." In resorting to patronage to build the party, however, Jackson gave his opponents an important issue. Revolutionary republicans feared a government of lackeys dependent on a powerful executive, and congressional opponents argued that Jackson was using appointments to "convert the entire body of those in office into corrupt and supple instruments of power."

JACKSONIAN DEMOCRACY AND THE SOUTH

In the 1828 election, even though Jackson ran strongly in every region but New England, the base of his support was in the South, where he won 8 of every 10 votes. Southerners had grown wary of an activist government in which they were in the minority. They looked to Jackson not only as a military hero but as a Tennessee planter who talked about getting back to republican fundamentals. But although southerners expected Jackson to look after southern interests, there was disagreement within the administration on how those interests should be protected. Some sided with Vice President Calhoun, who believed that any state had the right to veto federal legislation and even in extreme cases to secede from the Union. Others agreed with Secretary of State Van Buren that the Union was inviolable, and that the South's best safeguard was in a political party committed to states' rights within the Union. The differences were fought out in the contest between Calhoun and Van Buren for the right to succeed Jackson as president.

SOUTHERNERS AND INDIANS

When Jackson entered office, a final crisis between frontier whites and the native peoples of the eastern woodlands was under way. By the 1820s few Native Americans were left east of the Appalachians in the North. The Iroquois of New York were penned into tiny reservations, and the tribes of the Old Northwest were broken and scattered. But in the Old Southwest 60,000 Cherokees, Creeks, Choctaws, Chickasaws, and Seminoles were still living on their ancestral lands, with tenure guaranteed by federal treaties that (at least implicitly) recognized them as sovereign peoples. Congress had appropriated funds for schools, tools, seeds, and training to help these "Civilized Tribes" make the transition to farming. Most government officials assumed that the tribes would eventually trade their old lands and use their farming skills on new land west of the Mississippi.

Southwestern whites resented federal Indian policy as an affront to both white democracy and states' rights. The poorer farmers coveted the Indians' land, and states'-rights southerners denied that the federal government had the authority to make treaties or to recognize

TRAIL OF TEARS   In 1838 the U.S. Army marched 18,000 Cherokee men, women, and children, along with their animals and whatever they could carry, out of their home territory and into Oklahoma. At least 4,000—most of them old or very young—died on the march.

sovereign peoples within their states. Resistance centered in Georgia, where Governor George Troup brought native lands under the state's jurisdiction and then turned them over to poor whites by way of lotteries. At one point, Troup sent state surveyors onto Creek territory before federal purchase from the Indians was complete, telling President Adams that if he resisted state authority he would be considered a "public enemy." The Cherokees in Georgia pressed the issue in 1827 by declaring themselves a republic with its own constitution, government, courts, and police. But almost at the same time, a gold discovery on their land made it even more attractive to whites. The Georgia legislature promptly declared Cherokee law null and void, extended Georgia's authority into Cherokee country, and began surveying the lands for sale. Hinting at the old connection between state sovereignty and the protection of slavery, Governor Troup warned that the federal "jurisdiction claimed over one portion of our population may very soon be asserted over *another*." Alabama and Mississippi quickly followed Georgia's lead by extending state authority over Indian lands and denying federal jurisdiction.

INDIAN REMOVAL

President Jackson agreed that the federal government lacked the authority to recognize native sovereignty within a state and declared that he could not protect the Cherokees and the other Civilized Tribes from state governments. Instead, he offered to remove them to federal land west of the Mississippi, where they would be under the authority of the benevolent federal government. Congress made that offer official in the Indian Removal Act of 1830.

The Cherokees, with the help of New England missionaries, had taken their claims of sovereignty to court in the late 1820s. In 1830 John Marshall's Supreme Court ruled in *Cherokee Nation* v. *Georgia* that the Cherokees could not sue Georgia because they were not a sovereign people but "domestic dependent nations," thus dependents of the federal government, and not of the state of Georgia, though somehow "nations" as well. The Court's decision in *Worcester* v. *Georgia* (1832) declared that Georgia's extension of state law over Cherokee land was unconstitutional. President Jackson ignored the decision, however, reportedly telling a congressman, "John Marshall has made his decision: *now let him enforce it!*" In the end, Jackson sat back as the southwestern states encroached on the Civilized Tribes. In 1838 his successor, Martin Van Buren, sent the Army to march the 18,000 remaining Cherokee to Oklahoma. Along this "Trail of Tears," 4,000 of them died of exposure, disease, starvation, and white depredation.

Indian removal had profound political consequences. It violated Supreme Court decisions and thus strengthened Jackson's reputation as an enemy of the rule of law and a friend of local, "democratic" solutions; at the same time, it reaffirmed the link between racism and white democracy in the South and announced Jackson's commitment to state sovereignty and limited federal authority.

SOUTHERNERS AND THE TARIFF

In 1828 the Democratic Congress set about writing a tariff that would win votes for Jackson in the upcoming presidential election. Assured of support in the South, the creators of the tariff bill fished for votes in the Middle Atlantic states and in the Old Northwest by including protective levies on raw wool, flax, molasses, hemp, and distilled spirits. The result was a patchwork tariff that pleased northern and western farmers but that worried the South. Protective tariffs hurt the South by diminishing exports of cotton and other staples and by raising the price of manufactured goods. Calling the new bill a "Tariff of Abominations," the legislature of one southern state after another denounced it as "unconstitutional, unwise, unjust, unequal, and oppressive."

South Carolina took the lead in opposing the Tariff of 1828. During the War of 1812 and the ensuing Era of Good Feelings, South Carolina had favored the economic nationalism of the American System. But the Missouri debates had sent Carolinians looking for ways to safeguard slavery. And then the Denmark Vesey conspiracy of 1822 (see Chapter 10) had stirred fears among the outnumbered whites of coastal South Carolina; their fears grew more intense when federal courts shot down a state law forbidding black merchant seamen from moving about freely while their ships were docked at Charleston. Carolinians were disturbed too by persistent talk of gradual emancipation—at a time when their own commitment to slavery was growing stronger.

NULLIFICATION

As early as 1827 Calhoun had embraced the principle that the states had the right to nullify federal laws. In 1828, in his anonymously published essay *Exposition and Protest,* he argued that the Constitution was a compact between sovereign states, and that the states (not the federal courts) could decide the constitutionality of federal laws. A state convention (like the conventions that had ratified the Constitution) could nullify any federal law within state borders. *Exposition and Protest* anticipated the secessionist arguments of 1861: The Union was a voluntary compact between sovereign states, states were the ultimate judges of the validity of federal law, and states could break the compact if they wished.

Nullification was the strongest card held by the southern extremists, and they avoided playing it. They knew that President Jackson was a states'-rights slaveholder and assumed that Vice President Calhoun would succeed to the presidency in time and would protect southern interests. They were wrong on both counts. Jackson favored states' rights, but only within a perpetual and inviolable Union. His Indian policy was simply an acknowledgment of state jurisdiction over institutions within state boundaries. A tariff, on the other hand, was ultimately a matter of foreign policy, clearly within the jurisdiction of the federal government. To allow a state to veto a tariff would be to deny the legal existence of the United States.

Jackson aired his views at a program celebrating Jefferson's birthday on April 13, 1830. He listened quietly as speaker after speaker defended the extreme states'-rights position. After the formal speeches were over, the president rose to propose an after-dinner toast. It was a powerful denunciation of what he had just heard: "Our Federal Union," he said in measured tones, *"It must be preserved."* Dumb-struck, the southerners looked to Calhoun, who as vice president was to propose the second toast. Obviously shaken by Jackson's unqualified defense of the Union, Calhoun offered this toast: "The Union. Next to our liberties the most dear." They were strong words, but they had little meaning after Jackson's affirmation of the Union.

Having reaffirmed the Union and rejected nullification, Jackson asked Congress to reduce the tariff rates. The resulting Tariff of 1832 lowered the rates on many items but still affirmed the principle of protectionism. That, along with the Boston abolitionist William Lloyd Garrison's declaration of war on slavery in 1831, followed by Nat Turner's bloody slave uprising in Virginia that same year (see Chapter 10), led the whites of South Carolina and Georgia to intensify their distrust of outside authority and their insistence on the right to govern their own neighborhoods. South Carolina, now with Calhoun's open leadership and support, called a state convention that nullified the Tariffs of 1828 and 1832.

In Washington, President Jackson raged that nullification (not to mention the right of secession that followed logically from it) was illegal. Insisting that "Disunion . . . is *treason,*" he asked Congress for a Force Bill empowering him to personally lead a federal army into South Carolina. At the same time, however, he supported the rapid reduction of tariffs. When Democratic attempts at reduction bogged down, Henry Clay, now back in the Senate, took on the tricky legislative task of rescuing his beloved protective tariff while quieting southern fears. The result was the Compromise Tariff of 1833, which by lowering tariffs over the course of several years, gave southern planters the relief they demanded while maintaining moderate protectionism and allowing northern manufacturers time to adjust to the lower rates. Congress also passed the Force Bill. Jackson signed both into law on March 2, 1833.

With that, the nullification crisis came to a quiet end. No other southern state had joined South Carolina in nullifying the tariff, though some states had made vague pledges of support. The Compromise Tariff of 1833 isolated the South Carolina nullifiers. Deprived of their issue and most of their support, they declared victory and disbanded their convention—but not before nullifying the Force Bill. Jackson chose to overlook that last defiant gesture, and the crisis passed.

THE "PETTICOAT WARS"

The spoils system, Indian removal, nullification, and other heated questions of Jackson's first term were fought out against a backdrop of gossip, intrigue, and angry division within the inner circles of Jackson's government. The talk centered on Peggy O'Neal Timberlake, a Washington tavernkeeper's daughter who, in January 1829, had married John Henry Eaton, Jackson's old friend and soon to be his secretary of war. Timberlake's husband, a navy purser, had recently committed suicide; it was rumored that her affair with Eaton was the cause. Eaton was middle-aged; his bride was 29, pretty, flirtatious, and, according to Washington gossip, "frivolous, wayward, [and] passionate." Knowing that his marriage might cause trouble for the new administration, Eaton had asked for and received Jackson's blessings—and, by strong implication, his protection.

The marriage of John and Peggy Eaton came at a turning point in the history of both Washington society and elite sexual mores. Until the 1820s most officeholders had left their families at home. They took lodgings at taverns and boardinghouses and lived in a bachelor world of shirtsleeves, tobacco, card-playing, and occasional liaisons with local women. But in the 1820s the boardinghouse world was giving way to high society. Cabinet members, senators, congressmen, and other officials moved into Washington houses, and their wives presided over the round of dinner parties through which much of the government's business was done. As in other wealthy families, political wives imposed new forms of gentility and politeness upon these affairs, and they assumed the responsibility of drawing up the guest lists. Many of them determined to exclude Peggy Eaton from polite society.

The exclusion of Peggy Eaton split the Jackson administration in half. Jackson himself was committed to protect her. He had met his own beloved Rachel while boarding at her father's Nashville tavern, and their grand romance (as well as the gossip that surrounded it) was a striking parallel to the affair of John and Peggy Eaton. That, coupled with Jackson's honor-bound agreement to the Eaton marriage, ensured that he would protect the Eatons to the bitter end. Motivated by chivalry, personal loyalty, grief and rage over Rachel's death, and angry disbelief that political intrigue could sully the private life of a valued friend, Jackson insisted to his cabinet that Peggy Eaton was "as chaste as a virgin!" Jackson noted that the rumors were being spread not only by politicians' wives but by prominent clergymen and blamed the "conspiracy" on "females with clergymen at their head."

In fact, Mrs. Eaton's tormentors included most of the cabinet members as well as Jackson's own White House "family." Widowed and without children, Jackson had invited his nephew and private secretary, Andrew Jackson Donelson, along with his wife and her sister, to live in the White House. Donelson's wife, serving as official hostess, resolutely shunned Peggy Eaton. Jackson, who valued domestic harmony and personal loyalty, assumed that schemers had invaded and subverted his own household. Before long, his suspicions centered on Vice President Calhoun, whose wife, Floride Bonneau Calhoun, a haughty and powerful Washington matron, was a leader of the assault on Peggy Eaton. Only Secretary of State Van Buren, a widower and an eminently decent man, included the Eatons in official functions. Sensing that Jackson was losing his patience with Calhoun, Van Buren's friends showed Jackson a letter revealing that while serving in Monroe's cabinet Calhoun had favored censuring Jackson for his unauthorized invasion of Florida in 1818. An open break with Calhoun became inevitable.

THE FALL OF CALHOUN

Jackson resolved the Peggy Eaton controversy, as he would resolve nullification, in ways that favored Van Buren in his contest with Calhoun. He sent Donelson, his wife, and his sister-in-law back to Tennessee and invited his friend W. B. Lewis and his daughter to take their place. But he pointedly made Peggy Eaton the official hostess at the White House. In the spring of 1831 Van Buren offered to resign his cabinet post and engineered the resignations of nearly all other members of the cabinet—thus allowing Jackson to remake his administration without firing anyone. Many of those who left were southern supporters of Calhoun. Jackson replaced them with a mixed cabinet that included political allies of Van Buren. It was also at this time that President Jackson began to consult with an informal "Kitchen Cabinet" that included journalists Amos Kendall and Francis Preston Blair, along with Van Buren and a few others.

Van Buren's victory over Calhoun came to a quick conclusion. As part of his cabinet reorganization, Jackson appointed Van Buren minister to Great Britain. Calhoun, sitting as president of the Senate, rigged the confirmation so that he cast the deciding vote against Van Buren's appointment—a petty act that turned out to be his last exercise of national power. Jackson replaced Calhoun with Van Buren as the vice presidential candidate in 1832 and let it be known that he wanted Van Buren to succeed him as president.

Petitions, the Gag Rule, and the Southern Mails

Van Buren promised to protect slavery with a disciplined national coalition committed to states' rights within an inviolable Union. The rise of a northern antislavery movement (see Chapter 11) posed a direct challenge to that formulation. Middle-class evangelicals, who were emerging as the reformist core of the northern Whig Party, had learned early on that Jacksonian Democrats wanted to keep moral issues out of politics. In 1828 and 1829, when they petitioned the government to stop movement of the mail on Sundays, Jackson had turned them down. They then petitioned the government for humane treatment of the Civilized Tribes, whose conversion to Christianity had been accomplished largely by New England missionaries; again, the Jackson administration had refused. The evangelicals were appalled by his defense of Peggy Eaton. Most of all, they disliked the Democrats' rigid party discipline, which in each case had kept questions of morality from shaping politics.

In the early 1830s a radical minority of evangelicals formed societies committed to the immediate abolition of slavery, and they devised ways of making the national government confront the slavery question. In 1835 abolitionists launched a "postal campaign," flooding the mail with antislavery tracts that southerners and most northerners considered incendiary. From 1836 onward, they bombarded Congress with petitions—most of them for the abolition of slavery and the slave trade in the District of Columbia (where Congress had undisputed jurisdiction), others against the interstate slave trade, slavery in the federal territories, and the admission of new slave states.

Some Jacksonians, including Jackson himself, wanted to put a stop to the postal campaign with a federal censorship law. Calhoun and other southerners, however, argued that the states had the right to censor mail crossing their borders. Amos Kendall, who had become postmaster general in the cabinet shuffle, proposed an informal solution. Without changing the law, he would simply look the other way as local postmasters violated postal regulations and removed abolitionist materials from the mail. Almost all such materials were published in New York City and mailed from there. The New York postmaster, a loyal appointee, proceeded to sift them out of the mail and thus cut off the postal campaign at its source. The few tracts that made it to the South were destroyed by local postmasters.

The Democrats dealt in a similar manner with antislavery petitions to Congress. Southern extremists demanded that Congress disavow its power to legislate on slavery in the District of Columbia, but Van Buren declared that Congress did indeed have that power but should never use it. In dealing with the petitions, Congress simply voted at each session from 1836 to 1844 to table them without reading them—thus acknowledging that they had been received but sidestepping any debate on them. This procedure, which became known as the "gag rule," was passed by southern Whigs and southern Democrats with the help of most of the northern Democrats.

Thus the Jacksonians answered the question that had arisen with the Missouri debates: how to protect the slaveholding South within the federal Union. Whereas Calhoun and other southern radicals found the answer in nullification and other forms of state sovereignty, Jackson and the Democratic coalition insisted that the Union was inviolable, and that any attempt to dissolve it would be met with force. At the same time, a Democratic Party uniting northern and southern agrarians into a states'-rights, limited-government majority could guarantee southern rights within the Union. This answer to the southern question stayed in place until the breakup of the Democratic Party on the eve of the Civil War.

JACKSONIAN DEMOCRACY AND THE MARKET REVOLUTION

Jacksonian Democrats assumed power at the height of the market revolution, and they spent much of the 1830s and 1840s trying to reconcile the market and the ideal of the agrarian republic. They welcomed commerce as long as it served the independence and rough equality of white men on which republican citizenship rested. But paper currency and the dependence on credit that came with the market revolution posed problems. The so-called "paper economy" separated wealth from "real work" and encouraged an unrepublican spirit of luxury and greed. Worst of all, the new paper economy required government-granted privileges that the Jacksonians branded "corruption." For the same reasons, the protective tariffs and government-sponsored roads and canals of the American System were antirepublican and unacceptable. It was the goal of the Jackson presidency to curtail government involvement in the economy, to end special privilege, and thus to rescue the republic from the "Money Power."

Jacksonians were opposed by proponents of an activist central government. The opposition wished to encourage orderly economic development through the American System of protective tariffs, a federally-subsidized transportation network, and a national bank. Jacksonian rhetoric about the Money Power and the Old Republic, they argued, was little more than the demoguery of unqualified, self-seeking politicians.

THE SECOND BANK OF THE UNITED STATES

The argument between Jacksonians and their detractors came to focus on the Second Bank of the United States, a mixed public-private corporation chartered by Congress in 1816 (see Chapter 9). The national government deposited its revenue in the Bank, thus giving it an enormous capital base. The government deposits also included state banknotes that had been used to pay customs duties or to buy public land; the Bank of the United States had the power to demand redemption of these notes in specie (gold and silver), thus discouraging state banks from issuing inflationary notes that they could not back up. The Bank also issued notes of its own, and these served as the beginnings of a national paper currency. Thus with powers granted under its federal charter, the Bank of the United States exercised central control over the nation's monetary and credit systems.

Most members of the business community valued the Bank of the United States, for it promised a stable, uniform paper currency and competent, centralized control over the banking system. But millions of Americans resented and distrusted the national bank, citing its role in the Panic of 1819. President Jackson agreed with them. He insisted that both the Bank and paper money were unconstitutional, and that the only safe, natural, republican currency was gold and silver. Above all, Jackson saw the Bank of the United States as a government-sponsored concentration of power that threatened the republic.

THE BANK WAR

The charter of the Bank of the United States ran through 1836. But Senators Henry Clay and Daniel Webster encouraged Nicholas Biddle, the Bank's brilliant, aristocratic president, to apply for recharter in 1832. Clay and his friends hoped to provoke the hot-tempered and supposedly erratic Jackson into a response that could be used against him in the election.

Biddle applied to Congress for a recharter of the Bank of the United States in January 1832. Congress passed the recharter bill in early July and sent it on to the president. On July 4, Van Buren visited the White House and found Jackson sick in bed; Jackson took Van Buren's hand and said, "The bank, Mr. Van Buren, is trying to kill me, *but I will kill it!*" Jackson vetoed the bill.

Jackson's Bank Veto Message, sent to Congress on July 10, was a manifesto of Jacksonian Democracy. Jackson declared that the Bank was "unauthorized by the Constitution, subversive of the rights of the states, and dangerous to the liberties of the people." Its charter, Jackson complained, bestowed special privilege on the Bank and its stockholders. Having made most of its loans to southerners and westerners, the Bank was a huge monster that sucked resources out of the agrarian South and West and poured them into the pockets of wealthy, well-connected northeastern gentlemen and their English friends. The granting of special privilege to such people (or to any others) threatened the system of equal rights that was essential in a republic. Jackson concluded with a call to civic virtue and conservative, God-centered Protestantism: "Let us firmly rely on that kind Providence which I am sure watches with peculiar care over the destinies of our Republic, and on the intelligence and wisdom of our countrymen."

Henry Clay, Nicholas Biddle, and other anti-Jacksonians had expected the veto. And the Bank Veto Message was a long, rambling attack that, in their opinion, demonstrated Jackson's unfitness for office. "It has all the fury of a chained panther biting the bars of its cage," said Biddle. So certain were they that the public shared their views that Clay's supporters distributed Jackson's Bank Veto Message as *anti*-Jackson propaganda during the 1832 campaign. They were wrong: A majority of the voters agreed that the republic was in danger of subversion by parasites who grew rich by manipulating credit, prices, paper money, and government-bestowed privileges. Jackson portrayed himself as both the protector of the old republic and a melodramatic hero contending with illegitimate, aristocratic, privileged, secretive powers. With the Bank and Jackson's veto as the principal issues, Jackson won reelection by a landslide in 1832.

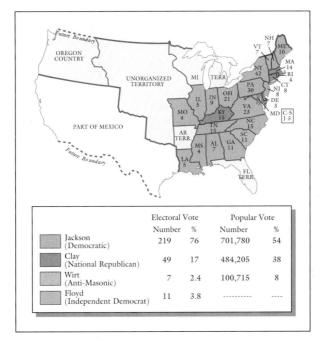

	Electoral Vote		Popular Vote	
	Number	%	Number	%
Jackson (Democratic)	219	76	701,780	54
Clay (National Republican)	49	17	484,205	38
Wirt (Anti-Masonic)	7	2.4	100,715	8
Floyd (Independent Democrat)	11	3.8	----------	----

PRESIDENTIAL ELECTION, 1832

Jackson began his second term determined to kill the Bank of the United States before Congress could reverse his veto. The Bank would be able to operate under its old charter until 1836. But Jackson was determined to speed its death by withdrawing government deposits as they were needed and by depositing new government revenues in carefully selected state banks. By law, the decision to remove the deposits had to be made by the secretary of the treasury, and Treasury Secretary Louis McLane doubted the wisdom if not the legality of withdrawing these funds. So Jackson transferred McLane to the vacant post of secretary of state and named William J. Duane as treasury secretary. Duane, too, refused to withdraw the deposits. Jackson fired him and appointed Roger B. Taney, the attorney general and a close adviser who had helped write the Bank Veto Message. A loyal Democrat who hated banks as much as Jackson did, Taney withdrew the deposits. In 1835, when the old Federalist John Marshall died, Jackson rewarded Taney by making him Chief Justice of the Supreme Court.

THE BEGINNINGS OF THE WHIG PARTY

It was over deposit removal and related questions of presidential power that the opposition to the Jacksonian Democrats coalesced into the Whig Party in 1834. Jackson, argued the Whigs, had transformed himself from the limited executive described in the Constitution into "King Andrew I." This had begun with Jackson's arbitrary uses of the executive patronage. It had become worse when Jackson began to veto congressional legislation. Jackson used the veto often—too often, said the Whigs, when a key component of the American

KING ANDREW   In this widely distributed opposition cartoon, King Andrew, with a scepter in one hand and a vetoed bill in the other, tramples on internal improvements, the Bank of the United States, and the Constitution.

System was at stake. In May 1830, for instance, Jackson vetoed an attempt by Congress to buy stock in a turnpike to run from the terminus of the National Road at Louisville to Maysville, Kentucky. Jackson questioned whether such federal subsidies were constitutional. More important, however, he announced that he was determined to reduce federal expenditures in order to retire the national debt—hinting strongly that he would oppose all federal public works.

The bank veto conveyed the same message even more strongly, and the withdrawl of the government deposits brought the question of "executive usurpation" to a head in 1834. Nicholas Biddle, announcing that he must clean up the affairs of the Bank of the United States before closing its doors, demanded that all its loans be repaid—a demand that undermined the credit system and produced a sharp financial panic. While Congress received a well-orchestrated petition campaign to restore the deposits, Henry Clay led an effort in the Senate to censure the president—which it did in March 1834. The old National Republican coalition became the new Whig Party. They were joined by southerners (including Calhoun) who resented Jackson's treatment of the South Carolina nullifiers and Biddle's bank. But it was Jackson's war on the Bank of the United States that did the most to separate parties. His withdrawal of the deposits chased lukewarm supporters into the opposition, while Democrats who closed ranks behind him could point to an increasingly sharp division between the Money Power and the Old Republic.

A Balanced Budget

One of the reasons Jackson had removed the deposits was that he anticipated a federal surplus revenue that, if handed over to the Bank of the United States, would have made it stronger than ever. The Tariffs of 1828 and 1832 produced substantial government revenue, and Jackson's frugal administration spent very little of it. The brisk sale of public lands was adding to the surplus. Without Jackson's removal of the deposits, a growing federal treasury would have gone into the Bank and would have found its way into the hated paper economy.

Early in his administration, Jackson had favored distributing surplus revenue to the states to be used for internal improvements. But he came to distrust even that minimal federal intervention in the economy, fearing that redistribution would encourage Congress to keep land prices and tariff rates high. Whigs, who by now despaired of ever creating a federally subsidized, coordinated transportation system, picked up the idea of redistribution. With some help from the Democrats, they passed the Deposit Act of 1836, which increased the number of banks receiving federal deposits and distributed any federal surplus to the states to be spent on roads, canals, and schools. Jackson feared that the new deposit banks would use their power to issue mountains of new banknotes. He demanded a provision limiting their right to print banknotes. With that provision, he reluctantly signed the Deposit Act.

Jackson and many members of his administration were deeply concerned about the inflationary boom that accompanied the rapid growth of commerce, credit, roads, canals, new farms, and the other manifestations of the market revolution in the 1830s. In 1836 Jackson issued a Specie Circular, which provided that speculators could buy large parcels of public land only with silver and gold coins while settlers could continue to buy farm-sized plots with banknotes. Henceforth, speculators would have to bring wagonloads of coins from eastern banks to frontier land offices. With this provision, Jackson hoped to curtail speculation and to reverse the flow of specie out of the South and West and into the Northeast. The Specie Circular was Jackson's final assault on the paper economy.

THE SECOND AMERICAN PARTY SYSTEM

In his farewell address in 1837 Jackson warned against a revival of the Bank of the United States and against all banks, paper money, the spirit of speculation, and every aspect of the "paper system." That system encouraged greed and luxury, which were at odds with republican virtue, he said. Worse, it thrived on special privilege, creating a world in which insiders meeting in "secret conclaves" could buy and sell elections. The solution, as always, was an arcadian society of small producers, a vigilant democratic electorate, and a chaste republican government that granted no special privileges.

"MARTIN VAN RUIN"

Sitting beside Jackson as he delivered his farewell address was his chosen successor, Martin Van Buren. In the election of 1836 the Whigs had acknowledged that Henry Clay, the leader of their party, could not win a national election. So they ran three sectional candidates—Daniel Webster in the Northeast, the old Indian fighter William Henry Harrison in the West, and Hugh Lawson White of Tennessee, a turncoat Jacksonian, in the South. With this ploy the Whigs hoped to deprive Van Buren of a majority and throw the election into the Whig-controlled House of Representatives.

The strategy failed. Van Buren had engineered a national Democratic Party that could avert the dangers of sectionalism, and he questioned the patriotism of the Whigs and their sectional candidates, asserting that "true republicans can never lend their aid and influence in creating geographical parties." That, along with his association with Jackson's popular presidency, won him the election.

Van Buren had barely taken office when the inflationary boom of the mid-1830s collapsed. Economic historians ascribe the Panic of 1837 and the ensuing depression largely to events outside the country. The Bank of England, concerned over the flow of British gold to American speculators, cut off credit to firms that did business in the United States. As a result, British demand for American cotton fell sharply, and the price of cotton dropped by half. With much of the speculative boom tied to cotton grown in the Southwest, the collapse of the economy was inevitable. The first business failures came in March 1837, just as Van Buren took office. By May, New York banks, unable to accommodate people who were demanding hard coin for their notes, suspended specie payments. Other banks followed suit, and soon banks all over the country went out of business. Although few American communities escaped the economic downturn, it was the commercial and export sectors of the economy that suffered most. In the seaport cities, one firm after another closed its doors, and about one-third of the workforce was unemployed.

Whigs blamed the depression on Jackson's hard-money policies. With economic distress the main issue, Whigs scored huge gains in the midterm elections of 1838, even winning control of Van Buren's New York with a campaign that castigated the president as "Martin Van Ruin." Democrats blamed the crash on speculation, luxury, and Whig paper money. While Whigs demanded a new national bank, Van Buren proposed the complete divorce of govern-

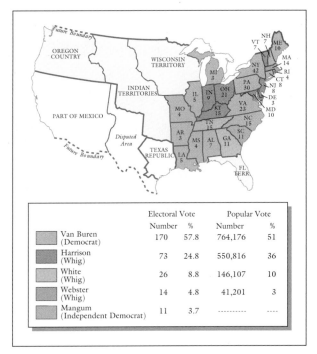

	Electoral Vote		Popular Vote	
	Number	%	Number	%
Van Buren (Democrat)	170	57.8	764,176	51
Harrison (Whig)	73	24.8	550,816	36
White (Whig)	26	8.8	146,107	10
Webster (Whig)	14	4.8	41,201	3
Mangum (Independent Democrat)	11	3.7	----------	----

PRESIDENTIAL ELECTION, 1836

ment from the banking system through what was known as the "Sub-Treasury," or "Independent Treasury." Under this plan, the federal government would simply hold and dispense its money without depositing it in banks; it would also require that tariffs and land purchases be paid in gold and silver coins or in notes from specie-paying banks, a provision that allowed government to regulate state banknotes without resorting to a central bank. Van Buren asked Congress to set up the Independent Treasury in 1837, and Congress spent the rest of Van Buren's time in office arguing about it. The Independent Treasury Bill was finally passed in 1840.

THE ELECTION OF 1840

Whigs were confident that they could blame Van Buren for the country's economic troubles and take the presidency away from him in the election of 1840. Trying to offend as few voters as possible, they passed over their best-known leaders, Senators Henry Clay and Daniel Webster, and nominated William Henry Harrison of Ohio as their presidential candidate. Harrison was the hero of the Battle of Tippecanoe (see Chapter 7), and a westerner whose Virginia origins made him palatable in the South. He was also a proven vote-getter. Best of all, he was a military hero who had expressed few opinions on national issues and who had no political record to defend. As his running mate, the Whigs chose John Tyler, a states'-rights Virginian who had joined the Whigs out of hatred for Jackson. To promote this baldly pragmatic ticket, the Whigs came up with a catchy slogan: "Tippecanoe and Tyler Too."

LOG CABINS AND HARD CIDER

Sloganeering, torchlight parades, and political theatricality by Whigs in the 1840 "Log Cabin Campaign" overwhelmed all attempts at serious discussion of the issues. Whigs, who had earlier been repelled by the boisterous electioneering techniques of the Democrats, filled the campaign with humor and noise, beating the Democrats at their own game. Whigs covered a great paper ball with slogans and, with music from a brass band and shouts of "Keep the ball rolling!" they rolled

A TIPPECANOE PROCESSION.

Early in the campaign a Democratic journalist, commenting on Harrison's political inexperience and alleged unfitness for the presidency, wrote, "Give [Harrison] a barrel of hard cider, and settle a pension of two thousand a year on him, and my word for it, he will sit out the remainder of his days in his log cabin." Whigs seized on the statement and launched what was known as the "Log Cabin Campaign." The log cabin, the cider barrel, and Harrison's folksiness and heroism constituted the entire Whig campaign, while Van Buren was pictured

the ball through the midwestern and northeastern states. They also hid their distaste for alcohol, tobacco, and other bad (but popular) habits associated with the Democrats. The pewter snuff box shown here (one of thousands of mementos from the campaign) was stamped with the image of a particularly bucolic log cabin—associating the candidate William Henry Harrison not only with the virtues of rural simplicity but with the male, democratic appetite that the contents of the box would satisfy. Another novelty distributed by the Whigs in 1840 was a cardboard picture of President Van Buren smiling at the taste of "White House Champagne." Viewers could pull a tab attached to the card to change the picture to one of Van Buren grimacing at the taste of hard cider from a mug emblazoned with Harrison's initials—thus accomplishing the campaign's transformation of Van Buren into a wine-drinking, extravagant aristocrat with a strong repugnance for the simple virtues and simple pleasures enjoyed by the Whigs.

A BEAUTIFUL GOBLET OF
WHITE HOUSE CHAMPAGNE

AN UGLY MUG OF
LOG CABIN HARD CIDER

as living in luxury at the public's expense. The Whigs conjured up an image of a nattily dressed President "Van Ruin" sitting on silk chairs and dining on gold and silver dishes while farmers and workingmen struggled to make ends meet.

Democrats howled that Whigs were peddling lies and refusing to discuss issues. But they knew they had been beaten at their own game. Harrison won only a narrow majority of the popular vote, but a landslide of 234 to 60 votes in the Electoral College.

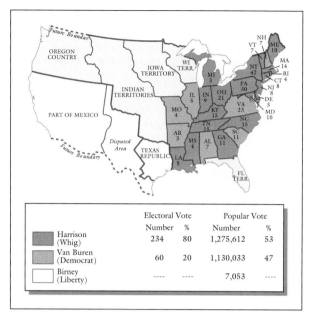

	Electoral Vote		Popular Vote	
	Number	%	Number	%
Harrison (Whig)	234	80	1,275,612	53
Van Buren (Democrat)	60	20	1,130,033	47
Birney (Liberty)	----	----	7,053	----

PRESIDENTIAL ELECTION, 1840

TWO PARTIES

The election of 1840 signaled the completion of the second party system. Andrew Jackson had won in 1828 with Jefferson's old southern and western agrarian constituency; in 1832 he had carried his old voters and had won added support in the Middle Atlantic states and in northern New England. In 1836, Whigs capitalized on southern resentment of Jackson's defeat of Calhoun and nullification and on southern mistrust of the New Yorker Van Buren to break the Democratic hold on the South. The election of 1840 completed the transition: Harrison and Van Buren contested the election in nearly every state; perhaps most significantly, they received nearly equal levels of support in the slave and free states.

The election of 1840 also witnessed the high-water mark of voter turnout. Whig and Democratic organizations focused on presidential elections, and prospective voters met a quadrennial avalanche of oratory, door-to-door canvassing, torchlight parades, and party propaganda. And as the contests became national, there was no state in the Union that Democrats or Whigs could take for granted. Both Whigs and Democrats maintained organizations and contested elections in nearly every neighborhood in the country, and the result was increased popular interest in politics. In 1824 about one in four adult white men had voted in the presidential election. Jackson's vengeful campaign of 1828 lifted the turnout to 56.3 percent, and it stayed at about that level in 1832 and 1836. The campaign of 1840 brought out 78 percent of the eligible voters, and the turnout remained at that high level throughout the 1840s and 1850s.

CHRONOLOGY

1804–1806	Lewis and Clark explore the northern regions of the Louisiana Purchase
1819	Controversy arises over Missouri's admission to the Union as a slave state • Panic of 1819 marks the first failure of the national market economy
1820	Missouri Compromise adopted
1823	Monroe Doctrine written by Secretary of State John Quincy Adams
1824–1825	Adams wins the presidency over Andrew Jackson • Adams appoints Henry Clay as secretary of state • Jacksonians charge a "Corrupt Bargain" between Adams and Clay
1827	Cherokees in Georgia declare themselves a republic
1828	Jackson defeats Adams for the presidency • "Tariff of Abominations" passed by Congress • John C. Calhoun's *Exposition and Protest* presents doctrine of nullification
1830	Congress passes the Indian Removal Act
1832	Jackson reelected over Henry Clay • *Worcester* v. *Georgia* exempts the Cherokee from Georgia law • Jackson vetoes recharter of the Bank of the United States
1833	Force Bill and Tariff of 1833 end the nullification crisis
1834	Whig Party formed in opposition to Jacksonians
1836	Congress adopts "gag rule" to table antislavery petitions • Van Buren elected president
1837	Financial panic ushers in a severe economic depression
1838	U.S. Army marches the remaining Cherokee to Indian Territory
1840	Whig William Henry Harrison defeats Van Buren for presidency

CONCLUSION

By 1840 American politics was conducted within a stable, national system of two parties—both of which depended on support in every section of the country. Whigs argued for the economic nationalism of the American System. Democrats argued for limited, inexpensive government. Democrats successfully fought off the American System: They dismantled the Bank of the United States, refused federal support for roads and canals, and revised the tariff in ways that mollified the export-oriented South. The result, however, was not the return to Jeffersonian agrarianism that many Democrats had wanted but an inadvertent experiment in laissez-faire capitalism: The stupendous growth of the American economy between 1830 and 1860 became a question of state and local—not national—government action. On the growing political problems surrounding slavery, the two-party system did what Van Buren had hoped it would do: Because the Whig and (especially) Democratic Parties needed both northern and southern support, they were careful to focus national political debates on economic development, avoiding any discussion of sectional questions. It worked that way until the party system disintegrated on the eve of the Civil War.

13

MANIFEST DESTINY: AN EMPIRE FOR LIBERTY— OR SLAVERY?

GROWTH AS THE AMERICAN WAY ∿ THE MEXICAN WAR
THE ELECTION OF 1848 ∿ THE COMPROMISE OF 1850 ∿ FILIBUSTERING

When William Henry Harrison took the oath as the first Whig president on March 4, 1841, the stage seemed set for the enactment of Henry Clay's American System. But Harrison came down with pneumonia after he delivered an interminable inaugural address outside during a storm of sleet and snow. He died a month later, and John Tyler became president. A states'-rights Virginian, Tyler had become a nominal Whig only because of his hatred of Andrew Jackson. Tyler proceeded to read himself out of the Whig Party by vetoing two bills to create a new national bank. Their domestic program a shambles, the Whigs lost control of the House in the 1842 midterm elections. Thereafter the political agenda shifted to the Democratic program of territorial expansion. By annexation, negotiation, and war the United States increased its size by 50 percent in the years between 1845 and 1848. But this achievement reopened the issue of slavery's expansion and planted the bitter seeds of civil war.

GROWTH AS THE AMERICAN WAY

By 1850, older Americans had seen the area of the United States quadruple in their own lifetime. During the 47 years since the Louisiana Purchase of 1803, the American population had also quadrupled. Many Americans took this prodigious growth for granted. They considered it evidence of God's beneficence to this virtuous republic. During the 1840s a group of expansionists affiliated with the Democratic Party began to call themselves the "Young America" movement. They proclaimed that it was the "Manifest Destiny" of the United States "to overspread and to possess the whole of the continent which Providence has given us for the development of the great experiment of liberty," wrote John L. O'Sullivan, editor of the *Democratic Review*, in 1845.

Not all Americans thought this unbridled expansion was a good thing. For the earliest Americans, whose ancestors had arrived on the continent thousands of years before the Europeans, it was a story of defeat and contraction. By 1850 the white man's diseases and guns had reduced the Indian population north of the Rio Grande to fewer than half a million, a fraction of the number who had lived there two or three centuries earlier. The relentless westward march of white settlements had pushed all but a few thousand Indians beyond the Mississippi. In the 1840s the U.S. government decided to create a "permanent Indian frontier" at about the

95th meridian (roughly the western borders of Iowa, Missouri, and Arkansas). But white emigrants were already violating that frontier on the overland trails to the Pacific, and settlers were pressing against the borders of Indian territory. In little more than a decade the idea of "one big reservation" in the West would give way to the policy of forcing Indians onto small reservations. Required to learn the white man's ways or perish, many Indians perished—of disease, malnutrition, and alcohol, and in futile efforts to break out of the reservations and regain their land.

MANIFEST DESTINY AND SLAVERY

If the manifest destiny of white Americans spelled doom for red Americans, it also presaged a crisis in the history of black Americans. Territorial acquisitions since 1803 had brought into the republic the slave states of Louisiana, Missouri, Arkansas, Florida, Texas, and parts of Alabama and Mississippi, while only Iowa, admitted in 1846, had joined the ranks of the free states.

The division between slavery and freedom in the rest of the Louisiana Purchase had supposedly been settled by the Missouri Compromise of 1820. However, the expansion of slavery into new territories was an explosive issue. The issue first arose with the annexation of Texas, which helped provoke war with Mexico in 1846—a war that many antislavery northerners considered an ugly effort to expand slavery.

THE WESTERING IMPULSE

For Americans of European descent, the future was to be found in the West. In the 1840s Horace Greeley urged, "Go West, young man." And to the West they went in unprecedented

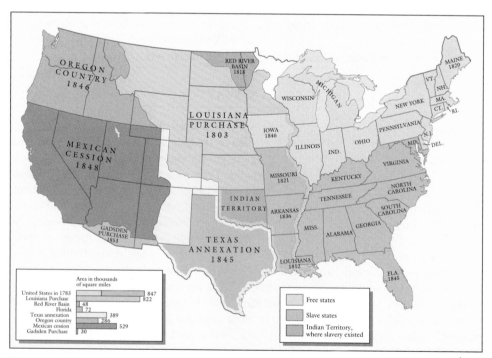

FREE AND SLAVE STATES AND TERRITORIES, 1848

numbers, driven in part by the depression of 1837–1843 that prompted thousands to search for cheap land and better opportunity. "The West is our object, there is no other hope left for us," declared one farmer as he and his family set out on the Oregon Trail. "There is nothing like a new country for poor folks."

An earlier wave of migration had populated the region between the Appalachians and the Missouri River. Reports from explorers, fur traders, missionaries, and sailors filtered back from California and the Pacific Northwest, describing the bounteous resources and benign climate of those wondrous regions. Richard Henry Dana's *Two Years before the Mast* (1840), the story of his experience in the cowhide and tallow trade between California and Boston, alerted thousands of Americans to this new Eden on the Pacific. Guidebooks rolled off the presses describing the boundless prospects that awaited settlers who would turn "those wild forests, trackless plains, untrodden valleys" into "one grand scene of continuous improvements, universal enterprise, and unparalleled commerce."

THE HISPANIC SOUTHWEST

Of course, another people of partial European descent already lived in portions of the region west of the 95th meridian. By the time Mexico won its independence from Spain in 1821, some 80,000 Mexicans lived in this region. Three-fourths of them had settled in the Rio Grande valley of New Mexico and most of the rest in California. Centuries earlier the Spaniards had introduced horses, cattle, and sheep to the New World. These animals became the economic mainstay of Hispanic society along New Spain's northern frontier.

Colonial society on New Spain's northern frontier had centered on the missions and the presidios. Intended to Christianize Indians, the missions also became an instrument to exploit their labor, while the presidios (military posts) protected the settlers from hostile Indians—and foreign nationals hoping to gain a foothold in Spanish territory. By the late 18th century, the mission system had fallen into decline, and a decade and a half after Mexican independence in 1821, it collapsed entirely. The presidios, underfunded and understaffed, also declined after Mexican independence, so that more and more the defense of Mexico's far northern provinces fell to the residents themselves. But by the 1830s, many residents of New Mexico and California were more interested in bringing American traders in than in keeping American settlers out. A flourishing trade over the Santa Fe Trail from Independence, Missouri, to Santa Fe brought American manufactured goods to New Mexico (and points south) in exchange for Mexican horses, mules, beaver pelts, and silver. New England ships carried American goods all the way around the horn of South America to San Francisco and other California ports in exchange for tallow and hides produced by *californio* ranchers.

THE OREGON AND CALIFORNIA TRAILS

In 1842 and 1843, "Oregon fever" swept the Mississippi valley. Thousands of farm families sold their land, packed their worldly goods in covered wagons along with supplies for five or six months on the trail, hitched up their oxen, and headed out from Independence or St. Joseph, Missouri, for the trek of almost 2,000 miles to the river valleys of Oregon or California. The land was occupied mostly by Indians, who viewed this latest intrusion with wary eyes. Few of the emigrants thought about settling down along the way, for this vast reach of arid plains, forbidding mountains, and burning wastelands was then known as "the Great

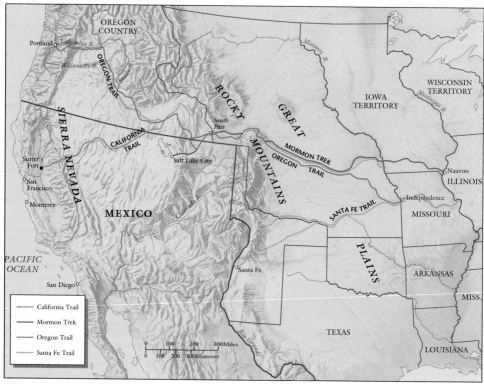

OVERLAND TRAILS, 1846

American Desert." White men considered it suitable only for Indians and the disappearing breed of mountain men who had roamed the region trapping beaver.

The migration of farm families to Oregon and California was followed in 1847 by the Mormon exodus to a new Zion in the basin of the Great Salt Lake and in 1849 by the gold rush to California. The story of all these migrants was one of triumph and tragedy, survival and death, courage and despair, success and failure. Most of them made it to their destination; some died on the way—victims of disease, exposure, starvation, suicide, or homicide by Indians or by fellow emigrants. Of those who arrived safely, a few struck it rich, most carved out a modest though hard living, and some drifted on, still looking for the pot of gold that had thus far eluded them.

Migration was mostly a male enterprise. Adult men outnumbered women on the Oregon Trail and on the California Trail before the gold rush by more than 2 to 1, and in the gold rush by more than 10 to 1. The quest for new land, a new start, and a chance to make a big strike represented primarily masculine ideals. Women, on the other hand, felt themselves more rooted in family, home, and community, less willing to pull up stakes to march into the wilderness. Yet even on the rough mining frontier of the West, men sought to replicate the homes and communities they had left behind. "We want families," wrote a Californian in 1858, "because their homes and hearth stones everywhere, are the only true and reliable basis of any nation." Except during the gold rush, family groups predominated on the overland trails. Half of the emigrants were mothers and children.

EMIGRANTS MAKING CAMP IN THE SNOW This drawing portrays the harsh conditions and dangers faced by many pioneers who crossed plains and mountains. Women often had to do a man's work as well as to cook and take care of children. One can only hope that this family did not suffer the fate of the Donner party, trapped by an early snowfall in the Sierra Nevada Mountains in October 1846. Nearly half of the 87 people in the Donner party died during the subsequent winter.

Many of the women were reluctant migrants. Men made the decision to go; women obeyed. Diaries kept by women on the trail testify to their unhappiness:

> What had possessed my husband, anyway, that he should have thought of bringing us away out through this God-forsaken country? . . . Oh, how I wish we never had started for the Golden Land. . . . I would make a brave effort to be cheerful and patient until the camp work was done. Then . . . I would throw myself down on the ground and shed tears, wishing myself back home with my friends and chiding myself for consenting to take this wild goose chase.

For many families it did turn out to be a wild goose chase. But for those who stayed the course and settled in the far West, it was a success story, made so in great measure by the women. They turned houses into homes, settlements into communities. But the frontier did not break down the separate spheres of men and women. Woman's sphere in the West was still the home and the family, the bearing and the nurturing of children, the management of the household economy.

THE MORMON MIGRATION

Patriarchal rule was strongest among those migrants with the most nearly equal sex ratio—the Mormons. Subjected to persecution that drove them from their original home in western New York, they went to Ohio, Missouri, and eventually Illinois, where they established a town that they named Nauvoo, a thriving community of 15,000 souls based on collective economic effort and theocratic discipline imposed by their founder and prophet, Joseph Smith. But the people of Illinois proved no more hospitable to the Mormons than the sect's previous neighbors had been. Smith did not make things any easier. His insistence that God spoke through him, his autocratic suppression of dissent, and his assertion that the Mormons were the only true Christians and would inherit the earth were not appreciated. When a dissident faction of Mormons published Smith's latest revelation, which sanctioned polygamy, he ordered their printing press destroyed. The county sheriff arrested him, and in June 1844 a mob broke into the jail and killed him.

Smith's martyrdom prompted yet another exodus. Under the leadership of Smith's successor, Brigham Young, the Mormons began the long trek westward that would eventually lead them to the Great Salt Lake basin. Arriving with the advance guard of Mormon pioneers at a pass overlooking the Great Basin on July 24, 1847, Young, ill with tick fever, struggled from his wagon and stared at the barren desert and mountains surrounding the lake. "This is the right place," he declared. Here the Mormons could build their Zion undisturbed.

They built a flourishing community, making the desert bloom with grain and vegetables irrigated by water diverted from mountain streams. Young reigned as leader of the church, and from 1850 to 1857 as governor of the newly created Utah Territory. But Zion did not remain undisturbed. Relations with the government in Washington and with territorial officials were never smooth, especially after Young's proclamation in 1852 authorizing polygamy. (Although Young himself married a total of 55 women, most Mormon men could afford to support no more than one wife and her children; only about one-sixth of Mormon marriages were polygamous.) When conflict between the Mormons and the U.S. Army broke out in 1857, Young surrendered his civil authority and made an uneasy peace with the government.

THE REPUBLIC OF TEXAS

As the Mormons were starting west, a crisis between Mexico and the United States was coming to a boil. Although the United States had renounced any claim to Texas in a treaty with Spain negotiated in 1819, many Americans believed that Texas had been part of the Louisiana Purchase. By the time the treaty was ratified in 1821, Mexico had won its independence from Spain. The new Republic of Mexico wanted to develop its northern borderlands in Texas by encouraging immigration and settlement there. Thus, Stephen F. Austin, a Missouri businessman, secured a large land grant from Mexico to settle 300 American families there.

The American settlers initially had very little contact with Mexican *tejanos,* but political events in Mexico City in 1835 had repercussions on the northern frontier. A new conservative national government seemed intent on consolidating its authority over the northern territories. In response, the Anglo-American settlers and the Mexican *tejanos* forged a political alliance. When the Mexican government responded militarily, the seeds of revolution were sown. Fighting flared fitfully for a year. Then, in March 1836, delegates from across Texas held a convention at which they declared Texas an independent republic.

It took the Texans less than seven months to win and consolidate their independence. On March 6, 1836, Mexican President Antonio López de Santa Anna led the Mexican army that captured the Alamo (a former mission converted to a fort) in San Antonio, killing all 187 of its defenders, including the legendary Americans Davy Crockett and Jim Bowie. Rallying to the cry "Remember the Alamo!" Texans swarmed to the revolutionary army commanded by Sam Houston. When the Mexican army slaughtered another force of more than 300 men after they had surrendered at Goliad on March 19, the Texans were further inflamed. A month later, Houston's army routed a larger Mexican force on the San Jacinto River and captured Santa Anna himself. Under duress, he signed a treaty granting Texas its independence. The Mexican congress later repudiated the treaty but could not muster enough strength to reestablish its authority north of the Nueces River. The victorious Texans elected Sam Houston president of their new republic and petitioned for annexation to the United States.

THE ANNEXATION CONTROVERSY

President Andrew Jackson, wary of provoking war with Mexico or quarrels with antislavery northerners, rebuffed the Texans. So did his successor, Martin Van Buren. Though disappointed, the Texans turned their energies to building their republic. The British government encouraged them in the hope that they would stand as a buffer against further U.S. expansion. Texas leaders made friendly responses to some of the British overtures, probably in the hope of provoking American annexationists to take action. They did.

Soon after Vice President John Tyler became president on the death of William Henry Harrison in 1841, he broke with the Whig Party that had elected him. Seeking to create a new coalition to reelect him in 1844, Tyler seized on the annexation of Texas as "the only matter that will take sufficient hold of the feelings of the South to rally it on a southern candidate."

Tyler named John C. Calhoun of South Carolina as secretary of state to negotiate a treaty of annexation. Calhoun concluded a treaty with the eager Texans. But then he made a mistake: He released to the press a letter he had written to the British minister to the United States, informing him that, together with other reasons, Americans wanted to annex Texas in order to protect slavery. This seemed to confirm abolitionist charges that annexation was a proslavery plot. Northern senators of both parties provided more than enough votes to defeat the treaty in June 1844.

By then, Texas had become the main issue in the forthcoming presidential election. Whig candidate Henry Clay had come out against annexation, as had the leading contender for the Democratic nomination, former president Martin Van Buren. Van Buren's stand angered southern Democrats, who were determined to have Texas. Through eight ballots at the Democratic national convention they blocked Van Buren's nomination; on the ninth, the southerners broke the stalemate by nominating one of their own, James K. Polk of Tennessee. Polk was a staunch Jacksonian who had served as Speaker of the House of Representatives. Southerners exulted in their victory. "We have triumphed," wrote one of Calhoun's lieutenants. Polk's nomination undercut President Tyler's forlorn hope of being reelected on the Texas issue, so he bowed out of the race.

Polk ran on a platform that called for not only the annexation of Texas but also the acquisition of all of Oregon up to 54°40′ (the Alaskan border). That demand was aimed at voters in the western free states, who felt that bringing Oregon into the Union would balance the expansion of slavery into Texas with the expansion of free territory in the Northwest.

"Texas fever" swept the South during the campaign. So powerful was the issue that Clay began to waver, stating that he would support annexation if it could be done without starting a war with Mexico. This concession won him a few southern votes but angered northern antislavery Whigs. Many of them voted for James G. Birney, candidate of the Liberty Party, which opposed any more slave territory. He probably took enough Whig votes from Clay in New York to give Polk victory there and in the electoral college.

ACQUISITION OF TEXAS AND OREGON

Although the election was extremely close, Democrats regarded it as a mandate for annexation. President Tyler submitted to Congress a joint resolution of annexation, which required only a simple majority in both houses instead of the two-thirds majority in the Senate that a treaty would have required. Congress passed the resolution in March 1845. Texas thus became the 15th slave state. Backed now by the United States, Texans claimed a southern and western border beyond the Nueces River all the way to the Rio Grande. Mexico responded by breaking off diplomatic relations with the United States. The stage was set for five years of bitter controversy.

Meanwhile, Polk lost no time in addressing his promise to annex Oregon. "Our title to the country of the Oregon is 'clear and unquestionable,'" he said in his inaugural address. The problem was to get Britain to recognize the title. Both countries had jointly "occupied" Oregon since 1818, overseeing the fur trade carried on by British and American companies. Chanting the slogan "Fifty-four forty or fight!" many Americans demanded all of Oregon, as pledged in the Democratic platform. But Americans had settled only in the region south of the Columbia River, at roughly the 46th parallel. In June 1846, Polk accepted a compromise treaty that split the Oregon country between the United States and Britain at the 49th parallel.

THE MEXICAN WAR

Having finessed a war with Britain, Polk provoked one with Mexico in order to get California and New Mexico. In 1845 he sent a special envoy to Mexico City with an offer to buy California and New Mexico for $30 million. To help Mexico make the right response, he ordered federal troops to the disputed border area between Mexico and Texas, dispatched a naval squadron to patrol the gulf coast of Mexico, and instructed the American consul at Monterey (the Mexican capital of California) to stir up annexation sentiment among settlers there. These strong-arm tactics provoked a political revolt in Mexico City that brought a militant anti-American regime to power.

Polk responded in January 1846 by ordering 4,000 soldiers under General Zachary Taylor to advance all the way to the Rio Grande. Recognizing that he could achieve his goals only through armed conflict, Polk waited for news from Texas that would justify a declaration of war, but none came. Finally, on May 9, 1846, word arrived that two weeks earlier Mexican troops had crossed the Rio Grande and had attacked an American patrol, killing 11 soldiers.

Polk had what he wanted. Most Whigs opposed war with Mexico. But on May 11, not wanting to be branded unpatriotic, all but a handful of them voted for the declaration of war, which passed the House by 174 to 14 and the Senate by 40 to 2.

The United States went to war with a tiny regular army of fewer than 8,000 men, supplemented by 60,000 volunteers in state regiments. Mexican soldiers outnumbered American in most of the battles. But the Americans had higher morale, better leadership, better weapons (especially artillery), a more determined, stable government, and a far richer, stronger economy. The U.S. forces won every battle—and the war—in a fashion that humiliated the proud Mexicans and left a legacy of national hostility and border violence. Especially remarkable was the prominent role played by Robert E. Lee, Ulysses S. Grant, Pierre G. T. Beauregard, George B. McClellan, Braxton Bragg, George H. Thomas, Thomas J. Jackson, George G. Meade, Jefferson Davis, and others whose names would become household words during the Civil War.

MILITARY CAMPAIGNS OF 1846

The Mexican War proceeded through three phases. The first phase was carried out by Zachary Taylor's 4,000 regulars on the Rio Grande. In two small battles on May 8 and 9, at Palo Alto and Resaca de la Palma, they routed numerically superior Mexican forces even before Congress had declared war. Reinforced by several thousand volunteers, Taylor pursued the retreating Mexicans 100 miles south of the Rio Grande to the Mexican city of Monterrey. The city was taken after four days of fighting in September 1846. Mexican resistance in the area had crumbled, and Taylor's force settled down as an army of occupation.

Meanwhile, the second phase of American strategy had gone forward. In June 1846 General Stephen Watts Kearny led an army of 1,500 tough frontiersmen and regulars west from Fort Leavenworth toward Santa Fe. Kearny bluffed and intimidated the New Mexico governor, who fled southward. Kearny's army occupied Santa Fe on August 18 without firing a shot.

After receiving reinforcements, Kearny left a small occupation force and divided the rest of his troops into two contingents, one of which he sent under Colonel Alexander Doniphan into the Mexican province of Chihuahua. In the most extraordinary campaign of the war, these 800 Missourians marched 3,000 miles, foraging supplies along the way; fought and beat two much larger enemy forces; and finally linked up with Zachary Taylor's army at Monterrey.

Kearny led the other contingent across deserts and mountains to California. Events there had anticipated his arrival. In June 1846 a group of American settlers backed by Captain John C. Frémont captured Sonoma and raised the flag of an independent California, displaying the silhouette of a grizzly bear. Marked by exploits both courageous and comic, this "bear-flag revolt" paved the way for the conquest of California by the *americanos*. The U.S. Pacific fleet seized California's ports and the capital at Monterey; sailors from the fleet and volunteer soldiers under Frémont subdued Mexican resistance.

MILITARY CAMPAIGNS OF 1847

The Mexican government refused to admit that the war was over. Early in 1847 Santa Anna raised new levies and marched north to attack Taylor's army near Monterrey.

Taylor, 62 years old, was not as ready to withstand a counteroffensive as he had been a few weeks earlier. After capturing Monterrey in September 1846, he had let the defeated Mexican army go and had granted an eight-week armistice in the hope that it would allow time for

PRINCIPAL CAMPAIGNS OF THE MEXICAN WAR, 1846–1847

peace negotiations. Angry at Taylor's presumption in making such a decision and suspicious of the general's political ambitions, Polk canceled the armistice and named General-in-Chief Winfield Scott to command the third phase of the war. Thus far Scott had fought the war from his desk in Washington. A large, punctilious man, he had acquired the nickname "Old Fuss and Feathers" for a military professionalism that contrasted with the homespun manner of "Rough and Ready" Zach Taylor. Scott decided to lead an invasion of Mexico's heartland from a beachhead at Veracruz and in January 1847 ordered the transfer of more than half of Taylor's troops to his own expeditionary force.

Left with fewer than 5,000 men, most of them untried volunteers, Taylor marched out to meet Santa Anna's army of 18,000. In a two-day battle on February 22 and 23 at Buena Vista, Taylor's little force inflicted twice as many casualties as they suffered in a fierce struggle highlighted by the brilliant counterattack of a Mississippi regiment commanded by Jefferson Davis. The bloodied Mexican army retreated toward the capital. When news of the victory reached the East, Taylor's popularity soared to new heights.

But the war was actually won by Scott. With a combined Army-Navy force, he took the coastal fortress at Veracruz in March 1847. Then over the next five months, his army, which never totaled more than 14,000 men, marched and fought its way over mountains and plains more than 200 miles to Mexico City. The risks were high. When Scott's forces reached the fortifications of Mexico City, held by three times their numbers, the Duke of Wellington predicted, "Scott is lost—he cannot capture the city and he cannot fall back upon his base." But capture it he did, on September 14, after fierce hand-to-hand combat in the battles of Contreras, Churubusco, Molino del Rey, and Chapultepec.

ANTIWAR SENTIMENT

The string of military victories prevented antiwar sentiment from winning even wider support. The war was enthusiastically supported in the South and West and among Democrats. But the Whigs and many people in the Northeast, especially in New England, considered it "a wicked and disgraceful war." Democrats and Whigs had different notions of "progress." Democrats believed in expanding American institutions over *space*—in particular, the space occupied by Mexicans and Indians. Whigs, on the other hand, believed in improving American institutions over *time*. "A nation cannot simultaneously devote its energies to the absorption of others' territories and the improvement of its own," said Horace Greeley.

Antislavery people raised their eyebrows when they heard rhetoric about "extending the blessings of American liberty" to benighted regions. They suspected that the real reason was the desire to extend slavery.

THE WILMOT PROVISO

The slavery issue overshadowed all others in the debate over the Mexican War. President Polk could not understand the reason for the fuss. "There is no probability," he wrote in his diary, "that any territory will ever be acquired from Mexico in which slavery would ever exist." But other Americans were not so sure. Many southerners hoped that slavery would spread into the fertile lowlands of Mexican territory. Many northerners feared that it might. The issue came to a head early in the war. On August 8, 1846, Pennsylvania Democratic Congressman David Wilmot offered an amendment to an Army appropriations bill: " . . . that, as an express and fundamental condition of the acquisition of any territory from the Republic of Mexico . . . neither slavery nor involuntary servitude shall ever exist in any part of said territory."

This famous "Wilmot Proviso" framed the national debate over slavery for the next 15 years. The House passed the amendment. Nearly all northern Democrats joined all northern Whigs in the majority, while southern Democrats and southern Whigs voted almost unanimously against it. This outcome marked the beginning of what came to be known as a *sectional* division between free and slave states.

Several factors underlay the split of northern Democrats from their own president on this issue. Ever since southern Democrats had blocked Van Buren's nomination in 1844, resentment had been growing in the party's Northern wing. Polk's acceptance of 49° latitude for Oregon's northern boundary exacerbated this feeling. "Our rights to Oregon have been

SLAVE AUCTION IN ST. LOUIS   The public buying and selling of human beings in cities like St. Louis made a mockery of American boasts of liberty and gave a powerful impetus to the drive to prohibit the expansion of slavery into the territories acquired from Mexico. This painting hints at the ugliest dimension of the slave trade, the sale of mothers and children apart from fathers and sometimes apart from each other.

shamefully compromised," fumed an Ohio Democrat. The reduced rates of the Walker tariff in 1846 (sponsored by Robert J. Walker of Mississippi, Polk's secretary of the treasury) annoyed Democrats from Pennsylvania's industrial districts. And Polk angered Democrats from the Old Northwest by vetoing a rivers and harbors bill that would have provided federal aid for transportation improvements in their districts. The Wilmot Proviso was in part the product of these pent-up frustrations. "The time has come," said a Democratic congressman in 1846, "when the Northern Democracy should make a stand. We must satisfy the Northern people . . . that we are not to extend the institution of slavery as a result of this war."

The issue of slavery hung like the sword of Damocles over Polk's efforts to negotiate peace with Mexico. Polk also came under pressure from expansionist Democrats who, excited by military victory, wanted more Mexican territory, perhaps even "all Mexico." Polk had sent a diplomat, Nicholas Trist, with Scott's army to negotiate the terms of Mexican surrender. Authorized to pay Mexico $15 million for California, New Mexico, and a Texas border on the Rio Grande, Trist worked out such a treaty. In the meantime, though, Polk had succumbed to the "all Mexico" clamor. He ordered Trist back to Washington, intending to replace him with someone who would exact greater concessions from Mexico. Trist ignored the recall, signed the treaty of Guadalupe Hidalgo on February 2, 1848, and sent it to Washington. Although angered by Trist's defiance, Polk nonetheless decided to end the controversy by submitting the treaty to the Senate, which approved it on March 10 by a vote of 38 to 14. The treaty sheared off half of Mexico and increased the size of the United States by one-fourth.

THE ELECTION OF 1848

The treaty did nothing to settle the question of slavery in the new territory, however. Mexico had abolished the institution two decades earlier; would the United States reintroduce it? Many Americans looked to the election of 1848 to decide the matter. Four positions on the issue emerged, each identified with a candidate for the presidential nomination.

The Wilmot Proviso represented the position of those determined to bar slavery from all territories. The Liberty Party endorsed the proviso and nominated Senator John P. Hale of New Hampshire for president.

Southern Democrat John C. Calhoun formulated the "southern-rights" position. Directly challenging the Wilmot Proviso, Calhoun introduced resolutions in the Senate in February 1847 affirming the right of slaveowners to take their human property into any territory, pointing out that the Constitution protected the right of property.

Although most southerners agreed with Calhoun, the Democratic Party sought a middle ground. The Polk administration endorsed the idea of extending the old Missouri Compromise line of 36°30′ to the Pacific. This would have excluded slavery from present-day Washington, Oregon, Idaho, Utah, Nevada, and the northern half of California, but would have allowed it in present-day New Mexico, Arizona, and southern California. Secretary of State James Buchanan, also a candidate for the Democratic presidential nomination (Polk did not seek renomination), embraced this position.

Another compromise position became known as "popular sovereignty." Identified with Senator Lewis Cass of Michigan, this concept proposed to let the settlers of each territory decide for themselves whether to permit slavery. This solution contained a crucial ambiguity: It did not specify *at what stage* the settlers of a territory could decide on slavery. Most northern Democrats assumed that a territorial legislature would make that decision as soon as it was organized. Most southerners assumed that it would not be made until the settlers had drawn up a state constitution. That would normally happen only after several years as a territory. So long as neither assumption was tested, each faction could support popular sovereignty.

The Democratic convention nominated Cass for president, thereby seeming to endorse popular sovereignty. In an attempt to maintain party unity, however, the platform made no mention of the matter. The attempt was not entirely successful: Two Alabama delegates walked out when the convention refused to endorse Calhoun's "southern-rights" position, and an antislavery faction from New York walked out when it failed to win a credentials fight.

The Whig convention tried to avoid a similar schism by adopting no platform at all. But the slavery issue would not die. In the eyes of many antislavery delegates ("Conscience Whigs"), the party made itself ridiculous by nominating Zachary Taylor for president. Desperate for victory, the Whigs chose a hero from a war that most of them had opposed. But the fact that Taylor was also a large slaveholder who owned several plantations in Louisiana and Mississippi was too much for the Conscience Whigs. They bolted from the party and formed a coalition with the Liberty Party and antislavery Democrats.

THE FREE SOIL PARTY

The "Free-Soilers" met in convention in August 1848. Speakers proclaimed slavery "a great moral, social, and political evil—a relic of barbarism which must necessarily be swept away in the progress of Christian civilization." The convention did not say how that would be done, but it did adopt a platform calling for "no more Slave States and no more Slave Territories." The Free Soil Party nominated former President Martin Van Buren, with Charles Francis Adams as his running mate.

The campaign was marked by futile efforts to bury the slavery issue. Free Soil pressure compelled both northern Democrats and Whigs to take a stand against slavery in the territories. Whigs pointed to their earlier support of the Wilmot Proviso, while Democrats said popular sovereignty would keep the territories free. In the South, though, the Democrats pointed with pride to the hundreds of thousands of square miles of territory they had brought to the nation—territory into which slavery might expand. But Taylor proved to be the strongest candidate in the South, because he was a southerner and a slaveholder.

Taylor carried 8 of the 15 slave states. Though he did less well in the North, he carried New York and enough other states to win the election. The Free-Soilers won no electoral votes but polled 14 percent of the popular vote in the North.

THE GOLD RUSH AND CALIFORNIA STATEHOOD

About the time Nicholas Trist was putting the finishing touches on a treaty to make California part of the United States, workers building a sawmill on the American River near Sacramento discovered flecks of gold in the riverbed. The news gradually leaked out, reaching the East in August 1848. In December, Polk's final message to Congress confirmed the "extraordinary" discoveries of gold. Two days later, a tea caddy containing 320 ounces of pure gold from California arrived in Washington. By the spring of 1849, 100,000 gold-seekers were poised to take off by foot on the overland trail, or by ship—either around Cape Horn or to the isthmus of Central America, where after a relatively short land crossing, they could board another ship to take them up the Pacific Coast to the new boom town of San Francisco. Some of the new arrivals struck it rich; most kept hoping to; more kept coming by the scores of thousands every year.

The political organization of California could not be postponed. The mining camps needed law and order; the settlers needed courts, land and water laws, mail service, and the like. In New Mexico, the 60,000 former Mexican citizens, now Americans, also needed a governmental structure for their new allegiance.

But the slavery question paralyzed Congress. In December 1848 Polk recommended extension of the Missouri Compromise 36°30′ line to the Pacific. The Whig-controlled House defied him, reaffirmed the Wilmot Proviso, drafted a bill to organize California as a free territory, and debated abolishing the slave trade and even slavery itself in the District of Columbia. However, the Democratic-controlled Senate quashed all the bills. A Southern caucus asked Calhoun to draft an "address" setting forth its position. He eagerly complied, producing in January 1849 a document that breathed fire against "unconstitutional" Northern efforts to keep slavery out of the territories.

But Calhoun's firebomb fizzled. Only two-fifths of the southern congressmen and senators signed it. The Whigs wanted nothing to do with it. "We do not expect an administration which we have brought into power [to] do any act or permit any act to be done [against] our safety," said Robert Toombs of Georgia, a leading Whig congressman.

They were in for a rude shock. President Taylor viewed matters as a nationalist, not as a southerner. He proposed to admit California and New Mexico (the latter comprising present-day New Mexico, Arizona, Nevada, Utah, and part of Colorado) immediately as *states*, skipping the territorial stage.

From the South came cries of outrage. Immediate admission would bring in two more free states, for slavery had not existed under Mexican law and most of the forty-niners were Free Soil in sentiment. Indeed, with the administration's support, Californians held a convention in October 1849, drew up a constitution excluding slavery, and applied to Congress for admission as a state. Taylor's end run would tip the existing balance of 15 slave and 15 free states in favor of the North, probably forever. "For the first time," said freshman Senator Jefferson Davis of Mississippi, "we are about permanently to destroy the balance of power between the sections." Southerners vowed never to "consent to be thus degraded and enslaved" by such a "monstrous trick and injustice" as admission of California as a free state.

THE COMPROMISE OF 1850

California and New Mexico became the focal points of a cluster of slavery issues. An earlier Supreme Court decision (*Prigg* v. *Pennsylvania*, 1842) had relieved state officials of any obligation to enforce the return of fugitive slaves who had escaped into free states, declaring that this was a federal responsibility. Southerners therefore demanded a strong national fugitive slave law. Antislavery northerners, on the other hand, were calling for an end to the disgraceful buying and selling of slaves in the national capital. And in the Southwest, a shooting war threatened to break out between Texas and New Mexico. Having won the Rio Grande as their southern border with Mexico, Texans insisted that the river must also mark their western border with New Mexico. This dispute also involved slavery, for the terms of Texas's annexation authorized the state to split into as many as five states, and the territory it carved out of New Mexico would create the potential for still another slave state.

These problems produced both a crisis and an opportunity. The crisis lay in the threat to break up the Union. From Mississippi had gone forth a call for a convention of southern states at Nashville in June 1850 "to devise and adopt some mode of resistance to northern aggression." Few doubted that the mode would be secession unless Congress met southern demands at least halfway. But sectional disputes prevented either major party from commanding a majority in electing a Speaker of the House. Through three weeks and 62 ballots, the contest went on. Finally, on the 63rd ballot, the exhausted legislators finally elected Howell Cobb of Georgia as Speaker by a plurality rather than a majority.

THE SENATE DEBATES

As he had in 1820 and 1833, Henry Clay hoped to turn the crisis into an opportunity. A veteran of 30 years in Congress, Clay was the most respected and still the most magnetic figure in the Senate. A nationalist from the border state of Kentucky, he hoped to unite North and South in a compromise. On January 29, 1850, he presented eight proposals to the Senate and supported them with an eloquent speech. Clay grouped the first six of his proposals into three

THE CALIFORNIA GOLD RUSH

Prospectors for gold in the foothills of California's Sierra Nevada came from all over the world, including China. The bottom photograph shows American-born and Chinese miners near Auburn, California, a year or two after the initial gold rush of 1849. It illustrates the original primitive technology of separating gravel from gold by panning or by washing the gravel away in a sluice box, leaving the heavier gold flakes behind. By 1853 most of the gold in streams and accessible gravel beds had been recovered,

so gold-seekers turned to hydraulic mining. They dammed a stream at an elevation high enough to create a powerful head of water pressure that blasted loose gold-bearing gravel from whole mountainsides, as shown in the photograph above. Hydraulic mining destroyed or reconfigured thousands of acres of California landscape and left scars still visible today.

pairs, each pair offering one concession to the North and one to the South. The first pair would admit California as a free state but would organize the rest of the Mexican cession without restrictions against slavery. The second would settle the Texas boundary dispute in favor of New Mexico but would compensate Texas to enable the state to pay off bonds it had sold when it was an independent republic. The third pair of proposals would abolish the slave trade in the District of Columbia but would guarantee the continued existence of slavery there unless both Maryland and Virginia consented to abolition. Of Clay's final two proposals, one affirmed that Congress had no jurisdiction over the interstate slave trade, while the other called for a strong national fugitive slave law.

The final shape of the Compromise of 1850 closely resembled Clay's package. But it required a long, grueling process of bargaining, including numerous set speeches in the Senate. The most notable were those of John C. Calhoun, Daniel Webster, and William H. Seward. Each senator spoke for one of the three principal viewpoints on the issues.

Calhoun went first, on March 4. Suffering from consumption, he sat shrouded in flannel as a colleague read his speech. Unless northerners returned fugitive slaves in good faith, he warned, unless they consented to the expansion of slavery into the territories and accepted a constitutional amendment "which will restore to the South, in substance, the power she possessed of protecting herself before the equilibrium between the two sections was destroyed," southern states could not "remain in the Union consistently with their honor and safety."

Webster's speech three days later was both a reply to Calhoun and an appeal for compromise. "I wish to speak to-day, not as a Massachusetts man, nor as a Northern man, but as an American," he announced. "I speak to-day for the preservation of the Union." Secession could no more take place "without convulsion," he said, than "the heavenly bodies [could] rush from their spheres . . . without causing the wreck of the universe!" He urged Yankees to forgo "taunt or reproach" of the South by insisting on the Wilmot Proviso. However, many of Webster's former antislavery admirers repudiated his leadership—especially since he also endorsed a fugitive slave law.

On March 11 Seward expressed the antislavery position in what came to be known as his "higher law" speech. Both slavery and compromise were "radically wrong and essentially vicious," he said. In reply to Calhoun's arguments for the constitutional protection of slavery in the territories, he invoked "a higher law than the Constitution," the law of God in whose sight all persons were equal. Instead of legislating the expansion of slavery or the return of fugitive slaves, the country should be considering how to bring slavery peacefully to an end.

PASSAGE OF THE COMPROMISE

While these speeches were being delivered, committee members worked ceaselessly behind the scenes to fashion compromise legislation. But, in reaching for a compromise, Clay chose what turned out to be the wrong tactic. He lumped most of his proposals together in a single bill, hoping that supporters of any given part of the compromise would vote for the whole in order to get the part they liked. Instead, most senators and representatives voted against the package in order to defeat the parts they disliked. President Taylor continued to insist on the immediate admission of California (and New Mexico, when it was ready) with no quid pro quo for the South. Exhausted and discouraged, Clay fled Washington's summer heat, leaving a young senator from Illinois, Stephen A. Douglas, to lead the forces of compromise.

Douglas reversed Clay's tactics. Starting with a core of supporters made up of Democrats from the Old Northwest and Whigs from the upper South, he built a majority for the Compromise by submitting each part of it separately and then adding its supporters to his core: northerners for a free California, southerners for a fugitive slave law, and so on. This effort benefited from Taylor's sudden death on July 9. The new president, Millard Fillmore, was a conservative Whig from New York who gave his support to the Compromise. One after another, in August and September, the separate measures became law. President Fillmore christened the Compromise of 1850 "a final settlement" of all sectional problems. Calhounites in the South and antislavery activists in the North branded the Compromise a betrayal of principle.

The consequences of the Compromise turned out to be different from what many anticipated. California came in as the 16th free state, but its senators turned out to be conservative Democrats who voted with the South on most issues. The territorial legislatures of Utah and New Mexico legalized slavery, but few slaves were brought there. And the fugitive slave law generated more trouble and controversy than all the other parts of this "final settlement" combined.

THE FUGITIVE SLAVE LAW

The Constitution required that a slave who escaped into a free state must be returned to his or her owner. But it did not specify how that should be done. Under a 1793 law, slaveowners could take their recaptured property before any state or federal court to prove ownership. This procedure worked well enough so long as officials in free states were willing to cooperate. But as the antislavery movement gained momentum in the 1830s, some officials proved uncooperative. And professional slave-catchers sometimes went too far— kidnapping free blacks and selling them. Several northern states responded by passing antikidnapping laws giving alleged fugitives the right of trial by jury. The laws also prescribed criminal penalties for kidnapping. In *Prigg* v. *Pennsylvania* (1842) the U.S. Supreme Court declared Pennsylvania's antikidnapping law unconstitutional. But it also ruled that enforcement of the Constitution's fugitive slave clause was entirely a federal responsibility, thereby absolving the states of any need to cooperate in enforcing it. Nine northern states thereupon passed personal liberty laws prohibiting the use of state facilities in the recapture of fugitives.

Fugitive slaves dramatized the poignancy and cruelties of bondage more vividly than anything else. A man or a woman risking all for freedom was a real human being whose plight invited sympathy and help. Consequently, many northerners who did not necessarily oppose slavery felt outrage at the idea of fugitives being seized and returned to slavery. The "underground railroad" that helped spirit slaves out of bondage took on legendary status. Stories of secret chambers where fugitives were hidden, dramatic trips in the dark between "stations" on the underground, and clever or heroic measures to foil pursuing bloodhounds exaggerated the legend.

Probably fewer than 1,000 of a total 3 million slaves actually escaped to freedom each year. But to southerners the return of those fugitives, like the question of the legality of slavery in California or New Mexico, was a matter of *honor* and *rights*. "Although the loss of property is felt," said Senator James Mason of Virginia, sponsor of the Fugitive Slave Act, "the loss of honor is felt still more." Southerners therefore regarded obedience to the fugitive slave law as a test of the North's good faith in carrying out the Compromise. President Millard Fillmore vowed to prove that good faith by strictly enforcing the law.

The provisions of that law were extraordinary. It created federal commissioners who could issue warrants for arrests of fugitives and before whom a slaveholder would bring a captured fugitive to prove ownership. All the slaveholder needed for proof was an affidavit from a slave-state court or the testimony of white witnesses. The fugitive had no right to testify in his or her own behalf. The federal Treasury would pay all costs of enforcement. The commissioner could call on federal marshals to apprehend fugitives, and the marshals in turn could deputize any citizen to help. Anyone who harbored a fugitive or obstructed his or her capture would be subject to imprisonment.

Abolitionists denounced the law and vowed to resist it. Opportunities soon came, as slave-owners sent agents north to recapture fugitives, some of whom had escaped years earlier. In February 1851 slave-catchers arrested a black man living with his family in Indiana and returned him to an owner who said he had run away 19 years before. Statistics show that the law was rigged in favor of the claimants. In the first 15 months of its operation, 84 fugitives were returned to slavery and only 5 were released.

THE SLAVE-CATCHERS

Unable to protect their freedom through legal means, many blacks, with the support of white allies, resorted to flight and resistance. Thousands of northern blacks fled to Canada. In February 1851 slave-catchers arrested a fugitive who had taken the name Shadrach when

RETURN OF THOMAS SIMS AND ANTHONY BURNS This symbolic woodcut depicts soldiers and marines returning two of the most famous fugitives to slavery while Bostonians vent their frustration and rage. Although the incidents were real, the Sims and Burns cases occurred three years apart, in 1851 and 1854.

he escaped from Virginia a year earlier. They rushed him to the federal courthouse, where a few deputy marshals held him, pending a hearing. But a group of black men broke into the courtroom, overpowered the deputies, and spirited Shadrach out of the country to Canada. This was too much for the Fillmore administration. In April 1851 another fugitive, Thomas Sims, was arrested in Boston, and the president sent 250 soldiers to help 300 armed deputies enforce the law and return Sims to slavery.

Continued rescues and escapes kept matters at fever pitch for the rest of the decade. In the fall of 1851 a Maryland slaveowner and his son accompanied federal marshals to Christiana, Pennsylvania, a Quaker village, where two of the man's slaves had taken refuge. The hunters ran into a fusillade of gunfire from a house where a dozen black men were protecting the fugitives. When the shooting stopped, the slaveowner was dead and his son was seriously wounded. Three of the blacks fled to Canada. This time Fillmore sent in the marines. They helped marshals arrest 30 black men and a half dozen whites, who were indicted for treason. But the U.S. attorney dropped charges after a jury acquitted the first defendant, a Quaker.

Another white man who aided slaves was not so lucky. Sherman Booth was an abolitionist editor in Wisconsin who led a raid in 1854 to free a fugitive from custody. Convicted in a federal court, Booth appealed for a writ of habeas corpus from the Wisconsin Supreme Court. The court freed him and declared the Fugitive Slave Law unconstitutional. That assertion of states' rights prompted the southern majority on the U.S. Supreme Court to overrule the Wisconsin court, assert the supremacy of federal law, and order Booth back to prison.

Two of the most famous fugitive slave cases of the 1850s ended in deeper tragedy. In the spring of 1854 federal marshals in Boston arrested a Virginia fugitive, Anthony Burns. Angry abolitionists poured into Boston to save him. But the new president, Franklin Pierce, was determined not to back down. After every legal move to free Burns had failed, Pierce sent a U.S. revenue cutter to carry Burns back to Virginia. While thousands of angry Yankees lined the streets, soldiers of the Army and Marine Corps marched this lone black man back into bondage.

Two years later Margaret Garner escaped from Kentucky to Ohio with her husband and four children. When a posse of marshals and deputies caught up with them, Margaret seized a kitchen knife and tried to kill her children and herself rather than return to slavery. She managed to cut her 3-year-old daughter's throat before she was overpowered. After complicated legal maneuvers, the federal commissioner remanded the fugitives to their Kentucky owner.

Such events had a profound impact on public emotions. Most northerners were not abolitionists, but millions of them moved closer to an antislavery position in response to the shock of seeing armed slave-catchers on their streets. Several northern states passed new personal liberty laws in defiance of the South. Although those laws did not make it impossible to recover fugitives, they made it so difficult, expensive, and time-consuming that many slaveowners gave up trying.

UNCLE TOM'S CABIN

A novel inspired by the plight of fugitive slaves further intensified public sentiment. Harriet Beecher Stowe, author of *Uncle Tom's Cabin,* was the daughter of Lyman Beecher, the most famous clergyman-theologian of his generation, and the sister of Henry Ward Beecher, the foremost preacher of the next generation. Having grown up in New England, Harriet lived for 18 years in Cincinnati, where she became acquainted with fugitive slaves who had escaped across the Ohio River. Outraged by the Fugitive Slave Law, she responded to her sister-in-law's suggestion: "Hattie, if I could use a pen as you can, I would write something that will make this nation feel what an accursed thing slavery is."

In 1851, writing by candlelight after putting the children to bed, Stowe turned out a chapter a week for serial publication in an antislavery newspaper. When the installments were published as a book in the spring of 1852, *Uncle Tom's Cabin* became a runaway best-seller and was eventually translated into 20 languages. Contrived in plot, didactic in style, steeped in sentiment, *Uncle Tom's Cabin* is nevertheless a powerful novel with unforgettable characters. Uncle Tom himself is a Christlike figure who bears the sins of white people and carries the salvation of black people on his shoulders. The novel's central theme is the tragedy of the breakup of families by slavery. Few eyes remained dry as they read about Eliza fleeing across the ice-choked Ohio River to save her son from the slave trader, or about Tom grieving for the wife and children he had left behind in Kentucky when he was sold.

Though banned in some parts of the South, *Uncle Tom's Cabin* found a wide but hostile readership there. Proslavery authors rushed into print with more than a dozen novels challenging Stowe's themes, but all of them together made nothing like the impact of *Uncle Tom's Cabin*. The book helped shape a whole generation's view of slavery. When Abraham Lincoln met Harriet Beecher Stowe a decade after its publication, he reportedly remarked, "So you're the little woman who wrote the book that made this great war."

FILIBUSTERING

If the prospects for slavery in New Mexico appeared unpromising, southerners could contemplate a closer region where slavery already existed—Cuba. Enjoying an economic boom based on slave-grown sugar, this Spanish colony only 90 miles from American shores had nearly 400,000 slaves in 1850. President Polk offered Spain $100 million for Cuba in 1848. The Spanish foreign minister spurned the offer, stating that he would rather see the island sunk in the sea than sold.

If money did not work, revolution might. Cuban planters intrigued with American expansionists in the hope of fomenting an uprising on the island. Their leader was Narciso Lopez, a Venezuelan-born Cuban soldier-of-fortune. In 1849 Lopez recruited several hundred American adventurers for the first "filibustering" expedition against Cuba (from the Spanish *filibustero*, a freebooter or pirate). When President Taylor ordered the Navy to prevent Lopez's ships from leaving New York, Lopez shifted his operations to New Orleans, where he raised a new force of filibusters. Port officials in New Orleans looked the other way when the expedition sailed in May 1850, but Spanish troops drove the filibusters into the sea after they had established a beachhead in Cuba.

Undaunted, Lopez escaped and returned to a hero's welcome in the South, where he raised men and money for a third try in 1851. This time, William Crittenden of Kentucky commanded the 420 Americans in the expedition. But the invasion was a fiasco. Spanish soldiers suppressed a local uprising timed to coincide with the invasion and then defeated the filibusters, killing 200 and capturing the rest. Lopez was garroted in the public square of Havana. Then 50 American prisoners, including Crittenden, were lined up and executed by firing squad.

These events dampened southerners' enthusiasm for Cuba, but only for a time. "Cuba must be ours," declared Jefferson Davis, in order to "increase the number of slaveholding constituencies." In 1852 the Democrats nominated Franklin Pierce of New Hampshire for president. Southern Democrats were delighted with his nomination. Pierce was "as reliable as Calhoun himself," wrote one. Especially gratifying was Pierce's support for annexing Cuba, which he made one of the top priorities of his new administration after winning a landslide victory.

Pierce tried again to buy Cuba, instructing the American minister in Madrid to offer Spain $130 million. The minister was Pierre Soulé, a flamboyant Louisianian who managed to alienate most Spaniards by his clumsy intriguing. Soulé's crowning act came in October 1854 at a meeting with the American ministers to Britain and France in Ostend, Belgium. He persuaded them to sign what came to be known as the Ostend Manifesto. "Cuba is as necessary to the North American republic as any of its present . . . family of states," declared this document. If Spain persisted in refusing to sell, then "by every law, human and divine, we shall be justified in wresting it from Spain."

This "manifesto of the brigands," as antislavery Americans called it, caused an international uproar. The administration repudiated the manifesto and recalled Soulé. Nevertheless, acquisition of Cuba remained an objective of the Democratic Party. The issue played a role in the 1860 presidential election and in the secession controversy during 1860 and 1861. Meanwhile, the focus of American filibustering shifted 750 miles south of Havana to Nicaragua. There, the most remarkable of the *filibusteros*, William Walker, had proclaimed himself president and had restored the institution of slavery.

THE GRAY-EYED MAN OF DESTINY

A native of Tennessee and a brilliant, restless man, Walker had earned a medical degree from the University of Pennsylvania and had studied and practiced law in New Orleans before joining the 1849 rush to California. Weighing less than 120 pounds, Walker seemed an unlikely fighter or leader of men. But his luminous eyes, which seemed to transfix his fellows, won him the sobriquet "gray-eyed man of destiny."

Walker found his true calling in filibustering. At the time, numerous raids were taking place back and forth across the border with Mexico. In 1853 Walker led a ragged "army" of footloose forty-niners into Baja California and Sonora and declared the region an independent republic. Exhaustion and desertion depleted his troops, however, and the Mexicans drove the survivors back to California.

Walker decided to try again, with another goal. Many southerners eyed the potential of tropical Nicaragua for growing cotton, sugar, coffee, and other crops. The instability of the Nicaraguan government offered a tempting target. In 1854 Walker signed a contract with rebel leaders. The following spring, he led an advance guard of filibusters to Nicaragua and proclaimed himself commander in chief of the rebel forces. At the head of 2,000 American soldiers, he gained control of the country and named himself president in 1856. The Pierce administration extended diplomatic recognition to Walker's regime.

The other Central American republics soon formed an alliance to invade Nicaragua and overthrow Walker. To win greater support from the southern states, Walker issued a decree in September 1856 reinstituting slavery in Nicaragua. A convention of southern economic promoters meeting in Savannah praised Walker's efforts "to introduce civilization in the States of Central America, and to develop these rich and productive regions by slave labor." Boatloads of new recruits arrived in Nicaragua from New Orleans. But in the spring of 1857 they succumbed to disease and to the Central American armies.

CHRONOLOGY

1844	Senate rejects Texas annexation • James K. Polk elected president
1845	Congress annexes Texas • Mexico spurns U.S. bid to buy California and New Mexico
1846	U.S. declares war on Mexico • U.S. forces under Zachary Taylor win battles of Palo Alto and Resaca de la Palma • U.S. and Britain settle Oregon boundary dispute • U.S. occupies California and New Mexico • House passes Wilmot Proviso • U.S. forces capture Monterrey, Mexico
1847	Americans win battle of Buena Vista • U.S. Army under Winfield Scott lands at Veracruz • Americans win battles of Contreras, Churubusco, Molino del Rey, and Chapultepec • Mexico City falls
1848	Treaty of Guadalupe Hidalgo ends Mexican War, fixes Rio Grande as border, cedes New Mexico and California to U.S. • Gold discovered in California • Spain spurns Polk's offer of $100 million for Cuba • Zachary Taylor elected president
1849	John C. Calhoun pens "Address of the Southern Delegates" • California seeks admission as a free state
1850	Taylor dies, Millard Fillmore becomes president • Bitter sectional debate culminates in Compromise of 1850 • Fugitive slave law empowers federal commissioners to recover escaped slaves
1851	Fugitive slave law provokes rescues and violent conflict in North • American filibusters executed in Cuba
1852	*Uncle Tom's Cabin* becomes best-seller • Franklin Pierce elected president
1854	Anthony Burns returned from Boston to slavery • William Walker's filibusters invade Nicaragua • Pierce tries to buy Cuba • Ostend Manifesto issued
1856	William Walker legalizes slavery in Nicaragua
1860	William Walker executed in Honduras

Walker escaped to New Orleans, where he was welcomed as a hero. Southern congressmen encouraged him to try again. On this expedition, however, his ship struck a reef and sank. Undaunted, he tried yet again. He wrote a book to raise funds for another invasion of Nicaragua, urging "the hearts of Southern youth to answer the call of honor. . . . The true field for the expansion of slavery is in tropical America." A few more southern youths answered the call, but they were stopped in Honduras. There, on September 12, 1860, the gray-eyed man met his destiny before a firing squad.

CONCLUSION

Within the three-year period from 1845 to 1848 the annexation of Texas, the settlement of the Oregon boundary dispute with Britain, and the acquisition by force of New Mexico and California from Mexico added 1,150,000 square miles to the United States. This expansion was America's "manifest destiny," according to Senator Stephen A. Douglas of Illinois. "Increase, and multiply, and expand, is the law of this nation's existence," proclaimed Douglas. "You cannot limit this great republic by mere boundary lines."

But other Americans feared that the country could not absorb such rapid growth without strains that might break it apart. At the outbreak of the war with Mexico, Ralph Waldo Emerson predicted that "the United States will conquer Mexico, but it will be as the man swallows the arsenic, which brings him down in turn."

Emerson proved to be right. The poison was the reopening of the question of slavery's expansion, which had supposedly been settled by the Missouri Compromise in 1820. The admission of Texas as a huge new slave state and the possibility that more slave states might be carved out of the territory acquired from Mexico provoked northern congressmen to pass the Wilmot Proviso. Southerners bristled at this attempt to prevent the further expansion of slavery. Threats of secession and civil war poisoned the atmosphere in 1849 and 1850.

The Compromise of 1850 defused the crisis and appeared to settle the issue once again. But events would soon prove that this "compromise" had merely postponed the crisis. The fugitive slave issue and filibustering expeditions to acquire more slave territory kept sectional controversies smoldering. In 1854 the Kansas-Nebraska Act would cause them to burst into a hotter flame than ever.

14

THE GATHERING TEMPEST, 1853–1860

KANSAS AND THE RISE OF THE REPUBLICAN PARTY

IMMIGRATION AND NATIVISM ～ BLEEDING KANSAS

THE ELECTION OF 1856 ～ THE ECONOMY IN THE 1850S

THE LINCOLN-DOUGLAS DEBATES

The wounds caused by the battle over slavery in the territories had barely healed when they were reopened. This time the strife was over the question of slavery in the Louisiana Purchase territory—though that question had presumably been settled 34 years earlier by the Missouri Compromise of 1820, which had admitted Missouri as a slave state but had banned slavery from the rest of the Purchase north of 36°30′. To obtain southern support for the organization of Kansas and Nebraska as territories, Senator Stephen Douglas consented to the repeal of this provision of the Missouri Compromise. Northern outrage at this repudiation of a "sacred contract" killed the Whig Party and gave birth to the antislavery Republican Party. In 1857 the Supreme Court added insult to injury with the Dred Scott decision, which denied the power of Congress to restrict slavery from the territories. The ominous reorientation of national politics along sectional lines was accompanied by a bloody civil war in Kansas.

KANSAS AND THE RISE OF THE REPUBLICAN PARTY

By 1853 land-hungry settlers had pushed up the Missouri River to its confluence with the Kansas and Platte rivers. But settlement of the country west of Missouri and land surveys for a railroad through this region would require that it be organized as a territory. Accordingly, in 1853 the House passed a bill creating the Nebraska Territory, embracing the area north of Indian Territory (present-day Oklahoma) up to the Canadian border. But the House bill ran into trouble in the Senate. Under the Missouri Compromise, slavery would be excluded from the new territory. Having lost California, the proslavery forces were determined to salvage something from Nebraska. Missourians were particularly adamant. Senator David R. Atchison of Missouri vowed to see Nebraska "sink in hell" before having it become free soil.

As president pro tem of the Senate, Atchison wielded great influence. A profane, gregarious man, he had inherited Calhoun's mantle as leader of the southern-rights faction. In the 1853–1854 session of Congress, he kept raising the asking price for southern support of a bill to organize the Nebraska Territory.

The sponsor of the Senate bill was Stephen A. Douglas, chairman of the Senate Committee on Territories. Only 5 feet 4 inches tall, Douglas had earned the nickname "Little Giant" for his parliamentary skill. In Douglas's opinion, the application of popular sovereignty to the slavery question in New Mexico and Utah had been the centerpiece of the Compromise of 1850. So the initial draft of his Nebraska bill merely repeated the language used for those territories, specifying that when any portion of the Nebraska Territory came in as a state, it could do so "with or without slavery, as its constitution may provide."

This was not good enough for Atchison and his southern colleagues. After talking with them, Douglas announced that because of a "clerical error," a provision calling for the territorial legislature to decide on slavery had been omitted from the draft. But Atchison raised the price once again, insisting on an explicit repeal of the Missouri Compromise. Sighing that this "will raise a hell of a storm," Douglas nevertheless agreed. He further agreed to divide the area in question into two territories: Kansas west of Missouri, and Nebraska west of Iowa and Minnesota. To many northerners this looked suspiciously like a scheme to mark Kansas out for slavery and Nebraska for freedom.

THE KANSAS-NEBRASKA ACT

The bill did indeed raise a hell of a storm. Douglas had failed to recognize the depth of northern opposition to the "slave power" and to the expansion of slavery. Douglas himself did not have firm moral convictions about slavery, but millions of Americans did care. They regarded the expansion of slavery as too important to be left to territorial voters. One of them was an old acquaintance of Douglas, Abraham Lincoln. An antislavery Whig who had served several terms in the Illinois legislature and one term in Congress, Lincoln was propelled back into politics by the shock of the Kansas-Nebraska bill. He acknowledged the constitutional right to hold slave property in the states where it already existed. But he believed slavery was "an unqualified evil to the negro, the white man, and to the state. . . . There can be no moral right in connection with one man's making a slave of another." Lincoln understood that race prejudice was a powerful obstacle to emancipation. Still, the country must face up to the problem. It must stop any further expansion of slavery as the first step on the long road to its "ultimate extinction."

Lincoln excoriated Douglas's "care not" attitude toward whether slavery was voted up or down. The assertion that slavery would never be imported into Kansas anyway, because of the region's unsuitable climate, Lincoln branded as a "LULLABY argument." The climate of eastern Kansas was similar to that of the Missouri River valley in Missouri, where slaves were busily raising hemp and tobacco. Missouri slaveholders were already poised to take their slaves into the Kansas River valley. In fact, the United States had become the world's largest slaveholding society, and Douglas's bill would permit slavery to expand even further.

Lincoln spoke vehemently against further expansion of slavery:

> The monstrous injustice of slavery . . . deprives our republican example of its just influence in the world—enables the enemies of free institutions, with plausibility, to taunt us as hypocrites. . . . Let us re-adopt the Declaration of Independence, and with it, the practices, and policy, which harmonize with it. . . . If we do this, we shall not only have saved the Union; but we shall have so saved it, as to make, and to keep it, forever worthy of the saving.

With this eloquent declaration, Lincoln gave voice to the feelings that fostered an uprising against the Kansas-Nebraska bill. Abolitionists, Free-Soilers, northern Whigs, and even many northern Democrats formed "anti-Nebraska" coalitions. But they could not stop passage of the bill. It cleared the Senate easily, supported by a solid South and 15 of the 20 northern Democrats. In the House, it passed by a vote of 113 to 100.

The Death of the Whig Party

These proceedings completed the destruction of the Whigs as a national party. In 1852 the Whig Party nominated General Winfield Scott for president. Though a Virginian, Scott took a national rather than a southern view. He was the candidate of the northern Whigs in the national convention, which nominated him on the 53rd ballot after a bitter contest. A mass exodus of southern Whigs into the Democratic Party enabled Franklin Pierce to carry all but two slave states in the election. The unanimous vote of northern Whigs in Congress against the Kansas-Nebraska bill was the final straw. The Whig Party never recovered its influence in the South.

It seemed to be on its last legs in the North as well. Antislavery Whig leaders like Seward and Lincoln hoped to channel the flood of anti-Nebraska sentiment through the Whig Party. But that was like trying to contain Niagara Falls. Free-Soilers and antislavery Democrats spurned the Whig label. Political coalitions arose under various names: Anti-Nebraska; Fusion; People's; Independent. But the name that caught on was Republican. The first use of this name seems to have been at an anti-Nebraska rally in a Congregational church at Ripon, Wisconsin, in May 1854.

The elections of 1854 were disastrous for northern Democrats. One-fourth of Democratic voters deserted the party. The Democrats lost control of the House of Representatives when 66 of 91 incumbent free-state Democratic congressmen went down to defeat. Combined with the increase in the number of Democratic congressmen from the South, this rout brought the party more than ever under southern domination.

But who would pick up the pieces of old parties in the North? The new Republican Party hoped to, but it suffered a shock in urban areas of the Northeast. Hostility to immigrants created a tidal wave of nativism that threatened to swamp the anti-Nebraska movement. Described as a "tornado," a "hurricane," and a "freak of political insanity," the anti-immigrant "Know-Nothings" won landslide victories in Massachusetts and Delaware, polled an estimated 40 percent of the vote in Pennsylvania, and did well elsewhere in the Northeast and border states. Who were these mysterious Know-Nothings? What did they stand for?

Immigration and Nativism

During the early 19th century, immigration was less pronounced than in most other periods of U.S. history. The volume of immigration (expressed as the number of immigrants during a decade in proportion to the whole population at its beginning) was little more than 1 percent in the 1820s, increasing to 4 percent in the 1830s. Three-quarters of the newcomers were Protestants, mainly from Britain. Most of them were skilled workers, farmers, or members of white-collar occupations.

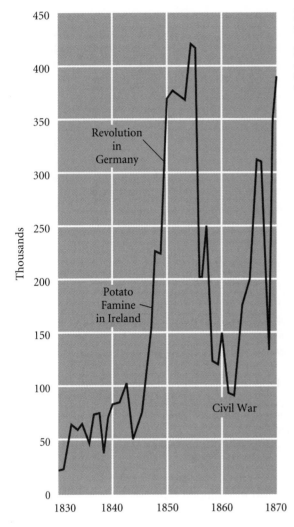

IMMIGRATION TO THE UNITED STATES

SOURCE: From *Division and the Stresses of Reunion 1845–1876,* by David M. Potter. Copyright © 1973 Scott, Foresman and Company. Reprinted by permission.

In the 1840s a combination of factors caused a sudden quadrupling in the volume of immigration and a change in its ethnic and occupational makeup. The pressure of expanding population on limited land in Germany and successive failures of the potato crop in Ireland impelled millions of German and Irish peasants to emigrate. A majority came to the United States. During the decade after 1845, 3 million immigrants entered the United States—15 percent of the total American population in 1845. Many of them, especially the Irish, joined the unskilled and semiskilled labor force in the rapidly growing eastern cities and in the construction of railroads.

Most of the new arrivals were Roman Catholics. However, fear of the Roman Catholic Church as autocratic and antirepublican was never far below the surface of American political culture. Several ethnic riots between Protestant and Catholic workers culminated in pitched battles and numerous deaths in Philadelphia in 1844. In several eastern cities nativist political parties sprang up in the early 1840s with the intent of curbing the political rights of immigrants.

Nativism appeared to subside with the revival of prosperity after 1844. But the decline was temporary, as the vast increase of immigration proved too much for the country to absorb. Not only were most of the new immigrants Catholics; many of them also spoke a foreign language and had alien cultural values. Older Americans perceived newer Americans as responsible for an increase of crime and poverty in the cities.

IMMIGRANTS IN POLITICS

The political power of immigrants also grew. Most of the immigrants became Democrats, because that party welcomed or at least tolerated them while many Whigs did not. Foreign-born voters leaned toward the proslavery wing of the Democratic Party, even though seven-eighths of them settled in free states. Mostly working-class and poor, they supported the Democratic Party as the best means of keeping blacks in slavery and out of the North. These attitudes sparked hostility toward immigrants among many antislavery people.

The Roman Catholic hierarchy did little to allay that hostility. The leading Catholic prelate, Archbishop John Hughes of New York, attacked abolitionists, Free-Soilers, and various Protestant reform movements. In 1850, in a widely publicized address titled "The Decline of Protestantism and Its Causes," Hughes noted proudly that Catholic Church membership in the United States had grown three times faster than Protestant membership over the previous decade, and he predicted an eventual Catholic majority.

Attitudes toward immigrants had political repercussions. Two of the hottest issues in state and local politics during the early 1850s were temperance and schools. The temperance crusaders had grown confident and aggressive enough to go into politics. The drunkenness and rowdiness they associated with Irish immigrants became one of their particular targets. Beginning with Maine in 1851, 12 states had enacted prohibition laws by 1855. Though several of the laws were soon weakened by the courts or repealed by legislatures, they exacerbated ethnic tensions.

So did battles over public schools versus parochial schools. Catholics resented the Protestant domination of public education and the reading of the King James Bible in schools. The Church began to build parochial schools for the faithful, and in 1852 the first Plenary Council of American bishops decided to seek tax support for these schools or tax relief for Catholic parents who sent their children to them. This effort set off heated election contests in numerous northern cities and states. "Free school" tickets generally won by promising to defend public schools against the "bold effort" of this "despotic faith" to "uproot the tree of Liberty."

THE RISE OF THE "KNOW-NOTHINGS"

It was in this context that the Know-Nothings (their formal name was the American Party) burst onto the political scene. This party was the result of the merger in 1852 of two secret fraternal societies that limited their membership to native-born Protestants: the Order of the Star-Spangled Banner and the Order of United Americans. Recruiting mainly young men in skilled blue-collar and lower white-collar occupations, the merged Order had a membership of 1 million or more by 1854. The Order supported temperance and opposed tax support for parochial schools. They wanted public office restricted to native-born men and sought to lengthen the naturalization period before immigrants could become citizens. Members were pledged to secrecy about the Order; if asked, they were to reply "I know nothing."

KNOW-NOTHINGS ON ELECTION DAY   In Baltimore, nativist political clubs called "Blood Tubs" and "Plug-Uglies" patrolled the streets at election time to intimidate foreign-born voters. An election riot in 1854 left 17 dead in Baltimore; similar riots in St. Louis and Louisville also resulted in many deaths. This cartoon satirizes Baltimore's Know-Nothing street gangs.

This was the tornado that swept through the Northeast in the 1854 elections. Although the American Party drew voters from both major parties, it cut more heavily into the Whig constituency. Many northern Whigs who had not already gone over to the Republicans flocked to the Know-Nothings.

When the dust of the 1854 elections settled, it was clear that those who opposed the Democrats would control the next House of Representatives. But who would control the opposition—antislavery Republicans or nativist Americans? In truth, some northern voters and the congressmen they elected adhered to both political faiths. In New England, several Know-Nothing leaders were actually Republicans in disguise who had jumped on the nativist bandwagon with the intention of steering it in an antislavery direction.

But many Republicans warned against flirting with bigotry. "How can any one who abhors the oppression of negroes, be in favor of degrading classes of white people?" asked Abraham Lincoln in a letter to a friend.

As a nation, we began by declaring that *"all men are created equal."* We now practically read it "all men are created equal, *except negroes.*" When the Know Nothings get control, it will read "all men are created equal, except negroes, *and foreigners, and catholics.*" When it comes to this I should prefer emigrating to some country where they make no pretense of loving liberty.

Other Republicans echoed Lincoln. Since "we are against Black Slavery, because the slaves are deprived of human rights," they declared, "we are also against . . . [this] system of Northern Slavery to be created by disfranchising the Irish and Germans."

THE DECLINE OF NATIVISM

In 1855 Republican leaders maneuvered skillfully to divert the energies of northern Know-Nothings from their crusade against Catholicism to a crusade against the slave power. Two developments helped them. The first was turmoil in Kansas, which convinced many northerners that the slave power was a greater threat than the pope. The second was an increase in nativist sentiment in the South. The American Party won elections in Maryland, Kentucky, and Tennessee and polled at least 45 percent of the votes in five other southern states. Violence in several southern cities with large immigrant populations preceded or accompanied these elections, evidencing a significant streak of nativism in the South.

These developments had important implications at the national level. Southern Know-Nothings were proslavery while many of their Yankee counterparts were antislavery. Just as the national Whig Party had foundered on the slavery issue, so did the American Party during 1855 and 1856. At the party's first national council in June 1855, most of the northern delegates walked out when southerners and northern conservatives joined forces to pass a resolution endorsing the Kansas-Nebraska Act. A similar scene occurred at an American Party convention in 1856. By that time, most northern members of the party had, in effect, become Republicans. At the convening of the House of Representatives in December 1855, a protracted fight for the speakership took place. The Republican candidate was Nathaniel P. Banks of Massachusetts, a former Know-Nothing who now considered himself a Republican. Banks finally won on the 133rd ballot with the support of about 30 Know-Nothings who thereby declared themselves Republicans.

By that time, nativism had faded. The volume of immigration suddenly dropped by more than half in 1855 and stayed low for the next several years. Ethnic tensions eased, and cultural issues like temperance and schools also seemed to recede. The real conflict turned out to be not the struggle between native and immigrant, or between Protestant and Catholic, but between North and South over the extension of slavery. That was the conflict that led to civil war—and the war seemed already to have begun in the territory of Kansas.

BLEEDING KANSAS

When it became clear that southerners had enough votes to pass the Kansas-Nebraska Act, William H. Seward told his southern colleagues: "Since there is no escaping your challenge, I accept it in behalf of the cause of freedom. We will engage in competition for the virgin soil of Kansas, and God give victory to the side which is stronger in numbers as it is in right." Senator David Atchison of Missouri wrote: "We are playing for a mighty stake. If we win we carry slavery to the Pacific Ocean; if we fail we lose Missouri, Arkansas, Texas and all the territories; the game must be played boldly."

Atchison did play boldly. At first, Missouri settlers in Kansas posted the stronger numbers. But as the year 1854 progressed, settlers from the North came pouring in and the scramble for the best lands in Kansas intensified. Alarmed by the growing numbers of northern settlers, bands of Missourians, labeled "border ruffians" by the Republican press, rode into Kansas prepared to vote as many times as necessary to install a proslavery government. In the fall of 1854 they cast at least 1,700 illegal ballots and sent a proslavery territorial delegate to Congress. When the time came for the election of a territorial legislature the following spring, Atchison led a contingent of border ruffians to Kansas for the election. "There are eleven hundred coming over from Platte County to vote," he told his followers, "and if that ain't enough, we can send five thousand."

His count was accurate. Five thousand was about the number who came and voted illegally to elect a proslavery territorial legislature. The territorial governor pleaded with President Pierce to nullify the election. But Pierce listened to Atchison and fired the governor. Meanwhile, the new territorial legislature legalized slavery and adopted a slave code that even authorized the death penalty for helping a slave to escape.

The "free state" party, outraged by these proceedings, had no intention of obeying laws enacted by this "bogus legislature." By the fall of 1855 they constituted a majority of bona fide settlers in Kansas. So they called a convention, adopted a free-state constitution, and elected their own legislature and governor. By January 1856 two territorial governments in Kansas stood with their hands at each other's throat.

Kansas now became the leading issue in national politics. The Democratic Senate and President Pierce recognized the proslavery legislature in Lecompton, while the Republican House recognized the antislavery legislature in Lawrence. Southerners saw the struggle as crucial to their future. "The admission of Kansas into the Union as a slave state is now a point of honor," wrote Congressman Preston Brooks of South Carolina. "The fate of the South is to be decided with the Kansas issue." On the other side, Charles Sumner of Massachusetts gave a well-publicized speech in the Senate on May 19 and 20. "Murderous robbers from Missouri," he charged, "from the drunken spew and vomit of an uneasy civilization" had committed the "rape of a virgin territory, compelling it to the hateful embrace of slavery." Among the southern senators whom Sumner singled out for special condemnation and ridicule was Andrew Butler of South Carolina, a cousin of Congressman Brooks. He accused Butler of having "chosen a mistress to whom he has made his vows . . . the harlot, Slavery."

THE CANING OF SUMNER

Sumner's speech incensed southerners, none more than Preston Brooks, who decided to avenge his cousin. Two days after the speech, Brooks walked into the Senate chamber and began beating Sumner with a heavy cane. His legs trapped beneath the desk bolted to the floor, Sumner wrenched it loose as he stood up to try to defend himself, whereupon Brooks clubbed him so ferociously that Sumner slumped forward, bloody and unconscious.

News of the incident sent a thrill of pride through the South and a rush of rage through the North. Brooks resigned from Congress after censure by the House and was unanimously reelected. From all over the South came gifts of new canes, some inscribed with such mottoes as "Hit Him Again." But, in the North, the Republicans gained thousands of voters as a result of the affair. It seemed to prove their contentions about "the barbarism of slavery." A veteran New York politician reported that he had "never before seen anything at all like the present state of deep, determined, & desperate feelings of hatred, & hostility to the further extension of slavery, & its political power."

At about the same time, an "army" of proslavery Missourians, complete with artillery, marched on the free-state capital of Lawrence, Kansas. On May 21 they shelled and sacked the town, burning several buildings. A rival force of free-state men arrived too late to intercept them. One of the free-state "captains" was John Brown, an abolitionist zealot who considered himself anointed by the Lord to avenge the sins of slaveholders. When he learned of the sack of Lawrence, he declared that "Something must be done to show these barbarians that we, too, have rights." Leading four of his sons and three other men to a proslavery settlement at Pottawatomie Creek on the night of May 24–25, 1856, Brown dragged five men from their cabins and split open their heads with broadswords.

Brown's murderous act set off a veritable civil war in Kansas. Not until President Pierce sent a tough new territorial governor and 1,300 federal troops to Kansas in September 1856 did the violence subside—just in time to save the Democrats from possible defeat in the presidential election.

THE ELECTION OF 1856

By 1856 the Republicans had become the largest party in the North. They were also the first truly sectional party in American history, for they had little prospect of carrying a single county in the slave states. At their first national convention, the Republicans wrote a platform that focused mainly on slavery but also incorporated the old Whig program of federal aid to internal improvements, including a railroad to California. For its presidential nominee, the party turned to John C. Frémont. This "Pathfinder of the West" had a dashing image as an explorer. With little political experience, he had few political enemies.

The Democrats chose as their candidate James Buchanan, a veteran of 30 years in various public offices. He had been minister to Britain during the Kansas-Nebraska controversy so was not tainted with its unpopularity. The Democratic platform endorsed popular sovereignty and condemned the Republicans as a "sectional party" that incited "treason and armed resistance in the Territories."

This would be a three-party election, for the American Party was still in the field. It nominated ex-Whig Millard Fillmore. The three-party campaign developed into a pair of two-party contests: Democrats versus Americans in the South; Democrats versus Republicans in the North. Fillmore, despite receiving 44 percent of the popular vote in the South, carried only Maryland. Considering Buchanan colorless but safe, the rest of the South gave him three-fourths of the electoral votes he needed for victory.

The real excitement was in the North. For many Republicans the campaign was a moral cause. Republican "Wide Awake" clubs marched in torchlight parades chanting "Free Soil, Free Speech, Free Men, Frémont!" The turnout of eligible voters in the North was a remarkable 83 percent. One awestruck journalist, anticipating a Republican victory, wrote that "the process now going on in the United States is a *Revolution*."

Not quite. Although the Republicans swept New England and the upper parts of New York state and the Old Northwest, the contest in the lower North was close. Buchanan needed only

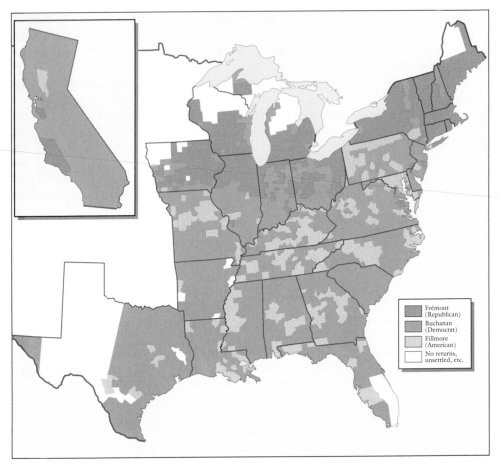

COUNTIES CARRIED BY CANDIDATES IN THE 1856 PRESIDENTIAL ELECTION

to carry Pennsylvania and either Indiana or Illinois to win the presidency, and the campaign focused on those states. The immigrant and working-class voters of the eastern cities and the rural voters of the lower Midwest were antiblack and antiabolitionist in sentiment. They were ripe for Democratic propaganda that accused Republicans of favoring racial equality. "Black Republicans," declared an Ohio Democratic newspaper, intended to "turn loose . . . millions of negroes, to elbow you in the workshops, and compete with you in fields of honest labor." Indiana Democrats organized parades, with young girls in white dresses carrying banners inscribed "Fathers, save us from nigger husbands."

The Republicans in these areas denied that they favored racial equality. They insisted that the main reason for keeping slavery out of the territories was to enable white farmers and workers to make a living there without competition from black labor. But their denials were in vain. Support for the Republican Party by prominent black leaders, including Frederick Douglass, convinced hundreds of thousands of voters that the "Black Republicans" were racial egalitarians.

POPULAR AND ELECTORAL VOTES IN THE 1856 PRESIDENTIAL ELECTION

	FREE STATES		SLAVE STATES		TOTAL	
Candidate	*Popular*	*Electoral*	*Popular*	*Electoral*	*Popular*	*Electoral*
Buchanan (Democrat)	1,227,000	62	607,000	112	1,833,000	174
Frémont (Republican)	1,338,000	114	0	0	1,338,000	114
Fillmore (American)	396,000	0	476,000	8	872,000	8

The charge that a Republican victory would destroy the Union was more effective. Buchanan set the tone in his instructions to Democratic Party leaders: "The Black Republicans must be . . . boldly assailed as disunionists, and the charge must be re-iterated again and again." It was. And southerners helped the cause by threatening to secede if Frémont won. Fears of disruption caused many conservative ex-Whigs in the North to support Buchanan. Buchanan carried Pennsylvania, New Jersey, Indiana, Illinois, and California and won the presidency.

THE DRED SCOTT CASE

The South took the offensive at the very outset of the Buchanan administration. Its instrument was the Supreme Court, which had a majority of five justices from slave states led by Chief Justice Roger B. Taney of Maryland. Those justices saw the Dred Scott case as an opportunity to settle once and for all the question of slavery in the territories.

Dred Scott was a slave whose owner, an army surgeon, had kept him at military posts in Illinois and in Wisconsin Territory for several years before taking him back to Missouri. After the owner's death, Scott sued for his freedom on the grounds of his prolonged stay in Wisconsin Territory, where slavery had been outlawed by the Missouri Compromise. The case worked its way up from Missouri courts through a federal circuit court to the U.S. Supreme Court.

The southern Supreme Court justices decided to declare that the Missouri Compromise ban on slavery in the territories was unconstitutional. But to avoid the appearance of a purely sectional decision, they sought the concurrence of a northern Democratic justice, Robert Grier of Pennsylvania. Having obtained Justice Grier's concurrence, Chief Justice Taney issued the Court's ruling stating that Congress did not have the power to keep slavery out of a territory, because slaves were property and the Constitution protects the right of property. Five other justices wrote concurring opinions. The two non-Democratic northern justices dissented vigorously. They cited the provision of the Constitution giving Congress power to make "all needful rules and regulations" for the territories.

Modern scholars agree with the dissenters. But in 1857 Taney had a majority and his ruling became law. Modern scholars have also demonstrated that Taney was motivated by his passionate commitment "to southern life and values" and by his determination to stop "northern aggression" by cutting the ground from under the hated Republicans.

Republicans denounced Taney's "jesuitical decision" as based on "gross perversion" of the Constitution. Several Republican state legislatures resolved that the ruling was "not binding in law and conscience." They probably did not mean to advocate civil disobedience. But they did look forward to the election of a Republican president who could "reconstitute" the Court and secure a reversal of the decision.

THE LECOMPTON CONSTITUTION

Instead of settling the slavery controversy, the Dred Scott decision intensified it. Meanwhile, the proslavery forces, having won legalization of slavery in the territories, moved to ensure that it would remain legal when Kansas became a state. That required deft maneuvering, because legitimate antislavery settlers outnumbered proslavery settlers by more than 2 to 1. In 1857 the proslavery legislature called for a constitutional convention at Lecompton to prepare Kansas for statehood. But because the election for delegates was rigged, Free Soil voters refused to participate in it. One-fifth of the registered voters thereupon elected convention delegates, who met at Lecompton and wrote a state constitution that made slavery legal.

Then a nagging problem arose. Buchanan had promised that the Lecompton constitution would be presented to the voters in a fair referendum. The problem was how to get the proslavery constitution approved given the antislavery majority of voters. The convention came up with an ingenious solution. Instead of a referendum on the whole constitution, it would allow the voters to choose between a constitution "with slavery" and one "with no slavery." But there was a catch. The constitution "with no slavery" guaranteed slaveowners' "inviolable" right of property in the 200 slaves already in Kansas and their progeny.

Free-state voters branded the referendum a farce and boycotted it. One-quarter of the eligible voters went to the polls in December 1857 and approved the constitution "with slavery." Meanwhile, in a fair election policed by federal troops, the antislavery party won control of the new territorial legislature and promptly submitted both constitutions to a referendum that was boycotted by proslavery voters. This time, 70 percent of the eligible voters went to the polls and overwhelmingly rejected both constitutions.

Which referendum would the federal government recognize? That question proved even more divisive than the Kansas-Nebraska debate four years earlier. President Buchanan faced a dilemma. He had promised a fair referendum. But southerners, who dominated both the Democratic Party and the administration, threatened secession if Kansas was not admitted to statehood under the Lecompton constitution "with slavery." Buchanan caved in. He sent the Lecompton constitution to Congress with a message recommending statehood.

What would Stephen Douglas do? If he endorsed the Lecompton constitution, he would undoubtedly be defeated in his bid for reelection to the Senate in 1858. And he regarded the Lecompton constitution as a travesty. So he broke with the administration on the issue. He could not vote to "force this constitution down the throats of the people of Kansas," he told the Senate, "in opposition to their wishes and in violation of our pledges."

The fight in Congress was long and bitter. The South and the administration had the votes they needed in the Senate and won handily there. But the Democratic majority in the House was so small that the defection of even a few northern Democrats would defeat the Lecompton constitution. At one point a wild fistfight erupted between Republicans and southern Democrats. "There were some fifty middle-aged and elderly gentlemen pitching into each other like so many Tipperary savages," wrote a bemused reporter.

When the vote was finally taken, two dozen northern Democrats defected, providing enough votes to defeat Lecompton. Both sides then accepted a compromise proposal to resubmit the constitution to Kansas voters, who decisively rejected it. This meant that while Kansas would not come in as a slave state, neither would it come in as a free state for some time yet. Nevertheless, the Lecompton debate had split the Democratic Party, leaving a legacy of undying enmity between southerners and Douglas. The election of a Republican president in 1860 was now all but assured.

The Economy in the 1850s

Beginning in the mid-1840s, the American economy enjoyed a dozen years of unprecedented growth and prosperity. Railroad construction provided employment for a large number of immigrants and spurred growth in industries that produced rails, rolling stock, and other railroad equipment. Most of the railroad construction took place in the Old Northwest, linking the region more closely to the Northeast and continuing the reorientation of transportation networks from a north-south river pattern to an east-west canal and rail pattern. This reinforced the effect of slavery in creating a self-conscious "North" and "South."

Although the Old Northwest remained predominantly agricultural, the rapid expansion of railroads there laid the basis for its industrialization. During the 1850s the growth rate of industrial output in the free states west of Pennsylvania was twice as great as the rate in the Northeast and three times as great as the rate in the South. In 1847 two companies that contributed to the rapid growth of agriculture during this era built their plants in Illinois: the McCormick reaper works at Chicago and the John Deere steel-plow works at Moline.

According to almost every statistical index available from that period, the rate of economic expansion considerably outstripped even the prodigious rate of population increase. While the number of Americans grew by 44 percent during these 12 years (1844–1856), the value of both exports and imports increased by 200 percent; the tonnage of coal mined by 270 percent; the amount of banking capital, industrial capital, and industrial output by approximately 100 percent; the value of farmland by 100 percent; and the amount of cotton, wheat, and corn harvested by about 70 percent. These advances meant a significant increase of per capita production and income—though the distance between rich and poor was widening, a phenomenon that has characterized all capitalist economies during stages of rapid industrial growth.

By the later 1850s the United States had forged ahead of most other countries to become the second-leading industrial producer in the world, behind only Britain. But the country was still in the early stages of industrial development, with the processing of agricultural products and raw materials still playing the dominant role. By 1860, the four leading industries, measured by value added in manufacturing, were cotton textiles, lumber products, boots and shoes, and flour milling.

"The American System of Manufactures"

The United States had pioneered in one crucial feature of modern industry: the mass production of interchangeable parts. High wages and a shortage of the skilled craftsmen who had traditionally fashioned guns, furniture, locks, watches, and other products had compelled American entrepreneurs to seek alternative methods. The "Yankee ingenuity" that was already world-famous came up with an answer: special-purpose machine tools that would cut and shape an endless number of parts that could be fitted together with other similarly produced parts to make whole guns, locks, clocks, and sewing machines in mass quantities. These products were less elegant and less durable than products made by skilled craftsmen. But they were also less expensive and thus more widely available to the "middling classes."

Such American-made products were the hit of the first World's Fair, the Crystal Palace Exhibition at London in 1851. British manufacturers were so impressed by Yankee techniques, which they dubbed "the American system of manufactures," that they sent two commissions to the United States to study them. The British firearms industry invited Samuel Colt of Connecticut, inventor of the famous six-shooting revolver, to set up a factory in England stocked with machinery from Connecticut. In testimony before a parliamentary committee in 1854, Colt summed up the American system of manufactures in a single sentence: "There is nothing that cannot be produced by machinery," thus expressing a philosophy that would enable the United States to surpass Britain as the leading industrial nation by 1880.

The British industrial commissions cited the American educational system as an important reason for the country's technological proficiency. By contrast, the British workman, trained by long apprenticeship "in the trade," rather than in school, lacked "the ductility of mind and the readiness of apprehension for a new thing" and was therefore "unwilling to change the methods he has been used to."

Whether this British commission was right in its belief that American schooling encouraged the "adaptative versatility" of Yankee workers, it was certainly true that public education and literacy were more widespread in the United States than in Europe. Almost 95 percent of adults in the free states were literate in 1860, compared with 65 percent in England and 55 percent in France. Nearly all children received a few years of schooling, and most completed at least six or seven years. This improvement in education coincided with the feminization of the teaching profession, which opened up new career opportunities for young women. By the 1850s nearly three-quarters of the public school teachers in New England were women (who worked for lower salaries than male teachers).

THE SOUTHERN ECONOMY

In contrast to the North, where only 6 percent of the population could not read and write, nearly 20 percent of the free population and 90 percent of the slaves in the South were illiterate. This was one of several differences between North and South that antislavery people pointed to as evidence of the backward, repressive, and pernicious nature of a slave society.

Still, the South shared in the economy's rapid growth following recovery from the depression of 1837–1843. Cotton prices and production both doubled between 1845 and 1855. Similar increases in price and output emerged in tobacco and sugar. The price of slaves also doubled during this decade. Southern crops provided three-fifths of all U.S. exports, with cotton alone supplying more than half.

But a growing number of southerners deplored the fact that the "colonial" economy of the South was so dependent on the export of agricultural products and the import of manufactured goods. The ships that carried southern cotton were owned by northern or British firms; financial and commercial services were provided mostly by Yankees or Englishmen. Around 1850, many southerners began calling for economic independence from the North. How could they obtain their "rights," they asked, if they were "financially more enslaved

THE COUNTRY SCHOOL   This famous painting by Winslow Homer portrays the typical one-room rural schoolhouse in which millions of American children learned the three R's in the 19th century. By the 1850s, elementary schoolteaching was a profession increasingly dominated by women, an important change from earlier generations.

than our negroes?" "Our slaves are clothed with Northern manufactured goods and work with Northern hoes, ploughs, and other implements," declared a southern newspaper. "The slaveholder dresses in Northern goods. . . . In Northern vessels his products are carried to market."

We must "throw off this humiliating dependence," declared James D. B. De Bow, the young champion of economic diversification in the South. In 1846 De Bow had founded a periodical, *De Bow's Review*. Proclaiming on its cover that "Commerce is King," the *Review* set out to make this slogan a southern reality. De Bow took the lead in organizing annual "commercial conventions" that met in various southern cities during the 1850s. In its early years, this movement encouraged southerners to invest in shipping lines, railroads, textile mills, and other enterprises.

Economic diversification in the South did make headway during the 1850s. The slave states quadrupled their railroad mileage, increased the amount of capital invested in manufacturing by 77 percent, and boosted their output of cotton textiles by 44 percent. But like Alice in Wonderland, the faster the South ran, the farther behind it seemed to fall—for northern industry was growing even faster. In 1860 the North had five times more industrial output per capita than the South, and it had three times the railroad capital and mileage per capita and per thousand square miles. Southerners had a larger percentage of their capital invested in land and slaves in 1860 than they had had 10 years earlier. By contrast, the northern economy developed a strong manufacturing and commercial sector whose combined labor force almost equaled that of agriculture by 1860.

KING COTTON

A good many southerners preferred to keep it that way. "That the North does our trading and manufacturing mostly is true," wrote an Alabama planter in 1858. "We are willing that they should. Ours is an agricultural people, and God grant that we may continue so." In the later 1850s King Cotton reasserted its primacy over King Commerce as cotton output *and* prices continued to rise, suffusing the South in a glow of prosperity. In a speech that became famous, James Hammond of South Carolina told his fellow senators in 1858 that "the slaveholding South is now the controlling power of the world. . . . No power on earth dares to make war on cotton. Cotton *is* king."

Even the commercial conventions in the South seem to have embraced this gospel. In 1854 they merged with a parallel series of planters' conventions. By the later 1850s, one of the main goals of these conventions was to reopen the African slave trade, prohibited by law since 1808. But many southerners rejected that goal, partly on moral and partly on economic grounds. Older slave states like Virginia, which profited from the sale of slaves to the booming cotton frontier of the Deep South, objected to any goal that would lower the price of their largest export.

Nowhere in the South, said defenders of slavery, did one see such "scenes of beggary, squalid poverty, and wretchedness" as one could find in any northern city. Black slaves, they insisted, enjoyed a higher standard of living than white "wage slaves" in northern factories. Black slaves never suffered from unemployment or wage cuts; they received free medical care; they were taken care of in old age.

This argument reached its fullest development in the writings of George Fitzhugh, a Virginia farmer-lawyer whose newspaper articles were gathered into two books published in 1854 and 1857, *Sociology for the South* and *Cannibals All*. Free-labor capitalism, said Fitzhugh, was a competition in which the strong exploited and starved the weak. Slavery, by contrast, was a paternal institution that guaranteed protection of the workers. "Capital exercises a more perfect compulsion over free laborers than human masters over slaves," wrote Fitzhugh, "for free laborers must at all times work or starve, and slaves are supported whether they work or not. . . . What a glorious thing is slavery, when want, misfortune, old age, debility, and sickness overtake [the slave]."

LABOR CONDITIONS IN THE NORTH

Some northern labor leaders did complain that the "slavery" of the wage system gave "bosses" control over the hours, conditions, and compensation of labor. But the use of this wage-slavery theme declined during the prosperous 1850s. And there is no evidence that a northern workingman ever offered to change places with a southern slave. Average per capita income was about 40 percent higher in the North than in the South. Although that average masked large disparities, those disparities were no greater, and probably less, in the North than in the South.

To be sure, substantial numbers of recent immigrants, day laborers, and young single women in large northern cities lived on the edge of poverty—or slipped over the edge. Many women seamstresses, shoe binders, milliners, and the like, who worked 60 or 70 hours a week in the outwork system, earned less than a living wage. The widespread adoption of the newly invented sewing machine in the 1850s did nothing to make life easier for seamstresses; it only lowered their per-unit piecework wages. Many urban working-class families could not have

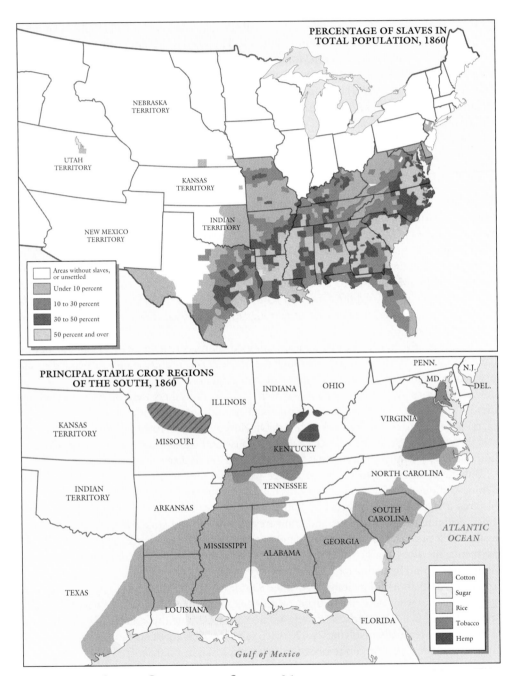

PERCENTAGE OF SLAVES IN TOTAL POPULATION, 1860

Areas without slaves, or unsettled

Under 10 percent

10 to 30 percent

30 to 50 percent

50 percent and over

PRINCIPAL STAPLE CROP REGIONS OF THE SOUTH, 1860

Cotton

Sugar

Rice

Tobacco

Hemp

Gulf of Mexico

ATLANTIC OCEAN

SLAVERY AND STAPLE CROPS IN THE SOUTH, 1860

survived on the wages of an unskilled or semiskilled father. The mother had to take in laundry, boarders, or outwork, and one or more children had to work. Much employment was seasonal or intermittent. The poverty, overcrowding, and disease in the tenement districts of large cities seemed to lend substance to proslavery claims that slaves were better off.

But they were not. Wages and opportunities for workers were greater in the North than anywhere else in the world, including the South. That was why 4 million immigrants came to the United States from 1845 to 1860 and why seven-eighths of them settled in free states. It was also why twice as many white residents of slave states migrated to free states as vice versa.

THE PANIC OF 1857

The relative prosperity of the North was interrupted by a financial panic that stemmed partly from the international economy and partly from domestic overexpansion. When the Crimean War in Europe (1854–1856) cut off Russian grain from the European market, U.S. exports mushroomed to meet the deficiency. Then they slumped in 1857 after the war ended. The sharp rise in interest rates in Britain and France, caused by the war, then spread to U.S. financial markets in 1857 and dried up sources of credit. Meanwhile, the economic boom of the preceding years had caused the American economy to overheat: Land prices had soared; railroads had built beyond the capacity of earnings to service their debts; banks had made too many risky loans.

This speculative house of cards came crashing down in September 1857. The failure of one banking house sent a wave of panic through the financial community. Banks suspended specie payments, businesses failed, railroads went bankrupt, construction halted, factories shut down. Hundreds of thousands of workers were laid off, and others went on part-time schedules or took wage cuts. Unemployed workers in several northern cities marched in parades carrying banners demanding work or bread. On November 10 a crowd gathered in Wall Street and threatened to break into the U.S. customs house and subtreasury vaults, where $20 million was stored. Soldiers and marines had to be called out to disperse the mob.

But the country got through the winter with little violence. No one was killed in the demonstrations. Charity and public works helped tide the poor over the winter, and the panic inspired a vigorous religious revival. Spontaneous prayer meetings arose in many northern cities, bringing together bankers and seamstresses, brokers and streetsweepers. Perhaps God heeded their prayers; the depression did not last long. By early 1858 banks had resumed specie payments; the stock market rebounded in the spring; factories reopened; railroad construction resumed; and by the spring of 1859 recovery was complete.

The modest labor-union activities of the 1850s revived after the depression, as workers in some industries went on strike to bring wages back to pre-panic levels. In February 1860 the shoemakers of Lynn, Massachusetts, began a strike that became the largest in U.S. history up to that time, eventually involving 20,000 workers in the New England shoe industry. Nevertheless, less than 1 percent of the labor force was unionized in 1860.

SECTIONALISM AND THE PANIC

The Panic of 1857 probably intensified sectional hostility. The South largely escaped the depression. After a brief dip, cotton and tobacco prices returned to high levels and production continued to increase: The cotton crop set new records in 1858 and 1859. Southern boasts took on added bravado. "Who can doubt, that has looked at recent events, that cotton is supreme?" asked Senator James Hammond in March 1858. "When thousands of the strongest commercial houses in the world were coming down," he told Yankees, "what brought you up? . . . We have poured in upon you one million six hundred thousand bales of cotton. . . . We have sold it for $65,000,000, and saved you."

Northerners were not grateful for their rescue. In fact, many blamed southern congressmen for blocking measures, especially higher tariffs, that would have eased the effects of the depression. They directed their arguments to workers as much as to manufacturers. "We demand that American laborers shall be protected against the pauper labor of Europe," they declared. Tariff revision would "give employment to thousands of mechanics, artisans, laborers, who have languished for months in unwilling idleness." In each session of Congress from 1858 through 1860, however, a combination of southerners and about half of the northern Democrats blocked Republican efforts to raise tariffs.

Three other measures acquired additional significance after the Panic of 1857. Republicans supported each of them as a means to promote economic health and to aid farmers and workers. But southerners perceived all of them as aimed at helping *northern* farmers and workers, and used their power to defeat them. One was a homestead act to grant 160 acres of public land to each farmer who settled and worked the land. Southern senators defeated this bill after the House had passed it in 1859. The following year both houses passed it, but Buchanan vetoed it and southern senators blocked an effort to pass it over his veto. A similar fate befell bills for land grants to a transcontinental railroad and for building agricultural and mechanical colleges to educate farmers and workers.

The Free-Labor Ideology

By the later 1850s the Republican antislavery argument had become a finely honed philosophy that historians have labeled a "free-labor ideology." It held that all work in a free society was honorable, but that slavery degraded the calling of manual labor by equating it with bondage. Slaves worked inefficiently, by compulsion; free men were stimulated to work efficiently by the desire to get ahead. Social mobility was central to the free-labor ideology. Free workers who practiced the virtues of industry, thrift, self-discipline, and sobriety could move up the ladder of success. "I am not ashamed to confess," Abraham Lincoln told a working-class audience in 1860, "that twenty-five years ago I was a hired laborer, mauling rails, at work on a flat-boat—just what might happen to any poor man's son!" But in the free states, said Lincoln, a man knows that "he can better his condition. . . . The *free* labor system opens the way for all—gives hope to all, and energy, and progress, and improvement of condition to all."

Lincoln drew too rosy a picture of northern *reality*, for large numbers of wage laborers in the North had little hope of advancing beyond that status. Still, he expressed a *belief* that was widely shared. "There is not a working boy of average ability in the New England states, at least," observed a visiting British industrialist in 1854, "who has not an idea of some mechanical invention or improvement in manufactures, by which, in good time, he hopes to better his condition." Americans could point to numerous examples of men who had achieved dramatic upward mobility. Belief in this "American dream" was most strongly held by Protestant farmers, skilled workers, and white-collar workers who had some real hope of getting ahead. These men tended to support the Republican Party and its goal of excluding slavery from the territories.

For slavery was the antithesis of upward mobility. Slaves could not hope to move up the ladder of success, nor could free men who lived in a society where they had to compete with slave labor. "Slavery withers and blights all it touches," insisted the Republicans. "It is a curse upon the poor, free, laboring white men." In the United States, social mobility often depended on geographic mobility. The main reason so many families moved into new territories was to get a new start, get ahead. But if slavery goes into the territories, "the free labor of all the states will not," declared a Republican editor. "If the free labor of the states goes there, the slave labor of the southern states will not, and in a few years the country will teem with an active and energetic population."

Southerners contended that free labor was prone to unrest and strikes. Of course it was, said Lincoln in a speech to a New England audience during the shoemakers' strike of 1860. "*I am glad to see that a system prevails in New England under which laborers CAN strike when they want to* (Cheers). . . . I *like* the system which lets a man quit when he wants to, and wish it might prevail everywhere (Tremendous applause)." Strikes were one of the ways in which free workers could try to improve their prospects. "I want every man," said Lincoln, "to have the chance— and I believe a black man is entitled to it—in which he can better his condition." That was why Republicans were determined to contain the expansion of slavery, for if the South got its way in the territories "free labor that *can* strike will give way to slave labor that *cannot!*"

THE IMPENDING CRISIS

From the South came a maverick voice that echoed the Republicans. Living in up-country North Carolina, a region of small farms and few slaves, Hinton Rowan Helper had brooded for years over slavery's retarding influence on southern development. In 1857, in a book entitled *The Impending Crisis of the South*, he pictured a South mired in economic backwardness, widespread illiteracy, poverty for the masses, and great wealth for the elite. He contrasted this dismal situation with the bustling, prosperous northern economy and its near-universal literacy, neat farms, and progressive institutions. "Slavery lies at the root of all the shame, poverty, ignorance, tyranny, and imbecility of the South," he wrote. Slavery monopolized the best land, degraded all labor to the level of bond labor, denied schools to the poor, and impoverished all but "the lords of the lash." The remedy? Non-slaveholding whites must organize and use their votes to overthrow "this entire system of oligarchical despotism."

The Impending Crisis was virtually banned in the South, and few southern whites read it. But the book made a huge impact in the North. The Republican Party subsidized an abridged edition and distributed thousands of copies as campaign documents. During the late 1850s, a war of books (Helper's *Impending Crisis* versus Fitzhugh's *Cannibals All*) exacerbated sectional tensions.

SOUTHERN NON-SLAVEHOLDERS

How accurate was Helper's portrayal of southern poor whites degraded by slavery and ready to revolt against it? The touchy response of many southern leaders suggested that the planters felt uneasy about that question. After all, slaveholding families constituted less than one-third of the white population in slave states, and the proportion was declining as the price of slaves continued to rise. Open hostility to the planters' domination of society and politics was evident in the mountainous and up-country regions of the South. These would become areas of Unionist sentiment during the Civil War and of Republican strength after it.

But Helper exaggerated the disaffection of most non-slaveholders in the South. Three bonds held them to the system: kinship, economic interest, and race. In the Piedmont and the low-country regions of the South, nearly half of the whites belonged to slaveholding families. Many of the rest were cousins or nephews or in-laws of slaveholders in the South's extensive and tightly knit kinship network. Moreover, many young, ambitious non-slaveholders hoped to buy slaves eventually. Some of them *rented* slaves. And because slaves could be made to do menial, unskilled labor, white workers monopolized the more skilled, higher-paying jobs.

Most important, even if they did not own slaves, white people owned the most important asset of all—a white skin. Race was a more important social distinction than class. The southern legal system, politics, and social ideology were based on the concept of "*herrenvolk* democracy" (the equality of all who belonged to the "master race"). Subordination was the Negro's fate, and slavery was the best means of subordination. Emancipation would loose a flood of free blacks on society and would undermine the foundations of white supremacy. Thus, many of the "poor whites" in the South and immigrant workers or poorer farmers in the North supported slavery.

The *herrenvolk* theme permeated proslavery rhetoric. "With us," said John C. Calhoun in 1848, "the two great divisions of society are not the rich and the poor, but white and black; and all the former, the poor as well as the rich, belong to the upper class, and are respected and treated as equals." True freedom as Americans understood it required equality of rights and status (though not of wealth or income). Slavery ensured that freedom for all whites. "Break down slavery," said a Virginia congressman, "and you would with the same blow destroy the great Democratic principle of equality among men."

THE LINCOLN-DOUGLAS DEBATES

Abraham Lincoln believed the opposite. For him, slavery and freedom were incompatible. This became the central theme of a memorable series of debates between Lincoln and Douglas in 1858.

The debates were arranged after Lincoln was nominated to oppose Douglas's reelection to the Senate. State legislatures elected U.S. senators at that time, so the campaign was technically for the election of the Illinois legislature. But the real issue was the senatorship, and Douglas's prominence gave the contest national significance. Lincoln launched his bid with one of his most notable speeches. "A house divided against itself cannot stand," he said. "I believe this government cannot endure, permanently half *slave* and half *free*. . . . It will become *all* one thing, or *all* the other." What, asked Lincoln, would prevent the Supreme Court from legalizing slavery in free states? (A case based on this question was then before the New York courts.) Advocates of slavery were trying to "push it forward, till it shall become lawful in *all* the States." But Republicans intended to keep slavery out of the territories, thus stopping its growth and placing it "where the public mind shall rest in the belief that it is in the course of ultimate extinction."

In response Douglas asked: Why could the country not continue to exist half slave and half free as it had for 70 years? Lincoln's talk about the "ultimate extinction" of slavery would provoke the South to secession. Douglas professed himself no friend of slavery—but if people in the southern states or in the territories wanted it, they had the right to have it. Lincoln's policy would not only free the slaves but would grant them equality. "Are you in favor of conferring upon the negro the rights and privileges of citizenship?" Douglas asked. "Do you desire to strike out of our State Constitution that clause which keeps slaves and free negroes out of the State . . . in order that when Missouri abolishes slavery she can send one hundred thousand emancipated slaves into Illinois, to become citizens and voters on an equality with yourselves?"

Douglas thus put Lincoln on the defensive. He responded with cautious denials that he favored "social and political equality" of the races. The "ultimate extinction" of slavery might take a century and would require the voluntary cooperation of the South. But come what may, freedom must prevail. Americans must reaffirm the principles of the founding fathers. In Lincoln's words, a black person was "entitled to all the natural rights enumerated in the Declaration of Independence, the right to life, liberty and the pursuit of happiness."

Lincoln deplored Douglas's "care not" attitude toward whether slavery was voted up or down. He *"looks to no end of the institution of slavery,"* said Lincoln. Indeed, by endorsing the Dred Scott decision he looks to its *"perpetuity and nationalization."* Douglas was thus "eradicating the light of reason and liberty in this American people." That was the real issue in the election, Lincoln insisted.

THE FREEPORT DOCTRINE

The popular vote for Republican and Democratic state legislators in Illinois was virtually even in 1858. But because apportionment favored the Democrats, they won a majority of seats and reelected Douglas. But Lincoln was the ultimate victor, for his performance in the debates lifted him from political obscurity, while Douglas further alienated southern Democrats. In the debate at Freeport, Lincoln had asked Douglas how he reconciled his support for the Dred Scott decision with his policy of popular sovereignty, which supposedly gave residents of a territory the power to vote slavery down. Douglas replied that even though the Court had legalized slavery in the territories, the enforcement of that right would depend on the people who lived there. This was a popular answer in the North. But it gave added impetus to southern demands for congressional passage of a federal slave code in territories like Kansas, where the Free Soil majority had by 1859 made slavery virtually null. In the next two sessions of Congress after the 1858 elections, southern Democrats, led by Jefferson Davis, tried to pass a federal slave code for all territories. Douglas and northern Democrats joined with Republicans to defeat it. Consequently, southern hostility toward Douglas mounted as the presidential election of 1860 approached.

The 1859–1860 session of Congress was particularly contentious. Once again a fight over the speakership of the House set the tone. Republicans had won a plurality of House seats, but without a majority they could not elect a Speaker without the support of a few border-state representatives from the American (Know-Nothing) Party. The problem was that the Republican candidate for Speaker was John Sherman, who, along with 67 other congressmen, had signed an endorsement of Hinton Rowan Helper's *The Impending Crisis of the South*. This was a red flag to southerners, who refused to vote for Sherman. Through 43 ballots and two months, the House remained deadlocked.

As usual, southerners threatened to secede if a Black Republican became Speaker. Several of them wanted a shootout on the floor of Congress. We "are willing to fight the question out," wrote one, "and to settle it right there." To avert a crisis, Sherman withdrew his candidacy and the House finally elected a conservative ex-Whig as Speaker on the 44th ballot.

JOHN BROWN　This modern mural of John Brown is full of symbolism. Holding an open Bible, Brown bestrides the earth like an Old Testament prophet while dead Union and Confederate soldiers lie at his feet. Other soldiers clash behind him, slaves struggle to break free, and God's wrath at a sinful nation sends a destructive tornado to earth in the background.

JOHN BROWN AT HARPERS FERRY

Southern tempers were frayed because of what had happened at Harpers Ferry, Virginia, the October before. After his exploits in Kansas, John Brown had disappeared from public view. But he had not been idle. He had worked up a plan to capture the federal arsenal at Harpers Ferry, arm slaves with the muskets he seized there, and move southward along the Appalachian Mountains, attracting more slaves to his army along the way until the "whole accursed system of bondage" collapsed.

Brown recruited five black men and 17 whites, including three of his sons, for this reckless scheme. On the night of October 16, 1859, Brown led his men across the Potomac and occupied the sleeping town of Harpers Ferry without resistance. Few slaves flocked to his banner, but the next day state militia units poured into town and drove Brown's band into the fire-engine house. At dawn on October 18 a company of U.S. marines commanded by Colonel Robert E. Lee and Lieutenant J. E. B. Stuart stormed the engine house and captured the surviving members of Brown's party. Four townsmen, one marine, and 10 of Brown's men (including two of his sons) were killed; not a single slave was liberated.

John Brown's raid lasted 36 hours; its repercussions resounded for years. Though no slaves had risen in revolt, it revived the fears of slave insurrection that were never far beneath the surface of southern consciousness. Exaggerated reports of Brown's network of abolitionist

CHRONOLOGY

1852	Plenary Council of Catholic Church seeks tax support for parochial schools
1853	American Party emerges
1854	Crimean War begins • Congress passes Kansas-Nebraska Act • Republican Party organized • Antebellum immigration reaches peak
1855	Ethnic riots in several cities • "Border Ruffian" legislature in Kansas legalizes slavery
1856	Civil war in Kansas • Preston Brooks canes Charles Sumner on Senate floor • Crimean War ends • Buchanan wins three-way presidential election
1857	Supreme Court issues Dred Scott decision • Lecompton constitution written in Kansas • Congress enacts lower tariff • Panic of 1857 • Helper's *Impending Crisis* published
1858	Kansas voters reject Lecompton constitution • Lincoln-Douglas debates
1859	Congress defeats federal slave code for territories • John Brown's raid at Harpers Ferry
1860	Shoemakers' strike in New England • Buchanan vetoes Homestead Act

supporters confirmed southern suspicions that a widespread northern conspiracy was afoot, determined to destroy their society. Although Republican leaders denied any connection with Brown and disavowed his actions, few southerners believed them.

Many northerners, impressed by Brown's dignified bearing and eloquence during his trial, considered him a martyr to freedom. On the day of Brown's execution, bells tolled in hundreds of northern towns, guns fired salutes, ministers preached sermons of commemoration. "The death of no man in America has ever produced so profound a sensation," commented one northerner. Ralph Waldo Emerson declared that Brown had made "the gallows as glorious as the cross."

This outpouring of northern sympathy for Brown shocked and enraged southerners and weakened the already frayed threads of the Union. "The Harper's Ferry invasion has advanced the cause of disunion more than any event that has happened since the formation of the government," observed a Richmond newspaper. "I have always been a fervid Union man," wrote a North Carolinian, but "the endorsement of the Harper's Ferry outrage . . . has shaken my fidelity."

Something approaching a reign of terror now descended on the South. Every Yankee seemed to be another John Brown; every slave who acted suspiciously seemed to be an insurrectionist. Hundreds of northerners were run out of the South in 1860, some wearing a coat of tar and feathers. Several "incendiaries," both white and black, were lynched. "Defend yourselves!" Senator Robert Toombs cried out to the southern people. "The enemy is at your door . . . meet him at the doorsill, and drive him from the temple of liberty, or pull down its pillars and involve him in a common ruin."

CONCLUSION

Few decades in American history witnessed a greater disjunction between economic well-being and political upheaval than the 1850s. Despite the recession following the Panic of 1857, the total output of the American economy grew by 62 percent during the decade. Railroad mileage more than tripled, value added by manufacturing nearly doubled, and gross farm product grew by 40 percent.

Yet a profound malaise gripped the country. Riots between immigrants and nativists in the mid-1850s left more than 50 people dead. Fighting in Kansas between proslavery and antislavery forces killed at least 200. A South Carolina congressman bludgeoned a Massachusetts senator to unconsciousness with a heavy cane. Representatives and senators came to congressional sessions armed with weapons as well as with violent words.

The nation proved capable of absorbing the large influx of immigrants. It might also have been able to absorb the huge territorial expansion of the late 1840s had it not been for the reopening of the slavery issue by the Kansas-Nebraska Act of 1854. This legislation, followed by the Dred Scott decision in 1857, seemed to authorize the unlimited expansion of slavery. But within two years of its founding in 1854, the Republican Party emerged as the largest party in the North on a platform of preventing all future expansion of slavery. By 1860 the United States had reached a fateful crossroads. As Lincoln had said, it could not endure permanently half slave and half free. The presidential election of 1860 would decide which road America would take into the future.

15

SECESSION AND CIVIL WAR, 1860–1862

THE ELECTION OF 1860 ∿ THE LOWER SOUTH SECEDES

CHOOSING SIDES ∿ THE BALANCE SHEET OF WAR

NAVIES, THE BLOCKADE, AND FOREIGN RELATIONS

CAMPAIGNS AND BATTLES, 1861–1862

CONFEDERATE COUNTEROFFENSIVES

As the year 1860 began, the Democratic Party was one of the few national institutions left in the country. The Methodists and Baptists had split into Northern and Southern churches in the 1840s over the issue of slavery; the Whig Party and the nativist American Party had been shattered by sectional antagonism in the mid-1850s. Even the Democratic Party, at its national convention in Charleston, South Carolina, in April 1860, split into Northern and Southern camps. This virtually assured the election of a Republican president. Such a prospect aroused deep fears among whites in the South. When Abraham Lincoln was elected president, the lower-South states seceded from the Union. When Lincoln refused to remove U.S. troops from Fort Sumter, South Carolina, the new Confederate States army opened fire on the fort. Lincoln called out the militia to suppress the insurrection. Four more slave states seceded, and the country drifted into a Civil War.

THE ELECTION OF 1860

A hotbed of southern-rights radicalism, Charleston turned out to be the worst possible place for the Democrats to hold their national convention. Sectional confrontations took place inside the convention hall and on the streets. Since 1836 the Democratic Party had required a two-thirds majority of delegates for a presidential nomination, a rule that in effect gave southerners veto power if they voted together. Although Stephen A. Douglas had the backing of a simple majority of the delegates, southern Democrats were determined to deny him the nomination, convinced that they would be unable to control a Douglas administration.

The first test came in the debate on the platform. Southern delegates insisted on a federal slave code for the territories. Douglas could not run on a platform that contained such a plank; and if the party adopted it, Democrats were sure to lose every state in the North. By a slim majority, the convention rejected the plank and reaffirmed the 1856 platform endorsing popular sovereignty. Fifty southern delegates thereupon walked out of the convention. Even after they

WIDE-AWAKE PARADE IN NEW YORK, OCTOBER 5, 1860   The Wide-Awakes were an organization of young Republicans who roused political enthusiasm by marching in huge torchlight parades during the political campaign of 1860. A year later, many of these same men would march down the same streets in army uniforms carrying rifles instead of torches on their way to the front.

left, Douglas could not muster a two-thirds majority, nor could any other candidate. After 57 futile ballots, the convention adjourned to meet in Baltimore six weeks later to try again.

But the party was so badly shattered that it could not be put back together. That pleased some proslavery radicals. The election of a "Black Republican" president, they felt, would provide the shock necessary to mobilize a southern majority for secession. Two of the most prominent secessionists were William L. Yancey and Edmund Ruffin. In 1858, they had founded the League of United Southerners to "fire the Southern heart . . . and at the proper moment, by one organized, concerted action, we can precipitate the Cotton States into a revolution."

In Baltimore an even larger number of delegates from southern states walked out of the convention. They formed the Southern Rights Democratic Party and nominated John C. Breckinridge of Kentucky (the incumbent vice president) for president. When regular Democrats nominated Douglas, the stage was set for what would become a four-party election. A coalition of former Whigs formed the Constitutional Union Party, which nominated John Bell of Tennessee. Bell had no chance of winning; the party's purpose was to exercise a conservative influence on a campaign that threatened to polarize the country.

THE REPUBLICANS NOMINATE LINCOLN

From the moment the Democratic Party broke apart, it became clear that 1860 could be the year when the Republican Party elected its first president. The Republicans could expect no electoral votes from the 15 slave states. But in 1856 they had won all but five northern states, and they needed only two or three of those five to win the presidency. The crucial states were Pennsylvania, Illinois, and Indiana. Douglas might still carry them and throw the presidential election into the House, where anything might happen. Thus the Republicans had to carry at least two of the swing states to win.

The Republicans' leading presidential prospect was William H. Seward of New York, an experienced politician who had served as governor and senator. However, in his long career Seward had made a number of enemies. His antinativist policies had alienated some former members of the American Party, and he had a reputation for radicalism that might drive away voters in the vital swing states.

Several of the delegates, uneasy about that reputation, staged a stop-Seward movement. The candidate who then came to the fore was Abraham Lincoln. Though he too had opposed nativism, he had done so less noisily than Seward. His reputation was that of a more moderate man. He was from one of the lower-North states where the election would be close, and his rise from a poor farm boy and rail-splitter to successful lawyer and political leader perfectly reflected the free-labor theme of social mobility extolled by the Republican Party. By picking up second-choice votes from states that switched from their favorite sons, Lincoln overtook Seward and won the nomination on the third ballot.

The Republican platform appealed to many groups in the North. Its main plank pledged exclusion of slavery from the territories. Other planks called for a higher tariff (especially popular in Pennsylvania), a homestead act (popular in the Northwest), and federal aid for construction of a transcontinental railroad and for improvement of river navigation. This blend of idealism and materialism proved especially attractive to young people; a large majority of first-time voters in the North voted Republican in 1860.

SOUTHERN FEARS

Militant enthusiasm in the North was matched by fear and rage in the South. Few people there could see any difference between Lincoln and Seward. Had not Lincoln branded slavery a moral, social, and political evil? Had he not said that the Declaration of Independence applied to blacks as well as whites? Had he not expressed a hope that excluding slavery from the

VOTING IN THE 1860 ELECTION

	ALL STATES		FREE STATES (18)		SLAVE STATES (15)	
	Popular	*Electoral*	*Popular*	*Electoral*	*Popular*	*Electoral*
Lincoln	1,864,735	180	1,838,347	180	26,388	0
Opposition to Lincoln	2,821,157	123	1,572,637	3	1,248,520	120
"Fusion" Tickets	595,846	—	580,426	—	15,420	—
Douglas	979,425	12	815,857	3	163,568	9
Breckinridge	669,472	72	99,381	0	570,091	72
Bell	576,414	39	76,973	0	499,441	39

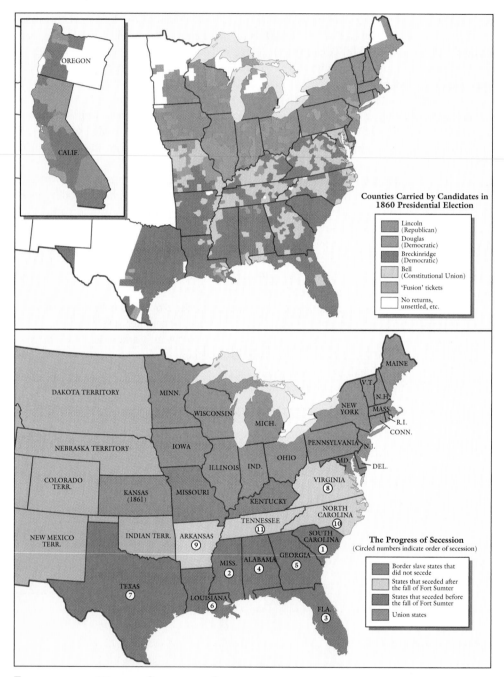

**Counties Carried by Candidates in
1860 Presidential Election**

- Lincoln
  (Republican)
- Douglas
  (Democratic)
- Breckinridge
  (Democratic)
- Bell
  (Constitutional Union)
- 'Fusion' tickets
- No returns,
  unsettled, etc.

The Progress of Secession
(Circled numbers indicate order of secession)

- Border slave states that
  did not secede
- States that seceded after
  the fall of Fort Sumter
- States that seceded before
  the fall of Fort Sumter
- Union states

ELECTION OF 1860 AND SOUTHERN SECESSION

territories would put it on the road to ultimate extinction? To southerners, the Republican pledge not to interfere with slavery in the states was meaningless.

A Republican victory in the presidential election would put an end to the South's control of its own destiny. Even southern moderates warned that the South could not remain in the Union if Lincoln won. "This Government and Black Republicanism cannot live together," said one. What about the three-quarters of southern whites who did not belong to slaveholding families? Lincoln's election, warned an Alabama secessionist, would show that "the North [means] to free the negroes and force amalgamation between them and the children of the poor men of the South."

Most whites in the South voted for Breckinridge, who carried 11 slave states. Bell won the upper-South states of Virginia, Kentucky, and Tennessee. Missouri went to Douglas—the only state he carried, though he came in second in the popular vote. While Lincoln received less than 40 percent of the popular vote, he won every free state and swept the presidency by a substantial margin in the electoral college.

THE LOWER SOUTH SECEDES

Lincoln's victory provided the shock that southern fire-eaters had craved. Seven states seceded. According to the theory of secession, when each state ratified the Constitution and joined the Union, it authorized the national government to act as its agent in the exercise of certain functions of sovereignty—but the states had never given away their fundamental underlying sovereignty itself. Any state, then, by the act of its own convention, could withdraw from its "compact" with the other states and reassert its individual sovereignty.

Many conservatives and former Whigs, including Alexander H. Stephens of Georgia, shrank from the drastic step of secession. Some state convention delegates tried to delay matters with vague proposals for "cooperation" among all southern states, or even with proposals to wait until after Lincoln's inauguration to see what course he would pursue. But those minority factions were overridden by those who favored immediate secession. One after another the conventions voted to take their states out of the Union: South Carolina on December 20, 1860, Mississippi on January 9, 1861, Florida on the 10th, Alabama on the 11th, Georgia on the 19th, Louisiana on the 26th, and Texas on February 1. Delegates from the seven seceding states met in Montgomery, Alabama, in February to create a new nation to be called the Confederate States of America.

NORTHERNERS AFFIRM THE UNION

Most people in the North considered secession unconstitutional and treasonable. In his final annual message to Congress, on December 3, 1860, President Buchanan insisted that the Union was not "a mere voluntary association of States, to be dissolved at pleasure by any one of the contracting parties." If secession was consummated, Buchanan warned, it would create a disastrous precedent that would make the United States government "a rope of sand."

European monarchists and conservatives were already expressing smug satisfaction at "the great smashup." They predicted that the United States would ultimately collapse into anarchy and revolution. That was precisely what northerners and even some upper-South Unionists feared. "The doctrine of secession is anarchy," declared a Cincinnati newspaper. "If any minority have the right to break up the Government at pleasure, because they have not had their way, there is an end of all government." Lincoln denied that the states had ever possessed independent sovereignty before becoming part of the United States. Rather, they had been colonies or territories that never would have become part of the United States had they not accepted unconditional sovereignty of the national government. "No State, upon its own mere motion, can lawfully get out of the Union. . . . They can only do so against law, and by revolution."

In that case, answered many southerners, we invoke the right of revolution to justify secession. After all, the United States itself was born of revolution. The secessionists maintained that they were merely following the example of their forefathers in declaring independence from a government that threatened their rights and liberties.

Northerners could scarcely deny the right of revolution. But "the right of revolution, is never a legal right," said Lincoln. "At most, it is but a moral right, when exercised for a morally justifiable cause. When exercised without such a cause revolution is no right, but simply a wicked exercise of physical power." The South, in Lincoln's view, had no morally justifiable cause. For southerners to cast themselves in the mold of 1776 was "a libel upon the whole character and conduct" of the Founding Fathers, said the antislavery poet and journalist William Cullen Bryant. They rebelled "to establish the rights of man . . . and principles of universal liberty," while southerners were rebelling to protect "a domestic despotism. . . . Their motto is not liberty, but slavery."

COMPROMISE PROPOSALS

Most people in the North agreed with Lincoln that secession was a "wicked exercise of physical power." The question was what to do about it. All kinds of compromise proposals came before Congress when it met in December 1860. To sort them out, the Senate and the House each set up a special committee. The Senate committee came up with a package of compromises sponsored by Senator John J. Crittenden of Kentucky. The Crittenden Compromise consisted of a series of proposed constitutional amendments: to guarantee slavery in the states perpetually against federal interference; to prohibit Congress from abolishing slavery in the District of Columbia or on any federal property; to deny Congress the power to interfere with the interstate slave trade; to compensate slaveholders who were prevented from recovering fugitive slaves; and, most important, to protect slavery south of latitude 36°30′ in all territories "now held *or hereafter acquired.*"

In the view of most Republicans, the latter clause might turn the United States into "a great slavebreeding and slavetrading empire." But some conservatives in the party were willing to accept it in the interest of peace and conciliation. Their votes, together with those of Democrats and upper-South Unionists whose states had not seceded, might have gotten the compromise through Congress. But President-elect Lincoln sent word to key Republican senators and congressmen to stand firm against compromise on the territorial issue. "Entertain no proposition for a compromise in regard to the *extension* of slavery," wrote Lincoln.

> Filibustering for all South of us, and making slave states would follow . . . to put us again on the high-road to a slave empire. . . . We have just carried an election on principles fairly stated to the people. Now we are told in advance, the government shall be broken up, unless we surrender to those we have beaten. . . . If we surrender, it is the end of us.

Lincoln's advice was decisive. The Republicans voted against the Crittenden Compromise. Most Republicans, though, went along with a proposal by Virginia for a "peace convention" of all the states to be held in Washington in February 1861. However, the convention came up with nothing better than a modified version of the Crittenden Compromise, which suffered the same fate as the original.

Nothing that happened in Washington would have made any difference to the seven states that had seceded. No compromise could bring them back. "We spit upon every plan to compromise," said one secessionist. No power could "stem the wild torrent of passion that is carrying everything before it," wrote former U.S. Senator Judah P. Benjamin of Louisiana. Secession "is a revolution" that "can no more be checked by human effort . . . than a prairie fire by a gardener's watering pot."

ESTABLISHMENT OF THE CONFEDERACY

While the peace convention deliberated in Washington, attention in the seceded states focused on a convention in Montgomery, Alabama, that drew up a constitution and established a government for the new Confederate States of America. The Confederate constitution contained clauses that guaranteed slavery in both the states and the territories, strengthened the principle of state sovereignty, and prohibited its Congress from granting government aid to internal improvements. It limited the president to a single six-year term. The convention delegates constituted themselves a provisional Congress until regular elections could be held in November 1861. To serve as its provisional president and vice president, the convention elected Jefferson Davis and Alexander Stephens.

Davis and Stephens were two of the ablest men in the South. Davis had commanded a regiment in the Mexican War and had been secretary of war in the Pierce administration. But perhaps the main reason they were elected was to present an image of moderation and respectability to the eight upper-South states that remained in the Union. The Confederacy needed those states—at least some of them—if it was to be a viable nation, especially if war came. Without the upper South, the Confederate states would have less than one-fifth of the population (and barely one-tenth of the free population) and only one-twentieth of the industrial capacity of the Union states.

Confederate leaders appealed to the upper South to join them because of the "common origin, pursuits, tastes, manners and customs" that "bind together in one brotherhood the . . . slaveholding states." The principal bond was slavery. In a speech at Savannah on March 21 aimed in part at the upper South, Vice President Alexander Stephens defined slavery as the "cornerstone" of the Confederacy.

Residents of the upper South were indeed concerned about preserving slavery. But the issue was less salient there. A strong heritage of Unionism competed with the commitment to slavery. Virginia had contributed more men to the pantheon of Founding Fathers than any other state. Tennessee took pride in being the state of Andrew Jackson, famous for his stern warning: "Our Federal Union—It must be preserved." Kentucky was the home of Henry Clay, the "Great Pacificator" who had put together compromises to save the Union on three occasions. These states would not leave the Union without greater cause.

THE FORT SUMTER ISSUE

As each state seceded, it seized the forts, arsenals, and other federal property within its borders. But still in federal hands were two remote forts in the Florida keys, another on an island off

Pensacola, and Fort Moultrie in the Charleston harbor. In December 1860 the self-proclaimed republic of South Carolina demanded that the United States Army evacuate Moultrie. An obsolete fortification, Moultrie was vulnerable to attack by the South Carolina militia. On the day after Christmas 1860 its commander, Major Robert Anderson, moved his men to Fort Sumter, located on an artificial island in the channel leading into Charleston Bay. Sympathetic to the South but loyal to the United States, Anderson hoped that moving the garrison would ease tensions by reducing the possibility of an attack. Instead, it lit a fuse that eventually set off the war.

South Carolina sent a delegation to President Buchanan to negotiate the withdrawal of the federal troops. Buchanan surprised them by saying no. He even tried to reinforce the garrison. On January 9 the unarmed merchant ship *Star of the West,* carrying 200 soldiers for Sumter, tried to enter the bay but was driven away by South Carolina artillery. Matters then settled into an uneasy truce. The Confederate government sent General Pierre G. T. Beauregard to take command of the troops ringing Charleston Bay with their cannons pointed at Fort Sumter, and waited to see what the incoming Lincoln administration would do.

When Abraham Lincoln took the oath of office as president of the *United* States, he knew that his inaugural address would be the most important in American history. On his words would hang the issues of union or disunion, peace or war. His goal was to keep the upper South in the Union while cooling passions in the lower South. In his address, he demonstrated firmness in purpose to preserve the Union, along with forbearance in the means of doing so. He repeated his pledge not "to interfere with the institution of slavery where it exists." He assured the Confederate states that "the government will not assail *you.*" But he also said that he would "hold, occupy, and possess the property, and places belonging to the government," without defining exactly what he meant or how he would do it.

Lincoln hoped to buy time with his inaugural address—time to demonstrate his peaceful intentions and to enable southern Unionists to regain the upper hand. But the day after his inauguration a dispatch from Major Anderson informed him that provisions for the soldiers at Fort Sumter would soon be exhausted. The garrison would have to be either resupplied or evacuated. Any attempt to send in supplies by force would undoubtedly provoke a response from Confederate guns at Charleston. And such an action would undoubtedly divide the North and unite the South, driving at least four more states into the Confederacy. Thus, most of the members of Lincoln's cabinet, along with the Army's General-in-Chief Winfield Scott, advised Lincoln to withdraw the troops from Sumter. But having pledged to "hold, occupy, and possess" national property, could Lincoln afford to abandon that policy during his first month in office?

Lincoln finally hit upon a solution. He decided to send in unarmed ships with supplies but to hold troops and warships outside the harbor with authorization to go into action only if the Confederates used force to stop the supply ships. And he would notify South Carolina officials in advance of his intention. This was a stroke of genius. If Confederate troops fired on the supply ships, the South would stand convicted of starting a war by attacking "a mission of humanity" bringing "food for hungry men." If Davis allowed the supplies to go in peacefully, the U.S. flag would continue to fly over Fort Sumter. The Confederacy would lose face at home and abroad, and southern Unionists would take courage.

Davis did not hesitate. He ordered General Beauregard to compel Sumter's surrender before the supply ships got there. At 4:30 A.M. on April 12, 1861, Confederate guns set off the Civil War by firing on Fort Sumter. After a 33-hour bombardment the burning fort lowered the U.S. flag in surrender.

Choosing Sides

News of the attack triggered an outburst of anger and war fever in the North. "The town is in a wild state of excitement," wrote a Philadelphia diarist. "The American flag is to be seen everywhere. . . . Men are enlisting as fast as possible." Because the tiny United States Army was inadequate to quell the "insurrection," Lincoln called on the states for 75,000 militia. The free states filled their quotas immediately. More than twice as many men volunteered as Lincoln had requested. Before the war was over, more than 2 million men would serve in the Union Army and Navy.

The eight slave states that were still in the Union rejected Lincoln's call for troops. Four of them—Virginia, Arkansas, Tennessee, and North Carolina—soon seceded and joined the Confederacy. As a former Unionist in North Carolina remarked, "The South must go with the South. . . . Blood is thicker than Water." Few found the choice harder to make than Robert E. Lee of Virginia. One of the most promising officers in the United States Army, Lee did not

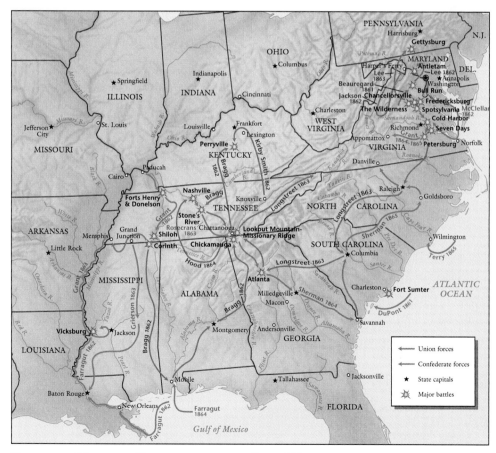

Principal Military Campaigns of the Civil War

believe that southern states had a legal right to secede. However, he felt compelled to resign after the Virginia convention passed an ordinance of secession on April 17. "I must side either with or against my section," Lee told a northern friend. "I cannot raise my hand against my birthplace, my home, my children."

Most southern whites embraced war against the Yankees with more enthusiasm. When news of Sumter's surrender reached Richmond, a huge crowd poured into the state capitol square and ran up the Confederate flag. "I never in all my life witnessed such excitement," wrote a participant. The London *Times* correspondent described crowds in North Carolina with "flushed faces, wild eyes, screaming mouths." No one in those cheering crowds could know that before the war ended at least 260,000 Confederate soldiers would lose their lives.

THE BORDER STATES

Except for Delaware, which remained firmly in the Union, the slave states that bordered free states were sharply divided by the outbreak of war. Leaders in these states talked of "neutrality," but they were to be denied that luxury—Maryland and Missouri immediately, and Kentucky in September 1861 when first Confederate and then Union troops crossed its borders.

The first blood was shed in Maryland on April 19 when a mob attacked part of a Massachusetts regiment traveling through Baltimore. The soldiers fired back, leaving 12 Baltimoreans and four soldiers dead. Confederate partisans burned bridges and tore down telegraph wires, cutting Washington off from the North for nearly a week until additional troops from Massachusetts and New York reopened communications and seized key points in Maryland. The troops also arrested many Confederate sympathizers. To prevent Washington from becoming surrounded by enemy territory, federal forces turned Maryland into an occupied state.

The same was true of Missouri. Aggressive action by the Union commander there, Nathaniel Lyon, provoked a showdown between Unionist and pro-Confederate militia that turned into a

SLAVERY AND SECESSION *The higher the proportion of slaves and slaveholders in the population of a southern state, the greater the intensity of secessionist sentiment.*

ORDER OF SECESSION	PERCENTAGE OF POPULATION WHO WERE SLAVES	PERCENTAGE OF WHITE POPULATION IN SLAVEHOLDING FAMILIES
Seven states that seceded December 1860–February 1861 (South Carolina, Mississippi, Florida, Alabama, Georgia, Louisiana, Texas)	47%	38%
Four states that seceded after the firing on Fort Sumter (Virginia, Arkansas, Tennessee, North Carolina)	32	24
Four border slave states remaining in Union (Maryland, Delaware, Kentucky, Missouri)	14	15

riot in St. Louis on May 10 and 11, 1861, in which 36 people were killed. Lyon then led his troops in a summer campaign that drove the Confederate militia into Arkansas. Reinforced by Arkansas regiments, these rebel Missourians invaded their home state and on August 10 defeated Lyon in the bloody battle of Wilson's Creek in the southwest corner of Missouri. The victorious Confederates marched northward all the way to the Missouri River, capturing a Union garrison at Lexington 40 miles east of Kansas City on September 20. By then, Union forces had regrouped and drove the ragged Missouri Confederates back into Arkansas.

From then until the war's end, military power enabled Unionists to maintain political control of Missouri. But continued guerrilla attacks by Confederate "bushwhackers" and counterinsurgency tactics by Unionist "jayhawkers" turned large areas of the state into a no-man's-land of hit-and-run raids, arson, ambush, and murder. During these years, the famous postwar outlaws Jesse and Frank James and Cole and Jim Younger rode with the notorious rebel guerrilla chieftains William Quantrill and "Bloody Bill" Anderson. More than any other state, Missouri suffered from a civil war within the Civil War, and its bitter legacy persisted for generations.

In elections held during the summer and fall of 1861, Unionists gained firm control of the Kentucky and Maryland legislatures. Kentucky Confederates, like those of Missouri, formed a state government in exile. When the Confederate Congress admitted both Kentucky and Missouri to full representation, the Confederate flag acquired its 13 stars. Nevertheless, two-thirds of the white population in the four border slave states favored the Union—though some of that support was undoubtedly induced by the presence of Union troops.

THE CREATION OF WEST VIRGINIA

The war itself produced a fifth Union border state: West Virginia. Most of the delegates from the portion of Virginia west of the Shenandoah Valley had voted against secession. A region of mountains, small farms, and few slaves, western Virginia was linked more closely to Ohio and Pennsylvania than to the South. Delegates who had opposed Virginia's secession returned home determined to secede themselves—from Virginia. Through a complicated process of conventions and referendums—carried out in the midst of raids and skirmishes—they created the new state of West Virginia, which entered the Union in 1863.

To the south and west of Missouri, civil war raged for control of the Indian Territory (present-day Oklahoma). The Native Americans, who had been resettled there in the generation before the war, chose sides and carried on bloody guerrilla warfare with each other. The more prosperous Indians of the five "civilized tribes" (Cherokees, Creeks, Seminoles, Chickasaws, and Choctaws), many of them of mixed blood and some of them slaveholders, tended to side with the Confederacy. However, aided by white and black Union regiments operating out of Kansas and Missouri, the pro-Union Indians gradually gained control of most of the Indian Territory.

In the meantime, a small army composed mostly of Texans pushed up the Rio Grande valley into New Mexico. In February 1862 they launched a deeper strike to capture Santa Fe. They hoped to push even farther westward and northward to the California and Colorado gold mines, which were helping to finance the Union war effort.

At first the Confederate drive up the Rio Grande went well. The Texans won the battle of Valverde, 100 miles south of Albuquerque, on February 21, 1862. They continued up the valley, occupied Albuquerque and Santa Fe, and pushed on toward Fort Union near Santa Fe. But

Colorado miners who had organized themselves into Union regiments met the Texans in the battle of Glorieta Pass on March 26–28. The battle itself ended in a draw, but a unit of Coloradans destroyed the Confederate wagon train, forcing the Southerners into a disastrous retreat back to Texas. Of the 3,700 who had started out to win the West for the Confederacy, only 2,000 made it back.

THE BALANCE SHEET OF WAR

If one counts three-quarters of the border state population (including free blacks) as pro-Union, the total number of people in Union states in 1861 was 22.5 million, compared with 9 million in the Confederate states. The North's advantage was even greater in military manpower, since the Confederate population total included 3.7 million slaves compared with 300,000 slaves in Union areas. At first, neither side expected to recruit blacks as soldiers. Eventually, the Union did enlist black soldiers and black sailors, but the Confederacy did not do so until the war was virtually over. Altogether, about 2.1 million men fought for the Union and 850,000 for the Confederacy. That was close to half of the North's male population of military age and three-quarters of the comparable Confederate white population. Since the labor force of the South consisted mainly of slaves, the Confederacy was able to enlist a larger proportion of its white population.

In economic resources, the North's superiority was even greater. The Union states possessed nine-tenths of the country's industrial capacity and registered shipping, four-fifths of its bank capital, three-fourths of its railroad mileage and rolling stock, and three-fourths of its taxable wealth. Thus, in a long war that mobilized the total resources of both sides, the North's advantages might prove decisive. But in 1861, few anticipated how long and intense the war would be. Both sides expected a short and victorious conflict. Confederates seemed especially confident. Many Southerners really did believe that one of their own could lick three Yankees.

Although this turned out to be a grievous miscalculation, the South did have some reason to believe that its martial qualities were superior. A higher proportion of southerners than northerners had attended West Point and other military schools, had fought in the Mexican War, or had served as officers in the regular army. As a rural people, southerners were proficient in hunting, riding, and other outdoor skills useful in military operations. Moreover, the South had begun to prepare for war earlier than the North. As each state seceded, it mobilized militia and volunteer military companies. Not until the summer of 1861 would the North's greater manpower begin to make itself felt in the form of a larger army.

STRATEGY AND MORALE

Even when fully mobilized, the North's superior resources did not guarantee success. The Confederacy had come into being in firm control of 750,000 square miles. To win the war, Union forces would have to invade, conquer, and occupy much of that vast territory and destroy its armies. To "win" the war, the Confederacy did not need to invade or conquer the Union or even to destroy its armies; it needed only to hold out long enough to convince Northerners that the cost of victory was too high.

The important factor of morale also seemed to favor the Confederacy. To be sure, Union soldiers fought for powerful symbols: Nation, Flag, Constitution. "We are fighting to maintain the best government on earth" was a common phrase in their letters and diaries. A Chicago newspaper declared that the South had "outraged the Constitution, set at defiance all law, and trampled under foot that flag which has been the glorious and consecrated symbol of American Liberty."

But Confederates, too, fought for Nation, Flag, Constitution, and Liberty—of whites. In addition, they fought to defend their land, homes, and families. An army fighting in defense of its homeland generally has the edge in morale. "We shall have the enormous advantage of fighting on our own territory and for our very existence," wrote a Confederate leader. "All the world over, are not one million of men defending themselves at home against invasion stronger in a mere military point of view, than five millions [invading] a foreign country?"

MOBILIZING FOR WAR

More than four-fifths of the soldiers on both sides were volunteers. In both North and South, patriotic rallies motivated the men of a county or town or city neighborhood to enlist in a company (100 men) organized by leading citizens in that locality. The recruits elected their own company officers (a captain and two lieutenants), who received their commissions from the state governor. A regiment consisted of 10 infantry companies, and each regiment was commanded by a colonel, with a lieutenant colonel and a major as second and third in command—all of them appointed by the governor. Cavalry regiments were organized in a similar manner. Field artillery units were known as "batteries," a grouping of four or six cannon with their caissons and limber chests (two-wheeled, horse-drawn vehicles) to carry ammunition; the full complement of a six-gun battery was 155 men and 72 horses.

Volunteer units received a state designation and number in the order of their completion— the 2nd Massachusetts Volunteer Infantry, the 5th Virginia Cavalry, and so on. In most regiments the men in each company mostly came from the same town or locality. Some Union regiments were composed of men of a particular ethnic group. By the end of the war, the Union Army had raised about 2,000 infantry and cavalry regiments and 700 batteries; the Confederates had organized just under half as many. As the war went on, the original 1,000-man complement of a regiment was whittled down by disease, casualties, desertions, and detachments, so that the average combat strength of a regiment after several months was 500 men or less. The states generally preferred to organize new regiments rather than keep the old ones up to full strength.

These were citizen soldiers, not professionals. They carried peacetime notions of democracy and discipline with them into the army. That is why the men elected their company officers and sometimes their field officers (colonel, lieutenant colonel, and major) as well. Political influence often counted for more than military training in the election and appointment of officers. These civilians in uniform were extremely awkward and unmilitary at first, and some regiments suffered battlefield disasters because of inadequate training, discipline, and leadership. In time, however, these raw recruits became battle-hardened veterans commanded by experienced officers.

As the two sides organized their field armies, both grouped four or more regiments into brigades, and three or more brigades into divisions. By 1862, they began grouping two or more divisions into corps, and two or more corps into armies. Each of these larger units was commanded by a general appointed by the president. Some of these generals turned out to be incompetent. But as the war went on, they too either learned their trade or were weeded out.

THE RICHMOND GRAYS   This photograph depicts a typical volunteer military unit that joined the Confederate army in 1861. Note the determined and confident appearance of these young men. By 1865, one-third of them would be dead and several others maimed for life.

In both the Union and the Confederate armies, the best officers (including generals) commanded from the front, not the rear. Combat casualties were higher among officers than among privates, and highest of all among generals, who were killed in action at a rate 50 percent higher than enlisted men.

WEAPONS AND TACTICS

In Civil War battles, the infantry rifle was the most lethal weapon. Muskets and rifles caused 80 to 90 percent of the combat casualties. From 1862 on, most of these weapons were "rifled"—that is, they had spiral grooves cut in the barrel to impart a spin to the cone-shaped lead bullet, whose base expanded upon firing to "take" the rifling of the barrel. This made it possible to load and fire a muzzle-loading rifle two or three times per minute. The rifle had greater accuracy and at least four times the effective range (400 yards or more) of the old smoothbore musket.

Civil War infantry tactics adjusted only gradually to the greater lethal range and accuracy of the new rifle, however. Close-order assaults against defenders equipped with rifles resulted in enormous casualties. The defensive power of the rifle became even greater when troops began digging into trenches. Massed frontal assaults became almost suicidal. Soldiers and their officers learned the hard way to adopt skirmishing tactics, taking advantage of cover and working around the enemy flank.

LOGISTICS

The Civil War is often called the world's first "modern" war because of the role played by railroads, steam-powered ships, and the telegraph. Railroads and steamboats transported supplies and soldiers with unprecedented speed and efficiency; the telegraph provided instantaneous communication between army headquarters and field commanders. Yet these modern forms of transport and communications were extremely vulnerable. Cavalry raiders and guerrillas could cut telegraph wires, burn railroad bridges, and tear up the tracks. Confederate cavalry became particularly skillful at sundering the supply lines of invading Union armies. The more deeply the Union armies penetrated into the South, the greater the number of men they had to detach to guard bridges, depots, and supply dumps.

Once the campaigning armies had moved away from their railhead or wharfside supply base, they were as dependent on animal-powered transport as earlier armies had been. Union armies required one horse or mule for every two or three men. Thus a large invading Union army of 100,000 men would need about 40,000 draft animals. Confederate armies, operating mostly in friendly territory closer to their bases, needed fewer. The poorly drained dirt roads typical of much of the South turned roads into a morass of mud in wet weather.

These logistical problems did much to offset the industrial supremacy of the North, particularly during the first year of the war. By 1862, though, the North's economy had fully geared up for war. The Union Army was the best-supplied army in history up to that time.

The South created war industries, especially munitions and gunpowder, but its industrial base was inadequate. Particularly troublesome for the Confederacy was its inability to replace rails and rolling stock. Although the South produced plenty of food, the railroads deteriorated to the point where they could not get that food to soldiers or civilians. As the war went into its third and fourth years, the Northern economy grew stronger and the Southern economy grew weaker.

FINANCING THE WAR

One of the greatest defects of the Confederate economy was finance. The Confederate Congress, wary of dampening patriotic ardor, was slow to raise taxes. And because most capital in the South was tied up in land and slaves, little was available for buying war bonds. Therefore, the Confederate Congress authorized a limited issue of treasury notes, to be redeemable in specie (gold or silver) within two years after the end of the war. The first modest issue was followed by many more because the notes declined sharply in value. By early 1863 it took eight dollars to buy what one dollar had bought two years earlier; just before the war's end the Confederate dollar was worth one U.S. cent.

In 1863 the Confederate Congress tried to stem this runaway inflation by passing a comprehensive law that taxed income, consumer purchases, and business transactions and included a "tax in kind" on agricultural products, allowing tax officials to seize 10 percent of a farmer's crops. This tax was extremely unpopular among farmers, many of whom hid their crops and livestock or refused to plant, thereby worsening the Confederacy's food shortages. The tax legislation was too little and too late to remedy the South's fiscal chaos. The Confederate government raised less than 5 percent of its revenue by taxes and less than 40 percent by loans, leaving 60 percent to be created by printing treasury notes (paper money)—a recipe for disaster.

In contrast, the Union government raised 66 percent of its revenue by selling war bonds, 21 percent by taxes, and only 13 percent by printing treasury notes. The Legal Tender Act authorizing these notes—the famous "greenbacks"—was passed in February 1862. Congress had enacted new taxes in 1861 and had authorized the sale of war bonds. But by early 1862 these measures had not yet raised enough revenue to pay for the rapid military buildup. So, to avert a crisis, Congress created the greenbacks. Instead of promising to redeem them in specie at some future date, as the South had done, Congress made them "legal tender"—that is, it required everyone to accept them as real money at face value. The North's economy suffered some inflation during the war, but it was mild compared with that experienced by the Confederacy.

The Union Congress also passed the National Banking Act of 1863. Before the war, the principal form of money had been notes issued by state-chartered banks. After Andrew Jackson's destruction of the Second Bank of the United States (Chapter 12), the number and variety of banknotes had skyrocketed until 7,000 different kinds of state banknotes were circulating in 1860. The National Banking Act of 1863 was an attempt to resurrect the centralized banking system and create a more stable banknote currency, as well as to finance the war. The act authorized the chartering of national banks, which could issue banknotes up to 90 percent of the value of the U.S. bonds they held. This provision created a market for the bonds and, in combination with the greenbacks, replaced the glut of state banknotes with a more uniform national currency.

National banknotes would be an important form of money for the next half-century. They had two defects, however: First, because the number of notes that could be issued was tied to each bank's holdings of U.S. bonds, the volume of currency available was dependent on the amount of federal debt rather than on the economic needs of the country; and second, the banknotes themselves tended to be concentrated in the Northeast, where most of the large national banks were located, leaving the South and West short. The creation of the Federal Reserve System in 1913 (Chapter 21) largely remedied these defects. But it was Civil War legislation that established the principle of a uniform national currency issued and regulated by the federal government.

Navies, the Blockade, and Foreign Relations

To sustain its war effort, the Confederacy needed to import large quantities of material from abroad, particularly from Britain. To shut off these imports, on April 19, 1861, Lincoln proclaimed a blockade of Confederate ports. The task was formidable; the Confederate coastline stretched for 3,500 miles, with two dozen major ports and another 150 bays and coves where cargo could be landed. The United States Navy recalled its ships from distant seas, took old sailing vessels out of mothballs, and bought or chartered merchant ships and armed them. Eventually it placed several hundred warships on blockade duty. But in 1861 the blockade was so thin that nine of every 10 vessels slipped through it on their way to or from Confederate ports.

KING COTTON DIPLOMACY

The Confederacy, however, inadvertently contributed to the blockade's success when it adopted "King Cotton diplomacy." Cotton was vital to the British economy because textiles were at the heart of British industry—and three-fourths of Britain's supply of raw cotton came from the South. If that supply was cut off, Southerners reasoned, British factories would shut down, unemployed workers would starve, and Britain would face the prospect of revolution. Rather than risk such a consequence, people in the South believed that Britain would recognize the Confederacy's independence and then use the powerful British navy to break the blockade.

Southerners were so firmly convinced of cotton's importance to the British economy that they kept the 1861 cotton crop at home rather than try to export it through the blockade. But the strategy backfired. Bumper crops in 1859 and 1860 had piled up a surplus of raw cotton in

CONFEDERATE BLOCKADE RUNNERS IN THE HARBOR AT HAMILTON, BERMUDA Confederate armies were heavily dependent on supplies brought in from abroad on blockade runners, paid for by cotton smuggled out through the Union naval cordon by these same blockade runners. The sleek, narrow-beamed ships with raked masts and smokestacks (which could be telescoped to deck level) pictured in this painting were designed for speed and deception to elude the blockade—a feat successfully accomplished on four-fifths of their voyages during the war.

British warehouses and delayed the anticipated "cotton famine" until 1862. In the end, the South's voluntary embargo of cotton cost them dearly. The Confederacy missed its chance to ship out its cotton and store it abroad, where it could be used to purchase war matériel.

Moreover, the Confederacy's King Cotton diplomacy contradicted its own foreign policy objective: to persuade the British and French governments to refuse to recognize the legality of the blockade. Under international law, a blockade must be "physically effective" to be respected by neutral nations. Confederate diplomats claimed that the Union effort was a mere "paper blockade," yet the dearth of cotton reaching European ports as a result of the South's embargo suggested to British and French diplomats that the blockade was at least partly effective. And indeed, by 1862 it was. Although most blockade runners got through, by 1862 the blockade had reduced the Confederacy's seaborne commerce enough to convince the British government to recognize it as legitimate. The blockade was also squeezing the South's economy. After lifting its cotton embargo in 1862, the Confederacy found it increasingly difficult to export enough cotton through the blockade to pay for the imports it needed.

Confederate foreign policy also failed to win diplomatic recognition by other nations. That recognition would have conferred international legitimacy on the Confederacy and might even have led to treaties of alliance or of foreign aid. The French Emperor Napoleon III expressed sympathy for the Confederacy, as did influential groups in the British Parliament. But Prime Minister Lord Palmerston and Foreign Minister John Russell did not want to recognize the Confederacy while it was engaged in a war it might lose, especially if recognition might jeopardize relations with the United States. The Union foreign policy team of Secretary of State Seward and Minister to England Charles Francis Adams did a superb job. Seward issued blunt warnings against recognizing the Confederacy; Adams softened them with the velvet glove of diplomacy. By 1862 it had become clear that Britain would withhold recognition until the Confederacy had virtually won its independence—but, of course, such recognition would have come too late to help the Confederacy win.

THE *TRENT* AFFAIR

If anything illustrated the frustrations of Confederate diplomacy, it was the "*Trent* Affair." In October 1861 Southern envoys James Mason and John Slidell slipped through the blockade; Mason hoped to represent the Confederacy in London and Slidell in Paris. However, on November 8, Captain Charles Wilkes of the U.S.S. *San Jacinto* stopped the British mail steamer *Trent,* with Mason and Slidell on board, near Cuba. Wilkes arrested the two Southerners and took them to Boston. When the news reached England, the government and the public were outraged by Wilkes's "high-handed" action. Britain demanded an apology and the release of Mason and Slidell. The popular press on both sides of the Atlantic stirred up war fever, but good sense soon prevailed. Britain softened its demands, and the Lincoln administration released Mason and Slidell the day after Christmas 1861, declaring that Captain Wilkes had acted "without instructions."

THE CONFEDERATE NAVY

Lacking the capacity to build a naval force at home, the Confederacy hoped to use British shipyards for the purpose. Through a loophole in the British neutrality law, two fast commerce raiders built in Liverpool made their way into Confederate hands in 1862. Named the

Florida and the *Alabama,* they roamed the seas for the next two years, capturing or sinking Union merchant ships and whalers. The *Alabama* sank 62 merchant vessels plus a Union warship before another warship, the U.S.S. *Kearsarge* sank it off Cherbourg, France, on June 19, 1864. Altogether, Confederate privateers and commerce raiders destroyed or captured 257 Union merchant vessels and drove at least 700 others to foreign registry. But this Confederate achievement, though spectacular, made only a tiny dent in the Union war effort.

The *Monitor* and the *Virginia*

Though plagued by shortages on every hand, the Confederate Navy Department demonstrated great skill at innovation. Southern engineers developed "torpedoes" (mines) that sank or damaged 43 Union warships in southern bays and rivers. Even more innovative (though less successful) was the building of ironclad "rams" to sink the blockade ships. The most famous of these was the C.S.S. *Virginia,* commonly called the *Merrimac* because it was rebuilt from the steam frigate U.S.S. *Merrimack.* Ready for its trial-by-combat on March 8, 1862, the *Virginia* steamed out to attack the blockade squadron at Hampton Roads. It sank one frigate with its iron ram and another with its 11 guns. Union shot and shells bounced off the *Virginia's* armor plate.

Panic seized Washington, but in the nick of time the Union's own ironclad sailed into Hampton Roads and saved the rest of the fleet. This was the U.S.S. *Monitor,* which had been completed just days earlier at the Brooklyn navy yard. Much smaller than the *Virginia,* with two 11-inch guns in a revolving turret (an innovation) set on a deck almost flush with the water, the *Monitor* looked like a "tin can on a shingle." It presented a small target and was capable of concentrating considerable firepower in a given direction with its revolving gun turret. Next day, the *Monitor* fought the *Virginia* in history's first battle between ironclads. It was a draw, but the *Virginia* limped home to Norfolk, never again to menace the Union fleet. Although the Confederacy built other ironclad rams, some never saw action and none achieved the initial success of the *Virginia.* By the war's end, the Union Navy had built or started 58 ships of the *Monitor* class, launching a new age in naval history.

Campaigns and Battles, 1861–1862

Wars can be won only by hard fighting. This was a truth that some leaders on both sides overlooked. One of them was Winfield Scott, General-in-Chief of the United States Army. Scott, a Virginian who had remained loyal to the Union, evolved a military strategy based on his conviction that there were a great many Southerners eager to be won back to the Union. The main elements of his strategy were a naval blockade and a combined Army-Navy expedition to take control of the Mississippi, thus sealing off the Confederacy on all sides. The Northern press ridiculed Scott's strategy as "the Anaconda Plan," after the South American snake that squeezes its prey to death.

The Battle of Bull Run

Most Northerners believed that the South could be overcome only by victory in battle. Virginia emerged as the most likely battleground, especially after the Confederate government moved its capital to Richmond in May 1861. "Forward to Richmond," clamored Northern newspapers. And forward toward Richmond moved a Union army of 35,000 men in July. They got no farther than Bull Run, a sluggish stream 25 miles southwest of Washington, where a Confederate army commanded by Beauregard had been deployed to defend a key rail junction at Manassas.

Another small Confederate army in the Shenandoah Valley under General Joseph E. Johnston had traveled to Manassas by rail to reinforce Beauregard. On July 21 the attacking Federals forded Bull Run and hit the rebels on the left flank, driving them back. By early afternoon, the Federals seemed to be on the verge of victory. But a Virginia brigade commanded by Thomas J. Jackson stood "like a stone wall," earning Jackson the nickname he carried ever after. By mid-afternoon Confederate reinforcements had grouped for a counterattack that drove the exhausted and disorganized Yankees back across Bull Run.

The Battle of Manassas (or Bull Run, as Northerners called it) made a profound impression on both sides. Of the 18,000 soldiers actually engaged on each side, Union casualties (killed, wounded, and captured) were about 2,800 and Confederate casualties 2,000. The victory exhilarated Confederates and confirmed their belief in their martial superiority. It also gave them a morale advantage in the Virginia theater that persisted for two years. And yet, Manassas also bred overconfidence. Some in the South thought the war was won. Northerners, by contrast, were jolted out of their expectations of a short war. Congress authorized the enlistment of up to a million 3-year volunteers. Hundreds of thousands flocked to recruiting offices in the next few months. Lincoln called General George B. McClellan to Washington to organize the new troops into the Army of the Potomac.

An energetic, talented officer only 34 years old, McClellan soon won the nickname "The Young Napoleon." He organized and trained the Army of the Potomac into a large, well-disciplined, and well-equipped fighting force. He was just what the North needed after its dispiriting defeat at Bull Run. When Scott stepped down as general-in-chief on November 1, McClellan took his place.

But as winter approached and McClellan did nothing to advance against the smaller Confederate army whose outposts stood only a few miles from Washington, his failings as a commander began to show. He was afraid to take risks; he never learned the military lesson that no victory can be won without risking defeat. He consistently overestimated the strength of enemy forces facing him and used these faulty estimates as a reason for inaction until he could increase his own force. When criticism of McClellan began to appear in the press, he accused his critics of political motives. Having built a fine fighting machine, he was afraid to start it up for fear it might break. Lincoln removed him from command in November 1862.

NAVAL OPERATIONS

Because of McClellan, no further action occurred in the Virginia theater until the spring of 1862. Meanwhile, the Union Navy won a series of victories over Confederate coastal forts at Hatteras Inlet on the North Carolina coast, Port Royal Sound in South Carolina, and other points along the Atlantic and Gulf coasts. These successes provided new bases from which to expand and tighten the blockade, as well as takeoff points for operations along the southern coast. In February and March 1862, an expeditionary force under General Ambrose Burnside occupied several crucial ports on the North Carolina sounds. Another Union force captured Fort Pulaski at the mouth of the Savannah River.

One of the Union Navy's most impressive achievements was the capture of New Orleans in April 1862. Most Confederate troops in the area had been called up the Mississippi to confront a Union invasion of Tennessee, leaving only some militia, an assortment of steamboats converted into gunboats, and two strong forts flanking the river 70 miles below the city. That was not enough to stop Union naval commander David G. Farragut, a native of Tennessee who had remained loyal to the U.S. Navy in which he had served for half a century. In a daring action on April 24, 1862, Farragut led his fleet upriver past the forts, scattering the Confederate fleet and fending off fire rafts. He lost four ships, but the rest got through and compelled the surrender of New Orleans.

FORT HENRY AND FORT DONELSON

These victories demonstrated the importance of seapower even in a civil war. Even more important were Union victories won by the combined efforts of the army and fleets of river gunboats on the Tennessee and Cumberland rivers, which flow through Tennessee and Kentucky and empty into the Ohio River just before it joins the Mississippi. The unlikely hero of these victories was Ulysses S. Grant, who had resigned from the military in 1854. Rejoining when war broke out, he demonstrated a quiet efficiency and a determined will that won him promotion from Illinois colonel to brigadier general. When Confederate units entered Kentucky in September, Grant moved quickly to occupy the mouths of the Cumberland and Tennessee rivers.

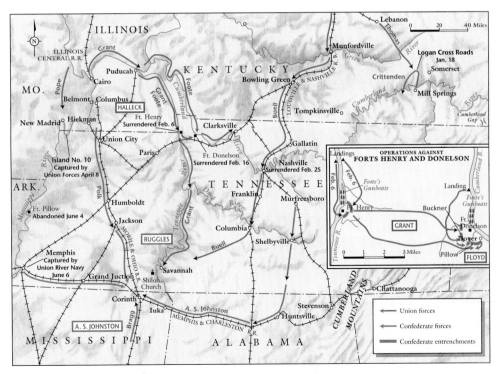

KENTUCKY-TENNESSEE THEATER, WINTER–SPRING 1862

CONFEDERATE DEAD ON THE BATTLEFIELD

The technology of photography was two decades old when the Civil War began. Professional photographers, who considered themselves artists, took thousands of pictures of Civil War scenes and soldiers. The most vivid and powerful of these were photographs of soldiers killed in battle, such as these pictures of Confederate soldiers on the Antietam battlefield, which conveyed "the terrible reality and suffering of war," as a reporter for *The New York Times* put it. But, he added, "there is one side of the picture that the sun did not catch, one phase that has escaped photographic skill. It is the background of widows and orphans, torn from the bosom of their natural protectors by the red remorseless hand of Battle. . . . All of this desolation imagination must paint— broken hearts cannot be photographed."

Military strategists on both sides understood the importance of these navigable rivers. The Confederacy had built forts at strategic points along the rivers and had begun to convert a few steamboats into gunboats and rams to back up the forts. The Union also converted steamboats into "timberclad" gunboats—so called because they were armored just enough to protect the engine and the paddle wheels. The Union also built a new class of ironclad gunboats designed for river warfare. Carrying 13 guns, these flat-bottomed, wide-beamed vessels drew only 6 feet of water. Their hulls and paddle wheels were protected by a sloping casemate sheathed in iron armor up to 2½ inches thick.

When the first of these strange-looking but formidable craft were ready in February 1862, Grant struck. His objectives were Forts Henry and Donelson on the Tennessee and Cumberland rivers just south of the Kentucky-Tennessee border. The gunboats knocked out Fort Henry on February 6. Fort Donelson proved a tougher nut to crack. Its guns repulsed a gunboat attack on February 14. Next day the 17,000-man Confederate army attacked Grant's besieging army, which had been reinforced to 27,000 men. With the calm decisiveness that became his trademark, Grant directed a counterattack that penned the defenders back up in their fort. Cut off from support by either land or river, the Confederate commander asked for surrender terms on February 16. Grant's reply made him instantly famous when it was published in the North: "No terms except an immediate and unconditional surrender can be accepted."

The strategic consequences of these victories were far-reaching. Union gunboats now ranged all the way up the Tennessee River to northern Alabama, enabling a Union division to occupy the region, and up the Cumberland to Nashville. Confederate military units pulled out of Kentucky and most of Tennessee and reassembled at Corinth in northern Mississippi. But by the end of March 1862 the Confederate commander in the western theater, Albert Sidney Johnston (not to be confused with Joseph E. Johnston in Virginia), had built up an army of 40,000 men at Corinth. His plan was to attack Grant's force of 35,000, which had established a base 20 miles away at Pittsburg Landing on the Tennessee River just north of the Mississippi-Tennessee border.

The Battle of Shiloh

On April 6 the Confederates attacked at dawn near a church called Shiloh, which gave its name to the battle. They caught Grant by surprise and drove his army toward the river. After a day's fighting with total casualties of 15,000, Grant's men brought the Confederate onslaught to a halt at dusk. One of the Confederate casualties was Johnston, the highest-ranking general on either side to be killed in the war. Beauregard, who had been transferred from Virginia to the West, took command after Johnston's death.

Some of Grant's subordinates advised retreat, but Grant would have none of it. Reinforced by fresh troops from a Union army commanded by General Don Carlos Buell, the Union counterattacked next morning (April 7) and, after 9,000 more casualties to the two sides, drove the Confederates back to Corinth. Although Grant had snatched victory from the jaws of defeat, his reputation suffered a decline because of the heavy casualties and the suspicion that he had been caught napping.

Union triumphs in the western theater continued. The combined armies of Grant and Buell, under the overall command of Henry W. Halleck, drove the Confederates out of Corinth at the end of May. Meanwhile, the Union gunboat fleet fought its way down the Mississippi, virtually wiping out the Confederate fleet in a spectacular battle at Memphis on June 6.

At Vicksburg the Union gunboats from the north connected with part of Farragut's fleet that had come up from New Orleans, taking Baton Rouge and Natchez along the way. The heavily fortified Confederate bastion at Vicksburg, however, proved too strong for the firepower of the Union naval fleet to subdue. Nevertheless, the dramatic succession of Union triumphs convinced the North that the war was nearly won. "Every blow tells fearfully against the rebellion," boasted the *New York Tribune* on May 23, 1862. "The rebels themselves are panic-stricken, or despondent."

THE VIRGINIA THEATER

In the western theater the broad rivers had facilitated the Union's invasion of the South, but in Virginia a half-dozen small rivers flowing west to east provided the Confederates with natural lines of defense. So McClellan, still in command of the Army of the Potomac, persuaded a reluctant Lincoln to approve a plan to transport his army down Chesapeake Bay to the tip of the Virginia peninsula. That would shorten the route to Richmond and give the Union Army a seaborne supply line.

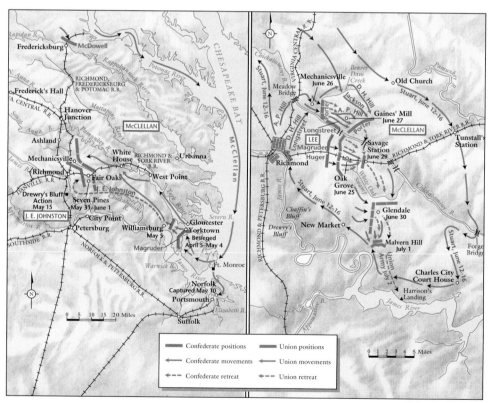

PENINSULA CAMPAIGN,
APRIL–MAY 1862

SEVEN DAYS' BATTLES,
JUNE 25–JULY 1, 1862

This was a good plan—in theory. But a small Confederate blocking force at Yorktown held McClellan for the entire month of April as he cautiously dragged up siege guns to blast through defenses that his large army could have punched through in days on foot. McClellan then slowly followed the retreating Confederate force up the peninsula to a new defensive line only a few miles east of Richmond.

Shortly thereafter, Stonewall Jackson's month-long campaign in the Shenandoah (May 8– June 9) demonstrated what could be accomplished through deception, daring, and mobility. With only 17,000 men, Jackson moved by forced marches, covering 350 miles in one month. During that month they won four battles against three separate Union armies, whose combined numbers surpassed Jackson's by more than 2 to 1.

Meanwhile McClellan's army continued toward Richmond. Although it substantially outnumbered the Confederate force defending Richmond, commanded by Joseph E. Johnston, McClellan overestimated Johnston's strength at double what it actually was. Even so, by the last week of May McClellan's army was within 6 miles of Richmond. A botched Confederate counterattack on May 31 and June 1 (the Battle of Seven Pines) produced no result except 6,000 Confederate and 5,000 Union casualties. But one of those casualties was Joseph Johnston, who had been wounded in the shoulder. Jefferson Davis named Robert E. Lee to replace him.

The Seven Days' Battles

That appointment marked a major turning point in the campaign. Lee's qualities as a commander manifested themselves when he took over what he renamed "The Army of Northern Virginia." While McClellan continued to dawdle, Lee sent his dashing cavalry commander, Jeb Stuart, to lead a reconnaissance around the Union army to discover its weak points, brought Jackson's army in from the Shenandoah Valley, and launched a June 25 attack on McClellan's right flank in what became known as the Seven Days' battles. Constantly attacking, Lee's army of 88,000 drove McClellan's 100,000 away from Richmond to a new fortified base on the James River. The offensive cost the Confederates 20,000 casualties (compared with 16,000 for the Union), but it reversed the momentum of the war.

Confederate Counteroffensives

The tide turned in the western theater as well. Union conquests there in the spring had brought 50,000 square miles of Confederate territory under Union control. But to occupy and administer this vast area many thousands of soldiers had to be drawn from combat forces. These depleted forces, deep in enemy territory, were vulnerable to cavalry raids. During the summer and fall of 1862 the cavalry commands of Tennesseean Nathan Bedford Forrest and Kentuckian John Hunt Morgan staged repeated raids in which they burned bridges, blew up tunnels, tore up tracks, and captured supply depots and the Union garrisons trying to defend them.

These raids paved the way for infantry counteroffensives. After recapturing some territory, Earl Van Dorn's Army of West Tennessee failed to retake Corinth on October 3 and 4. At the end of August, Braxton Bragg's Army of Tennessee launched a drive northward from Chattanooga through east Tennessee and Kentucky but was turned back at the Battle of Perryville on October 8. Even after these defeats, the Confederate forces in the western theater were in better shape than they had been four months earlier.

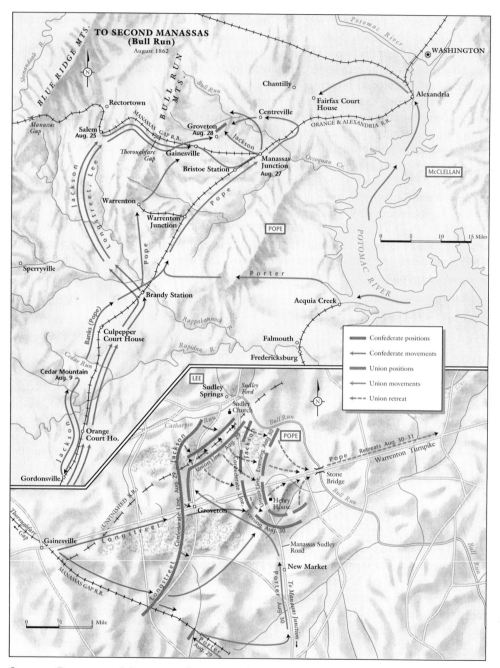

SECOND BATTLE OF MANASSAS (BULL RUN), AUGUST 29–30, 1862

CHRONOLOGY

1860	Lincoln elected president (November 6) • South Carolina secedes (December 20) • Federal troops transfer from Fort Moultrie to Fort Sumter (December 26)
1861	Rest of lower South secedes (January–February) • Crittenden Compromise rejected (February) • Jefferson Davis inaugurated as provisional president of new Confederate States of America (February 18) • Abraham Lincoln inaugurated as president of the United States (March 4) • Fort Sumter falls; Lincoln calls out troops, proclaims blockade (April) • Four more states secede to join Confederacy (April–May) • Battle of Bull Run (Manassas) (July 21) • Battle of Wilson's Creek (August 10) • The *Trent* affair (November–December)
1862	Union captures Forts Henry and Donelson (February 6 and 16) • Congress passes Legal Tender Act (February 25) • Battle of the *Monitor* and *Merrimac (Virginia)* (March 9) • Battle of Glorieta Pass (March 26–28) • Battle of Shiloh (April 6–7) • Union Navy captures New Orleans (April 25) • Stonewall Jackson's Shenandoah Valley camapign (May–June) • Seven Days' battles (June 25–July 1) • Second Battle of Manassas (Bull Run) (August 29–30) • Lee invades Maryland (September) • Battle of Corinth (October 3–4) • Battle of Perryville (October 8)
1863	Congress passes National Banking Act (February 25)

THE SECOND BATTLE OF BULL RUN

Most attention, though, focused on Virginia. Lincoln reorganized the Union corps near Washington into the Army of Virginia under General John Pope. In August, Lincoln ordered the withdrawal of the Army of the Potomac from the peninsula to reinforce Pope for a drive southward from Washington. Lee quickly seized the opportunity provided by the separation of the two Union armies. To attack Pope before McClellan could reinforce him, Lee shifted most of his army to northern Virginia, sent Jackson's "foot cavalry" on a deep raid to destroy the supply base at Manassas Junction, and then brought his army back together to defeat Pope's army near Bull Run on August 29 and 30. The demoralized Union forces retreated to Washington, where Lincoln reluctantly gave McClellan command of the two armies and told him to reorganize them into one.

Lee decided to keep up the pressure by invading Maryland. On September 4, his weary troops splashed across the Potomac 40 miles upriver from Washington. Momentous possibilities accompanied this move. Another victory by Lee might influence the U.S. congressional elections in November and help Democrats gain control of Congress, and would paralyze Lincoln's war effort. The invasion of Maryland, coming on top of other Confederate successes, might even persuade Britain and France to recognize the Confederacy and offer mediation to end the war. In September 1862 the British and French governments were indeed considering recognition and were awaiting the outcome of Lee's invasion to decide whether to proceed.

CONCLUSION

The election of 1860 had accomplished a national power shift of historic proportions. Southern political leaders had maintained effective control of the national government for most of the time before 1860. South Carolina's secession governor Francis Pickens described this leverage of power in a private letter to a fellow South Carolinian in 1857:

> We have the Executive [Buchanan] with us, and the Senate & in all probability the H[ouse of] R[epresentatives] too. Besides we have repealed the Missouri line & the Supreme Court in a decision of great power, has declared it . . . unconstitutional null and void. So, that before our enemies can reach us, they must first break down the Supreme Court—change the Senate & seize the Executive & . . . restore the Missouri line, repeal the Fugitive slave law & change the whole govern[men]t. As long as the Govt. is on our side I am for sustaining it, & using its power for our benefit.

In 1860 Pickens's worst-case scenario started to come true. With Lincoln's election as the first president of an antislavery party, the South lost control of the Executive—and also probably of the House. They feared that the Senate and Supreme Court would soon follow. The Republicans, Southerners feared, would launch a "revolution" to cripple slavery. The "revolutionary dogmas" of the Republicans, declared a South Carolina newspaper in 1860, were "active and bristling with terrible designs." Worst of all, the Northern "Black Republicans" would force racial equality on the South.

Thus the South seceded in order to forestall the feared revolution of liberty and equality that would be their fate if they remained in the Union. As the Confederate secretary of state put it in 1861, the southern states had formed a new nation "to preserve their old institutions" from "a revolution [that] threatened to destroy their social system."

Seldom has a preemptive counterrevolution so quickly brought on the very revolution it tried to prevent. If the Confederacy had lost the war in the spring of 1862, as appeared likely, the South might have returned to the Union with slavery still intact. But the success of Confederate counteroffensives in the summer of 1862 convinced Lincoln that the North could not win the war without striking against slavery.

16

A NEW BIRTH OF FREEDOM, 1862–1865

SLAVERY AND THE WAR ∾ A WINTER OF DISCONTENT

BLUEPRINT FOR MODERN AMERICA

THE CONFEDERATE TIDE CRESTS AND RECEDES

BLACK MEN IN BLUE ∾ THE YEAR OF DECISION

THE REELECTION OF LINCOLN AND THE END OF THE CONFEDERACY

One of the great issues awaiting resolution as the armies moved into Maryland in September 1862 was emancipation of the slaves. The war had become a "total war," requiring the mobilization or the destruction of every resource that might bring victory or inflict defeat. To abolish slavery would strike at a vital Confederate resource (slave labor). Slaves had already made clear their choice by escaping to Union lines by the tens of thousands. Lincoln had made up his mind to issue an emancipation proclamation and was waiting for a Union victory to give it credibility and potency.

This was a momentous decision that would polarize Northern public opinion and political parties. So long as the North fought simply for restoration of the Union, Northern unity had been impressive. But the events of 1862 and 1863 raised the divisive question of what kind of Union was to be restored. Would it be a Union without slavery, as abolitionists and radical Republicans hoped? Or "the Union as it was, the Constitution as it is," as Democrats desired?

SLAVERY AND THE WAR

At first, the leaders of both the Union and the Confederacy tried to keep the issue of slavery out of the war. For Southern leaders to proclaim that the defense of slavery was the aim of the war might prompt non-slaveholders to ask why they were risking their lives to protect their rich neighbors' property. So the Confederates proclaimed not slavery, but liberty as their war aim—including the liberty of whites to own blacks.

In the North, the issue of slavery was deeply divisive. Lincoln had been elected on a pledge to contain the expansion of slavery. But that pledge had provoked most of the southern states to quit the Union. For the administration to take action against slavery in 1861 would be to risk the breakup of the fragile coalition Lincoln had stitched together to fight the war: Republicans, Democrats, and border-state Unionists. In July 1861, with Lincoln's endorsement,

Congress passed a resolution affirming that Northern war aims intended only "to defend and maintain the supremacy of the Constitution and to preserve the Union."

But many Northerners did not see things that way. They insisted that a rebellion sustained *by* slavery in defense *of* slavery could be suppressed only by striking *against* slavery. As the black leader Frederick Douglass stated, "War for the destruction of liberty must be met with war for the destruction of slavery." A good many Union soldiers began to grumble about protecting the property of traitors in arms against the United States.

Wars tend to develop a logic and momentum that go beyond their original purposes. When Northerners discovered at Bull Run in July 1861 that they were not going to win an easy victory, many of them began to take a harder look at slavery. Slaves constituted the principal labor force in the South. They raised most of the food and fiber, built most of the military fortifications, worked on the railroads and in mines and munitions factories. Southern newspapers boasted that slavery was "a tower of strength to the Confederacy." Precisely, responded abolitionists. So why not convert this Confederate asset to a Union advantage by confiscating slaves as enemy property and using them to help the Northern war effort?

THE "CONTRABANDS"

The slaves themselves entered this debate in a dramatic fashion. As Union armies penetrated the South, a growing number of slaves voted with their feet for freedom. By twos and threes, by families, eventually by scores, they escaped from their masters and came over to the Union lines.

Although some commanders returned escaped slaves to their masters or prevented them from entering Union camps, most increasingly did not. Their rationale was first expressed by General Benjamin Butler. In May 1861 three slaves escaped to Butler's lines near Fortress Monroe at the mouth of the James River. Butler refused to return them, on the grounds that they were "contraband of war." For the rest of the war, slaves who came within Union lines were known as contrabands. On August 6, 1861, Congress passed an act that authorized the seizure of all property, including slaves, that was being used for Confederate military purposes. The following March, Congress forbade the return of slaves who entered Union lines.

THE BORDER STATES

On August 30, 1861, Major General John C. Frémont, who commanded Union forces in Missouri, issued an order freeing the slaves of all Confederate sympathizers in that state. This caused such a backlash among border-state Unionists that Lincoln revoked the order.

In the spring of 1862, Lincoln tried persuasion instead of force. At his urging, Congress passed a resolution offering federal compensation to states that voluntarily abolished slavery. Three times Lincoln summoned border-state congressmen to the White House to discuss the matter. He told them that the Confederate hope that their states might join the rebellion was helping to keep the war alive. Accept the proposal for compensated emancipation, he pleaded, and that hope would die. The pressure for a bold antislavery policy was growing stronger, he warned them. "You cannot," he said, "be blind to the signs of the times."

But they did seem to be blind. They complained that they were being coerced, bickered about the amount of compensation, and wrung their hands over the prospects of economic ruin and race war. At a final meeting, on July 12, Lincoln, in effect, gave them an ultimatum:

Accept compensated emancipation or face the consequences. "The incidents of the war cannot be avoided," he said. But again they failed to see the light and by a vote of 20 to 9, they rejected the proposal for compensated emancipation.

THE DECISION FOR EMANCIPATION

That very evening, Lincoln decided to issue an emancipation proclamation. Several factors, in addition to the recalcitrance of the border states, impelled him to this fateful decision. One was a growing demand from his own party for bolder action. Another was rising sentiment in the Army to "take off the kid gloves" when dealing with "traitors." From General Henry W. Halleck, who had been summoned to Washington as general-in-chief, went orders to General Grant in northern Mississippi instructing him on the treatment of rebel sympathizers inside Union lines: "Handle that class without gloves, and take their property for public use." Finally, Lincoln's decision reflected his sentiments about the "unqualified evil" and "monstrous injustice" of slavery.

The military situation, however, rather than his moral convictions, determined the timing and scope of Lincoln's emancipation policy. Northern hopes that the war would soon end had risen after the victories of early 1862 but had then plummeted amid the reverses of that summer. Three courses of action seemed possible. One, favored by the so-called Peace Democrats, urged an armistice and peace negotiations to patch together some kind of Union, but that would have been tantamount to conceding Confederate victory. Republicans therefore reviled the Peace Democrats as traitorous "Copperheads," after the poisonous snake. A second alternative was to keep on fighting—in the hope that with a few more Union victories, the rebels would lay down their arms and the Union could be restored. But such a policy would leave slavery intact. The third alternative was to mobilize all the resources of the North and to destroy all the resources of the South, including slavery—a war not to restore the old Union but to build a new one.

After his meeting with the border-state representatives convinced him there could be no compromise, Lincoln made his decision. A week later he notified the cabinet of his intention to issue an emancipation proclamation. It was "a military necessity, absolutely essential to the preservation of the Union," said Lincoln. "We must free the slaves or be ourselves subdued."

The cabinet agreed, except for Postmaster General Montgomery Blair, a resident of Maryland and a former Democrat, who warned that the border states and the Democrats would rebel against the proclamation and perhaps cost the administration the fall congressional elections. But Lincoln accepted the advice of Secretary of State Seward to delay the proclamation "until you can give it to the country supported by military success." Lincoln slipped his proclamation into a desk drawer and waited for a military victory.

NEW CALLS FOR TROOPS

Meanwhile, Lincoln issued a call for 300,000 new three-year volunteers for the Army. In July, Congress passed a militia act giving the president greater powers to mobilize the state militias into federal service and to draft men into the militia if the states failed to do so. This was not yet a national draft law, but it was a step in that direction. In August, Lincoln called up 300,000 militia for nine months of service, in addition to the 300,000 three-year volunteers. The Peace

Democrats railed against these measures and provoked antidraft riots in some localities. The government responded by arresting rioters and antiwar activists under the president's suspension of the writ of habeas corpus.[1]

Democrats denounced these "arbitrary arrests" and added this issue to others on which they hoped to gain control of the next House of Representatives in the fall elections. With the decline in Northern morale following the defeat at Second Bull Run and the early success of the Confederate invasion of Kentucky, prospects for a Democratic triumph seemed bright. One more military victory by Lee's Army of Northern Virginia might crack the North's will to continue the fighting. Lee's legions began crossing the Potomac into Maryland on September 4, 1862.

THE BATTLE OF ANTIETAM

The Confederate invasion ran into difficulties from the start. The people of western Maryland responded impassively to Lee's proclamation that he had come "to aid you in throwing off this foreign yoke" of Yankee rule. Lee split his army into five parts. Three of them, under the overall command of Stonewall Jackson, occupied the heights surrounding the Union garrison at Harpers Ferry, which lay athwart the Confederate supply route from the Shenandoah Valley. The other two remained on watch in the South Mountain passes west of Frederick. But on September 13, in a field near Frederick, two Union soldiers found a copy of Lee's orders for these deployments, apparently dropped by a careless officer. With this new information, Union commander George B. McClellan planned to pounce on the separated segments of Lee's army before they could reunite.

Union troops overwhelmed the Confederate defenders of the South Mountain passes on September 14. But they advanced too slowly to save the garrison at Harpers Ferry, which surrendered 12,000 men to Jackson on September 15. Lee then managed to reunite most of his army near the village of Sharpsburg by September 17, when McClellan finally crossed Antietam Creek to attack. The battle of Antietam (called Sharpsburg by the Confederates) proved to be the single bloodiest day in American history, with more than 23,000 casualties (killed, wounded, and captured) in the two armies.

Attacking from right to left on a 4-mile front, McClellan's Army of the Potomac achieved potential breakthroughs at a sunken road northeast of Sharpsburg and in the rolling fields southeast of town. But fearing counterattacks, McClellan held back 20,000 of his troops and failed to follow through. Thus the battle ended in a draw. The battered Confederates still clung to their precarious line, with the Potomac at their back, at the end of a day in which more than 6,000 men on both sides were killed or mortally wounded. Even though he received reinforcements the next day and Lee received none, McClellan did not renew the attack.

---

[1] The writ of habeas corpus is an order issued by a judge to law enforcement officers requiring them to bring an arrested person before the court to be charged with a crime so that the accused can have a fair trial. The Constitution of the United States, however, permits the suspension of this writ "in cases of rebellion or invasion," so that the government can arrest enemy agents, saboteurs, or any individual who might hinder the defense of the country, and hold such individuals without trial. Lincoln had suspended the writ, but political opponents charged him with usurping a power possessed only by Congress in order to curb the freedom of speech of antiwar opponents and political critics who were guilty of nothing more than speaking out against the war. This issue of "arbitrary arrests" became a controversial matter in both the Union and Confederacy (where the writ was similarly suspended during part of the war).

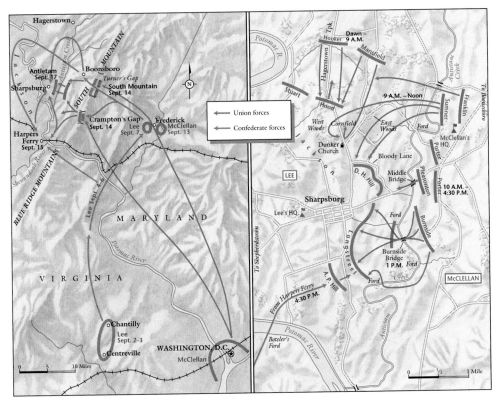

LEE'S INVASION OF MARYLAND, 1862

BATTLE OF ANTIETAM, SEPTEMBER 17, 1862

THE EMANCIPATION PROCLAMATION

Lincoln was not happy with this equivocal Union victory. But it was a victory with important consequences. Britain and France decided to withhold diplomatic recognition of the Confederacy. Northern Democrats failed to gain control of the House in the fall elections. And most significant of all, on September 22, Lincoln seized the occasion to issue his preliminary emancipation proclamation. It did not come as a total surprise. A month earlier, after Horace Greeley had written a strong editorial in the *New York Tribune* calling for action against slavery, Lincoln had responded with a public letter to Greeley. "My paramount object in this struggle," wrote Lincoln, "*is* to save the Union. . . . If I could save the Union without freeing *any* slave I would do it, and if I could save it by freeing *all* the slaves I would do it; and if I could save it by freeing some and leaving others alone I would also do that." Lincoln had crafted these phrases carefully to maximize public support for his proclamation. He portrayed emancipation not as an end in itself but only as an instrument, a *means* toward the end of saving the Union.

Lincoln's proclamation did not go into effect immediately. Rather, it stipulated that if any state, or part of a state, was still in rebellion on January 1, 1863, the president would proclaim the slaves therein "forever free." Confederate leaders scorned this warning, and by January 1 no Southern state had returned to the Union. On New Year's Day Lincoln signed the final proclamation.

The Emancipation Proclamation exempted the border states, plus Tennessee and those portions of Louisiana and Virginia that were already under Union occupation, since these areas were deemed not to be in rebellion, and Lincoln's constitutional authority for the proclamation derived from his power as commander in chief to confiscate enemy property. Although the proclamation could do nothing to liberate slaves in areas under Confederate control, it essentially made the Northern soldiers an army of liberation. The North was now fighting for freedom as well as for Union.

A WINTER OF DISCONTENT

Although Lee's retreat from Maryland and Braxton Bragg's retreat from Kentucky suggested that the Confederate tide might be ebbing, the tide soon turned. The Union could never win the war simply by turning back Confederate invasions. Northern armies would have to invade the South, defeat its armies, and destroy its ability to fight.

Displeased by McClellan's "slows" after Antietam, Lincoln replaced him on November 7, 1862, with General Ambrose E. Burnside. Burnside proposed to cross the Rappahannock River at Fredericksburg for a move on Richmond before bad weather forced both sides into winter quarters. Although Lee put his men into a strong defensive position on the heights behind Fredericksburg, Burnside nevertheless attacked on December 13. He was repulsed with heavy casualties that shook the morale of both the Army and the public.

News from the western theater did little to dispel the gloom in Washington. The Confederates had fortified Vicksburg on bluffs commanding the Mississippi River. This preserved transportation links between the states to the east and west. To sever those links was the goal of Grant, who in November 1862 launched a two-pronged drive against Vicksburg. With 40,000 men, he marched 50 miles southward from Memphis by land, while his principal subordinate William T. Sherman came down the river with 32,000 men accompanied by a gunboat fleet. But raids by Confederate cavalry destroyed the railroads and supply depots in his rear, forcing him to retreat to Memphis. Meanwhile, Sherman attacked the Confederates at Chickasaw Bluffs on December 29, with no more success than Burnside had enjoyed at Fredericksburg.

The only bit of cheer for the North came in central Tennessee. There, Lincoln had removed General Don Carlos Buell from command of the Army of the Cumberland and replaced him with William S. Rosecrans. On the Confederate side, Davis stuck with Braxton Bragg as commander of the Army of Tennessee.

On the day after Christmas Rosecrans moved from his base at Nashville to attack Bragg's force 30 miles to the south at Murfreesboro. The ensuing three-day battle (called Stones River by the Union and Murfreesboro by the Confederacy) resulted in Confederate success on the first day (December 31) but defeat on the last. Both armies suffered devastating casualties. The Confederate retreat to a new base 40 miles farther south enabled the North to call Stones River a victory.

Elsewhere, however, things went from bad to worse. Renewing the campaign against Vicksburg, Grant was bogged down in the swamps and rivers that protected that Confederate bastion on three sides. Only on the east, away from the river, was there high ground suitable for an assault on Vicksburg's defenses. Grant's problem was to get his army across the Mississippi to that high ground, along with supplies and transportation to support an assault. For three months, he floundered in the Mississippi-Yazoo bottomlands, while disease and exposure took a fearful toll of his troops.

THE RISE OF THE COPPERHEADS

Lincoln's reputation reached a low point during the winter of 1863. In this climate, the Copperhead faction of the Democratic Party found a ready audience for its message that the war was a failure and should be abandoned. Having won control of the Illinois and Indiana legislatures the preceding fall, Democrats there called for an armistice and a peace conference. They also demanded retraction of the "wicked, inhuman, and unholy" Emancipation Proclamation.

In Ohio, the foremost Peace Democrat, Congressman Clement L. Vallandigham, was planning to run for governor. What had this wicked war accomplished, Vallandigham asked Northern audiences. "Let the dead at Fredericksburg and Vicksburg answer." The Confederacy could never be conquered; the only trophies of the war were "debt, defeat, sepulchres." The solution was to "stop the fighting. Make an armistice. Withdraw your army from the seceded states." Above all, give up the unconstitutional effort to abolish slavery.

Vallandigham and other Copperhead spokesmen had a powerful effect on Northern morale. Alarmed by a wave of desertions, the army commander in Ohio had Vallandigham arrested in May 1863. A military court convicted him of treason for aiding and abetting the enemy. The court's action raised serious questions of civil liberties. Was the conviction a violation of Vallandigham's First Amendment right of free speech? Could a military court try a civilian under martial law in a state like Ohio where civil courts were functioning?

Lincoln was embarrassed by the swift arrest and trial of Vallandigham, which he learned about from the newspapers. To keep Vallandigham from becoming a martyr, Lincoln commuted his sentence from imprisonment to banishment. On May 15, Union cavalry escorted Vallandigham under a flag of truce to Confederate lines in Tennessee. He soon escaped to Canada on a blockade runner. There, from exile, Vallandigham conducted his campaign for governor of Ohio—an election he lost in October 1863.

ECONOMIC PROBLEMS IN THE SOUTH

Southerners were buoyed by their military success but were suffering from economic problems caused by the Union blockade, the weaknesses and imbalances of the Confederate economy, the escape of slaves to Union lines, and enemy occupation of some of the South's prime agricultural areas. Despite the conversion of hundreds of thousands of acres from cotton to food production, the deterioration of Southern railroads and the priority given to army shipments made food scarce in some areas. Prices rose much faster than wages. The price of salt—necessary to preserve meat in that pre-refrigeration age—shot out of sight. Even the middle class suffered, especially in Richmond, whose population had more than doubled since 1861. One man wrote that the rats in his kitchen were so hungry that they nibbled bread crumbs from his daughter's hand "as tame as kittens. Perhaps we shall have to eat them!"

Things were even worse for the poor—especially for the wives and children of non-slaveholders who were away in the army. By the spring of 1863, food supplies were virtually gone. "I have 6 little children and my husband in the armey and what am I to do?" wrote a North Carolina farm woman.

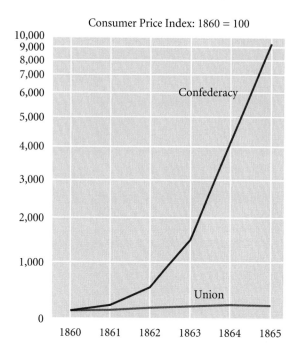

Consumer Price Index: 1860 = 100

WARTIME INFLATION IN THE CONFEDERACY AND THE UNION

Some women took matters into their own hands. Denouncing "speculators" who allegedly hoarded goods to drive up prices, they marched to stores, denounced "extortion," and took what they wanted without paying. On April 2, 1863, a mob of more than 1,000 women and boys looted several shops in Richmond before the militia forced them to disperse. The Confederate government subsequently released some emergency food stocks to civilians, and state and county governments aided the families of soldiers. Better crops in 1863 helped to alleviate the worst shortages, but serious problems persisted.

THE WARTIME DRAFT AND CLASS TENSIONS

In both South and North, the draft intensified social unrest and turned it in the direction of class conflict. In April 1862 the Confederacy enacted a draft that made all white men aged 18 to 35 liable to conscription. A drafted man could hire a substitute, but the price of substitutes soon rose beyond the means of the average Southern farmer or worker, giving rise to the bitter cry that it was "a rich man's war and a poor man's fight."

The cry grew louder in October 1862 when the Confederate Congress raised the draft age to 45 and added a clause exempting one white man from the draft on every plantation with 20 or more slaves. The purpose of this "overseer exemption" was to keep up production and prevent slave uprisings. But the so-called Twenty Negro Law was regarded as blatant discrimination against non-slaveholding farm families. Also, raising the age limit to 45 took away many fathers of children who were too young to work the farm. The law provoked widespread draft-dodging and desertions.

Similar discontent greeted the enactment of a conscription law in the North. In the summer of 1863, some 30,000 Union soldiers would be leaving military service, along with 80,000 of the nine-month militia called into service the preceding autumn. To meet the shortfall, Congress decreed in March that all male citizens aged 20 to 45 must enroll for the draft. Not all of them would necessarily be called, but all would be liable.

The law was intended more to encourage volunteers to come forward than it was to draft men directly. The War Department set a quota for every congressional district and gave it 50 days to meet its quota with volunteers before resorting to a draft lottery. Some districts avoided having to draft anyone by offering large bounties to volunteers. The bounty system produced glaring abuses, including "bounty jumpers" who enlisted and then deserted as soon as they got their money—often to enlist again under another name somewhere else.

The drafting process itself was also open to abuse. Like the Confederate law, the Union law permitted the hiring of substitutes. The Union law also allowed a drafted man the alternative of paying a "commutation fee" of $300 that exempted him from the current draft call (but not necessarily from the next one). That provision raised the cry of "rich man's war, poor man's fight" in the North as well. This sense of class resentment was nurtured by the Democratic Party. Democrats in Congress opposed conscription. Democratic newspapers told white workers that the draft would force them to fight a war to free the slaves, who would then come north to take their jobs. This volatile issue sparked widespread violence when the Northern draft got under way in the summer of 1863. The worst riot occurred in New York City on July 13 through 16, where huge mobs consisting mostly of Irish Americans demolished draft offices, lynched several blacks, and destroyed huge areas of the city in four days of looting and burning.

Draft riots in the North and bread riots in the South exposed alarming class fissures that were deepened by the strains of full-scale war. Labor unions sprang up in several Northern industries and struck for higher wages. In some areas, such as the anthracite coalfields of eastern Pennsylvania, labor organizations dominated by Irish Americans mounted violent strikes against industries owned by Protestant Republicans. Troops sent in to enforce the draft sometimes suppressed the strikes as well.

A Poor Man's Fight?

But the grievance that it was a rich man's war and a poor man's fight was more apparent than real. The principal forms of taxation to sustain the war were property, excise, and income taxes that bore proportionately more heavily on the wealthy than on the poor. In the South, the property of the rich suffered greater damage and confiscation than did the property of non-slaveholders. The war liberated 4 million slaves, the poorest class in America. Both the Union and Confederate armies were made up of men from all strata of society in proportion to their percentage of the population. If anything, among those who volunteered in 1861 and 1862, the planter class was overrepresented in the Confederate army and the middle class in the Union forces. Those volunteers—especially the officers—suffered the highest percentage of combat casualties.

Nor did conscription itself fall much more heavily on the poor than on the rich. Those who escaped the draft by decamping to the woods, the territories, or Canada came mostly from the poor. The Confederacy abolished substitution in December 1863 and made men who had previously sent substitutes liable to the draft. In the North, several city councils, political machines, and businesses contributed funds to pay the commutation fees of drafted men who were too poor to pay out of their own pockets. In the end, it was neither a rich man's war nor a poor man's fight. It was an all-American war.

BLUEPRINT FOR MODERN AMERICA

The 37th Congress (1861–1863)—the Congress that enacted conscription, passed measures for confiscation and emancipation, and created the greenbacks and the national banking system (see Chapter 15)—also enacted three laws that provided what one historian has called "a blueprint for modern America": the Homestead Act; the Morrill Land-Grant College Act; and the Pacific Railroad Act. The Homestead Act granted a farmer 160 acres of land virtually free after he had lived on the land for five years and had made improvements on it. The Morrill Land-Grant College Act gave each state thousands of acres to fund the establishment of colleges for the teaching of "agricultural and mechanical arts." The Pacific Railroad Act granted land and loans to railroad companies to spur the building of a transcontinental railroad from Omaha to Sacramento. These laws helped farmers settle some of the most fertile land in the world, studded the land with state colleges, and spanned it with steel rails in a manner that altered the landscape of the western half of the country.

WOMEN AND THE WAR

The war advanced many other social changes, particularly with respect to women. In factories and on farms women took the place of the men who had gone off to war. The war accelerated the entry of women into the teaching profession, a trend that had already begun in the Northeast and now spread to other parts of the country. It also brought significant numbers of women into the civil service. The huge expansion of government bureaucracies after 1861 and the departure of male clerks to the army provided openings that were filled partly by women. After the war the private sector began hiring women as clerks, bookkeepers, "typewriters," and telephone operators.

But women's most visible impact was in the field of medicine. The outbreak of war prompted the organization of soldiers' aid societies, hospital societies, and other voluntary associations, with women playing a leading role. Their most important function was to help the armies' medical branches provide more efficient, humane care for sick and wounded soldiers. Dr. Elizabeth Blackwell, the first American woman to earn an M.D. (1849), organized a meeting of 3,000 women in New York City on April 29, 1861. They put together the Women's Central Association for Relief, which became the nucleus for the most powerful voluntary association of the war, the United States Sanitary Commission.

The Sanitary Commission was an essential adjunct of the Union Army's medical bureau. Most of its local volunteers were women. So were most of the nurses it provided to army hospitals. Nursing was not a new profession for women—but it had not been a respectable wartime profession. The fame won by Florence Nightingale of Britain during the Crimean War a half-dozen years earlier had begun to change that perception. And the flocking of thousands of middle- and even upper-class women volunteers to army hospitals did a great deal to transform nursing from a menial occupation to a respected profession.

FEMALE SPIES AND SOLDIERS   In addition to working in war industries and serving as army nurses, some women pursued traditionally male wartime careers as spies and soldiers. One of the most famous Confederate spies was Rose O'Neal Greenhow, a Washington widow and socialite who fed information to officials in Richmond. Federal officers arrested her in August 1861 and deported her to Richmond in the spring of 1862. She was photographed with her daughter in the Old Capitol prison in Washington, D.C., while awaiting trial. In October 1864 she drowned in a lifeboat off Wilmington, North Carolina, after a blockade runner carrying her back from a European mission was run aground by a Union warship.

The second photograph shows a Union soldier who enlisted in the 95th Illinois Infantry under the name of Albert Cashier and fought through the war. Not until a farm accident in 1911 revealed Albert Cashier to be a woman, whose real name was Jennie Hodgers, was her secret disclosed. Most of the other estimated 400 women who evaded the superficial physical exams and passed as men to enlist in the Union and Confederate armies were more quickly discovered and discharged—six of them after they had babies while in the army. A few, however, served long enough to be killed in action.

The nurses had to overcome the deep-grained suspicions of army surgeons and the opposition of husbands and fathers who shared the cultural sentiment that the shocking, embarrassingly physical atmosphere of an army hospital was no place for a respectable woman. But many thousands of women did it, winning grudging and then enthusiastic admiration.

The war also bolstered the fledgling women's rights movement. It was no coincidence that Elizabeth Cady Stanton and Susan B. Anthony founded the National Woman Suffrage Association in 1869, only four years after the war. Although it did not win final victory for half a century, this movement could not have achieved the momentum that made it a force in American life without the work of women in the Civil War.

THE CONFEDERATE TIDE CRESTS AND RECEDES

The Army of Northern Virginia and the Army of the Potomac spent the winter of 1862–1863 on opposite banks of the Rappahannock River. With the coming of spring, Union commander Joe Hooker resumed the offensive. On April 30, Hooker crossed his men several miles upriver and came in on Lee's rear. But Lee quickly faced most of his troops about and confronted the enemy in dense woods near the crossroads hostelry of Chancellorsville. Nonplussed, Hooker lost the initiative.

THE BATTLE OF CHANCELLORSVILLE

Even though the Union forces outnumbered the Confederates by almost 2 to 1, Lee boldly went over to the offensive. On May 2, Stonewall Jackson led 28,000 men on a stealthy march through the woods to attack the Union right flank late in the afternoon. The surprise was complete, and Jackson's assault crumpled the Union flank. Lee resumed the attack next day. In three more days of fighting that brought 12,800 Confederate and 16,800 Union casualties (the largest number for a single battle in the war so far), Lee drove the Union troops back across the Rappahannock.

"My God!" exclaimed Lincoln when he heard the news of Chancellorsville. "What will the country say?" Copperhead opposition intensified. Southern sympathizers in Britain renewed efforts for diplomatic recognition of the Confederacy. Lee decided to parlay his tactical victory

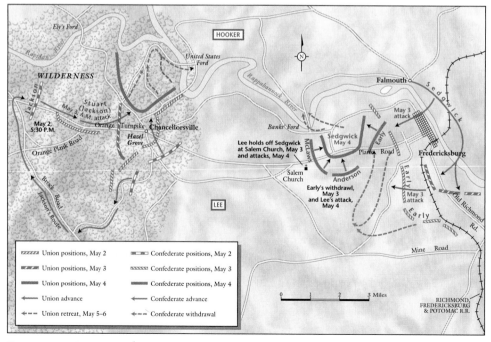

BATTLE OF CHANCELLORSVILLE, MAY 2–6, 1863

at Chancellorsville into a strategic offensive by again invading the North. A victory on Union soil would convince Northerners and foreigners alike that the Confederacy was invincible. As his army moved north in June 1863, Lee was confident of success.

THE GETTYSBURG CAMPAIGN

At first, all went well. The Confederates brushed aside or captured Union forces in the northern Shenandoah Valley and in Pennsylvania. Stuart's cavalry threw a scare into Washington by raiding behind Union lines into Maryland and Pennsylvania. But that very success led to trouble. With Stuart's cavalry separated from the rest of the army, Lee was deprived of vital intelligence.

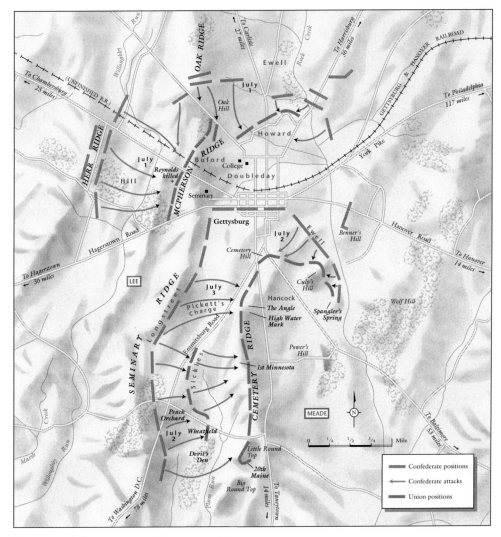

BATTLE OF GETTYSBURG, JULY 1–3, 1863

THE BATTLE OF GETTYSBURG   This is one of many paintings of Pickett's assault on the Union center on Cemetery Ridge at the climactic moment of the battle on July 3, 1863. The painting depicts "the high tide of the Confederacy" as Virginia and North Carolina troops pierce the Union line only to be shot down or captured—a fate suffered by half of the 13,000 Confederate soldiers who participated in Pickett's charge.

By June 28 several detachments of Lee's forces were scattered about Pennsylvania, far from their base and vulnerable to being cut off.

At this point, Lee learned that the Army of the Potomac was moving toward him, now under the command of George Gordon Meade. Lee immediately ordered his own army to reassemble in the vicinity of Gettysburg. There, on the morning of July 1, the vanguard of the two armies met in a clash that grew into the greatest battle in American history.

As the fighting spread west and north of town, reinforcements were summoned to both sides. The Confederates got more men into the battle and broke the Union lines late that afternoon, driving the survivors to a defensive position on Cemetery Hill south of town. Judging this position too strong to take with his own troops, General Richard Ewell chose not to press the attack as the sun went down on what he presumed would be another Confederate victory.

But when the sun rose next morning, the reinforced Union army was holding a superb defensive position from Culp's Hill and Cemetery Hill south to Little Round Top. Lee's principal subordinate, First Corps commander James Longstreet, advised against attack, but Lee believed his army invincible. Pointing to the Union lines, he said: "The enemy is there, and I am going to attack him there."

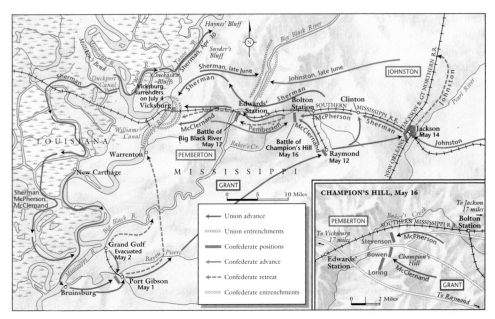

VICKSBURG CAMPAIGN, APRIL–JULY 1863

Longstreet reluctantly led the attack on the Union left. His men fought with fury, but the Union troops fought back with equal fury. By the end of the day, Confederate forces had made small gains at great cost, but the main Union line had held firm.

Lee was not yet ready to yield the offensive. Having attacked both Union flanks, he thought the center might be weak, so on July 3 he ordered a frontal attack on Cemetery Ridge, led by a fresh division under George Pickett. After a two-hour artillery barrage, Pickett's troops moved forward. "Pickett's Charge" was shot to pieces; scarcely half of the men returned unwounded to their own lines. It was the final act in an awesome three-day drama that left some 50,000 men killed, wounded, or captured.

Lee limped back to Virginia pursued by the Union troops. Lincoln was unhappy with Meade for not cutting off the Confederate retreat. Nevertheless, Gettysburg was a great Northern victory. And it came at the same time as other important Union successes in Mississippi, Louisiana, and Tennessee.

THE VICKSBURG CAMPAIGN

In mid-April, Grant had begun a move that would put Vicksburg in a vise. The Union ironclad fleet ran downriver past the big guns at Vicksburg with little damage. Grant's troops marched down the Mississippi's west bank and were ferried across the river 40 miles south of Vicksburg. There they kept the Confederate defenders off balance by striking east toward Jackson instead of marching north to Vicksburg. Grant's purpose was to scatter the Confederate forces in central Mississippi and to destroy the rail network so that his rear would be secure when he turned toward Vicksburg. It was a brilliant strategy, flawlessly executed. Grant's troops trapped 32,000 Confederate troops and 3,000 civilians in Vicksburg.

The Confederate army threw back Union assaults against the Vicksburg trenches on May 19 and 22. Grant then settled down for a siege. Running out of supplies, the Vicksburg garrison surrendered on July 4. On July 9, the Confederate garrison at Port Hudson, 200 river miles south of Vicksburg, surrendered to a besieging Union army. Northern forces now controlled the entire length of the Mississippi River. The Confederacy had been torn in two.

CHICKAMAUGA AND CHATTANOOGA

Northerners had scarcely finished celebrating the twin victories of Gettysburg and Vicksburg when they learned of an important—and almost bloodless—triumph. On June 24, Union commander Rosecrans assaulted the Confederate defenses in the Cumberland foothills of east-central Tennessee. He used his cavalry and a mounted infantry brigade armed with new repeating rifles to get around the Confederate flanks while his infantry threatened the Confederate front. In the first week of July, the Confederates retreated all the way to Chattanooga.

After a pause for resupply, Rosecrans's army advanced again in August, this time in tandem with a smaller Union army in eastern Tennessee commanded by Burnside. Again the outnumbered Confederates fell back, evacuating Knoxville on September 2 and Chattanooga on September 9. This action severed the South's only direct east-west rail link. Union forces now stood poised for a campaign into Georgia. For the Confederacy it was a stunning reversal of the situation only four months earlier, when the Union cause had appeared hopeless.

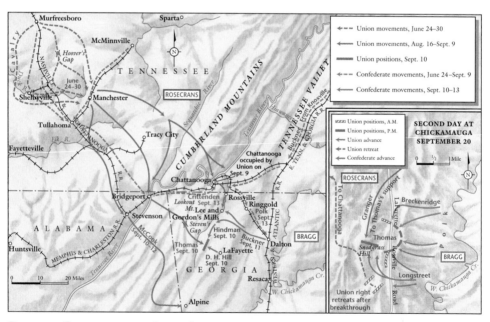

ROAD TO CHICKAMAUGA, JUNE–SEPTEMBER 1863

But Confederate General Braxton Bragg sent fake deserters into Union lines with tales of a Confederate retreat toward Atlanta. He then laid a trap for Rosecrans's troops as they advanced through the mountain passes south of Chattanooga. To help him spring it, Davis approved the detachment of Longstreet with two divisions from Lee's army to reinforce Bragg. On September 19, the Confederates turned and counterattacked Rosecrans's army in the valley of Chickamauga Creek.

Over the next two days, in ferocious fighting that produced more casualties (36,000) than any other single battle save Gettysburg, the Confederates finally scored a victory. On September 20 Longstreet's men broke through the Union line, sending part of the Union army reeling back to Chattanooga. Only a firm stand by corps commander George H. Thomas prevented a rout. Lincoln subsequently appointed Thomas commander of the Army of the Cumberland to replace Rosecrans.

Lincoln also sent two army corps from Virginia under Hooker and two from Vicksburg under Sherman to reinforce Thomas, whose troops in Chattanooga were under virtual siege by Bragg's forces, which held most of the surrounding heights. More important, Lincoln put Grant in overall command of the beefed-up Union forces there. When Grant arrived in late October, he welded the various Northern units into a new army and opened a new supply line into Chattanooga. On November 24, Hooker's troops drove Confederate besiegers off massive Lookout Mountain. Next day, an assault on Bragg's main line at Missionary Ridge east of Chattanooga drove the Confederates off the ridge and 20 miles south into Georgia.

These battles climaxed a string of Union victories in the second half of 1863. The Southern diarist Mary Boykin Chesnut described "gloom and unspoken despondency hang[ing] like a pall everywhere." Jefferson Davis replaced Bragg with Joseph E. Johnston. Lincoln summoned Grant to Washington and appointed him general-in-chief of all Union armies. The stage was set for a fight to the finish.

BLACK MEN IN BLUE

The events of the second half of 1863 also confirmed emancipation as a Union war aim. Northerners had not greeted the Emancipation Proclamation with great enthusiasm. Democrats and border-state Unionists continued to denounce it, and many Union soldiers resented the idea that they would now be risking their lives for black freedom. The Democratic Party had hoped to capitalize on this opposition, and on Union military failures, to win important off-year elections. Northern military victories knocked one prop out from under the Democratic platform, and the performance of black soldiers fighting for the Union knocked out another.

The enlistment of black soldiers was a logical corollary of emancipation. Free Negroes in the North had tried to enlist in 1861, but they were rejected. Proposals to recruit black soldiers, Democrats said, were part of a Republican plot to establish "the equality of the black and white races." In a way, that charge was correct. One consequence of black men fighting for the Union would be to advance the black race a long way toward equal rights. "Once let the black man get upon his person the brass letters, U.S.," said Frederick Douglass, "and a musket on his shoulder and bullets in his pocket, and there is no power on earth which can deny that he has earned the right to citizenship."

BLACK UNION ARTILLERYMEN   This photograph shows the crew of a gun in Battery A of the 2nd U.S. Colored Artillery, an outfit of freed slaves who served in the Tennessee theater and participated in the Battle of Nashville on December 15 and 16, 1864. They were among the 190,000 black soldiers and sailors who fought for the Union.

But it was pragmatism more than principle that pushed the North toward black recruitment. One purpose of emancipation was to deprive the Confederacy of black laborers and to use them for the Union. Some Union commanders in occupied portions of Louisiana, South Carolina, and Missouri began to organize black regiments in 1862. The Emancipation Proclamation legitimized this policy with its proposal to enroll able-bodied male contrabands in new black regiments. However, under this policy black soldiers would not serve as combat troops. They would be paid less than white soldiers, and their officers would be white.

BLACK SOLDIERS IN COMBAT

Continuing pressure from abolitionists, as well as military necessity, eroded discrimination somewhat. Congress enacted equal pay in 1864. The regiments themselves lobbied for the right to *fight* as combat soldiers. Even some previously hostile white soldiers came around to the notion that black men might just as well stop enemy bullets as white men. In May and June 1863, black regiments in Louisiana fought well at Milliken's Bend, near Vicksburg. "The bravery of the blacks in the battle of Milliken's Bend completely revolutionized the sentiment of the army with regard to the employment of negro troops," wrote the assistant secretary of war.

Even more significant was the action of the 54th Massachusetts Infantry, the first black regiment raised in the North. Its officers, headed by Colonel Robert Gould Shaw, came from prominent New England antislavery families. Shaw worked hard to win the right for the regiment to fight, and on July 18, 1863, he succeeded: The 54th was assigned to lead an assault on Fort Wagner, part of the network of Confederate defenses protecting Charleston. Though the attack failed, the 54th fought courageously, suffering 50 percent casualties, including Colonel Shaw, who was killed.

The battle took place just after the occurrence of draft riots in New York where white mobs had lynched blacks. Abolitionist and Republican commentators drew the moral: Black men who fought for the Union deserved more respect than white men who rioted against it. Lincoln made this point eloquently in a widely published letter to a political meeting in August 1863. When final victory was achieved, he wrote, "there will be some black men who can remember that, with silent tongue, and clenched teeth, and steady eye, and well-poised bayonet, they have helped mankind on to this great consummation; while, I fear, there will be some white ones, unable to forget that, with malignant heart, and deceitful speech, they have strove to hinder it."

Emancipation Confirmed

Lincoln's letter set the tone for Republican campaigns in state elections that fall. The party swept them all. In effect, the elections were a powerful endorsement of the administration's emancipation policy. But emancipation would not be assured of survival until it had been christened by the Constitution. On April 8, 1864, the Senate passed the Thirteenth Amendment to abolish slavery, but Democrats in the House blocked the required two-thirds majority there. Not until after Lincoln's reelection in 1864 would the House pass the amendment, which became part of the Constitution on December 6, 1865. In the end, though, the fate of slavery depended on the outcome of the war. And some of the heaviest fighting lay ahead.

The Year of Decision

Many Southerners succumbed to defeatism in the winter of 1863–1864. Desertions from Confederate armies increased. Inflation galloped out of control. According to a Richmond diarist, a merchant told a poor woman in October 1863 that the price of a barrel of flour was $70: "'My God!' exclaimed she, 'how can I pay such prices? I have seven children; what shall I do?' 'I don't know, madam,' said he, coolly, 'unless you eat your children.'"

The Davis administration, like the Lincoln administration a year earlier, had to face congressional elections during a time of public discontent, for the Confederate constitution mandated such elections in odd-numbered years. Political parties had ceased to exist in the Confederacy after Democrats and former Whigs had tacitly declared a truce in 1861. By 1863, however, significant hostility to Davis had emerged.

Some antiadministration candidates ran on a quasi-peace platform (analogous to that of the Copperheads in the North) that called for an armistice and peace negotiations. Left unresolved were the terms of such negotiations—reunion or independence. But any peace overture from a position of weakness was tantamount to conceding defeat. Still, antiadministration candidates made significant gains in the 1863 Confederate elections, though they fell about 15 seats short of a majority in the House and two seats short in the Senate.

OUT OF THE WILDERNESS

Shortages, inflation, political discontent, military defeat, high casualties, and the loss of thousands of slaves did not break the Southern spirit. The Confederate armies were no longer powerful enough to invade the North or to try to win the war with a knockout blow, but they were still strong enough to fight a war of attrition. If they could hold out long enough and inflict enough casualties on the Union armies, they might weaken the Northern will to continue fighting. And if they could just hold out until the Union presidential election in November, Northern voters might reject Lincoln and elect a Peace Democrat.

Northerners were vulnerable to this strategy. Military success in 1863 had created a mood of confidence, and people expected a quick, decisive victory in 1864. When Grant decided to remain in Virginia with the Army of the Potomac and to leave Sherman in command of the Union forces in northern Georgia, Northerners expected these two heavyweights to floor the Confederacy with a one-two punch. Lincoln was alarmed by this euphoria, fearing that disappointment might trigger despair.

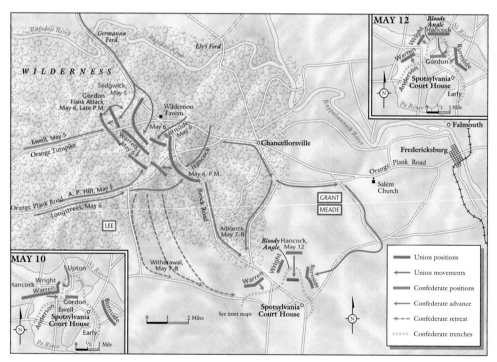

BATTLE OF THE WILDERNESS AND SPOTSYLVANIA, MAY 5–12, 1864

And that is what almost happened. Grant's strategic plan was elegant in its simplicity. While smaller Union armies in peripheral theaters carried out auxiliary campaigns, the two principal armies in Virginia and Georgia would attack the main Confederate forces under Lee and Johnston. Grant ordered simultaneous offensives on all fronts, to prevent the Confederates from shifting reinforcements from one theater to another.

Grant's offensives began in the first week of May. The heaviest fighting occurred in Virginia. When the Army of the Potomac crossed the Rapidan River, Lee attacked it in the flank while it was still in the Wilderness, a thick scrub forest where Union superiority in numbers and artillery would count for little. Lee's action brought on two days (May 5–6) of the most confused, frenzied fighting the war had yet seen. The battle surged back and forth, with the Confederates inflicting 18,000 casualties and suffering 12,000 themselves. Having apparently halted Grant's offensive, they claimed a victory.

Spotsylvania and Cold Harbor

But Grant did not retreat. Instead, he moved toward Spotsylvania Courthouse, a key crossroads 10 miles closer to Richmond. Skillfully, Lee pulled back to cover the road junction. Repeated Union assaults during the next 12 days (May 8–19) left another 18,000 Northerners and 12,000 Southerners killed, wounded, or captured. The Confederates fought from an elaborate network of trenches and log breastworks they had constructed virtually overnight.

Having achieved no better than stalemate around Spotsylvania, Grant moved south around Lee's right flank in an effort to force the outnumbered Confederates into an open fight. But Lee, anticipating Grant's moves, confronted him from behind formidable defenses at the North Anna River, Totopotomoy Creek, and near the crossroads inn of Cold Harbor, only 10 miles northeast of Richmond. Believing the Confederates must be exhausted and demoralized by their repeated retreats, Grant decided to attack at Cold Harbor on June 3—a costly mistake. Lee's troops were ragged and hungry but far from demoralized. Their withering fire inflicted 7,000 casualties in less than an hour.

Stalemate in Virginia

Now Grant moved all the way across the James River to strike at Petersburg, an industrial city and rail center 20 miles south of Richmond. If Petersburg fell, the Confederates could not hold Richmond. But once more Lee's troops raced southward and blocked Grant's troops. Four days of Union assaults (June 15–18) produced another 11,000 Northern casualties but no breakthrough.

Union losses in just six weeks had been so high that the Army of the Potomac had lost its offensive power. Grant reluctantly settled down for a siege along the Petersburg-Richmond front that would last more than nine grueling months.

Meanwhile, other Union operations in Virginia had achieved little success. Benjamin Butler bungled an attack up the James River against Richmond and was stopped by a scraped-together army under Beauregard. A Union thrust up the Shenandoah Valley was blocked at Lynchburg in June by Jubal Early. Early then led a raid all the way to the outskirts of Washington on July 11 and 12 before being driven back to Virginia. Union cavalry under Philip Sheridan inflicted considerable damage on Confederate resources in Virginia, but they did not strike a crippling blow. In the North, frustration set in.

THE ATLANTA CAMPAIGN

In Georgia, Sherman forced Johnston south toward Atlanta by constantly flanking him to the Union right, generally without bloody battles. By the end of June, Sherman had advanced 80 miles at the cost of 17,000 casualties to Johnston's 14,000—only one-third of the combined losses of Grant and Lee.

Davis grew alarmed by Johnston's apparent willingness to yield territory without a fight. Sherman again flanked the Confederate defenses at Kennesaw Mountain in early July. He crossed the Chattahoochee River and drove Johnston back to Peachtree Creek less than 5 miles from Atlanta. Fearing that Johnston would abandon the city, Davis replaced him with John Bell Hood.

Hood immediately prepared to counterattack against the Yankees. He did so three times, in late July. Each time, the Confederates reeled back in defeat, suffering a total of 15,000 casualties to Sherman's 6,000. At last, Hood retreated into the formidable earthworks ringing Atlanta and launched no more attacks. But his army did manage to keep Sherman's cavalry and infantry from taking the two railroads leading into Atlanta from the south. Like Grant at Petersburg, Sherman seemed to settle down for a siege.

PEACE OVERTURES

By August, the Confederate strategy of attrition seemed to be working. Union casualties on all fronts during the preceding three months totaled a staggering 110,000. "Who shall revive the withered hopes that bloomed at the opening of Grant's campaign?" asked the leading Democratic newspaper, the *New York World*. "STOP THE WAR!" shouted Democratic headlines. "All are tired of this damnable tragedy."

Even Republicans joined the chorus of despair. "Our bleeding, bankrupt, almost dying country longs for peace," wrote Horace Greeley of the *New York Tribune*. Greeley became involved in abortive "peace negotiations" spawned by Confederate agents in Canada. Those agents convinced Greeley that they carried peace overtures from Davis, but Lincoln was skeptical. Still, given the mood of the North in midsummer 1864, Lincoln could not reject any opportunity to stop the bloodshed. He deputized Greeley to meet with the Confederate agents in Niagara Falls on the Canadian side of the border. At almost the same time (mid-July), two other Northerners met under a flag of truce with Davis in Richmond. Lincoln had carefully instructed them—and Greeley—that his conditions for peace were "restoration of the Union and abandonment of slavery."

Of course, Davis would no more accept those terms than Lincoln would accept his. Although neither of the peace contacts came to anything, the Confederates gained a propaganda victory by claiming that Lincoln's terms had been the only obstacle to peace. Northern Democrats ignored the Southern refusal to accept reunion and focused on the slavery issue as the sole stumbling block. "Tens of thousands of white men must yet bite the dust to allay the negro mania of the President," ran a typical Democratic editorial. By August, even staunch Republicans were convinced that Lincoln's reelection was an impossibility. Lincoln thought so too. "I am going to be beaten," he told a friend, "and unless some great change takes place, *badly* beaten."

Lincoln faced enormous pressure to drop emancipation as a condition of peace, but he refused to yield. He would rather lose the election than go back on the promise he had made in the Emancipation Proclamation. Some 130,000 black soldiers and sailors were fighting for the Union. They would not do so if they thought the North intended to forsake them.

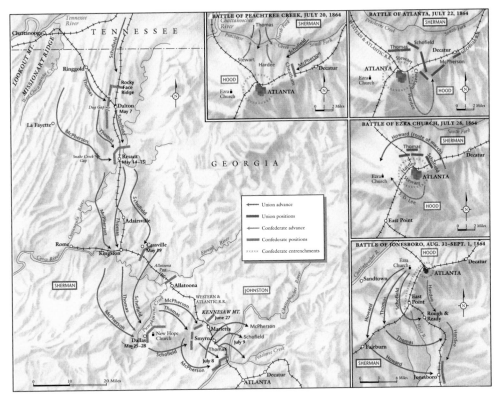

CAMPAIGN FOR ATLANTA, MAY–SEPTEMBER 1864

At the end of August, the Democrats nominated McClellan for president. The platform on which he ran declared that "after four years of failure to restore the Union by the experiment of war . . . [we] demand that immediate efforts be made for a cessation of hostilities." Southerners were jubilant. Democratic victory on that platform, said the *Charleston Mercury*, "must lead to peace and our independence" if "for the next two months *we hold our own and prevent military success by our foes.*"

THE PRISONER-EXCHANGE CONTROVERSY

The Democratic platform also raised another contentious matter. By midsummer 1864 the plight of Union and Confederate captives had become one of the most bitter issues of the war. Because of the upcoming presidential election, and also because conditions were generally worse in Southern prisons it was a political issue mainly in the North.

In 1862 the Union and Confederate armed forces had signed a cartel for the exchange of prisoners captured in battle. The arrangement had worked reasonably well for a year, making large prison camps unnecessary. But when the Union Army began to organize regiments of former slaves, the Confederate government announced that if they were captured, they and their white officers would be put to death. However, Lincoln threatened retaliation on

Confederate prisoners of war if it did so. Nevertheless, Confederate troops sometimes murdered black soldiers and their officers as they tried to surrender.

In most cases, though, Confederate officers returned captured black soldiers to slavery or put them to hard labor on Southern fortifications. Expressing outrage at this treatment, in 1863 the Lincoln administration suspended the exchange of prisoners until the Confederacy agreed to treat white and black prisoners alike. The Confederacy refused.

There matters stood as the heavy fighting of 1864 poured scores of thousands of captured soldiers into hastily contrived prison compounds that quickly became death camps. Prisoners were subjected to overcrowding, poor sanitation, contaminated water, scanty rations, inadequate medical facilities, and the exposure of Union prisoners to the heat of a deep-South summer and Confederate prisoners to the cold of a northern winter. The suffering of Northern prisoners was especially acute because of the deterioration of the Southern economy. Nearly 16 percent of all Union soldiers held in Southern prison camps died. Andersonville was the most notorious hellhole. A stockade camp of 26 acres with neither huts nor tents, designed to accommodate 15,000 prisoners, it held 33,000 in August 1864. They died at the rate of more than 100 a day. Altogether, 13,000 Union soldiers died at Andersonville.

The suffering of Union prisoners brought heavy pressure on the Lincoln administration to renew exchanges, but the Confederates would not budge on the question of exchanging black soldiers. After a series of battles on the Richmond-Petersburg front in September 1864, Lee proposed an informal exchange of prisoners. Grant agreed, on condition that black soldiers captured in the fighting be included "the same as white soldiers." Lee replied that "negroes belonging to our citizens are not considered subjects of exchange and were not included in my proposition." No exchange, then, responded Grant. Lincoln backed this policy. He would not sacrifice the principle of equal treatment of black prisoners, even though local Republican leaders warned that many in the North "will work and vote against the President."

THE ISSUE OF BLACK SOLDIERS IN THE CONFEDERATE ARMY

During the winter of 1864–1865 the Confederate government quietly abandoned its refusal to exchange black prisoners, and exchanges resumed. One reason for this reversal was a Confederate decision to recruit slaves to fight for the South. Two years earlier, Davis had denounced the North's arming of freed slaves. But by February 1865, Southern armies were desperate for manpower, and slaves constituted the only remaining reserve. Davis pressed the Confederate Congress to enact a bill for recruitment of black soldiers. The assumption that any slaves who fought for the South would have to be granted freedom generated bitter opposition. "What did we go to war for, if not to protect our property?" asked a Virginia senator. By three votes in the House and one in the Senate, the Confederate Congress finally passed the bill on March 13, 1865. Before any Southern black regiments could be organized, however, the war ended.

THE REELECTION OF LINCOLN AND THE END OF THE CONFEDERACY

Despite Republicans' fears, events on the battlefield, rather than political controversies, had the strongest impact on U.S. voters in 1864. In effect, the election became a referendum on whether to continue fighting for unconditional victory. And suddenly the military situation changed dramatically.

THE CAPTURE OF ATLANTA

After a month of apparent stalemate on the Atlanta front, Sherman's army again made a large movement by the right flank to attack the last rail link into Atlanta from the south. At the battle of Jonesboro on August 31 and September 1, Sherman's men captured the railroad. Hood abandoned Atlanta to save his army. On September 2, jubilant Union troops marched into Atlanta.

This news had an enormous impact on the election. A New York Republican wrote that the capture of Atlanta, "coming at this political crisis, is the greatest event of the war." The *Richmond Examiner* glumly concurred. The fall of Atlanta, it declared, "came in the very nick of time" to "save the party of Lincoln from irretrievable ruin."

THE SHENANDOAH VALLEY

If Atlanta was not enough to brighten the prospects for Lincoln's reelection, events in Virginia's Shenandoah Valley were. After Early's raid through the valley in July, Grant put Philip Sheridan in charge of a reinforced Army of the Shenandoah, telling him to "go after Early and follow him to the death." Sheridan infused the same spirit into the Army of the Shenandoah that he had previously imbued in his cavalry. On September 19 they attacked Early's force near Winchester and after a day-long battle sent the Confederates flying to the south. Sheridan pursued them, attacking again on September 22 at Fisher's Hill 20 miles south of Winchester. Early's line collapsed, and his routed army fled 60 more miles southward.

Sheridan now set about destroying the valley's crops and mills so thoroughly that "crows flying over it for the balance of the season will have to carry their provender with them." Sheridan boasted that by the time he was through, "the Valley, from Winchester up to Staunton, ninety-two miles, will have little in it for man or beast."

But Jubal Early was not yet willing to give up. Reinforced by a division from Lee, on October 19 he launched a dawn attack across Cedar Creek, 12 miles south of Winchester. He caught the Yankees by surprise and drove them back in disorder. At the time of the attack, Sheridan was returning to his army from Washington, where he had gone to confer on strategy. He jumped onto his horse and sped to the battlefield. By sundown, Sheridan's charisma and tactical leadership had turned the battle from a Union defeat into another Confederate rout.

The victories won by Sherman and Sheridan ensured Lincoln's reelection on November 8 by a majority of 212 to 21 in the Electoral College. Soldiers played a notable role in the balloting. Every Northern state except three whose legislatures were controlled by Democrats had passed laws allowing absentee voting by soldiers. Seventy-eight percent of the military vote went to Lincoln—compared with 54 percent of the civilian vote. The men who were doing the fighting had sent a clear message that they meant to finish the job.

FROM ATLANTA TO THE SEA

Many Southerners got the message. But not Davis. The Confederacy remained "as erect and defiant as ever," he told his Congress in November 1864. It was this last-ditch resistance that Sherman set out to break in his famous march from Atlanta to the sea.

Sherman had concluded that defeat of the Confederate armies was not enough to win the war; the railroads, factories, and farms that supported those armies must also be destroyed. The will of the civilians who sustained the war must be crushed. Sherman expressed more bluntly than anyone else the meaning of total war. "We cannot change the hearts of those people of the South," he said, "but we can make war so terrible and make them so sick of war that generations would pass away before they would again appeal to it."

In Tennessee and Mississippi, Sherman's troops had burned everything of military value that was within their reach. Now Sherman proposed to do the same in Georgia. He urged Grant to let him march through the heart of Georgia, living off the land and destroying all resources not needed by his army—the same policy Sheridan was carrying out in the Shenandoah Valley. Grant and Lincoln were reluctant to authorize such a risky move, especially with Hood's army of 40,000 men still intact in northern Alabama. But Sherman assured them that he would send George Thomas to take command of a force of 60,000 men in Tennessee who would be more than a match for Hood. With another 60,000, Sherman could "move through Georgia, smashing things to the sea."

Lincoln and Grant finally consented. On November 16, Sherman's avengers marched out of Atlanta after burning a third of the city, including some nonmilitary property. Southward they marched 280 miles to Savannah, wrecking everything in their path that could by any stretch of the imagination be considered of military value.

THE BATTLES OF FRANKLIN AND NASHVILLE

They encountered little resistance. Instead of chasing Sherman, Hood invaded Tennessee with the hope of recovering that state for the Confederacy. But this campaign turned into a disaster that virtually destroyed his army. On November 30, the Confederates attacked part of the Union force at Franklin, 20 miles south of Nashville. It was a slaughter. But instead of retreating, Hood moved on to Nashville, where on December 15 and 16 Thomas launched an attack that almost wiped out the Army of Tennessee. Its remnants retreated to Mississippi, where Hood resigned in January 1865.

FORT FISHER AND SHERMAN'S MARCH THROUGH THE CAROLINAS

News of Hood's defeat produced, in the words of a Southern diarist, "the darkest and most dismal day" of the Confederacy's short history. But worse was yet to come. Lee's army in Virginia drew its dwindling supplies overland from the Carolinas and through the port of Wilmington, North Carolina, the only city still accessible to blockade runners. That was because the mouth of the Cape Fear River below Wilmington was guarded by massive Fort Fisher, whose big guns kept blockade ships at bay and protected the runners. In January 1865, though, the largest armada of the war—58 ships with 627 guns—pounded Fort Fisher for two days, disabling most of its big guns. Army troops and marines landed and stormed the fort, capturing it on January 15. That ended the blockade running, and Sherman soon put an end to supplies from the Carolinas as well.

At the end of January, Sherman's soldiers headed north from Savannah, eager to take revenge on South Carolina, which to their mind had started the war. Here, they made even less distinction between civilian and military property than they had in Georgia, and left even less of Columbia standing than they had of Atlanta. Seemingly invincible, Sherman's army pushed into North Carolina and brushed aside the force that Joseph E. Johnston had assembled to stop them.

But the war would not end until the Confederate armies surrendered, as Lincoln made clear in his second inaugural address on March 4, 1865. In the best-known words from that address, he urged a binding up of the nation's wounds "with malice toward none" and "charity for all." But even more significant, given that the conflict still raged, were these words:

> American Slavery is one of those offences which, in the providence of God . . . He now wills to remove [through] this terrible war, as the woe due to those by whom the offence came. . . . Fondly do we hope—fervently do we pray—that this mighty scourge of war may speedily pass away.

THE ROAD TO APPOMATTOX

The Army of Northern Virginia was now the only entity that now kept the Confederacy alive, but it was on the verge of disintegration. Scores of its soldiers were deserting every day. On April 1, Sheridan's cavalry and an infantry corps smashed the right flank of Lee's line at Five Forks and cut off the last railroad into Petersburg. The next day, Grant attacked all along the line and forced Lee to abandon both Petersburg and Richmond. As the Confederate government fled its capital, its army set fire to all the military stores it could not carry. The fires spread and destroyed more of Richmond than the Northern troops had destroyed of Atlanta or Columbia.

Lee's starving men limped westward, hoping to turn south and join the remnants of Johnston's army in North Carolina. But Sheridan's cavalry raced ahead and cut them off at Appomattox, 90 miles from Petersburg, on April 8. When the weary Confederates tried a breakout attack the next morning, their first probe revealed solid ranks of Union infantry arrayed behind the cavalry. It was the end. "There is nothing left for me to do," said Lee, "but to go and see General Grant." Lee met with Grant at the house of Wilmer McLean. There, Grant dictated the terms of surrender.

CASUALTIES IN CIVIL WAR ARMIES AND NAVIES   *Confederate records are incomplete; the Confederate data listed here are therefore estimates. The actual Confederate totals were probably higher.*

	KILLED AND MORTALLY WOUNDED IN COMBAT	DIED OF DISEASE	DIED IN PRISON	MISCELLANEOUS DEATHS*	TOTAL DEATHS	WOUNDED, NOT MORTALLY	TOTAL CASUALTIES
Union	111,904	197,388	30,192	24,881	364,345	277,401	641,766
Confederate (estimated)	94,000	140,000	26,000	No Estimates	260,000	195,000	455,000
Both Armies (estimated)	205,904	337,388	56,192	24,881	624,365	472,401	1,096,766

*Accidents, drownings, causes not stated, etc.

Abraham Lincoln in 1865   This is the last photograph of Lincoln, taken on April 10, 1865, four days before his assassination. Four years of war had left their mark on the 56-year-old president; note the lines of strain, fatigue, and sadness in his face.

The terms were generous. Thirty thousand captured Confederates were allowed to go home on condition that they promise never again to take up arms against the United States. After completing the surrender formalities on April 9, Grant introduced Lee to his staff, which included Colonel Ely Parker, a Seneca Indian. As Lee shook hands with Parker, he stared for a moment at Parker's dark features and said: "I am glad to see one real American here." Parker replied solemnly: "We are all Americans."

The Assassination of Lincoln

Wild celebrations broke out in the North at the news of the fall of Richmond, followed soon by news of Appomattox. But almost overnight, the celebrations turned to mourning. On the evening of April 14, the careworn Abraham Lincoln sought to relax by attending a comedy at Ford's Theatre. In the middle of the play, John Wilkes Booth broke into Lincoln's box and shot

Chronology

1862	Confederacy enacts conscription (April 16) • Lincoln informs two cabinet members of intention to issue Emancipation Proclamation (July 13) • Battle of Antietam (September 17) • Lincoln issues preliminary Emancipation Proclamation (September 22) • Battle of Fredericksburg (December 13) • Battle of Stones River (December 31–January 2)
1863	Lincoln issues final Emancipation Proclamation (January 1) • Union enacts conscription (March 3) • Richmond bread riot (April 2) • Battle of Chancellorsville (May 1–5) • Battle of Gettysburg (July 1–3) • Vicksburg surrenders (July 4) • Port Hudson surrenders (July 9) • New York draft riot (July 13–16) • Assault on Fort Wagner (July 18) • Battle of Chickamauga (September 19–20) • Battles of Chattanooga (November 24–25)
1864	Battle of the Wilderness (May 5–6) • Battle of Spotsylvania (May 8–19) • Fighting at Petersburg leads to nine-month siege (June 15–18) • Fall of Atlanta (September 1) • Reelection of Lincoln (November 8) • Battle of Nashville (December 15–16)
1865	Capture of Fort Fisher (January 15) • Confederates evacuate Richmond (April 2) • Lee surrenders at Appomattox (April 9) • Booth assassinates Lincoln (April 14) • Last Confederate army surrenders (June 23) • Congress ratifies Thirteenth Amendment abolishing slavery (December 6)

the president fatally in the head. An aspiring actor, Booth was a native of Maryland and a frustrated, unstable egotist who hated Lincoln for what he had done to Booth's beloved South. As he jumped from Lincoln's box to the stage and escaped out a back door, he shouted Virginia's state motto at the stunned audience: "Sic semper tyrannis" ("Thus always to tyrants").

Lincoln's death in the early morning of April 15 produced an outpouring of grief throughout the North and among newly freed slaves in the South. The martyred president did not live to see the culmination of his great achievement in leading the nation to a victory that preserved its existence and abolished slavery. Within 10 weeks after Lincoln's death, his assassin was trapped and killed in a burning barn in Virginia (April 26), the remaining Confederate armies surrendered one after another (April 26, May 4, May 26, June 23), and Union cavalry captured the fleeing Jefferson Davis in Georgia (May 10). The trauma of the Civil War was over, but the problems of peace and reconstruction had just begun.

Conclusion

Northern victory in the Civil War resolved two fundamental questions that had been left unresolved by the Revolution of 1776 and the Constitution of 1789: whether this fragile experiment in federalism called the United States would survive as one nation; and whether that nation, founded on a charter of liberty, would continue to exist as the largest slaveholding country in the world. Before 1861 the question of whether a state could secede from the Union had remained open. Eleven states did secede, but their defeat in a war that cost 625,000 lives resolved the issue: Since 1865 no state has seriously threatened secession. And in 1865 the adoption of the Thirteenth Amendment to the Constitution confirmed the supreme power of the national government to abolish slavery and ensure the liberty of all Americans.

At the same time the Civil War accomplished a regional transfer of power from South to North. From 1800 to 1860 the slave states had used their leverage in the Jeffersonian Republican and Jacksonian Democratic parties to control national politics. A southern slaveholder was president of the United States during two-thirds of the years from 1789 to 1861. Most congressional leaders and Supreme Court justices during that period were southerners. But for half a century after 1861 no native of a southern state was elected president, only one served as Speaker of the House and none as president pro tem of the Senate, and only 5 of the 26 Supreme Court justices appointed during that half-century were from the South. In 1860 the South's share of the national wealth was 30 percent; in 1870 it was 12 percent. The institutions and ideology of a plantation society and a caste system that had dominated half of the country before 1861 went down with a great crash in 1865—to be replaced by the institutions and ideology of free-labor capitalism. Once feared as the gravest threat to liberty, the power of the national government sustained by a large army had achieved the greatest triumph of liberty in American history. With victory and peace in 1865, the reunited nation turned its attention to the issue of equality.

RECONSTRUCTION, 1863–1877

WARTIME RECONSTRUCTION

ANDREW JOHNSON AND RECONSTRUCTION

THE ADVENT OF CONGRESSIONAL RECONSTRUCTION

THE IMPEACHMENT OF ANDREW JOHNSON

THE GRANT ADMINISTRATION ∿ THE RETREAT FROM RECONSTRUCTION

From the beginning of the Civil War, the North fought to "reconstruct" the Union. At first Lincoln's purpose was to restore the Union as it had existed before 1861. But once the abolition of slavery became a Northern war aim, the Union could never be reconstructed on its old foundations. Instead, it must experience a "new birth of freedom," as Lincoln had said at the dedication of the military cemetery at Gettysburg.

But precisely what did "a new birth of freedom" mean? At the very least it meant the end of slavery. The slave states would be reconstructed on a free-labor basis. But what would be the dimensions of liberty for the 4 million freed slaves? Would they become citizens equal to their former masters in the eyes of the law? And on what terms should the Confederate states return to the Union? What would be the powers of the states and of the national government in a reconstructed Union?

WARTIME RECONSTRUCTION

Lincoln pondered these questions long and hard. At first he feared that whites in the South would never extend equal rights to the freed slaves. In 1862 and 1863, Lincoln encouraged freedpeople to emigrate to all-black countries like Haiti. But black leaders, abolitionists, and many Republicans objected to that policy. Black people were Americans. Why should they not have the rights of American citizens instead of being urged to leave the country?

Lincoln eventually was converted to the logic and justice of that view. But in beginning the process of reconstruction, Lincoln first reached out to southern *whites* whose allegiance to the Confederacy was lukewarm. On December 8, 1863, Lincoln issued his Proclamation of Amnesty and Reconstruction, which offered presidential pardon to southern whites who took an oath of allegiance to the United States and accepted the abolition of slavery. In any state where the number of white males aged 21 or older who took this oath equaled 10 percent of the number of voters in 1860, that nucleus could reestablish a state government to which Lincoln promised presidential recognition.

Because the war was still raging, this policy could be carried out only where Union troops controlled substantial portions of a Confederate state: Louisiana, Arkansas, and Tennessee in early 1864. Nevertheless, Lincoln hoped that once the process had begun in those areas, it might snowball as Union military victories convinced more and more Confederates that their cause was hopeless. As matters turned out, those military victories were long delayed, and reconstruction in most parts of the South did not begin until 1865.

Another problem that slowed the process was growing opposition within Lincoln's own party. Many Republicans believed that white men who had fought *against* the Union should not be rewarded with restoration of their political rights while black men who had fought *for* the Union were denied those rights. The Proclamation of Reconstruction stated that "any provision which may be adopted by [a reconstructed] State government in relation to the freed people of such State, which shall recognize and declare their permanent freedom, provide for their education, and which may yet be consistent, as a temporary arrangement, with their present condition as a laboring, landless, and homeless class, will not be objected to by the national Executive." This seemed to mean that white landowners and former slaveholders could adopt labor regulations and other measures to control former slaves, so long as they recognized their freedom.

RADICAL REPUBLICANS AND RECONSTRUCTION

These were radical advances over slavery, but for many Republicans they were not radical enough. If the freedpeople were landless, they said, provide them with land by confiscating the plantations of leading Confederates as punishment for treason. Radical Republicans also distrusted oaths of allegiance sworn by ex-Confederates. Rather than simply restoring the old ruling class to power, they asked, why not give freed slaves the vote, to provide a genuinely loyal nucleus of supporters in the South?

These radical positions did not command a majority of Congress in 1864. Yet the experience of Louisiana, the first state to reorganize under Lincoln's more moderate policy, convinced even nonradical Republicans to block that policy. Enough white men in the occupied portion of the state took the oath of allegiance to satisfy Lincoln's conditions. They adopted a new state constitution and formed a government that abolished slavery and provided a school system for blacks. But the new government did not grant blacks the right to vote. It also authorized planters to enforce restrictive labor policies on black plantation workers. Louisiana's actions alienated a majority of congressional Republicans, who refused to admit representatives and senators from the "reconstructed" state.

At the same time, though, Congress failed to enact a reconstruction policy of its own. This was not for lack of trying. In fact, both houses passed the Wade-Davis reconstruction bill (named for Senator Benjamin Wade of Ohio and Representative Henry Winter Davis of Maryland) in July 1864. That bill did not enfranchise blacks, but it did impose such stringent loyalty requirements on southern whites that few of them could take the required oath. Lincoln therefore vetoed it.

Lincoln's action infuriated many Republicans. Wade and Davis published a blistering "manifesto" denouncing the president. This bitter squabble threatened for a time to destroy Lincoln's chances of being reelected. But Union military success in the fall of 1864 reunited the Republicans behind Lincoln. The collapse of Confederate military resistance the following spring set the stage for compromise on a policy for the postwar South. Two days after Appomattox, Lincoln promised that he would soon announce such a policy. But three days later he was assassinated.

ANDREW JOHNSON AND RECONSTRUCTION

In 1864 Republicans had adopted the name "Union Party" to attract the votes of War Democrats and border-state Unionists who could not bring themselves to vote Republican. For the same reason, they also nominated Andrew Johnson of Tennessee as Lincoln's running mate.

Of "poor white" heritage, Johnson had clawed his way up in the rough-and-tumble politics of East Tennessee. This was a region of small farms and few slaves, where there was little love for the planters who controlled the state. Johnson denounced the planters as "stuck-up aristocrats" who had no empathy with the southern yeomen for whom Johnson became a self-appointed spokesman. Johnson was the only senator from a seceding state who refused to support the Confederacy. For this, the Republicans rewarded him with the vice presidential nomination, hoping to attract the votes of pro-war Democrats and upper-South Unionists.

Booth's bullet therefore elevated to the presidency a man who still thought of himself as primarily a Democrat and a southerner. The trouble this might cause in a party that was mostly Republican and northern was not immediately apparent, however. In fact, Johnson's enmity toward the "stuck-up aristocrats" whom he blamed for leading the South into secession prompted him to utter dire threats against "traitors." "Traitors must be impoverished," he said. "They must not only be punished, but their social power must be destroyed."

Radical Republicans liked the sound of this. It seemed to promise the type of reconstruction they favored—one that would deny political power to ex-Confederates and would enfranchise blacks. They envisioned a coalition between these new black voters and the small minority of southern whites who had never supported the Confederacy. These men could be expected to vote Republican. Republican governments in southern states would guarantee freedom and would pass laws to provide civil rights and economic opportunity for freed slaves.

JOHNSON'S POLICY

From a combination of pragmatic, partisan, and idealistic motives, therefore, radical Republicans prepared to implement a progressive reconstruction policy. But Johnson unexpectedly refused to cooperate. Instead of calling Congress into special session, he moved ahead on his own. On May 29, Johnson issued two proclamations. The first provided for a blanket amnesty for all but the highest-ranking Confederate officials and military officers, and those ex-Confederates with taxable property worth $20,000 or more. The second named a provisional governor for North Carolina and directed him to call an election of delegates to frame a new state constitution. Only white men who had received amnesty and taken an oath of allegiance could vote. Similar proclamations soon followed for other former Confederate states. Johnson's policy was clear. He would exclude both blacks and upper-class whites from the reconstruction process.

Many Republicans supported Johnson's policy at first. But the radicals feared that restricting the vote to whites would open the door to the restoration of the old power structure in the South. They began to sense that Johnson was as dedicated to white supremacy as any

Confederate. "White men alone must govern the South," he told a Democratic senator. After a tense confrontation with a group of black men led by Frederick Douglass, Johnson told his private secretary: "I know that damned Douglass; he's just like any nigger, and he would sooner cut a white man's throat than not."

Moderate Republicans believed that black men should participate to some degree in the reconstruction process, but in 1865 they were not yet prepared to break with the president. They regarded his policy as an "experiment" that would be modified as time went on. "Loyal negroes must not be put down, while disloyal white men are put up," wrote a moderate Republican. "But I am quite willing to see what will come of Mr. Johnson's experiment."

SOUTHERN DEFIANCE

As it happened, none of the state conventions enfranchised a single black. Some of them even balked at ratifying the Thirteenth Amendment (which abolished slavery). Reports from Unionists and army officers in the South told of neo-Confederate violence against blacks and their white sympathizers. Johnson seemed to encourage such activities by allowing the organization of white militia units in the South. "What can be hatched from such an egg," asked a Republican newspaper, "but another rebellion?"

Then there was the matter of presidential pardons. After talking fiercely about punishing traitors, and after excluding several classes of them from his amnesty proclamation, Johnson began to issue special pardons to many ex-Confederates, restoring to them all property and political rights. Moreover, under the new state constitutions southern voters were electing hundreds of ex-Confederates to state offices. Even more alarming to northerners, who thought they had won the war, was the election to Congress of no fewer than nine ex-Confederate congressmen, seven ex-Confederate state officials, four generals, four colonels, and even the former Confederate vice president, Alexander H. Stephens.

Somehow the aristocrats and traitors Johnson had denounced in April had taken over the reconstruction process. What had happened? Flattery was part of the answer. In applying for pardons, thousands of prominent ex-Confederates or their tearful female relatives had confessed the error of their ways and had appealed for presidential mercy. Reveling in his power, Johnson waxed eloquent on his "love, respect, and confidence" toward southern whites, for whom he now felt "forbearing and forgiving."

More important, perhaps, was the praise and support Johnson received from leading northern Democrats. Though the Republicans had placed him on their presidential ticket in 1864, Johnson was after all a Democrat. That party's leaders enticed Johnson with visions of reelection as a Democrat in 1868 if he could manage to reconstruct the South in a manner that would preserve a Democratic majority there.

THE BLACK CODES

That was just what the Republicans feared. Their concern was confirmed in the fall of 1865 when some state governments enacted "Black Codes."

One of the first tasks of the legislatures of the reconstructed states was to define the rights of 4 million former slaves who were now free. The option of treating them exactly like white citizens was scarcely considered. Instead, the states excluded black people from juries and the ballot box, did not permit them to testify against whites in court, banned interracial marriage, and punished them more severely than whites for certain crimes. Some states defined any un-employed black person as a vagrant and hired him out to a planter, forbade blacks to lease land, and provided for the apprenticing to whites of black youths who did not have adequate parental support.

These Black Codes aroused anger among northern Republicans, who saw them as a brazen attempt to reinstate a quasi-slavery. "We tell the white men of Mississippi," declared the *Chicago Tribune,* "that the men of the North will convert the State of Mississippi into a frog pond before they will allow such laws to disgrace one foot of the soil in which the bones of our soldiers sleep and over which the flag of freedom waves." And, in fact, the Union Army's occu-pation forces did suspend the implementation of Black Codes that discriminated on racial grounds.

LAND AND LABOR IN THE POSTWAR SOUTH

The Black Codes, though discriminatory, were designed to address a genuine problem. The end of the war had left black-white relations in the South in a state of limbo. The South's economy was in a shambles. Burned-out plantations, fields growing up in weeds, and railroads without tracks, bridges, or rolling stock marked the trail of war. Most tangible assets except the land itself had been destroyed. Law and order broke down in many areas. The war had ended early enough in the spring to allow the planting of at least some food crops. But who would plant and cultivate them? One-quarter of the South's white farmers had been killed in the war; the slaves were slaves no more. "We have nothing left to begin anew with," lamented a South Carolina planter. "I never did a day's work in my life, and I don't know how to begin."

But despite all, life went on. Slaveless planters and their wives, soldiers' widows and their children plowed and planted. Confederate veterans drifted home and went to work. Former slaveowners asked their former slaves to work the land for wages or shares of the crop, and many did so. But others refused, because for them to leave the old place was an essential part of freedom. "You ain't, none o' you, gwinter feel rale free," said a black preacher to his congre-gation, "till you shakes de dus' ob de Ole Plantashun offen yore feet" (dialect in original source).

Thus in the summer of 1865 the roads were alive with freedpeople on the move. Many of them signed on to work at farms just a few miles from their old homes. Others moved into town. Some looked for relatives who had been sold away during slavery or from whom they had been separated during the war. Some wandered aimlessly. Crime increased, and whites or-ganized vigilante groups to discipline blacks and force them to work.

THE FREEDMEN'S BUREAU

Into this vacuum stepped the United States Army and the Freedmen's Bureau. Tens of thou-sands of troops remained in the South until civil government could be restored. The Freed-men's Bureau (its official title was Bureau of Refugees, Freedmen, and Abandoned Lands), created by Congress in March 1865, became the principal agency for overseeing relations be-tween former slaves and owners. Staffed by army officers, the bureau established posts throughout the South to supervise free-labor wage contracts between landowners and freed-people. The Freedmen's Bureau also issued food rations to 150,000 people daily during 1865, one-third of them to whites.

THE FREEDMEN'S BUREAU Created in 1865, the Freedmen's Bureau stood between freed slaves and their former masters in the postwar South, charged with the task of protecting freedpeople from injustice and repression. Staffed by officers of the Union Army, the bureau symbolized the military power of the government in its efforts to keep peace in the South.

The Freedmen's Bureau was viewed with hostility by southern whites. But without it, the postwar chaos and devastation in the South would have been much greater. Bureau agents used their influence with black people to encourage them to sign free-labor contracts and return to work.

In negotiating labor contracts, the Bureau tried to establish minimum wages. Because there was so little money in the South, however, many contracts called for share wages—that is, paying workers with shares of the crop. At first, landowners worked their laborers in large groups called gangs. But many black workers resented this system. Thus, a new system evolved, called sharecropping, whereby a black family worked a specific piece of land in return for a share of the crop produced on it.

LAND FOR THE LANDLESS

Freedpeople, of course, would have preferred to farm their own land. "What's de use of being free if you don't own land enough to be buried in?" asked one black sharecropper (dialect in original). Some black farmers did manage to save up enough money to buy small plots of land. Demobilized black soldiers purchased land with their bounty payments, sometimes pooling their money to buy an entire plantation, on which several black families settled. Northern philanthropists helped some freedmen buy land. But for most ex-slaves the purchase of land was impossible. Few of them had money, and even if they did, whites often refused to sell.

Several northern radicals proposed legislation to confiscate ex-Confederate land and redistribute it to freedpeople. But those proposals got nowhere. And the most promising effort to put thousands of slaves on land of their own also failed. In January 1865, after his march through Georgia, General William T. Sherman had issued a military order setting aside thousands of acres of abandoned plantation land in the Georgia and South Carolina low-country for settlement by freed slaves. The army even turned over some of its surplus mules to black farmers. The expectation of "40 acres and a mule" excited freedpeople in 1865. But President Johnson's Amnesty Proclamation and his wholesale issuance of pardons restored most of this property to pardoned ex-Confederates. The same thing happened to white-owned land elsewhere in the South. Placed under the temporary care of the Freedmen's Bureau for subsequent possible distribution to freedpeople, by 1866 nearly all of this land had been restored to its former owners by order of President Johnson.

EDUCATION

Abolitionists were more successful in helping freedpeople get an education. During the war, freedmen's aid societies and missionary societies founded by abolitionists had sent teachers to

A BLACK SCHOOL DURING RECONSTRUCTION In the antebellum South, teaching slaves to read and write was forbidden. Thus, about 90 percent of the freedpeople were illiterate in 1865. One of their top priorities was education. At first, most of the teachers in the freedmen's schools established by northern missionary societies were northern white women. But as black teachers were trained, they took over the elementary schools, such as this one photographed in the 1870s.

Union-occupied areas of the South to set up schools for freed slaves. After the war, this effort was expanded with the aid of the Freedmen's Bureau. Two thousand northern teachers fanned out into every part of the South to train black teachers. After 1870 missionary societies concentrated on making higher education available to African Americans. They founded many of the black colleges in the South. These efforts reduced the southern black illiteracy rate to 70 percent by 1880 and to 48 percent by 1900.

THE ADVENT OF CONGRESSIONAL RECONSTRUCTION

The civil and political rights of freedpeople would be shaped by the terms of reconstruction. By the time Congress met in December 1865, the Republican majority was determined to take control of the process by which former Confederate states would be restored to full representation. Congress refused to admit the representatives and senators elected by the former Confederate states under Johnson's reconstruction policy, and set up a special committee to formulate new terms. The committee held hearings at which southern Unionists, freedpeople, and U.S. Army officers testified to abuse and terrorism in the South. Their testimony convinced Republicans of the need for stronger federal intervention to define and protect the civil rights of freedpeople. However, because racism was still strong in the North, the special committee decided to draft a constitutional amendment that would encourage southern states to enfranchise blacks but would not require them to do so.

SCHISM BETWEEN PRESIDENT AND CONGRESS

Meanwhile, Congress passed two laws to protect the economic and civil rights of freedpeople. The first extended the life of the Freedmen's Bureau and expanded its powers. The second defined freedpeople as citizens with equal legal rights and gave federal courts appellate jurisdiction to enforce those rights. But to the dismay of moderates who were trying to heal the widening breach between the president and Congress, Johnson vetoed both measures. He followed this action with a speech to Democratic supporters in which he denounced Republican leaders as traitors who did not want to restore the Union except on terms that would degrade white southerners. Democratic newspapers applauded the president for vetoing bills that would "compound our race with niggers, gypsies, and baboons."

THE FOURTEENTH AMENDMENT

Johnson had thrown down the gauntlet to congressional Republicans. But with better than a two-thirds majority in both houses, they passed the Freedmen's Bureau and Civil Rights bills over the president's vetoes. Then on April 30, the special committee submitted to Congress its proposed Fourteenth Amendment to the Constitution. After lengthy debate, the amendment received the required two-thirds majority in Congress on June 13 and went to the states for ratification. Section 1 defined all native-born or naturalized persons, including blacks, as American citizens and prohibited the states from abridging the "privileges and immunities" of citizens, from depriving "any person of life, liberty, or property without due process of law," and from denying to any person "the equal protection of the laws." Section 2 gave states the option of either enfranchising black males or losing a proportionate number of congressional seats and electoral votes. Section 3 disqualified a significant number of ex-Confederates from holding federal or state office. Section 4 guaranteed the national debt and repudiated the Confederate debt. Section 5 empowered Congress to enforce the Fourteenth Amendment by "appropriate legislation."

The Fourteenth Amendment had far-reaching consequences. Section 1 has become the most important provision in the Constitution for defining and enforcing civil rights. It vastly expanded federal powers to prevent state violations of civil rights. It also greatly enlarged the rights of blacks.

THE 1866 ELECTIONS

During the campaign for the 1866 congressional elections Republicans made clear that any ex-Confederate state that ratified the Fourteenth Amendment would be declared "reconstructed" and that its representatives and senators would be seated in Congress. Tennessee ratified the amendment, but Johnson counseled other southern legislatures to reject the amendment, and they did so. Johnson then created a "National Union Party" made up of a few conservative Republicans who disagreed with their party, some border-state Unionists who supported the president, and Democrats.

The inclusion of Democrats doomed the effort from the start. Many northern Democrats still carried the taint of having opposed the war effort, and most northern voters did not trust them. The National Union Party was further damaged by race riots in Memphis and New Orleans. The riots bolstered Republican arguments that national power was necessary to protect "the fruits of victory" in the South. Perhaps the biggest liability was Johnson himself. In a whistle-stop tour through the North, he traded insults with hecklers and embarrassed his supporters.

Republicans swept the election. Having rejected the reconstruction terms embodied in the Fourteenth Amendment, southern Democrats now faced far more stringent terms. "They would not cooperate in rebuilding what they destroyed," wrote an exasperated moderate Republican, so "we must remove the rubbish and rebuild from the bottom."

THE RECONSTRUCTION ACTS OF 1867

In March 1867 the new Congress enacted two laws prescribing new procedures for the full restoration of the former Confederate states to the Union. The Reconstruction acts of 1867 divided the 10 southern states into five military districts, directed army officers to register voters for the election of delegates to new constitutional conventions, and enfranchised males aged 21 and older (including blacks) to vote in those elections. When a state had adopted a new constitution that granted equal civil and political rights regardless of race and had ratified the Fourteenth Amendment, it would be declared reconstructed and its newly elected congressmen would be seated.

These measures embodied a true revolution. Just a few years earlier, southerners had been masters of 4 million slaves and part of an independent Confederate nation. Now they were shorn of political power, with their former slaves not only freed but also politically empowered.

Like most revolutions, the reconstruction process did not go smoothly. Many southern Democrats breathed defiance and refused to cooperate. The presence of the army minimized anti-black violence. But thousands of white southerners who were eligible to vote refused to do so, hoping that their nonparticipation would delay the process long enough for northern voters to come to their senses and elect Democrats to Congress.

Blacks and their white allies organized Union leagues to mobilize the new black voters into the Republican Party. Democrats branded southern white Republicans as "scalawags" and northern settlers as "carpetbaggers." By September 1867, there were 735,000 black voters and only 635,000 white voters registered in the 10 states. At least one-third of the registered white voters were Republicans.

President Johnson did everything he could to block Reconstruction. He replaced several Republican generals with Democrats. He had his attorney general issue a ruling that interpreted the Reconstruction acts narrowly, thereby forcing a special session of Congress to pass a supplementary act in July 1867. And he encouraged southern whites to obstruct the registration of voters and the election of convention delegates.

Johnson's purpose was to slow the process until 1868 in the hope that northern voters would repudiate Reconstruction in the presidential election of that year, when Johnson planned to run as the Democratic candidate. Indeed, in off-year state elections in the fall of 1867 Republicans suffered setbacks in several northern states. "I almost pity the radicals," chortled one of President Johnson's aides after the 1867 elections. "After giving ten states to the negroes, to keep the Democrats from getting them, they will have lost the rest."

THE IMPEACHMENT OF ANDREW JOHNSON

Johnson struck even more boldly against Reconstruction after the 1867 elections. In February 1868, he removed from office Secretary of War Edwin M. Stanton, who had administered the War Department in support of the congressional Reconstruction policy. This appeared to violate the Tenure of Office Act, passed the year before over Johnson's veto, which required Senate consent for such removals. By a vote of 126 to 47 along party lines, the House impeached Johnson on February 24. The official reason for impeachment was that he had violated the Tenure of Office Act, but the real reason was Johnson's stubborn defiance of Congress on Reconstruction.

Under the U.S. Constitution, impeachment by the House does not remove an official from office. It is more like a grand jury indictment that must be tried by a petit jury—in this case, the Senate, which sat as a court to try Johnson on the impeachment charges brought by the House. If convicted by a two-thirds majority of the Senate, he would be removed from office.

The impeachment trial proved to be long and complicated, which worked in Johnson's favor by allowing passions to cool. The Constitution specifies the grounds on which a president can be impeached and removed: "Treason, Bribery, or other high Crimes and Misdemeanors." The issue was whether Johnson was guilty of any of these acts. His able defense counsel exposed technical ambiguities in the Tenure of Office Act that raised doubts about whether Johnson had actually violated it. Behind the scenes, Johnson strengthened his case by promising to appoint the respected General John M. Schofield as secretary of war and to stop obstructing the Reconstruction acts. In the end, seven Republican senators voted for acquittal on May 16, and the final tally fell one vote short of the necessary two-thirds majority.

The Completion of Formal Reconstruction

The end of the impeachment trial cleared the poisonous air in Washington. Constitutional conventions met in the South during the winter and spring of 1867–1868. The constitutions they wrote were among the most progressive in the nation. The new state constitutions enacted universal male suffrage. Some disfranchised certain classes of ex-Confederates for several years, but by 1872 all such disqualifications had been removed. The constitutions mandated statewide public schools for both races for the first time in the South. Most states permitted segregated schools, but schools of any kind for blacks represented a great step forward. Most of the constitutions increased the state's responsibility for social welfare.

Violence in some parts of the South marred the voting on ratification of these state constitutions. A night-riding white terrorist organization, the Ku Klux Klan, made its first appearance during the elections. Nevertheless, voters in seven states ratified their constitutions and elected new legislatures that ratified the Fourteenth Amendment in the spring of 1868. That amendment became part of the United States Constitution the following summer, and the newly elected representatives and senators from those seven states, nearly all of them Republicans, took their seats in the House and Senate.

The Fifteenth Amendment

The remaining three southern states completed the reconstruction process in 1869 and 1870. Congress required them to ratify the Fifteenth as well as the Fourteenth Amendment. The Fifteenth Amendment prohibited states from denying the right to vote on grounds of race, color, or previous condition of servitude. Its purpose was not only to prevent any future revocation of black suffrage by the reconstructed states, but also to extend equal suffrage to the border states and to the North. But the challenge of enforcement lay ahead.

The Election of 1868

Just as the presidential election of 1864 was a referendum on Lincoln's war policies, so the election of 1868 was a referendum on the reconstruction policy of the Republicans. The Republican nominee was General Ulysses S. Grant. Though he had no political experience, Grant commanded greater authority and prestige than anyone else in the country. Grant agreed to run for the presidency in order to preserve in peace the victory for Union and liberty he had won in war.

The Democrats turned away from Andrew Johnson and nominated Horatio Seymour, the wartime governor of New York. They adopted a militant platform denouncing the Reconstruction acts as "a flagrant usurpation of power . . . unconstitutional, revolutionary, and void." The platform also demanded "the abolition of the Freedmen's Bureau, and all political instrumentalities designed to secure negro supremacy."

The vice presidential candidate, Frank Blair of Missouri, became the point man for the Democrats. In a public letter he proclaimed, "There is but one way to restore the Government and the Constitution, and that is for the President-elect to declare these [Reconstruction] acts null and void, compel the army to undo its usurpations at the South, disperse the carpet-bag State Governments, [and] allow the white people to reorganize their own governments."

The only way to achieve this bold counterrevolutionary goal was to suppress Republican voters in the South. This the Ku Klux Klan tried its best to do. Federal troops had only limited success in preventing the violence. In Louisiana, Georgia, Arkansas, and Tennessee, the Klan or Klan-like groups committed dozens of murders and intimidated thousands of black voters. The violence helped the Democratic cause in the South but probably hurt it in the North, where many voters perceived the Klan as an organization of neo-Confederate paramilitary guerrillas.

Seymour did well in the South, carrying five former slave states and coming close in others despite the solid Republican vote of the newly enfranchised blacks. But Grant swept the electoral vote 214 to 80. Seymour actually won a slight majority of the white voters nationally, so without black enfranchisement, Grant would have had a minority of the popular vote.

THE GRANT ADMINISTRATION

Grant is usually branded a failure as president. His two administrations (1869–1877) were plagued by scandals. His private secretary allegedly became involved in the infamous "Whiskey Ring," a network of distillers and revenue agents that deprived the government of millions of tax dollars; his secretary of war was impeached for selling appointments to army posts and Indian reservations; and his attorney general and secretary of the interior resigned under suspicion of malfeasance in 1875.

Honest himself, Grant was too trusting of subordinates. But not all of the scandals were Grant's fault. This was an era notorious for corruption at all levels of government. The Tammany Hall "Ring" of "Boss" William Marcy Tweed in New York City may have stolen more money from taxpayers than all the federal agencies combined. In Washington, one of the most widely publicized scandals, the Credit Mobilier affair, concerned Congress rather than the Grant administration. Several congressmen had accepted stock in the Credit Mobilier, a construction company for the Union Pacific Railroad, which received loans and land grants from the government in return for ensuring lax congressional supervision, thereby permitting financial manipulations by the company.

What accounted for this explosion of corruption in the postwar decade? The expansion of government contracts and the bureaucracy during the war had created new opportunities for the unscrupulous. Then came a relaxation of tensions and standards following the intense sacrifices of the war years. Rapid postwar economic growth, led by an extraordinary rush of railroad construction, encouraged greed and get-rich-quick schemes of the kind satirized by Mark Twain and Charles Dudley Warner in their 1873 novel *The Gilded Age,* which gave its name to the era.

CIVIL SERVICE REFORM

But some of the increase in corruption during the Gilded Age was more apparent than real. Reformers focused on the dark corners of corruption hitherto unilluminated because of the nation's preoccupation with war and reconstruction. Thus, the actual extent of corruption may have been exaggerated by the publicity that reformers gave it. In reality, during the Grant administration several government agencies made real progress in eliminating abuses that had flourished in earlier administrations.

One area of progress was civil service reform. Its chief target was the "spoils system." With the slogan "To the victor belong the spoils," the victorious party in an election rewarded party workers with appointments as postmasters, customs collectors, and the like. The hope of getting appointed to a government post was the glue that kept the faithful together when a party was out of power. The spoils system politicized the bureaucracy and staffed it with unqualified personnel who spent more time working for their party than for the government.

Civil service reformers wanted to separate the bureaucracy from politics by requiring competitive examinations for the appointment of civil servants. This movement gathered steam during the 1870s and finally achieved success in 1883 with the passage of the Pendleton Act, which established the modern structure of the civil service. When Grant took office, he seemed to share the sentiments of civil service reformers. Grant named a civil service commission headed by George William Curtis, a leading reformer and editor of *Harper's Weekly*. But many congressmen, senators, and other politicians resisted civil service reform because patronage was the grease of the political machines that kept them in office. They managed to subvert reform, sometimes using Grant as an unwitting ally and thus turning many reformers against the president.

FOREIGN POLICY ISSUES

A foreign policy fiasco added to Grant's woes. The irregular procedures by which his private secretary had negotiated a treaty to annex Santo Domingo (now the Dominican Republic) alienated leading Republican senators, who defeated ratification of the treaty. Grant's political inexperience led him to act like a general who needed only to give orders rather than as a president who must cultivate supporters. The fallout from the Santo Domingo affair widened the fissure in the Republican Party.

But the Grant administration had some solid foreign policy achievements to its credit. Hamilton Fish, the able secretary of state, negotiated the Treaty of Washington in 1871 to settle the vexing "Alabama Claims." These were damage claims against Britain for the destruction of American shipping by the C.S.S. *Alabama* and other Confederate commerce raiders built in British shipyards. The treaty established an international tribunal to arbitrate the U.S. claims, resulting in the award of $15.5 million in damages to U.S. shipowners and a British expression of regret.

The events leading to the Treaty of Washington also resolved another long-festering issue between Britain and the United States: the status of Canada. The seven separate British North American colonies were especially vulnerable to U.S. desires for annexation. In 1867 Parliament passed the British North America Act, which united most of the Canadian colonies into a new and largely self-governing Dominion of Canada.

The successful conclusion of the treaty cooled Canadian-American tensions. It also led to the resolution of disputes over American commercial fishing in Canadian waters. American demands for annexation of Canada faded away. These events gave birth to the modern nation of Canada, whose 3,500-mile border with the United States remains the longest unfortified frontier in the world.

RECONSTRUCTION IN THE SOUTH

During Grant's two administrations, the "Southern Question" was the most intractable issue. A phrase in Grant's acceptance of the presidential nomination in 1868 had struck a responsive chord in the North: "Let us have peace." With the ratification of the Fifteenth Amendment, many people breathed a sigh of relief at this apparent resolution of "the last great point that remained to be settled of the issues of the war." It was time to deal with other matters that had been long neglected.

But there was no peace. State governments elected by black and white voters were in place in the South, but Democratic violence protesting Reconstruction and the instability of the Republican coalition that sustained it portended trouble.

BLACKS IN OFFICE

In the North, the Republican Party represented the most prosperous, educated, and influential elements of the population; but in the South, most of its adherents were poor, illiterate, and propertyless. About 80 percent of southern Republican voters were black. Although most black leaders were educated and many had been free before the war, the mass of black voters were illiterate ex-slaves. Neither the leaders nor their constituents, however, were as ignorant as stereotypes have portrayed them. Of 14 black representatives and two black senators elected in the South between 1868 and 1876, all but three had attended secondary school and four had attended college. Several of the blacks elected to state offices were among the best-educated men of their day. For example, Jonathan Gibbs, secretary of state in Florida from 1868 to 1872 and state superintendent of education from 1872 to 1874, was a graduate of Dartmouth College and Princeton Theological Seminary.

It is true that some lower-level black officeholders, as well as their constituents, could not read or write. But illiteracy did not preclude an understanding of political issues for them any more than it did for Irish American voters in the North, many of whom also were illiterate. Southern blacks thirsted for education. Participation in the Union League and the experience of voting were themselves a form of education. Black churches and fraternal organizations proliferated during Reconstruction and tutored African Americans in their rights and responsibilities.

Linked to the myth of black incompetence was the legend of the "Africanization" of southern governments during Reconstruction. The theme of "Negro rule" was a staple of Democratic propaganda. It was enshrined in folk memory and textbooks. In fact, blacks held only 15 to 20 percent of public offices, even at the height of Reconstruction in the early 1870s. There were no black governors and only one black state supreme court justice. Nowhere except in South Carolina did blacks hold office in numbers anywhere near their proportion of the population.

"CARPETBAGGERS"

Next to "Negro rule," carpetbagger corruption and scalawag rascality have been the prevailing myths of Reconstruction. "Carpetbaggers" did hold a disproportionate number of high political offices in southern state governments during Reconstruction. A few did resemble the proverbial adventurer who came south with nothing but a carpetbag in which to stow the loot plundered from a helpless people. But most were Union Army officers who stayed on after the war as Freedmen's Bureau agents, teachers in black schools, or business investors.

Those who settled in the postwar South hoped to rebuild its society in the image of the free-labor North. Many were college graduates. Most brought not empty carpetbags but considerable capital, which they invested in what they hoped would become a new South. They also invested human capital—themselves—in a drive to modernize the region's social structure and democratize its politics. But they underestimated the hostility of southern whites, most of whom regarded them as agents of an alien culture.

"Scalawags"

Most of the native-born whites who joined the southern Republican Party came from the up-country Unionist areas of western North Carolina and Virginia and eastern Tennessee. Others were former Whigs. Republicans, said a North Carolina scalawag, were the "party of progress, of education, of development."

But Democrats were aware that the southern Republican Party they abhorred was a fragile coalition of blacks and whites, Yankees and southerners, hill-country yeomen and low-country entrepreneurs, illiterates and college graduates. The party was weakest along the seams where these disparate elements joined—especially the racial seam. Democrats attacked that weakness with every weapon at their command, including violence.

The Ku Klux Klan

The generic name for the secret groups that terrorized the southern countryside was the Ku Klux Klan. But some went by other names (the Knights of the White Camelia in Louisiana, for example). Part of the Klan's purpose was social control of the black population. Sharecroppers who tried to extract better terms from landowners, or black people who were considered too "uppity," were likely to receive a midnight whipping—or worse—from white-sheeted Klansmen. Scores of black schools, perceived as a particular threat to white supremacy, went up in flames.

But the Klan's main purpose was political: to destroy the Republican Party by terrorizing its voters and, if necessary, murdering its leaders. No one knows the number of politically motivated killings that took place, but it was certainly in the hundreds, probably in the thousands. Nearly all the victims were Republicans; most of them were black. In one notorious incident, the "Colfax Massacre" in Louisiana (April 18, 1873), a clash between black militia and armed whites left three whites and nearly 100 blacks dead.

In some places, notably Tennessee and Arkansas, militias formed by Republicans suppressed and disarmed many Klansmen. But in most areas the militias were outgunned and outmaneuvered by ex-Confederate veterans who had joined the Klan. Some Republican governors were reluctant to use black militia against white guerrillas for fear of sparking a racial bloodbath—as happened at Colfax.

The answer seemed to be federal troops. In 1870 and 1871 Congress enacted three laws intended to enforce the Fourteenth and Fifteenth Amendments. Interference with voting rights became a federal offense, and any attempt to deprive another person of civil or political rights became a felony. The third law, passed on April 20, 1871, and popularly called the Ku Klux Klan Act, gave the president power to suspend the writ of habeas corpus and send in federal troops to suppress armed resistance to federal law.

Armed with these laws, the Grant administration moved against the Klan. But Grant did so with restraint. He suspended the writ of habeas corpus only in nine South Carolina counties. Nevertheless, there and elsewhere federal marshals backed by troops arrested thousands of suspected Klansmen. Federal grand juries indicted more than 3,000, and several

TWO MEMBERS OF THE KU KLUX KLAN   Founded in Pulaski, Tennessee, in 1866 as a social organization similar to a college fraternity, the Klan evolved into a terrorist group whose purpose was intimidation of southern Republicans. The Klan, in which former Confederate soldiers played a prominent part, was responsible for the beating and murder of hundreds of blacks and whites alike from 1868 to 1871.

hundred defendants pleaded guilty in return for suspended sentences; the Justice Department dropped charges against nearly 2,000 others. About 600 Klansmen were convicted. Most of them received fines or light jail sentences, but 65 went to a federal penitentiary for terms of up to five years.

THE ELECTION OF 1872

These measures broke the back of the Klan in time for the 1872 presidential election. A group of dissident Republicans had emerged to challenge Grant's reelection. They believed that conciliation of southern whites rather than continued military intervention was the only way to achieve peace in the South. Calling themselves Liberal Republicans, these dissidents nominated Horace Greeley, the famous editor of the *New York Tribune*. Under the slogan "Anything to beat Grant," the Democratic Party also endorsed Greeley's nomination. On a platform denouncing "bayonet rule" in the South, Greeley urged his fellow northerners to put the issues of the Civil War behind them.

Most voters in the North were still not prepared to trust Democrats or southern whites, however. Anti-Greeley cartoons by Thomas Nast showed Greeley shaking the hand of a Klansman dripping with the blood of a murdered black Republican. On election day Grant swamped Greeley. Republicans carried every northern state and 10 of the 16 southern and border states. But this apparent triumph of Republicanism and Reconstruction would soon unravel.

THE PANIC OF 1873

The U.S. economy had grown at an unprecedented pace since 1867. The first transcontinental railroad had been completed on May 10, 1869, when a golden spike was driven at Promontory Point, Utah Territory, linking the Union Pacific and the Central Pacific. But it was the building of a second transcontinental line, the Northern Pacific, that precipitated a Wall Street panic in 1873 and plunged the economy into a five-year depression.

Jay Cooke's banking firm, fresh from its triumphant marketing of Union war bonds, took over the Northern Pacific in 1869. Cooke pyramided every conceivable kind of equity and loan financing to raise the money to begin laying rails west from Duluth, Minn. Other investment firms did the same as a fever of speculative financing gripped the country. In September 1873 the pyramid of paper collapsed. Cooke's firm was the first to go bankrupt. Like dominoes, hundreds of banks and businesses also collapsed. Unemployment rose to 14 percent and hard times set in.

THE RETREAT FROM RECONSTRUCTION

Democrats made large gains in the congressional elections of 1874, winning a majority in the House for the first time in 18 years. Public opinion also began to turn against Republican policies in the South. Intra-party battles among Republicans in southern states enabled Democrats to regain control of several state governments. Well-publicized corruption scandals also discredited Republican leaders. Although corruption was probably no worse in southern states than in many parts of the North, the postwar poverty of the South made waste and extravagance seem worse. White Democrats scored propaganda points by claiming that corruption proved the incompetence of "Negro-carpetbag" regimes.

Northerners grew increasingly weary of what seemed the endless turmoil of southern politics. Most of them had never had a very strong commitment to racial equality, and they were growing more and more willing to let white supremacy regain sway in the South. "The truth is," confessed a northern Republican, "our people are tired out with this worn out cry of 'Southern outrages'!!!"

By 1875 only four southern states remained under Republican control: South Carolina, Florida, Mississippi, and Louisiana. In those states, white Democrats had revived paramilitary organizations under various names: White Leagues (Louisiana); Rifle Clubs (Mississippi); and Red Shirts (South Carolina). Unlike the Klan, these groups operated openly. In Louisiana, they fought pitched battles with Republican militias in which scores were killed. When the Grant administration sent large numbers of federal troops to Louisiana, people in both North and South cried out against military rule. The protests grew even louder when soldiers marched onto the floor of the Louisiana legislature in January 1875 and expelled several Democratic legislators after a contested election.

THE MISSISSIPPI ELECTION OF 1875

The backlash against the Grant administration affected the Mississippi state election of 1875. Democrats there devised a strategy called the Mississippi Plan. The first step was to "persuade" the 10 to 15 percent of white voters still calling themselves Republicans to switch to the Democrats. Only a handful of carpetbaggers could resist the economic pressures, social ostracism, and threats that made it "too damned hot for [us] to stay out," wrote one white Republican who changed parties.

The second step in the Mississippi Plan was to intimidate black voters, for even with all whites voting Democratic, the party could still be defeated by the 55 percent black majority. Economic coercion against black sharecroppers and workers kept some of them away from the

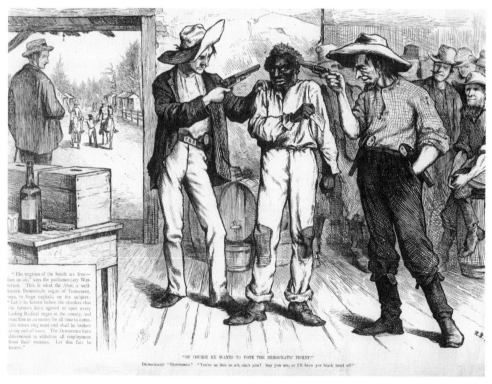

HOW THE MISSISSIPPI PLAN WORKED   This cartoon shows how black counties could report large Democratic majorities in the Mississippi state election of 1875. The black voter holds a Democratic ticket while one of the men, described in the caption as a "Democratic reformer," holds a revolver to his head and says: "You're as free as air, ain't you? Say you are, or I'll blow your black head off!"

polls. But violence was the most effective method. Democratic "rifle clubs" showed up at Republican rallies, provoked riots, and shot down dozens of blacks in the ensuing melees. Governor Adelbert Ames called for federal troops to control the violence. Grant intended to comply, but Ohio Republicans warned him that if he sent troops to Mississippi, the Democrats would exploit the issue of bayonet rule to carry Ohio in that year's state elections. Grant yielded—in effect giving up Mississippi for Ohio.

Governor Ames did try to organize a loyal state militia. But that proved difficult—and in any case, he was reluctant to use a black militia for fear of provoking a race war. "No matter if they are going to carry the State," said Ames with weary resignation, "let them carry it, and let us be at peace and have no more killing." The Mississippi Plan worked like a charm. What had been a Republican majority of 30,000 in 1874 became a Democratic majority of 30,000 in 1875.

THE SUPREME COURT AND RECONSTRUCTION

Even if Grant had been willing to continue intervening in southern state elections, Congress and the courts would have constricted such efforts. The new Democratic majority in the House threatened to cut any appropriations intended for use in the South. And in 1876 the Supreme Court handed down two decisions that declared parts of the 1870 and 1871 laws for enforcement of the Fourteenth and Fifteenth Amendments unconstitutional. In *U.S.* v. *Cruikshank* and *U.S.* v. *Reese,* the Court ruled that the Fourteenth and Fifteenth Amendments apply to actions by *states:* "No State shall . . . deprive any person of life, liberty, or property . . . nor deny to any person . . . equal protection of the laws"; the right to vote "shall not be denied . . . by any State." Therefore, the portions of these laws that empowered the federal government to prosecute *individuals* were unconstitutional. The Court did not say what could be done when states were controlled by white-supremacy Democrats who had no intention of enforcing equal rights.

Meanwhile, in the *Civil Rights Cases* (1883), the Court declared unconstitutional a civil rights law passed by Congress in 1875. That law banned racial discrimination in all forms of public transportation and public accommodations. If enforced, it would have effected a sweeping transformation of race relations—in the North as well as in the South. But even some of the congressmen who voted for the bill doubted its constitutionality, and the Justice Department had made little effort to enforce it. Several cases made their way to the Supreme Court, which in 1883 ruled the law unconstitutional—again on grounds that the Fourteenth Amendment applied only to states, not to individuals. Several states—all in the North—passed their own civil rights laws in the 1870s and 1880s, but less than 10 percent of the black population resided in those states. The mass of African Americans lived a segregated existence.

THE ELECTION OF 1876

In 1876 the Republican state governments that still survived in the South fell victim to the passion for "reform." The mounting revelations of corruption at all levels of government ensured that reform would be the leading issue in the presidential election. Both major parties gave their presidential nominations to governors who had earned reform reputations in their states: Democrat Samuel J. Tilden of New York and Republican Rutherford B. Hayes of Ohio.

Democrats entered the campaign as favorites for the first time in two decades. It seemed likely that they would be able to put together an electoral majority from a "solid South" plus

New York and two or three other northern states. To ensure a solid South, they looked to the lessons of the Mississippi Plan. In 1876 a new word came into use to describe Democratic techniques of intimidation: "bulldozing." To bulldoze black voters meant to trample them down or keep them away from the polls. In South Carolina and Louisiana, the Red Shirts and the White Leagues mobilized for an all-out bulldozing effort.

The most notorious incident, the "Hamburg Massacre," occurred in the village of Hamburg, South Carolina, where a battle between a black militia unit and 200 Red Shirts resulted in the capture of several militiamen, five of whom were shot "while attempting to escape." This time Grant did send in federal troops. He pronounced the Hamburg Massacre "cruel, bloodthirsty, wanton, unprovoked . . . a repetition of the course that has been pursued in other Southern States."

The federal government also put several thousand deputy marshals and election supervisors on duty in the South. Though they kept an uneasy peace at the polls, they could do little to prevent assaults, threats, and economic coercion in backcountry districts, which reduced the potential Republican tally in the former Confederate states by at least 250,000 votes.

DISPUTED RESULTS

When the results were in, Tilden had carried four northern states, including New York with its 35 electoral votes, and all the former slave states except—apparently—Louisiana, South Carolina, and Florida. From those three states came disputed returns. Since Tilden needed only one of them to win the presidency, while Hayes needed all three, and since Tilden seemed to have carried Louisiana and Florida, it appeared initially that he had won the presidency. But frauds and irregularities reported from several bulldozed districts in the three states clouded the issue. The official returns ultimately sent to Washington gave all three states—and therefore the presidency—to Hayes. But the Democrats refused to recognize the results—and they controlled the House.

The country now faced a serious constitutional crisis. Many people feared another civil war. The Constitution offered no clear guidance on how to deal with the matter. It required the concurrence of both houses of Congress in order to count the electoral votes of the states, but with a Democratic House and a Republican Senate such concurrence was not forthcoming. To break the deadlock, Congress created a special electoral commission consisting of five representatives, five senators, and five Supreme Court justices split evenly between the two parties, with one member, a Supreme Court justice, supposedly an independent—but in fact a Republican.

Tilden had won a national majority of 252,000 popular votes, and the raw returns gave him a majority in the three disputed states. But an estimated 250,000 southern Republicans had been bulldozed away from the polls. In a genuinely fair and free election, the Republicans might have carried Mississippi and North Carolina as well as the three disputed states. While the commission agonized, Democrats and Republicans in Louisiana and South Carolina each inaugurated their own separate governors and legislatures. Only federal troops in the capitals at New Orleans and Columbia protected the Republican governments in those states.

THE COMPROMISE OF 1877

In February 1877, three months after voters had gone to the polls, the electoral commission issued its ruling. By a partisan vote of 8 to 7—with the "independent" justice voting with the

CHRONOLOGY

1863	Lincoln issues Proclamation of Amnesty and Reconstruction
1864	Congress passes Wade-Davis bill; Lincoln kills it by pocket veto
1865	Congress establishes Freedmen's Bureau • Andrew Johnson becomes president, announces his reconstruction plan • Southern states enact Black Codes • Congress refuses to seat southern congressmen elected under Johnson's plan
1866	Congress passes civil rights bill and expands Freedmen's Bureau over Johnson's veto • Race riots in Memphis and New Orleans • Congress approves Fourteenth Amendment • Republicans increase congressional majority in fall elections
1867	Congress passes Reconstruction acts over Johnson's vetoes • Congress passes Tenure of Office Act over Johnson's veto
1868	Most southern senators and representatives readmitted to Congress under congressional plan of Reconstruction • Andrew Johnson impeached but not convicted • Ulysses S. Grant elected president • Congress ratifies Fourteenth Amendment
1870	Fifteenth Amendment is ratified
1871	Congress passes Ku Klux Klan Act
1872	Liberal Republicans defect from party • Grant wins reelection
1873	Economic depression begins with the Panic
1874	Democrats win control of House of Representatives
1875	Democrats implement Mississippi Plan • Congress passes civil rights act
1876	Centennial celebration in Philadelphia • Disputed presidential election causes constitutional crisis
1877	Compromise of 1877 installs Rutherford B. Hayes as president • Hayes withdraws troops from South
1883	Supreme Court declares civil rights act of 1875 unconstitutional

Republicans—it awarded all the disputed states to Hayes. The Democrats cried foul and began a filibuster in the House to delay the final electoral count beyond the inauguration date of March 4. But, behind the scenes, a compromise began to take shape. Hayes promised his support as president for federal appropriations to rebuild war-destroyed levees on the lower Mississippi and federal aid for a southern transcontinental railroad. Hayes's lieutenants also hinted at the appointment of a southerner as postmaster general, who would have a considerable amount of patronage at his disposal. Hayes also signaled his intention to end "bayonet rule." He believed that the goodwill and influence of southern moderates would offer better protection for black rights than federal troops could provide. In return for his commitment to withdraw the troops, Hayes asked for—and received—promises of fair treatment of freedpeople and respect for their constitutional rights.

The End of Reconstruction

Such promises were easier to make than to keep, as future years would reveal. In any case, the Democratic filibuster collapsed and Hayes was inaugurated on March 4. He soon fulfilled his part of the Compromise of 1877: ex-Confederate Democrat David Key of Tennessee became postmaster general; the South received more federal money in 1878 for internal improvements than ever before; and federal troops left the capitals of Louisiana and South Carolina. The last two Republican state governments collapsed. Any remaining voices of protest could scarcely be heard above the sighs of relief that the crisis was over.

Conclusion

Before the Civil War, most Americans had viewed a powerful government as a threat to individual liberties. That is why the first 10 amendments to the Constitution (the Bill of Rights) imposed strict limits on the powers of the federal government. But during the Civil War and especially during Reconstruction, it became clear that the national government would have to exert an unprecedented amount of power to free the slaves and guarantee their equal rights as free citizens. That is why the Thirteenth, Fourteenth, and Fifteenth Amendments to the Constitution contained clauses stating that "Congress shall have power" to enforce these provisions for liberty and equal rights.

During the post–Civil War decade, Congress passed civil rights laws and enforcement legislation to accomplish this purpose. Federal marshals and troops patrolled the polls to protect black voters, arrested thousands of Klansmen and other violators of black civil rights, and even occupied state capitals to prevent Democratic paramilitary groups from overthrowing legitimately elected Republican state governments. But by 1875 many northerners had grown tired of or alarmed by this continued use of military power to intervene in the internal affairs of states. The Supreme Court stripped the federal government of much of its authority to enforce certain provisions of the Fourteenth and Fifteenth Amendments.

The withdrawal of federal troops from the South in 1877 constituted both a symbolic and a substantive end of the 12-year postwar era known as Reconstruction. Reconstruction had achieved the two great objectives inherited from the Civil War: to reincorporate the former Confederate states into the Union, and to accomplish a transition from slavery to freedom in the South. But that transition was marred by the economic inequity of sharecropping and the social injustice of white supremacy. And a third goal of Reconstruction, enforcement of the equal civil and political rights promised in the Fourteenth and Fifteenth Amendments, was betrayed by the Compromise of 1877. In subsequent decades the freed slaves and their descendants suffered repression into segregated second-class citizenship.

18

FRONTIERS OF CHANGE, POLITICS OF STALEMATE, 1865–1890

AGENCIES OF WESTWARD EXPANSION ∿ THE LAST INDIAN FRONTIER
THE NEW SOUTH ∿ THE POLITICS OF STALEMATE

One of the most remarkable developments in the post–Civil War generation was the accelerating westward expansion. From 1865 to 1890 the white population of the West increased five times faster than that of the nation as a whole. Through the Homestead Act, land grants to railroads, the Morrill Act (which turned land over to states to finance "agricultural and mechanical colleges"), and other liberal land laws enacted during and after the Civil War, some 400 million acres passed into private ownership by farmers, ranchers, and other forms of enterprise. The number of American farms more than doubled. Their output of cattle, hogs, and hay more than doubled while the production of corn, wheat, and oats nearly tripled.

This growth enabled American farmers to increase agricultural exports tenfold. These exports were partly fueled by immigration. Many of the 4 million immigrants who came from Germany, the Czech region of the Austro-Hungarian empire, and the Scandinavian countries during this period settled in the Midwest or Far West and became farmers. To them the opportunity to obtain 160 acres in Minnesota or Nebraska seemed miraculous. The power of a generous government to make equality of opportunity available to them underpinned the extraordinary expansion of population and agricultural production after the Civil War.

But that growth and opportunity came at great cost. The Indians were herded onto reservations. Buffalo were hunted almost to extinction. Millions of acres of forest and native grasslands were cut down or plowed up, setting the stage for destructive erosion, floods, and dust bowls in future generations. The overproduction of American agriculture drove prices down and contributed to a worldwide agricultural depression.

AGENCIES OF WESTWARD EXPANSION

One of the main engines of this postwar growth was the railroad. Five transcontinental railroads went into service between 1869 and 1893. At the end of the Civil War, there had been only 3,272 miles of rail west of the Mississippi. By 1890 the total was 72,473 miles. The existence of this infrastructure spurred settlement and economic development.

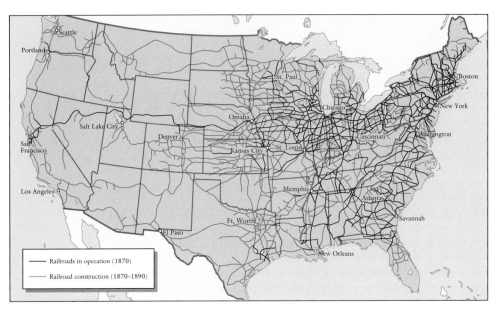

RAILROAD EXPANSION, 1870–1890

No longer did this region appear on maps as "The Great American Desert." There was plenty of desert, to be sure. But during the 1870s and early 1880s precipitation was heavier than normal, giving rise to the erroneous (as it turned out) notion that "rainfall follows the plow"—that settlement and cultivation somehow changed the weather.

This was the age of the "sodbuster," who adapted to the almost treeless prairies and plains by fencing with barbed wire (invented in 1874) and building his first house out of the sod that he broke with his steel plow. It was also the era of "bonanza farms" in the Red River Valley of Dakota Territory and the Central Valley of California—huge wheat farms cultivated with heavy machinery and hired labor.

Perhaps even more important to the growth of the West were the mining and ranching frontiers. This was the West of prospectors and boom towns that became ghost towns, of cowboys and cattle drives, of gold rushes and mother lodes, of stagecoach robbers and rustlers. It is a West so celebrated on stage, screen, radio, and television that it is hard to separate myth from reality—a reality in which thousands of black and Mexican American cowboys rode the Goodnight-Loving Trail, eastern capital and railroads came increasingly to control the mines and the grasslands, and gold or silver miners and cowboys came to resemble more closely the coal miners and farm laborers of the East than the romanticized independent spirits of legend.

THE MINING FRONTIER

Gold discoveries had propelled the first waves of western settlement, but in the 1870s silver eclipsed gold. Other minerals also increased in value. Rich copper mines opened in Montana at about the same time that Alexander Graham Bell's invention of the telephone (1876) and

THE SOD-HOUSE FRONTIER On the prairies and plains of the regions west of the Mississippi, trees were scarce and the cost of lumber was prohibitive until railroads crisscrossed the land. So the settlers built their first houses from the tough prairie sod, which baked in the sun to almost the hardness of bricks.

Thomas A. Edison's invention of the incandescent lightbulb (1879) and construction of a successful electrical generator (1881) created a demand for thousands of tons of copper wire.

Violence was never far from the surface in the mining frontier. In the early days, claim-jumping, robberies, and vigilante justice made life precarious. As placer mining of streams gave out, men ravaged the environment by hydraulic mining, deep bores, and strip-mining. Mining became a highly capitalized and mechanized industry in which the biggest and richest mines were owned by corporations with headquarters in the East. Capital-labor relations were savage. Violent strikes at Coeur d'Alene, Idaho, in 1892, at Cripple Creek, Colorado, in 1894 and again in 1903, and at other places caused western governors to call out the militia 10 times from 1892 to 1904.

THE RANCHING FRONTIER

Of course, the dominant symbol of the Old West is not the prospector or the hard-rock miner: It is the cowboy. The postwar boom in the range cattle industry had its beginnings in southern Texas. The Spaniards had introduced longhorn cattle there in the 18th century. This hardy breed multiplied rapidly; by the 1850s millions of them roamed freely on the Texas plains. Then the Civil War depleted the cattle supply in the older states, where prices rose to the unheard-of sum of $40 a head. The postwar explosion of population and railroads westward brought markets and railheads ever closer to western cattle that were free to anyone who rounded them up and branded them.

Astute Texans were not slow to see that the longhorns represented a fortune on the hoof—if they could be driven northward the 800 miles to the railhead at Sedalia, Missouri. In the spring of 1866, cowboys hit the trail with 260,000 cattle in the first of the great drives. However, disease, stampedes, bad weather, Indians, and irate farmers killed or ran off most of the cattle.

Only a few thousand head made it to Sedalia, but the prices they fetched convinced ranchers that the system would work, if only they could find a better route. By 1867 the rails of the Kansas Pacific had reached Abilene, Kansas, 150 miles closer to Texas, making it possible to drive the herds through a sparsely occupied portion of Indian Territory. About 35,000 longhorns reached Abilene that summer, where they were loaded onto cattle cars for the trip to Kansas City or Chicago. The development of refrigerated rail cars in the 1870s enabled Chicago to ship dressed beef all over the country.

More than a million longhorns bellowed their way north on the Chisholm Trail to Abilene over the next four years while the railhead crept westward to other Kansas towns, chiefly Dodge City, which became the most wide-open and famous of the cow towns. Cattle drives grew shorter as railroads inched forward. Ranchers grazed their cattle for free on millions of acres of open, unfenced government land. But clashes with "grangers" (the ranchers' contemptuous term for farmers) on the one hand and with a growing army of sheep ranchers on the other—not to mention rustlers—led to several "range wars." Most notable was the Johnson County War in Wyoming in 1892. Grangers and small ranchers there defeated the hired guns of the Stock Growers' Association, which represented larger ranchers.

By that time, however, the classic form of open-range grazing was already in decline. The boom years of the early 1880s had overstocked the range and driven down prices. Then came record cold and blizzards on the southern range in the winter of 1885–1886, followed by even

BLACK COWBOYS   Some studies of cowboys estimate that one-quarter of them were black. That estimate is probably too high for all cowboys, but it might be correct for Texas, where this photograph was taken.

worse weather on the northern plains the following winter. Hundreds of thousands of cattle froze or starved to death. These catastrophes spurred reforms that brought an end to open-range grazing.

Ranching and the cowboy survived, but in a form quite different from their Hollywood image. Most cowboys were small, wiry men; the mustangs they rode could not carry large men. In popular literature and movies, one seldom encounters a Mexican cowboy portrayed in a favorable light and even more rarely a black cowboy. But of the 40,000 cowboys who rode the range between 1865 and 1885, several thousand were blacks or Mexicans. Cowboys were tough and hardy, but hardly any of them became gunfighters. The work was hard, the pay was low, and their life was far from glamorous. Nevertheless, the romantic image of the cowboy, which began with the dime novels of the 19th century, has endured as a central myth of American popular culture.

THE LAST INDIAN FRONTIER

The westward expansion of the ranching and farming frontiers after 1865 doomed the free range of the Plains Indians and the buffalo. In the 1830s, the purpose of moving eastern tribes to preserves west of the Mississippi had been to end strife by separating whites and Indians. But in scarcely a decade, white settlers had penetrated these lands. In the 1850s, when the Kansas and Nebraska territories were opened to white settlement, the government forced a dozen of the tribes living there to cede 15 million acres, leaving them on reservations totaling less than 1.5 million acres. Thus began what historian Philip Weeks has called the "policy of concentration."

In the aftermath of the Civil War, the process of concentrating Indian tribes on reservations accelerated. Chiefs of the five "civilized tribes"—Cherokees, Creeks, Choctaws, Chickasaws, and Seminoles—had signed treaties of alliance with the Confederacy. At that time they were living in Indian Territory (most of present-day Oklahoma), where their economy was linked to the South. Many of them, especially members of the mixed-blood upper class, were slaveholders. But siding with the Confederacy proved to be a costly mistake for the "civilized tribes." The U.S. government "reconstructed" Indian Territory more quickly and with less contention than it reconstructed the former Confederate states. Treaties with the five tribes in 1866 required them to grant tribal citizenship to their freed slaves and reduced tribal lands by half.

CONFLICT WITH THE SIOUX

The Civil War had set in motion a generation of Indian warfare more violent and widespread than anything since the 17th century. Herded onto reservations along the Minnesota River by the Treaty of Traverse des Sioux in 1851, the Santee Sioux grew restive in the summer of 1862. Angry braves began to speak openly of reclaiming ancestral hunting grounds. Then on August 17, a robbery in which five white settlers were murdered seemed to open the floodgates. The braves persuaded Chief Little Crow to take them on the warpath, and over the next few weeks, at least 500 white Minnesotans were massacred.

Hastily mobilized militia and army units finally suppressed the uprising. A military court convicted 319 Indians of murder and atrocities and sentenced 303 of them to death. Appalled,

Lincoln personally reviewed the trial transcripts and reduced the number of executions to 38. The government evicted the remaining Sioux from Minnesota to Dakota Territory.

In the meantime, the army's pursuit of fleeing Santee Sioux provoked other Sioux tribes farther west. By 1864 and for a decade afterward, fighting flared between the army and the Sioux across the northern plains. It reached a climax after gold-seekers in 1874 and 1875 poured into the Black Hills of western Dakota, a sacred place to the Sioux. At the battle of Little Big Horn in Montana Territory on June 25, 1876, Sioux warriors led by Sitting Bull and Crazy Horse, along with their Cheyenne allies, wiped out George A. Custer and the 225 men with him in the 7th Cavalry. In retaliation, General Philip Sheridan carried out a winter campaign in which the Sioux and Cheyenne were crushed.

Largest and most warlike of the Plains tribes, the Sioux were confined to a reservation in Dakota Territory where poverty, disease, apathy, and alcoholism reduced this once proud people to desperation. In 1890 a current of hope arrived at the Sioux reservation in the form of a "Ghost Dance." The Ghost Dance expressed the belief that the Indians' god would destroy the whites and return their land. Alarmed by the frenzy of the dance, federal authorities sent soldiers to the Sioux reservation. A confrontation at Wounded Knee in the Dakota badlands led to a shootout that left 25 soldiers and at least 150 Sioux dead. Wounded Knee symbolized the death of 19th century Plains Indian culture.

SUPPRESSION OF OTHER PLAINS INDIANS

Just as the Sioux uprising in Minnesota had triggered war on the northern plains in 1862, a massacre of Cheyennes in Colorado in 1864 sparked a decade of conflict on the southern plains. The discovery of gold near Pike's Peak set off a rush to Colorado in 1858 and 1859. The government responded by calling several Cheyenne and Arapaho chiefs to a council and persuading them to sign a treaty giving up all claims to land in this region in exchange for a reservation at Sand Creek in southeast Colorado.

In 1864 hunger and resentment on the reservation prompted many of the braves to return to their old hunting grounds and to raid white settlements. Skirmishes soon erupted into open warfare. In the fall, Cheyenne Chief Black Kettle, believing that he had concluded peace with the Colorado settlers, returned to the reservation. There, at dawn on November 29, militia commanded by Colonel John Chivington surrounded and attacked Black Kettle's unsuspecting camp, killing 200 Indians.

The notorious Sand Creek massacre set a pattern for several similar attacks on Indian villages in subsequent years. Their purpose was to corral all the Indians onto the reservations that were being created throughout the West. In addition to trying to defeat the Indians in battle, the Army encouraged the extermination of the buffalo herds. Professional hunters slaughtered the large, clumsy animals by the millions for their hides, thus depriving Plains Indians of their principal source of food, shelter, and clothing.

The Indians were left with no alternative but to come into the reservations, and by the 1880s nearly all of them had done so. Chief Joseph of the Nez Percé pronounced the epitaph for their way of life when federal troops blocked the escape of his band from Montana to Canada in 1877:

> I am tired of fighting. Our chiefs are killed. The old men are all dead. It is cold and we have no blankets . . . no food. . . . The little children are freezing to death. . . . Hear me, my chiefs; I am tired; my heart is sick and sad. From where the sun now stands, I will fight no more forever.

THE "PEACE POLICY"

The iron fist of repression was one part of the government's Indian policy. The other was the velvet glove of reform. Reformers believed that Indians must be compelled to give up their nomadic culture and settle down as the first step toward being assimilated into the American polity as citizens. Just as reformers wanted to reconstruct the South by assimilating emancipated slaves into a free-labor society, so they wished to reconstruct Indian culture by means of schools and Christian missions.

President Grant, in his inaugural address in 1869, announced this new "Peace Policy" toward Indians. He urged "their civilization and ultimate citizenship." "Civilization" meant acceptance of white culture, including the English language, Christianity, and individual ownership of property. "Citizenship" meant allegiance to the United States rather than to a tribe. In 1869 Grant established a Board of Indian Commissioners and staffed it with humanitarian reformers. In 1871 Indians became "wards of the nation," to be civilized and prepared for citizenship.

Some Indians accepted this destruction of their culture as inevitable. Others resisted. That resistance fed the flames of frontier wars for nearly a decade after 1869. "I love the land and the buffalo," said the Kiowa Chief Satanta. "I love to roam over the wide prairie, and when I do, I feel free and happy, but when we settle down we grow pale and die."

But with their military power broken and the buffalo gone, most Indians by the 1880s had acquiesced in the "reconstruction" that offered them citizenship. Also in the 1880s, the reformers found themselves in a strange alliance with land-hungry westerners, who greedily eyed the 155 million acres of land tied up in reservations. If part of that land could be allotted directly to individual ownership by Indian families, the remainder would become available for purchase by whites. The Dawes Severalty Act did just that in 1887. This landmark legislation called for the dissolution of Indian tribes as legal entities, offered Indians the opportunity to become citizens, and allotted each head of family 160 acres of farmland or 320 acres of grazing land.

For whites eager to seize reservation land, the Dawes Act brought a bonanza. At noon on April 22, 1889, the government threw open specified parts of the Indian Territory to "Boomers," who descended on the region like locusts and by nightfall had staked claim to nearly 2 million acres. Eventually, whites gained title to 108 million acres of former reservation land.

For Indians, writes historian Philip Weeks, the Dawes Act "proved an unqualified failure." Although many Indians made a successful transition to the new order, others slipped further into depression, destitution, and alcoholism.

MEXICAN AMERICANS

Mexican Americans in the West were also forced to adjust to a new order. At the hands of Anglo-American settlers, Mexican Americans suffered dispossession of their land, loss of political influence, and suppression of their culture. Even as early as 1849 in the northern California gold fields, resentment of "foreigners" provoked violence against Mexican American miners—and the Foreign Miners Tax of 1850 effectively forced Mexican Americans out of the gold fields. As the 19th century progressed, hordes of Anglo-American "squatters" invaded the expansive holdings of the Mexican American elite, who were forced to seek relief in the courts. Although their claims were generally upheld, these legal proceedings often stretched on for years. After exorbitant legal fees and other expenses were taken into account, a legal triumph

DESTRUCTION OF THE BUFFALO

Historians estimate that as many as 30 million bison (popularly called buffalo) once roamed the grasslands of North America. By the mid-19th century, however, the expansion of European-American settlement, the demand for buffalo robes in the European and eastern U.S. markets, and competition from Indian horses for grazing lands had reduced the herds by many millions. Such pressures intensified after the Civil War—as railroads penetrated the West and new technology enabled tanners to process buffalo hides for leather. Professional hunters flocked to the range and systematically killed the bison; the hides were then shipped out by rail, as shown in the photograph at right. Passengers on trains sometimes shot buffalo from the cars as shown in the magazine illustration. The U.S. Army encouraged this slaughter in order to force the Plains Indians onto reservations by depriving them of their traditional sustenance from hunting bison. By the 1880s the buffalo were almost extinct, leaving behind millions of bones, which were gathered and piled, as in the photograph of buffalo skulls, for shipment to plants that ground them into fertilizer.

was often a Pyrrhic victory. In the end, most Mexican American landholders in northern California were forced to sell the very lands they had fought to keep. Similarly, the ranchers in southern California were forced to sell their lands after devastating droughts in the 1860s virtually destroyed the ranching industry. Forced off the land, California's Mexican Americans increasingly found themselves concentrated in segregated urban *barrios*.

The migration of Anglos into eastern Texas had played a role in fomenting the war for Texas independence and in bringing about the war with Mexico (see Chapter 13). By the latter half of the 19th century, eastern Texas was overwhelmingly Anglo; most Mexican Americans were concentrated in the Rio Grande valley of southern Texas. As in California, Anglos in Texas used force and intimidation to disfranchise the Mexican Americans. The vaunted Texas Rangers often acted as an Anglo vigilante force. Eventually, Mexican Americans in Texas were reduced to a state of peonage, dependent on their Anglo protectors for political and economic security.

Similar patterns prevailed in New Mexico, but the effects of Anglo-American settlement were mitigated somewhat because New Mexicans continued to outnumber Anglo-Americans. Earlier in the 19th century, international trade along the Santa Fe Trail had strengthened the political and economic status of the New Mexican elites. Now these same elites consolidated their position by acting as power brokers between poorer New Mexicans and wealthy Anglos.

Despite all these difficulties, Spanish-speaking peoples in the Southwest and California managed to preserve much of their distinctive culture. Moreover, Mexican American agricultural methods and mining techniques were adopted by Anglo-American immigrants to the region.

THE NEW SOUTH

Southern whites proved more resistant than western Indians to Yankee dominance. Nevertheless, after the North's retreat from Reconstruction, a Yankee presence did remain, in the form of investment and a "New South" ideology.

The Republican Party did not disappear from the South after 1877. Nor was the black vote immediately and totally suppressed. Republican presidential candidates won about 40 percent of the votes in former slave states through the 1880s, and a number of blacks continued to win elections to state legislatures until the 1890s. Down to 1901, every U.S. Congress but one had at least one black representative from the South.

But there was enough "bulldozing" of black voters (Chapter 17) to keep the southern states solid for the Democrats. In 1880 the Democratic Party hoped to build on this foundation to win the presidency. They nominated a Civil War hero, General Winfield Scott Hancock. His opponent was another Civil War general, James A. Garfield, who had served in Congress since the war. In an election with the closest popular vote in American history, Hancock carried every southern state, while Garfield won all but three northern states—and the election.

However, following this political defeat, a new spirit of enterprise quickened southern life in the 1880s. Some southerners even went so far as to acknowledge that the Yankees had shown them the way. And they welcomed northern investment. Henry Grady, editor of the *Atlanta Constitution,* was the leading spokesman for the New South ideology. In an 1886 speech to northern businessmen, Grady boasted of the New South's achievements: "We have sown towns and cities in the place of theories, and put business above politics. . . . We have established thrift in city and country. We have fallen in love with work."

Southern Industry

The South's textile industry expanded rapidly during the 1880s. Along the piedmont from Virginia to Alabama, new cotton mills sprang up. The labor force was almost entirely white. About 40 percent of the workers were women, and 25 percent were children aged 16 and younger. These "lintheads" labored long hours for wages about half the level prevailing in New England's mills. This cheap labor gave southern mill owners a competitive advantage. In 1880 the South had only 5 percent of the country's textile-producing capacity; by 1900 it had 23 percent.

Tobacco was another southern industry that developed from a regional crop. Unlike the textile industry, many of the workers in the tobacco factories were black. James B. Duke of North Carolina transformed the tobacco industry when he installed cigarette-making machines at Durham in 1885. In 1890 he created the American Tobacco Company, which controlled 90 percent of the market, with himself at its head.

Railroads and iron were two New South industries that were especially dependent on outside capital. During the 1880s, railroad construction in the South outpaced the national average. In 1886 southern railroads with a 5-foot gauge shifted to the national standard of 4 feet $8\frac{1}{2}$ inches. This change integrated southern lines into the national network and symbolized northern domination of the region's railroads. During those same years, northern capital helped fuel the growth of an iron and steel industry in the South. In 1880, the former slave states produced only 9 percent of the nation's pig iron; by 1890, that proportion had doubled. Most of the growth was concentrated in northern Alabama, where the proximity of coal, limestone, and ore made the new city of Birmingham the "Pittsburgh of the South."

The heavy northern investment in these industries meant that the South had less control over economic decisions that affected its welfare. Some historians have referred to the South's "colonial" relationship to the North in the late 19th century. And because of the low wages prevailing in the South, the economic benefits that accrued from industrial growth were inequitably distributed. Average southern per capita income remained only two-fifths of the average in the rest of the country well into the 20th century.

Southern Agriculture

The main reason for this relative poverty, however, was the weakness of the region's agriculture. A crucial reason for this retardation was the low level of investment in farming. One-crop specialization, overproduction, declining prices, and an exploitative credit system also contributed to the problem. The basic institution of the southern rural economy was the crop lien system, which came into being because of the shortage of money and credit. Few banks had survived the war, and land values had plummeted, so it was impossible for farmers to get a bank loan with their land as collateral. Instead, merchants provided farmers with supplies and groceries in return for a lien on their next crop.

This system might have worked well if the merchants had charged reasonable interest rates and if cotton and tobacco prices had remained high enough for the farmer to pay off his debts after harvest with a little left over. But the country storekeeper charged a credit price 50 or 60 percent above the cash price. And crop prices, especially for cotton, were dropping steadily. Cotton prices declined from an average of 12 cents a pound in the 1870s to 6 cents in the 1890s. As prices fell, many farmers went deeper and deeper into debt to the merchants. Sharecroppers and tenants incurred a double indebtedness: to the land-owner, whose land they sharecropped or rented, and to the merchant, who furnished them supplies on credit. Many sharecroppers, particularly blacks, fell into virtual peonage.

One reason for the fall of cotton prices was overproduction. Britain had encouraged the expansion of cotton growing in Egypt and India during the Civil War to make up for the loss of American cotton. So after the war, southern growers had to face international competition. From 1878 to 1898 output doubled. This overproduction drove prices ever lower. To get credit, farmers had to plant every acre with the most marketable cash crop—cotton. This practice exhausted the soil, required ever-increasing amounts of expensive fertilizer, and fed the cycle of overproduction and declining prices.

It also reduced the amount of land that could be used to grow food crops. Farmers who might otherwise have produced their own cornmeal and raised their own hogs for bacon became dependent on merchants for these supplies. By the 1890s they had to import nearly half their food at a price 50 percent higher than it would have cost to grow their own. Many southerners recognized that only diversification could break this dependency. But the crop lien system locked them into it.

RACE RELATIONS IN THE NEW SOUTH

The downward spiral of the rural southern economy caused frustration and bitterness in which blacks became the scapegoats of white rage. Lynching rose to an all-time high in the 1890s, averaging 188 per year. The viciousness of racist propaganda reached an all-time low. Serious antiblack riots broke out at Wilmington, North Carolina, in 1898 and in Atlanta in 1906. Several states adopted new constitutions that disfranchised most black voters by means of literacy or property qualifications (or both), poll taxes, and other clauses implicitly aimed at black voters. The new constitutions contained "understanding clauses" or "grandfather clauses" that enabled registrars to register white voters who were unable to meet the new requirements. In *Williams* v. *Mississippi* (1898), the U.S. Supreme Court upheld these disfranchisement clauses on the grounds that they did not discriminate "on their face" against blacks. State Democratic parties then established primary elections in which only whites could vote.

It was during these same years that most southern states passed "Jim Crow" laws, which mandated racial segregation in public facilities of all kinds. In the landmark case of *Plessy* v. *Ferguson* (1896), the Supreme Court sanctioned such laws so long as the separate facilities for blacks were equal to those for whites—which, in practice, they never were.

One of the worst features of race relations in the New South was the convict leasing system. The southern prison system was inadequate to accommodate the increase in convicted criminals after emancipation. Most states began leasing convicts to private contractors—coal-mining firms, railroad construction companies, planters, and so on. The state not only saved the cost of housing and feeding the prisoners but also received an income for leasing them; the lessees obtained cheap labor whom they could work like slaves. The cruelty and exploitation suffered by the convicts became a national scandal. Ninety percent of the convicts were black, the result in part of discriminatory law enforcement practices. The convicts were ill fed, ill clothed, victimized by sadistic guards, and worked to death. Annual mortality rates among convicts in several states ranged up to 25 percent.

Northern reformers condemned what they called "this newest and most revolting form of slavery." Thoughtful southerners agreed; reform groups, many of them led by white women, sprang up in the South to work for the abolition of convict leasing.

In 1895 a new black leader emerged. Booker T. Washington, a 39-year-old educator who had founded Tuskegee Institute in Alabama, gave a speech at the Atlanta Exposition that made him famous. In effect, Washington accepted segregation as a temporary accommodation between the races in return for white support of black efforts for education, social uplift, and economic progress. "In all things that are purely social we can be as separate as the fingers," said Washington, "yet one as the hand in all things essential to mutual progress."

Washington's goal was not permanent second-class citizenship for blacks, but improvement through self-help and uplift until they earned white acceptance as equals. Yet to his black critics, Washington's strategy and rhetoric seemed to play into the hands of white supremacists.

The Politics of Stalemate

During the years between the Panic of 1873 and the Panic of 1893, serious economic and social issues beset the American polity. As described in the next chapter, the strains of rapid industrialization, an inadequate monetary system, agricultural distress, and labor protest built up to potentially explosive force. But the two mainstream political parties seemed indifferent to these problems. Paralysis gripped the national government as the Civil War continued to cast its shadow into the future.

Knife-Edge Electoral Balance

The five presidential elections from 1876 through 1892, taken together, were the most closely contested elections in American history. No more than 1 percent separated the popular vote of the two major candidates in any of these contests except 1892, when the margin was 3 percent. The Democratic candidate won twice (Grover Cleveland in 1884 and 1892), and in two other elections carried a tiny plurality of popular votes (Tilden in 1876 and Cleveland in 1888) but lost narrowly in the Electoral College. During only six of those 20 years did the same party control the presidency and both houses, and then by razor-thin margins.

The few pieces of major legislation during these years—the Pendleton Civil Service Act of 1883, the Interstate Commerce Act of 1887, and the Sherman Antitrust Act of 1890—could be enacted only by bipartisan majorities, and only after they had been watered down by numerous compromises. Politicians often debated the tariff, but the tariff laws they passed had little real impact on the economy.

Divided government and the even balance between the two major parties accounted for the political stalemate. Neither party had the power to enact a bold legislative program; both parties avoided taking firm stands on controversial issues. Both parties practiced the politics of the past rather than the politics of the present. At election time, Republican candidates "waved the bloody shirt" to keep alive the memory of the Civil War. They castigated Democrats as former rebels or Copperheads who could not be trusted with the nation's destiny. Democrats, in turn, especially in the South, denounced racial equality and branded Republicans as the party of "Negro rule." From 1876 almost into the 20th century scarcely anyone but a Confederate veteran could be elected governor or senator in the South.

Availability rather than ability or a strong stand on issues became the prime requisite for presidential and vice presidential nominees. Geographical "availability" was particularly important. The solid Democratic South and the rather less solid Republican North gave each party a firm bloc of electoral votes in every election. But in three large northern states—New York, Ohio, and Indiana—the two parties were so closely balanced that the shift of a few thousand votes would determine the margin of victory for one or the other party in the state's electoral votes. And these three states alone represented 74 electoral votes, fully one-third of the total necessary for victory.

So it is not surprising that of 20 nominees for president and vice president by the two parties in five elections, 16 of them were from these three states. Only once did each party nominate a presidential candidate from outside these three states: Democrat Winfield Scott Hancock of Pennsylvania in 1880 and Republican James G. Blaine of Maine in 1884. Both lost.

CIVIL SERVICE REFORM

The most salient issue of national politics in the early 1880s was civil service reform. The Republicans split into three factions known as Mugwumps (the reformers), Stalwarts (who opposed reform), and Half-Breeds (who supported halfway reforms). Mugwumps and Half-Breeds combined to nominate James A. Garfield for president in 1880; Chester A. Arthur was nominated for vice president. Four months after Garfield took office, a man named Charles Guiteau approached the president at the railroad station in Washington and shot him. Garfield lingered for two months before dying on September 19, 1881.

Described by psychiatrists as a paranoid schizophrenic, Guiteau had been a government clerk and a supporter of the Stalwart faction of the Republican Party; he had lost his job under the new administration. As he shot Garfield he shouted: "I am a Stalwart and Arthur is president now!" This tragedy gave a final impetus to civil service reform. In 1883 Congress passed the Pendleton Act, which established a category of civil service jobs that were to be filled by competitive examinations. At first, only a tenth of government positions fell within that category, but a succession of presidential orders gradually expanded the list to about half by 1897. State and local governments began to emulate federal civil service reform in the 1880s and 1890s.

Like the other vice presidents who had succeeded presidents who died in office (John Tyler, Millard Fillmore, and Andrew Johnson), Arthur failed to achieve nomination for president in his own right. The Republicans in 1884 turned instead to Speaker of the House James G. Blaine of Maine. Blaine had made enemies over the years, however, especially among Mugwumps, who felt that his cozy relationship with railroad lobbyists while Speaker disqualified him for the presidency.

The Mugwumps had a tendency toward self-righteousness in their self-appointed role as spokesmen for political probity. They were small in number but large in influence. Many were editors, authors, lawyers, college professors, or clergymen. Concentrated in the Northeast, they admired the Democratic governor of New York, Grover Cleveland, who had gained a reputation as an advocate of reform and "good government." When Blaine won the Republican nomination, the Mugwumps defected to Cleveland.

In such a closely balanced state as New York, that shift could make a decisive difference. But Blaine hoped to neutralize it by appealing to the Irish vote. He made the most of his Irish ancestry on the maternal side. But that effort was rendered futile late in the campaign when a Protestant clergyman characterized the Democrats as the party of "Rum, Romanism, and Rebellion." Though Blaine was present when the Reverend Samuel Burchard made this remark, he failed to repudiate it. When the incident hit the newspapers, Blaine's hope for Irish support faded. Cleveland carried New York State by 1,149 votes (a margin of one-tenth of 1 percent) and thus became the first Democrat to be elected president in 28 years.

THE TARIFF ISSUE

Ignoring a rising tide of farmer and labor discontent, Cleveland decided to make or break his presidency on the tariff issue. He devoted his annual State of the Union message in December 1887 entirely to the tariff, maintaining that lower import duties would help all Americans by reducing the cost of consumer goods and expanding American exports. Republicans responded that low tariffs would flood the country with products from low-wage industries abroad, forcing American factories to close and throwing American workers out on the streets. The following year, the Republican nominee for president, Benjamin Harrison, pledged to retain the protective tariff. To reduce the budget surplus that had built up during the 1880s, the Republicans also promised more generous pensions for Union veterans.

The voters' response was ambiguous. Cleveland's popular-vote plurality actually increased from 29,000 in 1884 to 90,000 in 1888. But a shift of six-tenths of 1 percent put New York in

CHRONOLOGY

1862	Sioux uprising in Minnesota; 38 Sioux executed
1864	Colorado militia massacres Cheyenne in village at Sand Creek, Colorado
1866	Cowboys conduct first cattle drive north from Texas
1869	President Grant announces his "peace policy" toward Indians
1876	Sioux and Cheyenne defeat Custer at Little Big Horn
1880	James A. Garfield elected president
1881	Garfield assassinated; Chester A. Arthur becomes president
1883	Pendleton Act begins reform of civil service
1884	Grover Cleveland elected president
1887	Dawes Severalty Act dissolves Indian tribal units and implements individual ownership of tribal lands
1888	Benjamin Harrison elected president
1889	Government opens Indian Territory (Oklahoma) to white settlement
1890	Wounded Knee massacre • New Mississippi constitution pioneers black disfranchisement in South • Republicans try but fail to enact federal elections bill to protect black voting rights • Congress enacts McKinley Tariff
1892	Grover Cleveland again elected president
1895	Booker T. Washington makes his "Atlanta Compromise" address
1896	*Plessy* v. *Ferguson* legalizes "separate but equal" state racial segregation laws
1898	*Williams* v. *Mississippi* condones use of literacy tests and similar measures to restrict voting rights

the Republican column and Harrison in the White House. Republicans also gained control of both houses of Congress. They promptly made good on their campaign pledges by passing legislation that almost doubled Union pensions and by enacting the McKinley Tariff of 1890. Named for Congressman William McKinley of Ohio, this law raised duties on a large range of products to an average of almost 50 percent.

In the midterm congressional elections, the voters handed the Republicans a decisive defeat, converting a House Republican majority of six to a Democratic majority of 147, and a Senate Republican majority of eight to a Democratic majority of six. Nominated for a third time in 1892, Cleveland built on this momentum to win the presidency by the largest margin in 20 years. But this outcome was deceptive. On March 4, 1893, when Cleveland took the oath of office for the second time, he stood atop a social and economic volcano that would soon erupt.

CONCLUSION

In 1890 the superintendent of the U.S. Census made a sober announcement of dramatic import: "Up to and including 1880 the country had a frontier of settlement, but at present the unsettled area has been so broken into by isolated bodies of settlement that there can hardly be said to be a frontier line . . . any longer."

This statement prompted a young historian at the University of Wisconsin, Frederick Jackson Turner, to deliver a paper in 1893 that became the single most influential essay ever published by an American historian. For nearly 300 years, said Turner, the existence of a frontier of European-American settlement advancing relentlessly westward had shaped American character. To the frontier Americans owed their upward mobility, their high standard of living, and the rough equality of opportunity that made liberty and democracy possible. "American social development has been continually beginning over again on the frontier," declared Turner.

For many decades Turner's insight dominated Americans' perceptions of themselves and their history. Today, however, the Turner thesis is largely discredited as failing to explain the experiences of the great majority of people who lived and worked in older cities and towns or on plantations hundreds of miles or more from any frontier, and whose culture and institutions were molded more by their place of origin than by a "frontier."

But the significance of Turner's remarks is not whether he was right; in the 1890s he expressed a widely-shared belief among white Americans. They *believed* that liberty and equality were at least partly the product of the frontier, of the chance to go west and start a new life. And now that opportunity seemed to be coming to an end—at the same time that the Panic of 1893 was launching another depression, the worst that the American economy had yet experienced. This depression caused the social and economic tinder that had been accumulating during the two preceding decades to burst into flame.

19

ECONOMIC CHANGE AND THE
CRISIS OF THE 1890S

ECONOMIC GROWTH ❧ LABOR STRIFE ❧ FARMERS' MOVEMENTS
THE RISE AND FALL OF THE PEOPLE'S PARTY

Alexis de Tocqueville visited the United States in 1831 and published his famous analysis, *Democracy in America,* in 1835. At that time more than two-thirds of all Americans lived on farms and only 10 percent lived in towns or cities with populations larger than 2,500. The overwhelming majority of white males owned property and worked for themselves rather than for wages. What impressed Tocqueville most was the relative absence of both great wealth and great poverty; the modest prosperity of the broad middle class created the impression of equality.

During the next generation the North began to industrialize, cities grew much faster than rural areas, and inequality of wealth and income grew larger. The country's preoccupation with sectional issues prior to the Civil War and the gnawing problems of Reconstruction after the war diverted attention from the economic and social problems associated with industrialism and class inequality. With the depression that followed the Panic of 1873, however, these problems burst spectacularly into public view.

ECONOMIC GROWTH

During the 15 years between recovery from one depression in 1878 and the onset of another in 1893, the American economy grew at one of the fastest rates in its history. All sectors of the economy were expanding. The most spectacular growth was in manufacturing, which increased by 180 percent, while agriculture grew by 26 percent.

RAILROADS

The railroad was the single most important agent of economic growth during these years. Track mileage increased from 103,649 to 221,864 miles; the number of locomotives and revenue cars (freight and passenger) increased by a similar amount. Railroads converted from iron to steel rails and wheels, boosting steel production. Railroads were the largest consumers of coal, the largest carriers of goods and people, the largest single employer of labor.

The power wielded by the railroads inevitably aroused hostility. Companies often charged less for long hauls than for short hauls in areas with little or no competition. The rapid proliferation of tracks produced overcapacity in some areas. This caused rate-cutting wars that

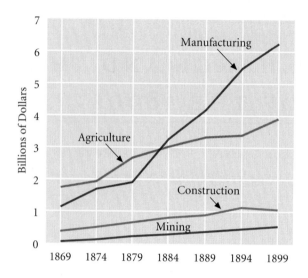

VALUE ADDED BY
ECONOMIC SECTOR,
1869–1899 (IN 1879 PRICES)

benefited some shippers at the expense of others—usually small ones. To avoid "ruinous competition" (as the railroads viewed it), companies formed "pools" by which they divided traffic and fixed their rates. Some of these practices made sound economic sense; others appeared discriminatory and exploitative. Railroads kept rates higher in areas with no competition (most farmers lived in areas served by only one line) than in regions with competition. Grain elevators, many of which were owned by railroad companies, came under attack for cheating farmers.

Farmers responded by organizing cooperatives to sell crops and buy supplies. The umbrella organization for many of these cooperatives was the Patrons of Husbandry, known as the Grange, founded in 1867. But farmers could not build their own railroads. So they organized "antimonopoly" parties and elected state legislators who enacted "Granger laws" in several states. These laws established railroad commissions that fixed maximum freight rates and warehouse charges. Railroads challenged the laws in court. Eight challenges made their way to the U.S. Supreme Court, which in *Munn* v. *Illinois* (1877) ruled that states could regulate businesses clothed with a "public interest"—including railroads.

The welter of different and sometimes conflicting state laws, plus rulings by the U.S. Supreme Court in the 1880s that states could not regulate interstate railroad traffic, brought a drive for federal regulation. After years of discussion, Congress passed the Interstate Commerce Act in 1887. This act, like most such laws, was a compromise that reflected the varying viewpoints of shippers, railroads, and other pressure groups. It outlawed pools, discriminatory rates, long-haul versus short-haul differentials, and rebates to favored shippers. It required that freight and passenger rates must be "reasonable and just." What that meant was not entirely clear, but the law created the Interstate Commerce Commission (ICC) to define it on a case-by-case basis. Because the ICC had minimal enforcement powers, however, federal courts frequently refused to issue the orders it requested. Nevertheless, the ICC had some effect on railroad practices. And freight rates continued to decline during this period as railroad operating efficiency improved.

The outstanding example of the railroads' impact on everyday life was the creation of standard time zones. Before 1883 many localities and cities kept their own time, derived from the sun's meridian in each locality. When it was noon in Chicago, it was 11:27 A.M. in Omaha, 11:56 A.M. in St. Louis, 12:09 P.M. in Louisville, and 12:17 P.M. in Toledo. This played havoc with railroad timetables. In 1883 a consortium of railroads established four standard time zones and put new timetables into effect for these zones. There was some grumbling about the arrogance of railroad presidents changing "God's time." For the most part, however, the public accepted the change, and Congress finally got around to sanctioning standard time zones in 1918.

Technology

Technological advances during this era had an enormous impact: automatic signals, air brakes, and knuckle couplers on the railroads; the Bessemer and then the open-hearth process in the steel mills; the telephone, electric light, and typewriter (all in the 1870s); the phonograph and motion pictures (1890s); the elevator and structural steel for buildings, which made possible the first "skyscrapers" (1880s); the electric dynamo (generator), which not only laid the basis for such household items as refrigerators and washing machines but also provided a new source of industrial power that gradually replaced water power and the steam engine; and the internal combustion engine, which made possible the first automobiles (1890s) and the first airplane flight by the Wright brothers in 1903.

Wealth and Inequality

All these wonders of economic growth and technological change were not accomplished without human cost. One such cost was a widening gulf between rich and poor. While the average per capita income of all Americans increased by 35 percent from 1878 to 1893, real wages advanced only 20 percent. And that advance masked sharp inequalities of wages by skill, region, race, and gender. Many unskilled and semiskilled workers made barely enough to support themselves, much less a family.

The perception of class inequality was even greater than the reality. Many wealthy people practiced what Thorstein Veblen described in his book *The Theory of the Leisure Class* (1899) as "conspicuous consumption." They sent agents to Europe to buy up paintings and tapestries from impoverished aristocrats. In their mansions on Fifth Avenue and their summer homes at Newport they entertained lavishly. These extravagant habits gave substance to the labeling of this era as the Gilded Age and sharpened the growing sense of class consciousness.

Some of the newly rich made their money by methods that critics considered predatory, and were labeled "robber barons." They included William Vanderbilt, Jay Gould, Jim Fisk, and Collis P. Huntington in railroading; John D. Rockefeller in oil; Andrew Carnegie and Henry Clay Frick in steel; James B. Duke in tobacco; and John Pierpont Morgan in banking.

Criticism of the "robber barons" sometimes focused more on the immense power commanded by their wealth than on the wealth itself. Fisk and Gould bribed legislators, manipulated the stock market, exploited workers, and cheated stockholders. Rockefeller either bought out or ruined his competitors, obtained rebates and drawbacks on rail shipments of oil, and created a monopoly in his determined efforts to gain control of oil refining. Carnegie and Frick pushed laborers to the limit in 72-hour workweeks, redefined skill levels and changed work rules, and sped up the pace in steel mills in a ceaseless quest for greater efficiency and lower labor costs. Morgan's banking firm built an empire of leveraged financing and interlocking corporate directorates.

These activities could be—and were—defended on grounds of entrepreneurial innovation and efficiency, and the enterprises these men created did enable the United States to leap ahead of Britain as an industrial power. By 1913 American manufacturing output equaled that of the next three industrial nations combined—Germany, Britain, and France. The "robber barons" created wealth for all Americans. And not all of them practiced conspicuous consumption. Professing a gospel of stewardship, Carnegie, Rockefeller, and others gave away much of their wealth to educational and philanthropic institutions.

THE ANTITRUST MOVEMENT

Nevertheless, many Americans feared the power wielded by these tycoons. Their monopoly or near-monopoly share of the market in oil, steel, tobacco, sugar, transportation, and other products seemed to violate the ideal of fair competition. To curb that power, an "antitrust" movement emerged in the 1880s. The word "trust" derived from an investment strategy in which the stockholders of several refining companies turned over their shares to Rockefeller's Standard Oil in return for so-called trust certificates. The term came to be applied to all large corporations that controlled a substantial share of any given market. In response to pressures to curb such "trusts," several states passed antitrust laws in the 1880s.

But because the larger corporations operated across state lines, reformers turned to Congress, which responded in 1890 by passing the Sherman Antitrust Act. The act stated that "Every contract, combination in the form of trust or otherwise, or conspiracy, in restraint of trade or commerce among the several States is hereby declared to be illegal." But what constituted "restraint of trade"? For that matter, what constituted a trust? Of eight cases against corporations brought before federal courts from 1890 to 1893, the government lost seven. In 1895 the Supreme Court dealt the Sherman Act a crippling blow in *U.S.* v. *E. C. Knight Company,* in which it ruled that manufacturing was not commerce and therefore did not fall under jurisdiction of the law.

LABOR STRIFE

The drive for even greater speed and productivity on railroads and in factories gave the United States the unhappy distinction of having the world's highest rate of industrial accidents. Many families were impoverished by workplace accidents that killed or maimed their chief breadwinner. This was one source of a rising tide of labor discontent. Another was the erosion of worker autonomy in factories, where managers made decisions about procedures and pace of operations that were once made by workers themselves. Many crafts that had once been a source of pride to those who practiced them became just a job that could be performed by anyone. Labor became increasingly a commodity to be bought for wages rather than a craft whereby the worker sold the product of his labor rather than the labor itself.

For skilled artisans, this was an alarming trend. In 1866 the leaders of several craft unions had formed the National Labor Union. Labor parties sprang up in several states, and several states established bureaus or departments of labor that had little substantive power but did begin to gather and report data. These pressures filtered up to Washington, where Congress created the

THE RAILROAD STRIKES OF 1877 This illustration shows striking workers on the Baltimore and Ohio Railroad forcing the engineer and fireman from a freight train at Martinsburg, West Virginia, on July 17, 1877.

Bureau of Labor in 1884 and elevated it to cabinet rank in 1903. In 1894 Congress also made the first Monday in September an official holiday—Labor Day—to honor working people.

The National Labor Union withered away in the depression of the 1870s. But industrial violence escalated. In the anthracite coal fields of eastern Pennsylvania, the Molly Maguires carried out guerrilla warfare against mine owners. In the later 1870s, the Greenbackers (a group that urged currency expansion) and labor reformers formed a coalition that elected several local and state officials plus 14 congressmen in 1878.

THE GREAT RAILROAD STRIKE OF 1877

Railroads became an early focal point of labor strife. Citing declining revenues during the depression that followed the Panic of 1873, several railroads cut wages by as much as 35 percent between 1874 and 1877. When the Baltimore and Ohio Railroad announced its third 10 percent wage cut on July 16, 1877, workers struck. The strike spread rapidly to other lines, and traffic from St. Louis to the East Coast came to a halt. Ten states called out their militias. Strikers and militia fired on each other, and workers set fire to rolling stock and roundhouses. By the time federal troops brought things under control in the first week of August, at least 100 strikers, militiamen, and bystanders had been killed, hundreds more had been injured, and uncounted millions of dollars of property had gone up in smoke.

THE KNIGHTS OF LABOR

The principal labor organization that emerged in the 1880s was the Knights of Labor. Founded in Philadelphia in 1869, the Knights were at first a secret fraternal society. But under the leadership of Terence V. Powderly, the Knights abandoned secrecy in 1879 and emerged as a potent national federation of unions. The Knights of Labor departed in several respects from the norm of labor organization at that time. Most of its unions were organized by industry rather than by craft, giving many unskilled and semiskilled workers union representation for the first time. Some admitted women; some also admitted blacks.

The goal of most members of the Knights was to improve their lot within the existing system through higher wages, shorter hours, and better working conditions. This meant collective bargaining with employers; it also meant strikes. But Powderly and the Knights' national leadership discouraged the members from calling strikes. One reason they did so was practical: A losing strike often destroyed a union as employers replaced strikers with strikebreakers, or "scabs."

Another reason was philosophical. Strikes constituted a tacit recognition of the legitimacy of the wage system. In Powderly's view, wages siphoned off to capital a part of the wealth created by labor. The Knights, Powderly said, intended "to secure to the workers the full enjoyment of the wealth they create." This was a goal grounded both in the past independence of skilled workers and in a radical vision of the future—a vision in which workers' cooperatives would own the means of production.

The Knights did sponsor several modest workers' cooperatives. Their success was limited, partly because of a lack of capital and of management experience and partly because even the most skilled craftsmen found it difficult to compete with machines. Ironically, the Knights gained their greatest triumphs through strikes. In 1884 and 1885 successful strikes against the Union Pacific and Missouri Pacific railroads won enormous prestige and a rush of new members, which by 1886 totaled 700,000. But defeat in a second strike against the two railroads in the spring of 1886 was a serious blow. Then came the Haymarket bombing in Chicago.

HAYMARKET

Chicago was a hotbed of labor radicalism. Anarchists infiltrated some trade unions in Chicago and leaped aboard the bandwagon of a national movement centered in that city for a general strike on May 1, 1886, to achieve the eight-hour workday. Chicago police were notoriously hostile to labor organizers and strikers, so the scene was set for a violent confrontation.

The May 1 showdown coincided with a strike at the McCormick farm machinery plant in Chicago. A fight outside the gates on May 3 brought a police attack on the strikers. Anarchists then organized a protest meeting at Haymarket Square on May 4. Toward the end of the meeting, the police suddenly arrived in force. When someone threw a bomb into their midst, the police opened fire. When the wild melee was over, 50 people lay wounded and 10 dead—six of them policemen.

This affair set off a wave of hysteria against labor radicals. Police in Chicago rounded up hundreds of labor leaders. Eight anarchists went on trial for conspiracy to commit murder—though no evidence turned up to prove that any of them had thrown the bomb. All eight were convicted; four were hanged on November 11, 1887. The case bitterly divided the country.

Many workers, civil libertarians, and members of the middle class branded the verdicts judicial murder. But the majority of Americans applauded them.

The Knights of Labor were caught in this antilabor backlash. Although the Knights had nothing to do with the Haymarket affair, Powderly's opposition to the wage system sounded suspiciously like anarchism. Membership in the Knights plummeted from 700,000 in the spring of 1886 to fewer than 100,000 by 1890.

As the Knights of Labor waned, a new national labor organization waxed. Founded in 1886, the American Federation of Labor (AFL) was a loosely affiliated association of unions organized by trade or craft: cigar-makers, machinists, carpenters, and so on. Under the leadership of Samuel Gompers, an immigrant cigar-maker, the AFL accepted capitalism and the wage system and worked for better conditions, higher wages, shorter hours, and occupational safety. Most of the members of the AFL unions were skilled workers. Its membership grew from 140,000 in 1886 to nearly a million by 1900.

HENRY GEORGE

Labor militancy did not die in the wake of Haymarket, however. Two best-selling books helped keep alive the vision of a more equalitarian social order. The first seemed an unlikely candidate for best-seller status. It was a book on economics titled *Progress and Poverty* (1879). Henry George, the self-educated author, had spent 15 years working as a sailor, printer, and prospector before becoming a newspaper editor in California. In his travels, George had been struck by the appalling contrast between wealth and poverty. He fixed on "land monopoly" as the cause: the control of land and resources by the few at the expense of the many. His solution was 100 percent taxation on the "unearned increment" in the value of land—that is, on the difference between the initial purchase price and the eventual market value (minus improvements), or what today we would call capital gains.

Progress and Poverty achieved astonishing success. By 1905 it had sold 2 million copies and been translated into several languages. However, few economists endorsed the single tax and the idea made little headway. The real impact of George's book came from its portrayal of the injustice of poverty in the midst of plenty. George became a hero to labor. He joined the Knights of Labor, moved to New York City, and ran for mayor as the candidate of the United Labor Party in 1886. He narrowly lost, but his campaign dramatized the grievances of labor and alerted the major parties to the power of that constituency.

EDWARD BELLAMY

The other book that found a wide audience was a novel, *Looking Backward,* by Edward Bellamy. Bellamy was a New England writer imbued with the tenets of Christian reform. *Looking Backward* takes place in the year 2000 and contrasts the America of that year with the America of 1887. In 2000 all industry is controlled by the national government, everyone works for equal pay, there are no rich and no poor, no strikes, no class conflict. Bellamy was not a Marxian socialist, and he preferred to call his collectivist order "Nationalism." His vision of a world without social strife appealed to middle-class Americans, who bought half a million copies of *Looking Backward* every year for several years in the early 1890s. More than 160 Nationalist clubs sprang up to support the idea of public ownership, if not of all industries, at least of public utilities.

Some of Bellamy's followers called themselves Christian Socialists. They formed the left wing of a broader movement, the Social Gospel, that deeply affected mainstream Protestant denominations in the rapidly growing cities of the Gilded Age. Shocked by poverty and over-crowding in the sprawling tenement districts, clergymen and laypeople associated with the Social Gospel embraced a theology which held that ameliorating the plight of the poor was as important as saving souls. They supported the settlement houses that were being established in many cities during the 1890s (see Chapter 21) and pressed for legislation to curb the ex-ploitation of the poor and provide them with opportunities for betterment.

THE HOMESTEAD STRIKE

Plenty of evidence was at hand to feed middle-class fears that America was falling apart. Strikes occurred with a frequency and a fierceness that made 1877 and 1886 look like mere preludes to the main event. The most dramatic confrontation took place in 1892 at the Homestead plant (near Pittsburgh) of the Carnegie Steel Company. Carnegie and his plant manager, Henry Clay Frick, were determined to break the power of the country's strongest union, the Amalgamated Association of Iron, Steel, and Tin Workers. Frick used a dispute over wages and work rules as an opportunity to close the plant (a "lockout") preparatory to reopening it with nonunion workers. When the union called a strike and refused to leave the plant (a "sitdown"), Frick called in 300 Pinkerton guards to oust them. A full-scale gun battle between strikers and Pinkertons erupted on July 6, leaving nine strikers and seven Pinkertons dead and scores wounded. Frick persuaded the governor to send in 8,000 militia to protect the strikebreakers, and the plant reopened.

PENNSYLVANIA MILITIA AT CARNEGIE'S HOMESTEAD STEEL MILL, 1892   After the shoot-out between striking workers and Pinkerton guards, the Pennsylvania militia reopened the mills and pro-tected strikebreakers from striking workers. This photograph shows the militia using steel beams manu-factured by the mill as a makeshift barricade.

THE DEPRESSION OF 1893–1897

By the 1890s the use of state militias to protect strikebreakers had become common. Events after 1893 brought an escalation of conflict. The most serious economic crisis since the depression of 1873–1878 was triggered by the Panic of 1893, a collapse of the stock market that plunged the economy into a severe four-year depression. The bankruptcy of the Reading Railroad and the National Cordage Company in early 1893 set off a process that by the end of the year had caused 491 banks and 15,000 other businesses to fail. By mid-1894 the unemployment rate had risen to more than 15 percent.

In Ohio, a reformer named Jacob Coxey conceived the idea of sending Congress a "living petition" of unemployed workers to press for appropriations to put them to work on road building and other public works. "Coxey's army" inspired other groups to hit the road and ride the rails to Washington during 1894. This descent of the unemployed on the capital provoked arrests by federal marshals and troops, and ended when Coxey and others were arrested for trespassing on the Capitol grounds.

THE PULLMAN STRIKE

Even more alarming to middle-class Americans was the Pullman strike of 1894. George M. Pullman had made a fortune in the manufacture of sleeping cars and other rolling stock for railroads. Workers in his large factory complex lived in the company town of Pullman just south of Chicago, where they enjoyed paved streets, clean parks, and decent houses rented from the company. But Pullman controlled every aspect of their lives, banned liquor from the town, and punished workers whose behavior did not suit his ideas of decorum. When the Panic of 1893 caused a sharp drop in orders for Pullman cars, the company laid off a third of its work force and cut wages for the rest by 30 percent. But it did not reduce rents in company houses or prices in company stores. Pullman refused to negotiate with a workers' committee, which called a strike and appealed to the American Railway Union (ARU) for help.

The Railway Union had been founded the year before by Eugene V. Debs. A native of Indiana, Debs had been elected secretary of the Brotherhood of Locomotive Firemen in 1875. By 1893 he had become convinced that the conservative stance of the railroad craft unions was contrary to the best interests of labor. So he formed the ARU to include all railroad workers in one union. When Pullman refused the ARU's offer to arbitrate the strike of Pullman workers, Debs launched a boycott by which ARU members would refuse to run any trains that included Pullman cars. When the railroads attempted to fire the ARU sympathizers, whole train crews went on strike. Rail traffic was paralyzed.

Over the protests of Governor John P. Altgeld of Illinois, President Grover Cleveland sent in federal troops. The U.S. attorney general also obtained a federal injunction against Debs under the Sherman Antitrust Act on grounds that the boycott and the strike were a conspiracy in restraint of trade. This creative use of the Sherman Act was upheld by the Supreme Court in 1895 and became a powerful weapon against labor unions.

For a week in July 1894 the Chicago railroad yards resembled a war zone. Millions of dollars of equipment went up in smoke. Thirty-four people were killed. Finally, state militia and federal troops restored order and broke the strike. Debs went to jail for six months.

The Pullman strike was only the most dramatic event of a year in which 750,000 workers went on strike and another 3 million were unemployed. But it was a surge of discontent from down on the farm that wrenched American politics off its foundations in the 1890s.

RETURNING TO ILLINOIS, 1894   This photograph shows one of the thousands of farm families who had moved into Kansas, Nebraska, and other plains states in the wet years of the 1870s and 1880s, only to give up during the dry years of the 1890s. Their plight added fuel to the fire of rural unrest and protest during those years.

FARMERS' MOVEMENTS

After the Civil War, farmers from the older states and immigrants from northern Europe poured into the territories and states of Dakota, Nebraska, Kansas, Texas, and—after 1889—Indian Territory. Some went on to the Pacific Coast states or stopped in the cattle-grazing and mining territories in between. This wave of settlement brought nine new states into the Union between 1867 and 1896 that almost equaled in total size all the states east of the Mississippi.

The vagaries of nature and weather were magnified in the West. Grasshopper plagues wiped out crops several times in the 1870s. Dry, searing summer winds alternated with violent hailstorms to scorch or level whole fields of wheat and corn. Winter blizzards intensified the isolation of farm families. Adding to these woes, the relatively wet years of the 1870s and early 1880s gave way to an abnormally dry cycle the following decade, causing many farmers to give up and return east.

Despite these problems, American grain production soared, increasing three times as fast as the American population from 1870 to 1890. Only rising exports could sustain such expansion in farm production. But by the 1880s the improved efficiency of large farms in eastern Europe brought intensifying competition and consequent price declines, especially for wheat. Prices on the world market fell about 60 percent from 1870 to 1895, while the wholesale price index for all commodities declined by 45 percent during the same period.

CREDIT AND MONEY

Victims of a world market largely beyond their control, farmers lashed out at targets nearer home: banks, commission merchants, railroads, and the monetary system. In truth, these institutions did victimize farmers, though not always intentionally. The long period of price deflation from 1865 to 1897, unique in American history, exacerbated the problem of credit. A price decline of 1 or 2 percent a year added that many points cumulatively to the nominal interest rate. If a farmer's main crop was wheat or cotton, whose prices declined even further, his real interest rate was that much greater.

The federal government's monetary policies worsened the problems of deflation. After the Civil War the Treasury's policy was to bring the greenback dollar to par with gold by reducing the amount of greenbacks in circulation. This limitation of the money supply produced deflationary pressures. Western farmers, who suffered from downward pressure on crop prices, were particularly vociferous in their protests against this situation, which introduced a new sectional conflict into politics—not North against South, but East against West. However, parity between greenbacks and gold would not be reached until 1879.

The benefits of parity were sharply debated then and remain controversial today. On the one hand, it strengthened the dollar, placed government credit on a firm footing, and helped create a financial structure for the remarkable economic growth that tripled the gross national product during the last quarter of the 19th century. On the other hand, the restraints on money supply hurt the rural economy in the South and West; they hurt debtors who found that deflation enlarged their debts by increasing the value of greenbacks; and they probably worsened the two major depressions of the era (1873–1878 and 1893–1897) by constraining credit.

THE GREENBACK AND SILVER MOVEMENTS

Many farmers in 1876 and 1880 supported the Greenback Party, whose platform called for the issuance of more U.S. Treasury notes (greenbacks). Even more popular was the movement for "free silver." Until 1873 government mints had coined both silver and gold dollars at a ratio of 16 to 1—that is, 16 ounces of silver were equal in value to one ounce of gold. However, when new discoveries of gold in the West after 1848 placed more gold in circulation relative to silver, that ratio undervalued silver, so that little was being sold for coinage. In 1873 Congress enacted a law, branded as "the Crime of 1873," that ended the coinage of silver dollars.

Soon after the law was passed, the production of new silver mines began to increase dramatically, which soon brought the price of silver below the old ratio of 16 to 1. Silver miners joined with farmers to demand remonetization of silver. In 1878 Congress responded by passing the Bland-Allison Act requiring the Treasury to purchase and coin not less than $2 million nor more than $4 million of silver monthly. Once again, silver dollars flowed from the mint. But the amounts issued did not absorb the increasing production of silver and did little, if anything, to slow deflation. The market price of silver dropped to a ratio of 20 to 1.

Pressure for "free silver"—that is, for government purchase of all silver offered for sale at a price of 16 to 1 and its coinage into silver dollars—continued through the 1880s. The admission of five new western states in 1889 and 1890 contributed to the passage of the Sherman Silver Purchase Act in 1890. That act increased the amount of silver coinage, but not at the 16-to-1 ratio. Even so, it went too far to suit the "gold bugs," who wanted to keep the United States on the international gold standard. President Cleveland blamed the Panic of 1893 on the Sherman

Silver Purchase Act, which caused a run on the Treasury's gold reserves triggered by uncertainty over the future of the gold standard. Cleveland called a special session of Congress in 1893 and persuaded it to repeal the Sherman Silver Purchase Act, setting the stage for the most bitter political contest in a generation.

THE FARMERS' ALLIANCE

Agrarian reformers supported the free silver movement, but many had additional grievances concerning problems of credit, railroad rates, and the exploitation of workers and farmers by the "money power." A new farmers' organization emerged in the 1880s. Starting in Texas as the Southern Farmers' Alliance, it expanded into other southern states and then into the North as well. By 1890 it had evolved into the National Farmers' Alliance and Industrial Union.

Reaching out to 2 million farm families, the Alliance set up marketing cooperatives. It served the social needs of farm families by bringing them together, especially in the sparsely settled regions of the West. It also gave farmers a sense of pride and solidarity to counter the image of "hick" and "hayseed."

The Farmers' Alliance developed a comprehensive political agenda. At a national convention in Ocala, Florida, in December 1890, it set forth these objectives: a graduated income tax; direct election of U.S. senators; free and unlimited coinage of silver at a ratio of 16 to 1; effective government control and, if necessary, ownership of railroad, telegraph, and telephone companies; and the establishment of "subtreasuries" (federal warehouses) for the storage of crops, with government loans at 2 percent interest on those crops. Of these goals, the most important was the setting up of "subtreasuries." Government storage would allow farmers to hold their crops until market prices were more favorable. Low-interest government loans on the value of these crops would enable farmers to pay their annual debts and thus escape the ruinous interest rates of the crop lien system in the South and bank mortgages in the West.

These were radical demands for the time. Nevertheless, most of them eventually became law: the income tax and the direct election of senators by constitutional amendments in 1913; government control of transportation and communications by various laws in the 20th century; and the "subtreasuries" in the form of the Commodity Credit Corporation in the 1930s.

Anticipating that the Republicans and the Democrats would resist these demands, many Alliancemen were eager to form a third party. In Kansas they had already done so, launching the People's Party (whose members were known as Populists) in 1890. But southerners opposed the idea of a third party. Most of them were Democrats who feared that a third party might open the way for the return of the Republican Party to power.

In 1890 farmers helped elect numerous state legislators and congressmen who pledged to support their cause. But the legislative results were thin. By 1892 many Alliance members were ready to take the third-party plunge.

THE RISE AND FALL OF THE PEOPLE'S PARTY

By 1892 the discontent of farmers in the West and South had reached the fever stage. Enthusiasm for a third party was particularly strong in the plains and mountain states. The most prominent leader of the Farmers' Alliance was Leonidas L. Polk of North Carolina. A Confederate veteran, Polk commanded support in the West as well as in the South. He undoubtedly would have been nominated for president by the newly organized People's Party had not death cut short his career in June 1892.

The first nominating convention of the People's Party met at Omaha a month later. The preamble of their platform expressed the grim mood of delegates. "We meet in the midst of a nation brought to the verge of moral, political, and material ruin," it declared. "The fruits of the toil of millions are boldly stolen to build up colossal fortunes for a few. . . . From the same prolific womb of governmental injustice we breed the two great classes—tramps and millionaires." The platform itself called for unlimited coinage of silver at 16 to 1; creation of the "subtreasury" program for crop storage and farm loans; government ownership of railroad, telegraph, and telephone companies; a graduated income tax; direct election of senators; and laws to protect labor unions against prosecution for strikes and boycotts. To ease the lingering tension between southern and western farmers, the party nominated Union veteran James B. Weaver of Iowa for president and Confederate veteran James G. Field of Virginia for vice president.

Despite winning 9 percent of the popular vote and 22 electoral votes, Populist leaders were shaken by the outcome. In the South most of the black farmers who were allowed to vote stayed with the Republicans. Democratic bosses in several southern states kept white farmers loyal to the party of white supremacy. Only in Alabama and Texas, among southern states, did the Populists get more than 20 percent of the vote. They did even less well in the older agricultural states of the Midwest, where the largest vote share they gained was 11 percent in Minnesota. Only in distressed wheat states like Kansas, Nebraska, and the Dakotas and in the silver states of the West did the Populists do well, carrying Kansas, Colorado, Idaho, and Nevada.

The party remained alive, however, and the anguish caused by the Panic of 1893 seemed to boost its prospects. In several western states, Populists or a Populist-Democratic coalition controlled state governments for a time, and a Populist-Republican coalition won the state elections of 1894 in North Carolina.

President Cleveland's success in getting the Sherman Silver Purchase Act repealed in 1893 drove a wedge into the Democratic Party. Southern and western Democrats turned against Cleveland. Senator Benjamin Tillman of South Carolina told his constituents: "When Judas betrayed Christ, his heart was not blacker than this scoundrel, Cleveland, in deceiving the Democracy. He is an old bag of beef and I am going to Washington with a pitchfork and prod him in his fat ribs."

THE SILVER ISSUE

Democratic dissidents stood poised to take over the party in 1896. They adopted free silver as the centerpiece of their program, raising the possibility of fusion with the Populists. Meanwhile, out of the West came a new and charismatic figure, a silver-tongued orator named William Jennings Bryan. Only 36 years old, Bryan came to the Democratic convention in 1896 as a delegate. Given the opportunity to make the closing speech in the debate on silver, he brought the house to its feet in a frenzy of cheering with his peroration: "You shall not press down upon the brow of labor this crown of thorns, you shall not crucify mankind upon a cross of gold."

This speech catapulted Bryan into the presidential nomination. He ran on a platform that not only endorsed free silver but also embraced the idea of an income tax, condemned trusts, and opposed the use of injunctions against labor. Bryan's nomination created turmoil in the People's Party. Though some Populists wanted to continue as a third party, most of them saw

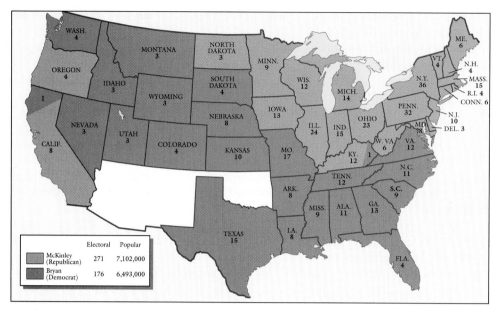

PRESIDENTIAL ELECTION OF 1896

fusion with silver Democrats as the road to victory. At the Populist convention, the fusionists got their way and endorsed Bryan's nomination.

THE ELECTION OF 1896

The Republicans nominated William McKinley, who would have preferred to campaign on his specialty, the tariff. But Bryan made that impossible. Crisscrossing the country, Bryan gave as many as 30 speeches a day, focusing almost exclusively on the free silver issue. Republicans responded by denouncing the Democrats as irresponsible inflationists. Free silver, they said, would demolish the workingman's gains in real wages achieved over the preceding 30 years.

Under the skillful leadership of Mark Hanna, an Ohio businessman who became chairman of the Republican National Committee, McKinley waged a "front-porch campaign" in which various delegations visited his home in Canton, Ohio, to hear carefully crafted speeches that were widely publicized in the mostly Republican press. Hanna sent out an army of speakers and printed pamphlets in more than a dozen languages to reach immigrant voters. His propaganda portrayed Bryan as a wild man from the prairie whose monetary schemes would further wreck an economy that had been plunged into depression during a Democratic administration. McKinley's election, by contrast, would maintain the gold standard, revive business confidence, and end the depression.

The 1896 election was the most impassioned and exciting in a generation. Many Americans believed that the fate of the nation hinged on the outcome. The number of voters jumped by 15 percent over 1892. Republicans won a substantial share of the urban, immigrant, and labor vote with the slogan of McKinley as "the advance agent of prosperity." McKinley rode to a convincing victory by carrying every state in the northeast quadrant of the country. Bryan carried

Chronology

1869	Knights of Labor founded
1873	"Crime of 1873" demonetizes silver
1877	Railroad strikes cost 100 lives and millions of dollars in damage
1878	Bland-Allison Act to remonetize silver passed over Hayes's veto
1879	Henry George publishes *Progress and Poverty*
1883	Railroads establish four standard time zones
1886	Knights of Labor membership crests at 700,000 • Haymarket riot causes antilabor backlash • American Federation of Labor founded
1887	Edward Bellamy publishes *Looking Backward* • Interstate Commerce Act creates the first federal regulatory agency
1890	Congress passes Sherman Antitrust Act • Congress passes Sherman Silver Purchase Act
1892	Homestead strike fails • Populists organize the People's Party
1893	Financial panic begins economic depression • Congress repeals Sherman Silver Purchase Act
1894	"Coxey's army" of the unemployed marches on Washington • Pullman strike paralyzes the railroads and provokes federal intervention
1896	William McKinley defeats William Jennings Bryan for the presidency

most of the rest. Republicans won decisive control of Congress as well as the presidency. They would maintain control for the next 14 years.

Whether by luck or by design, McKinley did prove to be the advance agent of prosperity. The economy pulled out of the depression during his first year in office and entered into a long period of growth—not because of anything the new administration did but because of the mysterious workings of the business cycle. With the discovery of rich new gold fields in the Yukon, in Alaska, and in South Africa, the silver issue lost potency and a cascade of gold poured into the world economy. The long deflationary trend since 1865 reversed itself in 1897. Farmers entered a new era of prosperity. Bryan ran against McKinley again in 1900 but lost even more emphatically. The nation seemed embarked on a placid sea of plenty. But below the surface, the currents of protest and reform still ran strong.

Conclusion

The 1890s were a major watershed in American history. On one side of that divide lay a largely rural society and agricultural economy. But the future belonged to the cities and to a commercial-industrial economy. Before the 1890s most immigrants had come from northern and western Europe and many became farmers. Then the principal origin of immigrants shifted to eastern and southern Europe and nearly all of them settled in cities. Before the 1890s the old sectional issues associated with slavery, the Civil War, and Reconstruction remained important forces in American politics; after 1900 racial issues would not play an important part in national politics for another 60 years. The election of 1896 ended 20 years of even balance between the two major parties and led to more than a generation of Republican dominance.

Most important of all, the social and political upheavals of the 1890s shocked many people into recognition that the liberty and equality they had taken for granted as part of the American dream was in danger of disappearing before the onslaught of wrenching economic changes. The strikes and violence and third-party protests of the decade were a wake-up call. As the forces of urbanization and industrialism continued to grow during the ensuing two decades, many middle-class Americans supported the enlargement of government power to carry out progressive reforms to cure the ills of an industrializing society.

An Industrial Society, 1890–1920

SOURCES OF ECONOMIC GROWTH ∼ "ROBBER BARONS" NO MORE

OBSESSION WITH PHYSICAL AND RACIAL FITNESS

IMMIGRATION ∼ BUILDING ETHNIC COMMUNITIES

AFRICAN AMERICAN LABOR AND COMMUNITY ∼ WORKERS AND UNIONS

THE JOYS OF THE CITY ∼ THE NEW SEXUALITY AND THE NEW WOMAN

With the collapse of populism in 1896 and the end of the depression in 1897, the American economy embarked on a remarkable stretch of growth. By 1910 America was unquestionably the world's greatest industrial power.

Corporations were changing the face of America. Their factories employed millions. Their production and management techniques became the envy of the industrialized world. A new kind of building—the skyscraper—came to symbolize America's corporate power. These modern towers were made possible by the use of steel rather than stone framework and by the invention of electrically powered elevators. Impelled upward by rising real estate values, they were intended to evoke the same sense of grandeur as Europe's medieval cathedrals. But these monuments celebrated man, not God; material wealth, not spiritual riches; science, not faith.

This chapter explores how the newly powerful corporations transformed America: how the jobs they generated attracted millions of European immigrants, southern blacks, and young single women to northern cities; and how they triggered an urban cultural revolution that made amusement parks, dance halls, vaudeville theater, and movies integral features of American life.

The power of the corporations dwarfed that of individual wage earners. But wage earners sought to limit corporate power through labor unions and strikes, or by organizing institutions of collective self-help within their own ethnic or racial communities. And significant numbers found opportunities and liberties they had not known before: Immigrant entrepreneurs invented ways to make money through legal and illegal enterprise; young, single, working-class women pioneered a sexual revolution; and radicals dared to imagine building a new society where no one suffered from poverty, inequality, and powerlessness.

SOURCES OF ECONOMIC GROWTH

A series of technological innovations in the late 19th century ignited the nation's economic engine. But technological breakthroughs alone do not fully explain the nation's spectacular economic boom. New corporate structures and new management techniques—in combination with the new technology—created the conditions that powered economic growth.

TECHNOLOGY

Two of the most important new technologies were the harnessing of electric power and the invention of the gasoline-powered internal combustion engine. Scientists had long been fascinated by electricity, but only in the late 19th century, through the work of Thomas Edison, George Westinghouse, and Nikola Tesla, did they produce the incandescent bulb that made electric lighting practical in homes and offices, and the alternating current (AC) that made electric transmission possible over long distances. Older industries switched from expensive and cumbersome steam power to more efficient and cleaner electrical power. The demand for electric generators and

Leading Industries

Cotton Goods	Sugar Refining	Marble and Stone Products
Copper Refining	Paper	Woolen Goods
Lumber Products	Shipbuilding	Diversified
Meatpacking	Automobiles	Rubber Products
Brass and Copper Products	Butter	Petroleum Refining
Leather Goods	Clothing	Lead Smelting
Iron and Steel	Products for Railroads	
Flour Mill Products	Tobacco Products	

Distribution of Factory Output, 1919
in thousands

Over $3,000,000
$1,000,000 to $2,999,000
$500,000 to $999,000
$100,000 to $499,000
Less than $99,000

Cities
o   Value of product over $1 billion
•   Value of product over $200 million

INDUSTRIAL AMERICA, 1900–1920

related equipment brought into being new sectors of metalworking and machine-tool industries. Between 1900 and 1920 virtually every major city built electric-powered transit systems to replace horse-drawn trolleys and carriages. In New York City electricity made possible the construction of the first subways. Electric lighting gave cities a new allure. The public also fell in love with the movies, which depended on electricity for the projection of images onto a screen.

The first gasoline engine was patented in the United States in 1878, and the first "horseless carriages" began appearing on European and American roads in the 1890s. But few thought of them as serious rivals to trains and horses; rather, they were seen as playthings for the wealthy. Then, in 1908, Henry Ford unveiled his Model T: an unadorned, even homely car, but reliable enough to travel hundreds of miles without servicing and cheap enough to be affordable to most working Americans. In the ensuing 20 years, Americans bought Model T vehicles by the millions. The stimulus this insatiable demand gave to the economy can scarcely be exaggerated. Millions of cars required millions of pounds of steel alloys, glass, rubber, petroleum, and other material. Millions of jobs in coal and iron-ore mining, oil refining and rubber manufacturing, steelmaking and machine tooling, road construction and service stations came to depend on automobile manufacturing.

CORPORATE GROWTH

Successful inventions such as the automobile required more than the mechanical ingenuity and social vision of inventors like Henry Ford. Corporations with sophisticated organizational

CHANGE IN DISTRIBUTION OF THE AMERICAN WORKFORCE, 1870–1920

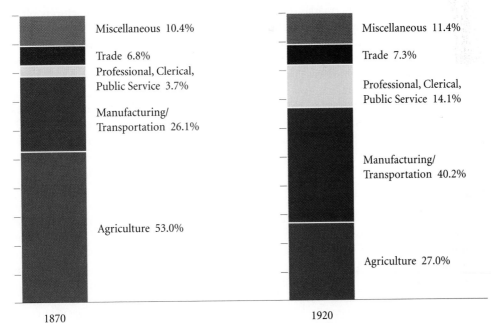

1870: Miscellaneous 10.4%; Trade 6.8%; Professional, Clerical, Public Service 3.7%; Manufacturing/Transportation 26.1%; Agriculture 53.0%

1920: Miscellaneous 11.4%; Trade 7.3%; Professional, Clerical, Public Service 14.1%; Manufacturing/Transportation 40.2%; Agriculture 27.0%

Source: Data from Alba Edwards, *Comparative Occupational Statistics for the United States 1870–1940*, U.S. Bureau of the Census, *Sixteenth Census of the United States, 1940, Population* (Washington, D.C., 1943).

and technical know-how were also required to mass-produce and mass-distribute the newly invented products. Corporations had played an important role in the nation's economic life since the 1840s, but in the late 19th and early 20th centuries they underwent significant changes.

The most obvious change was in their size. Delaware's DuPont Corporation, a munitions and chemical manufacturer, employed 1,500 workers in 1902 and 31,000 workers in 1920. Founded with a few hundred employees in 1903, the Ford Motor Company employed 33,000 at its Detroit Highland Park plant by 1916 and 42,000 by 1924.

This growth in scale was in part a response to the enormous size of the domestic market. By 1900 railroads provided the country with an efficient transportation system that allowed corporations to ship goods virtually anywhere in the United States. A national network of telegraph lines made it possible for buyers and sellers separated by thousands of miles to stay in constant communication. And the population, which was expanding rapidly, demonstrated an ever-growing appetite for goods and services.

Mass Production and Distribution

The size of this domestic market encouraged manufacturers to perfect mass-production techniques that increased the speed of production and lowered unit costs. Mass production required the coordination of machines to permit high-speed, uninterrupted production at every stage of the manufacturing process. Mass-production techniques had become widespread in basic steel manufacturing and sugar refining by the 1890s, and spread to the machine-tool industry and automobile manufacturing in the first two decades of the 20th century.

For such production techniques to be profitable, large quantities of output had to be sold. And although the domestic market offered a vast potential for sales, manufacturers often found that distribution systems were inadequate. This was the case with the North Carolina manufacturer of smoking tobacco, James Buchanan Duke. In 1885, Duke invested in several Bonsack cigarette machines, each of which manufactured 120,000 cigarettes a day. Then he advertised his product aggressively throughout the country. He also established regional sales offices so that his sales representatives could keep in touch with local jobbers and retailers. As the sales of cigarettes skyrocketed, more and more corporations sought to emulate Duke's techniques. Over the course of the next 20 years, the characteristics of American "big business" came to be defined by the corporations that were able to integrate mass production and mass distribution.

Corporate Consolidation

Corporate expansion also reflected a desire to avoid market instability. The rapid industrial growth of the late 19th century had proved deeply unsettling to industrialists. As promising economic opportunities arose, more and more industrialists sought to take advantage of them. But overexpansion and increasingly furious competition often turned rosy prospects into less-than-rosy results. Buoyant booms were quickly followed by bankrupting busts. Soon, corporations began looking for ways to insulate themselves from the harrowing course of the business cycle.

In tackling this problem, the railroads led the way. Rather than engaging in ruinous rate wars, railroads began cooperating. They shared information on costs and profits, established standardized rates, and allocated discrete portions of the freight business among themselves. These cooperative arrangements were variously called "pools," "cartels," or "trusts." The 1890 Sherman Antitrust Act declared such cartel-like practices illegal, but the law's enforcement proved to be short-lived (see Chapter 19). Still, the railroads' efforts rarely succeeded for long because they depended heavily on voluntary compliance.

Efforts by corporations to restrain competition and inject order into the economic environment continued unabated, however. Mergers now emerged as the favored instrument of control. By the 1890s powerful and sophisticated investment bankers, such as J. P. Morgan, possessed both the capital and the financial skills to engineer the complicated stock transfers and ownership renegotiations that mergers required. James Duke again led the way in 1890 when he and four competitors merged to form the American Tobacco Company.

The merger movement intensified as the depression of the 1890s lifted. In the years from 1898 to 1904, many of the corporations that would dominate American business throughout most of the 20th century acquired their modern form. The largest merger occurred in steel in 1901, when Andrew Carnegie and J. P. Morgan together fashioned the U.S. Steel Corporation from 200 separate iron and steel companies. U.S. Steel controlled 60 percent of the country's steelmaking capacity. Moreover, its ownership of 78 iron-ore boats and 1,000 miles of railroad gave it substantial control over the procurement of raw materials and the distribution of finished steel products.

Revolution in Management

The dramatic growth in the number and size of corporations revolutionized corporate management. The ranks of managers mushroomed, as elaborate corporate hierarchies defined both the status and the duties of individual managers. Increasingly, senior managers took over from owners the responsibility for long-term planning. Day-to-day operations were then placed in the hands of numerous middle managers who oversaw particular departments (purchasing, research, production, labor) in corporate headquarters, or who supervised regional sales offices, or directed particular factories. Middle managers also managed the people—accountants, clerks, foremen, engineers, salesmen—in these departments, offices, or factories. The rapid expansion within corporate managerial ranks created a new middle class, intensely loyal to their employers but at odds both with blue-collar workers and with the older middle class of shopkeepers, small businessmen, and independent craftsmen.

As management grew in importance, companies tried to make it more scientific. Firms introduced rigorous cost-accounting methods into departments (such as purchasing) charged with controlling the inflow of materials and the outflow of goods. Many corporations began requiring college or university training in science, engineering, or accounting for entry into middle management. Corporations that had built their success on a profitable invention or discovery sought to maintain their competitive edge by creating research departments and hiring professional scientists—those with Ph.D.'s from American or European universities—to come up with new technological and scientific breakthroughs.

Scientific Management on the Factory Floor

The most controversial and, in some respects, the most ambitious effort to introduce scientific practices into management occurred in production. Managers sought optimal arrangements

THE WORLD'S FIRST AUTOMOBILE ASSEMBLY LINE   Introduced by Henry Ford at his Highland Park plant in 1913, this innovation cut production time on Ford Model Ts by an astounding 90 percent, allowing Ford to reduce the price of his cars by more than half and to double the hourly wages of his workers.

of machines and deployments of workers that would achieve the highest speed in production with the fewest human or mechanical interruptions. Some of these managers, such as Frederick Winslow Taylor, methodically examined every human task and mechanical movement involved in each production process. In "time-and-motion studies," they recorded every distinct movement a worker made in performing his or her job, how long it took, and how often it was performed. They hoped thereby to identify and eliminate wasted human energy. Eliminating waste might mean reorganizing an entire floor of machinery so as to reduce "down time" between production steps; it might mean instructing workers to perform their tasks differently; or it might mean replacing uncooperative skilled workers with machines tended by unskilled, low-wage laborers. Regardless of the method chosen, the goal was the same: to make human labor emulate the smooth and apparently effortless operation of an automatic, perfectly calibrated piece of machinery.

Taylor shared his vision widely in the early 20th century, first through speeches to fellow engineers and managers, and then through his writings. By the time he published *The Principles of Scientific Management* (1911), his ideas had already captivated countless corporate managers and engineers, many of whom sought to introduce "Taylorism" into their own production systems.

But the introduction of scientific management practices rarely proceeded easily. Time-and-motion studies were costly, and Taylor's formulas for increasing efficiency and reducing waste

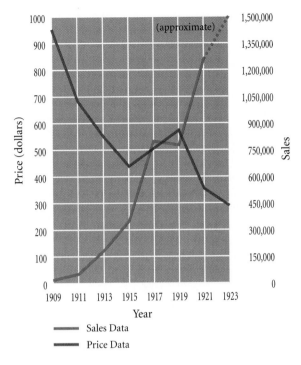

MODEL T PRICES AND SALES, 1909–1923

Source: From Alfred D. Chandler Jr., ed., *Giant Enterprise: Ford, General Motors, and the Automobile Industry* (New York: Harcourt, Brace and World, 1964), pp. 32–33.

were often far less scientific than he claimed. Taylor also overestimated the willingness of workers to play the mechanical role he assigned them. And the skilled workers and general foremen, whom Taylor sought to eliminate, used every available means of resistance. For these reasons, those managers and engineers who persisted in their efforts to apply scientific management invariably modified Taylor's principles.

Henry Ford led the way. His engineers initially adopted Taylorism wholeheartedly, with apparent success. By 1910 they had broken down automobile manufacturing into a series of simple, sequential tasks. Each worker performed only one task—adding a carburetor to an engine, inserting a windshield, mounting tires onto wheels. Then, in 1913 Ford's engineers introduced the first moving assembly line, a continuously moving conveyor belt that carried cars-in-production through each workstation. This innovation eliminated precious time previously wasted in transporting car parts (or partially built cars) by crane or truck from one work area to another. It also sharply limited the time available to workers to perform their assigned tasks.

The continuous assembly line allowed the potential of the factory's many other organizational and mechanical innovations to be fully realized. By 1913 the Ford Motor Company's new Highland Park plant was the most tightly integrated and continuously moving production system in manufacturing. The pace of production exceeded all expectations. A thousand Model Ts began rolling off the assembly line each day. This striking increase in the rate of production enabled Ford to slash the price of a Model T from $950 in 1909 to only $295 in 1923. The assembly line quickly became the most admired—and most feared—symbol of American mass production.

Problems immediately beset the system, however. Repeating a single motion all day long induced mental stupor, and managerial efforts to speed up the line produced physical exhaustion—both of which increased the incidence of error and injury. Some workers tried to organize a union to gain a voice in production matters. But most Ford workers expressed their dissatisfaction simply by quitting. By 1913 employee turnover at Highland Park had reached the astounding rate of 370 percent a year.

A problem of that magnitude demanded a dramatic solution. Ford provided it in 1914 by raising the wage he paid his assembly-line workers to $5 a day, double the average manufacturing wage then prevalent in American industry. The result: Workers, especially young and single men, flocked to Detroit.

Taylor himself had believed that improved efficiency would lead to dramatic wage gains. With his decision to raise wages, Ford was being true to Taylor's principles. But Ford went even further in his innovations. He set up a sociology department, forerunner of the personnel department, to collect job, family, and other information about his employees. He offered his employees housing subsidies, medical care, and other benefits. In short, Ford recognized that workers were more complex than Taylor had allowed, and that high wages alone would not transform them into the perfectly functioning parts of the mass-production system that Taylor had envisioned.

Ford's success impelled others to move in his direction. But it would take time for modern management to come of age. Not until the 1920s did a substantial number of corporations establish personnel departments, institute welfare and recreational programs for employees, and hire psychologists to improve human relations in the workplace.

"ROBBER BARONS" NO MORE

Innovations in corporate management were part of a broader effort among elite industrialists to shed their "robber baron" image. The swashbuckling entrepreneurs of the 19th century—men like Cornelius Vanderbilt, Jay Gould, and Leland Stanford—had wielded their economic power brashly and ruthlessly, while lavishing money on European-style palaces, private yachts, personal art collections, and extravagant entertainments. But the depression of the 1890s shook the confidence of the members of this elite. The anarchist Alexander Berkman's 1892 attempt to assassinate Henry Clay Frick, Andrew Carnegie's right-hand man, by marching into his office and shooting him at point-blank range (Frick survived), terrified industrialists. Although such physical assaults were rare, anger over ill-gotten and ill-spent wealth was widespread.

Seeking a more favorable image, some industrialists began to restrain their displays of wealth and use their private fortunes to advance the public welfare. As early as 1889 Andrew Carnegie had advocated a "gospel of wealth." The wealthy, he believed, should consider all income in excess of their needs as a "trust fund" for their communities. By the time he died in 1919, he had given away or entrusted to several Carnegie foundations 90 percent of his fortune. Among the projects he funded were New York's Carnegie Hall, Pittsburgh's Carnegie Institute (now Carnegie-Mellon University), and 2,500 public libraries throughout the country.

Other industrialists, including John D. Rockefeller, soon followed Carnegie's lead. Rockefeller's ruthless business methods in assembling the Standard Oil Company and in crushing his competition made him one of the most reviled of the robber barons. In the wake of the federal

FOUNDATION	DATE OF ORIGIN	ORIGINAL ENDOWMENT
Buhl Foundation	1927	$10,951,157
Carnegie Corporation of New York	1911	125,000,000
Carnegie Endowment for International Peace	1910	10,000,000
Carnegie Foundation for the Advancement of Teaching	1905	10,000,000
Carnegie Institution of Washington	1902	10,000,000
Duke Endowment	1924	40,000,000
John Simon Guggenheim Memorial Foundation	1925	3,000,000
W. K. Kellogg Foundation	1930	21,600,000
Rockefeller Foundation	1913	100,000,000
Rosenwald Fund	1917	20,000,000
Russell Sage Foundation	1907	10,000,000

Source: Joseph C. Kiger, *Operating Principles of the Larger Foundations* (New York: Russell Sage Foundation, 1957), p. 122.

government's prosecution of Standard Oil for monopolistic practices in 1906, Rockefeller transformed himself into a public-spirited philanthropist. Through the Rockefeller Foundation, which was officially incorporated in 1913, he had dispersed an estimated $500 million by 1919. His most significant gifts included money to establish the University of Chicago and the Rockefeller Institute for Medical Research (later renamed Rockefeller University).

OBSESSION WITH PHYSICAL AND RACIAL FITNESS

The fractious events of the 1890s also induced many wealthy Americans to engage in what Theodore Roosevelt dubbed "the strenuous life." In an 1899 essay with that title, Roosevelt exhorted Americans to live vigorously, to test their physical strength and endurance in competitive athletics, and to experience nature through hiking, hunting, and mountain climbing. He articulated a way of life that influenced countless Americans from a variety of classes and cultures.

The 1890s were indeed a time of heightened enthusiasm for competitive sports, physical fitness, and outdoor recreation. Millions of Americans began riding bicycles and eating healthier foods. A passion for athletic competition gripped American universities. The power and violence of football helped make it the sport of choice at the nation's elite campuses. In athletic competition, as in nature, one could discover and recapture one's manhood, one's virility. The words "sissy" and "pussyfoot" entered common usage in the 1890s as insults hurled at men whose masculinity was found wanting.

Ironically, this quest for masculinity had a liberating effect on women. In the vigorous new climate of the 1890s, young women began to engage in sports and other activities long considered too manly for "the fragile sex." They put away their corsets and long dresses and began wearing simple skirts, shirtwaists, and other clothing that gave them more comfort and freedom of movement.

In the country at large the new enthusiasm for athletics and the outdoor life reflected a widespread dissatisfaction with the growing regimentation of industrial society. But among wealthy Americans, the quest for physical superiority reflected a deeper and more ambiguous anxiety: These Americans worried about their *racial* fitness. Most of them were native-born Americans whose families had lived in the United States for several generations and whose ancestors had come from the British Isles, the Netherlands, or some other region of northwestern Europe. They liked to attribute their success and good fortune to their "racial superiority." They saw themselves as "natural" leaders, members of a noble Anglo-Saxon race endowed with uncommon intelligence, imagination, and discipline. But events of the 1890s had challenged the legitimacy of the elite's wealth and authority, and the ensuing depression mocked their ability to exert economic leadership. The immigrant masses laboring in factories, despite their poverty and alleged racial inferiority, seemed to possess a vitality that the "superior" Anglo-Saxons lacked.

Some rich Americans reacted to the immigrants' vigor and industry by calling for a halt to further immigration. But that would not do for the ebullient Roosevelt, who argued instead for a return to fitness, superiority, and numerical predominance of the Anglo-Saxon race. He called on American men to live the strenuous life and on women to devote themselves to reproduction. The only way to avoid "race suicide," he declared, was for every Anglo-Saxon mother to have at least four children.

Such racialist thought was not limited to wealthy elites. Many other Americans, from a variety of classes and regions, also thought that all people demonstrated the characteristics of their race. Racial stereotypes were used to describe not only blacks, Asians, and Hispanics, but Italians ("violent"), Jews ("nervous"), and Slavs and Poles ("slow"). Such aspersions flowed as easily from the pens of compassionate reformers, such as Jacob Riis, who wanted to help the immigrants, as from the pens of bitter reactionaries, such as Madison Grant, who argued in *The Passing of the Great Race* (1916) that America should rid itself of inferior races.

SOCIAL DARWINISM

Racialist thinking even received "scientific" sanction from distinguished biologists and anthropologists, who believed that racially inherited traits explained variations in the economic, social, and cultural lives of ethnic and racial groups. For a large number of the nation's intellectuals, human society developed according to the "survival of the fittest" principle articulated by the English naturalist Charles Darwin to describe plant and animal evolution. Human history could be understood in terms of an ongoing struggle among races, with the strongest and the fittest invariably triumphing. The wealth and power of the Anglo-Saxon race was ample testimony, in this view, to its superior fitness.

This view, which would become known as "Social Darwinism," was rooted in two developments of the late 19th century, one intellectual and one socioeconomic. Intellectually, it reflected a widely shared belief that human society operated according to principles every bit as scientific as those governing the natural world. The social sciences—economics, political science, anthropology, sociology, psychology—took shape in the late 19th century, each trying to discover the scientific laws governing individual and group behavior. Awed by the accomplishments of natural scientists, social scientists were prone to exaggerate the degree to which social life mimicked natural life; hence the appeal of Social Darwinism.

Social Darwinism was also rooted in the unprecedented interpenetration of the world's economies and peoples. Cheap and rapid ocean travel had bound together continents as never before. International trade, immigration, and imperial conquest made Americans more conscious of the variety of peoples inhabiting the earth. Although awareness of diversity sometimes encourages tolerance and cooperation, in the economically depressed years of the late 19th century, it encouraged intolerance and suspicion, fertile soil for the cultivation of Social Darwinism.

IMMIGRATION

Perhaps the most dramatic evidence of the nation's growing involvement in the international economy was the high rate of immigration. The United States had always been a nation of immigrants, but never had so many come in so short a time. Between 1880 and 1920, some 23 million immigrants came to a country that numbered only 76 million in 1900. In many cities of the Northeast and Midwest, immigrants and their children comprised a majority of the population. Everywhere in the country, except in the South, the working class was overwhelmingly ethnic.

European immigration accounted for approximately three-fourths of the total. Some states received significant numbers of non-European immigrants—Chinese, Japanese, and Filipinos in California; Mexicans in California and the Southwest; and French Canadians in New England—whose presence profoundly affected regional economies, politics, and culture. But their numbers, relative to the number of European immigrants, were small.

Most of the European immigrants who arrived between 1880 and 1914 came from eastern and southern Europe. Among them were 3 to 4 million Italians, 2 million Russian and Polish Jews, 2 million Hungarians, an estimated 4 million Slavs (including Poles, Bohemians, Slovaks, Russians, Ukrainians, Bulgarians, Serbians, Croatians, Slovenians, Montenegrins, and Macedonians), and 1 million from Lithuania, Greece, and Portugal. Hundreds of thousands came as well from Turkey, Armenia, Lebanon, Syria, and other Near Eastern lands abutting the European continent.

These post-1880 arrivals were called "new immigrants" to underscore the cultural gap separating them from the "old immigrants," who had come from northwestern Europe—Great Britain, Scandinavia, and Germany. "Old immigrants" were regarded as racially fit, culturally sophisticated, and politically mature. The "new immigrants," by contrast, were often regarded as racially inferior, culturally impoverished, and incapable of assimilating American values and traditions. This negative view of the "new immigrants" reflected in part a fear of their alien languages, religions, and economic backgrounds. Few spoke English. Most adhered to Catholicism, Greek Orthodoxy, or Judaism rather than Protestantism. And most, with the exception of the Jews, were peasants, unaccustomed to urban industrial life.

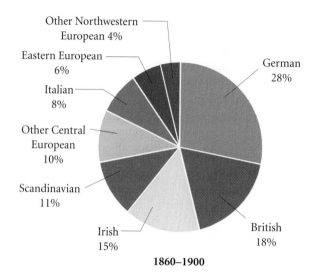

Other Northwestern European 4%
Eastern European 6%
Italian 8%
Other Central European 10%
Scandinavian 11%
Irish 15%
German 28%
British 18%

1860–1900

SOURCES OF IMMIGRATION

Source: Data from *Historical Statistics of the United States, Colonial Times to 1970* (White Plains, N.Y.: Kraus International, 1989), pp. 105–109.

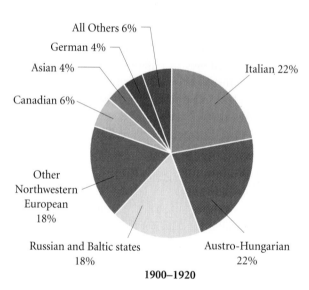

All Others 6%
German 4%
Asian 4%
Canadian 6%
Other Northwestern European 18%
Russian and Baltic states 18%
Italian 22%
Austro-Hungarian 22%

1900–1920

CAUSES OF IMMIGRATION

In fact, the "old" and "new" European immigrants were more similar than different. Both came to America for the same reasons: either to flee religious or political persecution or to escape economic hardship. It is true that the United States attracted a small but steady stream of political refugees throughout the 19th century. Many of these people possessed unusual talents as skilled workers, labor organizers, political agitators, and newspaper editors and thus exercised considerable influence in their ethnic communities. However, only the anti-Semitic policies of Russia in the late 19th and early 20th centuries triggered a mass emigration (in this case Jewish) of political refugees.

Most mass immigration was propelled instead by economic hardship. Europe's rural population was growing at a faster rate than the land could support. European factories absorbed some, but not all, of the rural surplus. And industrialization and urbanization were affecting the European countryside in ways that disrupted rural ways of life. As railroads penetrated the countryside, village artisans found themselves unable to compete with the cheap manufactured goods that arrived from city factories. These handicraftsmen were among the first to emigrate. Meanwhile, rising demand for food in the cities accelerated the growth of commercial agriculture in the hinterland. Some peasant families lost their land. Others turned to producing crops for the market, only to discover that they could not compete with larger, more efficient producers. In addition, by the last third of the 19th century, peasants faced competition from North American farmers. Prices for agricultural commodities plummeted everywhere. The economic squeeze that spread distress among American farmers in the 1880s and 1890s caused even more hardship among Europe's peasantry. These were the circumstances that triggered mass emigration.

PATTERNS OF IMMIGRATION

An individual's or family's decision to emigrate often depended on having a contact—a family member, relative, or fellow villager—already established in an American city. These were people who provided immigrants with a destination, with inspiration (they were examples of success in America), with advice about jobs, and with financial aid. Sometimes whole villages in southern Italy or western Russia—or at least all the young men—seemed to disappear, only to reappear in a certain section of Chicago, Pittsburgh, or New York.

A majority of immigrants viewed their trip to the United States as a temporary sojourn. They came not in search of permanent settlement but in search of the high wages that would enable them to improve their economic standing in their homeland. For them, America was a land of economic opportunity, not a land to call home. This attitude explains why men vastly outnumbered women and children in the migration stream. Some had left wives and children behind; more were single. Most wanted merely to make enough money to buy a farm in their native land. And, true to their dream, many did return home.

The rate of return was negligible among certain groups, however. Jews had little desire to return to the religious persecution they had fled. Most came as families, intending to make America their permanent home. Only 5 percent of them returned home. The rate of return was also low among the Irish, who saw few opportunities in their long-suffering (though much-loved) Emerald Isle. But in the early 20th century, such groups were exceptional. Most immigrants looked forward to returning to Europe.

Immigration tended to move in rhythm with the U.S. business cycle. It rose in boom years and fell off during depressions. It remained at a high level during the first 14 years of the new century when the U.S. economy was experiencing a period of sustained growth, broken only by the brief Panic of 1907–1908.

IMMIGRANT LABOR

In the first decade of the 20th century, immigrant men and their male children built the nation's railroads and tunnels; mined its coal, iron ore, and other minerals; stoked its hot and sometimes deadly steel furnaces; and slaughtered and packed its meat in Chicago's putrid packinghouses. In 1909 first- and second-generation immigrants comprised more than 96 percent of the labor force that built and maintained the nation's railroads. Of the 750,000 Slovaks who arrived in America before 1913, at least 600,000 headed for the coal mines and steel mills of western Pennsylvania. The steel mills of Pittsburgh, Buffalo, Cleveland, and Chicago attracted disproportionately large numbers of Poles and other Slavs as well.

Immigrants also performed "lighter" but no less arduous work. Jews and Italians predominated in garment manufacturing shops. In 1900 French Canadian immigrants and their children held one of every two jobs in New England's cotton textile industry. By 1920 the prosperity of California's rapidly growing agricultural industry depended primarily on Mexican and Filipino labor. In these industries, immigrant women and children, who worked for lower wages than men, formed a large part of the labor force.

Immigrants were as essential as fossil fuels to the smooth operation of the American economic machine. Sometimes, however, the "machine" consumed workers as well as coal and oil. Those who worked in heavy industry, mining, or railroading were especially vulnerable to accident and injury. Between the years 1906 and 1911, almost one-quarter of the recent immigrants employed at the U.S. Steel Corporation's South Works (Pittsburgh) were injured or killed on the job. Lax attention to safety rendered even light industry hazardous and sometimes fatal. In 1911 a fire broke out on an upper floor of the Triangle Shirtwaist Company, a New York City garment factory. The building had no fire escapes. The owners of the factory, moreover, had locked the entrances to each floor as a way of keeping their employees at work. A total of 146 workers perished in the fire or from desperate nine-story leaps to the pavement below.

Chronic fatigue and inadequate nourishment increased the risk of accident and injury. Workweeks averaged 60 hours—10 hours every day except Sunday. Workers who were granted

TRIANGLE SHIRTWAIST COMPANY FIRE   In 1911, a fire at the Triangle Shirtwaist Company in New York City claimed the lives of 146 workers, most of them young Jewish and Italian women. Many died because they could not escape the flames. There were no fire escapes and their employer had locked the entrances to each floor. The tragedy spurred the growth of unions and the movement for factory reform in New York.

Saturday afternoons off considered themselves fortunate. Steelworkers were not so lucky. They labored from 72 to 89 hours a week, and were required to work one 24-hour shift every two weeks.

Most workers had to labor long hours simply to eke out a meager living. In 1900 the annual earnings of American manufacturing workers averaged only $400 to $500 a year. Skilled workers who held higher-paying jobs earned far more than those doing comparable work in Europe. In theory, such well-paid work offered immigrants their greatest opportunities. But most of these jobs were held by Yankees and by the Germans, Irish, Welsh, and other Europeans who had come as part of the "old immigration." Through their unions, workers of northern European extraction also controlled access to new jobs that opened up and usually managed to fill them with a son, relative, or fellow countryman. Consequently, relatively few of the "new immigrants" rose into the prosperous ranks of skilled labor.

From the 1870s to 1910 real wages paid to factory workers and common laborers did rise, but not steadily. Wages fell sharply during depressions. And the hope for sharp increases during periods of recovery collapsed under the weight of renewed mass immigration, which brought hundreds of thousands of new job seekers into the labor market.

Most working families required two or three wage earners to survive. If a mother could not go out to work because there were small children at home, she might rent rooms to some of the many single men who had recently immigrated. But economic security was hard to attain. In his book, *Poverty*, published in 1904, the social investigator Robert Hunter conservatively estimated that 20 percent of the industrial population of the North lived in poverty.

Living Conditions

Strained economic circumstances confined many working-class families to cramped and dilapidated living quarters. Many of them lived in two- or three-room apartments, with several sleeping in each room. The lack of windows in city tenements allowed little light or air into these apartments, and few had their own toilets or running water. Crowding was endemic. Overcrowding and poor sanitation resulted in high rates of deadly infectious diseases, especially diphtheria, typhoid fever, and pneumonia.

By 1900 this crisis in urban living had begun to yield to the insistence of urban reformers that cities adopt housing codes and improve sanitation. Between 1880 and 1900, housing inspectors condemned the worst of the tenements and ordered landlords to make certain minimal improvements. City governments built reservoirs, pipes, and sewers to carry clean water to the tenements and to carry away human waste. Newly paved roads lessened the dirt, mud, and stagnant pools of water and thus further curtailed the spread of disease. As a result, urban mortality rates fell in the 1880s and 1890s. Nevertheless, improvements came far more slowly to the urban poor than they did to the middle and upper classes.

Building Ethnic Communities

The immigrants may have been poor, but they were not helpless. Migration itself had required a good deal of resourcefulness, self-help, and mutual aid—assets that survived in the new surroundings of American cities.

A NETWORK OF INSTITUTIONS

Each ethnic group quickly established a network of institutions that gave it a sense of community and multiplied the sources of communal assistance. Some people simply reproduced those institutions that had been important to them in the "Old Country." The devout established churches and synagogues. Lithuanian, Jewish, and Italian radicals reestablished Old World socialist and anarchist organizations. Irish nationalists set up clandestine chapters of the Clan Na Gael to keep alive the struggle to free Ireland from the English. Germans felt at home in their traditional *Turnevereins* (athletic clubs) and musical societies.

Immigrants developed new institutions as well. In the larger cities, foreign-language newspapers disseminated news, advice, and culture. Each ethnic group created fraternal societies to bring together immigrants who had known each other in the Old Country, or who shared the same craft, or who had come from the same town or region. Most of these societies provided members with a death benefit (ranging from a few hundred to a thousand dollars) that guaranteed the deceased a decent burial and the family a bit of cash. Some fraternal societies made small loans as well. Among those ethnic groups that prized home ownership, especially the Slavic groups, the fraternal societies also provided mortgage money. And all of them served as centers of sociability—places to have a drink, play cards, or simply relax with fellow countrymen.

THE EMERGENCE OF AN ETHNIC MIDDLE CLASS

Within each ethnic group, a sizable minority directed their talents and ambitions to economic gain. Some of these entrepreneurs first addressed their communities' needs for basic goods and services. Immigrants preferred to buy from fellow countrymen with whom they shared a language, a history, and presumably a bond of trust. Enterprising individuals responded by opening dry goods stores, food shops, butcher shops, and saloons in their ethnic neighborhoods. Those who could not afford to rent a store hawked their fruit, clothing, or dry goods from portable stands, wagons, or sacks carried on their back. The work was endless, the competition tough. Although many of these small businesses failed, enough survived to give some immigrants and their children a toehold in the middle class.

Other immigrants turned to industry, particularly the garment industry, truck farming, and construction. A clothing manufacturer needed only a few sewing machines to become competitive. Many Jewish immigrants, having been tailors in Russia and Poland, opened such facilities. Competition among these small manufacturers was fierce, and work environments were condemned by critics as "sweatshops": inadequate lighting, heat, and ventilation; 12-hour workdays and 70-hour workweeks during peak seasons, with every hour spent bent over a sewing machine; poor pay and no employment security, especially for the women and children who made up a large part of this labor force. Even at this level of exploitation, many small manufacturers failed. But over time, a good many of them managed to firm up their position as manufacturers and to evolve into stable, responsible employers. Their success contributed to the emergence of a Jewish middle class.

The story was much the same in urban construction, where Italians who had established themselves as labor contractors, or *padroni*, went into business for themselves to take advantage of the rapid expansion of American cities. Though few became general contractors on major downtown projects, many of them did well building family residences or serving as subcontractors on larger buildings.

Japanese Farmers on a Texas Seed Rice Farm, circa 1910 Unlike most immigrants of the early 20th century, Japanese immigrants found a niche in agriculture and used it as a route to middle-class status and income.

In southern California, Japanese immigrants chose agriculture as their route to the middle class. Working as agricultural laborers in the 1890s, they began to acquire their own land in the early years of the 20th century. Altogether, they owned only 1 percent of California's total farm acreage, but their specialization in fresh vegetables and fruits (particularly strawberries), combined with their labor-intensive agricultural methods (with family members supplying the labor), was yielding $67 million in annual revenues by 1919. That was one-tenth of the total revenue generated by California agriculture that year. Japanese farmers sold their produce to Japanese fruit and vegetable wholesalers in Los Angeles, who had chosen a mercantile route to middle-class status.

Each ethnic group created its own history of economic success and social mobility. From the emerging middle classes came many leaders who would provide their ethnic groups with identity, legitimacy, and power and would lead the way toward Americanization and assimilation. Their children tended to do better in school than the children of working-class ethnics, and academic success served as a ticket to upward social mobility in a society that depended more and more on university-trained engineers, managers, lawyers, doctors, and other professionals.

Political Machines and Organized Crime

The underside of this success story could be seen in the rise of government corruption and organized crime. Some ethnic entrepreneurs looked beyond their usual support networks and accepted the help of those who promised to ensure their economic survival. Sometimes the help came from honest unions and upright government officials, but sometimes it did not. Unions were generally weak, and some government officials were susceptible to bribery. Economic necessity became a breeding ground for government corruption and greed. A contractor eager to win a city contract would find it necessary to "pay off" government officials who could throw the contract his way. By 1900 such payments, referred to as graft, had become essential to the day-to-day operation of government in most large cities. The graft, in turn, made local officeholding a rich source of economic gain. Politicians began building political organizations called machines to guarantee their success in municipal elections. The machine "bosses" won the loyalty of urban voters—especially immigrants—by providing poor neighborhoods with paved roads and sewer systems. They helped newly arrived immigrants to get jobs (often on city payrolls) and occasionally provided food, fuel, or clothing to families in dire need.

The bosses who ran the political machines—including "King Richard" Croker in New York, James Michael Curley in Boston, Tom Pendergast in Kansas City, Martin Behrman in New Orleans, and Abe Ruef in San Francisco—served their own needs first. They saw to it that construction contracts went to those who offered the most graft, not to those who were likely to do the best job. They protected gamblers, pimps, and other purveyors of urban vice who contributed large amounts to their machine coffers. And they engaged in widespread election fraud: rounding up truckloads of newly arrived immigrants and paying them to vote a certain way; having their supporters vote two or three times; and stuffing ballot boxes with the votes of phantom citizens who had died, moved away, or never been born.

Big city machines, then, were both a positive and negative force in urban life. Reformers despised them for disregarding election laws and encouraging vice. Immigrants valued them for providing social welfare services and for creating opportunities for upward mobility.

The history of President John F. Kennedy's family offers a compelling example of the economic and political opportunities opened up by machine politics. Both of Kennedy's grandfathers, John Francis ("Honey Fitz") Fitzgerald and Patrick Joseph Kennedy, were the children of penniless Irish immigrants who arrived in Boston in the 1840s. Fitzgerald was the more talented of the two, excelling at academics and winning a coveted place in Harvard's Medical School. But Fitzgerald left Harvard that same year, choosing a career in politics instead. Between 1891 and 1905 he served as a Boston city councillor, Massachusetts state congressman and senator, U.S. congressman, and mayor of Boston. For much of this period, he derived considerable income and power from his position as the North End ward boss.

Patrick Kennedy, a tavern owner and liquor merchant in East Boston, became an equally important figure behind the scenes in Boston city politics. In addition to running the Democratic Party's affairs in Ward Two, he served on the Strategy Board, a secret council of Boston's machine politicians that met regularly to devise policies, settle disputes, and divide up the week's graft. Both Fitzgerald and Kennedy derived a substantial income from their political work and used it to lift their families into middle-class prosperity. Kennedy's son (and the future president's father), Joseph P. Kennedy, would go on to make a fortune as a Wall Street speculator and liquor distributor. But his rapid economic and social ascent had been made possible by his father's and father-in-law's earlier success in Boston machine politics.

Underworld figures, too, influenced urban life. In the early years of the 20th century, gangsterism was a scourge of Italian neighborhoods, where Sicilian immigrants had established outposts of the notorious Mafia, and in Irish, Jewish, Chinese, and other ethnic communities as well. Favorite targets of these gangsters were small-scale manufacturers and contractors, who were threatened with violence and economic ruin if they did not pay a gang for "protection." Gangsters enforced their demands with physical force, beating up or killing those who failed to abide by the "rules." By the 1920s petty extortion had escalated in urban areas, and underworld crime had become big business. Al Capone, the ruthless Chicago mobster who made a fortune from gambling, prostitution, and bootleg liquor during Prohibition, once claimed: "Prohibition is a business. All I do is to supply a public demand. I do it in the best and least harmful way I can." Mobsters like Capone were charismatic figures, both in their ethnic communities and in the nation at large. Few immigrants, however, followed their criminal path to economic success.

African American Labor and Community

Unlike immigrants, African Americans remained a predominately rural and southern people in the early 20th century. Most blacks were sharecroppers and tenant farmers. The markets for cotton and other southern crops had stabilized in the early 20th century, but black farmers remained vulnerable to exploitation. Landowners often forced sharecroppers to accept artificially low prices for their crops. At the same time, they charged high prices for seed, tools, and groceries at the local stores that they controlled. Few rural areas generated enough business to support more than one store, or to create a competitive climate that might force prices down. Those sharecroppers who traveled elsewhere to sell their crops or purchase their necessities risked retaliation. Thus, most remained beholden to their landowners, mired in poverty and debt.

Some African Americans sought a better life by migrating to industrial areas of the South and the North. In the South, they worked in iron and coal mines, in furniture and cigarette manufacture, as railroad track layers and longshoremen, and as laborers in the steel mills of Birmingham, Alabama. By the early 20th century, their presence was growing in the urban North as well, where they worked as janitors, elevator operators, teamsters, longshoremen, and servants of various kinds. Altogether, about 200,000 blacks left the South for the North and West between 1890 and 1910.

In southern industries, blacks were subjected to hardships and indignities that even the newest immigrants were not expected to endure. Railroad contractors in the South, for example, treated their black track layers like prisoners. Armed guards marched them to work in the morning and back at night. Track layers were paid only once a month and forced to purchase food at the company commissary, where the high prices claimed most of what they earned. Other employers of black laborers in the South usually did not discipline their workers so severely, but they did isolate them in the dirtiest and most grueling jobs. The "Jim Crow" laws passed by every southern state legislature in the 1890s legalized this rigid separation of the black and white races (see Chapter 18).

Although northern states did not pass Jim Crow laws, the nation's worsening racial climate adversely affected southern blacks who had come north. Industrialists generally refused to hire black migrants for manufacturing jobs, preferring the labor of European immigrants. Only when those immigrants went on strike did employers turn to African Americans.

African Americans who had long resided in northern urban areas also experienced intensifying discrimination in the late 19th and early 20th centuries. In 1870 about a third of the black men in many northern cities had been skilled tradesmen: blacksmiths, painters, shoemakers, and carpenters. But by 1910 only 10 percent of black men made a living in this way. In many cities, the number of barber shops and food catering businesses owned by blacks also went into sharp decline, as did black representation in the ranks of restaurant and hotel waiters. These barbers, food caterers, and waiters had formed a black middle class whose livelihood depended on the patronage of white clients. By the early 20th century, this middle class had been dissipated, the victim of growing racism. Whites were no longer willing to engage the services of blacks, preferring to have their hair cut, beards shaved, food prepared and served by European immigrants. The residential segregation of northern blacks also rose in these years.

Thus, blacks in the North at the turn of the 20th century had to cope with a marked deterioration in their working and living conditions. But they did not lack for resourcefulness. Urban blacks laced their communities with the same array of institutions—churches, fraternal societies, political organizations—that solidified ethnic neighborhoods. A new black middle class arose, comprised of ministers, professionals, and businesspeople who serviced the needs of their racial group. Black-owned realties, funeral homes, doctors' offices, newspapers, groceries, restaurants, and bars opened for business on the commercial thoroughfares of African American neighborhoods. Nevertheless, community-building remained a tougher task among African Americans than among immigrants. Black communities were often smaller and poorer than their white ethnic counterparts; economic opportunities were fewer, and the chance of gaining power or wealth through municipal politics almost nonexistent. Yet, some black entrepreneurs succeeded despite these odds. Madame C. J. Walker, for example, built a lucrative business from the hair and skin lotions she devised and sold to black customers throughout the country. In many cities, African American real estate agents achieved significant wealth and power. Still, most black businessmen could not overcome the obstacles posed by racial prejudice. Thus, the African American middle class remained smaller and more precarious than did its counterpart in ethnic communities, less able to lead the way toward affluence and assimilation.

WORKERS AND UNIONS

Middle-class success eluded most immigrants and blacks in the years prior to the First World War. Even among Jews, whose rate of social mobility was rapid, most immigrants were working class. For most workers, the path toward a better life lay in the improvement of working conditions, not in escape from the working class. Henry Ford's offering of the $5-a-day wage in 1914, double the average manufacturing wage, raised the hopes of many. But in the early decades of the century few other manufacturers were prepared to follow Ford's lead, and most factory workers remained in a fragile economic state.

SAMUEL F. GOMPERS AND THE AFL

For those workers, the only hope for economic improvement lay in organizing unions powerful enough to wrest wage concessions from reluctant employers. This was not an easy task. Federal and state governments, time and again, had shown themselves ready to use military force to break strikes. The courts, following the lead of the U.S. Supreme Court, repeatedly found unions in violation of the Sherman Antitrust Act, even though that act had been intended to control corporations, not unions. Judges in most states usually granted employer requests for injunctions—court orders that barred striking workers from picketing their place of employment (and thus from obstructing employer efforts to hire replacement workers). And prior to 1916 no federal laws protected the right of workers to organize or required employers to bargain with the unions to which their workers belonged.

This hostile legal environment retarded the growth of unions from the 1890s through the 1930s. It also made the major labor organization of those years, the American Federation of

Labor (AFL), more timid and conservative than it had been prior to the depression of the 1890s. In the aftermath of that depression, the AFL poured most of its energy into organizing craft, or skilled, workers such as carpenters, typographers, plumbers, painters, and machinists. Because of their skills, these workers commanded more respect from employers than did the unskilled. Employers negotiated contracts, or trade agreements, with craft unions that stipulated the wages workers were to be paid, the hours they were to work, and the rules under which new workers would be accepted into the trade. These agreements were accorded the same legal protection that American law bestowed on other commercial contracts.

As the AFL focused on these "bread-and-butter" issues, it withdrew from the political activism that had once occupied its attention. It no longer agitated for governmental regulation of the economy and the workplace. This "business" unionism was given its most forceful expression by the AFL's president, Samuel F. Gompers. A onetime Marxist and cigar-maker who had helped found the AFL in 1886, Gompers was reelected to the AFL presidency every year from 1896 until his death in 1924. The AFL showed considerable vitality under his leadership. Aware of the AFL's growing significance and conservatism, the National Civic Federation, a newly formed council of corporate executives, agreed to meet periodically with the organization's leaders to discuss the nation's industrial and labor policies.

Nevertheless, the AFL's success was limited. Its 2 million members represented only a small portion of the total industrial workforce. Its concentration among craft workers, moreover, distanced it from the majority of workers. Unskilled and semiskilled workers could only be organized into an industrial union that offered membership to *all* workers in a particular industry. Gompers understood the importance of such unions and allowed several of them to participate in the AFL. The most significant in the early 20th century were the United Mine Workers (UMW), the United Textile Workers, and the International Ladies Garment Workers Union (ILGWU). Within the AFL, these unions received support from socialist members, who were trying to make the organization more responsive to the needs of the unskilled and semiskilled. But members of the conservative craft unions resisted the socialists' efforts. Craftsmen's feelings of superiority over the unskilled were intensified by their ethnic background. Most were from "old immigrant" stock, and they shared the common prejudice against immigrants from southern and eastern Europe.

The prejudice demonstrated by AFL members toward black workers was even worse. In the early 20th century, nine AFL unions explicitly excluded African Americans from membership, while several others accomplished the same goal by declaring blacks ineligible for union initiation rituals. National unions that did not officially discriminate often permitted their union locals to segregate African American workers in Jim Crow locals or to bar them from membership altogether.

Nevertheless, white and black workers sometimes managed to set aside their suspicions of each other and cooperate. The UMW allowed black workers to join and to rise to positions of leadership. In New Orleans, black and white dockworkers constructed a remarkable experiment in biracial unionism that flourished from the 1890s through the early 1920s. Their unity gave them leverage in negotiations with their employers and allowed them to exercise a great deal of control over the conditions of work. But these moments of cooperation were rare.

Although blacks made up too small a percentage of the working class to build alternative labor organizations that would counteract the influence of the AFL, the "new immigrants" from eastern and southern Europe were too numerous to be ignored. Their participation in the UMW enabled that union to grow from only 14,000 in 1897 to more than 300,000 in 1914.

"Big Bill" Haywood and the IWW

When the AFL failed to help them organize, immigrants turned to other unions. The most important was the Industrial Workers of the World (IWW), led by the charismatic William "Big Bill" Haywood. The IWW rejected the principle of craft organization, hoping instead to organize all workers into "one big union." It scorned the notion that only a conservative union could survive in American society, declaring its commitment to revolution instead. The IWW refused to sign collective bargaining agreements with employers, arguing that such agreements only trapped workers in capitalist property relations. Capitalism had to be overthrown through struggles between workers and their employers at the point of production.

The IWW was too radical and reckless ever to attract a mass membership. Nevertheless, few organizations inspired as much awe and fear. The IWW organized the poorest and most isolated workers—lumbermen, miners, and trackmen in the West, textile workers and longshoremen in the East. Emboldened by IWW leaders, these workers waged strikes against employers who were not accustomed to having their authority challenged. Violence lurked beneath the surface of these strikes and occasionally erupted in bloody skirmishes between

The Radical Critique of Capitalism   This "Pyramid of the Capitalist System" humorously illustrates how radicals analyzed capitalism—as an economic system that oppressed workers, rewarded the wealthy, and worshipped money. In this pyramid, the police, political leaders, and clerics are all depicted as the servants of capital and the opponents of workers.

strikers and police, National Guardsmen, or the private security forces hired by employers. Some blamed the IWW for the violence, seeing it as a direct outgrowth of calls for a "class war." But others understood that the IWW was not solely responsible. Employers had shown themselves quite willing to resort to violence to enforce their will on employees. In 1913, for example, at Ludlow, Colorado, the Colorado Fuel and Iron Company brought in a private security force and then the local militia to break up a UMW strike. When the company evicted strikers and their families from their homes, the union set up 13 tent colonies to obstruct the entrances to the mines. The standoff came to a bloody conclusion in April 1914 when company police, firing randomly into one colony of tents, killed 66 men, women, and children.

The "Ludlow massacre" outraged and shamed the nation. The massacre revealed yet again what the IWW strikes had repeatedly demonstrated: that many American workers felt abused by their low wages and poor working conditions; that neither the government nor employers offered workers a mechanism that would allow their grievances to be openly discussed and peacefully settled; and that workers, as a result, felt compelled to protest through joining unions and waging strikes, even if it meant risking their lives.

THE JOYS OF THE CITY

Industrial workers might not have been getting their fair share of the nation's prosperity, but they were crowding the dance halls, vaudeville theaters, amusement parks, and ballparks offered by the new world of commercial entertainment. Above all, they were flocking to the movies.

Movies were well suited to poor city dwellers with little money, little free time, and little English. Initially, they cost only a nickel. The "nickelodeons" where they were shown were usually converted storefronts in working-class neighborhoods. Movies did not require much leisure time, for at first they lasted only 15 minutes on average. Those with more time on their hands could stay for a cycle of two or three films. And moviegoers needed no knowledge of English to understand what was happening on the "silent screen," a circumstance that made movies especially attractive to immigrants. By 1910, at least 20,000 nickelodeons dotted northern cities.

Every aspect of these early "moving pictures" was primitive by today's standards. But they were thrilling just the same. The figures appearing on the screen were realistic, yet "larger than life." Moviegoers could transport themselves to parts of the world they otherwise would never see, encounter people they would otherwise never meet, and watch boxing matches they could otherwise not afford to attend. The darkened theater provided a setting in which secret desires, especially sexual ones, could be explored.

No easy generalizations are possible about the content of these early films, more than half of which came from France, Germany, and Italy. Among those produced in the United States, slapstick comedies were common, as were adventure stories and romances. The Hollywood formula of happy endings had yet to be worked out. In 1914 the movies' first sex symbol, Theda Bara, debuted in a movie that showed her tempting an upstanding American ambassador into infidelity and then into ruin. She would be the first of the big screen's many "vamps," so-called because the characters they portrayed, like vampires, thrived on the blood (and death) of men.

NICKELODEONS IN MAJOR AMERICAN CITIES, 1910

CITIES	POPULATION	NICKELODEONS (ESTIMATE)	SEATING CAPACITY	POPULATION PER SEAT
New York	4,338,322	450	150,000	29
Chicago	2,000,000	310	93,000	22
Philadelphia	1,491,082	160	57,000	26
St. Louis	824,000	142	50,410	16
Cleveland	600,000	75	22,500	27
Baltimore	600,000	83	24,900	24
San Francisco	400,000	68	32,400	12
Cincinnati	350,000	75	22,500	16
New Orleans	325,000	28	5,600	58

Source: Garth Jowett, *Film: The Democratic Art* (Boston: Little, Brown, 1976), p. 46.

THE NEW SEXUALITY AND THE NEW WOMAN

The introduction of movies was closely bound up with a sexual revolution in American life. For most of the 19th century, the idea of "separate spheres" had dominated relations between the sexes. The male sphere was one of work, politics, and sexual passion. The female sphere, by contrast, was one of domesticity, moral education, and sexual reproduction. Men and women were not supposed to intrude into each other's spheres. It was "unnatural" for women to work, or to enter the corrupting world of politics, or to engage in pleasurable sex. It was equally "unnatural" for men to devote themselves to child-rearing, or to "idle" themselves with domestic chores, or to live a life bereft of sexual passion. Not only did this doctrine of separate spheres discriminate against women, it also meant that men and women spent substantial portions of their daily lives apart from each other. The ceremonial occasions, meals, and leisure activities that brought them together tended to be closely regulated. The lives of the young, in particular, were closely watched, guided, and supervised by parents, teachers, and ministers.

Although this doctrine, often referred to as Victorianism, never worked as well in practice as it did in theory, throughout the 1880s and 1890s it had a profound influence on gender identity and sexual practice. Then a revolt set in. That revolt came from many sources: from middle-class men who were tiring of a life devoted to regimented work with no time for play; from middle-class women who, after achieving first-rate educations at elite women's colleges, were told they could not participate in the nation's economic, governmental, or professional enterprises; from immigrants, blacks, and other groups who had never been fully socialized into the Victorian world; and from the ready availability of leisure activities far removed from parental supervision.

Among the most influential rebels in the new century were the young, single, working-class women who were entering the workforce in large numbers. The economy's voracious appetite

Theda Bara as Cleopatra (1917) Bara was the first movie actress to gain fame for her roles as a "vamp"—a woman whose irresistible sexual charm led men to ruin. Because little effort was made to censor movies prior to the early 1920s, movie directors were able to explore sexual themes and to film their female stars in erotic, and partially nude, poses.

for labor was drawing women out of the home and into factories and offices. Men who would have preferred to keep their wives and daughters at home were forced, given their own low wages, to allow them to go to work. Women's employment doubled between 1880 and 1900, and increased by 50 percent from 1900 to 1920. Meanwhile, the nature of female employment was undergoing a radical change. Domestic service had been the most common occupation for women during the 19th century. Female servants generally worked alone, or with one or two other servants. They worked long hours cooking, cleaning, and caring for their masters' children and received only part of their wages in cash, the rest being "paid" in the form of room and board. Their jobs offered them little personal or financial independence.

Now, women were taking different kinds of jobs. The jobs tended to be either industrial or clerical. In both cases, women worked both with one another and in proximity to men. Their places of work were distant from their homes and from parental supervision. They received all their pay in the form of wages, which, though low, heightened their sense of economic independence. Their ranks, however, included few black women, who, like black men, were largely excluded from the expanding job opportunities in the economy's manufacturing and clerical sectors.

Once the barriers against white women in the workforce had fallen, other barriers also began to weaken—especially the Victorian ban on close associations with men outside of marriage. Young women and men flocked to the dance halls that were opening in every major city. They rejected the stiff formality of earlier ballroom dances like the cotillion or the waltz for the freedom and intimacy of newer forms, like the fox trot, tango, and bunny-hug. They went to movies and to amusement parks together, and they engaged, far more than their parents had, in premarital sex. It is estimated that the proportion of women having sex before marriage rose from 10 percent to 25 percent in the generation that was coming of age between 1910 and 1920.

THE RISE OF FEMINISM

This movement toward sexual equality was one expression of women's dissatisfaction with their subordinate place in society. By the second decade of the 20th century, eloquent spokeswomen had emerged to make the case for full female equality. The writer Charlotte Perkins Gilman called for the release of women from domestic chores through the collectivization of housekeeping. Social activist Margaret Sanger insisted, in her lectures on birth control, that women should be free to enjoy sexual relations without having to worry about unwanted motherhood. The anarchist Emma Goldman denounced marriage as a kind of prostitution and embraced the ideal of "free love"—love unburdened by contractual commitment. Alice Paul, founder of the National Women's Party, brought a new militancy to the campaign for woman suffrage (see Chapter 21).

These women were among the first to use the term "feminism" to describe their desire for complete equality with men. Some of them came together in Greenwich Village, a community of radical artists and writers in lower Manhattan, where they found a supportive environment in which to express and live by their feminist ideals. Crystal Eastman, a leader of the feminist Greenwich Village group called Heterodoxy, defined the feminist challenge as "how to arrange the world so that women can be human beings, with a chance to exercise their infinitely varied gifts in infinitely varied ways, instead of being destined by the accident of their sex to one field of activity."

The movement for sexual and gender equality aroused considerable anxiety in the more conservative sectors of American society. Parents worried about the promiscuity of their children. Conservatives were certain that the "new women" would transform American cities into dens of iniquity. Vice commissions sprang up in every major city to clamp down on prostitution, drunkenness, and pornography. The campaign for prohibition—a ban on the sale of alcoholic beverages—gathered steam. Movie theater owners were pressured into excluding "indecent" films from their screens.

Cultural conservatism was strongest in those areas of the country least involved in the ongoing industrial and sexual revolutions—in farming communities and small towns; in the South, where industrialization and urbanization were proceeding at a slower rate than elsewhere; and among old social elites, who felt pushed aside by the new corporate men of power.

What conservatives shared with radicals was a conviction that the country could not afford to ignore its social problems—the power of the corporations; the poverty and powerlessness of wage earners; the role of women and African Americans. Conservatives were as determined to restore a Victorian morality as radicals were determined to achieve working-class emancipation and women's equality. But in politics, neither would become the dominant force. That role

Chronology

1897	Depression ends; prosperity returns
1899	Theodore Roosevelt urges Americans to live the "strenuous life"
1890s	Football becomes sport-of-choice in Ivy League • Young women put away their corsets
1900–1914	Immigration averages more than 1 million per year
1901	U.S. Steel is formed from 200 separate companies • Andrew Carnegie devotes himself to philanthropic pursuits • 1 of every 400 railroad workers dies on the job
1904	20 percent of the North's industrial population lives below poverty line
1905	Industrial Workers of World (IWW) founded
1908	Henry Ford unveils his Model T
1909	Immigrants and their children comprise more than 96 percent of labor force building and maintaining railroads
1910	Black skilled tradesmen in northern cities reduced to 10 percent of total skilled trades workforce • 20,000 nickelodeons dot northern cities
1911	Triangle Shirtwaist Company fire kills 146 workers • Frederick Winslow Taylor publishes *The Principles of Scientific Management*
1913	Henry Ford introduces the first moving assembly line; employee turnover reaches 370 percent a year • John D. Rockefeller establishes Rockefeller Foundation
1914	Henry Ford introduces the $5-a-day wage • 66 men, women, and children killed in "Ludlow massacre" • Theda Bara, movies' first sex symbol, debuts
1919	Japanese farmers in California sell $67 million in agricultural goods, 10 percent of state's total
1920	Nation's urban population outstrips rural population for first time

would fall to the so-called progressives, a widely diverse group of reformers who confidently and optimistically believed that they could bring both order and justice to the new society.

Conclusion

Between 1890 and 1920, corporate power, innovation, and demands had stimulated the growth of cities, attracted millions of immigrants from southern and eastern Europe, enhanced commercial opportunities, and created the conditions for a vibrant urban culture. Many Americans thrived in this new environment, taking advantage of business opportunities or, as in the case of women, discovering liberties for dress, employment, dating, and sex that they had not known. But millions of Americans were impoverished, unable to rise in the social order or to earn enough in wages to support their families. African Americans who had migrated to the North in search of economic opportunity suffered more than any other single group, as they found themselves shut out of most industrial and commercial employment.

Henry Ford, whose generous $5-a-day wage drew tens of thousands to his Detroit factories, was an exceptional employer. Although other employers had learned to restrain their crass displays of wealth and had turned toward philanthropy in search of a better public image, they were reluctant to follow Ford's lead.

Working-class Americans proved resourceful in creating self-help institutions to attend to their own and each other's needs. In some cities, they gained a measure of power through the establishment of political machines. Labor unions arose and fought for a society of greater equality and justice. But it remained unclear how successful these institutions would be in their efforts to inject greater equality and opportunity into an industrial society in which the gap between rich and poor had reached alarming proportions.

PROGRESSIVISM

PROGRESSIVISM AND THE PROTESTANT SPIRIT

MUCKRAKERS, MAGAZINES, AND THE TURN TOWARD "REALISM"

SETTLEMENT HOUSES AND WOMEN'S ACTIVISM

SOCIALISM AND PROGRESSIVISM ~ MUNICIPAL REFORM

POLITICAL REFORM IN THE STATES

ECONOMIC AND SOCIAL REFORM IN THE STATES

A RENEWED CAMPAIGN FOR CIVIL RIGHTS ~ NATIONAL REFORM

THE TAFT PRESIDENCY ~ ROOSEVELT'S RETURN

THE RISE OF WOODROW WILSON ~ THE ELECTION OF 1912

THE WILSON PRESIDENCY

Progressivism was a reform movement that took its name from individuals who left the Republican Party in 1912 to join Theodore Roosevelt's new party, the Progressive Party. But the term "progressive" refers to a much larger and more varied group of reformers than those who gathered around Roosevelt in 1912. Progressives wanted to cleanse politics of corruption, tame the power of the "trusts" and, in the process, inject more liberty into American life. They fought against prostitution, gambling, drinking, and other forms of vice. They first appeared in municipal politics, organizing movements to oust crooked mayors and to break up local gas or streetcar monopolies. They then carried their fights to the states and finally to the nation.

Progressivism was popular among a variety of groups who brought to the movement distinct, and often conflicting, aims. But on one issue most progressives agreed: the need for an activist government to right political, economic, and social wrongs. Some progressives wanted government to become active only long enough to clean up the political process, end drinking, upgrade the electorate, and break up trusts. But these problems were so difficult to solve that many progressives endorsed the notion of a permanently active government—with the power to tax income, regulate industry, protect consumers from fraud, safeguard the environment, and provide social welfare. Progressives, in other words, came to see the federal government as the institution best equipped to solve social problems.

Such positive attitudes toward government power marked an important change in American politics. Americans had long been suspicious of centralized government, viewing it as the enemy of liberty. The Populists had broken with that view (see Chapter 19), but they had been defeated. So the progressives had to build a new case for strong government as the protector of liberty and equality.

Progressivism and the Protestant Spirit

Progressivism emerged first and most strongly among young, mainly Protestant, middle-class Americans who felt alienated from their society. Many had been raised in devout Protestant homes in which religious conviction had often been a spur to social action. They were expected to become ministers or missionaries or to serve their church in some other way. They had abandoned this path, but they never lost their zeal for righting moral wrongs and for uplifting the human spirit. They were distressed by the immorality and corruption rampant in American politics, and by the gap that separated rich from poor. They became, in the words of one historian, "ministers of reform."

Other Protestant reformers retained their faith. This was true of William Jennings Bryan, the former Populist leader who became an ardent progressive and a prominent evangelical. Throughout his political career, Bryan always insisted that Christian piety and American democracy were integrally related. Billy Sunday, a former major league baseball player who became the most theatrical evangelical preacher of his day, elevated opposition to saloons and the "liquor trust" into a righteous crusade. And Walter Rauschenbusch led a movement known as the Social Gospel, which emphasized the duty of Christians to work for the social good.

Protestants, of course, formed a diverse population, large sections of which showed little interest in reform. Thus, it is important to identify smaller and more cohesive groups of reformers. Of the many that arose, three were of particular importance, especially in the early years: investigative journalists, who were called "muckrakers"; the founders and supporters of settlement houses; and socialists.

Muckrakers, Magazines, and the Turn toward "Realism"

The term "muckraker" was coined by Theodore Roosevelt, who had intended it as a criticism of newspaper and magazine reporters who wrote stories about scandalous situations. But it became a badge of honor among journalists who were determined to expose the seedy, sordid side of life in the United States. During the first decade of the 20th century, they presented the public with one startling revelation after another. Ida Tarbell revealed the shady practices by which John D. Rockefeller had transformed his Standard Oil Company into a monopoly. Lincoln Steffens unraveled the webs of bribery and corruption that were strangling local governments in the nation's great cities. George Kibbe Turner documented the extent of prostitution and family disintegration in the ethnic ghettos of those cities. These muckrakers wanted to shock the public into recognizing the shameful state of political, economic, and social affairs and to prompt "the people" to take action.

The tradition of investigative journalism reached back at least to the 1870s, when newspaper and magazine writers exposed the corrupt practices of New York City's Boss Tweed and his well-oiled Tammany Hall machine. But the rise of the muckrakers reflected two factors, one economic and the other intellectual, which transformed investigative reporting into something of national importance.

INCREASED NEWSPAPER AND MAGAZINE CIRCULATION

A dramatic expansion in newspaper and magazine circulation was the economic factor underlying the rise of the muckrakers. From 1870 to 1909 the number of daily newspapers rose from 574 to 2,600, and their circulation increased from less than 3 million to more than 24 million. During the 1890s magazines also underwent a revolution. Cheap, 10-cent periodicals such as *McClure's Magazine* and *Ladies Home Journal,* with circulations of 400,000 to 1 million, displaced genteel and relatively expensive 35-cent publications such as *Harper's* and *The Atlantic Monthly.* The expanded readership brought journalists considerably more money and prestige and attracted many talented and ambitious men and women to the profession. It also made magazine publishers more receptive to stories that might appeal to their newly acquired millions of readers.

THE TURN TOWARD "REALISM"

The intellectual factor favoring the muckrakers was the turn toward "realism" among the nation's middle class. "Realism" was a way of thinking that prized detachment, objectivity, and skepticism. Many people, for example, felt that constitutional theory had little to do with the way government in the United States actually worked. What could one learn about bosses, machines, and graft from studying the Constitution? There was also a sense that the nation's glorification of the "self-made man" and of "individualism" was preventing Americans from coping effectively with the sudden centrality of large-scale organizations—corporations, banks, labor unions—to the nation's economy and to society.

In the 1890s this impatience reached a crisis point. Intellectuals and artists of all sorts set about creating truer, more realistic ways of representing and analyzing American society. Many of them were inspired by the work of investigative journalists; some had themselves been newspapermen. Years of firsthand observation enabled them to describe American society as it "truly was." They brought shadowy figures vividly to life. They pictured for Americans the captain of industry who ruthlessly destroyed his competitors; the con artist who tricked young people new to city life; the innocent immigrant girl who fell prey to the white slave traders; the corrupt policeman under whose protection urban vice flourished.

A vast middle class, uneasy about the state of American society, applauded the muckrakers for telling these stories, and became interested in reform. Members of this class put pressure on city and state governments to send crooked government officials to jail and to stamp out the sources of corruption and vice. Between 1902 and 1916 more than 100 cities launched investigations of the prostitution trade. At the federal level, all three branches of government felt compelled to address the question of "the trusts"—the concentration of power in the hands of a few industrialists and financiers. Progressivism began to crystallize around the abuses the muckrakers had exposed.

SETTLEMENT HOUSES AND WOMEN'S ACTIVISM

Settlement houses, too, played a crucial role in fashioning the progressive agenda. Established by middle-class reformers, these institutions were intended to help the largely immigrant poor cope with the harsh conditions of city life. Much of the inspiration for them came from young, college-educated, Protestant women from comfortable but not particularly wealthy backgrounds. Highly educated and talented, these women rebelled against being relegated solely to the roles of wife and mother. For them, the settlement houses provided a way to assert their independence and apply their talents in socially useful ways.

HULL HOUSE

Jane Addams and Ellen Gates Starr established the nation's first settlement house, in Chicago, in 1889. The two women had been inspired by a visit the year before to London's Toynbee Hall, where a small group of middle-class men had been living and working with

JANE ADDAMS   The founder of the settlement house movement, Addams was the most famous woman reformer of the Progressive Era. This photograph (1930) shows her late in her career, by which time she had dedicated more than 40 years to helping immigrant children and their families.

that city's poor since 1884. Addams and Starr bought a decaying mansion that had once been the country home of a prominent Chicagoan, Charles J. Hull. By 1889 "Hull House" had been surrounded by factories, churches, saloons, and tenements inhabited by very poor, largely foreign-born working-class families.

Addams quickly emerged as the guiding spirit of Hull House. She moved into the building and demanded that all workers there do the same. She and Starr enlisted extraordinary women such as Florence Kelley, Alice Hamilton, and Julia Lathrop. They set up a nursery for the children of working mothers, a penny savings bank, and an employment bureau, soon followed by a baby clinic, a neighborhood playground, and social clubs. Determined to minister to cultural as well as economic needs, Hull House sponsored an orchestra, reading groups, and a lecture series. Members of Chicago's widening circle of reform-minded intellectuals, artists, and politicians contributed their energies to the enterprise. In 1893 Illinois Governor John P. Altgeld named Hull House's Florence Kelley as the state's chief factory inspector. Her investigations led to Illinois's first factory law, which prohibited child labor, limited the employment of women to eight hours a day, and authorized the state to hire inspectors to enforce the law.

There seemed to be no limit to the energy, imagination, and commitment of the Hull House principals. Julia Lathrop used her appointment to the State Board of Charities to agitate for improvements in the care of the poor, the handicapped, and the delinquent. With Edith Abbott and Sophonisba Breckinridge, she established the Department of Social Research at the University of Chicago.

The Hull House leaders did not command the instant fame accorded the muckrakers. Nevertheless, they were steadily drawn into the public arena. Thousands of women across the country were inspired to build their own settlement houses on the Hull House model. By 1910 Jane Addams had become one of the nation's most famous women.

THE CULTURAL CONSERVATISM OF PROGRESSIVE REFORMERS

In general, settlement house workers were much more sympathetic toward the poor, the illiterate, and the downtrodden than the muckrakers were. Jane Addams, though she disapproved of machine politics, saw firsthand the benefits machine politicians delivered to their constituents. She respected the cultural inheritance of the immigrants and admired their resourcefulness. Although she wanted them to become Americans, she encouraged them to preserve their "immigrant gifts" in their new identity. Those attitudes were more liberal than the attitudes of other reformers, who considered most immigrants culturally, even racially, inferior.

But there were limits even to Addams's sympathy for the immigrants. In particular, she disapproved of the new working-class entertainments that gave adolescents extensive and unregulated opportunities for intimate association. She was also troubled by the emergence of the "new woman" and her frank sexuality (see Chapter 20). Addams tended to equate female sexuality with prostitution. Such attitudes revealed the extent to which she still adhered to Victorian notions of "pure," asexual womanhood.

In fact, a good many champions of progressive reform were cultural conservatives. In addition to their position on women's sexuality, their conservatism was evident in their attitudes toward alcohol. Drinking was a serious problem in poor, working-class areas. Settlement house workers were well aware of the ill-effects of alcoholism and sought to combat it. They called on working people to refrain from drink and worked for legislation that would shut

WOMEN ENROLLED IN INSTITUTIONS OF HIGHER EDUCATION, 1870–1930

YEAR	WOMEN'S COLLEGES (THOUSANDS OF STUDENTS)	COED INSTITUTIONS (THOUSANDS OF STUDENTS)	TOTAL (THOUSANDS OF STUDENTS)	PERCENTAGE OF ALL STUDENTS ENROLLED
1870	6.5	4.6	11.1	21.0%
1880	15.7	23.9	39.6	33.4
1890	16.8	39.5	56.3	35.9
1900	24.4	61.0	85.4	36.8
1910	34.1	106.5	140.6	39.6
1920	52.9	230.0	282.9	47.3
1930	82.1	398.7	480.8	43.7

Source: From Mabel Newcomer, *A Century of Higher Education for American Women* (New York: Harper and Row, 1959), p. 46.

down the saloons. The progressives joined forces with the Women's Christian Temperance Union and the Anti-Saloon League. By 1916, through their collective efforts, these groups had won prohibition of the sale and manufacture of alcoholic beverages in 16 states. In 1919 their crowning achievement was the Eighteenth Amendment to the U.S. Constitution, making Prohibition the law of the land (see Chapter 23).

In depicting alcohol and saloons as unmitigated evils, however, the prohibition movement ignored the role saloons played in ethnic, working-class communities. On Chicago's South Side, for example, saloons provided tens of thousands of packinghouse workers with the only decent place to eat lunch. Some saloons catered to particular ethnic groups: They served traditional foods and drinks, provided meeting space for fraternal organizations, and offered camaraderie to men longing to speak in their native tongue. Saloonkeepers sometimes functioned as informal bankers, cashing checks and making small loans.

Alcohol figured in ethnic life in other ways, too. For Catholics, wine was central to Communion. Jews greeted each Sabbath and religious festival with a blessing over wine. For both groups, the sharing of wine or beer marked the celebration of births, marriages, deaths, and other major family events. Understandably, many of the nation's immigrants shunned the prohibition movement. Here was a gulf separating the immigrant masses from the Protestant middle class that even compassionate reformers such as Jane Addams could not bridge.

A NATION OF CLUBWOMEN

Settlement house workers comprised only one part of a vast network of female reformers. Hundreds of thousands of women belonged to local women's clubs. Conceived as self-help organizations in which women would be encouraged to sharpen their minds, refine their domestic skills, and strengthen their moral faculties, these clubs began taking on tasks of social reform. Clubwomen typically focused their energies on improving schools, building libraries and playgrounds, expanding educational and vocational opportunities for girls, and securing fire and sanitation codes for tenement houses. In so doing, they transformed traditional female concerns into questions of public policy and significantly increased public awareness of the problems afflicting children and families.

SOCIALISM AND PROGRESSIVISM

While issues such as women's sexuality and men's alcoholism drew progressives in a conservative direction, other issues drew them to socialism. In the early part of the 20th century, socialism stood for the transfer of control over industry from a few industrialists to the laboring masses. Socialists believed that such a transfer, usually defined in terms of government ownership and operation of economic institutions, would make it impossible for wealthy elites to control society.

The Socialist Party of America, founded in 1901, became a political force during the first 16 years of the century, and socialist ideas influenced progressivism. In 1912, at the peak of its influence, the party's presidential candidate, the charismatic Eugene Victor Debs, attracted almost 1 million votes—6 percent of the total votes cast that year. In that same year, 1,200 Socialists held elective office in 340 different municipalities. More than 300 newspapers and periodicals spread the socialist gospel. The most important socialist publication was *Appeal to Reason,* published by the Kansan Julius Wayland and sent out each week to 750,000 subscribers. In 1905 Wayland published, in serial form, a novel by an obscure muckraker named Upton Sinclair, which depicted the scandalous working conditions in Chicago's meatpacking industry. When it was later published in book form in 1906, *The Jungle* created such an outcry that the federal government was forced to regulate the meat industry.

THE MANY FACES OF SOCIALISM

Socialists came in many varieties. In Milwaukee, they consisted of predominantly German working-class immigrants and their descendants; in New York City, their numbers were strongest among Jewish immigrants from eastern Europe. In the Southwest, tens of thousands of disgruntled native-born farmers who had been Populists in the 1890s now flocked to the socialist banner. In the West, socialism was popular among miners, timber cutters, and others who labored in isolated areas where industrialists enjoyed extraordinary power. These radicals gravitated to the militant labor union, the Industrial Workers of the World (IWW) (Chapter 20), which from 1905 to 1913 found a home in the Socialist Party.

Socialists differed not only in their occupations and ethnic origins but also in their politics. The IWW was the most radical socialist group, with its incessant calls for revolution. By contrast, mainstream socialism was more respectful of American political, cultural, and religious traditions. Mainstream socialists saw themselves as the saviors rather than the destroyers of the American republic. Their confidence that the nation could be redeemed through conventional politics—through the election of Debs as president—is evidence of their affection for American democracy. Evolutionary socialists, led by Victor Berger of Milwaukee, abandoned talk of revolution altogether and chose instead an aggressive brand of reform

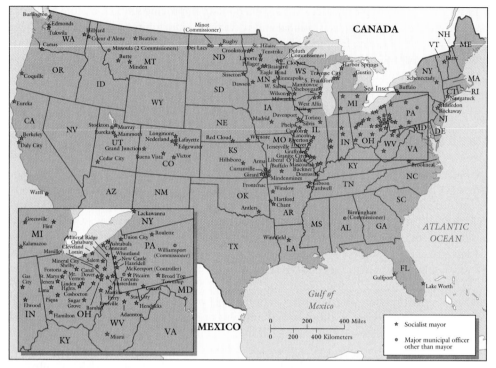

CITIES AND TOWNS ELECTING SOCIALIST MAYORS OR OTHER MAJOR MUNICIPAL
OFFICERS, 1911–1920

politics. They were dubbed "gas and water socialists" because of their interest in improving city services.

These differences would, after 1912, fragment the socialist movement. But for a decade or so, all these divergent groups managed to coexist in a single political party. That was due in no small measure to the eloquence of Debs. When he was released from a Chicago jail in 1895, where he had been imprisoned for his role in leading the strike against the Pullman Company (see Chapter 19), Debs declared to the 100,000 admirers who had gathered to celebrate his release: "Manifestly the spirit of '76 still survives. The fires of liberty and noble aspirations are not yet extinguished. . . . The vindication and glorification of American principles of government, as proclaimed to the world in the Declaration of Independence, is the high purpose of this convocation."

SOCIALISTS AND PROGRESSIVES

Debs's speeches both attracted and disturbed progressives. On the one hand, he spoke compellingly about the economic threats that concerned progressives. And his confidence that a strong state could bring the economic system under control mirrored the progressives' own faith in the positive uses of government. Indeed, progressives often worked hand-in-hand with socialists to win economic and political reforms, especially at the municipal and state lev-

THE RISE OF SOCIALISM The socialists hoped to bring economic security and dignity to working men and women. Under the leadership of Eugene V. Debs, pictured on the left in this 1904 campaign poster, they became a significant force in American politics. Their influence crested in the election of 1912, when Debs received nearly a million votes.

els, and many intellectuals and reformers moved easily back and forth between socialism and progressivism. Walter Lippmann, who would become a close adviser to President Wilson during the First World War, began his political career in 1912 as an assistant to the Socialist mayor of Schenectady. Several of the era's outstanding intellectuals, including John Dewey, Richard Ely, and Thorstein Veblen, also traveled back and forth between the socialist and progressive camps. So did Helen Keller, the country's leading spokesperson for the disabled.

On the other hand, Debs's talk of revolution scared progressives, as did his efforts to organize a working-class political movement independent of middle-class involvement or control. Although progressives wanted to tame capitalism, they did not want to eliminate it altogether. They wanted to improve the working and living conditions of the masses but not cede political control to them. The progressives hoped to offer a political program with enough socialist elements to counter the appeal of Debs's more radical movement. In this, they were successful.

MUNICIPAL REFORM

Progressive reform arose first in the cities. Early battles were over control of municipal transportation networks and utilities. Street railways were typically owned and operated by private corporations, as were electrical and gas systems. Many of the corporations used their monopoly power to charge exorbitant fares and rates, and often they won that power by bribing city officials who belonged to one of the political machines. Corporations achieved generous reductions in real estate taxes in the same way.

The assault on private utilities and their protectors in city government gained momentum in the mid-1890s. In Detroit, reform-minded Mayor Hazen S. Pingree led successful fights to control the city's gas, telephone, and trolley companies. In Chicago in 1896 and 1897, a group of middle-class reformers ousted a corrupt city council and elected a mayor, Carter Harrison Jr., who promised to protect Chicago's streetcar riders from exploitation. In St. Louis in 1900, middle-class consumers and small businessmen joined hands with striking workers to challenge the "streetcar trust." In Cleveland, the crusading reformer Tom Johnson won election as mayor in 1901, curbed the power of the streetcar interests, and brought honest and efficient government to the city.

Occasionally, a reform politician of Johnson's caliber would rise to power through one of the regular political parties. But this path to power was a difficult one, especially in cities where the political parties were controlled by machines. Consequently, progressives worked for reforms that would strip the parties of their power. Two of their favorite reforms were the city commission and the city manager forms of government.

THE CITY COMMISSION PLAN

First introduced in Galveston, Texas, in 1900, the city commission shifted municipal power from the mayor and his aldermen to five city commissioners, each responsible for a different department of city government. In Galveston and elsewhere, the impetus for this reform came from civic-minded businessmen determined to rebuild government on the same principles of efficient and scientific management that had energized the private sector. The results were often impressive. The Galveston commissioners restored the city's credit after a close brush with bankruptcy, improved the city's harbor, and built a massive seawall to protect the city from floods. And they accomplished all that on budgets only two-thirds the size of what they had been in the past. In Houston, Texas; Des Moines, Iowa; Dayton, Ohio; Oakland, California; and elsewhere, commissioners similarly improved urban infrastructures, expanded city services, and strengthened the financial health of the cities.

THE CITY MANAGER PLAN

The city commission system did not always work to perfection, however. Sometimes the commissioners used their position to reward electoral supporters with jobs and contracts; at other times, they pursued power and prestige for their respective departments. The city manager plan was meant to overcome such problems. Under this plan, the commissioners continued to set policy, but the implementation of policy now rested with a "chief executive." This official, who was appointed by the commissioners, was to be insulated from the pressures of running for office. The city manager would curtail rivalries between commissioners and ensure that no outside influences interfered with the expert, businesslike management of the city. The job of city manager was explicitly modeled after that of a corporation executive. First introduced in Sumter, South Carolina, in 1911 and then in Dayton, Ohio, in 1913, by 1919 the city manager plan had been adopted in 130 cities.

THE COSTS OF REFORM

Although these reforms limited corruption and improved services, they were not universally popular. Poor and minority voters, in particular, found that their influence in local affairs was weakened by the shift to city commissioners and city managers. Previously, candidates for municipal office (other than the mayor) competed in ward elections rather than in citywide elections. Voters in working-class wards commonly elected workingmen to represent them, and voters in immigrant wards made sure that fellow ethnics represented their interests on city councils. Citywide elections diluted the strength of these constituencies. Candidates from poor districts often lacked the money needed to mount a citywide campaign, and they were further hampered by the nonpartisan nature of such elections. Denied the support of a political party or platform, they had to make themselves personally known to voters throughout the city. That was a much easier task for the city's "leading citizens"—manufacturers, merchants, and lawyers—than it was for workingmen.

POLITICAL REFORM IN THE STATES

Political reform in the cities quickly spread to the states. As at the local level, political parties at the state level were often dominated by corrupt, incompetent politicians who did the bidding of powerful private lobbies. In New Jersey in 1903, for example, large industrial and financial interests, working through the Republican Party machine, controlled numerous appointments to state government, including the chief justice of the state supreme court, the attorney general, and the commissioner of banking and insurance. Such webs of influence ensured that New Jersey would provide large corporations such as the railroads with favorable political and economic legislation.

RESTORING SOVEREIGNTY TO "THE PEOPLE"

Progressives introduced reforms designed to undermine the power of party bosses, restore sovereignty to "the people," and encourage honest, talented individuals to enter politics. One such reform was the direct primary, a mechanism that enabled voters themselves, rather than party bosses, to choose party candidates. By 1916 all but three states had adopted the direct primary. Closely related was a movement to strip state legislatures of their power to choose U.S. senators. State after state enacted legislation that permitted voters to choose senate candidates in primary elections. In 1912 a reluctant U.S. Senate was obliged to approve the Seventeenth Amendment to the Constitution, mandating the direct election of senators.

The direct election of U.S. senators had first been proposed by the Populists back in the 1890s; so too had two other reforms, the initiative and the referendum, both of which were adopted first by Oregon in 1902 and then by 18 other states between 1902 and 1915. The initiative allowed reformers to put before voters in general elections legislation that state legislatures had yet to approve. The referendum gave voters the right in general elections to repeal an unpopular act that a state legislature had passed. Less widely adopted but important nevertheless was the recall, a device that allowed voters to remove from office any public servant who had betrayed their trust. As a further control over the behavior of elected officials, numerous states enacted laws that regulated corporate campaign contributions and restricted lobbying activities in state legislatures.

These laws did not eliminate corporate privilege or destroy the power of machine politicians. Nevertheless, they made politics more honest and strengthened the influence of ordinary voters.

CREATING A VIRTUOUS ELECTORATE

Progressive reformers focused as well on creating a responsible electorate that understood the importance of the vote and that resisted efforts to manipulate elections. To create this ideal electorate, reformers had to see to it that all those citizens who were deemed virtuous could cast their votes free of coercion and intimidation. At the same time, reformers sought to disfranchise all citizens who were considered irresponsible and corruptible. In pursuing these goals, progressives substantially altered the composition of the electorate and strengthened government regulation of voting. The results were contradictory. On the one hand, progressives enlarged the electorate by extending the right to vote to women; on the other hand, they either initiated or tolerated laws that barred large numbers of minority and poor voters from the polls.

THE AUSTRALIAN BALLOT

Government regulation of voting had begun back in the 1890s when virtually every state adopted the Australian, or secret, ballot. This reform required voters to vote in private rather than in public. It also required the government, rather than political parties, to print the ballots and supervise the voting. Prior to this time, each political party had printed its own ballot with only its candidates listed. At election time, each party mobilized its loyal supporters. Party workers offered liquor, free meals, and other bribes to get voters to the polls and to "persuade" them to cast the right ballot. Because the ballots were cast in public, few voters who had accepted gifts of liquor and food dared to cross watchful party officials. Critics argued that the system corrupted the electoral process. They also pointed out that it made "ticket-splitting"—dividing one's vote between candidates of two or more parties—virtually impossible.

The Australian ballot solved these problems. Although it predated progressivism, it reflected the progressives' determination to use government power to encourage citizens to cast their votes responsibly and wisely.

PERSONAL REGISTRATION LAWS

That same determination was apparent in the progressives' support for the personal registration laws that virtually every state passed between 1890 and 1920. These laws required prospective voters to appear at a designated government office with proper identification; only then would they be allowed to register to vote. Frequently, these laws also mandated a certain period of residence in the state prior to registration and a certain interval between registration and actual voting.

Personal registration laws were meant to disfranchise citizens who showed no interest in voting until election day when a party worker arrived with a few dollars and offered a free ride to the polls. They also excluded, however, many hard-working, responsible, poor people who wanted to vote but had failed to register, either because their work schedules made it impossible or because they were intimidated by the complex regulations. The laws were particularly frustrating for immigrants whose knowledge of American government and of the English language were limited.

DISFRANCHISEMENT

Some election laws promoted by the progressives were expressly designed to keep noncitizen immigrants from voting. In the 1880s, 18 states had passed laws allowing immigrants to vote without first becoming citizens. Progressives reversed this trend. At the same time, the newly formed Bureau of Immigration and Naturalization (1906) made it more difficult to become a citizen. Applicants for citizenship now had to appear before a judge who interrogated them, in the English language, on American history and civics. In addition, immigrants were required to provide two witnesses to vouch for their "moral character" and their "attachment to the principles of the Constitution." Finally, immigrants had to swear (and, if necessary, prove) that they were not anarchists or polygamists and that they had resided continuously in the United States for five years.

Most progressives defended the new rigor of the process. U.S. citizenship, they believed, carried great responsibilities; it was not to be bestowed lightly. This position was understandable, given the electoral abuses progressives had exposed. Nevertheless, the reforms also had the effect of denying the vote to a large proportion of the population. Nowhere was exclusion more startling than in the South, where between 1890 and 1904 every ex-Confederate state passed laws designed to strip blacks of their right to vote. Because laws explicitly barring blacks from voting would have violated the Fifteenth Amendment, this exclusion had to be accomplished indirectly—through literacy tests, property qualifications, and poll taxes. Any citizen who failed a reading test, or who could not sign his name, or who did not own a minimum amount of property, or who could not pay a poll tax, lost his right to vote. The citizens who failed these tests most frequently were blacks, who formed the poorest and least educated segment of the southern population, but a large portion of the region's poor whites also failed the tests.

Many progressives in the North bitterly criticized southern disfranchisement. Others joined in 1910 with the black intellectual W. E. B. Du Bois to found the National Association for the Advancement of Colored People (NAACP), an interracial political organization that made the struggle for black equality its primary goal. But in the South, white progressives rarely challenged disfranchisement. They had little difficulty using progressive ideology to justify disfranchisement. Because progressives everywhere believed that the franchise was a precious gift that was to be granted only to those who could handle its responsibilities, it obviously had to be withheld from any who were deemed racially or culturally unfit. Progressives in the North

LYNCHING   This grim photo records the death of five of the approximately 1,000 African Americans who were lynched between 1901 and 1914. The increase in lynching was one measure of the virulence of white racism in the early years of the 20th century.

VOTER PARTICIPATION IN 13 SOUTHERN STATES, 1876, 1892, 1900, 1912

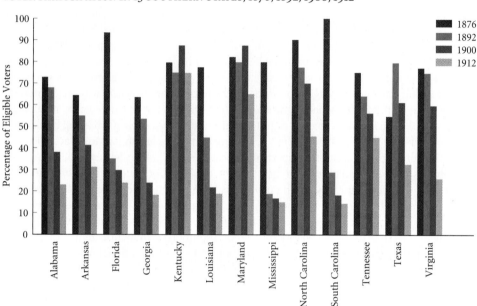

Source: Data from *Historical Statistics of the United States, Colonial Times to 1970* (White Plains, N.Y.: Kraus International, 1989).

excluded many immigrants on just those grounds. Progressives in the South saw the disfranchisement of African Americans in the same light.

DISILLUSIONMENT WITH THE ELECTORATE

In the process of identifying those groups "unfit" to hold the franchise, some progressives soured on the electoral process altogether. The more they looked for rational and virtuous voters, the fewer they found. In *Drift and Mastery* (1914), Walter Lippmann developed a theory that ordinary people had been overwhelmed by industrial and social changes. Because these changes seemed beyond their comprehension or control, they "drifted," unable to "master" the circumstances of modern life or take charge of their own destiny. Lippmann did not suggest that such ordinary people should be barred from voting. But he did argue that more political responsibility should be placed in the hands of appointed officials with the training and knowledge necessary to make government effective and just. The growing disillusionment with the electorate, in combination with intensifying restrictions on the franchise, created an environment in which fewer and fewer Americans actually went to the polls. Voting participation rates fell from 79 percent in 1896 to only 49 percent in 1920.

WOMAN SUFFRAGE

The major exception to this trend was the enfranchisement of women. This momentous reform was embraced by several states during the 1890s and the first two decades of the 20th

SUFFRAGISTS   After faltering in the 1870s and 1880s, the campaign for woman suffrage revived during the Progressive Era. Here suffragists campaign for the vote in New York City in 1912. By this time, women had already won the vote in many western states but in few eastern states.

century and then became federal law with the ratification of the Nineteenth Amendment to the Constitution in 1920.

Launched in 1848 at the famous Seneca Falls convention (see Chapter 11), the women's rights movement had floundered in the 1870s and 1880s. In 1890 suffragists came together in a new organization, the National American Woman Suffrage Association (NAWSA). Thousands of young, college-educated women campaigned door-to-door, held impromptu rallies, and pressured state legislators.

Wyoming, which attained statehood in 1890, became the first state to grant women the right to vote, followed in 1893 by Colorado and in 1896 by Idaho and Utah. The main reason for success in these sparsely populated western states was not egalitarianism but rather the conviction that women's supposedly gentler and more nurturing nature would tame and civilize the rawness of the frontier.

This notion reflected a subtle but important change in the thrust of the suffrage movement. Earlier generations had insisted that women were fundamentally equal to men, but the new suffragists argued that women were different from men. Women, they stressed, possessed a moral sense and a nurturing quality that men lacked. Consequently, they understood the civic obligations implied by the franchise and could be trusted to vote virtuously. Their experience as mothers and household managers, moreover, would enable them to guide local and state governments in efforts to improve education, sanitation, and the condition of women and children in the workforce.

Suffragists were slow to ally themselves with blacks, Asians, and other disfranchised groups. In fact, many suffragists, especially those in the South and West, vehemently opposed the franchise for Americans of color. They, like their male counterparts, believed that members of these groups lacked moral strength and thus did not deserve the franchise.

Washington, California, Kansas, Oregon, and Arizona followed the lead of the other western states by enfranchising women in the years from 1910 to 1912. After a series of setbacks in eastern and midwestern states, the movement regained momentum under the leadership of the strategically astute Carrie Chapman Catt, who became president of NAWSA in 1915, and the radical Alice Paul, who founded the militant National Women's Party in 1916. Aided by a heightened enthusiasm for democracy generated by America's participation in the First World War (see Chapter 23) and by the decision to shift the movement's focus from individual states to the nation at large, the suffragists achieved their goal of universal woman suffrage in 1920.

Predictions that suffrage for women would radically alter politics turned out to be false. Although the numbers of voters increased after 1920, voter participation rates continued to decline. Still, the extension of the vote to women, 144 years after the founding of the nation, was a great political achievement.

ECONOMIC AND SOCIAL REFORM IN THE STATES

In some states, progressive reform extended well beyond political parties and the electorate. Progressives also wanted to limit the power of the corporations, strengthen organized labor, and offer social welfare protection to the weak. State governments were pressured into passing such legislation by progressive alliances of middle-class and working-class reformers, and by dynamic state governors.

ROBERT LA FOLLETTE AND WISCONSIN PROGRESSIVISM

Nowhere else did the progressives' campaign for social reform flourish as it did in Wisconsin. The movement arose first in the 1890s as citizens began to mobilize against the state's corrupt Republican Party. These reform-minded citizens came from varied backgrounds. They were middle-class and working-class, urban and rural, male and female, intellectual and evangelical. Wisconsin progressivism had already gained considerable momentum by 1897, when Robert La Follette assumed its leadership.

La Follette was born into a prosperous farming family in 1855. He entered politics as a Republican in the 1880s and embraced reform in the late 1890s. Elected governor in 1900, he secured for Wisconsin both a direct primary and a tax law that stripped the railroad corporations of tax exemptions they had long enjoyed. In 1905 he pushed through a civil service law mandating that every state employee had to meet a certain level of competence.

A tireless campaigner and a spellbinding speaker, "Fighting Bob" won election to the U.S. Senate in 1906. Meanwhile, the growing strength of Wisconsin's labor and socialist movements forced progressive reformers to focus their legislative efforts on issues of corporate greed and social welfare. By 1910 reformers had passed state laws that regulated railroad and utility rates, instituted the nation's first state income tax, and provided workers with compensation for injuries, limitations on work hours, restrictions on child labor, and minimum wages for women.

Many of these laws were written by social scientists at the University of Wisconsin, with whom reformers had close ties. In the first decade of the 20th century, John R. Commons, University of Wisconsin economist, drafted Wisconsin's civil service and public utilities laws. In 1911 Commons designed and won legislative approval for the Wisconsin Industrial Commission, which brought together employers, trade unionists, and professionals and gave them broad powers to investigate and regulate relations between industry and labor throughout the state. Never before had a state government so plainly committed itself to the cause of industrial justice. For the first time, the rights of labor would be treated with the same respect as the rights of industry. Equally important was the responsibility the commission delegated to non-elected professionals: social scientists, lawyers, engineers, and others.

The "Wisconsin idea" was quickly adopted in Ohio, Indiana, New York, and Colorado; and in 1913 the federal government established its own Industrial Relations Commission and hired Commons to direct its investigative staff. In other areas, too, reformers began urging state and federal governments to shift the policymaking initiative away from political parties and toward administrative agencies staffed by professionals.

Progressive Reform in New York

New York was probably second only to Wisconsin in the vigor and breadth of its Progressive movement. As in Wisconsin, progressives in New York focused first on fighting political corruption. Startling revelations of close ties between leading Republican politicians and life insurance companies vaulted the reform lawyer Charles Evans Hughes into the governor's mansion in 1907. Hughes immediately established several public service commissions to regulate railroads and utility companies. As in Wisconsin, the growing strength of labor had an effect. Successful strikes by New York City's garment workers forced state legislators to treat the condition of workers more seriously than they might have otherwise. With the establishment of the Factory Investigating Committee, New York, like Wisconsin, became a pioneer in labor and social welfare policy.

New York state legislators also were being pressured by middle-class reformers whose work with the poor had convinced them that laws were needed to promote social justice. This combined pressure from working-class and middle-class constituencies impelled some state Democrats to convert from machine to reform politics. While they opposed prohibition, city commissions, voter registration laws, and other reforms whose intent seemed anti-immigrant and anti-Catholic, they now agitated for a minimum wage, factory safety, workmen's compensation, the right of workers to join unions, and the regulation of excessively powerful corporations. Their participation in progressivism accelerated the movement's shift away from a preoccupation with political reform and toward questions of economic justice and social welfare.

A Renewed Campaign for Civil Rights

As state legislators in New York and elsewhere were refocusing progressivism on economic and social issues, a new generation of African American activists began insisting that the issue of racial equality also be placed on the reform agenda.

The Failure of Accommodationism

Booker T. Washington's message—that blacks should accept segregation and disfranchisement as unavoidable and focus their energies instead on self-help and self-improvement—was increasingly criticized by black activists. Washington's accommodationist leadership (see Chapter 18), in their eyes, brought blacks in the South no reprieve from racism. More than 100 blacks had been lynched in 1900 alone; between 1901 and 1914 at least 1,000 others would be hanged. Increasingly, unsubstantiated rumors of black assaults on whites became occasions for white mobs to rampage through black neighborhoods and indiscriminately destroy life and property. In 1908 a mob in Springfield, Illinois, attacked black businesses and individuals; a force of 5,000 state militia was required to restore order. The troops were too late, however, to stop the lynching of two innocent black men.

Washington had long believed that blacks who educated themselves or who succeeded in business would be accepted as equals by whites and welcomed into their society. But as militants observed, white rioters made no distinction between rich blacks and poor, or between solid citizens and petty criminals. All that had seemed to matter was the color of one's skin. Similarly, many black militants knew from personal experience that individual accomplishment was not enough to overcome racial prejudice.

FROM THE NIAGARA MOVEMENT TO THE NAACP

Seeing no future in accommodation, W. E. B. Du Bois and other young black activists came together at Niagara Falls in 1905 to fashion their own aggressive political agenda. They demanded that African Americans be given the right to vote in states where it had been taken away; that segregation be abolished; and that the many discriminatory barriers placed in the path of black advancement be removed. They declared their commitment to freedom of speech, the brotherhood of all men, and respect for the working man.

The 1908 Springfield riot had shaken a sizable number of whites. Some, especially those already involved in matters of social and economic reform, now joined in common cause with the Niagara movement. A conference was planned for Lincoln's birthday in 1909 to revive, in the words of the writer William English Walling, "the spirit of the abolitionists" and to "treat the Negro on a plane of absolute political and social equality." The conference brought together a number of distinguished progressives, white and black. They drew up plans to establish an organization dedicated to fighting racial discrimination and prejudice. In May 1910 the National Association for the Advancement of Colored People (NAACP) was officially launched, with Moorfield Storey of Boston as president, Walling as chairman of the executive committee, and Du Bois as the director of publicity and research.

The formation of the NAACP marked the beginning of the modern civil rights movement. The organization immediately launched a magazine, *The Crisis,* edited by Du Bois, to publicize and protest the lynchings, riots, and other abuses directed against black citizens. Equally important was the Legal Redress Committee, which initiated lawsuits against city and state governments for violating the constitutional rights of African Americans. The committee scored its first major success in 1915, when the U.S. Supreme Court ruled that the so-called "grandfather" clauses of the Oklahoma and Maryland constitutions violated the Fifteenth Amendment. (These clauses allowed poor, uneducated whites—but not poor, uneducated blacks—to vote, even if they failed to pay their state's poll tax or to pass its literacy test, by exempting the descendants of men who had voted prior to 1867.)

By 1914, the NAACP had enrolled thousands of members in scores of branches throughout the United States. The organization's success also stimulated the formation of other groups committed to the advancement of blacks. Thus, the National Urban League, founded in 1911, worked to improve the economic and social conditions of blacks in cities. The Urban League pressured employers to hire blacks, distributed lists of available jobs and housing in African American communities, and developed social programs to ease the adjustment of rural black migrants to city life.

Attacking segregation and discrimination through lawsuits was, by its nature, a snail-paced strategy that would take decades to complete. The growing membership of the NAACP, although impressive, was not large enough to qualify it as a mass movement. And its interracial character made the organization seem dangerously radical to millions of whites. White NAACP leaders responded to this hostility by limiting the number and power of African Americans who worked for the organization. This conciliatory policy, in turn, outraged black militants, who argued that a civil rights organization should not be in the business of appeasing white racists.

Despite its limitations, the early work of the NAACP was significant. The NAACP gave Du Bois the security and visibility he needed to carry on his fight against Booker T. Washington's accommodationism. Even before his death in 1915, Washington's enormous influence in black and white communities had begun to recede. The NAACP, more than any other organization, was responsible for resurrecting the issue of racial equality at a time when many white Americans had accepted as normal the practices of racial segregation and discrimination.

NATIONAL REFORM

The more progressives focused on economic and social matters, the more they sought to increase their influence in national politics. Certain problems demanded national solutions. A patchwork of state regulations, for example, was not enough to curtail the power of the trusts, protect workers, or monitor the quality of consumer goods. Moreover, state and federal courts were often hostile toward progressive goals: They repeatedly struck down as unconstitutional reform laws regulating working hours or setting minimum wages, on the grounds that they impinged on the freedom of contract and trade. With a national movement, progressives could force the passage of laws less vulnerable to judicial veto or elect a president who could overhaul the federal judiciary through the appointment and confirmation of progressive-minded judges.

National leadership was not going to emerge from Congress. The Democratic Party had been badly scarred by the Populist challenge of the 1890s. Divided between the radical Bryanites and the conservative followers of Grover Cleveland, and consequently unable to speak with one voice on questions of social and economic policy, after 1896 the Democrats seemed incapable of winning a national election or offering a national agenda. The Republican Party was more unified and popular, but it was controlled by a conservative "Old Guard" that was resolutely pro-business and devoted to a 19th century style of backroom patronage.

National progressive leadership came from the executive rather than the legislative branch, and from two presidents in particular, the Republican Theodore Roosevelt and the Democrat Woodrow Wilson. These two presidents sponsored reforms that profoundly affected the lives of Americans.

THE ROOSEVELT PRESIDENCY

As governor of New York, Roosevelt had shown himself to be a moderate reformer. But even his modest efforts to rid the state's Republican Party of corruption and to institute civil service reform were too much for the state party machine, led by Thomas C. Platt. Consigning Roosevelt to the vice presidency seemed like a safe solution. McKinley was a young, vigorous

THEODORE ROOSEVELT CAMPAIGNING FOR THE PRESIDENCY IN 1912   This photograph captures some of the strength and exuberance that were central features of Roosevelt's public persona and critical to his popular appeal. Note the stuffed deer, eagle, and moosehead adorning the platform: These reminded voters of Roosevelt's love of the outdoors and of the "strenuous life."

politician, fully in control of his party and his presidency. Then in September 1901, less than a year into his second term, McKinley was shot by an anarchist assassin. The president clung to life for nine days, and then died. Upon succeeding McKinley, Theodore Roosevelt, aged 42, became the youngest chief executive in the nation's history.

Born to an aristocratic New York family, Roosevelt nevertheless developed an uncommon affection for "the people." Asthmatic, sickly, and nearsighted as a boy, he remade himself into a vigorous adult. With an insatiable appetite for high-risk adventure, he was also a voracious reader and an accomplished writer. Aggressive and swaggering in his public rhetoric, he was a skilled, patient negotiator in private. A devout believer in the superiority of his Anglo-Saxon race, he nevertheless appointed members of "inferior" races to important posts in his administration. Rarely has a president's personality so enthralled the American public.

REGULATING THE TRUSTS

It did not take long for Roosevelt to reveal his flair for the dramatic. In 1902 he ordered the Justice Department to prosecute the Northern Securities Company, a $400 million monopoly that had been set up by leading financiers and railroad tycoons to control all railroad lines and traffic in the Northwest from Chicago to Washington state. Never before had an American president sought to use the Sherman Antitrust Act to break up a monopoly. In 1903 a federal court ordered Northern Securities dissolved, and the U.S. Supreme Court upheld the decision the next year. Roosevelt was hailed as the nation's "trust-buster."

But Roosevelt did not believe in breaking up all, or even most, large corporations. Industrial concentration, he believed, brought the United States wealth, productivity, and a rising standard of living. The role of government should be to regulate these industrial giants, to punish those that used their power improperly, and to protect citizens who were at a disadvantage in their dealings with industry. This new role would require the federal government to expand its powers. The *strengthening* of the federal government—not a return to small-scale industry—was the true aim of Roosevelt's antitrust campaign.

Toward a "Square Deal"

Roosevelt displayed his willingness to use government power to protect the economically weak in a long and bitter 1902 coal miners' strike. Miners in the anthracite fields of eastern Pennsylvania wanted recognition for their union, the United Mine Workers (UMW). They also wanted a 10 to 20 percent increase in wages and an eight-hour day. When their employers, led by the uncompromising George F. Baer of the Reading Railroad, refused to negotiate, they went on strike. In October, the fifth month of the strike, Roosevelt summoned the mine owners and John Mitchell, the UMW president, to the White House. Baer expected Roosevelt to threaten the striking workers with arrest by federal troops if they failed to return to work. Instead, Roosevelt supported Mitchell's request for arbitration and warned the mine owners that if they refused to go along, 10,000 federal troops would seize their property. Stunned, the mine owners agreed to submit the dispute to arbitrators, who awarded the unionists a 10 percent wage increase and a nine-hour day.

The mere fact that the federal government had ordered employers to compromise with their workers carried great symbolic weight. Roosevelt enjoyed a surge of support from ordinary Americans convinced that he shared their dislike for ill-gotten wealth and privilege. He also raised the hopes of African Americans when, only a month into his presidency, he dined with Booker T. Washington at the White House. Blacks were impressed, too, by how easily Roosevelt brushed off the bitter protests of white southerners who accused him of striking a blow against segregation.

In his 1904 election campaign, Roosevelt promised that, if reelected, he would offer every American a "square deal." The slogan resonated with voters and helped carry Roosevelt to a victory over the lackluster, conservative Democrat Alton B. Parker. To the surprise of many observers, Roosevelt had aligned the Republican Party with the cause of reform.

Expanding Government Power: The Economy

Emboldened by his victory, the president intensified his efforts to extend government regulation of economic affairs. His most important proposal was to give the government power to set railroad shipping rates and thereby to eliminate the industry's discriminatory marketing practices. The government, in theory, already possessed this power through the Interstate Commerce Commission (ICC), a national regulatory body established by Congress in 1887. But the courts had so weakened the oversight and regulatory functions of the ICC as to render it virtually powerless. Roosevelt achieved his goal in 1906. Congress passed the Hepburn Act, which significantly increased the ICC's powers of rate review and enforcement. Roosevelt supported the Pure Food and Drug Act, passed by Congress that same year, which protected the public from fraudulently marketed and dangerous foods and medications. The uproar created by the publication of Sinclair's *The Jungle* in 1906 prompted Roosevelt to order a government investigation of conditions in the meatpacking industry. When the investigation corroborated Sinclair's findings, Roosevelt supported the Meat Inspection Act (1906), which committed the government to monitoring the quality and safety of meat being sold to American consumers.

EXPANDING GOVERNMENT POWER: THE ENVIRONMENT

Roosevelt also did more than any previous president to extend federal control over the nation's physical environment. Roosevelt was not a "preservationist" in the manner of John Muir, founder of the Sierra Club, who insisted that the beauty of the land and the well-being of its wildlife should be protected from all human interference. Roosevelt viewed the wilderness as a place to live strenuously, to test oneself against rough natural elements, and to match wits against strong and clever game. Roosevelt further believed that in the West—that land of ancient forests, lofty mountain peaks, and magnificent canyons—Americans could learn something important about their nation's roots and destiny. To preserve this West, Roosevelt oversaw the creation of 5 new national parks, 16 national monuments, and 53 wildlife reserves. The work of his administration led directly to the formation of the National Park Service in 1916.

Roosevelt also emerged a strong supporter of the "conservationist" movement. Conservationists cared little for national parks or grand canyons. They wanted to manage the environment, so as to ensure the most efficient use of the nation's resources for economic development. Roosevelt shared the conservationists' belief that the plundering of western timberlands, grazing areas, water resources, and minerals had reached crisis proportions. Only the institution of broad regulatory controls would restore the West's economic potential.

To that end, Roosevelt appointed a Public Lands Commission in 1903 to survey public lands, inventory them, and establish permit systems to regulate the kinds and numbers of users. Soon after, the Departments of Interior and Agriculture decreed that certain western lands rich in natural resources and waterpower could not be used for agricultural purposes. Government officials also limited waterpower development by requiring companies to acquire permits and then to pay fees for the right to generate electricity on their sites. When political favoritism and corruption within the Departments of the Interior and Agriculture threatened these efforts at regulation, Roosevelt authorized the hiring of university-trained bureaucrats to replace state and local politicians. Scientific expertise, rather than political connections, would now determine the distribution and use of western lands.

Gifford Pinchot, a specialist in forestry management, led the drive for expert and scientific management of natural resources. In 1905 he persuaded Roosevelt to relocate jurisdiction for the national forests from the Department of the Interior to the Department of Agriculture. The newly created National Forest Service quickly instituted a system of competitive bidding for the right to harvest timber on national forest lands. Pinchot and his expanding staff of college-educated foresters also implemented a new policy that exacted user fees from livestock ranchers who had previously used national forest grazing lands for free. Armed with new legislation and bureaucratic authority, Pinchot and fellow conservationists in the Roosevelt administration also declared vast stretches of federal land in the West off-limits to mining and dam construction.

The Old Guard in the Republican Party did not take kindly to these initiatives. When Roosevelt recommended the prosecution of cattlemen and lumbermen who were illegally using federal land for private gain, congressional conservatives struck back with legislation (in 1907) that curtailed the president's power to create new government land reserves. Roosevelt responded by seizing another 17 million acres for national forest reserves before the new law went into effect. To his conservative opponents, excluding commercial activity from public land was bad enough. But flouting the will of Congress with a 17-million-acre land grab was a violation of hallowed constitutional principles governing the separation of powers. Yet, to millions of American voters, Roosevelt's willingness to defy western cattle barons, mining tycoons, and other "malefactors of great wealth" added to his popularity.

PROGRESSIVISM: A MOVEMENT FOR THE PEOPLE?

Historians have long debated how much Roosevelt's economic and environmental reforms altered the balance of power between the "interests" and the people. Some have demonstrated that many corporations were eager for federal government regulation—that railroad corporations wanted relief from the ruinous rate wars that were driving them to the brink of bankruptcy, for example, and that the larger meatpackers believed that the costs of government food inspections would drive smaller meatpackers out of business. So, too, historians have shown that large agribusinesses, timber companies, and mining corporations in the West believed that government regulation would aid them and hurt smaller competitors. According to this view, government regulation benefited the corporations more than it benefited workers, consumers, and small businessmen.

This view has much to commend it. These early reforms did not go far enough in curtailing corporate power. Corporations fought with some success to turn the final versions of the reform laws to their advantage. But that does not mean that the corporations were the sponsors of reform, or that they dictated the content of reform measures.

Popular anger over the power of the corporations and over political corruption remained a driving force of progressivism. After 1906, the presence in the Senate of La Follette, Albert Beveridge of Indiana, and other anticorporate Republicans gave that anger a powerful national voice. Before he left office in 1909, Roosevelt would expand his reform program to include income and inheritance taxes, a national workmen's compensation law, abolition of child labor, and the eight-hour workday. Those proposals widened the rift between Roosevelt and the Old Guard. In 1907 the progressive program was still evolving. Whether the corporations or the people would benefit most remained unclear.

THE REPUBLICANS: A DIVIDED PARTY

The financial panic of 1907 further strained relations between Roosevelt reformers and Old Guard conservatives. A failed speculative effort by several New York banks to corner the copper market triggered a run on banks, a short but severe dip in industrial production, and widespread layoffs. Everywhere, people worried that a devastating depression was in the offing. Indeed, only the timely decision of J. P. Morgan and his fellow bankers to pour huge amounts of private cash into the collapsing banks saved the nation from a disastrous economic crisis. Prosperity quickly returned, but the jitters caused by the panic lingered. Conservatives blamed Roosevelt's "radical" economic policies for the fiasco. To Roosevelt and his fellow progressives, however, the panic merely pointed up how little impact their reforms had actually made on the reign of "speculation, corruption, and fraud."

Roosevelt now committed himself even more strongly to a reform agenda that included a drastic overhaul of the banking system and the stock market. The Republican Old Guard, meanwhile, was more determined than ever to run the "radical" Roosevelt out of the White House. Sensing that he might fail to win his party's nomination, and mindful of a rash promise he had made in 1904 not to run again in 1908, Roosevelt decided not to seek reelection. It was a decision that would soon come back to haunt him. Barely 50, he was too young and energetic to end his political career. And much of his reform program had yet to win Congressional approval.

THE TAFT PRESIDENCY

Roosevelt thought he had found in William Howard Taft, his secretary of war, an ideal successor. Taft had worked closely with Roosevelt on foreign and domestic policies. He had supported Roosevelt's progressive reforms and offered him shrewd advice on countless occasions. Roosevelt believed he possessed both the ideas and the skills to complete the reform Republican program.

To reach that conclusion, however, Roosevelt had to ignore some obvious differences between Taft and himself. Taft neither liked nor was particularly adept at politics. With the exception of a judgeship in an Ohio superior court, he had never held elective office. His greatest political asset was an ability to debate thorny constitutional questions. His respect for the Constitution and its separation of powers made him suspicious of the powers that Roosevelt had arrogated to the presidency. He was by nature a cautious and conservative man. As Roosevelt's anointed successor, Taft easily won the election of 1908, defeating the Democrat William Jennings Bryan with 52 percent of the vote. But his conservatism soon revealed itself in his choice of staid corporation lawyers, rather than freethinking reformers, for cabinet positions.

TAFT'S BATTLES WITH CONGRESS

Taft's troubles began when he appeared to side against progressives in two acrimonious congressional battles. The first was over tariff legislation, the second over the dictatorial powers of House Speaker "Uncle Joe" Cannon.

Progressives had long desired tariff reduction, believing that competition from foreign manufacturers would benefit American consumers and check the economic power of American manufacturers. Taft himself had raised expectations for tariff reduction when he called Congress into special session to consider a reform bill that called for a modest reduction of tariffs and an inheritance tax. The bill passed the House but was gutted in the Senate. When congressional progressives pleaded with Taft to use his power to whip conservative senators into line, he pressured the Old Guard into including a 2 percent corporate income tax in their version of the bill, but he did not insist on the tariff reductions. As a result, the Payne-Aldrich Tariff he signed into law on August 5, 1909, did nothing to encourage foreign imports. Progressive Republicans, bitterly disappointed, held Taft responsible.

They were further angered when Taft withdrew his support of their efforts to strip Speaker Cannon of his legislative powers, which (they felt) he was putting to improper use. By 1910

Republican insurgents no longer looked to Taft for leadership; instead they entered into an alliance with reform-minded congressional Democrats. This bipartisan coalition of insurgents first curbed Cannon's powers and then, over Taft's objections, diluted the pro-business nature of a railroad regulation bill. Relations between Taft and the progressive Republicans then all but collapsed in a bruising controversy over Taft's conservation policies.

THE BALLINGER-PINCHOT CONTROVERSY

Richard A. Ballinger, secretary of the interior, had aroused progressives' suspicions by reopening for private commercial use 1 million acres of land that the Roosevelt administration had previously brought under federal protection. Then, Gifford Pinchot, still head of the National Forest Service, obtained information implicating Ballinger in the sale of Alaskan coal deposits. Pinchot showed the information, including an allegation that Ballinger had personally profited from the sale, to Taft. When Taft defended Ballinger, Pinchot leaked the story to the press and publicly called on Congress to investigate the matter. Pinchot's insubordination cost him his job, but it riveted the nation's attention once again on corporate greed and government corruption. Taft's Old Guard allies controlled the investigation that followed, and Congress exonerated Ballinger. But Louis D. Brandeis, lawyer for the congressional reformers, kept the controversy alive by accusing Taft and his attorney general of tampering with information that had been sent to congressional investigators. Whatever hope Taft may have had of escaping political damage disappeared when Roosevelt, returning from an African hunting trip by way of Europe in the spring of 1910, staged a highly publicized rendezvous with Pinchot in England. In so doing, Roosevelt signaled his continuing support for his old friend Pinchot and his sharp displeasure with Taft.

ROOSEVELT'S RETURN

When Roosevelt arrived in the United States later that summer, he was still insisting that his political career was over. But his craving for the public eye and his conviction that the reform insurgency needed his leadership prompted a quick return from retirement. In September, Roosevelt embarked on a speaking tour, the high point of which was his elaboration at Osawatomie, Kansas, of his "New Nationalism," a far-reaching reform program that called for a strong federal government to stabilize the economy, protect the weak, and restore social harmony.

The 1910 congressional elections confirmed the popularity of Roosevelt's positions. Insurgent Republicans trounced conservative Republicans in primary after primary, and the embrace of reform by the Democrats brought them a majority in the House of Representatives. When Robert La Follette, who was challenging Taft for the Republican presidential nomination, seemed to suffer a nervous breakdown in February 1912, Roosevelt announced his own candidacy.

Although La Follette quickly recovered his health and resumed his campaign, there was little chance that he could beat Roosevelt in the fight for the Republican nomination. Taft, too, would have lost to Roosevelt had the decision been in the hands of rank-and-file Republicans. In the 13 states sponsoring preferential primaries, Roosevelt won nearly 75 percent of the delegates. But the party's national leadership remained in the hands of the Old Guard, and they were determined to deny Roosevelt the Republican nomination. Taft, angered by Roosevelt's behavior, refused to step aside. At the Republican convention in Chicago, Taft won renomination on the first ballot.

THE BULL MOOSE CAMPAIGN

Roosevelt had expected this outcome. The night before the convention opened, he had told a spirited assembly of 5,000 supporters that the party leaders would not succeed in derailing their movement. The next day, Roosevelt and his supporters withdrew from the convention and from the Republican Party. In August, the reformers reassembled as the new Progressive Party, nominated Roosevelt for president and the California governor Hiram W. Johnson for vice president, and hammered out the far-reaching reform platform they had long envisioned: sweeping regulation of the corporations, extensive protections for workers, a sharply graduated income tax, and woman suffrage. The new party constituted a remarkable assemblage of reformers, exhilarated by their defiance of party bosses. "I am as strong as a bull moose," Roosevelt roared as he readied for combat; his proud followers took to calling themselves "Bull Moosers."

Some of them, however, probably including Roosevelt himself, knew that their mission was futile. They had failed to enroll many of the Republican insurgents who had supported Roosevelt in the primaries but who now refused to abandon the GOP. Consequently, the Republican vote would be split between Roosevelt and Taft. And Roosevelt could not even be assured of a united progressive vote. The Democrats had nominated a powerful reform candidate of their own.

THE RISE OF WOODROW WILSON

Few would have predicted in 1908 that the distinguished president of Princeton University, Woodrow Wilson, would be the 1912 Democratic nominee for president of the United States. The son of a Presbyterian minister from Virginia, Wilson had practiced law for a short time after graduating from Princeton before settling on an academic career. Earning his doctorate in political science from Johns Hopkins in 1886, he taught history and political science at Bryn Mawr and Wesleyan (Connecticut) before returning to Princeton in 1890. He became president of Princeton in 1902, a post he held until he successfully ran for the governorship of New Jersey in 1910.

Throughout his almost 30 years in academia, however, Wilson had aspired to a career in politics. In 1885 he published *Congressional Government,* a brilliant analysis and critique of Congress. He had long admired the powerful leadership style of such British parliamentary giants as Benjamin Disraeli and William Gladstone. "I feel like a new prime minister getting ready to address his constituents," he remarked to his wife as he prepared for the Princeton presidency in 1902. The national reputation he won in that office rested less on his originality as an educator than on the leadership he displayed in transforming the humdrum College of New Jersey into a world-class university.

Wilson's public stature as a university president afforded him new opportunities to comment on political as well as educational matters. Identifying himself with the anti-Bryan wing of the Democratic Party, he attracted the attention of wealthy conservatives, who saw him as a potential presidential candidate. They convinced the bosses of the New Jersey Democratic ma-

WOODROW WILSON   Wilson entered politics after a long career in academia, where he had been a distinguished political scientist, historian, and university president. Here he strides across the Princeton campus in 1910, the last year of his college presidency.

chine to nominate Wilson for governor in 1910. Beset by growing opposition to his aggressive style of leadership from trustees and faculty members at Princeton, and eager to test his talents in a new arena, Wilson accepted the nomination and won the governorship handily. He then shocked his conservative backers by declaring his independence from the state's Democratic machine and moving New Jersey into the forefront of reform.

THE UNEXPECTED PROGRESSIVE

Wilson's Presbyterian upbringing had instilled in him a strong sense that society should be governed by God's moral law. As a young man in the 1880s, he had come to believe that the social consequences of unregulated industrialization were repugnant to Christian ethical principles. "The modern industrial organization," he wrote at the time, had "so distorted competition as to put it into the power of some to tyrannize over many, as to enable the rich and strong to combine against the poor and weak." And therefore, Wilson asked, "must not government lay aside all timid scruple and boldly make itself an agency for social reform as well as political control?" Wilson wanted reform to occur in an orderly, peaceful way; he recoiled from the labor and populist agitators who, in his eyes, showed no respect for existing social and political institutions. The more Wilson stressed the values of order, harmony, and tradition in his public speeches as president of Princeton, the more he attracted the attention of conservatives. But although Wilson's reform impulses had receded, they had not disappeared. Their presence in his thought helps to explain his emergence in 1911 and 1912 as one of the most outspoken progressives in the nation.

THE ELECTION OF 1912

At the Democratic convention of 1912, Wilson was something of a dark horse, running a distant second to House Speaker Champ Clark of Missouri. When the New York delegation gave Clark a simple majority of delegates, virtually everyone assumed that he would soon command the two-thirds majority needed to win the nomination. But Wilson's managers held onto Wilson's delegates and began chipping away at Clark's lead. On the fourth day, on the 46th ballot, Wilson finally won the nomination. The exhausted Democrats then closed ranks behind a candidate who pledged to renew the national campaign for reform.

The stage was now set for the momentous 1912 election. Given the split in Republican ranks, Democrats had their best chance in 20 years of regaining the White House. A Wilson victory, moreover, would give the country its first southern-born president in almost 50 years. Finally, whatever its outcome, the election promised to deliver a hefty vote for reform. Both Roosevelt and Wilson were running on reform platforms, and the Socialist Party candidate, Eugene V. Debs, was attracting larger crowds and generating greater enthusiasm than had been expected.

Debate among the candidates focused on the trusts. All three reform candidates agreed that corporations had acquired too much economic power. Debs argued that the only way to ensure popular control of that power was for the federal government to assume ownership of the trusts. Roosevelt called for the establishment of a powerful government that would regulate and, if necessary, curb the power of the trusts. This was the essence of his New Nationalism, the program he had been advocating since 1910.

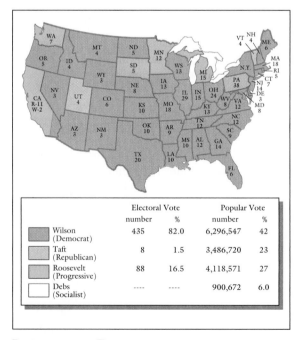

	Electoral Vote		Popular Vote	
	number	%	number	%
Wilson (Democrat)	435	82.0	6,296,547	42
Taft (Republican)	8	1.5	3,486,720	23
Roosevelt (Progressive)	88	16.5	4,118,571	27
Debs (Socialist)	----	----	900,672	6.0

PRESIDENTIAL ELECTION, 1912

Wilson, however, was too suspicious of centralized government to countenance such a program. Rather than regulate the trusts, he wanted to break them up. He wanted to reverse the tendency toward economic concentration and thus restore opportunity to the people. This philosophy, which Wilson labeled the "New Freedom," called for a temporary concentration of governmental power in order to dismantle the trusts. But once that was accomplished, Wilson promised, the government would relinquish its power.

Wilson won the November election with 42 percent of the popular vote to Roosevelt's 27 percent and Taft's 23 percent; Debs made a strong showing with 6 percent, the largest in his party's history. The three candidates who had pledged themselves to sweeping reform programs—Wilson, Roosevelt, and Debs—together won a remarkable 75 percent of the vote.

THE WILSON PRESIDENCY

The new president immediately put into practice the parliamentary-style leadership he had long admired. He assembled a cabinet of talented men who could be counted on for wise counsel, loyalty, and influence over vital Democratic constituencies. He cultivated a public image of himself as a president firmly in charge of his party and as a faithful tribune of the people.

TARIFF REFORM AND A PROGRESSIVE INCOME TAX

Like his predecessor, Wilson first turned his attention to tariff reform. Immediately after his inauguration, he called Congress into special session to consider the matter. The House passed a tariff reduction bill within a month. But the bill ran into trouble in the Senate, chiefly because of the pressure that protectionist lobbyists applied to key Democratic senators. Wilson outflanked them by appealing directly to the American people to destroy the influence of private interests on lawmakers. Wilson's plea to the public, together with an ensuing investigation of senator-lobbyist relations, humbled the Senate into complying with the president's wishes.

The resulting Underwood-Simmons Tariff of 1913 achieved the long-sought progressive aim of significantly reducing tariff barriers (from approximately 40 to 25 percent). Then, partly as a matter of expediency (new funds had to be found to make up for revenue lost to tariff reductions), another progressive ambition was achieved with passage of a law calling for an income tax. The Sixteenth Amendment to the Constitution, ratified by the states in 1913, had already given the government the right to impose an income tax; the income tax law passed by Congress made good on the progressive pledge to reduce the power and privileges of wealthy Americans by requiring them to pay taxes on a greater *percentage* of their income than the poor.

THE FEDERAL RESERVE ACT

Wilson continued to demonstrate his leadership by keeping Congress in session through the summer to consider various plans to overhaul the nation's financial system. Virtually everyone in both parties agreed on the need for greater federal regulation of banks and currency, but there were sharp differences over how to proceed. The banking interests and their congressional supporters wanted the government to give the authority to regulate credit and currency flows either to a single bank or to several regional banks. Progressives opposed the vesting of so much financial power in private hands and insisted that any reformed financial system must be publicly controlled. Wilson worked out a compromise plan that included both private and public controls and marshaled the votes to push it through both the House and the Senate. By the end of 1913 Wilson had signed the Federal Reserve Act, the most important law passed in his first administration.

The Federal Reserve Act established 12 regional banks, each controlled by the private banks in its region. Every private bank in the country was required to deposit an average of 6 percent of its assets in its regional Federal Reserve bank. The reserve would be used to make loans to member banks and to issue paper currency (Federal Reserve notes) to facilitate financial transactions. The regional banks were also instructed to use their funds to shore up member banks in distress and to respond to sudden changes in credit demands by easing or tightening the flow of credit. A Federal Reserve Board appointed by the president and responsible to the public rather than to private bankers would set policy and oversee activities within the 12 reserve banks.

The Federal Reserve system did a great deal to strengthen the nation's financial structure and was in most respects an impressive political achievement for Wilson. In its final form, however, it revealed that Wilson was retreating from his New Freedom pledge. The Federal Reserve Board was a less powerful and less centralized federal authority than a national bank would have been, but it nevertheless represented a substantial increase in government control of banking. Moreover, the bill authorizing the system made no attempt to break up private financial institutions that had grown too powerful. Because it sought to work with large banks rather than to break them up, the Federal Reserve system seemed more consonant with the principles of Roosevelt's New Nationalism than with those of Wilson's New Freedom.

FROM THE NEW FREEDOM TO THE NEW NATIONALISM

Wilson's failure to mount a vigorous antitrust campaign confirmed his drift toward the New Nationalism. For example, in 1914 Wilson swung his full support behind the Federal Trade Commission Act, which created a government agency by that name to regulate business practices. Because the act gave the Federal Trade Commission (FTC) wide powers to collect information on corporate pricing policies and on cooperation and competition among businesses, the FTC might have been used to prosecute trusts for "unfair trade practices." But the Senate stripped the FTC Act's companion legislation, the Clayton Antitrust Act, of virtually all provisions that would have allowed vigorous government prosecution of the trusts. Wilson supported this weakening of the Clayton Act, having decided that the breakup of large-scale industry was no longer practical or preferable. The purpose of the FTC, in Wilson's eyes, was to help businesses, large and small, to regulate themselves in ways that contributed to national well-being.

But would Wilson use government merely to assist businessmen and bankers to regulate themselves? Or would he use government to balance the claims of industry and finance against the claims of labor, farmers, and other disadvantaged groups?

In 1914 and 1915 Wilson favored the first approach: He intended the FTC to become as much a friend to business as a policeman. At this time, Wilson usually refused to use government powers to aid organized groups of workers and farmers. Nor did Wilson, at this time, view with any greater sympathy the campaign for African Americans' political equality. He

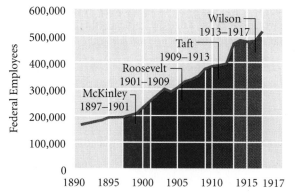

GROWTH IN FEDERAL EMPLOYEES, 1891–1917

Source: Reprinted by permission from *The Federal Government Service,* ed. W. S. Sayre (Englewood Cliffs, N.J.: Prentice-Hall, 1965), p. 41, The American Assembly.

supported efforts by white southerners in his cabinet to segregate their government departments, and he ignored pleas from the NAACP to involve the federal government in a campaign against lynching.

In late 1915, however, Wilson changed his tune, in part because he feared losing his reelection in 1916. The Bull Moosers of 1912 were retreating back to the Republican Party. To halt the progressives' rapprochement with the GOP, he made a stunning bid for their support. In January 1916 he nominated Louis Brandeis to the Supreme Court. Not only was Brandeis one of the country's most respected progressives, he was also the first Jew nominated to serve on the country's highest court. Congressional conservatives did everything they could to block the confirmation of a man they regarded as dangerously radical. But Wilson, as usual, was better organized, and by June his forces in the Senate had emerged victorious.

Wilson followed up this victory by pushing through Congress the first federal workmen's compensation law (the Kern-McGillicuddy Act, which covered federal employees), the first federal law outlawing child labor (the Keating-Owen Act), and the first federal law guaranteeing workers an eight-hour day (the Adamson Act, which covered the nation's 400,000 railway workers). The number of Americans affected by these acts was in fact rather small; nevertheless, Wilson had reoriented the Democratic Party to a New Nationalism that cared as much about the interests of the powerless as the interests of the powerful.

Trade unionists flocked to Wilson, as did most of the prominent progressives who had followed the Bull Moose in 1912. Meanwhile, Wilson had appealed to the supporters of William Jennings Bryan by supporting legislation that made large amounts of federal credit available to farmers in need. He had put together a reform coalition capable of winning a majority at the polls. In the process, he had transformed the Democratic Party. From 1916 on, the Democrats, rather than the Republicans, became the chief guardians of the American reform tradition.

That Wilson did so is a sign of the strength of the reform and radical forces in American society. By 1916 the ranks of middle-class progressives had grown broad and deep. Working-class protest had also accelerated in scope and intensity. In Lawrence, Massachusetts, in 1912, and in Paterson, New Jersey, in 1913, for example, the IWW organized strikes of textile workers that drew national attention, as did the 1914 strike by Colorado mine workers that ended with the infamous Ludlow massacre (see Chapter 20). These protests reflected the mobilization of those working-class constituencies—immigrants, women, the unskilled—long considered inconsequential both to American labor and party politics. Assisted by radicals, these groups had begun to fashion a more inclusive and politically contentious labor movement.

CHRONOLOGY

1889	Hull House established
1890–1904	All ex-Confederate states pass laws designed to disfranchise black voters • Virtually all states adopt the Australian (secret) ballot
1900	La Follette elected governor of Wisconsin • City commission plan introduced in Galveston, Texas
1901–1914	More than 1,000 African Americans lynched
1901	Johnson elected reform mayor of Cleveland • McKinley assassinated; Roosevelt becomes president
1902	Initiative and referendum introduced in Oregon • Roosevelt sides with workers in coal strike
1903	Federal court dissolves Northern Securities Company
1904	Roosevelt defeats Parker for presidency
1905	National Forest Service established
1906	La Follette elected to U.S. Senate • Congress passes Hepburn Act • Upton Sinclair publishes *The Jungle* • Congress passes Pure Food and Drug Act and Meat Inspection Act
1907	Reformer Hughes elected New York governor • Financial panic shakes economy
1908	Taft defeats Bryan for presidency
1909	Congress passes Payne-Aldrich tariff bill
1910	Ballinger-Pinchot controversy • NAACP founded • Wilson elected governor of New Jersey
1911	National Urban League founded • City manager plan introduced in Sumter, South Carolina • Wisconsin Industrial Commission established
1912	Roosevelt forms Progressive Party • Wilson defeats Roosevelt, Taft, and Debs for presidency
1913	Sixteenth and Seventeenth Amendments ratified • Congress passes Underwood-Simmons Tariff • Congress establishes Federal Reserve system
1914	Congress establishes Federal Trade Commission • Congress passes Clayton Antitrust Act
1916	Louis Brandeis appointed to Supreme Court • Kern-McGillicuddy Act, Keating-Owen Act, and Adamson Act passed • National Park Service formed • National Women's Party founded
1919	Eighteenth Amendment ratified
1920	Nineteenth Amendment ratified

CONCLUSION

By 1916, the progressives had accomplished a great deal. They exposed and curbed some of the worst abuses of the American political system. They enfranchised women and took steps to protect the environment. They broke the hold of laissez-faire economic policies on national politics and replaced it with the idea of a strong federal government committed to economic regulation and social justice. They enlarged the executive branch by establishing new commissions and agencies charged with administering government policies.

The progressives, in short, had presided over the emergence of a new national state, one in which power increasingly flowed away from municipalities and states and toward the federal government. There was a compelling logic to this reorientation: A national government stood a better chance of solving the problems of economic inequality, mismanagement of natural resources, and consumer fraud than did local and state governments.

The promise of effective remedies, however, brought new dangers. In particular, the new national state was giving rise to a bureaucratic elite whose power rested on federal authority rather than private wealth or political machines. The university-educated experts who staffed the new federal agencies, progressives argued, would bring to the political process the very qualities that party politicians allegedly lacked: knowledge, dedication, and honesty. But many of these new public servants were not entirely disinterested and unassuming. Some had close ties to the corporations and businesses that their agencies were expected to regulate. Others allowed their prejudices against women, immigrants, and minorities to shape social policy. Still others believed that "the people" could not be trusted to evaluate the government's work intelligently. For these reasons, the progressive state did not always enhance democracy or secure the people's sovereignty.

22

BECOMING A WORLD POWER, 1898–1917

THE UNITED STATES LOOKS ABROAD

THE SPANISH-AMERICAN WAR

THE UNITED STATES BECOMES A WORLD POWER

THEODORE ROOSEVELT, GEOPOLITICIAN

WILLIAM HOWARD TAFT, DOLLAR DIPLOMAT

WOODROW WILSON, STRUGGLING IDEALIST

For much of the 19th century, most Americans were preoccupied by continental expansion. Elections rarely turned on international events, and presidents rarely made their reputations as statesmen in the world arena. The diplomatic corps was small and inexperienced. The government projected its limited military power westward and possessed virtually no capacity or desire for involvement overseas.

The nation's rapid industrial growth in the late 19th century forced a turn away from such continentalism. Technological advances, especially the laying of transoceanic cables and the introduction of steamship travel, diminished America's physical isolation. The babel of languages one could hear in American cities testified to how much the Old World had penetrated the New. Then, too, Americans watched anxiously as England, Germany, Russia, Japan, and other industrial powers intensified their competition for overseas markets and colonies, and some believed America also needed to enter this contest.

A war with Spain in 1898 gave the United States an opportunity to upgrade its military and acquire colonies and influence in the Western Hemisphere and Asia. Under Presidents William McKinley and Theodore Roosevelt, the United States pursued these initiatives, with impressive results. But subjugating the peoples of Cuba, Puerto Rico, and the Philippines did not sit well with all Americans. It seemed as though the United States was becoming the kind of nation that many Americans had long despised—one that valued power more than liberty. Exercising imperial power did not trouble Roosevelt, who wanted to create an international system in which a handful of industrial nations pursued their global economic interests, dominated world trade, and kept the world at peace. It did concern Woodrow Wilson, however, who sought to devise a policy toward postrevolutionary Mexico that restrained American might and respected Mexican desires for liberty.

THE UNITED STATES LOOKS ABROAD

By the late 19th century, sizable numbers of Americans had become interested in extending their country's influence abroad. The most important groups were Protestant missionaries, businessmen, and imperialists.

PROTESTANT MISSIONARIES

Protestant missionaries were among the most active promoters of American interests abroad. Integration of the world economy made evangelical Protestants more conscious of the diversity of the world's peoples. Overseas missionary activity grew quickly between 1870 and 1900, most of it directed toward China. Convinced of the superiority of the Anglo-Saxon race, Protestant missionaries considered it their Christian duty to teach the Gospel to the "ignorant" Asian masses and save their souls. Missionaries also believed that their efforts would free those masses from their racial destiny, enabling them to become "civilized."

BUSINESSMEN

For different reasons, industrialists, traders, and investors also began to look overseas, sensing that they could make fortunes in foreign lands. Exports of American manufactured goods rose substantially after 1880. By 1914 American foreign investment equaled 7 percent of the nation's gross national product. Companies such as Kodak Camera, Singer Sewing Machine, Standard Oil, American Tobacco, and International Harvester had become multinational corporations with overseas branch offices.

Some industrialists became entranced by the prospect of clothing, feeding, and housing the 400 million people of China. James B. Duke, who headed American Tobacco, was selling 1 billion cigarettes a year in East Asian markets. Looking for ways to fill empty boxcars heading west from Minnesota to Tacoma, Washington, the railroad tycoon James J. Hill imagined stuffing them with wheat and steel destined for China and Japan. Although export trade with East Asia during this period never fulfilled the expectations of Hill and other industrialists, their talk about the "wealth of the Orient" convinced politicians that this part of the world was important to national well-being.

Events of the 1890s only intensified the appeal of foreign markets. First, the 1890 U.S. census announced that the frontier had disappeared; America had completed the task of westward expansion. Then, in 1893 a young historian named Frederick Jackson Turner published an essay, "The Significance of the Frontier in American History," that articulated what many Americans feared: that the frontier had been essential to the growth of the economy and to the cultivation of democracy. It was the wilderness, Turner argued, that had transformed the Europeans who settled the New World into Americans. They shed their European clothes, tools, social customs, and political beliefs, and acquired distinctively "American" characteristics—rugged individualism, egalitarianism, and a democratic faith. How, Turner wondered, could the nation continue to prosper now that the frontier had gone?

In recent years, historians of the American West have criticized Turner's "frontier thesis." They have argued that the very idea of the frontier as uninhabited wilderness overlooked the tens of thousands of Indians who occupied the region and that much else of what Americans believe about the West is based more on myth than on reality.

Leading U.S. Exports, 1875 and 1915

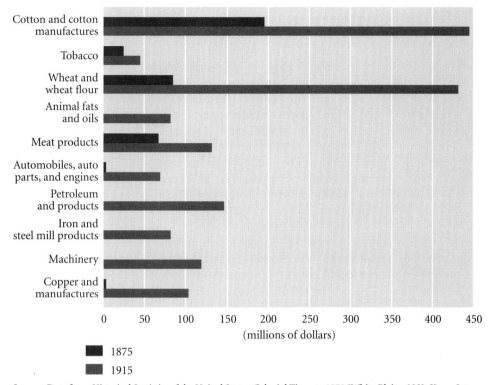

(millions of dollars)

■ 1875
■ 1915

Source: Data from *Historical Statistics of the United States, Colonial Times to 1970* (White Plains, N.Y.: Kraus International, 1989).

Even though these points are valid, they would have meant little to Americans living in Turner's time. For them, as for Turner, concern about the disappearing frontier expressed a fear that the increasingly urbanized and industrialized nation had lost its way. Turner's essay appeared just as the country was entering the deepest, longest, and most conflict-ridden depression in its history (see Chapter 19). What could the republic do to regain its economic prosperity and political stability? Where would it find its new frontiers? One answer to these questions focused on the pursuit of overseas expansion.

IMPERIALISTS

Eager to assist in the drive for overseas economic expansion was a group of politicians, intellectuals, and military strategists who viewed such expansion as a key ingredient in the pursuit of world power. They believed that the United States should build a strong navy, solidify a sphere of influence in the Caribbean, and extend markets into Asia. Their desire to control ports and territories beyond the continental borders of their own country made them imperialists. Many of them were also Social Darwinists, who believed that America's destiny required that it prove itself supreme in international affairs.

Perhaps the most influential imperialist was Admiral Alfred Thayer Mahan. In the 1880s Mahan had become convinced that all the world's great empires, beginning with Rome, had relied on their capacity to control the seas. In an influential book, *The Influence of Sea Power upon History, 1660–1783* (1890), Mahan called for the construction of a first-class navy with enough ships and firepower to make its presence felt everywhere in the world. To be effective, that global fleet would require a canal across Central America. It would also require a string of far-flung service bases. Mahan wanted the U.S. government to take possession of Hawaii and other strategically located Pacific islands with superior harbor facilities.

Presidents William McKinley and Theodore Roosevelt would eventually make almost the whole of Mahan's vision a reality. But in the early 1890s Mahan doubted that Americans would accept the responsibility and costs of empire. Many Americans still insisted that the United States should not aspire to world power by acquiring overseas bases and colonizing foreign peoples.

Mahan underestimated the government's alarm over the scramble of Europeans to extend their imperial control. Every administration from the 1880s on committed itself to a "big navy" policy. Already in 1878, the United States had secured rights to Pago Pago, a superb deep-water harbor in Samoa (a collection of islands in the southwest Pacific inhabited by Polynesians), and in 1885 it had leased Pearl Harbor from the Hawaiians. Both harbors were expected to serve as fueling stations for the growing U.S. fleet.

These attempts to project U.S. power overseas had already deepened the government's involvement in the affairs of distant lands. In 1889, the United States established a protectorate over part of Samoa. In the early 1890s, President Grover Cleveland's administration was increasingly drawn into Hawaiian affairs, as tensions between American sugar plantation owners and native Hawaiians upset the islands' economic and political stability. In 1891 the plantation owners succeeded in deposing the Hawaiian king and putting into power Queen Liliuokalani. But when Liliuokalani strove to establish her independence, the planters, assisted by U.S. sailors, overthrew her too. Cleveland declared Hawaii a protectorate in 1893, but he resisted the imperialists in Congress who wanted to annex the islands.

THE U.S. NAVY, 1890–1914: EXPENDITURES AND BATTLESHIP SIZE

FISCAL YEAR	TOTAL FEDERAL EXPENDITURES	NAVAL EXPENDITURES	NAVAL EXPENDITURES AS PERCENT OF TOTAL FEDERAL EXPENDITURES	SIZE OF BATTLESHIPS (AVERAGE TONS DISPLACED)
1890	$318,040,711	$22,006,206	6.9%	11,000
1900	520,860,847	55,953,078	10.7	12,000
1901	524,616,925	60,506,978	11.5	16,000
1905	657,278,914	117,550,308	20.7	16,000
1909	693,743,885	115,546,011	16.7	27,000 (1910)
1914	735,081,431	139,682,186	19.0	32,000

Sources: (for expenditures) E. B. Potter, *Sea Power: A Naval History* (Annapolis: Naval Institute Press, 1982), p. 187; (for size of ships) Harold Sprout, *Toward a New Order of Sea Power* (New York: Greenwood Press, 1976), p. 52.

By this time, imperialist sentiment in Congress and throughout the nation was being fueled by "jingoism." Jingoists were nationalists who thought that a swaggering foreign policy and a willingness to go to war would enhance their nation's glory. This predatory brand of nationalism emerged not only in the United States, but in Britain, France, Germany, and Japan as well. The anti-imperialist editor of *The Nation*, E. L. Godkin, exclaimed in 1894: "The number of men and officials of this country who are now mad to fight somebody is appalling." Spain's behavior in Cuba in the 1890s gave those men and officials the war they sought.

THE SPANISH-AMERICAN WAR

Relations between the Cubans and their Spanish rulers had long been deteriorating. A revolt in 1868 had taken the Spanish 10 years to subdue. In 1895 the Cubans staged another revolt. The fighting was brutal. Cuban forces destroyed large areas of the island to make it uninhabitable by the Spanish. The Spanish army, led by General Valeriano Weyler, responded in kind, forcing large numbers of Cubans into concentration camps. Denied adequate food, shelter, and sanitation, an estimated 200,000 Cubans died of starvation and disease.

Such tactics inflamed American opinion. Many Americans sympathized with the Cubans. Americans were kept well informed about the atrocities by accounts in the *New York Journal*, owned by William Randolph Hearst, and the *New York World*, owned by Joseph Pulitzer. Hearst and Pulitzer were transforming newspaper publishing in much the same way that other publishers had revolutionized the magazine business (see Chapter 21). To boost circulation they sought out the most sensational and shocking stories and then described them in lurid detail. They were accused of engaging in "yellow journalism"—embellishing stories with titillating details when the true reports did not seem dramatic enough.

The sensationalism of the yellow press and its frequently jingoistic accounts were not sufficient to bring about American intervention in Cuba, however. In the final days of his administration, President Cleveland resisted mounting pressure to intervene. William McKinley, who succeeded him in 1897, harshly denounced the Spanish, with the aim of forcing Spain into concessions that would satisfy the Cuban rebels and bring an end to the conflict. Initially, this strategy seemed to be working: Spain relieved "Butcher" Weyler of his command, stopped incarcerating Cubans in concentration camps, and granted Cuba limited autonomy. But the Spaniards who lived on the island refused to be ruled by a Cuban government, and the Cuban rebels continued to demand full independence. Late in 1897, when riots broke out in Havana, McKinley ordered the battleship *Maine* into Havana harbor to protect U.S. citizens and their property. Two unexpected events then set off a war.

The first was the February 9, 1898, publication in Hearst's *New York Journal* of a letter stolen from Depuy de Lôme, the Spanish minister to Washington, in which he described McKinley as "a cheap politician" and a "bidder for the admiration of the crowd." The de Lôme letter also implied that the Spanish were not serious about resolving the Cuban crisis through negotiation and reform. The news embarrassed Spanish officials and outraged U.S. public opinion. Then, only six days later, the *Maine* exploded in Havana harbor, killing 260 American sailors. Although subsequent investigations revealed that the most probable cause of the explosion was a malfunctioning boiler, Americans were certain that it had been the work of Spanish agents. "Remember the Maine!" screamed the headlines in the yellow press. On March 8, Congress responded to the clamor for war by authorizing $50 million to mobilize U.S. forces. In the meantime, McKinley

"**REMEMBER THE *MAINE!*"**   The explosion of the battleship *Maine* in Havana harbor on February 16, 1898, killed 260 American sailors and helped to drive the United States into war with Spain.

notified Spain of his conditions for avoiding war: Spain would pay an indemnity for the *Maine*, abandon its concentration camps, end the fighting with the rebels, and commit itself to Cuban independence. On April 9, Spain accepted all the demands but the last. Nevertheless, on April 11, McKinley asked Congress for authority to go to war. Three days later Congress approved a war resolution, which included a declaration (spelled out in the Teller Amendment) that the United States would not use the war as an opportunity to acquire territory in Cuba. On April 24, Spain responded with a formal declaration of war against the United States.

"A SPLENDID LITTLE WAR"

Secretary of State John Hay called the fight with Spain "a splendid little war." Begun in April, it ended in August. More than 1 million men volunteered to fight, while fewer than 500 were killed or wounded in combat. The American victory over Spain was complete, not just in Cuba but in the neighboring island of Puerto Rico and in the Philippines, Spain's strategic possession in the Pacific.

Actually, the war was more complicated than it seemed. The main reason for the easy victory was U.S. naval superiority. In the war's first major battle, a naval engagement in Manila harbor in the Philippines on May 1, a U.S. fleet commanded by Commodore George Dewey destroyed an entire Spanish fleet. On land, the story was different. On the eve of war the U.S. Army consisted of only 26,000 troops. A force of 80,000 Spanish regulars awaited them in Cuba. Congress immediately increased the Army to 62,000 and called for an additional 125,000 volunteers. The response to this call was astounding, but outfitting, training, and transporting the new recruits overwhelmed the Army's capacities. Its standard-issue, blue flannel uniforms proved too heavy for fighting in Cuba. Most of the volunteers had to make

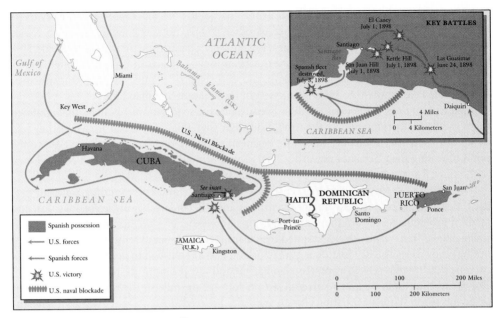

SPANISH-AMERICAN WAR IN CUBA, 1898

do with ancient Civil War rifles that still used black, rather than smokeless, powder. Moreover, the Army was unprepared for the effects of malaria and other tropical diseases.

That the Cuban revolutionaries were predominantly black also came as a shock to the U.S. forces. In their attempts to arouse support for the Cuban cause, U.S. newspapers had portrayed the Cuban rebels as fundamentally similar to white Americans, with an "Anglo-Saxon tenacity of purpose." The Spanish oppressors, by contrast, were depicted as dark complexioned and as possessing the characteristics of their "dark race": barbarism, cruelty, and indolence. The U.S. troops' first encounters with Cuban and Spanish forces dispelled these myths. Their Cuban allies appeared poorly outfitted, rough in their manners, and primarily black-skinned. The Spanish soldiers appeared well-disciplined, tough in battle, and light-complexioned.

The Cuban rebels were actually skilled guerrilla fighters, but racial prejudice prevented most U.S. soldiers and reporters from crediting their military accomplishments. Instead, they judged the Cubans harshly—as primitive, savage, and incapable of self-control or self-government. White U.S. troops preferred not to fight alongside the Cubans; increasingly, they refused to co-ordinate strategy with them.

At first, the U.S. Army's ineptitude and its racial misconceptions did little to diminish the soldiers' hunger for a good fight. No one was more eager for battle than Theodore Roosevelt who, along with Colonel Leonard Wood, led a volunteer cavalry unit comprised of Ivy League gentlemen, western cowboys, sheriffs, prospectors, Indians, and small numbers of Hispanics and ethnic European Americans. Roosevelt's "Rough Riders," as the unit came to be known, landed with the invasion force and played an active role in the three battles fought in the hills surrounding Santiago. Their most famous action was a furious charge up Kettle Hill into the teeth of Spanish defenses. Roosevelt's bravery was stunning, though his judgment was faulty.

Nearly 100 men were killed or wounded in the charge. Reports of Roosevelt's bravery over-shadowed the equally brave performance of other troops, notably the 9th and 10th Negro Cavalries, which played a pivotal role in clearing away Spanish fortifications on Kettle Hill. One Rough Rider commented: "If it had not been for the Negro cavalry, the Rough Riders would have been exterminated." The 24th and 25th Negro Infantry Regiments performed equally vital tasks in the U.S. Army's conquest of the adjacent San Juan Hill.

African American soldiers risked their lives despite the segregationist policies that confined them to all-black regiments. At the time, Roosevelt gave them full credit for what they had done. But soon after returning home, he began minimizing their contributions, even to the point of calling their behavior cowardly. Like most white American officers and enlisted men of the time, Roosevelt had difficulty believing that blacks could fight well.

The taking of Kettle Hill, San Juan Hill, and other high ground surrounding Santiago gave the U.S. forces a substantial advantage over the Spanish defenders. Nevertheless, logistical and medical problems nearly did them in. The troops were short of food, ammunition, and med-ical facilities. Their ranks were devastated by malaria, typhoid, and dysentery; more than 5,000 soldiers died from disease. Fortunately, the Spanish had lost the will to fight. On July 3 Spain's Atlantic fleet tried to retreat from Santiago harbor and was promptly destroyed by a U.S. fleet. The Spanish army in Santiago surrendered on July 16; on July 18 the Spanish government asked for peace. While negotiations for an armistice proceeded, U.S. forces overran the neigh-boring island of Puerto Rico. On August 12 the U.S. and Spanish governments agreed to an armistice. But before the news could reach the Philippines, the United States had captured Manila and had taken prisoner 13,000 Spanish soldiers.

The armistice required Spain to relinquish its claim to Cuba, cede Puerto Rico and the Pacific island of Guam to the United States, and tolerate the American occupation of Manila until a peace conference could be convened in Paris on October 1, 1898. At that conference, American diplomats startled their Spanish counterparts by demanding that Spain also cede the Philippines to the United States. After two months of stalling, the Spanish government agreed to relinquish its coveted Pacific colony for $20 million, and the transaction was sealed by the Treaty of Paris on December 10, 1898.

THE UNITED STATES BECOMES A WORLD POWER

America's initial war aim had been to oust the Spanish from Cuba—an aim supported by both imperialists and anti-imperialists, but for different reasons. Imperialists hoped to incor-porate Cuba into a new American empire; anti-imperialists hoped to see the Cubans gain their independence. But only the imperialists condoned the U.S. acquisition of Puerto Rico, Guam, and particularly the Philippines. Soon after the war began, President McKinley had cast his lot with the imperialists. First, he annexed Hawaii, giving the United States permanent control of Pearl Harbor. Then, he set his sights on establishing a U.S. naval base at Manila. Never before had the United States sought such a large military presence outside the Western Hemisphere.

In a departure of equal importance, McKinley announced his intent to administer much of this newly acquired territory as U.S. colonies. Virtually all the territory previously acquired by the United States had been settled by Americans, who had eventually petitioned for statehood and been admitted to the Union with the same rights as existing states. In the case of these new territories, however, only Hawaii would be allowed to follow a traditional path toward

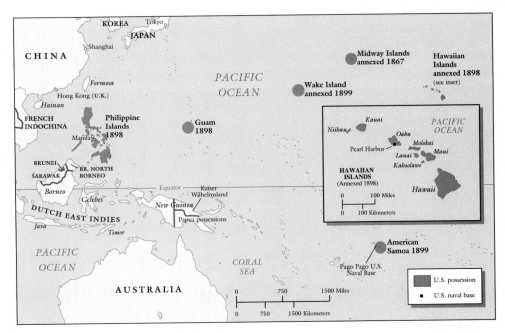

AMERICAN SOUTH PACIFIC EMPIRE, 1900

statehood. There, the powerful American sugar plantation owners prevailed on Congress to pass an act in 1900 extending U.S. citizenship to all Hawaiian citizens and putting Hawaii on the road to statehood. But no influential group of Americans resided in the Philippines. The decision to make the country an American colony was taken mainly to prevent other powers, such as Japan and Germany, from gaining a foothold somewhere in the 400-island archipelago and launching attacks on the American naval base in Manila.

The McKinley administration might have taken a different course. It might have negotiated a deal with Emilio Aguinaldo, the leader of the anticolonial movement, that would have given the Philippines independence in exchange for a U.S. naval base at Manila. An American fleet stationed there would have been able to protect both American interests and the fledgling Philippine nation from predatory assaults by Japan, Germany, or Britain. Alternatively, the United States might have annexed the Philippines outright and offered Filipinos U.S. citizenship as the first step toward statehood. But McKinley believed that self-government was beyond the capacity of the "inferior" Filipino people. The United States would undertake a solemn mission to "civilize" the Filipinos and thereby prepare them for independence. But until that mission was complete, the Philippines would be ruled by American governors appointed by the president.

THE DEBATE OVER THE TREATY OF PARIS

The proposed acquisition of the Philippines aroused opposition both in the United States and in the Philippines. The Anti-Imperialist League enlisted the support of several elder statesmen in McKinley's own party, as well as the former Democratic President Grover Cleveland, the industrialist Andrew Carnegie, and the labor leader Samuel Gompers. William Jennings Bryan,

KETTLE HILL IN BLACK AND WHITE

Theodore Roosevelt believed that the "Rough Rider" regiment that he commanded in the Spanish-American War (pictured below) was a melting pot of southwesterners, Ivy Leaguers, and Indians, with a smattering of Hispanics and ethnic European Americans. Combat, he further believed, would forge these many groups into one, as war had always done in the American past. African Americans and Asian immigrants were the two groups conspicuously absent from this mix.

meanwhile, marshaled a vigorous anti-imperialist protest among Democrats in the South and West. Some anti-imperialists believed that the subjugation of the Filipinos would violate the nation's most precious principle: the right of all people to independence and self-government.

Other anti-imperialists were motivated more by self-interest than by democratic ideals. U.S. sugar producers, for example, feared competition from Filipino producers. Trade unionists worried that poor Filipinos would flood the U.S. labor market and depress wage rates. Some businessmen warned that the costs of maintaining an imperial outpost would exceed

Yet the success of Roosevelt's charge up Kettle Hill and San Juan Hill had depended on the assistance of four regiments of regular Army troops, the 9th and 10th Cavalry and the 24th and 25th Infantry, which happened to be black. Some members of the 10th Cavalry who took part in the battle are pictured below. The fury of the fighting damaged the cohesion of the different regiments to the extent that by the time the troops reached the San Juan summit, they were all intermixed: Ivy Leaguers and southwesterners, Hispanics and European immigrants, even blacks and whites, all fighting side by side. Combat had brought blacks into the great American melting pot, a phenomenon that Roosevelt celebrated at the time by praising the black troops.

But Roosevelt did not truly believe that blacks were the equals of whites, or that they could be absorbed into the American nation. So, over time, he downplayed the role of black troops and questioned their ability to fight. The heroic role of black soldiers not only disappeared from Roosevelt's own memory, but from most paintings and other commemorations of the great charge.

any economic benefits that the colony might produce. Still other anti-imperialists feared the contaminating effects of contact with "inferior" Asian races.

The anti-imperialists almost dealt McKinley and his fellow imperialists a defeat in the U.S. Senate, where the Treaty of Paris had to be ratified. On February 6, 1899, the Senate voted 57 to 27 in favor of the treaty, only one vote beyond the minimum two-thirds majority required for ratification. Two last-minute developments may have brought victory. First, William Jennings Bryan, in the days just before the vote, abandoned his opposition and announced his support for the treaty. Second, on the eve of the vote, Filipinos rose in revolt against the U.S. army of occupation. With another war looming and the lives of American soldiers imperiled, a few senators who had been reluctant to vote for the treaty may have felt obligated to support the president.

THE AMERICAN-FILIPINO WAR

The acquisition of the Philippines immediately embroiled the United States in a long, brutal war to subdue the Filipino rebels. In four years of fighting, more than 120,000 American soldiers served in the Philippines and more than 4,200 of them died. The war brought Americans face-to-face with an unpleasant truth: that American actions in the Philippines were virtually indistinguishable from Spain's actions in Cuba. Like Spain, the United States refused to acknowledge a people's aspiration for self-rule. Like "Butcher" Weyler, American generals permitted their soldiers to use savage tactics. Whole communities suspected of harboring guerrillas were driven into concentration camps, while their houses, farms, and livestock were destroyed. American soldiers executed so many Filipino rebels that the ratio of Filipino dead to wounded reached 15 to 1. One New York infantryman wrote home that his unit had killed 1,000 Filipinos in retaliation for the murder of a single American soldier. Estimates of total Filipino deaths from gunfire, starvation, and disease range from 50,000 to 200,000.

The United States finally gained the upper hand after General Arthur MacArthur (father of Douglas) was appointed commander of the islands in 1900. MacArthur did not lessen the war's ferocity, but he understood that it could not be won by guns alone. He offered amnesty to Filipino guerrillas who agreed to surrender, and he cultivated close relations with the islands' wealthy elites. McKinley supported this effort to build a Filipino constituency sympathetic to the U.S. presence. To that end, he sent William Howard Taft to the islands in 1900 to establish a civilian government. In 1901 Taft became the colony's first "governor-general." He transferred many governmental functions to Filipino control and sponsored a vigorous program of public works (roads, bridges, schools) that would give the Philippines the infrastructure necessary for economic development and political independence. By 1902 this dual strategy of ruthless war against those who had taken up arms and concessions to those who were willing to live under benevolent American rule had crushed the revolt, though sporadic fighting continued until 1913.

CONTROLLING CUBA AND PUERTO RICO

Helping the Cubans achieve independence had been one of the major rationalizations for the war against Spain. But in 1900, when General Leonard Wood, now commander of American forces in Cuba, authorized a constitutional convention to write the laws for a Cuban republic, the McKinley administration made clear it would not easily relinquish control of the island. At McKinley's urging, the U.S. Congress attached to a 1901 army appropriations bill the Platt Amendment delineating three conditions for Cuban independence. First, Cuba would not be permitted to make treaties with foreign powers. Second, the United States would have broad authority to intervene in Cuban political and economic affairs. Third, Cuba would sell or lease land to the United States for naval stations. The delegates to Cuba's constitutional convention were so outraged by these conditions that they refused even to vote on them. But the dependence of Cuba's vital sugar industry on the U.S. market and the continuing presence of a U.S. army on Cuban soil rendered resistance futile. In 1901, by a vote of 15 to 11, the delegates reluctantly wrote the Platt conditions into their constitution.

Cuba's status differed little from that of the Philippines. Both were colonies of the United States. In the case of Cuba, economic dependence closely followed political subjugation. Between 1898 and 1914, American trade with Cuba increased more than tenfold, while investments more than quadrupled. The United States intervened in Cuban political affairs a total of five times between 1906 and 1921 to protect its economic interests and those of the indigenous ruling class with whom it had become closely allied. The economic, political, and military control that the United States imposed on Cuba would fuel anti-American sentiment there for years to come.

Puerto Rico received somewhat different treatment. The United States did not think independence appropriate. Nor did it follow its Cuban strategy by granting Puerto Rico nominal independence under informal economic and political controls. Instead, it annexed the island outright with the Foraker Act (1900). This act contained no provision for making the inhabitants citizens of the United States. Puerto Rico was designated an "unincorporated" territory, which meant that Congress would dictate the island's government and specify the rights of its inhabitants. Puerto Ricans were allowed no role in designing their government, nor was their consent requested. With the Foraker Act, Congress had, in effect, invented a new, imperial mechanism for ensuring sovereignty over lands deemed vital to U.S. economic and military security. The U.S. Supreme Court upheld the constitutionality of this mechanism in a series of historic decisions, known as the Insular Cases, in the years from 1901 to 1904.

In some respects Puerto Rico fared better than "independent" Cuba. Puerto Ricans were granted U.S. citizenship in 1917 and won the right to elect their own governor in 1947. Still, Puerto Ricans enjoyed fewer political rights than Americans in the 48 states. Moreover, throughout the 20th century they endured a poverty rate far exceeding that of the mainland.

The subjugation of Cuba and the annexation of Puerto Rico troubled Americans far less than the U.S. takeover in the Philippines. Since the first articulation of the Monroe Doctrine in 1823, the United States had, in effect, claimed the Western Hemisphere as its sphere of influence. Within that sphere, many Americans believed, the United States possessed the right to act unilaterally to protect its interests. Before 1900 most of its actions (with the exception of the Mexican War) had been designed to limit the influence of European powers. After 1900, however, it assumed a more aggressive role, seizing land, overturning governments it did not like, and forcing its economic and political policies on weaker neighbors.

CHINA AND THE "OPEN DOOR"

Except for the Philippines and Guam, the United States made no effort to take control of Asian lands. Such a policy might well have triggered war with other world powers already well established in the area. The United States opted for a diplomatic rather than a military strategy to achieve its foreign policy objectives. In China, in 1899 and 1900, it proposed the policy of the "Open Door."

The United States was concerned that the actions of the other world powers in China would block its own efforts to open up China's markets to American goods. Britain, Germany, Japan, Russia, and France—each coveted their own chunk of China, where they could monopolize trade, exploit cheap labor, and establish military bases. By the 1890s each of these powers was building a sphere of influence, either by wringing economic and territorial concessions from the weak Chinese government or by seizing outright the land and trading privileges they desired.

To prevent China's breakup and to preserve American economic access to the whole of China, McKinley's secretary of state, John Hay, sent "Open Door" notes to the major world powers. The notes asked each power to open its Chinese sphere of influence to the merchants of other nations and to grant them reasonable harbor fees and railroad rates. Hay also asked each power to respect China's sovereignty by enforcing Chinese tariff duties in the territory it controlled.

None of the world powers was eager to endorse either of Hay's requests, though Britain and Japan gave provisional assent. France, Germany, Russia, and Italy responded evasively, indicating their support for the Open Door policy in theory but insisting that they could not implement it until all the other powers had done so. Hay then put the best face on their responses by declaring that all the powers had agreed to observe his Open Door principles and that he regarded their assent as "final and definitive." The rival powers may have been impressed by Hay's diplomacy, but whether they intended to uphold the United States' Open Door policy was not at all clear.

The first challenge to Hay's policy came from the Chinese themselves. In May 1900 a nationalist Chinese organization, colloquially known as the "Boxers," sparked an uprising to rid China of all "foreign devils" and foreign influences. Hundreds of Europeans were killed, as were many Chinese men and women who had converted to Christianity. When the Boxers laid siege to the foreign legations in Beijing and cut off communication between that city and the outside world, the imperial powers raised an expeditionary force to rescue the diplomats and punish the Chinese rebels. The force broke the Beijing siege in August, and ended the Boxer Rebellion soon thereafter.

Hay now sent out a second round of Open Door notes, asking each power to respect China's political independence and territorial integrity, in addition to guaranteeing unrestricted access to its markets. Worried that the Chinese rebels might strike again, the imperialist rivals responded more favorably. Britain, France, and Germany endorsed Hay's policy outright. With that support, Hay was able to check Russian and Japanese designs on Chinese territory. Significantly, when the powers decided that the Chinese government should pay them reparations for their property and personnel losses during the Boxer Rebellion, Hay convinced them to accept payment in cash rather than in territory. By keeping China intact and open to free trade, the United States had achieved a major foreign policy victory.

DANCE WITH DEATH?   America's acquisition of the Philippines and other colonies in 1898 generated bitter debate at home. This anti-imperialist cartoon from 1899 portrays U.S. expansion as a dangerous dance with "Death." In the background is a spurned and forlorn "Lady Liberty" who is powerless to stop Uncle Sam's infatuation with war and empire.

THEODORE ROOSEVELT, GEOPOLITICIAN

Roosevelt had been a driving force in the transformation of U.S. foreign policy during the McKinley administration. As assistant secretary of the navy, as a military hero, as a vigorous speaker and writer, and then as vice president, Roosevelt worked tirelessly to remake the country into one of the world's great powers. He fervently believed that the Anglo-Saxon character of the nation destined it for supremacy in both economic and political affairs. He did not assume, however, that international supremacy would automatically accrue to the United States. A nation, like an individual, had to strive for greatness. It had to build a military force that could convincingly project power overseas. And it had to be prepared to fight.

Roosevelt's appetite for a good fight caused many people to rue the ascension of this "cowboy" to the White House after McKinley's assassination in 1901. But behind his blustery exterior was a shrewd analyst of international relations. As much as he craved power for himself and the nation, he understood that the United States could not rule every portion of the globe through military or economic means. Consequently, he sought to bring about a balance of power among the great industrial nations through negotiation rather than war. Such a balance would enable each imperial power to safeguard its key interests and contribute to world peace and progress.

Absent from Roosevelt's geopolitical thinking was concern for the interests of less powerful nations. Roosevelt had little patience with the claims to sovereignty of small countries or the human rights of weak peoples. In his eyes, the peoples of Latin America, Asia (with the exception of Japan), and Africa were racially inferior and thus incapable of self-government or industrial progress.

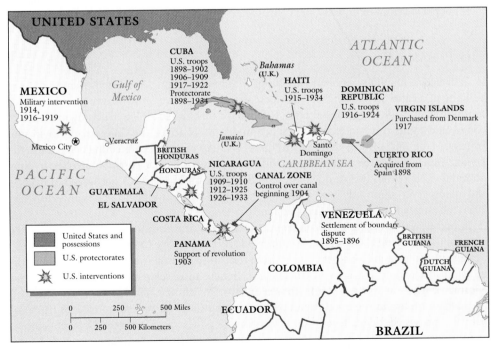

UNITED STATES PRESENCE IN LATIN AMERICA, 1895–1934

THE ROOSEVELT COROLLARY

Ensuring U.S. dominance in the Western Hemisphere ranked high on Roosevelt's list of foreign policy objectives. In 1904 he issued a "corollary" to the Monroe Doctrine, which had asserted the right of the United States to keep European powers from meddling in hemispheric affairs. In his corollary Roosevelt declared that the United States possessed a further right: the right to intervene in the domestic affairs of hemispheric nations to quell disorder and forestall European intervention. The Roosevelt corollary formalized a policy that the United States had already deployed against Cuba and Puerto Rico in 1900 and 1901. Subsequent events in Venezuela and the Dominican Republic had further convinced Roosevelt of the need to expand the scope of U.S. intervention in hemispheric affairs.

The governments of both Venezuela and the Dominican Republic were controlled by corrupt dictators. Both had defaulted on debts owed to European banks. Their delinquency prompted a German-led European naval blockade and bombardment of Venezuela in 1902 and a threatened invasion of the Dominican Republic by Italy and France in 1903. The United States forced the German navy to retreat from the Venezuelan coast in 1903. In the Dominican Republic, after a revolution had chased the dictator from power, the United States assumed control of the nation's customs collections in 1905 and refinanced the Dominican national debt through U.S. bankers.

The prevalence of corrupt, dictatorial regimes in Latin America and the willingness of European bankers to loan these regimes money had provided ideal conditions for bankruptcy, social turmoil, and foreign intervention. The United States now took aggressive actions to correct those conditions. But rarely in Roosevelt's tenure did the United States show a willingness to help the people who had suffered under these regimes to establish democratic institutions or achieve social justice. When Cubans seeking genuine national independence rebelled against their puppet government in 1906, the United States sent in the Marines to silence them.

THE PANAMA CANAL

In addition to maintaining order, Roosevelt's interest in Latin America also embraced the building of a canal across Central America. Central America's narrow width, especially in its southern half, made it the logical place to build a canal. In fact, a French company had obtained land rights and had begun construction of a canal across the Colombian province of Panama in the 1880s. But even though a "mere" 40 miles of land separated the two oceans, the French were stymied by technological difficulties and financial costs of literally moving mountains. Moreover, French doctors found they were unable to check the spread of malaria and yellow fever among their workers. By the time Roosevelt entered the White House in 1901, the French Panama Company had gone bankrupt.

Roosevelt was not deterred by the French failure. He first presided over the signing of the Hay-Pauncefote Treaty with Great Britain in 1901, releasing the United States from an 1850 agreement that prohibited either country from building a Central American canal without the other's participation. He then instructed his advisers to develop plans for a canal across Nicaragua. The Panamanian route chosen by the French was shorter than the proposed Nicaraguan route and the canal begun by the French was 40 percent complete, but the company that possessed the rights to it wanted $109 million for it, more than the United States was willing to pay. In 1902, however, the company reduced the price to $40 million, a sum that Congress approved. Secretary of State Hay quickly negotiated an agreement with Tomas Herran, the

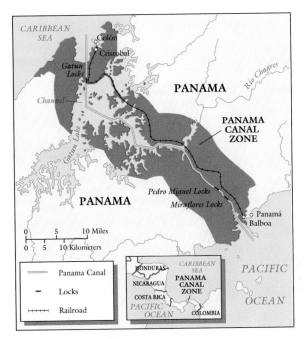

PANAMA CANAL ZONE, 1914

Colombian chargé d'affaires in Washington. The agreement, formalized in the Hay-Herran Treaty, accorded the United States a 6-mile-wide strip across Panama on which to build the canal. Colombia was to receive a onetime $10 million payment and annual rent of $250,000.

The Colombian legislature, however, rejected the proposed payment as insufficient and sent a new ambassador to the United States with instructions to ask for a onetime payment of $20 million and a share of the $40 million being paid to the French company. Actually, the Colombians (not unreasonably) were hoping to stall negotiations until 1904, when they would regain the rights to the canal zone and consequently to the $40 million sale price promised to the French company.

Although Colombia was acting within its rights, Roosevelt would not tolerate the delay. Unable to get what he wanted through diplomatic means, he encouraged the Panamanians to revolt against Colombian rule. The Panamanians had staged several rebellions in the previous 25 years, all of which had failed. But the 1903 rebellion succeeded, mainly because a U.S. naval force prevented Colombian troops from landing in Panama. Meanwhile, the U.S.S. *Nashville* put U.S. troops ashore to help the new nation secure its independence. The United States formally recognized Panama as a sovereign state only two days after the rebellion against Colombia began.

Philippe Bunau-Varilla, a director of the French company from which the United States had bought the rights to the canal, declared himself the new state's diplomatic representative. Even as the duly appointed Panamanian delegation embarked for the United States for negotiations over the canal, Bunau-Varilla rushed to Washington, where he and Secretary of State Hay signed the Hay–Bunau-Varilla Treaty (1903). It granted the United States a 10-mile-wide canal zone in return for $10 million down and $250,000 annually. Thus, the United States secured its

THE PANAMA CANAL UNDER CONSTRUCTION   This illustration shows the combination of machine and human labor that was used to move millions of tons of earth in the building of the Panama Canal, an undertaking that the British Ambassador James Bryce called "the greatest liberty Man has ever taken with Nature."

canal, not by dealing with the newly installed Panamanian government, but with Bunau-Varilla's French company. When the Panamanian delegation arrived in Washington, its hands were tied. If it objected to the counterfeit treaty, the United States might withdraw its troops from Panama, leaving the new country at the mercy of Colombia.

Roosevelt's severing of Panama from Colombia prompted angry protests in Congress. But Roosevelt was not perturbed. He later gloated, "I took the Canal Zone and let Congress debate!"

Roosevelt turned the building of the canal into a test of American ingenuity and willpower. Engineers overcame every obstacle; doctors developed drugs to combat malaria and yellow fever; armies of construction workers "made the dirt fly." The canal remains a testament to the labor of some 30,000 workers, imported mainly from the West Indies, who, over a 10-year period, labored 10 hours a day, six days a week, for 10 cents an hour. Completed in 1914, the canal shortened the voyage from San Francisco to New York by more than 8,000 miles and significantly enhanced the international prestige of the United States.

In 1921 the United States paid the Colombian government $25 million as compensation for its loss of Panama. It took Panama more than 70 years, however, to regain control of the 10-mile-wide strip of land that Bunau-Varilla, in connivance with the U.S. government, had bargained away in 1902. President Jimmy Carter signed a treaty in 1977 providing for the reintegration of the Canal Zone into Panama, and the canal itself was transferred to Panama in 2000.

KEEPING THE PEACE IN EAST ASIA

In Asia, Roosevelt's main objective was to preserve the Open Door policy in China and the balance of power throughout East Asia. The chief threats came from Russia and Japan, both of whom wanted to seize large chunks of China. At first, Russian expansion into Manchuria and Korea prompted Roosevelt to support Japan when in 1904 it launched a devastating attack on the Russian Pacific fleet anchored at Port Arthur, China. But once the ruinous effects of the war on Russia became clear, Roosevelt entered into secret negotiations to arrange a peace. He invited representatives of Japan and Russia to Portsmouth, New Hampshire, and prevailed on them to negotiate a compromise. The settlement, reached in 1905, favored Japan by perpetuating its control over most of the territories it had won during the brief Russo-Japanese War. Its chief prize was Korea, which became a protectorate of Japan, but Japan also acquired the southern part of Sakhalin Island, Port Arthur, and the South Manchurian Railroad. Russia avoided having to pay Japan a huge indemnity and it retained Siberia, thus preserving its role as an East Asian power. Finally, Roosevelt protected China's territorial integrity by inducing the armies of both Russia and Japan to leave Manchuria. Roosevelt's success in ending the Russo-Japanese War won him the Nobel Prize for Peace in 1906.

Although Roosevelt succeeded in negotiating a peace between these two world powers, he subsequently ignored, and even encouraged, challenges to the sovereignty of weaker Asian nations. In a secret agreement with Japan (the Taft-Katsura Agreement of 1905), for example, the United States agreed that Japan could dominate Korea in return for a Japanese promise not to attack the Philippines. And in the Root-Takahira Agreement of 1908, the United States recognized Japanese expansion into southern Manchuria.

In Roosevelt's eyes the overriding need to maintain peace with Japan justified ignoring the claims of Korea and, increasingly, of China. Roosevelt admired Japan's industrial and military might and regarded Japanese expansion into East Asia as a natural expression of its imperial ambition. The task of American diplomacy, he believed, was first to allow the Japanese to build a secure sphere of influence in East Asia and second to encourage them to join the United States in pursuing peace rather than war. This was a delicate diplomatic task that required both sensitivity and strength, especially when anti-Japanese agitation broke out in California in 1906.

White Californians had long feared the presence of Asian immigrants. They had pressured Congress into passing the Chinese Exclusion Act of 1882, which ended most Chinese immigration to the United States. Then they turned their racism on Japanese immigrants. In 1906 the San Francisco school board ordered the segregation of Asian schoolchildren so that they would not "contaminate" white children. In 1907 the California legislature debated a law to bar any more Japanese immigrants from entering the state. Anti-Asian riots erupted in San Francisco and Los Angeles, encouraged in part by hysterical stories in the press about the "Yellow Peril."

Militarists in Japan began talking of a possible war with the United States. Roosevelt assured the Japanese government that he too was appalled by the Californians' behavior. In 1907 he reached a "gentlemen's agreement" by which the Tokyo government promised to halt the immigration of Japanese adult male laborers to the United States in return for Roosevelt's pledge to end anti-Japanese discrimination. Roosevelt did his part by persuading the San Francisco school board to rescind its segregation ordinance.

At the same time, Roosevelt worried that the Tokyo government would interpret his sensitivity to Japanese honor as weakness. So he ordered the main part of the U.S. fleet to embark on a 45,000-mile world tour, including a splashy stop in Tokyo Bay. Many Americans deplored

ANTI-ASIAN HYSTERIA IN SAN FRANCISCO   In 1906, in the midst of a wave of anti-Asian prejudice in California, the San Francisco school board ordered the segregation of all Asian schoolchildren. Here, a 9-year-old Japanese student submits an application for admission to a public primary school and is refused by the principal, Miss M. E. Dean.

the cost of the tour and feared that the appearance of the U.S. Navy in a Japanese port would provoke military retaliation. But Roosevelt brushed his critics aside, and, true to his prediction, the Japanese were impressed by the "Great White Fleet's" show of strength. Their response seemed to lend validity to the African proverb Roosevelt often invoked: "Speak softly and carry a big stick." Roosevelt's policies lessened the prospect of a war with Japan while preserving a strong U.S. presence in East Asia.

WILLIAM HOWARD TAFT, DOLLAR DIPLOMAT

William Howard Taft brought impressive credentials to the job of president. He had gained valuable experience in colonial administration as the first governor-general of the Philippines. As Roosevelt's secretary of war and chief negotiator for the delicate Taft-Katsura agreement of 1905, he had learned a great deal about conducting diplomacy with imperialist rivals. Yet Taft lacked Roosevelt's grasp of balance-of-power politics and capacity for leadership in foreign affairs. Further, Taft's secretary of state, Philander C. Knox, a corporation lawyer from Pittsburgh, was without diplomatic expertise. Knox's conduct of foreign policy seemed to be

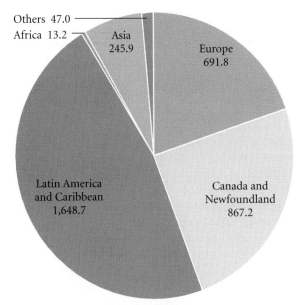

Others 47.0
Africa 13.2
Asia 245.9
Europe 691.8
Latin America and Caribbean 1,648.7
Canada and Newfoundland 867.2

U.S. Global Investments and Investments in Latin America, 1914

Source: From Cleona Lewis, *America's Stake in International Investments* (Washington, D.C.: The Brookings Institute, 1938), pp. 576–606.

Global investments (millions of dollars)

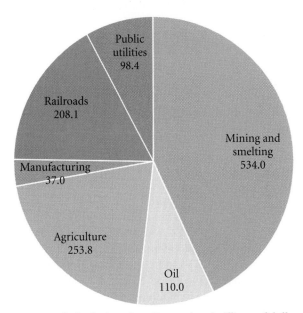

Public utilities 98.4
Railroads 208.1
Manufacturing 37.0
Mining and smelting 534.0
Agriculture 253.8
Oil 110.0

Investments in Latin American Enterprises (millions of dollars)

directed almost entirely toward expanding opportunities for corporate investment overseas, a disposition that prompted critics to deride his policies as "dollar diplomacy."

The inability of Taft and Knox to grasp the complexities of power politics led to a diplomatic reversal in East Asia. Knox, prodded by his banker friends, sought to expand American economic activities throughout China—even in Manchuria, where they encroached on the Japanese sphere of influence. In 1911 Knox proposed that a syndicate of European and American bankers buy the South Manchurian Railroad (then under Japanese control) to open up North China to international trade. Japan reacted by signing a friendship treaty with Russia, its former enemy, which signaled their joint determination to exclude American, British, and French goods from Manchurian markets. Knox's plans for a syndicate collapsed. Similar efforts by Knox to increase American trade with Central and South China triggered further hostile responses from the Japanese and the Russians and contributed to the collapse of the Chinese government and the onset of the Chinese Revolution in 1912.

Dollar diplomacy worked better in the Caribbean. Knox encouraged American investment in the region. Companies such as United Fruit of Boston, which established extensive banana plantations in Costa Rica and Honduras, grew so powerful that they were able to influence both the economies and the governments of Central American countries. When political turmoil threatened their investments, the United States simply sent in its troops. Thus, when Nicaraguan dictator José Santos Zelaya reportedly began negotiating with a European country to build a second trans-Isthmian canal in 1910, a force of U.S. Marines toppled his regime. Marines landed again in 1912 when Zelaya's successor, Adolfo Diaz, angered Nicaraguans with his pro-American policies. This time the Marines were instructed to keep the Diaz regime in power. Except for a brief period in 1925, U.S. troops would remain in Nicaragua continuously from 1912 until 1933.

WOODROW WILSON, STRUGGLING IDEALIST

Woodrow Wilson's foreign policy in the Caribbean initially appeared to be no different from that of his Republican predecessors. In 1915 the United States sent troops to Haiti to put down a revolution; they remained as an army of occupation for 21 years. In 1916, when the people of the Dominican Republic refused to accept a treaty making them more or less a protectorate of the United States, Wilson forced them to accept the rule of a U.S. military government. When German influence in the Danish West Indies began to expand, Wilson purchased the islands from Denmark, renamed them the Virgin Islands, and added them to the U.S. Caribbean empire.

But Wilson's relationship with Mexico in the wake of its revolution reveals that he was troubled by a foreign policy that took no account of a less powerful nation's right to determine its own future. In his dealings with Mexico, however, he was not motivated solely by his fondness for democracy. He also feared that political unrest could lead to violence, social disorder, and revolutionary governments hostile to U.S. economic interests. If a democratic government could be put in place in Mexico, property rights would be respected and U.S. investments would remain secure. Wilson's desire both to encourage democracy and to limit the extent of social change made it difficult to devise a consistent foreign policy toward Mexico.

The Mexican Revolution broke out in 1910 when dictator Porfirio Diaz was overthrown by democratic forces led by Francisco Madero. Madero's talk of democratic reform frightened many foreign investors. Thus, when Madero himself was overthrown early in 1913 by Victoriano Huerta, a conservative general who promised to protect foreign investments, the dollar diplomatists breathed a sigh of relief. Henry Lane Wilson, the U.S. ambassador to Mexico, had helped to engineer Huerta's coup. Before close relations between the United States and Huerta could be worked out, however, Huerta's men murdered Madero.

Woodrow Wilson, who became president shortly after Madero's assassination in 1913, might have overlooked it and entered into close ties with Huerta on condition that he protect American property. Instead, Wilson refused to recognize Huerta's "government of butchers" and demanded that Mexico hold democratic elections. Wilson favored Venustiano Carranza and Francisco ("Pancho") Villa, two enemies of Huerta who commanded rebel armies and who claimed to be democrats. In April 1914 Wilson seized upon the arrest of several U.S. sailors by Huerta's troops to send a fleet into Mexican waters. He then ordered the U.S. Marines to occupy the Mexican port city of Veracruz and to prevent a German ship there from unloading munitions meant for Huerta's army. In the resulting action between U.S. and Mexican forces, 19 Americans and 126 Mexicans were killed. The battle brought the two countries dangerously close to war. Eventually, however, American control over Veracruz weakened and embarrassed Huerta's regime to the point where Carranza was able to take power.

But Carranza did not behave as Wilson had expected. He rejected Wilson's efforts to shape a new Mexican government and announced a bold land-reform program. If the program went into effect, U.S. petroleum companies would lose control of their Mexican properties, a loss that Wilson deemed unacceptable. So Wilson now threw his support to Pancho Villa, who seemed more

CHRONOLOGY

1893	Frederick Jackson Turner publishes an essay announcing the end of the frontier
1898	Spanish-American War (April 14–August 12) • Treaty of Paris signed (December 10), giving U.S. control of Philippines, Guam, and Puerto Rico • U.S. annexes Hawaii
1899–1902	American-Filipino War
1899–1900	U.S. pursues "Open Door" policy toward China
1900	U.S. annexes Puerto Rico • U.S. and other imperial powers put down Chinese Boxer Rebellion
1901	U.S. forces Cuba to adopt constitution favorable to U.S. interests
1903	Hay–Bunau-Varilla Treaty signed, giving U.S. control of Panama Canal Zone
1904	"Roosevelt corollary" to Monroe Doctrine proclaimed
1905	Roosevelt negotiates end to Russo-Japanese War
1906–1917	U.S. intervenes in Cuba, Nicaragua, Haiti, Dominican Republic, and Mexico
1907	Roosevelt and Japanese government reach a "Gentlemen's Agreement" restricting Japanese immigration to U.S. and ending discrimination against Japanese schoolchildren in California
1907–1909	Great White Fleet circles the earth
1909–1913	William Howard Taft conducts "dollar diplomacy"
1910	Mexican Revolution
1914	Panama Canal opens
1914–1917	Wilson struggles to develop a policy toward Mexico
1917	U.S. purchases Virgin Islands from Denmark

willing to protect U.S. oil interests. When Carranza's forces defeated Villa's forces in 1915, Wilson reluctantly withdrew his support of Villa and prepared to recognize the Carranza government.

Furious that Wilson had abandoned him, Villa and his soldiers pulled 18 U.S. citizens from a train in northern Mexico and murdered them, along with another 17 in an attack on Columbus, New Mexico. Determined to punish Villa, Wilson got permission from Carranza to send a U.S. expeditionary force under General John J. Pershing into Mexico. Pershing's troops pursued Villa's forces 300 miles into Mexico but failed to catch them. The U.S. troops did, however, clash twice with Mexican troops under Carranza's command, bringing the countries to the brink of war once again. Because the United States was about to enter the First World War, Wilson could not afford a fight with Mexico. So, in 1917, he quietly ordered Pershing's troops home and grudgingly recognized the Carranza government.

Wilson's policies toward Mexico in the years from 1913 to 1917 seemed to have produced few concrete results, except to reinforce an already deep antagonism among Mexicans toward the United States. His repeated changes in strategy, moreover, seemed to indicate a lack of skill and decisiveness in foreign affairs. Actually, however, Wilson recognized something that Roosevelt and Taft had not: that more and more peoples of the world were determined to control their own destinies. Somehow the nation had to find a way to support their democratic aspirations while also safeguarding its own economic interests.

CONCLUSION

We can assess the dramatic turn in U.S. foreign policy after 1898 either in relation to the foreign policies of rival world powers or against America's own democratic ideals. By the first standard, U.S. foreign policy looks impressive. The United States achieved its major objectives in world affairs: It tightened its control over the Western Hemisphere and projected its military and economic power into Asia. It did so while sacrificing relatively few American lives and while constraining the jingoistic appetite for truly extensive military adventure and conquest. Relatively few foreigners were subjected to American colonial rule. By contrast, in 1900 the British Empire extended over 12 million square miles and embraced one-fourth of the world's population. At times, American rule could be brutal, but on the whole it was no more severe than British rule and significantly less severe than that of the French, German, Belgian, or Japanese imperialists. McKinley, Roosevelt, Taft, and Wilson all placed limits on American expansion and avoided, prior to 1917, extensive foreign entanglements and wars.

If measured against the standard of America's own democratic ideals, however, U.S. foreign policy after 1898 must be judged more harshly. It demeaned the peoples of the Philippines, Puerto Rico, Guam, Cuba, and Colombia as inferior, primitive, and barbaric and denied them the right to govern themselves. In choosing to behave like the imperialist powers of Europe, the United States abandoned its long-standing claim that it was a different kind of nation— one that valued liberty more than power.

Many Americans of the time judged their nation by both standards and thus faced a dilemma. On the one hand, they believed that the size, economic strength, and honor of the United States required it to accept the role of world power and policeman. On the other hand, they continued to believe that they had a mission to spread the values of 1776 to the farthest reaches of the earth. The Mexico example demonstrates how hard it was for the United States to reconcile these two very different approaches to world affairs.

War and Society, 1914–1920

The First World War broke out in Europe in August 1914. The Triple Alliance of Germany, Austria-Hungary, and the Ottoman Empire squared off against the Triple Entente of Great Britain, France, and Russia. The United States entered the war on the side of the Entente (the Allies, or Allied Powers, as they came to be called) in 1917. Over the next year and a half, the United States converted its immense and sprawling economy into a disciplined war production machine, raised a 5-million-man army, and provided both the war matériel and troops that helped propel the Allies to victory.

But the war also convulsed American society more deeply than any event since the Civil War. This war was the first "total" war, meaning that it required combatants to devote virtually all their resources to the fight. Thus the United States government had no choice but to pursue a degree of industrial control and social regimentation without precedent in American history. Needless to say, this drastic government buildup was itself a controversial measure in a society that had long distrusted state power. Moreover, significant numbers of Americans from a variety of constituencies opposed the war. To overcome this opposition, Wilson couched American war aims in disinterested and idealistic terms: The United States, he claimed, wanted a "peace without victory," a "war for democracy," and liberty for the world's oppressed peoples.

Many people in the United States and abroad responded enthusiastically to Wilson's ideals. But Wilson could not deliver a "peace without victory" without the support of the other victors (England and France), and this support was never forthcoming. At home, disadvantaged groups stirred up trouble by declaring that American society had failed to live up to its democratic and egalitarian ideals. Wilson supported repressive policies to silence these rebels and to enforce unity and conformity on the American people. In the process, he tarnished the ideals for which America had been fighting.

Europe's Descent into War

Europe began its descent into war on June 28, 1914, in Sarajevo, Bosnia, when a Bosnian nationalist assassinated Archduke Franz Ferdinand, heir to the Austro-Hungarian throne. This

THE ROAD TO WAR, SUMMER 1914

1 — June 28 Assassination at Sarajevo

2 — July 28 Austria-Hungary declares war on Serbia

3 — July 30 Russia begins mobilization

4 — August 1 Germany declares war on Russia

5 — August 3 Germany declares war on France

6 — August 4 Great Britain declares war on Germany

7 — August 6 Russia and Austria-Hungary at war

8 — August 12 Great Britain declares war on Austria-Hungary

Allied powers and possessions, 1916

♦♦♦♦♦ British naval blockade

Central powers, 1916

—— Trench line, Western front, 1915

Neutral countries

—— Eastern front, 1915

EUROPE GOES TO WAR

act was meant to protest the Austro-Hungarian imperial presence in the Balkans, and to encourage the Bosnians, Croatians, and other Balkan peoples to join the Serbs in establishing independent nations. Austria-Hungary responded to this provocation on July 28 by declaring war on Serbia, holding it responsible for the archduke's murder.

The conflict might have remained local had not an intricate series of treaties divided Europe into two hostile camps. Germany, Austria-Hungary, and Italy, the so-called Triple Alliance, had promised to come to each other's aid if attacked. Italy would soon opt out of this alliance, to be replaced by the Ottoman Empire. Arrayed against the nations of the Triple

Alliance were Britain, France, and Russia in the Triple Entente. Russia was obligated by another treaty to defend Serbia against Austria-Hungary, and consequently on July 30 it mobilized its armed forces to go to Serbia's aid. That brought Germany into the conflict to protect Austria-Hungary from Russian attack. On August 3 German troops struck not at Russia itself but at France, Russia's western ally. To reach France, German troops had marched through neutral Belgium. On August 4 Britain reacted by declaring war on Germany.

Complicated alliances and defense treaties of the European nations undoubtedly hastened the rush toward war. But equally important was the fierce competition that existed among the major powers to build the strongest economies, the largest armies and navies, and the grandest colonial empires. Britain and Germany, in particular, were engaged in a bitter struggle for European and world supremacy. Historians now believe that several advisers close to the German emperor, Kaiser Wilhelm II, were actually eager to engage Russia and France in a fight for supremacy on the European continent. They expected that a European war would be swift and decisive—in Germany's favor.

But there was to be no quick victory. The two camps were evenly matched. Moreover, the first wartime use of machine guns and barbed wire made it easier to defend against attack than to go on the offensive. On the western front, after the initial German attack narrowly failed to take Paris in 1914, the two opposing armies confronted each other along a battle line stretching from Belgium in the north to the Swiss border in the south. Troops dug trenches to protect themselves from artillery bombardment and poison gas attacks. Commanders on both sides mounted suicidal ground assaults on the enemy by sending tens of thousands of infantry, armed only with rifles, bayonets, and grenades, out of the trenches and directly into enemy fire. Barbed wire further retarded forward progress, enabling enemy artillery and machine guns to cut down appalling numbers of men. Many of those who were not killed in combat succumbed to disease that spread rapidly in the cold, wet, and rat-infested trenches. In eastern Europe the armies of Germany and Austria-Hungary squared off against those of Russia and Serbia. Though trench warfare was not employed there, the combat was no less lethal. By the time the First World War ended, total casualties, both military and civilian, had reached 37 million.

AMERICAN NEUTRALITY

Soon after the fighting began, Woodrow Wilson told Americans that this was a European war; neither side was threatening a vital American interest. The United States would therefore proclaim its neutrality and maintain normal relations with both sides. Normal relations meant that the United States would continue trading with both camps. Wilson's neutrality policy was greeted by lively opposition, but a majority of Americans applauded Wilson's determination to keep the country out of war.

It was easier to proclaim neutrality than it was to achieve it, however. Many Americans, especially those with economic and political power, identified culturally more with Britain than with Germany. They shared with the English a language, a common ancestry, and a commitment to liberty. Germany had no such attraction for U.S. policymakers. On the contrary, Germany's acceptance of monarchical rule, the prominence of militarists in German politics, and the weakness of democratic traditions inclined U.S. officials to judge Germany harshly.

The United States was tied to Great Britain by economics as well as culture. In 1914 the United States exported more than $800 million in goods to Britain and its allies, compared with $170 million to Germany and Austria-Hungary (which came to be known as the Central Powers). As soon as the war began, the British and then the French turned to the United States for food, clothing, munitions, and other war supplies. The U.S. economy, which had been languishing in 1914, enjoyed a great boom. Bankers began to issue loans to the Allied Powers, further knitting together the American and British economies and giving American investors a direct stake in an Allied victory. Moreover, the British navy had blockaded German ports, which further limited U.S. trade with Germany.

The British blockade of German ports clearly violated American neutrality. The Wilson administration vigorously protested the search and occasional seizure of American merchant ships by the British navy. But it never suspended loans or the export of goods to Great Britain in retaliation for the blockade. To do so would have plunged the U.S. economy into a severe recession. In failing to protect its right to trade with Germany, however, the United States compromised its neutrality and allowed itself to be drawn slowly into war.

SUBMARINE WARFARE

To combat British control of the seas, Germany unveiled a terrifying new weapon, the *Unterseeboot*, or U-boat, the first militarily effective submarine. On May 7, 1915, without warning, a German U-boat torpedoed the British passenger liner *Lusitania*, en route from New York to London. The ship sank in 22 minutes, killing 1,198 men, women, and children, 128 of them U.S. citizens. Americans were shocked by the sinking. The attack appeared to confirm what anti-German agitators were saying: that the Germans were by nature barbaric and uncivilized. The circumstances surrounding the sinking of the *Lusitania*, however, were more complicated than most Americans realized.

Prior to its sailing, the Germans had alleged that the *Lusitania* was secretly carrying a large store of munitions to Great Britain (a charge later shown to have been true) and that it therefore was subject to U-boat attack. Germany had explicitly warned American passengers not to travel on British passenger ships that carried munitions. Moreover, Germany claimed, with some justification, that the purpose of the U-boat attacks—the disruption of Allied supply lines—was no different from Britain's purpose in blockading German ports.

Wilson denounced the sinking of the *Lusitania* in harsh, threatening terms and demanded that Germany pledge never to launch another attack on the citizens of neutral nations, even when they were traveling in British or French ships. Germany acquiesced to Wilson's demand. The resulting lull in submarine warfare was short-lived, however. In early 1916 the Allies began to arm their merchant vessels with guns and depth charges capable of destroying German U-boats. Considering this a provocation, Germany renewed its campaign of surprise submarine attacks. In March 1916 a German submarine torpedoed the French passenger liner *Sussex*, causing a heavy loss of life and injuring several Americans. Again Wilson demanded that Germany spare civilians from attack. In the so-called *Sussex* pledge, Germany once again relented but warned that it might resume unrestricted submarine warfare if the United States did not prevail upon Great Britain to permit neutral ships to pass through the naval blockade.

THE SINKING OF THE *LUSITANIA* On May 7, 1915, a German U-boat torpedoed and sank the British passenger liner *Lusitania,* killing 1,198 people, 128 of them Americans. The event turned U.S. opinion sharply against the Germans, especially because the civilians on board had been given no chance to escape or surrender. Few Americans knew that the ship was secretly transporting a large munitions cache to the British.

The German submarine attacks strengthened the hand of Theodore Roosevelt and others who had been arguing that war with Germany was inevitable and that the United States must prepare itself to fight. By 1916 Wilson could no longer ignore these critics. Between January and September of that year, he sought and won congressional approval for bills to increase the size of the Army and Navy, tighten federal control over National Guard forces, and authorize the building of a merchant fleet. But although Wilson had conceded ground to the prowar agitators, he did not share their belief that war with Germany was either inevitable or desirable. To the contrary, he accelerated his diplomatic initiatives to forestall the necessity of American military involvement. He dispatched his closest foreign policy adviser, Colonel Edward M. House, to London in January 1916 to draw up a peace plan with the British foreign secretary, Lord Grey. This initiative resulted in the House-Grey memorandum of February 22, 1916, in which Britain agreed to ask the United States to negotiate a settlement between the Allies and the Central Powers. The British believed that the terms of such a peace settlement would be favorable to the Allies. They were furious when Wilson revealed that he wanted an impartial, honestly negotiated peace in which the claims of the Allies and Central Powers would be treated with equal respect and consideration. Britain now rejected U.S. peace overtures, and relations between the two countries grew unexpectedly tense.

THE PEACE MOVEMENT

Underlying Wilson's 1916 peace initiative was a vision of a new world order in which relations between nations would be governed by negotiation rather than war and in which justice would replace power as the fundamental principle of diplomacy. In a major foreign policy address on May 27, 1916, Wilson formally declared his support for an international parliament dedicated to the pursuit of peace, security, and justice for all the world's peoples.

In his effort to keep the United States out of war and to commit national prestige to the cause of international peace rather than conquest, Wilson enjoyed the support of a large number of Americans. In 1915 an international women's peace conference at The Hague (in the Netherlands) had drawn many participants from the United States. A substantial pacifist group emerged among the nation's Protestant clergy. Influential midwestern progressives urged that the United States steer clear of this European conflict, as did prominent socialists. In April 1916 many of the country's most prominent progressives and socialists joined hands in the American Union Against Militarism and pressured Wilson to continue pursuing the path of peace. Wilson's peace campaign also attracted support from the country's sizable Irish and German ethnic populations, who were determined to block any formal military alliance with Great Britain.

WILSON'S VISION: "PEACE WITHOUT VICTORY"

The 1916 presidential election revealed the breadth of peace sentiment. At the Democratic convention, Governor Martin Glynn of New York, the keynote speaker, praised the president for keeping the United States out of war. His portrayal of Wilson as the "peace president" electrified the convention and made "He kept us out of war" a campaign slogan. The slogan proved particularly effective against Wilson's Republican opponent, Charles Evans Hughes, whose close ties to Theodore Roosevelt seemed to place him in the pro-war camp. Combining the promise of peace with a pledge to push ahead with progressive reform, Wilson won a narrow victory.

Emboldened by his electoral triumph, Wilson intensified his quest for peace. On December 16, 1916, he sent a peace note to the belligerent governments, entreating them to consider ending the conflict and, to that end, to state their terms for peace. Although Germany refused to specify its terms and Britain and France announced a set of conditions too extreme for Germany ever to accept, Wilson pressed ahead, initiating secret peace negotiations with both sides. To prepare the American people for what he hoped would be a new era of international relations, Wilson appeared before the Senate on January 22, 1917, to outline his plans for peace. In his speech, he reaffirmed his commitment to an international parliament or League of Nations. But for such a league to succeed, Wilson argued, it would have to be handed a sturdy peace settlement. This entailed a "peace without victory." A peace settlement that did not favor the winners or losers would ensure the equality of the combatants, and "only a peace between equals can last."

Wilson then listed the crucial principles of a lasting peace: freedom of the seas; disarmament; and the right of every people to self-determination, democratic self-government, and security against aggression. Wilson was advocating a revolutionary change in world order, one that would allow all the earth's peoples, regardless of their size or strength, to achieve political independence and to participate as equals in world affairs. These were uncommon views coming from the leader of a world power, and they stirred the despairing masses of Europe and elsewhere who were caught in a deadly conflict.

GERMAN ESCALATION

But Wilson's oratory came too late to serve the cause of peace. Sensing the imminent collapse of Russian forces on the eastern front, Germany had decided to throw its full military might at France and Britain. On land it planned to launch a massive assault on the trenches, and at sea it prepared to unleash its submarines to attack all vessels heading for British ports. Germany knew that this last action would compel the United States to enter the war, but it was gambling on being able to strangle the British economy and leave France isolated before significant numbers of American troops could reach European shores.

On February 1 the United States broke off diplomatic relations with Germany. Wilson continued to hope for a negotiated settlement, however, until February 25, when the British intercepted and passed on to the president a telegram from Germany's foreign secretary, Arthur Zimmermann, to the German minister in Mexico. The infamous "Zimmermann telegram" instructed the minister to ask the Mexican government to attack the United States in the event of war between Germany and the United States. In return, Germany would pay the Mexicans a large fee and regain for them the "lost provinces" of Texas, New Mexico, and Arizona. Wilson, Congress, and the American public were outraged.

In March news arrived that Tsar Nicholas II's autocratic regime in Russia had collapsed and had been replaced by a liberal-democratic government under the leadership of Alexander Kerensky. As long as the tsar ruled Russia and stood to benefit from the Central Powers' defeat, Wilson could not honestly claim that America's going to war against Germany would bring democracy to Europe. Russia's fledgling democratic government's need for support gave Wilson the rationale he needed to justify American intervention.

Appearing before a joint session of Congress on April 2, Wilson declared that the United States must enter the war because "the world must be made safe for democracy." Inspired by his words, Congress broke into thunderous applause. On April 6, Congress voted to declare war by a vote of 373 to 50 in the House and 82 to 6 in the Senate.

The United States thus embarked on a grand experiment to reshape the world. Wilson had given millions of people around the world reason to hope. Although he was taking America to war on the side of the Allies, he stressed that America would fight as an "Associated Power," a phrase meant to underscore America's determination to keep its war aims pure and disinterested.

Still, there was ample cause to worry. Wilson himself understood all too well the risks of his undertaking. If the American people went to war, he predicted, "they'll forget there ever was such a thing as tolerance. To fight you must be brutal and ruthless, and the spirit of ruthless brutality will enter into the very fibre of our national life, infecting Congress, the courts, the policeman on the beat, the man in the street."

AMERICAN INTERVENTION

The entry of the United States into the war gave the Allies the muscle they needed to defeat the Central Powers, but it almost came too late. Germany's resumption of unrestricted submarine warfare took a frightful toll on Allied shipping. From February through July 1917, German subs sank almost 4 million tons of shipping. American intervention ended Britain's vulnerability in dramatic fashion. U.S. and British naval commanders now grouped merchant ships into convoys and provided them with warship escorts through the most dangerous stretches of the North Atlantic. Destroyers armed with depth charges were particularly effective as escorts. Their shallow draft made them invulnerable to torpedoes, and their great acceleration and speed allowed them to pursue slow-moving U-boats. The U.S. and British navies had begun to use sound waves (later called "sonar") to pinpoint the location of underwater craft, and this new technology increased the effectiveness of destroyer attacks. By the end of 1917, the tonnage of Allied shipping lost each month to U-boat attacks had declined by two-thirds. The increased flow of supplies stiffened the resolve of the exhausted British and French troops.

The French and British armies had bled themselves white by taking the offensive in 1916 and 1917 and had scarcely budged the trench lines. The Germans had been content in those years simply to hold their trench position in the West, for they were engaged in a huge offensive against the Russians in the East. The Germans intended first to defeat Russia and then to shift their eastern armies to the West for a final assault on the weakened British and French lines. Their opportunity came in the winter and spring of 1918.

A second Russian revolution in November 1917 had overthrown Kerensky's liberal-democratic government and had brought to power a revolutionary socialist government under Vladimir Lenin and his Bolshevik Party. Believing that the war was not in the best interests of the working classes, Lenin pulled Russia out of the war. In March 1918 he signed a treaty at Brest-Litovsk that added to Germany's territory and resources and enabled Germany to shift its eastern forces to the western front.

Russia's exit from the war hurt the Allies. Not only did it expose French and British troops to a much larger German force, it also challenged the Allied claim that they were fighting a just war against German aggression. Lenin had published the texts of secret Allied treaties showing that Britain and France, like Germany, had plotted to enlarge their nations and empires through war. The revelation that the Allies were fighting for land and riches rather than democratic principles outraged large numbers of people in France and Great Britain, demoralized Allied troops, and threw the French and British governments into disarray. The treaties also embarrassed Wilson, who had brought America into the war to fight for democracy, not territory. But Wilson quickly restored the Allies' credibility by unveiling, in January 1918, a concrete program for peace, the Fourteen Points, that removed territorial aggrandizement as a legitimate war aim.

In March and April 1918, Germany launched its huge offensive against British and French positions, sending Allied troops reeling. A ferocious assault against French lines on May 27 met with little resistance; German troops advanced 10 miles a day until they reached the Marne River, within striking distance of Paris. The French government prepared to evacuate the city. At this perilous moment, a large American army arrived to reinforce what remained of the French lines.

In fact, these American troops, part of the American Expeditionary Force (AEF) commanded by General John J. Pershing, had begun landing in France almost a year earlier. But it took many months to build up a sizable and disciplined force. The United States had had to create a modern army from scratch. Men had to be drafted, trained, supplied with food and equipment; ships for transporting them to Europe had to be found or built. In France, Pershing put his troops through additional training before committing them to battle. He was determined that the American soldiers—or "doughboys," as they were called—should acquit themselves well on the battlefield. The army he ordered into battle to counter the German spring offensive of 1918 fought well. Many American soldiers fell, but Paris was saved, and Germany's best chance for victory slipped from its grasp.

Buttressed by this show of AEF strength, the Allied troops staged a major offensive of their own in late September. Millions of Allied troops advanced across the 200-mile-wide Argonne forest in France, cutting German supply lines. By late October, they had reached the German border. Faced with an invasion of their homeland and with rapidly mounting popular dissatisfaction with the war, German leaders asked for an armistice, to be followed by peace negotiations based on Wilson's Fourteen Points. Having forced the Germans to agree to numerous concessions, the Allies ended the war on November 11, 1918.

MOBILIZING FOR "TOTAL" WAR

Compared to Europe, the United States suffered little from the war. The deaths of 112,000 American soldiers paled in comparison to European losses: 900,000 by Great Britain, 1.2 million by Austria-Hungary, 1.4 million by France, 1.7 million by Russia, and 2 million by Germany. The U.S. civilian population was also spared most of the war's ravages—the destruction of homes and industries, the shortages of food and medicine, the spread of disease—that afflicted millions of Europeans. Only with the flu epidemic that swept across the Atlantic from Europe in 1919 to claim approximately 500,000 American lives did Americans briefly experience wholesale suffering and death.

Still, the war had a profound effect on American society. Every military engagement the United States had fought since the Civil War had been limited in scope. The First World War was different. It was a "total" war to which every combatant had committed virtually all its resources. The scale of the effort for the United States became apparent early in 1917 when Wilson asked Congress for a conscription law that would permit the federal government to raise a multimillion-man army. The United States would also have to devote much of its agricultural, transportation, industrial, and population resources to the war effort if it wished to end the European stalemate. Who would organize this massive effort? Who would pay for it?

ORGANIZING INDUSTRY

Southern and midwestern Democrats, fearing the centralization of governmental authority, pushed for a decentralized approach to mobilization. Northeastern progressives, on the other hand, saw the war as an opportunity to realize their dream of establishing a strong state to regulate the economy, boost efficiency, and achieve social harmony. At first Wilson pursued decentralization, delegating the chore of mobilization to local defense councils throughout the country. When that effort failed, however, Wilson created several centralized federal agencies, each charged with supervising nationwide activity in its assigned economic sector.

The agencies exhibited varying success. The Food Administration, headed by mining engineer Herbert Hoover, was able to increase production of basic foodstuffs substantially through the use of economic incentives. Hoover also put in place an efficient distribution system that delivered food to millions of troops and European civilians. Treasury Secretary William McAdoo, as head of the U.S. Railroad Administration, also performed well in shifting the rail system from private to public control, coordinating dense train traffic, and making capital improvements that allowed goods to move rapidly to eastern ports, where they were loaded onto ships and sent to Europe. At the other extreme, the Aircraft Production Board and Emergency Fleet Corporation did a poor job of supplying the Allies with combat aircraft and merchant vessels. On balance, the U.S. economy performed wonders in supplying troops with uniforms, food, rifles, munitions, and other basic items; it failed badly, however, in producing more sophisticated weapons and machines such as artillery, aircraft, and ships.

At the time, the new government war agencies were thought to possess awesome power over the nation's economy. But most of them were more powerful on paper than in fact. Consider, for example, the War Industries Board (WIB). The WIB floundered for the first nine months of its existence, as it lacked the statutory authority to force manufacturers and the military to adopt its plans. Only the appointment of Wall Street investment banker Bernard Baruch as WIB chairman in March 1918 turned the agency around. Rather than attempting to force manufacturers to do the government's bidding, Baruch permitted industrialists to charge high prices for their products. He won exemptions from antitrust laws for corporations that complied with his requests. In general, he made war production too lucrative an activity to resist. However, he did not hesitate to unleash his wrath upon corporations that resisted WIB enticements.

Baruch's forceful leadership worked reasonably well throughout his nine months in office. War production increased substantially, and manufacturers discovered the financial benefits of cooperation between the public and private sectors. But Baruch's approach created problems, too. His favoritism toward the large corporations hurt smaller competitors. Moreover, the cozy relationship between government and corporate America violated the progressive pledge to protect the people against the "interests."

ORGANIZING CIVILIAN LABOR

The government worried as much about labor's cooperation as about industry's compliance. The outbreak of war in 1914 had strengthened the market power of workers, because war orders from Europe prompted manufacturers to expand their production facilities and workforces. Meanwhile, the number of European immigrants plummeted—from more than 1 million in 1914, to 200,000 in 1915, to 31,000 in 1918. That meant that 3 million potential workers were lost to U.S. industry. The economy lost another 5 million workers to military service in 1917 and 1918.

Manufacturers responded to the shortage by encouraging potential workers around the country to come to their factories in the North. From the rural South, 500,000 African Americans migrated to northern cities between 1916 and 1920. Another half-million white southerners followed the same path during that period. Hundreds of thousands of Mexicans fled their homeland for jobs in the Southwest and Midwest. Approximately 40,000 northern women found work as streetcar conductors, railroad workers, metalworkers, munitions makers, and other jobs customarily reserved for men. The number of female clerical workers doubled between 1910 and 1920, with many of these women finding work in the government war bureaucracies.

These workers alleviated but did not eliminate the nation's acute labor shortage. Workers were quick to recognize the benefits to be won from the tight labor market. White male workers quit jobs they did not like, confident that they could do better. Workers took part in strikes and other collective actions in unprecedented numbers. Union membership almost doubled, from 2.6 million in 1915 to 5.1 million in 1920. Workers commonly sought higher wages and shorter hours through strikes and unionization. Workers also struck in response to managerial attempts to speed up production and tighten discipline. As time passed, increasing numbers of workers began to wonder why the war for democracy in Europe was not being matched by democratization of power in their factories at home. "Industrial democracy" became the battle cry of an awakened labor movement.

Wilson's willingness to include labor in his 1916 progressive coalition reflected his awareness of labor's potential power (see Chapter 21). In 1918 he bestowed prestige on the newly formed National War Labor Board (NWLB) by appointing former president William Howard Taft as one of its two cochairmen. The NWLB brought together representatives of labor, industry, and the public to resolve labor disputes. The presence of Samuel Gompers, president of the American Federation of Labor, on the board gave unions a strong national voice in government affairs. In return for his appointment, Gompers was expected to mobilize workers behind Wilson, discredit socialists who criticized the war, and discourage strikes that threatened war production. Although, like most other federal wartime agencies, the NWLB lacked the ability to impose its will, it managed to pressure many manufacturers into improving wages and hours, reducing wage discrimination, and allowing their workers to join unions.

OCCUPATIONS WITH LARGEST INCREASE IN WOMEN, 1910–1920

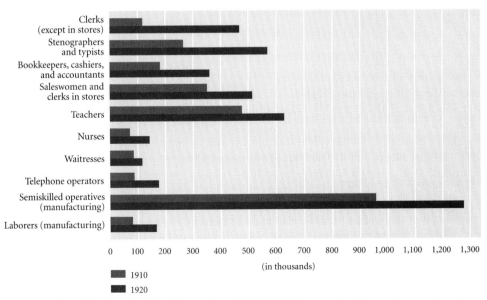

Source: Joseph A. Hill, *Women in Gainful Occupations, 1870–1920,* U.S. Bureau of the Census, Monograph no. 9 (Washington, D.C.: Government Printing Office, 1929), p. 33.

WOMEN DOING "MEN'S" WORK   Labor shortages during the war years allowed thousands of women to take industrial jobs customarily reserved for men. The two female lathe operators in this photograph (taken in an industrial plant in Portland, Oregon) had been schoolteachers before the war.

ORGANIZING MILITARY LABOR

Only when it came to raising an army did the federal government use its full power without hesitation. The Wilson administration committed itself to conscription—to the drafting of most men of a certain age, irrespective of their family's wealth, ethnic background, or social standing. The Selective Service Act of May 1917 empowered the administration to do just that. By war's end, local Selective Service boards had registered 24 million young men age 18 and older, and had drafted nearly 3 million of them into the military. Another 2 million volunteered for service.

There was relatively little resistance to the draft, even among recently arrived immigrants. Foreign-born men constituted 18 percent of the armed forces—a percentage greater than their share of the total male population. Almost 400,000 African Americans served, representing approximately 10 percent, the same as the percentage of African Americans in the total population.

The U.S. Army, under the command of Chief of Staff Peyton March and General John J. Pershing, faced the difficult task of fashioning these ethnically and racially diverse millions into a professional fighting force. Teaching raw recruits to fight was hard enough, Pershing and March observed; teaching them to put aside their racial and ethnic prejudices was a task they refused to tackle. Rather than integrate the armed forces, they segregated black soldiers from white. Virtually all African Americans were assigned to all-black units that were barred from combat. Being stripped of a combat role was particularly galling to blacks, who, in previous wars, had proven themselves to be among the best American fighters.

For a time, the military justified its intensified discrimination against blacks by referring to the results of rudimentary "IQ" (intelligence quotient) tests administered by psychologists to 2 million AEF soldiers. These tests allegedly "proved" that native-born Americans and immigrants from the British Isles, Germany, and Scandinavia were well endowed with intelligence, while African Americans and immigrants from southern and eastern Europe were poorly endowed. But these tests were scientifically so ill-conceived that their findings revealed nothing about the true distribution of intelligence in the population. In 1919 the military discontinued the IQ testing program.

Given the sharp racial and ethnic differences among American troops and the short time Pershing and his staff had to train recruits, the performance of the AEF was impressive. The most decorated soldier in the AEF was Sergeant Alvin C. York of Tennessee, who captured 35 machine guns and 132 prisoners and who killed 17 German soldiers with 17 bullets. York had learned his marksmanship hunting wild turkeys in the Tennessee hills. "Of course, it weren't no trouble nohow for me to hit them big [German] army targets," he later commented. "They were so much bigger than turkeys' heads."

One of the most decorated AEF units was New York's 369th Regiment, a black unit recruited in Harlem. Bowing to pressure from civil rights groups like the NAACP that some black troops be allowed to fight, Pershing had offered the 369th to the French army. The 369th entered the French front line and scored one major success after another. In gratitude for its service, the French government decorated the entire unit with one of its highest honors—the *Croix de Guerre*.

Paying the Bills

As chief purchaser of food, uniforms, munitions, weapons, vehicles, and sundry other items for the U.S. military, the government incurred huge debts. To help pay its bills, it sharply increased tax rates. The new taxes hit the wealthiest Americans the hardest: The richest were slapped with a 67 percent income tax and a 25 percent inheritance tax. Corporations were ordered to pay an "excess profits" tax. The revenues brought in by the taxes, however, provided only about one-third of the $33 billion that the government ultimately spent on the war. The rest came from the sale of "Liberty Bonds." These were 30-year bonds the government sold to individuals with a return of 3½ percent in annual interest.

The government offered five bond issues between 1917 and 1920 and all were quickly sold out. Their success was due in no small measure to a high-powered sales pitch, orchestrated by Treasury Secretary William G. McAdoo, that equated bond purchases with patriotic duty. McAdoo's agents blanketed the country with posters, sent bond "salesmen" into virtually every American community, enlisted Boy Scouts to go door-to-door, and staged rallies at which movie stars such as Mary Pickford, Douglas Fairbanks, and Charlie Chaplin stumped for the war.

Arousing Patriotic Ardor

The Treasury's bond campaign was only one aspect of an extraordinary government effort to arouse public support for the war. In 1917 Wilson set up a new agency, the Committee on Public Information (CPI), to publicize and popularize the war. Under the chairmanship of George Creel, a midwestern progressive and a muckraker, the CPI conducted an unprecedented propaganda campaign. It distributed 75 million copies of pamphlets explaining U.S. war aims in several languages. It trained a force of 75,000 "Four Minute Men" to deliver succinct, uplifting war speeches to numerous groups in their home cities and towns. It papered the walls of virtually every public institution (and many private ones) with posters, placed advertisements in mass-circulation magazines, sponsored exhibitions, and peppered newspaper editors with thousands of press releases on the progress of the war.

Faithful to his muckraking past, Creel wanted to give the people "the facts" of the war, believing that well-informed citizens would see the wisdom of Wilson's policies. He also felt his work gave him an opportunity to achieve the progressive goal of uniting all Americans into a single moral community. Americans everywhere were told that the United States had entered the war "to make the world safe for democracy," to help the world's weaker peoples achieve self-determination, to bring a measure of social justice into the conduct of international affairs. Americans were asked to affirm those ideals by doing everything they could to support the war.

This uplifting message had a profound effect on the American people. It imparted to many a deep love of country and a sense of participation in a grand democratic experiment. Workers, women, European ethnics, and African Americans began demanding that America live up to its democratic ideals at home as well as abroad. Workers rallied to the cry of "industrial democracy." Women seized upon the democratic fervor to bring their fight for suffrage to a successful conclusion (see Chapter 21). African Americans began to dream that the war might deliver them from second-class citizenship. European ethnics believed that Wilson's support of their countrymen's rights abroad would improve their own chances for success in the United States.

Although the CPI had helped to unleash it, this new democratic enthusiasm troubled Creel and others in the Wilson administration. The United States, after all, was still deeply divided along class, ethnic, and racial lines. Workers and industrialists regarded each other with suspicion. Cultural differences compounded this class division, for the working class was overwhelmingly ethnic in composition, while the industrial and political elites consisted mainly of the native-born whose families had been "Americans" for generations. Progressives had fought hard to overcome these divisions. They had tamed the power of capitalists, improved the condition of workers, encouraged the Americanization of immigrants, and articulated a new, more inclusive idea of American nationhood. But their work was far from complete when the war broke out, and the war itself opened up new social and cultural divisions. The decision to authorize the CPI's massive unity campaign is evidence that the progressives understood how widespread the discord was. Still, they had not anticipated that the promotion of democratic ideals at home would exacerbate, rather than lessen, existing social and cultural conflicts.

WARTIME REPRESSION

By early 1918 the CPI's campaign had developed a darker, more coercive side. Inflammatory advertisements called on patriots to report on neighbors, coworkers, and ethnics whom they suspected of subverting the war effort. Propagandists called on immigrants to repudiate all ties to their homeland, native language, and ethnic customs. The CPI aroused hostility to Germans by spreading lurid tales of German atrocities and encouraging the

Renamed German American Words

Original	"Patriotic" Name
hamburger	salisbury steak, liberty steak, liberty sandwich
sauerkraut	liberty cabbage
Hamburg Avenue, Brooklyn, New York	Wilson Avenue, Brooklyn, New York
Germantown, Nebraska	Garland, Nebraska
East Germantown, Indiana	Pershing, Indiana
Berlin, Iowa	Lincoln, Iowa
pinochle	liberty
German shepherd	Alsatian shepherd
Deutsches Hans of Indianapolis	Athenaeum of Indiana
Germania Maennerchor of Chicago	Lincoln Club
Kaiser Street	Maine Way

Source: From La Vern J. Rippley, *The German Americans* (Boston: Twayne Publishers, 1976), p. 186; and Robert H. Ferrell, *Woodrow Wilson and World War I, 1917–1921* (New York: Harper and Row, 1985), pp. 205–206.

public to see movies like *The Prussian Cur* and *The Beast of Berlin*. The Department of Justice arrested thousands of German and Austrian immigrants whom it suspected of subversive activities. Congress passed the Trading with the Enemy Act, which required foreign-language publications to submit all war-related stories to post office censors for approval.

German Americans became the objects of popular hatred. American patriots sought to expunge every trace of German influence from American culture. In Boston, performances of Beethoven's symphonies were banned. Libraries removed works of German literature from their shelves, while Theodore Roosevelt and others urged school districts to prohibit the teaching of the German language. Patriotic school boards burned the German books in their districts.

German Americans were at risk of being fired from work, losing their businesses, and being assaulted on the street. A St. Louis mob lynched an innocent German immigrant whom they suspected of subversion. After only 25 minutes of deliberation, a St. Louis jury acquitted the mob leaders, who had brazenly defended their crime as an act of patriotism. German Americans began hiding their ethnic identity, changing their names, speaking German only in the privacy of their homes, celebrating their holidays only with trusted friends.

The anti-German campaign escalated into a general anti-immigrant crusade. Congress passed the Immigration Restriction Act of 1917, which declared that all adult immigrants who

TURNING ENEMIES INTO APES

From the mid-19th to the mid-20th century, Americans frequently drew on simian imagery to describe and demean their enemies, both internal and external. Blacks and Asians were the groups most commonly depicted as apelike, a reflection in part of popular and pseudo-scientific notions that human beings belonged to a series of distinct and unequal "races" with varying capacities for intelligence, morality, and achievement. Africans and Asians often were thought to be the most primitive human races, closest to the apes, and northwest Europeans the most civilized.

But simian imagery was sometimes used against northwest and west Europeans themselves, as the images shown here demonstrate: one portrays Germany in the First World War; the other represents Spain as a brute who cruelly sank the battleship *Maine* in 1898. Both enemies were turned into "brutes" who were alleged to possess no self-control, no knowledge of right from wrong, and no respect for human life, pure womanhood, or law and order. To depict enemies in these terms was to justify America's obligation to use force against them. Brutes, like animals, could only be killed or beaten into submission; they would not respond—as would civilized peoples (such as Americans)—to reason or negotiation. In the case of the Spanish and the Germans, using force meant war.

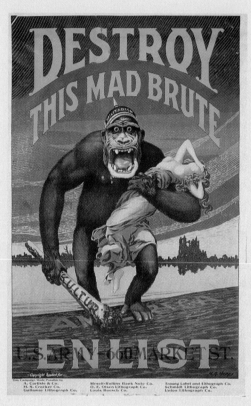

The Spanish Brute Adds Mutilation to Murder

failed a reading test would be denied admission to the United States. The act also banned the immigration of laborers from India, Indochina, Afghanistan, Arabia, the East Indies, and several other countries within an "Asiatic Barred Zone." Congress also passed the Eighteenth Amendment to the Constitution, which prohibited the manufacture and distribution of alcoholic beverages (see Chapter 21). The crusade for Prohibition was not new, but anti-immigrant feelings generated by the war gave it added impetus. Prohibitionists pictured the nation's urban ethnic ghettos as scenes of drunkenness, immorality, and disloyalty. The Eighteenth Amendment was quickly ratified by the states, and in 1919 Prohibition became the law of the land.

More and more, the Wilson administration relied on repression to achieve domestic unity. In the Espionage, Sabotage, and Sedition Acts passed in 1917 and 1918, Congress gave the administration sweeping powers to silence and even imprison dissenters. These acts went far beyond outlawing behavior such as spying for the enemy, sabotaging war production, and calling for the enemy's victory. By making it illegal to write or utter any statement that could be construed as profaning the flag, the Constitution, or the military, they constituted the most drastic restriction of free speech at the national level since enactment of the Alien and Sedition Acts of 1798 (see Chapter 8).

Government repression fell most heavily on the IWW and the Socialist Party. Both groups had opposed intervention before 1917. Although they subsequently muted their opposition, they continued to insist that the true enemies of American workers were to be found in the ranks of American employers, not in Germany or Austria-Hungary. The government responded by banning many socialist materials from the mails and by disrupting socialist and IWW meetings. By the spring of 1918 government agents had arrested 2,000 IWW members, including its entire executive board. Many of those arrested would be sentenced to long jail terms. Eugene V. Debs, the head of the Socialist Party, received a 10-year jail term for making an antiwar speech in Canton, Ohio, in the summer of 1918.

Citizens organized groups to enforce patriotism. The largest of these, the American Protective League, routinely spied on fellow workers and neighbors, opened the mail and tapped the phones of those suspected of disloyalty, and harassed young men who were thought to be evading the draft. Attorney General Thomas Gregory publicly endorsed the group and sought federal funds to support its "police" work.

The spirit of coercion even infected institutions that had long prided themselves on tolerance. In July 1917 Columbia University fired two professors for speaking out against U.S. intervention in the war. The National Americanization Committee, which prior to 1917 had pioneered a humane approach to the problem of integrating immigrants into American life, now supported surveillance, internment, and deportation of aliens suspected of anti-American sentiments.

Wilson himself bore significant responsibility for this climate of repression. On the one hand, he did attempt to block certain pieces of repressive legislation; for example, he vetoed both the Immigration Restriction Act and the Volstead Act (the act passed by Congress to enforce Prohibition), only to be overridden by Congress. But on the other hand Wilson did little to halt Attorney General Gregory's prosecution of radicals or Postmaster General Burleson's campaign to exclude Socialist Party publications from the mail. He ignored pleas from progressives that he intervene in the Debs case. His acquiescence in these matters cost him dearly among progressives and socialists. Wilson believed , however, that once the Allies won the war and arranged a just peace in accordance with the Fourteen

Points, his administration's wartime actions would be forgiven and the progressive coalition would be restored.

THE FAILURE OF THE INTERNATIONAL PEACE

In the month following Germany's surrender on November 11, 1918, Wilson was confident about the prospects of achieving a just peace. Both Germany and the Allies had publicly accepted the Fourteen Points as the basis for negotiations. Wilson's international prestige was enormous. To capitalize on his fame, Wilson broke sharply with diplomatic precedent and decided to head the American delegation to the Paris Peace Conference in January 1919 himself. Some 2 million French citizens lined the parade route in Paris to catch a glimpse of "Wilson, *le juste* [the just]."

In the Fourteen Points, Wilson had translated his principles for a new world order into specific proposals for world peace and justice. The first group of points called for all nations to abide by a code of conduct that embraced free trade, freedom of the seas, open diplomacy, disarmament, and the resolution of disputes through mediation. A second group, based on the principle of self-determination, proposed redrawing the map of Europe to give the subjugated peoples of the Austro-Hungarian, Ottoman, and Russian empires national sovereignty. The last point called for establishing a League of Nations, an assembly in which all nations would be represented and in which all international disputes would be given a fair hearing and an opportunity for peaceful solutions.

"THE SAVIOR OF HUMANITY" Wherever he went in Europe, Wilson was greeted by huge, delirious crowds eager to thank him for ending Europe's terrible war and to endorse his vision of a peaceful, democratic world. Here millions of Italians greet Wilson's arrival in Milan.

The Paris Peace Conference and the Treaty of Versailles

Although representatives of 27 nations began meeting in Paris on January 12, 1919, to discuss Wilson's Fourteen Points, negotiations were controlled by the "Big Four": Wilson, Prime Minister David Lloyd George of Great Britain, Premier Georges Clemenceau of France, and Prime Minister Vittorio Orlando of Italy. When Orlando quit the conference after a dispute with Wilson, the Big Four became the Big Three. Wilson quickly learned that his negotiating partners' support for the Fourteen Points was much weaker than he had believed. Indeed, Clemenceau and Lloyd George refused to include most of Wilson's points in the peace treaty. The points having to do with freedom of the seas and free trade were omitted, as were the proposals for open diplomacy and Allied disarmament. Wilson won partial endorsement of the

EUROPE AND THE NEAR EAST AFTER THE FIRST WORLD WAR

principle of self-determination: Belgian sovereignty was restored, Poland's status as a nation was affirmed, and the new nations of Czechoslovakia, Yugoslavia, Finland, Lithuania, Latvia, and Estonia were created. Some lands of the former Ottoman Empire—Armenia, Palestine, Mesopotamia, and Syria—were to be placed under League of Nations' trusteeships with the understanding that they would some day gain their independence. But Wilson failed in his efforts to block a British plan to transfer former German colonies in Asia to Japanese control, an Italian plan to annex territory inhabited by 200,000 Austrians, and a French plan to take from Germany its valuable Saar coal mines.

Nor was Wilson able to blunt the drive to punish Germany for its wartime aggression. In addition to awarding the Saar basin to France, the Allies gave portions of northern Germany to Denmark and portions of eastern Germany to Poland and Czechoslovakia. Germany was stripped of virtually its entire navy and air force, and forbidden to place soldiers or fortifications in western Germany along the Rhine. In addition, Germany was forced to admit its responsibility for the war. In accepting this "war guilt," Germany was, in effect, agreeing to compensate the victors in cash ("reparations") for the pain and suffering it had inflicted on them.

Lloyd George and Clemenceau brushed off the protests of those who viewed this desire to prostrate Germany as a cruel and vengeful act. That the German people, after their nation's 1918 defeat, had overthrown the monarch (Kaiser Wilhelm II) who had taken them to war, and had reconstituted their nation as a democratic republic won them no leniency. In 1921 an Allied commission notified the Germans that they were to pay the victors $33 billion, a sum well beyond what a defeated and economically ruined Germany could muster. The Treaty of Versailles was signed by Great Britain, France, the United States, Germany, and other European nations on June 28, 1919.

THE LEAGUE OF NATIONS

The Allies' single-minded pursuit of self-interest disillusioned many liberals and socialists in the United States. But Wilson seemed not to be dismayed, for he had won approval of the most important of his Fourteen Points—the point that called for the creation of the League of Nations. The League, whose structure and responsibilities were set forth in the Covenant attached to the peace treaty, would usher in Wilson's new world order. Drawing its membership from the signatories to the Treaty of Versailles (except, for the time being, Germany), the League would function as an international parliament and judiciary, establishing rules of international behavior and resolving disputes between nations through rational and peaceful means.

The League, Wilson believed, would redeem the failures of the Paris Peace Conference. Under its auspices, free trade and freedom of the seas would be achieved, reparations against Germany would be reduced or eliminated, disarmament of the Allies would proceed, and the principle of self-determination would be extended to peoples outside Europe. Moreover, the League would have the power to punish aggressor nations, which would be subject to economic isolation and military retaliation.

WILSON VERSUS LODGE: THE FIGHT OVER RATIFICATION

For the League to succeed, however, Wilson had to convince the U.S. Senate to ratify the Treaty of Versailles. Wilson knew that this would be no easy task. The Republicans had gained a majority in the Senate in 1918, and two groups within their ranks were determined to frustrate Wilson's ambitions. One group was a caucus of 14 midwesterners and westerners known as the "irreconcilables." Most of them were conservative isolationists who wanted the United States to preserve its separation from Europe, but a few were prominent progressives who had voted against the declaration of war in 1917. Under no circumstances would they support a plan that would embroil the United States in European affairs.

The second opposition group was led by Senator Henry Cabot Lodge of Massachusetts. Its members did not subscribe to Wilson's belief that every group of people on earth had a right to form their own nation; that every state, regardless of its size, should have a voice in world affairs; and that disputes between nations could be settled in open, democratic forums. They subscribed instead to Theodore Roosevelt's vision of a world controlled by a few great nations, each militarily strong, secure in its own sphere of influence, and determined to avoid war through a carefully negotiated balance of power. These Republicans preferred to let Europe return to the power politics that had prevailed before the war rather than experiment with a new world order that might constrain and compromise U.S. power and autonomy.

Of particular importance in the Republican critique were the questions it raised about the power given the League by Article X to undertake military actions against aggressor nations. Did Americans want to authorize an international organization to decide when the United States would go to war? Was this not a violation of the Constitution, which vested war-making power solely in Congress? Even if the constitutional problem could be solved, how could the United States ensure that it would not be forced into a military action that might damage its national interest?

It soon became clear, however, that a number of the Republicans, especially Lodge, were more interested in humiliating Wilson than in engaging in debate. They accused him of promoting socialism through his wartime expansion of government power. They were angry that he had failed to include any distinguished Republicans on the Paris peace delegation. And they were still bitter about the 1918 congressional elections, when Wilson had argued that a Republican victory would embarrass the nation abroad in a critical moment in world affairs. Though Wilson's electioneering had failed to sway the voters (the Republicans won a majority in both Houses), his suggestion that a Republican victory would injure national honor had infuriated Theodore Roosevelt and his supporters. Roosevelt died in 1919, but his close friend Lodge kept his rage alive.

As chairman of the Senate Foreign Relations Committee, which was charged with considering the treaty before reporting it to the Senate floor, Lodge had considerable power, and he did everything possible to obstruct ratification. When his committee finally reported the treaty to the full Senate, it came encumbered with nearly 50 amendments whose adoption Lodge made a precondition of his support. Some of the amendments expressed reasonable concerns—namely, that participation in the League not diminish the role of Congress in determining foreign policy, or compromise the sovereignty of the nation, or involve the nation in an unjust or ill-advised war. But many were meant only to complicate the task of ratification.

Despite Lodge's obstructionism, the treaty's chances for ratification by the required two-thirds majority of the Senate were still good. Many Republicans were prepared to vote for ratification if Wilson indicated his willingness to accept some of the proposed amendments.

Wilson possessed the political savvy to salvage the treaty and, along with it, U.S. participation in the League of Nations. But at this crucial moment in national and world history, he refused to compromise and announced that he would carry his case directly to the people. In September 1919 he undertook a whirlwind cross-country tour in which he addressed as many crowds as he could reach, sometimes speaking for an hour at a time, four times a day. However, in thinking that this "appeal to the country" would force Republican senators to change their votes, Wilson had gravely miscalculated. All he achieved was his own physical exhaustion.

On September 25, after giving a speech at Pueblo, Colorado, Wilson suffered excruciating headaches throughout the night. His physician ordered him back to Washington, where on October 2 he suffered a near-fatal stroke. Wilson hovered near death for two weeks and remained seriously disabled for another six. Wilson's wife, Edith Bolling Wilson, and his doctor isolated him from Congress and the press, withholding news they thought might upset him and preventing the public from learning how much his body and mind had deteriorated.

Many historians believe that the stroke impaired Wilson's political judgment. If so, that may explain his refusal to consider any of the Republican amendments to the treaty, even after it had become clear that compromise offered the only chance of winning U.S. participation in the League of Nations. When Lodge presented an amended treaty for a ratification vote on November 19, Wilson ordered Senate Democrats to vote against it; 42 (of 47) Democratic senators complied, and with the aid of 13 Republican irreconcilables, the Lodge version was defeated. Only moments later, the unamended version of the treaty—Wilson's version—received only 38 votes.

THE TREATY'S FINAL DEFEAT

As the magnitude of the calamity became apparent, supporters of the League in Congress, the nation, and the world urged the Senate and the president to reconsider. Wilson would not budge. A bipartisan group of senators desperately tried to work out a compromise without consulting him. When that effort failed, the Senate put to a vote, one more time, the Lodge version of the treaty. Because 23 Democrats, most of them southerners, still refused to break with Wilson, this last-ditch effort at ratification failed.

The judgment of history lies heavily upon these events, for the flawed treaty and the failure of the League are thought by many to have contributed to Adolf Hitler's rise and the outbreak of a second world war even more terrifying than the first. It is necessary to ask, then, whether American participation in the League would have significantly altered the course of world history.

The mere fact of U.S. membership in the League would not have magically solved Europe's postwar problems. The U.S. government was inexperienced in diplomacy and prone to mistakes. Its freedom to negotiate solutions to international disputes would have been limited by the large number of American voters who remained strongly opposed to American entanglement in European affairs. Even if such opposition could have been overcome, the United States would still have confronted European countries determined to go their own way.

Nevertheless, one thing is clear: No stable international order could have arisen after the First World War without the full involvement of the United States. The League of Nations required American authority and prestige in order to operate effectively as an international parliament. We cannot know whether the League, with American involvement, would have

WOODROW WILSON'S FOURTEEN POINTS, 1918: RECORD OF IMPLEMENTATION

1. Open covenants of peace openly arrived at	Not fulfilled
2. Absolute freedom of navigation upon the seas in peace and war	Not fulfilled
3. Removal of all economic barriers to the equality of trade among nations	Not fulfilled
4. Reduction of armaments to the level needed only for domestic safety	Not fulfilled
5. Impartial adjustments of colonial claims	Not fulfilled
6. Evacuation of all Russian territory; Russia to be welcomed into the society of free nations	Not fulfilled
7. Evacuation and restoration of Belgium	Fulfilled
8. Evacuation and restoration of all French lands; return of Alsace-Lorraine to France	Fulfilled
9. Readjustment of Italy's frontiers along lines of Italian nationality	Compromised
10. Self-determination for the former subjects of the Austro-Hungarian Empire	Compromised
11. Evacuation of Romania, Serbia, and Montenegro; free access to the sea for Serbia	Compromised
12. Self-determination for the former subjects of the Ottoman Empire; secure sovereignty for Turkish portion	Compromised
13. Establishment of an independent Poland with free and secure access to the sea	Fulfilled
14. Establishment of a League of Nations affording mutual guarantees of independence and territorial integrity	Compromised

Source: From G. M. Gathorne-Hardy, *The Fourteen Points and the Treaty of Versailles*, Oxford Pamphlets on World Affairs, no. 6 (1939), pp. 8–34; and Thomas G. Paterson et al., *American Foreign Policy: A History*, 2nd ed. (Lexington, Mass.: D. C. Heath, 1983), vol. 2, pp. 282–293.

offered the Germans a less humiliating peace, allowing them to rehabilitate their economy and salvage their national pride; nor whether an American-led League would have stopped Hitler's expansionism before it escalated into full-scale war in 1939. Still, it seems fair to suggest that American participation would have strengthened the League and improved its ability to bring a lasting peace to Europe.

THE POSTWAR PERIOD: A SOCIETY IN CONVULSION

The end of the war brought no respite from the forces that were convulsing American society. Workers were determined to regain the purchasing power they had lost to inflation. Employers were determined to halt or reverse the wartime gains labor had made. Radicals saw in this conflict between capital and labor the possibility of a socialist revolution. Conservatives were certain that the revolution had already begun. Returning white servicemen were nervous about regaining their civilian jobs and looked with hostility on the black, Hispanic, and female workers who had been recruited to take their places. Black veterans were in no mood to return to segregation and subordination.

LABOR-CAPITAL CONFLICT

Nowhere was the escalation of conflict more evident than in the workplace. In 1919, 4 million workers—one-fifth of the nation's manufacturing workforce—went on strike. In January 1919, a general strike paralyzed the city of Seattle when 60,000 workers walked off their jobs. By August, walkouts had been staged by 400,000 eastern and midwestern coal miners, 120,000 New England textile workers, and 50,000 New York City garment workers. Then came two strikes that turned public opinion sharply against labor. In September, Boston policemen walked off their jobs after the police commissioner refused to negotiate with their newly formed union. Rioting and looting soon broke out. Massachusetts Governor Calvin Coolidge, outraged by the policemen's betrayal of their sworn public duty, refused to negotiate with them, called out the National Guard to restore order, and then fired the entire police force.

Hard on the heels of the policemen's strike came a strike by more than 300,000 steelworkers in the Midwest. No union had established a footing in the steel industry since the 1890s, when Andrew Carnegie had ousted the ironworkers' union from his Homestead, Pennsylvania, mills. Most steelworkers labored long hours (the 12-hour shift was still standard) for low wages in workplaces where they were exposed to serious injury. The organizers of the 1919 strike had somehow managed to persuade steelworkers with varied skill levels and ethnic backgrounds to put aside their differences and demand an eight-hour day and union recognition. When the employers rejected those demands, the workers walked off their jobs. The employers responded by procuring armed guards to beat up the strikers and by hiring nonunion labor to keep the plants running. In many areas, local and state police prohibited union meetings, ran strikers out of town, and opened fire on those who disobeyed orders. In Gary, Indiana, a confrontation between unionists and armed guards left 18 strikers dead. To arouse public support for their antiunion campaign, industry leaders painted the strike leaders as dangerous and violent radicals bent on the destruction of political liberty and economic freedom. They succeeded in arousing public opinion against the steelworkers, and the strike collapsed in January 1920.

RADICALS AND THE RED SCARE

The steel companies succeeded in putting down the strike by fanning the public's fear that revolutionary sentiment was spreading among the workers. Radical sentiment was indeed on the rise. Mine workers and railroad workers had begun calling for the permanent nationalization of coal mines and railroads. Longshoremen in San Francisco and Seattle refused to load ships carrying supplies to the White Russians who had taken up arms against Lenin's Bolshevik government. Socialist trade unionists mounted the most serious challenge to Gompers' control of the AFL in 25 years. In 1920, nearly a million Americans voted for the Socialist presidential candidate Debs.

This radical surge did not mean, however, that leftists had fashioned themselves into a single movement or political party. On the contrary, the Russian Revolution had split the American Socialist Party. One faction, which would keep the name Socialist and would continue to be led by Debs, insisted that radicals follow a democratic path to socialism. The other group, which would take the name Communist, wanted to establish a Lenin-style "dictatorship of the proletariat." Small groups of anarchists, some of whom advocated campaigns of terror to speed the revolution, represented yet a third radical tendency.

The fact that the radical camp was in such disarray escaped the notice of most Americans, who assumed that radicalism was a single, coordinated movement bent on establishing a communist government on American soil. Beginning in 1919, this perceived "Red Scare" prompted government officials and private citizens to embark on yet another campaign of repression.

The postwar repression of radicalism closely resembled the wartime repression of dissent. Thirty states passed sedition laws to punish people who advocated revolution. Numerous public and private groups intensified Americanization campaigns designed to strip foreigners of their "subversive" ways and remake them into loyal citizens. A newly formed veterans' organization, the American Legion, took on the American Protective League's role of identifying seditious individuals and organizations and making sure that the public's devotion to "100 percent Americanism" did not abate.

The Red Scare reached its climax on New Year's Day 1920 when federal agents broke into the homes and meeting places of thousands of suspected revolutionaries in 33 cities. Directed by Attorney General A. Mitchell Palmer, these widely publicized "Palmer raids" were meant to expose the extent of revolutionary activity. Palmer's agents uncovered three pistols, no rifles, and no explosives. Nevertheless, they arrested 6,000 people and kept many of them in jail for weeks without formally charging them with a crime. Finally, those who were not citizens (approximately 500) were deported and the rest were released.

As Palmer's exaggerations of the Red threat became known, many Americans began to reconsider their near-hysterical fear of dissent and subversion. But the political atmosphere remained hostile to radicals, as the Sacco and Vanzetti case revealed. In May 1920, two Italian-born anarchists, Nicola Sacco and Bartolomeo Vanzetti, were arrested in Brockton, Massachusetts, and charged with armed robbery and murder. Both men proclaimed their innocence and insisted that they were being punished for their political beliefs. Indeed, their foreign accents and their defiant espousal of anarchist doctrines in the courtroom inclined many Americans, including the judge who presided at their trial, to view them harshly. Although the case against them was weak, they were convicted of first-degree murder and sentenced to death. Their lawyers attempted numerous appeals, all of which failed. Anger over the verdicts began to build, first among Italian Americans, then among radicals, and finally among liberal intellectuals. Protests compelled the governor of Massachusetts to appoint a commission to review the case, but no new trial was ordered. On August 23, 1927, Sacco and Vanzetti were executed, still insisting that they were innocent.

RACIAL CONFLICT AND THE RISE OF BLACK NATIONALISM

The more than 400,000 blacks who served in the armed forces believed that a victory for democracy abroad would help them achieve democracy for themselves at home. At first, the discrimination they encountered in the military did not weaken their conviction that they would be treated as full-fledged citizens upon their return. Thousands joined the NAACP, which was at the forefront of the fight for racial equality. By 1918, there were 100,000 African Americans subscribing to the NAACP's magazine, *The Crisis*, whose editor, W. E. B. Du Bois, had urged them to support the war.

MARCUS GARVEY, BLACK NATIONALIST   Marcus Garvey participates in a black nationalist parade in Harlem. Garvey wears a plumed hat and is seated on the right, in the car's back seat. He often appeared in public as he does here—in a showy military-style uniform complete with epaulets and an admiral's hat.

That wartime optimism made the discrimination and hatred African Americans encountered after the war hard to endure. Many black workers who had found jobs in the North were fired to make way for returning white veterans. Returning black servicemen, meanwhile, had to scrounge for poorly paid jobs as unskilled laborers. In the South, lynch mobs targeted black veterans who were no longer willing to tolerate the usual insults and indignities.

The worst antiblack violence that year occurred in the North, however. Crowded conditions during the war had forced black and white ethnic city dwellers into uncomfortably close proximity. Many ethnic whites regarded blacks with a mixture of fear and prejudice. These racial tensions escalated into race riots. The deadliest explosion occurred in Chicago in July 1919, when a black teenager who had been swimming in Lake Michigan was killed by whites after coming too close to a whites-only beach. Rioting soon broke out throughout the city, with white mobs invading black neighborhoods, torching homes and stores, and attacking innocent residents. Led by war veterans, some of whom were armed, the blacks fought back, turning the border areas between white and black neighborhoods into battle zones. Fighting raged for five days, leaving 38 dead (23 black, 15 white) and more than 500 injured. Race rioting in other cities pushed the death total to 120 before the summer of 1919 ended.

The riots made it clear to blacks that the North was not the Promised Land. Confined to unskilled jobs and to segregated neighborhoods with substandard housing and exorbitant rents, black migrants in Chicago, New York, and other northern cities suffered severe economic hardship throughout the 1920s. The NAACP carried on its campaign for civil rights and racial equality, but many blacks no longer shared its belief that they would one day be accepted as first-class citizens. They turned instead to a compelling leader from Jamaica, Marcus Garvey. Garvey called on blacks to give up their hopes for integration and to set about forging a separate black nation. He reminded blacks that they possessed a rich culture stretching back over the centuries that would enable them to achieve greatness as a nation. Garvey's grand vision was to build a black nation in Africa that would bring together all the world's people of African descent. In the short term, he wanted to help American and Caribbean blacks to achieve economic and cultural independence.

Garvey's call for black separatism and self-sufficiency—or, black nationalism, as it came to be called—elicited a remarkable response among blacks in the United States. In the early 1920s, the Universal Negro Improvement Association (UNIA), which Garvey had founded, enrolled millions of members. His newspaper, *The Negro World,* reached a circulation of 200,000. Garvey's most visible economic venture was the Black Star Line, a shipping company with three ships that proudly flew the UNIA flag from their masts.

This black nationalist movement did not endure for long, however. Garvey entered into bitter disputes with other black leaders, including W. E. B. Du Bois, who regarded him as a flamboyant, self-serving demagogue. Garvey sometimes showed poor judgment, as when he expressed support for the Ku Klux Klan on the grounds that it shared his pessimism about the possibility of racial integration. Inexperienced in economic matters as well, Garvey squandered a great deal of UNIA money on abortive business ventures. In 1923 he was convicted of mail fraud involving the sale of Black Star stocks and was sentenced to five years in jail. In 1927 he was deported to Jamaica and the UNIA folded. But Garvey's philosophy of black nationalism endured.

CHRONOLOGY

1914	First World War breaks out (July–August)
1915	German submarine sinks *Lusitania* (May 7)
1916	Woodrow Wilson unveils peace initiative • Wilson reelected as "peace president"
1917	Germany resumes unrestricted submarine warfare (February) • Tsar Nicholas II overthrown in Russia (March) • U.S. enters the war (April 6) • Committee on Public Information established • Congress passes Selective Service Act, Espionage Act, Immigration Restriction Act • War Industries Board established • Lenin's Bolsheviks come to power in Russia (Nov.)
1918	Lenin signs treaty with Germany, pulls Russia out of war (March) • Germany launches offensive on western front (March–April) • Congress passes Sabotage Act and Sedition Act • French, British, and U.S. troops repel Germans, advance toward Germany (April–October) • Eugene V. Debs jailed for making antiwar speech • Germany signs armistice (Nov. 11)
1919	Treaty of Versailles signed (June 28) • Chicago race riot (July) • Wilson suffers stroke (September 25) • Police strike in Boston
1919–1920	Steelworkers strike in Midwest • Red Scare prompts "Palmer raids" • Senate refuses to ratify Treaty of Versailles • Universal Negro Improvement Association grows under Marcus Garvey's leadership
1920	Anarchists Sacco and Vanzetti convicted of murder
1923	Marcus Garvey convicted of mail fraud
1924	Woodrow Wilson dies
1927	Sacco and Vanzetti executed

CONCLUSION

The resurgence of racism in 1919 and the consequent turn to black nationalism among African Americans were signs of how the high hopes of the war years had been dashed. Industrial workers, immigrants, and radicals also learned through bitter experience that the fear, intolerance, and repression unleashed by the war interrupted their pursuit of liberty and equality. Of the reform groups, only woman suffragists made enduring gains—especially the right to vote—but, for the feminists in their ranks, these steps forward did not compensate for the collapse of the progressive movement and, with it, their program of achieving equal rights for women across the board.

A similar disappointment engulfed those who had embraced and fought for Wilson's dream of creating a new and democratic world order. The world in 1919 appeared as volatile as it had been in 1914. More and more Americans—perhaps even a majority—were coming to believe that U.S. intervention had been a colossal mistake.

In other ways, the United States benefited a great deal from the war. By 1919, the American economy was by far the world's strongest. The nation's economic strength triggered an extraordinary burst of growth in the 1920s, and millions of Americans rushed to take advantage of the prosperity that this "people's capitalism" had put within their grasp. But the joy generated by affluence did not dissolve the class, ethnic, and racial tensions that the war had exposed. And the failure of the peace process added to Europe's problems, delayed the emergence of the United States as a leader in world affairs, and created the preconditions for another world war.

24

THE 1920S

PROSPERITY ∼ THE POLITICS OF BUSINESS

FARMERS, SMALL-TOWN PROTESTANTS, AND MORAL TRADITIONALISTS

ETHNIC AND RACIAL COMMUNITIES

THE "LOST GENERATION" AND DISILLUSIONED INTELLECTUALS

In 1920 Americans elected a president, Warren G. Harding, who could not have been more different from his predecessor, Woodrow Wilson. A Republican, Harding presented himself as a common man with common desires. In his 1920 campaign he called for a "return to normalcy." Although he died in office in 1923, his carefree spirit is thought to characterize the 1920s.

To many Americans, indeed, the decade was one of fun rather than reform, of good times rather than high ideals. It was, in the words of novelist F. Scott Fitzgerald, the "Jazz Age," a time when the quest for personal gratification seemed to replace the quest for public welfare.

CULTURE SHOCK This photo juxtaposes the short dresses and dance steps of young women alongside the longer dresses and formal bearing of the older generation. Here, older women seem enchanted with the young women, but many others of their generation were discomfited by the revolution in dance and female demeanor that they were witnessing.

Despite Harding's call for a return to a familiar past, America seemed to be rushing head-long into the future. The word "modern" began appearing everywhere: modern times, modern women, modern technology, the modern home, modern marriage. Although the word was rarely defined, it connoted certain beliefs: that science was a better guide to life than religion; that people should be free to choose their own lifestyles; that sex should be a source of plea-sure for women as well as men; that women and minorities should be equal to and enjoy the same rights as white men.

Many other Americans, however, reaffirmed their belief that God's word transcended sci-ence; that people should obey the moral code set forth in the Bible; that women were not equal to men; and that blacks, Mexicans, and eastern European immigrants were inferior to Anglo-Saxon whites. They made their voices heard in a resurgent Ku Klux Klan and the fun-damentalist movement, and on issues such as evolution and immigration.

Modernists and traditionalists confronted each other in party politics, in legislatures, in courtrooms, and in the press. Their battles make it impossible to think of the 1920s merely as a time for the pursuit of leisure. Nor were the 1920s free of economic and social problems that had troubled Americans for decades.

PROSPERITY

Despite the strains placed on the U.S. economy after the First World War, it remained strong and innovative during the 1920s. Its industries had emerged intact, even strength-ened, from the war. The war needs of the Allies had created an insatiable demand for American goods and capital. Manufacturers and bankers had exported so many goods and extended so many loans to the Allies that by war's end the United States was the world's leading creditor nation.

For a time after the war ended, the country did experience economic turmoil and depres-sion. From 1919 to 1921, it struggled to redirect industry from wartime production to civilian production. Workers went on strike to protest wage reductions or increases in the workweek. Farmers were hit by a severe depression as the overseas demand for American foodstuffs fell from its peak of 1918 and 1919. Disgruntled workers and farmers even joined forces to form statewide farmer-labor parties. In 1924 the two groups formed a national Farmer-Labor Party. Robert La Follette, their presidential candidate, received an impressive 16 percent of the vote that year. But then the third-party movement fell apart.

Its collapse reflected a rising public awareness of how vigorous and productive the econ-omy had become. Beginning in 1922, the nation embarked on a period of remarkable growth. From 1922 to 1929, gross national product grew at an annual rate of 5.5 percent. The unem-ployment rate never exceeded 5 percent—and real wages rose about 15 percent.

A CONSUMER SOCIETY

The rate of economic growth was matched by the variety of products being produced. In the 19th century economic growth had rested primarily on the production of capital goods, such as factory machinery and railroad tracks. In the 1920s, however, growth rested more on the proliferation of consumer goods. Some products, such as cars and telephones, had been available since the early 1900s, but in the 1920s their sales reached new levels. Other consumer goods became available for the first time—tractors, washing machines, refrigerators, electric irons, radios, and vacuum cleaners. The term "consumer durable" was coined to describe such goods, which, unlike food, clothing, and other "perishables," were meant to last. Even "perishables" took on new allure. Scientists had discovered the importance of vitamins in the diet and began urging Americans to consume more fresh fruits and vegetables. Improvements in refrigeration and in packaging, meanwhile, made it possible to transport fresh produce long distances and to extend its shelf life in grocery stores. And more and more stores were being operated by large grocery chains that could afford the latest refrigeration and packaging technology.

The public responded to these innovations with excitement. American industry had made fresh food and stylish clothes available to the masses. Refrigerators, vacuum cleaners, and washing machines would spare women much of the drudgery of housework. Radios would expand the public's cultural horizons. Automobiles, asphalt roads, service stations, hot dog stands, "tourist cabins" (the forerunners of motels), and traffic lights seemed to herald a wholly new civilization. By the middle of the decade the country was a network of paved roads. Camping trips and long-distance vacations became routine. Farmers and their families could now hop into their cars and head for the nearest town with its stores, movies, amusement parks, and sporting events. Suburbs proliferated, billed as the perfect mix of urban and rural life. Young men and women everywhere discovered that cars were a place where they could "make out," and even make love, without fear of reproach by prudish parents or prying neighbors.

In the 1920s Americans also discovered the benefits of owning stocks. The number of stockholders in AT&T, the nation's largest corporation, rose from 140,000 to 568,000. By 1929, as many as 7 million Americans owned stock, most of them people of ordinary, middle-class means.

A People's Capitalism

Capitalists boasted that they had created a "people's capitalism" in which virtually all Americans could participate. Now, everyone could have a share of luxuries and amenities. Poverty, capitalists claimed, had been banished, and the gap between rich and poor had been closed. If every American could own a car and house, buy quality clothes, own stock, take vacations, and go to the movies, then clearly there was no longer any significant inequality in society.

Actually, although wages were rising, millions of Americans still did not earn enough income to partake fully of the marketplace. Robert and Helen Lynd were social scientists who studied the people of Muncie, Indiana, a small industrial city of 35,000, and published their findings in a classic study entitled *Middletown*. They discovered that working-class families who bought a car often did not have enough money left for other goods. One housewife admitted, "We don't have no fancy clothes when we have the car to pay for. . . . The car is the only pleasure we have." But many industrialists were reluctant to increase wages, and workers lacked the organizational strength to force them to pay more.

One solution came with the introduction of consumer credit. Car dealers, home appliance salesmen, and other merchants began to offer installment plans that enabled consumers to purchase a product by making a down payment and promising to pay the rest in installments. By 1930, 15 percent of all purchases were made on the installment plan.

Even so, many poor Americans benefited little from the consumer revolution. Middle-class Americans acquired a disproportionate share of consumer durables. They also were the main consumers of fresh vegetables and the main buyers of stock.

THE RISE OF ADVERTISING AND MASS MARKETING

But even middle-class consumers had to be wooed. How could they be persuaded to buy another car only a few years after they had bought their first one? General Motors had the answer. In 1926 it introduced the concept of the annual model change. Its cars were given a different look every year as GM engineers changed headlights and chassis colors, streamlined bodies, and added new features. The strategy worked. GM leaped past Ford and became the world's largest car manufacturer.

Henry Ford reluctantly introduced his Model A in 1927 to provide customers with a colorful alternative to the drab Model T. Having spent his lifetime selling a product renowned for its utility and reliability, Ford could not believe that sales could be increased by appealing to the intangible hopes and fears of consumers. He was wrong. The desire to be beautiful, handsome, or sexually attractive; to exercise power and control; to demonstrate competence and success; to escape anonymity, loneliness, and boredom; to experience pleasure—all such desires, once activated, could motivate a consumer to buy a new car at a time when the old one was still serviceable, or to spend money on goods that might have once seemed frivolous to some.

Arousing such desires required more than bright colors, sleek lines, and attractive packaging. It called for advertising campaigns intended to make a product seem to be the answer to the consumer's desires. To create those campaigns, corporations turned to a new kind of company: professional advertising firms. The new advertising entrepreneurs believed that many Americans were bewildered by bureaucratic workplaces and the anonymity of urban living. This modern anomie, they argued, left consumers susceptible to suggestion.

In their campaigns, advertisers played upon the emotions and vulnerabilities of their target audiences. One cosmetics ad decreed: "Unless you are one woman in a thousand, you must use powder and rouge. Modern living has robbed women of much of their natural color." A mouthwash ad warned about one unsuspecting gentleman's bad breath—"the truth that his friends had been too delicate to mention"—while a tobacco ad matter-of-factly declared: "Men at the top are apt to be pipe-smokers. . . . It's no coincidence—pipe-smoking is a calm and deliberate habit—restful, stimulating. His pipe helps a man think straight. A pipe is back of most big ideas."

Advertising professionals believed they were helping people to manage their lives in ways that would increase their satisfaction and pleasure. By enhancing one's appearance and personality with the help of goods to be found in the marketplace, one would have a better chance of achieving success and happiness.

American consumers responded enthusiastically. The most enthusiastic of all were middle-class Americans, who could afford to buy what the advertisers were selling. Many of them were newcomers to middle-class ranks, searching for ways to affirm—or even create—their new identity. The aforementioned ad for pipe tobacco, for example, was certainly targeted at the new middle-class man—who held a salaried position in a corporate office or bank, or worked as a commission salesman.

As male wage earners moved into the new middle class, their wives were freed from the necessity of outside work. Advertisers appealed to the new middle-class woman, too, as she refocused her attention toward dressing in the latest fashion, managing the household, and raising the children. Vacuum cleaners and other consumer durables would make her more efficient. Cosmetics would aid women in their "first duty"—to be beautiful for the men in their lives—a beauty that would lead to sexual arousal and fulfillment for both men and women.

CHANGING ATTITUDES TOWARD MARRIAGE AND SEXUALITY

That husbands and wives were encouraged to pursue sexual satisfaction together was one sign of how much prescriptions for married life had changed since the 19th century, when women were thought to lack sexual passion and men were tacitly expected to satisfy their drives through extramarital liaisons. Modern husbands and wives were expected to share other leisure activities as well—dining out, playing cards with friends, going to the movies, attending concerts, and discussing the latest selection from the newly formed Book-of-the-Month Club.

The public pursuit of pleasure was also noticeable among young and single middle-class women. The so-called "flappers" of the 1920s donned short dresses, rolled their stockings down, wore red lipstick, and smoked in public. Flappers were signaling their desire for independence and equality; but they had no thought of achieving those goals through politics, as had their middle-class predecessors in the woman suffrage movement. Rather, those goals were to be achieved through the creation of a new female personality endowed with self-reliance, outspokenness, and a new appreciation for the pleasures of life.

CELEBRATING A BUSINESS CIVILIZATION

Industrialists, advertisers, and merchandisers now began to claim that what they were doing was at the heart of American civilization. In 1924 President Calvin Coolidge declared that "the business of America is business." Even religion became a business. Bruce Barton, in his best-seller *The Man That Nobody Knows* (1925), depicted Jesus as a business executive "who picked up twelve men from the bottom ranks of business and forged them into an organization that conquered the world."

Some employers set up employee cafeterias, hired doctors and nurses to staff on-site medical clinics, and engaged psychologists to counsel troubled employees. They built ball fields and encouraged employees to join industry-sponsored leagues. They published employee newsletters and gave awards to employees who did their jobs well and with good spirit. Some even gave employees a voice in determining working conditions. The real purpose of these measures—collectively known as welfare capitalism—was to encourage employee loyalty to the firm and to the capitalist system.

INDUSTRIAL WORKERS

Many industrial workers benefited from the nation's prosperity. A majority of them enjoyed rising wages and a reasonably steady income. Skilled craftsmen in the older industries of construction, railroad transportation, and printing fared especially well. The several million workers employed in the large mass-production industries also did well. Their wages were relatively high, and they enjoyed unprecedented benefits—paid sick leave, paid vacations, life insurance, stock options, subsidized mortgages, and retirement pensions. Although all workers in companies with these programs were eligible for such benefits, skilled workers were in the best position to claim them.

Semiskilled and unskilled industrial workers had to contend with a labor surplus throughout the decade. As employers replaced workers with machines, the aggregate demand for industrial labor increased at a lower rate than it had in the preceding 20 years. Despite a weakening demand for labor, rural whites, rural blacks, and Mexicans continued their migration to the cities, stiffening the competition for factory jobs. Employers could hire and fire as they saw fit and were therefore able to keep wage increases lagging behind increases in productivity.

This softening demand for labor helps to explain why many working-class families did not benefit much from the decade's prosperity or from its consumer revolution. An estimated 40 percent of workers remained mired in poverty, unable to afford a healthy diet or adequate housing, much less any of the more costly consumer goods.

The million or more workers who labored in the nation's two largest industries, coal and textiles, suffered the most during the 1920s. Throughout the decade, both industries experienced severe overcapacity. By 1926 only half of the coal mined each year was being sold. New England textile cities experienced levels of unemployment that sometimes approached 50 percent. One reason was that many textile industrialists had shifted their operations to the South, where taxes and wages were lower. But the southern textile industry also suffered from excess capacity, and prices and wages continued to fall. Plant managers put constant pressure on their workers to speed up production. Workers loathed the frequent "speed-ups" of machines and the "stretch-outs" in the number of spinning or weaving machines each worker was expected to tend. By the late 1920s, labor strife and calls for unionization were rising sharply among disgruntled workers in both the South and the North.

Unionization of textiles and coal, and of more prosperous industries as well, would have brought workers a larger share of the decade's prosperity. Moreover, progressive labor leaders, such as Sidney Hillman of the Amalgamated Clothing Workers, argued that unionization would actually increase corporate profits by compelling employers to observe uniform wage and hour schedules that would restrain ruinous competition. Hillman pointed out that rising wages would enable workers to purchase more consumer goods and thus increase corporate sales and revenues. But Hillman's views were ignored outside the garment industry.

Elsewhere, unions lost ground as business and government remained hostile to labor organization. A conservative Supreme Court whittled away at labor's legal protections. In 1921 it ruled that lower courts could issue injunctions against union members, prohibiting them from striking or picketing an employer. State courts also enforced what union members called "yellow dog" contracts, written pledges by which employees promised not to join a union while they were employed. Any employee who violated that pledge was subject to immediate dismissal. These measures crippled efforts to organize trade unions. Membership fell from a high of 5 million in 1920 to less than 3 million in 1929, a mere 10 percent of the nation's industrial workforce. Not all of the decline was the result of the hostile political climate, though. Many workers, especially those who were benefiting from welfare capitalist programs, decided they no longer needed trade unions. And the labor movement hurt itself by moving too slowly to open its ranks to semiskilled and unskilled factory workers.

THE POLITICS OF BUSINESS

Republican presidents governed the country from 1921 to 1933. In some respects, their administrations resembled those of the Gilded Age, when presidents were mediocre, corruption was rampant, and the government's chief objective was to remove obstacles to capitalist development. But in other respects, the state-building tradition of Theodore Roosevelt lived on, although in somewhat altered form.

HARDING AND THE POLITICS OF PERSONAL GAIN

Warren Gamaliel Harding defeated the Democrat James M. Cox for the presidency in 1920. From modest origins as a newspaper editor in the small town of Marion, Ohio, Harding had risen to the U.S. Senate chiefly because the powerful Ohio Republican machine knew it could count on him to do its bidding. His election to the presidency occurred for the same reason. The Republican Party bosses believed that almost anyone they nominated in 1920 could defeat the Democratic opponent; they chose Harding because they could control him. Harding's good looks and geniality made him a favorite with voters, and he swept into office with 61 percent of the popular vote.

Aware of his own intellectual limitations, Harding included talented men in his cabinet. But he did not possess the will to alter his ingrained political habits. He had built his political career on a willingness to please the lobbyists who came to his Senate office asking for favors and deals. He had long followed Ohio boss Harry M. Daugherty's advice and would continue to do so, now that he had made Daugherty his attorney general. Harding apparently did not think of men such as Daugherty as self-serving or corrupt. They were his friends; they had been with him since the beginning of his political career. He made sure the "boys" had jobs in his administration, and he continued to socialize with them.

It seems that Harding kept himself blind to the widespread use of public office for private gain that characterized his administration. His old friends, the "Ohio gang," got rich selling government appointments, judicial pardons, and police protection to bootleggers. By 1923 the corruption could no longer be concealed. Journalists and senators began to focus public attention on the actions of Secretary of the Interior Albert Fall, who had persuaded Harding to transfer control of large government oil reserves at Teapot Dome, Wyoming, and Elk Hills, California, from the Navy to the Department of the Interior. Fall had then immediately leased the deposits to two oil tycoons, Harry F. Sinclair and Edward L. Doheny, who were allowed to pump oil from the wells in exchange for providing the Navy with a system of fuel tank reserves. Fall had issued the leases secretly, without allowing other oil corporations to compete for them, and he had accepted almost $400,000 from Sinclair and Doheny.

Fall would pay for this shady deal with a year in jail. He was not the only Harding appointee to do so. Charles R. Forbes, head of the Veterans' Bureau, would go to Leavenworth Prison for swindling the government out of $200 million in hospital supplies. The exposure of Forbes's theft prompted his lawyer, Charles Cramer, to commit suicide; Jesse Smith, Attorney General Daugherty's close friend and housemate, also killed himself, apparently to avoid being indicted and brought to trial. Daugherty himself managed to escape conviction and incarceration for bribery by burning incriminating documents held by his brother's Ohio bank. Still, Daugherty was forced to leave government service in disgrace.

Harding grew depressed when he finally realized what had been going on. In the summer of 1923, in poor spirits, he left Washington for a West Coast tour. He fell ill in Seattle and died from a heart attack in San Francisco. The train returning his body to Washington attracted crowds of grief-stricken mourners who little suspected the web of corruption and bribery in which Harding had been caught.

Coolidge and the Politics of Laissez-Faire

Harding's successor, Vice President Calvin Coolidge, never socialized with the "boys." He believed that the best government was the government that governed least, and he took a nap every afternoon. The welfare of the country hinged on the character of its people—their willingness to work hard, to be honest, to live within their means. Coolidge quickly put to rest the anxiety aroused by the Harding scandals.

Born in Vermont and raised in Massachusetts, he gained national visibility in September 1919, when as governor of Massachusetts he took a firm stand against Boston's striking policemen (see Chapter 23). His reputation as a man who battled labor radicals earned him a place

A Stern Yankee   In sharp contrast to Harding, President Calvin Coolidge did not enjoy informality, banter, or carousing. Here he fishes alone and in formal attire.

on the 1920 national Republican ticket. His image as an ordinary man helped convince voters in 1920 that the Republican Party would return the country to its commonsensical ways after eight years of reckless reforms. Coolidge won his party's presidential nomination handily in 1924 and easily defeated his Democratic opponent, John W. Davis. Coolidge's popularity remained strong throughout his first full term, and he probably would have been renominated and reelected in 1928. But he chose not to run.

Coolidge took greatest pride in those measures that reduced the government's control over the economy. The Revenue Act of 1926 slashed the high income and estate taxes that progressives had pushed through Congress during the First World War. Coolidge twice vetoed the McNary-Haugen Bill, which would have compelled the government to pay subsidies to farmers when domestic farm prices fell below certain levels. He stripped the Federal Trade Commission of the powers it needed to regulate business affairs. And he supported Supreme Court decisions invalidating Progressive Era laws that had strengthened organized labor and protected children and women from exploitation.

Hoover and the Politics of "Associationalism"

Republicans in the 1920s did more than simply lift government restraints and regulations from the economy. Some Republicans, led by Secretary of Commerce Herbert Hoover, conceived of government as a dynamic, even progressive, economic force. Hoover did not want government to control industry, but he did want government to persuade private corporations to abandon their wasteful, selfish ways and turn to cooperation and public service. Hoover envisioned an economy built on the principle of association. Industrialists, wholesalers, retailers, operators of railroad and shipping lines, small businessmen, farmers, workers, doctors—each of these groups would form a trade association whose members would share economic information, discuss problems of production and distribution, and seek ways of achieving greater efficiency and profit. Hoover believed that the very act of associating in this way—an approach that historian Ellis Hawley has called "associationalism"—would convince participants of the superiority of cooperation over competition, of negotiation over conflict, of public service over selfishness.

During the war, Hoover had directed the government's Food Administration and had made it an outstanding example of public management. From that experience, he had come to appreciate the advantages of coordinating the activities of thousands of producers and distributors scattered across the country. Hoover's ambition as secretary of commerce was to make the department the grand orchestrator of economic cooperation. During his eight years in that post, from 1921 to 1929, he organized over 250 conferences around such themes as unemployment or the problems of a particular industry or economic sector. He brought together government officials, representatives of business, policymakers, and others who had a stake in strengthening the economy.

Hoover achieved some notable successes. He convinced steel executives to abandon the 12-hour day. His support of labor's right to organize contributed to the passage of the 1926 Railway Labor Act, one of the few acts of the 1920s that endorsed labor's right to bargain collectively. His efforts to persuade farmers to join together in marketing cooperatives, which he believed would solve problems of inefficiency and overproduction, led to the Cooperative Marketing Act of 1926. He worked to standardize the size and shape of a great variety of products so as to increase their usefulness and strengthen their sales. When the Mississippi River overflowed its banks in 1927, Hoover was the man Coolidge appointed to organize the relief effort. Hoover used this disaster as an opportunity to place credit operations in flood-affected areas on a sounder footing and to organize local banks into associations with adequate resources and expertise.

Hoover's dynamic conception of government brought him into conflict with Republicans whose economic philosophy began and ended with laissez-faire. Hoover found himself increasingly at odds with Coolidge, who declared in 1927: "That man has offered me unsolicited advice for six years, all of it bad."

THE POLITICS OF BUSINESS ABROAD

Republican domestic policy disagreements between laissez-faire and associationalism spilled over into foreign policy as well. Hoover had accepted the post of secretary of commerce thinking he would represent the United States in negotiations with foreign companies and governments. In fact, he intended to apply his concept of "associationalism" to international relations. He wanted the world's leading nations to meet regularly in conferences, to limit military buildups and to foster an international environment in which capitalism could flourish. Aware that the United States would have to contribute to the creation of such an environment, Hoover hoped to persuade American bankers to adopt investment and loan policies that would aid European recovery. If they refused to do so, he was prepared to urge the government to take an activist, supervisory role in foreign investment.

In 1921 and 1922 Hoover had some influence on the design of the Washington Conference on the Limitation of Armaments. Although he did not serve as a negotiator at the conference—Secretary of State Charles Evans Hughes reserved that role for himself and his subordinates—he did supply Hughes's team with a wealth of economic information. And he helped Hughes to use that information to design forceful, detailed proposals for disarmament. Those proposals gave U.S. negotiators a decided advantage over their European and Asian counterparts and helped them win a stunning accord, the Five-Power Treaty, by which the United States, Britain, Japan, France, and Italy agreed to scrap more than 2 million tons of their warships. Hughes also obtained pledges from all the signatories that they would respect the "Open Door" in China, long a U.S. foreign policy objective (see Chapter 22).

These triumphs redounded to Hughes's credit but not to Hoover's, and Hughes used it to consolidate his control over foreign policy. He rebuffed Hoover's efforts to put international economic affairs under the direction of the Commerce Department and rejected Hoover's suggestion to intervene in the international activities of U.S. banks. In so doing, Hughes revealed his affinity for the laissez-faire rather than the associational school of Republican politics. Hughes was willing to urge bankers to participate in Europe's economic recovery, and he was willing to use the power of government to protect their investments once they were made, but the bankers would be free to decide which loans would be appropriate.

Hughes put his policy into action in 1923 to resolve a crisis in Franco-German relations. The victorious Allies had imposed on Germany an obligation to pay $33 billion in war reparations (see Chapter 23). In 1923, when the impoverished German government suspended its payments, France sent troops to occupy the Ruhr valley, whose industry was vital to the German economy. German workers retaliated by going on strike, and the crisis threatened to undermine Europe's precarious economic recovery.

Hughes understood that the only way to relieve the situation was to convince the French to reduce German reparations to a reasonable level. To help them come to that decision, he demanded that France repay in full the money it had borrowed from the United States during the First World War. The only way France could pay off those loans was to get additional credit from U.S. bankers, but Hughes made it clear that this would not happen until France had agreed to reduce German reparations. At last France relented and sent representatives to a U.S.-sponsored conference in 1924 to restructure Germany's obligation.

At this point, Hughes suddenly withdrew the government from the conference proceedings and turned over negotiations to a group of American bankers. The conference produced the Dawes Plan (after the Chicago banker and chief negotiator, Charles G. Dawes), which sharply reduced German reparations from $542 million to $250 million annually and called on U.S. and foreign banks to stimulate the German economy with a quick infusion of $200 million in loans. Within a matter of days, banker J. P. Morgan Jr. raised more than $1 billion from eager American investors. Money poured into German financial markets, and the German economy was apparently stabilized.

The Dawes Plan won applause on both sides of the Atlantic. But it soon became apparent that the U.S. money flooding into Germany was creating its own problems. American investors were so eager to lend to Germany that their investments became speculative and unsound. At this point, a stronger effort by the U.S. government to direct loans to sound investments might have helped. But Hughes's successor as secretary of state, Frank Kellogg, was interested in no such initiatives; nor was Secretary of the Treasury Mellon.

In only two areas did Republicans depart from their hands-off approach to foreign affairs. The first was in their pursuit of disarmament and world peace. The Five-Power Treaty, negotiated by Hughes in 1921 and 1922, was a major success. Secretary of State Kellogg drew up a treaty with Aristide Briand, the French foreign minister, outlawing war as a tool of national policy. In 1928, representatives of the United States, France, and 13 other nations met in Paris to sign the Kellogg-Briand pact. Hailed as a great stride toward world peace, the pact soon attracted the support of 48 other nations.

Coolidge viewed the treaty as an opportunity to further reduce the size of the U.S. government. With the threat of war removed, the United States could scale back its military forces and eliminate much of the bureaucracy needed to support a large standing army and navy. Unfortunately, the pact contained no enforcement mechanism. It would do nothing to slow the next decade's descent into militarism and war.

The other area in which the Republican administrations of the 1920s took a hands-on approach was Latin America. U.S. investments in the region more than doubled from 1917 to 1929, and the U.S. government continued its policy of intervening in the internal affairs of Latin America to protect U.S. interests. Republican administrations did attempt to curtail American military involvement in the Caribbean. The Coolidge administration pulled American troops out of the Dominican Republic in 1924 and Nicaragua in 1925. But, in the case of Nicaragua, U.S. Marines were sent back in 1926 to end a war between liberal and conservative Nicaraguans and to protect American property; this time they stayed until 1934. U.S. troops, meanwhile, occupied Haiti continuously between 1919 and 1934, keeping in power governments friendly to U.S. interests.

Farmers, Small-Town Protestants, and Moral Traditionalists

Although many Americans benefited from the prosperity of the 1920s, others did not. Over-production was impoverishing substantial numbers of farmers. Beyond economic hardship, many white Protestants, especially those in rural areas and small towns, believed that the country was being overrun by racially inferior and morally suspect foreigners.

Agricultural Depression

The 1920s brought hard times to the nation's farmers after the boom period of the war years. During the war, domestic demand for farm products had risen steadily, and foreign demand had exploded as the war disrupted agricultural production in France, Ukraine, and other European food-producing regions. Soon after the war, however, Europe's farmers quickly resumed their customary levels of production. Foreign demand for American foodstuffs fell precipitously, creating an oversupply and depressing prices in the United States.

Contributing further to the plight of U.S. farmers was the sharp rise in agricultural productivity made possible by the tractor, which greatly increased the acreage that each farmer could cultivate. Produce flooded the market. Prices fell even further, as did farm incomes. By 1929, the annual per capita income of rural Americans was only $223, one-quarter that of the non-farm population. Millions were forced to sell their farms. Their choices were then to scrape together a living as tenants or to abandon farming altogether.

Those who stayed on the land grew increasingly vociferous in their demands. In the first half of the decade, radical farmers working through such organizations as the Nonpartisan League of North Dakota and farmer-labor parties in Minnesota, Wisconsin, and other midwestern states led the movement. By the second half of the decade, however, leadership of the farm movement had passed from farming radicals to farming moderates, and from small farmers in danger of dispossession to larger farmers and agribusinesses seeking to extend their holdings. By lobbying through such organizations as the Farm Bureau Federation, the more powerful agricultural interests brought pressure on Congress to set up economic controls that would protect them from failure. Their proposals, embodied in the McNary-Haugen Bill, called on the government to erect high tariffs on foreign produce and to purchase surplus U.S. crops at prices that enabled farmers to cover their production costs. The government would then sell the surplus crops in the world market for whatever prices they fetched. Any money lost in international sales would be absorbed by the government rather than by the farmers. The McNary-Haugen Bill passed Congress in 1926 and in 1928, only to be vetoed by President Coolidge both times.

Cultural Dislocation

Added to the economic plight of the farmers was a sense of cultural dislocation. Farmers had long perceived themselves as the backbone of the nation—hardworking, honest, God-fearing yeomen, guardians of independence and liberty.

The 1920 census challenged the validity of that view. For the first time, a slight majority of Americans now lived in urban areas. That finding did not in itself signify very much, for the census classified as "urban" those towns with a population as small as 2,500. But the census figures did reinforce the widespread perception that both the economic and cultural vitality of the nation had shifted from the countryside to the metropolis. Industry, the chief engine of prosperity, was an urban phenomenon. Leisure—the world of amusement parks, department stores, professional sports, movies, cabarets, and theaters—was to be enjoyed in cities; so too were flashy fashions and open sexuality. Cities also were the home of secular intellectuals who had scrapped their belief in Scripture and in God and had embraced science as their new, unimpeachable authority.

All through the Progressive Era rural Americans had believed that the cities could be redeemed, that city dwellers could be reformed, that the Protestant values of rural America would triumph. War had crushed that confidence and had replaced it with the fear that urban culture and urban people would undermine all that "true" Americans held dear.

These fears grew even more intense with the changes brought by prosperity. Urban-industrial America was obviously the most prosperous sector of society; its consumer culture and its commodities were penetrating the countryside as never before. Even small towns now sported movie theaters and automobile dealerships. Radio waves carried news of city life into isolated farmhouses. The growth in the circulation of national magazines also broke down the wall separating country from city.

Rural Americans were ambivalent about this cultural invasion. On the one hand, country dwellers were eager to participate in the consumer marketplace. On the other, they worried that by doing so they would expose the countryside to atheism, immorality, and radicalism. Their determination to protect their imperiled way of life was manifested by their support of Prohibition, the Ku Klux Klan, immigration restriction, and religious fundamentalism.

Prohibition

The Eighteenth Amendment to the Constitution, which prohibited the manufacture and sale of alcohol, went into effect in January 1920. At its inception it was supported by a large and varied constituency that included farmers, middle-class city dwellers, feminists, and progressive reformers. It soon became apparent, however, that Prohibition was doing more to encourage law-breaking than abstinence. With only 1,500 federal agents to enforce the law, the government could not possibly police the drinking habits of 110 million people. With little fear of punishment, those who wanted to drink did so, either brewing liquor at home or buying it from speakeasies and bootleggers. Because the law prevented legitimate businesses from manufacturing liquor, organized crime simply added alcohol to its business portfolio. Mobsters procured much of their liquor from Canadian manufacturers, smuggled it across the border, protected it in warehouses, and distributed it to speakeasies. Al Capone's Chicago-based mob alone employed 1,000 men to protect its liquor trafficking, which was so lucrative that Capone became the richest (and most feared) gangster in America.

These unexpected consequences caused many early advocates of Prohibition, especially in the cities, to withdraw their support. That was not the response of Prohibition's rural, Protestant supporters, however. The violence spawned by liquor trafficking confirmed their view that alcohol was an agent of evil that had to be eradicated. The high-profile participation of Italian, Irish, and Jewish gangsters in the bootleg trade merely reinforced their view that Catholics and Jews were threats to law and morality. Many rural Protestants became more, not less, determined to rid the country of liquor once and for all; many resolved to rid the country of Jews and Catholics as well.

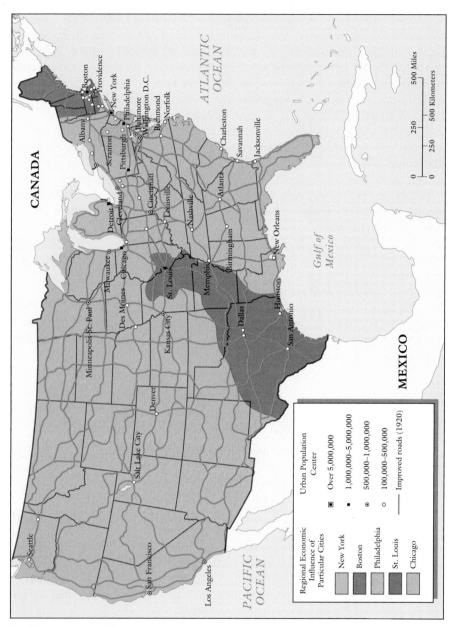

URBANIZATION, 1920

THE KU KLUX KLAN

The original Ku Klux Klan, formed in the South in the late 1860s, had died out with the defeat of Reconstruction and the reestablishment of white supremacy (see Chapter 17). The new Klan was created in 1915 by William Simmons, a white southerner who had been inspired by D. W. Griffith's racist film, *Birth of a Nation,* in which the early Klan was depicted as having saved the nation (and especially its white women) from predatory blacks. By the 1920s control of the Klan had passed from Simmons to a Texas dentist, Hiram Evans, and its ideological focus had expanded from a loathing of blacks to a hatred of Jews and Catholics as well. Evans's Klan propagated a nativist message that the country should contain—or better yet, eliminate—the influence of Jews and Catholics and restore "Anglo-Saxon" racial purity, Protestant supremacy, and traditional morality to national life. Evans's message swelled Klan ranks and expanded its visibility and influence in the North and South alike. By 1924, as many as 4 million Americans are thought to have belonged to the Klan, including the half-million members of its female auxiliary, Women of the Ku Klux Klan.

In some respects, the Klan functioned just as many other fraternal organizations did. It offered members friendship networks, social services, and conviviality. Its rituals, regalia, and mock-medieval language (the Imperial Wizard, Exalted Cyclops, Grand Dragons, etc.) gave initiates the same sense of superiority, valor, and mystery that so many other fraternal societies imparted to their members. But the Klan also stirred up hate. It thrived on lurid

WOMEN OF THE KU KLUX KLAN   Women comprised a substantial portion of the Klan's membership in the 1920s. Here a group marches in an "America First" parade in Binghamton, New York.

tales of financial extortion by Jewish bankers and sexual exploitation by Catholic priests. The accusations were sometimes general, as in the claim that an international conspiracy of Jewish bankers had caused the agricultural depression. More common, and more incendiary, however, were the seemingly plausible, yet totally manufactured, tales of Jewish or Catholic depravity. For example, Catholic priests and nuns were said to prey on Protestant girls and boys who had been forced into convents and Catholic orphanages. These outrageous stories sometimes provoked attacks on individual Jews and Catholics. More commonly, they prompted campaigns to boycott Jewish businesses and Catholic institutions, and to ruin reputations.

The emphasis on sexual exploitation in these stories reveals the anxiety Klan members felt about modern society's acceptance of sexual openness and sexual gratification. Many Klanspeople lived in towns like Muncie, Indiana, where, as the Lynds reported, life was suffused with modern attitudes. That such attitudes might reflect the yearnings of Protestant youth rather than the manipulation of deceitful Jews and Catholics was a truth some Protestant parents found difficult to accept.

IMMIGRATION RESTRICTION

Although the vast majority of Protestant Americans never joined the Klan, many of them did respond to the Klan's nativist argument that the country and its values would best be served by limiting the entry of outsiders. That was the purpose of the Johnson-Reed Immigration Restriction Act of 1924.

By the early 1920s most Americans believed that the country could no longer accommodate the million immigrants who had been arriving each year prior to the war and the more than 800,000 who arrived in 1921. Industrialists no longer needed unskilled European laborers to operate their factories, their places having been taken either by machines or by African American and Mexican workers. And most of the leaders of the labor movement were convinced that the influx of workers unfamiliar with English and with trade unions was weakening labor solidarity. Progressive reformers no longer believed that immigrants could be easily Americanized or that harmony between the native-born and the foreign-born could be readily achieved. Congress responded to constituents' concerns by passing an immigration restriction act in 1921. Then, in 1924, the more comprehensive Johnson-Reed Act imposed a yearly quota of 165,000 immigrants from countries outside the Western Hemisphere.

The sponsors of the 1924 act believed that certain groups—British, Germans, and Scandinavians, in particular—were racially superior and that, consequently, these groups should be allowed to enter the United States in greater numbers. However, because the Constitution prohibits the enactment of explicitly racist laws, Congress had to achieve this racist aim through subterfuge. Lawmakers established a formula to determine the annual immigrant quota for each foreign country, which was to be computed at 2 percent of the total number of immigrants from that country already resident in the United States in the year 1890. In 1890, immigrant ranks had been dominated by the British, Germans, and Scandinavians, so the new quotas would thus allow for a relatively larger cohort of immigrants from those countries. Immigrant groups that were poorly represented in the 1890 population—Italians, Greeks, Poles, Slavs, and eastern European Jews—were effectively locked out. The Johnson-Reed Act also reaffirmed the long-standing policy of excluding Chinese immigrants, and it added Japanese and other Asians to the list of groups that were altogether barred from entry. The act did not

ANNUAL IMMIGRANT QUOTAS UNDER THE JOHNSON-REED ACT, 1925–1927

NORTHWEST EUROPE AND SCANDINAVIA		EASTERN AND SOUTHERN EUROPE		OTHER COUNTRIES	
Country	*Quota*	*Country*	*Quota*	*Country*	*Quota*
Germany	51,227	Poland	5,982	Africa (other than Egypt)	1,100
Great Britain and Northern Ireland	34,007	Italy	3,845	Armenia	124
		Czechoslovakia	3,073		
Irish Free State (Ireland)	28,567	Russia	2,248	Australia	121
		Yugoslavia	671	Palestine	100
Sweden	9,561	Romania	603	Syria	100
Norway	6,453	Portugal	503	Turkey	100
France	3,954	Hungary	473	New Zealand and Pacific Islands	100
Denmark	2,789	Lithuania	344	All others	1,900
Switzerland	2,081	Latvia	142		
Netherlands	1,648	Spain	131		
Austria	785	Estonia	124		
Belgium	512	Albania	100		
Finland	471	Bulgaria	100		
Free City of Danzig	228	Greece	100		
Iceland	100				
Luxembourg	100				
Total (number)	142,483	Total (number)	18,439	Total (number)	3,745
Total (%)	86.5%	Total (%)	11.2%	Total (%)	2.3%

Note: Total annual immigrant quota was 164,667

Source: From *Statistical Abstract of the United States* (Washington, D.C.: Government Printing Office, 1929), p. 100.

officially limit immigration from nations in the Western Hemisphere, chiefly because agribusiness interests in Texas and California had convinced Congress that cheap Mexican laborers were indispensable to their industry's prosperity. Still, the establishment of a Border Patrol along the U.S.-Mexican border and the imposition of a $10 head tax on all prospective Mexican immigrants made entry into the United States more difficult for Mexicans than it had been.

The Johnson-Reed Act accomplished Congress's underlying goal. Annual immigration from transoceanic nations fell by 80 percent. The large number of available slots for English and German immigrants regularly went unfilled, while the smaller number of available slots for Italians, Poles, Russian Jews, and others prevented hundreds of thousands of them from entering the country. A "national origins" system put in place in 1927 reduced the total annual quota further, to 150,000, and reserved more than 120,000 of these slots for immigrants from northwestern Europe.

Remarkably few Americans, outside of the ethnic groups that were being discriminated against, objected to these laws at the time they were passed—an indication of how broadly acceptable racism and nativism had become.

FUNDAMENTALISM

Of all the forces reacting against urban life, Protestant fundamentalism was perhaps the most enduring. Fundamentalists regard the Bible as God's word and thus the source of all "fundamental" truth. They believe that every event depicted in the Bible, from the creation of the world in six days to the resurrection of Christ, happened exactly as the Bible describes it. For fundamentalists, God is a deity who intervenes directly in the lives of individuals and communities.

The rise of the fundamentalist movement from the 1870s through the 1920s roughly paralleled the rise of urban-industrial society. Fundamentalists recoiled from the "evils" of the city—from what they perceived as its poverty, its moral degeneracy, its irreligion, and its crass materialism. Fundamentalism took shape in reaction against two additional aspects of urban society: the growth of liberal Protestantism and the revelations of science.

Liberal Protestants believed that religion had to be adapted to the skeptical and scientific temper of the modern age. The Bible was to be mined for its ethical values rather than for its literal truth. Liberal Protestants removed God from his active role in history and refashioned him into a distant and benign deity who watches over the world but does not intervene to punish or to redeem. They turned religion away from the quest for salvation and toward the pursuit of good deeds, social conscience, and love for one's neighbor. Fundamentalism arose in part to counter the "heretical" claims of the liberal Protestants.

Liberal Protestants and fundamentalists both understood that science was the source of most challenges to Christianity. Scientists believed that rational inquiry was a better guide to the past and to the future than prayer and revelation. Scientists even challenged the ideas that God had created the world and had fashioned mankind in his own image. These were beliefs that many religious peoples, particularly fundamentalists, simply could not accept. Conflict was inevitable. It came in 1925, in Dayton, Tennessee.

THE SCOPES TRIAL

No aspect of science aroused more anger among fundamentalists than Charles Darwin's theory of evolution. There was no greater blasphemy than to suggest that man emerged from lower forms of life instead of being created by God himself. In Tennessee in 1925, fundamentalists succeeded in getting a law passed forbidding the teaching of "any theory that denies the story of the divine creation of man as taught in the Bible."

For Americans who accepted the authority of science, denying the truth of evolution was as ludicrous as insisting that the sun revolved around the earth. They ridiculed the fundamentalists, but they worried that the passage of the Tennessee law might signal the onset of a campaign to undermine First Amendment guarantees of free speech. The American Civil Liberties Union began searching for a teacher who would be willing to challenge the constitutionality of the Tennessee law. They found their man in John T. Scopes, a 24-year-old biology teacher in Dayton. After confessing that he had taught evolution to his students, Scopes was arrested. The case quickly attracted national attention. William Jennings Bryan announced that he would help to prosecute Scopes, and the famous liberal trial lawyer Clarence Darrow rushed to Dayton to lead Scopes's defense. That Bryan and Darrow had once been allies in the progressive movement only heightened the drama. A small army of journalists, led by H. L. Mencken, descended on Dayton.

The trial dragged on, and most of the observers expected Scopes to be convicted. (He was.) But it took an unexpected turn when Darrow persuaded the judge to let Bryan testify as an "expert on the Bible." Darrow knew that Bryan's testimony would have no bearing on the question of Scopes's innocence or guilt. His aim was to expose Bryan as a fool for believing that the Bible was a source of literal truth and thus to embarrass the fundamentalists. In a brilliant confrontation, Darrow made Bryan's defense of the Bible look silly, and he then led Bryan to admit that the "truth" of the Bible was not always easy to accept. In that case, Darrow asked, how could fundamentalists be so sure that everything in the Bible was literally true?

In his account of the trial, Mencken portrayed Bryan as a pathetic figure who had been devastated by his humiliating experience on the witness stand, a view popularized in the 1960 movie, *Inherit the Wind*. When Bryan died only a week after the trial ended, Mencken claimed that the trial had broken Bryan's heart.

Bryan deserved a better epitaph than the one Mencken had given him. Diabetes caused his death, not a broken heart. Nor was Bryan the innocent fool that Mencken made him out to be. He remembered when social conservatives had used Darwin's phrase "survival of the fittest" to prove that the wealthy and politically powerful were racially superior to the poor and powerless (see Chapter 20). His rejection of Darwinism evidenced his democratic faith that all human beings were creatures of God and thus capable of striving for perfection and equality.

The public ridicule attendant on the Scopes trial did take its toll on fundamentalists. Many of them retreated from politics and refocused their attention on purging sin from their own hearts rather than from the hearts of others. In the end, the fundamentalists were able to prevail on three more states to prohibit the teaching of evolution. But the controversy had even more far-reaching effects. Worried about losing sales, publishers quietly removed references to Darwin from their science textbooks, a policy that would remain in force until the 1960s.

Ethnic and Racial Communities

The 1920s were a decade of change for ethnic and racial minorities. Some minorities benefited from the prosperity of the decade; others created and sustained vibrant subcultures. All, however, experienced a surge in religious and racial discrimination that made them uneasy in Jazz Age America.

European Americans

European American immigrants were concentrated in the cities of the Northeast and Midwest. A large number were semiskilled and unskilled industrial laborers and suffered economic

DEMOCRATIC PRESIDENTIAL VOTING IN CHICAGO BY ETHNIC GROUPS,
1924 AND 1928

	PERCENT DEMOCRATIC	
	---	---
	1924	*1928*
Czechoslovaks	40%	73%
Poles	35	71
Lithuanians	48	77
Yugoslavs	20	54
Italians	31	63
Germans	14	58
Jews	19	60

Source: From John M. Allswang, *A House for All Peoples: Ethnic Politics in Chicago, 1890–1936* (Lexington: University Press of Kentucky), p. 42.

insecurity as a result. In addition, they faced cultural discrimination. Catholics generally opposed Prohibition, viewing it as a crude attempt by Protestants to control their behavior. Southern and eastern Europeans, particularly Jews and Italians, resented immigration restriction and the implication that they were unworthy of citizenship. Many Italians were outraged by the execution of Nicola Sacco and Bartolomeo Vanzetti in 1927 (Chapter 23). Had the two men been native-born Protestants, Italians argued, their lives would have been spared.

Southern and eastern Europeans everywhere were the objects of intensive Americanization campaigns. State after state passed laws requiring public schools to instruct children in the essentials of citizenship. Several states, including Rhode Island, extended these laws to private schools as well, convinced that immigrants' children who attended Catholic parochial schools were spending too much time learning about their native religion, language, and country. An Oregon law tried to eliminate Catholic schools altogether by ordering all children aged 8 to 16 to enroll in public schools. But attending a public school was no guarantee of acceptance, either—a lesson learned by Jewish children who had excelled in their studies only to be barred from Harvard, Columbia, and other elite universities.

Southern and eastern European Americans responded to these insults and attacks by strengthening the very institutions and customs Americanizers were trying to undermine. Ethnic associations flourished in the 1920s. Children learned their native languages and customs at home and at church if not at school, and joined with their parents to celebrate their ethnic heritage.

These immigrants and their children were not oblivious to the new consumer culture, however. They flocked to movies and amusement parks, to baseball games and boxing matches. Children usually entered more enthusiastically into the world of American mass culture than did their immigrant parents. Many ethnics found it possible to reconcile their own culture with American culture. Youngsters who went to the movies did so with friends from within their community. Ethnics also played sandlot baseball, but their leagues were customarily organized around churches or ethnic associations. In these early days of radio, ethnics living in large cities could always find programs in their native language and music from their native lands.

European American ethnics also resolved to develop the political muscle needed to defeat the forces of nativism and to turn government policy in a more favorable direction. One sign of this determination was a sharp rise in the number of immigrants who became U.S. citizens. Armed with the vote, ethnics turned out on election day to defeat unsympathetic city council-men, mayors, state representatives, and even an occasional governor. Their growing national strength first became apparent at the Democratic national convention of 1924, when urban-ethnic delegates almost won approval of planks calling for the repeal of Prohibition and con-demnation of the Klan. Then, after denying the presidential nomination to William G. McAdoo, they nearly secured it for their candidate, Alfred E. Smith, the Irish American gover-nor of New York. McAdoo represented the rural and southern constituencies of the Democra-tic Party. His forces ended up battling Smith's urban-ethnic forces for 103 ballots, until the two men gave up and supporters from each camp switched their votes to a compromise candi-date, the corporate lawyer John W. Davis.

The nomination fight devastated the Democratic Party in the short term, and the popular Coolidge easily defeated the little-known Davis. But the convention upheaval of 1924 also marked an important milestone in the bid by European Americans for political power. They would achieve a second milestone at the Democratic national convention of 1928 when, after another bitter nomination struggle, they were finally successful in securing the presidential nomination for Al Smith. Never before had a major political party nominated a Catholic for that high office. Herbert Hoover crushed Smith in the general election, as nativists stirred up anti-Catholic prejudice yet again, and as large numbers of southern Democrats either stayed home or voted Republican. But there were encouraging signs in the campaign, none more so than Smith's beating Hoover in the nation's 12 largest cities. European Americans would yet have their day.

African Americans

Despite the urban race riots of 1919 (see Chapter 23), African Americans continued to leave their rural homes for the industrial centers of the South and the North. In New York City and Chicago, their numbers grew so large that they formed cities unto themselves. Within these black metropolises, complex societies emerged consisting of workers, businessmen, profes-sionals, intellectuals, artists, and entertainers. Social differentiation intensified as various groups—long-resident northerners and newly arrived southerners, religious conservatives and cultural radicals, African Americans and African Caribbeans—found reason to disap-prove of one another's ways. Still, the diversity and complexity of urban black America were thrilling, nowhere more so than in Harlem, the "Negro capital."

Not even the glamour of Harlem could erase the reality of racial discrimination, how-ever. Most African Americans could find work only in New York City's least-desired and lowest-paying jobs. Because they could rent apartments only in areas that real estate agents and banks had designated as "colored," African Americans suffered the highest rate of resi-dential segregation of any minority group. Harlem became a black ghetto, an area set apart from the rest of the city by the skin color of its inhabitants, by its higher population den-sity and poverty rate, by its higher incidence of infectious diseases, and by the lower life ex-pectancy of its people. At the same time, substantial numbers of New York City's European

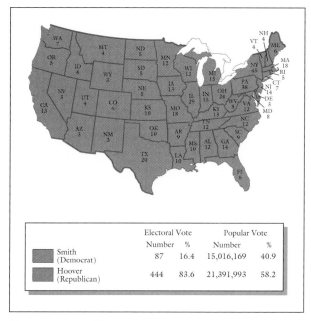

PRESIDENTIAL ELECTION, 1928

ethnics were leaving their lower Manhattan ghettos for the "greener" pastures of Brooklyn and the Bronx.

Blacks did enjoy some important economic breakthroughs in the 1920s. Henry Ford, for example, hired large numbers of African Americans to work in his Detroit auto factories. But even here a racist logic was operating, for Ford believed that black and white workers, divided along racial lines, would not challenge his authority.

African Americans grew pessimistic about achieving racial equality. After Marcus Garvey's black nationalist movement collapsed in the mid-1920s (see Chapter 23), no comparable organization arose to take its place. The NAACP continued to fight racial discrimination, and the Urban League carried on quiet negotiations with industrial elites to open up jobs to African Americans. But the victories were small; white allies were scarce. The political initiatives emerging among European ethnics had no counterpart in the African American community.

In terms of black culture, however, the 1920s were remarkably vigorous and productive. Black musicians coming north to Chicago and New York brought with them their distinctive musical styles, most notably the blues and ragtime. Influenced by the harmonies and techniques of European classical music, these southern styles metamorphosed into jazz. Urban audiences found this new music irresistible. In Chicago, Detroit, New York, New Orleans, and elsewhere, jazz musicians came together in cramped apartments, cabarets, and nightclubs to jam, compete, and entertain. Jazz seemed to express something quintessentially modern. Jazz musicians broke free of convention, improvised, and produced new sounds that gave rise to new sensations. Both blacks and whites found in jazz an escape from the routine, the predictability, and the conventions of their everyday lives.

DEATH RATES FROM SELECTED CAUSES FOR NEW YORK CITY RESIDENTS, 1925

CAUSE OF DEATH	TOTAL POPULATION	AFRICAN AMERICAN POPULATION
General death rate (per 1,000 population)	11.4	16.5
Pneumonia	132.8	282.4
Pulmonary tuberculosis	75.5	258.4
Infant mortality (per 1,000 live births)	64.6	118.4
Maternal mortality (per 1,000 total births)	5.3	10.2
Stillbirths (per 1,000 births)	47.6	82.7
Homicide	5.3	19.5
Suicide	14.8	9.7

Note: Rate is per 100,000 population, unless noted

Source: Cheryl Lynn Greenberg, *"Or Does It Explode?" Black Harlem in the Great Depression* (New York: Oxford University Press, 1991), p. 32.

THE HARLEM RENAISSANCE

Paralleling the emergence of jazz was a black literary and artistic awakening known as the Harlem Renaissance. Black novelists, poets, painters, sculptors, and playwrights set about creating works rooted in their own culture instead of imitating the styles of white Europeans and Americans. The movement had begun during the war, when blacks sensed that they might at last be advancing to full equality. It was symbolized by the image of the "New Negro," who would no longer be deferential to whites but who would display his or her independence through talent and determination. As racial discrimination intensified after the war, cultural activities took on special significance. The world of culture was the one place where blacks could express their racial pride and demonstrate their talent.

Langston Hughes, a young black poet, said of the Harlem Renaissance: "We younger Negro artists who create now intend to express our individual dark-skinned selves without fear or shame. If white people are pleased, we are glad. If they are not, it doesn't matter. We know we are beautiful. And ugly, too." In 1925, *Survey Graphic,* a white liberal magazine, devoted an entire issue to "Harlem—the Mecca of the New Negro."

But even these cultural advances did not escape white prejudice. The most popular jazz nightclubs in Harlem, most of which were owned and operated by whites, refused to admit black customers. The only African Americans who were permitted inside were the jazz musicians, singers and dancers, prostitutes, and kitchen help. Moreover, the musicians had to play what the white patrons wanted to hear. Duke Ellington, for example, featured "jungle music," which for whites revealed the "true" African soul—sensual, innocent, primitive.

Artists and writers experienced similar pressures. Many of them depended for their sustenance on the support of wealthy white patrons. Those patrons were generous, but they wanted a return on their investment. Charlotte Mason, the New York City matron who supported Hughes and another black writer, Zora Neale Hurston, for example, felt free to judge their work and expected them to entertain her friends by demonstrating "authentic Negritude."

MEXICAN AMERICANS

After the Johnson-Reed Act of 1924, Mexicans became the country's chief source of immigrant labor. A total of 500,000 Mexicans came north in the 1920s. Most settled in the Southwest. In Texas three of every four construction workers and eight of every 10 migrant farm workers were Mexicans. In California, Mexican immigrants made up 75 percent of the state's agricultural workforce.

Mexican farm laborers in Texas worked long hours for little money. They were usually barred from becoming machine operators or assuming other skilled positions. Forced to follow the crops, they had little opportunity to develop settled homes and communities. Farm

"Los Madrugadores"   Led by Pedro J. Gonzalez (seated, on left), this popular Mexican group sang *corridos* in live performances and on KMPC, a Spanish-language radio station in 1920s Los Angeles.

owners rarely required the services of Mexican workers for more than several days or weeks, and few were willing to spend the money required to provide decent homes and schools. Houses typically lacked even wooden floors or indoor plumbing. Mexican laborers found it difficult to protest these conditions. Their knowledge of English and American law was limited. Many were in debt to employers who had advanced them money and who threatened them with jail if they failed to fulfill the terms of their contract. Others feared deportation; they lacked visas, having slipped into the United States illegally rather than pay the immigrant tax or endure harassment from the Border Patrol.

Increasing numbers of Mexican immigrants, however, found their way to California. Some escaped agricultural labor altogether for construction and manufacturing jobs. Mexican men in Los Angeles worked in the city's large railroad yards, at the city's numerous construction sites, as unskilled workers in local factories, and as agricultural workers in the fruit and vegetable fields of Los Angeles County. Mexican women labored in the city's garment shops, fish canneries, and food processing plants.

The Los Angeles Mexican American community increased in complexity as it grew in size. By the mid-1920s it included a growing professional class, a proud group of *californios* (Spanish-speakers who had been resident in California for generations), a large number of musicians and entertainers, a small but energetic band of entrepreneurs and businessmen, conservative clerics and intellectuals who had fled or been expelled from revolutionary Mexico, and Mexican government officials who had been sent to counter the influence of the conservative exiles and to strengthen the ties of the immigrants to their homeland. This diverse mix gave rise to much internal conflict, but it also generated considerable cultural vitality. Indeed, Los Angeles became the same kind of magnet for Mexican Americans that Harlem had become for African Americans. Mexican musicians flocked to Los Angeles, as did Mexican playwrights. The city supported a vigorous Spanish-language theater. Mexican musicians performed on street corners, at ethnic festivals and weddings, at cabarets, and on the radio. Especially popular were folk ballads, called *corridos,* that spoke to the experiences of Mexican immigrants.

This flowering of Mexican American culture in Los Angeles could not erase the low wages, high rates of infant mortality, racial discrimination, and other hardships Mexicans faced; nor did it encourage Mexicans to mobilize themselves as a political force. Unlike European immigrants, Mexican immigrants showed little interest in becoming American citizens and acquiring the vote. Yet, the cultural vibrancy of the Mexican immigrant community did sustain many individuals who were struggling to survive in a strange, and often hostile, environment.

THE "LOST GENERATION" AND DISILLUSIONED INTELLECTUALS

Many native-born, white artists and intellectuals also felt uneasy in America in the 1920s. Their unease arose not from poverty or discrimination but from alienation. They despaired of American culture and regarded the average American as anti-intellectual, small-minded, materialistic, and puritanical. The novelist Sinclair Lewis ridiculed small-town Americans in *Main Street* (1920), "sophisticated" city dwellers in *Babbitt* (1922), physicians in *Arrowsmith* (1925), and evangelicals in *Elmer Gantry* (1927).

Before the First World War intellectuals and artists had been deeply engaged with "the people." Although they were critical of many aspects of American society, they believed that they could help bring about a new politics and improve social conditions. Some of them joined the war effort before the United States had officially intervened. Ernest Hemingway, John Dos Passos, and e. e. cummings, among others, sailed to Europe and volunteered their services to the Allies, usually as ambulance drivers carrying wounded soldiers from the front.

America's intellectuals were shocked by the effect the war had on American society. The wartime push for consensus created intolerance of radicals, immigrants, and blacks. Not only had many Americans embraced conformity for themselves, but they seemed determined to force conformity on others. The young critic Harold Stearns wrote in 1921 that "the most moving and pathetic fact in the social life of America today is emotional and aesthetic starvation." Before these words were published, Stearns had sailed for France. So many alienated young men like Stearns showed up in Paris that Gertrude Stein, an American writer whose Paris apartment became a gathering place for them, took to calling them the "Lost Generation."

These writers and intellectuals managed to convert their disillusionment into a new literary sensibility. The finest works of the decade focused on the psychological toll of living in what the poet T. S. Eliot referred to as *The Waste Land* (1922). F. Scott Fitzgerald's novel *The Great Gatsby* (1925) told of a man destroyed by his desire to be accepted into a world of wealth, fancy cars, and fast women. In the novel *A Farewell to Arms* (1929), Ernest Hemingway wrote of an American soldier overwhelmed by the senselessness and brutality of war who deserts the army for the company of a woman he loves. The playwright Eugene O'Neill created characters haunted by despair, loneliness, and unfulfilled longing. Writers created innovations in style as well as in content. Sherwood Anderson, in his novel *Winesburg, Ohio* (1919), blended fiction and autobiography. John Dos Passos, in *Manhattan Transfer* (1925), mixed journalism with more traditional literary methods. Hemingway wrote in an understated, laconic prose that somehow drew attention to his characters' rage and vulnerability.

White southern writers found a tragic sensibility surviving from the South's defeat in the Civil War that spoke to their own loss of hope. One group of writers, calling themselves "the Agrarians," argued that the enduring agricultural character of their region offered a more hopeful path to the future than did the mass-production and mass-consumption regime that had overtaken the North. In 1929 William Faulkner published *The Sound and the Fury,* the first in a series of novels set in northern Mississippi's fictional Yoknapatawpha County. Faulkner explored the violence and terror that marked relationships among family members and townspeople, while at the same time maintaining compassion and understanding.

DEMOCRACY ON THE DEFENSIVE

Their disdain for the masses led many intellectuals to question democracy itself. If ordinary people were as stupid, prejudiced, and easily manipulated as they seemed, how could they be entrusted with the fate of the nation? Walter Lippmann, a former radical and progressive, declared that modern society had rendered democracy obsolete. In his view, average citizens, buffeted by propaganda emanating from powerful opinion-makers, could no longer make the kind of informed, rational judgments that were needed to make democracy work. Lippmann's solution, and that of many other political commentators, was to shift government power from the people to educated elites. Those elites, who would be appointed rather than elected, would conduct foreign and domestic policy in an informed, intelligent way.

These antidemocratic views did not go uncontested. The philosopher John Dewey was the most articulate spokesman for the "prodemocracy" position. He acknowledged that the concentration of power in a few giant organizations had eroded the authority of Congress, the presidency, and other democratic institutions. But democracy was not doomed, he insisted. The people could reclaim their freedom by making big business subject to government control. The government could then use its power to democratize corporations and to regulate the communications industry to ensure that every citizen had access to the facts needed to make reasonable, informed political decisions.

Dewey's views attracted the support of a wide range of liberal intellectuals and reformers, including Robert and Helen Lynd, the authors of *Middletown;* Rexford Tugwell, professor of economics at Columbia; and Felix Frankfurter, a rising star at Harvard Law School. Some of these activists had ties to labor leaders and to New York Governor Franklin D. Roosevelt. They formed the vanguard of a new liberal movement that was committed to taking up the work the progressives had left unfinished.

But these reformers were utterly without power, except in a few states. The Republican Party had driven reformers from its ranks. The Democratic Party was a fallen giant, crippled by a split between its principal constituencies—rural Protestants and urban ethnics—over Prohibition, immigration restriction, and the Ku Klux Klan. The labor movement was moribund. The Socialist Party had never recovered from the trauma of war and Bolshevism.

CHRONOLOGY

1920	Prohibition goes into effect • Warren G. Harding defeats James M. Fox for presidency • Census reveals a majority of Americans live in urban areas • 8 million cars on road
1922	United States, Britain, Japan, France, and Italy sign Five-Power Treaty, agreeing to reduce size of their navies
1923	Teapot Dome scandal lands Secretary of the Interior Albert Fall in jail • Harding dies in office; Calvin Coolidge becomes president
1924	Dawes Plan to restructure Germany's war debt put in effect • Coolidge defeats John W. Davis for presidency • Ku Klux Klan membership approaches 4 million • Immigration Restriction Act cuts immigration by 80 percent and discriminates against Asians and southern and eastern Europeans
1925	Scopes trial upholds right of Tennessee to bar teaching of evolution in public schools • *Survey Graphic* publishes a special issue, *The New Negro,* announcing the Harlem Renaissance • F. Scott Fitzgerald publishes *The Great Gatsby* • U.S. withdraws Marines from Nicaragua
1926	Revenue Act cuts income and estate taxes • Coolidge vetoes McNary-Haugen bill, legislation meant to relieve agricultural distress • U.S. sends Marines back to Nicaragua to end civil war and protect U.S. property
1928	15 nations sign Kellogg-Briand pact, pledging to avoid war • Coolidge vetoes McNary-Haugen bill again • Herbert Hoover defeats Alfred E. Smith for presidency
1929	Union membership drops to 3 million • 27 million cars on road • William Faulkner publishes *The Sound and the Fury*
1930	Los Angeles's Mexican population reaches 100,000

La Follette's Farmer-Labor Party, after a promising debut, had stalled. John Dewey and his friends tried to launch yet another third party, but they failed to raise money or arouse mass support.

Reformers took little comfort in the presidential election of 1928. Hoover's smashing victory suggested that the trends of the 1920s—the dominance of the Republicans, the centrality of Prohibition to political debate, the paralysis of the Democrats, the growing economic might of capitalism, and the pervasive influence of the consumer culture—would continue unabated.

CONCLUSION

Signs abounded in the 1920s that Americans were creating a new and bountiful society. The increased accessibility of cars and other consumer durables; rising real wages, low unemployment, and installment buying; and the spread of welfare capitalism—all these pointed to an economy that had become more prosperous, more consumer-oriented, even somewhat more egalitarian. Moves to greater equality within marriage and to enhanced liberty for single women suggested that economic change was propelling social change as well.

But many working-class and rural Americans benefited little from the decade's prosperity. And the changes aroused resistance, especially from farmers and small-town Americans who feared that the rapid growth of cities was rendering their white, Protestant America unrecognizable.

In the Democratic Party, farmers, small-town Americans, and moral traditionalists fought bitterly against the growing power of urban, ethnic constituencies. Elsewhere, the traditionalists battled hard to protect religion's authority against the inroads of science and to purge the nation of "inferior" population streams. In the process they arrayed themselves against American traditions of liberty and equality.

Their resistance to change caused many of the nation's most talented artists and writers to turn away from their fellow Americans in disgust. Meanwhile, although ethnic and racial minorities experienced high levels of discrimination, they nevertheless found enough freedom to create vibrant ethnic and racial communities and to launch projects of cultural renaissance.

The Republican Party, having largely shed its reputation for reform, took credit for engineering the new economy of consumer plenty. It looked forward to years of political dominance. A steep and unexpected economic depression, however, would soon dash that expectation, revive the Democratic Party, and destroy Republican political power for a generation.

THE GREAT DEPRESSION AND THE NEW DEAL, 1929–1939

CAUSES OF THE GREAT DEPRESSION

HOOVER: THE FALL OF A SELF-MADE MAN

THE DEMOCRATIC ROOSEVELT ∾ THE FIRST NEW DEAL, 1933–1935

POLITICAL MOBILIZATION, POLITICAL UNREST, 1934–1935

THE SECOND NEW DEAL, 1935–1937

AMERICA'S MINORITIES AND THE NEW DEAL

THE NEW DEAL ABROAD ∾ STALEMATE, 1937–1940

The Great Depression began on October 29, 1929—"Black Tuesday"—with a spectacular stock market crash. On that one day, the value of stocks plummeted $14 billion. By the end of that year, stock prices had fallen 50 percent from their September highs. By 1932, the worst year of the depression, they had fallen another 30 percent. Meanwhile the unemployment rate had soared to 25 percent.

Many Americans who lived through the Great Depression were never able to forget the scenes of misery that they saw on every hand. In cities, the poor meekly awaited their turn at ill-funded soup kitchens. Scavengers poked through garbage cans for food, scoured railroad tracks for coal that had fallen from trains, and sometimes ripped up railroad ties for fuel. Hundreds of thousands of Americans built makeshift shelters out of cardboard, scrap metal, and whatever else they could find in the city dump. They called their towns "Hoovervilles," after the president whom they despised for his apparent refusal to help them.

The Great Depression brought cultural crisis as well as economic crisis. In the 1920s the leaders of American business had successfully redefined the national culture in business terms, as Americans' values became synonymous with the values of business: economic growth, freedom of enterprise and acquisitiveness. But with the prestige of business and business values in decline, how could Americans regain their hope and recover their confidence in the future?

The gloom broke in early 1933 when Franklin Delano Roosevelt became president and unleashed the power of government to regulate capitalist enterprises, to restore the economy to health, and to guarantee the social welfare of Americans unable to help themselves. Roosevelt called his pro-government program a "new deal for the American people." In the short term, the New Deal did not restore prosperity to America. But the "liberalism" that the New Deal championed found acceptance among millions, who agreed with Roosevelt that only a large and powerful government could guarantee Americans their liberty.

CAUSES OF THE GREAT DEPRESSION

There had been other depressions, or "panics," in American history, and no one would have been surprised had the boom of the 1920s been followed by an economic downturn lasting a year or two. No one was prepared, however, for the economic catastrophe of the 1930s.

STOCK MARKET SPECULATION

In 1928 and 1929 the New York Stock Exchange had undergone a remarkable run-up in prices. Money had poured into the market. But many investors were buying on 10 percent "margin"—putting up only 10 percent of the price of a stock and borrowing the rest from brokers or banks. They expected to be able to resell their shares within a few months at dramatically higher prices, pay back their loans from the proceeds, and still clear a handsome profit. And, for a while, that is exactly what they did. But the possibility of making a fortune with an investment of only a few thousand dollars only intensified investors' greed. Money flowed indiscriminately into all kinds of risky enterprises, as speculation became rampant. The stock market spiraled upward, out of control. When confidence in future earnings finally faltered, in October 1929, creditors began demanding that investors who had bought stocks on margin repay their loans. The market crashed from its dizzying heights.

Still, the crash, by itself, does not explain why the Great Depression lasted as long as it did. Poor decision making by the Federal Reserve Board, an ill-advised tariff that took effect soon after the depression hit, and a lopsided concentration of wealth in the hands of the rich deepened the economic collapse and made recovery more difficult.

MISTAKES BY THE FEDERAL RESERVE BOARD

In 1930 and 1931, the Federal Reserve curtailed the amount of money in circulation and raised interest rates, thereby making credit more difficult for the public to secure. This tight money policy was disastrous. What the economy needed was an expanded money supply, lower interest rates, and easier credit. Such a course would have enabled debtors to pay their creditors. Instead, by choosing the opposite course, the Federal Reserve plunged an economy starved for credit deeper into depression.

AN ILL-ADVISED TARIFF

The Tariff Act of 1930, also known as the Hawley-Smoot Tariff, accelerated economic decline abroad and at home. It not only raised tariffs on 75 agricultural goods; it also raised tariffs on 925 manufactured products. Industrialists had convinced their supporters in the Republican-controlled Congress that such protection would give American industry much needed assistance. But the legislation was a disaster. Angry foreign governments retaliated by raising their own tariff rates to keep out American goods. International trade, already weakened by the tight credit policies of the Federal Reserve, was dealt another blow at the very moment when it desperately needed a boost.

A MALDISTRIBUTION OF WEALTH

A serious maldistribution in the nation's wealth that had developed in the 1920s also stymied economic recovery. Between 1918 and 1929 the share of the national income that went to the wealthiest 20 percent of the population rose by more than 10 percent, while the share that went to the poorest 60 percent fell by almost 13 percent. The Coolidge administration contributed to this maldistribution by lowering taxes on the wealthy. The deepening inequality of income distribution slowed consumption and held back the growth of consumer-oriented industries. Even when the rich spent their money lavishly, they still spent a smaller proportion of their total incomes on consumption than wage earners did. Had more of the total increase in national income found its way into the pockets of average Americans during the 1920s, the demand for consumer goods would have been steadier and the newer consumer industries would have been correspondingly stronger. Such an economy might have recovered relatively quickly from the stock market crash of 1929. But recovery from the Great Depression did not come until 1941, more than a decade later.

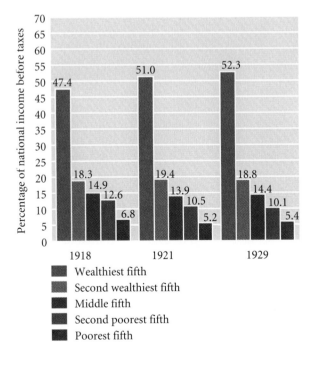

INCOME DISTRIBUTION BEFORE THE GREAT DEPRESSION

Source: From Gabriel Kolko, *Wealth and Power in America: An Analysis of Social Class and Income Distribution* (New York: Praeger, 1962), p. 14.

HOOVER: THE FALL OF A SELF-MADE MAN

In 1928 Herbert Hoover seemed to represent living proof that the American dream could be realized by anyone who was willing to work for it. At Stanford University he majored in geology. After graduation, he took part in mining expeditions to many parts of the world. As he rose quickly through corporate ranks, Hoover's managerial skills brought him more demanding and more handsomely rewarded tasks. Hoover's government service began during the First World War, when he won an international reputation for his expert management of agricultural production in the United States and his success in feeding millions of European soldiers and civilians. Then, in the 1920s, he served as an active and influential secretary of commerce (see Chapters 23 and 24). As the decade wound down, no American seemed better qualified to become president of the United States, an office that Hoover assumed in March 1929. Hoover was certain he could make prosperity a permanent feature of American life. "We in America today are nearer to the final triumph over poverty than ever before in the history of any land," he declared in August 1928. A little more than a year later, the Great Depression struck.

HOOVER'S PROGRAM

Within a short time after the stock market collapse, the depression had spread to nearly every sector of the economy. To cope with the crisis, Hoover first turned to the "associational" principles he had followed as secretary of commerce (see Chapter 24). He encouraged organizations of farmers, industrialists, and bankers to share information, bolster one another's spirits, and devise policies to aid economic recovery. Farmers would restrict output, industrialists would hold wages at predepression levels, and bankers would help each other remain solvent.

Hoover, to his credit, pursued a more aggressive set of economic policies once he realized that associationalism had failed to improve economic conditions. To ease a concurrent European crisis, Hoover secured a one-year moratorium on loan payments that European governments owed American banks. He steered through Congress the Glass-Steagall Act of 1932, intended to help American banks meet the demands of European depositors who wished to convert their dollars to gold. And to ease the crisis at home he began to expand the government's economic role. The Reconstruction Finance Corporation (RFC), created in 1932, made $2 billion available in loans to ailing banks and to corporations willing to build low-cost housing, bridges, and other public works. The Home Loan Bank Board, set up that same year, offered funds to savings and loans, mortgage companies, and other financial institutions that lent money for home construction.

Despite this new government activism, Hoover was uncomfortable with the idea that the government was responsible for restoring the nation's economic welfare. In 1932 RFC expenditures gave rise to the largest peacetime deficit in U.S. history, prompting Hoover to try to balance the federal budget. He supported the Revenue Act of 1932, which tried to increase government revenues by raising taxes, thus erasing the deficit. He also insisted that the RFC issue loans only to relatively healthy institutions that were capable of repaying them and that it favor public works, such as toll bridges, that were likely to become self-financing. As a result of these constraints, the RFC spent considerably less than Congress had mandated.

Hoover was especially reluctant to engage the government in providing relief to unemployed and homeless Americans. To give money to the poor, he insisted, would destroy their desire to work, undermine their sense of self-worth, and erode their capacity for citizenship.

The Bonus Army

In the spring of 1932 a group of army veterans mounted a particularly emotional challenge to Hoover's policies. In 1924 Congress had authorized a $1,000 bonus for First World War veterans in the form of compensation certificates that would mature in 1945. Now the veterans were demanding that the government pay the bonus immediately. A group of them from Portland, Oregon, decided to take action. Calling themselves the Bonus Expeditionary Force, they hopped onto empty boxcars of freight trains heading east, determined to stage a march on Washington. As the impoverished "army" moved eastward their ranks multiplied, so that by the time they reached Washington their number had swelled to 20,000. The so-called Bonus Army set up camp in the Anacostia Flats, southeast of the Capitol, and petitioned Congress for early payment of the promised bonus. The House of Representatives agreed, but the Senate turned them down. Hoover refused to meet with them. In July, federal troops led by Army Chief of Staff Douglas MacArthur and 3rd Cavalry Commander George Patton attacked the veterans' Anacostia encampment, set the tents and shacks ablaze, and dispersed the protestors. In the process, more than 100 veterans were wounded and one infant was killed.

News that veterans and their families had been attacked in the nation's capital served only to harden anti-Hoover opinion. In the 1932 elections, Hoover received only 39.6 percent of the popular vote and just 59 (of 531) electoral votes. When he left the presidency in 1933 Hoover was a bewildered man, reviled by Americans for what they took to be his indifference to suffering and his ineptitude in dealing with the economy's collapse.

The Bonus Army's Encampment Set Ablaze   U.S. troops under the command of General Douglas MacArthur torched the tents and shacks that housed thousands of First World War veterans who had come to Washington to demand financial assistance from the government.

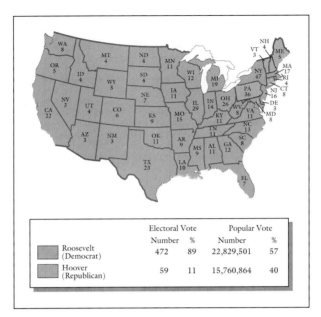

	Electoral Vote		Popular Vote	
	Number	%	Number	%
Roosevelt (Democrat)	472	89	22,829,501	57
Hoover (Republican)	59	11	15,760,864	40

PRESIDENTIAL ELECTION, 1932

THE DEMOCRATIC ROOSEVELT

The man who defeated Hoover, Franklin D. Roosevelt, was born in 1882 into a patrician family. On his father's side, Roosevelt was descended from Dutch gentry who in the 17th century had built large estates on the fertile land along the Hudson River. His mother's family—the Delanos—traced their ancestors back to the Mayflower. In short, Roosevelt was raised among people who were convinced of their superiority. His education at Groton, Harvard College, and Columbia Law School was typical of the path followed by the sons of America's elite.

The Roosevelt family was wealthy, although not spectacularly so by the standards of the late 19th century. His parents' net worth of more than $1 million was relatively small in comparison to the fortunes being amassed by the rising class of industrialists and railroad tycoons, many of whom commanded fortunes of $50 to $100 million or more. This widening gap in wealth disturbed families like the Roosevelts, who were concerned that the new industrial elite would dislodge them from their social position. Moreover, they were offended by the newcomers' vulgar displays of wealth, lack of taste and etiquette, and hostility toward those less fortunate than themselves. In 1899 Theodore Roosevelt, an older cousin of Franklin Roosevelt, had remarked that such people were "sunk in a scrambling commercialism, heedless of the higher life."

In 1921, at the age of 39, Franklin Roosevelt was stricken by polio and permanently lost the use of his legs. Before becoming paralyzed, Roosevelt had not distinguished himself either at school or in the practice of law, nor could he point to many significant political achievements. He owed his political ascent more to his famous name than to actual accomplishments or hard work. He was charming, gregarious, and popular among his associates in the New York Democratic Party. He enjoyed a good time and devoted a great deal of energy to sailing, partying, and enjoying the company of women other than his wife, Eleanor. After his illness, Roosevelt spent the next two years bedridden, and he seemed to acquire a new determination and seriousness.

Roosevelt's physical debilitation also transformed his relationship with Eleanor, with whom he had shared a testy and increasingly loveless marriage. Eleanor's dedication to nursing Franklin back to health forged a new bond between them. More conscious of his dependence on others, he now welcomed her as a partner in his career. Eleanor soon displayed a talent for political organization and public speaking. She would become an active, eloquent First Lady and an architect of American liberlism.

ROOSEVELT LIBERALISM

As governor of New York for four years (1929–1933), Roosevelt had initiated various reform programs, and his success made him the front-runner in the contest for the 1932 Democratic presidential nomination. It was by no means certain, however, that he would be the party's choice. Since 1924 the Democrats had been sharply divided between southern and midwestern agrarians on the one hand and northeastern ethnics on the other. The agrarians favored government regulation—both of the nation's economy and of the private affairs of its citizens. Their support of government intervention in the pursuit of social justice marked them as economic progressives, while their advocacy of Prohibition revealed a deep cultural conservatism as well as a nativistic strain. By contrast, urban ethnics opposed Prohibition and other forms of government interference in the private lives of its citizens. On the issue of whether the government should regulate the economy, urban ethnics were divided, with former New York governor Al Smith increasingly committed to a policy of laissez-faire and Senator Robert Wagner of New York and others supporting more federal control.

Roosevelt understood the need to carve out a middle ground. As governor of New York, and then as a presidential candidate in 1932, he surrounded himself with men and women who embraced the new reform movement called liberalism. Liberals shared with the agrarians and Wagner's supporters a desire to regulate capitalism, but agreed with Al Smith that the government had no business telling people how to behave.

But Roosevelt was by no means assured of the presidential nomination in 1932. At the Democratic convention in July, Smith worked to secure the nomination of the more conservative Newton Baker. William Gibbs McAdoo, hoping to deadlock the convention so that he could take the nomination himself, initially supported Speaker of the House John Nance Garner. As the balloting entered its third round, Roosevelt began to fall behind. At that point, however, McAdoo and Garner reevaluated their strategy. Recognizing that party unity and a victory in the general election might be more important than their own ambitions, they swung their support to Roosevelt, putting him over the top. Roosevelt, in gratitude, chose Garner as his vice presidential running mate. In a rousing call to action, he declared: "Ours must be the party of liberal thought, of planned action, of enlightened international outlook, and of the greatest good for the greatest number of citizens." He promised "a new deal for the American people."

In his campaign, Roosevelt sometimes spoke of using government programs to stabilize the economy, but he also spent much of his time wooing conservative Democrats. In point of fact, Roosevelt only made two outright promises during his presidential campaign: to repeal Prohibition and to balance the budget. Thus, the nation had to wait until March 4, 1933—the day Roosevelt was sworn in as president—to learn what the New Deal would bring.

THE FIRST NEW DEAL, 1933–1935

By the time Roosevelt assumed office, the economy lay in shambles. From 1929 to 1932 industrial production fell by 50 percent, while new investment declined from $16 billion to a mere fraction of $1 billion. The nation's banking system was on the verge of collapse. In 1931 alone, more than 2,000 banks had shut their doors. The unemployment rate was soaring. Some Americans feared that the opportunity for reform had already passed.

But not Roosevelt. "This nation asks for action, and action now," Roosevelt declared in his inaugural address. Roosevelt was true to his word. In his first "Hundred Days," from early March through early June 1933, Roosevelt persuaded Congress to pass 15 major pieces of legislation to help bankers, farmers, industrialists, workers, homeowners, the unemployed, and the hungry. He also prevailed on Congress to repeal Prohibition. Not all the new laws helped to relieve distress and promote recovery. But, in the short term, that seemed not to matter. Roosevelt had brought excitement and hope to the nation. He was confident, decisive, and defiantly cheery. "The only thing we have to fear is fear itself," he declared. He used the radio to reach out to ordinary Americans. On the second Sunday after his inaugural, he launched a series of radio addresses known as "fireside chats," speaking in a plain, friendly, and direct voice to the forlorn and discouraged.

DELIVERING A FIRESIDE CHAT   Soon after taking office, Roosevelt began using the radio airwaves to speak to the American people in an informal and friendly manner. His "fireside chats" substantially boosted his popularity.

To hear the president speaking warmly and conversationally—as though he were actually there in the room—was riveting. An estimated 500,000 Americans wrote letters to Roosevelt within days of his inaugural address. Millions more would write to him and to Eleanor Roosevelt over the next few years. Many of the letters were simply addressed to "Mr. or Mrs. Roosevelt, Washington, D.C."

Roosevelt was never the benign father figure he made himself out to be. His public image was skillfully crafted. Compliant news photographers agreed not to show him in a wheelchair. For his part, Roosevelt often sought to hide the true content of legislation he proposed with diverting rhetoric.

To his credit, Roosevelt used his popularity and executive power to strengthen American democracy at a time when democracy was crumbling in Europe. During his long tenure in office, however, he set in motion tendencies that would long plague American politics: a drift of power to the executive branch, a steady expansion of the size and reach of federal bureaucracies, and a widening gap between political appearance and political reality.

SAVING THE BANKS

Roosevelt's first order of business was to save the nation's financial system. By inauguration day, several states had already shut their banks. Roosevelt immediately ordered all the nation's banks closed—a bold move he brazenly called a "bank holiday." He then had Congress rush through an Emergency Banking Act (EBA) that made federal loans available to private bankers. He followed that with an Economy Act (EA) that committed the government to balancing the budget.

Both the EBA and the EA were fiscally conservative programs that Hoover had proposed earlier. The EBA made it possible for private bankers to retain financial control of their institutions, and the EA announced the government's intention of pursuing a fiscally prudent course. Only after the financial crisis had eased did Roosevelt turn to the structural reform of banking. A second Glass-Steagall Act (1933) separated commercial banking from investment banking. It also created the Federal Deposit Insurance Corporation (FDIC), which assured

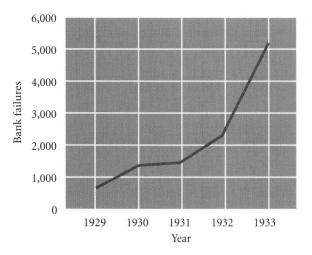

BANK FAILURES, 1929–1933

Source: From C. D. Bremer, *American Bank Failures* (New York: Columbia University Press, 1935), p. 42.

depositors that the government would protect up to $5,000 of their savings. The Securities Act (1933) and the Securities Exchange Act (1934) imposed long overdue regulation on the New York Stock Exchange, both by reining in buying on the margin and by establishing the Securities and Exchange Commission to enforce federal law.

SAVING THE PEOPLE

Roosevelt understood the need to temper financial prudence with compassion. Congress responded swiftly in 1933 to Roosevelt's request to establish the Federal Emergency Relief Administration (FERA), granting it $500 million for relief to the poor. To head it, Roosevelt appointed a brash young reformer, Harry Hopkins. Roosevelt then won congressional approval for the Civilian Conservation Corps (CCC), which put more than 2 million single young men to work planting trees, halting erosion, and otherwise improving the environment. The following winter, Roosevelt launched the Civil Works Administration (CWA), an ambitious work-relief program, also under Harry Hopkins's direction, that hired 4 million unemployed at $15 a week and put them to work on 400,000 small-scale government projects. For middle-class Americans threatened with the loss of their homes, Roosevelt won congressional approval for the Homeowners' Loan Corporation (1933) to refinance mortgages. These direct subsidies to millions of jobless and home-owning Americans lent credibility to Roosevelt's claim that the New Deal would set the country on a new course.

REPAIRING THE ECONOMY: AGRICULTURE

In 1933 Roosevelt expected economic recovery to come not from relief, but through agricultural and industrial cooperation. He regarded the Agricultural Adjustment Act, passed in May, and the National Industrial Recovery Act (NIRA), passed in June, as the most important legislation of his Hundred Days. Both were based on the idea that curtailing production would trigger economic recovery. By shrinking the supply of agricultural and manufactured goods, Roosevelt's economists reasoned, they could restore the balance of normal market forces. Then, as demand for scarce goods exceeded supply, prices would rise and revenues would climb. Farmers and industrialists, earning a profit once again, would increase their investment in new technology and hire more workers.

To curtail farm production, the Agricultural Adjustment Administration (AAA), set up by the Agricultural Adjustment Act, began paying farmers to keep a portion of their land out of cultivation and to reduce the size of their herds. The program was controversial, as many farmers did not readily accept the idea that they were to be paid more money for working less land and husbanding fewer livestock. But few refused to accept government payments.

The AAA had made no provision, however, for the countless tenant farmers and farm laborers who would be thrown out of work by the reduction in acreage. In the South, the victims were disproportionately black. A Georgia sharecropper wrote Harry Hopkins of his misery: "I have Bin farming all my life But the man I live with Has Turned me loose taking my mule [and] all my feed.... I can't get a Job so Some one said Rite you."

The programs of the AAA also proved inadequate to Great Plains farmers, whose economic problems had been compounded by ecological crisis. Just as the depression rolled in, the rain stopped falling on the plains. The land, stripped of its native grasses by decades of excessive plowing, dried up and turned to dust. And then the dust began to blow, sometimes traveling

Legislation Enacted during the "Hundred Days," March 9–June 16, 1933

Date	Legislation	Purpose
March 9	Emergency Banking Act	Provide federal loans to private bankers
March 20	Economy Act	Balance the federal budget
March 22	Beer-Wine Revenue Act	Repeal Prohibition
March 31	Unemployment Relief Act	Create the Civilian Conservation Corps
May 12	Agricultural Adjustment Act	Establish a national agricultural policy
May 12	Emergency Farm Mortgage Act	Provide refinancing of farm mortgages
May 12	Federal Emergency Relief Act	Establish a national relief system, including the Civil Works Administration
May 18	Tennessee Valley Authority Act	Promote economic development of the Tennessee Valley
May 27	Securities Act	Regulate the purchase and sale of new securities
June 5	Gold Repeal Joint Resolution	Cancel the gold clause in public and private contracts
June 13	Home Owners Loan Act	Provide refinancing of home mortgages
June 16	National Industrial Recovery Act	Set up a national system of industrial self-government and establish the Public Works Administration
June 16	Glass-Steagall Banking Act	Create Federal Deposit Insurance Corporation; separate commercial and investment banking
June 16	Farm Credit Act	Reorganize agricultural credit programs
June 16	Railroad Coordination Act	Appoint federal coordinator of transportation

Source: Arthur M. Schlesinger Jr., *The Coming of the New Deal* (Boston: Houghton Mifflin, 1959), pp. 20–21.

1,000 miles across open prairie. Dust became a fixed feature of daily life on the plains (which soon became known as the "Dust Bowl"), covering furniture, floors, and stoves, and penetrating people's hair and lungs.

The government responded to this calamity by establishing the Soil Conservation Service (SCS) in 1935. Recognizing that the soil problems of the Great Plains could not be solved simply by taking land out of production, SCS experts urged plains farmers to plant soil-conserving grasses and legumes in place of wheat. They taught them how to plow along contour lines and how to build terraces. Plains farmers were open to these suggestions, especially when the government offered to subsidize those willing to implement them. Bolstered by the new assistance, plains agriculture began to recover.

Still, the government offered little to the rural poor—the tenant farmers and sharecroppers. Nearly 1 million had left their homes by 1935, and another 2.5 million would leave after 1935. Most headed west, piling their belongings onto their jalopies, snaking along Route 66 until they reached California. They became known as Okies, because many, although not all, had come from Oklahoma.

In 1936 the Supreme Court ruled that AAA-mandated limits on farm production constituted illegal restraints of trade. Congress responded by passing the Soil Conservation and Domestic Allotment Act, which justified the removal of land from cultivation for reasons of conservation rather than economics. This new act also called upon landowners to share their government subsidies with sharecroppers and tenant farmers, although landowners managed to evade this and subsequent laws that required them to share federal funds.

The use of subsidies, begun by the AAA, did eventually bring stability and prosperity to agriculture. But the costs were high. Agriculture became the most heavily subsidized sector of the U.S. economy, and the Department of Agriculture grew into one of the government's largest bureaucracies. And the rural poor, black and white, never received a fair share of federal benefits.

REPAIRING THE ECONOMY: INDUSTRY

American industry was so vast that paying individual manufacturers direct subsidies to reduce, or even halt, production was never contemplated. Instead, the government decided to limit production through persuasion and association. To head the National Recovery Administration (NRA), authorized under the National Industrial Recovery Act, Roosevelt chose General Hugh Johnson. Johnson's first task was to persuade industrialists and businessmen to agree to raise employee wages to a minimum of 30 to 40 cents an hour and to limit employee hours to a maximum of 30 to 40 hours a week. The intent was to reduce the quantity of goods that any factory or business could produce.

Johnson launched a high-powered publicity campaign. He distributed pamphlets and pins throughout the country. He used the radio to exhort all Americans to do their part. He staged an elaborate NRA celebration in Yankee Stadium and organized a massive parade down New York City's Fifth Avenue. He sent letters to millions of employers asking them to place a "blue eagle"—the logo of the NRA—on storefronts, at factory entrances, and on company stationery to signal their participation in the campaign to limit production and restore prosperity. Blue eagles soon sprouted everywhere, usually accompanied by the slogan "We Do Our Part."

Johnson understood, however, that his propaganda campaign could not by itself guarantee recovery. So he brought together the largest producers in every sector of manufacturing and asked each group (or conference) to work out a code of fair competition that would specify prices, wages, and hours throughout the sector. He also asked each conference to restrict production.

In the summer and fall of 1933, the NRA codes drawn up for steel, textiles, coal mining, rubber, garment manufacture, and other industries seemed to be working. The economy picked up and people began to hope that an end to the depression might be near. But in the winter and spring of 1934, economic indicators plunged downward once again and manufacturers began to evade the provisions of the codes. Government committees set up to enforce the codes were powerless to punish violators. By the fall of 1934, it was clear that the NRA had failed. When the Supreme Court declared the NRA codes unconstitutional in May 1935, the Roosevelt administration allowed the agency to die.

REBUILDING THE NATION

In addition to establishing the NRA, the National Industrial Recovery Act launched the Public Works Administration (PWA). The PWA was given a $3.3 billion budget to sponsor internal improvements that would strengthen the nation's infrastructure of roads, bridges, sewage systems, hospitals, airports, and schools. The PWA authorized the building of three major dams in the West—the Grand Coulee, Boulder, and Bonneville—that opened up large stretches of Arizona, California, and Washington to industrial and agricultural development. It funded the construction of the Triborough Bridge in New York City and the 100-mile causeway linking Florida to Key West. It also appropriated money for the construction of thousands of new schools between 1933 and 1939.

THE TVA ALTERNATIVE

One piece of legislation passed during Roosevelt's First New Deal specified a strategy for economic recovery very different from the one promoted by the NRA. The Tennessee Valley Authority Act (1933) called for the government itself—rather than private corporations—to promote economic development throughout the Tennessee Valley, a vast river basin winding through parts of Kentucky, Tennessee, Mississippi, Alabama, Georgia, and North Carolina. The act created the Tennessee Valley Authority (TVA) to control flooding on the Tennessee River, harness its water power to generate electricity, develop local industry (such as fertilizer production), and improve river transportation. The extent of its control over economic development reflected the influence of Rexford Tugwell and other New Dealers

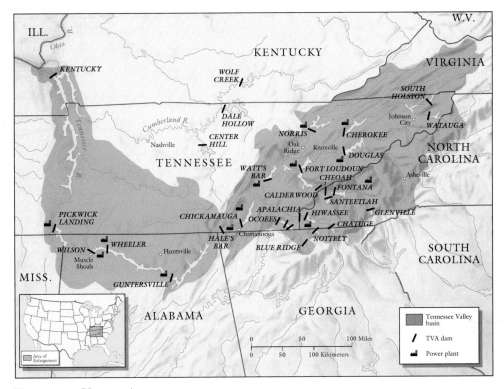

TENNESSEE VALLEY AUTHORITY

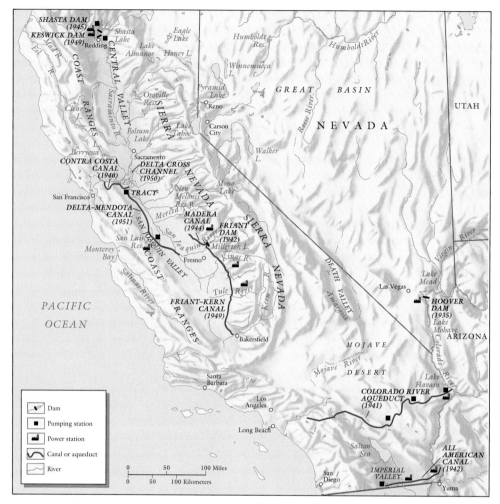

FEDERAL WATER PROJECTS IN CALIFORNIA BUILT OR FUNDED BY THE NEW DEAL

who were committed to a government-planned and government-operated economy. Although they rarely said so, these reformers were drawn to socialism.

The accomplishments of the TVA were many. It built, completed, or improved more than 20 dams. At several of the dam sites, the TVA built hydroelectric generators and soon became the nation's largest producer of electricity. Its low rates compelled private utility companies to reduce their rates as well. The TVA also constructed waterways to bypass unnavigable stretches of the river, reduced the danger of flooding, and taught farmers how to prevent soil erosion and use fertilizers.

Although the TVA was one of the New Deal's most celebrated successes, it generated little support for more ambitious experiments in national planning. For the government to have assumed control of established industries and banks would have been quite a different matter from bringing prosperity to an impoverished region. Like Roosevelt, few members of Congress or the public favored the radical growth of governmental power that such programs would entail. Thus, the New Deal never embraced the idea of the federal government as a substitute for private enterprise.

The New Deal and Western Development

As the example of the TVA suggests, New Deal programs could make an enormous difference to a particular region's welfare. The region that benefited most from the New Deal was the West. Between 1933 and 1939, per capita payments for public works projects, welfare, and federal loans in the Rocky Mountain and Pacific Coast states outstripped those of any other region.

Central to this western focus was the program of western dam building. Western real estate and agricultural interests wanted to dam the West's major rivers to provide water and electricity for urban and agricultural development. They found a government ally in the Bureau of Reclamation, a hitherto small federal agency that became, under the New Deal, a prime dispenser of infrastructural funds. Drawing on PWA monies, the bureau oversaw the building of the Boulder Dam (later renamed Hoover Dam), which provided drinking water for southern California, irrigation water for California's Imperial Valley, and electricity for Los Angeles and southern Arizona. It also authorized the Central Valley Project and the All-American Canal, vast water-harnessing projects in central and southern California meant to provide irrigation, drinking water, and electricity to California farmers and towns. The greatest construction project of all was the Grand Coulee Dam on the Columbia River in Washington, which created a lake 150 miles long. Together with the Bonneville Dam (also on the Columbia), the Grand Coulee gave the Pacific Northwest the cheapest electricity in the country and created the potential for huge economic and population growth.

These developments did not attract as much attention in the 1930s as did the TVA. The benefits of this dam building program were not fully realized until after the Second World War. Also, dam building in the West was not seen as a radical experiment in government planning and management. Unlike the TVA, the Bureau of Reclamation hired private contractors to do the work and made them rich. Moreover, the benefits of these dams were intended to flow first to large agricultural and real estate interests, not to the poor; they were intended to aid private enterprise, rather than bypass it. In political terms, then, dam building in the West was more conservative than it was in the Tennessee Valley.

Political Mobilization, Political Unrest, 1934–1935

Although Roosevelt and the New Dealers quickly dismantled the NRA in 1935, they could not stop the political forces it had set it in motion. Americans now believed that they themselves could make a difference. If the New Dealers could not achieve economic recovery, the people would find others who could.

Populist Critics of the New Deal

Some critics were disturbed by what they perceived as the conservative bent of New Deal programs. Banking reforms, the AAA, and the NRA, they alleged, all seemed to favor large economic interests. Ordinary people had been ignored.

In the South and Midwest, millions listened regularly to the radio addresses of Louisiana Senator Huey Long, a former governor of that state and a spellbinding orator. In attacks on New Deal programs, he alleged that "not a single thin dime of concentrated, bloated, pompous wealth, massed in the hands of a few people has been raked down to relieve the masses." Long offered a simple alternative: "Break up the swollen fortunes of America and . . . spread the wealth among all our people."

Long's rhetoric inspired hundreds of thousands of Americans to join the Share the Wealth clubs his supporters organized. A majority came from middle-class ranks, worried that the big business orientation of New Deal programs might undermine their economic and social status. Substantial numbers of Share the Wealth club members also came from highly skilled and white-collar sections of the working class. By 1935 Roosevelt regarded Long as the man most likely to unseat him in the presidential election of 1936. But before that campaign began, Long was murdered by an assassin.

Meanwhile, in the Midwest, Father Charles Coughlin, the "radio priest," delivered a message similar to Long's. Like Long, Coughlin appealed to anxious middle-class Americans and to privileged groups of workers who believed that middle-class status was slipping from their grasp. A devoted Roosevelt supporter at first, Coughlin had become a harsh critic. The New Deal was run by bankers, he claimed. The NRA was a program to resuscitate corporate profits. Coughlin called for a strong government to compel capital, labor, agriculture, professionals, and other interest groups to do its bidding. He founded the National Union of Social Justice (NUSJ) in 1934 as a precursor to a political party that would challenge the Democrats in 1936. Coughlin admired leaders, such as Italy's Benito Mussolini, who built strong states through decree rather than through democratic consent.

As Coughlin's disillusionment with the New Deal deepened, a strain of anti-Semitism became apparent in his radio talks, as in his accusation that Jewish bankers were masterminding a world conspiracy to dispossess the toiling masses. Although Coughlin was a compelling speaker, he failed to build the NUSJ into an effective force. Its successor, the Union Party, attracted only a tiny percentage of voters in 1936. Embittered, Coughlin moved further and further to the political right. By 1939 his denunciations of democracy and Jews had become so extreme that some radio stations refused to carry his addresses. But millions of ordinary Americans continued to believe that the "radio priest" was their savior.

Another popular figure was Francis E. Townsend, a California doctor who claimed that the way to end the depression was to give every senior citizen $200 a month. The Townsend Plan briefly garnered the support of an estimated 20 million Americans.

None of these self-styled reformers—Long, Coughlin, and Townsend—showed much skill at transforming his popularity into disciplined political parties that could compete in elections. Still, their attacks on New Deal programs deepened popular discontent and helped to legitimate other insurgent movements. The most important of them was the labor movement.

LABOR'S REBIRTH

The ranks of the working class were diverse: immigrant radicals and ethnic conservatives, northerners and southerners, blacks and whites, skilled and unskilled, factory workers and farm workers, men and women. But labor's diversity was not as great as it had been during the Progressive Era. Mass immigration had ended in 1921, and the trend toward Americanization

JOHN L. LEWIS The president of the United Mine Workers and principal founder of the CIO, Lewis was the most famous and charismatic labor leader of the 1930s. Lewis's large frame, dramatic features, and deep voice gave him a powerful and compelling presence, which he used to good effect. In this fresco, the artist Ben Shahn celebrates Lewis's physical power and appeal.

at school, at work, and in popular entertainment had broadened throughout the decade. The Great Depression itself further heightened the sense of shared experience.

This commonality of working-class sentiment first became apparent in 1932, when many workers voted for Roosevelt. Following his election, the NRA helped to transform their despair into hope. It set guidelines for wages and work hours that, if implemented by employers, would improve working conditions. Moreover, Clause 7(a) of the National Industrial Recovery Act granted workers the right to join labor unions of their own choosing, and obligated employers to recognize unions and bargain with them in good faith.

Millions of workers joined labor unions in 1933 and early 1934, encouraged by John L. Lewis, president of the United Mine Workers, who often declared in his rousing speeches and radio addresses: "The president wants you to join a union." Actually, Roosevelt did not favor the rapid growth of unions. But Lewis believed that by repeatedly invoking the president's name he could transform working-class support for Roosevelt into union strength.

The demands of union members were quite modest at first. They wanted employers to observe the provisions of the NRA codes. They wanted to be treated fairly by their foremen. And they wanted employers to recognize their unions. But few employers were willing to grant them any say in their working conditions. Many ignored the NRA's wage and hour guidelines altogether, and even used their influence over NRA code authorities to get worker requests for wage increases and union recognition rejected.

Workers flooded Washington with letters addressed to President Roosevelt, Labor Secretary Frances Perkins, and General Hugh Johnson asking them to force employers to comply with the law. When their pleas went unanswered, workers began to take matters into their own hands. In 1934 they staged 2,000 strikes in virtually every industry and region of the country. A few of those strikes escalated into armed confrontations between workers and police that shocked the nation. In Toledo in May, 10,000 workers surrounded the Electric Auto-Lite plant, declaring that they would block all exits and entrances until the company agreed to shut down operations and negotiate a union contract. A seven-hour pitched battle between strikers and police waged with water hoses, tear gas, and gunfire failed to dislodge the strikers. Ultimately, the National Guard was summoned, and two strikers were killed in an exchange of gunfire. In San Francisco in July, longshoremen fought employers and police in street skirmishes in which two were killed and scores wounded. Employers there had hoped that the use of force would break a two-month-old strike, but the violence provoked more than 100,000 additional workers in the transportation, construction, and service industries to walk off their jobs in a general strike. From July 5 to July 19, the city of San Francisco was virtually shut down.

The largest and most violent confrontation began on September 1, 1934, with the strike of 400,000 textile workers at mills from Maine to Alabama. Workers who had never acknowledged a common bond with their fellows now joined hands. They insisted that they were Americans bound together by class and national loyalties that transcended ethnic and religious differences. In the first two weeks of September, the strikers brought cotton production to a virtual standstill. Employers recruited replacement workers and hired private security forces to protect them. At many of the mills, the arrival of strikebreakers prompted violent confrontations between strikers and police. In northern communities, such as Saylesville and Woonsocket, Rhode Island, full-scale riots erupted. The result was several deaths, hundreds of injuries, and millions of dollars in property damage. Similar confrontations took place throughout the South.

ANGER AT THE POLLS

By late September, textile union leaders had lost their nerve and called off the strike. But workers took their anger to the polls. In Rhode Island, they broke the Republican Party's 30-year domination of state politics. In the country as a whole, Democrats won 70 percent of the contested seats in the Senate and House. The Democrats increased their majority, from 310 to 319 (out of 432) in the House, and from 60 to 69 (out of 96) in the Senate.

But the victory was not an unqualified one for Roosevelt and the First New Deal. The 74th Congress would include the largest contingent of radicals ever sent to Washington. Their support for the New Deal depended on whether Roosevelt delivered more relief, more income security, and more political power to farmers, workers, the unemployed, and the poor.

THE RISE OF RADICAL THIRD PARTIES

Radical critics of the New Deal also made an impressive showing in state politics in 1934 and 1936. They were particularly strong in states gripped by labor unrest. In Wisconsin, for example, Philip La Follette, the son of Robert La Follette (see Chapter 21), was elected governor in 1934 and 1936 as the candidate of the radical Wisconsin Progressive Party. In Minnesota, discontented agrarians and urban workers organized the Minnesota Farmer-Labor (MFL) Party and elected their candidate to the governorship in 1930, 1932, 1934, and 1936. And in California, the socialist and novelist Upton Sinclair and his organization, End Poverty in California (EPIC), came closer to winning the governorship than anyone had expected.

These impressive showings made it clear that many voters were prepared to abandon Democrats who refused to endorse a more comprehensive program of reform. A widespread movement to form local labor parties offered further evidence of voter volatility, as did the growing appeal of the Communist Party.

The American Communist Party (CP) had emerged in the early 1920s with the support of radicals who wanted to adopt the Soviet Union's path to socialism. They began to attract attention in the early 1930s. Confident that the Great Depression signaled the death throes of capitalism, party members dedicated themselves to marshaling the forces of socialism.

CP organizers spread out among the poorest and most vulnerable populations in America—homeless urban blacks in the North, black and white sharecroppers in the South, Chicano and Filipino agricultural workers in the West—and mobilized them in unions and unemployment leagues. CP members also played significant roles in the strikes described earlier, and they were influential in the Minnesota Farmer-Labor Party. Once they stopped preaching world revolution in 1935 and began calling instead for a "popular front" of democratic forces against fascism, their ranks grew even more. By 1938, approximately 80,000 Americans were thought to have been members of the Communist Party.

Although the Communist Party proclaimed its allegiance to democratic principles beginning in 1935, it nevertheless remained a dictatorial organization that took its orders from the Soviet Union. Many Americans feared the growing strength of the CP and began to call for its suppression. Actually, the CP was never strong enough to pose a real political threat. Membership turnover was high, as many left the party after learning about its undemocratic character. Its chief role in 1930s politics was to channel popular discontent into unions and political parties that would, in turn, force New Dealers to respond to the demands of the nation's dispossessed.

THE SECOND NEW DEAL, 1935–1937

The labor unrest of 1934 had taken Roosevelt by surprise, and for a time he kept his distance from the masses mobilizing in his name. But in the spring of 1935, with the presidential election coming up in 1936, he decided to place himself at their head. He called for the "abolition of evil holding companies," attacked the wealthy for their profligate ways, and called for new programs to aid the poor and downtrodden. Roosevelt had not become a socialist, as his critics have charged. Rather, he sought to reinvigorate his appeal among poorer Americans and turn them away from radical solutions.

PHILOSOPHICAL UNDERPINNINGS

To point the New Deal in a more populist direction, Roosevelt turned increasingly to a relatively new economic theory, underconsumptionism. Advocates of this theory held that a chronic weakness in consumer demand had caused the Great Depression. The path to recovery lay, therefore, not in restricting the output of producers but in boosting consumer expenditures through government support for strong labor unions (to force up wages), higher social welfare expenditures (to put more money in the hands of the poor), and vast public works projects (to create hundreds of thousands of new jobs).

Underconsumptionists did not worry that new welfare and public works programs might strain the federal budget. If the government found itself short of revenue, it could always borrow additional funds from private sources. Government borrowing, in fact, was viewed as a crucial antidepression tool. Those who lent the government money would receive a return on their investment; those who received government assistance would have additional income to spend on consumer goods; and manufacturers would profit from increases in consumer spending. Government borrowing, in short, would stimulate the circulation of money throughout the economy and would put an end to the depression.

Many politicians and economists rejected the notion that increased government spending and the deliberate buildup of federal deficits would lead to prosperity. Roosevelt himself remained committed to fiscal restraint and balanced budgets. But in 1935, as the nation entered its sixth year of the depression, he was willing to give the new ideas a try. Reform-minded members of the 1934 Congress were themselves eager for a new round of legislation directed more to the needs of ordinary Americans than to the needs of big business.

LEGISLATION OF THE SECOND NEW DEAL

Much of that legislation was passed by Congress from January to June 1935—a period that came to be known as the Second New Deal. Two of the acts were of historic importance. The Social Security Act, passed in May, required the states to set up welfare funds from which money would be disbursed to the elderly poor, the unemployed, unmarried mothers with dependent children, and the disabled. It also enrolled a majority of working Americans in a pension program that guaranteed them a steady income upon retirement. A federal system of employer and employee taxation was set up to fund the pensions.

Equally historic was the passage, in June, of the National Labor Relations Act (NLRA). This act delivered what the NRA had only promised: the right of every worker to join a union of his or her own choosing, and the obligation of employers to bargain with that union in good faith. The NLRA, also called the Wagner Act after its sponsor in the Senate, Robert Wagner of New York, set up a National Labor Relations Board (NLRB) to supervise union elections and to investigate claims of unfair labor practices. The NLRB was to be staffed by federal appointees, who would have the power to impose fines on employers who violated the law.

Congress also passed the Holding Company Act to break up the 13 utility companies that controlled 75 percent of the nation's electric power. It passed the Wealth Tax Act, which increased tax rates on the wealthy from 59 to 75 percent, and on corporations from 13¾ to 15 percent; and it passed the Banking Act, which strengthened the power of the Federal Reserve Board over its member banks. It created the Rural Electrification Administration (REA) to bring electric power to rural households. Finally, it passed the $5 billion Emergency Relief Appropriation Act. Roosevelt funneled part of this sum to the PWA and the CCC and used another part to create the National Youth Administration (NYA), which provided work and guidance to the nation's youth.

Selected WPA Projects in New York City, 1938

Construction and Renovation	Education, Health, and Art	Research and Records
East River Drive	Adult education: homemaking, trade and technical skills, and art and culture	Sewage treatment, community health, labor relations, and employment trends surveys
Henrik Hudson Parkway		
Bronx sewers	Children's education: remedial reading, lip reading, and field trips	Museum and library catalogs and exhibits
Glendale and Queens public libraries		Municipal office clerical support
King's County Hospital	Prisoners' vocational training, recreation, and nutrition	Government forms standardization
Williamsburg housing project		
School buildings, prisons, and firehouses	Dental clinics	
	Tuberculosis examination clinics	
Coney Island and Brighton Beach boardwalks	Syphilis and gonorrhea treatment clinics	
Orchard Beach	City hospital kitchen help, orderlies, laboratory technicians, nurses, doctors	
Swimming pools, playgrounds, parks, drinking fountains		
	Subsistence gardens	
	Sewing rooms	
	Central Park sculpture shop	

Source: John David Millet, *The Works Progress Administration in New York City* (Chicago: Public Administration Service, 1938), pp. 95–126.

Roosevelt directed most of the new relief money, however, to the Works Progress Administration (WPA). The WPA built or improved thousands of schools, playgrounds, airports, and hospitals. WPA crews were put to work raking leaves, cleaning streets, and landscaping cities. In the process, the WPA provided jobs to approximately 30 percent of the nation's jobless.

By the time the decade ended, the WPA, in association with an expanded Reconstruction Finance Corporation, PWA, and other agencies, had brought about the building of 500,000 miles of roads, 100,000 bridges, 100,000 public buildings, and 600 airports. The New Deal had transformed America's urban and rural landscapes. The awe generated by those great public works projects helped Roosevelt retain popular support at a time when the success of the New Deal's economic policies was uncertain. The WPA also funded a vast program of public art, supporting the work of thousands of painters, architects, writers, playwrights, actors, and intellectuals. Beyond extending relief to struggling artists, it fostered the creation of art that spoke to the concerns of ordinary Americans, adorned public buildings with colorful murals, and boosted public morale.

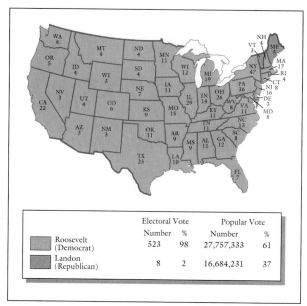

	Electoral Vote		Popular Vote	
	Number	%	Number	%
Roosevelt (Democrat)	523	98	27,757,333	61
Landon (Republican)	8	2	16,684,231	37

PRESIDENTIAL ELECTION, 1936

VICTORY IN 1936: THE NEW DEMOCRATIC COALITION

Roosevelt described his Second New Deal as a program to limit the power and privilege of the wealthy few and to increase the security and welfare of ordinary citizens. He called on voters to strip the corporations of their power and "save a great and precious form of government for ourselves and the world." American voters responded by handing Roosevelt a landslide victory. He received 61 percent of the popular vote; Alf Landon of Kansas, his Republican opponent, received only 37 percent.

The 1936 election won for the Democratic Party its reputation as the party of reform and the party of the "forgotten American." Of the 6 million Americans who went to the polls for the first time, 5 million voted for Roosevelt. Among the poorest Americans, Roosevelt received 80 percent of the vote. Black voters in the North deserted the Republican Party, calculating that their interests would best be served by the "Party of the Common Man." Roosevelt also did well among white middle-class voters, many of whom were grateful to him for pushing through the Social Security Act. These constituencies would constitute the "Roosevelt coalition" for most of the next 40 years.

RHETORIC VERSUS REALITY

Roosevelt's anticorporate rhetoric in 1935 and 1936 was more radical than the laws he supported. The Wealth Tax Act took considerably less out of wealthy incomes and estates than was advertised, and the utility companies that were to have been broken up by the Holding Company Act remained largely intact. Moreover, Roosevelt promised more than he delivered to the nation's poor. Farm workers, for example, were not covered by the Social Secu-

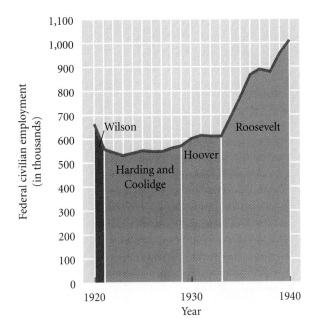

GROWTH IN FEDERAL CIVILIAN EMPLOYMENT, 1920–1940

Source: Data from *Historical Statistics of the United States, Colonial Times to 1970* (White Plains, N.Y.: Kraus International, 1989), p. 1102

rity Act or by the National Labor Relations Act. Consequently, thousands of African American sharecroppers in the South, along with substantial numbers of Chicano farm workers in the Southwest, were excluded from their protections and benefits. Moreover, the New Deal made little effort to restore voting rights to southern blacks or to protect their basic civil rights.

Roosevelt's populist stance in 1935 and 1936 also obscured the enthusiastic support that some capitalists were according the Second New Deal. In the West, Henry J. Kaiser headed a consortium of six companies that built the Hoover, Bonneville, and Grand Coulee dams. In the Midwest and the East, Roosevelt's corporate supporters included real estate developers, mass merchandisers, clothing manufacturers, and the like. These firms, in turn, had financial connections with recently established investment banks and with consumer-oriented banks such as the Bank of America. They were willing to tolerate strong labor unions, welfare programs, and high levels of government spending. But they had no intention of surrendering their wealth or power. The Democratic Party had become, in effect, the party of the masses and one section of big business. The conflicting interests of these two constituencies would create tensions within the Democratic Party throughout all the years of its political domination.

NEW DEAL MEN, NEW DEAL WOMEN

For the academics, policymakers, and bureaucrats who designed and administered the rapidly growing roster of New Deal programs and agencies, 1936 and 1937 were exciting years. Fired by idealism and dedication, they were confident they could make the New Deal work. They planned and won congressional approval for the Farm Security Administration (FSA),

IMAGES OF MEN AND WOMEN
IN THE GREAT DEPRESSION

Women played an important role in the New Deal. Eleanor Roosevelt set the tone through her visible involvement in numerous reform activities. She met with many different groups of Americans, including the miners depicted in the photo here, seeking to learn more about their condition and ways that the New Deal might assist them. But women also found their activism limited by a widespread hostility toward working women, who were thought to be taking scarce jobs away from men. In the popular movie, *Mr. Smith Goes to Washington* (1939), Jefferson Smith (Jimmy Stewart) helps a hardboiled career secretary, Clarissa Saunders (Jean Arthur), to realize that work has dam-

an agency designed to improve the economic lot of tenant farmers, sharecroppers, and farm laborers. They drafted and got passed laws that outlawed child labor, set minimum wages and maximum hours for adult workers, and committed the federal government to building low-cost housing. They investigated and tried to regulate concentrations of corporate power.

aged her sweet, womanly soul. By movie's end, Saunders is ready to leave her job and become Smith's wife and home-maker. Many other movies of the period also conveyed the sentiment that women belonged in the home.

Men, for their part, responded enthusiastically to the hypermasculinism that characterized much of the decade's mass culture. Images of strong, muscled work-ers were popular with trade unionists who feared that the Depression would strip them of their manly roles as workers and breadwinners. Boys and male adolescents, meanwhile, found a new hero in Superman, the "man-of-steel" comic-book hero who debuted in 1938. Super-man's strength, unlike that of so many men in the 1930s, could not be taken away—except by Kryptonite and Lois Lane, that "dangerous" working woman.

Although they worked on behalf of "the people," the New Dealers themselves constituted a new class of technocrats. But they did have noble aspirations. What fired their imagination was the prospect of building a strong state committed to prosperity and justice. They did not welcome interference from those they regarded as less intelligent or motivated by outworn ideologies.

This was particularly true of the men. Many had earned advanced degrees in law and economics at elite universities such as Harvard, Columbia, and Wisconsin. Not all had been raised among wealth and privilege, however, as was generally the case with earlier generations of reformers. To his credit, Franklin Roosevelt was the first president since his cousin Theodore Roosevelt to welcome Jews and Catholics into his administration. These were men who had to struggle to make their way, first on the streets and then in school and at work. They brought to the New Deal intellectual aggressiveness, quick minds, and mental toughness.

The profile of New Deal women was different. Although a few, notably Eleanor Roosevelt and Secretary of Labor Frances Perkins, were more visible than women in previous administrations had been, many of the female New Dealers worked in relative obscurity, in agencies like the Women's Bureau or the Children's Bureau (both in the Department of Labor). And women who worked on major legislation or directed major programs received less credit than men in comparable positions. Moreover, female New Dealers tended to be a generation older than their male colleagues and were more likely to be Protestant than Catholic or Jewish.

The New Deal offered these women little opportunity, however, to advance the cause of women's equality. Demands for greater economic opportunity, sexual freedom, and full equality for women and men were heard less often in the 1930s than they had been in the preceding two decades. One reason was that the women's movement had fragmented after suffrage had been achieved. Another was that prominent New Deal women did not vigorously pursue a campaign for equal rights. They concentrated instead on "protective legislation"—laws that safeguarded female workers, who were thought to be more fragile than men. Those who in-

RATES OF UNEMPLOYMENT IN SELECTED MALE AND FEMALE OCCUPATIONS, 1930

MALE OCCUPATIONS	PERCENTAGE MALE	PERCENTAGE UNEMPLOYED
Iron and steel	96%	13%
Forestry and fishing	99	10
Mining	99	18
Heavy manufacturing	86	13
Carpentry	100	19
Laborers (road and street)	100	13

FEMALE OCCUPATIONS	PERCENTAGE FEMALE	PERCENTAGE UNEMPLOYED
Stenographers and typists	96%	5%
Laundresses	99	3
Trained nurses	98	4
Housekeepers	92	3
Telephone operators	95	3
Dressmakers	100	4

Source: U.S. Department of Commerce, Bureau of the Census, *Fifteenth Census of the United States, 1930, Population* (Washington, D.C.: Government Printing Office, 1931).

sisted that women needed special protections could not easily argue that women were the equal of men in all respects.

But feminism was hemmed in on all sides by a male hostility that the depression had only intensified. Men had built their male identities on the value of hard work and the ability to provide economic security for their families. For them, the loss of work unleashed feelings of inadequacy. That the unemployment rates of men tended to be higher than those of women exacerbated male vulnerability. Many fathers and husbands resented wives and daughters who had taken over their breadwinning roles.

This male anxiety had political and social consequence. Several states passed laws outlawing the hiring of married women. The labor movement made the protection of the male wage earner one of its principal goals. The Social Security pension system did not cover waitresses, domestic servants, and other largely female occupations.

Many artists introduced a strident masculinism into their painting and sculpture. Mighty Superman, the new comic-strip hero of 1938, reflected the spirit of the times. Superman was depicted as a working-class hero who, on several occasions, saved workers from coal mine explosions and other disasters caused by the greed and negligence of villainous employers.

Superman's greatest vulnerability, however, other than kryptonite, was his attraction to the sexy and aggressive *working* woman, Lois Lane. He was never able to resolve his dilemma by marrying Lois and tucking her away in a safe domestic sphere, because the continuation of the comic strip demanded that Superman repeatedly be exposed to kryptonite and female danger. But the producers of male and female images in other mass media, like the movies, faced no such technical obstacles. Anxious men could take comfort from the conclusion of the movie *Woman of the Year,* in which Spencer Tracy persuades the ambitious Katharine Hepburn to exchange her successful newspaper career for the bliss of motherhood and homemaking.

LABOR ASCENDANT

In 1935 John L. Lewis of the United Mine Workers, Sidney Hillman of the Amalgamated Clothing Workers, and the leaders of six other unions that had seceded from the American Federation of Labor (AFL) cobbled together a new labor organization. The Committee for Industrial Organization (CIO—later renamed the Congress of Industrial Organizations) took as its goal the organization of millions of nonunion workers into effective unions that would strengthen labor's influence in the workplace. In 1936 Lewis and Hillman created a second organization, Labor's Non-Partisan League (LNPL), to develop a labor strategy for the 1936 elections. Although professing the league's nonpartisanship, Lewis intended from the start that LNPL's role would be to channel labor's money, energy, and talent into Roosevelt's reelection campaign. Roosevelt welcomed the league's help, and labor would become one of the most important constituencies of the new Democratic coalition. The passage of the Wagner Act and the creation of the NLRB in 1935 enhanced the labor movement's status and credibility. Membership in labor unions climbed steadily, and in short order union members began flexing their new muscles.

In late 1936 the United Auto Workers (UAW) took on General Motors, widely regarded as the mightiest corporation in the world. Workers occupied key GM factories in Flint, Michigan, declaring that their "sit-down" strike would continue until GM agreed to recognize the UAW and negotiate a collective bargaining agreement. Frank Murphy, the pro-labor governor of Michigan, refused to use National Guard troops to evict the strikers, and Roosevelt declined to send federal

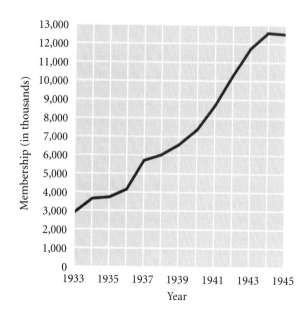

LABOR UNION MEMBERSHIP, 1933–1945

Source: From Christopher Tomlins, "AFL Unions in the 1930s," in Melvyn Dubofsky and Stephen Burwood, eds., *Labor* (New York: Garland, 1990), p. 1023.

troops. General Motors capitulated after a month of resistance. Soon, the U.S. Steel Corporation, which had defeated unionists in the bloody strike of 1919 (see Chapter 23), announced that it was ready to negotiate a contract with the newly formed CIO steelworkers union.

The labor movement's public stature grew along with its size. Many writers and artists depicted the labor movement as the voice of the people and the embodiment of the nation's values. Murals sprang up in post offices and other public buildings featuring portraits of blue-collar Americans at work. Broadway's most celebrated play in 1935 was Clifford Odets's *Waiting for Lefty,* a raw drama about taxi drivers who confront their bosses and organize an honest union. Audiences were so moved by the play that they often spontaneously joined in the final chorus of "Strike, Strike, Strike."

Similarly, many of the most popular novels and movies of the 1930s celebrated the decency, honesty, and patriotism of ordinary Americans. In *Mr. Deeds Goes to Town* (1936) and *Mr. Smith Goes to Washington* (1939) Frank Capra delighted movie audiences with fables of simple, small-town heroes vanquishing the evil forces of wealth and decadence. Likewise, in *The Grapes of Wrath,* the best-selling novel of 1939, John Steinbeck told an epic tale of an Oklahoma family's fortitude in surviving eviction from their land, migrating westward, and suffering exploitation in the "promised land" of California. In themselves and in one another, Americans seemed to discover the resolve they needed to rebuild a culture that had surrendered its identity to corporations and business.

AMERICA'S MINORITIES AND THE NEW DEAL

Reformers generally believed that issues of capitalism's viability, economic recovery, and the inequality of wealth and power outweighed problems of racial and ethnic discrimination. Because they were disproportionately poor, most minority groups did profit from the populist and pro-labor character of New Deal reforms. But the gains were distributed unevenly. Eastern and southern European ethnics benefited the most while African Americans and Mexican Americans advanced the least.

EASTERN AND SOUTHERN EUROPEAN ETHNICS

Eastern and southern European immigrants and their children had begun mobilizing politically in the 1920s in response to religious and racial discrimination (see Chapter 24). By the early 1930s, they had made themselves into a formidable political force in the Democratic Party. Roosevelt understood their importance well. He made sure that a significant portion of New Deal monies for welfare, infrastructural improvements, and unemployment relief reached the urban areas where most European ethnics lived. As a result, Jewish and Catholic Americans voted for Roosevelt in overwhelming numbers. The New Deal did not eliminate anti-Semitism and anti-Catholicism from American society, but it did allow millions of European ethnics to believe, for the first time, that they would overcome the second-class status they had long endured.

Southern and eastern European ethnics also benefited from their strong presence in the working-class. Forming one of the largest groups in the mass-production industries of the Northeast, Midwest, and West, they made crucial contributions to the labor movement's rebirth. Roosevelt accommodated himself to their wishes because he understood and feared the power they wielded through their labor organizations.

AFRICAN AMERICANS

The New Deal did more to reproduce patterns of racial discrimination than to advance the cause of racial equality. African Americans who belonged to CIO unions or who lived in northern cities benefited from New Deal programs, but the vast majority of blacks lived in rural areas of the South where they were barred from voting, largely excluded from AAA programs, and denied federal protection in their efforts to form agricultural unions. The TVA hired few blacks. Those enrolled in the CWA and other work-relief programs frequently received less pay than whites doing the same jobs. Roosevelt consistently refused to support legislation to make lynching a federal crime.

This failure to push a strong civil rights agenda did not mean that New Dealers were themselves racist. Eleanor Roosevelt spoke out frequently against racial injustice. In 1939 she resigned from the Daughters of the American Revolution when the organization refused to allow black opera singer Marian Anderson to perform in its concert hall. She then pressured the federal government into granting Anderson permission to sing from the steps of the Lincoln Memorial. On Easter Sunday, 75,000 people gathered to hear Anderson and to demonstrate their support for racial equality.

Franklin Roosevelt eliminated segregationist practices in the federal government that had been in place since Woodrow Wilson's presidency. He appointed African Americans to important second-level posts in his administration. Working closely with each other in what came to be known as the "Black Cabinet," these officials fought hard against discrimination in New Deal programs.

But Roosevelt was never willing to make the fight for racial justice a priority. He refused to support his black cabinet if it meant alienating white southern senators who controlled key congressional committees. This refusal revealed Roosevelt's belief that economic issues were more important than racial ones. It revealed, too, Roosevelt's pragmatism. His decisions to support particular policies often depended on his calculation of their potential political cost or gain. Roosevelt believed that pushing for civil rights would cost him the support of the white South. Meanwhile, African Americans and their suppporters were not yet strong enough as an electoral constituency or as a reform movement to force Roosevelt to accede to their wishes.

MEXICAN AMERICANS

The experience of Mexicans during the Great Depression was particularly harsh. In 1931, Hoover's secretary of labor, William N. Doak, announced a plan for repatriating illegal aliens (returning them to their land of origin) and giving their jobs to American citizens. The federal campaign quickly focused on Mexican immigrants in California and the Southwest. The U.S. Immigration Service staged a number of highly publicized raids, rounded up large numbers of Mexicans and Mexican Americans, and demanded that each detainee prove his or her legal status. Those who failed to produce the necessary documentation were deported.

Local governments pressured many more into leaving. Los Angeles County officials, for example, "persuaded" 12,000 unemployed Mexicans to leave by threatening to remove them from the relief rolls and offering them free railroad tickets to Mexico; Colorado officials secured the departure of 20,000 Mexicans through the use of similar techniques. The combined efforts of federal, state, and local governments created a climate of fear in Mexican communities that prompted 500,000 to return to Mexico by 1935. This total equaled the number of Mexicans who had come to the United States in the 1920s. Included in repatriate ranks were a significant number of legal immigrants who were unable to produce their immigration papers, the American-born children of illegals, and some Mexican Americans who had lived in the Southwest for generations.

The advent of the New Deal in 1933 eased but did not eliminate pressure on Chicano communities. New Deal agencies made more money available for relief, thereby lightening the burden on state and local governments. Some federal programs, moreover, prohibited the removal of illegal aliens from relief rolls. But federal laws, more often than not, failed to dissuade local officials from continuing their campaign against Mexican immigrants. Where Mexicans gained access to relief rolls, they received payments lower than those given to "Anglos" (whites) or were compelled to accept tough agricultural jobs that did not pay living wages.

Life grew harder in other ways for Mexicans who stayed in the United States. The Mexican cultural renaissance that had arisen in 1920s Los Angeles (see Chapter 24) could not continue. Hounded by government officials, Mexicans everywhere sought to escape public attention and scrutiny. In Los Angeles, where their influence had been felt throughout the city in the 1920s, they retreated into the separate community of East Los Angeles.

Mexicans and Mexican Americans who lived in urban areas and worked in blue-collar industries did benefit from New Deal programs. In Los Angeles, for example, Chicanos responded to the New Deal's pro-labor legislation by joining unions in large numbers and winning concessions from their employers. These Mexicans and Mexican Americans shared the belief of southern and eastern Europeans that the New Deal would bring them economic improvement and cultural acceptance. But most Chicanos lived in rural areas and labored in agricultural jobs. The National Labor Relations Act did not protect their right to organize unions, while the Social Security Act excluded them from the new federal welfare system.

NATIVE AMERICANS

From the 1880s until the early 1930s, federal policy had contributed to the elimination of Native Americans as a distinctive population. The Dawes Act of 1887 (see Chapter 18) had called for tribal lands to be broken up and allotted to individual owners in the hope that Indians would adopt the work habits of white farmers. But Native Americans had proved stubbornly loyal to their languages, religions, and cultures. Few of them succeeded as farmers, and many of them lost land to white speculators.

The shrinking land base in combination with a growing population deepened Native American poverty. The assimilationist pressures on Native Americans, meanwhile, reached a climax in the intolerant 1920s when the Bureau of Indian Affairs (BIA) outlawed Indian religious ceremonies, forced children from tribal communities into federal boarding schools, banned polygamy, and imposed limits on the length of men's hair.

Government officials working in the Hoover administration began to question this draconian policy, but its reversal had to await the New Deal and Roosevelt's appointment of John Collier as the commissioner of the BIA. Collier pressured the CCC, AAA, and other New Deal agencies to employ Indians on projects that improved reservation land and trained Indians in land conservation methods. He prevailed on Congress to pass the Pueblo Relief Act of 1933, which compensated Pueblos for land taken from them in the 1920s, and the Johnson-O'Malley Act of 1934, which funded states to provide for Indian health care, welfare, and education.

Collier also took steps to abolish federal boarding schools, encourage enrollment in local public schools, and establish community day schools. He insisted that Native Americans be allowed to practice their traditional religions, and he created the Indian Arts and Crafts Board in 1935 to nurture traditional Indian artists and to help them market their works.

The centerpiece of Collier's reform strategy was the Indian Reorganization Act (IRA, also known as the Wheeler-Howard Act) of 1934, which revoked the allotment provisions of the Dawes Act. The IRA restored land to tribes, granted Indians the right to establish constitutions and bylaws for self-government, and provided support for new tribal corporations that would regulate the use of communal lands. This was a landmark act that signaled the government's recognition that Native American tribes possessed the right to chart their own political, cultural, and economic futures. It reflected Collier's commitment to "cultural pluralism," a doctrine that celebrated the diversity of peoples and cultures in American society and sought to protect that diversity against the pressures of assimilation.

Collier encountered opposition everywhere: from Protestant missionaries and cultural conservatives who wanted to continue an assimilationist policy; from white farmers and businessmen who feared that the new legislation would restrict their access to Native American land; and even from a sizable number of Indian groups, some of which had embraced assimilation while others viewed the IRA as one more attempt by the federal government to impose "the white man's will" on the Indian peoples.

A vocal minority of Indians continued to oppose the act even after its passage. The most crushing blow came when the Navajo Indians voted to reject its terms. For a variety of reasons,

76 other tribes joined the Navajo in opposition. Still, a large majority of tribes supported Collier's reform and began organizing new governments under the IRA. Although their quest for independence would suffer setbacks, as Congress and the BIA continued to interfere with their economic and political affairs, these tribes gained significant measures of freedom and autonomy.

THE NEW DEAL ABROAD

When he first entered office, Roosevelt seemed to favor a nationalist approach to international relations. The United States, he believed, should pursue foreign policies to benefit its domestic affairs, without regard for the effects of those policies on world trade and international stability. Thus, in June 1933, Roosevelt abruptly pulled the United States out of the World Economic Conference in London, a meeting called by leading nations to strengthen the gold standard and thereby stabilize the value of their currencies. Roosevelt feared that the other nations would force the United States into an agreement designed to keep the gold content of the dollar high and commodity prices in the United States low. This would then frustrate the efforts of just-established New Deal agencies to inflate the prices of agricultural and industrial goods.

Soon after his withdrawal from the London conference, however, Roosevelt put the United States on a more internationalist course. In November 1933, he became the first president to recognize the Soviet Union and to establish diplomatic ties with its Communist rulers. In December 1933, he inaugurated a "Good Neighbor Policy" toward Latin America by formally renouncing the right of the United States to intervene in the affairs of Latin American nations. To back up his pledge, Roosevelt ordered home the Marines stationed in Haiti and Nicaragua, scuttled the Platt Amendment that had given the United States control over the Cuban government since 1901, and granted Panama more political autonomy and a greater administrative role in operating the Panama Canal.

None of this, however, meant that the United States had given up its influence over Latin America. When a 1934 revolution brought a radical government to power in Cuba, the United States ambassador there worked with conservative Cubans to put a regime more favorable to U.S. interests in its place. The United States did refrain from sending its troops to Cuba. It also kept its troops at home in 1936 when a radical government in Mexico nationalized a number of U.S.-owned and British-owned petroleum companies. The United States merely demanded that the new Mexican government compensate the oil companies for their lost property—a demand that Mexico eventually met.

The Roosevelt administration's recognition of the Soviet Union and embrace of the Good Neighbor Policy can be seen as an international expression of the liberal principles that guided its domestic policies. But these diplomatic initiatives also reflected Roosevelt's interest in stimulating international trade. American businessmen wanted access to the Soviet Union's market. Latin America was already a huge market for the United States, but one in need of greater stability.

Roosevelt's interest in building international trade was also evident in his support for the Reciprocal Trade Agreement, passed by Congress in 1934. This act allowed his administration to lower U.S. tariffs by as much as 50 percent in exchange for similar reductions by other nations. By the end of 1935, the United States had negotiated reciprocal trade agreements with

14 countries. Roosevelt's turn to free trade further solidified support for the New Deal in parts of the business community.

Actually increasing the volume of international trade turned out to be more difficult than passing legislation to encourage it. The supporters of free trade encountered vociferous opposition to tariff reduction both within the United States and abroad. In Germany and Italy, belligerent nationalists Adolf Hitler and Benito Mussolini told their people that the solution to their ills lay not in trade but in military strength and conquest. Throughout the world, similar appeals to national pride proved to be more popular than calls for tariff reductions and international trade.

STALEMATE, 1937–1940

By 1937 and 1938 the New Deal had begun to lose momentum. One reason was an emerging split between working-class and middle-class Democrats. After the UAW's victory over General Motors in 1937, other workers began to imitate the successful tactics pioneered by the Flint militants. The sit-down strike became ubiquitous across the nation. Many middle-class Americans, meanwhile, were becoming disturbed by labor's growing power.

THE COURT-PACKING FIASCO

The president's proposal on February 5, 1937, to alter the makeup of the Supreme Court exacerbated middle-class fears. Roosevelt asked Congress to give him the power to appoint one new Supreme Court justice for every member of the court who was over the age of 70 and who had served for at least 10 years. His stated reason was that the current justices were too old and feeble to handle the large volume of cases coming before them. But his real purpose was to prevent the conservative justices on the court from dismantling his New Deal. Roosevelt had not minded when, in 1935, the court had declared the NRA unconstitutional, but he was not willing to see the Wagner Act and the Social Security Act invalidated. His proposal, if accepted, would have given him the authority to appoint six additional justices, thereby securing a pro–New Deal majority.

What seems remarkable about this episode is Roosevelt's willingness to tamper with an institution that many Americans considered sacred. The president seemed genuinely surprised by the storm of indignation that greeted his "court-packing" proposal. Roosevelt's political acumen had apparently been dulled by the victory he had won in 1936. His inflated sense of power infuriated many who had previously been New Deal enthusiasts. Although working-class support for Roosevelt remained strong, many middle-class voters turned away from the New Deal. In 1937 and 1938 a conservative opposition took shape, uniting Republicans, conservative Democrats, and civil libertarians determined to protect private property and government integrity.

Ironically, Roosevelt's court-packing scheme may not have been necessary. In March 1937, just one month after he proposed his plan, Supreme Court Justice Owen J. Roberts, who had formerly opposed New Deal programs, decided to support them. In April and May, the Court upheld the constitutionality of the Wagner Act and Social Security Act, both by a 5-to-4 margin. Roosevelt allowed his court-reform proposal to die in Congress that summer. Within three years, five of the aging justices had retired, giving Roosevelt the

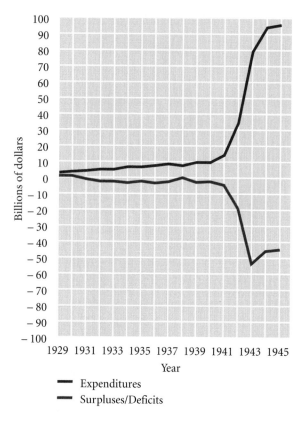

FEDERAL EXPENDITURES
AND SURPLUSES/DEFICITS,
1929–1945

Source: Data from *Historical Statistics of the United States, Colonial Times to 1970* (White Plains, N.Y.: Kraus International, 1989), p. 1105.

— Expenditures
— Surpluses/Deficits

opportunity to fashion a court more to his liking. But nonetheless, Roosevelt's reputation had suffered.

THE RECESSION OF 1937–1938

Whatever hope Roosevelt may have had for a quick recovery from the court-packing fiasco was dashed by a sharp recession that struck the country in late 1937 and 1938. The New Deal programs of 1935 had stimulated the economy. In 1937 production surpassed the highest level of 1929, and unemployment fell to 14 percent. Believing that the depression was easing at last, Roosevelt began to scale back relief programs. New payroll taxes took $2 billion dollars from wage earners' salaries to finance the Social Security pension fund. That withdrawal would not have hurt the economy had the money been returned to circulation as pensions for retirees. But no Social Security pensions were scheduled to be paid until 1941. Once again, the economy became starved for money, and once again the stock market crashed. By March 1938, the unemployment rate had soared to 20 percent. In the off-year elections later that year, voters elected many conservative Democrats and Republicans opposed to the New Deal. These conservatives were not strong enough to dismantle the New Deal reforms already in place, but they were able to block the passage of new programs.

CHRONOLOGY

1929	Herbert Hoover assumes the presidency • Stock market crashes on "Black Tuesday"
1930	Tariff Act (Hawley-Smoot) raises tariffs
1932	Unemployment rate reaches 25 percent • Reconstruction Finance Corporation established • Bonus Army marches on Washington • Roosevelt defeats Hoover for presidency
1933	Roosevelt assumes presidency • "Hundred Days" legislation defines First New Deal (March–June) • Roosevelt administration recognizes the Soviet Union • "Good Neighbor Policy" toward Latin America launched • Reciprocal Trade Agreement lowers tariffs
1934	Father Charles Coughlin and Huey Long challenge conservatism of First New Deal • 2,000 strikes staged across country • Democrats overwhelm Republicans in off-year election • Radical political movements emerge in Wisconsin, Minnesota, Washington, and California • Indian Reorganization Act restores tribal land, provides funds, and grants limited right of self-government to Native Americans
1935	Committee for Industrial Organization (CIO) formed • Supreme Court declares NRA unconstitutional • Roosevelt unveils his Second New Deal • Congress passes Social Security Act • National Labor Relations Act (Wagner Act) guarantees workers' right to join unions • Holding Company Act breaks up utilities' near-monopoly • Congress passes Wealth Tax Act • Emergency Relief Administration Act passed; funds Works Progress Administration and other projects • Rural Electrification Administration established • Number of Mexican immigrants returning to Mexico reaches 500,000
1936	Roosevelt defeats Alf Landon for second term • Supreme Court declares AAA unconstitutional • Congress passes Soil Conservation and Domestic Allotment Act to replace AAA • Farm Security Administration established
1937	United Auto Workers defeat General Motors in sit-down strike • Roosevelt attempts to "pack" the Supreme Court • Supreme Court upholds constitutionality of Social Security and National Labor Relations Acts • Severe recession hits
1938	Conservative opposition to New Deal does well in off-year election • Superman comic debuts
1939	75,000 gather to hear Marian Anderson sing at Lincoln Memorial

CONCLUSION

The New Deal reinvigorated American democracy. Some feared that Roosevelt, by accumulating more power into the hands of the federal government than had ever been done in peacetime, aspired to autocratic rule. But nothing of the sort happened. The New Dealers inspired millions of Americans who had never before voted to go to the polls. Groups that had been marginalized now felt that their political activism could make a difference.

Not everyone benefited to the same degree from the broadening of American democracy. Northern factory workers, farm owners, European ethnics, and middle-class consumers were among the groups who benefited most. In contrast, the socialist and communist elements of the labor movement failed to achieve their radical demands. Southern industrial workers, black and white, benefited little from New Deal reforms; so did farm laborers. Feminists made no headway. African Americans and Mexican Americans gained meager influence over public policy.

Of course, New Deal reforms might not have mattered to any group had not the Second World War rescued the New Deal economic program. With government war orders flooding factories from 1941 on, the economy grew vigorously, unemployment vanished, and prosperity finally returned. The architects of the Second New Deal, who had argued that large government expenditures would stimulate consumer demand and trigger economic recovery, were vindicated.

The war also solidified the political reforms of the 1930s: an increased role for the government in regulating the economy and in ensuring the social welfare of those unable to help themselves; strong state support of unionization, agricultural subsidies, and progressive tax policies; the use of government power and money to develop the West and Southwest. Voters returned Roosevelt to office for unprecedented third and fourth terms. And these same voters remained wedded for the next 40 years to Roosevelt's central idea: that a powerful state would enhance the pursuit of liberty and equality.

AMERICA DURING THE SECOND WORLD WAR

The Second World War, a struggle of unprecedented destruction, vastly changed American life. The United States abandoned isolationism, moved toward military engagement on the side of the Allies, and emerged triumphant in a global war in which U.S. forces fought and died in North Africa, Europe, and Asia.

The mobilization for war finally brought the United States out of the Great Depression and produced significant economic and social change. The nation's productive capacity—spurred by new technologies and by a new working relationship among government, business, labor, and scientific researchers—dwarfed that of every other nation and provided the economic basis for military victory.

At home, citizens considered the meaning of liberty and equality both in the international order and in their own lives. Although a massive propaganda effort heralded the war as a struggle to protect and preserve "the American way of life," the war inevitably raised significant questions. How would America, while striving for victory, reorder its economy, its culture, and the social patterns that had shaped racial, ethnic, and gender relationships during the 1930s? What process of international reconstruction might be required to build a prosperous and lasting peace?

THE ROAD TO WAR: AGGRESSION AND RESPONSE

The road to the Second World War began at least a decade before U.S. entry in 1941. In Japan, Italy, and Germany, economic collapse and rising unemployment created political conditions that nurtured ultranationalistic movements. Elsewhere in Europe and in the United States itself, economic problems made governments turn inward, concentrating upon domestic recovery and avoiding expensive foreign entanglements.

THE RISE OF AGGRESSOR STATES

On September 18, 1931, Japanese military forces seized Manchuria and created a puppet state called Manchukuo. This action violated the League of Nations charter, the Washington treaties, and the Kellogg-Briand Pact (see Chapter 24). Japanese military leaders won their gamble: The international community was too preoccupied with domestic economic ills to counter Japan's move. In the United States, the Hoover-Stimson Doctrine declared a policy of "nonrecognition" of Manchukuo, and the League of Nations also condemned Japan's action; but these stands were not backed by force, and Japan ignored them.

Meanwhile, ultranationalist states in Europe also sought to alleviate domestic ills through military aggression. Adolf Hitler's National Socialist (Nazi) Party came to power in Germany in 1933, instituting a fascist regime, a one-party dictatorial state. Hitler denounced the Versailles peace settlement of 1919, blamed Germany's plight on a Jewish conspiracy, claimed a genetic superiority for the "Aryan" race of German-speaking peoples, and promised to build a new empire (the "Third Reich"). The regime withdrew from the League of Nations and reinstituted compulsory military service. Another fascist government in Italy, headed by Benito Mussolini, also launched a military buildup and dreamed of empire. In October 1935 Mussolini's armies invaded Ethiopia. After meeting fierce resistance, Italy prevailed over Ethiopian forces.

ISOLATIONIST SENTIMENT AND AMERICAN NEUTRALITY

Many Americans wished to isolate their country from these foreign troubles. Antiwar movies, such as *All Quiet on the Western Front* and *The Big Parade,* popularized the notion that war was a power game played by business and governmental elites who used appeals to nationalism to dupe common people into serving as cannon fodder. Between 1934 and 1936 a Senate investigating committee headed by Republican Gerald P. Nye of North Dakota held well-publicized hearings. The Nye committee underscored claims that the nation had been maneuvered into the First World War to preserve the profits of American bankers and munitions makers. By 1935 public opinion polls suggested that Americans overwhelmingly opposed involvement in foreign conflicts.

To prevent a repetition of the circumstances that had supposedly drawn the United States into the First World War, Congress enacted neutrality legislation. The Neutrality Acts of 1935 and 1936 mandated an arms embargo against belligerents, prohibited loans to them, and curtailed Americans' travel on ships belonging to nations at war. The Neutrality Act of 1937 further broadened the embargo to cover all trade with belligerents, unless the nation at war paid in cash and carried the products away in its own ships.

The isolationist mood in the United States, matched by British policies of noninvolvement, encouraged Hitler's expansionist designs. In March 1936 Nazi troops seized the Rhineland. And a few months later, Hitler and Mussolini extended aid to General Francisco Franco, a fellow fascist who was seeking to overthrow Spain's republican government. Republicans in Spain appealed to antifascist nations for assistance, but only the Soviet Union responded. Britain, France, and the United States, fearing that the conflict would flare into world war if more nations took sides, adopted policies of noninvolvement.

GROWING INTERVENTIONIST SENTIMENT

Although the United States remained officially uninvolved, the Spanish Civil War did precipitate a major debate over foreign policy. Many conservative groups in the United States applauded Franco as a strong anticommunist whose fascist state would support religion and a stable social order in Spain. In contrast, the political left championed the cause of republican Spain and denounced the fascist repression that was sweeping Europe. Cadres of Americans, including the famed "Abraham Lincoln battalion," crossed the Atlantic and joined Soviet-organized, international brigades, which fought alongside republican forces. American peace groups split over how to respond. Some continued to advocate neutrality and isolation, but others argued for a strong stand against fascist militarism and aggression.

In October 1937 President Franklin Roosevelt called for international cooperation to "quarantine" aggressor states, and he gingerly suggested some modification of America's neutrality legislation. But congressional leaders were adamant in maintaining the policy of noninvolvement.

JAPAN'S INVASION OF CHINA

As Americans were debating strict neutrality versus cautious engagement, Japan launched an attack against China. In the summer of 1937, after an exchange of gunfire between Japanese and Chinese troops at the Marco Polo Bridge southwest of Beijing, Japanese armies invaded southward, capturing Beijing, Shanghai, Nanjing, and Shandong. The Japanese government demanded that China become subservient politically and economically to Tokyo. It also announced a plan for a greater East Asia Co-Prosperity Sphere, which would supposedly liberate peoples throughout Asia from Western colonialism and create a self-sufficient economic zone under Japanese leadership. Toward the end of 1937 Japanese planes sank the *Panay,* an American gunboat that was evacuating American officials from Nanjing, but Japan's quick apology defused the potential crisis. Even so, the *Panay* incident and Japanese brutality in occupying Nanjing alarmed Roosevelt.

Further aggression heightened the sense of alarm among interventionists in the United States. In October 1936 Germany and Italy agreed to cooperate as the "Axis Powers," and Japan joined them to form an alliance against the Soviet Union in November 1936. Italy followed Japan and Germany in withdrawing from the League of Nations. In March 1938 Hitler annexed Austria to the Third Reich and then announced his intention to annex the Sudetenland, a portion of Czechoslovakia inhabited by 3.5 million people of German descent.

THE OUTBREAK OF WAR IN EUROPE

The leaders of France and Britain, wishing to avoid a confrontation with Germany, met with Hitler in Munich in September of 1938. They acquiesced to Germany's seizure of the Sudetenland in return for Hitler's promise to seek no more territory. However, the promise of peace did not last. In March 1939 Germans marched into Prague and, within a few months, annexed the rest of Czechoslovakia. In August 1939 Hitler signed a nonaggression pact with the Soviet Union. In a secret protocol Stalin and Hitler plotted to divide Poland and the Baltic states. By the fall of 1939 Germany was clearly preparing for an attack on Poland.

Britain and France pledged to defend Poland, and on September 1, 1939, Hitler's invasion forced them into action. Two days after Hitler's armies stormed into Poland, Britain and France declared war on Germany. The Allies, however, were unable to mobilize in time to help the Poles, who were outnumbered and outgunned. With Soviet troops moving in simultaneously from the east, Poland fell within weeks. Once the occupation of Poland was completed, Hitler's troops waited out the winter of 1939–1940.

The lull proved only temporary. In April 1940 a German *blitzkrieg,* or "lightning war," began moving swiftly and suddenly, overrunning Denmark, Norway, the Netherlands, Belgium, Luxembourg, and then France. The speed with which Hitler's army moved shocked Allied leaders

GERMAN EXPANSION AT ITS HEIGHT

in Paris and London; Britain barely managed to evacuate its troops, but not its equipment, from the French coastal town of Dunkirk, just before it fell to the German onslaught that began in late May. Early in June, Italy joined Germany by declaring war on the Allies. In June 1940, France fell, and Hitler installed a pro-Nazi government at Vichy in southern France. In only six weeks, Hitler's army had seized complete control of Europe's Atlantic coastline, from the North Sea south to Spain, where Franco remained officially neutral but decidedly pro-Axis.

AMERICA'S RESPONSE TO WAR IN EUROPE

From 1939 to 1941 Roosevelt tried to mobilize public opinion against Congress's Neutrality Acts and in favor of what he called "measures short of war" that would bolster the Allied fight against the Axis. At Roosevelt's urging, late in 1939 Congress lifted the Neutrality Act's ban on selling arms to either side and substituted a "cash-and-carry" provision that permitted arms sales to belligerents who could pay cash for their purchases and carry them away in their own ships. Because Britain and France controlled the Atlantic sea lanes, they clearly benefited from this change in U.S. policy. Congress also passed the Selective Training and Service Act of 1940, the first peacetime draft in U.S. history. Abandoning any further pretense of neutrality, the United States began supplying war matériel directly to Great Britain.

Meanwhile, from August through October 1940 Germany's *Luftwaffe* subjected British air bases to daily raids, coming close to knocking Britain's Royal Air Force (RAF) out of the war. Just as he was on the verge of success, however, Hitler lost patience with this strategy and ordered instead the bombing of London and other cities. The bombing of Britain's cities aroused a sense of urgency about the war in the United States. The use of airpower against civilians in the Battle of Britain, as it was called, shocked Americans, who heard the news in dramatic radio broadcasts from London.

In September 1940 the president agreed to transfer 50 First World War–era naval destroyers to the British navy. In return, the United States gained the right to build eight naval bases in British territory in the Western Hemisphere. This "destroyers-for-bases" deal infuriated isolationist members of Congress. Even within the president's own party, opposition was strong. The opposition extended beyond Congress. The most formidable opposition came from the America First Committee, organized by General Robert E. Wood, head of Sears, Roebuck and Company.

Although the people who tried to keep the United States out of the war were generally lumped together as "isolationists," this single term obscures their ideological diversity. Some pacifists opposed all wars as immoral, even those against evil regimes. Some political progressives disliked fascism but feared even more the growth of centralized power that the conduct of war would require in the United States. On the other hand, some conservatives sympathized with fascism, and some Americans opposed Roosevelt's pro-Allied policies because they shared Hitler's anti-Semitism.

A current of anti-Semitism existed in the country at large. In 1939 congressional leaders had quashed the Wagner-Rogers Bill, which would have boosted immigration quotas in order to allow for the entry of 20,000 Jewish children otherwise slated for Hitler's concentration camps. Bowing to anti-Semitic prejudices, the United States adopted a restrictive refugee policy that did not permit even the legal quota of Jewish immigrants from eastern Europe to enter the country during the Second World War. The consequences of these policies became even graver after June of 1941, when Hitler established the death camps that would systematically exterminate millions of Jews, gypsies, homosexuals, and anyone else whom the Nazis deemed "unfit" for life in the Third Reich and its occupied territories.

To counteract the isolationists, those who favored supporting the Allies also organized. The Military Training Camps Association, for example, lobbied on behalf of the Selective Service Act. The Committee to Defend America by Aiding the Allies, headed by William Allen White, a well-known Republican newspaper editor, organized more than 300 local chapters in just a few weeks. Like the isolationists, interventionist organizations drew from an ideologically diverse group of supporters. All, however, sounded alarms about the dangerous possibility that fascist brutality, militarism, and racism might overrun Europe as Americans watched passively.

Presidential election politics in 1940 forced Roosevelt to tone down his pro-Allied rhetoric. The Republicans nominated Wendell Willkie, a lawyer and business executive with ties to the party's liberal, internationalist wing. The Democrats nominated Roosevelt for a third term. To differentiate his policies from Willkie's, the president played to the popular opposition to war. He promised not to send American boys to fight in "foreign wars." Once he had won an unprecedented third term, however, Roosevelt produced his most ambitious plan yet to support Britain's war effort.

AN "ARSENAL OF DEMOCRACY"

Britain was nearly out of money, so the president proposed an additional provision to the Neutrality Act. The United States would now loan, or "lend-lease," rather than sell munitions to the Allies. By making the United States a "great arsenal of democracy," FDR assured Americans, he would "keep war away from our country and our people." But not everyone in Congress felt as Roosevelt did, and debate over the Lend-Lease Act was bitter. Nevertheless, House Resolution 1776 was passed by Congress on March 11, 1941. When Germany turned its attention away from Britain and suddenly attacked its recent ally the Soviet Union in June, Roosevelt extended lend-lease to Joseph Stalin's communist regime, even though it had earlier cooperated with Hitler.

In September 1941 Senator Burton K. Wheeler of Montana created a special Senate committee to investigate whether Hollywood movies were being used to sway people in a pro-war direction. Some isolationists, pointing out that many Hollywood producers were Jewish, expressed blatantly anti-Semitic opinions.

Roosevelt next took steps to coordinate military strategy with Britain. Should the United States be drawn into a two-front war against both Germany and Japan, the president pledged to follow a Europe-first strategy. And to back up his promise, Roosevelt deployed thousands of marines to Greenland and Iceland to relieve British troops, which had occupied these strategic Danish possessions after Germany's seizure of Denmark.

Then, in August 1941, Roosevelt and British Prime Minister Winston Churchill, meeting on the high seas off the coast of Newfoundland, worked out the basis of what would shortly become a formal wartime alliance. An eight-point declaration of common principles, the so-called Atlantic Charter, disavowed territorial expansion, endorsed free trade and self-determination, and pledged the postwar creation of a new world organization that would ensure "general security." Roosevelt agreed to Churchill's request that the U.S. Navy convoy American goods as far as Iceland. This step, aimed at ensuring the safe delivery of lend-lease supplies to Britain, inched the United States even closer to belligerence. Soon, in an undeclared naval war, Germany was using its formidable submarine "wolfpacks" to attack U.S. ships.

By this time, Roosevelt and his advisers understood that in order to defeat Hitler the United States would have to enter the war, but public support for such a move was still lacking. The president urged Congress to repeal the Neutrality Act altogether to allow U.S. merchant ships to carry munitions directly to Britain. Privately, he may have hoped that Germany would commit some provocative act in the North Atlantic that would move public opinion toward further involvement. The October 1941 sinking of the U.S. destroyer *Reuben James* did just that, and Congress did repeal the Neutrality Act—but the vote was so close and the debate so bitter that Roosevelt knew he could not yet seek a formal declaration of war.

THE ATTACK AT PEARL HARBOR

As it turned out, America's formal entry into the war came about as a result of escalating tensions with Japan rather than Germany. In response to Japan's invasion of China in 1937, the

United States extended economic credits to China to bolster its efforts to defend itself. Then, in 1939 the United States abrogated its Treaty of Commerce and Navigation with Japan.

These measures did little to deter Japanese aggression, and by 1940 Germany's successes in Europe had further raised the stakes in Asia. Japan quickly mobilized to exploit the vacuum created by a weakened Europe. Japanese expansionists called for the incorporation of Southeast Asia into their East Asian Co-Prosperity Sphere.

The president hoped that a 1940 ban on the sale of aviation fuel and high-grade scrap iron to Japan would slow Japan's imminent military advance into Southeast Asia. But this act only intensified Japanese militancy. After joining the Axis alliance in September 1940, Japan pushed deeper into Indochina. When its occupation of French Indochina went unopposed, its military forces prepared to launch attacks on Singapore, the Netherlands East Indies (Indonesia), and the Philippines. Roosevelt expanded the trade embargo against Japan, promised further assistance to China, and accelerated the U.S. military buildup in the Pacific. Then, in mid-1941, Roosevelt froze Japanese assets in the United States, effectively bringing under presidential control all commerce between the two countries. With this action, Roosevelt hoped to bring Japan to the bargaining table. But faced with impending economic strangulation, the leaders of Japan began planning for a preemptive attack on the United States.

On December 7, 1941, nearly the entire U.S. Pacific fleet, stationed at Pearl Harbor in Hawaii, was destroyed by Japanese bombers. Only the fleet's aircraft carriers, which were out to sea at the time, were spared. Altogether, 19 ships were sunk or severely damaged; 188 planes were destroyed on the ground; and more than 2,200 Americans were killed. In a war message broadcast by radio on December 8, Roosevelt decried the Japanese attack and labeled December 7 "a date which will live in infamy," a phrase that served as a rallying cry throughout the war.

For the Japanese, the attack on Pearl Harbor was an act of desperation. With limited supplies of raw materials, Japan had little hope of winning a prolonged war. Japanese military strategists gambled that a crippling blow would so weaken U.S. military power that a long war would be avoided. Japanese leaders decided to risk a surprise attack.

A few Americans charged that Roosevelt had intentionally provoked Japan in order to open a "backdoor" to war. They pointed out that the fleet at Pearl Harbor lay vulnerable at its docks, not even in a state of full alert. In actuality, the American actions and inactions that led to Pearl Harbor were more confused than they were devious. Beginning in 1934 the United States had gradually enlarged its Pacific fleet, and Roosevelt had also increased the number of B-17 bombers based in the Philippines. The president hoped that the possibility of aerial attacks would intimidate Japan and slow its expansion. But the strategy of deterrence failed. It may also have contributed to the lack of vigilance at Pearl Harbor. American leaders doubted that Japan would risk a direct attack, and intelligence experts expected Japan to move toward Singapore or other British or Dutch possessions. Intercepted messages, along with visual sightings of Japanese transports, seemed to confirm preparations for a strike in Southeast Asia (a strike that did occur). A warning that Japan might also be targeting Pearl Harbor was not sent with sufficient urgency and was lost under a mountain of intelligence reports.

On December 8, 1941, Congress declared war against Japan. Japan's allies, Germany and Italy, declared war on the United States three days later. Hitler mistakenly assumed that war with Japan would keep the United States preoccupied in the Pacific. The three Axis Powers drastically underestimated America's ability to mobilize swiftly and effectively.

FIGHTING THE WAR IN EUROPE

The first few months after America's entry into the war proved to be discouraging. German forces already controlled most of Europe from Norway to Greece and had pushed rapidly eastward into the Soviet Union. Now they were rolling across North Africa. In the Atlantic, German submarines were endangering Allied supply lines. Japan seemed unstoppable in the Pacific. Japanese forces overran Malaya, the Dutch East Indies, and the Philippines and drove against the British in Burma and the Australians in New Guinea.

Long before December 7, 1941, the Roosevelt administration had expected war and had vainly tried to prepare for it. When war came, Army morale was low, industrial production was still on a peacetime footing, and labor-management relations were contentious. As the country faced the need for rapid economic and military mobilization, new government bureaucracies began to spring up everywhere.

The wartime growth in the size of government transformed American foreign policymaking. Military priorities superseded all other demands. The administration was being forced to settle on new policies overnight and then implement them on a global scale the following day. The newly formed Joint Chiefs of Staff, consisting of representatives from each of the armed services, became Roosevelt's major source of guidance on military strategy. The War Department's new Pentagon complex dwarfed the State Department's cramped quarters at "Foggy Bottom." The giant five-story, five-sided building was completed in January 1943, after 16 months of round-the-clock work.

In the Atlantic, German submarines sank 7 million tons of Allied shipping in the first 16 months after Pearl Harbor. In 1942 aircraft equipped with radar, a new technology developed in collaboration with Britain, proved effective against submarines. During 1943 Germany's submarine capability faded "from menace to problem," in the words of Admiral Ernest King.

CAMPAIGNS IN NORTH AFRICA AND ITALY

Military strategy became a contentious issue among the Allied Powers. All advisers agreed that their primary focus would be on Europe, and Roosevelt and his military strategists immediately established a unified command with the British. The Soviet Union pleaded with Roosevelt and Churchill to open a second front in western Europe to relieve Germany's pressure on the USSR. Many of Roosevelt's advisers agreed. They feared that if German troops forced the Soviet Union out of the war, Germany would then turn its full attention to defeating Britain. Churchill, however, urged instead the invasion of French North Africa, in order to peck away at the edges of enemy power rather than strike at its heart. At a meeting between Roosevelt and Stalin at Casablanca, Morocco, in January 1943, Roosevelt sided with Churchill, and the promised invasion of France was postponed. To assuage Stalin's fears that his two allies might sign a separate peace with Hitler, the two leaders did announce that they would stay in the fight until Germany agreed to an unconditional surrender.

The North African operation, code-named TORCH, began with Anglo-American landings in Morocco and Algeria in November 1942. To ease resistance against the Allies' North African invasion, U.S. General Dwight D. Eisenhower struck a deal with French Admiral Jean Darlan, the Vichy officer who controlled France's colonies in North Africa. Darlan agreed to break with the Vichy regime in return for Eisenhower's pledge that the United States would support him. The deal outraged some Americans who believed that it compromised the moral purpose of the war. Darlan's assassination in December 1942 put an end to the embarrassment. But the antagonism that Eisenhower's action had created between Americans and the Free French movement, led by General Charles de Gaulle, had lasting consequences after the war.

As TORCH progressed, the Soviets managed to turn the tide of battle at Stalingrad. Despite this defeat in the East, Hitler poured reinforcements into North Africa, but could not stop either TORCH or the British, who were driving west from Egypt. In the summer of 1943 Allied troops followed up the successful North African campaign by overrunning the island of Sicily and then fighting their way slowly north through Italy's mountains.

Some American officials increasingly worried about the postwar implications of wartime strategy. Secretary of War Henry Stimson, for example, warned that the peripheral campaigns through Africa and Italy might leave the Soviets dominating central Europe. Acting on their advice, Roosevelt finally agreed to set a date for the cross-Channel invasion that Stalin had long been promised.

Operation OVERLORD

Operation OVERLORD finally began on June 6, 1944, D-Day. During the months preceding D-Day, probably the largest invasion force in history had been assembled in England. Disinformation and diversionary tactics had led the Germans to expect a landing at the narrowest part of the English Channel rather than in the Normandy region. Allied intelligence officers knew from monitoring the cables sent to Tokyo by Japan's ambassador in Berlin that their ruse had worked. After several delays, due to the Channel's unpredictable weather, nervous commanders finally ordered the daring plan to begin. The night before, as naval guns pounded the Normandy shore, three divisions of paratroopers were dropped behind enemy lines to disrupt German communications. Then, at dawn, more than 4,000 Allied ships landed troops and supplies on Normandy's beaches. The first American troops to land at Omaha Beach met especially heavy German fire and took enormous casualties. But the waves of invading troops continued. Within three weeks, over 1 million people had landed, secured the Normandy coast, and opened the long-awaited second front.

Just as the Battle of Stalingrad had reversed the tide of the war in the East, so operation OVERLORD turned the tide in the West. Within three months, U.S., British, and Free French troops entered Paris. After turning back a desperate German counteroffensive in Belgium, at the Battle of the Bulge in December and January, Allied armies swept eastward, crossing the Rhine and heading toward Berlin.

The Allies disagreed on how the defeat of Germany should be orchestrated. British strategists favored a swift drive, so as to meet up with Soviet armies in Berlin or even farther east. General Eisenhower favored a strategy that was militarily less risky and politically less provocative to the Soviets. He was also eager to end the war on a note of trust and believed that racing the Soviets to Berlin would undermine the basis for postwar Soviet-American cooperation. In the end, Eisenhower's views prevailed. He moved cautiously along a broad front, halting his troops at the Elbe River, west of Berlin, and allowing Soviet troops to roll into the German capital.

As the war in Europe drew to a close, the horrors perpetrated by the Third Reich became visible to the world. Although only a military victory could put an end to German death camps, the Allies could have saved thousands of Jews by encouraging them to emigrate and helping them to escape. Allied leaders, however, worried about the impact large numbers of Jewish refugees would have on their countries, and they were also reluctant to use scarce ships to transport Jews to

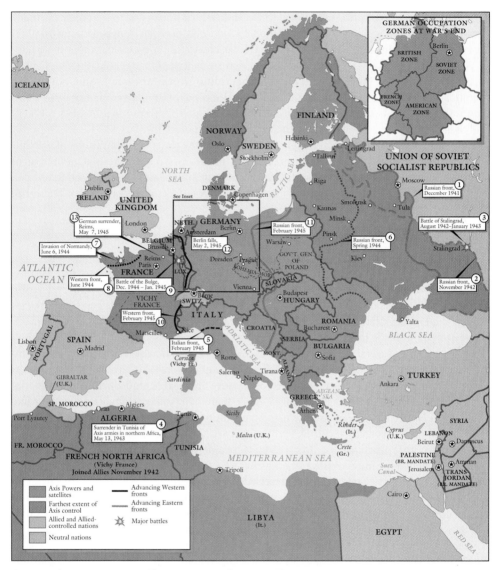

ALLIED ADVANCES AND COLLAPSE OF GERMAN POWER

neutral sanctuaries. In 1943, after Romania proposed permitting an evacuation of 70,000 Jews from its territory, Allied leaders avoided any serious discussion of the plan. The United States even refused to relax its strict policy on visas to admit Jews who might have escaped on their own.

Hitler's campaign of extermination, now called the Holocaust, killed between 5 and 6 million Jews out of Europe's prewar population of 10 million; hundreds of thousands more from various other groups were also murdered, especially gypsies, homosexuals, intellectuals, communists, and the physically and mentally handicapped. The Allies would, in 1945 and 1946, bring 24 high German officials to trial at Nuremburg for "crimes against humanity." Large quantities of money, gold, and jewelry that Nazi leaders stole from victims of the Holocaust and deposited in Swiss banks remained largely hidden from view for more than 50 years. Not until 1997 did Jewish groups and the U.S. government begin to force investigations of the Swiss banking industry and its relationship to stolen "Nazi gold."

With Hitler's suicide in April and Germany's surrender on May 8, 1945, the military foundations for peace in Europe were complete. Soviet armies controlled eastern Europe; British and U.S. forces predominated in Italy and the rest of the Mediterranean; Germany and Austria fell under divided occupation. Governmental leaders now needed to work out a plan for transforming these military arrangements into a comprehensive political settlement for the postwar era. Meanwhile, the war in the Pacific was still far from over.

THE PACIFIC THEATER

For six months after Pearl Harbor, nearly everything in the Pacific went Japan's way. Singapore fell easily. American naval garrisons in the Philippines and on Guam and Wake islands were overwhelmed, and American and Filipino armies were forced to surrender at Bataan and Corregidor in the Philippines. Other Japanese forces steamed southward to menace Australia. Then the tide turned.

SEIZING THE INITIATIVE IN THE PACIFIC

When Japan finally suffered its first naval defeat at the Battle of the Coral Sea in May 1942, Japanese naval commanders decided to hit back hard. They amassed 200 ships and 600 planes to destroy what remained of the U.S. Pacific fleet and to take Midway Island. U.S. intelligence, however, was monitoring Japanese codes and warned Admiral Chester W. Nimitz of the plan. Surprising the Japanese navy, U.S. planes sank four Japanese carriers and destroyed a total of 322 planes.

Two months later, American forces splashed ashore at Guadalcanal in the Solomon Islands. The bloody engagements in the Solomons continued for months on both land and sea, but they accomplished one major objective: seizing the initiative against Japan. This success, combined with the delay in opening a second front in Europe, also affected grand strategy. According to prewar plans, the war in Europe was to have received highest priority. But by 1943 the two theaters were receiving roughly equal resources.

The bloody engagements in the Pacific dramatically illustrated that the war was one in which racial prejudices reinforced brutality. For Japan, the Pacific conflict was a war to establish forever the superiority of the divine Yamato race. Prisoners taken by the Japanese were brutalized in unimaginable ways. The Japanese army's Unit 731 tested bacteriological weapons in China and conducted horrifying medical experiments on live subjects. American propaganda images also played upon themes of racial superiority, portraying the Japanese as animalistic subhumans. American troops often rivaled Japan's forces in their disrespect for the enemy dead and sometimes killed the enemy rather than take prisoners.

CHINA POLICY

U.S. policymakers hoped that China would fight Japan more effectively and then emerge after the war as a strong and united nation. Neither hope was realized.

General Joseph W. Stilwell undertook the job of turning China into an effective military force. Jiang Jieshi (formerly spelled Chiang Kai-shek) headed China's government and appointed Stilwell his chief of staff. But frictions between "Vinegar Joe" Stilwell and Jiang became so intense that in May 1943 Roosevelt bowed to Jiang's demand for Stilwell's dismissal. Meanwhile, Japan's advance into China continued, and in 1944 its forces captured seven of the principal U.S. air bases in China.

During the same period China was beset by civil war. Jiang's Nationalist government was incompetent, corrupt, and unpopular. It avoided engaging the Japanese invaders and still made extravagant demands for U.S. assistance. Meanwhile, a growing communist movement led by Mao Zedong was fighting effectively against the Japanese and enjoyed widespread support among Chinese peasants. Stilwell urged Roosevelt to cut off support to Jiang unless he fought with more determination. Roosevelt, however, feared that such actions would create even greater chaos. He continued to provide moral support and matériel to Jiang's armies. Moreover, pressed by a powerful "China lobby" of domestic conservatives, he insisted that Jiang's China be permitted to stand with the major powers after victory had been won. By tying U.S. policy to Jiang's leadership, Roosevelt and the "China lobby" prepared the way for great difficulties in forging a China policy in the postwar period.

PACIFIC STRATEGY

In contrast to the war in Europe, there was no unified command to guide the war in the Pacific; consequently, military actions often emerged from compromise. General Douglas MacArthur, commander of the army in the South Pacific, favored an offensive launched from his headquarters in Australia through New Guinea and the Philippines and on to Japan. After Japan drove him out of the Philippines in May 1942, he promised to return. Admiral Nimitz disagreed. He favored an advance across the smaller islands of the central Pacific, which would provide more direct access to Japan. Unable to decide between the two strategies, the Joint Chiefs of Staff authorized both.

Marked by fierce fighting and heavy casualties, both offensives moved forward. MacArthur took New Guinea, and Nimitz's forces liberated the Marshall Islands and the Marianas in 1943 and 1944. At about this point, an effective radio communication system conducted by a Marine platoon of Navajo Indians made a unique contribution to the war effort. Navajo, a language unfamiliar to both the Japanese and the Germans, provided a secure medium for sensitive communications. In late 1944 the fall of Saipan brought American bombers within range of Japan. The capture of the islands of Iwo Jima and Okinawa further shortened that distance during the spring of 1945.

As the seaborne offensive proceeded, the United States brought its airpower into play. In February 1944 General Henry Harley ("Hap") Arnold presented Roosevelt with a plan for strategic air assaults on Japanese cities. His proposal included a systematic campaign of destruction through the firebombing of urban targets. Roosevelt approved the plan. In the month before bombing began, the Office of War Information lifted its ban on atrocity stories about Japan's treatment of American prisoners. As grisly reports and racist anti-Japanese propaganda swept across the country, it was thought the public would become more accepting of the killing of Japanese civilians. Arnold's original air campaign, operating from bases in China, turned out to be cumbersome and ineffective; it was replaced by an even more lethal operation, running from Saipan, under the aegis of General Curtis LeMay.

NAVAJO SIGNAL CORPS Sending messages in their native language, which was unfamiliar to the Japanese, Navajo Indians in the Signal Corps made a unique contribution to preserving the secrecy of U.S. intelligence.

The official position on the incendiary raids on Japanese cities was that they constituted "precision" rather than "area" bombing. In actuality, the success of a mission was measured in terms of the number of square miles that had been left scorched and useless. The number of Japanese civilians killed in the raids is estimated to have been greater than the number of Japanese soldiers killed in battle. An attack on Tokyo on the night of March 9–10, 1945, inaugurated the new policy, inflicting 185,000 casualties.

By the winter of 1944–1945, a combined sea and air strategy had emerged: The United States would seek "unconditional surrender" by blockading Japan's seaports, continuing its bombardment of Japanese cities from the air, and perhaps invading Japan itself. Later critics of the policy of unconditional surrender have suggested that it may have hardened the determination with which Japan fought the war after its inevitable defeat had become obvious. With the unconditional surrender policy in place and Japan's determination to fight even in the face of certain defeat, the strategy of American leaders seemed to require massive destruction to achieve victory.

ATOMIC POWER AND JAPANESE SURRENDER

At Los Alamos, New Mexico, scientists from all across the United States had been secretly working on a weapon that promised just such massive destruction. Advances in theoretical

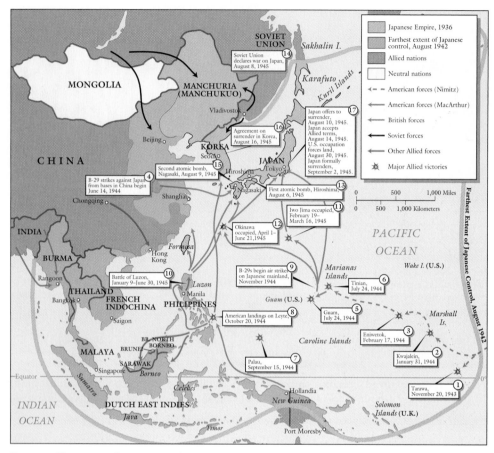

PACIFIC THEATER OFFENSIVE STRATEGY AND FINAL ASSAULT AGAINST JAPAN

physics during the 1930s had suggested that splitting the atom (fission) would release a tremendous amount of energy. Fearful that Germany was racing ahead in this effort, Albert Einstein, a Jewish refugee from Germany, urged President Roosevelt to launch a secret program to build a bomb based on atomic research. The government subsequently enlisted top scientists in the Manhattan Project, the largest and most secretive military project yet undertaken. On July 16, 1945, the first atomic weapon was successfully tested at Trinity Site, near Alamagordo, New Mexico. The researchers then notified the new president, Harry Truman, that the terrifying new weapon was ready.

Truman and his top policymakers assumed that the weapon should be put to immediate military use. They were eager to end the war, both because a possible land invasion of Japan might have cost so many American lives and also because the Soviet Union was planning to enter the Pacific theater, and Truman wished to limit Soviet power in that region. Churchill called the bomb a "miracle of deliverance" and a peace-giver. Truman later said that he had never lost a night's sleep over its use.

TOTAL WAR: DRESDEN AND HIROSHIMA   The effects of "total war" are graphically illustrated in these photographs—of the devastation of Dresden, Germany (top), by the British Bomber Command and the U.S. 8th Air Force on February 13 and 14, 1945, and that of Hiroshima, Japan (bottom), by the U.S. 509th Composite Group on August 6, 1945. In the initial attack on Dresden, 786 aircraft dropped 5,824,000 pounds (2,600 long tons) of bombs on the city, killing an estimated 60,000 people and injuring another 30,000. An area of more than 2.5 square miles in the town center was demolished, and some 37,000 buildings were destroyed. To critics, the bombing of Dresden, a target that many argued was of little strategic value, exemplified the excessive use of airpower.

In sobering comparison, the devastation of Hiroshima was created by one bomb weighing only 10,000 pounds (4.4 long tons)—an atomic bomb—which was dropped from one aircraft. The single U-235 bomb killed 68,000 people outright, injured another 30,000, and left 10,000 missing. (These figures do not include those who later developed diseases from deadly gamma rays.) Almost 5 square miles of the city's center was obliterated, and 40,653 buildings were destroyed. Truman reported the strike as "an overwhelming success." Many hailed the atomic bomb as a necessary step toward military victory; others worried about the dawn of the "nuclear age."

Other advisers had more qualms, and there was some disagreement over where and how the bomb should be deployed. A commission of atomic scientists recommended a "demonstration" that would impress Japan with the bomb's power yet cause no loss of life. But most of Truman's advisers agreed that simply demonstrating the bomb's power might not be enough. They believed that it would take massive destruction to bring unconditional surrender.

In the context of the earlier brutal aerial bombardment of Japanese cities, dropping atomic bombs on the previously unbombed cities of Hiroshima and Nagasaki on August 6 and 9, 1945, seemed simply an acceleration of existing policy rather than a departure from it. "Fat Man" and "Little Boy," as the two bombs were nicknamed, were merely viewed as bigger, more effective firebombs. Of course, atomic weapons did produce yet a new level of violence. Colonel Paul Tibbets, who piloted the plane that dropped the first bomb, reported that "the shimmering city became an ugly smudge . . . a pot of bubbling hot tar." Teams of U.S. observers who entered the cities in the aftermath were stunned at the immediate devastation, including the instantaneous incineration of both human beings and man-made structures, as well as the longer-lasting horror of radiation disease. The mushroom clouds over Hiroshima and Nagasaki would inaugurate a new "atomic age," in which dreams of peace were mingled with nightmares of Armageddon. But in those late summer days of 1945, most Americans sighed with relief. News reports on August 15 proclaimed Japan's surrender, VJ Day.

THE WAR AT HOME: THE ECONOMY

The success of the U.S. military effort in both Europe and Asia depended on mobilization at home. Ultimately, it was this mobilization that finally brought the depression of the 1930s to an end. But the war did more than restore prosperity. It transformed the nation's entire political economy—its government, its business and financial institutions, and its labor force.

GOVERNMENT'S ROLE IN THE ECONOMY

The federal bureaucracy nearly quadrupled in size during the war, as new economic agencies proliferated. The most powerful of these, the War Production Board, oversaw the conversion and expansion of factories, allocated resources, and enforced production priorities and schedules. The War Labor Board had jurisdiction over labor-management disputes, and the War Manpower Commission allocated labor to various industries. The Office of Price Administration regulated prices to control inflation and rationed such scarce commodities as gasoline, rubber, steel, shoes, coffee, sugar, and meat. Although most of the controls were abandoned after the war, the concept of greater governmental regulation of the economy survived.

From 1940 to 1945 the U.S. economy expanded rapidly. In each year of the war, GNP rose by 15 percent or more. When Roosevelt called for the production of 60,000 planes, shortly after Pearl Harbor, skeptics jeered. Yet within the next few years the nation produced nearly 300,000 planes. The Maritime Commission oversaw construction of more than 53 million tons of shipping. The previously stagnant economy spewed out prodigious quantities of other supplies, including 2.5 million trucks and 50 million pairs of shoes.

Striving to increase production, industry entered into an unprecedented relationship with government to promote scientific and technological research and development, "R&D." Government money subsidized new industries, such as electronics, and enabled others, such as rubber and chemicals, to transform their processes and products. The newly established Office of Scientific Research and Development entered into contracts for a variety of projects with universities and scientists. Under this program, radar, penicillin, rocket engines, and other new products were rapidly perfected for wartime use.

BUSINESS AND FINANCE

To finance the war effort, government spending rose from $9 billion in 1940 to $98 billion in 1944. In 1941 the national debt stood at $48 billion; by VJ Day it was $280 billion. With few goods to buy, Americans invested in war bonds, turning their savings into tanks and planes. Although war bonds provided a relatively insignificant contribution to defense spending, they did help drive the level of personal saving up to 25 percent of consumer income.

WOMEN ARE ENLISTED IN THE WAR EFFORT   This picture of a Jeep assembly line at Willys-Overland in Toledo, Ohio, illustrates the extent to which women during the Second World War took over manufacturing jobs traditionally held by men. It was usually stressed, however, that the trend would be merely temporary. Photographs such as this, in which carefully groomed women are attired in dresses and aprons, conveyed a double message: Women needed to fill in for men who were away during the war, but they should retain their traditional symbols of femininity and be ready to resume more traditional roles after victory.

CHILDREN ARE ENLISTED IN THE WAR EFFORT   These children, flashing the "V-for-Victory" sign, stand atop a pile of scrap metal. Collecting scrap of all kinds for war production helped to engage millions of Americans on the home front.

As production shifted from autos to tanks, from refrigerators to guns, many consumer goods became scarce. Essentials such as food, fabrics, and gasoline were rationed and, consequently, were shared more equitably than they had been before the war. Higher taxes on wealthier Americans tended to redistribute income and narrow the gap between the poor and the well-to-do. War bonds, rationing, and progressive taxation gave Americans a sense of shared sacrifice and helped ease the class tensions of the 1930s.

As the war fostered an increase in personal savings and promoted a measure of income redistribution, however, it also facilitated the dismantling of many of the New Deal agencies most concerned with the interests of the poor. A Republican surge in the off-year elections of 1942—the GOP gained 44 seats in the House and 7 new senators—helped strengthen an anti–New Deal, conservative coalition in Congress. In 1943 Congress abolished the job creation programs run by the Works Progress Administration (WPA), the Civilian Conservation Corps (CCC), and the National Youth Administration (NYA) (see Chapter 25). It also shut down the Rural Electrification Administration (REA) and Farm Security Administration (FSA), agencies that had assisted impoverished rural areas. As business executives flocked to Washington to run the new wartime bureaus, the Roosevelt administration shifted its attitude toward big business from one of guarded hostility to one of cooperation.

Social programs withered as big businesses that were considered essential to victory flourished under government subsidies. What was "essential," of course, became a matter of definition. Coca-Cola and Wrigley's chewing gum won precious sugar allotments by arguing that GIs overseas "needed" to enjoy their products. Both companies prospered. The Kaiser Corporation, whose spectacular growth in the 1930s had been spurred by federal dam contracts, now turned its attention to the building of ships, aircraft, and military vehicles. Federal subsidies, low-interest loans, and tax breaks enabled factories to expand and retool.

The war concentrated power in the largest corporations. The enforcement of antitrust laws was postponed at Roosevelt's request. Legal challenges that had been years in preparation, such as the case against America's great oil cartel, were now tucked away. Congressional efforts to investigate alleged collusion in the awarding of government contracts and to increase assistance to small businesses made little progress in Washington's crisis atmosphere. The top 100 companies, which had provided 30 percent of the nation's total manufacturing output in 1940, were providing 70 percent by 1943.

THE WORKFORCE

During the first two years of military buildup, many workers who had been idled during the Depression were called back to work. Employment in heavy industry invariably went to men, and most of the skilled jobs went to whites. But as military service drained the supply of white male workers, women and minorities became more attractive as candidates for production jobs. Soon, both private employers and government were encouraging women to go to work, southern African Americans to move to northern industrial cities, and Mexicans to enter the United States under the *bracero* guest worker program.

Women were hired for jobs that had never been open to them before. They became welders, shipbuilders, lumberjacks, miners. As major league baseball languished from a lack of players, female teams sprang up to give new life to the national pastime. Many employers hired married women, who, before the war, were often banned even from such traditionally female occupations as teaching. Minority women moved into clerical or secretarial jobs, where they had not previously been welcome. Most workplaces, however, continued to be segregated by sex.

The character of unpaid labor, long provided mostly by women, also underwent significant change. Volunteer activities such as Red Cross projects, civil defense work, and recycling drives claimed more and more of the time of women, children, and older people. In the home, conservation was emphasized. Government propaganda exhorted homemakers: "Wear it out, use it up, make it do, or do without." Both in the home and in the factory, women's responsibilities and workloads increased.

The new labor market improved the economic position of African Americans generally. By executive order in June 1941, the president created the Fair Employment Practices Commission (FEPC), which tried to ban discrimination in hiring. In 1943 the government announced that it would not recognize as collective bargaining agents any unions that denied admittance to minorities. The War Labor Board outlawed the practice of paying different wages to whites and nonwhites doing the same job. Before the war, the African American population had been mainly southern, rural, and agricultural; within a few years, a substantial percentage of African Americans had become northern, urban, and industrial. Although employment discrimination was hardly eliminated, twice as many African Americans held skilled jobs at the end of the war as at the beginning.

For both men and women, the war brought higher wages and longer work hours. Although in 1943 the government got labor unions to limit demands for wage increases to 15 percent, overtime often raised paychecks far more. During the war, average weekly earnings rose nearly 70 percent. Farmers, who had suffered through many years of low prices and overproduction, doubled their income and then doubled it again.

LABOR UNIONS

The scarcity of labor during the war substantially strengthened the labor union movement. Union membership rose by 50 percent. Women and minority workers joined unions in unprecedented numbers, but the main beneficiaries of labor's new power were white males.

Especially on the national level, the commitment of organized labor to female workers was weak. Not a single woman served on the executive boards of either the AFL or the CIO. The International Brotherhood of Teamsters even required women to sign a statement that their union membership could be revoked when the war was over. Unions did fight for contracts stipulating equal pay for men and women in the same job, but these benefited women only as long as they held "male" jobs. The unions' primary purpose in advocating equal pay was to maintain wage levels for the men who would return to their jobs after the war. During the first year of peace, as employers trimmed their workforces, both business and unions gave special consideration to returning veterans and worked to ease women out of the labor force. Unions based their wage demands on the goal of securing male workers a "family wage," one that would be sufficient to support an entire family.

Some unions, reflecting the interests of their white male members, also supported racial discrimination. Union members believed that the hiring of lower-paid, nonwhite workers would jeopardize their own, better-paid positions. Early in the war, most AFL affiliates in the aircraft and shipbuilding industries had refused to accept African Americans as members. They quarreled with the FEPC over this policy throughout the war. As growing numbers of African Americans were hired, racial tensions in the workplace increased. In various factories across the country white workers walked off the job to protest the hiring of African Americans. Beyond revealing deep-seated racism, such incidents reflected the union leaders' fears of losing the organizing gains and recognition they had fought so hard to win during the 1930s.

The labor militancy of the 1930s was muted by a wartime no-strike pledge, but it nonetheless persisted. Despite no-strike assurances, for example, the United Mine Workers union called a strike in the bituminous coal fields in 1943. When the War Labor Board took a hard line against the union's demands, the strike was prolonged. In Detroit, disgruntled aircraft workers roamed the factory floors, cutting off the neckties of their supervisors; wildcat strikes erupted in St. Louis, Detroit, and Philadelphia. Congress responded by passing the Smith-Connally Act of 1943, which empowered the president to seize plants or mines if strikes interrupted war production. Even so, the war helped to strengthen organized labor's place in American life.

ASSESSING ECONOMIC CHANGE

Overall, the impact of the war on America's political economy was significant. During the war, the workplace became more inclusive in terms of gender and race than ever before, and so did labor unions. More people entered the paid labor force, and many of them earned more money than rationing restrictions allowed them to spend. Although some of these changes proved to be short-lived, the new precedents and expectations arising from the wartime experience could not be entirely effaced at war's end.

More than anything else, the institutional scale of American life was transformed. Big government, big business, and big labor all grew even bigger during the war years. Science and technology forged new links of mutual interest among these three sectors. The old America of small farms, small businesses, and small towns did not disappear. But urban-based, bureaucratized institutions increasingly organized life in postwar America.

THE WAR AT HOME: SOCIAL ISSUES

Dramatic social changes accompanied the wartime mobilization. Ordered by military service or attracted by employment, many people moved away from the communities where they had grown up. Even on the home front, the war involved constant sacrifice. The war, most Americans believed, was being fought to preserve democracy and individual freedom. Yet for many, wartime ideals highlighted everyday inequalities.

WARTIME PROPAGANDA

During the First World War, government propagandists had asked Americans to fight for a more democratic world and a permanent peace. But such idealistic goals had little appeal for the skeptical generation of the 1930s and 1940s. Sensitive to popular attitudes, the Roosevelt administration asked Americans to fight to preserve the "American way of life"—not to save the world.

Hollywood studios and directors eagerly answered the government's call by shaping inspiring and sentimental representations of American life. Called to make a series of government films entitled *Why We Fight,* Frank Capra contrasted Norman Rockwell–type characters with harrowing portrayals of the mass obedience and militarism in Germany, Italy, and Japan. A hundred or so Hollywood personalities received commissions to make films for the Army's Pictorial Division.

Freedom from Want

Print advertising also contributed to the wartime propaganda effort. Roosevelt encouraged advertisers to sell the benefits of freedom. Most obliged, and "freedom" often appeared in the guise of new washing machines, ingenious kitchen appliances, improved automobiles, a wider range of lipstick hues, and automation in a hundred forms. As soon as the war was over, the ads promised, American technological know-how would usher in a consumer's paradise.

In the spring of 1942, Roosevelt created the Office of War Information (OWI) to coordinate policies related to propaganda and censorship. Liberals charged that the OWI was dominated by advertising professionals who dealt in slogans rather than substance. Conservatives blasted it as a purveyor of crass political advertisements for causes favored by Roosevelt and liberal Democrats. Despite such sniping, the OWI established branches throughout the world, published a magazine called *Victory,* and produced hundreds of films, posters, and radio broadcasts.

GENDER EQUALITY

As women took over jobs traditionally held by men, many people began to take more seriously the idea of gender equality. Some 350,000 women volunteered for military duty during the war; more than 1,000 women served as civilian pilots with the WASPs (Women's Airforce Service Pilots). Not everyone approved. But most in Congress came to support a women's corps, with full status, for each branch of the military, a step that had been thwarted during the First World War.

The military service of women, together with their new importance in the labor market, strengthened arguments for laws to guarantee equal treatment. But women's organizations themselves disagreed over how to advance women's opportunities. Organizations representing middle-class women strongly backed passage of an Equal Rights Amendment (ERA), but other groups, more responsive to the problems of poor women, opposed its passage. They saw it as a threat to the protective legislation, regulating hours and hazardous conditions, that women's rights crusaders had struggled to win earlier in the century. Should women continue to be accorded "protected" status in view of their vulnerability to exploitation in a male-directed workplace? Or should they fight for "equal" status?

Even as the war temporarily narrowed gender differences in employment, government policies and propaganda frequently framed changes in women's roles in highly traditional terms. Women's expanded participation in the workplace was often portrayed as a short-term sacrifice. Feminine stereotypes abounded. A typical ad suggesting that women take on farm work declared: "A woman can do anything if she knows she looks beautiful doing it." Despite the acceptance of women into the armed services, most were assigned to stateside clerical and supply jobs; only a relatively few women served overseas. Day care programs for mothers working outside their homes received reluctant and inadequate funding. The 3,000 centers set up during the war filled only a fraction of the need and were swiftly shut down after the war. Leading social scientists and welfare experts, mostly male, blamed working mothers for the apparent rise in juvenile delinquency and in the divorce rate during the war years.

The war also widened the symbolic gap between "femininity" and "masculinity." Military culture encouraged men to adopt a "pin-up" mentality toward women. Tanks and planes were decorated with symbols of female sexuality, and wartime fiction often associated manliness with brutality and casual sex. After the war, tough-guy fiction with a violent and misogynist edge, like Mickey Spillane's "Mike Hammer" series of detective novels, became one of the most successful formulas of popular culture.

RACIAL EQUALITY

Messages about race were as ambiguous as those related to gender. Before the Second World War, America had been a sharply segregated society. African Americans, disfranchised in the South and only beginning to achieve voting power in the North, had only limited access to the political, legal, or economic systems. The fight against fascism, however, challenged this old order in a number of ways.

Nazism, a philosophy based on the idea of racial inequality, exposed the racist underpinnings of much of 20th century social science theory. The view that racial difference was not a

"United We Win"   Government posters created during the Second World War attempted to mute class and racial divisions and to offer images of all Americans united against fascism.

function of biology but a function of culture gained wider popular acceptance during the war. The implication was that a democratic and pluralistic society could accommodate racial difference. This new thinking helped to lay the foundation for the postwar struggle against discrimination.

The northward migration of African Americans accelerated demands for equality. Drawn by the promise of wartime jobs, nearly 750,000 African Americans relocated to northern cities, where many sensed the possibility of political power for the first time in their lives. They found an outspoken advocate of civil rights within the White House itself. First Lady Eleanor Roosevelt repeatedly antagonized southern Democrats and members of her husband's administration by her advocacy of civil rights and her participation in integrated social functions.

African Americans understood the irony of fighting for a country that denied them equality and challenged the government to live up to its own rhetoric about freedom and democracy. The *Amsterdam News,* a Harlem newspaper, called for a "Double V" campaign—victory at home as well as abroad. In January 1941 labor leader A. Philip Randolph threatened to lead tens of thousands of frustrated black workers in a march on Washington to demand more defense jobs and integration of the military forces. President Roosevelt viewed the march as potentially embarrassing to his administration and urged that it be canceled. Randolph's persistence, however, forced Roosevelt to make concessions. In return for Randolph's canceling the march, the president created the FEPC in June of that year. The FEPC initially seemed a victory for equal rights, but Roosevelt gave the agency little power over discriminatory employers.

Roosevelt also let stand the policy of segregation in the armed forces. "A jim crow army cannot fight for a free world," proclaimed the NAACP newspaper *The Crisis*. Yet General George C. Marshall, Secretary of War Stimson, and others remained opposed to change. African Americans were relegated to inferior jobs in the military and excluded from combat status. Toward the end of the war, when manpower shortages forced the administration to put African American troops into combat, they performed with distinction.

RACIAL TENSIONS

In industrial cities, the wartime boom threw already overcrowded, working-class neighborhoods into turmoil. Many of the residents of these neighborhoods came from European immigrant backgrounds or had migrated from rural areas. Wartime work provided their first real opportunity to escape from poverty, and they viewed the minority newcomers as unwelcome rivals for jobs and housing. In 1943, for example, it was estimated that between 6,000 and 10,000 African Americans arrived in Los Angeles every month. Once there, their living options were effectively limited to a few overcrowded neighborhoods segregated by landlords' practices and by California's restrictive housing covenants—legal agreements prohibiting the sale of homes to certain religious or racial groups.

Around the country, public housing projects presented a particularly explosive dilemma to federal officials charged with administering the supply of desperately needed housing. Whites resisted the forced integration of public housing; nonwhites denounced the government for vacillating. In Buffalo, New York, threats of violence caused the cancellation of one housing project. In Detroit in June 1943, when police escorted African American tenants into a new complex, a full-scale race riot erupted.

Racial disturbances were not restricted to confrontations between whites and blacks. In Los Angeles, the so-called "zoot suit" incidents of 1943 pitted whites against Mexican Americans. Minor incidents between young Mexican American men wearing "zoot suits"—flamboyant outfits that featured oversized coats and trousers—and soldiers and sailors from nearby military bases escalated into virtual warfare between the zoot-suiters and local police. The Roosevelt administration feared that the zoot suit violence might have a negative effect on the Good Neighbor Policy in Latin America. The president's Coordinator of Inter-American Affairs, therefore, allocated federal money to train Spanish-speaking Americans for wartime jobs, to improve education in barrios, and to open up more opportunities in colleges throughout the American Southwest.

American Indians comprised a significant group of new migrants to urban areas during the war. The war introduced powerful pressures for migration and assimilation. By the end of the war, approximately 25,000 Indian men and several hundred Indian women had served in the armed forces, where Indians were fully integrated with whites. Some 40,000 other Indians found war work in nearby cities, many leaving their reservation for the first time. For Indians, the white-dominated towns and cities tended to be strange and hostile places. Many Indians moved back and forth between city and reservation, holding their urban jobs for only a few months at a time while seeking to live between two quite different worlds.

For African Americans, Latinos, and Indians, fighting for the "American way of life" represented a commitment not to the past but to the future. Increasingly, Americans of all backgrounds were realizing that racial grievances had to be addressed. In Detroit, for example, the local NAACP chapter emerged from the wartime years with a strong base from which to fight for jobs and political power. The Committee (later, Congress) on Racial Equality (CORE), an organization founded in 1942 and composed of whites and blacks who advocated nonviolent resistance to segregation, devised new strategies during the war. CORE activists staged sit-ins to integrate restaurants, theaters, and even prison dining halls in Washington, D.C.

However, of all the minority groups in the United States, Japanese Americans suffered most grievously during the war. In the two months following the attack on Pearl Harbor, West Coast communities became engulfed in hysteria against people of Japanese descent. One military report concluded that a "large, unassimilated, tightly knit racial group, bound to an enemy nation by strong ties of race, culture, custom, and religion . . . constituted a menace" that justified extraordinary action.

Despite lack of evidence of disloyalty, government officials in February 1942 issued Executive Order 9066, directing the relocation and internment of first- and second-generation Japanese Americans (called Issei and Nisei, respectively) at inland camps. Forced to abandon their possessions or sell them for a pittance, nearly 130,000 Japanese Americans were confined in flimsy barracks, enclosed by barbed wire and under armed guard. Two-thirds of the detainees were native-born U.S. citizens. Many had been substantial landowners in California's agricultural industries. In December 1944 a divided Supreme Court upheld the constitutionality of Japanese relocation in *Korematsu* v. *U.S.* (In 1988, however, Congress officially apologized for the injustice and authorized the payment of a cash indemnity to any affected person who was still living.)

Despite the internment, the suffering and sacrifice of Japanese American soldiers became legendary: The 100th Battalion, comprised of Nisei from Hawaii, was nearly wiped out; 57 percent of the famed 442nd Regimental Combat Team were killed or wounded in the mountains of Italy; and 6,000 members of the Military Intelligence Service provided invaluable service in the Pacific theater.

Racial hostilities reflected the underlying strains in America's social fabric, but there were other tensions pulling at Americans as well. Rifts developed between city dwellers and migrants from rural areas. Californians derided the "Okies," people who had fled the Dust Bowl of Oklahoma, as ignorant and dirty. In Chicago, migrants from Appalachia were met with a similar reception. Many ethnic communities, by preserving the language and culture of their homelands, also reflected social rivalries and divisions.

Despite the underlying fragmentation of American society, the symbol of the "melting pot," together with appeals to nationalism, remained powerful. Wartime propaganda stressed the theme of national unity. The Second World War was called a "people's war," and America's "melting pot" was purposefully contrasted with the German and Japanese obsessions with racial purity. Wartime movies, plays, and music reinforced a sense of national community by building on cultural nationalism and expressing pride in American historical themes.

The great movements of population during the war eroded geographical distinctions, and wartime demands for additional labor weakened the barriers to many occupations. As each of America's racial and ethnic minorities established records of distinguished military service, the claim of equality—"Americans All," in the words of a wartime slogan—took on greater moral force. The possibility for more equitable participation in the mainstream of American life, together with rhetoric extolling social solidarity and freedom, provided a foundation for the civil rights movements of the decades ahead.

SHAPING THE PEACE

On April 13, 1945, newspaper headlines across the country mourned, "President Roosevelt Dead." Sorrow and shock were widespread and profound—in the armed forces, in diplomatic conference halls, and among factory workers, farmers, and bureaucrats. Roosevelt had accumulated a host of critics and enemies, yet he had been the most popular president in modern history, and he left an enduring imprint on American life.

Compared with the legacy of Roosevelt, Vice President Harry Truman's stature seemed impossibly small. Born on a farm near Independence, Missouri, Harry Truman had served in France during the First World War. After the war, he went into politics in Kansas City. He was elected to the Senate in 1934 and was chosen as Roosevelt's running mate in 1944. Truman was poorly prepared for the job of president. He knew little about international affairs or about any informal understandings that Roosevelt may have made with foreign leaders.

Despite his inexperience, Truman built on Roosevelt's many wartime conferences and agreements to shape the framework of international relations for the next half-century.

THE UNITED NATIONS AND INTERNATIONAL ECONOMIC ORGANIZATIONS

In the Atlantic Charter of 1941 and at a conference in Moscow in October 1943, the Allies had already pledged to create an international organization to replace the defunct League of Nations. The new United Nations (UN) fulfilled Woodrow Wilson's vision of an international body to deter aggressor nations. At the Dumbarton Oaks Conference in Washington in August 1944 and a subsequent meeting in San Francisco in April 1945, the Allies worked out the organizational structure of the UN. It would have a General Assembly, in which each member nation would be represented and have one vote. And it would have a Security Council, whose makeup would include five permanent members—the United States, Great Britain, the Soviet Union, France, and China—and six rotating members. The Security Council would have primary responsibility for maintaining peace, but any individual member of the council could exercise an absolute veto over any council decision. Finally, a UN Secretariat would handle day-to-day business, and an Economic and Social Council would promote social and economic advancement throughout the world.

The U.S. Senate accepted the UN charter in July 1945 with only two dissenting votes. This resounding victory for internationalism contrasted sharply with the Senate's rejection of membership in the League of Nations after the First World War. Americans of an earlier generation had worried that internationalist policies might impinge on their country's ability to follow its own national interests. But following the Second World War, because U.S. power clearly dominated emerging organizations such as the UN, Americans thought it less likely that decisions of international bodies would clash with their nation's own foreign policies. In addition, Americans recognized that the war had partly resulted from the lack of a coordinated, international response to aggression during the 1930s.

Postwar economic settlements also illustrated a growing acceptance of new international organizations. In dealing with the world economy, U.S. policymakers endeavored to establish stable exchange rates for currency, create an international lending authority, and eliminate discriminatory trade practices.

At the Bretton Woods (New Hampshire) Conference of 1944, Americans had worked toward these objectives. The agreements reached at Bretton Woods created the International Monetary Fund (IMF), designed to maintain a stable system of international exchange by ensuring that each national currency could be converted into any other currency at a fixed rate. Exchange rates could be altered only with the agreement of the fund. The International Bank for Reconstruction and Development, later renamed the World Bank, was also created to provide loans to war-battered countries and to promote the resumption of world trade. In 1947 a General Agreement on Tariffs and Trade (GATT) created the institutional structure for implementing free and fair trade agreements.

Spheres of Interest and Postwar Political Settlements

In wartime conversations, Stalin, Churchill, and Roosevelt all had assumed that powerful nations would have special "spheres of influence" in the postwar world. As early as January 1942 the Soviet ambassador to the United States reported to Stalin that Roosevelt had tacitly assented to Soviet postwar control over the Baltic states of Lithuania, Latvia, and Estonia. In 1944 Stalin and Churchill agreed informally and secretly that Britain would continue its dominance in Greece and that the Soviets could dominate Romania and Bulgaria. Roosevelt understood why the Soviets wanted friendly states on their vulnerable western border, but, at the Teheran Conference of November 1943, he told Stalin that American voters of Polish, Latvian, Lithuanian, and Estonian descent expected their homelands to be independent after the war.

Precisely how Roosevelt intended to handle the issue of Soviet influence in the postwar world will never be known. As long as Soviet armies were essential to Germany's defeat, Roosevelt cooperated with Stalin whenever possible. After Roosevelt's death, however, the military results of the war, particularly the USSR's powerful position in eastern Europe, strongly influenced postwar settlements regarding territory. On issues of governance—particularly in Germany, Poland, and Korea—splits between U.S. and Soviet interests widened. Germany, especially, became a focus and a symbol of bipolar tensions.

Early in the war, both the United States and the Soviet Union had urged the dismemberment and deindustrialization of Nazi Germany after its defeat. At a conference held at Yalta, in Ukraine, in early February 1945, the three Allied powers agreed to divide Germany into four zones of occupation (with France as the fourth occupation force). Later, as relations among the victors cooled, this temporary division of Germany permanently solidified into a Soviet-dominated zone in the East and the three Allied zones in the West. Berlin, the German capital, also was divided, even though it lay totally within the Soviet zone.

Postwar rivalries also centered on Poland. At Yalta, the Soviets agreed to permit free elections in Poland after the war and to create a government "responsible to the will of the people," but Stalin also believed that the other Allied leaders had tacitly accepted the idea that Poland would fall within the Soviet's postwar sphere of influence. The agreement at Yalta was ambiguous at best. The war was still at a critical stage, and the western Allies chose to sacrifice clarity over the Polish issue in order to encourage cooperation with the Soviets. After Yalta, the Soviets assumed that Poland would be in their sphere of influence, but many Americans charged the Soviets with bad faith for failing to hold free elections and for not relinquishing control.

In Asia, military realities also influenced postwar settlements. At Teheran in November 1943 and again at Yalta, Stalin pledged to send troops to Asia as soon as Germany had been defeated. But when U.S. policymakers learned that the atomic bomb was ready for use against Japan, they became eager to limit Soviet involvement in the Pacific theater. The first atomic bomb fell on Hiroshima just one day before the Soviets were to enter the war against Japan, and the United States took sole charge of the occupation and postwar reorganization of Japan. The Soviet Union and the United States split Korea, which had been occupied by Japan, into separate zones of occupation. Here, as in Germany, the zones later emerged as two antagonistic states (see Chapter 27).

The fate of the European colonies that had been seized by Japan in Southeast Asia was another issue that remained unresolved in the planning for peace. The United States would have preferred to see the former British and French colonies become independent nations, but U.S. policymakers also worried about the left-leaning politics of many anticolonial nationalist movements. As the United States developed an anticommunist foreign policy, it moved to support Britain and France in their efforts to reassemble their colonial empires.

In the Philippines, the United States honored its long-standing pledge to grant independence. A friendly government that agreed to respect U.S. economic interests and military bases took power in 1946 and enlisted American advisers to help deal with leftist rebels. The Mariana, the Caroline, and the Marshall Islands, all of which had been captured by Japan during the war, were designated Trust Territories of the Pacific by the United Nations and placed under U.S. administration in 1947.

Although the countries of Latin America had not been very directly involved in the war or the peace settlements, U.S. relations with them were also profoundly affected by the war. During the 1930s Roosevelt's Good Neighbor Policy had helped to improve U.S.–Latin American relations. The Office of Inter-American Affairs (OIAA), created in 1937, began an aggressive and successful policy of expanding cultural and economic ties. Just weeks after the German invasion of Poland in 1939, at the Pan American Conference in Panama City, Latin American leaders showed that the hemisphere was nearly united on the side of the Allies. The conferees declared a 300-mile-wide band of neutrality in waters around the hemisphere (excepting Canada). After U.S. entry into the war, at a January 1942 conference in Rio de Janeiro, all the Latin American countries except Chile and Argentina broke off diplomatic ties with the Axis governments. When naval warfare in the Atlantic severed commercial connections between Latin America and Europe, Latin American countries became critical suppliers of raw materials to the United States, to the benefit of both.

Wartime conferences and settlements avoided clear decisions about creating a Jewish homeland in the Middle East. The Second World War prompted survivors of the Holocaust and Jews from around the world to take direct action. Zionism, the movement to found a Jewish state in their ancient homeland, drew thousands of Jews to Palestine, where they began to carve out the new state of Israel. Middle Eastern affairs, which had been of small concern to U.S. policymakers before 1941, would take on greater urgency after 1948, when the Truman administration recognized the new state of Israel.

CHRONOLOGY

1931	Japanese forces seize Manchuria
1933	Hitler takes power in Germany
1936	Spanish Civil War begins • Germany and Italy agree to cooperate as the Axis Powers
1937	Neutrality Act broadens provisions of Neutrality Acts of 1935 and 1936 • Roosevelt makes "Quarantine" speech • Japan invades China
1938	France and Britain appease Hitler at Munich
1939	Hitler and Stalin sign Soviet-German nonaggression pact • Hitler invades Poland; war breaks out in Europe • Congress amends Neutrality Act to assist Allies
1940	Paris falls after German *blitzkrieg* (June) • Battle of Britain carried to U.S. by radio broadcasts • Roosevelt makes "destroyers-for-bases" deal with Britain • Selective Service Act passed • Roosevelt wins third term
1941	Lend-Lease established • Roosevelt creates Fair Employment Practices Commission • Atlantic Charter proclaimed by Roosevelt and Churchill • U.S. engages in undeclared naval war in North Atlantic • Congress narrowly repeals Neutrality Act • Japanese forces attack Pearl Harbor (December 7)
1942	Rio de Janeiro Conference (January) • President signs Executive Order 9066 for internment of Japanese Americans (February) • General MacArthur driven from Philippines (May) • U.S. victorious in Battle of Midway (June) • German army defeated at Battle of Stalingrad (August) • Operation TORCH begins (November)
1943	Axis armies in North Africa surrender (May) • Allies invade Sicily (July) and Italy (September) • "Zoot suit" incidents in Los Angeles; racial violence in Detroit • Allies begin drive toward Japan through South Pacific islands
1944	Allies land at Normandy (D-Day, June 6) • Allied armies reach Paris (August) • Allies turn back Germans at Battle of the Bulge (September) • Roosevelt reelected to fourth term • Bretton Woods Conference creates IMF and World Bank • Dumbarton Oaks Conference establishes plan for UN
1945	U.S. firebombs Japan • Yalta Conference (February) • Roosevelt dies; Truman becomes president (April) • Germany surrenders (May) • Potsdam Conference (July) • Hiroshima and Nagasaki hit with atomic bombs (August) • Japan signs terms of surrender (September) • United Nations established (December)

CONCLUSION

The world changed dramatically during the Second World War. Wartime mobilization ended the Great Depression and shifted the New Deal's focus away from domestic social reform and toward international concerns. It brought a historic victory over dictatorial, brutal regimes, and the United States emerged as the world's preeminent power.

At home, the war brought significant change. A more powerful national government, concerned with preserving national security, assumed nearly complete power over the nation's economy. New, cooperative ties were forged among government, business, labor, and scientific researchers. All sectors worked together to provide the seemingly miraculous growth in productivity that ultimately won the war.

The early 1940s sharpened debates over the nature of liberty and equality. Many Americans saw the Second World War as a struggle to protect and preserve the power and liberties they already enjoyed. Others, inspired by a struggle against racism and injustice abroad, insisted that a war for freedom should help expand equal rights at home.

News of Japan's surrender prompted the largest celebration in the nation's history. International conferences established a structure for the United Nations and for new, global economic institutions. Still, Americans remained uncertain about post-war reconstruction of former enemies and about future relations with wartime allies, particularly the Soviet Union. Domestically, the wrenching dislocations of war took their toll. And, of course, the nation now faced the future without the charismatic leadership of Franklin D. Roosevelt.

THE AGE OF CONTAINMENT, 1946–1954

The Second World War, heralded as an effort to preserve and protect the fabric of American life, had ended up transforming it. The struggle against fascism had brought foreign policy issues to the center of political debate, and the international struggles of the postwar period kept them there. As the Second World War gave way to a "Cold War" between the United States and the Soviet Union, Washington adopted global policies to "contain" the Soviet Union and to enhance America's economic and military security. Preoccupation with national security abroad, however, raised calls for limiting dissent at home.

The Cold War years from 1946 to 1954 also produced questions about government power. What role should Washington play in planning the postwar economy? What should be its relationship to social policymaking, especially efforts to achieve equality? These broad questions first emerged during the presidency of Democrat Harry Truman, from 1945 to 1953. They would remain central concerns during the administration of his Republican successor, Dwight David Eisenhower.

CREATING A NATIONAL SECURITY STATE, 1945–1949

The wartime alliance between the United States and the Soviet Union had never been anything but a marriage of convenience. Defeat of the Axis Powers had demanded that the two governments cooperate, but collaboration scarcely lasted beyond VE Day. Relations between the United States and the Soviet Union steadily degenerated into a Cold War of suspicion and growing tension.

ONSET OF THE COLD WAR

Historians have discussed the origins of the Cold War from many different perspectives. The traditional interpretation focuses on Soviet expansionism, stressing a traditional Russian appetite for new territory, or an ideological zeal to spread international communism, or some interplay between the two. According to this view, the United States needed to take as hard a line as possible. Other historians—generally called revisionists—argue that the Soviet Union's obsession with securing its borders was an understandable response to the invasion of its territory during both world wars. The United States, in this view, should have tried to reassure the Soviets by seeking accommodation, instead of pursuing policies that intensified Stalin's fears. Still other scholars maintain that assigning blame obscures the clash of deep-seated rival interests that made postwar tensions between the two superpowers inevitable.

In any view, the role of Harry Truman proved important. Truman initially hoped that he could somehow cut a deal with Soviet Premier Joseph Stalin. However, as disagreements between the two former allies mounted, Truman came to rely on advisers hostile to Stalin's Soviet Union.

The atomic bomb provided an immediate source of friction. At the Potsdam Conference of July 1945, Truman had casually remarked to Stalin, "We have a new weapon of unusual destructive force." Stalin immediately ordered a crash program to develop atomic weapons of his own. Truman hoped that the bomb would scare the Soviets, and it did. Historians still debate whether it frightened the Soviets into more cautious behavior or made them more fearful and aggressive.

In 1946 Truman authorized Bernard Baruch, a presidential adviser and special representative to the United Nations, to offer a plan for the international control of atomic power. The Baruch plan called for full disclosure by all UN member nations of nuclear research and materials, creation of an international authority to ensure compliance, and destruction of all U.S. atomic weapons once these first steps were completed. Andrei A. Gromyko, the Soviet ambassador to the UN, countered by proposing that the United States unilaterally destroy its atomic weapons first, with international disclosure and control to follow. The United States refused. Both sides used this deadlock to justify a stepped-up arms race.

Other sources of Soviet-American friction involved U.S. loan policies and the Soviet sphere of influence in Eastern Europe. Truman abruptly suspended lend-lease assistance to the Soviet Union in early September 1945. Subsequently, Truman's administration linked extension of U.S. reconstruction loans to its goal of rolling back Soviet power in Eastern Europe. However, lack of capital and signs of Western hostility provided the Soviets with excuses for tightening their grip. A Soviet sphere of influence, which Stalin called defensive and Truman labeled proof of communist expansionism, emerged in Eastern Europe. Suspicion steadily widened into mutual distrust.

From 1947 on, Harry Truman placed his personal stamp on the presidency by focusing on the fight against the Soviet Union. The menace of an "international communist conspiracy" was said to justify extraordinary measures to ensure U.S. national security. The claim of protecting "national security" allowed Truman to justify policy initiatives, in both foreign and domestic affairs, that extended the reach and power of the executive branch of government.

CONTAINMENT ABROAD: THE TRUMAN DOCTRINE

In March 1947, the president announced what became known as the Truman Doctrine when he addressed Congress on the civil war in Greece, a conflict in which communist-led insurgents were trying to topple a corrupt but pro-Western government. Historically, Greece had fallen within Great Britain's sphere of influence. But Britain could no longer maintain its formerly strong presence there or in the Middle East. A leftist victory in Greece, Truman's advisers claimed, would open neighboring Turkey to Soviet subversion. Seeking to justify U.S. aid to Greece and Turkey, Truman addressed Congress on March 12, 1947, in dramatic terms.

U.S. security interests, according to this Truman Doctrine, were now worldwide. Truman declared that the fate of "free peoples" everywhere hung in the balance. Unless the United

States unilaterally aided countries "who are resisting attempted subversion by armed minorities or by outside pressures," totalitarian communism would spread around the world and threaten the security of the United States itself.

Initially, the Truman Doctrine's global vision of national security encountered skepticism. Henry Wallace, the president's most visible Democratic critic, chided Truman for exaggerating the expansive nature of Soviet foreign policy and its threat to the United States. Conservative Republicans looked suspiciously at the increase of executive power and the vast expenditures that the Truman Doctrine seemed to imply. If Truman wanted to win support for his position, Republican Senator Arthur Vandenberg had already advised, he would need to "scare hell" out of people, something that Truman proved quite willing to do.

The rhetorical strategy worked. With backing from both Republicans and Democrats, Truman's request for $400 million in assistance to Greece and Turkey, most of it in military aid, was passed by Congress in the spring of 1947. This vote signaled broad, bipartisan support for a national security policy that came to be called "containment."

The term "containment" was first used in a 1947 article in the influential journal *Foreign Affairs,* written under the pseudonym "X" by George Kennan, the State Department's leading expert on Soviet affairs. Kennan argued that the "main element" in any U.S. policy "must be that of a long-term, patient but firm and vigilant containment of Russian expansive tendencies." The article quickly became associated with the alarmist tone of the Truman Doctrine.

Containment thus became the catchphrase for a global, anticommunist, national security policy. In the popular view, containment linked all leftist insurgencies, wherever they occurred, to a totalitarian movement controlled from Moscow that directly threatened the United States. Although foreign policy debates regularly included sharp disagreements over precisely *how* to pursue the goal of containment, few Americans dared to question *why* the country needed a far-flung, activist foreign policy.

TRUMAN'S LOYALTY PROGRAM

Nine days after proclaiming the Truman Doctrine, the president issued Executive Order 9835, which called for a system of loyalty boards empowered to determine whether there were "reasonable grounds" for believing that any government employee belonged to an organization or held political ideas that might pose a "security risk" to the United States. People judged to be security risks would lose their government jobs. The Truman loyalty program also authorized the attorney general's office to identify organizations it considered subversive, and in December 1947 the first Attorney General's List was released.

In developing the loyalty program, the Truman administration needed to gauge the extent of Soviet espionage activities in the United States. Although few historians ever doubted that the Soviets carried on spy operations, scholars have disagreed about their scope and success. Were Soviet agents operating only at the fringes or had they penetrated the top levels of the U.S. government? Were they supplying information that might have been obtained almost anywhere or were they stealing vital national secrets? As early as 1943, an Army counterintelligence unit had begun secretly intercepting transmissions between Moscow and the United States. Collected (and finally released to the public in 1995) as the "Venona files," these intercepted messages suggested that the USSR had several agents in wartime government agencies, including the Office of War Information and the top-secret OSS. Moscow began obtaining secret information about U.S. atomic work in 1944. The issue of Soviet spies, in short, was a legitimate cause of concern.

Curiously, the national security bureaucrats who intercepted the Soviet messages seem to have told neither the president nor his attorney general anything about their own super-secret operation or the intelligence being gathered. Truman's apparent lack of clear information may help to explain his inconsistent justification for the loyalty program. On the one hand, the president claimed that there were only a few security risks in the government but that their potential to do harm demanded a response that was unprecedented in peacetime. On the other hand, the president's program also clashed with the argument that a limited internal security threat logically demanded a limited, carefully crafted governmental response. Truman's approach angered both civil libertarians, who charged the president with going too far, and staunch anticommunists, who accused him of doing too little to fight the Red Menace at home.

THE NATIONAL SECURITY ACT, THE MARSHALL PLAN, AND THE BERLIN CRISIS

The National Security Act of 1947 created several new bureaucracies. It began the process that transformed the old Navy and War departments into a new Department of Defense, finally established in 1949. It instituted another new arm of the executive branch, the National Security Council (NSC), with broad authority over the planning of foreign policy. It established the Air Force as a separate service equal to the Army and Navy. And it created the Central Intelligence Agency (CIA) to gather information and to undertake covert activities in support of the nation's newly defined security interests.

The CIA proved the most flexible arm of the national security bureaucracy. Shrouded from public scrutiny, it used its secret funds to finance and encourage anticommunist activities around the globe. The CIA cultivated ties with anti-Soviet groups in Eastern Europe and even within the Soviet Union itself. It helped finance pro-U.S. labor unions in Western Europe to curtail the influence of leftist organizations. It orchestrated covert campaigns to prevent the Italian Communist Party from winning an electoral victory in 1948 and to bolster anticommunist parties in France, Japan, and elsewhere.

Truman's administration also linked economic policies in Western Europe to the doctrine of containment. Concerned that the region's severe economic problems might embolden leftist, pro-Soviet political movements, Secretary of State George Marshall sought to strengthen the economies of Western Europe. Shortly after Congress approved funding for the Truman Doctrine, the secretary proposed the Marshall Plan, under which governments in Western Europe would coordinate their plans for postwar economic reconstruction with the help of funds provided by the United States. Between 1946 and 1951, nearly $13 billion in U.S. assistance was distributed to 17 Western European nations.

The Marshall Plan proved a stunning success. In response to charges that it was a "giveaway" program, the administration pointed out that it opened up both markets and investment opportunities in Western Europe to American businesses. Moreover, it helped stabilize the European economy by quadrupling industrial production within its first few years. Improved standards of living enhanced political stability and helped undermine left-wing political parties in Europe.

American policymakers believed that to revitalize Europe under the Marshall Plan they would first have to restore the economy of Germany, which was still divided into zones of occupation. In June 1948 the United States, Great Britain, and France announced a plan for currency reform that would be the first step in merging their sectors of occupation into a federal German republic. Soviet leaders were alarmed. Having twice been invaded by Germany during the preceding 35 years, they wanted a reunited but weak Germany. Hoping to sidetrack Western plans for Germany, in June 1948 the Soviets cut off all highways, railroads, and water routes linking West Berlin to West Germany.

This Soviet blockade of Berlin failed. Air routes to the city remained open, and American and British pilots, in what became known as the Berlin Airlift, delivered tons of supplies to the city's beleaguered residents. Truman reinstated the draft and sent two squadrons of B-29 bombers to Britain. Recognizing his defeat, Stalin abandoned the blockade in May 1949. The Soviets then created the German Democratic Republic out of their East German sector, and West Berlin survived as an enclave tied to the West.

THE ELECTION OF 1948

National security issues helped Harry Truman win the 1948 election, a victory that capped a remarkable political comeback. Truman had been losing the support of some Democrats, led by Henry A. Wallace, who thought his containment policies too militant. In the off-year national election of 1946, voters had given the Republicans control of Congress for the first time since 1928. Although his standing in public opinion polls had risen slowly in 1947 and 1948, most political pundits thought Truman had little chance to win the presidency in his own right in 1948. Challenged from the left by a new Progressive Party, which nominated Wallace, and from the right by both the Republican nominee, Thomas E. Dewey, and Strom Thurmond, the candidate of the States' Rights Party, or "Dixiecrats," Truman waged a vigorous campaign. He called Congress into special session, presented it with domestic policy proposals that were

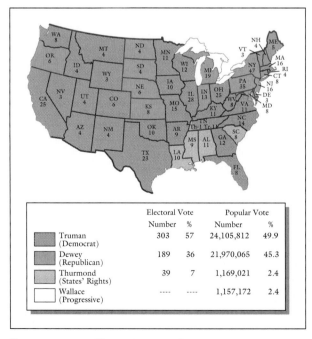

		Electoral Vote		Popular Vote	
		Number	%	Number	%
	Truman (Democrat)	303	57	24,105,812	49.9
	Dewey (Republican)	189	36	21,970,065	45.3
	Thurmond (States' Rights)	39	7	1,169,021	2.4
	Wallace (Progressive)	----	----	1,157,172	2.4

PRESIDENTIAL ELECTION, 1948

DEWEY DEFEATS TRUMAN?   Contrary to the predictions that had led to this newspaper headline, Harry Truman defeated Thomas Dewey in the close election of 1948. The "little man from Missouri" would continue to pursue containment abroad.

anathema to the GOP, and then denounced the "Republican Eightieth Congress, that do-nothing, good-for-nothing, worst Congress."

Thomas Dewey proved a cautious, lackluster campaigner. A pro-Democratic newspaper caricatured Dewey's standard speech as four "historic sentences: Agriculture is important. Our rivers are full of fish. You cannot have freedom without liberty. The future lies ahead." Truman, for his part, conducted an old-style campaign. He moved from town to town, stopping to denounce Dewey and Henry Wallace from the back of a railroad car. Dewey was plotting "a real hatchet job on the New Deal," and the Republican Party was controlled by a cabal of "cunning men" who were planning "a return of the Wall Street economic dictatorship," Truman charged. "Give 'em hell, Harry!" shouted enthusiastic crowds. In November, Truman won only 49.9 percent of the popular vote but gained a solid majority in the electoral college.

Truman's victory now seems less surprising to historians than it did to political analysts in 1948. Despite Republican electoral gains in the congressional elections of 1946, the Democratic Party was far from enfeebled. Indeed, the Democrats running for Congress in 1948, who identified themselves with Roosevelt rather than with Truman, generally polled a higher percentage of the popular vote in their districts than did Truman himself. Still, the loyalty of voters to the memory of Franklin Roosevelt and to his New Deal coalition helped Truman.

Meanwhile, Truman commanded a constituency of his own by virtue of his anticommunist policies. In this sense, Truman's presidency established a pattern that would persist for several decades: If Democratic candidates could avoid appearing "soft" or "weak" on national security issues, they stood a good chance of being elected president. Truman's hard-line national security credentials proved especially effective against Henry Wallace. Hampered by his refusal to reject the support of Communist Party members, Wallace failed to win a single electoral vote and received less than 3 percent of the popular tally.

The Era of the Korean War, 1949–1952

To carry out the containment policy, the Truman administration marshaled the nation's economic and military resources. A series of Cold War crises in 1949 heightened its anti-communist fervor and deepened its focus on national security issues.

NATO, China, and the Bomb

In April 1949 the United States, Canada, and 10 European nations formed the North Atlantic Treaty Organization (NATO). Members of NATO pledged that an attack against one would

The Cold War split Europe into two opposing alliances. Germany was divided into two countries: The Federal Republic of Germany (West Germany) and the German Democratic Republic (East Germany). Berlin, the former capital of Germany, was also divided. In 1949 NATO was formed, and in 1955 the Warsaw Pact came into existence.

THE DIVISION OF BERLIN

American Zone
British Zone
French Zone
Soviet Zone

(The American, British, and French zones were consolidated as West Berlin)

NATO Countries
Warsaw Pact Countries
Nonaligned Countries

Divided Germany and the NATO Alliance

automatically be considered an attack against all. Some U.S. leaders worried about the implications of NATO. Republican Senator Robert Taft of Ohio declared that it was a provocation to the Soviet Union and an "entangling alliance" that defied common sense, violated the traditional U.S. foreign policy of nonentanglement, and threatened constitutional government by eclipsing Congress's power to declare war. But the NATO concept prevailed, and the idea of pursuing containment through such "collective security" pacts expanded during the 1950s.

Meanwhile, events in China elevated Cold War tensions. Between 1945 and 1948 the United States extended to Jiang Jieshi's government a billion dollars in military aid and another billion in economic assistance. But Jiang steadily lost ground to the communist forces of Mao Zedong. Experienced U.S. diplomats privately predicted that Jiang's downfall was inevitable, but the Truman administration continued publicly to portray Jiang as a respected leader of "free China" and to prop up his regime.

In 1949, when Mao's armies forced Jiang off the mainland to the offshore island of Formosa (Taiwan), many Americans wondered how communist forces could have triumphed. Financed by conservative business leaders, a powerful "China lobby" excoriated Truman and his new secretary of state, Dean Acheson, for being "soft" on communism and spoke of a global communist conspiracy directed from Moscow. Responding to the criticism, Acheson and Truman escalated their anticommunist rhetoric. For more than 20 years, even after friction between China and the Soviet Union became evident, the United States refused to recognize or deal with Mao's "Red China."

Late in 1949 the threat became even more alarming. Word reached Washington in September that the Soviets had exploded a crude atomic device, marking the end of the U.S. nuclear monopoly. Already besieged by critics who saw a world filled with Soviet gains and American defeats, Truman authorized the development of a new bomb based upon the still unproven concept of nuclear fusion. The decision to build this "hydrogen bomb" wedded the doctrine of containment to the creation of ever more deadly nuclear technology.

NSC-68

Prompted by events of 1949, the Truman administration reviewed its foreign policy assumptions. The task of conducting this review fell to Paul Nitze, a hard-liner who produced a top-secret policy paper officially identified as National Security Council document number 68 (NSC-68). It opened with an emotional account of a global ideological clash between "freedom," spread by U.S. power, and "slavery," promoted by the Soviet Union as the center of "international communism." Warning against any negotiations with the Soviets, the report urged a full-scale offensive to enlarge U.S. power. It endorsed covert action, economic pressure, more vigorous propaganda efforts, and a massive military buildup. Because Americans might oppose larger military spending and budget deficits, the report warned, U.S. actions should be labeled as "defensive" and be presented as a stimulus to the economy rather than as a drain on national resources.

THE KOREAN WAR

The dire warnings of NSC-68 seemed confirmed in June 1950 when communist North Korea attacked South Korea. The Truman administration portrayed the move as a simple case of Soviet-inspired aggression against a "free" state. Truman invoked once again the policy of containment: "If aggression is successful in Korea, we can expect it to spread through Asia and Europe to this hemisphere." The Korean situation, however, defied such simplistic analysis. Korea had been occupied by Japan between 1905 and 1945, and after Japan's defeat in the Second World War, Koreans had expected to establish their own independent state. Instead, the Soviet and U.S. zones of occupation resulting from the war were transformed into political entities. Korea became two states, split at the 38th parallel. The Soviet Union supported a communist government in the North under the dictatorial Kim Il-sung; the United States backed Syngman Rhee to head the unsteady yet autocratic government in the South.

But Korea could not be easily split along an arbitrary geographic line. It remained a single society, though it was riven by political factions as well as by ethnic and religious divisions. Rhee's oppressive regime generated opposition in the South. As discontent spread, Kim moved troops across the 38th parallel on June 25, 1950, to attempt unification. Earlier, he had consulted both Soviet and Chinese leaders about his plans and received their support, after assuring them that a U.S. military response was highly unlikely.

The fighting in Korea soon escalated into an international conflict. The Soviets were boycotting the United Nations on the day the invasion was launched. Consequently, they were not present to veto a U.S. proposal to send a peacekeeping force to Korea. Under UN auspices, the United States rushed assistance to the dictatorial Rhee, who moved to eliminate disloyal civilians in the South as well as to repel the invading armies of the North.

U.S. goals in Korea were unclear. Should the United States seek to "contain" communism by driving the North Koreans back over the 38th parallel? Or should it try to reunify the country under Rhee's leadership? At first, that decision could be postponed because the war was going so badly. North Korean troops pushed their Soviet-made tanks rapidly southward; within three months, they took Seoul and reached the southern tip of the Korean peninsula. American troops seemed unprepared and, unaccustomed to the unusually hot Korean weather during these first months, fell sick. But American firepower gradually took its toll on the elite troops who had spearheaded North Korea's rapid move southward. North Korea had to send fresh, untrained recruits to replace seasoned fighters.

General Douglas MacArthur then devised a plan that most other commanders considered crazy: an amphibious landing behind enemy lines at Inchon. Those stunned by the riskiness of his proposed invasion were even more astounded by its results. On September 15, 1950, the Marines successfully landed 13,000 troops at Inchon, suffered only 21 deaths, and moved back into Seoul within 11 days.

As MacArthur's troops drove northward, Truman faced a crucial decision. MacArthur, emboldened by success, urged an all-out war of "liberation" and reunification. Other advisers warned that China would retaliate if U.S. forces approached its border. Cautiously, Truman allowed MacArthur to carry the war into the North but ordered him to avoid antagonizing China.

MacArthur pushed too far, advancing toward the Yalu River on the Chinese-Korean border. China responded by sending troops into North Korea and driving MacArthur back across the 38th parallel. With China now in the war, Truman again faced the question of military goals. When MacArthur's troops regained the initiative, Truman ordered his general to negotiate a truce at the 38th parallel. But MacArthur challenged the president, arguing instead for all-out victory over North Korea—and over China, too. Truman thereupon relieved him of his command in April 1951, pointing out that the Constitution specified that military commanders must obey the orders of the president, the commander in chief.

MacArthur returned home as a war hero. One poll reported that less than 30 percent of the U.S. public supported Truman's actions. The China lobby portrayed MacArthur as a martyr to Truman's "no-win," containment policy. But this outpouring of admiration reflected

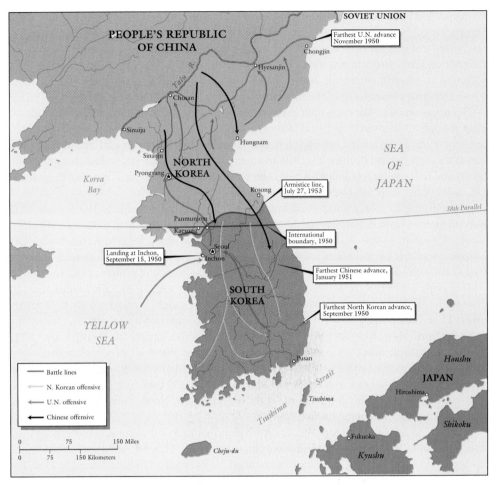

KOREAN WAR

MacArthur's personal charisma rather than any significant public support for a full-scale land war in Asia. During Senate hearings on the general's dismissal, military strategists expressed their opposition to such a war. And most Americans apparently preferred a negotiated settlement in Korea. Truman now set about convincing North Korea and South Korea to meet at the conference table. Eisenhower, the Republican candidate for president in 1952, promised to go to Korea to hasten the peace process. The negotiations that eventually reestablished the borderline at the 38th parallel emerged as a major foreign policy task for the new Eisenhower administration in 1953.

KOREA AND CONTAINMENT

The Korean War justified the global offensive that NSC-68 had recommended. The United States announced a plan to rearm West Germany, scarcely five years after Germany's defeat, and increased NATO's military forces. In 1951 the United States signed a formal peace treaty with Japan, and a Japanese-American security pact granted the United States a base on Okinawa and permission for U.S. troops to be stationed in Japan. The United States also acquired bases in Saudi Arabia and Morocco. In 1950 direct military aid to Latin American governments, which had been voted down in the past, slid through Congress. In French Indochina, Truman provided assistance to strengthen French efforts to put down a communist-led movement that was fighting for independence. In the Philippines, the United States stepped up military assistance for the suppression of the leftist Huk rebels. And in 1951 the ANZUS collective security pact linked the United States strategically to Australia and New Zealand. Throughout the world, economic pressure, covert activities by the CIA, and propaganda campaigns helped to forge anticommunist alliances. Truman's global "Campaign of Truth," an intensive informational and psychological offensive, used mass media and cultural exchanges to counter Soviet claims with pro-American perspectives.

While the Truman administration fortified America's strategic position throughout the world, U.S. military budgets increased. Strategic priorities linked Washington to ongoing weapons research and production. The Atomic Energy Commission had been created in 1946 to succeed the Manhattan Project in overseeing development of nuclear power; aviation had received special government funding for the first time in the 1946 budget; the Army had joined with aircraft manufacturers in an effort to develop surface-to-surface missiles. And to coordinate global strategy with the development of long-range weapons, a new "think tank"— RAND, an acronym for Research and Development—was created. Expensive contracts for the manufacture of military materials worried cost-conscious members of Congress, but the prospect that the contracts would create new jobs in their home districts muted their opposition. The Cold War thus brought what the historian Michael Sherry has called "the militarization of American life": a steady military buildup and an intermingling of military and economic policies.

As the emphasis on anticommunism intensified, U.S. policymakers became more suspicious of any movement that was left-leaning in its political orientation. The U.S. occupation government in Japan, for example, increasingly restricted the activities of labor unions and barred communists from government offices and universities. As in Germany, the United States tried to contain communism by strengthening industrial elites and promoting economic growth.

In Africa, as well, anticommunism shaped U.S. policies, bringing the United States into an alliance with South Africa. In 1948 the all-white (and militantly anticommunist) Nationalist Party instituted a legal system based on elaborate rules of racial separation and subordination of blacks (apartheid). Some State Department officials warned that supporting apartheid in South Africa would damage U.S. prestige, but the Truman administration decided to cement an alliance with South Africa nonetheless.

Containment relied on a rhetoric of defensiveness: The term "national security" replaced "national interest"; the "War Department" became the "Department of Defense." Yet the United States extended its power into the former British sphere of influence of Iran, Greece, and Turkey; initiated the Marshall Plan and NATO; transformed its former enemies—Italy, Germany, and Japan—into anti-Soviet bulwarks; assumed control of hundreds of Pacific islands; launched research for the development of the hydrogen bomb; winked at apartheid in order to win an anticommunist ally in South Africa; solidified its sphere of influence in Latin America; acquired bases around the globe; and devised a master plan for using military, economic, and covert action to achieve its goals. Beginning with the Truman Doctrine of 1947, the United States staked out global interests.

CONTAINMENT AT HOME

Although containment abroad generally gained bipartisan support, a strident debate over how best to counter alleged communist influences in the United States raged from the late 1940s through the middle 1950s. Conservative members of Congress and private watchdog groups, taking their cue from Truman's anticommunist rhetoric, launched their own search for evidence of internal communist subversion. Civil libertarians complained that a "witch-hunt" was being conducted against people whose only sins were dissent from the Truman administration's anticommunist measures or support for a leftist political agenda at home. Indeed, witch-hunters increasingly charged Truman's own anticommunist administration with harboring people who were disloyal or "soft" on communism. In time, even devoted anticommunists began to complain that wild-goose chases after unlikely offenders were hampering the search for authentic Soviet agents. Still, the search for supposed subversives continued, affecting many areas of postwar life. A particularly vitriolic group of anticommunists emerged in Congress.

ANTICOMMUNISM AND THE LABOR MOVEMENT

The labor movement became an obvious target for anticommunist legislators. After the end of the Second World War, militant workers had struck for increased wages and for a greater voice over workplace routines and production decisions. Strikes had brought both the auto industry and the electronics industry to a standstill. In Stamford, Connecticut, and Lancaster, Pennsylvania, general strikes had led to massive work stoppages that later spread to Rochester, Pittsburgh, Oakland, and other large cities. By 1947, however, labor militancy had begun to subside as Truman took a hard line. He threatened to seize mines and railroads that had been shut down by strikes and ordered the strikers back to work.

Still, in 1947 congressional opponents of organized labor effectively tapped anticommunist sentiment to help pass the Labor-Management Relations Act, popularly known as the Taft-Hartley Act. The law negated some of the gains that unions had made during the 1930s by limiting a union's power to conduct boycotts, to compel employers to accept "closed shops" in which only union members could be hired, and to conduct any strike that the president judged against the national interest. In addition, the law required that union officials sign affidavits stating that they did not belong to the Communist Party or to any other "subversive" organization. A union that refused to comply was effectively denied protection under national labor laws. Truman vetoed Taft-Hartley, but Congress swiftly overrode him.

The place of communists in the labor movement was becoming a national security issue. Anticommunist unionists had long charged that communists were more loyal to their party than to their unions; now they charged communists with disloyalty to the nation itself. Differences over whether to support the Democratic Party or Henry Wallace's third-party effort in 1948 heightened tensions within many unions, and in the years following Truman's victory the Congress of Industrial Organizations (CIO) expelled 13 unions. Meanwhile, many workers found their jobs at risk because of their political ideas. By the end of the

Truman era, some type of loyalty-security check had been conducted on about 20 percent of the American workforce. People who were especially outspoken on behalf of labor radicalism risked being labeled as pro-Communist.

HUAC AND THE LOYALTY PROGRAM

Anticommunists carefully scrutinized the Hollywood film industry. In 1947 the House Committee on Un-American Activities (popularly known as HUAC) opened hearings in Hollywood to expose alleged communist infiltration. Basking in the glare of newsreel cameras, its members seized on the refusal of 10 screen writers, producers, and directors who had been or still were Communist Party members to testify about their own political affiliations and those of other members of the film community. Known as "the Hollywood Ten," this group claimed that the First Amendment shielded their political activities from official scrutiny. But the federal courts upheld HUAC's inquisitional powers, and the Hollywood Ten eventually went to prison for contempt of Congress because of their defiance of HUAC.

Meanwhile, studio heads secretly drew up a "blacklist" of so-called subversives who could no longer work in Hollywood. By the mid-1950s hundreds of people in Hollywood and in the fledgling television industry were unable to find jobs unless they would agree to appear before HUAC and ritualistically name people whom they had seen at some "communist meeting" some time in the past.

Ronald Reagan and Richard Nixon first attracted the political spotlight through the HUAC hearings. Reagan, who was president of the Screen Actors Guild and also a secret informant for the FBI (identified as "T-10"), decried the presence of subversives in the movie industry. Nixon, then an obscure member of Congress from California, began his climb to national prominence in 1948 when Whittaker Chambers, a journalist who had once been active in the Communist Party, came before HUAC to charge Alger Hiss, a prominent liberal Democrat who had a long career in government, with having also been a party member and with passing classified documents to Soviet agents in the late 1930s.

The Hiss-Chambers-Nixon affair set off a raging controversy. Hiss maintained that he had been framed in an elaborate FBI plot, alleging that the Bureau rigged his typewriter so it would appear to be the source of incriminating evidence. Legal technicalities prevented Hiss from being prosecuted for espionage, but he was charged with lying to Congress about his activities and went to prison. To Nixon and other leaders of the anticommunist campaign, the exposure of Hiss proved the need to search out subversion with more vigor than was being shown by the Truman administration. But to civil libertarians, the cases of the Hollywood Ten and Alger Hiss suggested the consequences of overzealous witch-hunting. Debates over whether the Hiss case was an example of high-level espionage or anticommunist hysteria would continue for decades.

Meanwhile, the Truman administration continued to pursue its own hard-line policies. Under the president's loyalty program, hundreds of government employees were dismissed. Attorney General Tom Clark authorized J. Edgar Hoover, head of the FBI, to draw up his own list of alleged subversives and to detain them, without any legal hearing, in the event of a national security emergency. Clark's successor, Howard McGrath, proclaimed that communist subversives were lurking "in factories, offices, butcher stores, on street corners, in private business."

At the same time, the FBI was also accumulating dossiers on a wide range of artists and intellectuals, particularly prominent African Americans. Richard Wright (author of the novel

Native Son), W. E. B. Du Bois (the nation's most celebrated African American intellectual), and Paul Robeson (one of America's most prominent entertainer-activists) became special targets. Robeson and Du Bois were harassed by State Department and immigration officials because of their ties to the Communist Party and their identification with anti-imperialist and anti-racist struggles throughout the world.

Concern that people with subversive political affiliations and ideas might emigrate to the United States produced a new immigration law. In 1952 Congress passed the McCarran-Walter Act, which placed restrictions on immigration from areas outside northern and western Europe and on the entry of people who immigration officials suspected might threaten national security.

TARGETING DIFFERENCE

Homosexuals became special targets. During the Second World War more visible and assertive gay and lesbian subcultures had begun to emerge. After the war, Dr. Alfred Kinsey's research on sexual behavior—the first volume, on male sexuality, was published in 1948—claimed that homosexual behavior could be found throughout American society. At about the same time, gays themselves formed the Mattachine Society (in 1950) and lesbians founded the Daughters of Bilitis (in 1955), organizations that cautiously began to push for recognition of rights for homosexuals. The *Kinsey Report*'s implicit claim that homosexuality was a normal form of sexuality that should be tolerated, together with the discreet militancy among gays and lesbians, produced a backlash that became connected to the broader antisubversion crusade. The fact that several founders of the Mattachine Society had also been members of the Communist Party, coupled with a belief that homosexuals could be blackmailed by Soviet agents more easily than heterosexuals, helped to link homosexuality with subversion.

A connection between antihomosexual and anticommunist rhetoric developed. Radical political ideas and homosexuality were both portrayed as "diseases" that could be spread throughout the body politic by people who often looked no different from "ordinary" Americans. According to this logic, homosexuality was an acceptable basis for denying people government employment.

THE ROSENBERG CASE AND "THE GREAT FEAR"

Harry Truman's last years as president were played out against a backdrop of public anxiety that the historian David Caute has called "the Great Fear." Foreign policy events of 1949 and 1950 highlighted the issue of whether subversives were at work in the most sensitive recesses of the U.S. government. Suspicions arose about the loyalty of foreign policy personnel, and stories about Soviet agents having stolen U.S. nuclear secrets spread rapidly. In early 1950, Great Britain released evidence that a spy ring had been operating in the United States since the mid-1940s. Shortly afterward, the U.S. Justice Department arrested several alleged members of this ring, including two members of the Communist Party, Julius and Ethel Rosenberg.

The Rosenberg case became a Cold War melodrama. The trial, the verdicts of guilty, the sentences of death at Sing Sing prison, the numerous legal appeals, the worldwide protests, and the executions in 1953—all provoked intense controversy. Were the Rosenbergs guilty of having been involved in the theft of important nuclear secrets? And even so, were their death sentences on the charge of espionage the constitutionally appropriate punishment? To their supporters, the Rosenbergs (who steadfastly maintained their innocence) had fallen victim to the Great Fear. Many believed that the government seemed more intent on punishing scapegoats than in conducting a fair trial. To others, the evidence showed that information had been channeled to the Soviets.

More than 45 years after the Rosenbergs' deaths, debates still rage over their case. Intelligence reports from the Cold War era not released until the 1990s strongly suggest that Julius Rosenberg had been engaged in espionage and that Ethel Rosenberg, though not directly involved, may have known of his activities. Yet, the government declined to prosecute others who almost certainly, according to a 1997 report, "were atomic spies." Only Julius and Ethel Rosenberg were charged with a crime that carried the death penalty.

The manner in which the courts responded to the anticommunist crusade sparked controversy. During the Justice Department's 1949 prosecution of Communist Party leaders for sedition, for example, the trial judge allowed the government a wide latitude to introduce evidence against the defendants. In effect, he accepted the claim that, by definition, the American Communist Party was simply the arm of an international conspiracy. Its Marxist ideology and its theoretical publications, even in the absence of any proof of subversive *acts* against national security, justified convictions against the party's leaders. In contrast, civil libertarians insisted that the government lacked any evidence that the publications and speeches of Communist Party members, by themselves, posed any "clear and present danger" to national security. In this view, the Communist Party's abstract political beliefs, which should enjoy the protection of the First Amendment, were unconstitutionally put on trial.

When the convictions of the Communist Party leaders were appealed to the Supreme Court, in the case of *Dennis* v. *U.S.* (1951), civil libertarians renewed their arguments that this prosecution violated constitutional guarantees for the protection of speech. The Supreme Court, however, modified the "clear and present danger" doctrine and upheld the lower court. The defendants, a majority of the Court declared, had been constitutionally convicted.

By 1952, the Truman administration itself became a primary target of anticommunist zealots. In Congress, Republicans and conservative Democrats condemned the administration's handling of anticommunist initiatives and introduced their own legislation, the McCarran Internal Security Act of 1950. It authorized the detention, during any national emergency, of alleged subversives in special camps, and created the Subversive Activities Control Board (SACB) to investigate organizations suspected of being affiliated with the Communist Party and to administer the registration of organizations allegedly controlled by communists.

The Truman administration responded ambiguously to the McCarran Act. Although the president vetoed the law, a futile response that Congress quickly overrode, his administration secretly allowed Hoover to plan a covert detention program. Still, Truman could never defuse the charges leveled at his own administration.

McCarthyism

Republican Senator Joseph McCarthy of Wisconsin became Truman's prime accuser. Charging in 1950 that communists were at work in Truman's State Department, McCarthy put the administration on the defensive. The nation was in a precarious position, according to McCarthy, "not because our only powerful potential enemy has sent men to invade our shores, but rather because of the traitorous actions of those who have been treated so well by this Nation." Among those people, McCarthy named Alger Hiss, Secretary of State Dean Acheson, and former Secretary of State George C. Marshall.

Truman's efforts to contain McCarthy failed. Although McCarthy never substantiated his charges, he lacked neither imagination nor targets. The main targets of McCarthy and his imitators were former members of the Communist Party of the United States and people associated with "communist front" organizations, supposedly legitimate political groups secretly manipulated by communists. In most of the cases McCarthy cited, the affiliations had been perfectly legal. He also made vague charges against the entertainment industry and academic institutions. And despite his claims that hundreds of communist subversives were working in the State Department, he produced no credible evidence to support his case.

Nevertheless, McCarthy seemed unstoppable. In the summer of 1950, a subcommittee of the Senate Foreign Relations Committee, after examining State Department files in search of the damning material, concluded that McCarthy's charges amounted to "the most nefarious campaign of half-truths and untruths in the history of this republic." McCarthy simply charged that the files had been "raped," and he broadened his mudslinging to include Millard Tydings, the Maryland senator who had chaired the subcommittee. In the November 1950 elections, Tydings was defeated, in part, because of a fabricated photo that linked him to an alleged Communist Party member.

Despite McCarthy's recklessness, influential people tolerated, even supported, his crusade. Conservative, anticommunist leaders of the Roman Catholic Church endorsed McCarthy, himself a Catholic. Leading Republicans welcomed McCarthy's attacks on their Democratic rivals. As head of a special Senate Subcommittee on Investigations, popularly known as the "McCarthy committee," McCarthy enjoyed broad subpoena power and legal immunity from libel suits. He bullied witnesses and encouraged self-styled "experts" to offer outlandish estimates of a vast Red Menace.

In the long run, growing concern about national security subtly altered the nation's constitutional structure. Except for the Twenty-second and the Twenty-third Amendments (adopted in 1951 and 1961, respectively), which barred future presidents from serving more than two terms and allowed the District of Columbia a vote in presidential elections, there were no formal modifications of the written Constitution during these years. But legislative enactments, especially the National Security Act of 1947, and the growing power of the executive branch of government, particularly of agencies like the CIA and the FBI, brought important informal changes to the nation's unwritten constitution. As the Truman administration sought to contain communism and conduct a global foreign policy, older ideas about a constitutional structure of limited governmental powers gave way to the idea that broader executive authority was necessary to protect national security.

DOMESTIC POLICY: TRUMAN'S FAIR DEAL

Although the Truman administration placed its greatest priority on containment, it also reconstructed the domestic legacy of Franklin Roosevelt. Many supporters of FDR's New Deal still endorsed the "Second Bill of Rights" that FDR had proclaimed in his State of the Union address of 1944. According to this vision, all Americans had the "right" to a wide range of substantive liberties, including employment, food and shelter, education, and health care. Whenever people were unable to obtain these "rights," the national government was responsible for providing access to them. Such governmental largesse required constant economic and social planning—and government spending—for the general welfare.

Talk about government planning and increased spending proved highly controversial. Even before the Second World War, the pace of domestic legislation had begun to slow, and throughout the war critics had assailed economic planning as meddlesome interference in private decision making. Government programs, Republicans charged, were an unconstitutional intrusion into people's private affairs and posed a threat to individual initiative and responsibility.

During Truman's presidency, opposition to dramatic innovations in social policymaking hardened. The National Association of Manufacturers (NAM) warned that new domestic programs would destroy the private, free enterprise system. Southern Democrats in Congress joined Republicans in blocking new programs that they feared might weaken white supremacy in their region. Even before Truman succeeded Roosevelt, these conservative forces had succeeded in abolishing several New Deal agencies that might have contributed to economic planning after the war, and had flatly rejected FDR's Second Bill of Rights.

THE EMPLOYMENT ACT OF 1946 AND THE PROMISE OF ECONOMIC GROWTH

Faced with such intense opposition to FDR's 1944 agenda, Truman needed to find a different approach to domestic policymaking. The 1946 debate over the Full Employment Bill helped identify one. The Full Employment Bill, as initially conceived, would have increased government spending and empowered Washington to intervene aggressively in the job market, so as to ensure employment for all citizens seeking work. To the bill's opponents, these provisions and the phrase "full employment" resembled socialism.

As the effort to enact the bill stalled, a scaled-down vision of domestic policymaking gradually emerged. The law that Congress finally passed, renamed the Employment Act of 1946, called for "maximum" (rather than "full") employment and specifically acknowledged that private enterprise, not government, bore primary responsibility for economic decision making. The act nonetheless recognized that the national government would play an ongoing role in economic management. It created a new executive branch body, the Council of Economic Advisers, to help formulate long-range policy recommendations and signaled that government policymakers would assume some responsibility for the performance of the economy.

A crucial factor in the gradual acceptance of Washington's new role was a growing faith that *advice* from economic experts, as an alternative to government *planning*, could help guarantee a constantly expanding economy. An influential group of theorists, many of them disciples of the British economist John Maynard Keynes, insisted that the United States no longer needed to endure the boom-and-bust cycles that had afflicted the nation during the 1920s and 1930s. Instead of leaving the economy to the uncoordinated decisions of private individuals and business firms, policymakers and citizens alike were urged to trust in the theoretical expertise of economists. They would advise government and private business on the policies most likely to produce uninterrupted economic growth.

The promise of economic growth as a permanent condition of American life dazzled postwar business and government leaders. Corporate executives viewed economic growth as a guarantee of social stability. Members of the Truman administration embraced the idea that the government should encourage economic growth not through centralized governmental planning but by updating, through measures such as the Employment Act of 1946, the cooperative relationship with both big business and organized labor that the Roosevelt administration had introduced during the Second World War.

In fact, Truman's closest advisers believed that such cooperation would actually make domestic policymaking easier. Economic growth would produce increased tax revenues and, in turn, give Washington the money to fund domestic programs. Using the relatively new measure of a "gross national product" (or GNP), postwar experts could actually calculate the nation's growing economic bounty. Developed in 1939, the concept of GNP—defined as the total dollar value of all the goods and services produced in the nation during a given year—became the standard gauge of economic health.

By the end of 1948 Truman and his advisers were preaching the gospel of economic growth. Indeed, that ideal fitted nicely with their foreign policy programs, such as the Marshall Plan, which were designed to create markets and investment opportunities overseas. Economic growth at home was linked to development in the world at large—and to the all-pervasive concern with national security.

TRUMAN'S FAIR DEAL

In his inaugural address of January 5, 1949, Truman unveiled a domestic agenda he labeled the "Fair Deal." He called for the extension of popular New Deal programs such as Social Security and minimum wage laws; enactment of civil rights and national health care legislation; federal aid for education; and repeal of the Taft-Hartley Act of 1947. Charles Brannan, Truman's secretary of agriculture, proposed an ambitious new plan for supporting farm prices by means of additional governmental subsidies, and the president himself urged substantial spending on public housing projects.

Two prominent government programs suggested the approach to domestic policymaking that dominated the Fair Deal years. The first, the so-called GI Bill (officially entitled the Serviceman's Readjustment Act of 1944), had always enjoyed strong support in Congress. After previous wars, Congress had simply voted veterans cash pensions or bonuses. But, this time, Congress worked out a comprehensive program of benefits for the several million men and the 40,000 women who had served in the armed forces. The GI Bill encompassed several different programs, including immediate financial assistance for college and job-training programs for veterans of the Second World War. In other provisions, veterans received preferential treatment when applying for government jobs; generous terms on loans when purchasing homes or businesses; and, eventually, comprehensive medical care in veterans' hospitals. The Veterans' Readjustment Assistance Act of 1952, popularly known as the "GI Bill of Rights," extended these programs to veterans of the Korean War.

Meanwhile, Social Security, the most popular part of Roosevelt's New Deal, expanded under Truman's Fair Deal. Fighting a rearguard attack by conservatives, the Social Security Administration defended its program, which also included support for the disabled and the blind, as a system that simply provided "income security" that older people had themselves earned through years of work and monetary contributions that had been withheld from their paychecks.

Under the Social Security Act of 1950 the level of benefits was increased significantly; the retirement portions of the program were expanded; and coverage was extended to more than 10 million people, including agricultural workers.

The more expansive (and expensive) Fair Deal proposals either failed or were scaled back. For instance, Truman's plan for a comprehensive national health insurance program ran into strong opposition. The American Medical Association (AMA) and the American Hospital Association (AHA) blocked any government intervention in the traditional fee-for-service medical system. Opinion polls suggested that most voters, many of whom were enrolling in private health insurance plans such as Blue Cross and Blue Shield, were simply apathetic, or confused, about Truman's national health proposals.

Because of the continued shortage of affordable housing in urban areas, polls showed greater support for home-building programs, another part of Truman's Fair Deal. Private construction firms and realtors welcomed extension of federal home loan guarantees, such as those established under the GI Bill and through the Federal Housing Administration, but they lobbied against publicly financed housing projects. Yet even conservatives recognized the housing shortage and supported the Housing Act of 1949. This law authorized construction of 810,000 public housing units and provided federal funds for "urban renewal" zones, areas to be cleared of run-down dwellings and built up again with new construction. The Housing Act of 1949 set forth relatively bold goals but provided only modest funding for its public housing program.

Domestic policymaking during the Truman era, then, ultimately focused on specific groups, such as veterans of the Second World War and older Americans, rather than on more extensive programs for all, such as a national health care plan and a large-scale commitment to government-built, affordable housing projects. Opponents of economic planning and greater spending by government considered the broader proposals of the Fair Deal to be "welfare," and the Truman administration found it easier to defend more narrowly targeted programs, which could be hailed as economic "security" measures for specific groups.

CIVIL RIGHTS

During his 1948 presidential campaign, Truman had strongly endorsed proposals that had been advanced by a civil rights committee he established in 1946. The committee's report called for federal legislation against lynching; a special civil rights division within the Department of Justice; antidiscrimination initiatives in employment, housing, and public facilities; and desegregation of the military. Although these proposals prompted many white southern Democrats to bolt to the short-lived Dixiecrat Party, they won Truman significant support from African Americans.

The Dixiecrat Party episode, a reaction to Truman's stance on civil rights, portended significant political change among southern whites who had voted overwhelmingly Democratic since the late 19th century. Strom Thurmond, the Dixiecrats' presidential candidate, denounced Truman for offering a "civil wrongs" program. Although Thurmond insisted that southern Democrats did not oppose all civil rights measures, he also argued that the Constitution required this kind of legislation to come from state governments and not from Washington. Moreover, white southern Democrats pledged to fight any effort to end racial segregation. Thurmond carried only four states in 1948, but his candidacy showed that, because of the issue of race, lifelong southern Democrats were willing to desert the party in national presidential elections.

Despite discord within his own party, Truman generally supported the efforts of the civil rights movement. When successive Congresses failed to enact any civil rights legislation—including an antilynching law and a ban on the poll taxes that prevented most southern blacks from voting—the movement turned to a sympathetic White House and to the federal courts. After A. Philip Randolph threatened to organize protests against continued segregation in the military, Truman issued an executive order calling for desegregation of the armed forces. Truman also endorsed the efforts of the Fair Employment Practices Commission (FEPC) to end racial discrimination in federal hiring.

Meanwhile, Truman's Justice Department regularly appeared in court on behalf of litigants who were contesting government-backed segregation of public schools and "restrictive covenants" (legal agreements that prevented racial or religious minorities from acquiring real estate). In 1946, the Supreme Court declared restrictive covenants illegal and began chipping away at the "separate but equal" principle that had been used since *Plessy* v. *Ferguson* (1898) to justify segregated schools. In 1950, the Court ruled that under the Fourteenth Amendment racial segregation in state-financed graduate and law schools was unconstitutional. In light of these decisions, all the traditional legal arguments that had been used since *Plessy* to legitimate racial segregation in all public schools seemed open to successful challenge—which would finally come in 1954 (see Chapter 28).

In summary, the years immediately after the Second World War marked a turning point in domestic policymaking. The New Deal's hope for comprehensive socioeconomic planning gave way to a view of social policy based on the assumption that the nation could expect uninterrupted economic growth. Henceforth, Washington could reap, through taxation, its own steady share of a growing economy, so the government could finance a set of targeted programs to assist specific groups. As one supporter of this new approach argued, postwar policymakers were sophisticated enough to embrace "partial remedies," such as the GI Bill, rather than to wait for fanciful "cure-alls," such as FDR's Second Bill of Rights.

SOCIAL CHANGE AND CONTAINMENT

The postwar years brought dramatic changes in the daily life of most Americans. Encouraged by the advertising industry, most people seemed, at one level, to believe that virtually any kind of change automatically meant "progress." Yet at another level the pace and scope of social change during these years brought a feeling of uneasiness into American life, prompting many people to try to contain the impact of new developments. Containment abroad sometimes paralleled a similar stance toward containing social innovation at home.

JACKIE ROBINSON AND THE BASEBALL "COLOR LINE"

The interplay between these two forces could be seen in the integration of organized baseball during the 1940s and 1950s. In 1947, major league baseball's policy of racial segregation finally changed when Jackie Robinson, who had played in the Negro National League, became the Brooklyn Dodgers' first baseman. A number of players, including several on Robinson's own club, had talked about boycotting any game in which Robinson appeared. Baseball's leadership, aware of the steady stream of African American fans coming out to the parks, crushed the opposition by threatening to suspend any player who refused to play with Robinson.

The pressure to integrate the national pastime became inexorable. Several months after Robinson's debut, the Cleveland Indians signed center fielder Larry Doby, and a number of other African American stars quickly left the Negro leagues for the American and National circuits. Eventually, the talent of Robinson—named Rookie of the Year in 1947 and the National League's Most Valuable Player in 1949—and of the other African American players carried the day. By 1960 every major league team fielded black players, and some had begun extensive recruiting in Puerto Rico and in the nations of the Caribbean. In 1997, the 50th anniversary of Robinson's debut, Major League Baseball staged elaborate memorial ceremonies

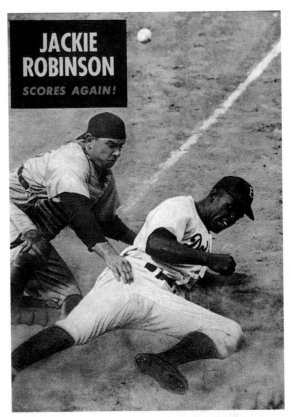

JACKIE ROBINSON In 1947 Jackie Robinson joined the Brooklyn Dodgers and became the first African American since the 19th century to play Major League baseball. He had served as a lieutenant in the Army during the Second World War. The racial integration of the national pastime of baseball became a powerful symbol of progress in race relations, and Robinson himself was a favorite of fans, both white and black.

for Robinson, who had died in 1972—and congratulated the sport for having led the fight against racial prejudice during the Cold War years.

Yet, during the late 1940s and early 1950s, baseball's leaders had worked to contain the participation of African Americans. Several teams waited for years before fielding any black players, claiming they could find no talented prospects. More commonly, teams restricted the number of nonwhite players they would take on and kept their managers, coaches, and front-office personnel solidly white.

THE POSTWAR SUBURBS

Suburbia was another place where the celebration of change and efforts to contain its effects were both constant themes. Suburban living had long been a feature of the "American dream." The new Long Island, New York, suburb of Levittown, which welcomed its first residents in October 1947, seemed to make that dream a reality, at affordable prices, for middle-income families.

Nearly everything about Levittown seemed unprecedented. A construction company that had mass-produced military barracks during the Second World War, Levitt & Sons could complete a five-room bungalow every 15 minutes. Architectural critics sneered at these "little boxes," but potential buyers stood in long lines hoping to get one. By 1950, Levittown consisted of more than 10,000 homes and 40,000 residents. By then, bulldozers and construction crews were sweeping into other suburban developments across the country.

To help buyers purchase their first home, the government offered an extensive set of programs. The Federal Housing Administration (FHA), which had been established during the New Deal, helped private lenders extend credit to mass-production builders, who could then sell the houses they built on generous financing terms. Typically, people who bought FHA-financed homes needed only 5 percent of the purchase price as a down payment; they could then finance the rest with a long-term, government-insured mortgage. Millions of war veterans enjoyed even more favorable terms under the GI loan program operated by the Veterans Administration. These government programs made it cheaper to buy a new house in the average suburb than to rent a comfortable apartment in most cities. Moreover, families could deduct from their federal income tax the interest they paid on their mortgages. This deduction was a disguised form of governmental subsidy.

Suburban homes promised greater privacy and more amenities than crowded city neighborhoods. Builders soon began to offer larger houses, including the sprawling, one-level "ranch style" model. The joys of "easy and better" living often came with the house. Levitt homes, for

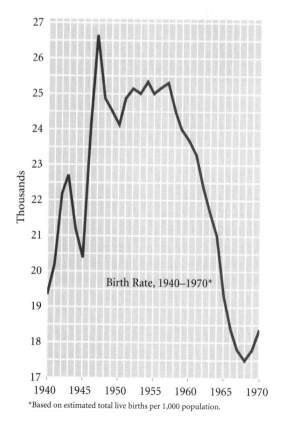

THE BABY BOOM

Birth Rate, 1940–1970*

*Based on estimated total live births per 1,000 population.

example, contained an automatic washer and a built-in television set. By being attached to the house itself, even the TV qualified as a "structural" component and could be financed under federally guaranteed loan programs.

Suburbs enjoyed the reputation for being ideal places in which to raise children, and families were having babies in much larger numbers. After the war, a complex set of factors, including early marriages and rising incomes, helped produce a "baby boom" that would last well into the next decade. With houses generally occupying only about 15 percent of suburban lots, large lawns served as private playgrounds. Nearby schools were as new as the rest of the neighborhood, and suburban school boards used the lure of modern, well-equipped buildings to attract both skilled teachers and middle-income families.

In many respects, the new suburban lifestyle epitomized an optimistic spirit of new possibilities, confidence in the future, and acceptance of change. In other respects, though, it represented an effort to contain some of the effects of rapid change by creating a material and psychological refuge. Most obviously, buying a new suburban home seemed a way of cushioning the impact of social and demographic changes. With African American families leaving the rural South in search of work in northern cities, "white flight" to suburbia quickened.

Government and private housing policies helped to structure and maintain the segregationist pattern of white suburbs and increasingly nonwhite urban neighborhoods. Federal laws allowed local groups to veto public housing projects in their communities. Although land and building costs would have been cheaper in the suburbs, public housing projects were concentrated on relatively expensive, high-density urban sites. More important, the lending industry channeled government loan guarantees away from most urban neighborhoods, and private lenders generally denied credit to nonwhites seeking new suburban housing.

No one in the postwar housing industry admitted intentional complicity in these discriminatory patterns. William Levitt might identify his private housing projects with the public crusade against communism. He held himself blameless, however, for racial issues. He could help solve the nation's housing problem, but he deceptively claimed that his "private" construction had nothing to do with the public issue of race.

Similarly, the architects of suburbia saw nothing problematic with postwar gender patterns. The lending industry made loan guarantees available only to men. Single women simply could not obtain FHA-backed loans, a policy that the agency justified on the grounds that women rarely made enough money to qualify as good credit risks.

THE SUBURBAN FAMILY AND GENDER ISSUES

Because the new suburbs generally lacked mass transit facilities, life revolved around the automobile. But if the male breadwinner needed the "family" car to commute to work, the wife spent the day at home. Until car ownership expanded in the mid-1950s, even a trip to the supermarket could prove difficult.

Still, wives and mothers found plenty of work at home. New appliances and conveniences— automatic clothes washers, more powerful vacuum cleaners, frozen foods, and home freezers—eased old burdens but created new ones. Contrary to what the ads promised, women were actually spending as much time on housework after the war as their grandmothers had spent at the turn of the century. The time spent on domestic tasks was reallocated but not reduced. Moreover, because child care facilities were not generally available in the new suburbs, mothers spent a great deal of time taking care of their children.

Daily life in the suburbs fell into a fairly rigid pattern of "separate spheres"—a public sphere of work and politics dominated by men and a private sphere of housework and child care reserved for women. Because few jobs of any kind initially were available in postwar suburbia, the distance between home and the workplace became greater for suburban men, and women who wanted to work found nearby job opportunities about as scarce as child care facilities.

Without mothers and grandmothers living close by, suburban mothers increasingly turned to child care manuals for advice. Dr. Benjamin Spock's *Baby and Child Care,* first published in 1946, sold millions of copies. Like earlier manuals, Spock's book assigned virtually all child care duties to women and underscored the importance of their nurturing role by stressing the need constantly to oversee a child's psychological growth. Other manuals picked up where Dr. Spock left off and counseled mothers on the care and feeding of teenagers. The alarmist tone of many of these books reflected—and also helped to generate—widespread concern over "juvenile delinquency."

The crusade against an alleged increase in juvenile crime soon attracted the attention of government officials. J. Edgar Hoover, director of the FBI, and Attorney General Tom Clark coupled their pleas for containing communism with pleas for containing juvenile delinquency. In a 1953 report, Hoover claimed that the first of the war babies were about to enter their teenage years, "the period in which some of them will inevitably incline toward juvenile delinquency and, later, full-fledged criminal careers."

How could this threat be contained? Many authorities suggested cures that focused on the individual family. Delinquents, according to one study in the early 1950s, sprang from a "family atmosphere not conducive to development of emotionally well-integrated, happy youngsters, conditioned to obey legitimate authority." It was up to parents, especially mothers, to raise good kids. The ideal mother, according to most advice manuals, did not work outside the home but devoted herself to rearing her own segment of the baby boom generation. Women who sought careers outside the home risked being labeled as lost, maladjusted, guilt-ridden, man-hating, or all of the above.

Even the nation's prestigious women's colleges offered instruction that was assumed to lead to marriage, not to work or careers. In his 1955 commencement address at Smith, a women's college, Adlai Stevenson, the Democratic Party's urbane presidential candidate in 1952 and 1956, told the graduates that it was the duty of each to keep her husband "truly purposeful, to keep him whole." Postwar magazines, psychology, and popular culture were filled with concerns about the reintegration and stability of returned war veterans.

Discussions about the ideal postwar family did not always offer such a one-dimensional view of gender relationships. When interviewed by researchers, most men reported they did not want a "submissive, stay-at-home" wife. Even popular TV shows, such as *Father Knows Best* or *Leave It to Beaver,* suggested a hope that middle-class fathers would become more involved in family life than their own fathers had been. And although experts on domestic harmony still envisioned suburban men earning their family's entire income, they also urged them to be "real fathers" at home. Literature on parenting emphasized "family togetherness," and institutions like the YMCA began to offer courses on how to achieve it.

In another sense, the call for family togetherness was a reaction against what some cultural historians have seen as an incipient "male revolt" against "family values." Hugh Hefner's *Playboy* magazine, which first appeared in 1953, preached that men who neglected their own happiness in order to support a wife and children were not saints but suckers. In *Playboy's* very first issue, Hefner proclaimed: "We aren't a 'family magazine.'" In Hefner's version of the good life, the man rented a "pad" rather than owned a home; drove a sports car rather than a sedan or a station wagon; and courted the Playmate of the Month rather than the Mother of the Year.

WOMEN'S CHANGING ROLES

Despite all of the media images that depicted the "average woman" as a homebound wife and mother, economic realities were propelling more and more women into the job market. Female employment rose steadily during the late 1940s and throughout the 1950s. Moreover, increasing numbers of married women were entering the labor force, many of them as part-time workers in the expanding clerical and service sectors. In 1948, about 25 percent of married mothers had jobs outside the home; at the end of the 1950s, nearly 40 percent did.

If more women were holding jobs outside their homes, their employment opportunities nevertheless remained largely contained within well-defined, sex-segregated areas. In 1950, for example, more than 90 percent of all nurses, telephone operators, secretaries, and elementary school teachers were women. As low-paid jobs for women expanded, professional opportunities actually narrowed. Medical and law schools and many professional societies admitted few, if any, women; the number of women on college faculties shrank back even from the low levels of the 1920s and 1930s.

Although the notion of the "family wage" was still invoked in order to excuse the disparity of pay and opportunity based on gender, more and more women were trying to support a family on their paychecks. This was especially true for women of color; by 1960 slightly more than 20 percent of black families were headed by women. Recognizing that stereotypical images of domesticity hardly fit the experience of African American women, *Ebony* magazine celebrated women who were able to combine success in parenting and in work. One story, for example, highlighted the only female African American mechanic at American Airlines.

Postwar magazines targeted to white women also carried somewhat ambiguous messages about domesticity. Although pursuing activities outside the home was stigmatized by some social commentators as "unnatural," magazines that depended on a broad, popular readership generally gave more positive portrayals of women who were participating in public life. Women's magazines, while being deferential to the dominant ideal of domesticity, still published articles that sensitively chronicled the difficulties of running a home and raising children and often ran stories on prominent career women.

The great fear of communism during the years from 1947 to 1954 accentuated pressures for conformity and often made it difficult to advocate significant social change. Yet, despite efforts to "contain" change at home, demographic shifts, new expectations stemming from the war, and robust prosperity inevitably transformed many social and cultural patterns. The everyday lives of Americans were inexorably changing.

FROM TRUMAN TO EISENHOWER

Emphasis on anticommunism and containment continued into the presidency of Republican Dwight D. Eisenhower. The election of 1952 marked few fundamental shifts in either foreign

FEMMES FATALES FROM FILM NOIR

During the 1940s and 1950s Hollywood released a cycle of motion pictures that came to be called film noir. These movies, nearly always filmed in black-and-white and often set at night in large cities, peeked into the dark corners of postwar America. They hinted at deep-seated anxieties and fears, especially about the possibility of men and women living together happily and harmoniously.

Many film noir pictures featured alluring femmes fatales: beautiful but dangerous women who challenged the prevailing social order. The femme fatale represented the opposite of the nurturing, safely contained wife and mother. Usually unmarried and childless, she posed a threat to both men and other women. In *The File on Thelma Jordan* (1949), for instance, the title character, played by Barbara Stanwyck, cynically destroys the marriage of a young, weak-willed district attorney. She initiates an illicit affair with him not because of love, or even lust, but as part of a complicated plot

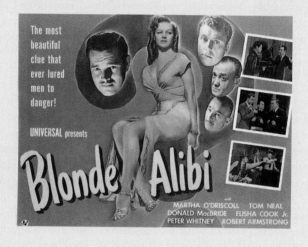

The most beautiful clue that ever lured men to danger!

UNIVERSAL presents

Blonde Alibi

MARTHA O'DRISCOLL   TOM NEAL
DONALD MacBRIDE   ELISHA COOK Jr.
PETER WHITNEY   ROBERT ARMSTRONG

or domestic policies. Containing communism overseas and at home continued to be central issues, especially during the first two years of the Eisenhower presidency.

THE ELECTION OF 1952

By 1952, Harry Truman and the Democrats were on the defensive. Denunciations of the communist threat remained the order of the day. Adlai Stevenson of Illinois, the Democratic presidential candidate, denounced Joseph McCarthy but used McCarthy-like rhetoric in his anticommunist pronouncements: "Soviet secret agents and their dupes" had "burrowed like moles" into governments throughout the world. Stevenson approved of the prosecution of the Communist Party's leaders and the dismissal of schoolteachers who were party members.

to use him in manipulating the criminal justice system. The postwar era's most prominent female stars—such as Stanwyck, Joan Crawford, Rita Hayworth, and Lana Turner—achieved both popular and critical acclaim by playing such roles.

What is the significance of the many femme fatale characters in postwar film culture? It is tempting, of course, to view them as nothing more than negative symbols, part of a Cold War culture that exalted family life and stressed the subordination of women to male heads-of-households. Film noir features, however, developed a loyal audience among women, and some students of Hollywood films have suggested that the femme fatale—who sought independence and power—might have provided an exaggerated symbol of repressed dissatisfaction among female filmgoers with tightly contained women's roles.

But a strong anticommunist stance was not enough to save Stevenson or the Democratic Party in 1952. The GOP's vice presidential candidate, Senator Richard Nixon, called Stevenson "Adlai the appeaser." Democrats faced criticism over Truman's handling of the Korean War and over revelations about favoritism and kickbacks on government contracts. The Republicans' successful election formula could be reduced to a simple equation, "K^1C^2": "Korea, corruption, and communism."

For their presidential candidate the Republicans turned to the hero of the Second World War, Dwight David Eisenhower, who was popularly known as "Ike." Eisenhower had neither sought elective office nor even been identified with a political party before 1952, but nearly a half-century of military service had made him a skilled politician. Ike grew up in Kansas; graduated from West Point; rose through the Army ranks under the patronage of General George

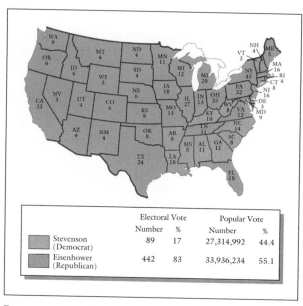

	Electoral Vote		Popular Vote	
	Number	%	Number	%
Stevenson (Democrat)	89	17	27,314,992	44.4
Eisenhower (Republican)	442	83	33,936,234	55.1

PRESIDENTIAL ELECTION, 1952

Marshall; directed the Normandy invasion of 1944 as Supreme Allied Commander; served as Army Chief of Staff from 1945 to 1948; and, after an interim period as president of Columbia University, returned to active duty as the commander of NATO, a post he held until May 1952.

Eisenhower seemed an attractive candidate. Although his partisan affiliations were vague, he finally declared himself a Republican. Initially reluctant to seek the presidency, he became convinced that Robert Taft, his main GOP rival, leaned too far to the right on domestic issues and might abandon Truman's aggressive containment policies. Perceived as a middle-of-the-roader, Ike seemed able to lead the nation through a Cold War as firmly as he had during a hot one.

In the 1952 election, the Eisenhower-Nixon ticket received almost 7 million more popular votes than the Democrats and won in the Electoral College by a margin of 442 to 89. The Republican Party itself made less spectacular gains. The GOP gained only a one-vote majority in the Senate and an eight-vote majority in the House of Representatives. The electoral coalition Franklin Roosevelt had put together during the 1930s still survived, even though it showed signs of fraying, especially in the South. There, many of the white votes that had gone to the Dixiecrats in 1948 began swinging over to the Republicans.

EISENHOWER TAKES COMMAND

Eisenhower's "moderate Republicanism" initially brought few fundamental changes in either foreign or domestic policies. Eisenhower honored his campaign pledge to travel to Korea as a means of bringing an end to U.S. military involvement there. However, armistice talks stalled when an impasse developed over whether North Korean and Chinese prisoners of war who had asked to remain in the South should be forcibly returned to North Korea and China. Hoping to end the diplomatic stalemate, Eisenhower began to threaten, in vague messages that

CHRONOLOGY

1946	Baruch plan for atomic energy proposed • Employment Act passed • Republicans gain control of Congress in November elections • Dr. Benjamin Spock's *Baby and Child Care* published
1947	Truman Doctrine announced • HUAC begins hearings on communist infiltration of Hollywood • George Kennan's "Mr. X" article published • National Security Act passed (CIA and NSC established) • Marshall Plan adopted • Truman's loyalty order announced • Taft-Hartley Act passed over Truman's veto • Jackie Robinson and Larry Doby break major league baseball's color line
1948	Berlin Airlift begins • Truman wins reelection • The *Kinsey Report* published
1949	NATO established • "Fall" of China to communism occurs • NSC-68 drafted • Soviet Union explodes atomic device • Truman outlines his Fair Deal
1950	Korean War begins • Senator Joseph McCarthy charges communist infiltration of state department • McCarran Internal Security Act passed
1951	Truman removes General MacArthur as commander in Korea
1952	GI Bill of Rights passed • Dwight Eisenhower elected president
1953	Korean War ends • Julius and Ethel Rosenberg executed • *Playboy* magazine debuts
1954	Joseph McCarthy censured by U.S. Senate • Communist Control Act passed

quickly reached China and North Korea, the use of nuclear weapons if negotiations failed. Talks resumed, and on July 27, 1953, both sides signed a truce that established a special commission of neutral nations to rule on the POW cases. (The POWs themselves were subsequently allowed to determine whether they wished to be repatriated.) So finally ended the fighting in which more than 2 million Asians, mostly noncombatants, and 33,000 Americans had died. A formal peace treaty remained unsigned, however, and the 38th parallel remained one of the most heavily armed borders in the world.

In both foreign and domestic policy, Eisenhower stood near the center. This strategy not only helped Eisenhower pursue his foreign policies but eventually allowed him to wrest control of the issue of national security at home from Senator McCarthy and the other extreme anticommunists in Congress. The Republican-controlled Congress did pass the Communist Control Act of 1954, which barred the Communist Party from entering candidates in elections and extended the registration requirements established by the McCarran Act of 1950. But with a Republican administration now in charge, many members of the GOP began to see McCarthy more as a liability than an asset.

McCarthy finally careened out of control when he claimed that the U.S. Army was harboring subversives within its ranks. During the spring of 1954, a televised Senate committee investigation into McCarthy's fantastic claim finally brought him down. Under the glare of TV lights during the Army-McCarthy hearings, the senator appeared as a crude, desperate bully who was flinging slanders in every direction. In December 1954 a majority of McCarthy's colleagues voted to censure him for conduct "unbecoming" a member of the Senate.

With McCarthyism discredited, Eisenhower could proceed with the expansion of the national security state. Following the excesses of McCarthyism, Ike's low-key approach seemed eminently reasonable. Indeed, the demonstrated unreliability of Congress's anticommunist zealots strengthened Eisenhower's own position when he claimed the constitutional privilege to withhold from Congress secret information on national security matters. Relatively free from congressional oversight, the Eisenhower administration quietly proceeded to extend Truman's earlier programs of domestic surveillance, wiretapping, and covert action overseas.

Many historians now see Eisenhower as a skilled leader who increased the power of the executive branch while seeming to do the opposite. According to one scholar, the crafty Eisenhower conducted a "hidden hand presidency." Mindful of how the mercurial Truman had become personally linked to unpopular policies, Ike tried to stay in the background and to project an air of calm steadiness. On matters of foreign policy, he usually had John Foster Dulles take center stage; on domestic issues, he let people assume that White House policies were being shaped by George Humphrey, his secretary of the treasury, and by Sherman Adams, his chief of staff.

Eisenhower's presidency helped to lower the pitch of the shrill anticommunist crusade that characterized American domestic and international policy from 1946 to 1954. With Eisenhower's presidency symbolizing tranquillity, a new sense of calm was settling over life in the United States in the middle 1950s—or so it seemed on the surface.

CONCLUSION

Efforts at "containing" communism dominated both domestic and foreign policy during the years after the Second World War. As worsening relations between the United States and the Soviet Union reached the stage of a Cold War, the Truman administration pursued policies that expanded the power of the government to counter the threat. The militarization of foreign policy intensified when the United States went to war in Korea in 1950. At home, anticommunism focused on containing the activities and ideas of alleged subversives. These initiatives raised difficult issues about how to protect the liberty of those who were suspected of being subversives or of simply being insufficiently zealous anticommunists.

Within this Cold War climate, struggles to achieve greater equality still emerged. Truman's Fair Deal promised that new economic wisdom would be able to guarantee economic growth and thereby provide the tax revenue to expand domestic programs. Truman himself pressed for national measures to end racial discrimination.

The election of a Republican president, Dwight D. Eisenhower, in 1952 brought few immediate changes in the Cold War climate. A moderate on most issues and a skillful political strategist, Eisenhower projected the image of an elder statesperson who kept above day-to-day partisan battles. In time, his style of presidential leadership helped to lower the shrillness of anticommunist rhetoric and to offer the prospect of calmer times.

AFFLUENCE AND ITS
DISCONTENTS, 1954–1963

Beginning in 1954 the Cold War tensions that had prevailed since 1947 began to abate. President Dwight Eisenhower lowered the pitch of superpower rivalry. Yet he and his successor, John F. Kennedy, still directed a determined anticommunist foreign policy. At home, Eisenhower's relaxed presidential style and Kennedy's youthful charisma helped them cautiously extend some of the domestic programs initiated during the Roosevelt and Truman eras. The economic growth of the late 1950s and early 1960s encouraged talk about an age of affluence.

Nevertheless, the era's general affluence also generated apprehension about a presumed conformity, the emergence of a "youth culture," and the impact of a mass commercial culture. At the same time, a broad-based movement against racial discrimination and new attention to economic inequities prompted renewed debate over the meaning of liberty, how to achieve equality, and the use of governmental power.

FOREIGN POLICY, 1954–1960

By 1954 the shrill anticommunist rhetoric associated with McCarthyism and the Korean War era was beginning to subside. The dominant assumption of Cold War policy—that the United States had to protect the "free world" and fight communism everywhere—remained unchanged, but the focus of that policy shifted. Bipolar confrontations between the United States and the Soviet Union over European issues gave way to greater reliance on nuclear deterrence and to more subtle and complex power plays in the "Third World"—the Middle East, Asia, Latin America, and Africa.

THE NEW LOOK AND SUMMITRY

One reason for this shift was a change of leadership in Moscow after the death of Joseph Stalin in 1953. Nikita Khrushchev, the new Soviet leader, talked of "peaceful coexistence." Seeking to free up resources to produce more consumer goods, Khrushchev began reducing Soviet armed forces.

The political climate in the United States also was changing. In December 1953, Admiral Arthur Radford, chairman of the Joint Chiefs of Staff, called for a reduction of the military budget and a revision of defense strategy. Radford's "New Look" reflected Eisenhower's belief that massive military expenditures would eventually impede the nation's economic growth. The new strategy would rely less on expensive ground forces and more on airpower, advanced nuclear capabilities, and covert action.

According to the Eisenhower administration's doctrine of "massive retaliation," the threat of U.S. atomic weaponry would hold communism in check. To make America's nuclear umbrella more effective worldwide, Eisenhower expanded NATO to include West Germany in 1955 and added two other mutual defense pacts with noncommunist nations in Central and Southeast Asia. The Southeast Asia Treaty Organization (SEATO), formed in 1954, was a mutual defense pact among Australia, France, Great Britain, New Zealand, Pakistan, the Philippines, and Thailand. The weakly bonded Central Treaty Organization (CENTO), formed in 1959, linked Pakistan, Iran, Turkey, Iraq, and Britain.

The Eisenhower administration also elevated psychological warfare and "informational" programs into major Cold War weapons. The government-run Voice of America extended its radio broadcasts globally and programmed in more languages. Covertly, the government also funded Radio Free Europe, Radio Liberation (directly to the Soviet Union), and Radio Asia. In 1953 Eisenhower persuaded Congress to create the United States Information Agency (USIA) to coordinate anticommunist informational and propaganda campaigns.

In an effort to improve relations, the superpowers resumed high-level "summit" meetings. In May 1955 an agreement was reached to end the postwar occupation of Austria and to transform that country into a neutral state. Two months later the United States, the Soviet Union, Britain, and France met in Geneva. In the fall of 1959, to soothe a crisis that had developed over Berlin, Khrushchev toured the United States, met with Eisenhower, and paid well-publicized visits to farmers in Iowa and to Disneyland in California. But a summit scheduled for 1960 in Paris was canceled after the Soviets shot down an American U-2 spy plane over their territory. Still, the tone of Cold War rhetoric had grown less strident.

The superpowers even began to consider arms limitation. In Eisenhower's "open skies" proposal of 1955, the president proposed that the two nations verify disarmament efforts by reconnaissance flights over each other's territory. The Soviets refused. But some progress was made in limiting atomic tests. Responding to worries about the health hazards of atomic fallout, both countries slowed their above-ground testing and discussed some form of test-ban agreement. For many Americans, concerns about the impact of nuclear testing came too late. Government documents declassified in the 1980s finally confirmed what antinuclear activists had long suspected: Many people who had lived "downwind" from rural nuclear test sites during the 1940s and 1950s had suffered an unusual number of atomic-related illnesses. Worse, in the 1990s it was revealed that Washington had conducted tests with radioactive materials on American citizens, who had no knowledge of these experiments.

Events in Eastern Europe accentuated American policymakers' caution about being drawn into a military confrontation with the Soviet Union. There, the reluctant satellites of the Soviet Union were chafing under the managed economy and police-state control imposed by the Soviets. Seizing on the post-Stalin thaw, Poland's insurgents staged a three-day rebellion in

June 1956 and forced the Soviets to accept Wladyslaw Gomulka, an old foe of Stalin, as head of state. Hungarians then began to demonstrate in support of Imre Nagy, an anti-Stalinist communist, who formed a new government and pledged a multiparty democracy. Hungarian revolutionaries appealed for American assistance, but the United States could hardly launch a military effort so close to Soviet power. Soviet armies crushed the uprising and killed thousands of Hungarians, including Nagy.

COVERT ACTION AND ECONOMIC LEVERAGE

Increasingly, the focus of the U.S. battle against communism began to shift from Europe to the Third World, with covert action and economic leverage replacing overt military confrontation as primary diplomatic tools. These techniques were less expensive than military action and provoked less public controversy because they were less visible.

In 1953 the CIA helped to bring about the election of the anticommunist leader Ramón Magsaysay as president in the Philippines. That same year, the CIA helped execute a coup to overthrow Mohammad Mossadegh's constitutional government in Iran, restoring to power Shah Reza Pahlavi. The increasingly dictatorial Shah remained a firm ally of the United States and a friend of American oil interests in Iran until his ouster by Moslem fundamentalists in 1979. In 1954 the CIA, working closely with the United Fruit Company, helped topple President Jacobo Arbenz Guzmán's elected government in Guatemala. Officials of the Eisenhower administration and officers of the fruit company regarded Arbenz as a communist because he sought to nationalize and redistribute large tracts of land, including some owned by United Fruit itself.

After these "successes" the CIA, under the direction of John Foster Dulles's brother Allen, grew in influence and power. In 1954 the National Security Council widened the CIA's mandate, and by 1960 it had approximately 15,000 agents deployed around the world.

Eisenhower also employed economic strategies—trade and aid—to fight communism and win converts in the Third World. Those strategies were aimed at opening more opportunities for American enterprises overseas, discouraging other countries from adopting state-directed economic systems, and encouraging expansion of commerce. New governmental assistance programs offered economic aid to friendly nations, and military aid rose sharply as well. Under the Mutual Security Program and the Military Assistance Program, the United States spent $3 billion a year, and 225,000 representatives from nations around the world were trained in anticommunism and police tactics. The buildup of military forces in friendly Third World nations strengthened anticommunist forces but also contributed to the development of military dictatorships.

AMERICA AND THE THIRD WORLD

In applying these new anticommunist measures, the Eisenhower administration employed a very broad definition of "communist." In many countries, communist political parties had joined other groups in fighting to bring about changes in labor laws and land ownership that would benefit the poor. Meanwhile, U.S. companies doing business abroad joined forces with local elites to resist the redistribution of power that such programs implied. Consequently, the

United States often found itself supporting "anticommunist" measures that simply suppressed political and social change.

LATIN AMERICA

In Latin America, Eisenhower talked about encouraging democracy but regularly supported dictatorial regimes as long as they welcomed U.S. investment and suppressed leftist movements. Eisenhower awarded the Legion of Merit to unpopular dictators in Peru and Venezuela and privately confessed his admiration for the anticommunism of Paraguay's General Alfredo Stroessner, who sheltered ex-Nazis and ran his country as a private fiefdom. The CIA established a training program for Cuban dictator Fulgencio Batista's repressive security forces.

Such policies offended many Latin Americans, and "yankeephobia" spread. Events in Cuba dramatized the growing anti-American hostility. After Fidel Castro overthrew Batista in 1959 and tried to curtail Cuba's dependence on the United States, the Eisenhower administration imposed an economic boycott of the island. Castro turned to the Soviet Union, declared himself a communist, and pledged to support leftist insurgencies throughout Latin America. At the same time the Eisenhower administration ordered a review of the policies that had sparked such ill will throughout Latin America. The review recommended that policymakers should place more emphasis on democracy, human rights, and economic growth.

NASSERISM AND THE SUEZ CRISIS OF 1956

In the Middle East, distrust of nationalism, neutralism, and social reform also influenced U.S. policy. In 1954, when Gamal Abdel Nasser overthrew a corrupt monarchy and took power in Egypt, he promised to rescue Arab nations from imperialist domination and guide them toward "positive neutralism." Nasser strengthened Egypt's economic and military power. Then he purchased advanced weapons from communist Czechoslovakia and extended diplomatic recognition to communist China. Those actions prompted the United States to cancel loans for the building of the huge Aswan Dam, a project designed to improve agriculture along the Nile River and provide power for new industries. Nasser retaliated in July 1956 by nationalizing the British-controlled Suez Canal. Suez was of major economic and symbolic importance to Britain, and the British government, joined by France and Israel, attacked Egypt in October to retake the canal.

Although Eisenhower distrusted Nasser, he decried Britain's blatant attempt to retain its imperial position. Denouncing the Anglo-French-Israeli action, Eisenhower threatened to destabilize the British currency unless the invasion was terminated. In the end, a plan supported by the United States and the United Nations allowed Nasser to retain the Suez Canal. But American prestige and power in the area suffered as the Soviet Union took over financing of the Aswan Dam.

With Nasser-style nationalism now more closely aligned with the Soviets, the Eisenhower administration feared the spread of "Nasserism" throughout the oil-rich Middle East. In the spring of 1957, his "Eisenhower Doctrine" pledged to defend Middle Eastern countries "against overt armed aggression from any nation controlled by international communism." When elites in Lebanon and Jordan, fearful of revolts by forces friendly to Nasser, asked the United States and Britain to stabilize their countries, Eisenhower sent U.S. marines to set up an anti-Nasser government in Beirut, and Britain simultaneously restored King Hussein to the throne in Jordan. These actions were part of Eisenhower's policy to support friendly, conservative governments in the Middle East, but Western military intervention also intensified Arab nationalism and anti-Americanism.

The Eisenhower administration tried to thwart revolutionary political movements elsewhere in the world. In 1958 the president approved a plan for the CIA to support an uprising against Achmed Sukarno, the president of Indonesia, who drew support from Indonesia's large Communist Party. But when the rebellion failed, the United States abandoned its Indonesian allies, and Sukarno tightened his grip on power. In the next few years, CIA activities included various schemes to assassinate Fidel Castro (these efforts failed) and Patrice Lumumba, a popular black nationalist in the Congo (Lumumba was killed in 1961, although the degree of CIA involvement in his death is still debated by scholars).

Vietnam

Eisenhower's strategy of thwarting communism and neutralism in the Third World set the stage for U.S. involvement in Vietnam, where communist-nationalist forces led by Ho Chi Minh were fighting for independence from France. Ho Chi Minh had studied in France and in the Soviet Union before returning to lead his country's anticolonial insurgency. At the end of the Second World War, Ho Chi Minh appealed in vain to the United States to support Vietnamese independence rather than allow the return of French colonial administration. But U.S. leaders backed France and its ally in the South, the government of Bao Dai. Ho Chi Minh went to war against the French who, after a major defeat at Dien Bien Phu in 1954, decided to withdraw. The subsequent Geneva Peace Accords of 1954 ended French control over all of Indochina and divided it into Laos, Cambodia, and Vietnam. Vietnam itself was split into two jurisdictions—North Vietnam and South Vietnam—until an election could be held to unify the country under one leader.

Eisenhower's advisers felt that Ho Chi Minh's powerful communist-nationalist appeal might set off a geopolitical chain reaction. The Eisenhower administration took the position that "the loss of any of the countries of Southeast Asia to Communist aggression" would ultimately "endanger the stability and security of Europe" and of Japan. This became known as the "domino theory." As Ho Chi Minh's government established itself in North Vietnam, Eisenhower supported a noncommunist government in the South.

Colonel Edward Lansdale, who had directed CIA efforts against a leftist insurgency in the Philippines from 1950 to 1953, arrived in Saigon, capital of the South, in 1954. Lansdale was to mastermind the building of a pro-U.S. government in South Vietnam under Ngo Dinh Diem, an anticommunist Catholic. Diem's government, with U.S. concurrence, denounced the Geneva Peace Accords and refused to take part in elections to create a unified government for Vietnam. It extended control over the South, redistributed land formerly owned by the French, built up its army, and launched a program of industrialization. But Diem alienated much of South Vietnam's predominantly Buddhist population and, as time passed, grew more and more isolated from his own people and almost totally dependent on the United States. By 1960 the United States had sent billions of American dollars and 900 advisers to prop up Diem's government.

The opposition to Diem in the South coalesced in the National Liberation Front (NLF). The NLF, formed in December 1960, was an amalgam of nationalists who resented Diem's dependence on the United States, communists who demanded more extensive land reform, and politicians who decried Diem's corruption and cronyism. It was allied with the Viet Minh communists of the North, from which it gradually received more and more supplies.

Although Eisenhower warned that military intervention in Indochina would be a "tragedy," he committed more and more aid and national prestige to South Vietnam and tied America's honor to Diem's diminishing political fortunes. The decision of whether to turn these commitments into a large-scale military intervention would fall to Eisenhower's successors in the White House.

In his farewell address of 1961, Eisenhower warned that the greatest danger to the United States was not communism but the nation's own "military-industrial complex." Despite his desire to limit militarism and lower the pitch of Cold War rivalries, however, Eisenhower and Secretary of State Dulles had nevertheless directed a resolutely anticommunist foreign policy that helped fuel the nuclear arms race and accelerate superpower contests in the Third World.

AFFLUENCE—A "PEOPLE OF PLENTY"

Writing in 1954, the historian David Potter called Americans a "people of plenty." The 1950s marked the midpoint of a period of generally steady economic growth that began during the Second World War and continued until the early 1970s. Corporations turned out vast quantities of consumer goods and enjoyed rising rates of profit. Investments and business ventures overseas boosted corporate profits at home. The domestic economy intersected with an international marketplace that was dominated by firms based in the United States. National security policies helped to keep the economy growing by facilitating access to raw materials and energy from the Third World.

Refrigerator-Freezers!

THE FINAL FROST BARRIER!

You'll feel like a queen ...

DESIGNED WITH YOU IN MIND!

Newer industries, such as chemicals and electronics, became particularly dominant in the world market. The Corning Glass Company reported that most of its sales in the mid-1950s came from products that had not even existed in 1940. General Electric proclaimed that "progress is our most important product." Government spending on national security pumped money into the general economy and stimulated specific industries.

HIGHWAYS AND WATERWAYS

Eisenhower was a fiscal conservative. His administration kept nonmilitary spending under tight control. After 1955 even the Pentagon's budget was reduced; and for several years, the federal government itself ran a balanced budget.

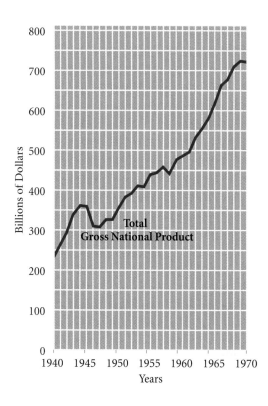

STEADY GROWTH OF GROSS NATIONAL PRODUCT, 1940–1970

Eisenhower did, however, support the Highway Act of 1956. Financed by a national tax on gasoline and other highway-related products, the Highway Act provided funds for the construction of a national system of limited-access, high-speed expressways. Touted as the largest public works project in the history of the world, this program provided steady work for construction firms and boosted the interstate trucking business. It was the first centrally planned transportation system in the nation's history.

By the mid-1950s, U.S. highways were crowded with automobiles that rivaled suburban homes as symbols of abundance. Automakers touted their annual model changes and their increasingly larger engines. Detroit's auto industry helped to support other domestic industries such as steel. In 1956 the steel industry could boast of being three and a half times more efficient than its fledgling Japanese rival.

The Eisenhower administration also supported river-diversion projects in the Far West. The Army Corps of Engineers and the Bureau of Reclamation spent billions of dollars on dams, irrigation canals, and reservoirs. Irrigation turned desert into crop land, and elaborate pumping systems even allowed rivers to flow uphill. By 1960, the western states had access to trillions of gallons of water per year, and the basis for new economic growth in Texas, California, and Arizona was established.

These water projects came at a high price. Technologically complicated and costly, they generated similarly complex and expensive bureaucracies to sustain them. As a consequence, ordinary people lost power to government agencies and private entrepreneurs. Increasingly, large corporate-style operations pushed out smaller farmers and ranchers. In addition, American

Indians found portions of their tribal lands being flooded or being purchased by agribusinesses or by large ranching interests. Finally, the vast water projects laid the basis for ecological problems. Plans to divert surface waters, to tap into groundwater tables, and to dot the West with dams and reservoirs began to take their toll upon the land. Worse, the buildup of salt byproducts in the water and the soil was accompanied by the disastrous overuse of pesticides such as DDT.

LABOR-MANAGEMENT ACCORD

Most corporate leaders, having accepted the kind of government involvement required to build interstate highways and water projects, were learning to live with labor unions as well. The auto industry led the way.

Closer cooperation with corporate management, labor leaders reasoned, could guarantee employment stability and political influence for their unions. Taking their cue from the United Auto Workers, labor dropped the demand for greater union involvement in corporate decision making. In exchange for recognizing "management prerogatives" over crucial issues—such as the organization of the daily work routine, the introduction of new technologies, and investment priorities—union leaders could still bargain aggressively for wages and fringe benefits.

Moreover, union leaders guaranteed management that rank-and-file workers would abide by the terms of their union contracts and disavow the wildcat tactics used in the 1930s and 1940s. To police this new labor-management détente, both sides looked to the federal government's National Labor Relations Board (NLRB). Meanwhile, in 1955, the AFL and the CIO merged—another sign of declining militancy within the labor movement.

Business leaders regarded this labor-management accord as a substantial victory. *Fortune* magazine noted that General Motors had paid a price in terms of more costly employee benefit packages and higher wages in the 1950s, but that "it got a bargain" in terms of labor peace. To safeguard their control over management functions, corporations regularly expanded their supervisory staffs. That practice drove up consumer prices and deprived workers of active participation in planning the work process. This accord may also have helped to divide industrial workers from one another, as those who worked in the more prosperous sectors of the economy, such as the auto industry, were able to bargain more effectively than those who worked in peripheral areas.

Most workers, however, did make economic gains. During the 1950s and early 1960s, real wages (what workers make after their paychecks are adjusted for inflation) steadily rose; the rate of industrial accidents dropped; fringe benefits (what workers receive in terms of health insurance, paid vacation time, and pension plans) improved; and job security was generally high.

Economic growth had made the United States the envy of the world. Widespread ownership of kitchen appliances, television sets, and automobiles supported the claim that American consumers were enjoying a culture of abundance. Harvard's celebrated economist John Kenneth Galbraith had simply entitled his 1952 study of the economy *American Capitalism;* his 1958 follow-up was *The Affluent Society,* a book that topped the best-seller lists for nearly six months.

Although Galbraith's second study was actually much more critical of economic affairs than his first, the term "affluence" fit nicely with the vision of constant economic growth. It also directed attention away from the deeply rooted inequalities that persisted in American society. Talking about affluence, for example, meant that one could avoid using the word "wealth," which might suggest its opposite, "poverty," a term seldom used in economic analyses of the mid-1950s. And by shifting the focus from what people *actually owned*— their accumulated wealth—to their affluence—what they could, with the aid of generous credit terms, *consume*—observers found that the "American way of life" was constantly improving.

POLITICAL PLURALISM

Many observers also credited economic affluence with giving rise to a new political structure. Galbraith, for example, suggested that unions, consumer lobbies, farm organizations, and other noncorporate groups could exert effective "countervailing power" against corporations. Only a few mavericks, such as the sociologist C. Wright Mills, disagreed. Mills saw corporate leaders as members of a small "power elite" that dominated American life. He claimed that this elite had made all of the big decisions on foreign and domestic policy in the decade since the Second World War.

In Mills's critique, the nation's Cold War policies represented an unwise, potentially disastrous, extension of government power at home and overseas. And in the vaunted affluent society, work was becoming more regimented and jobs were bringing little satisfaction. Although Mills anticipated and inspired critics of the 1960s and early 1970s, most of his contemporaries dismissed his power elite thesis as a simplistic conspiracy theory.

To those who subscribed to the dominant view, called "pluralism," no power elite could ever dominate the political process. According to pluralist accounts, public policymaking proceeded from wide participation in public debate by a broad range of different interest groups. Short-term conflicts over specific issues would obviously continue to arise, but as a professor at Harvard Law School put it, constant economic growth meant that "in any conflict of interest," it was "always possible to work out a solution" because affluence guaranteed that all interests would be "better off than before." Pluralists praised postwar leaders for finding "realistic" solutions to difficult problems.

A RELIGIOUS PEOPLE

The celebration of political pluralism dovetailed with an exaltation of the role of religion in American life. Congress emphasized religious values by constructing a nondenominational prayer room on Capitol Hill; by adding the phrase "under God" to the Pledge of Allegiance; and declaring the phrase "In God We Trust" the official national motto.

The emphasis on a pluralistic, transdenominational religious faith was not simply a product of anticommunism. Intense religious commitments, most analysts insisted, no longer divided people as much as in the past. President Eisenhower urged people to practice their own religious creed, whatever it might be. "Our government makes no sense," he declared "unless it is founded in a deeply felt religious faith—and I don't care what it is."

Religious leaders echoed this theme. Will Herberg's *Protestant-Catholic-Jew* (1955) argued that these three faiths were really "'saying the same thing' in affirming the 'spiritual ideals' and 'moral values' of the American Way of Life." Rabbi Morris Kretzer, head of the Jewish Chaplain's Organization, reassured Protestants and Catholics that they and their Jewish neighbors shared "the same rich heritage of the Old Testament . . . the sanctity of the Ten Commandments, the wisdom of the prophets, and the brotherhood of man." Religious commentators increasingly talked about the "Judeo-Christian traditon."

Individual religious leaders became national celebrities. Norman Vincent Peale, a Protestant minister who emphasized the relationship between religious faith and "peace of mind," sold millions of books declaring that belief in a Higher Power could reinvigorate daily life "with health, happiness, and goodness." His *The Power of Positive Thinking* (1952) remained a best-seller throughout the 1950s. The Catholic Bishop Fulton J. Sheen hosted an Emmy-winning, prime-time, TV program called *Life Is Worth Living*. Oral Roberts and Billy Graham—two younger, more charismatic TV ministers—began to spread their fiery brand of Protestant evangelism during the 1950s.

Peale, Sheen, Roberts, and Graham identified themselves with conservative, anticommunist causes, but an emphasis on religious faith was hardly limited to the political right. Dorothy Day, who had been involved in grass-roots activism since the early 1930s, continued to crusade for world peace and for a program aimed at redistributing wealth at home through the pages of *The Catholic Worker*. Church leaders and laypeople from all of the three major denominations supported the antidiscrimination cause and came to play important roles in the civil rights movement. Even so, the revival of religious faith during the 1950s remained closely identified with the culture of affluence.

DISCONTENTS OF AFFLUENCE

Alongside the celebrations of economic affluence, political pluralism, and religious faith, the 1950s still produced a good deal of social criticism—especially about conformity, youth, mass culture, discrimination, and inequality.

CONFORMITY IN AN AFFLUENT SOCIETY

In *The Organization Man* (1956), the sociologist William H. Whyte Jr. indicted the business corporation for contributing to one of the problems produced by affluence: conformity. Whyte saw middle-class corporate employees accepting the values of their employers, at the expense of their own individuality. The security of knowing what the corporate hierarchy wanted outweighed the organization man's concerns about a loss of individuality, Whyte argued.

In *The Lonely Crowd* (1950), David Riesman, another sociologist, wrote of a shift from an "inner-directed" society, in which people looked to themselves and to their immediate families for a sense of identity and self-worth, to an "other-directed" society, in which people looked to peer groups for approval and measured their worth against mass-mediated models. To illustrate the subtle manner in which conformist values were taught to children, Riesman pointed to *Tootle the Engine,* a popular children's book of the 1950s. When Tootle showed a preference for frolicking in the fields beside the tracks, people came to him to exert peer pressure on him as a means of getting him to conform. If Tootle stayed on tracks laid down by others, they assured him, he would grow up to be a powerful and fast-moving streamliner. This message of unprotesting adjustment to peer expectations, Riesman argued, contrasted vividly with the conflict-filled fairy tales, such as *Little Red Riding Hood,* on which earlier generations of young people had been raised.

The critique of conformity reached a broad audience through the best-selling books of journalist Vance Packard. *The Hidden Persuaders* (1957) argued that advertising produced conformity. The book, Packard wrote his publisher, was designed to show "how to achieve a creative life in these conforming times" when so many people "are left only with the roles of being consumers or spectators."

Critics such as Whyte, Riesman, and Packard wrote primarily about the plight of middle-class men, but other writers, such as Betty Friedan, claimed to find a similar psychological malaise among many women. Corporation managers, for example, were criticized for expecting the wives of their male executives to help their husbands deal with the demands of corporate life, including the need for frequent relocation. The organization man, it was said, found that his ascent up the corporate ladder depended on how well his wife performed her informal corporate duties in an equally conformist social world.

Youth Culture

Concerns about young people also intensified during the 1950s. Many criminologists linked burgeoning sales of comic books to an alleged rise in juvenile delinquency. The psychologist Frederick Wertham, in *The Seduction of the Innocent* (1954), blamed comics displaying sex and violence for "mass-conditioning" children and for stimulating juvenile unrest. Responding to local legislation and to calls for federal regulation, the comic book industry resorted to self-censorship. Publishers who adhered to new guidelines for the portrayal of violence and deviant behavior could display a seal of approval, and the great comic book scare soon faded away.

Critics of the youth culture, however, easily found other worrisome signs. In 1954 Elvis Presley, a former truck driver from Memphis, rocked the pop music establishment with a string of hits on the tiny Sun record label. Presley's sensual, electric stage presence thrilled his youthful admirers and outraged critics. Presley ("The King") and other youthful rock stars—such as Buddy Holly from West Texas, Richard Valenzuela (Richie Valens) from East Los Angeles, and Frankie Lymon from Spanish Harlem—crossed cultural and ethnic barriers and shaped new musical forms from older ones, especially African American rhythm and blues (R&B) and the "hillbilly" music of southern whites.

The first rock 'n' rollers inspired millions of fans and thousands of imitators. They sang about the joys of "having a ball tonight"; the pain of the "summertime blues"; the torment of being "a teenager in love"; and the hope of deliverance, through the power of rock, from "the days of old." Songs such as "Roll over Beethoven" by Chuck Berry became powerful teen anthems.

Guardians of older, family-oriented forms of mass culture found rock 'n' roll music even more frightening than comic books. They denounced its sparse lyrics, pulsating guitars, and screeching saxophones as an assault on the very idea of music. Religious groups condemned it as the "devil's music"; red-hunters detected a communist plan to corrupt youth; and segregationists found it to be part of a sinister plot to mix the races. The dangers of rock 'n' roll were abundantly evident in *The Blackboard Jungle* (1955), a film in which a racially mixed gang of high school students terrorized teachers and mocked adult authority.

Some rock 'n' roll music looked critically at daily life in the 1950s. The satirical song "Charley Brown" contrasted pieties about staying in school with the bleak educational opportunities open to many students. Chuck Berry sang of alienated teenagers riding around "with no particular place to go." This kind of implied social criticism, which most older listeners failed to decode, anticipated the more overtly rebellious rock music of the 1960s.

But rock music and the larger youth culture gradually merged into the mass-consumption economy of the 1950s. Top-40 radio stations and the producers of 45-rpm records identified middle-class teenagers as a market worth targeting. By 1960, record companies and disk jockeys promoted songs and performers exalting the pursuit of "fun, fun, fun" with the help of clothes, cars, and rock 'n' roll records. Rock music had come to celebrate the ethic of a people of plenty.

The Mass Culture Debate

Criticism of conformity and of youth culture merged into a wider debate over the effects of mass culture. Much of the anxiety about the decline of individualism and the rise of rock 'n' roll could be traced to fears that "hidden persuaders" were now conditioning millions of people.

Custodians of culture decried mass-marketed products. According to the cultural critic Dwight MacDonald, "bad" art—such as rock music and Mickey Spillane's best-selling "Mike Hammer" series—was driving "good" art from the marketplace and making it difficult for people to distinguish between them. MacDonald and other critics of mass culture argued that entrepreneurs, by treating millions of consumers as if they were all the same, obscured difficult social issues with a blur of pleasant, superficial imagery.

Television became a prominent target. Evolving out of network radio, television was dominated by three major corporations (NBC, CBS, and ABC) and sustained by advertisers. Picturing millions of seemingly passive viewers gathered around "the boob tube," critics decried both the quality of mass-produced programming and its impact on the public. Situation comedies, such as *Father Knows Best,* generally featured middle-class, consumption-oriented suburban families. At the same time, network television responded to pressure from advertisers and avoided programs with contemporary themes in favor of ones that, according to TV's critics, encouraged retreat into unrealities such as the mythical, heroic Old West.

These critics also worried about how mass culture seemed to be transforming the fabric of everyday life. Architects were calling for the rearrangement of living space within middle-class homes so that the television set could become the new focal point for family life. Entire new lines of products—such as the frozen TV dinner and the influential magazine *TV Guide*—became extensions of the new televisual culture. The TV set itself became an important symbol of postwar affluence.

THE LIMITS OF THE MASS CULTURE DEBATE

Most critics of mass culture acknowledged that mass culture was closely linked to the economic system. Was it really possible to cure the ills of mass culture while still enjoying the benefits of affluence? Convinced that the nation was on the right track, critics of mass culture refused to question the distribution of political and economic power in the United States. Radical critiques of industrial capitalism, heard so often during the 1930s, were no longer in vogue during the 1950s.

Moreover, the most obvious cures for the disease of mass culture clashed with the critics' own commitment to an open, pluralistic society. If, on the one hand, Congress were encouraged to legislate against "dangerous" cultural products, censorship might end up curtailing freedom of expression. On the other hand, if local communities were to step in, the results might be even worse. The prospect of southern segregationists censoring civil rights literature or of local censorship boards banning movies produced in Hollywood or books published in New York City hardly appealed to the cosmopolitan critics of mass culture.

Meanwhile, amid the concern about mass culture, a number of other questions about the direction of postwar life were beginning to emerge. Americans remained especially divided over issues related to race and to the role of government.

THE FIGHT AGAINST DISCRIMINATION, 1954–1960

Following the death in 1953 of Chief Justice Fred Vinson, Eisenhower rejected more conservative candidates to replace him on the Supreme Court and chose Earl Warren, a former governor of California. Under Warren, the Court would come to play an important role in the civil rights struggle, the most significant movement for change in the postwar period.

BROWN V. BOARD

In 1954 Warren wrote the Court's unanimous opinion in *Brown* v. *Board of Education of Topeka,* which declared that segregation of public schools violated the constitutional right of African American students to equal protection of the law. Although it technically applied only to educational facilities, *Brown* implied that all segregated public facilities, not simply schools, were open to legal challenge.

The job of carrying out the broader implications of *Brown* tested the nation's political and social institutions. The crusade against racial discrimination had long centered on the South, but demographic changes meant that national leaders could no longer treat the issue as simply a regional one.

The 1950s marked the beginning of a period in which the South was becoming more like the rest of the country. New cultural forces, such as network television, were linking the South more closely with a nationally based culture. Economic forces were also at work. Machines were replacing the region's predominantly black field workers, and the absence of strong labor

"THE PROBLEM WE ALL LIVE WITH" Eighty years after federal troops withdrew from enforcement of Reconstruction in southern states in 1877, they returned to enforce school desegregation against resistance by southern whites. This 1960 painting by Norman Rockwell shows a young black girl being escorted by U.S. marshals to a newly desegregated school in New Orleans, while an unseen mob screams obscenities and threats. Despite the affluence enjoyed by most of U.S. society in the decade following the Korean War, some members of the population were still fighting for their most basic rights.

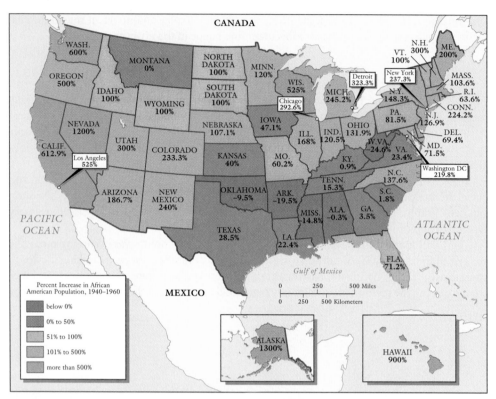

SHIFTS IN AFRICAN AMERICAN POPULATION PATTERNS, 1940–1960

unions and the presence of favorable tax laws were attracting national chain stores, business franchises, and northern-based industries to the South.

At the same time, the racial composition of cities in the West, Midwest, and Northeast was becoming more like that of the South. Accelerating the pattern begun during the Second World War, African Americans left the rural South and settled in cities like Los Angeles, Chicago, New York, and Cleveland during the late 1940s and early 1950s. In the mid-1950s this demographic shift helped to quicken "white flight" to the suburbs and to transform political alignments. With African American voters becoming increasingly important in the North, for example, urban Democrats came to support the drive to end racial discrimination. Meanwhile, the Republicans were making small electoral gains in what had long been the Democratic Party's "solid South." Most important, African Americans themselves mounted a new attack on segregation and racial discrimination in the South.

The battle against racial discrimination was coming to dominate domestic politics. Segregationists in the South pledged "massive resistance" to the Supreme Court ruling in *Brown* v. *Board of Education.* This strategy seemed to be succeeding when in 1955 the Supreme Court ruled that school desegregation should proceed with "all deliberate speed." In the following year, 100 members of the U.S. House and Senate signed a "Southern Manifesto" in which they promised to support any state that intended "to resist forced integration by any lawful means."

Rosa Parks Ignites Desegregation Campaign   Rosa Parks's refusal to sit at the back of a segregated bus in 1955 sparked a campaign to integrate public transit in Montgomery, Alabama. Here, following a successful boycott, Rosa Parks rides in the front seat on the first day of desegregated bus travel.

Defiance went beyond the courtroom. Vigilantes donned the white robes of the Ku Klux Klan, which was joined by new racist organizations, such as the White Citizens Council. As a result, antidiscrimination activists constantly risked injury and death. In August 1955 two white Mississippians murdered 14-year-old Emmett Till, a visitor from Chicago, for acting "disrespectful" to a white woman. Mamie Till Bradley demanded that her son's maimed corpse be displayed publicly for "the whole world to see" and that young Till's killers be punished. When their case came to trial, an all-white jury found the killers—who would subsequently confess their part in the murder—not guilty.

The Montgomery Bus Boycott and Martin Luther King Jr.

In response to the uncertainty of judicial remedies, African Americans began supplementing legal maneuvering with aggressive campaigns of direct action. In Montgomery, Alabama, Rosa Parks, a member of the local NAACP, was arrested in 1955 for refusing to obey a state segregation law that required black passengers to give up their seats to whites and sit at the back of the bus. Montgomery's black community responded to her arrest by boycotting public transportation. The resulting financial losses convinced the city's public transit system to reconsider its segregationist policy.

The Montgomery boycott vaulted the Reverend Martin Luther King Jr., one of its leaders, into the national spotlight. King followed up the victory in Montgomery by joining with other black ministers to form the Southern Christian Leadership Conference (SCLC). In addition to pressing for the desegregation of public facilities, the SCLC launched an effort to register

African American voters throughout the South. More activist than the NAACP, the SCLC served to spread King's broad vision of social change—integration forced by passive civil disobedience—throughout the nation. The purpose of civil disobedience, according to King, was to persuade people of the moral evil of racial discrimination. Aided by the national media, especially network television, King's powerful presence and religiously rooted rhetoric carried the message of the antidiscrimination movement in the South to the entire nation.

THE POLITICS OF CIVIL RIGHTS

But political institutions in Washington responded very slowly. The Supreme Court expanded its definition of civil rights but generally backed away from mandating the sweeping institutional changes needed to make these rights meaningful. Congress, meanwhile, remained deeply divided on racial issues. With southern segregationists, all of them members of the Democratic majority, holding key posts on Capitol Hill, antidiscrimination legislation faced formidable obstacles.

Even so, Congress passed its first civil rights measures in more than 80 years. The Civil Rights Act of 1957 set up a procedure for expediting lawsuits by African Americans who claimed their right to vote had been abridged. It also created a permanent Commission on Civil Rights to study alleged violations and recommend new remedies. In 1960, another act promised additional federal support for blacks who were being barred from voting in the South. These civil rights initiatives, which became law against fierce opposition from southern Democrats, dramatized the difficulty of getting even relatively limited antidiscrimination measures through Congress.

President Eisenhower appeared largely indifferent to the issue of racial discrimination. When liberal Republicans urged him to take action, he did nothing. He regarded the fight against discrimination as primarily a local matter, and he publicly doubted that any federal civil rights legislation could change the attitudes of people opposed to the integration of public facilities or job sites.

Indeed, Eisenhower's grasp of domestic issues seemed to grow more uncertain during his second term as president. In the election of 1956, he achieved another landslide victory over Democrat Adlai Stevenson, but his personal appeal did relatively little to help his party. In 1956 the Republicans failed to win back control of Congress from the Democrats. In fact, in this presidential election and in the off-year races of 1958, the GOP lost congressional seats as well as state legislatures and governors' mansions to the Democrats. Meanwhile, Eisenhower, who had suffered a mild heart attack prior to the 1956 election, seemed progressively enfeebled, physically as well as politically. He appeared especially weak in his handling of racial issues.

In 1957, however, Eisenhower was forced to act. Orval Faubus, the segregationist governor of Arkansas, ordered his state's National Guard to block enforcement of a federal court order mandating integration of Little Rock's Central High School. Responding to this direct challenge to national authority, Eisenhower put the Arkansas National Guard under federal control and augmented it with members of the U.S. Army. Black students, escorted by armed troops, then were able to enter the high school.

AMERICAN INDIAN POLICY

The Eisenhower administration also lacked coherent policies on issues affecting American Indians. It attempted to implement two programs, "termination" and "relocation," that had been proposed during the Truman years. The termination policy called for the national government to end its oversight of tribal affairs and to treat American Indians as individuals rather than as members of tribes. Its long-term goals were to abolish reservations, to liquidate assets of the tribes, and to end the kinds of federal services offered by the Bureau of Indian Affairs (BIA). In 1954, one year after this general policy had received congressional approval, six bills of termination were enacted, affecting more than 8,000 Native Americans.

Under the relocation program, Indians were encouraged to leave their rural reservations and take jobs in urban areas. In 1954 the BIA intensified its earliest relocation efforts, with Minneapolis, St. Louis, Dallas, and several other cities joining Denver, Salt Lake City, and Los Angeles as relocation sites. This program, like the termination policy, encouraged American Indians to migrate to urban areas and become assimilated into the social mainstream.

Both programs were deeply flawed. As several more termination bills were enacted during the Eisenhower years, almost 12,000 people lost their status as tribal members, and the bonds of communal life for many Indians grew weaker. At the same time, nearly 1.4 million acres of tribal lands were lost, often falling into the hands of real estate speculators. Indians from terminated tribes lost both their exemptions from state taxation and the social services provided by the BIA and gained almost nothing in return. Most terminated Indians sank into even deeper poverty. Relocation went no better. Most of the relocated Indians found only low-paying, dead-end jobs and racial discrimination. In the mid-1950s, Indian children who had been relocated from reservations found it difficult even to enter *segregated,* let alone integrated, public schools in some cities. Despite its problems, the program nevertheless continued throughout the Eisenhower years.

Gradually, however, both Indians and civil rights activists mobilized against the termination and relocation policies. By 1957 the BIA had scaled back its initial timetable for liquidating every tribe within five years, and in 1960 the party platforms of both the Republicans and Democrats repudiated the termination policy entirely. In 1962 this disastrous policy was itself terminated. Meanwhile, however, the relocation program continued, and by 1967 almost

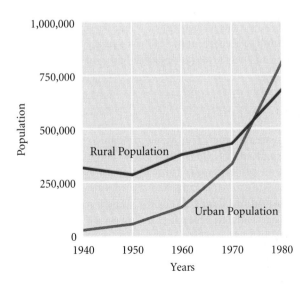

TOTAL URBAN AND RURAL INDIAN
POPULATION IN THE UNITED
STATES, 1940–1980

half of the nation's Indians were living in relocation cities. The policy hardly touched the deeply rooted problems that many Indians confronted, including a life expectancy only two-thirds that of whites, nor did it ever provide significantly better opportunities for employment or education.

THE GROWTH OF SPANISH-SPEAKING POPULATIONS

The millions of new Spanish-speaking people, many of whom had recently arrived in the United States, also highlighted the issue of discrimination. In the 1950s Puerto Ricans began moving to the mainland in large numbers. Finding only low-paying jobs and settling in older urban neighborhoods, these new arrivals were U.S. citizens but often spoke only Spanish. In 1960 New York City's Puerto Rican community was nearly 100 times greater than it had been before the Second World War.

Meanwhile, large numbers of Spanish-speaking people from Mexico were moving into the Southwest, where they joined already sizable Mexican American communities. Beginning during the Second World War and continuing until 1967, the U.S. government sponsored the *bracero* (or farmhand) program, which brought nearly 5 million Mexicans northward to serve as agricultural laborers. Many of the *braceros* remained in the United States after their contracts expired. Joining them were legal immigrants from Mexico and growing numbers of people who illegally filtered across the border. The illegal Mexican immigrants, derisively labeled "wetbacks" because they supposedly swam across the Rio Grande, became the target of a government dragnet called "Operation Wetback." During the early 1950s, the government rounded up and deported to Mexico nearly 4 million people.

Leaders in long-established Mexican American communities mobilized to fight discrimination. Labor organizers sought higher wages and better working conditions in the factories and fields, although the FBI labeled many of these efforts as "communist-inspired" and harassed unions that had large Mexican American memberships. Middle-class organizations, such as the League of United Latin American Citizens (LULAC) and the Unity League, also sought to desegregate schools, public facilities, and housing in southern California and throughout the Southwest. In 1940 Mexican Americans had been the most rural of all the major ethnic groups; by 1950, in contrast, more than 65 percent of Mexican Americans were living in urban areas, a figure that would climb to 85 percent by 1970. As a result of this fundamental demographic shift, Mexican Americans began to gain political clout in many southwestern cities.

URBAN ISSUES

The growth of new, largely white, suburban areas in the 1950s was accompanied by new urban issues, many of them related to race. Throughout the 1950s, both public and private institutions were shifting money and construction projects away from the cities, especially away from neighborhoods in which Latinos and African Americans had settled. Adopting a policy called "redlining," many banks and loan institutions denied funds for home buying and business expansion in neighborhoods that were considered "decaying" or "marginal" because they contained aging buildings, dense populations, and growing numbers of nonwhites. Meanwhile, the Federal Housing Authority and other government agencies channeled most of their funds toward the new suburbs.

"Urban renewal" programs, authorized by the Housing Act of 1949 (see Chapter 27), often amounted to "urban removal." Although federal housing laws called for "a feasible method for the temporary relocation" of persons displaced by urban renewal projects, developers often ignored the housing needs of the people they displaced. People with low-income jobs were evicted so that their apartments and homes could be replaced by office buildings and freeways.

Public housing projects, which had been designed to provide affordable housing for low- and moderate-income families, proved an especially grave disappointment. Although the suburbs, where land was abundant and relatively inexpensive, seemed an obvious place in which to build public housing, middle-income suburbanites blocked such construction. Consequently, the few public projects built were in the cities, where population density was high and land was expensive. Originally conceived as a temporary alternative for families who would rather quickly move out to their own homes, public housing facilities became stigmatized as "the projects," housing of last resort for people with little prospect for economic advancement.

By the end of the 1950s, the urban policies of both the Fair Deal and the Eisenhower era were widely regarded as failures. Urban renewal projects not only disrupted housing patterns but also helped to dislocate industries that had long provided entry-level jobs for unskilled workers. Both major presidential candidates in 1960 pledged to create a new cabinet office for urban affairs and to expand the federal government's role.

Debates over Government's Role in the Economy

Controversy over urban issues was related to larger debates over the role that government should play in economic life. Although Eisenhower sometimes hinted to conservative Republicans that he wanted to roll back the New Deal and the Fair Deal, he lacked both the will and the political support to do so. Actually, Eisenhower presided over an expanded Social Security system, higher minimum wages, better unemployment benefits, and a new Department of Health, Education, and Welfare (HEW). Still, as his stance on urban and racial issues showed, he took few steps to enlarge governmental power. His popularity seemed to rest on his personality rather than on the specifics of his policies.

Eisenhower and the New Conservatives

As a result of his centrist position on most domestic issues, Eisenhower attracted the ire of a growing group of political conservatives. Eisenhower, of course, was the first Republican president since Herbert Hoover, but did his administration really represent basic GOP principles?

Not to Arizona's Barry Goldwater. A fervent anticommunist, Goldwater was elected to the U.S. Senate in 1952. In his book *Conscience of a Conservative* (1960), Goldwater criticized postwar U.S. leaders, including Eisenhower, for failing to take stronger military measures against the Soviet Union. At the same time, Goldwater decried almost all domestic programs, especially civil rights legislation, as grave threats to individual liberty.

While Goldwater was working to push the GOP to the right of Eisenhower's moderate Republicanism, William F. Buckley Jr. was trying to reshape a broader right-wing message for the country at large. Buckley, a devout Roman Catholic, first gained national attention while still in his twenties with a 1952 book, *God and Man at Yale,* that detected a "collectivist" and antireligious tilt in American higher education. Three years later, Buckley helped found the

National Review, a magazine that attracted a talented group of writers. The *National Review* moved away from extremist positions, particularly the hysterical anticommunism of groups such as the John Birch Society. Although this "new conservatism" began amid considerable doubts about its immediate prospects for success, Buckley's own *Up from Liberalism* (1959), Goldwater's *Conscience of a Conservative,* and other books looked to a long-term strategy for building a right-of-center movement.

ADVOCATES OF A MORE ACTIVE GOVERNMENT

While the new conservatives were criticizing the Eisenhower administration for failing to break decisively with the policies of the Roosevelt and Truman years, liberals were grumbling that it was failing to address pressing public issues through the more active use of government power. They were especially critical of Eisenhower's relatively passive approach to questions involving racial discrimination. Moreover, critics ridiculed Eisenhower's commitment to a balanced budget as evidence of his 19th century approach. After Eisenhower suffered a second heart attack and a mild stroke during his second term, many critics talked about the need for more vigorous presidential leadership. Liberal advocates of greater governmental intervention in the economy urged deficit spending by Washington as a way to stimulate continued economic expansion.

Other critics recommended dramatic increases in spending for national security. The 1957 Gaither Report, prepared by prominent people with close ties to defense industries, warned that the Soviet Union's GNP was growing even more quickly than that of the United States and that much of this expansion came in the military sector. It urged an immediate increase of about 25 percent in the Pentagon's budget and long-term programs for building fallout shelters, for developing intercontinental ballistic missiles (ICBMs), and for expanding conventional military forces.

Eisenhower reacted cautiously. Although he agreed to accelerate the development of ICBMs, he opposed any massive program for building fallout shelters or for fighting limited, nonnuclear wars around the globe. In fact, he reduced the size of several Army and Air Force units and kept his defense budget well below the levels his critics were proposing. Eisenhower could confidently take such steps because secret flights over the USSR by U-2 surveillance planes, which had begun in 1956, revealed that the Soviets were lagging behind, rather than outpacing, the United States in military capability.

Concerns about national security and calls for greater governmental spending also surfaced in the continuing controversy over education. Throughout the 1950s, some critics complained that schools were emphasizing "life adjustment" skills—getting along with others and accommodating to social change—instead of teaching the traditional academic subjects. Rudolf Flesch's best-selling book of 1955 wondered *Why Johnny Can't Read.* Other books suggested that Johnny and his classmates couldn't add or subtract very well either and that they lagged behind their counterparts in the Soviet Union in their mastery of science. These arguments gained new intensity when, in October 1957, the Soviets launched the world's first artificial satellite, a 22-inch sphere called *Sputnik.*

Using the magical phrase "national security," school administrators and university researchers sought and won more federal dollars. The National Defense Education Act of 1958 funneled money to college-level programs in science, engineering, foreign languages, and the social sciences. This act marked a milestone in the long battle to overcome congressional opposition to federal aid to education.

Other critics urged the Eisenhower administration to seek increased federal spending for social welfare programs. Writing in 1958, in *The Affluent Society,* John Kenneth Galbraith found a dangerous tilt in the "social balance," away from "public goods." Affluent families could travel in air-conditioned, high-powered automobiles, Galbraith observed, but they must pass "through cities that are badly paved, made hideous by litter, blighted buildings," and billboards. While the researcher who develops a new carburetor or an improved household cleanser is well rewarded, the "public servant who dreams up a new public service is [labeled] a wastrel."

Galbraith's musings seemed mild in comparison to the jeremiads of Michael Harrington. In 1959, *Commentary,* one of several influential magazines that featured social criticism during the late 1950s, published an article in which Harrington argued that the problem of economic inequality remained as urgent as it had been during the 1930s. At least one-third of the population was barely subsisting in a land of supposed affluence. Avoiding statistics and economic jargon, Harrington told dramatic stories about the ways in which poverty could ravage the bodies and spirits of people who had missed out on the affluence of the 1940s and 1950s.

During the early 1960s, when domestic policymaking became a priority of John F. Kennedy and Lyndon Baines Johnson, critics such as Galbraith and Harrington became political celebrities. But their critique should be seen as a product of the political culture of the late 1950s. The Kennedy presidency of 1961–1963 would be firmly rooted in the critique of both foreign and domestic policymaking that had emerged during the Eisenhower years.

THE KENNEDY YEARS: FOREIGN POLICY

John Fitzgerald Kennedy had been groomed for the White House by his politically ambitious father. After his graduation from Harvard in 1940, Kennedy pursued a life devoted to public service. After winning military honors while serving in the U.S. Navy during the Second World War, Kennedy entered politics. In 1946 he won election from Massachusetts to the House of Representatives, and in 1952 he captured a seat in the Senate. In Washington, Kennedy gradually gained a national political reputation, largely on the basis of his charm and youthful image. He was aided by his 1953 marriage to Jacqueline Bouvier. In 1956, he narrowly missed winning the Democratic vice presidential nomination.

THE ELECTION OF 1960

Between 1956 and 1960, Kennedy barnstormed the country, speaking at party functions and rounding up supporters for a presidential bid. This early campaigning, along with his talented political advisers and his family's vast wealth, helped Kennedy overwhelm his primary rivals, including the more liberal Senator Hubert Humphrey of Minnesota and Lyndon Johnson.

Richard Nixon remained on the defensive throughout the campaign of 1960. Nixon seemed notably off balance during the first of several televised debates in which political pundits credited the cool, tanned Kennedy with a stunning victory over the pale, nervous Nixon. Despite chronic and severe health problems, which his loyal staff effectively concealed, Kennedy projected the image of a youthful, vigorous leader.

During the 1960 campaign, Kennedy stressed four issues that together made up what he called his "New Frontier" proposals. On civil rights and social programs, he pledged support for antidiscrimination efforts. In an important symbolic act, he sent his aides to Georgia to

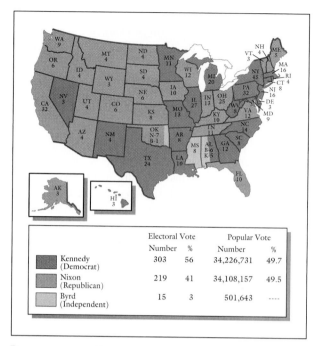

		Electoral Vote		Popular Vote	
		Number	%	Number	%
	Kennedy (Democrat)	303	56	34,226,731	49.7
	Nixon (Republican)	219	41	34,108,157	49.5
	Byrd (Independent)	15	3	501,643	----

PRESIDENTIAL ELECTION, 1960

assist Martin Luther King Jr., who had been sentenced to six months in jail for a minor traffic violation. Moreover, Kennedy endorsed the sort of social programs that liberals had been advocating. Although his proposals remained vague, he did mention greater federal spending to rebuild rural communities, to increase educational opportunities, and to improve urban conditions.

Kennedy also highlighted two other issues that had provoked debate during the 1950s: stimulating greater economic growth and conducting a more aggressive foreign policy. He surrounded himself with advisers who spoke of stimulating the economy by means of tax cuts and deficit spending measures. On Cold War issues, he criticized Eisenhower for failing to rid the hemisphere of Castro in Cuba and for allowing a "missile gap" to develop in U.S. defenses against the Soviet Union. By spending heavily on defense, he claimed, he would create a "flexible response" against communism, especially in the Third World.

The 1960 election defied easy analysis. Kennedy defeated Nixon by only about 100,000 popular votes and won the electoral votes of several states, including Illinois, by a razor-thin margin. Apparently hurt by his Catholicism, especially in the South, Kennedy won a smaller percentage of the popular vote than most other Democrats running for lesser offices. Clearly, his victory owed a great deal to his vice presidential running mate, Lyndon Johnson, whose appeal to southern whites helped the ticket carry the Deep South and Johnson's home state of Texas.

From the outset, the president and his wife Jacqueline riveted media attention on the White House. They hobnobbed with movie stars and brought prominent intellectuals into the administration. In his inaugural address, Kennedy challenged people to "ask not what your country can do for you; ask what you can do for your country." The "best and the brightest," the hard-driving people who joined Kennedy's New Frontier, promised to launch exciting new crusades, even to the ultimate frontier of outer space.

KENNEDY'S FOREIGN POLICY GOALS

In foreign policy, Kennedy boasted of making a break with the past to wage the Cold War more vigorously. Military assistance programs, propaganda agencies, and covert action plans all received strong support from the White House. In one of his most popular initiatives, the president created the Peace Corps, a new program that sent Americans to nations around the world to work on development projects that were supposed to undercut the appeal of communism.

Kennedy, however, also built upon many of Eisenhower's policies. Eisenhower's last-minute efforts to reorient Latin American policies away from reliance on dictators and toward support of more progressive programs were elaborated on and repackaged as Kennedy's "Alliance for Progress." Proposed in the spring of 1961 as a way to prevent the spread of anti-Americanism and communist insurgencies, the Alliance offered $20 billion in loans over a 10-year period to Latin American countries that would undertake land reform and democratic development measures. The Alliance, based on a naive assessment of the obstacles to social and economic development, rapidly failed.

CUBA AND BERLIN

The worst fiasco of the Kennedy presidency, a daring but ill-conceived CIA mission against Cuba, also had its roots in the Eisenhower administration. The CIA was planning a secret invasion to topple Fidel Castro, Cuba's revolutionary leader. On April 17, 1961, when U.S.-backed and trained forces (mainly anticommunist Cuban exiles) landed at the Bahia de Cochinas (the Bay of Pigs) on the southern coast of Cuba, however, the expected popular uprising against Castro did not occur. The invaders were quickly surrounded and imprisoned. Kennedy refused to provide the air support that Cuban exiles had been led to expect and at first even tried to deny that the United States had been involved in the invasion, but the CIA's role quickly became public, and anti-Yankee sentiment mounted in Latin America. Castro tightened his grip over Cuba and strengthened his ties with the Soviet Union. "I have made a tragic mistake," Kennedy told Clark Clifford, an adviser. Yet, stung by the failed invasion, the Kennedy administration continued to target Castro with a covert program called Operation Mongoose, which consisted of economic destabilization activities and futile assassination plots.

Another dramatic confrontation loomed in Berlin. In June 1961, Nikita Khrushchev and Kennedy met in Vienna, where Khrushchev proposed ending the Western presence in Berlin and reuniting the city as part of East Germany. His proposal was motivated by the steady flow of immigrants from East Germany into West Berlin, a migration that was both embarrassing and economically draining to the German communist regime. Kennedy was forceful in his refusal to abandon West Berlin, but the East German government continued to press Khrushchev to help solve their problems. On August 13, 1961, the communist regime began to erect a wall to separate East from West Berlin. East Germans attempting to escape into the West were shot. The Berlin Wall became a symbol of communist repression. Kennedy's assertion, *"Ich bin ein Berliner"* ("I am a Berliner"), delivered in front of the wall to a massive crowd, became one of the most memorable lines of his presidency.

THE CUBAN MISSILE CRISIS   During the Cuban Missile Crisis of October 1962, these Cuban refugees, like most people, were riveted to their television sets to obtain the latest update from President Kennedy. In this nuclear confrontation, the fate of the world seemed at stake.

Superpower confrontation escalated to its most dangerous level during the Cuban Missile Crisis of 1962. The Soviet Union, responding to Castro's request, sent sophisticated weapons to Cuba. In October, after spy-plane flights confirmed the existence of missile launching sites there, the Kennedy administration publicly warned that it would not allow nuclear warheads to be installed so close to American shores. Kennedy demanded that the Soviets dismantle the missile silos they had already prepared and turn back some supply ships that were heading for Cuba. After dramatic meetings with his top advisers, Kennedy rejected an outright military strike. Instead, he ordered the U.S. Navy to "quarantine" the island. The Strategic Air Command was put on full alert for possible nuclear war. Meanwhile, both sides engaged in complicated, secret diplomatic maneuvers to prevent a nuclear confrontation.

The maneuvers succeeded. On October 28, 1962, Khrushchev ordered the missiles dismantled and the Soviet supply ships brought home; Kennedy promised not to invade Cuba and secretly assured Khrushchev that he would complete the previously ordered withdrawal of U.S. Jupiter missiles from Turkey. In the mid-1990s, with the opening of some Soviet archives, Americans learned that the crisis had been even more perilous than they had imagined. Unknown to Kennedy's circle at the time, the Soviets already had tactical nuclear weapons in Cuba that could have been launched.

After the Cuban Missile Crisis, both superpowers seemed to recognize the perils of direct conflict. A direct phone line was established between Moscow and Washington to ensure the kind of communication that might forestall a nuclear confrontation or an accident in the future. And both nations became a bit more cautious.

Southeast Asia and "Flexible Response"

In Southeast Asia, Kennedy followed Eisenhower's policy of trying to build South Vietnam into a viable, noncommunist state. After the Bay of Pigs disaster, in which the attempt to overthrow an already established pro-communist government had failed, Kennedy decided that the U.S. must put down communist-led "wars of national liberation" before they succeeded.

Kennedy viewed Vietnam as a test case for "flexible response," which aimed at implementing a variety of methods to combat the growth of communist movements. Elite U.S. special forces known as Green Berets were trained in "counterinsurgency" tactics to use against communist guerrillas; cadres of social scientists charged with "nation building" were sent as advisers. When these efforts brought nothing but greater corruption and a deeper sense of isolation to the Diem regime, the CIA gave the South Vietnamese army the green light to orchestrate Diem's overthrow. Just weeks before Kennedy himself would be assassinated, Diem was run out of his palace and murdered. The coup against Diem brought a military leader to power, but this seemed only to breed even greater political instability.

The Kennedy Years: Domestic Policy

Despite his campaign promises, Kennedy was slow to depart from Eisenhower's cautious fiscal policies. He was fearful of running federal budget deficits greater than those of the Eisenhower years. Relations with corporate leaders nevertheless turned ugly in 1962, when Kennedy publicly clashed with the president of U.S. Steel over that company's decision to raise prices beyond the guidelines suggested by the administration.

Policymaking under Kennedy

Eventually, though, Kennedy endorsed tax breaks as a means of promoting economic growth. According to prevailing theory, lower tax rates for everyone and special deductions for corporations that invested in new plants and equipment would free up money for investment. In 1962 he urged Congress to change the complex tax code. Despite opposition from those who thought the tax breaks would unfairly benefit corporations and the wealthy, the bill seemed headed for passage in the fall of 1963.

On matters of social welfare, the Kennedy administration advanced policies that had been initiated by the Fair Deal of the 1940s—namely, a higher minimum wage and continuation of urban renewal programs. It also lent its support to the Area Redevelopment Bill of 1961, which called for directing federal grants and loans to areas that had missed out on the general economic prosperity of the postwar years. Meanwhile, under the urban renewal programs begun during the 1940s, bulldozers were still razing large parts of urban America so that low-income housing continued to be replaced by business and freeway construction projects aimed at middle- and upper-income people. Finally, the Kennedy administration made the fight against organized crime a top priority—much more so (at least initially) than the fight for racial equality.

THE CIVIL RIGHTS CRUSADE, 1960–1963

Although JFK talked about new civil rights legislation, he tried to placate segregationist Democrats by doing little to press the issue for nearly the first two years of his presidency. Meanwhile, the president and his brother Robert, the attorney general, listened sympathetically to complaints from J. Edgar Hoover, director of the FBI, about the allegedly suspicious political activities of Martin Luther King Jr. and his associates. To keep tabs on King's activities and gather information that it might use against him, the FBI used surveillance and, ultimately, illegal wiretaps of his private conversations.

Rising dissatisfaction over the slow pace of the campaign against racial discrimination, however, gradually forced the Kennedy administration to consider new initiatives. In early 1960 young African American students at North Carolina A & T College in Greensboro sat down at a dimestore lunch counter, defied state segregation laws, and asked to be served in the same manner as white patrons. It was the beginning of the "sit-in" movement, a new phase in the civil rights movement in which groups of young activists challenged legal segregation by demanding equal access to hitherto segregated public facilities. All across the South, demon-

RACIAL CONFLICT IN BIRMINGHAM   Images such as this 1963 photograph of a confrontation in Birmingham, Alabama, in which segregationists turned dogs on youthful demonstrators, helped rally public support for civil rights legislation. Events in Birmingham, however, also presaged the increasingly violent clashes that would punctuate the efforts to end racial discrimination.

strators staged nonviolent sit-in demonstrations at restaurants, bus and train stations, and other public facilities.

The courage and commitment of the demonstrators gave the antidiscrimination movement new momentum. With songs such as "We Shall Overcome" and "Oh Freedom" inspiring solidarity, young people pledged their talents and resources—indeed their lives—to the civil rights struggle. In 1961 interracial activists from the Congress of Racial Equality (CORE) and the Student Non-Violent Coordinating Committee (SNCC), a student group that had grown out of the sit-in movement, risked racist retaliation in "freedom rides" across the South; the freedom riders were determined that a series of federal court decisions, which had declared segregation on buses and in waiting rooms to be unconstitutional, would not be ignored by southern officials.

The new grass-roots activism forced the Kennedy administration to respond. In 1961 it sent federal marshals into the South in order to protect freedom riders. In 1962 and again the following year, it called on National Guard troops and federal marshals to prevent segregationists from stopping racial integration at several educational institutions in the Deep South, including the universities of Mississippi and Alabama. In November 1962, Kennedy issued a long-promised executive order that banned racial discrimination in housing financed by the national government. In February 1963, Kennedy sent Congress a moderate civil rights bill, which focused on providing faster trial procedures in voting rights cases.

But events were outpacing Kennedy's policies. Racial conflict convulsed Birmingham, Alabama, in 1963. White police officers used dogs and high-power water hoses on young African Americans who were demanding an end to segregation in the city. Four children were later murdered (and 20 injured) when racists bombed Birmingham's Sixteenth Street Baptist Church, a center of the antisegregation campaign. When thousands of blacks took to the streets in protest—and two more children were killed, this time by police officers—the Kennedy administration finally took more vigorous action.

During the last six months of the Kennedy presidency, civil rights issues dominated domestic politics. Kennedy himself made an emotional plea on television for a national commitment to the cause of antidiscrimination. However, the administration still hoped to shape the direction and pace of change by passing new laws to get demonstrators "off the streets and into the courts." Thus, it supported stronger civil rights legislation, including a ban on racial discrimination in all public facilities and housing and new federal laws to guarantee the vote to millions of African Americans who were being kept from polls in the South.

On August, 28, 1963, an integrated group of more than 200,000 people marched through the nation's capital. Leaders of the march endorsed Kennedy's new civil rights bill, but they also pressed a broader agenda. In addition to more effective civil rights legislation, the marchers' formal demands included a higher minimum wage and a federal program to guarantee new jobs. Standing in front of the Lincoln Memorial, Martin Luther King Jr. delivered his eloquent "I Have a Dream" speech. The march on Washington, which received favorable coverage from the national media, put considerable pressure on the White House and Congress to offer new legislative initiatives.

WOMEN'S ISSUES

The seeds of a resurgent women's movement were also being sown, although more quietly, during the Kennedy years. All across the political spectrum, women were speaking out on contemporary issues. The new conservative movement benefited from the energy of women

CHRONOLOGY

1954	*Brown v. Board of Education of Topeka* decision • SEATO formed • Arbenz government overthrown in Guatemala • Elvis Presley releases first record on Sun label • Geneva Peace Accords in Southeast Asia
1955	Montgomery bus boycott begins • *National Review* founded
1956	Suez Crisis • Anti-Soviet uprisings occur in Poland and Hungary • Federal Highway Act passed • Eisenhower reelected
1957	Eisenhower sends troops to Lebanon • Eisenhower sends troops to Little Rock • Congress passes Civil Rights Act, first civil rights legislation in 80 years • Soviets launch *Sputnik* • Gaither Report urges more defense spending
1958	National Defense Education Act passed by Congress • *The Affluent Society* published
1959	Khrushchev visits United States • Castro overthrows Batista in Cuba
1960	Civil Rights Act passed • U-2 incident ends Paris summit • Kennedy elected president • Sit-in demonstrations begin
1961	Bay of Pigs invasion fails • Berlin Wall erected • Freedom rides begin in the South • Kennedy announces Alliance for Progress
1962	Cuban Missile Crisis • Kennedy sends troops to University of Mississippi to enforce integration
1963	Civil rights activists undertake march on Washington • Betty Friedan's *The Feminine Mystique* published • Kennedy assassinated (November 22); Lyndon Johnson becomes president

such as Phyllis Schlafly, whose book *A Choice, Not an Echo* (1964) became one of the leading manifestos of the Republican Party's right wing. African American activists such as Bernice Johnson Reagon (whose career with the Freedom Singers combined music and social activism) and Fannie Lou Hamer (who helped to organize an integrated Mississippi Freedom Democratic Party) fought discrimination based on both race and gender. And during Kennedy's final year in office, 1963, Betty Friedan published *The Feminine Mystique*. Generally credited with helping to spark a new phase of the feminist movement, Friedan's book articulated the dissatisfactions that many middle-class women felt about the narrow confines of domestic life and the lack of public roles available to them.

To address women's issues, Kennedy appointed the Presidential Commission on the Status of Women, chaired by Eleanor Roosevelt. Negotiating differences between moderate and more militant members, the commission issued a report that documented discrimination against women in employment opportunities and wages. Kennedy responded with a presidential order designed to eliminate gender discrimination within the federal civil service system. His administration also supported the Equal Pay Act of 1963, which made it a federal crime for employers to pay lower wages to women who were doing the same work as men.

THE ASSASSINATION OF JOHN F. KENNEDY

By the fall of 1963 the Kennedy administration was preparing initiatives on civil rights and economic opportunity. Then, on November 22, 1963, John F. Kennedy was shot down as his presidential motorcade moved through Dallas, Texas. Police quickly arrested Lee Harvey Oswald as the alleged assassin. Oswald had ties to the Marcello crime family, had once lived in the Soviet Union, and had a bizarre set of political affiliations, especially with groups interested in Cuba. Oswald declared his innocence, but he was never brought to trial. Instead, Oswald himself was killed, while in the custody of the Dallas police, by Jack Ruby, a nightclub owner who also had links to powerful crime figures. A lengthy but flawed investigation by a special commission headed by Chief Justice Earl Warren concluded that both Oswald and Ruby had acted alone—but these claims came under increasing scrutiny. In 1978 a special panel of the House of Representatives claimed that Kennedy might have been the victim of an assassination plot, perhaps involving organized crime.

A variety of other theories about Kennedy's assassination sprang up, including one, which pointed toward the CIA, advanced in Oliver Stone's film, *JFK* (1991). Although most historians ridiculed Stone's scenario, his film reignited controversy over the report issued by the Warren commission. In response, Congress created the Assassinations Records Review Board as a means of preserving from destruction information about Kennedy's death.

CONCLUSION

After 1954, the Cold War fears associated with McCarthyism began to abate. Presidents Dwight Eisenhower and John F. Kennedy cautiously eased tensions with the Soviet Union, especially after Kennedy found himself on the brink of nuclear war over the presence of Soviet weapons in Cuba in 1962. Even so, both presidents continued to pursue anticommunist foreign policies that focused on the buildup of nuclear weapons, economic pressure, and covert activities. Developments in the Third World, particularly in Cuba and Southeast Asia, became of growing concern.

At home, the period from 1954 to 1963 was one of generally steady economic growth. A cornucopia of new consumer products encouraged talk about an age of affluence but also produced apprehension about conformity, mass culture, and the problems of youth. At the same time, the concerns of racial minorities and other people who were missing out on this period's general affluence increasingly moved to the center of public debates over the meaning of liberty and equality. The Eisenhower administration, many critics charged, seemed too reluctant to use the power of government to fight segregation or to create economic conditions that would distribute the benefits of affluence more widely.

Although Kennedy did not rush to deal with domestic issues, the press of events gradually forced his administration to use government power to confront racial discrimination and advance the cause of equality at home. When Kennedy was killed in November 1963, a new kind of insurgent politics, growing out of the battle against racial discrimination in the Deep South, was beginning to transform political life in the United States.

In the post-Kennedy era, debates would become riveted around issues related to the government's exercise of power: Was the U.S. spreading liberty in Vietnam? Was it sufficiently active in pursuing equality for racial minorities and the poor? Lyndon Johnson's troubled presidency would grapple with these questions.

AMERICA DURING ITS LONGEST WAR, 1963–1974

THE GREAT SOCIETY ∽ ESCALATION IN VIETNAM

THE WAR AT HOME ∽ THE NIXON YEARS, 1969–1974

FOREIGN POLICY UNDER NIXON AND KISSINGER

THE WARS OF WATERGATE

Lyndon Baines Johnson promised to finish what John F. Kennedy had begun. Ultimately though, Johnson's troubled presidency bore little resemblance to John Kennedy's thousand days of "Camelot."

In Southeast Asia, Johnson faced a crucial decision: Should the United States introduce its own forces and weaponry in order to prop up its South Vietnamese ally? If Johnson did this, what would be the consequences?

At home, Johnson enthusiastically mobilized the federal government's power in order to promote greater equality. But could federal action produce the Great Society that Johnson envisioned?

Many Americans, particularly young people, began to dissent from Johnson's foreign and domestic policies. As a result of a war overseas and dissent at home, the late 1960s and early 1970s became a time of increasingly sharp political and cultural polarization. Richard Nixon's presidency contributed to this polarization. By the end of America's longest war and the Watergate crisis that caused Nixon's resignation, the nation's political culture and social fabric differed significantly from what Johnson had inherited from Kennedy in 1963.

THE GREAT SOCIETY

Johnson lacked Kennedy's charisma, but he possessed political assets of his own. As a member of the House of Representatives during the late 1930s and early 1940s and majority leader of the U.S. Senate in the 1950s, the gangling Texan became the consummate legislative horse trader. Few issues, Johnson believed, defied consensus. Nearly everyone could be flattered, cajoled, even threatened into lending him their support. During his time in Congress, LBJ's wealthy Texas benefactors gained valuable oil and gas concessions and lucrative construction contracts, while Johnson himself acquired a personal fortune. At the same time, the growth of Dallas, Houston, and other cities and the economic boom throughout the Southwest owed much to Johnson's skill in pushing measures such as federally funded irrigation and space-exploration projects through Congress.

Kennedy's death gave Johnson the opportunity to fulfill his dreams of transforming the nation, just as he had transformed Dallas and Houston. Confident that he could use the tactics he had employed in the Senate to build a national consensus for the expansion of government power, Johnson began by urging Congress to honor JFK's memory by passing legislation that Kennedy's administration had originated.

COMPLETING KENNEDY'S INITIATIVES

More knowledgeable in the ways of Congress than Kennedy, Johnson quickly completed the major domestic goals of JFK's New Frontier. Working behind the scenes, Johnson secured passage of Kennedy's proposed $10 billion tax cut, a measure intended to stimulate the economy. Although historians differ on how much this tax cut contributed to the economic boom of the mid-1960s, it *appeared* to work. GNP rose 7 percent in 1964 and 8 percent the following year; unemployment dropped to about 5 percent; and consumer prices rose by less than 3 percent.

Johnson also built on Kennedy-era plans for addressing the problem of poverty. In his January 1964 State of the Union address, Johnson announced that his administration was declaring "an unconditional war on poverty in America." In August 1964 Congress created the Office of Economic Opportunity (OEO) to coordinate the various elements of a multifaceted program. The Economic Opportunity Act of 1964, in addition to establishing OEO, mandated loans for rural and small-business development; established a program of work training called the Jobs Corps; created a domestic version of the Peace Corps program, called VISTA; provided low-wage jobs, primarily in urban areas, for young people; began a work-study plan to assist college students; and, most important, authorized the creation of additional federally funded social programs that were to be designed in concert with local community groups.

Finally, Johnson secured passage of civil rights legislation. In 1964 he helped push an expanded version of Kennedy's civil rights bill through Congress. Championing the bill as a memorial to Kennedy, he nevertheless recognized that southern segregationists in the Democratic Party would try to delay and dilute the measure. Consequently, he successfully lobbied key Republicans for their support. Passed in July 1964 after lengthy delaying tactics by southerners, the Civil Rights Act of 1964, administered by a new Equal Employment Opportunity Commission (EEOC), strengthened federal remedies for fighting job discrimination. It also prohibited racial discrimination in public accommodations connected with interstate commerce, such as hotels and restaurants. Moreover, Title VII, a provision added to the bill during the legislative debates, barred discrimination based on sex, a provision that became extremely important to the women's movement.

THE ELECTION OF 1964

Civil rights legislation was also a testimony to the moral power of civil rights workers. During the summer of 1964 a coalition of civil rights organizations enlisted nearly a thousand volunteers to help register voters in Mississippi—an operation they called "Freedom Summer." During that violent summer, six volunteers were murdered by segregationists, but their fellow civil rights workers pressed forward, only to see their political work frustrated at the Democratic national convention. Pressured by Johnson, who used the FBI to gather information on dissidents, party leaders seated Mississippi's "regular" all-white delegates rather than members of the alternative (and racially diverse) "Freedom Democratic Party."

After this rebuff, civil rights activists recalled their earlier suspicions about Lyndon Johnson and the national Democratic Party. Johnson did seem more committed to change than John Kennedy had been, but would LBJ—and Hubert Humphrey, Johnson's personal choice for his vice presidential running mate—continue to press for antidiscrimination measures after the election? This question became all the more important once it became apparent that Johnson would win the 1964 presidential race.

The Republicans nominated Senator Barry Goldwater of Arizona to oppose Johnson. Goldwater's strategists believed that an unabashedly conservative campaign would attract the millions of voters who were thought to be dissatisfied with both Democratic liberalism and moderate Republicanism. Goldwater denounced Johnson's foreign policies as too timid and Johnson's domestic programs as destructive of individual freedoms. Goldwater, one of eight Republican senators who had voted against the Civil Rights Act of 1964, had criticized the measure as a dangerous extension of power by the national government.

Goldwater's penchant for blurting out ill-considered opinions allowed critics to picture him as fanatical, unpredictable, and reactionary. Goldwater suggested that people who feared nuclear war were "silly and sissified." U.S. weapons were so accurate, he once quipped, that the military could target the men's room in the Kremlin. Reinforcing his "radical-right" image, Goldwater declared in his acceptance speech at the 1964 Republican convention that "extremism in the pursuit of liberty is no vice" and "moderation in the pursuit of justice is no virtue."

Even many Republican voters came to view Goldwater as too extreme, and he led the GOP to a crushing defeat in November. Johnson carried 44 states and won more than 60 percent of the popular vote; in addition, Democrats gained 38 new seats in Congress. Most political pundits immediately hailed the 1964 election as a triumph for Johnson's vision of domestic policymaking.

In retrospect, however, the 1964 election presaged significant political changes that would eventually erode support for Johnson. During the Democratic primaries, for example, Alabama's segregationist governor, George Wallace, had run strongly against the president in several northern states. An opponent of civil rights legislation, Wallace attacked federal "meddling" in local affairs and demonstrated the potential of a "white backlash" movement. The 1964 election was the last time the Democratic Party would capture the White House by hewing to the New Deal–Fair Deal tradition of urging expanded use of governmental power at home.

Goldwater's defeat seemed to invigorate his conservative supporters. His youthful campaign staff had pioneered several innovative stratagems such as direct mail fund-raising. By refining these tactics in future campaigns, conservative strategists helped to make the 1964 election the beginning, not the end, of the Republican Party's movement to the right. Moreover, Goldwater's stand against the Civil Rights Act of 1964 helped him carry five southern states, and these victories convinced Republicans that opposition to antidiscrimination measures by Washington would continue to attract white voters in the South who had once been solidly Democratic.

The Goldwater effort also propelled an attractive group of conservative leaders into national politics. Ronald Reagan, the actor and corporate spokesperson, proved such an effective campaigner in 1964 that conservative Republicans began to groom him for a political career. Other prominent conservatives such as William Rehnquist also entered national politics through the 1964 campaign. In the immediate aftermath of Goldwater's defeat, however, the prospect that a President Ronald Reagan would one day nominate William

Rehnquist to be Chief Justice of the United States seemed beyond any conservative's wildest dream (see Chapter 31).

LYNDON JOHNSON'S GREAT SOCIETY

Lyndon Johnson wanted to capitalize quickly on his electoral victory. Enjoying broad support in Congress, Johnson announced his plans for a "Great Society," an array of programs funded by the national government, that he envisioned would bring economic opportunity to all the people who had missed the prosperity of the 1950s and early 1960s. Some of the Great Society programs fulfilled the dreams of Johnson's Democratic predecessors. Nationally funded medical coverage for the elderly (Medicare) and for low-income citizens (Medicaid) culminated efforts begun during the New Deal and revived during the Fair Deal. Similarly, an addition to the president's cabinet, the Department of Housing and Urban Development (HUD), built upon earlier plans for coordinating urban revitalization programs. Finally, the Voting Rights Act of 1965, which mandated federal oversight of elections in the South, seemed to cap federal efforts begun during the 1930s to end racial discrimination in political life.

The array of initiatives developed under Johnson's "War on Poverty" heartened his supporters and appalled his conservative critics. The "Model Cities Program" was intended to demonstrate how to reconstruct cities without the inequality that had marked the urban renewal efforts of the 1950s; rent supplements were designed to help low-income families maintain and eventually upgrade their living conditions; the expanded Food Stamp program was aimed at improving nutritional levels; Head Start was to help preschool youngsters from low-income families climb the educational ladder; a variety of other federally financed educational programs would upgrade classroom instruction throughout the nation, especially in low-income neighborhoods; and a legal services program would provide legal advice and access to the court system for those who could not afford private attorneys. These initiatives were intended to build services, funded by federal tax dollars, to help people fight their own way out of economic distress.

The Great Society's Community Action Program (CAP) also promised to empower grassroots activists. It encouraged citizens, working through local organizations, to design community-based projects that would be financed from Washington. By promoting "maximum feasible participation" by citizens themselves, CAP was supposed to spark the kind of community-based democracy that could transform the entire political system.

EVALUATING THE GREAT SOCIETY

Why did the Great Society become so controversial? Most obviously, Johnson's dramatic extension of Washington's power rekindled old debates about the proper role of the national government. In addition, the president's extravagant rhetoric, with its promise of an "unconditional" victory over poverty, raised expectations that could not be met in one presidency, or even in one generation. Most important, the faith that economic growth would generate the tax revenues needed to fund expanding social programs simply collapsed with the onset of economic problems during the late 1960s. In 1964 Lyndon Johnson assumed that continued prosperity would allow him to build a consensus for the Great Society; worsening economic conditions, however, made greater federal spending for domestic programs a highly divisive policy.

Historians have evaluated Lyndon Johnson's Great Society programs in a variety of ways. Conservatives have subjected them to harsh criticism. Charles Murray's influential *Losing*

Ground (1984) set the tone by charging that massive government expenditures during the Johnson years had encouraged antisocial behavior. Lured by welfare payments, he argued, many people with low incomes had abandoned the goals of marrying, settling down, and seeking jobs. According to this view, the Great Society's spending had also created huge government deficits that slowed economic growth. Had the nation's economic structure not been weakened by the Great Society, virtually everyone in America could have come to enjoy a middle-class lifestyle. This conservative argument condemned Johnson's program as the cause, not the remedy, for persistent economic inequality in America.

Historians more sympathetic to Johnson's approach have vigorously rejected the conservative argument. They find scant evidence for the claim that low-income people preferred welfare to meaningful work. Spending on the military sector far outstripped that for social programs and seemed the principal cause of burgeoning government deficits. Moreover, they note, expenditures on Great Society programs neither matched Johnson's promises nor commanded the massive amounts claimed by conservatives.

Historians on the left have criticized the Great Society's failure to challenge the prevailing distribution of political and economic power. The Johnson administration, they argue, remained closely wedded to large-scale bureaucratic solutions for problems that had many local variations. In addition, they point out, the Great Society never sought a redistribution of wealth and income. For these critics, the Great Society was a noble ideal that was never seriously implemented.

Although historians evaluate the impact of the Great Society in very different ways, there is broad agreement that Johnson's domestic agenda left its mark on American life. It represented the first significant new outlay of federal dollars for domestic social programs since the New Deal. Spending on such programs increased more than 10 percent in every year of Johnson's presidency. Within a decade of the beginning of the Great Society, programs such as Medicaid, legal services, and job training provided low-income individuals with some of the services more affluent Americans had long taken for granted.

The Great Society, by extending the reach of the welfare state that had begun to appear in the United States during the 1930s, ignited increasingly intense public debate over how best to use the power and resources of the national government. In seeking to extend tangible assistance to the poor, how could policymakers follow the distinction between people who seemed to deserve assistance and those who seemed to be, in Lyndon Johnson's own formulation, seeking a "hand-out" rather than a "hand-up"? Partisan debates over government's social welfare policies would continue throughout the rest of the century.

Escalation in Vietnam

Johnson's crusade to build a Great Society at home had its counterpart in an ambitious extension of U.S. power abroad. The escalation of the war in Vietnam demanded increasingly more of the administration's energy and resources. Eventually, it alienated many Americans, especially the young, and divided the entire nation.

The Tonkin Gulf Resolution

Immediately after John Kennedy's assassination in November 1963, Johnson had avoided widening the war in Vietnam. But he did not wish to appear "soft" on communism. Seeing no alternative to backing the government in South Vietnam, he accepted his military advisers' recommendation to forestall enemy offensives in the South by staging air strikes against the North. He prepared a congressional resolution authorizing such an escalation of hostilities.

Events in the Gulf of Tonkin, off the coast of North Vietnam, provided him with a rationale for taking the resolution to Congress. On August 1, 1964, the U.S. destroyer *Maddox* exchanged fire with North Vietnamese torpedo boats while conducting an intelligence-gathering mission. Three days later, the *Maddox* returned with the destroyer *Turner Joy* and, amid severe weather conditions, reported a torpedo attack. Although the *Maddox*'s commander radioed that the "attack" might have been a false report, Johnson proclaimed that U.S. forces had been the target of "unprovoked aggression." He rushed the resolution to Congress, where he received overwhelming approval to take "all necessary measures to repel armed attack." Johnson subsequently used this Tonkin Gulf Resolution as tantamount to a congressional declaration of war.

Despite his moves in the Gulf of Tonkin, the president was still able to position himself as a cautious moderate during the presidential campaign of 1964. When Goldwater urged stronger measures against North Vietnam and mentioned the possible use of tactical nuclear weapons, Johnson's campaign managers portrayed Goldwater as a threat to the survival of civilization. A TV commercial depicted a little girl picking the petals from a daisy as a nuclear bomb exploded onscreen. The implication was that a Goldwater victory would bring nuclear holocaust. Johnson promised not to commit American troops to fight a land war in Asia.

Soon after the election, however, Johnson further escalated the war. The 1963 coup against Diem (see Chapter 28) had left a political vacuum in the South. The incompetence of the South's new military-led government sparked growing discontent. Soldiers deserted at an alarming rate. In January 1965, the regime fell, and factionalism prevented any stable government from emerging in its wake.

Without any credible or effective government in South Vietnam, Johnson increasingly worried over his options. Should the pursuit of anticommunism turn the Vietnamese struggle into "America's war"? What would be the public backlash against a possible communist victory? Could the United States escalate and win the war without provoking a deadly clash with China or even the Soviet Union?

Johnson's advisers offered conflicting views. National Security Adviser McGeorge Bundy predicted inevitable defeat unless the United States sharply escalated its military role. Walt Rostow assured Johnson that a determined effort would bring a clear-cut victory. If all routes to victory are denied the enemy, he advised, they will give up. Undersecretary of State George Ball, by contrast, warned that greater Americanization of the war would bring defeat, not victory. "The South Vietnamese are losing the war," he wrote, and "no one has demonstrated that a white ground force of whatever size can win a guerrilla war . . . in jungle terrain in the midst of a population that refuses cooperation to the white forces." The Joint Chiefs of Staff, afflicted by interservice rivalries, provided differing military assessments and no clear advice.

Although privately doubting the long-term prospects for success, Johnson nonetheless feared the immediate political hazards of a U.S. pullout from Vietnam. Domestic criticism of a communist victory in South Vietnam, he believed, would certainly endanger his Great Society programs. Moreover, to those who argued that Vietnam had little strategic importance to the United States, Johnson countered that U.S. withdrawal would set off a "domino effect": encouraging Castro-style insurgencies in Latin America, increasing pressure on West Berlin, and damaging American credibility around the world.

Swayed by political calculations, Johnson decided on a sustained campaign of bombing in North Vietnam, code-named "Rolling Thunder." While the bombing was going on, he deployed

U.S. ground forces to regain territory in the South, expanded covert operations, and stepped up economic aid to the beleaguered Saigon government. Only six months into his new term, with both civilian and military advisers divided in their recommendations, Johnson committed the United States to full-scale war against North Vietnam.

THE WAR WIDENS

The war grew more intense throughout 1965. U.S. military commanders called for an all-out effort to escalate the number of casualties inflicted. Accordingly, the administration authorized the use of napalm, a chemical that charred both foliage and people, and allowed the Air Force to bomb new targets. Additional combat troops arrived to secure enclaves in the South. Each escalation seemed to make further escalation inevitable. North Vietnam's rejection of an unrealistic "peace plan," outlined by Johnson in a speech in April 1965, became a pretext for again raising the levels of U.S. military spending and action. North Vietnam's leader, Ho Chi Minh, was playing the same game of escalation and attrition, convinced that Johnson commanded meager public and congressional support for continuing the costly war.

In April 1965, Johnson brought his anticommunist crusade closer to home. Prompted by exaggerated reports of a communist threat in the Dominican Republic, Johnson sent American troops to unseat a left-leaning, elected president and to install a government favorable to U.S. economic interests. This U.S. incursion violated a long-standing, "good neighbor" pledge not to intervene militarily in the Western Hemisphere. Although the action was criticized throughout Latin America, the seemingly successful military ouster of a leftist regime boosted the administration's determination to hold the line against communism in Vietnam.

During the spring of 1965, as the fifth government since Diem's death took office in Saigon, U.S. strategists were still puzzling over how to prop up its South Vietnamese ally. The commander in charge of the American effort, General William Westmoreland, recommended moving U.S. forces out of their enclaves and sending them on "search and destroy" missions. In July, Johnson dispatched 50,000 additional troops to Vietnam. He also approved saturation bombing of the countryside in the South and intensified bombing of the North.

Some of his advisers urged Johnson to admit candidly to the public that the scope of the war was being steadily enlarged. They also recommended either an outright declaration of war or emergency legislation that would formally put the United States on a wartime footing, so that the president could wield the economic and informational controls that past administrations had used in conflicts of this magnitude. But Johnson feared that assuming the formal status of a belligerent would provoke the Soviet Union or China. He also worried about arousing greater protests from Congress and the public. Rather than risk open debate that might reveal his shallow political support, Johnson decided to stress the administration's efforts to negotiate and to pretend that the war was not a war.

Over the next three years, the number of American troops increased from 50,000 to 535,000. Operation RANCHHAND scorched South Vietnam's crop lands and defoliated half its forests in an effort to eliminate the natural cover for enemy troop movements. Bombs leveled North Vietnamese cities and pummeled the villages and inhabitants of "free-fire zones" (designated areas in which anything was considered a fair target) in the South. Still, Johnson was careful to avoid bombing too close to the Chinese border or doing anything else that might provoke either Chinese or Soviet entry into the war.

The weekly body count of enemy dead became the measure by which the Johnson administration gauged the war's progress. Estimates that a kill ratio of 10 to 1 would force the North to

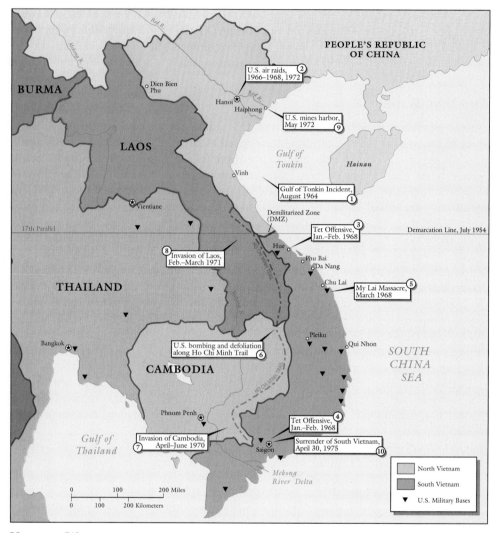

VIETNAM WAR

surrender encouraged the military to inflate body count figures and to engage in indiscriminate killing. Johnson welcomed figures suggesting that "victory was around the corner." Actually, North Vietnam was controlling its losses by concealing troops under the jungle canopy that remained. The North was able to channel a constant flow of supplies into the South through a shifting network of jungle paths called the Ho Chi Minh Trail. The war had reached a stalemate, but few members of Johnson's administration would admit it.

The extent of the destruction wreaked by the U.S. effort gave North Vietnamese leaders a decided propaganda advantage. Critics around the world condemned the escalation of American attacks. The Soviet Union and China increased their aid to Ho Chi Minh. Both at home and abroad, Johnson administration officials were hounded by protesters almost everywhere they went.

Meanwhile, the government in Saigon was reeling under the devastation of its countryside, the destabilizing effect of the flood of U.S. dollars on its economy, and the corruption of its politicians. So-called "pacification" and "strategic hamlet" programs, which brought Vietnamese farmers together in tightly guarded villages, sounded viable in Washington but caused further chaos by uprooting one in four South Vietnamese from their villages and ancestral lands. Buddhist priests persistently demonstrated against foreign influence. When Generals Nguyen Van Thieu and Nguyen Cao Ky, who had led the government since 1965, held elections in 1967 to legitimate their regime, their narrow margin of victory merely highlighted their weakness.

THE MEDIA AND THE WAR

Criticism against the war continued to mount. In most earlier wars, Congress had imposed strict controls on what journalists could report to the public. Because the Vietnam War was undeclared, Johnson had to resort to informal ways of managing information. With television coverage making Vietnam a "living room war," Johnson kept three TV sets playing in his office in order to monitor the major networks. Sometimes he would phone the news anchors after their broadcasts and castigate them for their stories. Increasingly sensitive to criticism, Johnson equated any question or doubt about his policy in Vietnam with a lack of patriotism.

Antiwar activists were equally disturbed by what they regarded as the media's uncritical reporting on the war. Most of the reporters, they claimed, relied on official handouts for their stories and took pains to avoid offending anyone at the White House. Indeed, especially in the early years, few reporters filed hard-hitting stories. In time, however, news coverage and its impact became more critical. The unrelenting images of destruction on the nightly news turned people against the war. In addition, a few journalists forthrightly expressed their opposition. Harrison Salisbury of *The New York Times* sent reports from Vietnam that dramatized the destructiveness of U.S. bombing missions. Gloria Emerson wrote reports picturing the war as a class-based effort in which the United States used poor and disproportionately nonwhite fighting forces, while rich men with draft-exempt sons raked in war profits.

As the war dragged on, Americans became polarized into "hawks" and "doves." Johnson insisted that he was merely following the policy of containment favored by Eisenhower and Kennedy. Secretary of State Dean Rusk spoke of the dangers of "appeasement." But influential senators warned of misplaced priorities and an "arrogance of power." Meanwhile, antiwar protestors began to challenge the structure of American society itself.

THE WAR AT HOME

Millions came to oppose the war in Southeast Asia, and backing eroded for the Great Society at home. Tensions that had been slowly building over recent years appeared to be reaching a critical point.

THE RISE OF THE NEW LEFT

During the early 1960s small groups of young people, many of them college students, came to reject the welfare-state policies of the postwar years. In 1962, two years after activists on the right had formed Young Americans for Freedom (YAF), insurgents on the left established a political organization called Students for a Democratic Society (SDS). Although SDS endorsed familiar causes, especially the fight against racial discrimination, its founding "Port Huron Statement" also spoke of new issues: the "loneliness, estrangement, isolation" of postwar society.

SDS became part of a new political initiative, popularly known as the "New Left," that tried to distance itself from both the welfare-state policies of the Great Society and the "old" communist-inspired Left. By confronting the dominant culture, which allegedly valued bureaucratic expertise over citizen engagement and conspicuous consumption over meaningful work, members of the New Left sought to create an alternative social vision. They called for "participatory democracy," grass-roots politics responsive to the wishes of local communities rather than the preferences of national elites.

During the early 1960s, many young, white college students found inspiration from the antidiscrimination movement in the Deep South. Risking racist violence, they went to the South where they forged bonds of community with African American activists. Some stayed in the South or moved on to political projects in northern neighborhoods. Others returned to their college campuses and joined protests against both the war in Southeast Asia and social conditions at home.

These dissenting students denounced the nation's prestigious colleges and universities as part of a vast "establishment" that resisted significant change. Giant universities, they claimed, seemed oblivious to the social and moral implications of their war-related research. Student dissidents charged faculty and administrators with ignoring the relevant issues of the day in favor of traditional, required courses. Moreover, restrictions on personal freedoms, such as student dress codes and mandatory dormitory hours, were labeled as relics of an authoritarian past in which colleges and universities acted *in loco parentis* (in place of parents). During the Berkeley "student revolt" of 1964 and 1965, students and sympathetic faculty protested the university administration's restrictions on political activity on campus and then moved on to broader issues such as Vietnam and racism.

By 1966 the war in Vietnam had come to dominate the agenda of student protesters. For young men, the antiwar movement became, in part, a matter of self-interest; when they reached age 18 they were required by federal law to register for possible military service. Local draft boards usually granted men who were attending college a student deferment, but these expired upon graduation. The burning of draft cards, as a symbolic protest against both the war and universal military service for men, became a central feature of many antiwar protests.

Meanwhile, many campuses became embroiled in bitter strife. At "teach-ins," supporters and opponents of the war presented their positions and debated the morality of the involvement of universities in national security policies. Teach-ins soon gave way to less-structured demonstrations. As antiwar sentiments grew more intense, campus supporters of the war claimed that *their* right to free speech was being threatened. Conservatives, along with many moderates, pressured college administrators to crack down on "troublemakers" and made opposition to campus protests a prominent part of their new agenda.

THE COUNTERCULTURE

Accompanying the spread of New Left politics was the rise of an antiestablishment "counterculture." Even though only a relatively small percentage of young people fully embraced countercultural values, they came to symbolize the youthful ferment of the late 1960s. Ridiculing

AMERICAN ATTITUDES TOWARD THE VIETNAM WAR   Responses to the question: "Do you think that the United States made a mistake in sending troops to fight there?"

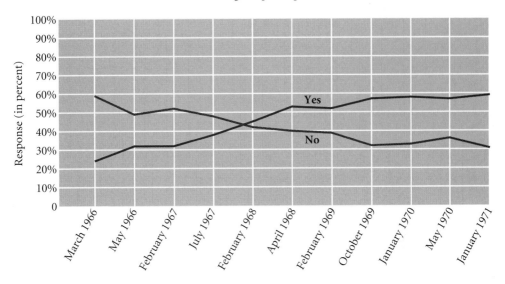

traditional attitudes on such matters as clothing, hair styles, and sexuality, devotees of the counterculture sought an open and experimental approach to daily life. Caricatured as "hippies," they dabbled with mind-altering drugs, communal living arrangements, and new forms of folk-rock music. Bob Dylan's "Like a Rolling Stone" (1965) exploded onto the Top 40 chart of AM radio. Although Dylan never sought the role, members of the counterculture and the media cast him as the musical prophet for an entire generation.

The trappings of the counterculture soon found a ready market among middle-class consumers. Impressed by the success of hippie bands like San Francisco's Grateful Dead and the Jefferson Airplane, the mass culture industry welcomed the youth rebellion. The Rolling Stones made big money with their ode to a "Street Fighting Man" (1968). The Beatles made even more money and attracted critical acclaim with *Sgt. Pepper's Lonely Hearts Club Band* (1967) and *The White Album* (1968). Hollywood tapped the youth culture market with *The Graduate* (1967) and *Bonnie and Clyde* (1967) and followed up with films, such as *Easy Rider* (1969) and *Wild in the Streets* (1968), that portrayed adult authority figures as vampirish ravagers of youth.

A lively debate arose over the media's coverage of the counterculture. Critics of the youth culture charged the media with spreading dangerous, antisocial images. According to conservative critics, the media's extensive coverage of demonstrations in which young radicals and countercultural musicians joined with older opponents of the war helped to exaggerate the strength of the antiwar movement. At the same time, ironically, veterans of earlier New Left protests claimed that the media's unrelenting attention to the counterculture actually undercut antiwar politics.

The media's coverage of an antiwar march on the Pentagon in 1967 crystallized this debate. Rejecting political speeches and the ritualistic burning of draft cards as too dull, some of the marchers amused themselves by trying to levitate the Pentagon. Abbie Hoffman, self-proclaimed leader of the fictitious Youth International Party (the "Yippies"), facetiously urged "loot-ins at department stores to strike at the property fetish that underlies genocidal war" in Vietnam. Although the Pentagon march played well as a media spectacle, its impact on political events was uncertain. At best, dramatic television clips conveyed the passion of dissenters; at worst, a colorful mélange of media-conscious demonstrators helped to fuel polarization throughout American society.

FROM CIVIL RIGHTS TO BLACK POWER

A similar debate developed over media images of the increasingly militant protests against racial discrimination. Early on, leaders in the fight against discrimination, notably Dr. Martin Luther King Jr., had recognized the benefits to be derived from media coverage. During King's 1965 drive to win access to the ballot box for African Americans, TV pictures of the racist violence in Selma, Alabama, helped to galvanize support for federal legislation. President Johnson used television to dramatize his support for voting-rights legislation.

At the same time, the media became the forum for fierce debates over what was increasingly being called a "racial crisis." Conservatives argued that subversive agitators were provoking conflict and violence and that only a good dose of law and order would ease urban racial tensions. Social activists argued that a complex mix of racism, lack of educational and

VIOLENCE IN DETROIT, 1967   Outbreaks of violence, rooted in economic inequality and racial tension, swept through many U.S. cities between 1965 and 1969. The 1967 violence in Detroit, which federal troops had to quell, left many African American neighborhoods in ruin.

employment opportunities, and inadequate government responses were producing the frustration and despair that burst forth in sporadic racial violence. This debate intensified in 1965 in the wake of a devastating racial conflict in Los Angeles. A confrontation between a white Highway Patrol officer and a black motorist escalated into six days of urban violence, centered in the largely African American community of Watts in South-Central Los Angeles. Thirty-four people died; hundreds of businesses and homes were burned; the National Guard patrolled the streets of Los Angeles; and TV cameras framed the conflagration as an ongoing media spectacle. Violence erupted in many other U.S. cities during the remainder of the decade.

Meanwhile, a radical "Black Power" movement emerged. A charismatic preacher named Malcolm X had heralded its arrival. A spokesperson for the Nation of Islam, Malcolm X preached a message fundamentally at odds with that of the leaders of the civil rights movement. He proclaimed that integration was unworkable. Although he never called for violent confrontation, he did endorse self-defense "by any means necessary."

Malcolm X offered more than angry rhetoric. He called for renewed pride in the African American heritage and for vigorous efforts at community reconstruction. In order to revitalize their contemporary institutions, he urged African Americans to "launch a cultural revolution to unbrainwash an entire people." Seeking to forge a broader movement, Malcolm X eventually broke from the Nation of Islam and established his own Organization of Afro-American Unity. Murdered in 1965 by political enemies from the Nation of Islam, Malcolm X remained a powerful symbol of both militant politics and a renewed pride in African American culture.

A new generation of African Americans picked up the mantle of Malcolm X. Disdaining the older integrationist agenda, the youthful militants embraced the word "black." "Black power" advocates soon caught the media's attention and began to gain support within African American communities. "Black Is Beautiful" became the watchword. James Brown captured this new spirit. His "Say It Loud, I'm Black and Proud" encapsulated the cultural message of the Black Power movement.

The Black Power crusade raised philosophical and tactical disagreements within the antidiscrimination movement. Angered by the slow pace of civil rights litigation, some younger African Americans, including Stokely Carmichael, who became head of the Student Non-Violent Coordinating Committee (SNCC) in 1966, and members of the Black Panther Party, escalated attacks on the gradualist and nonviolent methods of the established civil rights organizations such as King's Southern Christian Leadership Conference. A Black Panther manifesto, for example, called for community "self-defense" groups as protection against police harassment, the release from jail of all African American prisoners (on the assumption that none had received fair trials in racist courts), and guaranteed employment for all citizens. Although opinion surveys suggested that the vast majority of African Americans still supported the integrationist agenda, the new modes of insurgency were unraveling the established civil rights alliance.

Within this social context, the Civil Rights Act of 1968 passed Congress. One provision of this omnibus law, popularly known as the Fair Housing Act, sought to eliminate racial discrimination in housing. But in response to charges that antidiscrimination legislation could illegally infringe on the rights of landlords and real estate agents, the act provided certain exemptions that rendered the law's enforcement provisions weak. Moreover, another section in the law made it a crime to cross state lines in order to incite a "riot." This antiriot provision was widely understood to be aimed at using the power of the federal government against radical political activists, particularly those connected with the Black Power movement.

1968: THE VIOLENCE OVERSEAS

In 1968, several shocking and violent events worsened political polarization. The first came in Vietnam. At the end of January, during a truce in observance of Tet, the lunar new year celebration, troops of the National Liberation Front (NLF) joined North Vietnamese forces in a series of coordinated surprise attacks throughout South Vietnam. During two weeks of intense fighting, they suffered heavy casualties and made no significant military gains. But Tet turned out to be a serious psychological defeat for the United States because it suggested that Johnson's claims about an imminent South Vietnamese–United States victory were not to be trusted. When General Westmoreland asked for 206,000 additional troops, most of Johnson's closest advisers urged that South Vietnamese troops be required to assume more of the military burden. Johnson accepted these arguments, realizing that such a large troop increase would have fanned antiwar opposition at home. In a way, Tet contributed to the beginning of a policy that would later be referred to as the "Vietnamization" of the war.

Although some analysts blamed the media for turning the Tet "victory" into a "defeat" by exaggerating the effect of the early attacks and by ignoring the heavy losses suffered by the NLF and the North Vietnamese, others pointed out that communist strength had caught the U.S. off guard. Faced with revolt in his own party, led by Senator Eugene McCarthy of Minnesota, Johnson suddenly declared on March 31, 1968, that he would not run for reelection. He halted the bombing of North Vietnam and promised to devote his remaining time in office to seeking an end to the war. McCarthy, campaigning on a peace platform, continued his election bid against Johnson's vice president and party stalwart, Hubert H. Humphrey.

1968: THE VIOLENCE AT HOME

One person who rejoiced at Johnson's withdrawal was Martin Luther King Jr. King hoped that the Democratic Party would now turn to an antiwar candidate, preferably Senator Robert Kennedy of New York, who could advance King's new vision of economic transformation for the United States. But on an April 4, 1968, trip to Memphis, Tennessee, in support of a strike by African American sanitation workers, King was assassinated, allegedly by a lone gunman named James Earl Ray.

As news of King's assassination spread, violence swept through black neighborhoods around the country. More than 100 cities and towns witnessed outbreaks; 39 people died; 75,000 regular and National Guard troops were called to duty. When Johnson proclaimed Sunday, April 7, as a day of national mourning for the slain civil rights leader, parts of Washington, D.C., were still ablaze.

Meanwhile, Robert Kennedy had entered the race for the Democratic presidential nomination. Campaigning at a feverish pace, Kennedy battled McCarthy in a series of primary elections, hoping to gain a majority of the convention delegates that had not already been pledged to Hubert Humphrey by the party's old-line bosses such as Richard J. Daley, mayor of Chicago. Then, on June 5, Kennedy fell victim to an assassin's bullets. Kennedy's nationally televised funeral was a disturbing reminder of King's recent murder and the assassination of his own brother nearly five years earlier.

The violence of 1968 continued. During the Republican national convention in Miami, as presidential candidate Richard Nixon was promising to restore "law and order," racial violence in that city killed four people. Later that summer, in Chicago, thousands of antiwar demonstrators converged on the Democratic Party's convention to protest the expected nomination of Humphrey, who was still supporting Johnson's policy in Vietnam. Responding to acts of provocation by demonstrators who seemed to welcome confrontation, members of the Chicago police department struck back with indiscriminate violence. Hubert Humphrey easily captured the Democratic nomination, but controversy over Johnson's Vietnam policies and the response to the antiwar demonstrations left the Democratic Party badly divided.

The Election of 1968

Both Humphrey and Nixon faced a serious challenge from the political right, spearheaded by Alabama's George Wallace. After running successfully in several northern Democratic primaries, Wallace decided to seek nationwide support as a third-party candidate. A grass-roots campaign eventually placed his American Independent Party on the presidential ballot in every state. Because Wallace's opposition to racial integration was well established, he could concentrate his fire on other controversial targets, particularly the counterculture and the antiwar movement. Moreover, Wallace recognized that many voters were beginning to lose faith in welfare-state programs and to see themselves as victims of an aloof, tax-and-spend bureaucracy in Washington.

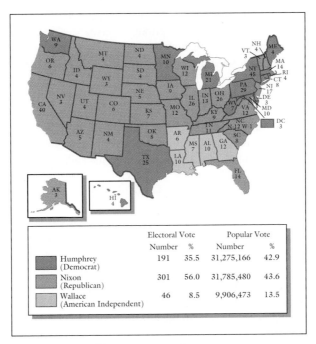

	Electoral Vote		Popular Vote	
	Number	%	Number	%
Humphrey (Democrat)	191	35.5	31,275,166	42.9
Nixon (Republican)	301	56.0	31,785,480	43.6
Wallace (American Independent)	46	8.5	9,906,473	13.5

Presidential Election, 1968

Wallace's candidacy exacerbated the political polarization of 1968. By threatening to prevent either major-party candidate from winning a majority of the electoral votes, it raised the possibility that the choice of the nation's president would rest with the House of Representatives and that Wallace himself could act as a power broker between Democrats and Republicans. In order to capitalize on right-wing dissent against U.S. foreign policy, Wallace chose the hawkish Air Force General Curtis LeMay as his running mate. LeMay quickly inflamed political passions when he complained that too many Americans had a "phobia" about the use of nuclear weapons. Political pundits immediately labeled Wallace and LeMay the "Bombsey Twins."

Nixon narrowly prevailed in November. Although he won 56 percent of the electoral vote, he out-polled Humphrey in the popular vote by less than 1 percent. Humphrey had benefited when Johnson ordered a pause in the bombing of North Vietnam and pledged to begin peace talks in Paris; and he helped his own cause with a belated decision to distance himself from Johnson's Vietnam policies. Still, Humphrey carried only Texas in the South. George Wallace picked up 46 electoral votes, all from the Deep South, and 13.5 percent of the popular vote. Nixon won five key southern states. Hinting that he had a plan for ending the war in Vietnam, he claimed to be the candidate most likely to restore tranquillity to the domestic front. But soon after taking office, Nixon embraced policies that proved every bit as divisive as those of Lyndon Johnson.

THE NIXON YEARS, 1969–1974

Raised in a modest Quaker home in southern California, Richard Nixon graduated from Whittier College, a small Quaker school near his hometown. Three years at Duke Law School, a hitch in the Navy during the Second World War, and a job in Franklin Roosevelt's wartime bureaucracy gave Nixon a taste of new, cosmopolitan worlds. After the war, however, he returned to his small-town California law practice before beginning a meteoric political career that took him to the House of Representatives in 1946, the Senate in 1950, and the vice presidency in 1952.

Nixon seemed to thrive on seeking enemies, at home and abroad, and on confronting a constant series of personal challenges. He titled an early memoir of his political life *Six Crises*. Devastated by his narrow defeat by Kennedy in 1960, Nixon seemed crushed politically when, in 1962, he failed to win the governorship of California. At a postelection press conference, a bitter Nixon announced his political retirement. But Barry Goldwater's 1964 defeat and Johnson's problems helped to revive his political fortunes. During his presidency (1969–1974) the "new" Nixon seemed increasingly like the old Nixon in his ability to inflame, rather than to calm, political passions.

THE ECONOMY

Nixon's presidency coincided with a series of economic problems unthinkable only a decade earlier. No simple cause can account for these difficulties, but most analyses begin with the war in Vietnam. This expensive military commitment, along with fundamental changes in the world economy, brought an end to the economic growth of the previous two decades.

Lyndon Johnson, determined to stave off defeat in Indochina without cutting Great Society programs, had concealed the rising costs of the war from his own advisers. Johnson bequeathed Nixon a deteriorating (though still favorable) balance of trade and a rising rate of inflation. Between 1960 and 1965, consumer prices had risen on average only about 1 percent a year; by 1968, the rate exceeded 4 percent.

Nixon pledged to cut war costs by reducing troop levels, but this strategy continued to drain economic resources. Moreover, although Nixon spoke of reducing domestic spending, he soon discovered that many federal programs still enjoyed support in the Democrat-controlled Congress and among voters. During his first years in office, the percentage of federal funds spent on domestic programs increased steadily.

Meanwhile, unemployment soared, topping 6 percent by 1971. According to conventional wisdom, expressed in a technical economic concept called "the Phillips curve," when unemployment rises, prices should remain constant or even decline. Yet *both* unemployment and inflation were rising. Economists invented the term "stagflation" to describe this puzzling, unprecedented convergence of economic stagnation and price inflation. Along with stagflation, U.S. exports were becoming less competitive in international markets, and in 1971, for the first time in the 20th century, the United States ran a trade deficit, importing more products than it exported.

Long identified as an opponent of government regulation of the economy but fearful of the political consequences of stagflation and the trade deficit, Nixon searched for a cure for the nation's economic ills. Suddenly he proclaimed himself a believer in greater government management of the economy. In August 1971 he announced a "new economic policy" that mandated a 90-day freeze on any increase in wages and prices, to be followed by government monitoring to detect "excessive" increases in either.

To try to reverse the trade deficit, Nixon also revised the U.S. relationship to the world monetary structure. Ever since the 1944 Bretton Woods agreement (see Chapter 26), the value of the dollar had been tied to the value of gold at $35 for every ounce. This meant that the United States was prepared to exchange U.S. dollars for gold at that rate if any other nation's central bank requested it to do so. Other countries had fixed their own exchange rates against the dollar. But U.S. trade deficits undermined the value of the American dollar, enabling foreign banks to exchange dollars for gold at highly favorable rates. Consequently, in August 1971 the Nixon administration abandoned the fixed gold-to-dollar ratio, announcing that the dollar would be free to "float" against the prevailing market price of gold and against all other currencies. In 1973, the Nixon administration devalued the dollar, cheapening the price of American goods in foreign markets in order to make them more competitive. The strategy fundamentally altered the international economic order but did little to arrest the deterioration of U.S. trade balances.

SOCIAL POLICY

At the urging of Daniel Patrick Moynihan, a Democrat who became Nixon's chief adviser on domestic policy, Nixon began to consider a drastic revision of the nation's welfare programs. After heated debates within his inner circle, Nixon unveiled his Family Assistance Plan (FAP) during a TV address in August 1969. The centerpiece of this complex policy package was the replacement of most welfare programs, including the controversial Aid to Families with Dependent Children (AFDC), with a guaranteed annual income for all families. AFDC provided government payments to cover basic costs of care for low-income children who had lost the support of a bread-winning parent. By 1970, half of all persons in families headed by women were receiving AFDC payments.

Under Nixon's proposal, the government would guarantee a family of four an annual income of $1,600, with the possibility of further assistance depending on how much income the family earned. In one bold stroke, FAP would replace the post–New Deal welfare system, which provided services and assistance *only* to those in particular circumstances, such as low-income mothers with small children or people who were unemployed, with a system that offered government aid to *all* low-income families.

Conservatives blasted FAP, especially its provisions for supplementing the income of families that had a regularly employed, though low-paid, wage earner. In contrast, proponents of more generous government assistance programs criticized its guaranteed income of $1,600 as too miserly. The House of Representatives approved a modified version of FAP in 1970, but a curious alliance of senators to the right and to the left of Nixon blocked its passage.

Some changes in domestic programs were enacted during the Nixon years, however. For example, Congress passed the president's revenue-sharing plan, which provided for the return of a certain percentage of federal tax dollars to state and local governments in the form of "block grants." Instead of Washington specifying how the funds were to be used, the block grant concept left the state and local governments free, within broad limits, to spend the funds as they saw fit.

Congress stitched together a revised welfare program in the early 1970s. It included rent subsidies for people at the lowest income levels and Supplementary Security Insurance (SSI) payments for those who were elderly, blind, or disabled. The Medicare and Medicaid programs, established under Johnson's Great Society, were gradually expanded during Nixon's presidency. In 1972 Social Security benefits were "indexed," which meant they would rise with the rate of inflation. More cautious than Nixon's FAP proposals, these congressional initiatives substantially extended the nation's income-support programs, albeit only for specific groups. Between 1970 and 1980 the federal government's spending for social welfare rose from 40.1 percent of total government outlays to slightly over 53 percent.

CONTROVERSIES OVER RIGHTS

These legislative initiatives came against the backdrop of a much broader debate over how to define the federal government's responsibility to protect basic constitutional rights. The struggle to define those rights embroiled the U.S. Supreme Court in controversy. Under the leadership of Chief Justice Earl Warren and Associate Justice William Brennan, both appointees of Dwight Eisenhower, an "activist" majority that was devoted to recognizing a broad range of constitutionally protected rights had dominated the Court during the 1960s. Although nearly all the Warren Court's rights-related decisions drew critical fire, the most emotional cases involved the rights of persons accused of violent crime. In *Miranda v. Arizona* (1966), the Court's activists held that the Constitution required police officers to advise people arrested for a felony offense of their constitutional rights to remain silent and to consult an attorney. While civil libertarians defended decisions such as *Miranda* as the logical extension of settled principles, the Court's numerous critics attacked the activist justices for allegedly inventing new rights that could not be found in the text of the Constitution. Amid rising public concern over crime, conservatives made *Miranda* a symbol of the judicial "coddling" of criminals.

Richard Nixon had campaigned for president in 1968 as an opponent of the Warren Court's activist stance. Before the election, Chief Justice Warren had announced his resignation, and incoming President Nixon was therefore able to appoint a moderately conservative Republican, Warren Burger, as Chief Justice. Pledged to select only judges who would interpret rights claims narrowly, Nixon also appointed three new associate justices to the Supreme Court during his presidency—Harry Blackmun, William Rehnquist, and Lewis Powell. The Supreme Court, meanwhile, continued to face controversial new cases involving the issue of rights.

Considerable discussion focused on the constitutional status of social welfare programs. Activist lawyers argued that access to adequate economic assistance from the federal government should be recognized as a national right. Many observers expected that the Court might soon take this step. In 1970, however, in *Dandridge* v. *Williams,* the Court rejected the argument that laws capping the amount a state would pay to welfare recipients violated the Constitution's requirement that the government must extend equal protection of the laws to all citizens. The Court drew a sharp distinction between the government's responsibility to respect the individual liberties of all citizens, such as the right to vote and freedom of speech, and its discretionary ability to make distinctions in the administration of spending programs such as AFDC. In short, the Court refused to hold that welfare was a national right.

Another controversial aspect of the rights debate involved issues of health and safety. A vigorous consumer rights movement, which had initially drawn inspiration from Ralph Nader's exposé about auto safety, titled *Unsafe at Any Speed* (1965), attracted immediate political support. Under Nader's leadership, consumer advocates lobbied for federal legislation to protect the right to safety in the workplace, the right to safe consumer products, and the right to a healthy environment. This effort found expression in such legislation as the Occupational Safety Act of 1973, stronger consumer protection laws, and new environmental legislation (see Chapter 30).

At the same time, a newly energized women's rights movement pushed its own set of issues. The National Organization for Women (NOW), founded in 1966, backed an Equal Rights Amendment (ERA) that would explicitly guarantee women the same legal rights as men. After having been passed by Congress in 1972 and quickly ratified by more than half the states, the ERA suddenly emerged as one of the most divisive domestic issues of the early 1970s. Conservative women's groups, such as Phyllis Schlafly's "Stop ERA," charged that equal rights would undermine traditional "family values." As a result of such opposition, the ERA, which once seemed assured of passage, failed to attain approval from the three-quarters of states needed for ratification. Ultimately, women's groups abandoned the ERA effort in favor of urging the courts to recognize equal rights on a case-by-case, issue-by-issue basis.

One of these specific issues, involving a woman's right to a safe and legal abortion, became even more controversial than the ERA. In *Roe* v. *Wade* (1973), the Supreme Court ruled that a state law making abortion a criminal offense violated a woman's right of privacy. The *Roe* decision outraged conservatives. Rallying under the "Right to Life" slogan and focusing on the rights of the unborn fetus, antiabortion groups labeled *Roe* v. *Wade* as another threat to family values, and in 1976 they succeeded in persuading Congress to ban the use of federal funds to finance abortions for women with low incomes. Feminist groups made the issue of individual choice in reproductive decisions a principal rallying point.

Nixon had promised an administration that, in contrast to Johnson's, would "bring us together." Instead, bitter divisions over economic policies, government spending programs, and the meaning of basic constitutional guarantees made the Nixon presidency a period of increasing, rather than decreasing, polarization.

Foreign Policy under Nixon and Kissinger

While attempting to deal with divisive domestic concerns, the Nixon administration was far more preoccupied with international affairs. Nixon appointed Henry Kissinger, a political scientist from Harvard, as his national security adviser. Under Kissinger, the National Security

Council (NSC) emerged as the most powerful shaper of foreign policy within the government. In 1973 Kissinger was appointed Secretary of State, a position that he continued to hold until 1977. With Nixon, Kissinger orchestrated a grand strategy for foreign policy: détente with the Soviet Union, normalization of relations with China, and disengagement from direct military involvement in Southeast Asia and other parts of the world.

DÉTENTE

Although Nixon had built his political career on hard-line anticommunism, the Nixon-Kissinger team mapped a foreign policy that aimed at easing tensions with the two major communist nations, the Soviet Union and China. Kissinger surmised that, as both nations began to seek favor with the United States, they might ease up on their support for North Vietnam, facilitating America's ability to withdraw from the war that was dividing the nation.

Arms control talks took top priority in U.S.-Soviet relations. In 1969 the two superpowers opened the Strategic Arms Limitation Talks (SALT), and after several years of high-level diplomacy they signed an agreement (SALT I) that limited further development of both antiballistic missiles (ABMs) and offensive intercontinental ballistic missiles (ICBMs). The impact of SALT I on the arms race was negligible because it did not limit the number of warheads that could be carried by each missile. Still, the very fact that the Soviet Union and the United States had concluded high-level discussions on arms control signaled a shift.

Nixon's overtures toward the People's Republic of China brought an even more dramatic break with the Cold War past. Tentative conversations arranged through the embassies of both countries in Poland led to a slight easing of U.S. trade restrictions against China in early 1971 and then to an invitation from China for Americans to compete in a Ping-Pong tournament. This celebrated exhibition became a prelude to more significant exchange. In 1972 Nixon himself visited China. Relations between the two countries remained difficult, especially over the status of Taiwan, which the United States still recognized as the legitimate government of China. A few months after Nixon's visit, however, the United Nations admitted the People's Republic as the representative of China, and in 1973 the United States and China exchanged informal diplomatic missions.

VIETNAMIZATION

Meanwhile, the Nixon administration continued to wage war in Vietnam. Nixon and Kissinger decided to start the withdrawal of U.S. ground forces (the policy called "Vietnamization") while stepping up the air war and intensifying diplomatic efforts to reach a settlement. In July of 1969 the president publicly announced the "Nixon Doctrine," which pledged that the United States would provide military assistance to anticommunist governments in Asia but would leave it to them to provide their own military forces.

The goal of Vietnamization was to withdraw U.S. ground troops without accepting compromise or defeat. While officially adhering to Johnson's 1968 bombing halt over the North, Nixon and Kissinger accelerated both the ground war and the air war by launching new offensives in the South and approving a military incursion into Cambodia, an ostensibly neutral country.

The move set off a new wave of protest at home. Campuses exploded in anger, and bomb threats led many colleges to close early for the 1970 summer recess. White police officers killed two students at the all-black Jackson State College in Mississippi, and National Guard troops

IMAGES THAT SHOCKED The war in Indochina produced a spiral of violence that also found its way back to the United States. In the photo at left, a military officer in the South Vietnamese Army summarily executes a prisoner suspected of being a member of the Viet Cong. At right, an anguished antiwar activist bends over the body of a college student killed by Ohio National Guard troops at Kent State University in 1970.

at Kent State University in Ohio fired on demonstrators and killed four students. As growing numbers of protestors took to the streets, moderate business and political leaders became alarmed by how Vietnam was dividing the country. Disillusionment with the war also grew from revelations that, a month after Tet, troops led by U.S. Lieutenant William Calley had entered a small hamlet called My Lai and shot more than 200 people, mostly women and children. This massacre of South Vietnamese civilians had become public in 1969; in 1971 a military court convicted Calley and sentenced him to life imprisonment.

The Cambodian incursion of 1970 was part of a widening secret war in Cambodia and Laos. Although the U.S. government denied that it was waging any such war, large areas of those rich agricultural countries were disrupted by American bombing. As the number of Cambodian refugees swelled and food supplies dwindled, the communist guerrilla force in Cambodia—the Khmer Rouge—grew into a well-disciplined army. The Khmer Rouge would later seize the government and, in an attempt to eliminate potential dissent, turn Cambodia into a "killing field." While peace negotiations with North Vietnam proceeded in Paris, the Vietnam War actually broadened into a war that destabilized the entire region of Indochina.

Even greater violence was yet to come. In the spring of 1972 a North Vietnamese offensive approached within 30 miles of Saigon. Nixon responded by resuming the bombing of North Vietnam and by mining its harbors. Just weeks before the 1972 election, Kissinger again promised peace and announced a cease-fire. After the election, however, the United States unleashed even greater firepower. In the so-called Christmas bombing of December 1972, B-52 bombers pounded North Vietnamese military and civilian targets around the clock.

By this time, however, much of the media, Congress, and the public had become sickened by the violence. In response, Nixon proceeded with full-scale Vietnamization of the war. In January 1973 North Vietnam and the United States signed peace accords in Paris that provided for the withdrawal of U.S. troops. As U.S. troops pulled out, the South Vietnamese government, headed by Nguyen Van Thieu, continued to fight, though it was growing increasingly demoralized and disorganized.

In the spring of 1975, South Vietnam's army was no longer able to withstand the advance of North Vietnam's skilled general Nguyen Giap. Thieu's government collapsed, North Vietnamese armies entered Saigon, and U.S. helicopters scrambled to airlift the last remaining officials out of the besieged U.S. embassy.

THE AFTERMATH OF WAR

Between 1960 and 1973, approximately 3.5 million American men and women served in Vietnam: 58,000 died; 150,000 were wounded; 2,000 remain missing. In the aftermath of the long, costly war, many Americans struggled to find meaning. Why had their country failed to

THE VIETNAM WAR MEMORIAL   This memorial, a kind of wailing wall that bears the names of all Americans who were killed in action in Vietnam, was dedicated on the Mall in Washington, D.C., in 1982.

prevail over a small, barely industrialized nation? Conservatives blamed the uncensored and irresponsible media, the coddling of dissenters, and the "failure of will" in Congress. The goals of the war, they believed, were laudable; politicians, setting unrealistic limits on the war, had denied the military the means to attain victory. By contrast, those who had opposed the war stressed the misguided belief that the United States was unbeatable, the deceitfulness of governmental leaders, and the incompetence of bureaucratic processes. For them, the war was in the wrong place and waged for the wrong reasons; and the human costs to Indochina outweighed any possible gain.

Regardless of their positions on the war, most Americans could agree on one proposition: There should be "no more Vietnams." The United States should not undertake future military involvements unless there were clear and compelling political objectives, demonstrable public support, and the provision of adequate means to accomplish the goal.

THE NIXON DOCTRINE

In molding foreign policy, Henry Kissinger relied increasingly on pro-U.S. anticommunist allies to police their own regions of the world. Kissinger made it clear that the United States would not dispatch troops to oppose revolutionary insurgencies but would give generous assistance to anticommunist regimes or factions that were willing to fight the battle themselves.

During the early 1970s, America's Cold War strategy came to rely on supporting staunchly anticommunist regional powers: nations such as Iran under Shah Reza Pahlavi, South Africa with its apartheid regime, and Brazil with its repressive military dictatorship. All of these states built large military establishments trained by the United States. U.S. military assistance, together with covert CIA operations, also incubated and protected anticommunist dictatorships in South Korea, in the Philippines, and in much of Latin America. In one of its most controversial foreign policies, the Nixon administration employed covert action against the elected socialist government of Salvador Allende Gossens in Chile. In 1973 Allende was overthrown by the Chilean military, who immediately suspended democratic rule and began a policy of political repression.

Critics charged that the United States, in the name of anticommunism, had too often wedded its diplomatic fortunes to such questionable covert actions and unpopular military governments. In 1975 Senator Frank Church conducted widely-publicized Senate hearings into abuses by the CIA. But supporters of the Nixon Doctrine applauded the administration's strengthening of a system of allies and its tough anticommunism. In many circles, Nixon received high marks for a pragmatic foreign policy that combined détente toward the communist giants with strong containment against the further global spread of revolutionary regimes.

THE WARS OF WATERGATE

Nixon's presidency ultimately collapsed as a result of horrendous decisions made in the president's own Oval Office. From the time Nixon entered the White House, he had been deeply suspicious of nearly every person and institution in Washington. Such suspicions centered on antiwar activists and old political opponents but even extended to likely allies, such as J. Edgar Hoover, the staunchly conservative director of the FBI. Isolated behind a close-knit group of advisers, Nixon ultimately set up his own secret intelligence unit.

During the summer of 1971 Daniel Ellsberg, a dissident member of the national security bureaucracy, leaked to the press a top-secret history of U.S. involvement in the Vietnam War, subsequently known as the "Pentagon Papers." Nixon responded by seeking, unsuccessfully, a court injunction to stop publication of the study and, more ominously, by unleashing his secret intelligence unit, now dubbed "the plumbers," to stop the leaking of information to the media. Looking for materials that might discredit Ellsberg, the plumbers burglarized his psychiatrist's office. Thus began a series of "dirty tricks" and outright illegalities, often financed by funds illegally solicited for Nixon's 1972 reelection campaign, that would culminate in the political scandal and constitutional crisis known as "Watergate."

THE ELECTION OF 1972

As the 1972 election approached, Nixon's political strategists worried that economic troubles and the war might deny the president reelection. Creating a campaign organization separate from that of the Republican Party, with the ironic acronym of CREEP (Committee to Re-Elect the President), they secretly raised millions of dollars, much of it from illegal contributions.

As the 1972 campaign proceeded, Nixon's chances of reelection dramatically improved. An assassin's bullet crippled George Wallace. Meanwhile, Democratic Senator Edmund Muskie of Maine made a series of blunders (some of them precipitated by Republican "dirty tricksters") that derailed his campaign. Eventually, Senator George McGovern of South Dakota, an outspoken opponent of the Vietnam War, won the Democratic nomination.

During the campaign, McGovern called for higher taxes on the wealthy, a guaranteed minimum income for all Americans, amnesty for Vietnam War draft resisters, and the decriminalization of marijuana—positions significantly to the left of the views of many traditional Democrats. In foreign policy, McGovern called for deep cuts in defense spending and for vigorous efforts to achieve peace in Vietnam—positions that Nixon successfully portrayed as signs of weakness.

Nixon won an easy victory in the November elections. The president received the Electoral College votes of all but one state and the District of Columbia, won more than 60 percent of the popular vote, and carried virtually every traditional Democratic bloc except the African American vote. His margin of victory was one of the largest in U.S. history.

NIXON PURSUED

In achieving that victory, however, the president's team left a trail of corruption that cut short Nixon's second term. In June 1972 a surveillance team with links to both CREEP and the White House had been arrested while adjusting some eavesdropping equipment that it had installed earlier in the Democratic Party's headquarters in Washington's Watergate office complex. In public, Nixon's spokespersons dismissed the Watergate break-in as an insignificant "third-rate burglary"; privately, Nixon and his closest aides immediately launched an illegal cover-up. They paid hush money to the Watergate burglars and had the CIA falsely warn the FBI that any investigation into the break-in would jeopardize national security.

While reporters from *The Washington Post* took the lead in pursuing the taint of scandal, members of Congress and the federal judiciary sought evidence on possible violations of the law. In January 1973 Judge John Sirica, a Republican appointee who was presiding over the trial of the Watergate burglars, refused to accept their claim that neither CREEP nor the White House had been involved in the break-in. While Sirica pushed for more information, Senate leaders convened a special Watergate Committee, headed by North Carolina's conservative Democratic Senator Sam Ervin, to investigate the 1972 campaign. Meanwhile, federal prosecutors uncovered evidence that seemed to link key administration and White House figures, including John Mitchell, Nixon's former attorney general and later the head of CREEP, to illegal activities.

Nixon's political and legal difficulties grew steadily worse during 1973. In March, under unyielding pressure from Judge Sirica, one of the Watergate burglars finally broke his silence. By May, he joined other witnesses who testified before the Senate's Watergate Committee about various illegal activities committed by CREEP and the White House. Nixon's closest aides were soon called before the committee. John Dean, who had been Nixon's chief legal counsel, gave testimony that linked the president himself to an elaborate Watergate cover-up and to other illegal activities.

Along the way, Senate investigators discovered that a voice-activated taping machine had recorded every conversation held in Nixon's Oval Office. Now it was possible to determine whether the president or John Dean was lying. Nixon claimed an "executive privilege" to keep the tapes from being released to other branches of government, but Judge Sirica, Archibald Cox (who had been appointed as a special, independent prosecutor in the Watergate case), and Congress all launched legal moves to gain access to them.

If Nixon's own problems were not enough, his vice president, Spiro Agnew, resigned in October 1973 after pleading "no contest" to income tax evasion. He agreed to a plea-bargain arrangement in order to avoid prosecution for having accepted illegal kickbacks while he was in Maryland politics. Acting under the Twenty-fifth Amendment (ratified in 1967), Nixon appointed—and both houses of Congress confirmed—Representative Gerald Ford of Michigan, a Republican Party stalwart, as the new vice president.

NIXON'S FINAL DAYS

By the early summer of 1974, the nation's legal-constitutional system was closing in on Nixon, and the president's inept attempts to sidetrack his pursuers only redounded against him. During the previous autumn, for example, Nixon had clumsily orchestrated the firing of Archibald Cox. When this rash action was greeted by a public outcry—the affair came to be known as Nixon's "Saturday Night Massacre"—the president was obliged to appoint another independent prosecutor, Leon Jaworski. Similarly, Nixon's own release of edited, and occasionally garbled, transcripts of a series of Watergate-related conversations merely prompted people to demand the original tape recordings. Finally, by announcing that he would only obey a "definitive" Supreme Court decision on the tapes' legal status, Nixon was all but inviting the justices to reach a unanimous decision. And on July 24, 1974, the Court did just that in the case of *U.S. v. Nixon*. By this time, Nixon was in desperate straits. While the Supreme Court was unanimously ruling that Nixon's claim of "executive privilege" over the tapes could not justify his refusal to release evidence needed in a criminal investigation, the Judiciary Committee of the House of Representatives was already moving toward a vote on impeachment.

At the end of July, after nearly a full week of televised deliberations, a majority of the House Judiciary Committee voted three formal articles of impeachment against the president for

CHRONOLOGY

1963	Johnson assumes presidency and pledges to continue Kennedy's initiatives
1964	Congress passes Kennedy's tax bill, the Civil Rights Act of 1964, and the Economic Opportunity Act • Gulf of Tonkin Resolution gives Johnson authority to conduct undeclared war • Johnson defeats Barry Goldwater in presidential election
1965	Johnson announces plans for the Great Society • Malcolm X assassinated • U.S. intervenes in Dominican Republic • Johnson announces significant U.S. troop deployments in Vietnam • Congress passes Voting Rights Act • Violence rocks Los Angeles and other urban areas
1966	Black Power movement emerges • *Miranda* v. *Arizona* decision guarantees rights of criminal suspects • U.S. begins massive air strikes in North Vietnam
1967	Large antiwar demonstrations begin • Beatles release *Sgt. Pepper's Lonely Hearts Club Band*
1968	Tet offensive (January) • Martin Luther King Jr. assassinated (April) • Robert Kennedy assassinated (June) • Violence at Democratic national convention in Chicago • Civil Rights Act of 1968 passed • Vietnam peace talks begin in Paris • Richard Nixon elected president
1969	Nixon announces "Vietnamization" policy • Pictures of My Lai massacre become public
1970	U.S. troops enter Cambodia • Student demonstrators killed at Kent State and Jackson State
1971	"Pentagon Papers" published; White House "plumbers" formed • Military court convicts Lieutenant Calley for My Lai incident
1972	Nixon crushes McGovern in presidential election
1973	Paris peace accords signed • *Roe* v. *Wade* upholds women's right to abortion • Nixon's Watergate troubles begin to escalate
1974	House votes impeachment, and Nixon resigns • Ford assumes presidency
1975	Saigon falls to North Vietnamese forces

obstruction of justice, violation of constitutional liberties, and refusal to produce evidence requested during the impeachment process. Nixon boasted that he would fight these accusations before the Senate, the body authorized by the Constitution (Article I, Section 3) to render a verdict of guilty or innocent after the House votes impeachment.

Nixon's closest aides, however, were already making ready for his departure. One of his own attorneys had discovered that a tape Nixon had been withholding contained the long-sought "smoking gun": a 1972 conversation confirming that Nixon himself had agreed to a plan by which the CIA would advance the fraudulent claim of national security in order to stop the FBI from investigating the Watergate burglary. At this point, Nixon's secretary of defense ordered all military commanders to ignore any order from the president unless it was countersigned by the secretary. Abandoned by almost every prominent Republican and about to confront a Senate prepared to vote him guilty on the impeachment charges, Nixon went on television on August 8, 1974, to announce that he would resign from office. On August 9, Gerald Ford became the nation's 38th president.

In 1974, most people believed that Watergate was one of the gravest crises in the history of the republic. As time passed, though, the public's recollection and knowledge of the Watergate illegalities and Nixon's forced resignation faded. Opinion polls conducted on the 20th anniversary of Nixon's resignation suggested that most Americans retained only a dim memory of Watergate.

One reason may be that although nearly a dozen members of the Nixon administration were convicted of criminal activities, the president himself escaped punishment. Only a month after Nixon's resignation, Gerald Ford granted Nixon an unconditional presidential pardon. The nation was spared the spectacle of witnessing a former president undergoing a lengthy, perhaps divisive trial; but it was also denied an authoritative accounting, in a court of law, of the full range of Nixon's misdeeds.

Another reason for the fading memory of Watergate may be the popular penchant for linking it to nearly every political scandal of the post-Nixon era. The suffix "-gate" became attached to grave constitutional episodes (such as Ronald Reagan's "Iran-Contragate" affair) and to the most trivial of political events (such as the brief "Nannygate" controversy that eliminated one of President Bill Clinton's nominees for attorney general in 1993). By the end of the 20th century, popular political discourse, it seemed, framed the dramatic events of 1973 and 1974 as another example of routine political corruption rather than as a unique, serious constitutional crisis.

Finally, what the historian Stanley Kutler has called the "wars of Watergate" may have been overshadowed by the enormity of the turmoil and loss Americans experienced as a result of America's longest war. In this sense, Watergate tends to blend into a broader pattern of political, social, economic, and cultural turmoil that emerged during the lengthy, increasingly divisive war in Southeast Asia.

CONCLUSION

The power of the national government expanded during the 1960s. Lyndon Johnson's Great Society created a blueprint for an expanding welfare state and a War on Poverty. The Great Society, however, was quickly overshadowed by the escalation of the war in Vietnam, a struggle that consumed increasingly more of the nation's wealth in order to prevent communism from gaining a victory in Southeast Asia.

This growth of governmental power—both the enlargement of domestic social programs and the waging of war abroad—prompted divisive debates that polarized the country. Johnson left the presidency a broken man. And his Republican successor, Richard Nixon, in trying to control the divisions at home, let loose an abuse of power that ultimately drove him from office in disgrace. The exalted hopes of the early 1960s—that the U.S. government would be able to enhance liberty and equality both in America and throughout the rest of the world—ended in frustration and defeat.

The era of America's longest war was a time of high political passions, of generational and racial conflict, of differing definitions of patriotism. It saw the slow convergence of an antiwar movement, along with the emergence of a youthful counterculture, of "Black Power," of "women's liberation," and of a variety of contests over what constituted basic rights for Americans. Different groups assigned different causes to explain the failures of both the Great Society and the war, and the polarization from these years shaped the fault lines of politics for years to come. Nearly all Americans, however, became much more reserved, many even cynical, about further enlarging the power of the federal government in the name of expanding liberty and equality.

30

AMERICA IN TRANSITION: ECONOMICS, CULTURE, AND SOCIAL CHANGE IN THE LATE 20TH CENTURY

A CHANGING PEOPLE ∾ ECONOMIC TRANSFORMATIONS
THE ENVIRONMENT ∾ MEDIA AND CULTURE ∾ SOCIAL ACTIVISM
RACE, ETHNICITY, AND SOCIAL ACTIVISM ∾ THE NEW RIGHT

At the end of the 20th century historians tried to assess several decades of remarkable economic and cultural changes. The 1960s—fraught with political assassinations, a lengthy foreign war, and domestic dissent—had once seemed a period peculiar for its upheavals. In fact, the decades that followed brought even more far-reaching, although less violent, changes. Increasing immigration, urbanization, and movement of people southward and westward altered the demographics of American life. A transformation from manufacturing to postindustrial employment swept the economy. A digital revolution transfigured systems of information and entertainment. And social movements associated with environmentalism, women's rights, gay pride, racial and ethnic solidarity, and the New Right affected both politics and the ways that Americans defined themselves.

A CHANGING PEOPLE

In demographic terms, the post-1970 period marked a watershed in American life. The population was becoming older, more urban, and more ethnically and racially diverse. Moreover, the nation's center of power was shifting away from the Northeast and toward the South and West.

AN AGING POPULATION

After about 1970 the birth rate slowed dramatically. During the 1970s and 1980s, even with a wave of new immigration and longer life expectancy, the growth rate was only about 1 percent a year. Most young people were delaying marriage until well into their twenties, and the number of women in their mid-thirties who had never married tripled between 1970 and 1990 to 16 percent.

As a result of declining birth rates, rising life expectancy, and the aging of the baby boom generation, the median age of the population rose steadily. Advertising agencies and TV serials turned to midlife appeals. As aging baby boomers pondered retirement, policymakers grew concerned that the projected payouts in Social Security and Medicare benefits would bequeath a staggering cost burden to the smaller post–baby boom generation of workers. During the 1990s, halting the rise of health care costs, revamping health payment systems, and guaranteeing Social Security benefits became major public policy issues.

THE RISE OF THE SUNBELT

Not only did population growth slow in the 1970s and 1980s, but the regional pattern of population distribution began to shift political and economic power within the country. Between 1970 and 1990, 90 percent of the nation's population growth came in the South and the West. The census of 1980 revealed that for the first time more Americans were living in the South and the West than were living in the North and the East.

The population shift profoundly reshaped national politics. In the late 1960s, Republican political analyst Kevin Phillips looked at the region extending from Florida to California—the Sunbelt—and predicted that its voters would join together in a conservative coalition. It was

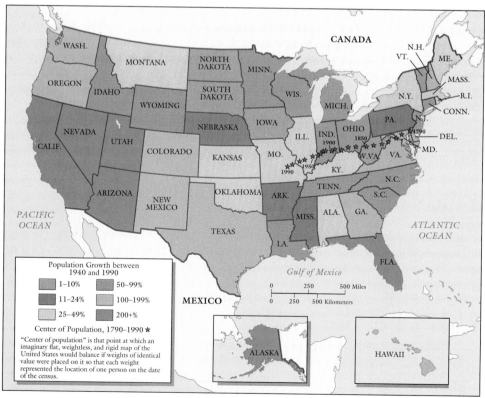

POPULATION SHIFTS TOWARD THE "SUNBELT"

just such a coalition that elected Californian Ronald Reagan president in 1980. The South, once solidly Democratic, finally developed a two-party system. And in the reapportionment of seats in the House of Representatives during the early 1990s, California gained seven seats, Florida gained four, New York lost three, and several other northeastern states lost two.

There were many reasons for this demographic shift. One was the availability of affordable air-conditioning for homes and offices. Another was the rise of tourism and the proliferation of new retirement communities in Nevada, California, Arizona, and Florida. Also, lower labor costs and the absence of strong unions prompted manufacturers to build new plants and relocate old ones in the Sunbelt. Equally important was the growth of high-tech industries with their economic fortunes tied to military-industrial spending. Those industries attracted highly skilled engineers and scientists. Silicon Valley in Santa Clara County near San Francisco, for example, had been a rural area until 1940. From then on, it doubled its population every decade. This spectacular growth was triggered by the new semiconductor industry and its network of electronics-related suppliers.

Government spending on the space program also helped shift research and technology to the Sunbelt. After the Soviet Union's launch of its *Sputnik* satellite in 1957, the United States stepped up its own space program under the newly formed National Aeronautics and Space Administration (NASA). In 1961 President Kennedy announced plans for the Apollo program, promising a manned mission to the moon by 1970. In July 1969 astronauts Neil Armstrong and Edwin ("Buzz") Aldrin stepped from their spacecraft onto the moon, planted the American flag, and gathered 47 pounds of lunar rocks for later study.

In the 1980s NASA began launching a series of "space shuttles," manned rockets that served as scientific laboratories and could be flown back to earth for reuse. This progression of ever more innovative, and costly, advances in space technology spurred economic development in the Sunbelt states.

New Immigration

Another reason for the sharp rise in the population of the Sunbelt was a dramatic increase in immigration. During the 1970s and 1980s, 10 million immigrants from Asia and Latin America arrived in the United States, six times the number of European immigrants arriving over the same period. (If illegal immigrants were included, the count would be far higher.)

The largest number of non-European immigrants came from Mexico. Many Americans of Mexican ancestry, of course, were not recent immigrants. Immigration became significant in the 20th century, spurred by the Mexican revolution after 1910 (see Chapter 24) and responding to U.S. labor shortages during the First World War, the Second World War, and the Korean War. In every decade of the postwar period, immigration from Mexico rose substantially. Many migrants came as seasonal agricultural workers; many others formed permanent communities. Ninety percent of all Mexican Americans lived in the Southwest.

Although Mexican Americans comprised the majority of the Spanish-speaking population across the country in the late 20th century, Puerto Ricans were more numerous on the East Coast. The United States annexed Puerto Rico after the Spanish-American War of 1898 (see Chapter 22) and in 1917 granted U.S. citizenship to its inhabitants. Puerto Ricans, therefore, were not really immigrants but could come and go freely from island to mainland. Before the Second World War, the Puerto Rican population in the United States was small and centered in New York City. After the war, however, immigration rose significantly (see Chapter 28). By

NEW AMERICANS   These new Americans, who are taking the oath of citizenship, are part of the upsurge in immigration that began in the mid-1960s. Before obtaining citizenship, applicants must demonstrate knowledge of basic English and pass a test on public rights and responsibilities.

the 1970s, more Puerto Ricans were living in New York City than in San Juan, Puerto Rico's capital. Sizable Puerto Rican communities also developed in Chicago and in industrial cities in New England and Ohio. By 1990 the Puerto Rican population had grown to over 2 million.

Cubans comprised the third most numerous Spanish-speaking group in the U.S. population. In 1962 congressional action designated Cubans who were fleeing Fidel Castro's regime as refugees eligible for admittance. Over the next 30 years, 800,000 Cubans quickly established themselves in South Florida. By 1990 Cubans comprised one-third of the population in Miami.

The Immigration Act of 1965 sharply altered national policy. Since the 1920s, rates of immigration had been determined by quotas based on national origins (see Chapter 24). The 1965 act ended these quotas and laid the basis not only for a resumption of high-volume immigration but also for a substantial shift in region of origin. The law placed a ceiling of 20,000 immigrants for every country, gave preference to those with close family ties in the United States, and accorded priority to those with special skills and those classified as "refugees." Under the new act, large numbers of people immigrated from Korea, China, the Philippines, the Dominican Republic, Colombia, and countries in the Middle East. In the aftermath of the Vietnam War, Presidents Ford and Carter ordered the admittance of many Vietnamese, Cambodians, Laotians, and Hmong (an ethnically distinct people who inhabited lands extending across the borders of all three countries) who had assisted the United States during the war.

In response to the surge in number of refugees, Congress passed the Refugee Act of 1980. It specified that political refugees would be admitted but that refugees who were seeking simply to improve their economic lot would be denied entry. In practice, the terms "political" and "economic" tended to be applied in such a way that people fleeing communist regimes were usually admitted but those fleeing right-wing oppression were turned away. For example,

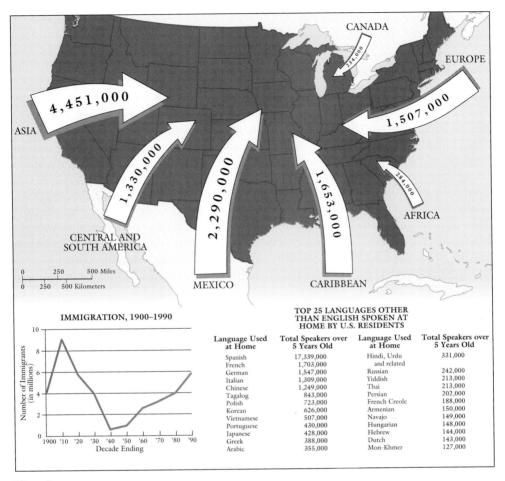

IMMIGRATION, 1900–1990

TOP 25 LANGUAGES OTHER
THAN ENGLISH SPOKEN AT
HOME BY U.S. RESIDENTS

Language Used at Home	Total Speakers over 5 Years Old	Language Used at Home	Total Speakers over 5 Years Old
Spanish	17,339,000	Hindi, Urdu and related	331,000
French	1,703,000	Russian	242,000
German	1,547,000	Yiddish	213,000
Italian	1,309,000	Thai	213,000
Chinese	1,249,000	Persian	202,000
Tagalog	843,000	French Creole	188,000
Polish	723,000	Armenian	150,000
Korean	626,000	Navajo	149,000
Vietnamese	507,000	Hungarian	148,000
Portuguese	430,000	Hebrew	144,000
Japanese	428,000	Dutch	143,000
Greek	388,000	Mon-Khmer	127,000
Arabic	355,000		

NEW IMMIGRANTS, 1970–1990

Cubans and Soviet Jews were admitted, but Haitians were often denied immigrant status. Many Guatemalans and Salvadorans, trying to escape the repressive military governments backed by the United States during the 1980s, stood little chance of being admitted as legal immigrants. Some of them, however, were helped into the U.S. and then harbored by a church-based "sanctuary movement" that opposed U.S. policies in Central America.

As illegal immigration became a major political issue in the mid-1980s, Congress passed another immigration law. The Immigration Reform and Control Act of 1987 imposed penalties on businesses employing illegal aliens and granted residency to workers who could prove that they had been living in the United States since 1982. Although this law may have temporarily reduced the number of illegal aliens entering the country, it became increasingly ineffective during the 1990s.

Los Angeles became a microcosm of world cultures. By the mid 1990s, fewer than half of the schoolchildren in Los Angeles were proficient in English, and some 80 different languages were spoken in homes there. The slogan "A City Divided and Proud of It" described Los Angeles's ambivalence about the issue of separate versus common identities.

URBANIZATION AND SUBURBANIZATION

Urban-suburban demographics were also in a state of flux. By 1990 nearly 80 percent of Americans were living in metropolitan areas. As those areas continued to expand, the suburbs melded into "urban corridors," metropolitan strips often running between older cities, as between Los Angeles and San Diego, Washington and Baltimore, Seattle and Tacoma, or into "edge cities," former suburban areas such as the Galleria area west of Houston, the Perimeter Center south of Atlanta, and Tysons Corner near Washington, D.C.

Meanwhile, central cities became centers primarily of financial, administrative, and entertainment activity. During the 1970s and 1980s, the percentage of upper- and middle-income residents within city boundaries fell, and tax bases declined at the same time that an influx of low-income populations placed greater demands on public services. Higher rates of homelessness and crime, together with deteriorating schools and urban infrastructures (such as sewer and water systems), plagued most large cities. Although many central cities began to revive during the mid-1990s—as a result of general economic growth, lower crime rates, better

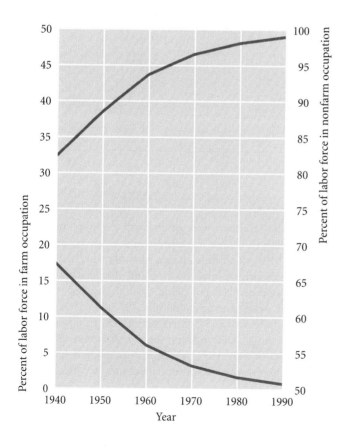

DECREASING NUMBER OF FARMERS, 1940–1990

During the late 20th century, Americans continued to leave farms and small towns for cities and suburbs. In 1990 only a few states retained a preponderance of rural population.

policing, and the renewed desire to enjoy the amenities of an urban lifestyle—the population growth of urban corridors continued to outpace that of traditional cities.

ECONOMIC TRANSFORMATIONS

A typical American adult of the 1990s would likely awake to a digital alarm clock, pop break-fast into a microwave oven, work at a desktop computer, and relax with a movie or TV pro-gram taped earlier on the VCR, while the children amused themselves with Nintendo or surfed the Internet. None of these products or activities had been known in the early 1960s. The pace of technological change had brought an astonishing transformation in consumer products, production processes, and the structure of the labor force.

NEW TECHNOLOGIES

The most noteworthy technological advances were made in biotechnology, high-performance computing, and communications systems. As scientists deepened their understanding of DNA and genetic engineering, they devised new techniques of gene transfer, embryo manipulation, tissue regeneration, and even cloning. Those techniques led the way to possible breakthroughs in cancer treatment, alteration of genetically inherited diseases, new and improved crops, waste conversion, and toxic cleanup. But biotechnology, especially genetic engineering, also raised fears about the decline in the variety of biological organisms, what scientists called "biodiver-sity," and prompted ethical questions about the role of science in manipulating reproduction.

The computer revolution, which began after the Second World War, entered a new phase during the 1970s, when the availability of microchips boosted the capability and reduced the size and cost of computer hardware. Sales of home computers soared. High-performance computers with powerful memory capabilities and "parallel processors," which allow many operations to run simultaneously, began to transform both industry and information systems. Computerized factories and robotics streamlined business operations. "Artificial intelligence" capabilities emerged, along with voice interaction between people and machines.

The computer revolution, enhanced by new communications technologies such as fiber-optic networks and satellite transmission, fueled an "information revolution." Libraries re-placed card catalogs with computer networks. Electronic mail, fax transmissions, voice mail, and the World Wide Web rapidly came to supplement posted (sometimes called "snail") mail and telephone conversations. Cellular phones became widespread. The variety of ways in which people could speedily communicate with other people or with information-bearing machines changed the patterns of human interaction and work. "Telecommuting" from home became common as electronic networks made it less necessary for workers to appear in per-son at an office.

BIG BUSINESS

Computerized communications helped transform ways of doing business by enabling the growth of electronic banking, far-flung business franchising, and huge globalized industries.

Although buying on credit had been widespread in the United States since the 1920s, Bank of America's introduction of its Visa credit card lifted credit-buying to new levels. From the

1970s on, use of bank-issued credit cards mounted. Private debt and personal bankruptcies also soared, and the rate of personal savings fell. Other innovations in electronic banking—automatic teller machines (ATMs), checking (or debit) cards, automatic depositing, and electronic bill-paying—moved Americans closer to a cashless economy where electronic impulses would substitute for currency.

Franchising and chain stores also changed the way consumer products were bought and sold. McDonald's and Holiday Inn pioneered nationwide standardization in the fast-food and travel industries during the 1950s. Other chain restaurants soon copied the McDonald's model, and some even showed that franchise food need not be inexpensive. Similarly, Starbuck's parlayed a simple dietary staple, coffee, into a pricey designer commodity. And Sam Walton's success in building his Wal-Mart chain symbolized the transformation that was engulfing the entire retailing industry. By the late 20th century, books, videotapes, records, electronics equipment, shoes, groceries, travel accommodations, and just about every other consumer item were made available by chains that brought a greater array of merchandise and lower prices—but often offered only low-wage or part-time jobs. Amazon.com became the darling of another innovation—e-commerce (buying over the Internet).

American chain businesses expanded overseas as well as at home. Especially after the collapse of communist regimes in the Soviet Union and Eastern Europe, they rushed to supply consumers with long-denied, American-style goods and services. McDonald's opened to great fanfare in Moscow and Budapest, while the Hilton chain opened new hotels in Eastern European capitals. Pepsi and Coke carried on with their "cola wars" for dominance in foreign markets.

Production, as well as consumption, turned international. U.S. automakers, for example, moved many of their production and assembly plants outside of the United States. Moreover, the trend toward "privatization" (the sale of government-owned industries to private business) in many economies worldwide provided American companies with new opportunities for acquisition. Foreign interests also purchased many U.S. companies and real estate holdings. So many industrial giants had become globalized by the late 20th century that it was difficult to define what constituted an American or a foreign company.

POSTINDUSTRIAL RESTRUCTURING

New technologies and economic globalization brought structural changes to American business and the workforce. Many companies cut their workforces and trimmed their management staffs. In the 1970s more than a dozen major steel plants closed, and the auto industry laid off thousands of workers. The Chrysler Corporation managed to survive only after the federal government took the unprecedented step of guaranteeing loans to the company. The steel and auto industries regained profitability in the 1980s and 1990s, but other giant corporations also began to "downsize." As employment in traditional manufacturing and extractive sectors decreased, jobs in service, high-technology, and the information-entertainment sector increased. By the end of the 1990s, the unemployment rate was at its lowest point in several decades, but the kinds of jobs held by Americans had shifted. Computing and other high-tech jobs brought high salaries, but jobs in the expanding service sector—clerks, servers, cleaners—tended to remain low-paid.

Union membership, always highest in the manufacturing occupations, fell to under 15 percent of the labor force by the late 1990s. While union membership rolls and political power steadily slipped, efforts to expand the base of the union movement into new sectors of the

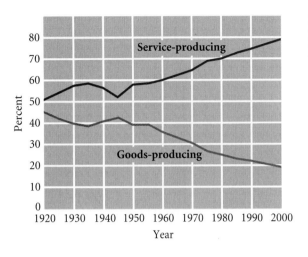

PERCENTAGES OF GOODS-PRODUCING AND SERVICE-PRODUCING U.S. JOBS, 1920–2000

SOURCE: U.S. Census Bureau.

economy initially met with little success. For example, some union locals around the country attempted to organize restaurant and hotel workers, a sector that employed many women. But businesses adamantly fought unionization, claiming that it would raise labor costs.

Cesar Chavez's efforts during the late 1960s and early 1970s to organize agricultural workers also dramatized the difficulties of expanding the base of the union movement. Chavez, a charismatic leader, vaulted the United Farm Workers (UFW) into public attention. As the union president, Chavez instituted several well-publicized consumer boycotts of lettuce and grapes as means of pressuring growers to bargain with the UFW. He won a major contract victory in 1970. During the late 1970s and the 1980s, however, the UFW steadily lost ground. Strong stands by growers to keep out union organizers and the continued influx of new immigrants eager for work undercut the UFW's efforts.

The major growth for organized labor came among government employees and workers in the health care industry. But these gains did not offset the losses in union membership in the old industrial sectors.

Some economists warned that the shift to a "postindustrial" economy was "deskilling" the labor force and worsening technological unemployment—people out of work because the jobs for which they were trained no longer exist. Critics of the new trends expressed alarm over statistics revealing that well over half the new jobs created in the U.S. economy during the 1980s paid less than $7,000 per year. Some analysts warned that the widening gulf between highly paid, highly skilled positions and minimum-wage jobs might ultimately undermine the middle-class nature of American society. By the late 1990s, the labor movement was trying to redress this trend.

More optimistic observers pointed out that internationalization and corporate downsizing might temporarily mean lost jobs for some people but that gains in productivity would eventually translate into lower consumer prices and rising living standards. Indeed, real wages did begin to rise in the 1990s. Moreover, new technologies promised to create business opportunities for future generations. New high-tech businesses turned many computer mavens into millionaires. Product innovation paved a broad avenue of upward economic mobility for those with computer-age skills.

These revolutionary changes in technology and the economy had profound effects on the lives of Americans. Skilled workers of earlier generations had tended to stick to one profession or place of employment throughout their working life. But by the end of the 20th century, even middle-income professionals were likely to switch occupations several times before retiring.

THE ENVIRONMENT

The modern environmental movement began during the 1970s, but its roots reached back to the earlier conservation and preservation movements. During the first four decades of the 20th century, the conservation movement promoted "wise use" of water, forests, and farmlands by urging government to promote scientific resource management and to designate areas as national parks and forests (see Chapter 21). A preservation movement—led by the Sierra Club, the Audubon Society, the Wilderness Society, and others—was primarily concerned with the aesthetics of nature and wanted to protect and enjoy the natural environment in a state as pristine as possible. Landmark legislation during the 1960s—the Wilderness Act of 1964, the National Wild and Scenic Rivers Act of 1968, and the National Trails Act of 1968—set aside new areas, protecting them from development.

ENVIRONMENTAL ACTIVISM AND GOVERNMENT POLICY

The conservation and preservation movements broadened into an "environmental movement." In 1962 Rachel Carson had published *Silent Spring,* which warned that the pesticides used in agriculture, especially DDT, threatened bird populations. Air pollution in major cities such as Los Angeles became so bad that simply breathing urban air was equivalent to smoking several packs of cigarettes a day. Industrial processes polluted water systems, and fears of overexposure to radiation mounted as a result of the testing of atomic weapons and the proliferation of nuclear power plants. In response to these concerns, environmentalists tried to focus national attention on toxic chemicals and the adverse impact of industrial development on air, water, and soil quality. The Environmental Defense Fund, a private organization formed in 1967, took the crusade against DDT and other dangerous toxins to the courts. And in 1970 activitists came together for Earth Day, organized largely by college students, to raise awareness about environmental degradation.

During the 1970s combating environmental hazards and maintaining ecological balances emerged as major concerns of public policy. During Richard Nixon's presidency, the federal government established the Environmental Protection Agency (EPA) in 1970 and enacted major pieces of environmental legislation: the Resources Recovery Act of 1970 (dealing with waste management), the Clean Air Act of 1970, the Water Pollution Control Act of 1972, the Pesticides Control Act of 1972, and the Endangered Species Act of 1973. National parks and wilderness areas were further expanded, and a new law required that "environmental impact statements" be prepared in advance of any major government project. Administering environmental policies became a complex task requiring sophisticated research and negotiations among conflicting interest groups. It also prompted heated public debates. Environmentalist groups grew in size, resources, and expertise, while businesses opposed to these types of bureaucracies attacked government regulation and branded environmentalism an elitist cause that destroyed jobs and impeded economic growth.

New standards brought some significant improvements. The Clean Air Act's restrictions on auto and smokestack emissions, for example, reduced the amount of six major airborne pollutants by one-third in a single decade. The emission of lead into the atmosphere declined by 95 percent. But the remedies could also create new problems. Requiring higher smokestacks to eliminate smog helped to clear city skies but also elevated pollutants into the atmosphere, where they produced damaging "acid rain."

In the late 1970s families living at Love Canal, a housing development near Buffalo, New York, learned that the soil under their homes was contaminated by chemical wastes produced 30 years earlier. The finding explained why residents of the area suffered from high levels of cancer and had children with genetic defects. The costs of resettlement and cleanup of wastes prompted Congress to create a cleanup "Superfund" to be financed by taxes imposed on polluting industries. The most heavily contaminated areas, designated as Superfund sites, were slated for special cleanup efforts.

Environmental legislation prompted a backlash. President Ronald Reagan denounced the environmental regulations of the 1970s. James Watt, Reagan's first secretary of the interior, angered environmentalists by supporting the "sagebrush rebellion," in which western states demanded fewer restrictions on the use of public land within their borders. Emotional battles broke out during the 1980s over private use of resources in federal wilderness areas and over whether protection of endangered species should take priority over economic activities.

The acrimony of environmental debates lessened somewhat during the 1990s. Alternative approaches to environmental management sought to promote change through incentives rather than penalties. In 1997, for example, the Conservation Reserve Program, a farm subsidy program that previously paid farmers to remove land from tillage, now stipulated payment to farmers who would restore wetlands on their properties in order to decrease polluted runoff into streams and preserve wildlife habitat.

The U.S. government itself, however, turned out to be one of the country's most flagrant polluters. In 1988 Secretary of Energy John Harrington admitted that the government's nuclear facilities had been lax on safety measures and estimated that cleanup would cost more than $1 billion. The revelation of hazardous conditions at sites where atomic weapons had been produced shocked nearby residents, who feared that they might have been victims of radiation poisoning. Medical records, long suppressed by the government, revealed that people living downwind of nuclear test sites in the 1940s and 1950s had experienced an abnormally high incidence of cancer, leukemia, and thyroid disorders. In 1993 President Bill Clinton's energy secretary, Hazel O'Leary, finally released records relating to radiation testing and experimentation and promised programs to inform and compensate victims.

The environmental movement increasingly focused on international, as well as national, ecological dangers. Those hazards included global warming (the "greenhouse effect"); holes in the ozone layer caused by chlorofluorocarbons (CFCs); massive deforestation and desertification; pollution of the oceans; and the rapid decline of biological diversity. Solutions to these global problems required worldwide cooperation. International meetings on environmental issues became more frequent. Conventions in Vienna in 1985, Montreal in 1987, London in 1990, and Kyoto in 1997 worked toward establishing international standards on emissions of CFCs and greenhouse gases. A so-called Earth Summit was held in Brazil in 1992, and a conference in Cairo in 1994 took up global population issues. Fear that environmental restrictions could harm economic growth and the lack of mechanisms to enforce internationally agreed-on targets, however, slowed the progress of the international environmental crusade.

ENERGY

The problem of global warming stemmed largely from patterns of energy use. The United States obtained 90 percent of its energy from the burning of fossil fuels, a major source of the carbon dioxide that creates the greenhouse effect. The nation's dependence on fossil fuels aroused serious public concern during the 1970s. Part of the concern was simply economic. In 1973 and again in 1976 the Organization of Petroleum Exporting Countries (OPEC), a cartel dominated by the oil-rich nations of the Middle East, sharply raised the price of oil and precipitated acute shortages in the industrialized world. As Americans wearied of high prices and long lines at gas stations, President Jimmy Carter (1976–1980) promised to make the United States less dependent on imported fossil fuel. He created a new cabinet-level Department of Energy in 1977 and gave some support to conservation efforts and to the development of renewable energy sources.

But Carter also continued to support the use of nuclear power generated by giant reactors. Boosters of the nation's atomic research program had promised that nuclear reactors would provide a cheap, almost limitless supply of energy. The cost of building and maintaining the reactors, however, far exceeded the original estimates, and critics charged that the reactors posed a grave safety risk. The danger was illustrated in 1979 by a malfunction at a reactor at Three Mile Island in Pennsylvania that nearly produced a nuclear meltdown. In response to growing public alarm, power companies canceled orders for new nuclear reactors. During the 1980s, expansion of the nuclear power industry halted.

Meanwhile, the cost of OPEC oil was skyrocketing, helping to boost U.S. inflation rates during Carter's presidency. On taking office as president in 1981, Ronald Reagan promised to break OPEC's oil monopoly by encouraging the development of new sources of supply. Reagan and his successor George Bush followed a "cheap oil" energy policy throughout the 1980s. The tapping of new supplies of oil, together with rivalries among OPEC members, weakened OPEC's hold over the world market and reduced energy costs. But little progress was made in breaking U.S. reliance on fossil fuels, and the United States government assumed little leadership in pushing for international standards on carbon dioxide emissions.

MEDIA AND CULTURE

Innovations in electronic technologies transformed America's culture as well as its economy. By 1995 virtually every residential unit in the country had at least one TV, 99 percent had a VCR, and about 80 percent had a personal computer. More than one-third of the population needed a computer in their daily work, and more than half of all schoolchildren used one in the classroom. The video screen seemed the preeminent symbol of the nation's mass culture.

THE VIDEO REVOLUTION

Video monitors were everywhere. Visitors to museums and historical sites could access information about a particular display simply by pressing spots on an interactive video screen.

Sports bars lined their walls with video monitors, enabling patrons to follow favorite teams. Meanwhile, TV screens were replacing last year's magazines in doctors' waiting rooms and auto repair shops. Air travelers could catch the latest news updates and weather conditions by watching a special Airport Channel.

The kind of specially targeted programming found in many airports highlighted the increasingly fragmented nature of cultural production. The 1970s represented the last decade in which the three major television networks—CBS, NBC, and ABC—were able to command the daily attention of a nation of loyal viewers.

At the beginning of the 1970s, the three major TV networks still offered a range of general-interest programming that was designed to attract a mass audience. A typical 30-minute episode of a top-rated situation comedy might draw more viewers in a single evening than a hit motion picture attracted over an entire year. The networks could promise advertisers that a cross section of the American public would be watching their sales pitches. Various ratings devices, including the venerable Nielsen system, tracked the number of viewers who were tuning in.

The networks began to modify this mass-market strategy during the 1970s. Early in the decade, CBS jettisoned a number of highly rated programs and targeted shows at younger urban and suburban viewers. This shift in strategy, CBS assured potential advertisers, would allow them concentrate on the consumers most likely to spend money on new products.

In line with this strategy of targeting specific groups, CBS began using its comedy lineup to offer more controversial programming. *All in the Family,* a sitcom that highlighted generational conflict within a blue-collar family from Queens, allowed Archie Bunker, the show's bigoted protagonist, to serve as a lightning rod for controversial issues involving race and gender. Although *The Mary Tyler Moore Show* rarely took positions that seemed overtly "feminist," this popular sitcom featured a woman who worked in a fictional TV newsroom. It portrayed the personal politics of working women of the 1970s. TV critics joined viewers in applauding new CBS shows, such as *M*A*S*H,* for integrating comedy with social commentary. NBC soon joined the trend; in 1975 *Saturday Night Live* brought the barbed humor of the 1960s counterculture to network television.

Choosing a strategy different from that of CBS or NBC, ABC cultivated the teenage audience. Aware that young people generally controlled at least one of the family's TV sets, ABC increased its ratings with sex-and-action programs *(Charlie's Angels),* mildly risqué sitcoms *(Three's Company),* fast-paced police shows *(Kojak),* and a variety of upbeat programs such as the nostalgic *Happy Days* and the escapist *Fantasy Island.*

All three networks enjoyed rising profits during the 1970s. At the end of the decade, 9 of every 10 TV sets were still tuned to a network program during prime-time viewing hours.

During the 1980s, however, the networks began to confront a slow yet steady loss of viewers. One reason was that programmers found it increasingly difficult to create successful prime-time programs. Although NBC found great success with *The Bill Cosby Show,* which featured an affluent African American family, and *Cheers,* a sitcom set in a Boston tavern where "everybody knows your name," most of its other offerings had significantly less audience appeal. NBC, like the other networks, adjusted by slashing budgets and spicing its prime-time programs with sexually oriented themes.

Meanwhile, independent stations began to compete in local markets. At a time when the number of daily newspapers was steadily shrinking, 200 independent TV stations went on the air during the 1980s. Lacking access to new network programs, these independents targeted small but lucrative markets by strategically scheduling Hollywood films, sporting events, and reruns of canceled network programs.

Capitalizing on the rise of the independents, Rupert Murdoch's Fox television network debuted in 1988. Fox broke new ground by offering a limited program schedule to previously independent stations. One of its first hit series, *The Simpsons,* a cartoon send-up of the venerable family sitcom, became a mass-marketing bonanza. Fox gradually expanded its nightly offerings and in 1993 shocked the TV industry by outbidding CBS for the rights to carry the National Football League's NFC conference games. In the 1990s, two other communication conglomerates, Paramount and Time-Warner, set up networks based on the Fox model and aimed much of their prime-time programming at younger, urban viewers.

New technologies were also undermining the monopoly of the major networks. At the simplest level, the remote-control device gave rise to a new TV aesthetic, called "zapping" or "channel surfing," in which viewers rapidly switch from program to program, usually during commercial breaks. The mass-marketing of VCRs also gave people new control over their television viewing habits.

But the greatest impact on viewing patterns came from the growth of cable television (CATV). By 1995 nearly 65 percent of the nation's homes were wired for CATV. Capable of carrying scores of different programs, most of which were aimed at very specific audiences, CATV further fragmented TV viewership. Ted Turner, one of the first to recognize the potential of CATV with his "Superstation" WTBS, later added Cable News Network (CNN), and several movie channels before his communications empire merged with that of Time-Warner. Cable operations—whether they featured news, cartoons, sports, public affairs, commercial-free movies, round-the-clock weather, or home shopping programs—steadily expanded. By 1998, the percentage of television viewers watching programs on ABC, CBS, and NBC had fallen to less than 60 percent.

HOLLYWOOD AND THE "MTV AESTHETIC"

The new media environment affected nearly every aspect of mass culture. With movie ticket sales remaining about the same in 1980 as they had been in 1960, Hollywood studios raised the price of each ticket and concentrated on turning out a handful of blockbuster epics, such as *Star Wars* (1977), and an occasional surprise hit, such as Sylvester Stallone's original *Rocky* (1976). But for every *Star Wars* or *Rocky,* Hollywood moguls seemed equally able to produce expensive box-office duds like *Waterworld* (1995). Thus, filmmakers increasingly tended to play it safe and use the kind of story lines and special effects that had made money in the past. Classic TV series, such as *Batman* and *Leave It to Beaver,* became motion pictures. Blockbuster hits such as *Jurassic Park* (1993) spawned sequels such as *Lost World* (1996). And following ABC's TV strategy, Hollywood also made teenagers a major target for films such as *The Breakfast Club* (1985), *Ferris Bueller's Day Off* (1986), and *Clueless* (1995). CATV and VCRs did, however, provide Hollywood with new sources of revenue. Although huge multiplex movie theaters opened in suburban shopping areas throughout the 1980s and early 1990s, video rental stores surpassed them in number, and VCR sales soared. During the late 1990s, most of the smaller video stores faced often-fatal competition from giant chains like Blockbuster and from corner gas-marts and convenience stores. More and more people were using VCRs and the various all-movie CATV channels to convert their TV sets into home movie theaters.

CATV and VCRs helped to transform the pop music industry as well. Music Television (MTV), initially offering a 24-hour supply of rock videos, was launched in 1981. Critics charged it with consistently portraying women as sex objects and with excluding artists of color. Eventually, however, MTV defused complaints—especially after airing Michael Jackson's 29-minute video based on his hit single "Thriller" (1983). Several years later, Madonna used MTV to create a new relationship between music and visual image. A decade later, Madonna's first MTV videos migrated to VH-1, the CATV channel whose musical format catered to older, post-MTV viewers. By the late 1990s, the entertainment industry was releasing VHS and CD-ROM musical packages, as well as singles and albums on tape and compact disc (CD), and was introducing new mini-disk and DVD technologies.

THE NEW MASS CULTURE DEBATE

Mass commercial culture generated controversy. In 1975 the Federal Communications Commission (FCC) ordered the TV networks to dedicate the first 60 minutes of prime time each evening to "family" programming free of violence or "mature" themes. Several TV production companies challenged this requirement, and a federal court ruled that it was a violation of the First Amendment's guarantee of free speech. Demands that the government regulate rock lyrics and album covers also ran afoul of complaints that this constituted illegal censorship. Although governmental efforts faltered, private organizations were more successful in pressing media companies to practice self-censorship. In 1992 pressure on Time-Warner resulted in the withdrawal of a song titled "Cop Killer" by the African American rap artist Ice-T; television networks subsequently adopted a rating system designed to inform parents about the amount of violence and sexual content in prime-time programs.

Meanwhile, a new generation of writers, reviewers, and university professors were paying serious attention to mass culture. Unlike the critics of the 1950s, who dismissed mass culture as trivial and condemned its effects on American life, the critics of the 1980s and 1990s often became fans of the cultural products they were reviewing. Instead of comparing mass culture to "high" culture (the so-called classical works of Western civilization), many abandoned the distinction between lowbrow and highbrow. They insisted that music of the Beatles should be studied along with that of Beethoven and argued that the lyrics of Chuck Berry and Bob Dylan merited academic analysis.

These new analysts also studied the ways in which consumers integrated the products of mass culture into their daily lives. Again rejecting the cultural criticism of the 1950s, they stressed ordinary people's creative interaction with mass culture. Much of this analysis came from professors in the new field of "cultural studies," who focused on how people reworked images from the mass media. Scholarly studies of *Star Trek,* for example, explored the ways in which loyal fans had kept this popular TV series of the 1960s alive in syndication and had subsequently prompted a succession of Hollywood motion pictures and several new *Star Trek* television series. Moreover, through conventions, self-produced magazines (called "fanzines"), and Web sites, fans of *Star Trek* ("Trekkies") and of shows such as *Xena* created a grass-roots subculture that used TV programs as vehicles for discussing social and political issues, especially ones that touched on race, gender, and sexuality. Those who advocated cultural studies argued that students should study such popular phenomena and also that they should be exposed to a range of works by women, people of color, and political outsiders.

Political and social conservatives condemned the introduction of cultural studies into the college curriculum and viewed such teaching as evidence of "the closing of the American mind" (which became the title of a best-selling 1987 book by Allan Bloom) and of the "opening" of students' minds only to what was trendy and "politically correct" (or "PC"). They

TV's FAMILY VALUES

Television sitcoms have always provided visual representations of the "typical" family. During the 1940s, when most viewers resided in urban areas, TV families also lived in cities and often held blue-collar jobs. Chester A. Riley, played by Jackie Gleason and later William Bendix, worked in an aircraft factory on *The Life of Riley.* Ralph Kramden, also portrayed by Gleason, drove a bus on *The Honeymooners.* By the mid-1950s, however, most sitcom families had moved to the suburbs and upward on the socioeconomic scale. Ward Cleaver of *Leave It to Beaver* and Jim Anderson of *Father Knows Best* were prosperous professionals who provided their wives and children with all of the amenities appropriate to the age of affluence. Other sitcom families—such as those portrayed on *I Love Lucy, The Adventures of Ozzie and Harriet,* and *Make Room for Daddy*—featured a husband who worked in show business and a wife who dominated home life from her command post in the kitchen.

Although most of these classic sitcom families continued to appear on television during the 1980s and 1990s through syndication to local stations or on cable channels such as NICK-at-

Nite, they were joined by a new and very different generation of TV families. The Huxtables (Bill Cosby and Phylicia Rashad), although as middle-class and affluent as the Andersons or Cleavers, represented a successful African American family that was coheaded by two well-educated professionals. The title character of *Murphy Brown* (Candice Bergen) worked in the media, but her family was composed of coworkers rather than a spouse. When the unmarried Murphy gave birth to a baby, Dan Quayle, the vice president of the United States, condemned her for endangering family values. The resultant flap only increased *Murphy Brown*'s ratings.

The Simpsons also drew critical fire from defenders of the traditional sitcom family. Although Homer and Marge were married with children, *The Simpsons,* especially during its early years, drew humor by portraying a dysfunctional family. Bart was "an underachiever—and proud of it," and Homer spent more time at Moe's Tavern than with his children. Gradually, the show gained cult status, particularly as viewers came to appreciate the subtle ways in which it playfully parodied TV and movie conventions.

charged that such fascination with mass culture represented a debasement of intellectual life that was also spreading beyond the classroom.

THE DEBATE OVER MULTICULTURAL EDUCATION

Debates over mass culture often merged with controversies over educational policies. Cultural studies, multiculturalism, and political correctness became fighting words. During the late 1970s, the government-funded National Endowment for the Humanities (NEH) and the National Endowment for the Arts (NEA) began to provide financial backing for projects that focused on America's cultural diversity and on politically sensitive reinterpretations of traditional works. In the 1980s conservative Republicans launched a counterattack. Ronald Reagan's secretary of education, William Bennett, used his office to crusade against multicultural education, while Lynn Cheney, head of the NEH, championed traditional programs. Seeking to placate conservatives such as North Carolina's Senator Jesse Helms, President George Bush's administration pressured the NEA to cancel grants to controversial artistic projects, especially those relating to feminism or homosexuality. Controversies over the funding, and even the continued survival, of the NEA and the NEH continued through the 1990s. On college campuses, meanwhile, faculty and students heatedly debated the value of multicultural curricula.

Conservative pressure groups mounted a parallel critique of educational practices in public schools. This phase of the conservative movement, which had initially begun in response to the Supreme Court decisions of the 1960s that barred state-sponsored prayers and Bible-reading in public schools, argued that cultural and educational innovations were manifestations of an antireligious philosophy they called "secular humanism." In the 1950s and 1960s, liberal opponents of Bible-reading and prayer in public schools had insisted that students should not be forced to participate in religious activities. In the 1980s conservatives adapted this argument for their cause and insisted that children should not be coerced into participating in secular-humanist activities that contradicted the religious teachings of their families and churches.

Originating in a complex and electronically mediated environment, the controversy over mass culture extended from the White House to the local schoolhouse. During the 1992 presidential campaign, Bill Clinton eagerly appeared on MTV. The Republican Party's national platform, in contrast, strongly attacked the new cultural climate. Meanwhile, in communities across the country, militant conservatives mobilized to elect school boards that opposed multicultural curricula and other educational changes. As the United States became the home to increasingly fragmented and highly politicized cultures, people debated the complex meanings of multiculturalism and tolerance for difference.

SOCIAL ACTIVISM

The legacy of activism from the 1960s became deeply embedded in American life and rippled through the decades that followed. The mass demonstration remained a tool of social activists representing all kinds of causes. Washington, D.C., continued to provide a favorite stage where huge rallies could attract the attention of national lawmakers and the media, but activists also mounted smaller rallies and protests that recalled the demonstrations of the 1960s. In the early 1980s the Clamshell Alliance mounted a campaign of civil disobedience against a nuclear reactor being built in Seabrook, New Hampshire. Women's groups staged annual "Take Back the Night" marches in major cities to protest the rising tide of sexual assaults, and both pro-choice and anti-abortion groups sponsored demonstrations in Washington, D.C., and in local communities. In October 1995, the "Million Man March" in Washington, D.C., sought to mobilize African American men behind a campaign of social reconstruction in black communities, and two years later an evangelical men's group called the "Promise Keepers" filled Washington's Mall.

Mass demonstrations, however, had lost much of their power to attract media attention by the end of the 20th century. During a period of violence in May 1991 in Los Angeles, 30,000 Korean Americans staged a march for peace. Although it was the largest demonstration ever conducted by any Asian American group, even the local media ignored it.

WOMEN'S ISSUES

Older ideologies of domesticity increasingly clashed with the situations in which millions of women found themselves. More and more women were working outside the home, postponing marriage, remaining single, or getting divorced. Moreover, the development of the birth-control pill gave women more control over reproduction and significantly changed the nature of sexual relationships.

As they pursued activities outside their homes, women came to realize the extent of gender discrimination and to ask new questions about the gender-based division of both public and private power arrangements. Even many of the men who were involved in movements for social change saw no contradiction between women's second-class status and men's positions of authority and leadership. Some male leaders of these movements expected female members to provide secretarial or sexual services and complained that raising issues of sexual equality "interfered" with the movements' primary tasks of redirecting racial and foreign policies. As a result, struggles for gender equality emerged within various older insurgency movements. African American women advocated black feminism; Chicana groups coalesced within Mexican American organizations; radical feminists split off from the antiwar movement; other women challenged the ethics of capitalism by forming new, female-directed cooperatives.

Throughout the 1970s groups of women came together in "consciousness-raising" sessions to discuss issues and share perspectives. These discussions produced a growing conviction that women's larger *political* concerns about the maldistribution of power in the United States could not be separated from the very *personal* power relationships that shaped their own lives. "The personal is political" became the watchword for this new generation of feminists.

Economic self-sufficiency became a pressing issue for many women. Although women increasingly entered the professions and gained unionized positions, the average female worker throughout the 1970s and 1980s continued to earn about 60 cents for every dollar earned by the average male worker. During the 1960s, social welfare benefits for single mothers with children had been boosted by higher AFDC payments and by the Food Stamp program. But in the 1970s and 1980s, the real monetary value of these benefits, measured in constant dollars, steadily decreased. Homeless shelters, which once catered primarily to single men, increasingly had to address the needs of women and children. Throughout the 1970s and 1980s, this "feminization of poverty," and the growing number of children raised in low-income, female-headed families, became a fact of life.

Feminism grew into a highly diverse movement. Women from all sectors of society built new institutions to address needs that had been long ignored by male leaders. American life was greatly influenced by an explosion of female-oriented organizations: battered-women's shelters, clinics specializing in women's medicine, rape crisis centers, economic development counseling for women-owned businesses, union-organizing efforts led by women, women's studies programs in colleges and universities, and academic journals devoted to research on women.

Pressure to end gender discrimination changed existing institutions as well. Previously all-male bastions, such as country clubs and service organizations, were pressured into admitting women. Most mainline Protestant churches and Reform Jewish congregations were challenged to accept women into the ministry. Educational institutions began to adopt "gender-fair" hiring practices and curricula. The everyday lives of most American women by the end of the 20th century took place in an institutional environment very different from that of their mothers a generation earlier.

Sexual harassment, to take only one of the new concerns, became a significant issue among women. Some feminists argued that to focus on sexual harassment would tend to identify feminism with a kind of sexual puritanism that the women's movement had once promised to end. Others, however, continued to push government organizations and private employers to ban behavior that demeaned women and exploited their lack of power vis-à-vis male supervisors and coworkers. In 1986 the U.S. Supreme Court ruled that sexual harassment constituted a form of discrimination covered under the 1964 Civil Rights Act.

In 1991 the issue of sexual harassment attracted national attention when Clarence Thomas, an African American nominee for the Supreme Court, was accused by Anita Hill, an African American law professor, of sexually harassing her when both had worked for the Office of Economic Opportunity. Feminists were angered when the all-male Senate Judiciary Committee seemed unable to understand the issues raised by Hill's charges. When the Senate confirmed Thomas's nomination, women's groups gained new converts to their views on sexual harassment. In addition, political observers credited anger over the Thomas-Hill hearings with helping to mobilize female voters to elect four women to the U.S. Senate in 1992.

Sexual harassment also became a controversial issue within the U.S. military. The service academies began accepting female cadets, and women seemed to be finding places within the military establishment. Front-page revelations about harassment and even sexual assaults against female naval officers by their male comrades at the 1991 "Tailhook" convention, however, highlighted problems. Attempts by Navy officials to cover up the incident provoked outrage, and several high-ranking officers were forced to step down.

SEXUAL POLITICS

Debates over gender and sexuality became extremely divisive when it came to issues involving gays and lesbians. Some homosexuals had already begun to claim rights on the basis of their sexuality in the 1950s (see Chapter 27). A new spirit of insurgence and self-assurance emerged toward the end of the 1960s. In 1969, New York City police raided the Stonewall Inn, a gay bar in Greenwich Village. "Stonewall" marked a turning point in homosexual politics. Within a decade after Stonewall, thousands of gay and lesbian advocacy groups sprang up, and many homosexuals came "out of the closet," proudly proclaiming their sexual orientation.

Soon, newspapers, theaters, nightspots, and religious groups identifying themselves with the homosexual community became part of daily life in cities and large towns. Specific forms of popular entertainment, such as the disco craze of the 1970s, became closely identified with the gay and lesbian subcultures. As a cultural movement, homosexuality benefited significantly at the end of the 20th century from a general relaxation of legal and cultural controls over the portrayal and practice of *all* forms of explicit sexuality.

Homosexuals pressured state and local governments to enact laws prohibiting discrimination in housing and jobs on the basis of sexual preference. Moreover, they demanded that the police treat attacks on homosexuals no less seriously than they treated other forms of violent crime. By the 1990s gays and lesbians had gained some political power. Activism by homosexuals, however, was also met with either indifference or determined opposition, especially by conservatives.

In addition to battling traditional forms of discrimination, broadly labeled as "homophobia," gays faced a new issue: acquired immunodeficiency syndrome (AIDS), a fatal and contagious condition that attacks a person's immune system. First identified in the early 1980s, AIDS quickly became an intensely emotional and often misunderstood medical and political issue. Epidemiologists correctly recognized AIDS as a health problem for the general public. The disease could be transmitted through the careless use of intravenous drugs, tainted blood supplies, and "unprotected" heterosexual intercourse. At first, however, its incidence in the United States was limited almost solely to gay men. As a consequence of this association, gay activists charged, the Reagan and Bush administrations placed a low priority on medical efforts to check the spread of AIDS or to find a cure for it. The controversy over AIDS and medical funding galvanized gay and lesbian activists to assert their concerns more forcefully.

RACE, ETHNICITY, AND SOCIAL ACTIVISM

The emphasis on group identity as the basis for activism grew especially strong among various racial and ethnic communities in the late 20th century. Groups emphasized pride in their distinctive traditions and declared that cultural differences among Americans should be celebrated rather than simply tolerated. Especially with the influx of new immigrants, multiculturalism became a contentious issue.

DEBATES WITHIN AFRICAN AMERICAN CULTURE

African Americans had developed a strong sense of cultural identity during the 1960s (see Chapters 28 and 29). Battles against discrimination continued in the post-Vietnam era. Controversies over future directions, however, also emerged.

During the 1970s a movement called "Afrocentrism" began to attract a number of African American intellectuals and professionals. In contrast to the cold rationality of "Eurocentrists," it was argued, African Americans understood people and knowledge in broader, more empathetic ways. Afrocentrists encouraged blacks to take pride in heroic figures from the recent past, especially Malcolm X (see Chapter 29). A trend that one African American writer called "Malcolmania" accelerated with the appearance of Spike Lee's film *Malcolm X* (1992). The stress on racial pride was also prominent in rap and hip-hop music. By 1990 more than 300 private schools and even some public systems were offering black students an "Afrocentric" curriculum.

Pride in racial identity and an African heritage became a complex, contested proposition. African American women who identified with feminist issues tended to view Afrocentrism and some male rap music as infected with misogyny. Queen Latifah sang songs like "Ladies First," which criticized what she saw to be the gender stereotyping and the romanticizing of a mythical African past in many rap lyrics. African American women's groups organized to pressure record companies and radio stations to censor some rap music, especially "gangsta rap," which they considered misogynistic.

Similarly in academia, most programs in African American studies veered away from a strict Afrocentric approach in order to acknowledge the diversity and complexity of a heritage that stemmed from a multiplicity of African and American cultural influences. African American scholars such as Henry Lewis Gates Jr., who became head of Harvard's Afro-American studies department in 1991, made pride in the black experience one part of a larger multicultural vision. Gates urged that African American authors, such as Toni Morrison (who won the Nobel Prize for Literature in 1993) and Alice Walker, be viewed as writers who take "the blackness of the culture for granted, as a springboard to write about those human emotions that we share with everyone else, and that we have always shared with each other." Although African American cultures could be seen as unique and different, said Gates, they should not be considered apart from their interaction with American culture generally.

This issue of whether African Americans should cultivate separateness or seek more interaction with the broader American culture surfaced at the NAACP convention in 1997. Leaders opened for debate the possibility that the NAACP should no longer adhere to its long-standing agenda favoring school integration. Although the organization did not change its stance, the very discussion of returning to separatist schools illustrated both frustration over the test scores of African American children in integrated public education and the impact of Afrocentric influences.

Other developments underscored the fact that a broad spectrum of views existed among African Americans. The controversy over the appointment of Clarence Thomas to the U.S. Supreme Court divided African Americans, just as it divided whites. Some, especially African American feminists, saw Anita Hill's testimony against Thomas as evidence of pervasive sexism within black culture, but many other African Americans remained focused on race. No white nominee, they argued, would ever have faced the kind of personal scrutiny that Thomas confronted.

The 1996 trial of sports star O. J. Simpson raised another important debate about the place of African Americans in American life. On this issue, African Americans were less divided. In the "trial of the century," Simpson was prosecuted for two brutal murders, including that of his former wife. Simpson's defense team, headed by the African American attorney Johnnie Cochran Jr., successfully refocused the trial on alleged misconduct by racist officers within the Los Angeles police department, and a largely black jury returned a verdict of not-guilty. Opinion polls indicated a significant division along racial lines: Whites were solidly convinced of Simpson's guilt, and African Americans overwhelmingly believed he was innocent. Quite apart from whatever the trial proved about Simpson's guilt or innocence, it indicated an enormous gulf between whites and African Americans because of the distrust of police and the legal system in African American communities.

AMERICAN INDIANS

American Indians pursued a variety of strategies for social change from the 1970s to the 1990s. In 1969 activists began a two-year sit-in, designed to dramatize a history of broken

INDIAN GAMING AT MYSTIC LAKE CASINO IN MINNESOTA By the mid-1990s, legal gambling had become one of the nation's leading recreational enterprises. Native Americans saw casinos as an important way to generate jobs and capital on Indian reservations.

treaty promises over land claims, at the former federal prison on Alcatraz Island in San Francisco harbor. Expanding on this tactic, the American Indian Movement (AIM), which had been created in 1968 by young activists from several Northern Plains tribes, adopted a confrontational approach. Clashes erupted in early 1973 on the Pine Ridge Reservation in South Dakota. In response, the FBI and federal prosecutors targeted members of AIM for illegal surveillance and criminal prosecutions.

Many American Indians, like other ethnic groups, emphasized building a stronger sense of identity through traditional cultural practices. To forestall the disappearance of their languages, Indian activists urged bilingualism and the revival of traditional rituals. AIM denounced the use of stereotypical Indian names in amateur and professional sports. Teams that had long called themselves "Chiefs" or "Redskins" were pressured to seek new names.

Meanwhile, important legal changes were taking place. The omnibus Civil Rights Act of 1968 contained six sections that became known as the "Indian Bill of Rights." In these, Congress finally extended most of the provisions of the constitutional Bill of Rights to reservation Indians while still upholding the legitimacy of tribal laws. Federal legislation and several Supreme Court decisions in the 1970s subsequently reinforced the broad principle of tribal self-determination.

Many tribes used the courts to press demands derived from old treaties with the U.S. government and the unique status of tribal nations. Some tribal representatives insisted that their traditional fishing and agricultural rights be restored, a demand that often provoked resentment among non-Indians. Indians also sued to protect tribal water rights and traditional religious ceremonies (some of which include the ritual use of drugs such as peyote) and to secure repatriation of Native American skeletal remains from museums across the country. Pressure from Indian rights groups led several states and finally Congress to pass laws that provided for the repatriation of both Indian remains and sacred religious artifacts.

Claiming exemption from state gaming laws, Indians opened bingo halls and then full-blown gambling casinos. In 1988 the Supreme Court ruled that states could not prohibit gambling operations on tribal land, and Congress soon passed the Indian Gaming Regulatory Act, which gave a seal of approval to their casino operations. In states such as Connecticut, Minnesota, and Wisconsin, Indian gaming establishments became a major source of employment for Indians and non-Indians alike. Vividly underscoring the contradictions within Indian culture, the glitzy postmodernism of Las Vegas–style casinos existed alongside tribal powwows and efforts to revive older tribal practices.

SPANISH-SPEAKING AMERICANS

The media proclaimed the 1980s the "decade of the Hispanics." (Many Spanish-speaking people preferred the term "Latino.") Whether "Hispanic" or "Latino," the designation signified a population that soon would comprise America's largest minority group. Beneath this designation and a common language, however, was enormous diversity. For example, Cuban Americans generally enjoyed greater access to education and higher incomes than did other Latinos. Émigrés from Puerto Rico were already U.S. citizens and focused some of their political energies on the persistent "status" question—that is, whether Puerto Rico should hope for independence, strive for statehood, or retain a "commonwealth" connection to the mainland. Immigrants from the Dominican Republic and Central America generally were the most recent and most impoverished newcomers.

Mexican Americans comprised the oldest and most numerous Spanish-speaking group in the United States. Among them, a spirit of *Chicanismo,* a populistic pride in a heritage that could be traced back to the ancient civilizations of Middle America, emerged in the late 1960s. Young activists made "Chicano," once a term of derision, a rallying cry. In cities in the Southwest, advocates of *Chicanismo* gained considerable cultural influence. Attempts by the police to crack down on Chicano activism during the 1970s backfired, and increasing numbers of young Mexican Americans came to identify with the new insurgent spirit.

The La Raza Unida movement, founded in 1967, began to win local elections in the Southwest during the early 1970s. At the same time, *Chicanismo* continued to stimulate a cultural flowering. Catholic priests opened their churches to groups devoted to ethnic dancing, mural painting, poetry, and literature. And Spanish-language newspapers, journals, and Chicano studies programs reinforced the growing sense of pride.

In the 1970s Ernesto Cortes Jr. took the lead in founding COPS (Communities Organized for Public Service), a group that focused on achieving concrete, tangible changes that touched the everyday lives of ordinary citizens. In San Antonio, a city with a large Mexican American population, this strategy meant that Mexican American activists worked with Anglo business leaders and with Democratic politicians like Henry Cisneros, who became the city's mayor in 1981. COPS brought many Mexican Americans, particularly women, into the public arena for the first time.

By the 1990s Mexican American politics was becoming increasingly diverse. La Raza Unida continued its activities during the 1980s but never became a national force. Instead, the Mexican American Legal Defense and Educational Fund (MALDEF) emerged as the most visible national group ready to lobby or litigate on behalf of Mexican Americans. At the local level, organizations formed on the model of COPS, such as UNO (United Neighborhood Organization) in Los Angeles, continued to work on community concerns. Meanwhile, as the U.S. economy of the 1990s offered expanding employment and educational opportunities, many Mexican Americans were encouraged to pursue their own career advancement. For example, the National Network of Hispanic Women, founded in the 1970s, represented Chicanas who had obtained positions in the professions and business corporations. Linda Chavez, who had moved from the business world to the Reagan administration and then to a prominent public-policy institute, symbolized the possibility of mobility for Mexican American professionals and businesspeople.

Asian Americans

Diverse people with ancestral roots in Asia increasingly used the term "Asian American" as a way of signifying a new ethnic consciousness. Especially at colleges and universities on the West Coast, courses and then programs in Asian American studies were established during the 1970s. By the early 1980s political activists were gaining influence, and a number of Asian American politicians were elected to office during the late 1980s and early 1990s. During the 1970s, older Japanese Americans finally began to talk about their experiences in internment camps during the Second World World (see Chapter 26). Talk eventually turned to political action, and in 1988 Congress issued a formal apology and voted a reparations payment of $20,000 to every living Japanese American who had been confined in the camps.

The new Asian American vision encouraged Americans of Chinese, Japanese, Korean, Filipino, and other backgrounds to join together in a single pan-Asian movement. Organizations such as the Asian Pacific Planning Council (APPCON) lobbied to obtain government funding for projects that benefited Asian American communities. The Asian Law Caucus and the Committee Against Anti-Asian Violence mobilized to fight a wide range of legal battles. And in 1997, the National Asian Pacific American Network Council began to lobby on issues related to immigration and education.

Emphasis on ethnic identity, however, raised problems of inclusion and exclusion. Activists who were Filipino American, the second largest Asian American group in the United States in 1990, often resisted the Asian American label because they felt that Chinese Americans and Japanese Americans dominated groups such as APPCON. As a result of complex pressures from different ethnic groups, the federal government finally decided to designate "Asian or Pacific Islanders" (API) as a single pan-ethnic category in the 1990 census, but it also provided nine specifically enumerated subcategories (such as Hawaiian or Filipino) and allowed other API groups (such as Hmong and Thai) to write in their respective ethnic identifications.

Socioeconomic differences also divided Asian Americans. Although in the late 1980s and early 1990s many Asian American groups showed remarkable upward mobility, others struggled to find jobs that paid more than the minimum wage. Thus, the term "Asian American" both reflected and was challenged by the new emphasis on ethnic identity.

Dilemmas of Antidiscrimination Efforts

The assertion of racial and ethnic solidarity raised difficult questions about the meaning of equality. Between the end of the Second World War and about 1970, the antidiscrimination movement had demanded that the government not be permitted to categorize people according to group identities based on race or ethnicity. On matters such as education, housing, or employment, the law must remain "color-blind," and government should strike down discriminatory laws and practices and enact measures that effectively secure equality of opportunity for all individuals.

In the 1960s this agenda began to be modified as ethnic groups embraced the politics of group identity. With people taking new pride in their ethnic heritage, there was a shift of emphasis in social programs away from individual advancement and toward ethnic-group interests. By the 1970s this shift helped to produce a new vision of antidiscrimination in which government was to move beyond simply eliminating discriminatory barriers to *individual* opportunity. Social justice, according to the new antidiscrimination credo, required government to take "affirmative action" so that *groups* that had historically faced discrimination would now receive an equitable share of the nation's jobs, public spending, and educational programs. Affirmative action, supporters argued, would help compensate for historic discrimination and hidden racial attitudes that continued to disadvantage members of minority groups.

Affirmative action sparked fierce controversy. Many people who had supported previous policies against discrimination found affirmative action a dangerous form of racialist thought. Setting aside jobs or openings in educational institutions for certain racial or ethnic groups smacked of racist "quotas," they charged. Moreover, was not affirmative action *on behalf of* some groups inevitably also "reverse discrimination" *against* others? The issue of reverse discrimination became particularly emotional when members of one ethnic group received jobs or entry to educational institutions despite lower scores on admissions exams. Even some beneficiaries of affirmative action programs began to claim that the "affirmative action" label devalued their individual talents.

Meanwhile, courts found it difficult to square affirmative action programs with already mandated antidiscrimination policies. As a general rule, courts tended to strike down plans that seemed to contain inflexible ethnic quotas but to uphold plans that intended to remedy past patterns of discrimination and to make ethnicity only one of several criteria in hiring or educational decisions.

But the movement to scale back affirmative action plans gained momentum during the 1990s. In 1996, voters in California passed Proposition 209, which aimed at ending most affirmative action measures in California by abolishing racial or gender "preference" in state hiring, contracting, and college admissions. The number of African Americans and Latinos admitted to the state's most prestigious law and medical schools precipitously dropped, and proponents of affirmative action immediately challenged Proposition 209 as discriminatory.

Ironically, the late 20th century debates over identity politics and affirmative action coincided with a rise in racial and ethnic intermarriage. In the 1990s, growing numbers of people identified themselves as "mixed race." In 1997, the media hailed Eldrick ("Tiger") Woods as the first African American golfer to win the prestigious Masters tournament. But Woods, whose mother was from Thailand, fiercely resisted being assigned any particular ethnic identification. In an official statement to the media, he said he was "EQUALLY PROUD" to be "both African American and Asian!" But he hoped that he could also "be just a golfer and a human being."

THE NEW RIGHT

The most successful social and cultural movement to emerge during the late 20th century was a newly militant conservatism, "the New Right." Beginning in the mid-1970s, a diverse coalition mobilized on behalf of the conservative reconstruction of American life. By the 1980s and 1990s this new conservative vision had captured the imagination of millions.

Several different constituencies comprised the New Right. Older activists contributed continuity (see Chapter 28). Espousing anticommunism and denouncing domestic spending programs, they also spoke out on an ever wider range of social issues. Phyllis Schlafly assumed a prominent role in mobilizing opposition to ratification of the Equal Rights Amendment, and William F. Buckley's broad-ranging *Firing Line* became one of public television's most successful programs.

NEOCONSERVATIVES

These established activists were joined by a group of intellectuals called the "neoconservatives." Many had been anticommunist liberals during the 1950s and early 1960s. They had criticized the Democratic Party for retreating from an anticommunist foreign policy. In 1968 most had still supported Democrat Hubert Humphrey over Republican Richard Nixon, but the left-leaning candidacy of George McGovern in 1972 prompted a rush to the right.

Although neoconservatives remained true to their Cold War roots, many simultaneously renounced their support of domestic social programs. Their lively essays denounced any movement associated with the 1960s, especially affirmative action. Neoconservatives offered intellectual sustenance to a new generation of conservative thinkers who worked to reinvigorate the nation's anticommunist foreign policy and celebrate its capitalist economic system.

A new militancy among conservative business leaders contributed to this movement. They advocated that the United States rededicate itself to "economic freedom." Generous funding by corporations and philanthropic organizations helped to staff conservative research institutions (such as the American Enterprise Institute and Heritage Foundation) and to finance new lobbying organizations (such as the Committee on the Present Danger). Conservatism also gained considerable ground on college campuses.

THE NEW RELIGIOUS RIGHT

The New Right of the 1970s also attracted much grass-roots support from Protestants who belonged to fundamentalist and evangelical churches. The Supreme Court's abortion decision in *Roe* v. *Wade* (1973) mobilized fundamentalist and evangelical leaders. Since the 1920s, fundamentalist and evangelical Protestants had generally stayed clear of partisan politics. Now they formed the core of this "New Religious Right" and united with Catholic conservatives over opposition to abortion and other social and cultural issues. Leaders of the New Religious Right also embarked on a lengthy legal battle to prevent the Internal Revenue Service from denying tax-exempt status to private Christian colleges and academies, particularly in the South, that allegedly discriminated against students of color.

CONSERVATIVE POLITICS

Political developments of the 1970s also contributed to the emergence of the New Right. The declining political fortunes of George Wallace left many conservatives looking for new leadership. The end of Richard Nixon's presidency in 1974 intensified the desire for a "real" conservative leader. This desire became a crusade after Nixon's successor, Gerald Ford, selected the standard-bearer of Republican liberalism, Nelson Rockefeller, as his vice president.

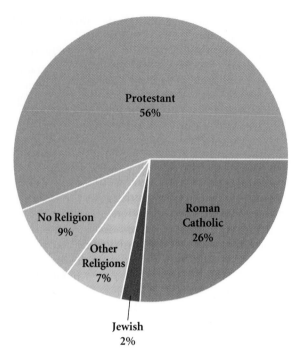

RELIGIOUS PREFERENCES IN
THE UNITED STATES (PERSONS
18 YEARS OF AGE AND OLDER)

SOURCE: *Statistical Abstract*, 1995.

George Wallace's campaigns had indicated that conservative politics could excite millions of voters. Eventually, activists organized the National Conservative Political Action Committee in 1975, the first of a number of organizations, including the Conservative Caucus, The Committee for the Survival of a Free Congress, and the Moral Majority. Although these organizations initially focused on lobbying in Washington and electing conservative Republicans, they also had broader cultural and social goals.

Increasingly, this crusading spirit became phrased in terms of defending "family values" and of opposing what the religious right considered to be "degenerate lifestyles," particularly those espoused by feminists and homosexuals. Jerry Falwell's *Listen America!* (1980) suggested that the nation's military establishment was "under the complete control of avid supporters of the women's liberation movement." Because homosexuality was "one of the gravest sins condemned in the Scriptures," argued Paul Weyrich, the issue of gay and lesbian rights was not a matter of private lifestyles but a "question of morality which . . . affects the society as a whole." American institutions, particularly the male-headed nuclear family, needed protection. Similarly, parents needed to be able to protect their children from educational "experiments." School boards and liberal educators, religious conservatives argued, were not only challenging Biblical precepts by teaching evolution but were advancing dangerous new ideas such as multiculturalism and gender-fair educational curricula.

The New Right proved adept in publicizing its crusade. Conservative foundations funded conferences and radio and TV programs. The New Religious Right mastered the media, and

CHRONOLOGY

1965	Congress passes Immigration Act of 1965
1968	Indian Bill of Rights extends most provisions of the Constitution's Bill of Rights to Native Americans
1970	First Earth Day observed • Environmental Protection Act passed • Clean Air Act passed
1973	*Roe v. Wade* decision upholds women's right to abortion • Endangered Species Act passed • Sudden rise in oil prices as result of OPEC action
1981	MTV debuts
1986	Supreme Court holds that sexual harassment qualifies as "discrimination"
1987	Immigration Reform and Control Act toughens laws against illegal aliens
1992	"Earth Summit" held in Brazil
1995	Million Man March takes place in Washington, D.C.
1996	O. J. Simpson tried and acquitted of murder • California's Proposition 209 curtails affirmative action

preachers such as Pat Robertson capitalized on the expansion of CATV in the 1970s and early 1980s. Robertson built a multimedia empire that included the 24-hour Christian Broadcasting Network (later renamed "The Family Channel"). During the 1980s, scandals and financial problems overtook some religious broadcasters, but Robertson's *700 Club,* a program that adapted his conservative evangelicalism to the talk-show and morning-news formats, grew steadily. At the same time, broadcasters associated with the New Right used talk-radio programs at both the local and national levels to spread the conservative message.

On its fringes, the New Right attracted support from ultralibertarian paramilitary groups who denounced gun control laws, taxes, and the federal government. Violent confrontations between such groups and federal authorities, especially the government's assault on the Branch Davidian group in Texas (in which 78 people were killed), left supporters of paramilitary politics feeling besieged. Any symbol of the federal government, one paramilitary leader claimed, could be considered a *"strategic military target."* In April 1995, on the second anniversary of the government's attack on the Branch Davidians, the Alfred P. Murrah Federal Building in Oklahoma City became such a target. A powerful bomb ripped through the building and killed 168 people. This bombing, for which a paramilitary loner named Timothy McVeigh was convicted and sentenced to death in 1997 (and for which accomplice Terry Nichols was convicted of conspiracy), discredited the extremist, antigovernment movement. Conservatives and liberals alike denounced the violent tendencies of paramilitary groups.

The New Right, a coalition of disparate parts, became a powerful force in American culture and, increasingly, in American politics. After the middle of the 1970s, the many strains of the new conservatism helped to challenge New Deal–Great Society liberalism and to remap the ways in which the nation's political system dealt with questions of liberty and power.

Conclusion

Sweeping changes occurred in demographics, economics, culture, and society during the last quarter of the 20th century. The nation aged, and more of its people gravitated to the Sunbelt. Sprawling "urban corridors" and "edge cities" challenged older central cities as sites for commercial, as well as residential, development. Rapid technological change fueled the growth of globalized industries, restructuring the labor force to fit a "postindustrial" economy. Americans also developed a new environmental consciousness.

In American mass culture, the most prominent development was the proliferation of the video screen. Television and motion pictures increasingly targeted specific audiences, and the fragmented nature of cultural reception was exemplified by the rise of new, particularistic media ventures such as CNN and MTV.

Meanwhile, American society itself also seemed to fragment. Social activism often organized around sexual, ethnic, and racial identities: the women's movement, gay and lesbian pride, Afrocentrism, Indian rights, and movements that represented people of Latino and Asian ancestry. Multiculturalists celebrated this fragmentation while another activist movement, the New Right, argued that it was dividing the nation. The New Right's stress on conservative social values and the necessity for limiting the power of government increasingly came to set the terms for political debate during the 1980s and 1990s.

31

WINDS OF CHANGE: POLITICS AND FOREIGN POLICY FROM FORD TO CLINTON

THE FORD PRESIDENCY ∽ THE CARTER PRESIDENCY: DOMESTIC ISSUES

THE CARTER PRESIDENCY: FOREIGN POLICY

REAGAN'S "NEW MORNING IN AMERICA" ∽ RENEWING THE COLD WAR

FROM REAGAN TO BUSH ∽ FOREIGN POLICY UNDER BUSH

TOWARD THE 21ST CENTURY

The power of the national government continually expanded during the three decades after the Second World War. Most people supported augmenting the government's military and intelligence capabilities so that the United States could play a dominant role in world affairs. They also generally endorsed the use of government power to cushion against economic downturns and to assist needy families.

The Vietnam War and the Watergate scandals (see Chapter 29), however, shook faith in government. Disillusionment with secrecy, corruption, and bloated budgets bred cynicism about the use of government power. Social and economic changes bred a feeling that the national government no longer operated effectively.

In this environment, divisive debates punctuated political life. How might a stagnating economy and a beleaguered welfare system be reshaped? Should there be more governmental activism in addressing persistent problems of poverty and inequality, or would conditions improve if government's role were reduced?

Disagreements also focused on foreign policy. Should the United States set aside anticommunism to pursue other goals, or should it wage the Cold War even more vigorously? Then, in 1989, the Cold War came to an unexpected end, and the United States faced the task of reorienting its foreign policy in a world without a Soviet threat.

The post–Cold War environment also affected domestic politics. Americans still debated the proper relationship of government power to the preservation of liberty and equality, but as the economy strengthened during the mid-1990s, domestic issues seemed less divisive than they had been only a decade earlier.

THE FORD PRESIDENCY

Gerald Ford, the first person to become vice president and then president without having been elected to either office, promised to mend the divisions that had split the nation during the 1960s and early 1970s. But Ford's ability to "heal the land," as he put it, proved limited. A genial, unpretentious person, Ford could not shake the impression that he was a weak, indecisive chief executive.

DOMESTIC ISSUES UNDER FORD

Ford quickly ran into trouble. Needing to appoint a new vice president (subject to congressional approval), Ford picked New York's Nelson Rockefeller. The choice of Rockefeller, one of the GOP's most liberal figures, infuriated conservatives within the Republican Party. Granting a presidential pardon to former President Nixon, in September 1974, proved even more controversial, and Ford's approval rating sharply plummeted.

Economic problems soon dominated the domestic side of Ford's presidency. Focusing on rising prices, rather than on increasing unemployment, Ford touted a program he called "Whip Inflation Now" (WIN). It offered a one-year income tax surcharge and cuts in federal spending as solutions to inflation. But escalating prices were accompanied by a sharp recession. As both prices and unemployment continued to rise, creating the condition known as "stagflation," Ford abandoned WIN.

Meanwhile, Ford and the Democratic-controlled Congress differed over how to deal with stagflation. Ford vetoed 39 spending bills during his brief presidency. He eventually acquiesced to an economic program that included a tax cut, an increase in unemployment benefits, an unbalanced federal budget, and a limited set of controls over oil prices.

FOREIGN POLICY UNDER FORD

While struggling with economic problems at home, Ford steered the nation through its final involvement in the war in Southeast Asia. Upon assuming office, Ford assured South Vietnam that the United States would renew its military support if the government in Saigon ever became directly menaced by North Vietnamese troops. The antiwar mood in Congress and throughout the country, however, made fulfilling this commitment impossible. North Vietnam's armies, sensing final victory, moved rapidly through the South in March 1975, and Congress refused to reintroduce U.S. military power. In early April, Khmer Rouge forces in Cambodia drove the American-backed government from the capital of Phnom Phen, and on April 30, 1975, North Vietnamese troops overran the South Vietnamese capital of Saigon, renaming it Ho Chi Minh City. The final defeat reignited the debate over U.S. policy in Indochina: Former "doves" lamented the lives lost and money wasted, while former "hawks" derided their country's "failure of will."

Within this charged atmosphere, Ford immediately sought to demonstrate that the United States could still conduct an assertive foreign policy. In May 1975, the Khmer Rouge boarded a U.S. ship, the *Mayaguez*, and seized its crew. Secretary of State Henry Kissinger convinced Ford to order a mission to rescue the *Mayaguez*'s crew and bombing strikes against Cambodia. This military response, along with pressure on the Khmer Rouge from China, secured the release of the *Mayaguez* and its crew. The president's approval ratings briefly shot up, but the incident did little to allay growing doubts about Ford's ability to handle complex foreign policy issues. The president's other foreign policy initiatives, which included extending Nixon's policy of détente with the Soviet Union and pursuing a peace treaty for the Middle East, achieved little.

THE ELECTION OF 1976

Conservative Republicans rallied behind Ronald Reagan, the former governor of California. Reagan's campaign initially floundered, but it suddenly caught fire when his advisers urged him to forgo specific proposals and to highlight his image as a true conservative who, unlike Ford, was not beholden to Washington insiders. By this time, however, Ford had already won just enough delegates in the early primaries to eke out a narrow, first-ballot victory at the Republican Party's national convention.

The Democrats turned to an outsider, James Earl (Jimmy) Carter, the former governor of Georgia. Carter had graduated from the Naval Academy with a degree in nuclear engineering and had worked on the nuclear submarine program. His military career had been cut short in the early 1950s, when he returned to Plains, Georgia, to run his family's peanut farming business following the death of his father. Later, Carter had entered state politics, gaining the reputation of being a moderate on racial issues and a fiscal conservative. When he announced his intention to run for the presidency in 1976, few people took him seriously; no governor had captured the White House since Franklin Roosevelt in 1932.

Carter campaigned as a person of many virtues. He emphasized his personal character and the fact that most of his life had been spent outside of politics. Highlighting his small-town roots, he pledged to "give the government of this country back to the people of this country." A devout Baptist, Carter campaigned as a born-again Christian. He also touted his record as a successful governor. In order to counterbalance his own status as a Washington outsider, he picked a member of the Senate, Walter Mondale, as his running mate. Although economic conditions seemed to be improving, it was not enough to secure Ford's reelection. In November, Carter won a narrow victory over Ford.

Carter owed his election to a diverse, transitory coalition. Capitalizing on his regional appeal, he carried every southern state except Virginia. He ran well among southern whites, but his victory in the South rested on a strong turnout among African Americans. Meanwhile, Carter courted the youth vote by promising to pardon most of the young men who had resisted the draft during the Vietnam War. Mondale's appeal to traditional Democrats helped Carter narrowly capture three key states—New York, Pennsylvania, and Ohio. Even so, Carter won by less than 2 million popular votes, and by the close margin of 297 to 241 in the electoral vote.

THE CARTER PRESIDENCY: DOMESTIC ISSUES

Jimmy Carter's lack of a popular mandate and his image as an outsider proved serious handicaps. Powerful constituencies, including both labor unions and multinational corporations, feared that Carter might prove to be an unpredictable leader. Moreover, many Democratic members of Congress stressed their independence from the White House, even though it was now occupied by a president from their own party. Carter also failed to develop the aura of a national leader. Although he brought some people with long experience in government into his cabinet, he relied mainly on the Georgians on his White House staff, a small cadre of advisers whom the Washington press corps dubbed the "Georgia Mafia."

Welfare and Energy

In trying to frame his agenda, Carter found himself caught between those who claimed that the power of the national government had already expanded too much and those who argued that Washington was doing too little to address social and economic problems. Unlike Richard Nixon, who had unveiled a bold Family Assistance Plan (FAP) in 1969 (Chapter 29), Carter temporized on what to do about social welfare policy. His advisers were divided between those who favored a more complicated version of FAP, which would have granted greater monetary assistance to low-income families, and those who thought the national government should create several million new public service jobs. Carter, while opposing any increase in the federal budget, asked Congress for a program that included both additional cash assistance and more jobs. He presented his proposal to Congress in 1977, where it quickly died in committee.

Carter pushed harder on energy issues. In response to soaring Middle East oil prices (see Chapter 30), he delegated James Schlesinger to develop a sweeping energy plan. Schlesinger, Carter's secretary of energy, came up with a set of ambitious goals: a decrease in U.S. reliance on foreign oil and natural gas; the expansion of domestic energy production through new tax incentives and the repeal of regulations on the production of natural gas; the levying of new taxes to discourage use of gasoline; the fostering of conservation by encouraging greater reliance on energy-saving measures; and the promotion of alternative sources of energy, especially coal and nuclear power. Neither Carter nor Schlesinger consulted Congress. Instead, Carter went on national television, in April 1977, to announce the new energy plan.

Congress quickly rejected the plan. Legislators from oil-producing states opposed the proposal for higher taxes on gasoline, and critics of the big oil companies blocked the idea of rapid deregulation of oil and natural gas production. Meanwhile, environmentalists opposed any increase in coal production. And most Americans simply ignored Carter's claim that the nation's struggle with its energy problems amounted to "the moral equivalent of war."

Economic Policy

Carter had no greater success with economic policy. He inherited the economic problems—especially stagflation—that had bedeviled Nixon and Ford. He pledged to lower both unemployment and inflation, to stimulate greater economic growth, and to balance the federal budget. Instead, by 1980 the economy had almost stopped expanding, unemployment (after dipping to a rate of under 6 percent in 1979) was beginning to rise again, and inflation topped 13 per cent. Most voters believed that economic conditions were deteriorating.

The economic difficulties of the 1970s were not limited to individuals. New York City, beset by long-term economic and social problems and short-term fiscal mismanagement, faced bankruptcy. It could neither meet its financial obligations nor borrow money through the usual channels. Finally, private bankers and public officials collaborated on congressional legislation to provide the nation's largest city with federal loan guarantees. New York's troubles were symptomatic of a broader urban crisis. According to one estimate, New York City lost 600,000 manufacturing jobs in the 1970s; Chicago lost 200,000. As a consequence, increasing

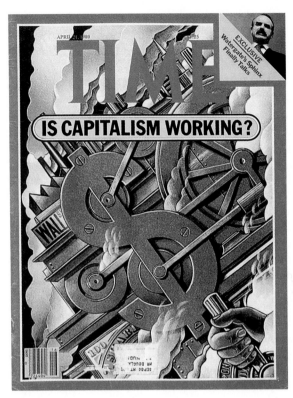

"Is Capitalism Working?" In 1980 *Time* magazine wondered about the future of the United States. Unprecedented economic problems—in particular, high rates of inflation and unemployment—dominated the Ford and Carter presidencies.

numbers of people living in central cities could find only low-paying, short-term jobs that carried no fringe benefits. Many found no jobs at all. Rising crime rates and deteriorating downtown neighborhoods afflicted most American cities, just when the impact of inflation further eroded city budgets.

What went wrong? Tax cuts and increased spending on public works projects had temporarily lowered the unemployment rate. And the Federal Reserve Board had permitted a growth in the supply of money. Those very measures, which were designed to stimulate recovery, fueled price inflation. Meanwhile, the continued rise in international oil prices triggered a series of increases for gasoline and home heating fuel that rippled through the economy. Inflation and high interest rates choked off productivity and economic growth.

Conservative economists and business groups argued that the domestic programs favored by most congressional Democrats also contributed to the spiral of rising prices. By increasing the minimum wage and by vigorously enforcing safety and antipollution regulations, conservatives argued, the national government had driven up the cost of doing business and had forced companies to pass on this increase to consumers in the form of higher prices. During the last two years of his presidency, Carter himself seemed to agree with some of this analysis when he reduced spending for a variety of social programs, supported a law that reduced the capital gains taxes paid by wealthier citizens, and began a process of deregulating transportation industries.

THE CARTER PRESIDENCY: FOREIGN POLICY

In foreign policy, as in domestic policy, Carter promised a significant change of direction. On his first day in office, he extended amnesty to those who had resisted the draft in the Vietnam War. After four years, however, his foreign policy initiatives were in disarray. Carter himself, although skillful in handling small-group negotiations, had little experience working with long-term foreign policy issues. Furthermore, his top policy advisers—Cyrus Vance as secretary of state and Zbigniew Brzezinski as national security adviser—often had contradictory approaches to policymaking. Brzezinski favored a hard-line, anti-Soviet policy with an emphasis on military muscle; Vance preferred avoiding public confrontations and emphasized the virtues of quiet diplomacy. Pulled in divergent directions, Carter's policy often seemed to waffle. Still, Carter set some important new directions, emphasizing negotiation in particular trouble spots of the world and elevating a concern for human rights into a foreign policy priority.

NEGOTIATIONS IN PANAMA AND THE MIDDLE EAST

One of the first concerns of the Carter administration involved the Panama Canal treaties. U.S. ownership of the canal, a legacy of turn-of-the-century imperialism, had sparked growing anti-Yankee sentiment throughout Latin America. Moreover, Carter argued, the canal was no longer the economic and strategic necessity it had once been. Despite strong opposition, Carter adroitly managed public and congressional relations to obtain ratification of treaties that granted Panama increasing jurisdiction over the canal, with full control after the year 2000.

Carter's faith in negotiations, and in his personal skill as a facilitator, again emerged in the Camp David peace accords of 1978. Relations between Egypt and Israel had been strained ever since the Yom Kippur War of 1973. Reviving Henry Kissinger's earlier efforts to mediate Arab-Israeli conflicts, Carter brought Menachem Begin and Anwar Sadat, leaders of Israel and Egypt, respectively, to the Camp David presidential retreat. After 13 days of bargaining, the three leaders announced the framework for a negotiating process and a peace treaty. Although Middle East tensions hardly vanished, the Camp David accords kept high-level discussions alive, lowered the level of acrimony between Egypt and Israel, and bound both sides to the United States through its promises of economic aid.

In Asia and Africa, the Carter administration also emphasized accommodation. Building on Nixon's initiative, Carter expanded economic and cultural relations with China and finally established formal diplomatic ties with the People's Republic on New Year's Day 1979. In Africa, Carter abandoned Kissinger's reliance on white colonial regimes and supported the transition of Zimbabwe (formerly Rhodesia) to a government run by the black majority.

HUMAN RIGHTS POLICY

Carter's foreign policy became best known for its emphasis on human rights. Cold War alliances with anticommunist dictatorships, Carter believed, were undermining U.S. influence in the world. In the long run, Carter's policy helped to raise consciousness around the world about human rights issues. The trend toward democratization that occurred in many nations during the 1980s and 1990s was partially triggered by the rising awareness associated with Carter's stress on human rights.

The immediate impact of the human rights policy, however, was ambiguous. Because Carter applied the policy inconsistently, many of America's most repressive allies, such as Ferdinand Marcos in the Philippines, felt little pressure to change their ways. Moreover, Carter's rhetoric about human rights helped spark revolutionary movements against America's long-standing dictator-allies in Nicaragua and Iran. These revolutions brought anti-American regimes to power and presented Carter with thorny policy dilemmas. In Nicaragua, for example, the Sandinista revolution toppled dictator Anastasio Somoza, whom the United States had long supported. The Sandinistas, initially a coalition of moderate democrats and communists, quickly drifted toward a more militant Marxism and began to expropriate property. Carter opposed Nicaragua's movement to the left but could not change the revolution's course. The president's Republican critics charged that his policies had given a green light to communism in Central America and pledged that they would work to oust the Sandinista government.

The Hostage Crisis in Iran

Events in Iran dramatically eroded Carter's standing. Shah Reza Pahlavi had regained his throne with the help of Western intelligence agencies in a 1953 coup, and the United States had subsequently provided him with a steady supply of military hardware. The overthrow of the Shah by an Islamic fundamentalist revolution in January 1979 thus signaled a massive rejection of U.S. influence in Iran. When the Carter administration bowed to political pressure and allowed the deposed and ailing Shah to enter the United States for medical treatment in November 1979, a group of Iranians took 66 Americans hostage at the U.S. embassy compound in Teheran; they demanded the return of the Shah in exchange for the release of the hostages.

As the hostage incident gripped the country, Carter's critics cited it as evidence of how weak and impotent the United States had become. Carter talked tough; levied economic reprisals against Iran; and sent a military mission to rescue the hostages. But the mission proved an embarrassing failure, and Carter never managed to resolve the situation. After his defeat in the 1980 election, diplomatic efforts finally brought the hostages home, but the United States and Iran remained at odds.

Meanwhile, criticism of Carter intensified when the Soviet Union invaded Afghanistan in December 1979. Many Americans interpreted the invasion as a simple sign that the Soviets now dismissed the United States as too weak to contain their expansionism. Carter could never shake the charge that he was afflicted with "post-Vietnam syndrome," a failure to act strongly in foreign affairs. Carter halted grain exports to the Soviet Union, organized a boycott of the 1980 Olympic Games in Moscow, withdrew a new Strategic Arms Limitation Treaty (SALT) from the Senate, and revived registration for the military draft. Still, conservatives charged Carter with presiding over a decline of American power and prestige, and Ronald Reagan made constant reference to Iran and Afghanistan as he prepared for the 1980 elections.

The Election of 1980

For a time, when Senator Edward Kennedy of Massachusetts entered the party's 1980 presidential primaries, it seemed that the Democrats might not even allow Carter to run for a second term. Kennedy's campaign underscored Carter's vulnerability and popularized anti-Carter themes that Republicans gleefully embraced. "It's time to say no more hostages, no more high interest rates, no more high inflation, and no more Jimmy Carter," went one of Kennedy's stump speeches. More than one-third of the people who supported Kennedy in the final eight Democratic primaries (five of which Kennedy won) were conservative Democrats who told pollsters they would likely vote Republican in the general election. As Carter entered the fall campaign against the Republicans, he seemed a likely loser.

Republican challenger Ronald Reagan exuded confidence. He stressed his opposition to federal social programs and his support for a stronger national defense. His successful primary campaign highlighted an optimistic vision of a rejuvenated America. To remind voters of the alleged failures of the Carter presidency, he asked repeatedly, "Are you better off now than you were four years ago?" He quickly answered his own question by invoking what he called a "misery index," which added the rate of inflation to the rate of unemployment.

Reagan's optimism allowed him to seize an issue that Democrats had long regarded as their own: economic growth. Reagan promised that tax cuts would bring back the kind of economic expansion the nation had enjoyed during the 1950s and 1960s. During a crucial television debate, when Carter tried to criticize Reagan's promises for their lack of specificity, a smiling Reagan spotlighted Carter's apparent pessimism by repeatedly quipping, "There you go again!"

Reagan won the November presidential election with only slightly more than 50 percent of the popular vote. (Moderate Republican John Anderson, who ran an independent campaign for the White House, won about 7 percent.) But Reagan's margin over Carter in the Electoral College was overwhelming: 489 to 49. Moreover, Republicans took 12 Senate seats away from Democrats, gaining control of the Senate for the first time since 1954.

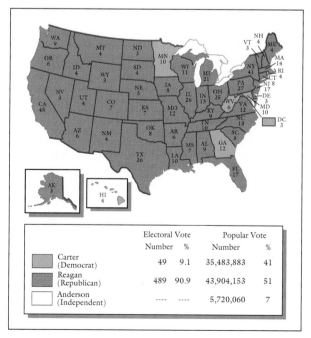

	Electoral Vote		Popular Vote	
	Number	%	Number	%
Carter (Democrat)	49	9.1	35,483,883	41
Reagan (Republican)	489	90.9	43,904,153	51
Anderson (Independent)	----	----	5,720,060	7

PRESIDENTIAL ELECTION, 1980

Noting Reagan's slim majority in the popular vote, many Democrats portrayed 1980 as more of a defeat for Carter than a victory for the Republicans. By reducing expenditures for domestic programs and lowering taxes on capital gains, according to this analysis, Carter had alienated traditional Democratic voters. Moreover, Reagan's sophisticated media campaign was credited with temporarily misleading voters; in due course, these Democrats claimed, Reagan would be unmasked as a media-manufactured president.

Democrats, however, failed to recognize that their own domestic agenda had been steadily losing support. The real income of the average American family, which had risen at an annual rate of just under 3 percent per year between 1950 and 1965, rose only 1.7 percent a year between 1965 and 1980. In such a stagnant economic climate, middle-income taxpayers found Democratic social welfare programs far less palatable than they had found them in more prosperous times.

During the 1970s, then, the United States had entered a new, more conservative era in social policymaking. Liberals continued to talk about how to improve welfare-state initiatives. But conservatives advocated a radical reduction in government spending programs, denouncing AFDC (Aid to Families with Dependent Children) and food stamps as socially debilitating for their recipients and a drag on the national economy. More and more voters came to identify with the position championed by Ronald Reagan.

REAGAN'S "NEW MORNING IN AMERICA"

Tapping anxieties about declining national power and eroding living standards, Reagan promised a "new morning in America," especially in the area of taxation. A taxpayer revolt, which had emerged in California in the late 1970s, provided a model for Reagan's attack on federal spending for domestic programs. Across the country, people responded to Reagan's tax-reduction message.

In addition, Reagan courted the New Right with opposition to abortion, support for prayer in school, and the endorsement of traditional "family values." Conservative religious figures, including Jerry Falwell and Pat Robertson, onetime Democrats, joined Reagan's new Republican coalition. Reagan also found a way to reach white (especially male) voters, who were upset over affirmative action, while avoiding being charged with making racial appeals. Reagan himself proclaimed a commitment to "color-blind" social policies. "Guaranteeing equality of treatment is the government's proper function," Reagan proclaimed at one of his first presidential press conferences.

REAGAN'S FIRST TERM: ECONOMIC ISSUES

To justify cutting taxes, Reagan touted a theory called "supply-side economics." This theory held that tax reductions would stimulate the economy by putting more money in the hands of investors and consumers, thereby reversing the economic stagnation of the 1970s. Reagan pushed his tax plan through Congress during the summer of 1981. The new law significantly reduced taxes for people who earned high incomes and already possessed significant wealth. Taxes on businesses were also slashed to encourage investment in new facilities and equipment. At the same time, the Federal Reserve Board pursued a policy of keeping interest rates high in order to drive down inflation.

After a severe recession in 1981 and 1982, the worst since the Great Depression of the 1930s, the economy rebounded and entered a period of noninflationary growth. By 1986, the GNP was steadily climbing, while the rate of inflation had plunged to less than 2 percent; unemployment figures, however, stubbornly refused to drop. Still, Reagan's supporters called the turnaround an "economic miracle" and hailed the "Reagan Revolution."

The economic revival of the 1980s sparked debate over the cumulative impact of annual federal budget deficits and the consequences of the economic expansion. On the first issue—budget deficits—Reagan's critics pointed out that his tax cuts had not been matched by budget reductions. Although Reagan constantly inveighed against budget deficits and big spenders, during his presidency the annual deficits tripled to nearly $300 billion. To finance such spending, the United States borrowed abroad and piled up the largest foreign debt in the world. Reagan's "Revolution," critics charged, brought short-term recovery for some people by courting a long-term budget crisis that would harm people with low incomes, who relied on government programs, and would imperil future generations, who would have to pay for the soaring government debt.

On the second issue—the soundness of the U.S. economy—critics complained that Reagan's policies were creating a "Swiss-cheese" economy, one that was full of holes. Farmers in the Midwest were especially battered during the recession of 1981–1982, as falling crop prices made it difficult for them to make payments on the high-interest loans contracted during the inflation-ridden 1970s. A series of mortgage foreclosures hit farm states, and the ripple effect decimated many small-town businesses. At the same time, urban families, who were struggling to get by on low-paying jobs and declining welfare benefits, were also puzzled by talk about a "Reagan boom." Many of the jobs created in the 1980s offered relatively low wages and few, if any, fringe benefits. The minimum wage, when measured in constant dollars, fell throughout Reagan's presidency.

In communities of color, this uneven pattern was especially glaring. From the late 1960s on, people of color with educational credentials and marketable skills had made significant economic gains. The number of African American families making a solid middle-class income more than doubled between 1970 and 1990. African American college graduates could expect incomes comparable to those of white college graduates. Many persons of color, therefore, could afford to move away from inner-city neighborhoods. But the story of mobility was very different for an "underclass" of people who were persistently unemployed and trapped in declining urban centers. At the end of the 1980s, one-third of all black families lived in poverty. In inner cities, less than half of African American children were completing high school, and more than 60 percent were unemployed. Throughout America, the gap between rich and poor widened significantly.

Implementing a Conservative Agenda

Meanwhile, Reagan made changes in other areas. In 1981 he fired the nation's air traffic controllers when their union refused to halt a nationwide strike. Overall, union membership continued to decline, as both the Reagan administration and many large businesses pursued aggressive antiunion strategies during the 1980s. The percentage of non-farmworkers who were unionized fell to just 16 percent by the end of Reagan's presidency. Workers, who recognized that the balance of power was tilting against them, increasingly turned away from strikes as an economic weapon.

Reagan also placed a conservative stamp on the federal court system. Almost immediately, he was able to nominate a Supreme Court justice, Sandra Day O'Connor, the first woman to sit on the High Court. During Reagan's first term, when the Republican Party controlled the Senate, Reagan also named other prominent conservative jurists, such as Robert Bork and Antonin Scalia, to lower federal courts. Conservatives welcomed the influx of judges from the political right. Civil libertarians complained that the federal courts were becoming less hospitable to legal claims made by criminal defendants, labor unions, and political dissenters. Because of the retirement of a number of older judges, by 1989 about 50 percent of the federal judiciary had been nominated and confirmed during Ronald Reagan's presidency.

In his non-judicial appointments, Reagan also looked for staunch conservatives. He filled the Justice Department with lawyers who were eager to end the "rights revolution" and affirmative action programs. He appointed James Watt, an outspoken critic of environmental legislation, as secretary of the interior. Reagan's first two appointees to the Department of Energy actually proposed eliminating the department they headed—an idea that Congress successfully blocked. Finally, having staffed most of the administrative agencies with conservatives, Reagan sought to ease regulations on businesses by relaxing enforcement of safety and environmental laws. The administration also eased the enforcement of affirmative action laws, in line with Reagan's call for a "color-blind" approach on racial issues.

In addition, Reagan eliminated some social welfare programs, most notably the Comprehensive Employment and Training Act (CETA), and reduced funding for others, such as food stamps. Nevertheless, he pledged that Washington would still maintain a "safety net" for those who were really in need of governmental assistance.

Critics complained, however, about the number of people whose total package of income and government benefits still fell below what economists considered the "poverty" level. Conditions would have been worse if the nation's most popular welfare program, Social Security, had not been redesigned in the 1970s so that its benefits automatically increased along with the rate of inflation (an arrangement called "indexing"). Rising Social Security payments, along with Medicare benefits, enabled millions of older Americans who might otherwise have fallen below the official poverty line to hold their own economically during the Reagan years. The burden of the growing poverty, then, fell disproportionately on female-headed households and especially on children. By the end of the 1980s, one of every five children was being raised in a household whose total income fell below the official poverty line.

Amid the controversies over the growing budget deficit and the inequalities in wealth, Reagan became known as the "Teflon president." No matter what problems beset his administration, nothing negative ever seemed to stick to Reagan himself. His genial optimism seemed unshakable. He even appeared to rebound quickly after being shot by a would-be assassin in March 1981.

THE ELECTION OF 1984

Democrats continued to underestimate Reagan's popular appeal—a miscalculation that doomed their 1984 presidential campaign. Walter Mondale, Jimmy Carter's vice president from 1976 to 1980, ran on a platform that called for "the eradication of discrimination in all aspects of American life" and for an expansion of domestic spending programs by the national government. Mondale's running mate, Representative Geraldine Ferraro of New York, was the first woman ever to run for president or vice president on a major-party ticket. Convinced that Reagan's "economic miracle" would eventually self-destruct, Mondale stuck to his basic themes. Reagan would soon have to raise taxes to cover the burgeoning federal deficit, Mondale bravely declared, and "so will I. He won't tell you; I just did."

The Republicans ran a textbook-perfect campaign. The president labeled Mondale's support by labor and civil rights groups as a vestige of the old politics of "special interests" and denounced Mondale's tax proposal as a reminder of the "wasteful tax-and-spend policies" that he claimed had precipitated the stagflation of the 1970s. Mondale's selection of Ferraro was criticized as another example of his kowtowing to special interests. Reagan himself continued to sketch the picture of a bright, conservative future for America. In his campaign films, the United States appeared as a glowing landscape of bustling small towns and lush farmland. His campaign slogan was "It's Morning Again in America." The 1984 presidential election ended with Mondale carrying only his home state of Minnesota and the District of Columbia.

Reagan and his conservative supporters succeeded in giving new meaning to many traditional political terms. "Liberal" no longer meant a set of government programs that would stimulate the economy and help people to buy new homes and more consumer goods. Instead, Republicans made "liberalism" a code word for supposedly wasteful social programs devised by a bloated federal government that gouged hardworking people and gave their dollars to people who were undeserving and lazy. The term "conservative," as used by Republicans, came to mean economic growth through limited government and support for traditional social-cultural values.

RENEWING THE COLD WAR

Reagan quickly established foreign policy themes that dominated both of his terms in office. Under Carter, he claimed, the nation's power had been eroded by the "Vietnam syndrome" of passivity and "loss of will." Reagan promised to reverse that trend. Although he did not repudiate Carter's human rights policy, he called it into the service of a renewed Cold War against the Soviet Union, highlighting the Soviet Union's mistreatment of its Jewish population and ethnic minorities.

THE DEFENSE BUILDUP

The United States, Reagan claimed, had "unilaterally disarmed" during the 1970s, while the Soviets were staging a massive military buildup. He called for a new battle against what he called the "evil empire" of the Soviet Union. Closing what Reagan called America's "window of vulnerability" against Soviet military power, however, would be expensive. Although his tax cuts would inevitably reduce government revenues, Reagan nonetheless asked Congress for dramatic increases in military spending. The Pentagon launched programs to enlarge the Navy and to modernize strategic nuclear forces, concentrating especially on missile systems. It also deployed new missiles throughout Western Europe.

In 1984 Reagan surprised even his closest advisers by proposing the most expensive defense system in history—a space-based shield against incoming missiles. The Strategic Defense Initiative (SDI) soon had its own agency in the Pentagon that projected a need for $26 billion over five years, just for start-up research. Critics dubbed the program "Star Wars," and many members of Congress shuddered at its astronomical costs. Although most scientists considered the project impractical, Congress voted appropriations for SDI, and throughout his presidency Reagan clung to the idea of a defensive shield. SDI dominated both the strategic debate at home and arms talks with the Soviet Union.

Greater defense spending had another strategic dimension. Secretary of Defense Caspar Weinberger suggested that, as the Soviets increased the burden on their own faltering economy in order to compete in the accelerating arms race, the Soviet Union itself might collapse under the economic strain. This had been an implicit goal of the containment policy since NSC-68 was drafted in 1949 (see Chapter 27).

Military Actions in Lebanon, Grenada, Nicaragua, and Libya

In waging the renewed Cold War, Reagan promised vigorous support to "democratic" revolutions around the globe. Reagan's UN representative, Jeane Kirkpatrick, wrote that "democratic" forces included almost any movement, no matter how autocratic, that was noncommunist. The United States thus funded opposition movements in countries that were aligned with the Soviet Union: Ethiopia, Angola, South Yemen, Cambodia, Grenada, Cuba, Nicaragua, and Afghanistan. Reagan called the participants in such movements "freedom fighters," although few had any visible commitment to liberty or equality.

The Reagan administration also displayed a new willingness to unleash U.S. military power. The first occasion was in southern Lebanon, where Israeli troops were facing off against Lebanese Moslems supported by Syria and the Soviet Union. Alarmed by the gains the Moslems were achieving, the Reagan administration in 1982 convinced Israel to withdraw and sent 1,600 American marines as part of a "peacekeeping force" to restore stability. But Moslem fighters then turned their wrath against the Americans. After a suicide commando mission into a U.S. military compound killed 241 marines, Reagan pulled out U.S. troops and disengaged from the conflict.

Although the debacle in Lebanon raised questions about Reagan's policies, another military intervention restored his popularity. In October 1983 Reagan sent 2,000 U.S. troops to the tiny Caribbean island of Grenada, whose socialist leader was forging ties with Castro's Cuba. U.S. troops overthrew the government and installed one friendly to American interests. Tight military control over news coverage shielded the administration from criticism and allowed it to declare Grenada a complete foreign policy victory.

Buoyed by events in Grenada, the Reagan administration fixed its sights on the Central American country of Nicaragua. The socialist government, led by the Sandinista Party, was trying to build ties with Cuba. The United States augmented its military forces in neighboring Honduras and conducted training exercises throughout the area. But Reagan decided to use covert means to topple the Sandinista regime. The United States tightened its economic stranglehold on Nicaragua and launched a propaganda offensive to discredit the Sandinistas. These measures were designed to give the United States time to train and equip an opposition military force of Nicaraguans, the *contras*. Meanwhile, the administration supported murderous dictatorships in nearby El Salvador and Guatemala to prevent other leftist insurgencies from gaining ground in Central America.

U.S. initiatives in Central America became the most controversial aspect of Reagan's foreign policy. U.S. backed regimes were clearly implicated in abuses of human rights. Mounting evidence of the brutality and corruption of the Nicaraguan *contras* brought growing public criticism. In 1984, the Democratic-controlled Congress denied further military aid to the *contras*.

The Reagan administration quickly sought ways around the congressional ban. One solution was to encourage wealthy U.S. conservatives and other governments to donate money to the *contras*. In June 1984, at a top secret meeting of the National Security Planning Group, Reagan and his top advisers discussed the legality of pressing "third parties" to contribute to the *contra* cause.

Meanwhile, violence continued to escalate throughout the Middle East. Militant Islamic groups stepped up the use of terrorism against Israel and Western powers; bombings and the kidnapping of Western hostages became more frequent. Apparently, such activities were being encouraged by Libyan leader Muammar al-Qaddafi as well as by Iran. In the spring of 1986 the United States launched an air strike into Libya aimed at Qaddafi's personal compound. The bombs did serious damage and killed Qaddafi's young daughter, but Qaddafi and his government survived. Despite some public criticism of this action, Americans generally approved of using strong measures against sponsors of terrorism and hostage-taking.

OTHER INITIATIVES

Reagan's foreign policy included initiatives other than military incursions. In a new "informational" offensive, the administration funded a variety of conservative groups around the world and established Radio Martí, a Florida radio station beamed at Cuba and designed to discredit Fidel Castro. When the United Nations agency UNESCO criticized the global dominance of the U.S. media and called for a "New World Information Order" that would reduce the overwhelming influence of U.S.-originated news and information, Reagan cut off U.S. contributions to UNESCO and demanded changes in the organization and operation of the UN. Reagan also championed free markets, urging other nations to minimize tariffs and restrictions on foreign investment. His Caribbean Basin Initiative, for example, rewarded with U.S. aid those small nations in the Caribbean region that adhered to free-market principles.

THE IRAN-CONTRA AFFAIR

In November 1986, a magazine in Lebanon reported that the Reagan administration was selling arms to Iran as part of a secret deal to secure the release of Americans being held hostage by Middle Eastern factions friendly to Iran's government. The story quickly became front-page news in the United States because such a deal would be in clear conflict with the Reagan administration's stated policies that it would not sell arms to Iran and that it would not reward hostage-taking by negotiating for the release of any captives.

As Congress began to investigate the arms-for-hostages story, matters turned even more bizarre. Profits from secret arms sales to Iran had been channeled to the *contra* forces in Nicaragua as a means of circumventing the congressional ban on U.S. military aid. Oliver North, a lieutenant colonel who worked in the office of the national security adviser, had directed the effort. Responsibility for carrying out the deal had been entrusted to a secret unit in the National Security Council, shadowy international arms dealers, and private go-betweens. North had been running a covert operation that violated both the stated policy of the White House and the ban legislated by Congress.

The arms-for-hostages idea dovetailed with Reagan's foreign policy priorities. During the 1980 campaign, Reagan had made hostages a symbol of U.S. weakness under Carter; as Iranian-backed groups continued to kidnap Americans, Reagan began to worry that the hostage issue might be as disastrous for his presidency as it had been for Carter's. Meanwhile, Iran was waging a prolonged war with Iraq. Although the United States allowed arms sales to Iraq, it had organized a ban on the sale of arms to Iran by Western powers because of Iran's connection with hostage-taking. The arms-for-hostages deal thus evolved out of mutual interests and fears: Despite the public enmity between the two nations, Iran needed arms to fight its war with Iraq, and the United States needed to show that it could bring hostages home. The secret deal satisfied both countries. Even better, the Reagan administration could use the profits from the sale secretly to fund other projects—such as the *contra* cause—that had to be hidden from Congress and the public.

This scheme seemed to cut at the heart of democratic processes, but everyone involved escaped accountability. Reagan maintained that he could not remember any details about either the release of the hostages or the funding of the *contras*. His management style might deserve criticism, he admitted, but no legal issues were involved. Vice President George Bush also escaped censure by claiming ignorance. Oliver North and National Security Adviser John Poindexter were convicted of felonies, including falsification of documents and lying to Congress, but their convictions were overturned on appeal. Six years later George Bush pardoned six former officials who had been involved in the Iran-*Contra* affair.

The Beginning of the End of the Cold War

Although Reagan's first six years in office had revived the Cold War confrontation, his last two years saw a sudden thaw in U.S.-Soviet relations and a movement toward détente. The economic cost of superpower rivalry was burdening both nations. Moreover, changes within the Soviet Union were eliminating the reasons for confrontation. Mikhail Gorbachev, who became general secretary of the Communist Party in 1985, was a new style of Soviet leader. He realized that his isolated country was facing economic stagnation and an environmental crisis brought on by decades of poorly planned industrial development. To redirect his country's course, he withdrew Soviet troops from Afghanistan, reduced commitments to Cuba and Nicaragua, proclaimed a policy of *glasnost* ("openness"), and began to implement *perestroika* ("economic liberalization") at home.

Soon Gorbachev was pursuing policies that stirred winds of change throughout the Soviet empire. He began summit meetings with the United States on arms control. At Reykjavik, Iceland, in October 1986, Reagan shocked both Gorbachev and his own advisers by proposing a wholesale ban on nuclear weapons. In December 1987 Reagan and Gorbachev signed a major arms treaty that reduced the number of intermediate-range missiles held by each nation and allowed for on-site verification, something the Soviets had never before permitted. The next year, Gorbachev scrapped the policy that forbade any nation under Soviet influence from renouncing communism. In effect, Gorbachev was declaring an end to the Cold War. And within the next few years, the Soviet sphere of influence—and then the Soviet Union itself—would cease to exist.

From Reagan to Bush

Even before the Iran-*Contra* affair, Reagan's image and influence were beginning to fade. Members of the New Right came to criticize the president for failing to support their agendas vigorously enough, while economic problems—especially the growing federal deficit—sparked broader-based calls for more assured leadership from the White House.

DOMESTIC POLICY DURING REAGAN'S SECOND TERM

During Reagan's second term, the White House and Congress began to address two long-term domestic issues: reduction of the federal budget and reform of the welfare system. First, the Gramm-Rudman-Hollings Act of 1985 mandated a balanced federal budget by 1991, but neither Congress nor the Reagan administration seemed eager to implement that goal. Second, the Family Support Act of 1988 required states to inaugurate work training programs and to move people off the welfare rolls. But this law did little to guarantee that people would actually find—and then keep—jobs. Without a plan to create new employment opportunities, the Family Support Act seemed to have more to do with the desire to cut domestic programs and less to do with finding actual alternatives to the existing welfare system. Yet, despite their limitations, Gramm-Rudman-Hollings and the Family Support Act set policymakers on a course of action that would culminate in a comprehensive budget-reduction and welfare-reform package nearly a decade later.

Meanwhile, many of Reagan's supporters became disappointed by domestic developments during his second term. In 1986, following the resignation of Warren Burger, the Senate confirmed William Rehnquist as chief justice of the Supreme Court and Antonin Scalia, another staunch conservative, to replace Rehnquist as associate justice. But in 1987 the Senate rebuffed Reagan's attempt to elevate Robert Bork, another conservative, to the Court. Bork's rejection sparked discord among conservatives, many of whom blamed Reagan for not working hard enough to secure his confirmation. Members of the Religious Right chafed at what they considered Reagan's tepid support for their antiabortion crusade, while his massive spending for military programs undermined the conservative dream of decreasing the federal budget.

Reagan's second term was also marked by charges of mismanagement and corruption. The process of banking deregulation became linked to malfeasance in financial circles and to risky speculation. Problems in the savings and loan industry reached crisis proportions. During a period of lax oversight by federal regulators, many savings and loan institutions (S&Ls) had extended too much money to risky ventures and had incurred financial obligations far beyond their means. As hundreds of S&Ls fell insolvent, the people and the businesses to whom they had lent money also faced financial disaster. The agency that regulated S&Ls predicted an impending crisis as early as the spring of 1985, but the Reagan administration and most members of Congress dismissed the warning.

Finally, in 1989 Congress enacted an expensive bailout plan, designed to save some institutions and to provide a means of transferring the assets of failed S&Ls to those that were still solvent. Even as taxpayers began paying for the plan, corruption plagued its execution; large, well-connected commercial banks purchased the assets of bankrupt S&Ls at bargain prices. By the time the Treasury Department stepped in, early in 1994, most of the larger S&Ls had already been sold.

THE ELECTION OF 1988

Despite the growing criticism of Reagan's leadership at home, Cold War détente boosted the 1988 presidential prospects of his heir-apparent, Vice President George Bush, who easily gained the Republican nomination. Part of a prominent Republican family from Connecticut, Bush had gone to Texas and entered the oil business as a young man. He had served in the House of Representatives and as director of the CIA. Bush chose as his running mate Senator J. Danforth Quayle, a staunch conservative. The selection of Quayle delighted political comedians, who found the bumbling Quayle a rich source for new comic material.

Governor Michael Dukakis of Massachusetts emerged from the primaries as the Democratic presidential candidate. Dukakis avoided talk of new domestic programs and higher taxes. Instead, he pledged to bring competence and honesty to the White House and boasted of how he had mobilized private experts to help streamline the government and stimulate the economy of Massachusetts. By running a cautious campaign and avoiding controversial domestic issues, Dukakis gambled that he could defeat Bush, who was burdened by Reagan's domestic failures.

The election of 1988 was dominated by negative campaigning, especially on behalf of George Bush. Pro-Bush television commercials usually presented Dukakis bathed in shadows and always showed him with a frown on his face. In the campaign's most infamous ad, Dukakis was linked to Willie Horton, an African American prison inmate who had committed a rape while on furlough from a Massachusetts prison. Clearly designed to play on racial fears, the ad also implied that Dukakis was soft on crime. Rising rates of violent crime during the late 1980s alarmed Americans across the country. As one pundit put it, the Bush campaign made it seem that Willie Horton was Dukakis's running mate.

Bush won a solid majority in both the popular vote and the Electoral College. Yet, he carried so many states by such small margins that relatively minor shifts in voter turnouts could have given the victory to Dukakis. Dukakis did better in 1988 than Mondale had done in 1984, winning 111 electoral votes. Outside the South, which went heavily for Bush, Dukakis carried more than 500 counties that had supported Reagan in 1984. Overall, voter turnout was the lowest it had been in any national election since 1924.

Although conservatives hoped Bush would build on the Reagan presidency, many doubted his commitment to their cause. Might not his campaign pledge of a "kinder, gentler America" be meant as a veiled criticism of Reagan's domestic policies? Bush angered many conservatives by agreeing to an increase in the minimum wage and by failing to veto the Civil Rights Act of 1991, a law they wrongly claimed set up quotas for the preferential hiring of women and people of color in business and government. Most important, in 1990 he broke his campaign promise of "no new taxes" and accepted a tax increase as a means of dealing with the rising federal deficit.

Meanwhile, there was a growing popular perception that the national government, divided between a Democratic-controlled Congress and a Republican-occupied White House, was suffering from "gridlock." Little seemed to be getting done on domestic issues. Moreover, the economic growth of the Reagan years was slowing, and the budget deficit was expanding. George Bush's chances for a second term would depend on his record in foreign, rather than domestic, policy.

FOREIGN POLICY UNDER BUSH

During Bush's presidency Soviet communism collapsed. As communist states fell like dominoes, the international order underwent its greatest transformation since the end of the Second World War.

The End of the Cold War

Beginning in 1989, political change swept through Eastern and Central Europe. In Poland, the anticommunist labor party, Solidarity, ousted the pro-Soviet regime. The pro-Soviet government in East Germany fell in November 1989, and Germans from both West and East hacked down the Berlin Wall. Divided since the Second World War, Germany began the difficult process of reunification. In Czechoslovakia, Hungary, Romania, and Bulgaria, public demonstrations forced out communist governments. Yugoslavia disintegrated, and warfare ensued as ethnic groups tried to re-create the separate states of Slovenia, Serbia, Bosnia, and Croatia. The Baltic countries of Latvia, Lithuania, and Estonia, which had been under Soviet control

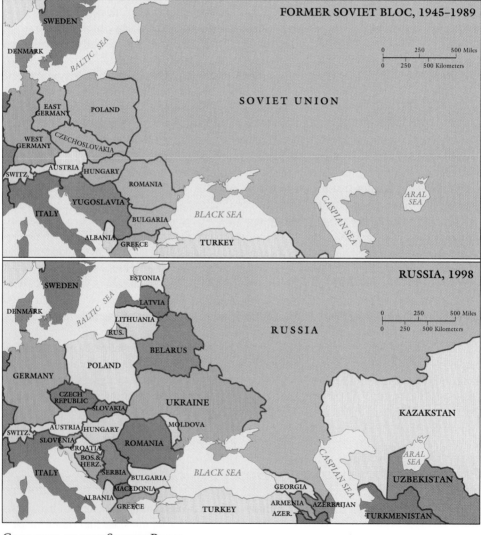

Collapse of the Soviet Bloc

since the Second World War, declared their independence. And most dramatic, the major provinces that had comprised the Soviet Union itself assumed self-government. The president of the new state of Russia, Boris Yeltsin, put down a coup by hard-line communists in August 1991, and his popularity rapidly eclipsed that of Mikhail Gorbachev. Yeltsin urged that the Soviet Union be abolished and replaced with 11 republics, loosely joined in a Commonwealth of Independent States. In December 1991, the Russian Parliament ratified that plan.

As the map of Europe changed, the United States faced the task of establishing diplomatic relations with many new and reconfigured countries. In December 1991 Congress authorized $400 million to help the Soviet Union's successor states dismantle their nuclear weaponry, and it allotted an equivalent amount the next year for promoting democracy in the new European republics. Critics charged that these sums for peace-building were minuscule compared to the funds that had been appropriated for military containment. But Bush, who feared being charged with slighting domestic problems, felt reluctant to press for more assistance.

Meanwhile, the international economic picture was improving. In the mid-1980s, huge debts that Third World nations owed to U.S. banks had threatened to shake the international banking system, but by the end of the decade most of these obligations had been renegotiated. Free-market economies began to emerge in the former communist states, and Western Europe moved toward economic integration. The nations of the Pacific Rim continued to prosper, and Bush pressed for a North American Free Trade Agreement (NAFTA) that would bring Canada, the United States, and Mexico together to form the largest free-market zone in the world.

As the likelihood of armed conflict with the Soviet Union faded, the Bush administration set about redefining "national security." In Central America, the Sandinistas were voted out of office in Nicaragua and became just another political party in a multiparty state. Supported by the United States, the United Nations began to assist both El Salvador and Guatemala in charting a course that would turn armed conflicts into electoral ones. The Pentagon thus began to consider new missions for its military forces. Future action, its planners predicted, would take the form of rapid, sharply targeted strikes rather than lengthy campaigns. Military troops might even be used to fight a "war against drugs." In Latin America, the Bush administration sponsored missions to destroy drug crops and interdict drug shipments.

Panama, whose government was headed by General Manuel Noriega, was deeply involved in the drug trade. The Reagan administration had secured an indictment in the United States against Noriega for drug trafficking and had tried to force him from power through economic pressure. But this had only deepened Noriega's reliance on drug revenues. Deciding how to deal with Noriega was a significant problem for U.S. policymakers. First, there was the embarrassing fact that Noriega had been recruited as a CIA "asset" in the mid-1970s, when Bush himself was the agency's director. In addition, the United States needed a friendly, responsible government in Panama in order to complete the transfer of the Panama Canal to Panamanian sovereignty by the end of the century. Bush finally decided to topple Noriega. In a military incursion called "Operation Just Cause," U.S. marines landed in Panama in December 1989, pinpointed Noriega's whereabouts, and put him under siege. Soon he surrendered and was extradited to stand trial in Florida. In April 1992 he was convicted of cocaine trafficking and imprisoned.

Seizing the leader of a foreign government in this manner raised questions of international law, and the resort to military force in a region long sensitive to U.S. intervention sparked controversy. Still, this military action, which involved 25,000 troops but only about two dozen U.S. casualties, boosted Bush's popularity at home. It also provided a new model for post–Cold War military action. The Pentagon firmed up plans for phasing out its older military bases, particularly in Germany and the Philippines, and for creating highly mobile, rapid-deployment forces. A test of this new strategy came in the Persian Gulf War.

THE PERSIAN GULF WAR

On August 2, 1990, President Saddam Hussein of Iraq ordered his troops to occupy the small neighboring emirate of Kuwait. Within a day, Iraq's forces had taken control of Kuwait, a move that caught the United States off guard. Although Iraq had been massing troops on Kuwait's border and denouncing Kuwaiti oil producers, U.S. intelligence forecasters had doubted that it was about to take over the country. Now, however, they warned that Iraq might make Saudi Arabia its next target.

Moving swiftly, Bush convinced the Saudi government to accept a U.S. military presence. Four days after Iraq's invasion of Kuwait, Bush launched operation "Desert Shield" by sending 230,000 troops to protect Saudi Arabia. After consulting with European leaders, he took the matter to the United Nations. The UN denounced Iraqi aggression, ordered economic sanctions against Saddam Hussein's regime, and authorized the United States to lead an international force to restore the government of Kuwait if Saddam Hussein had not withdrawn his troops by January 15, 1991. Bush assembled an international coalition and persuaded Congress to approve a resolution backing the use of force. Although Bush claimed a moral obligation to rescue Kuwait, his policymakers spoke frankly about the economic peril Hussein's aggression posed for the United States and other oil-dependent economies.

Just after the January 15 deadline passed, the United States launched an air war on Iraq. "Pools" of journalists, whose movements were carefully controlled by the military, focused mainly on new military technology, especially the antimissile missile called the "Patriot." The media also highlighted the new role that women played in America's modernized military. After six weeks of devastating aerial bombardment and economic sanctions against Iraq, General Colin Powell ordered a ground offensive on February 24. Over the next four days Saddam Hussein's armies were shattered. The United States, with its control of the skies, kept its casualties relatively light (148 deaths in battle). Estimates of Iraq's casualties ranged from 25,000 to 100,000 deaths. Although the conflict had lasted scarcely six weeks, the destruction of highways, bridges, communications, and other infrastructure in both Iraq and Kuwait was enormous.

In a controversial decision, Bush decided not to force Saddam Hussein's ouster. Instead, the United States, backed by the UN, maintained its economic pressure, worked to dismantle Iraq's nuclear and bacteriological capabilities, and enforced a "no-fly" zone over northern Iraq to protect the Kurdish population, which was being persecuted by Saddam Hussein. The government of Iraq survived, still headed by Saddam Hussein. Even so, the Persian Gulf War boosted George Bush's popularity and seemed to assure his reelection.

The end of the Cold War had eliminated some foreign policy issues, but new ones emerged. Turmoil broke out in some of the former Soviet provinces, and Russia struggled to develop a private-property, free-market economy. Full-scale warfare erupted among the states of the former Yugoslavia, with Serbians launching a brutal campaign against Bosnian Muslims. In the Far East, Japan's economic strength prompted Americans to grumble about unfair competition. In Africa, when severe famine struck the country of Somalia, Bush ordered American troops to establish humanitarian supply lines, but the American public remained wary of this military mission.

In confronting such diverse global issues, Bush met with mixed success. He could claim significant foreign policy accomplishments: He had assembled and held together an international coalition against Iraq, had constructively assisted the transition in Russia and Eastern Europe at the end of the Cold War, and had begun a process of trade liberalization. But when Bush spoke about creating a "new world order," neither he nor his advisers could explain just what that meant. The old reference points that had defined national security, especially containment of the Soviet enemy, had disappeared, and Bush never effectively articulated a new vision that could firmly establish his reputation as a foreign policy leader.

TOWARD THE 21ST CENTURY

The unraveling of George Bush's presidency and the meteoric rise of Democrat Bill Clinton in 1992 was followed, in congressional elections two years later, by a surprising Republican triumph. These abrupt swings suggested, among other things, a suspicion of national political leaders and a declining loyalty to political parties, particularly among people who had come to oppose many of the domestic policies that had been championed by the Democratic Party since the 1930s.

THE ELECTION OF 1992

The inability to portray a coherent vision of either foreign or domestic policy threatened Bush's reelection and forced him to make concessions to the New Right. Dan Quayle returned as his running mate, and the president allowed conservative activists to dominate the 1992 Republican national convention. They talked about "a religious war" for "the soul of America" and pictured Democrats as the enemies of "family values." But conservative Democrats and independents found this rhetoric no substitute for policies that addressed domestic problems, particularly the sluggish economy.

Bush's Democratic challenger, Governor Bill Clinton of Arkansas, concentrated on economic issues, pledging to increase government spending for job creation and long-term economic growth. Addressing a concern that apparently cut across partisan lines, Clinton promised a comprehensive revision of the nation's health care system. On other domestic issues, Clinton almost sounded like a Republican. "It's time to end this [welfare] system as we know it," Clinton insisted. He claimed to be a "new Democrat" who would reduce taxes for middle-class Americans, cut the federal deficit, and shrink the size of government. Clinton, in short, highlighted economic issues while making it difficult for Bush to label him as a "big government" liberal.

This focus on economics also helped to deflect attention from social-cultural issues on which Clinton appeared vulnerable. As a college student in the 1960s, he had not only avoided service in Vietnam but also had participated in antiwar demonstrations while in England as a Rhodes Scholar. When Bush, a decorated veteran of the Second World War, challenged Clinton's patriotism, Clinton countered by emphasizing, rather than repudiating, his roots in the Vietnam War generation. He became the first presidential candidate to campaign on MTV. In addition, he chose Senator Albert Gore, who had served in Vietnam, as his running mate. And when Clinton's personal life drew fire, Bill and Hillary Rodham Clinton defended their marriage as an effective, ongoing partnership. Hillary Rodham Clinton's

BILL CLINTON PLAYS THE SAXOPHONE   During the 1992 presidential campaign, Clinton eagerly identified himself as a baby boomer who had grown up with rock 'n' roll.

career as a lawyer and advocate for children's issues, the couple insisted, would be an asset to a Clinton presidency.

The 1992 presidential campaign was enlivened by the third-party candidacy of Ross Perot, a billionaire from Texas. A blunt, folksy speaker, Perot claimed that political insiders in Washington, both Republicans and Democrats, had created a "mess" that satisfied only special interests. If people would only come together in the 1990s as they had done in the 1940s, he argued, they could "take back our country." After suddenly dropping out of the presidential race in July, the unpredictable Perot returned in October with a media blitz that apparently hurt Bush more than Clinton.

Clinton won by a comfortable margin. He garnered 43 percent of the popular vote and won 370 electoral votes. Perot gained no electoral votes but did attract 19 million popular votes. Bush won a majority only among white Protestants in the South. In contrast, Clinton carried the Jewish, African American, and Latino vote by large margins, and he even gained a plurality among people who had served in the Vietnam War. He also ran very well among independents, voters whom Reagan and Bush had carried during the 1980s and on whom Perot had counted in 1992. Perhaps most surprising, about 55 percent of eligible voters went to the polls, a turnout that reversed 32 years of steady decline in voter participation.

CLINTON'S DOMESTIC POLICIES

Bill Clinton, the first Democratic president in 12 years, brought an emphasis on youth, vitality, and cultural diversity to Washington. The African American author Maya Angelou delivered a poem especially commissioned for his inauguration, and there were different inaugural balls for different musical tastes. Clinton's first cabinet included three African Americans and two Latinos; three cabinet posts went to women. As his first nomination to the Supreme Court, he chose Ruth Bader Ginsburg, only the second woman to sit on the Court. And as representative to the United Nations, Clinton named Madeleine Albright, who would become the country's first female secretary of state during his second term.

On social issues, Clinton claimed several victories during his first term. He ended the Reagan era's ban on abortion counseling in family planning clinics; pushed a family leave program for working parents through Congress; established a program, Americorps, that allowed students to repay their college loans through community service; and secured passage of the Brady Bill, which instituted a five-day waiting period for the purchase of handguns.

But health care reform collapsed. Hillary Rodham Clinton led a task force that produced a plan so complex that few understood it; worse, it pleased virtually no one. Republicans used the health care fiasco to paint Clinton as an advocate of "big government" spending. The administration's health care proposal died in Congress.

Meanwhile, Clinton faced problems of his own. Hillary Rodham Clinton's prominent role in the failed heath care effort fueled criticism of her public activities, and the Clintons' joint involvement in financial dealings in Arkansas—particularly those connected to a bankrupt S&L and to a failed land development called "Whitewater"—drew renewed criticism. In August 1994 Kenneth Starr, a Republican, was appointed as an independent prosecutor charged with investigating the allegations. Starr soon negotiated guilty pleas from several people in Arkansas who were connected to Whitewater and pressed forward with an investigation that seemed aimed at securing an indictment against at least one of the Clintons. Conservative talk show hosts leveled a nonstop barrage of criticism against the president.

The 1994 elections brought a dramatic GOP victory. Republicans secured control of both houses of Congress for the first time in 40 years; they won several new governorships; gained ground in most state legislatures; and made significant headway in many city and county elections. Led by Representative Newt Gingrich of Georgia, conservative Republicans hailed these gains as a mandate for their new agenda called the "Contract with America," which aimed at rolling back federal spending and a variety of governmental programs and regulations.

Congressional Republicans, however, overplayed their hand. Opinion polls suggested that people found Gingrich less trustworthy and competent than the president. Moreover, surveys also showed little support for the kind of thoroughgoing "revolution" against federal programs that was being proposed by the conservatives in Congress. When conflict between the Democratic president and GOP Congress over budget issues led to two brief shutdowns of many government agencies (November 14–20, 1995, and December 16, 1995–January 4, 1996), most people blamed the Republicans in Congress, rather than the White House.

Most important, a revived U.S. economy benefited Clinton. As low rates of inflation accompanied steady economic growth, new jobs were created at a rate that surpassed the president's

POLITICS ON THE WEB

Although the World Wide Web has begun to transform many aspects of daily life, especially at colleges and universities, the Web's impact on American politics remains uncertain. Candidates who have tried to use the Internet to distribute information have run into great difficulty because recipients have generally considered e-mail from politicians to be a form of "spam," or junk mail. In some cases, angry constituents have retaliated by flooding the Web servers used by politicians with their own "junk replies."

Political commentary on the World Wide Web has also been slow to develop. Internet sites still suffer from the stigma of disseminating too many rumors and too little verifiable information.

most optimistic predictions. The stock market, buoyed by technology companies, soared to new heights. Although the specific benefits of this general expansion were distributed unequally—the gap between the pay of corporate executives and ordinary workers grew steadily larger and the wealthiest 10 percent of households still owned 90 percent of the nation's stock holdings—many people did see their economic fortunes improve significantly.

During independent prosecutor Kenneth Starr's investigation of President Bill Clinton, the "Drudge Report," an iconoclastic Web site generally viewed as being hostile to the Clinton administration, gained wider attention for daring to publish information that more traditional political publications hesitated to release. But it also attracted a libel suit by one of the president's advisers for posting claims that were later retracted. Similarly, several newspapers posted stories on their Web sites containing rumors that would likely not have been printed in their "hard copies" and that were later withdrawn from the Internet.

As a result of these and other problems, one of the most popular uses of the World Wide Web for politics has been the relatively traditional sites maintained by the Democratic and Republican parties. What effects might the Web revolution have on modern political culture? Visit these two sites and surf others to see for yourself.

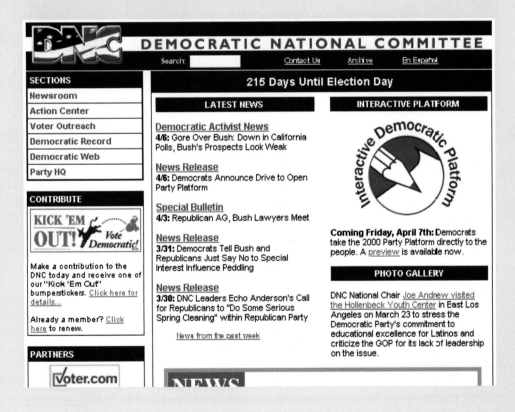

A backlash against the budget gridlock of 1995, together with the signs of continued economic growth, inclined both the White House and Congress to cooperate on overhauling the welfare system. The Personal Responsibility and Work Opportunity Reconciliation Act of 1996 represented a series of compromises that pleased conservatives more than liberals. Relatively noncontroversial sections of the law tightened collection of child support payments and reorganized nutrition and child care programs. Clinton, while voicing concern about provisions that cut the Food Stamp program and benefits for recent immigrants, embraced the law's central feature: the replacement of the AFDC program, which had promised a minimum level of funds and social services to poor families headed by single unemployed women, by a flexible system of block grants to individual states. Under the new program, entitled Temporary Assistance to Needy Families (TANF), states were to design their own welfare-to-work programs under broad federal guidelines.

TANF, which effectively ended the welfare system that had been in place since the New Deal, provoked bitter controversy. Its proponents claimed it would encourage states to experiment with new programs that would reduce their welfare costs. Critics worried that its provisions, including those that limited a person to five years of government assistance during his or her lifetime and authorized states to cut off support if recipients did not find employment within two years, ignored the difficulty that people without job skills faced. They also feared the impact that TANF might have on daily lives of children, especially if states provided inadequate child care, nutritional, and medical care programs. Studies showed that one of every five children already lived in poverty. By pushing further debate over such issues into the future, however, the new welfare law helped to remove a number of potential domestic issues from the political campaign of 1996.

Clinton's Foreign Policy

For nearly half a century, anticommunism and rivalry with the Soviet Union had shaped policy-making. The United States now had to redefine national security to fit a multipolar world. Clinton often articulated an expansive, internationalist vision: improving relations with the UN, expanding NATO, advancing human rights and democracy abroad, reducing nuclear threats, working on global environmental concerns, and promoting free-market policies. During both of his presidential campaigns, however, Clinton focused primarily on domestic issues, and the public seemed suspicious of new international commitments.

One of the most perplexing issues involved revamping the U.S. military for the post–Cold War world. Under what conditions should U.S. troops participate in "peacekeeping" missions? Some people saw any reluctance to use military power as a "new isolationism." Others cautioned against drifting into long-term, ill-defined commitments.

Several trouble spots sparked debate. In the African country of Somalia, U.S. troops had been assisting a humanitarian effort to provide food and relief supplies since May 1992. Caught in factional fighting, however, U.S. troops suffered well-publicized casualties, and Clinton ordered a pullout during the spring of 1994. In Haiti, Clinton vowed to help reestablish the elected president, Jean-Bertrand Aristide. In September 1994, U.S. troops landed in Haiti, and last-minute negotiations by former president Jimmy Carter persuaded the Haitian military to step aside. After six months, with Aristide in power and political institutions functioning again, U.S. soldiers handed over the responsibility for keeping civil order to UN forces. In the former Yugoslavia, the United States committed troops to halt the massacre of Bosnian Muslims by Bosnian Serbs and to oversee a cease-fire and peace-building process that all parties to the conflict had accepted in the U.S.-brokered Dayton (Ohio) accords of 1995.

In March 1999, President Clinton supported a bombing campaign by NATO in Kosovo, a province of Serbia. NATO leaders and Clinton insisted that this controversial use of military force was necessary to protect Muslims of Albanian descent, who comprised nearly 90 percent of Kosovo's population, from an "ethnic cleansing" program directed by Serbia's president,

Slobodan Milosevic. Although NATO's bombs systematically decimated Serbia's economic infrastructure, Milosevic stepped up his campaign and forced hundreds of thousands of ethnic Albanians to flee from Kosovo into neighboring countries. Finally, in June 1999, after 78 days of bombardment, Serbia agreed to withdraw its forces and permit troops under NATO command to oversee the return of ethnic Albanians to Kosovo.

Meanwhile, other post–Cold War concerns drew Clinton's attention. In February 1994, the CIA was rocked by scandal when a high-ranking official, Aldrich Ames, and his wife were arrested on charges of selling information to the Soviet Union and Russia over the preceding decade, contributing to the deaths of several CIA agents. Ames subsequently pled guilty to espionage and was sentenced to life in prison; his wife received a lesser sentence. A year later, it was revealed that the CIA had maintained connections to death squads in Guatemala. Mindful of calls for reform, the CIA tried to chart new, post–Cold War missions. International drug traffickers and other criminal syndicates posed potential threats. And the CIA also targeted international terrorism. In early 1993, a bomb rocked the World Trade Center in New York City, killing 6 people and injuring nearly 1,000. Investigators arrested four Muslims, who had links to previous terrorist acts.

Clinton also shaped new policies on weapons of mass destruction. He dismantled some of the U.S. nuclear arsenal and tried to curtail the potential danger from other nuclear powers. When the Soviet Union collapsed and its nuclear weapons became dispersed among several independent states, the Clinton administration feared these might be sold on the black market to terrorists. In early 1994 Clinton increased economic aid for Ukraine in return for promises to disarm its 1,600 warheads. In the same year, a highly secret "Project Sapphire" transferred enriched uranium stocks from Kazakstan to storage facilities in the United States. Jimmy Carter helped negotiate a complicated agreement with North Korea over nuclear weapons, signed in 1994. North Korea agreed to begin dismantling its nuclear program and permit international inspections as soon as the United States helped it construct safer, light-water nuclear reactors for its energy needs. Throughout the rest of the world, the United States successfully pressed many nations to sign a new Nuclear Nonproliferation Treaty in the spring of 1995. In early 1998, Clinton went to the brink of war with Iraq to maintain international inspections of Saddam Hussein's weapons programs, but after enduring punishing air strikes, Iraq expelled the investigators.

A principal goal of Clinton's foreign policy was to lower trade barriers and expand global markets. Building on the Reagan-Bush legacy, Clinton argued that such policies would boost prosperity and foster democracy around the world. His administration consummated several historic trade agreements. Despite opposition from labor unions and other groups, Clinton strongly backed the North American Free Trade Agreement (NAFTA), which projected cutting tariffs and eliminating other trade barriers among the United States, Canada, and Mexico over a 15-year period. After adding new provisions on labor and environmental issues, in December 1993 he muscled the bill through Congress in a close vote. NAFTA took effect on January 1, 1994. Then, in early 1995, Mexico's severe debt crisis and a dramatic devaluation of its peso prompted Clinton to extend a $20 billion loan from America's Exchange Stabilization Fund. Clinton's trade negotiators completed the so-called "Uruguay Round" of the General Agreement on Tariffs and Trade (GATT) in late 1993, and in early 1995 GATT was replaced by a new World Trade Organization (WTO), a group created to enlarge world trade by implementing new agreements and mediating disputes. Clinton also granted China, despite its dismal record on human rights, equal trading status with other nations and in October 1999 agreed to back China's entry into the WTO in exchange for a promise to liberalize its policies toward the United States and other potential trading partners. To justify this action, he argued that increased trade with China

PROTESTS AGAINST THE WORLD TRADE ORGANIZATION   Police used pepper spray and tear gas to clear thousands of protesters from downtown Seattle streets during demonstrations against the World Trade Organization conference on November 30, 1999.

would contribute to long-term pressures for democratization there. Similarly, in February 1994, the United States ended its 19-year-old trade embargo against Vietnam.

Clinton claimed that all of these measures on behalf of market expansion, along with the emergence of free-market economies in Eastern Europe and Latin America, provided the framework for a new era of global prosperity. When Asian economies faltered during 1998, the president strongly supported acting with the International Monetary Fund to provide huge emergency credits to reform and restore financial systems from Korea to Indonesia.

THE ELECTION OF 1996 AND ITS AFTERMATH

The election of 1996 brought few political changes. The special Whitewater prosecutor had failed to secure any new indictments, and corruption in the White House never became a major issue. The Clinton-Gore team, benefiting from the burgeoning economy, defeated the Republican ticket of Bob Dole and Jack Kemp by about the same margin that it had beaten Bush and Quayle in 1992. Clinton and most other Democrats ran particularly well among African Americans, women, and Hispanic voters. Republicans retained control of Congress and gained several new governorships, but Democrats still held a majority of the seats in state legislatures, a sign that many voters found ticket-splitting (voting for both Democrats and Republicans) a desirable course. After the election, Clinton and congressional Republicans re-

CHRONOLOGY

1974	Nixon resigns and Ford becomes president; Ford soon pardons Nixon
1975	South Vietnam falls to North Vietnam • Ford asserts U.S. power in *Mayaguez* incident
1976	Jimmy Carter elected president
1978	Carter helps negotiate Camp David peace accords on Middle East
1979	Soviet Union invades Afghanistan • Sandinista Party comes to power in Nicaragua • U.S. hostages seized in Iran
1980	Reagan elected president
1981	Reagan tax cut passed • U.S. hostages in Iran released
1983	U.S. troops removed from Lebanon • U.S. troops invade Grenada • Reagan announces SDI ("Star Wars") program
1984	Reagan defeats Walter Mondale
1986	Reagan administration rocked by revelation of Iran-*Contra* affair
1988	George Bush defeats Michael Dukakis in presidential election
1989	Communist regimes in Eastern Europe collapse; Berlin Wall falls • Cold War, in effect, ends
1990	Bush angers conservative Republicans by agreeing to a tax increase
1991	Bush orchestrates Persian Gulf War against Iraq
1992	Bill Clinton defeats Bush and third-party candidate Ross Perot in presidential race
1993	Congress approves North American Free Trade Agreement (NAFTA) and the General Agreement on Tariffs and Trade (GATT)
1994	Republicans gain control of both houses of Congress and pledge to enact their "Contract with America"
1995	Special prosecutor Kenneth Starr takes over the investigation of "Whitewater" allegations
1996	Personal Responsibility and Work Opportunity Reconciliation Act becomes first major overhaul of the national welfare system since the 1930s • Clinton defeats Robert Dole in the presidential race
1998	Congress votes two articles of impeachment against Clinton
1999	Impeachment trial in Senate fails to convict the president • NATO bombs Serbia to stop persecution of Albanians in Kosovo

sponded by cooperating to pass legislation that promised broadly distributed tax cuts and phased reductions in the federal deficit. In his 1998 State of the Union address, Clinton proudly proclaimed that the budget deficit would soon move to zero.

After the election of 1996, however, national politics increasingly came to revolve around Kenneth Starr's investigations of the president and his administration. The White House had hoped to focus Clinton's second term on a new "national conversation" about racial issues and on programs to improve education, but the media highlighted a seemingly endless array of legal allegations leveled against the president and his associates. While Starr continued to press forward on matters related to the involvement of the Clintons in the Whitewater land deal, he broadened his inquiry to include claims that the president had made inappropriate sexual advances to female employees and that he had later engaged in an effort to obstruct justice either by committing perjury himself or by pressuring others to offer false accounts of his behavior with a young White House intern, Monica Lewinsky.

Clinton's presidency, though still judged a success by a majority of people in public opinion surveys, came under intense scrutiny. Republicans charged the White House with impeding Starr's investigation and the president of lying, and some began to talk about impeaching the president for obstruction of justice. The president's defenders charged Starr's office with engaging in a partisan vendetta against Clinton, leaking secret testimony to the media, and working in concert with the conservative political action committees that were financing a private lawsuit against the president by Paula Corbin Jones for an incident of sexual harassment that had allegedly occurred while Clinton had been governor of Arkansas. And with economic statistics continuing to show improvement, Clinton's approval rating went up, while that of Starr plummeted. Although the GOP surprisingly lost five seats in the House during the off-year election of 1998, the lame-duck 105th Congress voted, in December 1998, two articles of impeachment against the still-popular president. After a month of proceedings, which concluded on February 12, 1999, Republican senators could not muster the two-thirds vote required by the Consititution (nor even a bare majority) to remove Clinton, only the second president in U.S. history to have faced an impeachment trial in the Senate.

Partisan rancor marked post-impeachment politics as both major parties prepared for the election of 2000. Republicans rebuffed the White House's effort to secure Senate ratification of a nuclear test ban treaty and to expand entitlement spending at home, while Clinton vetoed the GOP's sweeping tax-cut bill. This political stalemate, which was broken only by congressional repeal of New Deal–era regulations that had barred banks from entering the insurance and securities businesses, prevented the two parties from fulfilling earlier promises to overhaul the Social Security and Medicare programs. Meanwhile, the continued revenue surplus, a result of the sustained economic boom and the partisan deadlock over tax policy, meant that the once-massive federal debt, which had been a pressing concern only a decade earlier, was steadily disappearing.

Conclusion

Winds of change swept over American life during the final 25 years of the 20th century. In foreign policy, people had to adjust to the trauma of Vietnam, to the sudden end of the Cold War, and to a global environment in which U.S. economic and strategic interests seemed in a state of constant flux. How and where should U.S. military and economic power be exercised?

At home, the Watergate scandal and the economic problems of the 1970s helped to breed cynicism about government. Support for extending the power of the national government in order to address domestic problems slowly eroded. Meanwhile, the "Reagan Revolution" of the 1980s marked the emergence of a new conservative movement. The strength of the Republican Party, which by 1996 could claim nearly as many supporters as the once-dominant Democratic Party, and the presidency of Bill Clinton, a "new Democrat" who declared that the era of "big government" had ended, suggested that many people now rejected the idea that increasing the power of the government meant progress. But how else could a diverse nation confront economic and social problems? As the United States entered the 21st century, Americans continued to debate how to negotiate the difficult balance among liberty, equality, and power.

Appendix

CANADA

Mt. Olympus
2424 m
(7954 ft)▲

Olympia ★

Mt. Rainier
4392 m
(14,410 ft)▲

WASHINGTON

Salem ★

Columbia R.

Blue Mts.

Bitterroot Range

Helena ★

Missouri R.

NORTH DAKO

MONTANA

Bighorn Mts.

Bismarck ★

Badlands

Cascade Ranges

OREGON

Columbia Plateau

Snake R.

Boise ★

IDAHO

R O C K Y

Absaroka Range

Wind River Range

WYOMING

Black Hills

SOUTH DAKOT

Pierre ★

Badlands

Klamath Mts.

Coast Ranges

Sierra Nevada

Central Valley

Sacramento R.

Carson City ★

Great Basin

Great Salt Lake

Salt Lake City ★

Uinta Mts.

Wyoming Basin

Cheyenne ★

M O U N T A I N S

Sand Hills

NEBRASK

Platte R.

Sacramento ★

San Francisco ★

Lake Tahoe

San Joaquin R.

NEVADA

UTAH

Denver ★

COLORADO

Mt. Elbert
4399 m
(14,433 ft)▲

Pikes Peak
4301 m
(14,110 ft)▲

Smoky Hills

KAN

Arkansas R.

Mt. Whitney
4418 m
(14,494 ft)▲

Death Valley

Colorado R.

Lake Powell

Colorado Plateau

Sangre de Cristo Mts.

CALIFORNIA

Point Conception

Coast Ranges

Lake Mead

Great Basin

Grand Canyon

Black Mesa

Santa Fe ★

Channel Islands

Los Angeles ★

Mojave Desert

Salton Sea

Colorado R.

ARIZONA

Painted Desert

NEW MEXICO

Llano Estacado

Guadalupe Mts.

Oklah

OKLAH

Red R.

PACIFIC OCEAN

Sonoran Desert

Phoenix ★

Rio Grande

Stockton Plateau

TEX

Austi

Austin C Cli

MEXICO

Rio Grande

HAWAII

Kauai

Niihau

Oahu

Honolulu ★

Molokai

Lanai

Maui

Kahoolawe

Hawaii

PACIFIC OCEAN

0   75   150 Miles

0   75   150 Kilometers

ARCTIC OCEAN

Chukchi Sea

Beaufort Sea

RUSSIA

Brooks Range

MacKenzie R.

ALASKA

Mt. McKinley
6194 m
(20,320 ft)▲

CANADA

Bering Strait

St. Lawrence I.

Yukon R.

Alaska Range

Yukon R.

Juneau ★

Bering Sea

Koyukuk R.

Alaska Peninsula

Kodiak I.

Gulf of Alaska

Alexander Archipelago

Aleutian Islands

0   150   300 Miles

0   150   300 Kilometers

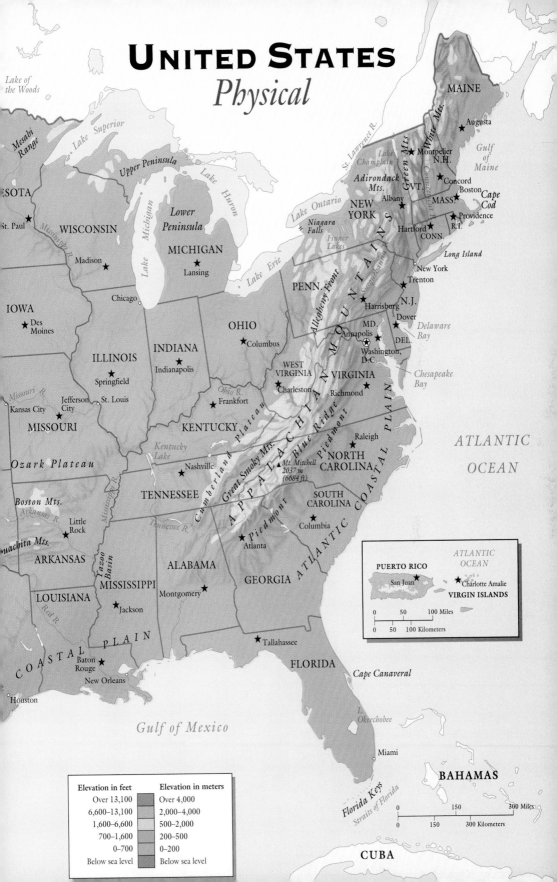

UNITED STATES
Physical

Lake of the Woods

MAINE

Augusta

Mesabi Range

Lake Superior

Gulf of Maine

St. Lawrence R.

Lake Champlain

Montpelier
N.H.

Green Mts.

White Mts.

Upper Peninsula

Adirondack Mts.

Concord

Boston

Cape Cod

-SOTA

Lake Huron

Lake Michigan

Lower Peninsula

Lake Ontario

NEW YORK

Albany

MASS.

Providence

St. Paul

WISCONSIN

MICHIGAN

Niagara Falls

Finger Lakes

Hartford

R.I.

CONN.

Madison

Lansing

Lake Erie

Long Island

Chicago

PENN.

New York

Trenton

IOWA

Des Moines

OHIO

Columbus

Harrisburg

N.J.

Dover

Delaware Bay

ILLINOIS

INDIANA

Indianapolis

Allegheny Front

MD.

Annapolis

DEL.

Springfield

Jefferson City

St. Louis

Frankfort

WEST VIRGINIA

Charleston

VIRGINIA

Richmond

Washington, D.C.

Chesapeake Bay

Kansas City

MISSOURI

Ohio R.

KENTUCKY

Piedmont

Missouri R.

Ozark Plateau

Kentucky Lake

Cumberland Plateau

Great Smoky Mts.

NORTH CAROLINA

Raleigh

ATLANTIC OCEAN

Boston Mts.

Nashville

Mt. Mitchell 2037 m (6684 ft)

Blue Ridge

COASTAL PLAIN

Arkansas R.

Little Rock

TENNESSEE

Tennessee R.

Piedmont

SOUTH CAROLINA

Columbia

-uachita Mts.

ARKANSAS

Yazoo Basin

ALABAMA

Atlanta

ATLANTIC

PUERTO RICO

ATLANTIC OCEAN

LOUISIANA

MISSISSIPPI

Jackson

GEORGIA

Montgomery

San Juan

Charlotte Amalie

VIRGIN ISLANDS

Red R.

Baton Rouge

Tallahassee

COASTAL PLAIN

0   50   100 Miles

0   50   100 Kilometers

New Orleans

Houston

FLORIDA

Cape Canaveral

Gulf of Mexico

L. Okeechobee

Miami

BAHAMAS

Florida Keys

Straits of Florida

0   150   300 Miles

0   150   300 Kilometers

CUBA

Elevation in feet	Elevation in meters
Over 13,100	Over 4,000
6,600–13,100	2,000–4,000
1,600–6,600	500–2,000
700–1,600	200–500
0–700	0–200
Below sea level	Below sea level

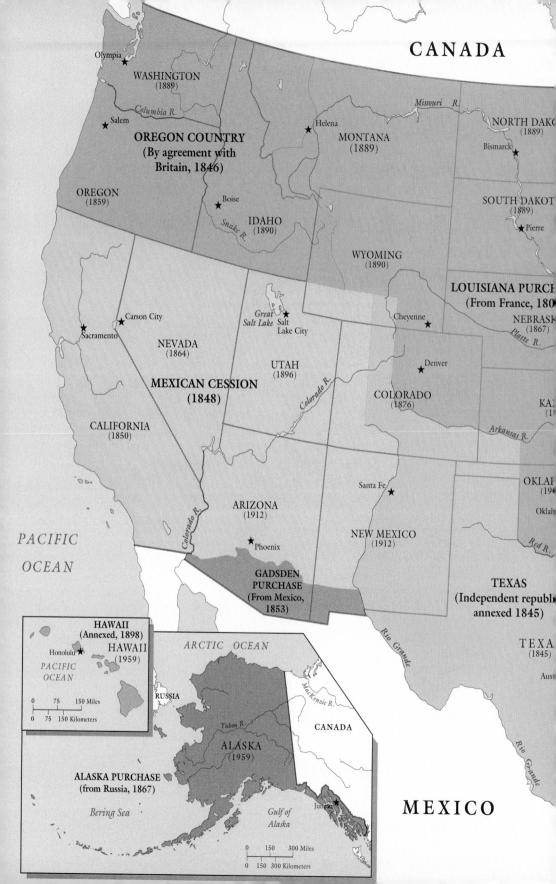

CANADA

Olympia ★
WASHINGTON
(1889)

Columbia R.

Salem ★

OREGON COUNTRY
(By agreement with
Britain, 1846)

OREGON
(1859)

★ Helena
MONTANA
(1889)

Missouri R.

NORTH DAKO
(1889)

Bismarck
★

★ Boise
IDAHO
(1890)

Snake R.

WYOMING
(1890)

SOUTH DAKOT
(1889)

★ Pierre

LOUISIANA PURCH
(From France, 180

★ Carson City
Sacramento ★

NEVADA
(1864)

Great
Salt Lake Salt ★
Lake City

UTAH
(1896)

Cheyenne
★

NEBRAS
(1867)

Platte R.

MEXICAN CESSION
(1848)

CALIFORNIA
(1850)

Colorado R.

Denver
★

COLORADO
(1876)

Arkansas R.

KA
(1

ARIZONA
(1912)

Colorado R.

★ Phoenix

Santa Fe ★

NEW MEXICO
(1912)

OKLA
(19

Oklah

PACIFIC

OCEAN

GADSDEN
PURCHASE
(From Mexico,
1853)

TEXAS
(Independent republi
annexed 1845)

Rio Grande

TEXA
(1845)

Aust

HAWAII
(Annexed, 1898)
HAWAII
(1959)

Honolulu ★

PACIFIC
OCEAN

0   75   150 Miles
0   75   150 Kilometers

ARCTIC OCEAN

RUSSIA

MacKenzie R.

CANADA

Yukon R.

ALASKA
(1959)

ALASKA PURCHASE
(from Russia, 1867)

Bering Sea

Gulf of
Alaska

Juneau ★

MEXICO

Rio Grande

0   150   300 Miles
0   150   300 Kilometers

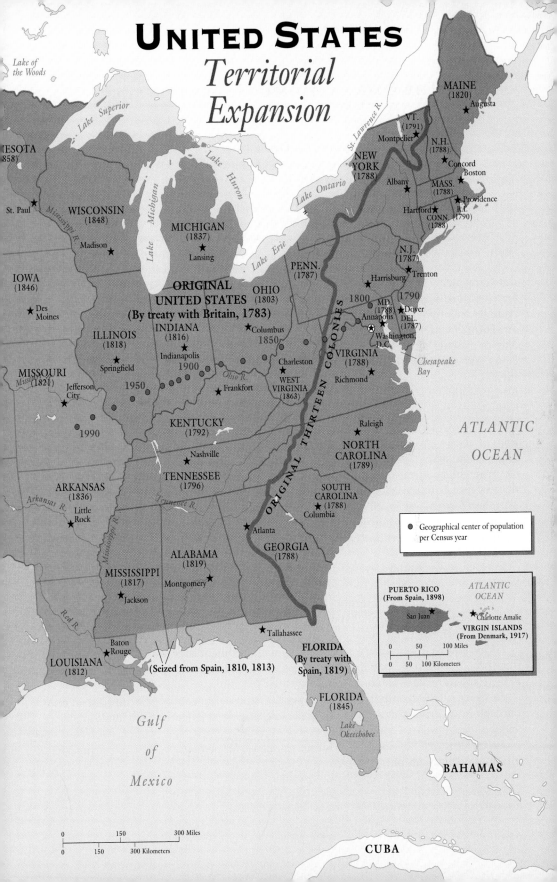

UNITED STATES
Territorial Expansion

Lake of the Woods

Lake Superior

St. Lawrence R.

MAINE (1820)
Augusta

VT. (1791)
Montpelier

N.H. (1788)
Concord
Boston

[M]ESOTA [1]858)

Lake Huron

NEW YORK (1788)
Albany

MASS. (1788)

Lake Michigan

St. Paul

Mississippi R.

WISCONSIN (1848)

Madison

MICHIGAN (1837)
★ Lansing

Lake Ontario

Hartford
CONN. (1788)

Providence
R.I. (1790)

Lake Erie

PENN. (1787)
Harrisburg
Trenton

N.J. (1787)

IOWA (1846)

Des Moines

ORIGINAL UNITED STATES
(By treaty with Britain, 1783)

OHIO (1803)

1800

MD. (1788)
Annapolis

1790

Dover
DEL. (1787)

ILLINOIS (1818)

INDIANA (1816)
Indianapolis

★ Columbus
1850

Washington, D.C.

Chesapeake Bay

MISSOURI (1821)

Missouri R.

Springfield

1900

Ohio R.

Frankfort

Charleston

WEST VIRGINIA (1863)

VIRGINIA (1788)

Richmond

Jefferson City

1950

KENTUCKY (1792)

ATLANTIC OCEAN

1990

Nashville

Raleigh

NORTH CAROLINA (1789)

ARKANSAS (1836)

Arkansas R.

TENNESSEE (1796)

Tennessee R.

ORIGINAL THIRTEEN COLONIES

Little Rock

SOUTH CAROLINA (1788)
Columbia

Mississippi R.

★ Atlanta

GEORGIA (1788)

ALABAMA (1819)

Montgomery

MISSISSIPPI (1817)
Jackson

	Geographical center of population per Census year

Red R.

Baton Rouge

(Seized from Spain, 1810, 1813)

★ Tallahassee

FLORIDA
(By treaty with Spain, 1819)

PUERTO RICO
(From Spain, 1898)
San Juan

ATLANTIC OCEAN

Charlotte Amalie
VIRGIN ISLANDS
(From Denmark, 1917)

0	50	100 Miles
0	50	100 Kilometers

LOUISIANA (1812)

FLORIDA (1845)

Lake Okeechobee

Gulf

of

Mexico

BAHAMAS

0	150	300 Miles
0	150	300 Kilometers

CUBA

THE DECLARATION OF INDEPENDENCE

THE UNANIMOUS DECLARATION OF THE
THIRTEEN UNITED STATES OF AMERICA

When in the Course of human events it becomes necessary for one people to dissolve the political bands which have connected them with another, and to assume among the Powers of the earth, the separate and equal station to which the Laws of Nature and of Nature's God entitle them, a decent respect to the opinions of mankind requires that they should declare the causes which impel them to the separation.

We hold these truths to be self-evident, that all men are created equal, that they are endowed by their Creator with certain unalienable Rights, that among these are Life, Liberty and the pursuit of Happiness. That to secure these rights, Governments are instituted among Men, deriving their just Powers from the consent of the governed. That whenever any Form of Government becomes destructive of these ends, it is the Right of the People to alter or to abolish it, and to institute new Government, laying its foundation on such principles and organizing its Powers in such form, as to them shall seem most likely to effect their Safety and Happiness. Prudence, indeed, will dictate that Governments long established should not be changed for light and transient causes; and accordingly all experience hath shewn, that mankind are more disposed to suffer, while evils are sufferable, than to right themselves by abolishing the forms to which they are accustomed. But when a long train of abuses and usurpations, pursuing invariably the same Object evinces a design to reduce them under absolute Despotism, it is their right, it is their duty, to throw off such Government, and to provide new Guards for their future security. Such has been the patient sufferance of these Colonies; and such is now the necessity which constrains them to alter their former Systems of Government. The history of the present King of Great Britain is a history of repeated injuries and usurpations, all having in direct object the establishment of an absolute Tyranny over these States. To prove this, let Facts be submitted to a candid world.

He has refused his Assent to Laws, the most wholesome and necessary for the public good.

He has forbidden his Governors to pass Laws of immediate and pressing importance, unless suspended in their operation till his Assent should be obtained; and when so suspended, he has utterly neglected to attend to them.

He has refused to pass other Laws for the accommodation of large districts of people, unless those people would relinquish the right of Representation in the Legislature, a right inestimable to them and formidable to tyrants only.

He has called together legislative bodies at places unusual, uncomfortable, and distant from the depository of their Public Records, for the sole Purpose of fatiguing them into compliance with his measures.

He has dissolved Representative Houses repeatedly, for opposing with manly firmness his invasions on the rights of the People.

Text is reprinted from the facsimile of the engrossed copy in the National Archives. The original spelling, capitalization, and punctuation have been retained. Paragraphing has been added.

He has refused for a long time, after such dissolutions, to cause others to be elected; whereby the Legislative Powers, incapable of Annihilation, have returned to the People at large for their exercise; the State remaining in the mean time exposed to all the dangers of invasion from without, and convulsions within.

He has endeavoured to prevent the Population of these States; for that purpose obstructing the Laws for Naturalization of Foreigners; refusing to pass others to encourage their migrations hither, and raising the conditions of new Appropriations of Lands.

He has obstructed the Administration of Justice, by refusing his Assent to Laws for establishing Judiciary Powers.

He has made Judges dependent on his Will alone, for the tenure of their offices, and the amount and payment of their salaries.

He has erected a multitude of New Offices, and sent hither swarms of Officers to harass our People, and eat out their substance.

He has kept among us, in times of peace, Standing Armies without the Consent of our legislatures.

He has affected to render the Military independent of and superior to the Civil Power.

He has combined with others to subject us to a jurisdiction foreign to our constitution, and unacknowledged by our laws; giving his Assent to their Acts of pretended Legislation:

For Quartering large bodies of armed troops among us:

For protecting them, by a mock Trial, from Punishment for any Murders which they should commit on the Inhabitants of these States:

For cutting off our Trade with all parts of the world:

For imposing Taxes on us without our Consent:

For depriving us in many cases, of the benefits of Trial by Jury:

For transporting us beyond Seas to be tried for pretended offences:

For abolishing the free System of English Laws in a neighbouring Province, establishing therein an Arbitrary government, and enlarging its Boundaries so as to render it at once an example and fit instrument for introducing the same absolute rule into these Colonies:

For taking away our Charters, abolishing our most valuable Laws, and altering fundamentally the Forms of our Governments:

For suspending our own Legislatures, and declaring themselves invested with Power to legislate for us in all cases whatsoever.

He has abdicated Government here, by declaring us out of his Protection, and waging War against us.

He has plundered our seas, ravaged our Coasts, burnt our towns, and destroyed the lives of our people.

He is at this time transporting large Armies of foreign Mercenaries to compleat the works of death, desolation and tyranny, already begun with circumstances of Cruelty and perfidy scarcely paralleled in the most barbarous ages, and totally unworthy the Head of a civilized nation.

He has constrained our fellow Citizens taken Captive on the high Seas to bear Arms against their Country, to become the executioners of their friends and Brethren, or to fall themselves by their Hands.

He has excited domestic insurrections amongst us, and has endeavoured to bring on the inhabitants of our frontiers, the merciless Indian Savages, whose known rule of warfare, is an undistinguished destruction of all ages, sexes and conditions.

In every stage of these Oppressions We have Petitioned for Redress in the most humble terms: Our repeated Petitions have been answered only by repeated injury. A Prince, whose character is thus marked by every act which may define a Tyrant, is unfit to be the ruler of a free People.

Nor have We been wanting in attentions to our British brethren. We have warned them from time to time of attempts by their legislature to extend an unwarrantable jurisdiction over us. We have reminded them of the circumstances of our emigration and settlement here. We have appealed to their native justice and magnanimity, and we have conjured them by the ties of our common kindred to disavow thee usurpations, which, would inevitably interrupt our connections and correspondence. They too have been deaf to the voice of justice and of consanguinity. We must, therefore, acquiesce in the necessity, which denounces our Separation, and hold them, as we hold the rest of mankind, Enemies in War, in Peace Friends.

We, THEREFORE, the Representatives of the UNITED STATES of AMERICA, in General Congress, Assembled, appealing to the Supreme Judge of the world for the rectitude of our intentions, do, in the Name, and by Authority of the good People of these Colonies, solemnly publish and declare, That these United Colonies are, and of Right ought to be FREE AND INDEPENDENT STATES; that they are Absolved from all Allegiance to the British Crown, and that all political connection between them and the State of Great Britain, is and ought to be totally dissolved; and that, as Free and Independent States, they have full Power to levy War, conclude Peace, contract Alliances, establish Commerce, and to do all other Acts and Things which Independent States may of right do. And for the support of this Declaration, with a firm reliance on the protection of divine Providence, we mutually pledge to each other our Lives, our Fortunes and our sacred Honor.

THE CONSTITUTION OF THE UNITED STATES OF AMERICA

We the People of the United States, in Order to form a more perfect Union, establish Justice, insure domestic Tranquility, provide for the common defence, promote the general Welfare, and secure the Blessings of Liberty to ourselves and our Posterity, do ordain and establish this Constitution for the United States of America.

ARTICLE I.

SECTION 1. All legislative Powers herein granted shall be vested in a Congress of the United States, which shall consist of a Senate and House of Representatives.

SECTION 2. The House of Representatives shall be composed of Members chosen every second Year by the People of the several States, and the Electors in each State shall have the Qualifications requisite for Electors of the most numerous Branch of the State Legislature.

No Person shall be a Representative who shall not have attained to the Age of twenty five Years, and been seven Years a Citizen of the United States, and who shall not, when elected, be an Inhabitant of that State in which he shall be chosen.

Text is from the engrossed copy in the National Archives. Original spelling, capitalization, and punctuation have been retained.

Representatives and direct Taxes[1] shall be apportioned among the several States which may be included within this Union, according to their respective Numbers, which shall be determined by adding to the whole Number of free Persons, including those bound to Service for a Term of Years, and excluding Indians not taxed, three fifths of all other Persons.[2] The actual Enumeration shall be made within three Years after the first Meeting of the Congress of the United States, and within every subsequent Term of ten Years, in such Manner as they shall by Law direct. The Number of Representatives shall not exceed one for every thirty Thousand, but each State shall have at Least one Representative; and until such enumeration shall be made, the State of New Hampshire shall be entitled to chuse three; Massachusetts eight; Rhode Island and Providence Plantations one; Connecticut five; New York six; New Jersey four; Pennsylvania eight; Delaware one; Maryland six; Virginia ten; North Carolina five; South Carolina five; and Georgia three.

When vacancies happen in the Representation from any State, the Executive Authority thereof shall issue Writs of Election to fill such Vacancies.

The House of Representatives shall chuse their Speaker and other Officers; and shall have the sole Power of Impeachment.

SECTION 3. The Senate of the United States shall be composed of two Senators from each State, chosen by the Legislature thereof, for six Years; and each Senator shall have one Vote.[3]

Immediately after they shall be assembled in Consequence of the first Election, they shall be divided as equally as may be into three Classes. The Seats of the Senators of the first Class shall be vacated at the Expiration of the second Year, of the second Class at the Expiration of the fourth Year, and of the third Class at the Expiration of the sixth Year, so that one third may be chosen every second Year; and if Vacancies happen by Resignation, or otherwise, during the Recess of the Legislature of any State, the Executive thereof may make temporary Appointments until the next Meeting of the Legislature, which shall then fill such Vacancies.[4]

No Person shall be a Senator who shall not have attained to the Age of thirty Years, and been nine Years a Citizen of the United States, and who shall not, when elected, be an Inhabitant of that State for which he shall be chosen.

The Vice President of the United States shall be President of the Senate, but shall have no Vote, unless they be equally divided.

The Senate shall chuse their other Officers, and also a President pro tempore, in the Absence of the Vice President, or when he shall exercise the Office of President of the United States.

The Senate shall have the sole Power to try all Impeachments. When sitting for that Purpose, they shall be on Oath or Affirmation. When the President of the United States is tried, the Chief Justice shall preside: And no Person shall be convicted without the Concurrence of two thirds of the Members present.

Judgment in Cases of Impeachment shall not extend further than to removal from Office, and disqualification to hold and enjoy any Office of honor, Trust or Profit under the United

---

[1]Modified by the Sixteenth Amendment.
[2]Replaced by the Fourteenth Amendment.
[3]Superseded by the Seventeenth Amendment.
[4]Modified by the Seventeenth Amendment.

States: but the Party convicted shall nevertheless be liable and subject to Indictment, Trial, Judgment and Punishment, according to Law.

SECTION 4. The Times, Places and Manner of holding Elections for Senators and Representatives, shall be prescribed in each State by the Legislature thereof, but the Congress may at any time by Law make or alter such Regulation, except as to the Places of chusing Senators.

The Congress shall assemble at least once in every Year, and such Meeting shall be on the first Monday in December, unless they shall by Law appoint a different Day.[5]

SECTION 5. Each House shall be the Judge of the Elections, Returns and Qualifications of its own Members, and a Majority of each shall constitute a Quorum to do Business; but a smaller Number may adjourn from day to day, and may be authorized to compel the Attendance of absent Members, in such Manner, and under such Penalties as each House may provide.

Each House may determine the Rules of its Proceedings, punish its Members for disorderly Behaviour, and, with the Concurrence of two thirds, expel a Member.

Each House shall keep a Journal of its Proceedings, and from time to time publish the same, excepting such Parts as may in their Judgment require Secrecy; and the Yeas and Nays of the Members of either House on any question shall, at the Desire of one fifth of those Present, be entered on the Journal.

Neither House, during the Session of Congress, shall, without the Consent of the other, adjourn for more than three days, nor to any other Place than that in which the two Houses shall be sitting.

SECTION 6. The Senators and Representatives shall receive a Compensation for their Services, to be ascertained by Law, and paid out of the Treasury of the United States. They shall in all Cases, except Treason, Felony and Breach of the Peace, be privileged from Arrest during their Attendance at the Session of their respective Houses, and in going to and returning from the same; and for any Speech or Debate in either House, they shall not be questioned in any other Place.

No Senator or Representative shall, during the Time for which he was elected, be appointed to any civil Office under the Authority of the United States, which shall have been created, or the Emoluments whereof shall have been encreased during such time; and no Person holding any Office under the United States, shall be a Member of either House during his Continuance in Office.

SECTION 7. All Bills for raising Revenue shall originate in the House of Representatives; but the Senate may propose or concur with Amendments as on other Bills.

Every Bill which shall have passed the House of Representatives and the Senate shall, before it become a Law, be presented to the President of the United States; If he approve he shall sign it, but if not he shall return it, with his Objections to that House in which it shall have originated, who shall enter the Objections at large on their Journal, and proceed to reconsider it. If after such Reconsideration two thirds of that House shall agree to pass the Bill, it shall be sent, together with the Objections, to the other House, by which it shall likewise be reconsidered, and if approved by two thirds of that House, it shall become a Law. But in all such Cases the Votes of both Houses shall be determined by yeas and Nays, and the Names of the Persons

---

[5]Superseded by the Twentieth Amendment.

voting for and against the Bill shall be entered on the Journal of each House respectively. If any Bill shall not be returned by the President within ten Days (Sundays excepted) after it shall have been presented to him, the Same shall be a Law, in like Manner as if he had signed it, unless the Congress by their Adjournment prevent its Return, in which Case it shall not be a Law.

Every Order, Resolution, or Vote to which the Concurrence of the Senate and House of Representatives may be necessary (except on a question of Adjournment) shall be presented to the President of the United States; and before the Same shall take Effect, shall be approved by him, or being disapproved by him shall be repassed by two thirds of the Senate and House of Representatives, according to the Rules and Limitations prescribed in the Case of a Bill.

SECTION 8. The Congress shall have power To lay and collect Taxes, Duties, Imposts and Excises, to pay the Debts and provide for the common Defence and general Welfare of the United States; but all Duties, Imposts and Excises shall be uniform throughout the United States;

To borrow Money on the credit of the United States;

To regulate Commerce with foreign Nations, and among the several States, and with the Indian Tribes;

To establish an uniform Rule of Naturalization, and uniform Laws on the subject of Bankruptcies throughout the United States;

To coin Money, regulate the Value thereof, and of foreign Coin, and fix the Standard of Weights and Measures;

To provide for the Punishment of counterfeiting the Securities and current Coin of the United States;

To establish Post Offices and post Roads;

To promote the Progress of Science and useful Arts, by securing for limited Times to Authors and Inventors the exclusive Right to their respective Writings and Discoveries;

To constitute Tribunals inferior to the supreme Court;

To define and punish Piracies and Felonies committed on the high Seas, and Offences against the Law of Nations;

To declare War, grant Letters of Marque and Reprisal, and make Rules concerning Captures on Land and Water;

To raise and support Armies, but no Appropriation of Money to that Use shall be for a longer Term than two Years;

To provide and maintain a Navy;

To make Rules for the Government and Regulation of the land and naval Forces;

To provide for calling forth the Militia to execute the Laws of the Union, suppress Insurrections and repel Invasions;

To provide for organizing, arming, and disciplining, the Militia, and for governing such Part of them as may be employed in the Service of the United States, reserving to the States respectively, the Appointment of the Officers, and the Authority of training the Militia according to the discipline prescribed by Congress;

To exercise exclusive Legislation in all Cases whatsoever, over such District (not exceeding ten Miles square) as may, by Cession of particular States, and the Acceptance of Congress, become the Seat of the Government of the United States, and to exercise like Authority over all

Places purchased by the Consent of the Legislature of the State in which the Same shall be, for the Erection of Forts, Magazines, Arsenals, dock-Yards, and other needful Buildings;—And

To make all Laws which shall be necessary and proper for carrying into Execution the foregoing Powers, and all other Powers vested by this Constitution in the Government of the United States, or in any Department or Officer thereof.

SECTION 9. The Migration or Importation of such Persons as any of the States now existing shall think proper to admit, shall not be prohibited by the Congress prior to the Year one thousand eight hundred and eight, but a Tax or duty may be imposed on such Importation, not exceeding ten dollars for each Person.

The Privilege of the Writ of Habeas Corpus shall not be suspended, unless when in Cases of Rebellion or Invasion the public Safety may require it.

No Bill of Attainder or ex post facto Law shall be passed.

No Capitation, or other direct, Tax shall be laid, unless in Proportion to the Census or Enumeration herein before directed to be taken.

No Tax or Duty shall be laid on Articles exported from any State.

No Preference shall be given by any Regulation of Commerce or Revenue to the Ports of one State over those of another: nor shall Vessels bound to, or from, one State, be obliged to enter, clear, or pay Duties in another.

No Money shall be drawn from the Treasury, but in Consequence of Appropriations made by Law, and a regular Statement and Account of the Receipts and Expenditures of all public Money shall be published from time to time.

No Title of Nobility shall be granted by the United States: And no Person holding any Office of Profit or Trust under them, shall, without the Consent of the Congress, accept of any present, Emolument, Office, or Title, of any kind whatever, from any King, Prince, or foreign State.

SECTION 10. No State shall enter into any Treaty, Alliance, or Confederation; grant Letters of Marque and Reprisal; coin Money; emit Bills of Credit; make any Thing but gold and silver Coin a Tender in Payment of Debts; pass any Bill of Attainder, ex post facto Law, or Law impairing the Obligation of Contracts, or grant any Title of Nobility.

No State shall, without the Consent of the Congress, lay any Imposts or Duties on Imports or Exports, except what may be absolutely necessary for executing its inspection Laws: and the net Produce of all Duties and Imposts, laid by any State on Imports or Exports, shall be for the Use of the Treasury of the United States; and all such Laws shall be subject to the Revision and Controul of the Congress.

No State shall, without the Consent of Congress, lay any Duty of Tonnage, keep Troops, or Ships of War in time of Peace, enter into any Agreement or Compact with another State, or with a foreign Power, or engage in War, unless actually invaded, or in such imminent Danger as will not admit of delay.

ARTICLE II.

SECTION 1. The executive Power shall be vested in a President of the United States of America. He shall hold his Office during the Term of four Years, and, together with the Vice President, chosen for the same Term, be elected, as follows:

Each State shall appoint, in such Manner as the Legislature thereof may direct, a Number of Electors, equal to the whole Number of Senators and Representatives to which the State may be entitled in the Congress: but no Senator or Representative, or Person holding an Office of Trust or Profit under the United States, shall be appointed an Elector.

The Electors shall meet in their respective States, and vote by Ballot for two Persons, of whom one at least shall not be an Inhabitant of the same State with themselves. And they shall make a List of all the Persons voted for, and of the Number of Votes for each; which List they shall sign and certify, and transmit sealed to the Seat of the Government of the United States, directed to the President of the Senate. The President of the Senate shall, in the Presence of the Senate and House of Representatives, open all the Certificates, and the Votes shall then be counted. The Person having the greatest Number of Votes shall be the President, if such Number be a Majority of the whole Number of Electors appointed; and if there be more than one who have such Majority, and have an equal Number of Votes, then the House of Representatives shall immediately chuse by Ballot one of them for President; and if no Person have a Majority, then from the five highest on the List the said House shall in like Manner chuse the President. But in chusing the President, the Votes shall be taken by States, the Representation from each State having one Vote; A quorum for this Purpose shall consist of a Member or Members from two thirds of the States, and a Majority of all the States shall be necessary to a Choice. In every Case, after the Choice of the President, the Person having the greatest Number of Votes of the Electors shall be the Vice President. But if there should remain two or more who have equal Votes, the Senate shall chuse from them by Ballot the Vice President.[6]

The Congress may determine the Time of chusing the Electors, and the Day on which they shall give their Votes; which Day shall be the same throughout the United States.

No Person except a natural born Citizen, or a Citizen of the United States, at the time of the Adoption of this Constitution, shall be eligible to the Office of President, neither shall any Person be eligible to that Office who shall not have attained to the Age of thirty five Years, and been fourteen Years a Resident within the United States.

In Case of the Removal of the President from Office, or of his Death, Resignation, or Inability to discharge the Powers and Duties of the said Office, the Same shall devolve on the Vice President, and the Congress may by Law provide for the Case of Removal, Death, Resignation or Inability, both of the President and Vice President, declaring what Officer shall then act as President, and such Officer shall act accordingly, until the Disability be removed, or a President shall be elected.[7]

The President shall, at stated Times, receive for his Services, a Compensation, which shall neither be encreased nor diminished during the Period for which he shall have been elected, and he shall not receive within that Period any other Emolument from the United States, or any of them.

Before he enter on the Execution of his Office, he shall take the following Oath or Affirmation:— "I do solemnly swear (or affirm) that I will faithfully execute the Office of President of the United States, and will to the best of my Ability, preserve, protect and defend the Constitution of the United States."

SECTION 2. The President shall be Commander in Chief of the Army and Navy of the United States, and of the Militia of the several States, when called into the actual Service of the United States; he may require the Opinion, in writing, of the principal Officer in each of the executive Departments, upon any Subject relating to the Duties of their respective Offices, and he shall have Power to grant Reprieves and Pardons for Offences against the United States, except in Cases of Impeachment.

[6]Superseded by the Twelfth Amendment.
[7]Modified by the Twenty-fifth Amendment.

He shall have Power, by and with the Advice and Consent of the Senate, to make Treaties, provided two thirds of the Senators present concur; and he shall nominate, and by and with the Advice and Consent of the Senate, shall appoint Ambassadors, other public Ministers and Consuls, Judges of the supreme Court, and all other Officers of the United States, whose Appointments are not herein otherwise provided for, and which shall be established by Law; but the Congress may by Law vest the Appointment of such inferior Officers, as they think proper, in the President alone, in the Courts of Law, or in the Heads of Departments.

The President shall have Power to fill up all Vacancies that may happen during the Recess of the Senate, by granting Commissions which shall expire at the End of their next Session.

SECTION 3. He shall from time to time give the Congress Information of the State of the Union, and recommend to their Consideration such Measures as he shall judge necessary and expedient; he may, on extraordinary Occasions, convene both Houses, or either of them, and in Case of Disagreement between them, with Respect to the Time of Adjournment, he may adjourn them to such Time as he shall think proper; he shall receive Ambassadors and other public Ministers; he shall take Care that the Laws be faithfully executed, and shall Commission all the Officers of the United States.

SECTION 4. The President, Vice President and all civil Officers of the United States, shall be removed from Office on Impeachment for, and Conviction of, Treason, Bribery, or other high Crimes and Misdemeanors.

ARTICLE III.

SECTION 1. The judicial Power of the United States, shall be vested in one supreme Court, and in such inferior Courts as the Congress may from time to time ordain and establish. The Judges, both of the supreme and inferior Courts, shall hold their Offices during good Behaviour, and shall, at stated Times, receive for their Services, a Compensation, which shall not be diminished during their Continuance in Office.

SECTION 2. The judicial Power shall extend to all Cases, in Law and Equity, arising under this Constitution, the Laws of the United States, and Treaties made, or which shall be made, under their Authority;—to all Cases affecting Ambassadors, other public Ministers and Consuls;—to all Cases of admiralty and maritime Jurisdiction;—to Controversies to which the United States shall be a Party;—to Controversies between two or more States;—between a State and Citizens of another State;[8]—between Citizens of different States,—between Citizens of the same State claiming Lands under Grants of different States, and between a State, or the Citizens thereof, and foreign States, Citizens or Subjects.

In all Cases affecting Ambassadors, other public Ministers and Consuls, and those in which a State shall be Party, the supreme Court shall have original Jurisdiction. In all the other Cases before mentioned, the supreme Court shall have appellate Jurisdiction, both as to Law and Fact, with such Exceptions, and under such Regulations as the Congress shall make.

The Trial of all Crimes, except in Cases of Impeachment, shall be by Jury; and such Trial shall be held in the State where the said Crimes shall have been committed; but when not committed within any State, the Trial shall be at such Place or Places as the Congress may by Law have directed.

SECTION 3. Treason against the United States, shall consist only in levying War against

[8]Modified by the Eleventh Amendment.

them, or in adhering to their Enemies, giving them Aid and Comfort. No Person shall be convicted of Treason unless on the Testimony of two Witnesses to the same overt Act, or on Confession in open Court.

The Congress shall have Power to declare the Punishment of Treason, but no Attainder of Treason shall work Corruption of Blood, or Forfeiture except during the Life of the Person attainted.

ARTICLE IV.

SECTION 1. Full Faith and Credit shall be given in each State to the public Acts, Records, and judicial Proceedings of every other State. And the Congress may by general Laws prescribe the Manner in which such Acts, Records and Proceedings shall be proved, and the Effect thereof.

SECTION 2. The Citizens of each State shall be entitled to all Privileges and Immunities of Citizens in the several States.

A Person charged in any State with Treason, Felony, or other Crime, who shall flee from Justice, and be found in another State, shall on Demand of the executive Authority of the State from which he fled, be delivered up, to be removed to the State having Jurisdiction of the Crime.

No Person held to Service or Labour in one State, under the Laws thereof, escaping into another, shall, in Consequence of any Law or Regulation therein, be discharged from such Service or Labour, but shall be delivered up on Claim of the Party to whom such Service or Labour may be due.

SECTION 3. New States may be admitted by the Congress into this Union; but no new State shall be formed or erected within the Jurisdiction of any other State, nor any State be formed by the Junction of two or more States, or Parts of States, without the Consent of the Legislatures of the States concerned as well as of the Congress.

The Congress shall have Power to dispose of and make all needful Rules and Regulations respecting the Territory or other Property belonging to the United States; and nothing in this Constitution shall be so construed as to Prejudice any Claims of the United States, or of any particular State.

SECTION 4. The United States shall guarantee to every State in this Union a Republican Form of Government, and shall protect each of them against Invasion; and on Application of the Legislature, or of the Executive (when the Legislature cannot be convened) against domestic Violence.

ARTICLE V.

The Congress, whenever two thirds of both Houses shall deem it necessary, shall propose Amendments to this Constitution, or, on the Application of the Legislatures of two thirds of the several States, shall call a Convention for proposing Amendments, which, in either Case, shall be valid to all Intents and Purposes, as Part of this Constitution, when ratified by the Legislatures of three fourths of the several States, or by Conventions in three fourths thereof, as the one or the other Mode of Ratification may be proposed by the Congress; Provided that no Amendment which may be made prior to the Year One thousand eight hundred and eight shall in any Manner affect the first and fourth Clauses in the Ninth Section of the first Article; and that no State, without its Consent, shall be deprived of its equal Suffrage in the Senate.

ARTICLE VI.

All Debts contracted and Engagements entered into, before the Adoption of this Constitution, shall be as valid against the United States under this Constitution, as under the Confederation.

This Constitution, and the Laws of the United States which shall be made in Pursuance thereof; and all Treaties made, or which shall be made, under the Authority of the United States, shall be the supreme Law of the Land; and the Judges in every State shall be bound thereby, any Thing in the Constitution or Laws of any State to the Contrary notwithstanding.

The Senators and Representatives before mentioned, and the Members of the several State Legislatures, and all executive and judicial Officers, both of the United States and of the several States, shall be bound by Oath or Affirmation, to support this Constitution; but no religious Test shall ever be required as a Qualification to any Office or public Trust under the United States.

ARTICLE VII.

The Ratification of the Conventions of nine States, shall be sufficient for the Establishment of this Constitution between the States so ratifying the Same.

Done in Convention by the Unanimous Consent of the States present the Seventeenth Day of September in the Year of our Lord one thousand seven hundred and Eighty seven and of the Independence of the United States of America the Twelfth. In witness whereof We have hereunto subscribed our Names,

Articles in Addition to, and Amendment of, the Constitution of the United States of America, Proposed by Congress, and Ratified by the Legislatures of the Several States, Pursuant to the Fifth Article of the Original Constitution.

AMENDMENT I[9]

Congress shall make no law respecting an establishment of religion, or prohibiting the free exercise thereof; or abridging the freedom of speech, or of the press; or the right of the people peaceably to assemble, and to petition the Government for a redress of grievances.

AMENDMENT II

A well regulated Militia, being necessary to the security of a free State, the right of the people to keep and bear Arms shall not be infringed.

AMENDMENT III

No Soldier shall, in time of peace, be quartered in any house, without the consent of the Owner, nor in time of war, but in a manner to be prescribed by law.

---

[9]The first ten amendments were passed by Congress September 25, 1789. They were ratified by three-fourths of the states December 15, 1791.

AMENDMENT IV

The right of the people to be secure in their persons, houses, papers, and effects, against unreasonable searches and seizures, shall not be violated, and no Warrants shall issue, but upon probable cause, supported by Oath or affirmation, and particularly describing the place to be searched, and the persons or things to be seized.

AMENDMENT V

No person shall be held to answer for a capital or otherwise infamous crime, unless on a presentment or indictment of a Grand Jury, except in cases arising in the land or naval forces, or in the Militia, when in actual service in time of War or public danger; nor shall any person be subject for the same offence to be twice put in jeopardy of life or limb; nor shall be compelled in any criminal case to be a witness against himself, nor be deprived of life, liberty, or property, without due process of law; nor shall private property be taken for public use, without just compensation.

AMENDMENT VI

In all criminal prosecutions, the accused shall enjoy the right to a speedy and public trial, by an impartial jury of the State and district wherein the crime shall have been committed, which district shall have been previously ascertained by law, and to be informed of the nature and cause of the accusation; to be confronted with the witnesses against him; to have compulsory process for obtaining witnesses in his favor, and to have the Assistance of Counsel for his defence.

AMENDMENT VII

In suits at common law, where the value in controversy shall exceed twenty dollars, the right of trial by jury shall be preserved, and no fact tried by a jury, shall be otherwise reexamined in any Court of the United States, than according to the rules of the common law.

AMENDMENT VIII

Excessive bail shall not be required, nor excessive fines imposed, nor cruel and unusual punishments inflicted.

AMENDMENT IX

The enumeration in the Constitution, of certain rights, shall not be construed to deny or disparage others retained by the people.

AMENDMENT X

The powers not delegated to the United States by the Constitution; nor prohibited by it to the States, are reserved to the States respectively, or to the people.

AMENDMENT XI[10]

The Judicial power of the United States shall not be construed to extend to any suit in law or equity, commenced or prosecuted against one of the United States by Citizens of another State, or by Citizens or Subjects of any Foreign State.

AMENDMENT XII[11]

The Electors shall meet in their respective States and vote by ballot for President and Vice-President, one of whom, at least, shall not be an inhabitant of the same State with themselves; they shall name in their ballots the person voted for as President, and in distinct ballots the person voted for as Vice-President, and they shall make distinct lists of all persons voted for as President, and of all persons voted for as Vice-President, and of the number of votes for each, which lists they shall sign and certify, and transmit sealed to the seat of the government of the United States, directed to the President of the Senate;—The President of the Senate shall, in the presence of the Senate and House of Representatives, open all the certificates and the votes shall then be counted;—The person having the greatest number of votes for President, shall be the President, if such number be a majority of the whole number of Electors appointed; and if no person have such majority, then from the persons having the highest numbers not exceeding three on the list of those voted for as President, the House of Representatives shall choose immediately, by ballot, the President. But in choosing the President, the votes shall be taken by states, the representation from each state having one vote; a quorum for this purpose shall consist of a member or members from two-thirds of the states, and a majority of all the states shall be necessary to a choice. And if the House of Representatives shall not choose a President whenever the right of choice shall devolve upon them, before the fourth day of March next following, then the Vice-President shall act as President, as in the case of the death or other constitutional disability of the President.—The person having the greatest number of votes as Vice-President, shall be the Vice-President, if such number be a majority of the whole number of Electors appointed, and if no person have a majority, then from the two highest numbers on the list, the Senate shall choose the Vice-President; a quorum for the purpose shall consist of two-thirds of the whole number of Senators, and a majority of the whole number shall be necessary to a choice. But no person constitutionally ineligible to the office of President shall be eligible to that of Vice-President of the United States.

AMENDMENT XIII[12]

SECTION 1. Neither slavery nor involuntary servitude, except as a punishment for crime whereof the party shall have been duly convicted, shall exist within the United States, or any place subject to their jurisdiction.

SECTION 2. Congress shall have power to enforce this article by appropriate legislation.

---

[10]Passed March 4, 1794. Ratified January 23, 1795.
[11]Passed December 9, 1803. Ratified June 15, 1804.
[12]Passed January 31, 1865. Ratified December 6, 1865.

AMENDMENT XIV[13]

SECTION 1. All persons born or naturalized in the United States, and subject to the jurisdiction thereof, are citizens of the United States and of the State wherein they reside. No State shall make or enforce any law which shall abridge the privileges or immunities of citizens of the United States; nor shall any State deprive any person of life, liberty, or property, without due process of law; nor deny to any person within its jurisdiction the equal protection of the laws.

SECTION 2. Representatives shall be apportioned among the several States according to their respective numbers, counting the whole number of persons in each State, excluding Indians not taxed. But when the right to vote at any election for the choice of electors for President and Vice-President of the United States, Representatives in Congress, the Executive and Judicial officers of a State, or the members of the Legislature thereof, is denied to any of the male inhabitants of such State, being twenty-one years of age, and citizens of the United States, or in any way abridged, except for participation in rebellion, or other crime, the basis of representation therein shall be reduced in the proportion which the number of such male citizens shall bear to the whole number of male citizens twenty-one years of age in such State.

SECTION 3. No person shall be a Senator or Representative in Congress, or elector of President and Vice-President, or hold any office, civil or military, under the United States, or under any State, who, having previously taken an oath, as a member of Congress, or as an officer of the United States, or as a member of any State legislature, or as an executive or judicial officer of any State, to support the Constitution of the United States, shall have engaged in insurrection or rebellion against the same, or given aid or comfort to the enemies thereof. But Congress may by a vote of two-thirds of each House, remove such disability.

SECTION 4. The validity of the public debt of the United States, authorized by law, including debts incurred for payment of pensions and bounties for services in suppressing insurrection or rebellion, shall not be questioned. But neither the United States nor any State shall assume or pay any debt or obligation incurred in aid of insurrection or rebellion against the United States, or any claim for the loss or emancipation of any slave; but all such debts, obligations, and claims shall be held illegal and void.

SECTION 5. The Congress shall have the power to enforce, by appropriate legislation, the provisions of this article.

AMENDMENT XV[14]

SECTION 1. The right of citizens of the United States to vote shall not be denied or abridged by the United States or by any State on account of race, color, or previous conditions of servitude—

SECTION 2. The Congress shall have power to enforce this article by appropriate legislation.

[13]Passed June 13, 1866. Ratified July 9, 1868.
[14]Passed February 26, 1869. Ratified February 2, 1870.

AMENDMENT XVI[15]

The Congress shall have power to lay and collect taxes on incomes, from whatever source derived, without apportionment among the several States, and without regard to any census or enumeration.

AMENDMENT XVII[16]

The Senate of the United States shall be composed of two Senators from each State, elected by the people thereof, for six years; and each Senator shall have one vote. The electors in each State shall have the qualifications requisite for electors of the most numerous branch of the State legislatures.

When vacancies happen in the representation of any State in the Senate, the executive authority of such State shall issue writs of election to fill such vacancies: *Provided,* That the legislature of any State may empower the executive thereof to make temporary appointments until the people fill the vacancies by election as the legislature may direct.

This amendment shall not be so construed as to affect the election or term of any Senator chosen before it becomes valid as part of the Constitution.

AMENDMENT XVIII[17]

SECTION 1. After one year from the ratification of this article the manufacture, sale, or transportation of intoxicating liquors within, the importation thereof into, or the exportation thereof from the United States and all territory subject to the jurisdiction thereof for beverage purposes is hereby prohibited.

SECTION 2. The Congress and the several States shall have concurrent power to enforce this article by appropriate legislation.

SECTION 3. This article shall be inoperative unless it shall have been ratified as an amendment to the Constitution by the legislatures of the several States, as provided in the Constitution, within seven years from the date of the submission hereof to the States by the Congress.

AMENDMENT XIX[18]

The right of citizens of the United States to vote shall not be denied or abridged by the United States or by any State on account of sex.

Congress shall have power to enforce this article by appropriate legislation.

AMENDMENT XX[19]

SECTION 1. The terms of the President and Vice-President shall end at noon on the 20th day of January, and the terms of Senators and Representatives at noon on the 3d day of January, of

[15]Passed July 12, 1909. Ratified February 3, 1913.
[16]Passed May 13, 1912. Ratified April 8, 1913.
[17]Passed December 18, 1917. Ratified January 16, 1919.
[18]Passed June 4, 1919. Ratified August 18, 1920.
[19]Passed March 2, 1932. Ratified January 23, 1933.

the years in which such terms would have ended if this article had not been ratified; and the terms of their successors shall then begin.

SECTION 2. The Congress shall assemble at least once in every year, and such meeting shall begin at noon on the 3d day of January, unless they shall by law appoint a different day.

SECTION 3. If, at the time fixed for the beginning of the term of the President, the President elect shall have died, the Vice-President elect shall become President. If a President shall not have been chosen before the time fixed for the beginning of his term, or if the President elect shall have failed to qualify, then the Vice-President elect shall act as President until a President shall have qualified; and the Congress may by law provide for the case wherein neither a President elect nor a Vice-President elect shall have qualified, declaring who shall then act as President, or the manner in which one who is to act shall be selected, and such person shall act accordingly until a President or Vice-President shall have qualified.

SECTION 4. The Congress may by law provide for the case of the death of any of the persons from whom the House of Representatives may choose a President whenever the right of choice shall have devolved upon them, and for the case of the death of any of the persons from whom the Senate may choose a Vice-President whenever the right of choice shall have devolved upon them.

SECTION 5. Sections 1 and 2 shall take effect on the 15th day of October following the ratification of this article.

SECTION 6. This article shall be inoperative unless it shall have been ratified as an amendment to the Constitution by the legislatures of three-fourths of the several States within seven years from the date of its submission.

AMENDMENT XXI[20]

SECTION 1. The eighteenth article of amendment to the Constitution of the United States is hereby repealed.

SECTION 2. The transportation or importation into any State, Territory, or possession of the United States for delivery or use therein of intoxicating liquors, in violation of the laws thereof, is hereby prohibited.

SECTION 3. This article shall be inoperative unless it shall have been ratified as an amendment to the Constitution by conventions in the several States, as provided in the Constitution, within seven years from the date of the submission hereof to the States by the Congress.

AMENDMENT XXII[21]

No person shall be elected to the office of the President more than twice, and no person who has held the office of President, or acted as President, for more than two years of a term to which some other person was elected President shall be elected to the office of the President more than once.

But this Article shall not apply to any person holding the office of President when this Article was proposed by the Congress, and shall not prevent any person who may be holding the

---

[20]Passed February 20, 1933. Ratified December 5, 1933.
[21]Passed March 12, 1947. Ratified March 1, 1951.

office of President, or acting as President, during the term within which this Article becomes operative from holding the office of President or acting as President during the remainder of such term.

AMENDMENT XXIII[22]

SECTION 1. The District constituting the seat of Government of the United States shall appoint in such manner as the Congress may direct:

A number of electors of President and Vice President equal to the whole number of Senators and Representatives in Congress to which the District would be entitled if it were a State, but in no event more than the least populous State; they shall be in addition to those appointed by the States, but they shall be considered, for the purposes of the election of President and Vice President, to be electors appointed by the State; and they shall meet in the District and perform such duties as provided by the twelfth article of amendment.

SECTION 2. The Congress shall have power to enforce this article by appropriate legislation.

AMENDMENT XXIV[23]

SECTION 1. The right of citizens of the United States to vote in any primary or other election for President or Vice President, or for Senator or Representative in Congress, shall not be denied or abridged by the United States or any State by reason of failure to pay any poll tax or other tax.

SECTION 2. The Congress shall have power to enforce this article by appropriate legislation.

AMENDMENT XXV[24]

SECTION 1. In case of the removal of the President from office or of his death or resignation, the Vice President shall become President.

SECTION 2. Whenever there is a vacancy in the office of the Vice President, the President shall nominate a Vice President who shall take office upon confirmation by a majority vote of both Houses of Congress.

SECTION 3. Whenever the President transmits to the President pro tempore of the Senate and the Speaker of the House of Representatives his written declaration that he is unable to discharge the powers and duties of his office, and until he transmits them a written declaration to the contrary, such powers and duties shall be discharged by the Vice President as Acting President.

SECTION 4. Whenever the Vice President and a majority of either the principal officers of the executive department or of such other body as Congress may by law provide, transmit to the President pro tempore of the Senate and the Speaker of the House of Representatives their written declaration that the President is unable to discharge the powers and duties of his office, the Vice President shall immediately assume the powers and duties of the office of Acting President

---

[22]Passed June 16, 1960. Ratified April 3, 1961.
[23]Passed August 27, 1962. Ratified January 23, 1964.
[24]Passed July 6, 1965. Ratified February 11, 1967.

Thereafter, when the President transmits to the President pro tempore of the Senate and the Speaker of the House of Representatives his written declaration that no inability exists, he shall resume the powers and duties of his office unless the Vice President and a majority of either the principal officers of the executive department or of such other body as Congress may by law provide, transmit within four days to the President pro tempore of the Senate and the Speaker of the House of Representatives their written declaration that the President is unable to discharge the powers and duties of his office. Thereupon Congress shall decide the issue, assembling within forty-eight hours for that purpose if not in session. If the Congress, within twenty-one days after receipt of the latter written declaration, or, if Congress is not in session, within twenty-one days after Congress is required to assemble, determines by two-thirds vote of both Houses that the President is unable to discharge the powers and duties of his office, the Vice President shall continue to discharge the same as Acting President; otherwise, the President shall resume the powers and duties of his office.

AMENDMENT XXVI[25]

SECTION 1. The right of citizens of the United States, who are eighteen years of age or older, to vote shall not be denied or abridged by the United States or by any State on account of age.

SECTION 2. The Congress shall have power to enforce this article by appropriate legislation.

AMENDMENT XXVII[26]

No law, varying the compensation for the service of the Senators and Representatives, shall take effect, until an election of Representatives shall have intervened.

[25]Passed March 23, 1971. Ratified July 5, 1971.
[26]Passed September 25, 1789. Ratified May 7, 1992

Admission of States

Order of admission	State	Date of admission	Order of admission	State	Date of admission
1	Delaware	December 7, 1787	26	Michigan	January 26, 1837
2	Pennsylvania	December 12, 1787	27	Florida	March 3, 1845
3	New Jersey	December 18, 1787	28	Texas	December 29, 1845
4	Georgia	January 2, 1788	29	Iowa	December 28, 1846
5	Connecticut	January 9, 1788	30	Wisconsin	May 29, 1848
6	Massachusetts	February 6, 1788	31	California	September 9, 1850
7	Maryland	April 28, 1788	32	Minnesota	May 11, 1858
8	South Carolina	May 23, 1788	33	Oregon	February 14, 1859
9	New Hampshire	June 21, 1788	34	Kansas	January 29, 1861
10	Virginia	June 25, 1788	35	West Virginia	June 20, 1863
11	New York	July 26, 1788	36	Nevada	October 31, 1864
12	North Carolina	November 21, 1789	37	Nebraska	March 1, 1867
13	Rhode Island	May 29, 1790	38	Colorado	August 1, 1876
14	Vermont	March 4, 1791	39	North Dakota	November 2, 1889
15	Kentucky	June 1, 1792	40	South Dakota	November 2, 1889
16	Tennessee	June 1, 1796	41	Montana	November 8, 1889
17	Ohio	March 1, 1803	42	Washington	November 11, 1889
18	Louisiana	April 30, 1812	43	Idaho	July 3, 1890
19	Indiana	December 11, 1816	44	Wyoming	July 10, 1890
20	Mississippi	December 10, 1817	45	Utah	January 4, 1896
21	Illinois	December 3, 1818	46	Oklahoma	November 16, 1907
22	Alabama	December 14, 1819	47	New Mexico	January 6, 1912
23	Maine	March 15, 1820	48	Arizona	February 14, 1912
24	Missouri	August 10, 1821	49	Alaska	January 3, 1959
25	Arkansas	June 15, 1836	50	Hawaii	August 21, 1959

Population of the United States

Year	Total Population	Number per Square Mile	Year	Total Population	Number per Square Mile	Year	Total Population	Number per Square Mile
1790	3,929	4.5	1817	8,899		1844	19,569	
1791	4,056		1818	9,139		1845	20,182	
1792	4,194		1819	9,379		1846	20,794	
1793	4,332		1820	9,618	5.6	1847	21,406	
1794	4,469		1821	9,939		1848	22,018	
1795	4,607		1822	10,268		1849	22,631	
1796	4,745		1823	10,596		1850	23,261	7.9
1797	4,883		1824	10,924		1851	24,086	
1798	5,021		1825	11,252		1852	24,911	
1799	5,159		1826	11,580		1853	25,736	
1800	5,297	6.1	1827	11,909		1854	26,561	
1801	5,486		1828	12,237		1855	27,386	
1802	5,679		1829	12,565		1856	28,212	
1803	5,872		1830	12,901	7.4	1857	29,037	
1804	5,065		1831	13,321		1858	29,862	
1805	6,258		1832	13,742		1859	30,687	
1806	6,451		1833	14,162		1860	31,513	10.6
1807	6,644		1834	14,582		1861	32,351	
1808	6,838		1835	15,003		1862	33,188	
1809	7,031		1836	15,423		1863	34,026	
1810	7,224	4.3	1837	15,843		1864	34,863	
1811	7,460		1838	16,264		1865	35,701	
1812	7,700		1839	16,684		1866	36,538	
1813	7,939		1840	17,120	9.8	1867	37,376	
1814	8,179		1841	17,733		1868	38,213	
1815	8,419		1842	18,345		1869	39,051	
1816	8,659		1843	18,957		1870	39,905	13.4

Figures are from *Historical Statistics of the United States, Colonial Times to 1957* (1961), pp. 7, 8; *Statistical Abstract of the United States: 1974*, p. 5, Census Bureau for 1974 and 1975; and *Statistical Abstract of the United States: 1988*, p. 7.

Note: Population figures are in thousands. Density figures are for land area of continental United States.

(continued)

Population of the United States, continued

Year	Total Population	Number per Square Mile	Year	Total Population	Number per Square Mile	Year	Total Population[1]	Number per Square Mile
1871	40,938		1900	76,094	25.6	1929	121,700	
1872	41,972		1901	77,585		1930	122,775	41.2
1873	43,006		1902	79,160		1931	124,040	
1874	44,040		1903	80,632		1932	124,840	
1875	45,073		1904	82,165		1933	125,579	
1876	46,107		1905	83,820		1934	126,374	
1877	47,141		1906	85,437		1935	127,250	
1878	48,174		1907	87,000		1936	128,053	
1879	49,208		1908	88,709		1937	128,825	
1880	50,262	16.9	1909	90,492		1938	129,825	
1881	51,542		1910	92,407	31.0	1939	130,880	
1882	52,821		1911	93,868		1940	131,669	44.2
1883	54,100		1912	95,331		1941	133,894	
1884	55,379		1913	97,227		1942	135,361	
1885	56,658		1914	99,118		1943	137,250	
1886	57,938		1915	100,549		1944	138,916	
1887	59,217		1916	101,966		1945	140,468	
1888	60,496		1917	103,414		1946	141,936	
1889	61,775		1918	104,550		1947	144,698	
1890	63,056	21.2	1919	105,063		1948	147,208	
1891	64,361		1920	106,466	35.6	1949	149,767	
1892	65,666		1921	108,541		1950	150,697	50.7
1893	66,970		1922	110,055		1951	154,878	
1894	68,275		1923	111,950		1952	157,553	
1895	69,580		1924	114,113		1953	160,184	
1896	70,885		1925	115,832		1954	163,026	
1897	72,189		1926	117,399		1955	165,931	
1898	73,494		1927	119,038		1956	168,903	
1899	74,799		1928	120,501		1957	171,984	

[1]Figures after 1940 represent total population including armed forces abroad, except in official census years.

Year	Total Population[1]	Number per Square Mile	Year	Total Population[1]	Number per Square Mile	Year	Total Population[1]	Number per Square Mile
1958	174,882		1972	208,842		1986	241,596	
1959	177,830		1973	210,396		1987	234,773	
1960	178,464	60.1	1974	211,894		1988	245,051	
1961	183,672		1975	213,631		1989	247,350	
1962	186,504		1976	215,152		1990	250,122	
1963	189,197		1977	216,880		1991	254,521	
1964	191,833		1978	218,717		1992	245,908	
1965	194,237		1979	220,584		1993	257,908	
1966	196,485		1980	226,546	64.0	1994	261,875	
1967	198,629		1981	230,138		1995	263,434	
1968	200,619		1982	232,520		1996	266,096	
1969	202,599		1983	234,799		1997	267,901	
1970	203,875	57.5[2]	1984	237,001		1998	269,501	
1971	207,045		1985	239,283		1999	274,114	

[1]Figures after 1940 represent total population including armed forces abroad, except in official census years.
[2]Figure includes Alaska and Hawaii.

YEAR	NUMBER OF STATES	CANDIDATES[1]
1789	11	**George Washington** John Adams Minor candidates
1792	15	**George Washington** John Adams George Clinton Minor candidates
1796	16	**John Adams** Thomas Jefferson Thomas Pinckney Aaron Burr Minor candidates
1800	16	**Thomas Jefferson** Aaron Burr John Adams Charles C. Pinckney John Jay
1804	17	**Thomas Jefferson** Charles C. Pinckney
1808	17	**James Madison** Charles C. Pinckney George Clinton
1812	18	**James Madison** DeWitt Clinton
1816	19	**James Monroe** Rufus King
1820	24	**James Monroe** John Quincy Adams
1824	24	**John Quincy Adams** Andrew Jackson William H. Crawford Henry Clay
1828	24	**Andrew Jackson** John Quincy Adams

[1]Before the passage of the Twelfth Amendment in 1804, the Electoral College voted for two presidential candidates; the runner-up became vice president. Figures are from *Historical Statistics of the United States, Colonial Times to 1957* (1961), pp. 682–683; and the U.S. Department of Justice.

Parties	Popular vote	Electoral vote	Percentage of popular vote[2]
No party designations		69	
		34	
		35	
No party designations		132	
		77	
		50	
		5	
Federalist		71	
Democratic-Republican		68	
Federalist		59	
Democratic-Republican		30	
		48	
Democratic-Republican		73	
Democratic-Republican		73	
Federalist		65	
Federalist		64	
Federalist		1	
Democratic-Republican		162	
Federalist		14	
Democratic-Republican		122	
Federalist		47	
Democratic-Republican		6	
Democratic-Republican		128	
Federalist		89	
Democratic-Republican		183	
Federalist		34	
Democratic-Republican		231	
Independent Republican		1	
Democratic-Republican	108,740	84	30.5
Democratic-Republican	153,544	99	43.1
Democratic-Republican	46,618	41	13.1
Democratic-Republican	47,136	37	13.2
Democratic	647,286	178	56.0
National Republican	508,064	83	44.0

[2]Candidates receiving less than 1 percent of the popular vote have been omitted. For that reason the percentage of popular vote given for any election year may not total 100 percent.

YEAR	NUMBER OF STATES	CANDIDATES
1832	24	**Andrew Jackson** Henry Clay William Wirt John Floyd
1836	26	**Martin Van Buren** William H. Harrison Hugh L. White Daniel Webster W. P. Mangum
1840	26	**William H. Harrison** Martin Van Buren
1844	26	**James K. Polk** Henry Clay James G. Birney
1848	30	**Zachary Taylor** Lewis Cass Martin Van Buren
1852	31	**Franklin Pierce** Winfield Scott John P. Hale
1856	31	**James Buchanan** John C. Frémont Millard Fillmore
1860	33	**Abraham Lincoln** Stephen A. Douglas John C. Breckinridge John Bell
1864	36	**Abraham Lincoln** George B. McClellan
1868	37	**Ulysses S. Grant** Horatio Seymour
1872	37	**Ulysses S. Grant** Horace Greeley
1876	38	**Rutherford B. Hayes** Samuel J. Tilden

Parties	Popular vote	Electoral vote	Percentage of popular vote[1]
Democratic	687,502	219	55.0
National Republican	530,189	49	42.4
Anti-Masonic		7	
National Republican	33,108	11	2.6
Democratic	765,483	170	50.9
Whig		73	
Whig		26	
Whig	739,795	14	
Whig		11	
Whig	1,274,624	234	53.1
Democratic	1,127,781	60	46.9
Democratic	1,338,464	170	49.6
Whig	1,300,097	105	48.1
Liberty	62,300		2.3
Whig	1,360,967	163	47.4
Democratic	1,222,342	127	42.5
Free Soil	291,263		10.1
Democratic	1,601,117	254	50.9
Whig	1,385,453	42	44.1
Free Soil	155,825		5.0
Democratic	1,832,955	174	45.3
Republican	1,339,932	114	33.1
American	871,731	8	21.6
Republican	1,865,593	180	39.8
Democratic	1,382,713	12	29.5
Democratic	848,356	72	18.1
Constitutional Union	592,906	39	12.6
Republican	2,206,938	212	55.0
Democratic	1,803,787	21	45.0
Republican	3,013,421	214	52.7
Democratic	2,706,829	80	47.3
Republican	3,596,745	286	55.6
Democratic	2,843,446	2	43.9
Republican	4,036,572	185	48.0
Democratic	4,284,020	184	51.0

[1]Candidates receiving less than 1 percent of the popular vote have been omitted. For that reason the percentage of popular vote given for any election year may not total 100 percent.

[2]Greeley died shortly after the election; the electors supporting him then divided their votes among minor candidates.

YEAR	NUMBER OF STATES	CANDIDATES
1880	38	**James A. Garfield** Winfield S. Hancock James B. Weaver
1884	38	**Grover Cleveland** James G. Blaine Benjamin F. Butler John P. St. John
1888	38	**Benjamin Harrison** Grover Cleveland Clinton B. Fisk Anson J. Streeter
1892	44	**Grover Cleveland** Benjamin Harrison James B. Weaver John Bidwell
1896	45	**William McKinley** William J. Bryan
1900	45	**William McKinley** William J. Bryan John C. Wooley
1904	45	**Theodore Roosevelt** Alton B. Parker Eugene V. Debs Silas C. Swallow
1908	46	**William H. Taft** William J. Bryan Eugene V. Debs Eugene W. Chafin
1912	48	**Woodrow Wilson** Theodore Roosevelt William H. Taft Eugene V. Debs Eugene W. Chafin
1916	48	**Woodrow Wilson** Charles E. Hughes A. L. Benson J. Frank Hanly

PARTIES	POPULAR VOTE	ELECTORAL VOTE	PERCENTAGE OF POPULAR VOTE[1]
Republican	4,453,295	214	48.5
Democratic	4,414,082	155	48.1
Greenback-Labor	308,578		3.4
Democratic	4,879,507	219	48.5
Republican	4,850,293	182	48.2
Greenback-Labor	175,370		1.8
Prohibition	150,369		1.5
Republican	5,477,129	233	47.9
Democratic	5,537,857	168	48.6
Prohibition	249,506		2.2
Union Labor	146,935		1.3
Democratic	5,555,426	277	46.1
Republican	5,182,690	145	43.0
People's	1,029,846	22	8.5
Prohibition	264,133		2.2
Republican	7,102,246	271	51.1
Democratic	6,492,559	176	47.7
Republican	7,218,491	292	51.7
Democratic; Populist	6,356,734	155	45.5
Prohibition	208,914		1.5
Republican	7,628,461	336	57.4
Democratic	5,084,223	140	37.6
Socialist	402,283		3.0
Prohibition	258,536		1.9
Republican	7,675,320	321	51.6
Democratic	6,412,294	162	43.1
Socialist	420,793		2.8
Prohibition	253,840		1.7
Democratic	6,296,547	435	41.9
Progressive	4,118,571	88	27.4
Republican	3,486,720	8	23.2
Socialist	900,672		6.0
Prohibition	206,275		1.4
Democratic	9,127,695	277	49.4
Republican	8,533,507	254	46.2
Socialist	585,113		3.2
Prohibition	220,506		1.2

[1]Candidates receiving less than 1 percent of the popular vote have been omitted. For that reason the percentage of popular vote given for any election year may not total 100 percent.

YEAR	NUMBER OF STATES	CANDIDATES
1920	48	**Warren G. Harding** James N. Cox Eugene V. Debs P. P. Christensen
1924	48	**Calvin Coolidge** John W. Davis Robert M. La Follette
1928	48	**Herbert C. Hoover** Alfred E. Smith
1932	48	**Franklin D. Roosevelt** Herbert C. Hoover Norman Thomas
1936	48	**Franklin D. Roosevelt** Alfred M. Landon William Lemke
1940	48	**Franklin D. Roosevelt** Wendell L. Willkie
1944	48	**Franklin D. Roosevelt** Thomas E. Dewey
1948	48	**Harry S Truman** Thomas E. Dewey J. Strom Thurmond Henry A. Wallace
1952	48	**Dwight D. Eisenhower** Adlai E. Stevenson
1956	48	**Dwight D. Eisenhower** Adlai E. Stevenson
1960	50	**John F. Kennedy** Richard M. Nixon
1964	50	**Lyndon B. Johnson** Barry M. Goldwater
1968	50	**Richard M. Nixon** Hubert H. Humphrey George C. Wallace

Parties	Popular Vote	Electoral Vote	Percentage of popular vote[1]
Republican	16,143,407	404	60.4
Democratic	9,130,328	127	34.2
Socialist	919,799		3.4
Farmer-Labor	265,411		1.0
Republican	15,718,211	382	54.0
Democratic	8,385,283	136	28.8
Progressive	4,831,289	13	16.6
Republican	21,391,993	444	58.2
Democratic	15,016,169	87	40.9
Democratic	22,809,638	472	57.4
Republican	15,758,901	59	39.7
Socialist	881,951		2.2
Democratic	27,752,869	523	60.8
Republican	16,674,665	8	36.5
Union	882,479		1.9
Democratic	27,307,819	449	54.8
Republican	22,321,018	82	44.8
Democratic	25,606,585	432	53.5
Republican	22,014,745	99	46.0
Democratic	24,105,812	303	49.5
Republican	21,970,065	189	45.1
States' Rights	1,169,063	39	2.4
Progressive	1,157,172		2.4
Republican	33,936,234	442	55.1
Democratic	27,314,992	89	44.4
Republican	35,590,472	457	57.6
Democratic	26,022,752	73	42.1
Democratic	34,227,096	303	49.9
Republican	34,108,546	219	49.6
Democratic	43,126,506	486	61.1
Republican	27,176,799	52	38.5
Republican	31,785,480	301	43.4
Democratic	31,275,165	191	42.7
American Independent	9,906,473	46	13.5

[1]Candidates receiving less than 1 percent of the popular vote have been omitted. For that reason the percentage of popular vote given for any election year may not total 100 percent.

YEAR	NUMBER OF STATES	CANDIDATES
1972	50	**Richard M. Nixon** George S. McGovern
1976	50	**Jimmy Carter** Gerald R. Ford
1980	50	**Ronald W. Reagan** Jimmy Carter John B. Anderson Ed Clark
1984	50	**Ronald W. Reagan** Walter F. Mondale
1988	50	**George H. Bush** Michael Dukakis
1992	50	**William Clinton** George H. Bush Ross Perot
1996	50	**William Clinton** Robert Dole Ross Perot

Parties	Popular vote	Electoral vote	Percentage of popular vote[1]
Republican	47,169,911	520	60.7
Democratic	29,170,383	17	37.5
Democratic	40,827,394	297	50.0
Republican	39,145,977	240	47.9
Republican	43,899,248	489	50.8
Democratic	35,481,435	49	41.0
Independent	5,719,437		6.6
Libertarian	920,859		1.0
Republican	54,281,858	525	59.2
Democratic	37,457,215	13	40.8
Republican	47,917,341	426	54.0
Democratic	41,013,030	112	46.0
Democratic	44,908,254	370	43.0
Republican	39,102,343	168	37.4
Independent	19,741,065		18.9
Democratic	45,628,667	379	49.2
Republican	37,869,435	159	40.8
Reform	7,874,283	0	8.5

[1]Candidates receiving less than 1 percent of the popular vote have been omitted. For that reason the percentage of popular vote given for any election year may not total 100 percent.

Justices of the U.S. Supreme Court

Name	Term of Service	Years of Service	Appointed By
John Jay	1789–1795	5	Washington
John Rutledge	1789–1791	1	Washington
William Cushing	1789–1810	20	Washington
James Wilson	1789–1798	8	Washington
John Blair	1789–1796	6	Washington
Robert H. Harrison	1789–1790	—	Washington
James Iredell	1790–1799	9	Washington
Thomas Johnson	1791–1793	1	Washington
William Paterson	1793–1806	13	Washington
John Rutledge[1]	1795–	—	Washington
Samuel Chase	1796–1811	15	Washington
Oliver Ellsworth	1796–1800	4	Washington
Bushrod Washington	1798–1829	31	J. Adams
Alfred Moore	1799–1804	4	J. Adams
John Marshall	1801–1835	34	J. Adams
William Johnson	1804–1834	30	Jefferson
H. Brockholst Livingston	1806–1823	16	Jefferson
Thomas Todd	1807–1826	18	Jefferson
Joseph Story	1811–1845	33	Madison
Gabriel Duval	1811–1835	24	Madison
Smith Thompson	1823–1843	20	Monroe
Robert Trimble	1826–1828	2	J. Q. Adams
John McLean	1829–1861	32	Jackson
Henry Baldwin	1830–1844	14	Jackson
James M. Wayne	1835–1867	32	Jackson
Roger B. Taney	1836–1864	28	Jackson
Philip P. Barbour	1836–1841	4	Jackson
John Catron	1837–1865	28	Van Buren
John McKinley	1837–1852	15	Van Buren

Note: Chief Justices appear in bold type.

[1]Acting Chief Justice; Senate refused to confirm appointment.

NAME	TERM OF SERVICE	YEARS OF SERVICE	APPOINTED BY
Peter V. Daniel	1841–1860	19	Van Buren
Samuel Nelson	1845–1872	27	Tyler
Levi Woodbury	1845–1851	5	Polk
Robert C. Grier	1846–1870	23	Polk
Benjamin R. Curtis	1851–1857	6	Fillmore
John A. Campbell	1853–1861	8	Pierce
Nathan Clifford	1858–1881	23	Buchanan
Noah H. Swayne	1862–1881	18	Lincoln
Samuel F. Miller	1862–1890	28	Lincoln
David Davis	1862–1877	14	Lincoln
Stephen J. Field	1863–1897	34	Lincoln
Salmon P. Chase	1864–1873	8	Lincoln
William Strong	1870–1880	10	Grant
Joseph P. Bradley	1870–1892	22	Grant
Ward Hunt	1873–1882	9	Grant
Morrison R. Waite	1874–1888	14	Grant
John M. Harlan	1877–1911	34	Hayes
William B. Woods	1880–1887	7	Hayes
Stanley Matthews	1881–1889	7	Garfield
Horace Gray	1882–1902	20	Arthur
Samuel Blatchford	1882–1893	11	Arthur
Lucius Q. C. Lamar	1888–1893	5	Cleveland
Melville W. Fuller	1888–1910	21	Cleveland
David J. Brewer	1890–1910	20	B. Harrison
Henry B. Brown	1890–1906	16	B. Harrison
George Shiras, Jr.	1892–1903	10	B. Harrison
Howell E. Jackson	1893–1895	2	B. Harrison
Edward D. White	1894–1910	16	Cleveland
Rufus W. Peckham	1895–1909	14	Cleveland

Name	Term of Service	Years of Service	Appointed By
Joseph McKenna	1898–1925	26	McKinley
Oliver W. Holmes, Jr.	1902–1932	30	T. Roosevelt
William R. Day	1903–1922	19	T. Roosevelt
William H. Moody	1906–1910	3	T. Roosevelt
Horace H. Lurton	1910–1914	4	Taft
Charles E. Hughes	1910–1916	5	Taft
Willis Van Devanter	1911–1937	26	Taft
Joseph R. Lamar	1911–1916	5	Taft
Edward D. White	1910–1921	11	Taft
Mahlon Pitney	1912–1922	10	Taft
James C. McReynolds	1914–1941	26	Wilson
Louis D. Brandeis	1916–1939	22	Wilson
John H. Clarke	1916–1922	6	Wilson
William H. Taft	1921–1930	8	Harding
George Sutherland	1922–1938	15	Harding
Pierce Butler	1922–1939	16	Harding
Edward T. Sanford	1923–1930	7	Harding
Harlan F. Stone	1925–1941	16	Coolidge
Charles E. Hughes	1930–1941	11	Hoover
Owen J. Roberts	1930–1945	15	Hoover
Benjamin N. Cardozo	1932–1938	6	Hoover
Hugo L. Black	1937–1971	34	F. Roosevelt
Stanley F. Reed	1938–1957	19	F. Roosevelt
Felix Frankfurter	1939–1962	23	F. Roosevelt
William O. Douglas	1939–1975	36	F. Roosevelt
Frank Murphy	1940–1949	9	F. Roosevelt
Harlan F. Stone	1941–1946	5	F. Roosevelt
James F. Byrnes	1941–1942	1	F. Roosevelt
Robert H. Jackson	1941–1954	13	F. Roosevelt
Wiley B. Rutledge	1943–1949	6	F. Roosevelt
Harold H. Burton	1945–1958	13	Truman

Name	Term of Service	Years of Service	Appointed By
Fred M. Vinson	1946–1953	7	Truman
Tom C. Clark	1949–1967	18	Truman
Sherman Minton	1949–1956	7	Truman
Earl Warren	1953–1969	16	Eisenhower
John Marshall Harlan	1955–1971	16	Eisenhower
William J. Brennan, Jr.	1956–1990	34	Eisenhower
Charles E. Whittaker	1957–1962	5	Eisenhower
Potter Stewart	1958–1981	23	Eisenhower
Byron R. White	1962–1993	31	Kennedy
Arthur J. Goldberg	1962–1965	3	Kennedy
Abe Fortas	1965–1969	4	Johnson
Thurgood Marshall	1967–1994	24	Johnson
Warren E. Burger	1969–1986	18	Nixon
Harry A. Blackmun	1970–1994	24	Nixon
Lewis F. Powell, Jr.	1971–1987	15	Nixon
William H. Rehnquist[2]	1971–	—	Nixon
John P. Stevens III	1975–	—	Ford
Sandra Day O'Connor	1981–	—	Reagan
Antonin Scalia	1986–	—	Reagan
Anthony M. Kennedy	1988–	—	Reagan
David Souter	1990–	—	Bush
Clarence Thomas	1991–	—	Bush
Ruth Bader Ginsburg	1993–	—	Clinton
Stephen G. Breyer	1994–	—	Clinton

[2]Chief Justice from 1986 on (Reagan administration).

⁓ SUGGESTED READINGS ⁓

Chapter 1

PRE-COLUMBIAN AMERICA General discussions of pre-Columbian America are found in Brian M. Fagan, *The Great Journey: The Peopling of Ancient America* (1987); Alfred M. Josephy, ed., *America in 1492: The World of the Indian Peoples before the Arrival of Columbus* (1993); and Francis Jennings, *The Founders of America: How Indians Discovered the Land, Pioneered in It, and Created Great Classical Civilizations . . .* (1993). Joseph H. Greenberg, *Language in the Americas* (1987), and William M. Denevan, ed., *The Native Population of the Americas in 1492* (1976), are standard. Philip Kopper, *The Smithsonian Book of North American Indians before the Coming of the Europeans* (1986), is accurate, accessible, and wonderfully illustrated. Michael Coe, Dean Snow, and Elizabeth Benson, *Atlas of Ancient America* (1986), provides a narrative and maps for the major cultures of North and South America. Lynda Norene Shaffer, *Native Americans before 1492: The Moundbuilding Centers of the Eastern Woodlands* (1992), provides a brief survey that covers thousands of years, while Thomas E. Emerson and R. Barry Lewis, eds., *Cahokia and the Hinterlands: Middle Mississippian Cultures of the Midwest* (1991), gives a series of detailed studies of the last cycle of mound building. Some important continuities between the pre-Columbian and post-Columbian eras are established in Neal Salisbury, "The Indians' Old World: Native Americans and the Coming of Europeans," *William and Mary Quarterly*, 3rd ser., 53 (1996): 435–458. Frederich Katz, *The Ancient American Civilizations* (1972), remains an excellent introduction. Michael D. Coe, *The Olmec World: Ritual and Rulership* (1995), is superb. Esther Pasztory's *Teotihuacan: An Experiment in Living* (1997), provides a bold and original interpretation of the Classic era's greatest metropolis. The complex cultures of Mesoamerica are covered in Norman Hammond, *Ancient Maya Civilization* (1982); Michael D. Coe, *The Maya*, 3rd ed. (1984); Linda Schele and Mary Ellen Miller, *The Blood of Kings: Dynasty and Ritual in Maya Art* (1986); Linda Schele and David Freidel, *A Forest of Kings: The Untold Story of the Ancient Maya* (1990); and Inga Clendinnen, *Aztecs: An Interpretation* (1991). For a comprehensive coverage of Andean cultures, compare Richard L. Burger, *Chavin and the Origins of Andean Civilization* (1992); Alan L. Kolata, *The Tiwanaku: Portrait of an Andean Civilization* (1993); Evan Hadingham, *Lines to the Mountain Gods: Nazca and the Mysteries of Peru* (1987); Thomas C. Patterson, *The Inca Empire: The Formation and Disintegration of a Pre-Capitalist State* (1991); and Nigel Davies, *The Incas* (1995). For the prehistory of the Pacific and Hawaii, see Peter Bellwood, *The Polynesians: Prehistory of an Island People*, rev. ed. (1987); and David E. Stannard, *Before the Horror: The Population of Hawai'i on the Eve of Western Contact* (1989).

THE EXPANSION OF EUROPE Works that trace the early expansion of Europe are G. V. Scammell, *The First Imperial Age: European Overseas Expansion c. 1400–1715* (1989); Carlo M. Cipolla, *Guns, Sails, and Empire: Technological Innovation and the Early Phases of European Expansion 1400–1700* (1965); Charles Verlinden, *The Beginnings of Modern Colonization: Eleven Essays with an Introduction* (1970); and Samuel Eliot Morison, *The European Discovery of America: The Northern Voyages, A.D. 500–1600* (1971), and *The European Discovery of America: The Southern Voyages, A.D. 1492–1616* (1974). P. E. Russell's elegant lecture, *Prince Henry the Navigator* (1960), greatly reduces Henry's importance. William D. Phillips Jr. and Carla Rahn Phillips, *The Worlds of Christopher Columbus* (1992), is a strong, recent biography. The religious motives of Columbus are explored in Pauline Moffitt Watts, "Prophecy and Discovery: On the Spiritual Origins of Christopher Columbus's 'Enterprise of the Indies,'" *American Historical Review* 90 (1985): 73–102, while Arthur Davies argues that Columbus scuttled his flagship in "The Loss of the *Santa Maria*, Christmas Day, 1492," *American Historical Review* 58 (1952–1953): 854–865. Alfred W. Crosby analyzes the long-term consequences of expansion in *The Columbian Exchange: Biological and Cultural Consequences of 1492* (1972) and in *Ecological Imperialism: The Biological Expansion of Europe, 900–1900* (1986).

AFRICA AND THE ATLANTIC SLAVE TRADE J. D. Fage, *A History of West Africa: An Introductory Survey*, 4th ed. (1969), although aging, is still useful. John Thornton, *Africa and Africans in the Making of the Modern World*,

1400–1680 (1992), insists that Africans retained control of their affairs, including the slave trade, before 1700. Patrick Manning, *Slavery and African Life: Occidental, Oriental, and African Slave Trades* (1990), emphasizes the devastating impact of the slave trade in the 18th and 19th centuries. Philip D. Curtin, *The Atlantic Slave Trade: A Census* (1969), is a classic, although it is modified by Paul E. Lovejoy, "The Volume of the Atlantic Slave Trade: A Synthesis," *Journal of African History* 23 (1982): 473–501. For a strong introduction to this topic, also see Lovejoy, "The Impact of the African Slave Trade on Africa: A Review of the Literature," *Journal of African History* 30 (1989): 365–394. Hugh Thomas, *The Slave Trade: The Story of the Atlantic Slave Trade, 1440–1870* (1997), is comprehensive and detailed. Robin Blackburn, *The Making of New World Slavery: From the Baroque to the Modern, 1492–1800* (1997), is a lucid and comprehensive synthesis, the best yet written. David Brion Davis, *Slavery and Human Progress* (1984), is a meditation on the changing significance of slavery between the onset of European expansion and the abolition of the institution.

THE IBERIAN EMPIRES James Lockhart and Stuart B. Schwartz, *Early Latin America: A History of Colonial Spanish America and Brazil* (1983), is a superb survey. Charles R. Boxer, *The Portuguese Seaborne Empire: 1415–1825* (1969), is excellent. David E. Stannard, *American Holocaust: Columbus and the Conquest of the New World* (1992), is an angry account of the European conquest. Major studies of the early Spanish Empire include J. H. Parry, *The Spanish Seaborne Empire* (1966); Carl O. Sauer, *The Early Spanish Main* (1966); Tzvetan Todorov, *The Conquest of America* (1984); Charles Gibson, *The Aztecs under Spanish Rule: A History of the Indians of the Valley of Mexico, 1519–1810* (1964); John Hemming, *The Conquest of the Incas* (1970); James Lockhart, *Spanish Peru, 1532–1560: A Colonial Society* (1968); David Noble Cook, *Demographic Collapse: Indian Peru, 1520–1620* (1981); and James Lockhart, "Encomienda and Hacienda: The Evolution of the Great Estate in the Spanish Indies," *Hispanic American Historical Review* 49 (1969): 411–429. David J. Weber, *The Spanish Frontier in North America* (1992), is excellent on the Franciscan missions in Florida and New Mexico. John Hemming, *Red Gold: The Conquest of the Brazilian Indians, 1500–1760* (1978), is careful and sobering.

THE FIRST GLOBAL ECONOMY Immanuel Wallerstein, *The Modern World System: Capitalist Agriculture and the Origins of the European World Economy in the Sixteenth Century* (1974), and Fernand Braudel, *Capitalism and Material Life, 1400–1800* (1967), both explore the emergence of a global economy. Charles A. Levinson, ed., *Circa 1492: Art in the Age of Exploration* (1991), provides a global view of art in the same era.

VIDEOS The *Nova* series on PBS has produced two outstanding documentaries on pre-Columbian America. *Search for the First Americans* (1992) assembles evidence for very early occupancy of the Americas. *Secrets of the Lost Red Paint People* (1987) is a fascinating example of how archaeologists reconstruct the distant past and the surprises that this process creates. Another challenging program is *The Sun Dagger* (1982), narrated by Robert Redford, on Anasazi astronomy, available through Pacific Arts Publishing.

Chapter 2

FRENCH AND DUTCH EXPANSION W. J. Eccles, *The French in North America, 1500–1783*, rev. ed. (1998), is a concise and authoritative survey. Also helpful are Peter N. Moogk, "Reluctant Exiles: The Problem of Colonization in French North America," *William and Mary Quarterly* 3rd ser., 46 (1989): 463–505; Morris Altman, "Economic Growth in Canada: Estimates and Analysis," *William and Mary Quarterly*, 3rd ser., 45 (1988): 684–711; and Winstanley Briggs, "Le Pays des Illinois," *William and Mary Quarterly*, 3rd ser., 47 (1990): 30–56. Superb overviews are found in Jonathan I. Israel, *The Dutch Republic: Its Rise, Greatness, and Fall* (1995); Simon Schama, *The Embarrassment of Riches: An Interpretation of Dutch Culture in the Golden Age* (1987); and Charles R. Boxer, *The Dutch Seaborne Empire: 1600–1800* (1965). George Masselman, *The Cradle of Colonialism* (1963), and Jonathan I. Israel, *Dutch Primacy in World Trade, 1585–1740* (1989), are more specialized. Oliver A. Rink, *Holland on the Hudson: An Economic and Social History of Dutch New York* (1986), and S. G. Nissenson, *The Patroon's Domain* (1937), cover New Netherland.

ELIZABETHAN EXPANSION David B. Quinn, *England and the Discovery of America, 1481–1620* (1974), and Kenneth R. Andrews, *Trade, Plunder, and Settlement: Maritime Enterprise and the Genesis of the British Empire, 1480–1630* (1984), offer fine narratives. Karen O. Kupperman's *Roanoke: The Abandoned Colony* (1984) is briefer than David B. Quinn's *Set Fair for Roanoke: Voyages and Colonies, 1584–1606* (1985); both are excellent. Nicholas P. Canny places the conquest of Ireland in a broad, Atlantic context in *The Elizabethan Conquest of*

Ireland: A Pattern Established, 1565–76 (1976) and *Kingdom and Colony: Ireland in the Atlantic World, 1560–1800* (1988).

THE 13 COLONIES: GENERAL STUDIES Jack P. Greene, *Pursuits of Happiness: The Social Development of Early Modern British Colonies and the Formation of American Culture* (1988), surveys all 13 colonies within the context of Britain's other Atlantic provinces, including Ireland and the West Indies. David Hackett Fischer, *Albion's Seed: Four British Folkways in America* (1989), traces the regional identities of New England, the upper South, the Mid-Atlantic, and the early backcountry to specific subcultures within the British Isles. Bernard Bailyn, *The Peopling of British North America: An Introduction* (1985), is a broadly conceived overview of the settlement process. Mary Beth Norton, *Founding Mothers and Fathers: Gendered Power and the Forming of American Society* (1996), sees very different gender relationships taking shape in the early Chesapeake colonies from what she finds in early New England. Some major interpretative essays are found in Stanley N. Katz, John M. Murrin, and Douglas Greenberg, eds., *Colonial America: Essays in Politics and Social Development*, 5th ed. (2000), and Jack P. Greene and J. R. Pole, eds., *Colonial British America: Essays in the New History of the Early Modern Era* (1984).

THE CHESAPEAKE AND WEST INDIAN COLONIES Edmund S. Morgan, *American Slavery, American Freedom: The Ordeal of Colonial Virginia* (1975), remains the best history of any American colony. For a sobering essay, see J. Frederick Fausz, "An 'Abundance of Blood Shed on Both Sides': England's First Indian War, 1609–1614," *Virginia Magazine of History and Biography* 98 (1990): 3–56. For perspectives on the social history of the Chesapeake colonies, see Thad W. Tate and David L. Ammerman, eds., *The Chesapeake in the Seventeenth Century: Essays on Anglo-American Society* (1979); Lois Green Carr, Philip D. Morgan, and Jean B. Russo, eds., *Colonial Chesapeake Society* (1988); and Aubrey Land, Lois Green Carr, and Edward C. Papenfuse, eds., *Law, Society, and Politics in Early Maryland* (1977). Kathleen M. Brown, *Good Wives, Nasty Wenches, and Anxious Patriarchs: Gender, Race, and Power in Colonial Virginia* (1996), is fresh and imaginative. Darrett and Anita Rutman, *A Place in Time* (1984), is a community study of Middlesex County, Virginia. On the role of younger sons in shaping cultural values, see Martin H. Quitt, "Immigrant Origins of the Virginia Gentry: A Study of Cultural Transmission and Innovation," *William and Mary Quarterly*, 3rd ser., 45 (1988): 629–655. Strong studies of Maryland include Gloria L. Main, *Tobacco Colony: Life in Early Maryland, 1650–1720* (1982); Russell R. Menard, *Economy and Society in Early Colonial Maryland* (1985); and David W. Jordan, *Foundations of Representative Government in Maryland, 1632–1715* (1987). On the West Indies, see Carl and Roberta Bridenbaugh, *No Peace beyond the Line: The English in the Caribbean, 1624–1690* (1972), and Richard S. Dunn, *Sugar and Slaves: The Rise of the Planter Class in the English West Indies, 1624–1713* (1972). Karen O. Kupperman, *Providence Island, 1630–1641: The Other Puritan Colony* (1993), tells the story of Puritan colonization in the tropics. Winthrop Jordan, *White over Black: American Attitudes toward the Negro, 1550–1812* (1968), and Orlando Patterson, *Slavery and Social Death: A Comparative Study* (1982), are classics. Ira Berlin, *Many Thousands Gone: The First Two Centuries of Slavery in North America* (1998), is essential.

NEW ENGLAND Three indispensable studies of New England Puritanism are Perry Miller, *The New England Mind: The Seventeenth Century* (1939); Edmund S. Morgan, *Visible Saints: The History of a Puritan Idea* (1963); and David D. Hall, *Worlds of Wonder, Days of Judgment: Popular Religious Belief in Early New England* (1989). Other major contributions include Sacvan Bercovitch, *The Puritan Origins of the American Self* (1975); Charles L. Cohen, *God's Caress: The Psychology of Puritan Religious Experience* (1986); Harry S. Stout, *The New England Soul: Preaching and Religious Culture in Colonial New England* (1986); and Andrew Delbanco, *The Puritan Ordeal* (1989). Darren Stoloff, *The Making of an American Thinking Class: Intellectuals and Intelligentsia in Puritan Massachusetts* (1998), is original and provocative. The best edition of an American classic is William Bradford, *Of Plymouth Plantation, 1620–1647*, edited by Samuel Eliot Morison (1959).

David Hall, John M. Murrin, and Thad W. Tate, eds., *Saints and Revolutionaries: Essays on Early American History* (1984), contains several important contributions on early New England. Virginia D. Anderson, *New England's Generation: The Great Migration and the Formation of Society and Culture in the Seventeenth Century* (1991), is the best study of the migration process. Major community and demographic studies include Darrett B. Rutman, *Winthrop's Boston: A Portrait of a Puritan Town, 1630–1649* (1965); John Demos, *A Little Commonwealth: Family Life in Plymouth Colony* (1970); Philip J. Greven Jr., *Four Generations: Population, Land and Family in Colonial Andover, Massachusetts* (1970); Kenneth A. Lockridge, *A New England Town, the First Hundred Years: Dedham, Massachusetts, 1636–1736*, rev. ed. (1985); and Stephen Innes, *Labor in a New Land: Economy and Society in Seventeenth-Century Springfield* (1983). Laurel T. Ulrich, *Good Wives: Images and*

Reality in the Lives of Women in Northern New England, 1650–1750 (1982), has been pathbreaking. Another important study is Amanda Porterfield, *Female Piety in Puritan New England: The Emergence of Religious Humanism* (1992).

Major studies of the New England economy include Bernard Bailyn, *The New England Merchants in the Seventeenth Century* (1955); Elaine Forman Crane, *Ebb Tide in New England: Women, Seaports, and Social Change, 1630–1800* (1998); Stephen Innes, *Creating the Commonwealth: The Economic Culture of Puritan New England* (1995); and Daniel Vickers, *Farmers and Fishermen: Two Centuries of Work in Essex County, Massachusetts, 1630–1850* (1994). John Frederick Martin, *Profits in the Wilderness: Entrepreneurship and the Founding of New England Towns in the Seventeenth Century* (1991), tries to integrate economic history with community studies.

Studies of dissent in New England include Edmund S. Morgan, *Roger Williams: The Church and the State* (1967); Emery Battis, *Saints and Sectaries: Anne Hutchinson and the Antinomian Controversy in the Massachusetts Bay Colony* (1962); and Carla G. Pestana, *Quakers and Baptists in Colonial Massachusetts* (1991). Robert E. Wall shows how the political and legal systems of Massachusetts took shape in response to dissent and controversy in *Massachusetts Bay: The Crucial Decade, 1640–1650* (1972). Robert G. Pope, *The Half-Way Covenant: Church Membership in Puritan New England* (1969), is insightful and thorough.

THE LOWER SOUTH Peter H. Wood, *Black Majority: Negroes in Colonial South Carolina from 1670 through the Stono Rebellion* (1974), remains the best book on early South Carolina. Charles Hudson, *The Southeastern Indians* (1976), and James H. Merrell, *The Indians' New World: Catawbas and Their Neighbors from European Contact through the Era of Removal* (1989), are superb studies of southern Indians. Other contributions on South Carolina include Peter A. Coclanis, *The Shadow of a Dream: Economic Life and Death in the South Carolina Low Country, 1670–1920* (1989); Richard Waterhouse, *A New World Gentry: The Making of a Merchant and Planter Class in South Carolina, 1670–1770* (1989); David C. Littlefield, *Rice and Slaves: Ethnicity and the Slave Trade in Colonial South Carolina* (1981); and M. Eugene Sirmans, *Colonial South Carolina: A Political History, 1663–1763* (1966).

ENGLAND'S MID-ATLANTIC COLONIES For a look at Restoration New York, see Robert C. Ritchie, *The Duke's Province: A Study of New York Politics and Society, 1664–1691* (1977); Joyce D. Goodfriend, *Before the Melting Pot: Society and Culture in Colonial New York City, 1664–1730* (1992); and Donna Merwick, *Possessing Albany, 1630–1710: The Dutch and English Experiences* (1990). Still standard are John E. Pomfret's *The Province of East New Jersey, 1609–1702* (1962) and *The Province of West New Jersey, 1609–1702* (1956). Melvin B. Endy, *William Penn and Early Quakerism* (1973), and the essays in Richard S. Dunn and Mary Maples Dunn, eds., *The World of William Penn* (1986), are comprehensive. Barry J. Levy, *Quakers and the American Family: British Settlement in the Delaware Valley* (1988), is strong on family life, while Gary B. Nash, *Quakers and Politics: Pennsylvania, 1681–1726* (1968), is one of the best political histories of any American colony.

VIDEOS *Black Robe*, a 1991 Canadian film based on Brian Manning's novel of the same name, is a powerful evocation of the early Jesuit missions in New France. The PBS miniseries *Roanoak* (1986) explores tensions between settlers and Indians in England's first sustained attempt to colonize North America.

Chapter 3

Two strong overviews of public events in England during these years are Derek Hirst, *Authority and Conflict: England, 1603–1658* (1986), and J. R. Jones, *Country and Court: England, 1658–1714* (1978). Wesley F. Craven, *The Colonies in Transition, 1660–1713* (1968), remains a strong survey of colonial developments. Edmund S. Morgan, *Inventing the People: The Rise of Popular Sovereignty in England and America* (1988), connects political thought in the English civil wars with the American Revolution more than a century later. Another influential work is J. G. A. Pocock, "Machiavelli, Harrington, and English Political Ideologies in the Eighteenth Century," *William and Mary Quarterly*, 3rd ser., 22 (1965): 549–583. Pocock's *The Machiavellian Moment: Florentine Political Thought and the Atlantic Republican Tradition* (1975) is difficult but essential.

MERCANTILISM Albert O. Hirschman, *The Passions and the Interests: Political Arguments for Capitalism before Its Triumph* (1977), is brief and brilliant. Important studies of trade wars and the Navigation Acts include Charles Wilson, *Profit and Power: A Study of England and the Dutch Wars* (1957); Charles M. Andrews, *The Colonial Period of American History*, vol. 4 (1938); Lawrence A. Harper, *The English Navigation Acts: A Seventeenth-Century Experiment in Social Engineering* (1939); and Michael Kammen's brief *Empire and Interest: The American Colonies and the Politics of Mercantilism* (1969).

INDIANS AND SETTLERS Colin G. Calloway, *New Worlds for All: Indians, Europeans, and the Remaking of Early America* (1997), surveys settler-Indian relations to about 1800. Daniel K. Richer, *The Ordeal of the Longhouse: The Peoples of the Iroquois League in the Era of European Colonization* (1992); Matthew Dennis, *Cultivating a Landscape of Peace: Iroquois-European Encounters in Seventeenth-Century America* (1993); and Francis Jennings, *The Ambiguous Iroquois Empire: The Covenant Chain Confederation of Indian Tribes with English Colonies from Its Beginnings to the Lancaster Treaty of 1744* (1984), are all essential. A brief and up-to-date account of Puritan missions is Richard W. Cogley, *John Eliot's Mission to the Indians before King Philip's War* (1999). Jill Lepore, *The Name of War: King Philip's War and the Origins of American Identity* (1998), Patrick M. Malone, *The Skulking Way of War: Technology and Tactics among the New England Indians* (1991), and Richard I. Melvoin, *New England Outpost: War and Society in Colonial Deerfield* (1989), are transforming the way that historians approach Metacom's War. Edmund S. Morgan, *American Slavery, American Freedom: The Ordeal of Colonial Virginia* (1975), provides the strongest analysis of Bacon's Rebellion, but also useful is Wilcomb Washburn, *The Governor and the Rebel: A History of Bacon's Rebellion in Virginia* (1957).

ROYAL GOVERNMENT Stephen S. Webb analyzes the origins of royal government through the Glorious Revolution in *The Governors General: The English Army and the Definition of Empire, 1569–1681* (1979) and in his *Lord Churchill's Coup: The Anglo-American Empire and the Glorious Revolution Reconsidered* (1995). Still impressive is Winfred T. Root, "The Lords of Trade, 1675–1696," *American Historical Review* 23 (1917–1918): 20–41.

THE GLORIOUS REVOLUTION AND ITS AFTERMATH The following works lay out various aspects of the transformation of English politics between 1660 and 1720: John Miller, *Popery and Politics in England, 1660–1688* (1973); Robert Willman, "The Origins of 'Whig' and 'Tory' in English Political Language," *Historical Journal* 17 (1974): 247–264; Clayton Roberts, *The Growth of Responsible Government in Stuart England* (1966); W. A. Speck, *Reluctant Revolutionaries: Englishmen and the Revolution of 1688* (1989); J. H. Plumb, *The Growth of Political Stability in England, 1675–1725* (1967); John Brewer, *The Sinews of Power: War, Money, and the English State, 1688–1783* (1989); P. G. M. Dickson, *The Financial Revolution in England: A Study in the Development of Public Credit, 1688–1756* (1967); Geoffrey Holmes, *The Electorate and the National Will in the First Age of Party* (1976); and Isaac Kramnick, *Bolingbroke and his Circle: The Politics of Nostalgia in the Age of Walpole* (1968). For an unusually thoughtful essay, consult Peter Laslett, "John Locke, the Great Recoinage, and the Origins of the Board of Trade: 1695–1698," *William and Mary Quarterly*, 3rd ser., 14 (1957): 370–402. Ian K. Steele, *The English Atlantic, 1675–1740: An Exploration of Communication and Community* (1986), is careful and original. John M. Murrin looks for similarities and differences in the English and American Revolutions in "The Great Inversion, or Court versus Country: A Comparison of the Revolution Settlements in England (1688–1721) and America (1776–1816)," in J. G. A. Pocock, ed., *Three British Revolutions: 1641, 1688, 1776* (1980), pp. 368–453.

David S. Lovejoy, *The Glorious Revolution in America* (1972), covers all the colonies. For more specific studies of the Glorious Revolution in New England, New York, and Maryland, see Richard R. Johnson, *Adjustment to Empire: The New England Colonies, 1675–1715* (1981); John M. Murrin, "The Menacing Shadow of Louis XIV and the Rage of Jacob Leisler: The Constitutional Ordeal of Seventeenth Century New York," in Stephen L. Schechter and Richard B. Bernstein, eds., *New York and the Union: Contributions to the American Constitutional Experience* (1990), pp. 29–71; and Lois G. Carr and David W. Jordan, *Maryland's Revolution of Government, 1689–1692* (1974). Imaginative and distinctive perspectives on the Salem witch trials are found in Paul Boyer and Stephen Nissenbaum, *Salem Possessed: The Social Origins of Witchcraft* (1974); John P. Demos, *Entertaining Satan: Witchcraft and the Culture of Early New England* (1982); Richard Weisman, *Witchcraft, Magic, and Religion in 17th Century Massachusetts* (1984); and Bernard Rosenthal, *Salem Story: Reading the Witch Trials of 1692* (1993)—but Carol F. Karlsen, *The Devil in the Shape of a Woman: Witchcraft in Colonial New England* (1987), and Elizabeth Reis, *Damned Women: Sinners and Witches in Puritan New England* (1997), are conceptual breakthroughs.

THE SPANISH AND FRENCH COLONIES Ramón A. Gutiérrez, *When Jesus Came, the Corn Mothers Went Away: Marriage, Sexuality, and Power in New Mexico, 1500–1846* (1991), has a strong account of the Pueblo revolt. David J. Weber, *The Spanish Frontier in North America* (1992), treats the Florida missions and Texas. Richard White, *The Middle Ground: Indians, Empires, and Republics in the Great Lakes Region, 1650–1815* (1991), and Eric Hinderaker, *Elusive Empires: Constructing Colonialism in the Ohio Valley, 1673–1800* (1997), are both superb. Daniel H. Usner, *Indians, Settlers, and Slaves in a Frontier Exchange Economy: The Lower Mississippi Valley before 1783* (1992), nicely covers Louisiana.

THE HOUSEHOLDER ECONOMY Important studies of the 18th century household are James A. Henretta, "Families and Farms: Mentalite in Pre-Industrial America," *William and Mary Quarterly*, 3rd ser., 35 (1978): 3–32; Daniel Vickers, "Competency and Competition: Economic Culture in Early America," *William and Mary Quarterly*, 3rd ser., 47 (1990): 3–27; Mary M. Schweitzer, *Custom and Contract: Household, Government, and the Economy in Colonial Pennsylvania* (1987); and Laurel Thatcher Ulrich, *Good Wives: Images and Reality in the Lives of Women in Northern New England* (1982).

VIDEOS The PBS miniseries *Three Sovereigns for Sarah* (1986), starring Vanessa Redgrave, is a superb dramatization of the Salem witch trials.

Chapter 4

IMMIGRATION AND ECONOMIC CHANGE The best studies of immigration during the 18th century are Bernard Bailyn, *Voyagers to the West: A Passage in the Peopling of America on the Eve of the Revolution* (1986); A. G. Roeber, *Palatines, Liberty, and Property: German Lutherans in Colonial British America* (1993); Aaron S. Fogleman, *Hopeful Journeys: German Immigration, Settlement, and Political Culture in Colonial America, 1717–1775* (1996); R. J. Dickson, *Ulster Emigration to Colonial America, 1718–1775* (1966); Alan L. Karras, *Sojourners in the Sun: Scottish Migrants in Jamaica and the Chesapeake, 1740–1800* (1992); and A. Roger Ekirch, *Bound for America: The Transportation of British Convicts to the Colonies, 1718–1775* (1987).

Ian K. Steele, *The English Atlantic, 1675–1740: An Exploration of Communication and Community* (1986), discusses the quickening pace of Atlantic commerce. Richard L. Bushman, *The Refinement of America: Persons, Houses, Cities* (1992), and Rhys Isaac, *The Transformation of Virginia* (1982), explore the rise of elegance and of gentry culture. Three works that deal with the decline of opportunity for 18th century householders are Toby L. Ditz, "Ownership and Obligation: Inheritance and Patriarchal Households in Connecticut, 1750–1820," *William and Mary Quarterly*, 3rd ser., 47 (1990): 235–265; Lucy Simler, "The Landless Worker: An Index of Economic and Social Change in Chester County, Pennsylvania, 1750–1820," *Pennsylvania Magazine of History and Biography* 94 (1990): 163–199; and Allan Kulikoff, *Tobacco and Slaves: The Development of Southern Culture in the Chesapeake, 1680–1800* (1986). John J. McCusker and Russell R. Menard, *The Economy of British America, 1607–1789* (1985), covers most economic patterns and questions. Joyce E. Chaplin, *An Anxious Pursuit: Agricultural Innovation and Modernity in the Lower South, 1730–1815* (1993), is thoughtful and important.

THE ENLIGHTENMENT AND THE GREAT AWAKENING Henry F. May, *The Enlightenment in America* (1976), needs to be supplemented by Norman Fiering, "The First American Enlightenment: Tillotson, Leverett, and Philosophical Anglicanism," *New England Quarterly* 54 (1981): 307–344; and by Charles E. Clark, *The Public Prints: The Newspaper in Anglo-American Culture, 1665–1740* (1994); Michael Warner, *The Letters of the Republic: Publication and the Public Sphere in Eighteenth-Century America* (1990); David S. Shields, *Civil Tongues & Polite Letters in British America* (1997); and Ned Landsman, *From Colonials to Provincials: Thought and Culture in America, 1680–1760* (1998). On the rise of the professions, contrast Daniel J. Boorstin, *The Americans: The Colonial Experience* (1958), with John M. Murrin, "The Legal Transformation: The Bench and Bar in Eighteenth-Century Massachusetts," in Stanley N. Katz and John M. Murrin, eds., *Colonial America: Essays in Politics and Social Development*, 3rd ed. (1983), pp. 540–572. Phinzey Spalding, *Oglethorpe in America* (1977), and Harold E. Davis, *The Fledgling Province: Social and Cultural Life in Colonial Georgia, 1733–1776* (1976), are standard.

Indispensable studies of the Great Awakening include John Walsh, "Origins of the Evangelical Revival," in G. V. Bennett and J. D. Walsh, eds., *Essays in Modern English Church History in Honor of Norman Sykes* (1966), pp. 132–162; W. R. Ward, *The Protestant Evangelical Awakening* (1992); Susan O'Brien, "A Transatlantic Community of Saints: The Great Awakening and the First Evangelical Network, 1735–1755," *American Historical Review* 91 (1986): 811–832; and Frank J. Lambert, *"Pedlar in Divinity": George Whitefield and the Transatlantic Revivals* (1994). Perry Miller, *Jonathan Edwards* (1949), is brilliant and controversial. Other important studies are Richard Warch, "The Shephard's Tent: Education and Enthusiasm in the Great Awakening," *American Quarterly* 30 (1978): 177–198; Martin E. Lodge, "The Crisis of the Churches in the Middle Colonies, 1720–1750," *Pennsylvania Magazine of History and Biography* 95 (1971): 195–220; Milton J Coalter, *Gilbert Tennent, Son of Thunder* (1986); Leigh Eric Schmidt, "'The Grand Prophet,' Hugh Bryan: Early Evangelicalism's Challenge to the Establishment and Slavery in the Colonial South," *South Carolina Historical Magazine* 87 (1986): 238–250; and Mark A. Noll, *Princeton and the Republic, 1768–1822: The Quest for a Christian Enlightenment in the Era of Samuel Stanhope Smith* (1989). To explore links between revivalism and revolution, see Harry S. Stout, "Religion, Communications, and the Ideological Origins of the American Revolution," *William and Mary Quarterly*, 3rd ser., 34 (1977): 519–541; and Nathan O. Hatch, *The Sacred Cause of Liberty: Republican Thought and the Millennium in Revolutionary New England* (1977).

Colonial Politics   For two views that clash sharply over provincial politics, compare Bernard Bailyn, *The Origins of American Politics* (1968), and Jack P. Greene, "Political Mimesis: A Consideration of the Historical and Cultural Roots of Legislative Behavior in the British Colonies in the Eighteenth Century," *American Historical Review* 75 (1969): 337–367. Greene elaborates his position in *Peripheries and Center: Constitutional Development in the Extended Polities of the British Empire and the United States, 1607–1788* (1987). More specialized studies include David Alan Williams, *Political Alignments in Colonial Virginia Politics* (1989); Robert M. Weir, "'The Harmony We Were Famous For': An Interpretation of Pre-Revolutionary South Carolina Politics," *William and Mary Quarterly*, 3rd ser., 26 (1969): 473–501; W. W. Abbot, *The Royal Governors of Georgia, 1754–1775* (1959); Alan Tully, *William Penn's Legacy: Politics and Social Structure in Provincial Pennsylvania, 1726–1755* (1977); Patricia U. Bonomi, *A Factious People: Politics and Society in Colonial New York* (1971); Stanley N. Katz, *Newcastle's New York: Anglo-American Politics, 1732–1753* (1968); William Pencak, *War, Politics, and Revolution in Provincial Massachusetts* (1981); Richard L. Bushman, *King and People in Provincial Massachusetts* (1985); and Jere R. Daniell, "Politics in New Hampshire under Governor Benning Wentworth," *William and Mary Quarterly*, 3rd ser., 23 (1966): 76–105. Two recent studies examine middle-colony politics on a regional scale. They are Alan Tully, *Forming American Politics: Ideals, Interests, and Institutions in Colonial New York and Pennsylvania* (1994); and Benjamin H. Newcombe, *Political Partisanship in the American Middle Colonies, 1700–1776* (1995).

The Renewal of Imperial Conflict   Richard Harding, *Amphibious Warfare in the Eighteenth Century: The British Expeditions to the West Indies* (1991), is the best account of the Caribbean theater during the War of Jenkins's Ear. For important perspectives on the crisis in the Deep South from 1739 to 1742, see Jane Landers, "Gracia Real de Santa Teresa de Mose: A Free Black Town in Spanish Colonial Florida," *American Historical Review* 95 (1990): 9–30; John Thornton, "African Dimensions of the Stono Rebellion," *American Historical Review* 96 (1991): 1101–1113; and Larry E. Ivers, *British Drums on the Southern Frontier: The Military Colonization of Georgia, 1733–1749* (1974). T. J. Davis, *A Rumor of Revolt: The "Great Negro Plot" in Colonial New York* (1985), is standard. John A. Schutz, *William Shirley, King's Governor of Massachusetts* (1961), is a good introduction to King George's War. Strong specialized studies include Robert E. Wall Jr., "Louisbourg, 1745," *New England Quarterly* 37 (1964): 64–83; and John Lax and William Pencak, "The Knowles Riot and the Crisis of the 1740s in Massachusetts," *Perspectives in American History* 10 (1976): 163–214.

The War for North America   Fred Anderson, *Crucible of War: The Seven Years' War and the Fate of Empire in British North America, 1754–1766* (2000) is a brilliant narrative and compelling synthesis. Lawrence H. Gipson, *The British Empire before the American Revolution*, 15 vols. (1936–1972), is the most detailed narrative ever written for the period 1748–1776 and is ardently pro-empire. Volumes 4 and 5 cover the background to the fourth Anglo-French war, which Gipson calls "the Great War for the Empire." Volumes 6 and 7 cover the war in North America. Three other standard works are Robert C. Newbold, *The Albany Congress and Plan of Union of 1754* (1955); Alison G. Olson, "The British Government and Colonial Union in 1754," *William and Mary Quarterly*, 3rd ser., 17 (1960): 22–34; and Paul E. Kopperman, *Braddock at the Monongahela* (1977). Francis Jennings, *Empire of Fortune: Crowns, Colonies, and Tribes in the Seven Years War in America* (1988), tries to put Indians at the center of the conflict, not on the margins, as do earlier narratives. Two much-needed Canadian perspectives, both of which are highly critical of Montcalm, can be found in Guy Frégault, *Canada: The War of the Conquest* (1968), and D. Peter MacLeod, "The Canadians against the French: The Struggle for Control of the Expedition to Oswego in 1756," *Ontario History* 80 (1988): 143–157. Ian K. Steele, *Betrayals: Fort William Henry and the "Massacre"* (1990), is innovative and persuasive. Victor L. Johnson explores some of the dilemmas of smuggling in "Fair Traders and Smugglers in Philadelphia, 1754–1763," *Pennsylvania Magazine of History and Biography* 83 (1959): 125–149. Fred Anderson, *A People's Army: Massachusetts Soldiers and Society in the Seven Years' War* (1984), emphasizes the contractual principles of colonial soldiers at the outset of the war. In *Empire and Liberty: American Resistance to British Authority, 1755–1763* (1974), Alan Rogers overstates the confrontation between colonists and imperial officials by failing to notice that it had largely been resolved by 1758. Harold E. Selesky, *War and Society in Colonial Connecticut* (1990), argues that the colonists became more soldierly as the war progressed. Tom Hatley, *The Dividing Paths: Cherokees and South Carolinians through the Era of Revolution* (1993), covers the Cherokee War.

Chapter 5

GENERAL HISTORIES Good general histories of the American Revolution include Robert M. Calhoon's moderate *Revolutionary America: An Interpretive Overview* (1976), Edward Countryman's more radical *The American Revolution* (1985), and Colin Bonwick's recent British perspective in *The American Revolution* (1991). Major attempts to understand the broader significance of the Revolution include Robert R. Palmer, *The Age of the Democratic Revolution, 1760–1800*, 2 vols. (1959–1964), which sees a close affinity between the American and French Revolutions; Lester D. Langley, *The Americas in the Age of Revolution, 1750–1850* (1996), which compares the American Revolution with Haiti's successful slave revolt and with the Latin American struggles for independence; Marc Egnal, *A Mighty Empire: The Origins of the American Revolution* (1988), which argues that westward expansion provided the underlying thrust for independence; and Gordon S. Wood, *The Radicalism of the American Revolution* (1992), which insists that the Revolution was the most important defining event in American history and the most successful revolution in world history. Merrill Jensen's *The Founding of a Nation: A History of the American Revolution, 1763–1776* (1968) remains the best one-volume history of the coming of the Revolution. Robert W. Tucker and David C. Hendrickson, *The Fall of the First British Empire: Origins of the War of American Independence* (1982), is intelligent but argumentative. Bernard Bailyn's *The Ideological Origins of the American Revolution* (1967) has had an enormous impact on studies of the Revolution and the early republic.

PONTIAC'S WAR Howard H. Peckham, *Pontiac and the Indian Uprising* (1947), although aging badly, remains the standard narrative. Gregory E. Dowd, *A Spirited Resistance: The North American Indian Struggle for Unity, 1745–1815* (1992), explores the religious roots of pan-Indian identity; and Dowd offers a fresh perspective on the goals of the uprising in "The French King Wakes Up in Detroit: 'Pontiac's War' in Rumor and History," *Ethnohistory* 37 (1990): 254–278. Bernhard Knollenberg sets out to refute the allegation of germ warfare but ends up affirming it in "General Amherst and Germ Warfare," *Mississippi Valley Historical Review* 41 (1954–1955): 489–494, 762–763. Alden T. Vaughan describes the murderous violence that followed the war in "Frontier Banditti and the Indians: The Paxton Boys' Legacy, 1763–1775," *Pennsylvania History,* 51 (1984): 1–29.

BRITISH POLITICS AND THE REVOLUTION Important recent studies of British politics and policy beginning in the late 1750s include Marie Peters, *Pitt and Popularity: The Patriot Minister and London Opinion during the Seven Years' War* (1981); Richard Middleton, *The Bells of Victory: The Pitt-Newcastle Ministry and the Conduct of the Seven Years' War, 1757–1762* (1985); John Brewer, *Party, Ideology, and Popular Politics at the Accession of George III* (1976); John L. Bullion, *A Great and Necessary Measure: George Grenville and the Genesis of the Stamp Act, 1763–1765* (1982); Paul Langford, *The First Rockingham Administration, 1765–1766* (1973); George F. E. Rudé, *Wilkes and Liberty: A Social Study of 1763 to 1774* (1962); Peter D. G. Thomas, *British Politics and the Stamp Act Crisis: The First Phase of the American Revolution, 1763–1767* (1975); Thomas, *John Wilkes: A Friend to Liberty* (1996); Thomas, *The Townshend Duties Crisis: The Second Phase of the American Revolution, 1767–1773* (1987); and Thomas, *Tea Party to Independence: The Third Phase of the American Revolution, 1773–1776* (1991).

THE FIRST TWO IMPERIAL CRISES Alison G. Olson, *Making the Empire Work: London and American Interest Groups, 1690–1790* (1992), is very perceptive on the breakdown of imperial authority after 1760. Edmund S. and Helen M. Morgan, *The Stamp Act Crisis, Prologue to Revolution,* 3rd ed. (1953, 1995), has become a classic. Pauline Maier, *From Resistance to Revolution: Colonial Radicals and the Development of American Opposition to Britain, 1765–1776* (1972), emphasizes the links between the Sons of Liberty and the English Wilkite movement. The best studies of merchants and the resistance movement are John W. Tyler, *Smugglers and Patriots: Boston Merchants and the Advent of the American Revolution* (1986), and Thomas H. Doerflinger, *A Vigorous Spirit of Enterprise: Merchants and Economic Development in Revolutionary Philadelphia* (1986). Hiller Zobel's *The Boston Massacre* (1970) is the standard study, but Jesse Lemisch's review in *The Harvard Law Review* 84 (1970–1971) makes some telling criticisms. Richard D. Brown, *Revolutionary Politics in Massachusetts: The Boston Committee of Correspondence and the Towns* (1970), is a fine study of the growth of disaffection. John Shy's *Toward Lexington: The Role of the British Army in the Coming of the American Revolution* (1965) remains indispensable.

Internal Discontent Gary B. Nash, *The Urban Crucible: Social Change, Political Consciousness, and the Origins of the American Revolution* (1979), is a superb study of social tensions in Boston, New York, and Philadelphia. Rowland Berthoff and John M. Murrin, "Feudalism, Communalism, and the Yeoman Freeholder: The American Revolution considered as a Social Accident," in Stephen G. Kurtz and James H. Hutson, eds., *Essays on the American Revolution* (1973), pp. 256–288, lays out the feudal revival. Conflicting views about the New York manor lords emerge from Sung Bok Kim's favorable portrait in *Landlord and Tenant in Colonial New York: Manorial Society, 1664–1775* (1978) and from Edward Countryman's more negative analysis in *A People in Revolution: The American Revolution and Political Society in New York, 1760–1790* (1981). An excellent study of the New Jersey riots is Thomas L. Purvis, "Origins and Patterns of Agrarian Unrest in New Jersey," *William and Mary Quarterly*, 3rd ser., 39 (1982): 600–627. James H. Hutson, *Pennsylvania Politics, 1746–1770: The Movement for Royal Government and Its Consequences* (1972), explores the Quaker Party's assault on Pennsylvania's proprietary regime. Ronald Hoffman's *A Spirit of Dissension: Economics, Politics, and the Revolution in Maryland* (1973) is the best study of internal tensions in revolutionary Maryland. Woody Holton imaginatively explores the onset of revolution in Virginia in his *Forced Founders: Indians, Debtors, Slaves, and the Making of the American Revolution in Virginia* (1999). On North Carolina's internal tensions, see A. Roger Ekirch, *"Poor Carolina": Politics and Society in Colonial North Carolina, 1729–1776* (1981); James P. Whittenburg, "Planters, Merchants, and Lawyers: Social Change and the Origins of the North Carolina Regulation," *William and Mary Quarterly*, 3rd ser., 34 (1977): 214–238; and E. Merton Coulter, "The Granville District," *James Sprunt Historical Studies* 13 (1913): 33–56. Three excellent South Carolina studies are Richard M. Brown, *The South Carolina Regulators* (1963); Rachel N. Klein, *Unification of a Slave State: The Rise of the Planter Class in the South Carolina Backcountry, 1760–1808* (1990); and Jack P. Greene, "Bridge to Revolution: The Wilkes Fund Controversy in South Carolina, 1769–1775," *Journal of Southern History* 29 (1963): 19–52. Alan Taylor, *Liberty Men and Great Proprietors: The Revolutionary Settlement on the Frontier, 1760–1820* (1990), finds strong backcountry resentments in Maine, although they peaked rather later.

David Grimsted, "Anglo-American Racism and Phillis Wheatley's 'Sable Veil,' 'Length'ned Chain,' and 'Knitted Heart,'" in Ronald Hoffman and Peter J. Albert, eds., *Women in the Age of the American Revolution* (1989), pp. 338–444, is a superb study of the emerging antislavery movement and the role of women in it.

The Third Imperial Crisis Benjamin W. Labaree's *The Boston Tea Party* (1964) is the fullest study of that event. David Ammerman's *In the Common Cause: American Response to the Coercive Acts of 1774* (1974) carefully traces the aftermath. Philip Lawson, *The Imperial Challenge: Quebec and Britain in the Age of the American Revolution* (1989), ends with the Quebec Act. David Hackett Fischer, *Paul Revere's Ride* (1994), is a brilliant study of how the Revolutionary War began. Jerrilyn Greene Marston, *King and Congress: The Transfer of Political Legitimacy from the King to the Continental Congress, 1774–76* (1987), is fresh and insightful. Together, Richard A. Ryerson's *The Revolution Is Now Begun: The Radical Committees of Philadelphia, 1765–1776* (1978); Larry R. Gerlach's *Prologue to Revolution: New Jersey in the Coming of the American Revolution* (1976); and Joseph S. Tiedemann's *Reluctant Revolutionaries: New York City and the Road to Independence, 1763–1776* (1997) analyze the radicalization of politics in three critical colonies. Explorations of other aspects of the movement toward independence can be found in Eric Foner's *Tom Paine and Revolutionary America* (1976), Jack N. Rakove's *The Beginnings of National Politics: An Interpretive History of the Continental Congress* (1979), and James H. Hutson's "The Partition Treaty and the Declaration of American Independence," *Journal of American History* 58 (1971–1972): 877–896. Garry Wills, *Inventing America: Jefferson's Declaration of Independence* (1978), and Jay Fliegelman, *Declaring Independence: Jefferson, Natural Language, and the Culture of Performance* (1993), are imaginative studies by literary scholars. Pauline Maier, *American Scripture: Making the Declaration of Independence* (1997), uses 90 local declarations in the spring of 1776 to give context to Jefferson's famous text.

Videos The musical *1776* (1972), while it makes no claim to serious historical reconstruction of events, has many delightful scenes, even if it burlesques Richard Henry Lee and gives John Adams more credit than Thomas Jefferson for American independence.

Chapter 6

The Revolutionary War Major histories of the Revolutionary War include Piers Mackesy, *The War for America, 1775–1783* (1964), which argues that Britain could have won; Don Higgenbotham, *The War of American Independence: Military Attitudes, Policies, and Practices, 1763–1789* (1971); Marshall Smelser, *The Winning of*

Independence (1972); Jeremy Black, *War for America: The Fight for Independence, 1775–1783* (1991), which is nicely illustrated; and Stephen Conway, *The War of American Independence* (1995). For differing views on the Continental Army, compare Charles Royster, *A Revolutionary People at War: The Continental Army and American Character, 1775–1783* (1979), and James Kirby Martin and Mark E. Lender, *A Respectable Army: The Military Origins of the Republic, 1763–1789* (1982). John Shy, *A People Numerous and Armed: Reflections on the Military Struggle for American Independence,* rev. ed. (1990), contains several provocative essays, especially on the political role of the militia. Mark V. Kwasny, *Washington's Partisan War, 1775–1783* (1996), argues that effective use of the militia became a major component of Washington's strategy. Howard H. Peckham, ed., *The Toll of Independence: Engagements and Battle Casualties of the American Revolution* (1974), documents the war's high mortality rate. Outstanding studies of the wartime experience of particular states include John E. Selby, *The Revolution in Virginia, 1775–1783* (1988), Richard Buel, *Dear Liberty: Connecticut's Mobilization for the Revolutionary War* (1981), and Buel *In Irons: Britain's Naval Supremacy and the American Revolutionary Economy* (1998).

Strong studies of major campaigns include Ira D. Gruber, *The Howe Brothers and the American Revolution* (1972); Thomas Fleming, *1776: Year of Illusions* (1975); Alfred H. Bill, *The Campaign of Princeton, 1776–1777* (1948); John S. Pancake, *1777: The Year of the Hangman* (1977); Pancake, *This Destructive War: The British Campaign in the Carolinas, 1780–1782* (1985); Max M. Mintz, *The Generals of Saratoga: John Burgoyne and Horatio Gates* (1990); David G. Martin, *The Philadelphia Campaign, June 1777–July 1778* (1993); Thomas Fleming, *The Forgotten Victory: The Battle for New Jersey* (1975), on Springfield in 1780; Russell F. Weigley, *The Partisan War: The South Carolina Campaign of 1780–1782* (1970), which is brief but brilliant; and Thomas Fleming, *Beat the Last Drum: The Siege of Yorktown, 1781* (1963). The essays in Ronald Hoffman, Thad W. Tate, and Peter J. Albert, eds., *An Uncivil War: The Southern Backcountry during the American Revolution* (1985), offer a variety of perspectives on the region most fiercely divided by the Revolution. Diplomacy is well covered in Jonathan R. Dull, *A Diplomatic History of the American Revolution* (1985), and Richard B. Morris, *The Peacemakers: The Great Powers and American Independence* (1965). Lee Kennett, *The French Forces in America, 1780–1783* (1977), is standard. Still offering the fullest studies of army discontent are Carl Van Doren, *Mutiny in January: The Story of a Crisis in the Continental Army* (1943), and Richard H. Kohn, "The Inside History of the Newburgh Conspiracy: America and the Coup d'État," *William and Mary Quarterly,* 3rd ser., 27 (1970): 187–220.

BIOGRAPHIES Most major men of the Revolutionary Era have attracted multiple and often multivolume biographies. Among the more accessible are John Ferling, *John Adams: A Life* (1992); James T. Flexner, *The Traitor and the Spy: Benedict Arnold and John André* (1953, or 1975 illustrated ed.); Isabel T. Kelsay, *Joseph Brant, 1743–1807: Man of Two Worlds* (1984); John Mack Faragher, *Daniel Boone: The Life and Legend of an American Pioneer* (1992); Theodore Thayer, *Nathanael Greene: Strategist of the American Revolution* (1960); John C. Miller, *Alexander Hamilton, Portrait in Paradox* (1959); Joseph J. Ellis, *American Sphinx: The Character of Thomas Jefferson* (1997); Lance Banning, *The Sacred Fire of Liberty: James Madison and the Founding of the Federal Republic* (1995); Marcus Cunliffe, *George Washington: Man and Monument* (1958); and Garry Wills, *George Washington and the Enlightenment: Images of Power in Early America* (1984).

LOYALISM Robert M. Calhoon's *The Loyalists in Revolutionary America* (1973) is comprehensive, while Wallace Brown's *The Good Americans: Loyalists in the American Revolution* (1969) is briefer. Important specialized studies include Paul H. Smith, "The American Loyalists: Notes on Their Organization and Numerical Strength," *William and Mary Quarterly,* 3rd ser., 25 (1968): 259–277; Smith, *Loyalists and Redcoats: A Study in British Revolutionary Policy* (1964); Mary Beth Norton, *The British Americans: Loyalist Exiles in England, 1774–1789* (1972); Norton, "The Fate of Some Black Loyalists of the American Revolution," *Journal of Negro History* 58 (1973): 202–226; Charles Royster, "'The Nature of Treason': Revolutionary Virtue and American Reactions to Benedict Arnold," *William and Mary Quarterly,* 3rd ser., 36 (1979): 163–193; Janice Potter, *The Liberty We Seek: Loyalist Ideology in Colonial New York and Massachusetts* (1983); Ann G. Condon, *The Envy of the American States: The Loyalist Dream for New Brunswick* (1984); and Jane Errington, *The Lion, the Eagle, and Upper Canada: A Developing Colonial Ideology* (1987).

REPUBLICANISM AND CONSTITUTIONALISM The fullest study of an emerging American identity is David Waldstreicher, *In the Midst of Perpetual Fetes: The Making of American Nationalism, 1776–1820* (1997). Gordon S. Wood, *The Creation of the American Republic, 1776–1787* (1969), has been the most influential study of early American republicanism and constitutionalism. Thomas L. Pangle dissents sharply from Wood in *The Spirit of Modern Republicanism: The Moral Vision of the American Founders and the Philosophy of Locke* (1988). Other important contributions include Willi Paul Adams, *The First American Constitutions: Republican Ideology and the Making of the State Constitutions in the Revolutionary Era* (1980), and H. James Henderson, *Party Politics in the Continental Congress* (1974). Two standard works on hyperinflation and its consequences during the revolutionary era are E. James Ferguson, *The Power of the Purse: A History of American Public Finance, 1776–1790* (1961), and John K. Alexander, "The Fort Wilson Incident of 1779: A Study of the Revolutionary Crowd," *William and Mary Quarterly*, 3rd ser., 31 (1974): 589–612.

INDIANS, THE WEST, AND THE REVOLUTION On the eastern woodland Indian nations during the Revolution, see Gregory E. Dowd, *A Spirited Resistance: The North American Indian Struggle for Unity, 1745–1815* (1992); Colin B. Calloway, *The American Revolution in Indian Country: Crisis and Diversity in Native American Communities* (1995); and Barbara Graymont, *The Iroquois in the American Revolution* (1972). Stephen Aron, *How the West Was Lost: The Transformation of Kentucky from Daniel Boone to Henry Clay* (1995), and R. Douglas Hurt, *The Ohio Frontier: Crucible of the Old Northwest* (1996), are fresh and challenging.

SOCIAL TRANSFORMATIONS John F. Jameson, *The American Revolution Considered as a Social Movement* (1925), remains provocative. Other indispensable studies of slavery and emancipation include Benjamin Quarles, *The Negro in the American Revolution* (1961, 1996); Ira Berlin and Ronald Hoffman, eds., *Slavery and Freedom in the Age of the American Revolution* (1983); Sylvia R. Frey, *Water from the Rock: Black Resistance in a Revolutionary Age* (1991); Arthur Zilversmit, *The First Emancipation: The Abolition of Slavery in the North* (1967); Gary B. Nash, *Forging Freedom: The Formation of Philadelphia's Black Community, 1720–1840* (1988); and Shane White, *Somewhat More Independent: The End of Slavery in New York City, 1770–1810* (1991).

For comprehensive studies of gender and age relations in the era, see Mary Beth Norton, *Liberty's Daughters: The Revolutionary Experience of American Women, 1750–1800* (1979); Linda Kerber, *Women of the Republic: Intellect and Ideology in Revolutionary America* (1980); Rosemarie Zagarrie, "Morals, Manners, and the Republican Mother," *American Quarterly* 44 (1992): 192–215; Ronald Hoffman and Peter J. Albert, eds., *Women in the Age of the American Revolution* (1989); and David Hackett Fischer, *Growing Old in America* (1978). More specialized but highly significant studies include Laurel Thatcher Ulrich, *A Midwife's Tale: The Life of Martha Ballard, Based on Her Diary, 1785–1812* (1990); Barbara Clark Smith, "Food Rioters and the American Revolution," *William and Mary Quarterly*, 3rd ser., 51 (1994): 3–38; Judith A. Klinghoffer and Lois Elkis, "The Petticoat Electors: Women's Suffrage in New Jersey, 1776–1807," *Journal of the Early Republic* 12 (1992): 159–193; Cathy N. Davidson, *Revolution and the Word: The Rise of the Novel in America* (1986); and Joel Perlman and Dennis Shirley, "When Did New England Women Acquire Literacy?" *William and Mary Quarterly*, 3rd ser., 48 (1991): 50–67.

For religious changes, see Ronald Hoffman and Peter J. Albert, eds., *Religion in a Revolutionary Age* (1994); Hamilton J. Eckenrode, *Separation of Church and State in Virginia: A Study in the Development of the Revolution* (1910); Thomas O. Hanley, *Their Rights and Liberties: The Beginnings of Religious and Political Freedom in Maryland* (1959); Frank Baker, *From Wesley to Asbury: Studies in Early American Methodism* (1976); Stephen A. Marini, *Radical Sects of Revolutionary New England* (1982); and Susan Juster, *Disorderly Women: Sexual Politics and Evangelicalism in Revolutionary New England* (1994).

CONFEDERATION AND CONSTITUTION General histories of the Confederation era include Merrill Jensen, *The New Nation: A History of the United States during the Articles of Confederation* (1950); Forrest McDonald, *E Pluribus Unum: The Formation of the American Republic* (1965); and Richard B. Morris, *The Forging of the Union, 1781–1789* (1987). Jackson Turner Main, *Political Parties before the Constitution* (1973), is a comprehensive study of state politics; also essential is his "Government by the People: The American Revolution and the Democratization of the Legislatures," *William and Mary Quarterly*, 3rd ser., 23 (1966): 354–367. On events from the rise of the Berkshire Constitutionalists through Shays's Rebellion, consult Robert J. Taylor, *Western Massachusetts in the Revolution* (1954), and John L. Brooke, "To the Quiet of the People: Revolutionary Settlements and Civil Unrest in Western Massachusetts, 1774–1789," *William and Mary Quarterly*, 3rd ser., 46 (1989): 425–462. For challenging perspectives on the Northwest Ordinance, see Peter S. Onuf, *Statehood and Union: A History of the Northwest Ordinance* (1987), and Staughton Lynd, "The Compromise of 1787," *Political Science Quarterly* 71 (1966): 225–250.

Jack N. Rakove, *Original Meanings: Politics and Ideas in the Making of the Constitution* (1996), won a Pulitzer Prize. Robert A. Rutland's *The Ordeal of the Constitution: The Antifederalists and the Ratification Struggle of 1787–1788* (1966) is still the fullest history of the ratification struggle, but two other works with telling points to make are Saul Cornell, *The Other Founders: Anti-Federalism and the Dissenting Tradition in America* (1999);

and Kenneth R. Bowling, "'A Tub to the Whale': The Founding Fathers and the Adoption of the Federal Bill of Rights," *Journal of the Early Republic* 8 (1988): 223–251.

Chapter 7

For good introductions to social and economic trends in these years, see Melvyn Stokes and Stephen Conway, eds., *The Market Revolution in America* (1996), and the *Journal of the Early Republic* 16 (Summer 1996). James A. Henretta, *The Origins of American Capitalism: Collected Essays* (1991), and Alan Kulikoff, *The Agrarian Origins of American Capitalism* (1992), are theoretically sophisticated social histories of the American economy in these years. Still essential is Douglass C. North, *The Economic Growth of the United States, 1790–1860* (1961).

THE NORTHEAST On rural society after the Revolution, the most thorough regional study is Christopher Clark, *The Roots of Rural Capitalism: Western Massachusetts, 1780–1860* (1990). Laurel Thatcher Ulrich, *A Midwife's Tale: The Life of Martha Ballard, Based on Her Diary, 1785–1812* (1990), is a beautiful and insightful account. Jack Larkin, *The Reshaping of Everyday Life, 1790–1840* (1988), is a valuable synthesis of scholarship on material culture, particularly in the Northeast. Also valuable are Winifred Barr Rothenberg, *From Market-Places to Market Economy: The Transformation of Rural Massachusetts, 1750–1850* (1994); Thomas Dublin, *Transforming Women's Work: New England Lives in the Industrial Revolution* (1994); Joan M. Jensen, *Loosening the Bonds: Mid-Atlantic Farm Women, 1750–1850* (1986); Toby L. Ditz, *Property and Kinship: Inheritance in Early Connecticut, 1750–1820* (1986); and the essays in Stephen Innes, ed., *Work and Labor in Early America* (1988). Other relevant studies are cited in the Suggested Readings for Chapter 9.

THE WEST Study of the postrevolutionary frontier begins with the final chapters of Richard White's magesterial *The Middle Ground: Indians, Empires, and Republics in the Great Lakes Region, 1650–1815* (1991). Other graceful and thoughtful accounts of Native Americans in these years include R. David Edmunds, *The Shawnee Prophet* (1983); Anthony F. C. Wallace, *The Death and Rebirth of the Seneca* (1969); William G. McLoughlin, *Cherokee Renaissance in the New Republic* (1986); Joel W. Martin, *Sacred Revolt: The Muskogees' Struggle for a New World* (1991); and Gregory Evans Dowd, *A Spirited Resistance: The North American Indian Struggle for Unity, 1745–1815* (1992). White settler societies are ably treated in John Mack Faragher, *Daniel Boone: The Life and Legend of an American Pioneer* (1992); Stephen Aron, *How the West Was Lost: The Transformation of Kentucky from Daniel Boone to Henry Clay* (1996); Andrew R. L. Cayton, *The Frontier Republic: Ideology and Politics in the Ohio Country, 1780–1825* (1986); Alan Taylor, *Liberty Men and Great Proprietors: The Revolutionary Settlement on the Maine Frontier, 1760–1820* (1990); *William Cooper's Town: Power and Persuasion on the Frontier of the Early American Republic* (1995); and Thomas P. Slaughter, *The Whiskey Rebellion: Frontier Epilogue to the American Revolution* (1986).

THE SOUTH Economic and demographic change in the plantation South is traced in Robert William Fogel and Stanley L. Engerman, *Time on the Cross: The Economics of American Negro Slavery*, 2 vols. (1974); Robert William Fogel, *Without Consent or Contract: The Rise and Fall of American Slavery* (1989); and Peter A. Coclanis, *The Shadow of a Dream: Economic Life and Death in the South Carolina Lowcountry, 1670–1920* (1989). The essays in Ira Berlin and Ronald Hoffman, eds., *Slavery and Freedom in the Age of the American Revolution* (1983), are essential, as are Barbara Jeanne Fields, *Slavery and Freedom on the Middle Ground: Maryland during the Nineteenth Century* (1985); Ira Berlin, *Slaves without Masters: The Free Negro in the Antebellum South* (1974); and Robert McColley, *Slavery and Jeffersonian Virginia*, 2nd ed. (1973). The limits of southern antislavery in these years are traced in David Brion Davis, *The Problem of Slavery in the Age of Revolution, 1770–1823* (1975), and in the relevant essays in Peter S. Onuf, ed., *Jeffersonian Legacies* (1993). Further studies of economic and social life in the South are listed in the Suggested Readings for Chapter 9.

CITIES David T. Gilchrist, ed., *The Growth of the Seaport Cities, 1790–1825* (1967), ably treats its subject. Thomas C. Cochran, *Frontiers of Change: Early Industrialization in America* (1981), synthesizes urban economic development. For the social history of cities in these years, see Howard B. Rock, *Artisans of the New Republic: The Tradesmen of New York City in the Age of Jefferson* (1979); Charles G. Steffen, *The Mechanics of Baltimore: Workers and Politics in the Age of Revolution, 1763–1812* (1984); the early chapters of Sean Wilentz, *Chants Democratic: New York City and the Rise of the American Working Class* (1984), and Christine Stansell, *City of Women: Sex and Class in New York, 1789–1860* (1986); Stuart M. Blumin, *The Emergence of the Middle Class:*

Social Experience in the American City, 1760–1900 (1989); and Elizabeth Blackmar, *Manhattan for Rent, 1785–1850* (1989). For other relevant studies, see the Suggested Readings for Chapter 9.

CULTURAL TRENDS A stirring introduction to the "democratization of mind" in these years is the concluding section of Gordon S. Wood, *The Radicalism of the American Revolution* (1992). On suffrage, see Chilton Williamson, *American Suffrage from Property to Democracy* (1960). On print culture, see Cathy N. Davidson, *Revolution and the Word: The Rise of the Novel in America* (1986); Davidson, ed., *Reading in America: Literature and Social History* (1989); and William J. Gilmore, *Reading Becomes a Necessity of Life: Material and Cultural Life in Rural New England, 1780–1835* (1989). On drinking, W. J. Rorabaugh, *The Alcoholic Republic: An American Tradition* (1979).

RELIGION The study of American religion in the postrevolutionary years begins with two books: Nathan O. Hatch, *The Democratization of American Christianity* (1989), and Jon Butler, *Awash in a Sea of Faith: Christianizing the American People* (1990). More specialized accounts include Christine Leigh Heyrman, *Southern Cross: The Beginnings of the Bible Belt* (1997); Paul K. Conkin, *Cane Ridge: America's Pentecost* (1990); John B. Boles, *The Great Revival, 1787–1805* (1972); and Stephen A. Marini, *Radical Sects of Revolutionary America* (1982). Religious developments among slaves and free blacks are treated in Sylvia R. Frey, *Water from the Rock: Black Resistance in a Revolutionary Age* (1991); Albert J. Raboteau, *Slave Religion: The 'Invisible Institution' in the Antebellum South* (1978); and the early essays in Paul E. Johnson, ed., *African-American Christianity: Essays in History* (1994). Douglas R. Egerton, *Gabriel's Rebellion: The Virginia Slave Conspiracies of 1800 & 1802* (1993), is imaginative and thorough. The "republicanization" of slave resistance is described in Eugene D. Genovese, *From Rebellion to Revolution: Afro-American Slave Revolts in the Making of the Modern World* (1979). Other works on early 19th century religion are listed in the Suggested Readings for Chapter 10.

Chapter 8

Stanley Elkins and Eric McKitrick, *The Age of Federalism: The Early American Republic, 1788–1800* (1993), is the best study of politics in the 1790s. James Roger Sharp, *American Politics in the Early Republic: The New Nation in Crisis* (1993), is an extended interpretive essay; John C. Miller, *The Federalist Era, 1789–1801* (1960), remains the best brief account. Stephen G. Kurtz, *The Presidency of John Adams* (1957), is a valuable study of the second Federalist presidency.

POLITICS, 1790–1800 Federalist approaches to government and administration are the subjects of Ralph Ketcham, *Presidents above Party: The First American Presidency, 1789–1829* (1984); Leonard D. White, *The Federalists: A Study in Administrative History* (1948); and Carl E. Prince, *The Federalists and the Origins of the U.S. Civil Service* (1977). Specific issues are handled ably in Robert A. Rutland, *The Birth of the Bill of Rights, 1776–1791* (1955); Thomas G. Slaughter, *The Whiskey Rebellion: Frontier Epilogue to the American Revolution* (1986); Richard H. Kohn, *Eagle and Sword: The Federalists and the Creation of the Military Establishment in America, 1783–1802* (1975); and James M. Smith, *Freedom's Fetters: The Alien and Sedition Laws and American Civil Liberties*, rev. ed. (1967). The rise of Jeffersonian opposition is treated in Richard Hostadter, *The Idea of a Party System: The Rise of Legitimate Opposition in the United States, 1780–1840* (1970); Lance Banning, *The Jeffersonian Persuasion: Evolution of a Party Ideology* (1980); and Joyce Appleby, *Capitalism and a New Social Order: The Republican Vision of the 1790s* (1984).

POLITICS, 1800–1815 The classic work on national politics from 1801 to 1815 is Henry Adams, *History of the United States of America during the Administrations of Thomas Jefferson and of James Madison*, 9 vols. (1889–1891; reprint, 2 vols., 1986). Marshall Smelser, *The Democratic Republic, 1801–1815* (1968), is a solid modern account, while Forrest McDonald, *The Presidency of Thomas Jefferson* (1976), is both critical and thoughtful. Drew R. McCoy, *The Elusive Republic: Political Economy in Jeffersonian America* (1980), is a stimulating essay on Jeffersonian economic policy. See also John R. Nelson Jr., *Liberty and Property: Political Economy and Policymaking in the New Nation, 1789–1812* (1987). The court controversies are treated in Richard E. Ellis, *The Jeffersonian Crisis: Courts and Politics in the Young Republic* (1971); Mary K. B. Tachau, *Federal Courts in the Early Republic: Kentucky, 1789–1816* (1978); Robert Lowry Clinton, *Marbury vs. Madison and Judicial Review* (1989); and R. Kent Newmyer, *The Supreme Court under Marshall and Taney* (1968). Other studies of domestic questions during the Jefferson and Madison administrations include Leonard B. White, *The Jeffersonians: A Study in Administrative History, 1801–1829* (1951); R. M. Johnstone, *Jefferson and the Presidency* (1978); and Robert W. Tucker and David C. Hendrickson, *Empire of Liberty: The Statecraft of Thomas Jefferson* (1990). Opposition to the Jeffersonians is treated in Norman K. Risjord, *The Old Republicans: Southern Conservatism in the Age of Jefferson* (1965); Robert E. Shalhope, *John Taylor of Caroline: Pastoral Republican* (1980); Linda K. Kerber, *Federalists in Dissent: Imagery and Ideology in Jeffersonian America* (1970); and James M. Banner Jr., *To the Hartford Convention: The Federalists and the Origins of Party Politics in Massachusetts, 1789–1815* (1969).

FOREIGN AFFAIRS A convenient introduction to foreign policy under the Federalists and Jeffersonians is Bradford Perkins, *The Creation of a Republican Empire, 1776–1860,* vol. 1 of *The Cambridge History of American Foreign Relations* (1993). Also helpful is Reginald Horsman, *The Diplomacy of the New Republic, 1776–1815* (1985). More specialized accounts include Harry Ammon, *The Genêt Mission* (1973); Samuel F. Bemis's classic studies, *Jay's Treaty,* 2nd ed. (1962), and *Pinckney's Treaty,* 2nd ed. (1960); Jerald A. Combs, *The Jay Treaty* (1970); Wiley Sword, *President Washington's Indian War: The Struggle for the Old Northwest, 1790–1795* (1985); Alexander DeConde, *The Quasi-War: Politics and Diplomacy of the Undeclared War with France, 1797–1801* (1966), and *This Affair of Louisiana* (1976); William Stinchcombe, *The XYZ Affair* (1981); Lawrence Kaplan, *"Entangling Alliances with None": American Foreign Policy in the Age of Jefferson* (1987); and Bradford Perkins, *The First Rapproachement: England and the United States, 1795–1805* (1967). On the diplomatic, political, and military history of the War of 1812, the essential accounts are Bradford Perkins, *Prologue to War: England and the United States, 1805–1812* (1961); Clifford L. Egan, *Neither Peace nor War: Franco-American Relations, 1803–1812* (1983); J. C. A. Stagg, *Mr. Madison's War: Politics, Diplomacy, and Warfare in the Early Republic, 1783–1830* (1983); and Donald R. Hickey, *The War of 1812: A Forgotten Conflict* (1989).

BIOGRAPHIES National politics under the Federalists and Jeffersonians can be approached through a number of excellent biographies. The multivolume works of Douglas Southall Freeman on Washington, Dumas Malone on Jefferson, and Irving Brant on Madison are definitive. The following are good single-volume studies of individuals: John R. Alden, *George Washington: A Biography* (1984); Marcus Cunliffe, *George Washington: Man and Monument* (1958); Gerald Stourzh, *Alexander Hamilton and the Idea of a Republican Government* (1970); Forrest McDonald, *Alexander Hamilton: A Biography* (1979); Peter Shaw, *The Character of John Adams* (1976); Joseph J. Ellis, *American Sphinx: The Character of Thomas Jefferson* (1997); Merrill Peterson, *Thomas Jefferson and the New Nation* (1960); Nobel E. Cunningham, *In Pursuit of Reason: The Life of Thomas Jefferson* (1987); Ralph Ketcham, *James Madison: A Biography* (1971); and Drew R. McCoy, *The Last of the Fathers: James Madison and the Republic Legacy* (1989).

Chapter 9

Works on the earlier phases of most questions covered in this chapter are included in the Suggested Readings for Chapter 7.

THE AMERICAN ECONOMY Charles G. Sellers, *The Market Revolution: Jacksonian America, 1815–1848* (1991), is a broad synthesis of economic, cultural, and political development. More narrowly economic surveys include Douglass C. North, *The Economic Growth of the United States, 1790–1860* (1961); George Rogers Taylor, *The Transportation Revolution, 1815–1860* (1951); Allan R. Pred, *Urban Growth and the Circulation of Information: The United States System of Cities, 1790–1840* (1973); Harry N. Scheiber, *Ohio Canal Era: A Case Study of Government and the Economy, 1820–1861,* 2nd ed. (1987); Ronald E. Shaw, *Erie Water West* (1966); Albert Fishlow, *American Railroads and the Transformation of the Ante-Bellum Economy* (1965); and Erik F. Haites, James Mak, and Gary M. Walton, *Western River Transportation: The Era of Early Internal Development, 1810–1860* (1975). On the role of federal and state courts, see R. Kent Newmeyer, *The Supreme Court under Marshall and Taney* (1968); Francis N. Stites, *John Marshall: Defender of the Constitution* (1981); and, especially, Morton J. Horwitz, *The Transformation of American Law, 1780–1860* (1977).

FARMERS The market revolution in northern and western agriculture is treated in Christopher Clark, *The Roots of Rural Capitalism: Western Massachusetts, 1780–1860* (1990); Carolyn Merchant, *Ecological Revolutions: Nature, Gender, and Science in New England* (1989); John Mack Faragher, *Sugar Creek: Life on the Illinois Prairie* (1986); Joan M. Jensen, *Loosening the Bonds: Mid-Atlantic Farm Women, 1750–1850* (1986); and Jack Larkin,

The Reshaping of Everyday Life, 1790–1840 (1988). Still very useful is R. Carlyle Buley, *The Old Northwest: Pioneer Period, 1815–1840,* 2 vols. (1950).

INDUSTRY Solid studies of early industrial communities include Thomas Dublin, *Women at Work: The Transformation of Work and Community in Lowell, Massachusetts, 1826–1860* (1979); Jonathan Prude, *The Coming of Industrial Order: Town and Factory Life in Rural Massachusetts, 1810–1860* (1983); Anthony F. C. Wallace, *Rockdale: The Growth of an American Village in the Early Industrial Revolution* (1978); Alan Dawley, *Class and Community: The Industrial Revolution in Lynn* (1976); and Mary H. Blewett, *Men, Women, and Work: Class, Gender, and Protest in the New England Shoe Industry, 1780–1910* (1990). On the transformation of cities, see Stuart M. Blumin, *The Emergence of the Middle Class: Social Experience in the American City, 1760–1900* (1989); Edward Pessen, *Riches, Class, and Power before the Civil War* (1973); Bruce Laurie, *Working People of Philadelphia, 1800–1850* (1980); Sean Wilentz, *Chants Democratic: New York City & the Rise of the American Working Class, 1788–1850* (1984); and Christine Stansell, *City of Women: Sex and Class in New York, 1789–1860* (1986).

THE SLAVE SOUTH Economic studies of the plantation South begin with Robert William Fogel and Stanley Engerman, *Time on the Cross: The Economics of American Negro Slavery,* 2 vols. (1974), and R. W. Fogel, *Without Consent or Contract: The Rise and Fall of American Slavery* (1989). Other useful studies include Orville Vernon Burton, *In My Father's House Are Many Mansions: Family and Community in Edgefield, South Carolina* (1985); Eugene D. Genovese, *The Political Economy of Slavery: Studies in the Economy and Society of the Slave South,* 2nd ed. (1989); James Oakes, *The Ruling Race: A History of American Slaveholders* (1982); Gavin Wright, *The Political Economy of the Cotton South: Households, Markets, and Wealth in the Nineteenth Century* (1978); and Elizabeth Fox-Genovese, *Within the Plantation Household: Black and White Women of the Old South* (1988). On the southern yeomanry, see Stephanie McCurry, *Masters of Small Worlds: Yeoman Households, Gender Relations, & the Political Culture of the Antebellum South Carolina Lowcountry* (1995); Steven Hahn, *The Roots of Southern Populism: Yeomen Farmers and the Transformation of the Georgia Upcountry, 1850–1890* (1983); J. William Harris, *Plain Folk and Gentry in a Slave Society: White Liberty and Black Slavery in Augusta's Hinterlands* (1985); and Grady McWhiney, *Cracker Culture: Celtic Folkways in the Old South* (1988).

Chapter 10

THE MIDDLE CLASSES Stuart M. Blumin, *The Emergence of the Middle Class: Social Experience in the American City, 1760–1900* (1989), is a thorough study of work and material life among the urban middle class. Studies that treat religion, family, and sentimental culture include Paul E. Johnson, *A Shopkeeper's Millennium: Society and Revivals in Rochester, New York, 1815–1837* (1978); Mary P. Ryan, *Cradle of the Middle Class: The Family in Oneida County, New York, 1790–1865* (1981); Carroll Smith-Rosenberg, *Disorderly Conduct: Visions of Gender in Victorian America* (1985); Karen Halttunen, *Confidence Men and Painted Women: A Study of Middle-Class Culture in America, 1830–1870* (1982); and Jane Tompkins, *Sensational Designs: The Cultural Work of American Fiction, 1790–1860* (1985). On art and artists, see Neil Harris, *The Artist in American Society: The Formative Years, 1790–1860* (1966); Barbara Novak, *Nature and Culture: American Landscape and Painting, 1825–1875* (1980); Angela Miller, *The Empire of the Eye: Landscape Representation and American Cultural Politics, 1825–1875* (1993); and Elizabeth McKinsey, *Niagara Falls: Icon of the American Sublime* (1985).

POPULAR RELIGION Lewis O. Saum, *The Popular Mood of Pre–Civil War America* (1980), is a valuable study of the unsentimental culture of antebellum plain folk. The most thorough treatments of popular evangelicalism are the works of Jon Butler and Nathan Hatch listed in the Suggested Readings for Chapter 7. See also Curtis D. Johnson, *Redeeming America: Evangelicals and the Road to Civil War* (1993); Michael Barkun, *Crucible of the Millennium: The Burned-Over District of New York in the 1840s* (1986); David L. Rowe, *Thunder and Trumpets: Millerites and Dissenting Religion in Upstate New York, 1800–1850* (1985); Paul E. Johnson and Sean Wilentz, *The Kingdom of Matthias: A Story of Sex and Salvation in 19th-Century America* (1994); and John L. Brooke, *The Refiner's Fire: The Making of Mormon Cosmology, 1644–1844* (1994).

POPULAR ENTERTAINMENTS Studies of popular literature and entertainments in these years include Elliott J. Gorn, *The Manly Art: Bare-Knuckle Prize Fighting in America* (1986); Melvin L. Adelman, *A Sporting Time: New*

York City and the Rise of Modern Athletics (1986); Alexander P. Saxton, *The Rise and Fall of the White Republic: Class Politics and Mass Culture in Nineteenth-Century America* (1990); Eric Lott, *Love & Theft: Blackface Minstrelsy and the American Working Class* (1993); Michael Denning, *Mechanic Accents: Dime Novels and Working-Class Culture in America* (1987); David S. Reynolds, *Beneath the American Renaissance: The Subversive Imagination in the Age of Emerson and Melville* (1988); and *Walt Whitman's America: A Cultural Biography* (1995). New directions in literary criticism in these years can be sampled in Sacvan Bercovitch and Myra Jehlen, eds., *Ideology and Classic American Literature* (1986).

SOUTHERN WHITES Peter Kolchin's *American Slavery, 1619–1877* (1993) is a brilliant synthesis of recent scholarship on the Old South. On the family culture of southern whites, see Bertram Wyatt-Brown, *Southern Honor: Ethics & Behavior in the Old South* (1982); Elizabeth Fox-Genovese, *Within the Plantation Household: Black and White Women in the Old South* (1988); Kenneth S. Greenberg, *Honor & Slavery* (1996); and Steven W. Stowe, *Intimacy and Power in the Old South* (1987). Eugene D. Genovese, *The Slaveholder's Dilemma: Southern Conservative Thought, 1820–1860* (1992), demonstrates the pervasive paternalism of southern social thought. Donald G. Matthews, *Religion in the Old South* (1977), is a valuable introduction to its subject. Other studies of southern religion are listed in the Suggested Readings to Chapter 7.

SLAVE CULTURE A now-classic overview of slave culture is Eugene D. Genovese, *Roll, Jordan, Roll: The World the Slaves Made* (1974). Also essential are Lawrence W. Levine, *Black Culture and Black Consciousness: Afro-American Folk Thought from Slavery to Freedom* (1977), and Charles Joyner, *Down by the Riverside: A South Carolina Slave Community* (1984). Study of the slave family begins with Herbert G. Gutman, *The Black Family in Slavery and Freedom, 1750–1925* (1976), which can now be supplemented with Ann Patton Malone, *Sweet Chariot: Slave Family and Household Structure in Nineteenth-Century Louisiana* (1992). John Michael Vlach, *Back of the Big House: The Architecture of Plantation Slavery* (1993), is a valuable cultural study. Slave religion is treated in Mechal Sobel, *Travelin' On: The Slave Journey to an Afro-Baptist Faith* (1979), and Margaret Washington Creel, *"A Peculiar People": Slave Religion and Community-Culture among the Gullahs* (1988). Other essential studies on these and related topics are cited in the Suggested Readings for Chapters 7 and 9.

Chapter 11

CONSTITUENCIES There are a number of careful studies of constituencies and issues at the state and local levels during the Jacksonian era. Students should consult Lee Benson, *The Concept of Jacksonian Democracy: New York as a Test Case* (1961); John L. Hammond, *The Politics of Benevolence: Revival Religion and American Voting Behavior* (1979); Ronald P. Formisano, *The Transformation of Political Culture: Massachusetts Parties, 1790s–1840s* (1983), and *The Birth of Mass Political Parties: Michigan, 1827–1861* (1971); John L. Brooke, *The Heart of the Commonwealth: Society and Political Culture in Worcester County, Massachusetts, 1713–1861* (1989); Amy Bridges, *A City in the Republic: Antebellum New York and the Origins of Machine Politics* (1984); Paul Bourke and Donald DeBats, *Washington County: Politics and Community in Antebellum America* (1995); Harry L. Watson, *Jacksonian Politics and Community Conflict: The Emergence of the Second American Party System in Cumberland County, North Carolina* (1981); Lacy K. Ford Jr., *Origins of Southern Radicalism: The South Carolina Upcountry, 1800–1860* (1988); and David W. Crofts, *Old Southampton: Politics and Society in a Virginia County, 1834–1869* (1992). Richard J. Carwardine, *Evangelicals and Politics in Antebellum America* (1993), is a good study of relations between religion and politics in these years.

IDEOLOGIES On party ideologies and political culture, see John Ashworth, *"Agrarians & Aristocrats": Party Political Ideology in the United States, 1837–1846* (1983); Daniel Walker Howe, *The Political Culture of the American Whigs* (1979); Anne Norton, *Alternative Americas: A Reading of Antebellum Political Culture* (1986); and Jean H. Baker, *Affairs of Party: The Political Culture of Northern Democrats in the Mid-Nineteenth Century* (1983). Aging but still very valuable are John William Ward, *Andrew Jackson: Symbol for an Age* (1953), and Marvin Meyers, *The Jacksonian Persuasion: Politics and Belief* (1957).

ECONOMIC ISSUES Party debates on banking and internal improvements are discussed in James Roger Sharp, *The Jacksonians versus the Banks: Politics in the States after the Panic of 1837* (1970); Harry N. Scheiber, *Ohio Canal Era: A Case Study of Government and the Economy, 1820–1861,* 2nd ed. (1987); L. Ray Gunn, *The Decline of Authority: Public Economic Policy and Political Development in New York, 1800–1860* (1988); and Oscar

Handlin's now-classic *Commonwealth: A Study of the Role of Government in the American Economy: Massachusetts, 1774–1861,* rev. ed. (1969).

Social Questions Political controversies surrounding schools are the subject of Carl F. Kaestle, *Pillars of the Republic: Common Schools and American Society, 1780–1860* (1983), and Kaestle's *The Evolution of an Urban School System: New York City, 1750–1850* (1973). An influential study of prisons and asylums is David J. Rothman, *The Discovery of the Asylum: Social Order and Disorder in the New Republic* (1971). It should be supplemented with W. David Lewis, *From Newgate to Dannemora: The Rise of the Penitentiary in New York, 1796–1848* (1965); Michael Meranze, *Laboratories of Virtue: Punishment, Revolution, and Authority in Philadelphia, 1760–1835* (1996); and Edward L. Ayers, *Vengeance and Justice: Crime and Punishment in the 19th-Century South* (1984). Drinking and temperance are the subjects of W. J. Rorabaugh, *The Alcoholic Republic: An American Tradition* (1979), and Ian Tyrrell, *Sobering Up: From Temperance to Prohibition in Ante-Bellum America, 1800–1860* (1979). The best discussion of Washingtonianism is in Teresa Anne Murphy, *Ten Hours' Labor: Religion, Reform, and Gender in Early New England* (1992).

Race and Gender The standard study of northern free blacks is Leon F. Litwack, *North of Slavery: The Negro in the Free States, 1790–1860* (1960). It can be supplemented by Gary B. Nash, *Forging Freedom: The Formation of Philadelphia's Black Community, 1720–1840* (1988). James Brewer Stewart, *Holy Warriors: The Abolitionists and American Slavery* (1976), is a graceful overview of the crusade against slavery. Students should also consult Robert H. Abzug, *Cosmos Crumbling: American Reform and the Religious Imagination* (1994); Thomas Bender, ed., *The Antislavery Debate: Capitalism and Abolitionism as a Problem in Historical Interpretation* (1992); and Lewis Perry, *Radical Abolitionism: Anarchy and the Government of God in Antislavery Thought* (1973).

On the origins of the women's rights movement, students should consult Ellen Carol DuBois, *Feminism and Suffrage: The Emergence of an Independent Women's Movement in America, 1848–1869* (1978); Jean Fagan Yellin, *Women & Sisters: The Antislavery Feminists in American Culture* (1989); and Lori D. Ginzberg, *Women and the Work of Benevolence: Morality, Politics, and Class in the 19th-Century United States* (1990).

Chapter 12

General Arthur M. Schlesinger Jr., *The Age of Jackson* (1945), is a now-classic overview of politics from the 1820s to the 1840s. Charles Sellers, *The Market Revolution: Jacksonian America, 1815–1846* (1991), synthesizes social, economic, and cultural history, while Harry L. Watson, *Liberty and Power: The Politics of Jacksonian America* (1990), is an excellent account of politics. Aging but still valuable (and friendlier to the Whigs) is Glyndon G. Van Deusen, *The Jacksonian Era, 1828–1848* (1959). This period has been particularly well served by biographers. See especially Robert V. Remini's *Andrew Jackson and the Course of American Freedom, 1822–1833* (1981); *Andrew Jackson and the Course of American Democracy, 1833–1845* (1984); and *Henry Clay: Statesman for the Union* (1991). Also valuable are Merrill D. Peterson, *The Great Triumvirate: Webster, Clay, and Calhoun* (1987); John Niven, *Martin Van Buren: The Romantic Age of American Politics* (1983), and *John C. Calhoun and the Price of Union* (1988); Irving H. Bartlett, *Daniel Webster* (1978); and Samuel Flagg Bemis, *John Quincy Adams and the Foundations of American Foreign Policy* (1949), and *John Quincy Adams and the Union* (1956).

Government On presidential elections in these years, the best place to start is with the essays in Arthur M. Schlesinger Jr. and Fred J. Israels, eds., *History of American Presidential Elections, 1789–1968,* 3 vols. (1971). George Dangerfield, *The Era of Good Feelings* (1953), and Glover Moore, *The Missouri Controversy, 1819–1821* (1953), are the standard treatments of their subjects. On Jacksonian administrative policies and the spoils system, see Leonard D. White, *The Jacksonians: A Study in Administrative History, 1829–1861* (1954); Sidney H. Aronson, *Status and Kinship in the Higher Civil Service* (1964); and Matthew A. Crenson, *The Federal Machine: Beginnings of Bureaucracy in Jacksonian America* (1975).

The South and National Politics William W. Freehling, *The Road to Disunion: Secessionists at Bay, 1776–1854* (1990), provides an interpretive overview of the South and slavery in national politics. On nullification, see Freehling, *Prelude to Civil War: The Nullification Controversy in South Carolina, 1816–1836* (1965); Richard E. Ellis, *The Union at Risk: Jacksonian Democracy, States' Rights and the Nullification Crisis* (1987); and Merrill D. Peterson, *Olive Branch and Sword: The Compromise of 1833* (1982). Michael Paul Rogin, *Fathers and*

Children: Andrew Jackson and the Subjugation of the American Indian (1975), is an imaginative essay, although students should also consult the works in Native American history cited in the Suggested Readings for Chapter 7. The fullest account of Congress's dealings with the abolitionists is William Lee Miller, *Arguing about Slavery: The Great Battle in the United States Congress* (1995). Students should also consult Leonard L. Richards, *The Life and Times of Congressman John Quincy Adams* (1986).

THE BANK WAR Study of the bank war still begins and ends with Bray Hammond, *Banks and Politics in America from the Revolution to the Civil War* (1957). Students should also consult Peter Temin, *The Jacksonian Economy* (1969), and Robert V. Remini, *Andrew Jackson and the Bank War* (1967).

POLITICAL PARTIES On party development, see Richard Hofstadter, *The Idea of a Party System: The Rise of Legitimate Opposition in the United States, 1780–1840* (1969); Richard P. McCormick, *The Second American Party System: Party Formation in the Jacksonian Era* (1966), and *The Presidential Game: The Origins of American Presidential Politics* (1982); and Joel H. Silbey, *The Partisan Imperative: The Dynamics of American Politics before the Civil War* (1985), and *The American Political Nation, 1838–1893* (1991).

Chapter 13

MANIFEST DESTINY For the West and the rise of Manifest Destiny, the best introductions are Malcolm J. Rohrbough, *The Trans-Appalachian Frontier: People, Societies, and Institutions 1775–1850* (1978), and Ray Allen Billington, *The Far Western Frontier, 1830–1860* (1956). Two books by Frederick Merk, *Manifest Destiny and Mission in American History* (1963) and *The Monroe Doctrine and American Expansion 1843–1849* (1967), explore the expansionism of the 1840s, while Norman A. Graebner, *Empire on the Pacific: A Study of American Continental Expansionism* (1955), traces its results.

CALIFORNIA AND OREGON Westward migration on the overland trails is chronicled and analyzed in John D. Unruh Jr., *The Plains Across: The Overland Emigrants and the Trans-Mississippi West, 1840–1860* (1979); John Mack Faragher, *Women and Men on the Overland Trail* (1978); and Julie Roy Jeffries, *Frontier Women: The Trans-Mississippi West, 1840–1860* (1979). Migration to Oregon is treated in Malcolm Clark, *Eden Seekers: The Settlement of Oregon, 1812–1862* (1981), while the California gold rush and its consequences are described by Malcolm J. Rohrbough, *Days of Gold: The California Gold Rush and the American Nation* (1997). For the harrowing story of the Donner party, see George R. Stewart, *Ordeal by Hunger: The Story of the Donner Party* (1960).

MORMONS For the Mormon migration and the creation of their Zion in Utah, see Wallace Stegner, *The Gathering of Zion: The Story of the Mormon Trail* (1964); Leonard J. Arrington, *Brigham Young: American Moses* (1985); and Leonard J. Arrington and Davis Bitton, *The Mormon Experience: A History of the Latter-Day Saints* (1979).

INDIANS A fine introduction to the impact of American expansion westward on the Indian residents of this region is Philip Weeks, *Farewell, My Nation: The American Indian and the United States, 1820–1890* (1990). Other important studies include Ronald M. Satz, *American Indian Policy in the Jacksonian Era* (1975); Robert A. Trennert Jr., *Alternatives to Extinction: Federal Indian Policy and the Beginnings of the Reservation System, 1846–1851* (1975); and Robert M. Utley, *The Indian Frontier of the American West, 1846–1890* (1984).

TEXAS For Texas and the northern frontier of Mexico that became part of the United States in 1848, see David J. Weber, *The Mexican Frontier, 1821–1846: The American Southwest under Mexico* (1982). American settlement in Texas and its annexation by the United States are described in Frederick Merk, *Slavery and the Annexation of Texas* (1972); Marshall De Bruhl, *Sword of San Jacinto: A Life of Sam Houston* (1993); and John Hoyt Williams, *Sam Houston* (1993). The impact of settlement of these regions by Anglo-Americans and the absorption of the region into the United States are analyzed by Leonard Pitts, *The Decline of the Californios: A Social History of the Spanish-Speaking Californians, 1846–1890* (1970), and Arnoldo De León, *The Tejano Community, 1836–1900* (1982).

MEXICAN WAR A good study of the relationship between American expansion and the coming of the war with Mexico is David Pletcher, *The Diplomacy of Annexation: Texas, Oregon, and the Mexican War* (1973). Mexican viewpoints are described in Gene M. Brack, *Mexico Views Manifest Destiny: An Essay on the Origins of the Mexican War* (1975). Glen M. Price, *Origins of the War with Mexico: The Polk-Stockton Intrigue* (1967), charges Polk with deliberately provoking Mexico to war, while Charles G. Sellers, *James K. Polk, Continentalist 1843–1846* (1966), is more sympathetic to the American president. The most detailed study of the Mexican War is still Justin H. Smith, *The War with Mexico,* 2 vols. (1919). Modern studies include Seymour V. Connor and Odie B. Faulk, *North America Divided: The Mexican War, 1846–1848* (1971); K. Jack Bauer, *The Mexican War* (1974); and John S. D. Eisenhower, *So Far from God: The U.S. War with Mexico 1846–1848* (1989). John H. Schroeder, *Mr. Polk's War: American Opposition and Dissent, 1846–1848* (1973), documents antislavery and Whig opposition, while Robert W. Johannsen, *To the Halls of the Montezumas: The Mexican War in the American Imagination* (1985), focuses on the popularity of the war among Democrats and expansionists. For the experiences of American soldiers in the Mexican War, see George Winston Smith and Charles Judah, eds., *Chronicles of the Gringos: The U.S. Army in the Mexican War* (1968), and James M. McCaffrey, *Army of Manifest Destiny: The American Soldier in the Mexican War* (1992).

SLAVERY AND EXPANSION There is a huge literature on the sectional conflict provoked by the issue of slavery's expansion into the territory acquired from Mexico. For an introduction, consult David M. Potter, *The Impending Crisis 1848–1861* (1976), and Allan Nevins, *Ordeal of the Union,* 2 vols. (1947). The best single study of antislavery politics in this era is Richard H. Sewell, *Ballots for Freedom: Antislavery Politics in the United States 1837–1860* (1976). For northern Democrats and the Wilmot Proviso, see Chaplain Morrison, *Democratic Politics and Sectionalism: The Wilmot Proviso Controversy* (1967). The divisive impact of the slavery issue on Whigs is treated in Kinley J. Brauer, *Cotton versus Conscience: Massachusetts Whig Politics and Southwestern Expansion 1843–1848* (1967). The Free Soil Party and the 1848 presidential election are treated in Joseph Rayback, *Free Soil: The Election of 1848* (1970), and Frederick J. Blue, *The Free Soilers: Third Party Politics 1848–1854* (1973). For the South and the sectional controversy over slavery's expansion, see William J. Cooper Jr., *The South and the Politics of Slavery, 1828–1856* (1978); William W. Freehling, *The Road to Disunion: Secessionists at Bay, 1776–1854* (1990); John Barnwell, *Love of Order: South Carolina's First Secession Crisis* (1982); and a study of nine southern nationalists, Eric H. Walther, *The Fire-Eaters* (1992).

COMPROMISE OF 1850 The fullest studies of the Compromise of 1850 are Holman Hamilton, *Prologue to Conflict: The Crisis and Compromise of 1850* (1964), and Mark J. Stegmaier, *Texas, New Mexico, and the Compromise of 1850* (1996). The careers of the three great senators who played such an important part in the compromise debate are portrayed in Merrill Peterson, *The Great Triumvirate: Webster, Clay, and Calhoun* (1987). For these and other key figures, see the following biographies: Robert F. Dalzell, *Daniel Webster and the Trial of American Nationalism 1843–1852* (1972); Robert V. Remini, *Henry Clay: Statesman for the Union* (1991); John Niven, *John C. Calhoun and the Price of Union* (1988); Robert W. Johannsen, *Stephen A. Douglas* (1973); Glyndon G. Van Deusen, *William Henry Seward* (1967); and K. Jack Bauer, *Zachary Taylor: Soldier, Planter, Statesman of the Old Southwest* (1985). The failed efforts of fire-eaters to capitalize on resentment of events that surrounded the compromise are treated in Thelma Jennings, *The Nashville Convention: Southern Movement for Unity 1848–1850* (1980), while the destructive impact of these events on the southern Whigs is narrated in Arthur C. Cole, *The Whig Party in the South* (1913).

FUGITIVE SLAVES The basic study of the passage and enforcement of the Fugitive Slave Act is Stanley W. Campbell, *The Slave Catchers* (1970). See also Paul Finkelman, *An Imperfect Union: Slavery, Federalism, and Comity* (1980). For northern personal liberty laws, see Thomas D. Morris, *Free Men All: The Personal Liberty Laws of the North 1780–1861* (1974). A scholarly study of the underground railroad is Larry Gara, *Liberty Line: The Legend of the Underground Railroad* (1961). One of the most dramatic fugitive slave confrontations is treated in Thomas P. Slaughter, *Bloody Dawn: The Christiana Riot and Racial Violence in the North* (1991). For the hostility of many northern states toward blacks—fugitive or otherwise—see Eugene Berwanger, *The Frontier against Slavery: Western Anti-Negro Prejudice and the Slavery Extension Controversy* (1971). The powerful impact of Harriet Beecher Stowe's novel is measured by Thomas F. Gossett, *Uncle Tom's Cabin and American Literature* (1985).

FILIBUSTERING The best accounts of southern expansionism and filibustering in the 1850s are Robert E. May, *The Southern Dream of a Caribbean Empire 1854–1861* (1971), and Charles H. Brown, *Agents of Manifest Destiny: The Lives and Times of the Filibusters* (1979). For licit as well as illicit attempts to obtain Cuba, see Basil Rauch, *American Interest in Cuba 1848–1855* (1948), and Tom Chaffin, *Fatal Glory: Narciso Lopez and the*

First Clandestine U.S. War against Cuba (1996). The remarkable career of William Walker is chronicled in William O. Scroggs, *Filibusters and Financiers: The Story of William Walker and His Associates* (1916), and Albert Z. Carr, *The World and William Walker* (1963).

Chapter 14

For general studies of the mounting sectional conflict during the 1850s, see David M. Potter, *The Impending Crisis 1848–1861* (1976); Allan Nevins, *Ordeal of the Union*, 2 vols. (1947), and *The Emergence of Lincoln*, 2 vols. (1950); Avery Craven, *The Coming of the Civil War*, 2nd ed. (1957); Michael F. Holt, *The Political Crisis of the 1850s* (1978); and James M. McPherson, *Battle Cry of Freedom: The Civil War Era* (1988).

THE KANSAS CONTROVERSY The Kansas-Nebraska Act and the ensuing conflict in Kansas are treated in Gerald W. Wolff, *The Kansas-Nebraska Bill: Party, Section, and the Coming of the Civil War* (1977); James A. Rawley, *Race and Politics: "Bleeding Kansas" and the Coming of the Civil War* (1969); and Alice Nichols, *Bleeding Kansas* (1954). Biographies of key figures in this controversy include Robert W. Johannsen, *Stephen A. Douglas* (1973), and Larry Gara, *The Presidency of Franklin Pierce* (1991).

NATIVISM AND IMMIGRATION The foregoing books contain a great deal of material about the relationship between the Kansas conflict and the origins of the Republican Party. For the crosscutting issue of nativism and the Know-Nothings, see especially William E. Gienapp, *The Origins of the Republican Party, 1852–1856* (1987), and Tyler Anbinder, *Nativism and Politics: The Know Nothing Party in the Northern United States* (1992). Other important studies of immigration and the nativist response include Oscar Handlin, *Boston's Immigrants* (1941); Robert Ernst, *Immigrant Life in New York City, 1825–1863* (1949); Jay P. Dolan, *The Immigrant Church: New York's Irish and German Catholics 1815–1865* (1975); and Dale T. Knobel, *Paddy and the Republic: Ethnicity and Nationality in Antebellum America* (1985). The best general narrative of nativism is still Ray Allen Billington, *The Protestant Crusade 1800–1861* (1938). See also Ira M. Leonard and Robert D. Parmet, *American Nativism, 1830–1860* (1971).

POLITICS AND SECTIONALISM Three of the numerous state studies of the political transformation in northern states are Mark L. Berger, *The Revolution in the New York Party Systems, 1840–1860* (1973); Steven E. Maizlish, *The Triumph of Sectionalism: The Transformation of Ohio Politics, 1844–1856* (1983); and Dale Baum, *The Civil War Party System: The Case of Massachusetts, 1848–1876* (1984). The Kansas-Nebraska Act brought Abraham Lincoln back into the political arena; for a fine study of Lincoln's role in the rise of the Republican Party, see Don E. Fehrenbacher, *Prelude to Greatness: Lincoln in the 1850's* (1962). A somewhat different interpretation is provided by Robert W. Johannsen, *Lincoln, the South, and Slavery* (1991). Two other valuable biographical studies are David Donald, *Charles Sumner and the Coming of the Civil War* (1960), and Frederick Blue, *Salmon P. Chase: A Life in Politics* (1987).

The southern response to these events in the North is chronicled in Avery Craven, *The Growth of Southern Nationalism 1848–1861* (1953); John McCardell, *The Idea of a Southern Nation* (1979); William L. Barney, *The Road to Secession: A New Perspective on the Old South* (1972); William J. Cooper Jr., *The South and the Politics of Slavery 1828–1856* (1978); and Eric H. Walther, *The Fire-Eaters* (1992). The widening North-South fissure in the Democratic Party is treated in Philip S. Klein, *President James Buchanan* (1962); Elbert B. Smith, *The Presidency of James Buchanan* (1975); and Roy F. Nichols, *The Disruption of American Democracy* (1948). The year 1857 witnessed a convergence of many of these events; for a stimulating book that pulls together the threads of that year of crisis, see Kenneth M. Stampp, *America in 1857: A Nation on the Brink* (1990). Another account of an important issue during this period is Mark W. Summers, *The Plundering Generation: Corruption and the Crisis of the Union, 1849–1861* (1987).

THE ECONOMY AND EDUCATION For economic developments during this era, a still valuable classic is George Rogers Taylor, *The Transportation Revolution, 1815–1860* (1951). Agriculture is treated in Paul W. Gates, *The Farmer's Age: Agriculture, 1815–1860* (1960). Important studies of railroads include Albert Fishlow, *American Railroads and the Transformation of the Antebellum Economy* (1965), and John F. Stover, *Iron Road to the West: American Railroads in the 1850s* (1978). For the "American System of Manufactures," see Nathan Rosenberg, ed., *The American System of Manufactures* (1969); David A. Hounshell, *From the American System to Mass Production, 1800–1932* (1983); and Donald R. Hoke, *Ingenious Yankees: The Rise of the American System of*

Manufactures in the Private Sector (1990). For the relationship of education to social and economic change, see Frederick M. Binder, *The Age of the Common School 1830–1865* (1974); Lee Soltow and Edward Stevens, *The Rise of Literacy and the Common School in the United States* (1981); Carl F. Kaestle, *Pillars of the Republic: Common Schooling and American Society, 1780–1860* (1983); and Carl F. Kaestle and Maris A. Vinovskis, *Education and Social Change in Nineteenth-Century Massachusetts* (1980).

THE SOUTHERN ECONOMY For the southern economy in these years, see Gavin Wright, *The Political Economy of the Cotton South* (1978), and Fred Bateman and Thomas Weiss, *A Deplorable Scarcity: The Failure of Industrialization in the Slave Economy* (1981). Herbert Wender's *Southern Commercial Conventions 1837–1859* (1930) chronicles the efforts of southerners to promote economic diversification. Other important studies include Harold D. Woodman, *King Cotton and His Retainers: Financing and Marketing the Cotton Crop of the South* (1968), and Laurence Shore, *Southern Capitalists: The Ideological Leadership of an Elite, 1832–1885* (1986). The Panic of 1857 and its sectional and political consequences are treated in James L. Huston, *The Panic of 1857 and the Coming of the Civil War* (1987).

ANTISLAVERY AND PROSLAVERY IDEOLOGY The best study of the Republican free-labor ideology is Eric Foner, *Free Soil, Free Labor, Free Men: The Ideology of the Republican Party before the Civil War* 2nd ed. (1995). Howard Floan's *The South in Northern Eyes 1831–1861* (1953) summarizes various northern images of the South. Still the fullest account of the southern defense of slavery and its way of life is William S. Jenkins, *Pro-Slavery Thought in the Old South* (1935), which should be supplemented by Drew Gilpin Faust, ed., *The Ideology of Slavery: Proslavery Thought in the Antebellum South* (1981).

SOUTHERN YEOMEN The numerous studies of white social structure and non-slaveholders in the South include Frank L. Owsley, *Plain Folk of the Old South* (1949); Bruce Collins, *White Society in the Antebellum South* (1985); Steven Hahn, *The Roots of Southern Populism: Yeoman Farmers and the Transformation of the Georgia Upcountry, 1850–1890* (1983); Paul D. Escott, *Many Excellent People: Power and Privilege in North Carolina, 1850–1900* (1985); J. William Harris, *Plain Folk and Gentry in a Slave Society: White Liberty and Black Slavery in Augusta's Hinterlands* (1985); Bill Cecil-Fronsman, *Common Whites: Class and Culture in Antebellum North Carolina* (1992); and Stephanie McCurry, *Masters of Small Worlds: Yeoman Households, Gender Relations, and the Political Culture of the Antebellum South Carolina Low Country* (1995).

DRED SCOTT, THE LINCOLN-DOUGLAS DEBATES, AND JOHN BROWN The best single study of the Dred Scott case is Don E. Fehrenbacher, *The Dred Scott Case: Its Significance in American Law and Politics* (1978), which was published in an abridged version with the title *Slavery, Law, and Politics: The Dred Scott Case in Historical Perspective* (1981). There are several editions of the Lincoln-Douglas debates; the fullest is Paul M. Angle, ed., *Created Equal? The Complete Lincoln-Douglas Debates of 1858* (1958). For analyses of the debates, see Harry F. Jaffa, *Crisis of the House Divided* (1959), and David Zarefsky, *Lincoln, Douglas and Slavery in the Crucible of Public Debate* (1990). See also Damon Wells, *Stephen Douglas: The Last Years, 1857–1861* (1971), and William E. Baringer, *Lincoln's Rise to Power* (1937). For John Brown's raid on Harpers Ferry, see Stephen B. Oates, *To Purge This Land with Blood: A Biography of John Brown* (1970); Jeffrey S. Rossback, *Ambivalent Conspirators: John Brown, the Secret Six, and a Theory of Slave Violence* (1982); and Benjamin Quarles, *Allies for Freedom: Blacks and John Brown* (1974).

Chapter 15

The most comprehensive one-volume study of the Civil War years is James M. McPherson, *Battle Cry of Freedom: The Civil War Era* (1988). The same ground is covered in greater detail by Allan Nevins, *The War for the Union*, 4 vols. (1959–1971). For single-volume accounts of the Confederacy and the Union that emphasize the home fronts, see Emory M. Thomas, *The Confederate Nation, 1861–1865* (1979); George C. Rable, *The Confederate Republic* (1994); and Phillip Shaw Paludan, *"A People's Contest": The Union and Civil War, 1861–1865* (1988). Two multivolume classics that concentrate mainly on military campaigns and battles are Bruce Catton, *The Centennial History of the Civil War*, vol. 1: *The Coming Fury* (1961), vol. 2: *Terrible Swift Sword* (1963), vol. 3: *Never Call Retreat* (1965); and Shelby Foote, *The Civil War: A Narrative*, 3 vols. (1958–1974).

WOMEN AND THE WAR The important roles of women in many facets of the war effort are described by Mary Elizabeth Masset, *Bonnet Brigades* (1966); Agatha Young, *Women and the Crisis: Women of the North* *in the Civil War* (1959); Elizabeth D. Leonard, *Yankee Women: Gender Battles in the Civil War* (1994); George C. Rable, *Civil Wars: Women and the Crisis of Southern Nationalism* (1989); and Drew Gilpin Faust, *Mothers of Invention: Women of the Slaveholding South in the American Civil War* (1996). Social history is the main focus of two collections of essays: Maris A. Vinovskis, ed., *Toward a Social History of the American Civil War* (1990), and Catherine Clinton and Nina Silber, eds., *Divided Houses: Gender and the Civil War* (1992).

ARMIES AND SOLDIERS For penetrating studies of the officers and men in three of the Civil War's most famous armies, see Bruce Catton's three volumes on the Army of the Potomac: *Mr. Lincoln's Army* (1951), *Glory Road* (1952), and *A Stillness at Appomattox* (1953); Douglass Southall Freeman's study of officers in the Army of Northern Virginia: *Lee's Lieutenants: A Study in Command,* 3 vols. (1942–1944); Thomas L. Connelly's two works on the Army of Tennessee: *Army of the Heartland* (1967) and *Autumn of Glory* (1971); and Larry J. Daniel's *Soldiering in the Army of Tennessee: A Portrait of Life in the Confederate Army* (1991). The classic studies of Civil War soldiers by Bell Irvin Wiley are *The Life of Johnny Reb* (1943) and *The Life of Billy Yank* (1952). For additional insights into the character and experience of soldiers, see Reid Mitchell, *Civil War Soldiers* (1988) and *The Vacant Chair: The Northern Soldier Leaves Home* (1993); James M. McPherson, *What They Fought For, 1861–1865* (1994) and *For Cause and Comrades: Why Men Fought in the Civil War* (1997); and Earl J. Hess, *The Union Soldier in Battle: Enduring the Ordeal of Combat* (1997).

BIOGRAPHIES Biographies of leading Civil War figures are of great value for understanding the period. For Abraham Lincoln, see especially Benjamin P. Thomas, *Abraham Lincoln* (1952); Stephen B. Oates, *With Malice toward None: The Life of Abraham Lincoln* (1977); Mark E. Neely Jr., *The Last Best Hope of Earth: Abraham Lincoln and the Promise of America* (1993); James G. Randall, *Lincoln the President,* 4 vols. (1945–1955; vol. 4 completed by Richard N. Current); James M. McPherson, *Abraham Lincoln and the Second American Revolution* (1991); Philip S. Paludan, *The Presidency of Abraham Lincoln* (1994); and David Herbert Donald, *Lincoln* (1995). For Jefferson Davis, the best one-volume biography is William C. Davis, *Jefferson Davis: The Man and His Hour* (1991). See also Hudson Strode, *Jefferson Davis,* 3 vols. (1955–1964). The classic biography of Robert E. Lee is Douglass Southall Freeman, *R. E. Lee: A Biography,* 3 vols. (1934–1935), which has been condensed into a one-volume abridgement by Richard Harwell, *Lee* (1961). For revisionist interpretations of Lee, see Thomas L. Connelly, *The Marble Man: Robert E. Lee and His Image in American Society* (1977); Alan T. Nolan, *Lee Considered: General Robert E. Lee and Civil War History* (1991); and Emory M. Thomas, *Robert E. Lee: A Biography* (1995). Biographies of two other leading Confederate generals are Grady McWhiney, *Braxton Bragg and Confederate Defeat* (1969); Judith Lee Hallock, *Braxton Bragg and Confederate Defeat* (1991); and Craig L. Symonds, *Joseph E. Johnston: A Civil War Biography* (1992). On the Union side, two biographies of Ulysses S. Grant are William S. McFeely, *Grant: A Biography* (1981), and Geoffrey Perret, *Ulysses S. Grant: Soldier and President* (1997). For a fuller account of Grant during the war, see Bruce Catton, *Grant Moves South* (1960) and *Grant Takes Command* (1969), and Brooks D. Simpson, *Let Us Have Peace: Ulysses S. Grant and the Politics of War and Reconstruction, 1861–1868* (1991). There are many biographies of William T. Sherman; two of the most valuable are Basil H. Liddell Hart, *Sherman: Soldier, Realist, American* (1929), and John F. Marszalek, *Sherman: A Soldier's Passion for Order* (1993). For George B. McClellan, the best biography is Stephen W. Sears, *George B. McClellan: The Young Napoleon* (1988).

ELECTION OF 1860 AND SECESSION The election of 1860 and the crisis of secession have been the subject of numerous studies: Emerson D. Fite, *The Presidential Campaign of 1860* (1911); Reinhard H. Luthin, *The First Lincoln Campaign* (1944); Ollinger Crenshaw, *The Slave States in the Presidential Election of 1860* (1945); William E. Baringer, *Lincoln's Rise to Power* (1937); Dwight L. Dumond, *The Secession Movement 1860–1861* (1931); Ralph Wooster, *The Secession Conventions of the South* (1962); Donald E. Reynolds, *Editors Make War: Southern Newspapers in the Secession Crisis* (1970); Steven A. Channing, *A Crisis of Fear: Secession in South Carolina* (1970); William L. Barney, *The Secessionist Impulse: Alabama and Mississippi in 1860* (1974); Michael P. Johnson, *Toward a Patriarchal Republic: The Secession of Georgia* (1977); Daniel W. Crofts, *Reluctant Confederates: Upper South Unionists in the Secession Crisis* (1989); David M. Potter, *Lincoln and His Party in the Secession Crisis* (1942; new ed. 1962); and Kenneth M. Stampp, *And the War Came: The North and the Secession Crisis, 1860–1861* (1950). The best accounts of the standoff at Fort Sumter that led to war are Richard N. Current, *Lincoln and the First Shot* (1963), and Maury Klein, *Days of Defiance: Sumter, Secession, and the Coming of the Civil War* (1997).

THE BORDER STATES The bitter experiences of the border states in the war are chronicled by William E. Parrish, *Turbulent Partnership: Missouri and the Union 1861–1865* (1963); Jean H. Baker, *The Politics of Continuity: Maryland Political Parties from 1858 to 1870* (1973); William H. Townsend, *Lincoln and the Bluegrass: Slavery and Civil War in Kentucky* (1955); and Lowell Harrison, *The Civil War and Kentucky* (1975). For guerrilla warfare along the border, particularly in Missouri, the best studies are Jay Monaghan, *Civil War on the Western Border 1854–1865* (1955), and Michael Fellman, *Inside War: The Guerrilla Conflict in Missouri during the Civil War* (1989). For the creation of West Virginia, see Richard O. Curry, *A House Divided: A Study of Statehood Politics and the Copperhead Movement in West Virginia* (1964).

WAR AND FINANCE The problem of Confederate war finance is treated in Richard C. Todd, *Confederate Finance* (1954), and Douglas B. Ball, *Financial Failure and Confederate Defeat* (1990). For Union war finance, see Bray Hammond, *Sovereignty and an Empty Purse: Banks and Politics in the Civil War Era* (1970).

THE NAVAL WAR There is a large literature on Civil War navies and the blockade. Perhaps the best place to begin is with William M. Fowler Jr., *Under Two Flags: The American Navy in the Civil War* (1990), and Ivan Musicant, *Divided Waters: The Naval History of the Civil War* (1995). The fullest account of naval warfare is Virgil C. Jones, *The Civil War at Sea*, 3 vols. (1960–1962). For the river war, see H. Allen Gosnell, *Guns on the Western Waters: The Story of River Gunboats in the Civil War* (1949); John D. Milligan, *Gunboats down the Mississippi* (1965); and James M. Merrill, *Battle Flags South: The Story of the Civil War Navies on Western Waters* (1970). A good general history of the Confederate navy is Raimundo Luraghi, *A History of the Confederate Navy* (1996). For the blockade and blockade running, see Robert Carse, *Blockade: The Civil War at Sea* (1958), and Stephen R. Wise, *Lifeline of the Confederacy: Blockade Running during the Civil War* (1988). The story of Confederate commerce raiding is told in George W. Dalzell, *The Flight from the Flag* (1943), and Edward C. Boykin, *Ghost Ship of the Confederacy: The Story of the "Alabama" and Her Captain* (1957).

FOREIGN POLICY Foreign policy complications caused by Confederate shipbuilding in Britain are treated in Frank J. Merli, *Great Britain and the Confederate Navy* (1970). The most concise account of Civil War diplomacy is David P. Crook, *The North, the South, and the Powers 1861–1865* (1974), an abridged version of which was published with the title *Diplomacy during the Civil War* (1975). The classic study of Confederate diplomacy is Frank L. Owsley, *King Cotton Diplomacy* (1931; rev. ed. 1959). British-American and British-Confederate relations have received exhaustive attention; the fullest studies are Ephraim D. Adams, *Great Britain and the American Civil War*, 2 vols. (1925); Brian Jenkins, *Britain and the War for the Union*, 2 vols. (1974–1980); and Howard Jones, *The Union in Peril: The Crisis over British Intervention in the Civil War* (1992). For the *Trent* Affair, consult Gordon H. Warren, *Fountains of Discontent: The "Trent" Affair and the Freedom of the Seas* (1981). For relations between France and the two warring parties, see Lynn M. Case and Warren F. Spencer, *The United States and France: Civil War Diplomacy* (1970).

Chapter 16

For works that cover the whole period of the Civil War, including the years encompassed by this chapter, see the books cited in the first four paragraphs of the Suggested Reading for Chapter 15. In addition, for analyses of military strategy and leadership that focus mainly on the period 1862–1865, consult T. Harry Williams, *Lincoln and His Generals* (1952); Archer Jones, *Civil War Command and Strategy* (1992); Joseph T. Glatthaar, *Partners in Command: The Relationships between Leaders in the Civil War* (1993); Steven E. Woodworth, *Jefferson Davis and His Generals* (1990); and Steven E. Woodworth, *Davis and Lee at War* (1995). Richard M. McMurry, *Two Great Rebel Armies* (1989), analyzes the reasons for the success of the Army of Northern Virginia and the relative failure of the Army of Tennessee, while Michael C. Adams, *Our Masters the Rebels: A Speculation on Union Military Defeat in the East, 1861–1865* (1978), reissued under the title *Fighting for Defeat* (1992), offers an interpretation of the Army of the Potomac's problems. Charles W. Royster, *The Destructive War: William Tecumseh Sherman, Stonewall Jackson, and the Americans* (1991), and Mark Grimsley, *The Hard Hand of War: Union Military Policy toward Southern Civilians, 1981–1865* (1995), focus on the escalating destructiveness of the war. Six studies canvass various explanations for Union victory: David Donald, ed., *Why the North Won the Civil War* (1960); Herman Hattaway and Archer Jones, *How the North Won: A Military History of the Civil War* (1983); Richard E. Beringer, Herman Hattaway, Archer Jones, and William N. Still Jr., *Why the South Lost the Civil War* (1986), an abridged version of which was published with the title *The Elements of Confederate Defeat*

(1988); Grady McWhiney and Perry D. Jamieson, *Attack and Die: Civil War Military Tactics and the Southern Heritage* (1982); Gabor S. Boritt, ed., *Why the Confederacy Lost* (1992); and Gary W. Gallagher, *The Confederate War* (1997). See also Drew Gilpin Faust, *The Creation of Confederate Nationalism* (1988).

SLAVERY AND EMANCIPATION On the issues of slavery and emancipation in the war, the best place to begin is Ira Berlin, Barbara J. Fields, Steven F. Miller, Joseph P. Reidy, and Leslie S. Rowland, *Slaves No More: Three Essays on Emancipation and the Civil War* (1992). An older but still useful study is Bell I. Wiley, *Southern Negroes 1861–1865* (1938). A superb study of one Confederate state is Clarence L. Mohr, *On the Threshold of Freedom: Masters and Slaves in Civil War Georgia* (1986), while a classic account of the experience of emancipation on the South Carolina Sea Islands is Willie Lee Rose, *Rehearsal for Reconstruction: The Port Royal Experiment* (1964). Two books on Maryland provide the best studies of slavery and emancipation in a border state: Charles L. Wagandt, *The Mighty Revolution: Negro Emancipation in Maryland 1862–1864* (1964), and Barbara Jeanne Fields, *Slavery and Freedom on the Middle Ground: Maryland during the Nineteenth Century* (1985). See also Victor B. Howard, *Black Liberation in Kentucky: Emancipation and Freedom, 1862–1884* (1983). For the hopes and realities of freedom as experienced by the slaves, see Leon F. Litwack, *Been in the Storm So Long: The Aftermath of Slavery* (1979). A fine study of the Emancipation Proclamation is John Hope Franklin, *The Emancipation Proclamation* (1963). Two books by James M. McPherson analyze the role of Northern abolitionists and black leaders in the achievement of emancipation: *The Struggle for Equality: Abolitionists and the Negro in the Civil War and Reconstruction* (1964), and *The Negro's Civil War* (1965; new ed. 1991). The impact of the loss of slavery on the slaveholding class is chronicled by James L. Roark, *Masters without Slaves: Southern Planters in the Civil War and Reconstruction* (1977).

BLACK SOLDIERS For black soldiers in the Union Army, the best studies are Dudley T. Cornish, *The Sable Arm: Negro Troops in the Union Army* (1956), and Joseph T. Glatthaar, *Forged in Battle: The Civil War Alliance of Black Soldiers and White Officers* (1990). A classic account by a white officer of a black regiment is Thomas Wentworth Higginson, *Army Life in a Black Regiment* (1869; reprinted 1961). For the Confederate debate about arming and freeing slaves, see Robert Durden, *The Gray and the Black: The Confederate Debate on Emancipation* (1972).

COPPERHEADS AND DEMOCRATS Antiblack and antiemancipation sentiments in the North are the focus of V. Jacque Voegeli, *Free but Not Equal: The Midwest and the Negro during the Civil War* (1967), and Forrest G. Wood, *Black Scare: The Racist Response to Emancipation and Reconstruction* (1968). Hostility to emancipation was at the core of Copperheadism in the North, a phenomenon provocatively interpreted in three books by Frank L. Klement: *The Copperheads in the Middle West* (1960), *The Limits of Dissent: Clement L. Vallandigham and the Civil War* (1970), and *Dark Lanterns: Secret Political Societies, Conspiracies, and Treason Trials in the Civil War* (1984). See also Wood Gray, *The Hidden Civil War: The Story of the Copperheads* (1942). For the Northern Democrats, one should also consult Joel Silbey, *A Respectable Minority: The Democratic Party in the Civil War Era* (1977).

POLITICS AND THE CONSTITUTION Three studies of the Lincoln administration's record on civil liberties and related constitutional issues are important: Mark E. Neely Jr., *The Fate of Liberty: Abraham Lincoln and Civil Liberties* (1990); Dean Sprague, *Freedom under Lincoln* (1965); and James G. Randall, *Constitutional Problems Under Lincoln* (rev. ed., 1951). Other studies of constitutional issues during the war include Harold M. Hyman, *A More Perfect Union: The Impact of the Civil War and Reconstruction on the Constitution* (1973), and Phillip S. Paludan, *A Covenant with Death: The Constitution, Law, and Equality in the Civil War Era* (1975). William B. Hesseltine, *Lincoln and the War Governors* (1948), is a valuable study of federal-state relations in the crucible of war.

ECONOMICS AND LOGISTICS Still a useful book on the Confederate economy is Charles W. Ramsdell, *Behind the Lines in the Southern Confederacy* (1944), while for the Union, the same can be said of Emerson D. Fite, *Social and Economic Conditions in the North during the Civil War* (1910). Railroads in North and South are treated in George E. Turner, *Victory Rode the Rails* (1953); Thomas Weber, *The Northern Railroads in the Civil War* (1952); and Robert C. Black, *The Railroads of the Confederacy* (1952). Robert V. Bruce, *Lincoln and the Tools of War* (1956), is a fascinating study of Northern technology in the war, while Edward Hagerman, *The American Civil War and the Origins of Modern Warfare* (1988), and Richard Goff, *Confederate Supply* (1969), are the best studies of logistics.

DISSENT AND CLASS CONFLICT Class conflict and political dissent in the Confederacy are discussed in Paul D. Escott, *After Secession: Jefferson Davis and the Failure of Confederate Nationalism* (1978); Bell I. Wiley, *The Plain*

People of the Confederacy (1943); Fred Arthur Bailey, *Class and Tennessee's Confederate Generation* (1987); Wayne K. Durrill, *War of Another Kind: A Southern Community in the Great Rebellion* (1990); and Frank L. Owsley, *State Rights in the Confederacy* (1966). The most dramatic manifestation of class conflict in the North was the New York draft riot. Two important studies of it are Adrian Cook, *The Armies of the Streets: The New York City Draft Riots of 1863* (1974), and Iver Bernstein, *The New York City Draft Riots: Their Significance for American Society and Politics in the Age of the Civil War* (1990). For the conflict in the Pennsylvania coal fields, see Grace Palladino, *Another Civil War: Labor, Capital, and the State in the Anthracite Regions of Pennsylvania* (1990).

CONSCRIPTION Controversies about conscription lay at the root of much wartime class conflict. For studies of the draft in South and North, see Albert B. Moore, *Conscription and Conflict in the Confederacy* (1924); Eugene C. Murdock, *One Million Men: The Civil War Draft in the North* (1971); and James W. Geary, *We Need Men: The Union Draft in the Civil War* (1991). The modernizing legislation of the Union Congress that drafted a "blueprint for modern America" is analyzed by Leonard P. Curry, *Blueprint for Modern America: Non-Military Legislation of the First Civil War Congress* (1968). For a provocative interpretation of the Confederacy's attempted crash program of modernization and industrialization, see Emory M. Thomas, *The Confederacy as a Revolutionary Experience* (1971; new ed. 1991).

CIVIL WAR MEDICINE For Civil War medicine, in addition to the books about women in the war cited in the Suggested Readings for Chapter 15, see Paul E. Steiner, *Disease in the Civil War* (1968); George W. Adams, *Doctors in Blue: The Medical History of the Union Army in the Civil War* (1952); and Horace H. Cunningham, *Doctors in Gray: The Confederate Medical Service* (1958). The basic history of the U.S. Sanitary Commission is William Q. Maxwell, *Lincoln's Fifth Wheel: The Political History of the United States Sanitary Commission* (1956). A stimulating interpretation of the Sanitary Commission in the context of wartime transformations in Northern attitudes toward other social and cultural issues is George M. Fredrickson, *The Inner Civil War: Northern Intellectuals and the Crisis of the Union* (1965).

THE PEACE ISSUE The complex relationships between peace negotiations and the Union presidential election of 1864 are discussed in Edward C. Kirkland, *The Peacemakers of 1864* (1927); William F. Zornow, *Lincoln and the Party Divided* (1954); David E. Long, *The Jewel of Liberty: Abraham Lincoln's Re-Election and the End of Slavery* (1994); and Larry E. Nelson, *Bullets, Ballots, and Rhetoric: Confederate Policy for the United States Presidential Contest of 1864* (1980). The best analysis of Lincoln's assassination and of the many unsubstantiated conspiracy theories to explain it is William Hanchett, *The Lincoln Murder Conspiracies* (1983). See also William A. Tidwell, James O. Hall, and David Winfred Gaddy, *Come Retribution: The Confederate Secret Service and the Assassination of Lincoln* (1988).

Chapter 17

The most comprehensive and incisive general history of Reconstruction is Eric Foner, *Reconstruction: America's Unfinished Revolution 1863–1877* (1988). For a skillful abridgement of this book, see Eric Foner, *A Short History of Reconstruction* (1990). A more concise survey of this era can be found in James M. McPherson, *Ordeal by Fire: The Civil War and Reconstruction,* 3rd ed. (2000), Part 3. Still valuable are Kenneth M. Stampp, *The Era of Reconstruction, 1865–1877* (1965), and John Hope Franklin, *Reconstruction: After the Civil War* (1961). The essays in Eric Anderson and Alfred A. Moss Jr., eds., *The Facts of Reconstruction: Essays in Honor of John Hope Franklin* (1991), offer important insights. The constitutional issues involved in the era are analyzed by Harold M. Hyman, *A More Perfect Union: The Impact of the Civil War and Reconstruction on the Constitution* (1973).

For the evolution of federal Reconstruction policies during the war and early postwar years, see three books by Herman Belz: *Reconstructing the Union: Theory and Policy during the Civil War* (1969), *A New Birth of Freedom: The Republican Party and Freedmen's Rights* (1976), and *Emancipation and Equal Rights: Politics and Constitutionalism in the Civil War Era* (1978). Also valuable is David Donald, *The Politics of Reconstruction 1863–1867* (1965). Important for their insights on Lincoln and the Reconstruction question are Peyton McCrary, *Abraham Lincoln and Reconstruction: The Louisiana Experiment* (1978), and LaWanda Cox, *Lincoln and Black Freedom: A Study in Presidential Leadership* (1981). A superb study of the South Carolina Sea Islands as a laboratory of Reconstruction is Willie Lee Rose, *Rehearsal for Reconstruction: The Port Royal Experiment* (1964).

Johnson versus Congress For the vexed issues of Andrew Johnson, Congress, and Reconstruction from 1865 to 1868, the following are essential: Eric L. McKitrick, *Andrew Johnson and Reconstruction* (1960); LaWanda Cox and John H. Cox, *Politics, Principle, and Prejudice 1865–1866* (1963); William R. Brock, *An American Crisis: Congress and Reconstruction 1865–1867* (1963); Michael Les Benedict, *A Compromise of Principle: Congressional Republicans and Reconstruction* (1974); David Warren Bowen, *Andrew Johnson and the Negro* (1989); and Hans L. Trefousse, *The Radical Republicans: Lincoln's Vanguard for Racial Justice* (1969), *Thaddeus Stevens: Nineteenth-Century Egalitarian* (1997), and *Andrew Johnson: A Biography* (1989). The two best studies of Johnson's impeachment are Michael Les Benedict, *The Impeachment and Trial of Andrew Johnson* (1973), and Hans L. Trefousse, *Impeachment of a President: Andrew Johnson, the Blacks, and Reconstruction* (1975).

The Fourteenth and Fifteenth Amendments For the political and judicial dimensions of the Fourteenth and Fifteenth Amendments and their enforcement, see Joseph B. James, *The Framing of the Fourteenth Amendment* (1956), and *The Ratification of the Fourteenth Amendment* (1984); Michael Kent Curtis, *No State Shall Abridge: The Fourteenth Amendment and the Bill of Rights* (1986); William E. Nelson, *The Fourteenth Amendment: From Political Principle to Judicial Doctrine* (1988); William Gillette, *The Right to Vote: Politics and Passage of the Fifteenth Amendment* (1965); and Robert J. Kaczorowski, *The Politics of Judicial Interpretation: The Federal Courts, Department of Justice and Civil Rights, 1866–1876* (1985).

Reconstruction Society, Politics, and Economics For the social and political scene in the South during Reconstruction, a good introduction is Howard N. Rabinowitz, *The First New South, 1865–1920* (1991). Dan T. Carter, *When the War Was Over: the Failure of Self-Reconstruction in the South, 1865–1867* (1985), and Michael Perman, *Reunion without Compromise: The South and Reconstruction, 1865–1868* (1973), portray the early postwar years, while Michael Perman, *The Road to Redemption: Southern Politics, 1868–1879* (1984), is a provocative interpretation. Otto H. Olsen, ed., *Reconstruction and Redemption in the South* (1980), contains essays on the Reconstruction process in a half-dozen states. For the role of the Ku Klux Klan and other white paramilitary organizations, see Allen W. Trelease, *White Terror: The Ku Klux Klan Conspiracy and Southern Reconstruction* (1974), and George C. Rable, *But There Was No Peace: The Role of Violence in the Politics of Reconstruction* (1984). For a fresh and intelligent look at the carpetbaggers, see Richard Nelson Current, *Those Terrible Carpetbaggers: A Reinterpretation* (1988). Economic issues are the subject of Mark W. Summers, *Railroads, Reconstruction, and the Gospel of Prosperity: Aid under the Radical Republicans, 1865–1877* (1984), and Terry L. Seip, *The South Returns to Congress: Men, Economic Measures, and Intersectional Relationships, 1868–1879* (1983).

Freedpeople during Reconstruction Two classics that portray sympathetically the activities of freedpeople during Reconstruction are W. E. Burghardt Du Bois, *Black Reconstruction* (1935), and Leon F. Litwack, *Been in the Storm So Long: The Aftermath of Slavery* (1979). A challenging brief interpretation is provided by Eric Foner, *Nothing but Freedom: Emancipation and Its Legacy* (1983). Howard N. Rabinowitz, *Race Relations in the Urban South, 1865–1890* (1978), and Howard N. Rabinowitz, ed., *Southern Black Leaders of the Reconstruction Era* (1982), add important dimensions to the subject. There are many good studies of black social and political life in various states during Reconstruction; three of the best deal with the state in which African Americans played the most active part: Joel Williamson, *After Slavery: The Negro in South Carolina during Reconstruction 1861–1877* (1965); Thomas Holt, *Black over White: Negro Political Leadership in South Carolina during Reconstruction* (1977); and Laura F. Edwards, *Gendered Strife and Confusion: The Political Culture of Reconstruction* (1997). See also Eric Foner, *Freedom's Lawmakers: A Directory of Black Officeholders during Reconstruction* (1993).

For the evolution of sharecropping and other aspects of freedpeople's economic status, see Roger L. Ransom and Richard Sutch, *One Kind of Freedom: The Economic Consequences of Emancipation* (1977), and William Cohen, *At Freedom's Edge: Black Mobility and the Southern White Quest for Racial Control, 1861–1915* (1991). Two sound studies of the Freedmen's Bureau are George R. Bentley, *A History of the Freedmen's Bureau* (1955), and Donald G. Nieman, *To Set the Law in Motion: The Freedmen's Bureau and the Legal Rights of Blacks 1865–1868* (1979). For the education of freedpeople, see especially William Preston Vaughan, *Schools for All: The Blacks & Public Education in the South 1865–1877* (1974); Joe M. Richardson, *Christian Reconstruction, The American Missionary Association and Southern Blacks, 1861–1890* (1986); and James M. McPherson, *The Abolitionist Legacy: From Reconstruction to the NAACP* (1975).

The End of Reconstruction The national political scene in the 1870s and the retreat from Reconstruction are the subject of William Gillette, *Retreat from Reconstruction: A Political History 1867–1878* (1979). The issues of corruption and civil service reform receive exhaustive treatment in Mark Wahlgren Summers, *The Era of Good Stealings* (1993). The classic analysis of the disputed election of 1876 and the Compromise of 1877 is C. Vann Woodward, *Reunion and Reaction: The Compromise of 1877 and the End of Reconstruction,* rev. ed., (1956); for challenges to aspects of Woodward's thesis see Keith I. Polakoff, *The Politics of Inertia: The Election of 1876 and the End of Reconstruction* (1973), and Michael Les Benedict, "Southern Democrats in the Crisis of 1876–1877: A Reconsideration of Reunion and Reaction," *Journal of Southern History* 46 (1980): 489–524.

Chapter 18

WESTWARD EXPANSION Classic accounts of the post–Civil War West can be found in Walter Prescott Webb, *The Great Plains* (1931), and Wallace Stegner, *Beyond the Hundredth Meridian* (1954). Also valuable are Rodman Paul, *The Far West and the Great Plains in Transition* (1988), and Howard Lamar, *The Far Southwest, 1846–1912* (1970). The best modern general study of the history of the West from the first contact between Europeans and Indians down to the present is Richard White, *"It's Your Misfortune and None of My Own": A History of the American West* (1991).

RAILROADS The role of railroads in westward expansion is treated in Robert R. Riegel, *The Story of the Western Railroads* (1926), and Oscar O. Winther, *The Great Iron Trail: The Story of the First Transcontinental Railroad* (1963).

THE FARMING FRONTIER The farmers' frontier is chronicled in Gilbert C. Fite, *The Farmer's Frontier, 1865–1900* (1966), and Fred Shannon, *The Farmers' Last Frontier, 1860–1897* (1945). The important part played by immigrants in western settlement is treated in Frederick C. Luebke, *Ethnicity on the Great Plains* (1980). Farmers' wives and other frontier women are the subject of Sandra Myres, *Western Women and the Frontier Experience, 1880–1915* (1982); Julie Roy Jeffrey, *Frontier Women: The Trans-Mississippi West, 1840–1880* (1979); and Christiane Fischer, *Let Them Speak for Themselves: Women in the American West, 1849–90* (1977). The experience of children is discussed in Elliott West, *Growing Up with the Country: Childhood on the Far Western Frontier* (1989).

THE MINING FRONTIER For the mining frontier, the following are valuable: William Greever, *The Bonanza West: The Story of the Western Mining Rushes* (1963); Rodman Paul, *Mining Frontiers of the Far West, 1848–1880* (1963); Richard Lingenfelter, *The Hardrock Miners: A History of the Mining Labor Movement in the American West, 1863–1893* (1974); and Mark Wyman, *Hard Rock Epic: Western Miners and the Industrial Revolution, 1860–1910* (1979).

THE RANCHING FRONTIER The saga of the ranching frontier and the cowboy is the subject of many books, including Lewis Atherton, *The Cattle Kings* (1961); Edward E. Dale, *The Range Cattle Industry,* rev. ed. (1969); Robert Dykstra, *The Cattle Towns* (1968); Ernest S. Osgood, *The Day of the Cattleman* (1929); Joe B. Frantz and Julian Choate, *The American Cowboy: The Myth and Reality* (1955); and William Savage, *The Cowboy Hero: His Image in American History and Culture* (1979). For black cowboys, see William L. Katz, *The Black West* (1971).

INDIANS AND THE WEST The best brief survey of Indians and Indian-white relations in this period is Philip Weeks, *Farewell, My Nation: The American Indian and the United States, 1820–1890* (1990). Other valuable works include Ralph K. Andrist, *The Long Death: The Last Day of the Plains Indians* (1964); and Robert M. Utley, *The Indian Frontier of the American West 1846–1890* (1984), and *The Last Days of the Sioux Nation* (1963). For the reformers and the Dawes Act, see Robert Mardock, *Reformers and the American Indian* (1971), and Leonard A. Carlson, *Indians, Bureaucrats, and Land* (1981). Two books by Francis Paul Prucha contain valuable material on this period: *The Great Father: The United States Government and the American Indians* (1984), and *The Indians in American Society from the Revolutionary War to the Present* (1985).

THE NEW SOUTH The classic study of the New South is C. Vann Woodward, *Origins of the New South, 1877–1913* (1951). It can be supplemented by Paul M. Gaston, *The New South Creed: A Study in Southern Mythmaking* (1970), and Edward L. Ayres, *The Promise of the New South: Life after Reconstruction* (1992). For the economy of the New South, see Gavin Wright, *Old South, New South: Revolutions in the Southern Economy Since the Civil War* (1986); Pete Daniel, *Breaking the Land: The Transformation of Cotton, Tobacco, and Rice*

Cultures Since 1880 (1985); John F. Stover, *The Railroads of the South, 1865–1900* (1955); Patrick H. Hearden, *Independence and Empire: The New South's Cotton Mill Campaign, 1865–1901* (1982); and David L. Carlton, *Mill and Town in South Carolina, 1880–1920* (1982).

RACE RELATIONS The politics of race in the New South is the subject of Vincent P. DeSantis, *Republicans Face the Southern Question . . . 1877–1897* (1959); Stanley P. Hirshson, *Farewell to the Bloody Shirt: Northern Republicans and the Southern Negro 1877–1893* (1962); and J. Morgan Kousser, *The Shaping of Southern Politics: Suffrage Restriction and the Establishment of the One-Party South 1880–1910* (1974). The rising tide of racism and segregation is treated in C. Vann Woodward, *The Strange Career of Jim Crow*, 3rd rev. ed. (1974); Joel Williamson, *The Crucible of Race: Black-White Relations in the American South Since Emancipation* (1984), which was also published in an abridged edition with the title *A Rage for Order: Black-White Relations in the American South Since Emancipation* (1986); and Howard B. Rabinowitz, *Race Relations in the Urban South 1865–1890* (1978). The horrors of lynching and the convict lease system are analyzed in Fitzhugh Brundage, *Lynching in the New South: Georgia and Virginia, 1880–1930* (1993), and Matthew J. Mancini, *One Dies, Get Another: Convict Leasing in the American South, 1866–1928* (1996). For responses by black leaders to these developments, see August Meier, *Negro Thought in America, 1880–1915* (1963), and Louis R. Harlan, *Booker T. Washington: The Making of a Black Leader, 1856–1901* (1972).

THE POLITICS OF STALEMATE Two useful political narratives of this period are John A. Garraty, *The New Commonwealth, 1877–1890* (1968), and John M. Dobson, *Politics in the Gilded Age* (1972). For the continuing impact of Civil War issues and memories in politics, see Mary R. Dearing, *Veterans in Politics: The Story of the G.A.R.* (1952); Stuart McConnell, *Glorious Contentment: The Grand Army of the Republic, 1865–1900* (1992); and Gaines M. Foster, *Ghosts of the Confederacy: Defeat, the Lost Cause, and the Emergence of the New South* (1987). Other useful studies include Paul Kleppner, *The Third Electoral System, 1853–1892* (1979); Robert Marcus, *Grand Old Party: Political Structure in the Gilded Age* (1971); H. Wayne Morgan, *From Hayes to McKinley* (1969); and Ari Hoogenboom, *Outlawing the Spoils: A History of the Civil Service Reform Movement* (1961).

Chapter 19

For stimulating overviews of this period and the Progressive Era that followed, consult Richard Hofstadter, *The Age of Reform* (1955); Robert H. Wiebe, *The Search for Order 1877–1920* (1967); and Nell Irvin Painter, *Standing at Armageddon: The United States, 1877–1919* (1987).

RAILROADS AND INDUSTRIAL GROWTH For the impact of the railroad on the Gilded Age economy and culture, see George R. Taylor and Irene D. Neu, *The American Railroad Network, 1861–1890* (1956); Albro Martin, *Railroads Triumphant: The Growth, Rejection, and Rebirth of a Vital American Force* (1992); and Alfred D. Chandler Jr., *The Railroads: The Nation's First Big Business* (1965). For the rise of industry and "big business," the following are useful: Glen Porter, *The Rise of Big Business, 1860–1910* (1973); Edward C. Kirkland, *Industry Comes of Age . . . 1860–1897* (1961); Harold G. Vatter, *The Drive to Industrial Maturity: The U.S. Economy, 1865–1914* (1975); Robert Higgs, *The Transformation of the American Economy, 1865–1914* (1971); and Alfred D. Chandler, *The Visible Hand: The Managerial Revolution in American Business* (1977). An old and entertaining (although biased and outmoded) portrait of the financial and industrial leaders of the era is Matthew Josephson, *The Robber Barons: The Great American Capitalists 1861–1901* (1934).

THE RESPONSE TO INDUSTRIALISM The response to industrialism and the rise of a regulatory antitrust movement are treated in Samuel P. Hays, *The Response to Industrialism, 1885–1914* (1957); Sidney Fine, *Laissez Faire and the General Welfare State: A Study of Conflict in American Thought, 1865–1900* (1956); George H. Miller, *Railroads and the Granger Laws* (1971); Gabriel Kolko, *Railroads and Regulation, 1877–1915* (1965); and Ari and Olive Hoogenboom, *A History of the ICC* (1976).

LABOR For the labor movement and labor strife, the following are particularly useful: Melvin Dubofsky, *Industrialism and the American Worker, 1865–1920* (1975); Walter Licht, *Working for the Railroad* (1983); Herbert G. Gutman, *Work, Culture, and Society in Industrializing America* (1976); Bruce Laurie, *Artisans into Workers: Labor in Nineteenth-Century America* (1989); David Montgomery, *The Fall of the House of Labor . . . 1865–1925* (1987); David Montgomery, *Workers' Control in America: Studies in the History of Work, Technology, and Labor Struggles* (1979); Leon Fink, *Workingmen's Democracy: The Knights of Labor and American Politics* (1983); Robert E. Weir, *Beyond Labor's Veil: The Culture of the Knights of Labor* (1996); Stuart Kaufman, *Samuel Gompers and the Origins of the American Federation of Labor* (1973); David Brody, *Steelworkers in America: The Nonunion Era* (1960); Robert V. Bruce, *1877: Year of Violence* (1959); Paul Avrich, *The Haymarket Tragedy* (1984); Leon Wolff, *Lockout, the Story of the Homestead Strike of 1892* (1965); and Almont Lindsey, *The Pullman Strike* (1971).

POPULISM AND THE ELECTION OF 1896   The classic history of the Populist movement, still valuable as a narrative, is John D. Hicks, *The Populist Revolt* (1931). The best modern survey of the movement is Lawrence Goodwyn, *Democratic Promise: The Populist Moment in America* (1976), which was published in an abridged edition with the title *The Populist Moment* (1978). Among the many other fine books about populism, the following are especially useful: C. Vann Woodward, *Tom Watson, Agrarian Rebel* (1938); Peter Argersinger, *Populism and Politics* (1974); Steven Hahn, *The Roots of Southern Populism* (1983); Sheldon Hackney, *Populism to Progressivism in Alabama* (1969); Robert McMath, *Populist Vanguard: A History of the Southern Farmers' Alliance* (1975); and Gerald H. Gaither, *Blacks and the Populist Revolt* (1977). The complexities of the silver issue are unraveled in Allen Weinstein, *Prelude to Populism: Origins of the Silver Issue* (1970).

The politics of the 1890s culminating in the climactic election of 1896 are treated in J. Rogers Hollingsworth, *The Whirligig of Politics: The Democracy of Cleveland and Bryan* (1963); Richard J. Jensen, *The Winning of the Midwest: Social and Political Conflict, 1888–1896* (1971); R. Hal Williams, *Years of Decision: American Politics in the 1890s* (1978); Paul W. Glad, *McKinley, Bryan, and the People* (1964); Stanley Jones, *The Presidential Election of 1896* (1964); and Robert F. Durden, *The Climax of Populism: The Election of 1896* (1965).

Chapter 20

For a general overview of the period, Alan Dawley, *Struggles for Justice: Social Responsibility and the Liberal State* (1991), and Nell Irvin Painter, *Standing at Armageddon: The United States, 1877–1919* (1987), are excellent accounts that are particularly strong on issues of social history.

ECONOMIC GROWTH AND TECHNOLOGICAL INNOVATION   On economic growth in the late 19th and early 20th centuries, see Harold G. Vatter, *The Drive to Industrial Maturity: The United States Economy, 1860–1914* (1975); Elliot Brownlee, *Dynamics of Ascent: A History of the American Economy*, 2nd ed. (1979); David Hounshell, *From the American System to Mass Production, 1800–1932: The Development of Manufacturing Technology in the United States* (1984); Nathan Rosenberg, *Technology and American Economic Growth* (1972); Charles Singer et al., eds., *History of Technology*, vol. 5: *The Late Nineteenth Century* (1958); and Harold I. Sharlin, *The Making of the Electrical Age* (1963). David Nye, *Electrifying America: Social Meanings of a New Technology, 1890–1940* (1990), is a fascinating account of the social consequences of technological change. For an older but lively history on this theme, see Frederick Lewis Allen, *The Big Change: America Transforms Itself, 1900–1950* (1952). Robert Conot, *A Streak of Luck* (1979), and Matthew Josephson, *Edison* (1959), assess Thomas Edison's contributions to the electrical revolution.

THE RISE OF THE MODERN CORPORATION   Alfred D. Chandler Jr., *The Visible Hand: The Managerial Revolution in American Business* (1977), is the classic work. See also Richard Tedlow, *The Rise of the American Business Corporation* (1991); Naomi Lamoreaux, *The Great Merger Movement in American Business, 1895–1904* (1985); and Glenn Porter, *The Rise of Big Business, 1860–1910* (1973). On the emerging alliance between corporations and science, see David F. Noble, *America by Design: Science, Technology and the Rise of Corporate Capitalism* (1977); Frederick A. White, *American Industrial Research Laboratories* (1961); and Leonard S. Reich, *The Making of Industrial Research: Science and Business at GE and Bell, 1876–1926* (1985). On the legal and political changes that undergirded the corporation's triumph, see Martin J. Sklar, *The Corporate Reconstruction of American Capitalism, 1890–1916: The Market, the Law and Politics* (1988). Olivier Zunz, *Making America Corporate, 1870–1920* (1990), is one of the first social histories to focus on the middle managers who comprised the new corporate middle class. A provocative exploration of the paths to economic development shut off by the triumph of mass production is found in Michael J. Piore and Charles F. Sabel, *The Second Industrial Divide: Possibilities for Prosperity* (1984). For an equally provocative critique of this interpretation, consult Philip Scranton, *Endless Novelty: Specialty Production and American Industrialization, 1865–1925* (1997).

SCIENTIFIC MANAGEMENT Any examination of this topic must start with Frederick Winslow Taylor, *The Principles of Scientific Management* (1911), and Robert Kanigel, *The One Best Way: Frederick Winslow Taylor and the Enigma of Efficiency* (1997). Daniel Nelson, *Frederick W. Taylor and the Rise of Scientific Management* (1980), and David Montgomery, *The Fall of the House of Labor: The Workplace, the State, and American Labor Activism, 1865–1925* (1987), are important. For its broader political ramifications, see Samuel Haber, *Efficiency and Uplift: Scientific Management in the Progressive Era* (1964). Allan Nevins and Frank E. Hill, *Ford* (1954–1963), is still the best biography of Henry Ford, but on Ford's labor policies, Stephen Meyer III, *The Five Dollar Day: Labor Management and Social Control in the Ford Motor Company, 1908–1921* (1981), and Nelson Lichtenstein and Stephen Meyer III, eds., *On the Line: Essays in the History of Auto Work* (1989), are essential reading. For a general perspective on the changes in work and management in this period, consult Sanford M. Jacoby, *Employing Bureaucracy: Managers, Unions, and the Transformation of Work in American Industry, 1900–1945* (1985).

ROBBER BARONS AND THE TURN TO PHILANTHROPY The classic work on the robber barons themselves is Matthew Josephson, *The Robber Barons* (1934). On the industrialists' turn to philanthropy, see Andrew Carnegie, *The Gospel of Wealth* (1889), and *Autobiography* (1920); Robert H. Bremner, *American Philanthropy* (1988); George E. Pozzetta, ed., *Americanization, Social Control and Philanthropy* (1991); Barry D. Karl and Stanley N. Katz, "The American Private Philanthropic Foundation and the Public Sphere, 1890–1930," *Minerva* 19 (Summer 1981): 236–270; and Ellen Condliffe Lagemann, *The Politics of Knowledge: The Carnegie Corporation, Philanthropy, and Public Policy* (1989).

"RACIAL FITNESS" AND SOCIAL DARWINISM On America's growing obsession with physical and racial fitness during this period, see John Higham, "The Reorientation of American Culture in the 1890s," in John Horace Weiss, ed., *The Origins of Modern Consciousness*, pp. 25–48 (1965), and Higham, *Strangers in the Land: Patterns of American Nativism*, rev. ed. (1992). For an assessment of the influence of Darwinist thinking on American culture, see Richard Hofstadter, *Social Darwinism in American Thought*, rev. ed. (1955); Robert Bannister, *Social Darwinism: Science and Myth in Anglo-American Social Thought* (1979); and Carl N. Degler, *In Search of Human Nature: The Decline and Revival of Darwinism in American Social Thought* (1991).

IMMIGRATION: GENERAL HISTORIES The best single-volume history of European immigrants is John Bodnar, *The Transplanted: A History of Immigrants in Urban America* (1985). Maldwyn Allen Jones, *American Immigration* (1974), and Alan M. Kraut, *The Huddled Masses: The Immigrant in American Society, 1880–1921* (1982), are also useful. Ronald Takaki, *A Different Mirror: A History of Multicultural America* (1993), Roger Daniels, *Coming to America: A History of Immigration and Ethnicity in American Life* (1990), and Leonard Dinnerstein, Roger L. Nichols, and David Reimers, *Natives and Strangers: Ethnic Groups and the Building of America* (1979), integrate the story of European immigrants with that of African, Asian, and Latin American newcomers. Stephan Thernstrom, ed., *Harvard Encyclopedia of American Ethnic Groups* (1980), is indispensable on virtually all questions pertaining to immigration and ethnicity. Frank Thistlewaite, "Migration from Europe Overseas," in Stanley N. Katz and Stanley I. Kutler, eds., *New Perspectives on the American Past* (1969), vol. 2, pp. 152–181, is a pioneering article on patterns of European migration. On European immigrants' encounters with racial patterns in the United States, see Matthew Frye Jacobson, *Whiteness of a Different Color: European Americans and the Alchemy of Race* (1998).

HISTORIES OF PARTICULAR IMMIGRANT GROUPS Irving Howe, *World of Our Fathers: The Journey of the East European Jews to America and the Life They Found and Made* (1976), is the best work on Jewish immigration, although it must be supplemented by Susan A. Glenn, *Daughters of the Shtetl: Life and Labor in the Immigrant Generation* (1990). For work on the Irish, see Kerby A. Miller, *Emigrants and Exiles: Ireland and the Irish Exodus to North America* (1985), and Hasia A. Diner, *Erin's Daughters in America: Irish Immigrant Women in the Nineteenth Century* (1983). Other excellent works on particular ethnic groups include Ewa Morawska, *For Bread with Butter: The Life-Worlds of East Central Europeans in Johnstown, Pennsylvania, 1890–1940* (1985); John J. Bukowczyk, *And My Children Did Not Know Me: A History of Polish Americans* (1987); Virginia Yans-McLaughlin, *Family and Community: Italian Immigrants in Buffalo, 1880–1930* (1977); Yuji Ichioka, *The Issei: The World of the First Japanese Immigrants, 1895–1924* (1988); Sucheng Chan, *Asian Americans: An Interpretive History* (1991); and Mario T. Garcia, *Desert Immigrants: The Mexicans of El Paso, 1880–1920* (1981). Olivier Zunz, *The Changing Face of Inequality: Urbanization, Industrial Development and Immigrants in Detroit, 1880–1920* (1982), and S. J. Kleinberg, *The Shadow of the Mills: Working-Class Families in Pittsburgh, 1870–1907* (1989), compare the experiences of several European American groups in one city.

IMMIGRANT LABOR Essential sources on both immigrant and nonimmigrant labor are Herbert Gutman, *Work, Culture and Society in Industrializing America* (1976); Montgomery, *The Fall of the House of Labor* (previously cited); and Alice Kessler-Harris, *Out of Work: A History of Wage-Earning Women in the United States* (1982). For a brief but incisive survey of working conditions in this period, consult Melvyn Dubofsky, *Industrialism and the American Worker, 1865–1920*, 2nd ed. (1985). Tamara Hareven, *Family Time and Historical Time: The Relationship between the Family and Work in a New England Industrial Community* (1982), and James R. Barrett, *Work and Community in the Jungle: Chicago's Packinghouse Workers, 1894–1922* (1990), are excellent local studies. Leon Stein, *The Triangle Fire* (1962), and John F. McClymer, *The Triangle Strike and Fire* (1998), chronicle that industrial disaster; and Alexander Keyssar, *Out of Work: The First Century of Unemployment in Massachusetts* (1986), offers the best analysis of unemployment in this period.

IMMIGRANTS, AFRICAN AMERICANS, AND SOCIAL MOBILITY Good sources on this topic include Stephan Thernstrom, *The Other Bostonians: Poverty and Progress in the American Metropolis* (1973); Joel Perlman, *Ethnic Differences: Schooling and Social Structure among the Irish, Italians, Jews, and Blacks in an American City, 1880–1935* (1988); Thomas Kessner, *The Golden Door: Italian and Jewish Mobility in New York City, 1880–1915* (1977); Edna Bonacich and John Modell, *The Economic Basis of Ethnic Solidarity: Small Businessmen in the Japanese-American Community* (1980); Stephen Steinberg, *The Ethnic Myth: Race, Ethnicity, and Class in America* (1981); Thomas Sowell, *Ethnic America: A History* (1981); and Stanley Lieberson, *A Piece of the Pie: Blacks and White Immigrants Since 1880* (1980).

IMMIGRANTS, POLITICAL MACHINES, AND ORGANIZED CRIME Steven P. Erie, *Rainbow's End: Irish Americans and the Dilemmas of Urban Machine Politics, 1840–1945* (1988), insightfully examines the benefits and costs of big city machines. See also Harold Zink, *City Bosses in the United States: A Study of Twenty Municipal Bosses* (1930); M. Craig Brown and Charles N. Halaby, "Machine Politics in America, 1870–1945," *Journal of Interdisciplinary History* 8 (1987): 587–612; John M. Allswang, *Bosses, Machines, and Urban Voters* (1977); Alexander B. Callow, ed., *The City Boss in America* (1976); and William L. Riordon, *Plunkitt of Tammany Hall: A Series of Very Plain Talks on Very Practical Politics* (1994). On organized crime, consult Joseph Albini, *The American Mafia* (1971); Humbert Nelli, *The Business of Crime* (1976); and Jenna Weissman Joselit, *Our Gang: Jewish Crime and the New York Jewish Community* (1983). Doris Kearns Goodwin, *The Fitzgeralds and the Kennedys* (1987), chronicles the history of President John F. Kennedy's family.

AFRICAN AMERICANS John Hope Franklin and Alfred A. Moss Jr., *From Slavery to Freedom: A History of Negro Americans*, 7th ed. (1994), offers a masterful overview. Gavin Wright, *Old South, New South: Revolutions in the Southern Economy since the Civil War* (1986), analyzes the southern sharecropping economy, while William H. Harris, *The Harder We Run: Black Workers since the Civil War* (1982), assesses the experiences of black industrial workers, South and North. On black female workers, consult Jacqueline Jones, *Labor of Love, Labor of Sorrow: Black Women, Work and the Family from Slavery to the Present* (1985). Kenneth L. Kusmer, *A Ghetto Takes Shape: Black Cleveland, 1870–1930* (1978), is the best work on the formation of urban black communities in the North prior to the Great Migration (1916–1920), but it should be supplemented with Elizabeth Hafkin Pleck, *Black Migration and Poverty: Boston, 1865–1900* (1979); Allan H. Spear, *Black Chicago: The Making of a Negro Ghetto, 1890–1920* (1967); and Theodore Hershberg et al., *Philadelphia: Work, Space, Family, and Group Experience in the Nineteenth Century* (1981). On the rise of a new black middle class, see Evelyn Brooks Higginbotham, *Righteous Discontent: The Women's Movement in the Black Baptist Church, 1880-1920* (1993), and Kevin K. Gaines, *Uplifting the Race: Black Leadership, Politics, and Culture in the Twentieth Century* (1996).

WORKERS AND UNIONS Indispensable sources are Montgomery, *The Fall of the House of Labor* (previously cited); David Brody, *Workers in Industrial America: Essays on the Twentieth Century Struggle* (1980); and Melvyn Dubofsky, *We Shall Be All: A History of the Industrial Workers of the World* (1969). Samuel Gompers's career can be traced through Stuart Kaufman, *Samuel Gompers and the Origins of the American Federation of Labor* (1973), and Gompers's own *Seventy Years of Life and Labor: An Autobiography*, ed. Nick Salvatore (1984). Michael Kazin, *Barons of Labor: The San Francisco Building Trades and Union Power in the Progressive Era* (1987), is a sterling study of AFL craftsmen at work and in local politics; and Gwendolyn Mink, *Old Labor and New Immigrants in American Political Development: Union, Party, and State, 1875–1920* (1986), offers a provocative interpretation of the AFL's role in national politics. Christopher Tomlins, *The State and the Unions: Labor Relations, Law, and the Organized Labor Movement in America, 1880–1960* (1985), carefully analyzes the effect of law on the labor movement's development.

David A. Corbin, *Life, Work, and Rebellion in the Coal Fields: The Southern West Virginia Miners, 1880–1922* (1981), examines the rise of the United Mine Workers; and Howe, *World of Our Fathers* (previously cited), treats the early years of the ILGWU in New York City. Sterling D. Spero and Abram L. Harris, *The Black Worker: The Negro and the Labor Movement* (1931), and James R. Grossman, *Land of Hope: Chicago, Black Southerners, and the Great Migration* (1989), analyze AFL attitudes toward black workers. Eric Arnesen, *Waterfront Workers of New Orleans: Race, Class and Politics, 1863–1923* (1991), probes that city's remarkable experiment in biracial unionism. Graham Adams Jr., *Age of Industrial Violence, 1910–1915: The Activities and Findings of the United States Commission on Industrial Relations* (1966), chronicles the Ludlow massacre and other labor-capital confrontations in these years. See also J. Anthony Lukas, *Big Trouble: A Murder in a Small Western Town Sets Off a Struggle for the Soul of America* (1997), a remarkable study of class conflict in the West during the early years of the 20th century.

THE RISE OF MASS CULTURE On the rise of mass culture, see David Nasaw, *Going Out: The Rise and Fall of Public Amusements* (1993); William Leach, *Land of Desire: Merchants, Power, and the Rise of a New American Culture* (1993); Roy Rosenzweig, *Eight Hours for What We Will: Workers and Leisure in an Industrial City, 1870–1920* (1983); and Lewis A. Erenberg, *Steppin' Out: New York Nightlife and the Transformation of American Culture, 1890–1930* (1981). Warren I. Susman, *Culture as History: The Transformation of American Society in the Twentieth Century* (1984), is essential reading for any student of this subject. Excellent studies of the rise of movies are Rosenzweig, *Eight Hours for What We Will* (previously cited); Lary May, *Screening Out the Past: The Birth of Mass Culture and the Motion Picture Industry* (1980); Robert Sklar, *Movie-Made America: A Social History of the American Movies* (1975); and Steven J. Ross, *Working-Class Hollywood: Silent Film and the Shaping of Class in America* (1998).

THE "NEW WOMAN" On the emergence of the "new woman," see Kathy Peiss, *Cheap Amusements: Working Women and Leisure in Turn-of-the-Century New York* (1986); Elaine Tyler May, *Great Expectations: Marriage and Divorce in Post-Victorian America* (1980); Leslie Woodcock Tentler, *Wage-Earning Women: Industrial Work and Family Life in the United States, 1900–1930* (1979); Joanne Meyerowitz, *Women Adrift: Independent Wage-Earners in Chicago, 1870–1930* (1988); and Elizabeth Lunbeck, *The Psychiatric Persuasion: Knowledge, Gender and Politics in Modern America* (1994).

FEMINISM Nancy F. Cott, *The Grounding of Modern Feminism* (1987), is the most important study of the movement's origins. Linda Gordon, *Woman's Body, Woman's Right: A Social History of Birth Control in America* (1976), and James Reed, *The Birth Control Movement and American Society: From Private Vice to Public Virtue* (1983), are important works on the history of birth control. Also see the following first-rate biographies: David M. Kennedy, *Birth Control in America: The Career of Margaret Sanger* (1970); Alice Wexler, *Emma Goldman: An Intimate Life* (1984); and Christine A. Lunardini, *From Equal Suffrage to Equal Rights: Alice Paul and the National Women's Party, 1912–1928* (1986). For a brief biography of Charlotte Perkins Gilman, see Gary Scharnhorst, *Charlotte Perkins Gilman* (1985). Leslie Fishbein, *Rebels in Bohemia: The Radicals of "The Masses," 1911–1917* (1982), deftly recreates the politics and culture of Greenwich Village.

Chapter 21

No topic in 20th century American history has generated as large and rapidly changing a scholarship as has progressivism. Today, few scholars treat this political movement in the terms set forth by the progressives themselves: as a movement of "the people" against the "special interests." In *The Age of Reform: From Bryan to FDR* (1955), Richard Hofstadter argues that progressivism was the expression of a declining Protestant middle class at odds with the new industrial order. In *The Search for Order, 1877–1920* (1967), Robert Wiebe finds the movement's core in a rising middle class, closely allied to the corporations and bureaucratic imperatives that were defining this new order. Gabriel Kolko, *The Triumph of Conservatism: A Reinterpretation of American History* (1963), and James Weinstein, *The Corporate Ideal in the Liberal State, 1900–1918* (1969), both argue that progressivism was the work of industrialists themselves, who were eager to ensure corporate stability and profitability in a dangerously unstable capitalist economy. Without denying the importance of this corporate search for order, Nell Irvin Painter, *Standing at Armageddon: The United States, 1877–1919,* (1987), and Alan Dawley, *Struggles for Justice: Social Responsibility and the Liberal State* (1991), insist on the role of the working class, men and women, whites and blacks, in shaping the progressive agenda. James T. Kloppenberg, *Uncertain*

Victory: Social Democracy and Progressivism in European and American Thought, 1870–1920 (1986), and Thomas J. Knock, *To End All Wars: Woodrow Wilson and the Quest for a New World Order* (1992), emphasize the influence of socialism on progressive thought, while Martin J. Sklar, *The Corporate Reconstruction of American Capitalism, 1900–1916: The Market, the Law and Politics* (1988), stresses the role of progressivism in "containing" or taming socialism. Paul Boyer, *Urban Masses and Moral Order in America, 1820–1920* (1978), treats progressivism as a cultural movement to enforce middle-class norms on an unruly urban and immigrant population. Theda Skocpol, *Protecting Soldiers and Mothers: The Political Origins of Social Policy in the United States* (1992), reconstructs the central role of middle-class Protestant women in shaping progressive social policy, while Robert M. Crunden, *Ministers of Reform: The Progressives' Achievement in American Civilization, 1889–1920* (1982), stresses the religious roots of progressive reform. Summaries of some of these various interpretations of progressivism—but by no means all—can be found in Arthur S. Link and Richard L. McCormick, *Progressivism* (1983).

Muckrakers, Settlement Houses, and Women Reformers On the muckrakers, see Walter M. Brasch, *Forerunners of Revolution: Muckrakers and the American Social Conscience* (1990); Harold S. Wilson, *McClure's Magazine and the Muckrakers* (1970); and Justin Kaplan, *Lincoln Steffens* (1974). On the settlement houses and women reformers, consult Jane Addams, *Twenty Years at Hull House* (1910); Kathryn Kish Sklar, *Florence Kelley and the Nation's Work: The Rise of Women's Political Culture, 1830–1900* (1995); Allen F. Davis, *Spearheads for Reform: The Social Settlements and the Progressive Movement, 1890–1914* (1967); Mina Julia Carson, *Settlement Folk: Social Thought and the American Settlement Movement, 1885–1930* (1990); and Rivka Shpak Lissak, *Pluralism and the Progressives: Hull House and the New Immigrants, 1890–1919* (1989). Ruth Borden, *Women and Temperance* (1980), is useful on the role of women in the prohibition movement. Paula Baker, "The Domestication of Politics: Women and American Political Society, 1780–1920," *American Historical Review* 89 (June 1984): 620–647, and Robyn Muncy, *Creating a Female Dominion in American Reform, 1890–1935* (1991), are important for understanding women's political activism in the years before they gained the vote.

Socialism For general histories, see James Weinstein, *The Decline of Socialism in America, 1912–1925* (1967), and Irving Howe, *Socialism in America* (1985). Mari Jo Buhle, *Women and American Socialism, 1870–1920* (1981), expertly analyzes the experiences of women who became socialists. Nick Salvatore, *Eugene V. Debs: Citizen and Socialist* (1982), is a superb biography of the charismatic Debs; Melvyn Dubofsky, *We Shall Be All: A History of the Industrial Workers of the World* (1969), offers the most thorough treatment of the IWW. James R. Green, *Grass-Roots Socialism: Radical Movements in the Southwest, 1895–1943* (1978), and Elliott Shore, *Talkin' Socialism: J. A. Wayland and the Role of the Press in American Radicalism, 1890–1912* (1988), analyze socialist movements in the Southwest.

Political Reform in the Cities Melvin Holli, *Reform in Detroit: Hazen S. Pingree and Urban Politics* (1969), is an exemplary study of a progressive mayor. On efforts to reform municipal governments, see David C. Hammack, *Power and Society: Greater New York at the Turn of the Century* (1982); Bradley R. Rice, *Progressive Cities: The Commission Government Movement in America, 1901–1920* (1977); and Martin J. Schiesl, *The Politics of Efficiency: Municipal Administration and Reform in America* (1977).

Reform in the States Richard L. McCormick, *The Party Period and Public Policy* (1986), is indispensable on the roots of state reform. Thomas E. Cronin, *Direct Democracy: The Politics of Initiative, Referendum and Recall* (1989), examines the various movements to limit the power of party bosses and private interests in state politics. David P. Thelen, *The New Citizenship: Origins of Progressivism in Wisconsin, 1885–1900* (1972) and *Robert M. La Follette and the Insurgent Spirit* (1976), offer the best introduction to Wisconsin progressivism. For New York progressivism, consult Richard L. McCormick, *From Realignment to Reform: Political Change in New York State, 1893–1910* (1981); J. Joseph Huthmacher, *Senator Robert F. Wagner and the Rise of Urban Liberalism* (1971); Oscar Handlin, *Al Smith and His America* (1958); and Irvin Yellowitz, *Labor and the Progressive Movement in New York State* (1965). On social and economic reform movements more generally, see John D. Buenker, *Urban Liberalism and Progressive Reform* (1973). George E. Mowry, *The California Progressives* (1951), and Michael Kazin, *Barons of Labor: The San Francisco Building Trades and Union Power in the Progressive Era* (1987), examine the complexities of progressivism in California. On progressivism in the South, consult Sheldon Hackney, *Populism to Progressivism in Alabama* (1969); Jack Temple Kirby, *Darkness at the Dawning: Race and Reform in the Progressive South* (1972); and Dewey Grantham, *Southern Progressivism: The Reconciliation of Progress and Tradition* (1983).

RECONFIGURING THE ELECTORATE AND THE REGULATION OF VOTING On progressive efforts to reform and reconfigure the electorate, see Michael E. McGerr, *The Decline of Popular Politics: The American North, 1865–1928* (1986); L. E. Fredman, *The Australian Ballot: The Story of an American Reform* (1968); Paul Kleppner, *Who Voted? The Dynamics of Electoral Turnout, 1870–1980* (1982); and John Francis Reynolds, *Testing Democracy: Electoral Behavior and Progressive Reform in New Jersey, 1880–1920* (1988). J. Morgan Kousser, *The Shaping of Southern Politics: Suffrage Restriction and the Establishment of the One-Party South, 1880–1910* (1974), is indispensable on black disfranchisement. On the campaign for woman suffrage, see Anne Firor Scott and Andrew MacKay Scott, *One Half the People: The Fight for Woman Suffrage* (1982); Aileen Kraditor, *Ideas of the Woman Suffrage Movement* (1965); David Morgan, *The Suffragists and Democrats: The Politics of Woman's Suffrage in America* (1972); and Christine Lunardini, *From Equal Suffrage to Equal Rights: Alice Paul and the National Women's Party, 1912–1920* (1986).

CIVIL RIGHTS On the renewed campaign for black civil rights, see Charles F. Kellogg, *NAACP: The History of the National Association for the Advancement of Colored People* (1967); Louis R. Harlan, *Booker T. Washington: Wizard of Tuskegee, 1901–1915* (1983); David Levering Lewis, *W. E. B. Du Bois: Biography of a Race, 1868–1919* (1993); and Nancy Weiss, *The National Urban League, 1910–1940* (1974).

NATIONAL REFORM George E. Mowry, *The Era of Theodore Roosevelt* (1958), and Arthur Link, *Woodrow Wilson and the Progressive Era* (1954), are comprehensive overviews of progressivism at the national level. On the conservation movement, see Samuel P. Hays, *The Gospel of Efficiency: The Progressive Conservation Movement, 1890–1920* (1962); Stephen R. Fox, *The American Conservation Movement: John Muir and His Legacy* (1981); and Alfred Runte, *National Parks: The American Experience* (1979). On conflicts within the Republican Party, consult Horace S. Merrill and Marion G. Merrill, *The Republican High Command* (1971). On the Federal Reserve Act, see Robert T. McCulley, *Banks and Politics during the Progressive Era: The Origins of the Federal Reserve System* (1992), and James Livingston, *Origins of the Federal Reserve System: Money, Class and Corporate Capitalism, 1890–1913* (1986). On Louis Brandeis, consult Phillippa Strum, *Louis D. Brandeis* (1984), and Melvin Urofsky, *Louis D. Brandeis and the Progressive Tradition* (1981).

THEODORE ROOSEVELT Good biographies of Roosevelt include Henry F. Pringle, *Theodore Roosevelt* (1931); William H. Harbaugh, *The Life and Times of Theodore Roosevelt* (1975); G. Wallace Chessman, *Theodore Roosevelt and the Politics of Power* (1969); Robert V. Friedenberg, *Theodore Roosevelt and the Rhetoric of Militant Decency* (1990); and H. W. Brands, *TR: The Last Romantic* (1997). John M. Blum, *The Republican Roosevelt* (1954), is a brief but interpretively significant account of Roosevelt's career, and Edmund Morris, *The Rise of Theodore Roosevelt* (1979), is a lively account of Roosevelt's early years.

WILLIAM HOWARD TAFT The fullest biography is still Henry F. Pringle, *The Life and Times of William Howard Taft*, 2 vols. (1939). For more critical views of Taft, see Paolo E. Coletta, *The Presidency of Taft* (1973), and Donald E. Anderson, *William Howard Taft* (1973). On the Pinchot-Ballinger affair, consult James Penich Jr., *Progressive Politics and Conservation: The Ballinger-Pinchot Affair* (1968), and Harold T. Pinkett, *Gifford Pinchot: Private and Public Forester* (1970).

WOODROW WILSON The premier biography and chronicle of Wilson's life from birth until the First World War is Arthur S. Link, *Woodrow Wilson*, 5 vols. (1947–1965). Other important biographies include Arthur Walworth, *Woodrow Wilson*, 2 vols. (1958); John M. Blum, *Woodrow Wilson and the Politics of Morality* (1962); August Heckscher, *Woodrow Wilson* (1991); Kendrick A. Clements, *The Presidency of Woodrow* Wilson (1992); and John Milton Cooper Jr., *The Warrior and the Priest: Woodrow Wilson and Theodore Roosevelt* (1983).

Chapter 22

General works on America's imperialist turn in the 1890s and early years of the 20th century include John Dobson, *America's Ascent: The United States Becomes a Great Power, 1880–1914* (1978); H. Wayne Morgan, *America's Road to Empire* (1965); David F. Healy, *U.S. Expansionism: Imperialist Urge in the 1890s* (1970); Ernest R. May, *Imperial Democracy: The Emergence of America as a Great Power* (1961); Robert L. Beisner, *From the Old Diplomacy to the New, 1965–1900* (1986); and Walter LaFeber, *The Cambridge History of Foreign Relations: The Search for Opportunity, 1865–1913* (1993).

MOTIVES FOR EXPANSION Patricia Hill, *The World Their Household: The American Woman's Foreign Mission Movement and Cultural Transformation, 1870–1920* (1984), and Jane Hunter, *The Gospel of Gentility: American Women Missionaries in Turn-of-the-Century China* (1984), are very good on the overseas work of female Protestant missionaries. William Appleman Williams, *The Tragedy of American Diplomacy*, rev. ed. (1972), is still indispensable on the economic motives behind imperialism, but it should be supplemented with Emily Rosenberg, *Spreading the American Dream: American Economic and Cultural Expansion, 1890–1945* (1982). For an important critique of Frederick Jackson Turner's notion that the year 1890 marked the end of the frontier, consult Patricia Nelson Limerick, *The Legacy of Conquest: The Unbroken Past of the American West* (1987). William E. Livezey, *Mahan on Sea Power* (1981), analyzes Admiral Mahan's strategy for transforming the United States into a world power, and Walter R. Herrick, *The American Naval Revolution* (1966), examines the emergence of a "Big Navy" policy. Julius W. Pratt, *Expansionists of 1898* (1936), is an important account of mounting jingoist fever in the 1890s.

THE SPANISH-AMERICAN WAR David F. Trask, *The War with Spain in 1898* (1981), is a comprehensive study of the Spanish-American War, but it should be supplemented with Philip S. Foner, *The Spanish-Cuban-American War and the Birth of American Imperialism*, 2 vols. (1972). See also James E. Bradford, *Crucible of Empire: The Spanish-American War and Its Aftermath* (1993). Joyce Milton, *The Yellow Journalists* (1989), discusses the role of the press in whipping up war fever, and Michael Blow, *A Ship to Remember: The Maine and the Spanish-American War* (1992), analyzes the battleship sinking that became the war's catalyst. Graham A. Cosmas, *An Army for Empire: The United States Army in the Spanish-American War* (1971), examines the achievements and failures of the army. Edmund Morris, *The Rise of Theodore Roosevelt* (1979), captures the daring of Roosevelt's Rough Riders and their charge up Kettle Hill, while William B. Gatewood Jr., *"Smoked Yankees": Letters from Negro Soldiers, 1898–1902* (1971), examines the important and unappreciated contributions of black soldiers. Gerald F. Linderman, *The Mirror of War: American Society and the Spanish-American War* (1974), brilliantly recaptures the shock that overtook Americans who discovered that their Cuban allies were black and the Spanish enemies were white.

BUILDING AN EMPIRE Julius W. Pratt, *America's Colonial Empire* (1950), analyzes steps the United States took to build itself an empire in the wake of the Spanish-American War. The annexation of Hawaii can be followed in Merze Tate, *The United States and the Hawaiian Kingdom* (1965), and William A. Russ Jr., *The Hawaiian Republic, 1894–1898, and Its Struggle to Win Annexation* (1961). The acquisition of Guam and Samoa is examined in Paul Carano and Pedro Sanchez, *A Complete History of Guam* (1964), and Paul M. Kennedy, *The Samoan Tangle* (1974). The anti-imperialist movement is analyzed in E. Berkeley Tompkins, *Anti-Imperialism in the United States, 1890–1920: The Great Debate* (1970); Robert L. Beisner, *Twelve against Empire: The Anti-Imperialists, 1898–1900* (1968); and Daniel B. Schirmer, *Republic or Empire? American Resistance to the Philippine War* (1972). Richard E. Welch Jr., *Response to Imperialism: The United States and the Philippine War, 1899–1902* (1979), and Stuart Creighton Miller, *"Benevolent Assimilation": The American Conquest of the Philippines, 1899–1903* (1982), analyze the Filipino-American war, while Peter Stanley, *A Nation in the Making: The Philippines and the United States, 1899–1921* (1974), examines the fate of the Philippines under the first 20 years of U.S. rule. James H. Hitchman, *Leonard Wood and Cuban Independence, 1898–1902* (1971), and Louis A. Perez, *Cuba under the Platt Amendment, 1902–1934* (1986), analyze the extension of U.S. control over Cuba, while Raymond Carr, *Puerto Rico: A Colonial Experiment* (1984), examines the history of Puerto Rico following its annexation by the United States. For the unfolding of the Open Door policy toward China, consult Marilyn B. Young, *The Rhetoric of Empire: American China Policy, 1895–1901* (1968); Warren I. Cohen, *America's Response to China* (1971); and Thomas J. McCormick, *China Market: America's Quest for Informal Empire, 1890–1915* (1971).

THEODORE ROOSEVELT Howard K. Beale, *Theodore Roosevelt and the Rise of America to World Power* (1956), is still a crucial work on Roosevelt's foreign policy, although it should be supplemented with David H. Burton, *Theodore Roosevelt: Confident Imperialist* (1968), and Frederick Marks III, *Velvet on Iron: The Diplomacy of Theodore Roosevelt* (1979). Richard H. Collin, *Theodore Roosevelt's Caribbean: The Panama Canal, the Monroe Doctrine and the Latin American Context* (1990), examines Roosevelt's Caribbean policy. Of the many books written on the Panama Canal, two stand out: Walter LaFeber, *The Panama Canal* (1978), and David McCullough, *The Path between the Seas* (1977), a lively account of the canal's construction. See also Michael L. Conniff, *Black Labor on a White Canal: Panama, 1904–1981* (1985). For Roosevelt's policy in East Asia, consult Akira Iriye, *Pacific Estrangement: Japanese and American Expansion, 1897–1911* (1972); Charles Neu, *An Uncertain Friendship:*

Theodore Roosevelt and Japan, 1906–1909 (1967); and Charles Neu, *The Troubled Encounter* (1975). On the treatment of the Japanese in California, see Jules Becker, *The Course of Exclusion, 1882–1924: San Francisco Newspaper Coverage of the Chinese and Japanese in the United States* (1991).

WILLIAM HOWARD TAFT   Ralph E. Minger, *William Howard Taft and American Foreign Policy* (1975), and Walter V. Scholes and Marie V. Scholes, *The Foreign Policies of the Taft Administration* (1970), are the standard works on William Howard Taft's foreign policies. For a comprehensive look at his "dollar diplomacy" and its effects on the Caribbean, see Dana G. Munro, *Intervention and Dollar Diplomacy in the Caribbean, 1900–1920* (1964). See also Emily Rosenberg, *Financial Missionaries to the World: The Politics and Culture of Dollar Diplomacy, 1900–1930* (1999).

WOODROW WILSON   Two books by Arthur Link, *Wilson the Diplomatist* (1957) and *Woodrow Wilson: Revolution, War, and Peace* (1979), sympathetically treat Wilson's struggle to fashion an idealistic foreign policy. These works must be supplemented with Thomas J. Knock, *To End All Wars: Woodrow Wilson and the Quest for a New World Order* (1992). Lloyd C. Gardner, *Safe for Democracy: The Anglo-American Response to Revolution, 1913–1923* (1984), offers a more critical appraisal of Wilson's policies. On U.S. responses to the Mexican Revolution, see John S. D. Eisenhower, *Intervention: The United States and the Mexican Revolution, 1913–1917* (1993); Peter Calvert, *The Mexican Revolution, 1910–1914* (1968); Kenneth J. Grieb, *The United States and Huerta* (1969); and Robert E. Quirk, *An Affair of Honor: Woodrow Wilson and the Occupation of Veracruz* (1962).

Chapter 23

On the factors leading to the outbreak of war in Europe in 1914, see James Joll, *The Origins of the First World War* (1984), and Fritz Fisher, *Germany's War Aims in the First World War* (1972). On the horrors of trench warfare, see John Keegan, *The Face of Battle* (1976), and Erich Maria Remarque's classic novel, *All Quiet on the Western Front* (1929). Paul Fussell, *The Great War and Modern Memory* (1973), is indispensable for understanding the effects of the First World War on European culture.

AMERICAN NEUTRALITY AND INTERVENTION   On American neutrality, see Arthur S. Link, *Woodrow Wilson: Revolution, War and Peace* (1979); John Milton Cooper Jr., *The Vanity of Power: American Isolationism and the First World War, 1914–1917* (1969); and Ernest R. May, *The World War and American Isolation, 1914–1917* (1959). Roland C. Marchand, *The American Peace Movement and Social Reform, 1898–1918* (1972), reconstructs the large and influential antiwar movement, while Ross Gregory, *The Origins of American Intervention in the First World War* (1971), analyzes the events that triggered America's intervention. Daniel R. Beaver, *Newton D. Baker and the American War Effort, 1917–1919* (1966), and John W. Chambers, *To Raise an Army: The Draft Comes to Modern America* (1987), analyze efforts to raise a multimillion-man fighting machine. Russell Weigley, *The American Way of War* (1973), examines the combat experiences of the American Expeditionary Force, while David F. Trask, *The AEF and Coalition Warmaking, 1917–1918* (1973), looks at relations between the AEF and the Allied armies. On the soldiers themselves, consult J. Garry Clifford, *The Citizen Soldiers* (1972), and A. E. Barbeau and Florette Henri, *The Unknown Soldiers: Black American Troops in World War I* (1974). Frank E. Vandiver, *Black Jack: The Life and Times of John J. Pershing* (1977), chronicles the life of the AEF's commander. Daniel H. Kevles, "Testing the Army's Intelligence: Psychologists and the Military in World War I," *Journal of American History* 55 (December 1968): 565–582, examines the military's use and misuse of IQ tests.

THE HOME FRONT   David Kennedy, *Over Here: The First World War and American Society* (1980), is a superb account of the effects of war on American society, but it should be supplemented with Robert H. Ferrell, *Woodrow Wilson and World War I, 1917–1921* (1985), and Ronald Schaffer, *America in the Great War: The Rise of the War Welfare State* (1991). On industrial mobilization, see Robert D. Cuff, *The War Industries Board: Business-Government Relations during World War I* (1973), and the pertinent sections of Jordan Schwarz, *The Speculator* (1981), an excellent biography of Bernard Baruch. Efforts to secure labor's cooperation are examined in Valerie J. Connor, *The National War Labor Board* (1983); Keith Grieves, *The Politics of Manpower, 1914–1918* (1988); and Frank L. Grubb, *Samuel Gompers and the Great War* (1982). On the migration of African Americans to northern industrial centers and the movement of women into war production, see Florette Henri, *Black Migration: Movement North, 1900–1920* (1975); Joe William Trotter Jr., ed., *The Great Migration in Historical*

Perspective: New Dimensions of Race, Class, and Gender (1991); James R. Grossman, *Land of Hope: Chicago, Black Southerners, and the Great Migration* (1989); and Maurine W. Greenwald, *Women, War and Work* (1980). David Montgomery, *The Fall of the House of Labor: The Workplace, the State, and American Labor Activism, 1865–1925* (1987), expertly reconstructs the escalation of labor-management tensions during the war, but it should be read alongside Joseph A. McCartin, *Labor's Great War: The Struggle for Industrial Democracy and the Origins of Modern Labor Relations, 1912–1921* (1997). Charles Gilbert, *American Financing of World War I* (1970), is indispensable on wartime tax and bond policies. See also Sidney Ratner, *Taxation and Democracy in America* (1967), and Dale N. Shook, *William G. McAdoo and the Development of National Economic Policy, 1913–1918* (1987).

GOVERNMENT PROPAGANDA AND REPRESSION Stephen Vaughn, *Holding Fast the Inner Lines: Democracy, Nationalism, and the Committee on Public Information* (1980), is an important account of the CPI, the government's central propaganda agency. See also George Creel, *How We Advertised America* (1920); John A. Thompson, *Reformers and War: Progressive Publicists and the First World War* (1987); and Walton Rawls, *Wake Up, America! World War I and the American Poster* (1987). The government's turn to repression as a way of achieving social unity can be followed in Zechariah Chafee Jr., *Free Speech in the United States* (1941); Harry N. Scheiber, *The Wilson Administration and Civil Liberties, 1917–1921* (1960); Harold C. Peterson and Gilbert Fite, *Opponents of War, 1917–1918* (1968); and William Preston Jr., *Aliens and Dissenters: Federal Suppression of Radicals, 1903–1933* (1966). John Higham, *Strangers in the Land: Patterns of American Nativism, 1865–1925* (1955), and Frederick C. Luebke, *Bonds of Loyalty: German-Americans and World War I* (1974), analyze the effects of this repression on European ethnic communities. Carol S. Gruber, *Mars and Minerva: World War I and the Uses of Higher Learning in America* (1975), discusses the effect of war on universities.

WOODROW WILSON AND THE LEAGUE OF NATIONS The best introduction is Thomas J. Knock, *To End All Wars: Woodrow Wilson and the Quest for a New World Order* (1992). For a more critical view of Wilson's motives, however, consult Arno Mayer, *The Politics and Diplomacy of Peacemaking: Containment and Counterrevolution at Versailles, 1918–1919* (1967); N. Gordon Levin Jr., *Woodrow Wilson and World Politics: America's Response to War and Revolution* (1968); and Lloyd C. Gardner, *Safe for Democracy: The Anglo-American Response to Revolution, 1913–1923* (1984). On Republican opposition to the League of Nations, see Ralph Stone, *The Irreconcilables: The Fight against the League of Nations* (1970), and William C. Widenor, *Henry Cabot Lodge and the Search for an American Foreign Policy* (1980).

POSTWAR STRIKES AND RADICALISM Nell Irvin Painter, *Standing at Armageddon: The United States, 1877–1919* (1987), offers a good overview of the class and racial divisions that convulsed American society in 1919. Consult Dana Frank, *Purchasing Power: Consumer Organizing, Gender, and the Seattle Labor Movement, 1919–1929* (1994), on the Seattle general strike; Francis Russell, *A City in Terror* (1975), on the Boston police strike; and David Brody, *Labor in Crisis: The Steel Strike of 1919* (1965), on the steel strike. James Weinstein, *The Decline of Socialism in America, 1912–1925* (1967), and Theodore Draper, *The Roots of American Communism* (1957), analyze the effects of the Bolshevik Revolution on American socialism. On the Red Scare, consult Robert K. Murray, *Red Scare: A Study in National Hysteria* (1955); Stanley Coben, *A. Mitchell Palmer: Politician* (1963); and Richard Polenberg, *Fighting Faiths: The Abrams Case, the Supreme Court, and Free Speech* (1987). Roberta Strauss Feuerlicht, *Justice Crucified* (1977), and Francis Russell, *Tragedy in Dedham* (1962), offer divergent interpretations of the Sacco-Vanzetti affair. Paul Avrich, *Sacco-Vanzetti: The Anarchist Background* (1991), reconstructs the anarchist milieu from which Sacco and Vanzetti emerged.

RACE RIOTS AND BLACK NATIONALISM William Tuttle Jr., *Race Riot: Chicago in the Red Summer of 1919* (1970), and Elliott M. Rudwick, *Race Riot at East St. Louis* (1964), examine the two most notorious race riots of 1919. On the emergence of Marcus Garvey and the Universal Negro Improvement Association, see Judith Stein, *The World of Marcus Garvey: Race and Class in Modern Society* (1986), and David Cronon, *Black Moses* (1955).

Chapter 24

OVERVIEWS See William Leuchtenberg, *The Perils of Prosperity, 1914–1932* (1958); Geoffrey Perrett, *America in the Twenties* (1982); and Ellis Hawley, *The Great War and the Search for a Modern Order: A History of the American People and Their Institutions, 1917–1933* (1979). Frederick Lewis Allen, *Only Yesterday* (1931), remains the most entertaining account of the Jazz Age.

Prosperity and a Consumer Society George Soule, *Prosperity Decade: From War to Depression, 1917–1929* (1947), offers a thorough analysis of the decade's principal economic developments. Alfred D. Chandler Jr., *Strategy and Structure: Chapters in the History of the American Enterprise* (1962), and Adolph A. Berle Jr. and Gardiner F. Means, *The Modern Corporation and Private Property* (1932), examine changes in the structure and management of corporations. Important works on the consumer revolution include Robert S. Lynd and Helen Merrell Lynd, *Middletown: A Study in Modern American Culture* (1929); Warren I. Susman, *Culture as History: The Transformation of American Society in the Twentieth Century* (1984); Stewart Ewen, *Captains of Consciousness: Advertising and the Social Roots of the Consumer Culture* (1976); Roland Marchand, *Advertising the American Dream: Making Way for Modernity, 1920–1940* (1985); Richard Wightman Fox and T. J. Jackson Lears, eds., *The Culture of Consumption: Critical Essays in American History, 1880–1980* (1983); Kathy Lee Peiss, *Hope in a Jar: The Making of America's Beauty Culture* (1998); and Jackson Lears, *Fables of Abundance: A Cultural History of Advertising in America* (1994). The ways in which consumer ideals reshaped gender roles and family life can be followed in Ruth Schwartz Cowan, *More Work for Mother* (1982); William Chafe, *The American Woman: Her Changing Social, Economic, and Political Role* (1972); Dorothy M. Brown, *Setting a Course: American Women in the 1920s* (1987); Paula S. Fass, *The Damned and the Beautiful: American Youth in the 1920s* (1977); and Ben B. Lindsay and Wainright Evans, *The Companionate Marriage* (1927).

Republican Politics John D. Hicks, *Republican Ascendancy, 1921–1933* (1960), and Arthur M. Schlesinger Jr., *The Crisis of the Old Order* (1957), are excellent introductions to national politics during the 1920s. On Harding, see Robert K. Murray, *The Politics of Normalcy: Governmental Theory and Practice in the Harding-Coolidge Era* (1973), and Eugene Trani and David Wilson, *The Presidency of Warren G. Harding* (1977). William Allen White, *A Puritan in Babylon* (1939), is a colorful portrait of Calvin Coolidge; but see also Donald McCoy, *Calvin Coolidge: The Quiet President* (1967), and Thomas B. Silver, *Coolidge and the Historians* (1982). On Hoover's efforts to substitute "associational" politics for laissez-faire, two indispensable sources are Ellis Hawley, ed., *Herbert Hoover as Secretary of Commerce: Studies in New Era Thought and Practice* (1974), and Joan Hoff Wilson, *Herbert Hoover: Forgotten Progressive* (1975); see also David Burner, *Herbert Hoover: A Public Life* (1979). On Republican foreign policy, see Thomas Buckley, *The United States and the Washington Conference* (1970); Dexter Perkins, *Charles Evans Hughes and American Democratic Statesmanship* (1953); Joan Hoff Wilson, *American Business and Foreign Policy, 1920–1933* (1971); Warren I. Cohen, *Empire without Tears* (1987); Derek A. Aldcroft, *From Versailles to Wall Street, 1919–1929* (1977); and Robert H. Ferrell, *Peace in Their Time* (1952).

Agricultural Distress and Prohibition On agricultural distress and protest, see Gilbert Fite, *George Peek and the Fight for Farm Parity* (1954), and Theodore Saloutos and John D. Hicks, *Twentieth Century Populism: Agricultural Discontent in the Middle West, 1900–1939* (1951). For an examination of the economic and social effects of Prohibition, consult Andrew Sinclair, *The Era of Excess* (1962); Norman Clark, *Deliver Us from Evil: An Interpretation of American Prohibition* (1976); Mark Thornton, *The Economics of Prohibition* (1991); and John C. Burnham, *Bad Habits: Drinking, Smoking, Taking Drugs, Gambling, Sexual Misbehavior, and Swearing in American History* (1993).

Nativism, Ku Klux Klan, and Immigration Restriction John Higham, *Strangers in the Land: Patterns of American Nativism, 1865–1925* (1955), remains the best work on the spirit of intolerance that gripped America in the 1920s. On the 1920s resurgence of the Ku Klux Klan, consult David Chalmers, *Hooded Americanism: The History of the Ku Klux Klan* (1965); Kenneth Jackson, *The Ku Klux Klan in the City* (1965); Nancy MacLean, *Behind the Mask of Chivalry: The Making of the Second Ku Klux Klan* (1994); Leonard J. Moore, *Citizen Klansmen: The Ku Klux Klan in Indiana, 1921–1928* (1991); Katherine M. Blee, *Women of the Klan: Racism and Gender in the 1920s* (1991); and Shawn Lay, ed., *The Invisible Empire in the West: Toward a New Historical Appraisal of the Ku Klux Klan of the 1920s* (1992). The movement for immigration restriction is examined in William S. Bernard, *American Immigration Policy: A Reappraisal* (1950); Robert A. Divine, *American Immigration Policy* (1957); and Henry B. Leonard, *The Open Gates: The Protest Against the Movement to Restrict Immigration, 1896–1924* (1980).

Liberal and Fundamentalist Protestantism Ferenc Morton Szasz, *The Divided Mind of Protestant America, 1880–1930* (1982), expertly analyzes the split in Protestant ranks between liberals and fundamentalists. On the fundamentalist movement itself, consult George S. Marsden, *Fundamentalism in American Culture* (1980); Norman Furniss, *The Fundamentalist Controversy, 1918–1931* (1954); and William G. McLoughlin, *Modern Revivalism* (1959). Ray Ginger, *Six Days or Forever? Tennessee versus John Thomas Scopes* (1958), is a colorful account of the Scopes trial, while Lawrence Levine, *Defender of the Faith: William Jennings Bryan: The Last Decade, 1915–1925* (1965), offers a sympathetic portrait of Bryan during his final years. For a provocative reading of the Scopes trial, see Garry Wills, *Under God: Religion and American Politics* (1990).

INDUSTRIAL WORKERS Irving Bernstein, *The Lean Years: A History of the American Worker, 1920–1933* (1960), remains the most thorough examination of 1920s workers, but it should be supplemented with Robert H. Zeiger, *American Workers, American Unions, 1920–1985* (1986); Melvyn Dubofsky and Warren Van Tine, *John L. Lewis: A Biography* (1977); Leslie Tentler, *Wage-Earning Women* (1979); and Jacquelyn Hall et al., *Like a Family: The Making of a Southern Cotton Mill World* (1987). Siegfried Giedion, *Mechanization Takes Command: A Contribution to Anonymous History* (1948), is an insightful account of the effects of mechanization.

EUROPEAN AMERICAN ETHNIC COMMUNITIES On ethnic communities and Americanization in the 1920s, see Gary Gerstle, *Working-Class Americanism: The Politics of Labor in a Textile City, 1914–1960* (1989); Lizabeth Cohen, *Making a New Deal: Industrial Workers in Chicago, 1919–1939* (1990); and Stephen J. Shaw, *The Catholic Parish as a Way-Station of Ethnicity and Americanization: Chicago's Germans and Italians, 1903–1939* (1991). Leonard Dinnerstein, *Antisemitism in America* (1994), analyzes the resurgence of antisemitism in the 1920s and the use of quotas by universities to limit the enrollment of Jews. On the growing political strength of European American ethnics, see David Burner, *The Politics of Provincialism* (1967); Oscar Handlin, *Al Smith and His America* (1958); Paula Elder, *Governor Alfred E. Smith: The Politician as Reformer* (1983); and Kristi Andersen, *The Creation of a Democratic Majority, 1928–1936* (1979).

AFRICAN AMERICANS Good studies of the African American experience in the 1920s include Gilbert Osofsky, *Harlem: The Making of a Ghetto: Negro New York, 1890–1930* (1963); Kenneth L. Kusmer, *A Ghetto Takes Shape: Black Cleveland, 1870–1930*; Joe William Trotter Jr., *Black Milwaukee: The Making of an Industrial Proletariat, 1915–1945* (1985); and August Meier and Elliott Rudwick, *Black Detroit and the Rise of the UAW* (1979). Kathy H. Ogren, *The Jazz Revolution: Twenties America and the Meaning of Jazz* (1989), offers a probing analysis of jazz's place in 1920s culture. On the Harlem Renaissance, see Nathan Huggins, *Harlem Renaissance* (1971); Cary D. Mintz, *Black Culture and the Harlem Renaissance* (1988); and Jervis Anderson, *This Was Harlem: A Cultural Portrait, 1900–1950* (1981). Arnold Rampersand, *The Life of Langston Hughes,* 2 vols. (1986–1988), and Robert E. Hemenway, *Zora Neale Hurston: A Literary Biography* (1977), are important biographical works on two leading African American literary figures.

MEXICAN AMERICANS On the 1920s experience of Mexican immigrants and Mexican Americans, see George J. Sánchez, *Becoming Mexican American: Ethnicity, Culture and Identity in Chicano Los Angeles, 1900–1945* (1993); David Montejano, *Anglos and Mexicans in the Making of Texas, 1836–1986* (1987); Ricardo Romo, *East Los Angeles: History of a Barrio* (1983); Mark Reisler, *By the Sweat of Their Brow: Mexican Immigrant Labor in the United States, 1900–1940* (1976); and Manuel Gamio, *The Life Story of the Mexican Immigrant* (1931).

THE "LOST GENERATION" AND DISILLUSIONED INTELLECTUALS Malcolm Cowley, *Exiles Return* (1934), is a marvelous account of the writers and artists who comprised the "lost generation." See also Arlen J. Hansen, *Expatriate Paris* (1990), and William Wiser, *The Great Good Place: American Expatriate Women in Paris* (1991). On the southern "Agrarians," see John Stewart, *The Burden of Time* (1965), and Paul K. Conkin, *Southern Agrarians* (1988). Frederick J. Hoffman, *The Twenties: American Writing in the Postwar Decade,* rev. ed. (1962), is a fine sampler of the decade's best fiction. For biographical treatments of some of the decade's notable writers, consult Cleanth Brooks, *William Faulkner: The Yoknapathwapha County* (1963); Joel Williamson, *William Faulkner and Southern History* (1993); Carlos Baker, *Hemingway: The Writer as Artist* (1965); Kim Townshend, *Sherwood Anderson* (1987); and Virginia S. Carr, *Dos Passos: A Life* (1984). For a provocative interpretation of the intertwined character of white and black literary cultures in 1920s New York, see Ann Douglas, *Terrible Honesty: Mongrel Manhattan in the 1920s* (1995).

POLITICAL THOUGHT Robert Crunden, *From Self to Society: Transition in American Thought, 1919–1941* (1972), and Roderick Nash, *The Nervous Generation: American Thought, 1917–1930* (1969), are superior analyses of intellectual thought during the decade. On Mencken, see George H. Douglas, *H. L. Mencken* (1978), and Edward A. Martin, *H. L. Mencken and the Debunkers* (1984). Ronald Steel, *Walter Lippmann and the American Century* (1980), and Robert Westbrook, *John Dewey and American Democracy* (1991), are the best biographies of these two critical thinkers. On the new reform vanguard that began to form around Sidney Hillman, Franklin Roosevelt, and others, see Steven Fraser, *Labor Will Rule: Sidney Hillman and the Rise of American Labor* (1991), and Kenneth S. Davis, *FDR: The New York Years, 1928–1933* (1985).

Chapter 25

T. H. Watkins, *The Great Depression: America in the 1930s* (1993), provides a broad overview of society and politics during the 1930s. No work better conveys the tumult and drama of that era than Arthur M. Schlesinger Jr.'s three-volume *The Age of Roosevelt: The Crisis of the Old Order* (1957), *The Coming of the New Deal* (1958), and *The Politics of Upheaval* (1960).

CAUSES OF THE GREAT DEPRESSION On causes of the depression, consult John Kenneth Galbraith, *The Great Crash* (1955); Milton Friedman and Anna J. Schwartz, *The Great Contraction, 1929–1933* (1965); Michael A. Bernstein, *The Great Depression: Delayed Recovery and Economic Change in America, 1929–1939* (1987); Charles Kindelberger, *The World in Depression* (1973); and John A. Garraty, *The Great Depression* (1986).

HERBERT HOOVER On Hoover's failure to restore prosperity and popular morale, see Albert U. Romasco, *The Poverty of Abundance: Hoover, the Nation, the Depression* (1965), and David Burner, *Herbert Hoover: A Public Life* (1979). Roger Daniels, *The Bonus March* (1971), analyzes the event that became a symbol of Hoover's indifference to the depression's victims. More sympathetic treatments of Hoover's efforts to cope with the depression can be found in Harris G. Warren, *Herbert Hoover and the Great Depression* (1959); Joan Hoff Wilson, *Herbert Hoover: Forgotten Progressive* (1975); and Martin L. Fausold, *The Presidency of Herbert C. Hoover* (1985). Hoover offered his own spirited defense of his policies and a critique of the New Deal in his *Memoirs: The Great Depression* (1952).

FRANKLIN D. ROOSEVELT AND ELEANOR ROOSEVELT No 20th century president has attracted more scholarly attention than Franklin Roosevelt. The most detailed biography is Frank Freidel, *Franklin D. Roosevelt* (1952–1973), four volumes that cover Roosevelt's life from birth through the Hundred Days of 1933. The most complete biography, and one that is remarkably good at balancing Roosevelt's life and times, is Kenneth S. Davis, *FDR* (1972–1993), also in four volumes. Anyone interested in Roosevelt's youth and prepresidential career should consult Geoffrey Ward's *Before the Trumpet: Young Franklin Roosevelt, 1882–1905* (1985) and *A First-Class Temperament: The Emergence of Franklin Roosevelt* (1989). James McGregor Burns, *Roosevelt: The Lion and the Fox* (1956), offers an intriguing portrait of Roosevelt as president.

On Eleanor Roosevelt, see Lois Scharf, *Eleanor Roosevelt: First Lady of American Liberalism* (1987); Joseph P. Lash, *Eleanor and Franklin* (1981); and, most importantly, Blanche Wiesen Cook, *Eleanor Roosevelt*, vol. 1 (1992), which chronicles her life from birth until she moved into the White House in 1933.

NEW DEAL OVERVIEWS William E. Leuchtenberg, *Franklin D. Roosevelt and the New Deal, 1932–1940* (1963), is still an authoritative account of the New Deal, although it should be supplemented with Robert S. McElvaine, *The Great Depression* (1984). Both books treat the New Deal as a transformative moment in American politics and economics. For more critical interpretations of the New Deal, stressing the limited nature of the era's reforms, see Barton J. Bernstein, "The New Deal: The Conservative Achievements of Liberal Reform," in Barton J. Bernstein, ed., *Toward a New Past: Dissenting Essays in American History* (1968); Paul K. Conkin, *The New Deal* (1975); and Anthony J. Badger, *The New Deal: The Depression Years, 1933–1940* (1989). Barry D. Karl, *The Uneasy State: The United States from 1915–1945* (1983), and the essays in Steve Fraser and Gary Gerstle, eds., *The Rise and Fall of the New Deal Order, 1930–1980* (1989), offer new perspectives on the achievements and limitations of the New Deal.

FIRST NEW DEAL See Susan E. Kennedy, *The Banking Crisis of 1933* (1973), and Michael Parrish, *Securities Regulation and the New Deal* (1970), on the First New Deal's efforts to restructure the nation's financial institutions. On New Deal relief efforts, consult George T. McJimsey, *Harry Hopkins: Ally of the Poor and Defender of Democracy* (1987); John Salmond, *The Civilian Conservation Corps, 1933–42* (1967); Percy H. Merrill, *Roosevelt's Forest Army: A History of the Civilian Conservation Corps, 1933–1942* (1981); and Bonnie Fox Schwartz, *The Civilian Works Administration: The Business of Emergency Employment in the New Deal 1933–1934* (1984). James T. Patterson, *America's Struggle against Poverty, 1900–1980* (1981), contains a substantial section on New

Deal poor relief. For the New Deal's role in rebuilding the nation's infrastructure, see T. H. Watkins, *Righteous Pilgrim: The Life and Times of Harold Ickes, 1874–1952* (1990), and James S. Olson, *Saving Capitalism: The Reconstruction Finance Corporation and the New Deal, 1933–1940* (1988). Albert V. Romasco, *The Politics of Recovery: Roosevelt's New Deal* (1983), provides a useful overview of the First New Deal's efforts to restore prosperity.

FIRST NEW DEAL, AGRICULTURAL POLICY Van Perkins, *Crisis in Agriculture* (1969), and Theodore M. Saloutos, *The American Farmer and the New Deal* (1982), examine efforts to revive agriculture; David E. Conrad, *The Forgotten Farmers: The Story of Sharecroppers in the New Deal* (1965), and Paul Mertz, *The New Deal and Southern Rural Poverty* (1978), focus on groups ignored by New Deal programs. Donald Worster, *Dust Bowl: The Southern Plains in the 1930s* (1979), and James N. Gregory, *American Exodus: The Dust Bowl Migration and Okie Culture in California* (1989), are indispensable on the crisis in plains agriculture and the ensuing "Okie" migration.

FIRST NEW DEAL, INDUSTRIAL POLICY Ellis Hawley, *The New Deal and the Problem of Monopoly* (1966), is essential to understand the First New Deal's industrial policy. See also Bernard Bellush, *The Failure of the NRA* (1975); Michael Weinstein, *Recovery and Redistribution under the NRA* (1980); and Donald R. Brand, *Corporatism and the Rule of Law: A Study of the National Recovery Administration* (1988). On the TVA alternative, see Thomas K. McCraw, *TVA and the Power Fight, 1933–1939* (1971), and Walter L. Creese, *TVA's Public Planning: The Vision, the Reality* (1990).

POPULAR UNREST On populist critics of the New Deal, see Alan Brinkley, *Voices of Protest: Huey Long, Father Coughlin and the Great Depression* (1982); Michael Kazin, *The Populist Persuasion: An American History* (1995); and Abraham Holtzman, *The Townsend Movement* (1963). For the rebirth of the labor movement, consult Irving Bernstein, *The Turbulent Years: A History of the American Worker, 1933–1941* (1969); Lizabeth Cohen, *Making a New Deal: Industrial Workers in Chicago, 1919–1939* (1990); Gary Gerstle, *Working-Class Americanism: The Politics of Labor in a Textile City, 1914–1960* (1989); Jacquelyn Hall et al., *Like a Family: The Making of a Southern Cotton Mill World* (1987); Bruce Nelson, *Workers on the Waterfront: Seamen, Longshoremen, and Unionism in the 1930s* (1988); and Joshua B. Freeman, *In Transit: The Transport Workers Union in New York City, 1933–1966* (1989).

RADICAL POLITICS Richard M. Vallely, *Radicalism in the States: The Minnesota Farmer-Labor Party and the American Political Economy* (1989), and Greg Mitchell, *The Campaign of the Century: Upton Sinclair's EPIC Race for Governor of California and the Birth of Media Politics* (1992), analyze the upheaval in state politics that followed closely upon labor's resurgence. Irving Howe and Lewis Coser, *The American Communist Party: A Critical History, 1919–1957* (1957), is still the best single-volume history of the Communist Party during the 1930s. On the work of communists among the nation's dispossessed, see Mark Naison, *Communists in Harlem during the Depression* (1983); Robin D. G. Kelley, *Hammer and Hoe: Alabama Communists during the Great Depression* (1990); Dorothy Ray Healey and Maurice Isserman, *California Red: A Life in the American Communist Party* (1990); and Vicki Ruiz, *Cannery Women/Cannery Lives: Mexican Women, Unionization, and the California Food Processing Industry, 1930–1950* (1987).

THE SECOND NEW DEAL Steven Fraser, *Labor Will Rule: Sidney Hillman and the Rise of American Labor* (1991), is indispensable for understanding the ideology, programs, and personalities of the Second New Deal. On the forging of the 1936 Democratic coalition, see Kristi Andersen, *The Creation of a Democratic Majority, 1928–1936* (1979), and Nancy J. Weiss, *Farewell to the Party of Lincoln: Black Politics in the Age of FDR* (1983). Roy Lubove, *The Struggle for Social Security* (1968), and J. Joseph Huthmacher, *Senator Robert Wagner and the Rise of Urban Liberalism* (1968), provide in-depth analyses of the Social Security Act, Wagner Act, and other crucial pieces of Second New Deal legislation. For critical perspectives on these reforms that stress their limitations as well as their achievements, consult Christopher Tomlins, *The State and the Unions: Labor Relations, Law and the Organized Labor Movement in America, 1880–1960* (1985), and Mark Leff, *The Limits of Symbolic Reform: The New Deal and Taxation, 1933–1939* (1984). Important for understanding the role of capitalists and money in the New Deal coalition are Jordan A. Schwarz, *The New Dealers: Power Politics in the Age of Roosevelt* (1993); Robert A. Caro, *The Years of Lyndon Johnson: The Path to Power* (1981); and Colin Gordon, *New Deals: Business, Labor, and Politics in America, 1920–1935* (1994).

NEW DEAL MEN, NEW DEAL WOMEN On the political and cultural style of New Deal men, see Peter H. Irons, *The New Deal Lawyers* (1982); Samuel I. Rosenman, *Working with Roosevelt* (1952); Joseph P. Lash, *Dealers and*

Dreamers: A New Look at the New Deal (1988); and Katie Louchheim, ed., *The Making of the New Deal: The Insiders Speak* (1983). On New Deal women, consult Susan Ware, *Beyond Suffrage: Women in the New Deal* (1981), and *Partner and I: Molly Dewson, Feminism and New Deal Politics* (1987); also see Linda Gordon, *Pitied but Not Entitled: Single Mothers and the History of Welfare, 1890–1935* (1994). On feminist weakness and male anxiety during the depression, see Lois Scharf, *To Work and to Wed: Female Employment, Feminism, and the Great Depression* (1980); Winifred Wandersee, *Women's Work and Family Values, 1920–1940* (1981); and Alice Kessler-Harris, *Out to Work: A History of Wage-Earning Women in the United States* (1982). Elizabeth Faue, *Community of Suffering and Struggle: Women, Men, and the Labor Movement in Minneapolis, 1915–1945* (1991), is illuminating on the strident masculinism that dominated 1930s labor and popular culture.

LABOR AND THE CIO Melvyn Dubofsky and Warren Van Tine, *John L. Lewis: A Biography* (1977), is important on the birth of the CIO and labor's growing power in 1936 and 1937. Sidney Fine, *Sit-Down: The General Motors Strike of 1936–1937* (1967), is the most complete study of that pivotal event, but Nelson Lichtenstein, *"The Most Dangerous Man in Detroit": Walter Reuther and the Fate of American Labor* (1995), should be consulted for the broader industrial and union context in which it occurred. The best work on the centrality of labor and the "common man" to literary and popular culture in the 1930s is that of Michael Denning, *The Cultural Front: The Laboring of American Culture in the Twentieth Century* (1996); see also Richard H. Pells, *Radical Visions and American Dreams: Culture and Social Thought in the Depression Years* (1973). On the government's role in supporting public art through the WPA and other federal agencies, see William F. McDonald, *Federal Relief Administration and the Arts* (1968); Richard D. McKinzie, *The New Deal for Artists* (1973); and Barbara Melosh, *Engendering Culture: Manhood and Womanhood in New Deal Public Art and Theater* (1991).

MINORITIES AND THE NEW DEAL Harvard Sitkoff, *A New Deal for Blacks* (1978), is a wide-ranging examination of the place of African Americans in New Deal reform. See also John B. Kirby, *Black Americans in the Roosevelt Era: Liberalism and Race* (1980); Robert L. Zangrando, *The NAACP Crusade against Lynching, 1909–1950* (1980); and James Goodman, *Stories of Scottsboro* (1994). Abraham Hoffman, *Unwanted Mexican Americans in the Great Depression: Repatriation Pressures, 1929–1939* (1974), is the best introduction to the repatriation campaign. George J. Sánchez, *Becoming Mexican American: Ethnicity, Culture and Identity in Chicano Los Angeles, 1900–1945* (1993), reconstructs the experience of the largest Mexican urban settlement in 1930s America; and Cletus E. Daniel, *Bitter Harvest: A History of California Farmworkers, 1870–1941* (1981), shows how little Chicanos and other groups of agricultural laborers benefited from New Deal reform. On Native Americans, consult Francis Paul Prucha, *The Great Father: The United States Government and the American Indians* (1984), and Christine Bolt, *American Indian Policy and American Reform* (1987). The importance of John Collier and the Indian Reorganization Act are treated well in Lawrence C. Kelly, *The Assault on Assimilation: John Collier and the Origins of Indian Policy Reform* (1983), and Graham D. Taylor, *The New Deal and American Indian Tribalism: The Administration of the Indian Reorganization Act, 1934–1945* (1980). For more detailed examinations of particular tribes' encounters with the New Deal, see Donald L. Parman, *The Navajos and the New Deal* (1976), and Harry A. Kersey Jr., *The Florida Seminoles and the New Deal, 1933–1942* (1989).

EBBING OF NEW DEAL James T. Patterson, *Congressional Conservatism and the New Deal* (1967), expertly analyzes the growing congressional opposition to the New Deal in the late 1930s. See also Frank Freidel, *FDR and the South* (1965). Leonard Baker, *Back to Back: The Duel between FDR and the Supreme Court* (1967), chronicles the court-packing fight. Alan Brinkley, *The End of Reform: New Deal Liberalism in Recession and War* (1995), provocatively examines the efforts of New Dealers to adjust their beliefs and programs as they lost support, momentum, and confidence in the late 1930s.

Chapter 26

U.S ENTRY INTO THE SECOND WORLD WAR The U.S entry into the Second World War is analyzed in Arnold A. Offner, *The Origins of the Second World War: American Foreign Policy and World Politics, 1917–1941* (1975); Waldo H. Heinrichs, *Threshold of War: Franklin D. Roosevelt and American Entry into World War II* (1988); Michael A. Barnhart, *Japan Prepares for Total War: The Search for Economic Security* (1987); Robert Dallek, *Franklin D. Roosevelt and American Foreign Policy, 1932–1945* (1979); Robert Divine, *The Reluctant Belligerent: American Entry into World War II* (1965); Akira Iriye, *The Origins of the Second World War in Asia and the Pacific* (1987); Ralph E. Schaffer, ed., *Towards Pearl Harbor: The Diplomatic Interchange between Japan and the*

United States, 1899–1941 (1991); and Sabura Ienaga, *The Pacific War: World War II and the Japanese* (1978). On isolationism, see Manfred Jonas, *Isolationism in America, 1935–1941* (1966); Wayne S. Cole, *Roosevelt and the Isolationists, 1932–45* (1983); and Goeffrey S. Smith, *To Save a Nation: American "Extremism," the New Deal, and the Coming of World War II* (1992).

PEARL HARBOR Pearl Harbor itself is the subject of several books by Gordon N. Prange, including *At Dawn We Slept: The Untold Story of Pearl Harbor* (1981); and *December 7, 1941: The Day the Japanese Attacked Pearl Harbor* (1988). See also John Toland, *Infamy: Pearl Harbor and Its Aftermath* (1982), and Michael Slackman, *Target–Pearl Harbor* (1990).

CONDUCT AND DIPLOMACY OF THE WAR The conduct and diplomacy of the war can be surveyed in Alastair Parker, *The Second World War: A Short History* (1997); Gerhard L. Weinberg, *A World at Arms: A Global History of World War II* (1994); and Stephen E. Ambrose, *The American Heritage New History of World War II* (rev. ed., 1997) and *Citizen Soldiers* (1997). Other important studies include Martin Gilbert, *The Second World War: A Complete History* (1989); John Ellis, *Brute Force: Allied Strategy and Tactics in the Second World War* (1990); Michael J. Lyons, *World War II: A Short History* (1989); Gary R. Hess, *The United States at War, 1941–1945* (1986); Gaddis Smith, *American Diplomacy during the Second World War* (2nd ed., 1985); John Keegan, *The Second World War* (1989); Robert A. Divine, *Roosevelt and World War II* (1969) and *Second Chance: The Triumph of Internationalism in America during World War II* (1967); Mark Stoler, *The Politics of the Second Front: American Military Planning and Diplomacy in Coalition Warfare, 1941–1943* (1977); Ronald Schaffer, *Wings of Judgment: American Bombing in World War II* (1985); Michael S. Sherry, *The Rise of American Air Power: The Creation of Armageddon* (1987); D. Clayton James, *A Time for Giants: Politics of the American High Command in World War II* (1987); and Nathan Miller, *War at Sea: A Naval History of World War II* (1995). David Wyman, *The Abandonment of the Jews: America and the Holocaust, 1941–1945* (1984), and William B. Rubinstein, *The Myth of Rescue: Why the Democracies Could Not Have Saved More Jews from the Nazis* (1997), offer very different views of U.S. policy toward the Holocaust. See also Eric Markusen and David Kopf, *The Holocaust and Strategic Bombing: Genocide and Total War in the Twentieth Century* (1995), and Verne W. Newton, ed., *FDR and the Holocaust* (1996). Paul Fussell, *Wartime: Understanding and Behavior in the Second World War* (1989), examines life in the military, and David R. Segal, *Recruiting for Uncle Sam: Citizenship and Military Manpower Policy* (1989), discusses the selective service.

WAR IN THE PACIFIC On the war in the Pacific, see Christopher Thorne, *Allies of a Kind: The United States, Britain, and the War against Japan, 1941–1945* (1978); Ronald Lewin, *The American Magic: Codes, Ciphers, and the Defeat of Japan* (1983); Ronald H. Spector, *Eagle against the Sun: The American War with Japan* (1985); John Dower, *War without Mercy: Race and Power in the Pacific War* (1986); Akira Iriye, *Power and Culture: The Japanese-American War, 1941–1945* (1981); Michael Schaller, *The U.S. Crusade in China, 1938–1945* (1979) and *Douglas MacArthur: The Far Eastern General* (1989); Sheldon H. Harris, *Factories of Death: Japan's Biological Warfare 1932–45 and the American Cover-Up* (1994); Edward J. Drea, *MacArthur's ULTRA: Code Breaking and the War against Japan* (1992); Bartlett E. Kerr, *Flames over Tokyo* (1991); Kenneth P. Werrell, *Blankets of Fire: U.S. Bombers over Japan during World War II* (1996); John D. Chappell, *Before the Bomb: How America Approached the End of the Pacific War* (1997); and Gunter Bischof and Robert L. Dupont, eds., *The Pacific War Revisited* (1997).

INDIVIDUAL POLICYMAKERS Individual policymakers are treated in Warren Kimball, *The Juggler: Franklin Roosevelt as Wartime Statesman* (1991); Forrest C. Pogue, *George C. Marshall*, vols. 2 and 3 (1966, 1973); Stephen E. Ambrose, *Eisenhower* (1983); Michael Schaller, *Douglas MacArthur: The Far Eastern General* (1989); and James Hershberg, *James B. Conant: Harvard to Hiroshima and the Making of the Nuclear Age* (1993).

THE HOME FRONT The home front receives attention in John Morton Blum's *V Was for Victory: Politics and American Culture during World War II* (1976); William L. O'Neill, *A Democracy at War: America's Fight at Home and Abroad in World War II* (1993); Richard Polenberg's *War and Society: The United States 1941–1945* (1972); Allan M. Winkler, *Home Front U.S.A.: America during World War II* (1986); Gerald D. Nash, *The Great Depression and World War II: Organizing America, 1933–1945* (1979); William Tuttle, *Daddy's Gone to War: The Second World War in the Lives of America's Children* (1993); Michael C. C. Adams, *The Best War Ever: America and World War II* (1994); and John W. Jeffries, *Wartime America: The World War II Home Front* (1996). Geoffrey Perret, *Days of Sadness, Years of Triumph: The American People, 1939–1945* (1973), remains good reading; Studs Terkel, *"The Good War": An Oral History of World War II* (1984), is a classic. Helpful works on the economy and labor include Paul A. C. Koistinen, *The Military-Industrial Complex: A Historical Perspective* (1980); Stephen B. Adams, *Mr. Kaiser Goes to War* (1998); James B. Atleson, *Labor and the Wartime State: Labor Relations and Law during World War II* (1998); Nelson Lichtenstein, *Labor's War at Home: The CIO in World War II* (1982); Bartholomew H. Sparrow, *From the Outside In: World War II and the American State* (1996); and George Lipsitz, *Rainbow at Midnight: Labor and Culture in the 1940s* (1994).

CHANGING GENDER RELATIONS ON THE HOME FRONT Major studies on the changing gender relations on the home front include Leila J. Rupp, *Mobilizing Women for War: German and American Propaganda, 1939–1945* (1978), a comparative study of the United States and Germany; Karen Anderson, *Wartime Women: Sex Roles, Family Relations, and the Status of Women during World War II* (1981); D'Ann Campbell, *Women at War with America: Private Lives in a Patriotic Era* (1984); Susan Hartman *The Home Front and Beyond: American Women in the 1940s* (1982); Ruth Milkman, *Gender at Work: The Dynamics of Job Segregation during World War II* (1987); and Sherna Berger Gluck, *Rosie the Riveter Revisited: Women, the War, and Social Change* (1988). See also Glen Jeansonne, *Women of the Far Right: The Mothers' Movement and World War II* (1996). Judy Barrett Litoff and David C. Smith, eds., *Since You Went Away: World War II Letters from American Women on the Home Front* (1991), is a moving compilation. John Costello, *Virtue under Fire: How World War II Changed Our Social and Sexual Attitudes* (1985), and Allan Berube, *Coming Out Under Fire: The History of Gay Men and Women in World War II* (1990), discuss changing sexual politics.

RACE AND THE HOME FRONT On issues of race and the home front, see Peter Irons *Justice at War* (1993); Roger Daniels, *Concentration Camps U.S.A.: Japanese Americans and World War II* (1989); Mauricio Mazon, *The Zoot-Suit Riots: The Psychology of Symbolic Annihilation* (1984); Neil Wynn, *The Afro-American and the Second World War* (1993); Dominic J. Capeci Jr. and Martha Wilkerson, *Layered Violence: The Detroit Rioters of 1943* (1991); Alison Bernstein, *American Indians and World War II: Toward a New Era in Indian Affairs* (1991); Clete Daniel, *Chicano Workers and the Politics of Fairness* (1991); and Merl E. Reed, *Seedtime for the Modern Civil Rights Movement: The President's Committee on Fair Employment Practice, 1941–1946* (1991).

THE PEACE MOVEMENT AND PACIFISM The peace movement and pacifism are examined in Lawrence Wittner, *Rebels against War: The American Peace Movement, 1941–1960* (1969); Cynthia Eller, *Conscientious Objectors and the Second World War: Moral and Religious Arguments in Support of Pacifism* (1991); Heather T. Frazier and John O'Sullivan, "*We Have Just Begun to Not Fight": An Oral History of Conscientious Objectors in Civilian Public Service during World War II* (1996); and Rachel Waltner Goosen, *Women against the Good War* (1998).

CULTURE DURING THE WAR On culture during the war, see Lewis A. Erenberg and Susan E. Hirsch, eds., *The War in American Culture: Society and Consciousness during World War II* (1996), and Lawrence Samuel, *Pledging Allegiance: American Identity and the Bond Drive of World War II* (1997). Thomas Patrick Doherty, *Projections of War: Hollywood, American Culture, and World War II* (1993), Clayton Koppes and Gregory D. Black, *Hollywood Goes to War; How Politics, Profits & Propaganda Shaped World War II Movies* (1987), and John Whiteclay Chambers II and David Culbert, *World War II, Film, and History* (1996), concentrate on film. Allan M. Winkler, *The Politics of Propaganda: The Office of War Information, 1942–1945* (1978), covers propaganda; Frank W. Fox, *Madison Avenue Goes to War* (1975), describes wartime advertising; and Robin Winks *Cloak and Gown: Scholars in the Secret War, 1939–1961* (1987), describes academic ties to government policy. Karl Ann Marling and John Wetenhall, *Iwo Jima: Monuments, Memory, and the American Hero* (1991), and George H. Roeder Jr., *The Censored War: American Visual Experience during World War II* (1993), both deal with the popular memory of the war.

WARTIME DIPLOMACY AND POSTWAR SETTLEMENTS On wartime diplomacy and postwar settlements, see Gabriel Kolko, *The Politics of War: The World and the United States Foreign Policy, 1943–1945* (1990); Remi Nadeau, *Stalin, Churchill and Roosevelt Divide Europe* (1990); Randall B. Woods and Howard Jones, *Dawning of the Cold War: The United States' Quest for Order* (1991); Diane S. Clemens, *Yalta* (1970); Randall B. Woods, *A Changing of the Guard: Anglo-American Relations, 1941–1946* (1990); and Michael Schaller, *The American Occupation of Japan: The Origins of the Cold War in Asia* (1985).

DROPPING OF THE ATOMIC BOMB The dropping of the atomic bomb has attracted a large and impressive literature. Good starting places for understanding the various controversies are Michael J. Hogan, ed., *Hiroshima in History and Memory* (1996); Edward J. Linenthal and Tom Engelhardt, *History Wars: The Enola Gay and*

Other Battles for the American Past (1996); and J. Samuel Walker, *Prompt and Utter Destruction: Truman and the Use of Atomic Bombs against Japan* (1997). Major works on this topic, from various perspectives, include Martin Sherwin, *A World Destroyed: The Atomic Bomb and the Grand Alliance* (1975); Barton J. Bernstein, *The Atomic Bomb: The Critical Issues* (1976); Michael Mandelbaum, *The Nuclear Revolution: International Politics before and after Hiroshima* (1981); John Ray Skates, *The Invasion of Japan: Alternative to the Bomb* (1994); Peter Wyden, *Day One: Before Hiroshima and After* (1984); Richard Rhodes, *The Making of the Atomic Bomb* (1986); Gar Alperowitz, *The Decision to Use the Bomb and the Architecture of an American Myth* (1995); Robert Jay Lifton, *Hiroshima in America: Fifty Years of Denial* (1995); and Ronald Takaki, *Hiroshima: Why America Dropped the Atomic Bomb* (1995).

Videos There are many video sources on the Second World War. *How Hitler Lost the War* (1990) and *The Call to Glory* (1991) are useful. The original "Why We Fight" series, produced by Frank Capra during the war, remains an important primary source. *WW II—The Propaganda Battle* is a fascinating entry in the "Walk through the 20th Century" series, hosted by Bill Moyers. *Rosie the Riveter* (1980) is a documentary of women workers during the war. *Without Due Process* (1991) is a video account of the evacuation of Japanese Americans. On the development of the atomic bomb, see *Day after Trinity* (1980) and *J. Robert Oppenheimer: Father of the Atomic Bomb* (1995). *The Promised Land* (1995) is a three-part documentary on the African American migration from the Deep South to Chicago.

Chapter 27

U.S. Foreign Policy and the Origins of the Cold War For overviews of U.S. foreign policy and the origins of the Cold War, see Thomas G. Paterson, *Meeting the Communist Threat: Truman to Reagan* (1988); Thomas J. McCormick, *America's Half-Century: United States Foreign Policy in the Cold War and After* (2nd ed., 1995); Warren I. Cohen, *America in the Age of Soviet Power* (1993); Fraser J. Harbutt, *The Iron Curtain: Churchill, America, and the Origins of the Cold War* (1986); John Lewis Gaddis, *Strategies of Containment: A Critical Appraisal of Postwar American National Security Policy* (1982), his *The Long Peace: Inquiries into the History of the Cold War* (1987), and his *We Now Know: Rethinking Cold War History* (1997); Thomas G. Paterson, *On Every Front: The Making and Unmaking of the Cold War* (rev. ed., 1992); Walter LaFeber, *America, Russia, and the Cold War, 1945–1992* (7th ed., 1993); Stephen Ambrose, *Rise to Globalism: American Foreign Policy since 1938* (8th ed., 1997); H. W. Brands, *The Devil We Knew: Americans and the Cold War* (1993); Melvin Leffler, *The Specter of Communism* (1994); Deborah Welch Larson, *Anatomy of Mistrust: U.S.-Soviet Relations during the Cold War* (1997); and Ronald E. Powaksi, *The Cold War: The United States and the Soviet Union, 1917–1991* (1998).

Specific Issues and Incidents of the Cold War Era For the history of specific issues and incidents of the Cold War era, see Gregg Herken, *The Winning Weapon: The Atomic Bomb in the Cold War, 1945–1950* (1980); Walter Hixson, *George F. Kennan: Cold War Iconoclast* (1989); Bruce R. Kuniholm, *The Origins of the Cold War in the Near East: Great Power Conflict and Diplomacy in Iran, Turkey, and Greece* (1980); Michael Schaller, *The American Occupation of Japan: The Origins of the Cold War in Asia* (1985); Frank Ninkovich, *Germany and the United States: The Transformation of the German Question since 1945* (1988); Robert A. Pollard, *Economic Security and the Origins of the Cold War, 1945–1950* (1985); Michael J. Hogan, *The Marshall Plan: America, Britain, and the Reconstruction of Western Europe, 1949–52* (1987); Louis Liebovich, *The Press and the Origins of the Cold War, 1944–1947* (1988); Howard Jones, *"A New Kind of War": America's Global Strategy and the Truman Doctrine in Greece* (1989); Sallie Pisani, *The CIA and the Marshall Plan* (1991); Lawrence S. Wittner, *One World or None: A History of the World Nuclear Disarmament Movement through 1953* (1993); Steven Hugh Lee, *Outposts of Empire: Korea, Vietnam, and the Origins of the Cold War in Asia, 1949–84* (1995); Robert Accinelli, *Crisis and Commitment: United States Policy toward Taiwan, 1950–55* (1996); Michael L. Krenn, *The Chains of Interdependence: U.S. Policy toward Central America, 1945–1954* (1996); Richard Rhodes, *Dark Sun: The Making of the Hydrogen Bomb* (1995); and Justus D. Doenecke, *Not to the Swift: The Old Isolationists in the Cold War Era* (1979). A superb political history of the early Cold War years is James T. Patterson, *Grand Expectations: The United States, 1945–74* (1996).

National Security Policy On national security policy during the late 1940s and early 1950s consult Daniel Yergin, *Shattered Peace: The Origins of the Cold War and the National Security State* (1977); Melvyn Leffler, *A Preponderance of Power: National Security, the Truman Administration, and the Cold War* (1992); and Michael S. Sherry, *In the Shadow of War: The United States since the 1930s* (1995). See also Walter Isaacson and Evan

Thomas, *The Wise Men: Six Friends and the World They Made: Acheson, Bohlen, Harriman, Kennan, Lovett, McCloy* (1986), and Evan Thomas, *The Very Best Men: Four Who Dared; The Early Years of the CIA* (1995).

CULTURAL INTERPRETATIONS OF NATIONAL SECURITY POLICIES For cultural interpretations of national security policies see the relevant chapters of Richard Slotkin, *Gunfighter Nation: The Myth of the Frontier in Twentieth-Century America* (1992), and Robert J. Corber, *In the Name of National Security: Hitchcock, Homophobia, and the Political Construction of Gender in Postwar America* (1993). For broader views of the cultural climate of the early Cold War see Lary May, ed., *Recasting America: Culture and Politics in the Age of the Cold War* (1989); Stephen J. Whitfield, *The Culture of the Cold War* (2nd ed., 1996); William Graebner, *The Age of Doubt: American Thought and Culture in the 1940s* (1991); Paul Boyer, *By the Bomb's Early Light* (1985); Tom Englehardt, *The End of Victory Culture: Cold War America and the Disillusioning of a Generation* (1994); Guy Oakes, *The Imaginary War: Civil Defense and American Cold War Culture* (1994); Mark Jancovich, *Rational Fears: American Horror in the 1950s* (1996); Alan Nadel, *Containment Culture: American Narrative, Postmodernism, and the Atomic Age* (1995); and Margot A. Henriksen, *Dr. Strangelove's America: Society and Culture in the Atomic Age* (1997).

PRESIDENT TRUMAN Harry Truman enjoys a number of good biographical treatments. See Robert H. Ferrell, *Harry S Truman and the Modern American Presidency* (1983) and *Harry S. Truman: A Life* (1994); Donald R. McCoy, *The Presidency of Harry S. Truman* (1984); William E. Pemberton, *Harry S. Truman: Fair Dealer and Cold Warrior* (1988); David G. McCullough, *Truman* (1992); Alonzo L. Hamby, *Man of the People: A Life of Harry S. Truman* (1995); and Sean J. Savage, *Truman and the Democratic Party* (1998). Michael J. Lacey, ed., *The Truman Presidency* (1989), offers interpretive essays, while Alonzo L. Hamby, *Beyond the New Deal: Harry S Truman and American Liberalism* (1973), remains a useful look at Truman's Fair Deal that should be supplemented by the relevant chapter of the same author's *Liberalism and Its Challengers: Liberalism from FDR to Bush* (2nd ed., 1992). Steve Fraser and Gary Gerstle, eds., *The Rise and Fall of the New Deal Order, 1930–1980* (1989), takes a longer view of postwar themes.

DOMESTIC POLICYMAKING DURING THE FAIR DEAL On domestic policymaking during the Fair Deal, see R. Alton Lee, *Truman and Taft-Hartley: A Question of Mandate* (1966); Kevin Boyle, *The UAW and the Heyday of American Liberalism, 1945–1968* (1997); Allen J. Matusow, *Farm Policies and Politics in the Truman Years* (1967); Richard O. Davies, *Housing Reform during the Truman Administration* (1966); Susan M. Hartmann, *Truman and the 80th Congress* (1971); Monte M. Poen, *Harry S. Truman versus the Medical Lobby: The Genesis of Medicare* (1979); Andrew J. Dunar, *The Truman Scandals and the Politics of Morality* (1984); the relevant chapters of Edward D. Berkowitz, *America's Welfare State: From Roosevelt to Reagan* (1991); and Sheryl R. Tynes, *Turning Points in Social Security: From "Cruel Hoax" to "Sacred Entitlement"* (1996).

ANTICOMMUNISM Anticommunism is the subject of M. J. Heale, *American Anticommunism: Combating the Enemy Within, 1880–1970* (1990), and Richard Gid Powers, *Not without Honor: The History of American Anticommunism* (1995), both of which take the long view. Fred Inglis, *The Cruel Peace: Everyday Life in the Cold War* (1991), offers an international perspective. Allen Weinstein's *Perjury: The Hiss Chambers Case* (rev. ed., 1997) is an important, once controversial study which is now bolstered by, among other recent works, Joseph Albright and Marcia Kunstel, *Bombshell: The Secret Story of America's Unknown Atomic Spy Conspiracy* (1997); Sam Tanenhaus, *Whittaker Chambers: A Biography* (1997); and *Secrecy: Report of the Commission on Protecting and Reducing Government Secrecy* (1997). Richard M. Fried, *Nightmare in Red: The McCarthy Era in Perspective* (1990), and Ellen Schrecker, *The Age of McCarthyism: A Brief History with Documents* (1994), are solid syntheses, but David Caute's *The Great Fear: The Anti-Communist Purge under Truman and Eisenhower* (1978) remains the most detailed account. See also Michael R. Belknap, *Cold War Political Justice: The Smith Act, the Communist Party, and American Civil Liberties* (1977); Stanley I. Kutler, *The American Inquisition: Justice and Injustice in the Cold War* (1982); Marjorie Garber and Rebecca L. Walkowitz, eds., *Secret Agents: The Rosenberg Case, McCarthyism, and Fifties America* (1995); and John F. Neville, *The Press, the Rosenbergs, and the Cold War* (1995).

SOCIAL CHANGES OF THE EARLY COLD WAR YEARS The social changes of the early Cold War years have drawn the attention of many recent historical works. For an interesting view, see Wendy Kozol, *Life's America: Family and Nation in Postwar Photojournalism* (1994). The baby boom is the focus of Richard A. Easterlin, *Birth and Fortune: The Impact of Numbers on Personal Welfare* (2nd ed., 1987), and Landon Y. Jones, *Great Expectations: America and the Baby Boom Generation* (1980). See also the relevant chapters of John Modell, *Into One's Own: From Youth to Adulthood in the United States, 1920–1975* (1989). On women's issues, see the final chapters of

Susan Strasser, *Never Done: A History of American Housework* (1982); Alice Kessler-Harris, *Out to Work: A History of Wage-Earning Women in the United States* (1982); Jacqueline Jones, *Labor of Love, Labor of Sorrow: Black Women, Work and the Family, from Slavery to the Present* (1985); Eugenia Kaledin, *Mothers and More: American Women in the 1950s* (1984); Leila Rupp and Verta Taylor, *Survival in the Doldrums: The American Women's Rights Movement, 1945 to the 1960s* (1990); and Cynthia Harrison, *On Account of Sex: The Politics of Women's Issues, 1945–68* (1988). Family and gender issues are nicely tied to Cold War culture in Elaine Tyler May, *Homeward Bound: American Families in the Cold War Era* (1989), and in Stephanie Coontz, *The Way We Never Were: American Families and the Nostalgia Trip* (1992). On issues related to sexuality and gender, see the relevant chapters of John D'Emilio and Estelle B. Freedman, *Intimate Matters: A History of Sexuality in America* (1988); Wini Breines, *Young, White, and Miserable: Growing Up Female in the Fifties* (1992); Graham McCann, *Rebel Males: Clift, Brando and Dean* (1993); and Joanne Meyerowitz, ed., *Not June Cleaver: Women and Gender in Postwar America, 1945–1960* (1994).

SUBURBAN AND URBAN ISSUES On suburban and urban issues, see Robert A. Caro, *The Power Broker: Robert Moses and the Fall of New York* (1974); Mark Gelfand, *A Nation of Cities: The Federalist Government and Urban America, 1933–1945* (1975); Herbert Gans, *The Levittowners: Ways of Life and Politics in a New Suburban Community* (2nd ed., 1982); the relevant chapters of Kenneth T. Jackson, *Crabgrass Frontier: The Suburbanization of the United States* (1985); Barbara M. Kelly, *Expanding the American Dream: Building and Rebuilding Levittown* (1993); and Rob Kling, Spencer Olin, and Mark Poster, *Postsuburban California: The Transformation of Orange County since World War II* (1991). See also John M. Findlay, *Magic Lands: Western City Scapes and American Culture after 1940* (1992); David L. Kirp, John P. Dwyer, and Larry A. Rosenthal, *Our Town: Race, Housing and the Soul of Suburbia* (1995); John R. Gillis, *A World of their Own: Myth, Ritual, and the Quest for Family Values* (1996); Jon C. Teaford, *The Rough Road to Renaissance: Urban Revitalization in America, 1940–85* (1990) and *Post-Suburbia: Government and the Politics in the Edge Cities* (1997); Alan Ehrenhalt, *The Lost City: Discovering the Forgotten Virtues of Community in the Chicago of the 1950s* (1995); Michael F. Logan, *Fighting Sprawl and City Hall: Resistance to Urban Growth in the Southwest* (1995); and James Hudnut-Beumler, *Looking for God in the Suburbs: the Religion of the American Dream and Its Critics, 1945–1965* (1994). Thomas J. Sugrue, *The Origins of the Urban Crisis: Race and Inequality in Postwar Detroit* (1996), is a recent, award-winning study.

THE KOREAN WAR On the Korean War, Burton I. Kaufman, *The Korean War: Challenges in Crisis, Credibility, and Command* (1986), is a brief synthesis. More detailed analyses may be found in several volumes by Bruce Cumings: *The Origins of the Korean War* (1981); *Child of Conflict: The Korean-American Relationship, 1943–53* (1983), a series of essays that he edited; and *Korea: The Unknown War* (coauthored with Jon Halliday) (1988). See also William Stueck, *The Korean War: An International History* (1995); Chen Jian, *China's Road to the Korean War: The Making of the Sino-American Confrontation* (1994); Shu Guang Zhang, *Mao's Military Romanticism: China and the Korean War, 1950–1953* (1995); and William T. Bowers, William M. Hammond, and George L. MacGarrigle, *Black Soldier, White Army: The 24th Infantry Regiment in Korea* (1996).

THE EISENHOWER YEARS The Eisenhower years received an early scholarly synthesis in Charles C. Alexander, *Holding the Line: The Eisenhower Era, 1952–1960* (1975), which can be updated with Chester Pach Jr. and Elmo Richardson, *The Presidency of Dwight D. Eisenhower* (rev. ed., 1991); Robert F. Burk, *Dwight David Eisenhower* (1986); William B. Pickett, *Dwight David Eisenhower and American Power* (1995); the relevant chapter of Hamby, *Liberalism and Its Challengers* (2nd ed., 1992); and Jeff Broadwater, *Eisenhower and the Anti-Communist Crusade* (1992). Stephen E. Ambrose's massive two-volume study *Eisenhower* (1983, 1984) contains a wealth of information. *Adlai Stevenson and American Politics: The Odyssey of a Cold War Liberal* (1994), by Jeff Broadwater, is a solid biography of the man twice defeated by Eisenhower for the presidency. Fred I. Greenstein, *The Hidden-Hand Presidency: Eisenhower as Leader* (rev. ed., 1994) helped to begin the trend toward a new view of Eisenhower's presidency.

VIDEOS *March of Time: American Lifestyles* (1987) is a five-video compilation taken from newscasts of the period. *Post-War Hopes, Cold War Fears*, from the "Walk through the 20th Century" series, offers an interesting overview. For a visual recounting of the beginning of U.S. involvement in the Vietnam War, see *The First Vietnam War (1946–1954)*, a one-hour video documentary in the series "Vietnam: A Television History." *The Rise of J. Edgar Hoover* (1991) is a superb video documentary in the "American Experience" series. *The Forgotten War* (1987) is a three-part video documentary on Korea. *Truman* (1997) and *Ike*, formally titled *Eisenhower* (1993), are solid entries in PBS's "The White House Collection." *George Marshall and the American Century* (1993) offers a sweeping overview of Eisenhower's important military benefactor, while *The Marshall Plan: Against All Odds* (1997) covers Marshall's most important Cold War initiative. *Adlai Stevenson: The Man from Libertyville* (1992) is a video portrait of the Democrat who was twice defeated by Eisenhower for the presidency. *Seeing Red* (1993) looks, with considerable compassion, on the people who supported the Communist Party. The anticommunist crusade in Hollywood is the subject of *Hollywood on Trial* (1976) and *Legacy of the Hollywood Blacklist* (1987). *Point of Order: A Documentary of the Army-McCarthy Hearings* (1964) is a classic documentary on the congressional hearings that marked the beginning of McCarthy's demise.

Chapter 28

EISENHOWER'S FOREIGN POLICY Robert Divine, *Eisenhower and the Cold War* (1981), and Blanche Wiesen Cook, *The Declassified Eisenhower* (1981), offer differing interpretations of Eisenhower's foreign policies. See also Joann P. Krieg, ed., *Dwight D. Eisenhower: Soldier, President and Statesman* (1987), and H. W. Brands, *Cold Warriors: Eisenhower's Generation and American Foreign Policy* (1988). See also the many works on Eisenhower which are cited in Chapter 27.

SPECIALIZED STUDIES ON FOREIGN POLICY More specialized studies on foreign policy include Robert Divine, *Blowing in the Wind: The Nuclear Test-Ban Debate* (1978) and *The Sputnik Challenge: Eisenhower's Response to the Soviet Satellite* (1993); Allan M. Winkler, *Life under a Cloud: American Anxiety about the Atom* (1993); Stuart W. Leslie, *The Cold War and American Science: The Military-Industrial-Academic Complex at MIT and Stanford* (1993). Regional studies include Stephen G. Rabe, *Eisenhower and Latin America: The Foreign Policy of Anticommunism* (1988); Zhang Shu Guang, *Deterrence and Strategic Culture Culture: Chinese-American Confrontations, 1949–1958* (1992); Robert J. McMahon, *The Cold War on the Periphery: The United States, India and Pakistan* (1994); Kenton J. Clymer, *Quest for Freedom: The United States and India's Independence* (1995); Isaac Alteras, *Eisenhower and Israel: U.S.-Israeli Relations, 1953–1960* (1993); Thomas G. Paterson, *Contesting Castro: The United States and the Triumph of the Cuban Revolution* (1994); Bonnie F. Saunders, *The United States and Arab Nationalism: The Syrian Case, 1953–1960* (1996); Saki Dockrill, *Eisenhower's New-Look National Security Policy, 1953–61* (1996); G. Wyn Rees, *Anglo-American Approaches to Alliance Security, 1955–60* (1996); and Cole C. Kingseed, *Eisenhower and Suez Crisis of 1956* (1995). The growing importance of intelligence agencies in foreign policy is examined in Stephen Ambrose and Richard H. Immerman, *Ike's Spies: Eisenhower and the Espionage Establishment* (1981) and *The CIA in Guatemala: The Foreign Policy of Intervention* (1982); Michael R. Beschloss, *Mayday: Eisenhower, Khrushchev, and the U-2 Affair* (1986); Rhodri Jeffreys-Jones, *The CIA and American Democracy* (1989); Loch K. Johnson, *America's Secret Power: The CIA in a Democratic Society* (1989); Thomas F. Troy, *Donovan and the CIA: A History of the Establishment of the Central Intelligence Agency* (1981); John Prados, *President's Secret Wars: CIA and Pentagon Covert Operations since World War II* (1986); Audrey R. Kahin and George McT. Kahin, *Subversion as Foreign Policy: The Secret Eisenhower and Dulles Debacle in Indonesia* (1995); and Nicholas Cullather, *Operation PSSUCCESS: The United States and Guatemala 1952–54* (1997). African Americans and foreign policy are discussed in Brenda Gayle Plummer, *Rising Wind: Black Americans and U.S. Foreign Affairs, 1935–1960* (1996), and Penny M. Von Eschen, *Race against Empire: Black Americans and Anticolonialism, 1937–1957* (1997). On cultural diplomacy, see especially Walter L. Hixson, *Parting the Curtain: Propaganda,Culture, and the Cold War, 1945–1961* (1997), and Robert H. Haddow, *Pavilions of Plenty: Exhibiting American Culture Abroad in the 1950s* (1997).

U.S. INVOLVEMENT IN VIETNAM On the deepening U.S. involvement in Vietnam, see David L. Anderson, *Trapped by Success: The Eisenhower Administration and Vietnam, 1953–1961* (1991); George Herring, *America's Longest War: The United States and Vietnam, 1950–1975* (1986); Andrew J. Rotter, *The Path to Vietnam: Origins of the American Commitment to Southeast Asia* (1987); Lloyd C. Gardner, *Approaching Vietnam: From World War II through Dien Bien Phu* (1988); James Arnold, *The First Domino: Eisenhower, the Military, and America's Intervention in Vietnam* (1991); and Melanie Billings-Yun, *Decision against War: Eisenhower and Dien Bien Phu, 1954* (1988).

DOMESTIC POLITICS Domestic politics are treated in Mark Rose, *Interstate: Express Highway Politics, 1941–1956* (1979); R. Alton Lee, *Eisenhower and Landrum Griffin: A Study in Labor-Management Politics* (1990); Richard Kluger, *Simple Justice: The History of* Brown v. Board of Education *and Black America's Struggle for Equality* (1975); Austin Sarat, ed., *Race, Law, and Culture: Reflections on* Brown v. Board of Education

(1996); and Tom Lewis, *Divided Highways: Building the Interstate Highways, Transforming American Life* (1997). Clarence G. Lasby, *Eisenhower's Heart Attack: How Ike Beat Heart Disease and Held on to the Presidency* (1996), is an interesting account.

POSTWAR MASS CULTURE For overviews of postwar mass culture, see Andrew Ross, *No Respect: Intellectuals and Popular Culture* (1989); W. T. Lhamon Jr., *Deliberate Speed: The Origins of a Cultural Style in the American 1950s* (1990); Karal Ann Marling, *As Seen on TV: The Visual Culture of Everyday Life in the 1950s* (1994); and James L. Baughman, *The Republic of Mass Culture: Journalism, Filmmaking, and Broadcasting in America since 1941* (2nd ed., 1996). The debates over mass culture in the 1950s can be sampled in Bernard Rosenberg and David Manning White, *Mass Culture* (1957) and *Mass Culture Revisited* (1971). James Gilbert, *A Cycle of Outrage: America's Reaction to the Juvenile Delinquent in the 1950s* (1986), critiques this debate and relates it to an emerging youth culture. On TV, see Cecelia Tichi, *The Electronic Hearth* (1991), and Michael Curtin, *Redeeming the Wasteland: Television Documentary and Cold War Politics* (1995). On rock music, see Greil Marcus, *Mystery Train: Images of America in Rock n' Roll* (3rd ed., 1990); Charley Gillet, *Sound of the City: The Rise of Rock and Roll* (rev. ed., 1984); and Nelson George, *The Death of Rhythm and Blues* (1988). On the diversity of the youth culture, see William Graebner, *Coming of Age in Buffalo: Youth and Authority in the Postwar Era* (1989).

SOCIAL ISSUES On social issues, see Michael Harrington's classic *The Other America: Poverty in the United States* (1962); James T. Patterson, *America's Struggle against Poverty, 1900–1980* (1981); Doug McAdam, *Political Process and the Development of Black Insurgency, 1930–1970* (1982); Harvard Sitkoff, *The Struggle for Black Equality, 1954–1992* (1993); Larry Burt, *Tribalism in Crisis: Federal Indian Policy, 1953–1961* (1982); Donald L. Fixico, *Termination and Relocation: Federal Indian Policy, 1945–1960* (1986); Manuel Alers-Montalvo, *The Puerto Rican Migrants of New York* (1985); David Garrow, *Bearing the Cross: Martin Luther King, Jr., and the Southern Christian Leadership Conference* (1986); Joseph P. Fitzpatrick, *Puerto Rican Americans: The Meaning of Migration to the Mainland* (2nd ed., 1987); Taylor Branch, *Parting the Waters: America in the King Years, 1954–1963* (1988); Steven J. Whitfield, *A Death in the Delta: The Story of Emmett Till* (1988); Mario Garcia, *Mexican-Americans: Leadership, Ideology, Identity, 1930–1960* (1989); Ricardo Romo, *East Los Angeles: History of a Barrio* (1989); Armstead L. Robinson and Patricia Sullivan, eds., *New Directions in Civil Rights Studies* (1991); the relevant chapters of Jacqueline Jones, *The Dispossessed: America's Underclass from the Civil War to the Present* (1992); Mark V. Tushnet, *Making Civil Rights Law: Thurgood Marshall and the Supreme Court, 1936–1961* (1993); James F. Findlay, *Church People in the Struggle: The National Council of Churches and the Black Freedom Movement, 1950–1970* (1993); Maria Cristina Garcia, *Havana USA: Cuban Exiles and Cuban Americans in South Florida, 1959–1994* (1996); and David G. Gutierrez, *Walls and Mirrors: Mexican Americans, Mexican Immigrants, and the Politics of Ethnicity* (1995). Clayborne Carson, ed., *The Papers of Martin Luther King, Jr.* (vol 3, 1997) focuses on struggles during the Montgomery bus boycott; see also Richard Lischer, *The Preacher King: Martin Luther King, Jr. and the Words that Moved America* (1995); and Glenn T. Eskew, *But for Birmingham: The Local and National Movements in the Civil Rights Struggle* (1997). On civil rights issues during the Kennedy years, see Howard Zinn, *SNCC: The New Abolitionists* (1965); William Chafe, *Civilities and Civil Rights: Greensboro, North Carolina and the Black Struggle for Freedom* (1980); John Walton Cotman, *Birmingham, JFK, and the Civil Rights Act of 1963* (1989); Kenneth O'Reilly, *Racial Matters: The FBI's Secret Files on Black America, 1960–72* (1989); Mark Stern, *Calculating Visions: Kennedy, Johnson, and Civil Rights* (1992); and many of the works listed in Chapter 29.

JOHN F. KENNEDY Garry Wills, *Nixon Agonistes: The Crisis of the Self-Made Man* (rev. ed., 1980) and *The Kennedy Imprisonment: A Meditation on Power* (1983) offer critical viewpoints on John F. Kennedy, as does Thomas C. Reeves, *A Question of Character: A Life of John F. Kennedy* (1991). Seymour M. Hersh, *The Dark Side of Camelot* (1997), is an attempt to obliterate the Kennedy mystique. More favorable, though not uncritical, is David Burner, *John F. Kennedy and a New Generation* (1988). James N. Giglio's *The Presidency of John F. Kennedy* (1991) provides a reliable overview. For more detail, see Herbert J. Parmet's two volumes: *Jack: The Struggle of John F. Kennedy* (1980) and *JFK: The Presidency of John F. Kennedy* (1983). There are many sympathetic accounts of Kennedy's presidency by close associates; by far the best is Arthur Schlesinger Jr., *A Thousand Days* (1965). Specific policy decisions are the subject of Jim F. Heath, *John Kennedy and the Business Community* (1969); Victor Navasky, *Kennedy Justice* (1971); Carl M. Brauer, *John F. Kennedy and the Second Reconstruction* (1977); James R. Williamson, *Federal Antitrust Policy during the Kennedy-Johnson Years* (1995).

KENNEDY'S FOREIGN POLICY On Kennedy's foreign policy, see Thomas G. Paterson, ed., *Kennedy's Quest for Victory: American Foreign Policy, 1961–1963* (1989); Michael R. Beschloss, *The Crisis Years: Kennedy and Khrushchev, 1960–1963* (1991); and Noam Chomsky, *Rethinking Camelot: JFK, the Vietnam War, and U.S. Political Culture* (1993). A huge literature on the missile crisis in Cuba includes Graham T. Allison, *Essence of Decision: Explaining the Cuban Missile Crisis* (1971); Trumbell Higgins, *The Perfect Failure: Kennedy, Eisenhower, and the CIA at the Bay of Pigs* (1989); Dino A. Brugioni, *Eyeball to Eyeball: The Inside Story of the Cuban Missile Crisis* (1991); James Blight, *Cuba on the Brink: Castro, the Missile Crisis, and the Soviet Challenge* (1993); Mark J. White, *The Cuban Missile Crisis* (1996); John C. Ausland, *Kennedy, Khrushchev, and the Berlin-Cuba Crisis, 1961–1964* (1996); Timothy Naftali and Aleksandr Fursenko, *"One Hell of a Gamble": Khrushchev, Castro, and Kennedy, 1958–1964* (1997); and Ernest R. May and Philip D. Zelikow, eds., *The Kennedy Tapes: Inside the White House during the Cuban Missile Crisis* (1997).

KENNEDY'S DEATH Events surrounding Kennedy's death have attracted almost as much attention as his life. Michael J. Kurtz, *The Crime of the Century: The Kennedy Assassination from an Historian's Perspective* (1982), tries to offer historical grounding, while Barbie Zelizer, *Covering the Body: The Kennedy Assassination, the Media, and the Shaping of Collective Memory* (1992), is a superb cultural study. Theories of the assassination itself include Peter Dale Scott, *Deep Politics and the Death of JFK* (1993), which is critical of the Warren Commission's findings, and Gerald L. Posner, *Case Closed: Lee Harvey Oswald and the Assassination of JFK* (1993), which defends them. See also John Newman, *Oswald and the CIA* (1995).

VIDEOS *Eisenhower* (1993) is an excellent documentary in the "American Experience" series. *America's Mandarin (1954–1967)* is a one-hour video documentary of U.S. involvement in Vietnam, from Eisenhower to Johnson, in the series "Vietnam: A Television History" (1983). *The Quiz Show Scandal* (1991) and *That Rhythm, Those Blues* (1988) are solid entries in the "American Experience" series. The multipart documentary series "Eyes on the Prize" (1987) provides a dramatic, visual representation of the struggle for African American civil rights. *The Road to Brown* (1990) offers a a more limited, but still important, view. See also, *Dr. Martin Luther King Jr.: A Historical Perspective* (1993) and *Southern Justice: The Murder of Medger Evers* (1994). *The Kennedys* (1992) is a four-hour video documentary in the "American Experience" series. *Spy in the Sky* (1996) is the story of the U.S. reconnaissance program during the Eisenhower years. *Crisis: Missiles in Cuba* (1989) offers a brief, 30-minute overview.

Chapter 29

LYNDON JOHNSON On Lyndon Johnson see Paul K. Conkin, *Big Daddy from the Pedernales: Lyndon Baines Johnson* (1986); Robert Caro, *The Path to Power* (1982) and *Means of Ascent* (1990); Robert J. Dallek, *Lone Star Rising: Lyndon Johnson and His Times, 1908–1960* (1991); and Irving Bernstein, *Guns or Butter: The Presidency of Lyndon Johnson* (1996). Other titles include Vaughn Davis Bornet, *The Presidency of Lyndon Baines Johnson* (1993), which is relatively sympathetic, and Doris Kearns Goodwin, *Lyndon Johnson and the American Dream* (1976). Joseph A. Califano Jr., *The Triumph and Tragedy of Lyndon Johnson: The White House Years* (1991), is an interesting memoir, and Michael R. Beschloss, ed., *Taking Charge: The Johnson White House Tapes, 1963–1964* (1997), offers fascinating insights. On the Warren Court see Morton J. Horwitz, *The Warren Court and the Pursuit of Justice* (1998).

CIVIL RIGHTS Civil rights issues are treated in David Garrow, *Protest at Selma: Martin Luther King, Jr., and the Voting Rights Act of 1965* (1980); Clayborne Carson, *In Struggle: SNCC and the Black Awakening of the 1960s* (1981); Doug McAdam, *Freedom Summer* (1988); Emily Stoper, *The Student Non-Violent Coordinating Committee: The Growth of Radicalism in a Civil Rights Organization* (1989); Mark Stern, *Calculating Visions: Kennedy, Johnson, and Civil Rights* (1992); William L. Van Deburg, *New Day in Babylon: The Black Power Movement and American Culture, 1965–1975* (1992); Gerald Horne, *Fire This Time: The Watts Uprising and the 1960s* (1995); David J. Armor, *Forced Justice: School Desegregation and the Law* (1995); Richard Griswold del Castillo and Richard A. Garcia, *Cesar Chavez: A Triumph of Spirit* (1995); Louis A. DeCaro Jr., *On the Side of My People: A Religious Life of Malcolm X* (1996); Michael Eric Dyson, *Making Malcolm: The Myth and Meaning of Malcolm X* (1995); Charles M. Payne, *I've Got the Light of Freedom: The Organizing Tradition and the Mississippi Freedom Struggle* (1995); and Taylor Branch, *Pillar of Fire: America in the King Years, 1963–65* (1998).

THE GREAT SOCIETY AND THE WAR ON POVERTY The Great Society and the War on Poverty receive a critical assessment in Alan J. Matusow, *The Unraveling of America: A History of Liberalism in the 1960s* (1984). The most influential analysis from the right of Great Society liberalism has been Charles Murray's *Losing Ground: American Social Policy, 1950–1980* (1984), which can be compared with Christopher Jencks, *Rethinking Social Policy: Race, Poverty and the Underclass* (1992). A recent overview is Gareth Davies, *From Opportunity to Entitlement: The Transformation and Decline of Great Society Liberalism* (1996). See also Michael L. Gillette, *Launching the War on Poverty: An Oral History* (1996).

JOHNSON'S FOREIGN POLICIES Johnson's foreign policies are treated in Bernard Firestone and Robert C. Vogt, eds., *Lyndon Baines Johnson and the Uses of Power* (1988); Warren I. Cohen and Nancy Bernkopf Tucker, eds., *Lyndon Johnson Confronts the World: American Foreign Policy, 1963–1968* (1994); and Diane Kunz, ed., *The Diplomacy of the Crucial Decade: American Foreign Relations during the 1960s* (1994). On the Dominican intervention see Bruce Palmer Jr., *Intervention in the Caribbean: The Dominican Crisis of 1965* (1989), and Abraham F. Lowenthal, *The Dominican Intervention* (1995).

JOHNSON'S POLICIES IN VIETNAM Johnson's policies in Vietnam have attracted an immense literature. Representative titles include George Herring, *America's Longest War: The United States and Vietnam, 1950–1975* (1986); Marilyn Blatt Young, *The Vietnam-American Wars, 1945–1990* (1991); David L. DiLeo, *George Ball, Vietnam, and the Rethinking of Containment* (1991); Melvin Small, *Johnson, Nixon, and the Doves* (1988); Larry Berman, *Lyndon Johnson's War: The Road to Stalemate in Vietnam* (1989); Marilyn Young and Jon Livingston, *The Vietnam War: How the United States Intervened in the History of Southeast Asia* (1990); Gabriel Kolko, *Anatomy of War: Vietnam, The United States, and the Modern Historical Experience* (1994); Lloyd C. Gardner, *Approaching Vietnam: From World War II through Dien Bien Phu* (1988); George McT. Kahin, *Intervention: How America Became Involved in Vietnam* (1986); R. B. Smith, *An International History of the Vietnam War* (1983); James J. Wirtz, *The Tet Offensive: Intelligence Failure in War* (1991); Ronald Spector, *After Tet: The Bloodiest Year in Vietnam* (1993); David M. Barrett, *Uncertain Warriors: Lyndon Johnson and His Vietnam Advisors* (1993); David L. Anderson, ed., *Facing My Lai: Moving beyond the Massacre* (1997); Michael Hunt, *Lyndon Johnson's War: America's Cold War Crusade in Vietnam, 1945–1968* (1996); Robert Buzzanco, *Masters of War: Military Dissent and Politics in the Vietnam Era* (1996); Richard A. Hunt, *Pacification: The American Struggle for Vietnam's Hearts and Minds* (1995); Edwin Moise, *Tonkin Gulf and the Escalation of the Vietnam War* (1996); Roger Warner, *Back Fire: The CIA's Secret War in Laos and Its Link to the Vietnam War* (1995); and Robert D. Schulzinger, *A Time for War: The United States and Vietnam, 1941–1975* (1997).

CULTURAL DEBATES GENERATED BY THE WAR IN VIETNAM For cultural debates generated by the war in Vietnam, see Loren Baritz, *Backfire: A History of How American Culture Led Us into Vietnam and Made Us Fight the Way We Did* (1985); Kathleen Turner, *Lyndon Johnson's Dual War: Vietnam and the Press* (1985); Susan Jeffords, *The Remasculinization of America: Gender and the Vietnam War* (1989); Albert Auster and Leonard Quart, *How the War Was Remembered: Hollywood and Vietnam* (1988); John Carlos Rowe and Rick Berg, eds., *The Vietnam War and American Culture* (1991); Michael Gregg, ed., *Inventing Vietnam: The War in Film and Television* (1991); David W. Levy, *The Debate over Vietnam* (2nd ed., 1995); and Fred Turner, *Echoes of Combat: The Vietnam War in American Memory* (1996).

POLITICAL INSURGENCY OF THE 1960S On the political insurgency of the 1960s see W. J. Rorbaugh, *Berkeley at War: The 1960s* (1989); Barbara Tischler, ed., *Sights on the Sixties* (1992); David Chalmers, *And the Crooked Place Made Straight: The Struggle for Social Change in the 1960s* (1996); Timothy Miller, *The Hippies and American Values* (1991); Peter Collier and David Horowitz, *Destructive Generation: Second Thoughts about the Sixties* (1996); Paul Berman, *A Tale of Two Utopias: The Political Journey of the Generation of 1968* (1998); David Farber, ed., *The Sixties: From Memory to History* (1994); Alexander Bloom and Wini Breines, eds., *"Takin It to the Streets": A Sixties Reader* (1995); Paul Lyons, *New Left, New Right, and the Legacy of the Sixties* (1996); Jonah Raskin, *For the Hell of It: The Life and Times of Abbie Hoffman* (1996); and David Burner, *Making Peace with the Sixties* (1996). The conservative insurgency is the subject of Mary C. Brennan, *Turning Right in the Sixties: The Conservative Capture of the GOP* (1995); Robert Alan Goldberg, *Barry Goldwater* (1995); and John A. Andrew III, *The Other Side of the Sixties: Young Americans for Freedom and the Rise of Conservative Politics* (1997).

OPPOSITION TO THE WAR On opposition to the war, see Charles De Benedetti, *An American Ordeal: The Anti-War Movement of the Vietnam Era* (1990); Melvin Small and William D. Hoover, eds., *Give Peace a Chance* (1992); Kenneth J. Heineman, *Campus Wars: The Peace Movement at American State Universities in the Vietnam Era* (1993); Amy Swerdlow, *Women Strike for Peace: Traditional Motherhood and Radical Politics in the 1960s* (1993); Tom Wells, *The War Within: America's Battle over Vietnam* (1993); and Adam Garfinkle, *Telltale Hearts: The Origins and Impact of the Vietnam Antiwar Movement* (1995). Todd Gitlin indicts the media for speeding the fall of opposition efforts in *The Whole World Is Watching: Mass Media in the Making and Unmaking of the New Left* (1980), while Maurice Isserman's *If I Had a Hammer: The Death of the Old Left and the Birth of the New Left* (1987) looks at the general conflict among radicals. See also Wini Breines, *Community and Organization in the New Left, 1962–1968* (1982); Jim Miller, *Democracy Is in the Streets: From Port Huron to the Siege of Chicago* (1987); Todd Gitlin, *The Sixties: Years of Hope, Days of Rage* (1987); and Douglas Knight, *Streets of Dreams: The Nature and Legacy of the 1960s* (1989). On the politics of 1968 see Lewis Gould, *1968: The Election That Changed America* (1993).

RICHARD NIXON AND HIS POLICIES On Richard Nixon and his policies, see Garry Wills, *Nixon Agonistes* (rev. ed., 1980); Bruce Odes, ed., *From the President: Richard Nixon's Secret Files* (1989); Stephen Ambrose, *Nixon* (1989); Roger Morris, *Richard Milhous Nixon: The Rise of an American Politician* (1990); Joan Hoff, *Nixon Reconsidered* (1994); and Terry Terriff, *The Nixon Administration and the Making of U.S. Nuclear Strategy* (1995). On economic policy see Diane B. Kunz, *Butter and Guns: America's Cold War Economic Policy* (1997), and Allen J. Matusow, *Nixon's Economy: Booms, Busts, Dollars, and Votes* (1997).

WATERGATE On Watergate and the broader ethos of secret government, see Peter Schrag, *Test of Loyalty: Daniel Ellsberg and the Rituals of Secret Government* (1974); Theodore White, *Breach of Faith: The Fall of Richard Nixon* (1975); Athan Theoharis, *Spying on Americans: Political Surveillance from Hoover to the Huston Plan* (1978); Frank J. Donner, *The Age of Surveillance: The Aims and Methods of America's Surveillance System* (1980); L. H. LaRue, *Political Discourse: A Case Study of the Watergate Affair* (1988); Stanley I. Kutler, *The Wars of Watergate: The Last Crisis of Richard Nixon* (1990) and *Abuse of Power: The New Nixon Tapes* (1998); and Michael Schudson, *Watergate in American Memory: How We Remember, Forget, and Reconstruct the Past* (1992).

VIDEOS *LBJ* (1991) is a four-hour video documentary in the "American Experience" series; *Chicago, 1968* (1995) is a solid, one-hour entry in the same series. There are a number of video accounts of Malcolm X, including *Malcolm X: Make It Plain* (1993) and *The Real Malcolm X: An Intimate Portrait of the Man* (1992). On civil rights, also consult the appropriate one-hour segments in the longer "Eyes on the Prize" series. On the political insurgency of the 1960s, see *Making Peace with the Sixties* (1991), a three-part series, and the more limited, but more insightful, *Berkeley in the Sixties* (1990). *Watergate* (1994) is a multipart documentary produced in Great Britain.

Chapter 30

SOCIAL, ECONOMIC, AND DEMOGRAPHIC DEVELOPMENTS On social, economic, and demographic developments, see Raymond Mohl, ed., *Searching for the Sunbelt: Historical Perspectives on a Region* (1990); Mike Davis, *City of Quartz: Excavating the Future in Los Angeles* (1990); Alejandro Portes and Alex Stepick, *City on the Edge: The Transformation of Miami* (1993); Merry Ovnick, *Los Angeles: The End of the Rainbow* (1994); Nathan Glazer, ed., *Clamor at the Gates: The New American Immigration* (1985); Michael D'Innocenzo and Josef P. Sirefman, eds., *Immigration and Ethnicity* (1992); Alejandro Portes and Ruben G. Rumbaut, *Immigrant America: A Portrait* (1996); Norman L. Zucker and Naomi Flink Zucker, *Desperate Crossings: Seeking Refuge in America* (1996); Robert J. Samuelson, *The American Dream in the Age of Entitlement, 1945–1995* (1996); Steven P. Dandaneau, *A Town Abandoned: Flint, Michigan, Confronts Deindustrialization* (1996); Ruth Milkman, *Farewell to the Factory: Auto Workers in the Late Twentieth Century* (1997); Charles Noble, *Welfare as We Knew It: A Political History of the American Welfare State* (1997); and Allen J. Scott and Edward W. Soja, *The City: Los Angeles and Urban Theory at the End of the Twentieth Century* (1996).

CHANGES IN TECHNOLOGY AND THE ENVIRONMENT On changes in technology and the environment, see Robert Reich, *The Work of Nations: Preparing Ourselves for 21st Century Capitalism* (1991); Kirkpatrick Sale, *The Green Revolution; The Environmental Movement* (1993); James W. Cortada, *The Computer in the United*

States: From Laboratory to Market, 1930–1960 (1993); Daniel Yergin, *The Prize: The Epic Quest for Oil, Money, and Power* (1991) and *The Commanding Heights: The Battle between Government and the Marketplace That Is Remaking the Modern World* (1998); Samuel P. Hays, *Beauty, Health, and Permanence: Environmental Politics in the United States, 1955–1985* (1987); Craig E. Coltren and Peter N. Skinner, *The Road to Love Canal: Managing Industrial Waste before the EPA* (1996); Michele Stenehjem Gerber, *On the Home Front: The Cold War Legacy of the Hanford Nuclear Site* (1992); Terence Kehoe, *Cleaning Up the Great Lakes: From Cooperation to Confrontation* (1997); Ann Markusen et al., *The Rise of the Gunbelt: The Military Remapping of Industrial America* (1991); and Philip Shabecoff, *A Fierce Green Fire: The American Environmental Movement* (1993).

CHANGES IN THE MEDIA ENVIRONMENT AND MASS CULTURE On changes in the media environment and mass culture, see Todd Gitlin, *Inside Prime Time* (1983); John Fiske, *Television Culture* (1987); Mark Crispin Miller, *Boxed-In: The Culture of TV* (1988); Robert Kolker, *Cinema of Loneliness: Penn, Kubrick, Scorcese, Spielberg, Altman* (rev. ed., 1988); Marsha Kinder, *Playing with Power in Movies, Television, and Video Games* (1991); Elizabeth G. Traube, *Dreaming Identities: Class, Gender, and Generation in the 1980s Hollywood Movies* (1992); Andrew Goodwin, *Dancing in the Distraction Factory: Music Television and Popular Culture* (1992); Henry Jenkins, *Textual Poachers: Television Fans & Participatory Culture* (1992); Anne Friedberg, *Window Shopping: Cinema and the Postmodern* (1993); Jane Feuer, *Seeing through the Eighties: Television and Reaganism* (1995); Alan Nadel, *Flatlining on the Field of Dreams: Cultural Narratives in the Films of President Reagan's America* (1997); Henry A. Giroux, *Channel Surfing: Race Talk and the Destruction of Today's Youth* (1997); and Joseph Turow, *Breaking Up America: Advertisers and the New Media World* (1997).

CONTINUATION OF POLITICAL INSURGENCY On the continuation of political insurgency, begin with Barbara Epstein, *Political Protest and Cultural Revolution: Non-Violent Direct Action in the 1970s* (1991). See also Paul Chaat Smith and Robert Allen Warrior, *Like a Hurricane: The Indian Movement from Alcatraz to Wounded Knee* (1996). Sara Evans, *Personal Politics: The Roots of Women's Liberation in the Civil Rights Movement and the New Left* (1979); Alice Echols, *Daring to Be Bad: Radical Feminism in America, 1967–1975* (1989); and Nancy Whittier, *Feminist Generations: the Persistence of the Radical Women's Movement* (1995), seek to trace the emergence of a new feminism out of the male-dominated ethos of the New Left and the counterculture and to suggest that the 1960s did not represent a sudden end to insurgent movements. See also Jane J. Mansbridge, *Why We Lost the Era* (1986); Mary Frances Berry, *Why ERA Failed: Politics, Women's Rights, and the Amending Process of the Constitution* (1986); Johnnetta B. Cole, ed., *All American Women: Lines That Divide, Ties That Bind* (1986); Catherine MacKinnon, *Feminism Unmodified: Discourses on Life and Law* (1988); Susan Staggenborg, *The Pro-Choice Movement: Organization and Activism in the Abortion Conflict* (1991); and the relevant chapters of Leslie Reagan, *When Abortion Was a Crime: Women, Medicine, and Law in the United States, 1867–1973* (1997). On the gay and lesbian rights movement, see John D'Emilio and Estelle B. Freedman, *Intimate Matters: A History of Sexuality in America* (1988); Randy Shilts, *And the Band Played On: Politics, People, and the AIDS Epidemic* (1987); and Steven Epstein, *Impure Science: AIDS, Aids Activism, and the Politics of Science* (1996).

RACE AND MULTICULTURALISM On the dilemmas of race and multiculturalism see Russell Ferguson et al., eds., *Out There: Marginalization and Contemporary Cultures* (1990); Toni Morrison, ed., *Race-ing Justice, En-Gendering Power: Essays on Anita Hill, Clarence Thomas, and the Construction of Social Reality* (1992); Andrew Hacker, *Two Nations: Black and White, Separate, Hostile, and Unequal* (1992); bell books, *Black Looks: Race and Representation* (1992); Michael Eric Dyson, *Reflecting Black: African-American Cultural Criticism* (1993); Cornel West, *Race Matters* (1993) and *Beyond Eurocentrism and Multiculturalism* (1993); Celeste Olalquiaga, *Megalopolis: Contemporary Cultural Sensibilities* (1992); James Davison Hunter, *Culture Wars: The Struggle to Define America* (1991); Henry Louis Gates Jr., *Loose Canons: Notes on the Culture Wars* (1992); Patricia Turner, *I Heard It through the Grapevine: Rumor in African-American Culture* (1993); Russell A. Potter, *Spectacular Vernaculars: Hip-Hop and the Politics of Postmodernism* (1995); David A. Hollinger, *Post-Ethnic America: Beyond Multiculturalism* (1995); Robert C. Smith, *Racism in the Post–Civil Rights Era; Now You See It, Now You Don't* (1995); Roger Waldinger, *Still the Promised City? African-Americans and New Immigrants in Postindustrial New York* (1996); Mattias Gardell, *In the Name of Elijah Muhammed: Louis Farrakhan and the Nation of Islam* (1996); Michael Eric Dyson, *Between God and Gangsta Rap: Bearing Witness to Black Culture* (1996); Jennifer L. Hochschild, *Facing Up to the American Dream: Race, Class, and the Soul of the Nation* (1995); Toni Morrison ed., *Birth of a Nation 'Hood: Gaze, Script, and Spectacle in the O. J. Simpson Case* (1997); Elaine Bell Kaplan, *Not Our Kind of Girl: Unravelling the Myths of Black Teenage Motherhood* (1997); Pyong Gap Min, *Caught in the Middle: Korean Merchants in America's Multiethnic Cities* (1996); Fergus M. Bordewich, *Killing the White Man's*

Indian: Reinventing Native Americans at the End of the Twentieth Century (1996); Ambrose I. Lane Sr., *Return of the Buffalo: The Story behind America's Indian Gaming Explosion* (1995); Raymond Tatalovich, *Nativism Reborn? The Official English Language Movement and the American States* (1995); Gary Y. Okihiro, *Margins and Mainstreams: Asians in American History and Culture* (1994); John William Sayer, *Ghost Dancing and the Law: The Wounded Knee Trials* (1997); Joane Nagel, *American Indian Ethnic Revival: Red Power and the Resurgence of Identity and Culture* (1996); Rennard Strickland, *Tonto's Revenge: Reflections on American Indian Culture and Policy* (1997); and Pierrette Hondagneu-Sotelo, *Gendered Transitions: Mexican Experiences of Immigration* (1994). Alan Klein, *Baseball on the Border: A Tale of Two Laredos* (1997), offers a unique look, through the American pastime, of multiculturalism.

CONSERVATIVE POLITICS The growth of the "new conservatism" may be traced in David Reinhard, *The Republican Right since 1945* (1983); Jerome Himmelstein, *To the Right: The Transformation of American Conservatism* (1990); Walter Capps, *The New Religious Right: Piety, Patriotism, and Politics* (1990); Walter Hixson, *Searching for the American Right* (1992); Michael Lienesch, *Redeeming America: Piety and Politics in the New Christian Right* (1993); Mary C. Brennan, *Turning Right in the Sixties: The Conservative Capture of the GOP* (1995); Robert Alan Goldberg, *Barry Goldwater* (1995); Dan T. Carter, *The Politics of Rage: George C. Wallace, the Origins of the New Conservatism, and the Transformation of American Politics* (1995); Catherine McNicol, *Stock, Rural Radicals: Righteous Rage in the American Grain* (1996); James D. Tabor and Eugene V. Gallagher, *Why Waco? Cults and the Battle for Religious Freedom in America* (1995); Mark J. Rozell and Clyde Wilcox, *Second Coming: The New Christian Right in Virginia Politics* (1996); Raymond Wolters, *Right Turn: William Bradford Reynolds, the Reagan Administration, and Black Civil Rights* (1996); and Didi Herman, *The Antigay Agenda: Orthodox Vision and the Christian Right* (1997).

VIDEOS *DreamWorlds II: Desire, Sex, and Power in Music Video* (1996) is an award-winning critique of the images in rock videos, while Michael Eric Dyson's *Material Witness: Race, Identity and the Politics of Gangsta Rap* (1996) offers a more complex view. *The Myth of the Liberal Media* (1994) is a three-part critique, by Noam Chomsky and Edward Herman, of how the U.S. media shape popular understandings.

Chapter 31

GENERAL SURVEYS OF RECENT POLITICAL TRENDS General surveys of recent political trends include Martin T. Wattenberg, *The Decline of American Political Parties, 1952–1980* (1984); Ryan Barilleaux, *The Post-Modern Presidency: The Office after Ronald Reagan* (1988); Kathleen Hall Jamieson, *Packaging the Presidency: A History and Criticism of Presidential Campaign Advertising* (3rd ed., 1996); William Greider, *Who Will Tell the People: The Betrayal of American Democracy* (1992); Thomas Byrne and Mary D. Edsall, *Chain Reaction: The Impact of Race, Rights, and Taxes on American Politics* (1992); Kevin Phillips, *Boiling Point: Republicans, Democrats, and the Decline of Middle Class Prosperity* (1993); William C. Berman, *America's Right Turn: From Nixon to Bush* (1994); Ronald Radosh, *Divided They Fell: The Demise of the Democratic Party, 1964–1996 (1996)*; and Philip John Davies, *An American Quarter Century: U.S. Politics from Vietnam to Clinton* (1995).

FOREIGN POLICY On general trends and specific episodes in foreign policy, see Paul Kennedy, *The Rise and Fall of the Great Powers: Economic Change and Military Conflict from 1500 to 2000* (1987); Walter LaFeber, *Inevitable Revolutions: The United States in Central America* (1983); Raymond Garthoff, *Detente and Confrontation: American-Soviet Relations from Nixon to Reagan* (1985); Gaddis Smith, *Morality, Reason, and Power: American Diplomacy in the Carter Years* (1986) and *The Last Years of the Monroe Doctrine, 1945–1993*; Herbert D. Rosenbaum and Alexej Ugrinsky, eds. *Jimmy Carter: Foreign Policy and Post-Presidential Years* (1994); Richard C. Thornton, *The Carter Years: Toward a New Global Order* (1991); David Skidmore, *Reversing Course: Carter's Foreign Policy, Domestic Politics, and the Failure of Reform* (1996); Timothy P. Maga, *The World of Jimmy Carter: U.S. Foreign Policy, 1977–1981* (1994); Joanna Spear, *Carter and Arms: Implementing the Carter Administration's Arms Transfer Restraint Policy* (1995); John Dumbrell, *American Foreign Policy: Carter to Clinton* (1996); Robert A. Pastor, *Whirlpool: U.S. Foreign Policy toward Latin America and the Caribbean* (1992); Raymond Garthoff, *The Great Transition: America-Soviet Relations and the End of the Cold War* (1994); Keith L. Nelson, *The Making of Detente: Soviet-American Relations in the Shadow of Vietnam* (1995); Michael R. Beschloss and Strobe Talbott, *At the Highest Levels: The Inside Story of the End of the Cold War* (1993); Theodore Draper, *A Very Thin Line: The Iran-Contra Affairs* (1991); Gary Sick, *October Surprise: America's Hostages in Iran and the Election of Ronald Reagan* (1991); Morris H. Morley, ed., *Crisis and Confrontation: Ronald Reagan's Foreign Policy* (1988);

H. Bruce Franklin, *War Stars: The Superweapon and the American Imagination* (1988); John Lewis Gaddis, *The United States and the End of the Cold War: Implications, Reconsiderations, Provocations* (1991) and *We Now Know* (1997); and Michael Hogan, ed., *The End of the Cold War: Its Meaning and Implications* (1992).

THE GULF WAR For the Gulf War, specifically, see Lawrence Freedman and Efraim Karsh, *The Gulf Conflict, 1990–1991: Diplomacy and War in the New World Order* (1993); Dilip Hiro, *Desert Shield to Desert Storm: The Second Gulf War* (1992); Douglas Kellner, *The Persian Gulf TV War* (1992); Richard Hallion, *Storm over Iraq: Air Power and the Gulf War* (1992); Susan Jeffords and Lauren Rabinovitz, eds., *Seeing through the Media: The Persian Gulf War* (1994); and Frank N. Schubert and Theresa L. Kraus, *The Whirlwind War: The United States Army in Operations Desert Shield and Desert Storm* (1995).

THE BRIEF FORD PRESIDENCY On the brief Ford presidency, see Edward L. and Frederick H. Schapsmeier, *Gerald R. Ford's Date with Destiny: A Political Biography* (1989); James Cannon, *Time and Chance: Gerald Ford's Appointment with History* (1994); John R. Greene, *The Presidency of Gerald R. Ford* (1995); and John F. Guilmartin Jr., *A Very Short War: The Mayaguez and the Battle of Koh Tang* (1995).

THE CARTER YEARS On the Carter years, see Burton I. Kaufman, *The Presidency of James Earl Carter Jr.* (1993); Betty Glad, *Jimmy Carter: In Search of the Great White House* (1980); Erwin C. Hargrove, *Jimmy Carter as President* (1988); Garland Haas, *Jimmy Carter and the Politics of Frustration* (1992); Kenneth Morris, *Jimmy Carter: American Moralist* (1996); Anthony S. Campagna, *Economic Policy in the Carter Administration* (1995); and Gary M. Fink and Hugh Davis Graham, *The Carter Presidency: Policy Choices in the Post–New Deal Era* (1998).

THE REAGAN ERA On the Reagan era, see Sidney Blumenthal and Thomas Byrne Edsall, eds., *The Reagan Legacy* (1988); Robert Dallek, *Ronald Reagan: The Politics of Symbolism* (1984); Garry Wills, *Reagan's America: Innocents at Home* (1987); Robert E. Denton Jr., *The Primetime Presidency of Ronald Reagan* (1988); Michael Schaller, *Reckoning with Reagan* (1992); James E. Combs, *The Reagan Range: The Nostalgic Myth in American Politics* (1993); William Pemberton, *Exit with Honor: The Life and Presidency of Ronald Reagan* (1997); John Lofand, *Polite Protesters: The American Peace Movement of the 1980s* (1993); Raymond Wolters, *Right Turn: William Bradford Reynolds, the Reagan Administration, and Black Civil Rights* (1996); Diane Vaughan, *The Challenger Launch Decision: Risky Technology, Culture and Deviance at NASA* (1997); and Beth A. Fischer, *The Reagan Reversal: Foreign Policy at the End of the Cold War* (1998).

THE BUSH PRESIDENCY On the Bush presidency see Michael Duffy and Dan Goodgame, *Marching in Place: The Status Quo Presidency of George Bush* (1992); David Mervin, *George Bush and the Guardian Presidency* (1996); John Podhoretz, *Hell of a Ride: Backstage at the White House Follies 1989–1993* (1993); Charles Kolb, *White House Daze: The Unmaking of Domestic Policy in the Bush Years* (1994); and Herbert S. Parmet, *George Bush: The Life of a Lone Star Yankee* (1997).

POLITICS OF THE 1990S On the politics of the 1990s, see Jack W. Germond and Jules Witcover, *Mad as Hell: Revolt at the Ballot Box 1992* (1993); David Maraniss, *First in His Class: A Biography of Bill Clinton* (1995); Bob Woodward, *The Agenda: Inside the Clinton White House* (1994); Michael Lienesch, *Redeeming America: Piety and Politics in the New Christian Right* (1993); James Gibson, *Warrior Dreams: Paramilitary Culture in Post Vietnam America* (1994); Sara Diamond, *Roads to Dominion: Right-Wing Power and Political Power in the United States* (1995); Catherine McNicol Stock, *Rural Radicals: Righteous Rage in the American Grain* (1996); Kathryn S. Olmsted, *Challenging the Secret Government: The Post-Watergate Investigations of the CIA and the FBI* (1996); Theda Skocpol, *Boomerang: Clinton's Health Security Effort and the Turn against Government in U.S. Politics* (1996); Jacob S. Hacker, *The Road to Nowhere: The Genesis of President Clinton's Plan for Health Security* (1997); John Hohenberg, *Reelecting Bill Clinton: Why America Chose a "New" Democrat* (1997); and Robert Reich, *Locked in the Cabinet* (1997).

VIDEOS The A&E "Biography" series contains a number of videos appropriate for these years, including *Jimmy Carter: To the White House and Beyond* (1995). The Gulf War is covered in *A Line in the Sand* (1990); *Desert Triumph* (1991), a three-part series; and *The Gulf War* (1997), also a three-part series. *Rush to Judgment: The Anita Hill Story* (1997) offers interviews with both advocates and critics of Justice Clarence Thomas's chief accuser. *The War Room* (1994) provides a candid, behind-the-scenes look at the 1992 Clinton campaign. *An American Journey: The Great Society to the Reagan Revolution* (1998) is a five-part overview of the period.

~ CREDITS ~

Images not referenced below are in the public domain

Chapter 1 p. 2 © John Maier, Jr/JB Pictures. **p. 7** Jon Adkins © National Geographic Society. **p. 10** © British Museum. **p. 14** © Mexico, Cat. #140–San Felipe de Jesus. SEDUE, Catedral Metropolitana, Mexico City. **p. 15** Courtesy of the John Carter Brown Library at Brown University. **p. 19** Boltin Picture Library. **p. 21** Boltin Picture Library. **p. 24** © David Muench 1998. **p. 25** Moctezuma's Mexico, by David Carrasco and Eduardo Mato Moctezuma, © 1992 University Press of Colorado. Photographs by Salvador Guil'liem Arroyo.

Chapter 2 p. 46 William C. Clements Library, University of Michigan, Ann Arbor. **p. 50** © Wendell Metzen/Bruce Coleman Inc. **p. 66** Corbis/Bettmann Archives

Chapter 3 p. 76 © copyright British Museum. **p. 81** Patrick M. Malone, The Skulking Way of War, Madison Books © 1991. **p. 87** Thomas B. Macaulay, History of England from the Accession of James II, ed. by Charles H. Firth (London: Macmillan, 1914). **p. 94** Archives Nationales

Chapter 4 p. 103 1963.6.1 (1904)/PA: Copley, John Singelton, "Watson and the Shark," Ferdinand Lammot Belin Fund © 1998 Board of Trustees, National Gallery of Art, Washington, 1778, oil on canvas, 1.82 × 2.297 (71 3/4 × 90 1/2); framed: 2.413 × 2.642 × .101 (95 × 104 × 4). **p. 117** Colonial Williamsburg Foundation. **p. 122** Peabody Museum, Harvard University. Photograph by Hillel Burger. **p. 126** North Wind Picture Archives

Chapter 5 p. 142 Courtesy of the John Carter Brown Library at Brown University. **p. 146** The Granger Collection, New York. **p. 154** American Antiquarian Society. **p. 158** Clements Library, University of Michigan, Ann Arbor. **p. 159** Yale University Art Gallery. Trumbull Collection. **p. 161** Engraving, hand colored, "Plate UV. A View of South Part of Lexington," engraved by Amos Doolittle after a drawing by Ralph Earl; New Haven, Conn., 1775. Chicago Historical Society

Chapter 6 p. 171 Lewis Walpole Library, Yale University. **p. 179** Courtesy, American Antiquarian Society. **p. 192** (top)Harvard Law Art Collection. Oil on canvas, 56-3/16 × 77-3/4. Gift of Dr. George Stevens Jones, Mar. 31, 1879. **p. 192** (bottom) Nicolino Calyo, The Richard K. Haight Family, ca. 1848. Museum of the City of New York. Gift of Elizabeth Cushing Iselin.

Chapter 7 p. 206 Old Dartmouth Historical Society/New Bedford Whaling Museum. **p. 209** The Granger Collection, New York. **p. 213** Collection of the Maryland Historical Society, Baltimore. **p. 217** John Lewis Krimmel, American, 1786–1821 Village Tavern, 1813–14, oil on canvas, 16 7/8 × 22 1/2 in. (42.8 × 56.9 cm) The Toledo Museum of Art, Toledo, Ohio; Purchased with funds from the Florence Scott Libbey Bequest in Memory of he Father, Maurice A. Scott. **p. 221** Old Dartmouth Historical Society/New Bedford Whaling Museum

Chapter 8 p. 228 National Portrait Gallery, Smithsonian Institution/Art Resource, NY. **p. 233** (both) North Wind Picture Archives. **p. 240** Corbis/Bettmann. **p. 242** The Granger Collection, New York. **p. 249** Courtesy of the Royal Ontario Museum, Toronto, Canada. **p. 251** The Field Museum, Neg.#A93581c

Chapter 9 p. 261 Corbis/Bettmann. **p. 264** (all) Smithsonian Institution. **p. 265** Old Sturbridge Village, Photo by: Thomas Neill, #25.K74if.1994.2.1. **p. 268** Corbis/Bettmann . **p. 271** American Textile History Museum. Lowell, Mass. **p. 276** The Historic New Orleans Collection, Accession #1975.931 & 2

Chapter 10 p. 284 Abby Aldrich Rockefeller Folk Art Center, Williamsburg, VA. **p. 286** Frederic Edwin Church NIAGARA, 1857. Oil on canvas, 42 1/2 × 90 1/2 in. (107.95 × 229.87 cm) In the Collection of the Corcoran Gallery of Art, Museum Purchase, Gallery Fund. 76.15. **p. 292** The Granger Collection, New York. **p. 295** Hunter Museum of American Art, Chattanooga, Tennessee, Gift of Mr. and Mrs. Thomas B. Whiteside. **p. 298** Reproduced from the collection of the Library of Congress, B811 152

Chapter 11 p. 311 Reproduced from the collection of the Library of Congress, B811 152. **p. 317** A Black Oyster Seller in Philadelphia, 1814, Watercolor by John Lewis Krimmel. The Metropolitan Museum of Art, Rogers Fund, 1942. (42.95.18). **p. 318** from J.C. Nott and George R. Gliddon, types of Mankind; or, Ethnological Researches (1845). **p. 321** Old Sturbridge Village, photo by Henry E. Peach

Chapter 12 p. 328 National Museum of American Art, Washington DC/Art Resource, NY. **p. 336** The Hermitage: Home of President Andrew Jackson, Nashville, TN. **p. 338** White House Collection. **p. 352** (top) Reproduced from the collections of the Library of Congress. **p. 352** (bottom) The Smithsonian Institution, Division of Political History. **p. 353** (both) The Smithsonian Institution, Division of Political History. **p. 340** Woolaroc Museum. . **p. 348** Collection of The New-York Historical Society

Chapter 13 p. 361 North Wind Picture Archives. **p. 368** Missouri Historical Society. MHS art acc# 1939.3.1. **p. 361** (top) The Granger Collection, New York. **p. 361** (bottom) Courtesy of the California History Room, California State Library, Sacramento, California. **p. 375** North Wind Picture Archives

Chapter 14 p. 386 Maryland Historical Society, Baltimore. **p. 395** Corbis/Bettmann. **p. 403** Kansas State Historical Society

Chapter 15 p. 408 From the Ralph E. Becker Collection of Political Americana, The Smithsonian Institution. **p. 420** Cook Collection, Valentine Museum, Richmond, Virginia. **p. 423** The West Point Museum Collections, United States Military Academy, West Point, New York. **p. 428** (top) Reproduced from the Collections of the Library of Congress, LC-B8171-0560DLC; (middle) Reproduced from the Collections of the Library of Congress, LC-B8171-0563DLC; (bottom) Corbis/Bettmann

Chapter 16 p. 445 (left) Reproduced from the Collections of the Library of Congress; (right) Courtesy of the Illinois State Historical Library. **p. 449** National Park Service, Harpers Ferry Center. **p. 452** Chicago Historical Society. **p. 462** Reproduced from the Collections of the Library of Congress.17299-3479

Chapter 17 p. 470 Reproduced from the Collections of the Library of Congress. **p. 471** Reproduced from the Collections of the Library of Congress #LCUSZ26229112/412312. **p. 480** Corbis/Bettmann. **p. 482** Corbis/Bettmann

Chapter 18 p. 489 Nebraska State Historical Society. **p. 490** Erwin E. Smith Collection of the Library of Congress on deposit at the Amon Carter Museum, Fort Worth. **p. 494** Burton Historical Collection, Detroit Public Library. **p. 495** (top) Kansas State Historical Society, Topeka, Kansas; (bottom) The Granger Collection, New York

Chapter 19 p. 507 Corbis/Bettmann. **p. 510** North Wind Picture Archives. **p. 512** Kansas State Historical Society

Chapter 20 p. 524 Corbis/Bettmann. **p. 532** Victor Joseph Gatto, Triangle Fire, March 25, 1911. Oil on canvas, 19 x 28 inches. Museum of the City of New York, 54.75, Gift of Mrs. Henry L. Moses. **p. 535** Brown Brothers. **p. 540** The Granger Collection, New York. **p. 543** Corbis/Bettmann

Chapter 21 p. 550 Corbis/Bettmann. **p. 555** The Granger Collection, New York. **p. 559** The Granger Collection, New York. **p. 561** Corbis/Bettmann. **p. 566** Reproduced from the Collections of the Library of Congress. **p. 573** Archives of the University, Department of Rare Books and Special Collections. Princeton University Library

Chapter 22 p. 586 Chicago Historical Society. **p. 590** Corbis/Bettmann. **p. 591** The Granger Collection. **p. 594** William H. Walker. Life, 1899. **p. 598** The Granger Collection, New York. **p. 600** North Wind Picture Archives

Chapter 23 p. 609 Mary Evans Picture Library. **p. 616** Brown Brothers. **p. 620** (top) Imperial War Museum; (bottom) Grant Hamilton. Judge, 1898. **p. 622** *The New York Times,* 1919. **p. 630** Stock Montage, Inc.

Chapter 24 p. 633 © Underwood Photo Archives, Inc. **p. 640** Brown Brothers. **p. 647** Corbis/Bettmann. **p. 656** Chicano Studies Research Library, University of California, Los Angeles

Chapter 25 p. 665 Corbis/Bettmann. **p. 668** Brown Brothers. **p. 667** Ben Shahn mural at Jersey Homesteads, Hightstown, New Jersey, 1936. WPA. **p. 684** AP/Wide World Photos. **p. 685** (top) Corbis-Springer/Bettmann Film Archive; (bottom) Michael Barson Collection/Past Perfect

Chapter 26 p. 709 National Archives #127-N-69559-A. **p. 711** (both) Corbis-UPI/Bettmann. **p. 713** AP/Wide World Photos. **p. 714** Reproduced from the Collection of the Library of Congress. **p. 717** National Archives Photo # 44-PA-189. **p. 719** Hoover Institute Archives, Stanford University. U56031

Chapter 27 p. 732 © Archive Photos. **p. 747** Michael Barson Collection/Past Perfect. **p. 752** Michael Barson Collection/Past Perfect. **p. 753** Michael Barson Collection/Past Perfect

Chapter 28 p. 762 The Granger Collection, New York. **p. 769** Printed by permission of the Norman Rockwell Family Trust. Copyright © 1964 the Norman Rockwell Family Trust. Photo courtesy of The Norman Rockwell Museum at Stockbridge. **p. 771** Corbis-UPI/Bettmann. **p. 780** Corbis-UPI/Bettmann. **p. 782** AP/Wide World Photos

Chapter 29 p. 798 Corbis-UPI/Bettmann. **p. 807** (left) AP/Wide World Photos; (right) © John Filo, *Valley Daily News,* Tarentum, PA. **p. 808** © Paul Conklin/PhotoEdit

Chapter 30 p. 818 © 1996 Andrew Holbrooke. **p. 830** Photofest. **p. 831** (both) © Archive Photos/Fotos International. **p. 837** Bill Pugliano/Gamma-Liaison Network

Chapter 31 p. 849 © 1980 Time Inc., Reprinted by permission. **p. 866** AP/Wide World. **p. 868** Republican National Committee. **p. 869** Democratic National Committee. **p. 872** Corbis/Reuters Newsmedia Inc.

~ INDEX ~